UNIVERSITY CASEBOOK SERIES

HUMAN RIGHTS

By

LOUIS HENKIN
University Professor Emeritus and Special Service Professor
Columbia University

GERALD L. NEUMAN
Herbert Wechsler Professor of Federal Jurisprudence
Columbia Law School

DIANE F. ORENTLICHER
Professor of Law
Washington College of Law, American University

DAVID W. LEEBRON
Dean and Lucy G. Moses Professor of Law
Columbia Law School

NEW YORK, NEW YORK
FOUNDATION PRESS
1999

COPYRIGHT © 1999 by FOUNDATION PRESS
                    11 Penn Plaza, Tenth Floor
                    New York, NY 10001
                    Phone (212) 760–8700
                    Fax (212) 760–8705

 TEXT IS PRINTED ON 10% POST
CONSUMER RECYCLED PAPER

To Alice, Joshua, David, and Daniel.

To Carol.

To the memory of Herman Israel Orentlicher,
who believed that law served the deepest interests of humanity.

To Ping.

*

PREFACE

This volume of cases and other materials is designed principally for use by law students in the United States in a course on Human Rights.

We expect, as has been our experience, that students who enroll in a course on human rights bring a special interest in "international human rights." We share and respond to that interest, and this volume provides materials for a comprehensive course in international human rights.

Some teachers and students, however, may seek a course that pursues a broader, *holistic* conception of human rights, which sees the intimate relation between the idea of human rights and its domestic, foreign and international applications at the end of the Twentieth Century. We have therefore included materials, and organized them, so as to facilitate study in a holistic course in Human Rights. (Hence, too, the title of this volume, the more inclusive *Human Rights* rather than *International Human Rights*). Our aim is to afford students (and teachers) the intellectual foundation and the materials for ploughing the rich field of human rights, whether in the academy or in practice, whether in an international or domestic context.

Human rights are commonly identified with the International Human Rights Movement, conceived and born during the Second World War and confirmed and certified at Nuremberg and in the United Nations Charter. A holistic approach to human rights might begin with human rights as an idea and an ideology, reflecting particular moral and political values, and a particular conception of the good society.

The human rights idea, growing out of centuries of philosophical speculation, laws, and institutions, became an ideology during the Seventeenth and Eighteenth Centuries, and was given expression in the American Declaration of Independence and in the French Declaration of the Rights of Man and of the Citizen, in the early bills of rights of the American States and in the U.S. Bill of Rights, and in subsequent European and Latin American constitutions. In the second half of the Twentieth Century, the International Human Rights Movement built on that idea and ideology and on those national constitutional foundations a growing edifice of international instruments, laws, and institutions. Like the human rights movement, both national and international laws of human rights have focused on the rights of the individual, but, increasingly, the idea of rights has been recognized as applying to individuals as members of groups and has been extended to the groups themselves.

A comprehensive study of human rights recognizes that the international law and institutions of human rights depend heavily on national rights systems. In a real sense, there are no "international human rights"; human rights are claims by human beings upon and within their national societies. International human rights law and institutions seek to promote and secure for the individual the protection of an array of agreed rights in his/her national society. (Indeed, in an "ideal" world of states, human rights would be protected by enlightened, effective national legal systems, and there would be no need for any international law of human rights or for international institutions to help promote and secure them.)

A holistic perspective on human rights is not merely faithful to the intellectual and political history of the human rights idea; it reflects the relationship in principle, in law and in fact, between national and international human rights in today's world. It seeks to locate where human rights stand in the lives of six billion human beings in an international political-legal system of states as we enter the Twenty-First Century. The national character of rights in a world of states today is the reality for the advocate, for the lawyer, and for the student. The individual will see his/her rights, and the lawyer or advocate would seek to protect those rights, primarily through national laws and institutions. In the United States, for example, rights are determined, defined, and protected by layers of domestic law—municipal and State law, federal law, federal and State constitutional law. The individual, the advocate, the lawyer, will turn to international law and institutions in order to enhance support for and to vindicate his/her rights under U.S. and State law, including international law that has become part of U.S. law.

For the student as for the citizen, then, human rights are both national and international, national before—and after—they are international. The laws of virtually every country purport to protect fundamental rights of individuals; there is also a rich and growing body of international law and agreements that have both national and international applications. International human rights derived their content from national human rights systems; in time, the international human rights movement provided ideas, principles, standards, for adoption by national rights systems. Thus, the sources of human rights law are many: common law, statutes, constitutional law and international law; the sources and nature of available remedies, both legal and political, are also varied. Whether representing an individual client or attempting to remedy repressive state practices, lawyers will make the best use of all the tools at their disposal.

The materials in this volume are arranged in four parts:

1. Historical and theoretical background of the idea and ideology of individual rights;

2. Individual rights in the United States, as a notable—for the people of the United States the notable—national rights system;

3. International human rights norms and remedies; and

4. Comparative human rights.

We have arranged the materials so that the teacher (and the student) who is so inclined can omit, condense, or reorder—for example, by moving earlier to International Human Rights, and by reducing study of the idea and ideology of human rights, or of national constitutional rights, to occasional notes.

Part I, *Human Rights: Idea and Ideology*, develops the origins of the idea of human rights and of the political-legal human rights movement, particularly in the United States and Europe. By characterizing them as rights, proponents sought a place for them in moral and legal philosophy. By denominating them "human rights," the human rights ideology declares some legal-moral rights to be universal, the responsibility of every society to realize for all its members through its domestic constitutional system. (At the end of the Twentieth Century, there have been challenges to the idea of universal human rights, flying banners of "cultural relativism" and "Asian values." See Part I, Chapter 2(C).) We set forth philosophical perspectives offering alternatives to the ideology of rights in conceptions of "the good society," including those of Marxism and religion (Part I, Chapter 1(C)), and of "Critical Legal Studies" (Part I, Chapter 2(C)).

The holistic perspective on the relation of national and international rights suggests presenting national rights as the gateway to international rights, and—for U.S. law students—an understanding of rights in the United States in particular as conducive to the effective study of the international rights system. From this perspective, Part II, *Human Rights in National Law: The United States*, has two principal functions. It sketches the development of rights in the United States (familiarity with which is crucial to understanding modern human rights), and it introduces students to the relationship between constitutionalism and rights. Part II also serves to develop the doctrinal framework of rights—the sources of rights, the limitations on rights, the problems of conflicting rights. U.S. materials are widely accessible and contain the most detailed consideration of rights, but the principles that emerge apply to rights generally, in any country and in any context. Students of rights in other national systems may substitute (or add) materials from those systems. (We provide some materials in respect of particular rights in Part IV.)

As summarized in Part II, U.S. constitutional and other U.S. law constitute the principal law governing individual rights in the United States. The U.S. law of rights will also help the student understand international human rights law, which in its development drew heavily on U.S. sources; it will permit meaningful comparison of an individual's rights under the U.S. legal system and under international covenants and conventions (and under customary international law), and will help determine whether the condition of human rights in the United States measures up to international human rights standards at the end of the Twentieth Century. The U.S. law of rights will also provide guidance as to how inhabitants of the United States may enhance respect for their rights by invoking applicable international human rights norms. Citizens, students, lawyers, and judges will be able to judge the extent to which the law of human rights in the United

States has been modified by U.S. adherence to international covenants and conventions, and help determine the significance of reservations, understandings and declarations which the United States has attached to U.S. ratification of international human rights treaties. See Part III, Chapter 4(B).

Some of the materials in Part II will be familiar to students in the United States from courses on U.S. Constitutional Law, but we provide some that may be unfamiliar, and they serve a different purpose here. Many courses in Constitutional Law tend to neglect the history and theory of rights and their place in the history of constitutionalism. We do not attempt to cover the substantive law of each of the many individual rights that have been held to be protected by the U.S. Constitution, not even those now recognized as universal human rights. The materials we provide are intended to help develop the analytical framework for human rights, and in particular the legal sources and structure of rights. (Teachers who are persuaded that their students have a good grounding in the theory and history of U.S. rights may decide to omit some of this Part or teach it as review and refresher.)

Part III presents *International Human Rights*. (A course limited to International Human Rights may concentrate on this Part and on Part IV with perhaps only a glance at Part II.) There are different reasons for the study of international human rights in the United States—the human rights ideology as a major development in human rights history, in intellectual, political, cultural history. We study international human rights law and institutions to determine whether the condition of human rights and human rights law in the United States measures up to international human rights standards at the end of the Twentieth Century; to what extent the United States has incorporated, or might incorporate, international human rights law into U.S. law, to be invoked by citizens and officials, lawyers, and courts. We study international human rights law and institutions for their relevance to U.S. concern with the condition of human rights in all other countries of the world, and to U.S. foreign policy generally.

Part III begins with the history of the International Human Rights movement, and covers the basic international agreements and other instruments, as well as the customary international law of human rights, and their implementation and justification by national and international courts and other bodies. Chapter 2(F) elaborates specially on women's rights as human rights. Other sections in Part III set forth what have been called "second and third generation" rights, as well as collective rights and group rights, such as the rights of "peoples" to self-determination, and to economic self-determination, and the right to development.

We consider remedies separately in Chapters 3 and 4 of Part III. This section presents the spectrum of remedial actions—international and domestic, legal and political. We set forth the remedies provided by the major international human rights instruments and the role of "remedies" provided by the network of non-governmental organizations and nonlegal institutions. We provide U. S. materials to explore the basic conceptual issues of remedies, and we also include U.S. legal remedies to protect international rights.

Finally, in Part IV, *Selected Rights Compared*, we elaborate the substantive law of selected human rights. The conception and structure of Parts I to III render it pedagogically awkward to pursue any particular substantive rights in depth and in comparative perspective. We have therefore added Part IV to allow more comprehensive treatment of particular rights, such as the right to life, to liberty and autonomy, to equality before the law, and we have provided a basis for comparative studies, and materials from different fora, including different domestic (national) courts, international courts, and human rights committees established by treaty. These materials raise questions not only regarding the "relativism" of human rights, but also of "pluralism": different nations may adopt differing configurations of rights in pursuit of the same or a similar vision of the good society. Of course, the teacher (or student) might choose to refer to some of the materials in Part IV earlier, in discussion of particular rights in the United States or under a particular international agreement. To supplement (or substitute for) the materials in this part, the teacher may also wish to hand out materials for one contemporary, topical case study.

International human rights suggest that the relation between the individual and society can, and have, become a subject of international politics and international law. By that development, the international system abandoned the traditional view that how a society treats its own inhabitants is no one else's business. But the idea dies hard, and the end of the Twentieth Century continues to witness recurrent challenge to international human rights, flying banners of "state sovereignty." The tension between "domestic jurisdiction" and "international concern" is reflected throughout the materials in Part III, and in specific contexts in Part IV—as indeed it permeates all the law and all of the politics of international human rights as well as the study of Human Rights as we enter the Twenty-First Century.

*

ACKNOWLEDGEMENTS

We acknowledge and are indebted to a large number of colleagues, students and friends who generously contributed their time, effort and counsel to make this book possible.

We extend our warm thanks to Jason Abel, Afra Afsharipour, Reena Agrawal, Mar Aguilera, Kelly Dawn Askin, Amjad H. Atallah, Farah Brelvi, Holly Burkhalter, Lisa Courtney, Lori Damrosch, Anne-Marie Devereux, Alexia Dorszynski, Claudio Grossman, Carrie Gustafson, Laura Guthrie, Sarah Herbert, Kevin Huff, Kathryn Ivers, David Kassebaum, Christine Klein, Antti Korkeakivi, Miriam Lefkowitz, Stephen Marks, Claudia Martin, Bartolomeo Migone, Jason Miller, Rosemary Nidiry, Jelena Pejic, Robert Phay, Catherine Powell, Aaron Saiger, Oscar Schachter, Brian D. Tittemore, Jonathan Todres, Mariann Wang, Laurent Wiesel, and Elizabeth Jane Williamson.

We would also like to thank Hilda Daniels, Lillian Hoffman, Linda Hughes, and Mark Williams for their dedication and assistance with the manuscript.

Finally, we acknowledge our indebtness to the following authors and publishers who granted us permission to reprint copyrighted material:

T. Alexander Aleinikoff, The Yale Law Journal Company, and Fred B. Rothman & Company for T. Alexander Aleinikoff, *Constitutional Law in the Age of Balancing*, 96 Yale L.J. 943 (1987). Reprinted by permission of The Yale Law Journal Company and Fred B. Rothman & Company from *The Yale Law Journal*, Vol. 96, pages 943-1005.

The American Law Institute, for excerpts from the Restatement (Third) of the Foreign Relations Law of the United States (1987), (c) 1987, reprinted by permission.

The American Society of International Law, for Karen Engle, *After the Collapse of the Public/Private Distinction: Strategizing Women's Rights*, in Reconceiving Reality: Women and International Law (Dorinda Dallmeyer ed. 1993) (c) The American Society of International Law.

Blackwell Publishers, for Antonio Cassese, *Reflections on International Criminal Justice*, 61 Mod. L. Rev. 1 (1998), (c) 1998, reprinted by permisison.

Carl Heymanns Verlag KG, for Rudolph Bernhardt, *Thoughts on the Interpretation of Human Rights Treaties*, in Protecting Human Rights: the

European Dimension: Studies in honor of Gerard J. Wiarda (1988), (c) 1988, reprinted by permission.

The Center for Strategic and International Studies of the Massachusetts Institute of Technology, for Peter J. Spiro, *New Global Communities: Nongovernmental Organization in International Decision-Making Institutions*, 18 Wash Q. 45 (1994).

The Center for the Study of Human Rights, for Louis Henkin, <u>The Rights of Man Today</u> (1988), reprinted by permission.

Columbia Human Rights Law Review, for Michael H. Posner & Candy Whittome, *The Status of Human Rights NGOs,* 25 Colum. Hum. Rts. L. Rev. 269 (1994), (c) 1994, reprinted by permission.

Columbia Law Review, for H.L.A. Hart, *Between Utility and Rights*, 79 Colum. L. Rev. 828 (1979), (c) 1979, reprinted by permission.

Columbia University Press, for excerpts from "The Age of Rights," by Louis Henkin. Copyright (c) 1990 Columbia University Press. Reprinted with the permission of the publisher; and for excerpts from "The International Bill of Rights," edited by Louis Henkin. Copyright (c) 1981 Columbia University Press. Reprinted with the permission of the publisher.

Cornell University and Fred B. Rothman & Company, for Abdullahi A. An-Na'im, Islamic Law, International Relations, and Human Rights: Challenge and Response, 20 Cornell Int'l L.J. 317 (1987), (c) Copyright 1987 by Cornell University, All Rights Reserved.

David Philip Publishers (Pty) Ltd, for John Dugard: *Sanctions against South Africa: An international law perspective*, in Sanctions Against Apartheid (Mark Orkin ed. 1989), (c) 1989, reprinted by permission.

Foundation Press, for Laurence Tribe, *American Constitutional Law* (2d ed. 1988), (c) 1988, reprinted by permission.

Harvard Civil Rights-Civil Liberties Law Review, for Patricia Williams, *Alchemical Notes: Reconstructed Ideals from Deconstructed Rights*, 22 Harv. C.R.-C.L. L. Rev. 401 (1987), (c) 1987, by the President and Fellows of Harvard College.

Harvard Human Rights Journal, for Hope Lewis, *Between Irua and "Female Genital Mutilation": Feminist Human Rights Discourse and the Cultural Divide*, 8 Harv. Hum. Rts. J. 1 (1995), (c) 1995, reprinted by permission.

Harvard Human Rights Yearbook, for Diane F. Orentlicher, *Bearing Witness: The Art and Science of Human Rights Fact-finding,* 3 Harv. Hum. Rts. Y.B. 83 (1990), (c) 1990, reprinted by permission.

Harvard International Law Journal, for Gregory H. Fox and Georg Nolte, *Intolerant Democracies*, 36 Harv. Int'l L.J. 1 (1995), (c) 1995, reprinted by permission.

Harvard University Press, for excerpts from TAKING RIGHTS SERIOUS-LY by Ronald Dworkin. Copyright (c) 1977, 1978 by Ronald Dworkin. Reprinted by permission of Harvard University Press.

Hastings Comparative and International Law Review, for Peter Quint, *The Comparative Law of Flag Desceration: The United States and the Federal Republic of Germany*, in 15 Hastings Comp. & Intl'l L. Rev. 613 (1992), (c) 1992, reprinted by permission.

Human Rights Watch, for Americas Watch Committee et al., Critique: Review of the Department of State's Country Reports on Human Rights Practices for 1984 (1985), and Human Rights Watch, World Report 1999 (1999), used with the permission of Human Rights Watch.

Johns Hopkins University Press, for Jack Donnelly, Universal Human Rights in Theory and Practice (1989), (c) 1989, reprinted by permission.

Juris Publishing for the translation of The Declaration of the Rights of Man and of the Citizen, in Bermann, et al., French Law: Constitution and Selective Legislation (1998). Reprinted with the permission of Juris Publishing, Inc. Executive Park, One Odell Plaza, Yonkers, NY 10701.

Kluwer Law International, for Evelyn A. Ankumah, The African Commission on Human and Peoples' Rights: Practice and Procedures (1996), (c) 1996, with kind permission of Kluwer Law International; for Asbjørn Eide, *Economic, Social and Cultural Rights as Human Rights*, in Economic, Social and Cultural Rights: A Textbook (Asbjørn Eide et al. eds. 1995), (c) 1995, with kind permission of Kluwer Law International; for Louis Henkin, International Law: Politics and Values (1995), (c) 1995, with kind permission of Kluwer Law, International; for R. St. J. Macdonald, *The Margin of Appreciation,* in The European System for the Protection of Human Rights 83 (R. St. J. Macdonald et al., eds. 1993), (c) 1993, with kind permission of Kluwer Law International; and for Hans Thoolen & Berth Verstappen, Human Rights Missions: A Study of the Fact-Finding Practice of Non-Governmental Organizations (1986), (c) 1986, with kind permission of Kluwer Law International.

Lawyers Committee for Human Rights, for Lawyers Committee for Human Rights, Critique: Review of the U.S. Department of State's Country Reports on Human Rights Practices for 1994 (1995), (c) 1995, reprinted by permission.

Michigan Journal of International Law for Alan W. Lepp, *The Death Penalty in Late Imperial, Modern, and Post-Tiananmen China*, in 11 Mich. J. Int'l L. 987 (1990), (c) 1990, reprinted by permission; and for Gregory H. Fox, *Self-Determination in the Post-Cold War Era: A New Internal Focus?*, 16 Mich. J. Int'l L. 733 (1995), (c) (1995), reprinted by permission.

The New Republic, Inc., for Michael Sandel, *Morality and the Liberal Ideal,* The New Republic, May 7, 1984. Reprinted by permission of THE NEW REPUBLIC, (c) 1984, The New Republic, Inc.

The New York Times, for Seble Dawit and Salem Mekuria, *The West Just Doesn't Get It*, N.Y. Times, Dec. 7, 1993. (c) 1993 by The New York Times. Reprinted by permission. For Bill Keller, *South Africa's Sanctions May Have Worked, at a Price*, N.Y. Times, Sep. 12, 1993. (c) 1993 by The New York Times. Reprinted by permission. And for Aryeh

Neier, *Not All Human Rights Groups are Equal*, N.Y. Times, May 27, 1989. (c) 1989 by The New York Times. Reprinted by permission.

New York University Journal of International Law and Politics, for Donna J. Sullivan, *Gender Equality and Religious Freedom: Toward a Framework for Conflict Resolution*, 24 N.Y.U. J. Int'l L. & Pol. 795 (1992), (c) 1992, reprinted by permission.

New York University Law Review, for William J. Brennan, Jr., *The Bill of Rights and the States: The Revival of State Constitutions as Guardians of Individual Rights*, 61 N.Y.U. L. Rev. 535, 537-38, 546-52 (1986), reprinted by permission.

Random House, Inc., for excerpts from A MIRACLE, A UNIVERSE by Lawrence Weschler. Copyright (c) 1990 by Lawrence Weschler. Reprinted by permission of Pantheon Books, a division of Random House, Inc.

Amartya Sen and The New Republic, Inc., for *Human Rights and Asian Values*, The New Republic, July 14, 1997. Reprinted by permission of Amartya Sen and THE NEW REPUBLIC, (c) 1987, The New Republic, Inc.

Southern Texas Law Review, for William J. Brennan, Jr., *The Constitution of the United States: Contemporary Ratification*, 27 Southern Tex. L. Rev. 433 (1986), (c) 1986, reprinted by permission.

Stanford Journal of International Law, for Michael J. Bazyler, *Reexamining the Doctrine of Humanitarian Intervention in Light of the Atrocities in Kampuchea and Ethiopia,* 23 Stan. J. Int'l L. 547 (1987), (c) 1987, reprinted by permission.

University of California at Los Angeles Law Review, for Eugenie Anne Gifford, *The Courage to Blaspheme": Confronting Barriers to Resisting Female Genital Mutilation*, 4 UCLA Women's L.J. 329 (1994), (c) 1994, reprinted by permission.

Temple Law Review, for Sarah Ramsey & Daan Braveman, "Let Them Starve": Government's Obligation to Children in Poverty, 68 Temp. L. Rev. 1607 (1995), (c) 1995, reprinted by permission.

United States Holocaust Memorial Museum, for Diane F. Orentlicher, Genocide and Crimes Against Humanity: The Legal Regime (1998), (c) 1998, reprinted by permission.

University of Chicago Press, for David P. Currie, *Lochner Abroad: Substantive Due Process and Equal Protection in the Federal Republic of Germany*, 1989 Sup. Ct. Rev. 333 (1990), (c) 1990, reprinted by permission.

Vanderbilt Law Review, for Peter Enrich, *Leaving Equality Beyond: New Directions in School Finance Reform*, 48 Vand. L. Rev. 101, 105-110 (1995), (c) 1995, reprinted by permission.

The Washington Post, for Dana Priest, *New Human Rights Law Triggers Policy Debate*, Washington Post, Dec. 31, 1998, (c) 1998, reprinted by permission.

Yale Journal of International Law, for Diane F. Orentlicher, Separation Anxiety: International Responses to Ethno-Separatist Claims, in 23 Yale L.J. 1 (1998), (c) 1998, reprinted by permission.

The Yale Law Journal Company and Fred B. Rothman & Company, for Laurence R. Helfer & Anne-Marie Slaughter, *Toward a Theory of Effective Supranational Adjudication,* 107 Yale L.J. 273 (1997). Reprinted by permission of The Yale Law Journal Company and Fred B. Rothman & Company from The Yale Law Journal, Vol. 107, pages 273-391.

Additional acknowledgements accompany the reprinted texts.

The authors have been unable to identify the current holders of the copyright, if any, for Oscar Janowsky, Nationalities and National Minorities, published by Macmillan & Co. in 1945, and for the translation of Karl Marx, "On the Jewish Question," reprinted in The Marx-Engels Reader (Robert C. Tucker, ed., 2d ed. 1978), published by W.W. Norton & Co.

In reproducing texts, the authors have omitted unnecessary footnotes and citations, but have attempted to preserve the original numbering of footnotes that are retained.

*

SUMMARY OF CONTENTS

TABLE OF CONTENTS

Section

TABLE OF CASES

Principal cases are in bold type. Non-principal cases are in roman type. References are to Pages.

*

HUMAN RIGHTS

*

PART I

HUMAN RIGHTS: IDEA AND IDEOLOGY

In the United States, and elsewhere, many consider the idea of human rights axiomatic, "self-evident." (See, for example, the American Declaration of Independence, *infra* Part I, Chapter 1(B).) The idea of human rights, however, is a particular idea in moral, legal, and political philosophy, and a particular political ideology. Notably, it differs from ideologies based on duties: the Bible, for example, represents an ideology of duties; even "thou shalt love thy neighbor as thyself," for example, does not give my neighbor a "right" to be loved. My neighbor, one might say, is the third party beneficiary of my duty to God to obey his commandment.

As the materials in this Part will suggest, the idea of human rights grew in opposition to historic forms of authoritarianism such as the divine right of kings, and, more recently, to totalitarian ideologies such as National Socialism (Nazism) and other forms of absolutist state socialism (Stalinism). These regimes sometimes conferred benefits on the individual, but these benefits were not seen as belonging to the individual "as of right."

The idea of human rights is related to, but different from, and sometimes in tension with, "democracy," "the rule of law," "constitutionalism." The ideology of rights needs to be understood also in relation to contemporary criticism. Communitarianism (Part I, Chapter 2(C)), for example, does not reject the idea of human rights but is disturbed by its individualistic emphasis, and by applications that give individual rights absolute (or near-absolute) preference in relation to community and communal interests. "Cultural relativism" generally, and "Asian values" recently invoked, do not claim to reject the idea of human rights, but insist that its interpretation, its content and application, and its relation to the public interest, may differ with time, place, and local culture. See Part I, Chapter 2(C).

CHAPTER 1

THE HUMAN RIGHTS IDEA

Louis Henkin, *The Age of Rights*

1–5 (1990).

The contemporary idea of human rights was formulated and given content during the Second World War and its aftermath. During the War, the Allied powers had proclaimed that assuring respect for human rights was their war aim. In 1945, at Nuremberg, the Allies included crimes against humanity among the charges on which Nazi leaders were tried. The United Nations Charter declared that promoting respect for human rights was a principal purpose of the United Nations Organization. The human rights idea found its contemporary expression in the Universal Declaration of Human Rights adopted by the United Nations General Assembly in 1948, and in the numerous covenants and conventions derived from it.

"Rights" have figured prominently in moral, legal, and political theory. The idea of rights is related to theories of "the good," of "the right," of "justice," and to conceptions of the "the good society." In contemporary philosophical literature the idea of rights is often considered an alternative to various brands of utilitarianism.

Individual rights as a political idea draws on natural law and its offspring, natural rights. In its modern manifestation that idea is traced to John Locke, to famous articulations in the American Declaration of Independence and in the French Declaration of the Rights of Man and of the Citizen, and to realizations of the idea in the United States Constitution and its Bill of Rights and in the constitutions and laws of modern states.

The idea of human rights that has received currency and universal (if nominal) acceptance in our day owes much to these antecedents but it is discrete and different from them. The contemporary version does not ground or justify itself in natural law, in social contract, or in any other political theory. In international instruments, representatives of states declare and recognize human rights, define their content, and ordain their consequences within political societies and in the system of nation-states. The justification of human rights is rhetorical, not philosophical. Human rights are self-evident, implied in other ideas that are commonly intuited and accepted. Human rights are derived from accepted principles, or are required by accepted ends—societal ends such as peace and justice; individual ends such as human dignity, happiness, fulfillment.

What the pattern of declared norms amounts to, the idea it reflects, is nowhere articulated. I attempt to do so here, not as a philosophical construct, but as a distillation of what underlies national and international instruments.

Human rights are rights of individuals in society. Every human being has, or is entitled to have, "rights"—legitimate, valid, justified claims—upon his or her society; claims to various "goods" and benefits. Human rights are not some abstract, inchoate "good";* they are defined, particular claims listed in international instruments such as the Universal Declaration of Human Rights and the major covenants and conventions. They are those benefits deemed essential for individual well-being, dignity, and fulfillment, and that reflect a common sense of justice, fairness, and decency. In the constitutional jurisprudence of the United States, as we shall see, individual rights have long been thought of as consisting only of "immunities," as limitations on what government might do *to* the individual. Human rights, on the other hand, include not only these negative "immunity claims" but also positive "resource claims," claims to what society is deemed required to do *for* the individual. They include liberties—freedom *from* (for example, detention, torture), and freedom *to* (speak, assemble); they include also the right to food, housing, and other basic human needs.

Human rights are universal: they belong to every human being in every human society. They do not differ with geography or history, culture or ideology, political or economic system, or stage of societal development. To call them "human" implies that all human beings have them, equally and in equal measure, by virtue of their humanity—regardless of sex, race, age; regardless of high or low "birth," social class, national origin, ethnic or tribal affiliation; regardless of wealth or poverty, occupation, talent, merit, religion, ideology, or other commitment.[**] Implied in one's humanity, human rights are inalienable and imprescriptible: they cannot be transferred, forfeited, or waived; they cannot be lost by having been usurped, or by one's failure to exercise or assert them.

Human rights are *rights*; they are not merely aspirations, or assertions of the good. To call them rights is not to assert, merely, that the benefits indicated are desirable or necessary; or, merely, that it is "right" that the individual shall enjoy these goods; or even, merely, that it is the duty of

---

* Human rights are not equivalent to, or interchangeable with, "justice," although some conceptions of justice—commutative, distributive, or retributive justice, or justice as fairness—are reflected in human dignity and in the particular rights human dignity requires. Human rights are not equivalent to, or interchangeable with, "democracy." The contemporary articulation of the idea of rights includes some democracy, declaring that the will of the people is the foundation of government, and that every human being has the right to authentic participation in his or her government. But democracy thus defined is one human right of many. The will of the people, surely the will of the majority, is subject to the human rights of the individual, although in some respects rights are limited by the common interest in security, public order, health, and general welfare as democratically determined.

[**] A person may have additional rights in a given society by virtue of such extraneous qualities, or of others, such as citizenship, residence, or having been elected to office, but those are not everybody's "human rights."

society to respect the immunity or provide the benefits. To call them "rights" implies that they are claims "as of right," not by appeal to grace, or charity, or brotherhood, or love; they need not be earned or deserved. The idea of rights implies entitlement on the part of the holder in some order under some applicable norm; the idea of human rights implies entitlement in a moral order under a moral law, to be translated into and confirmed as legal entitlement in the legal order of a political society. When a society recognizes that a person has a right, it affirms, legitimates, and justifies that entitlement, and incorporates and establishes it in the society's system of values, giving it important weight in competition with other societal values.

Human rights imply the obligation of society to satisfy those claims. The state must develop institutions and procedures, must plan, must mobilize resources as necessary to meet those claims. Political and civil rights require laws, institutions, procedures, and other safeguards against tyranny, against corrupt, immoral, and inefficient agencies or officials. Economic and social rights in modern society require taxation and spending and a network of agencies for social welfare. The idea of human rights implies also that society must provide some system of remedies to which individuals may resort to obtain the benefits to which they are entitled or be compensated for their loss.[†] Together, the affirmation of entitlement, the recognition by society of an obligation to mobilize itself to discharge it, and the implication of remedy, all enhance the likelihood that the right will be realized, that individuals will actually enjoy the benefits to which they are entitled.

Human rights are claims upon society. These claims may derive from moral principles governing relations between persons, but it is society that bears the obligation to satisfy the claims. Of course, the official representatives of society must themselves respect individual freedoms and immunities; political society must also act to protect the individual's rights against private invasion. As regards claims to economic and social benefits, society must act as insurer to provide them if individuals cannot provide them for themselves. Thus, government must protect me from assault by my neighbor, or from wolves, and must ensure that I have bread or hospitalization; in human rights terms my rights are against the state, not against the neighbor or the wolves, the baker, or the hospital. The state may arrange to satisfy my claims by maintaining domestic laws and institutions that give me, say, rights and remedies in tort against my neighbor, or administrative remedies against a corrupt, misguided, or inefficient bureaucrat, or access to public schools or health services. Those legal rights and remedies against individuals or agencies within society give effect to my human rights claims upon society.

The idea of human rights has implications for the relation of the individual's rights to other public goods. It is commonly said that human

---

† In some circumstances the idea of rights may also legitimate some measure of "self-help" to realize one's entitlement, for example, by resisting repressive behavior when no effective societal protection or remedy is available.

rights are "fundamental." That means that they are important, that life, dignity, and other important human values depend on them; it does not mean that they are "absolute," that they may never be abridged for any purpose in any circumstances. Human rights enjoy a prima facie, presumptive inviolability, and will often "trump" other public goods. Government may not do some things, and must do others, even though the authorities are persuaded that it is in the society's interest (and perhaps even in the individual's own interest) to do otherwise; individual human rights cannot be lightly sacrificed even for the good of the greatest number, even for the general good of all. But if human rights do not bow lightly to public concerns, they may be sacrificed if countervailing societal interests are important enough, in particular circumstances, for limited times and purposes, to the extent strictly necessary. The Universal Declaration recognizes that rights are subject to limitations determined by law "for the purpose of securing due recognition and respect for the rights and freedoms of others and of meeting the just requirements of morality, public order, and the general welfare in a democratic society" (Art. 29[2]).

The idea of rights accepts that some limitations on rights are permissible but the limitations are themselves strictly limited. Public emergency, national security, public order are weighty terms, bespeaking important societal interests, but they are not to be lightly or loosely invoked, and the conception of national security or public order cannot be so large as to swallow the right. Derogations are permitted only in time of a public emergency that threatens the life of the nation, not as a response to fears (warranted or paranoid) for other values, or for the security of a particular regime. Even in an authentic emergency, a society may derogate from rights only to the extent strictly required by the exigencies of the situation, and even such necessary derogations must not involve invidious inequalities, and may not derogate from basic rights: they must not invade the right to life, or involve torture or cruel, inhuman punishment, slavery or servitude, conviction of crime under ex post facto laws, denial of rights as a person before the law, or violate freedom of thought, conscience, or religion. Moreover, considerations of public emergency permitting derogations, or of national security or public order permitting limitations on certain rights, refer to a universal standard, monitored by external scrutiny and judgment.

In sum, the idea of human rights is that the individual counts—independent of and in addition to his or her part in the common good. Autonomy and liberty must be respected, and the individual's basic economic-social needs realized, as a matter of entitlement, not of grace or discretion (even by wise and benevolent authority, or even by "the people"). The individual has obligations to others and to the community, and society may ask all individuals to give up some of their rights for the rights of others and for the common good, but there is a core of individuality that cannot be invaded or sacrificed. And all individuals count equally. An individual's right can be sacrificed to another's right only when choice is inevitable, and only according to some principle of choice reflecting the comparative value of each right. No particular individual can be singled out for particular sacrifice, except at random or by some other "neutral principle," consistent with the spirit of equal protection of the laws.

I have referred to rights as claims *upon* society, not *against* society. In the ideology of rights, human rights are not "against society," against the interest of society; on the contrary, the good society is one in which individual rights flourish, and the promotion and protection of every individual's rights are a public good. There is an aura of conflict between individual and society only in that individual rights are asserted against government, against those who represent society officially, and because the human rights idea often requires that an individual's right be preferred to some other public good. But this apparent conflict between individual and society is specious; in the longer, deeper view, the society is better if the individual's rights are respected.

Human rights, as conceived by and specified in the Universal Declaration and other international instruments, are the rights of individuals. They include the individual's right to associate with others and to form groups of varying character for various purposes. The individual has the right to marry and create a family, to join a religious community and to pursue religious, cultural, or social activities with them, to identify with an ethnic or other group and to pursue their common interests, to join a political party or trade union. But the essential human rights idea addresses the rights of the individual, not of any group or collectivity.

Groups may have rights in domestic legal systems but, at least at its origin, the human rights movement did not address them. Later, the principal international human rights covenants declared the rights of "peoples" to self-determination and to sovereignty over their natural resources, but those provisions were an exceptional addition to the general conception in the covenants that human rights are claims of a person upon his or her own society.* There has been a movement to recognize other "generations of rights"—a right to peace, to development, to a healthy environment—but none of these has been incorporated into any legally binding human rights agreement.

1. THE FIRST TWO HUNDRED YEARS

Louis Henkin, *The Rights of Man Today*
3–13 (1988 Reprint of 1978 Ed.).
Origins and Antecedents

The conception of human rights as an individual's political-legal claims, implying limitations and obligations upon society and government, is a product of modern history. It reflects particular political theories and rejects others. Both the recent history and the prevailing theory reflect their antecedents.

---

* Western states resisted those provisions on the ground that they dealt with matters that were not individual rights.

The origins and ancestry of ideas are rarely single or simple, or readily disentangled. Many can claim patent to the ideas of human rights, with some warrant, yet all claims include some exaggeration, for the various elements of human rights have different ancestry, and attempts to correlate contemporary with ancient concepts court anachronism and other distortion. The Bible, for example, stressed not rights but duties—and these were essentially duties to God, although fellow man was the beneficiary of many of them. "Society" and "government" were not central conceptions in the life of a people governed by God through his prophets, judges, and others chosen, ordained, or anointed. (The people's desire for a king was decried as a rejection of God's kingship.) The "higher law," God's law, was in principle the only law. The individual had free will and freedom of choice; but he was, a priori, not autonomous but subject to God's law, and he was not to do "that which was right in his own eyes." On the other hand, the major religions, philosophies, and poetic traditions can surely claim some ideas and values central to human rights: right and wrong, good and evil; law, legality, and illegality, justice and fairness; the equal protection of the laws; the significance of individual man and the essential dignity and equality of men. In the Bible, justice is particularized in various precepts but is also prescribed generally, undefined but intuitive, and is required of God as of man. The equality and dignity of man are supported by the Genesis story of the common ancestor of mankind and by the fatherhood of God to all men. For the principle of limited, "constitutional" government—that there is a higher law binding on the governor as on the governed, and that man-made law is valid and to be respected only insofar as it is consistent with that higher law—we cite Sophocles's Antigone, the midwives resisting Pharaoh's order to kill all male Israelite babies, King Saul's servants refusing to kill the priests, or the story of Daniel.

Immediately, human rights derive from "natural rights" flowing from "natural law." The Stoics, Cicero, and their jurist successors did not perceive natural law as a higher law invalidating and justifying disobedience to man-made laws that did not measure up, but as a standard for making, developing, and interpreting law: law should be made and developed so that it will correspond to nature. Later the church christianized Roman ideas, rooted natural law in divine authority, and gave it the quality of highest law. Although some of this law was revealed, most of it was left to man to uncover and develop by his God-given "right reason."

Natural law theory emphasized duties imposed by God on every human society in an orderly cosmos. In time, society's duties came to be seen as natural rights for the individual. It was difficult, however, to fill early natural rights with agreed content, other, perhaps, than the rights of "conscience"—to worship the true God and to refuse to commit "unjust" acts.

Currents of natural law and natural rights run deep in human rights even today. Politically as well as intellectually, however, human rights today trace their authentic origins to seventeenth- and eighteenth-century concepts. Although no idea is nicely confined within dates, although each recent century saw variety in ideas, one might see human rights today as a kind of twentieth-century synthesis of an eighteenth-century thesis and a nineteenth-century antithesis.

The Eighteenth–Century Thesis

The American and French revolutions, and the declarations that expressed the principles that inspired them, took "natural rights" and made them secular, rational, universal, individual, democratic, and radical. For divine foundations for the rights of man they substituted (or perhaps only added) a social-contractual base. Consider these famous lines:

> We hold these truths to be self-evident, that all men are created equal, that they are endowed by their creator with certain unalienable rights, that among these are life, liberty and the pursuit of happiness. That to secure these rights, governments are instituted among men, deriving their just powers from the consent of the governed, that ... it is the right of the people ... to institute new government, laying its foundation on such principles, and organizing its power in such form, as to them shall seem most likely to effect their safety and happiness.

The Virginia Declaration of Rights begins:

> 1.   That all men are by nature equally free and independent, and have certain inherent rights, of which, when they enter into a state of society, they cannot, by any compact, deprive or divest their posterity; namely, the enjoyment of life and liberty, with the means of acquiring and possessing property, and pursuing and obtaining happiness and safety.
>
> 2.   That all power is vested in, and consequently derived from, the people; that magistrates are their trustees and servants, and at all times amenable to them.
>
> 3.   That government is, or ought to be, instituted for the common benefit, protection, and security of the people, nation, or community; of all the various modes and forms of government, that is best which is capable of producing the greatest degree of happiness and safety, and is most effectually secured against the danger of maladministration; and that, when any government shall be found inadequate or contrary to these purposes, a majority of the community hath an undubitable, inalienable, and indefeasible right to reform, alter, or abolish it, in such manner as shall be judged most conducive to the public weal.

The rights of man, it will be noted, are not (or not necessarily) divinely ordained, not (or not necessarily) divinely conceived: they are God's gift in that they result from his creation.* They are natural in the sense that

---

* The relation of these rights to God is ambiguous. In the American declaration, men are endowed with rights by their creator. That may mean what Paine meant when he referred to the "illuminating and divine principle of equal rights of man, (for it has its origin from the Maker of man)"; therefore, "all men are born equal, and with equal natural right." The French Declaration was made only "in the presence and under the auspices of the Supreme Being."

nature (and nature's God) created and inspired man's reason and judgment. They are natural in the sense that every man is born with them. They are natural also in a different sense, in that they are man's in the "state of nature," and he brings them with him into society. The individual was autonomous, sovereign, before government was established, and he, and other individuals taken together—"the people"—remain sovereign under any government, for their sovereignty is inalienable, and government is only by the consent of the governed. (The logical leap from autonomy of the individual to the sovereignty of the people and majority rule was not commonly noted or explained; presumably that was deemed implicit in the social compact.)

The people gave up some of their autonomy to government for limited purposes, retaining the rest as rights and freedoms under government. (Paine distinguished "that class of natural rights which man retains after entering society, and those which he throws into common stock as a member of society" because he cannot execute them by himself.) Rights originate with and are retained by the people; they are not granted to them.* "Society *grants* him nothing. Every man is a proprietor in society, and draws on the capital as a matter of right." Some rights, indeed, could not be subordinated to government even if the people wished, because these rights are inalienable.

Man retains rights against government in principle by virtue of his social contract, though that, we know, is a hypothetical construct, not a historical fact; a justification, not an explanation. In any particular society, the rights retained may be determined by "the people" in an actual contract with their government. In the United States, for example, we look for our rights in the people's contract with their governors, in the Constitution, which "We the people . . . ordain and establish."

Inevitably the rights retained are the preferred, contemporary values, though the founding fathers, and the people they represent, may deem and justify them as "natural," the inspiration of nature and of nature's God. Although in principle the people must retain those rights that are "inalienable," which rights are inalienable will be determined by what the people (or those who draft their constitutions) in fact decide to retain. Whatever the source from which rights draw their inspiration, then, in this view the authority for rights, and their content, are contractual.

The people, of course, may deem and justify their values as eternal and their rights as timeless, valid for their children's children as for themselves.

---

* Compare the Ninth Amendment to the United States Constitution: "The enumeration in the Constitution, of certain rights, shall not be construed to deny or disparage others retained by the people." Explicit provisions of the Bill of Rights also reflect the view that rights are not bestowed by the Constitution but are antecedent to it; the Bill of Rights only commands the government to respect those antecedent rights. E.g., "Congress shall make no law . . . abridging the freedom of speech, or of the press." "The right of the people to be secure . . . shall not be violated." Amendments I, IV. The Supreme Court has written of "implied reservations of individual rights, without which the social compact could not exist."

But in principle, surely, the autonomy and sovereignty of our ancestors did not include the right to impose their values on their descendants.[†] Later generations might decide that their ancestors improperly alienated the inalienable, or that they might delegate to their government new kinds of authority and new responsibilities and retain less autonomy for themselves. It was perhaps permissible for our ancestors to make the United States Constitution valid indefinitely, and even difficult to amend. But we are as autonomous as our ancestors, our reason is as right as theirs, and their own principles would warrant us in tearing up the Constitution and substituting our own terms with government, terms that would reflect our views of its proper purposes and retain the rights and liberties that we would not alienate.

The American fathers of rights were not legal philosophers. They were not troubled to debate against whom an individual has these rights, what duties they imply, and upon whom they fell. They did not ask whether they were only moral rights or also legal rights, and if the latter, under what system of law. They did not consider it relevant to indicate how such legal rights could be enforced. Presumably they saw these rights as implying duties of restraint upon their chosen governors, and some restraints might be mandated by the courts of law. We know they saw their rights as justifying "self-determination," independence from Great Britain. In principle "the people"—though not particular individuals—could vindicate their rights by revolution and reconstitution.

The Content of Eighteenth–Century Rights

The eighteenth-century birth date of human rights, of course, shaped their content. They were the rights that the wise men thought the people wished to retain, or thought they should retain and persuaded them to do so, the rights that reflected their views of the purposes of government and the desirable division of authority between government and individual. For these views, those who drafted the various declarations and constitutions and those—like Thomas Paine—who preached and propagated their principles drew principally on John Locke (perhaps filtered through Blackstone), Montesquieu, and Rousseau,* with perspective, detail, and emphasis from their own experience.

Locke gave us essential ideas out of English antecedents,** including probably those of the Levellers. Some go back to the hallowed Great

[†] Thomas Paine rejected Burke's notion that the people were bound by agreements made by their ancestors, whether with king or with parliament: "The vanity and presumption of governing beyond the grave, is the most ridiculous and insolent of all tyrannies."

* To Rousseau one might trace the view that men were created equal, that they were autonomous before they entered into society,

and that their submission to society is governed by the social contract.

** Although the eighteenth century drew immediately on the seventeenth, more or less authentic antecedents for the several doctrines reflected in the Declaration of Independence have been traced back to old sources. One author found the creation of government as a conscious act, and the social compact, in Protagoras and the Sophists (as

Charter, to Magna Carta, to what it was, perhaps more to what it was perceived, even misperceived, to be. Perhaps all that happened in 1215 at Runnymede was that some nobles stood up to King John, broke his autarchy, and exacted some concessions for themselves. Even that, obviously, was a limitation on monarchy and a seed of constitutionalism. Rights that the nobles obtained for themselves, later, slowly, spread to others: unknowing, the nobles laid the foundations for parliament. A perhaps innocent, incidental phrase in Magna Carta, providing that a freeman shall be punished only "by the lawful judgment of his peers or by the law of the land," came to establish the rule of law; later that became the "due process of law," with its luxuriant growth in U. S. constitutional jurisprudence. From subsequent components of the British constitution—the Petition of Rights (1628), the Agreement of the People (1647), the Bill of Rights (1688)—the eighteenth century developed representative government, expanded suffrage and increased protections for those whom authority accused of crime, and established some freedom of religion and some freedom from religious discrimination.

The rights of man were born in revolution, against Great Britain here, against the *ancien régime* in France. Inevitably they were political rights, and self-government and the consent to be governed were their essential character. To Thomas Paine, representative government was *the* human right: "*representative government is freedom.*" But the framers of rights were not content with democracy, even with representative government, for parliament, too, they had learned, could be despotic: "The accumulation of all powers, legislative, executive, and judiciary, in the same hands, whether of one, a few, or many, and whether hereditary, self-appointed, or elective, may justly be pronounced the very definition of tyranny." Hence the separation of powers and checks and balances that have remained our particular U.S. hallmark—not, Justice Brandeis reminded us, to promote efficiency, but to prevent tyranny. Our federalism, too, was a "vertical separation," which by dividing authority guarded against too much, too concentrated governmental power. And against any and all government the individual retains his other inviolable rights.*

Locke wrote of the rights of life, liberty, and property; the Declaration of Independence spoke of life, liberty, and the pursuit of happiness. (Locke sometimes spoke of property as including individual autonomy and it is not

reflected in Plato's *Republic*); government as based on the consent of the governed, and the right of revolution, in St. Augustine; natural, inalienable rights in Cicero and the Roman jurists Gaius and Ulpian; equality in the Stoics and in Wycliffe; and the combination of the various doctrines, as in the Declaration of Independence, in Nicholas of Cusa.

* Compare Mr. Justice Miller: "A government which recognized no such rights, which held the lives, the liberty, and the property of its citizens subject at all times to the absolute disposition and unlimited control of even the most democratic depository of power, is after all but a despotism. It is true it is a despotism of the many, of the majority, if you choose to call it so, but it is none the less a despotism. It may well be doubted if a man is to hold all that he is accustomed to call his own, all in which he has placed his happiness, and the security of which is essential to that happiness, under the unlimited dominion of others, whether it is not wiser that this power should be exercised by one man than by many."

implausible to argue that even when used more narrowly, *property* did not reflect narrow concern for the property of "men of property," but regarded rights to personal possessions and the fruits of one's labor as aspects of individuality and autonomy—and the pursuit of happiness?—for all.) The United States Constitution guaranteed neither of these formulas of rights, for the Constitution, as conceived, was not essentially a charter of rights and liberties, but a blueprint of government.** The Constitution, moreover, largely governed only the new federal government, which at our beginnings was not the principal government on these shores, but only a small superstructure on the governments of the states. It was the states that governed individual lives intimately, every day, and it is primarily to the states' constitutions and bills and declarations of rights that one must go to see what rights the people had. These, and those included later in the national Bill of Rights, contained the political rights we know—political freedom, security and privacy, rights for those accused of crime. They reflected an ideology of rights that implied original individual autonomy subject only to limited government for limited purposes.* Government, and every act of government, had to be justified. The individual was protected against his government; there was no suggestion that he could make claim on government to contribute to his economic and social welfare. The Constitution was ordained, inter alia, "to promote the general welfare," and Congress could lay and collect taxes to provide for "the general welfare." But neither the framers of the federal constitution nor those who established the governments of the states considered it to be a purpose of government to provide the citizen with food or work or social security. (Only the obligation to provide or promote education found its way early into some state constitutions.)

Note a glaring (and unhappy) omission. The original U.S. Constitution did not ordain equality. Some of the early state constitutions did declare the equality of all men, but such declarations had no normative significance. States that declared equality maintained slavery. (The Indians also enjoyed less than equality, although their situation was more ambiguous since in many respects they were autonomous and not part of U.S. society.)

** We tend to couple the Declaration and the Constitution in our national hagiography, but they are, of course, different in inspiration, purpose, tone, and character. The Declaration was a ringing manifesto heralding and justifying revolution; the Constitution was a blueprint of government. Perhaps all postrevolutionary constitutions are inherently "conservative," seeking to conserve and to establish what antecedent revolutions fought for, although ours has impressed many as strikingly removed from the spirit of 1776, responding to years of frustration with the difficulties of self-governance and hammered out in careful compromise. Originally, the Constitution did not even have a bill of rights because the framers thought it unnecessary, since the limited powers of the federal government would hardly impinge on the individual and his rights. The bill of rights was added by amendment under the new government, as promised, the price of ratification in several states.

* Compare Jefferson's First Inaugural Address: "Still one thing more, fellow citizens—a wise and frugal Government, which shall restrain men from injuring one another, shall leave them otherwise free to regulate their own pursuits of industry and improvement, and shall not take from the mouth of labor the bread it has earned. This is the sum of good government, and this is necessary to close the circle of our felicities."

There was not full equality even among freemen, between propertied and propertyless, between men and women, even in the measure we know today.

Note, on the other hand, what today might seem a striking but happy omission. A constitution ordained by the people to prescribe and limit their government does not provide for its suspension, or for government by decree even in emergency. It does not declare the people's duties or make their rights contingent on the performance of duties.

The French Legacy

Americans tend to think of human rights as their special gift to the world. Even if we include our English ancestors and cousins in that self-congratulation, it is egoistically blind at least by half. The eighteenth-century ideology of rights drew on French as well as English ideas, and the French Revolution and Declaration were probably more influential than ours in spreading them in many parts of the world. The French Declaration, moreover, articulated some ideas that were at best implicit with us, such as the presumption of innocence. It propagated also ideas more "advanced" than our own, some of which took long to reach and take root in the United States. "Liberty consists in the power to do anything that does not injure another." "The law has the right to forbid only such actions as are injurious to society." "All citizens ... are equally eligible to all public dignities, places and employments, according to their capacities and without other distinction than their virtues and their talents." Taxes should be "equally apportioned among all the citizens according to their means." And the French constitution of 1791 provided for public relief for the poor and free public education—"economic and social rights" unknown in early U.S. constitutions.

Notes

Henkin's essays were published in 1978 and 1990. Developments since then suggest postscripts:

1. Recent years have witnessed the strengthening of the women's rights movement and the emergence of a children's rights movement. Many believe that there is still far more to be done to establish gender equality and the rights of women. See Part III, Chapter 2(F). The international system is beginning to recognize children as human beings of young age, with their own rights, including rights independent of those of parents and family, even rights against abuse and neglect by parents and family.

2. The end of the Cold War and the break-up of the Soviet empire and the Soviet Union led to political convulsions that have made it difficult to contain issues of human rights within the framework of relations between the individual and his/her own state. These claims have given new urgency to developing norms and institutions focusing on issues of self-determination, minority and other group rights, and the rights of individuals as they

may be modified by their ethnic or religious identity. See Part III, Chapter 2(H).

3.   The movement to recognize additional rights has continued, including, notably, a legally binding "right to development," but, as of 1998, no international agreement on the right to development has come into effect. Part III, Chapter 2(I). Agreements on the environment are also under consideration, but it does not appear likely that they will soon include a legally binding individual right to a healthful environment.

4.   A Declaration on the Elimination of all Forms of Intolerance and of Discrimination Based on Religion or Belief was proclaimed by the UN General Assembly on 25 November 1981. As of 1998, it has not been converted into a legally-binding convention.

5.   In 1998, the Fiftieth Anniversary of the Universal Declaration was widely celebrated, confirming it as the "birth certificate" of contemporary human rights, and as the authoritative definition of the human rights idea. See *infra* Part III, Chapter 1. See, for example, The Universal Declaration of Human Rights: Fifty Years and Beyond (Y. Danieli, E. Stamatopoulou, and C. Dias eds., 1999).

For discussion of the theory of the Universal Declaration, see Part I, Chapter 2(B). For the significance of the Universal Declaration for the International Human Rights Movement and the development of the international law on human rights, and analysis of the rights declared, see Part III, Chapters 1 and 2(B).

2.   THE IDEA OF "RIGHTS": WESLEY HOHFELD

Behind the idea of human rights are, of course, the idea of rights and the ways in which that idea differs from, and relates to, other "jural relations." Professor Hohfeld, of Yale Law School, published the following in 1913. It has become a "classic."

Wesley Hohfeld, *Some Fundamental Legal Conceptions as Applied in Judicial Reasoning*

23 Yale L.J. 16, 28–32 (1913)

One of the greatest hindrances to the clear understanding, the incisive statement, and the true solution of legal problems frequently arises from the express or tacit assumption that all legal relations may be reduced to "rights" and "duties," and that these latter categories are therefore adequate for the purpose of analyzing even the most complex legal interests, such as trusts, options, escrows, "future" interests, corporate interests, etc. Even if the difficulty related merely to inadequacy and ambiguity of terminology, its seriousness would nevertheless be worthy of definite recognition and persistent effort toward improvement; for in any closely reasoned problem, whether legal or non-legal, chameleon-hued words are a peril both to clear thought and to lucid expression. As a matter of fact, however, the above mentioned inadequacy and ambiguity of terms unfortunately reflect, all too often, corresponding paucity and confusion as regards actual legal conceptions. That this is so may appear in some measure from the discussion to follow.

The strictly fundamental legal relations are after all, *sui generis*; and thus it is that attempts at formal definition are always unsatisfactory, if not altogether useless. Accordingly, the most promising line of procedure seems to consist in exhibiting all of the various relations in a scheme of "opposites" and "correlatives," and then proceeding to exemplify their individual scope and application in concrete cases. An effort will be made to pursue this method:

Jural Opposites	rights	privilege	power	immunity
	no-rights	duty	disability	liability
Jural Correlatives	right	privilege	power	immunity
	duty	no-right	liability	disability

Rights and Duties. As already intimated, the term "rights" tends to be used indiscriminately to cover what in a given case may be a privilege, a power, or an immunity, rather than a right in the strictest sense; and this looseness of usage is occasionally recognized by the authorities....

. . .

Recognizing, as we must, the very broad and indiscriminate use of the term, "right," what clue do we find, in ordinary legal discourse, toward limiting the word in question to a definite and appropriate meaning? That clue lies in the correlative "duty," for it is certain that even those who use the word and the conception "right" in the broadest possible way are accustomed to thinking of "duty" as the invariable correlative. As said in *Lake Shore & M. S. R. Co. v. Kurtz* [37 N.E. 303, 304 (Ind. App. 1894)]:

> "A duty or a legal obligation is that which one ought or ought not to do. 'Duty' and 'right' are correlative terms. When a right is invaded, a duty is violated."

In other words, if X has a right against Y that he shall stay off the former's land, the correlative (and equivalent) is that Y is under a duty toward X to stay off the place. If, as seems desirable, we should seek a synonym for the term "right" in this limited and proper meaning, perhaps the word "claim" would prove the best. The latter has the advantage of being a monosyllable....

Notes

1.   That a right implies a correlative duty is commonly accepted; can there be a duty without a right? In the example given *supra* p. 1, there is a duty to love thy neighbor; who has the right? God? In political ideologies that stress duties, any correlative right would presumably be indeterminate, a right of "the state," "society," "the people."

2.   In the idea of human rights, the insistence on a correlative duty is related to the desire to help realize the right, to ensure that it is enjoyed in fact and that remedies are available to give effect to the right or to compensate for its violation. See Henkin, *supra* p. 4. And see Note: Rights and Duties, *infra* p. 86.

3.   Jerome Shestack, in his summary of "The Philosophic Foundations of Human Rights," *infra* Part I, p. 79, seeks to apply Hohfeld to international human rights.

A.   THE WESTERN INDIVIDUAL RIGHTS TRADITION

Like some other concepts and terms that are prominent in characterizations of the international political system today—statehood, sovereignty, nationality, as well as popular sovereignty, democracy, constitutionalism—the idea of human rights grew in and out of "the West," out of a tradition that included the monotheistic religions, Greece and Rome, Europe and its political offspring. That is not to suggest that their contributions did not draw on other civilizations—Egyptian, Sumerian; or that ideas of justice and the good society were unknown in other traditions, for example in China, India and elsewhere in Asia. But it is difficult to identify notions of "rights" in what is known about relations between rulers and subjects, say, in Confucianism. See generally, Confucianism and Human Rights (de Bary and Tu Weiming eds., 1998). And it is difficult to find evidence of transcultural influence generally as contributing to the idea of human rights that grew in Western Europe in the Seventeenth and Eighteenth Centuries.

The Western origin of rights was a source of some political resentment after the end of colonialism and became a political issue towards the end of the Twentieth Century, leading, for example, to the invocation of "cultural relativism." "Asian values," in particular, were invoked to challenge the universality of rights. See Part I, Chapter 2(C). Even proponents of cultural relativism do not question the Western origins of human rights as a matter of intellectual and political history, or the Western prominence in bringing human rights and constitutionalism onto the world stage in the Twentieth Century. But they have insisted on the role of non-Western states in the development of the human rights idea in the second half of the Twentieth Century and their right to adapt it to their own culture and conditions.

1.   AUTHORITY SUBJECT TO LAW: MAGNA CARTA

The modern idea of human rights was conceived, born and developed in the Seventeenth and Eighteenth Centuries, in England and Europe. But some elements of the idea had earlier antecedents. In the English-speaking world, surely, the primary human rights document is *Magna Carta*—the Charter which a group of barons extracted from King John in 1215 at Runnymede.

Magna Carta (1215)

John, by the grace of God, king of England, lord of Ireland, duke of Normandy and Aquitaine, and count of Anjou, to the archbishops, bishops, abbots, earls, barons, justiciars, foresters, sheriffs, stewards, servants, and to all his bailiffs, and liege subjects, greeting. Know that, having regard to God and for the salvation our soul, and those of all our ancestors and heirs, and unto the honour of God and the advancement of holy Church, and for the reform of our realm, [we have granted as underwritten] by advice of our venerable fathers, Stephen, archbishop of Canterbury, primate of all England and cardinal of the holy Roman church, Henry, archbishop of Dublin, William of London, Peter of Winchester, Jocelyn of Bath and Glastonbury, Hugh of Lincoln, Walter of Worcester, William of Coventry, Benedict of Rochester, bishops; of master Pandulf, subdeacon and member of the household of our lord the Pope, of brother Aymeric, master of the Knights of the Temple in England, and of the illustrious men William Marshal, earl of Pembroke, William, earl of Salisbury, William, earl of Warenne, William, earl of Arundel, Alan of Galloway, constable of Scotland, Waren Fitz Gerald, Peter Fitz Herbert, Hubert de Burgh, seneschal of Poitou, Hugh de Neville, Matthew Fitz Herbert, Thomas Basset, Alan Basset, Philip d'Aubigny, Robert of Roppesley, John Marshal, John Fitz Hugh, and others, our liegemen.

1.   In the first place we have granted to God, and by this our present charter confirmed for us and our heirs for ever that the English church shall be free, and shall have her rights entire, and her liberties inviolate; and we will that it be thus observed; which is apparent from this that the freedom of elections, which is reckoned most important and very essential to the English church, we, of our pure and unconstrained will, did grant, and did by our charter confirm and did obtain the ratification of the same from our lord, Pope Innocent III, before the quarrel arose between us and our barons: and this we will observe, and our will is that it be observed in good faith by our heirs for ever. We have also granted to all freemen of our kingdom, for us and our heirs forever, all the underwritten liberties, to be had and held by them and their heirs, of us and our heirs forever.

. . .

7.   A widow, after the death of her husband, shall forthwith and without difficulty have her marriage portion and inheritance; nor shall she give anything for her dower, or for her marriage portion, or for the inheritance which her husband and she held on the day of the death of that husband; and she may remain in the house of her husband for forty days after his death, within which time her dower shall be assigned to her.

8.   No widow shall be compelled to marry, so long as she prefers to live without a husband; provided always that she gives security not to marry without our consent, if she holds of us, or without the consent of the lord of whom she holds, if she holds of another.

9.   Neither we nor our bailiffs shall seize any land or rent for any debt, so long as the chattels of the debtor are sufficient to repay the debt;

nor shall the sureties of the debtor be distrained so long as the principal debtor is able to satisfy the debt; and if the principal debtor shall fail to pay the debt, having nothing wherewith to pay it, then the sureties shall answer for the debt; and let them have the lands and rents of the debtor, if they desire them, until they are indemnified for the debt which they have paid for him, unless the principal debtor can show proof that he is discharged thereof as against the said sureties.

10.   If anyone who has borrowed a sum of money from Jews dies before the debt has been repaid, his heir shall pay no interest on the debt for so long as he remains under age, irrespective of whom he holds his lands. If such a debt falls into the hands of the Crown, it will take nothing except the principal sum specified in the bond.

11.   If a man dies owing money to Jews, his wife may have her dower and pay nothing towards the debt from it. If he leaves children that are under age, their needs may also be provided for on a scale appropriate to the size of his holding of lands. The debt is to be paid out of the residue, reserving the service due to his feudal lords. Debts owed to persons other than Jews are to be dealt with similarly.

12.   No scutage nor aid shall be imposed on our kingdom, unless by common counsel of our kingdom, except for ransoming our person, for making our eldest son a knight, and for once marrying our eldest daughter; and for these there shall not be levied more than a reasonable aid. In like manner it shall be done concerning aids from the city of London.

. . .

20.   A freeman shall not be amerced for a slight offence, except in accordance with the degree of the offence; and for a grave offense he shall be amerced in accordance with the gravity of the offense, yet saving always his "contenement" and a merchant in the same way, saving his "merchandise", and a villein shall be amerced in the same way, saving his "wainage"—if they have fallen into our mercy: and none of the aforesaid amercements shall be imposed except by the oath of honest men of the neighbourhood.

21.   Earls and barons shall not be amerced except through their peers, and only in accordance with the degree of the offense.

. . .

28.   No constable or other bailiff of ours shall take corn or other provisions from anyone without immediately tendering money therefor, unless he can have postponement thereof by permission of the seller.

29.   No constable shall compel any knight to give money in lieu of castle guard, when he is willing to perform it in his own person, or if he himself cannot do it from any reasonable cause then by another responsible man. Further, if we have led or sent him upon military service, he shall be relieved from guard in proportion to the time during which he has been on service because of us.

30. No sheriff or bailiff of ours, or other person, shall take the horses or cars of any freeman for transport duty, against the will of the said freeman.

31. Neither we nor our bailiffs shall take, for our castles or for any other work of ours, wood which is not ours, against the will of the owner of that wood.

32. We will not retain beyond one year and one day, the lands of those who have been convicted of felony, and the lands shall thereafter be handed over to the lords of the fiefs.

. . .

34. The writ which is called *praecipe* shall not for the future be issued to anyone, regarding any tenement whereby a freeman may lose his court.

. . .

38. No bailiff for the future shall, upon his own unsupported complaint, put anyone to his "law," without credible witnesses brought for this purpose.

39. No freeman shall be taken or [and] imprisoned or disseised or exiled or in any way destroyed, nor will we go upon him or send upon him, except by the lawful judgment of his peers or [and] by the law of the land.

40. To no one will we sell, to no one will we refuse or delay, right or justice.

. . .

42. It shall be lawful in future for anyone excepting always those imprisoned or outlawed in accordance with the law of the kingdom, and natives of any country at war with us, and merchants, who shall be treated as is above provided to leave our kingdom and to return, safe and secure by land and water, except for a short period in time of war, on grounds of public policy—reserving always the allegiance due to us.

. . .

46. All barons who have founded abbeys, concerning which they hold charters from the kings of England, or of which they have long-continued possession, shall have the wardship of them, when vacant, as they ought to have.

47. All forests that have been made such in our time shall forthwith be disafforested; and a similar course shall be followed with regard to river-banks that have been placed "in defence" by us in our time.

48. All evil customs connected with forests and warrens, foresters and warreners, sheriffs and their officers, river-banks and their wardens, shall immediately be inquired into in each county by twelve sworn knights of the same county chosen by the honest men of the same county, and shall, within forty days of the said inquest, be utterly abolished, so as never to be

restored, provided always that we previously have intimation thereof, or our justiciar, if we should not be in England.

49.   We will immediately restore all hostages and charters delivered to us by Englishmen, as sureties of the peace or of faithful service.

. . .

52.   If anyone has been dispossessed or removed by us, without the legal judgment of his peers, from his lands, castles, franchises, or from his right, we will immediately restore them to him; and if a dispute arise over this, then let it be decided by the five-and-twenty barons of whom mention is made below in the clause for securing the peace. Moreover, for all those possessions, from which anyone has, without the lawful judgment of his peers, been disseised or removed, by our father, King Henry, or by our brother, King Richard, and which we retain in our hand or which are possessed by others, to whom we are bound to warrant them, we shall have respite until the usual term of crusaders; excepting those things about which a plea has been raised, or an inquest made by our order, before our taking of the cross; but as soon as we return from our expedition or if perchance we desist from the expedition we will immediately grant full justice therein.

. . .

54.   No one shall be arrested or imprisoned upon the appeal of a woman, for the death of any other than her husband.

55.   All fines made with us unjustly and against the law of the land, and all amercements imposed unjustly and against the law of the land, shall be entirely remitted, or else it shall be done concerning them according to the decision of the five-and-twenty barons of whom mention is made below in the clause for securing the peace, or according to the judgment of the majority of the same, along with the aforesaid Stephen, archbishop of Canterbury, if he can be present, and such others as he may wish to bring with him for this purpose, and if he cannot be present the business shall nevertheless proceed without him, provided always that if any one or more of the aforesaid five-and-twenty barons are in a similar suit, they shall be removed as far as concerns this particular judgment, others being substituted in their places after having been selected by the rest of the same five-and-twenty for this purpose only, and after having been sworn.

. . .

61.   Since, moreover, for God and the amendment of our kingdom and for the better allaying of the quarrel that has arisen between us and our barons, we have granted all these concessions desirous that they should enjoy them in complete and firm endurance for ever, we give and grant to them the underwritten security, namely that the barons choose five-and-twenty barons of the kingdom, whosoever they will, who shall be bound with all their might, to observe and hold, and cause to be observed, the peace and liberties we have granted and confirmed to them by this our

present Charter, so that if we, or our justiciar, or our bailiffs, or any of our officers, shall in anything be at fault towards any one, or shall have broken any one of the articles of the peace or of this security, and the offence be notified to four barons of the foresaid five-and-twenty, the said four barons shall repair to us or our justiciar, if we are out of the realm, and, laying the transgression before us, petition to have that transgression redressed without delay. And if we shall not have corrected the transgression or, in the event of our being out of the realm, if our justiciar shall not have corrected it within forty days, reckoning from the time it has been intimated to us or to our justiciar, if we should be out of the realm, the four barons aforesaid shall refer that matter to the rest of the five-and-twenty barons, and those five-and-twenty barons shall, together with the community of the whole land, distrain and distress us in all possible ways, namely, by seizing our castles, lands, possessions, and in any other way they can, until redress has been obtained as they deem fit, saving harmless our own person, and the persons of our queen and children; and when redress has been obtained, they shall resume their old relations towards us. And let whoever in the country desires it, swear to obey the orders of the said five-and-twenty barons for the execution of all the aforesaid matters, and along with them, to molest us to the utmost of his power, and we publicly and freely grant leave to every one who wishes to swear, and we shall never forbid any one to swear. All those, moreover, in the land who of themselves and of their own accord are unwilling to swear to the twenty-five to help them in constraining and molesting us, we shall by our command compel the same to swear to the effect foresaid. And if any one of the five-and-twenty barons shall have died or departed from the land, or be incapacitated in any other manner which would prevent the foresaid provisions being carried out, those of the said twenty-five barons who are left shall choose another in his place according to their own judgment, and he shall be sworn in the same way as the others. Further, in all matters, the execution of which is entrusted to these twenty-five barons, if perchance these twenty-five are present and disagree about anything, or if some of them, after being summoned, are unwilling or unable to be present, that which the majority of those present ordain or command shall be held as fixed and established exactly as if the whole twenty-five had concurred in this; and the said twenty-five shall swear that they will faithfully observe all that is aforesaid, and cause it to be observed with all their might. And we shall procure nothing from any one, directly or indirectly, whereby any part of these concessions and liberties might be revoked or diminished; and if any such thing has been procured, let it be void and null, and we shall never use it personally or by another.

· · ·

63.   Wherefore it is our will, and we firmly enjoin, that the English Church be free, and that the men in our kingdom have and hold all the aforesaid, liberties, rights, and concessions, well and peaceably, freely and quietly, fully and wholly, for themselves and their heirs, of us and our heirs, in all respects and in all places for ever, as is aforesaid. An oath,

moreover, has been taken, as well on our part as on the part of the barons, that all these conditions aforesaid shall be kept in good faith and without evil intent. Given under our hand—the above-named and many others being witnesses—in the meadow which is called Runnymede, between Windsor and Staines, on the fifteenth day of June, in the seventeenth year of our reign.

Notes

Does *Magna Carta* deserve its repute as a founding instrument of human rights? It reflects no ideology, it is argued, only a struggle for power between king and nobles who contract to resolve that struggle. It recognizes the rights of nobles and some rights of others, but it is hardly a universalist document applicable to all human beings everywhere, or even a charter of liberties for all the inhabitants of England. Champions of the great Charter, however, honor it as a limitation on monarchy and therefore as a necessary step in the development of an ideology of individual rights. *Magna Carta* has also been seen as a step toward representative government and democracy, an important element in the human rights ideology. Some have suggested that the significance of *Magna Carta* is less in what it provided than in how it was later perceived and in what it came to represent. Laying the foundation for a broad conception of rights, *Magna Carta* also fed the common law, which became the expression and implementation of the rights of Englishmen. See Blackstone Part I, infra p. 28.

Magna Carta is credited with contributing to the establishment of a right to a jury trial ("the lawful judgment of his peers"), *habeas corpus*, and a right to due process of law. (Compare paragraph 39.) One can also plausibly trace to *Magna Carta* rights of property, freedom of religion, some rights for women, rights to the equal protection of the laws, freedom from cruel and unusual punishment, and even an embryonic judicial review. (Compare paragraph 61.)

2.   NATURAL RIGHTS AND THE SOCIAL CONTRACT: JOHN LOCKE

In addition to developing rights for Englishmen following *Magna Carta*, through the common law, England contributed to the ideology of human rights through the writings of John Locke in the Seventeenth Century and Thomas Paine in the Eighteenth Century.

John Locke, an English political philosopher, is commonly recognized as the father of human rights. One can trace the development of the human rights idea from Locke through the common law; the growth of "the liberties of Englishmen," as summarized in Blackstone; and the idea of rights articulated in the American Declaration of Independence, and in American bills of rights. See Part II, Chapter 1(A).

Locke here introduces the concept of "the state of nature," before society, as well as "the law of nature," the principle of equality, and the development of political society by a "social contract." That term was spread and popularized later by Jean–Jacques Rousseau who made it the title of his book. See Part I, Chapter 1(B). But, for the idea of human rights, the differences between Locke's conception and Rousseau's may be greater than the similarities between them.

John Locke, *The Second Treatise of Civil Government*

§§ 4, 14, 87–89, 95, 135–38, 228–29 (1690).

4.   To understand political power aright, and derive it from its original, we must consider what state all men are naturally in, and that is a state of perfect freedom to order their actions and dispose of their possessions and persons as they think fit, within the bounds of the law of nature, without asking leave, or depending upon the will of any other man.

A state also of equality, wherein all the power and jurisdiction is reciprocal, no one having more than another; there being nothing more evident than that creatures of the same species and rank, promiscuously born to all the same advantages of nature, and the use of the same faculties, should also be equal one amongst another without subordination or subjection, unless the Lord and Master of them all should by any manifest declaration of His will set one above another, and confer on him by an evident and clear appointment an undoubted right to dominion and sovereignty.

· · ·

14.   'Tis often asked as a mighty objection, Where are, or ever were there, any men in such a state of nature? To which it may suffice as an answer at present: That since all princes and rulers of independent governments all through the world are in a state of nature, 'tis plain the world never was, nor ever will be, without numbers of men in that state. I have named all governors of independent communities, whether they are or are not in league with others. For 'tis not every compact that puts an end to the state of nature between men, but only this one of agreeing together mutually to enter into one community, and make one body politic; other promises and compacts men may make one with another, and yet still be in the state of nature. The promises and bargains for truck, etc., between the two men in Soldania, in or between a Swiss and an Indian, in the woods of America, are binding to them, though they are perfectly in a state of nature in reference to one another. For truth and keeping of faith belong to men as men, and not as members of society.

· · ·

87.   Man being born, as has been proved, with a title to perfect freedom and uncontrolled enjoyment of all the rights and privileges of the law of nature equally with any other man or number of men in the world, has by nature a power not only to preserve his property—that is, his life, liberty, and estate—against the injuries and attempts of other men, but to judge of and punish the breaches of that law in others as he is persuaded

the offense deserves, even with death itself in crimes where the heinous-
ness of the fact in his opinion requires it. But because no political society
can be, nor subsist, without having in itself the power to preserve the
property and, in order thereunto, punish the offenses of all those of that
society, there and there only is political society where every one of the
members has quitted his natural power, resigned it up into the hands of the
community in all cases that exclude him not from appealing for protection
to the law established by it. And thus all private judgment of every
particular member being excluded, the community comes to be umpire by
settled standing rules, indifferent and the same to all parties; and by men
having authority from the community for the execution of those rules
decides all the differences that may happen between any members of that
society concerning any matter of right; and punishes those offenses which
any member has committed against the society, with such penalties as the
law has established; whereby it is easy to discern who are, and who are not,
in political society together. Those who are united into one body, and have
a common established law and judicature to appeal to, with authority to
decide controversies between them, and punish offenders, are in civil
society one with another; but those who have no such common appeal, I
mean on earth, are still in the state of nature, each being, where there is no
other, judge for himself, and executioner, which is, as I have before shown
it, the perfect state of nature.

88.   And thus the commonwealth comes by a power to set down what
punishment shall belong to the several transgressions which they think
worthy of it, committed among the members of that society (which is the
power of making laws) as well as it has the power to punish any injury
done unto any of its members, by anyone that is not of it (which is the
power of war and peace): and all this for the preservation of the property of
all the members of that society as far as is possible. But though every man
who has entered into civil society, and is become a member of any
commonwealth, has thereby quitted his power to punish offenses against
the law of nature, in prosecution of his own private judgment; yet, with the
judgment of offenses, which he has given up to the legislative in all cases,
where he can appeal to the magistrate, he has given a right to the
commonwealth to employ his force for the execution of the judgments of
the commonwealth, whenever he shall be called to it; which, indeed, are his
own judgments, they being made by himself or his representative. And
herein we have the original of the legislative and executive power of civil
society, which is to judge by standing laws how far offenses are to be
punished when committed within the commonwealth, and also to determine, by occasional judgments founded on the present circumstances of the
fact, how far injuries from without are to be vindicated; and in both these
to employ all the force of all the members, when there shall be need.

89.   Whenever, therefore, any number of men are so united into one
society, as to quit every one his executive power of the law of nature, and to
resign it to the public, there and there only is a political or civil society.
And this is done wherever any number of men, in the state of nature, enter
into society to make one people, one body politic, under one supreme

government; or else when any one joins himself to, and incorporates with, any government already made; for hereby he authorizes the society or, which is all one, the legislative thereof, to make laws for him, as the public good of the society shall require, to the execution whereof his own assistance (as to his own decrees) is due. And this puts men out of a state of nature into that of a commonwealth by setting up a judge on earth, with authority to determine all the controversies, and redress the injuries that may happen to any member of the commonwealth; which judge is the legislative, or magistrate appointed by it. And wherever there are any number of men, however associated, that have no such decisive power to appeal to, there they are still in the state of nature.

. . .

95. Men, being, as has been said, by nature all free, equal, and independent, no one can be put out of this estate and subjected to the political power of another without his own consent. The only way whereby anyone divests himself of his natural liberty and puts on the bonds of civil society is by agreeing with other men to join and unite into a community for their comfortable, safe, and peaceable living one among another, in a secure enjoyment of their properties and a greater security against any that are not of it. This any number of men may do, because it injures not the freedom of the rest; they are left as they were in the liberty of the state of nature. When any number of men have so consented to make one community or government, they are thereby presently incorporated and make one body politic wherein the majority have a right to act and conclude the rest.

. . .

135. Though the legislative, whether placed in one or more, whether it be always in being, or only by intervals, though it be the supreme power in every commonwealth; yet:

First, it is not, nor can possibly be absolutely arbitrary over the lives and fortunes of the people, for it being but the joint power of every member of the society given up to that person or assembly which is legislator, it can be no more than those persons had in a state of nature before they entered into society and gave up to the community; for nobody can transfer to another more power than he has in himself, and nobody has an absolute arbitrary power over himself, or over any other, to destroy his own life, or take away the life or property of another. A man, as has been proved, cannot subject himself to the arbitrary power of another; and having in the state of nature no arbitrary power over the life, liberty, or possession of another, but only so much as the law of nature gave him for the preservation of himself and the rest of mankind, this is all he does or can give up to the commonwealth, and by it to the legislative power, so that the legislative can have no more than this. Their power, in the utmost bounds of it, is limited to the public good of the society. It is a power that has no other end but preservation, and therefore can never have a right to destroy, enslave, or designedly to impoverish the subjects. The obligations of the law of nature cease not in society but only in many cases are drawn closer and have by human laws known penalties annexed to them to enforce their observation. Thus the law of nature stands as an eternal rule to all men, legislators as well as others. The rules that they make for other men's actions must, as well as their own and other men's actions be conformable to the law of nature, i.e., to the will of God, of which that is a declaration, and the fundamental law of nature being the preservation of mankind, no human sanction can be good or valid against it.

136. *Secondly*, the legislative or supreme authority cannot assume to itself a power to rule by extemporary, arbitrary decrees, but is bound to dispense justice, and to decide the rights of the subject by promulgated, standing laws, and known authorized judges. For the law of nature being unwritten, and so nowhere to be found but in the minds of men, they who through passion or interest shall mis-cite or misapply it, cannot so easily be convinced of their mistake where there is no established judge; and so it serves not, as it ought, to determine the rights and fence the properties of those that live under it, especially where everyone is judge, interpreter, and executioner of it too, and that in his own case; and he that has right on his side, having ordinarily but his own single strength, has not force enough to defend himself from injuries or to punish delinquents. To avoid these inconveniences which disorder men's properties in the state of nature, men unite into societies that they may have the united strength of the whole society to secure and defend their properties, and may have standing rules to bound it by which everyone may know what is his. To this end it is that men give up all their natural power to the society which they enter into, and the community put the legislative power into such hands as they think fit with this trust, that they shall be governed by declared laws, or else their peace, quiet, and property will still be at the same uncertainty as it was in the state of nature.

137. Absolute arbitrary power or governing without settled standing laws can neither of them consist with the ends of society and government which men would not quit the freedom of the state of nature for, and tie themselves up under, were it not to preserve their lives, liberties, and fortunes, and by stated rules of right and property to secure their peace and quiet. It cannot be supposed that they should intend, had they power so to do, to give to any one, or more, an absolute arbitrary power over their persons and estates, and put a force into the magistrate's hand to execute his unlimited will arbitrarily upon them. This were to put themselves into a worse condition than the state of nature, wherein they had a liberty to defend their right against the injuries of others, and were upon equal terms of force to maintain it, whether invaded by a single man or many in combination. Whereas, by supposing they have given up themselves to the absolute arbitrary power and will of a legislator, they have disarmed themselves, and armed him, to make a prey of them when he please; he being in a much worse condition who is exposed to the arbitrary power of one man, who has the command of 100,000, than he that is exposed to the arbitrary power of 100,000 single men, nobody being secure that his will, who has such a command, is better than that of other men, though his force be 100,000 times stronger. And therefore, whatever form the com-

monwealth is under, the ruling power ought to govern by declared and received laws and not by extemporary dictates and undetermined resolutions; for then mankind will be in a far worse condition than in the state of nature if they shall have armed one or a few men with the joint power of a multitude, to force them to obey at pleasure the exorbitant and unlimited decrees of their sudden thoughts, or unrestrained, and till that moment unknown wills, without having any measures set down which may guide and justify their actions. For all the power the government has being only for the good of the society, as it ought not to be arbitrary and at pleasure, so it ought to be exercised by established and promulgated laws; that both the people may know their duty and be safe and secure within the limits of the law; and the rulers, too, kept within their bounds, and not be tempted by the power they have in their hands to employ it to such purposes and by such measures as they would not have known, and own not willingly.

138. *Thirdly*, the supreme power cannot take from any man part of his property without his own consent; for the preservation of property being the end of government, and that for which men enter into society, it necessarily supposes and requires, that the people should have property; without which they must be supposed to lose that, by entering into society, which was the end for which they entered into it—too gross an absurdity for any man to own.

. . .

228. But if they who say "it lays a foundation for rebellion" mean that it may occasion civil wars or intestine broils, to tell the people they are absolved from obedience when illegal attempts are made upon their liberties or properties, and may oppose the unlawful violence of those who were their magistrates when they invade their properties contrary to the trust put in them, and that therefore this doctrine is not to be allowed, being so destructive to the peace of the world; they may as well say, upon the same ground, that honest men may not oppose robbers or pirates because this may occasion disorder or bloodshed. If any mischief come in such cases, it is not to be charged upon him who defends his own right, but on him that invades his neighbor's. If the innocent honest man must quietly quit all he has, for peace's sake, to him who will lay violent hands upon it, I desire it may be considered, what a kind of peace there will be in the world, which consists only in violence and rapine, and which is to be maintained only for the benefit of robbers and oppressors. Who would not think it an admirable peace betwixt the mighty and the mean when the lamb without resistance yielded his throat to be torn by the imperious wolf? Polyphemus' den gives us a perfect pattern of such a peace and such a government, wherein Ulysses and his companions had nothing to do but quietly to suffer themselves to be devoured. And no doubt Ulysses, who was a prudent man, preached up passive obedience, and exhorted them to a quiet submission by representing to them of what concernment peace was to mankind, and by showing the inconveniences which might happen if they should offer to resist Polyphemus, who had now the power over them.

229. The end of government is the good of mankind. And which is best for mankind: that the people should be always exposed to the boundless will of tyranny, or that the rulers should be sometimes liable to be opposed when they grow exorbitant in the use of their power and employ it for the destruction and not the preservation of the properties of their people?

Notes

Contrast Locke's theory of natural law and the social contract with an address to Parliament by James I:

> The monarchical state is the most supreme on earth, for kings are not only God's lieutenants on earth and sit upon God's throne, but are called gods even by God himself.... Kings are justly called gods, because they exercise a manner or resemblance of divine power on earth, for if you consider the attributes of God, you will see how they are found in the person of a king.... Now a father of a family may dispose of his inheritance to his children at his pleasure.... He may make them beggars or rich at his pleasure. He can restrain them, or banish them from his presence if he finds them offensive, or he may restore them to favor again like penitent sinners: so may the King deal with his subjects....

James I, *Address to Parliament*, reprinted in Human Rights in Western Civilization 1600–Present 17 (John A. Maxwell & James J. Friedberg eds., 2d ed. 1994).

3.   RIGHTS AND THE COMMON LAW

Magna Carta had launched embryonic rights for Englishmen, rights protected by the laws of England, but Locke declared a theory of universal rights for mankind, everywhere, at all times. By the Eighteenth Century, these rights of all mankind, "in most other countries of the world being now more or less debased and destroyed, they at present may be said to remain, in a peculiar and emphatical manner, the rights of the people of England," protected by the laws of England.

The "restatement" of the common law, authoritative in England and in the United States, was Blackstone's Commentaries.

William Blackstone, *Commentaries on the Laws of England*

Book 1, Chapter 1 (1769).

. . .

Thus much for the *declaration* of our rights and liberties. The rights themselves thus defined by these several statutes, conflict in a number of private immunities; which will appear, from what has been premised, to be indeed no other, than either that *residuum* of natural liberty, which is not required by the laws of society to be sacrificed to the public convenience; or else those civil privileges, which society hath engaged to provide, in lieu of the natural liberties so given up by individuals. These therefore were formerly, either by inheritance or purchase, the rights of all mankind; but, in most other countries of the world being now more or less debased and destroyed, they at present may be said to remain, in a peculiar and emphatical manner, the rights of the people of England. And these may be reduced to three principal or primary articles; the right of personal security, the right of personal liberty; and the right of private property: because as there is no other known method of compulsion, or of abridging man's natural free will, but by an infringement or diminution of one or other of these important rights, the preservation of these, inviolate, may justly be said to include the preservation of our civil immunities in their largest and most extensive sense.

. . .

In these several articles consist the rights, or, as they are frequently termed, the liberties of Englishmen: liberties more generally talked of, than thoroughly understood; and yet highly necessary to be perfectly known and considered by every man of rank or property, lest his ignorance of the points whereon it is founded should hurry him into faction and licentiousness on the one hand, or a pusillanimous indifference and criminal submission on the other. And we have seen that these rights consist, primarily, in the free enjoyment of personal security, of personal liberty, and of private property. So long as these remain inviolate, the subject is perfectly free; for every species of compulsive tyranny and oppression must act in opposition to one or other of these rights, having no other object upon which it can possibly be employed. To preserve these from violation, it is necessary that the constitution of parliaments be supported in its full vigor; and limits certainly known, be set to the royal prerogative. And, lastly, to vindicate these rights, when actually violated or attacked, the subjects of England are entitled, in the first place, to the regular administration and free course of justice in the courts of law; next to the right of petitioning the king and parliament for redress of grievances; and lastly to the right of having and using arms for self-preservation and defence. And all these rights and liberties it is our birthright to enjoy entire; unless where the laws of our country have laid them under necessary restraints. Restraints in themselves so gentle and moderate, as will appear upon farther enquiry, that no man of sense or probity would wish to see them slackened. For all of us have it in our choice to do every thing that a good man would desire to do; and are restrained from nothing, but what would be pernicious either to ourselves or our fellow citizens. So that this review of our situation may fully justify the observation of a learned French author, who indeed generally both thought and wrote in the spirit of genuine freedom; and who hath not scrupled to profess, even in the very bosom of his native country, that the English is the only nation in the world, where political or civil liberty is the direct end of its constitution. Recommending therefore to the student in our laws a farther and more accurate search into this extensive and important title, I shall close my remarks upon it with the expiring wish of the famous father Paul to his country, "ESTO PERPETUA!"

Notes

For Blackstone's elaboration of these rights at common law, see Part II, Chapter 1(A). For a perspective on rights at common law in the United States, see Thomas M. Cooley, A Treatise on the Law of Torts (1879).

4.   INALIENABLE RIGHTS AND THE PURPOSES OF GOVERNMENT

The American colonies valued their rights as British subjects, as protected by the common law. See Burke, *infra* section C. But the American Declaration of Independence and the early bills of rights of the American States returned to Locke and universal human rights. In time, after the American Revolution, rights came to be protected in America by the common law which the States maintained, by State constitutions and State laws, and later, and above all, by the U.S. Constitution and its Bill of Rights as supplemented by U.S. federal law. See Part II, Chapter 1(A).

An eloquent, famous expression of John Locke's theory is Thomas Jefferson's in the American Declaration of Independence. The idea of rights in the Declaration of Independence had been expressed a few weeks earlier in the Virginia Bill of Rights, *infra* Part II, Chapter 1(A); both instruments influenced the French Declaration of the Rights of Man and of the Citizen, *infra* p. 32.

The American Declaration of Independence (1776)

When, in the course of human events, it becomes necessary for one people to dissolve the political bands which have connected them with another, and to assume among the Powers of the earth, the separate and equal station to which the Laws of Nature and of Nature's God entitle them, a decent respect to the opinions of mankind requires that they should declare the causes which impel them to the separation.

We hold these truths to be self-evident, that all men are created equal, that they are endowed by their Creator with certain unalienable Rights, that among these are Life, Liberty and the pursuit of Happiness. That to secure these rights, Governments are instituted among Men, deriving their just powers from the consent of the governed. That whenever any Form of Government becomes destructive of these ends, it is the Right of the People to alter or to abolish it, and to institute new Government, laying its foundation on such principles and organizing its powers in such form, as to them shall seem most likely to effect their Safety and Happiness.

. . .

We, therefore, the Representatives of the United States of America, in General Congress, Assembled, appealing to the Supreme Judge of the world for the rectitude of our intentions, do, in the Name, and by Authority of the good People of these Colonies, solemnly publish and declare, That these United Colonies are, and of Right ought to be Free and Independent States; that they are Absolved from all Allegiance to the British Crown, and that all political connection between them and the State of Great Britain, is and ought to be totally dissolved; and that as Free and Independent States, they have full Power to levy War, conclude Peace, contract Alliances, establish Commerce, and to do all other Acts and Things, which Independent States may of right do. And for the support of this Declaration, with a firm reliance on the Protection of Divine Providence, we mutually pledge to each other our Lives, our Fortunes and our sacred Honor.

Notes

Locke wrote of man's "natural right" to preserve his "property—that is, his life, liberty, and estate." Jefferson highlighted inalienable rights to life, liberty, and the pursuit of happiness. Is the difference between Locke and Jefferson significant? Is Locke's conception of property broader than that later reflected in the Fifth Amendment to the U.S. Constitution? What does "pursuit of happiness" add to "liberty" in Jefferson's formula? Is the right to property included in the pursuit of happiness? Did Jefferson omit property, perhaps, because for him it was not a right in the state of nature before political society, but a right dependent on (if not granted by) society? Or was property omitted not on theoretical grounds, but as an act of political compromise lest a reference to "property" be construed to affirm the rights of slaveholders?

5.   THE FRENCH DECLARATION OF RIGHTS

It is reported that the Marquis de Lafayette, leaving the American colonies after contributing to their victory in the War of Independence, brought with him to France a copy of the Virginia Bill of Rights, the predecessor and close kin of the American Declaration of Independence.

The Declaration of the Rights of Man and of the Citizen was proclaimed by the French National Assembly in 1789 and was prefixed to the French Constitution of 1791. With the end of the French Revolution and the rise of Napoleon, the Declaration of 1791 ceased to have legal or constitutional character, though it remained part of French hagiography. It was revived and given constitutional character by reference in the constitutions of France following the Second World War. See the Preambles to the French Constitutions of 1946 and 1958.

Lord Acton, the British historian, is reported to have said that "the single confused page of the French Declaration outweighs libraries and is stronger than all the armies of Napoleon." See Hersch Lauterpacht, International Law and Human Rights 126 (1950).

Compare, for their character and content, the French Declaration with the Virginia Bill of Rights (Part II, Chapter 1(A)), with the American

Declaration of Independence, and with the U.S. Bill of Rights (Part II, Chapter 1(C)).

*The Declaration of the Rights of Man and of the Citizen (1789)**

The Representatives of the French people, formed into a National Assembly, considering that ignorance, neglect, or contempt of the rights of man are the sole causes of public misfortunes and the corruption of governments, have resolved to set forth, in a solemn declaration, these natural, inalienable and sacred rights of man, to the end that this declaration, being constantly before the members of the body social, may serve as a constant reminder of their rights and duties; to the end that the acts of the legislative power and those of the executive power, being susceptible of being at any moment compared with the end of every political institution, may be more respected; to the end that the future claims of the citizens, founded henceforth upon simple and incontestable principles, may always tend to the maintenance of the Constitution, and the general happiness.

For these reasons, the National Assembly recognizes and declares, in the presence and under the auspices of the Supreme Being, the following rights of Man and of the Citizen:

I.   Men are born and remain free and equal in respect of their rights (*en droit*). Social distinctions, therefore, may be founded only on common utility.

II.   The end of every political association is the preservation of the natural and imprescriptible rights of man. These rights are liberty, property, security and resistance to oppression.

III.   The principle of all sovereignty resides essentially in the Nation. No body and no individual may exercise authority which does not derive expressly therefrom.

IV.   Liberty consists in being able to do anything which does not injure another: therefore, the exercise of the natural rights of each man has no limits other than those which assure to the other members of society the enjoyment of these same rights. These limits may be determined only by the law (*loi*).

V.   The law may prohibit only those actions which are harmful to society. What is not prohibited by the law may not be prevented; and no one may be compelled to do what is not required by law.

VI.   The law is an expression of the general will. All the citizens have a right to concur personally, or by their representatives, in its formation. It must be the same for all, whether it protects or punishes. All the citizens being equal in its sight are equally eligible to all honors, offices and public

* As translated in George A. Bermann, et al., French Law: Constitution and Selected Legislation (1998).

employments, according to their ability; and without distinction other than those of their virtues and talents.

VII.   No man may be accused, arrested or detained except as determined by the law, and according to the forms which it has prescribed. Those who solicit, promote, execute or cause to be executed arbitrary orders must be punished; but every citizen summoned or apprehended by virtue of the law must obey instantly; he renders himself culpable by resistance.

VIII.   The law must impose no penalties other than those which are absolutely and clearly necessary, and no one may be punished except by virtue of a law enacted and promulgated prior to the offense, and lawfully applied.

IX.   Every man being presumed innocent until he has been declared guilty, if it becomes unavoidable to arrest him, any severity which is not necessary to secure his person must be strictly repressed by law.

X.   No one may be harassed because of his opinions, even his religious opinions, provided their expression does not disturb the public order established by law.

XI.   The free communication of thoughts and opinions is one of the most precious rights of man; every citizen may therefore speak, write and publish freely, provided he shall be liable for the abuse of this freedom in such cases as are determined by law.

XII.   The security of the rights of man and of the citizen necessitate a public force; this force is thus created for the benefit of all, and not for the special benefit of those to whom it is entrusted.

XIII.   For the maintenance of the public force and for the expenses of the administration, a common contribution is indispensable; it must be divided equally among all the citizens, in accordance with their abilities.

XIV.   All the citizens have a right to determine the necessity of the public contribution, either in person or by their representatives, to consent freely thereto, to watch over its use, and to determine the amount, base, collection and duration thereof.

XV.   Society has the right to demand of every public officer an account of his administration.

XVI.   Every society in which the guaranty of rights is not assured or the separation of powers established, has no Constitution.

XVII.   Property being an inviolable and sacred right, no one may be deprived thereof except where a public need, lawfully established, clearly requires, and on condition of a just and prior indemnity.

Notes

1.   Both in the original French text and in the common translations into English, the Declaration suffers the ambiguity of the term *"homme."*

It is commonly assumed that, in principle, the French Declaration applied to human beings, not only to masculine human beings. Some have noted similar ambiguity in the American Declaration of Independence which declared, "All *men* are created equal." See p. 30 above.

Two years after the Declaration of the Rights of Man, Olympe de Gouges penned a Declaration of the Rights of Woman and the Female Citizen to voice her discontent with the continuing political and social inequality of women:

> [B]elieving that ignorance, omission, or scorn for the rights of woman are the only causes of public misfortunes and of the corruption of governments, [the women] have resolved to set forth in a solemn declaration the natural, inalienable, and sacred rights of woman in order that this declaration, constantly exposed before all the members of the society, will ceaselessly remind them of their rights and duties....

Preamble, Declaration of the Rights of Woman and the Female Citizen, reprinted in Human Rights in Western Civilization 1600–Present 34–35 (John A. Maxwell & James J. Friedberg eds., 2d ed. 1994). De Gouges' document, framed in twenty-seven articles, parallels the more famous Declaration of the Rights of Man, and largely addresses the same rights and concerns.

2. The French Declaration declares "the Rights of Man and of the Citizen." Which are rights of all human beings, which of citizens only? Compare Articles 6 and 14 with the right to vote in the United States, *infra* Part II, Chapter 1(C), and Article 25 of the International Covenant on Civil and Political Rights, Part IV, Chapter 2. Compare Article 13 of the French Declaration which, incidentally, apparently declares it to be a right that taxation be graduated according to one's ability to pay.

3. The U.S. Constitution is seen as an expression of "popular sovereignty" as implied in the opening phrase, "We the people." The French Declaration declares sovereignty to be in "the Nation." Is the difference significant?

6. THE RIGHTS OF MAN: THOMAS PAINE

Perhaps the most influential proponent of the idea and ideology of human rights in the Eighteenth Century was Thomas Paine. Paine defended the ideas of the French Revolution against the attack on them in Edmund Burke's Reflections on the Revolution in France (1790), excerpted *infra* Section C.

Note Paine's reiteration of the idea of natural rights and his distinction between natural rights and civil rights. "Natural rights are those which appertain to man in right of his existence.... Civil rights are those which appertain to man in right of his being a member of society." Note also his restatement of the social contract as a contract among individuals to form a society: any contract between citizens and political authority must come later, after political society and governments are established.

Paine also contributed to "constitutionalism," offering a definition of a "constitution" and its relation to popular sovereignty and to representative government.

Thomas Paine, *The Rights of Man*
66–69, 71 (1791, Penguin Classics Reprint 1985).

Though I mean not to touch upon any sectarian principle of religion, yet it may be worth observing, that the genealogy of Christ is traced to Adam. Why then not trace the rights of man to the creation of man? I will answer the question. Because there have been upstart governments, thrusting themselves between, and presumptuously working to *un-make* man.

If any generation of men ever possessed the right of dictating the mode by which the world should be governed for ever, it was the first generation that existed; and if that generation did it not, no succeeding generation can show any authority for doing it, nor can set any up. The illuminating and divine principle of the equal rights of man, (for it has its origin from the Maker of man) relates, not only to the living individuals, but to generations of men succeeding each other. Every generation is equal in rights to the generations which preceded it, by the same rule that every individual is born equal in rights with his contemporary.

Every history of the creation, and every traditionary account, whether from the lettered or unlettered world, however they may vary in their opinion or belief of certain particulars, all agree in establishing one point, *the unity of man*; by which I mean, that men are all of *one degree*, and consequently that all men are born equal, and with equal natural right, in the same manner as if posterity had been continued by *creation* instead of *generation*, the latter being only the mode by which the former is carried forward; and consequently, every child born into the world must be considered as deriving its existence from God. The world is as new to him as it was to the first man that existed, and his natural right in it is of the same kind.

. . .

Hitherto we have spoken only (and that but in part) of the natural rights of man. We have now to consider the civil rights of man, and to show how the one originates from the other. Man did not enter into society to become *worse* than he was before, nor to have fewer rights than he had before, but to have those rights better secured. His natural rights are the foundation of all his civil rights. But in order to pursue this distinction with more precision, it will be necessary to mark the different qualities of natural and civil rights.

A few words will explain this. Natural rights are those which appertain to man in right of his existence. Of this kind are all the intellectual rights, or rights of the mind, and also all those rights of acting as an individual for his own comfort and happiness, which are not injurious to the natural rights of others. Civil rights are those which appertain to man in right of his being a member of society. Every civil right has for its foundation some natural right pre-existing in the individual, but to the enjoyment of which his individual power is not, in all cases, sufficiently competent. Of this kind are all those which relate to security and protection.

From this short review, it will be easy to distinguish between that class of natural rights which man retains after entering into society, and those which he throws into the common stock as a member of society.

The natural rights which he retains, are all those in which the *power* to execute is as perfect in the individual as the right itself. Among this class, as is before mentioned, are all the intellectual rights, or rights of the mind: consequently, religion is one of those rights. The natural rights which are not retained, are all those in which, though the right is perfect in the individual, the power to execute them is defective. They answer not his purpose. A man, by natural right, has a right to judge in his own cause; and so far as the right of mind is concerned, he never surrenders it: but what availeth it him to judge, if he has not power to redress? He therefore deposits this right in the common stock of society, and takes the arm of society, of which he is a part, in preference and in addition to his own. Society *grants* him nothing. Every man is a proprietor in society, and draws on the capital as a matter of right.

.   .   .

But it will be first necessary to define what is meant by a *constitution*. It is not sufficient that we adopt the word; we must fix also a standard signification to it.

A constitution is not a thing in name only, but in fact. It has not an ideal, but a real existence; and wherever it cannot be produced in a visible form, there is none. A constitution is a thing *antecedent* to a government, and a government is only the creature of a constitution. The constitution of a country is not the act of its government, but of the people constituting a government. It is the body of elements, to which you can refer, and quote article by article; and which contains the principles on which the government shall be established, the manner in which it shall be organized, the powers it shall have, the mode of elections, the duration of parliaments, or by what other name such bodies may be called; the powers which the executive part of the government shall have; and, in fine, everything that relates to the complete organization of a civil government, and the principles on which it shall act, and by which it shall be bound. A constitution, therefore, is to a government, what the laws made afterwards by that government are to a court of judicature. The court of judicature does not make the laws, neither can it alter them; it only acts in conformity to the laws made: and the government is in like manner governed by the constitution.

.   .   .

Notes

1. In Part Two of *The Rights of Man*, Chapter 5, Paine proposed an elaborate plan (and justification) for remission of taxes on the poor, and for

subventions to them for support of their families, notably their children, including their education, and for the aged. For Paine this was not a matter of charity but of right, apparently because the poor paid direct and indirect taxes.

2.   In The Rights of Man Today 134–36 (1988 reprint of 1978 ed.), Professor Henkin wrote:

> So many of the issues of our time were addressed by Paine—colonialism and self-determination, the values and the costs of stability and of revolution, the essentials of individual liberty and of democratic government, the welfare state, international peace, even (as someone put it) how people can make sense of their lives without the consolations of revealed religion.... He was a democrat and libertarian, meliorist, and even something of a socialist (small *s*, before the word was common and acquired Marxist connotations)....

> . . .

> Thomas Paine had proclaimed constitutionalism as *the* right of man and as the foundation of all rights of man: today constitutionalism is accepted by virtually all, at least in principle. Paine argued hotly the sovereignty of the people; today popular sovereignty is accepted almost everywhere, at least in principle. For Paine, "representative government is freedom"; today suffrage is universal, and government is representative everywhere, at least in principle. For Paine, man's rights were natural, inherent in the equality of God's human creations, and retained by them pursuant to their social contract. Today human rights—whether natural, contractual, psychological, or political as positive law—are accepted by all, at least in principle.

> Paine would be delighted that the purpose of government has expanded, that government's responsibility for the economic and social welfare of all the people is now axiomatic; that his program for social security financed by progressive taxation is taken for granted in Europe and America; that the tenets, libertarian as well as socialist, of the French Revolution and the French Declaration, revolutionary then, are commonplace now, at least in constitutional principle. Paine would glow at the realization that self-determination (our word for his idea) is a prominent principle of our times, that international institutions, reflecting universal commitment, try to keep peace between nations (another of his interests) and promote other common goals and ideas— all of them Rights of Man.

7.   HUMAN RIGHTS AND HUMAN DIGNITY: IMMANUEL KANT

For the international human rights movement, the human rights idea has an additional ancestor, Immanuel Kant. Kant also accepted "the social contract" but he wrote principally and famously not from the perspective of "natural law" but of morality. One might look at Kant within the Social Contract tradition, or one might consider Kant independently, as the modern progenitor of contemporary concern with "human dignity" which, in the second half of the Twentieth Century, has become the source and the justification for the ideology of human rights. See the Universal Declaration of Human Rights, *infra* Part III, Chapter 1.

Although the idea of "human dignity" was old before Locke's time, Locke had no particular need of the concept for his purpose. Locke derived human rights from natural law, and it needed no other justification: human rights were natural, "self-evident"; they needed no support from other ideas, not from dignity, not even from "justice." Kant, a hundred years later, was concerned with ethics; he arrived at law and politics from ethics, and at physical and social liberty from moral autonomy, from human worth, worthiness, "dignity." Rights (and the social contract) were rooted, implicit, in Kant's concept of human dignity, but they were not his central concern.

In the following excerpts, note Kant's "categorical imperative"—human beings "should always judge their actions by such maxims as they themselves could will to serve as universal laws," and act so as to treat humanity "always as an end and never as a means only." The second excerpt presents Kant's contribution to "human dignity."

Immanuel Kant, *Foundations of the Metaphysics of Morals*

49–54 (Lewis W. Beck trans., 1959)*

The question then is: Is it a necessary law for all rational beings that they should always judge their actions by such maxims as they themselves could will to serve as universal laws? . . .

But suppose that there were something the existence of which in itself had absolute worth, something which, as an end in itself, could be a ground of definite laws. In it and only in it could lie the ground of a possible categorical imperative, i.e., of a practical law.

Now, I say, man and, in general, every rational being exists as an end in himself and not merely as a means to be arbitrarily used by this or that will. In all his actions, whether they are directed to himself or to other rational beings, he must always be regarded at the same time as an end. . . . Beings whose existence does not depend on our will but on nature, if they are not rational beings, have only a relative worth as means and are therefore called "things"; on the other hand, rational beings are designated "persons" because their nature indicates that they are ends in themselves, i.e., things which may not be used merely as means. Such a being is thus an object to respect and, so far, restricts all [arbitrary] choice. Such beings are not merely subjective ends whose existence as a result of our action has a worth for us, but are objective ends, i.e., beings whose existence in itself is an end. Such an end is one for which no other end can be substituted, to which these beings should serve merely as means. For, without them, nothing of absolute worth could be found, and if all worth is conditional

* Foundations of the Metaphysics of Morals Z/E. by Kant (trans. L.W. Beck), © 1990. Reprinted by permission of Prentice-Hall, Inc., Upper Saddle River, NJ.

and thus contingent, no supreme practical principle for reason could be found anywhere.

Thus if there is to be a supreme practical principle and a categorical imperative for the human will, it must be one that forms an objective principle of the will from the conception of that which is necessarily an end for everyone because it is an end in itself. Hence this objective principle can serve as a universal practical law. The ground of this principle is: rational nature exists as an end in itself. Man necessarily thinks of his own existence in this way; thus far it is a subjective principle of human actions. Also every other rational being thinks of his existence by means of the same rational ground which holds also for myself; thus it is at the same time an objective principle from which, as a supreme practical ground, it must be possible to derive all laws of the will. The practical imperative, therefore, is the following: Act so that you treat humanity, whether in your own person or in that of another, always as an end and never as a means only. Let us now see whether this can be achieved.

. . .

The concept of each rational being as a being that must regard itself as giving universal law through all the maxims of its will, so that it may judge itself and its actions from this standpoint, leads to a very fruitful concept, namely, that of a *realm of ends.*

By "realm" I understand the systematic union of different rational beings through common laws. Because laws determine ends with regard to their universal validity, if we abstract from the personal difference of rational beings and thus from all content of their private ends, we can think of a whole of all ends in systematic connection, a whole of rational beings as ends in themselves as well as of the particular ends which each may set for himself. This is a realm of ends, which is possible on the aforesaid principles. For all rational beings stand under the law that each of them should treat himself and all others never merely as means but in every case also as an end in himself. Thus there arises a systematic union of rational beings through common objective laws. This is a realm which may be called a realm of ends (certainly only an ideal), because what these laws have in view is just the relation of these beings to each other as ends and means.

A rational being belongs to the realm of ends as a member when he gives universal laws in it while also himself subject to these laws. He belongs to it as sovereign when he, as legislat[or], is subject to the will of no other. The rational being must regard himself always as legislat[or] in a realm of ends possible through the freedom of the will, whether he belongs to it as member or as sovereign. He cannot maintain the latter position merely through the maxims of his will but only when he is a completely independent being without need and with power adequate to his will.

Morality, therefore, consists in the relation of every action to that legislation through which alone a realm of ends is possible. This legislation, however, must be found in every rational being. It must be able to arise from his will, whose principle then is to take no action according to any maxim which would be inconsistent with its being a universal law and thus to act only so that the will through its maxims could regard itself at the same time as universally lawgiving. If now the maxims do not by their nature already necessarily conform to this objective principle of rational beings as universally lawgiving, the necessity of acting according to the principle is called practical constraint, i.e., duty. Duty pertains not to the sovereign in the realm of ends, but rather to each member, and to each in the same degree.

The practical necessity of acting according to this principle, i.e., duty, does not rest at all on feelings, impulses, and inclinations; it rests merely on the relation of rational beings to one another, in which the will of a rational being must always be regarded as legislative, for otherwise it could not be thought of as an end in itself. Reason, therefore, relates every maxim of the will as giving universal laws to every other will and also to every action toward itself; it does so not for the sake of any other practical motive or future advantage but rather from the idea of the dignity of a rational being who obeys no law except that which he himself also gives.

In the realm of ends everything has either a *price* or a *dignity*. Whatever has a price can be replaced by something else as its equivalent; on the other, whatever is above all price, and therefore admits of no equivalent, has a dignity.

That which is related to general human inclinations and needs has a *market price*. That which, without presupposing any need, accords with a certain taste, i.e., with pleasure in the mere purposeless play of our faculties, has an *affective price*. But that which constitutes the condition under which alone something can be an end in itself does not have mere relative worth, i.e., a price, but an intrinsic worth, i.e., *dignity*.

Now morality is the condition under which alone a rational being can be an end in itself, because only through it is it possible to be a legislative member in the realm of ends. Thus morality and humanity, so far as it is capable of morality, alone have dignity. Skill and diligence in work have a market value; wit, lively imagination, and humor have an affective price; but fidelity in promises and benevolence on principle (not from instinct) have intrinsic worth. Nature and likewise art contain nothing which could replace their lack, for their worth consists not in effects which flow from them, nor in advantage and utility which they procure; it consists only in intentions, i.e., maxims of the will which are ready to reveal themselves in this manner through actions even though success does not favor them. These actions need no recommendation from any subjective disposition or taste in order that they may be looked upon with immediate favor and satisfaction, nor do they have need of any immediate propensity or feeling directed to them. They exhibit the will which performs them as the object of an immediate respect, since nothing but reason is required in order to impose them on the will. The will is not to be cajoled into them, for this, in the case of duties, would be a contradiction. This esteem lets the worth of such a turn of mind be recognized as dignity and puts it infinitely beyond any price, with which it cannot in the least be brought into competition or comparison without, as it were, violating its holiness.

And what is it that justifies the morally good disposition or virtue in making such lofty claims? It is nothing less than the participation it affords the rational being in giving universal laws. He is thus fitted to be a member in a possible realm of ends to which his own nature already destined him. For, as an end in himself, he is destined to be legislative in the realm of ends, free from all laws of nature and obedient only to those which he himself gives. Accordingly, his maxims can belong to a universal legislation to which he is at the same time also subject. A thing has no worth other than that determined for it by the law. The legislation which determines all worth must therefore have a dignity, i.e., unconditional and incomparable worth. For the esteem which a rational being must have for it, only the word "respect" is a suitable expression. Autonomy is thus the basis of the dignity of both human nature and every rational nature.

. . .

Note

John Locke and Immanuel Kant are both credited as "ancestors" of the human rights idea. Are their contributions different? Cumulative? What has each contributed to the theory of the modern human rights idea? To the content of rights? To the principle and content of limitations on rights?

8.   RIGHTS AND LIBERTY: JOHN STUART MILL

The idea of rights has strong roots in individual "liberty," and "liberty" resounds in Locke and Jefferson and in the French Declaration. There has been less attention to how much liberty man retains after entering into the social contract. (For Rousseau, man retains none at all, except as granted by the "general will". See p. 45.) The U.S. Constitution, we shall see, exalts "the Blessings of Liberty" in its preamble, the First Amendment famously guarantees several "freedoms," and the Fifth Amendment guarantees that no one shall be deprived of "liberty" without due process of law. See *infra* p. 160. But in the Nineteenth Century "liberty," as a cardinal right, was sometimes subordinated to other values, including equality, democracy and representative government, the rule of law, socialism, economic and social welfare.

But not for John Stuart Mill.

John Stuart Mill, English political philosopher, is commonly thought of as a "Utilitarian," and utilitarianism is commonly thought of as an unfriendly alternative to the rights idea. See Section C. But John Stuart Mill is perhaps most famous for his Essay on Liberty and its defense of freedom of expression and freedom of the press. For Mill, however, these are aspects of a larger freedom which includes liberty of conscience, of thought and feeling, opinion and sentiment, and of individual autonomy—

freedoms that underlie the human rights idea and contemporary concepts of civil and political rights generally. His ideas are commonly invoked, particularly in discussions of the freedoms guaranteed by the First Amendment to the U.S. Constitution.

John Stuart Mill, *On Liberty*

Chapters I and II (1849).

CHAPTER I

. . .

But there is a sphere of action in which society, as distinguished from the individual, has, if any, only an indirect interest; comprehending all that portion of a person's life and conduct which affects only himself, or if it also affects others, only with their free, voluntary, and undeceived consent and participation. When I say only himself, I mean directly, and in the first instance: for whatever affects himself, may affect others *through* himself; and the objection which may be grounded on this contingency, will receive consideration in the sequel. This, then, is the appropriate region of human liberty. It comprises, first, the inward domain of consciousness; demanding liberty of conscience, in the most comprehensive sense; liberty of thought and feeling; absolute freedom of opinion and sentiment on all subjects, practical or speculative, scientific, moral, or theological. The liberty of expressing and publishing opinions may seem to fall under a different principle, since it belongs to that part of the conduct of an individual which concerns other people; but, being almost of as much importance as the liberty of thought itself, and resting in great part on the same reasons, is practically inseparable from it. Secondly, the principle requires liberty of tastes and pursuits; of framing the plan of our life to suit our own character; of doing as we like, subject to such consequences as may follow; without impediment from our fellow-creatures, so long as what we do does not harm them, even though they should think our conduct foolish, perverse, or wrong. Thirdly, from this liberty of each individual, follows the liberty, within the same limits, of combination among individuals; freedom to unite, for any purpose not involving harm to others: the persons combining being supposed to be of full age, and not forced or deceived.

No society in which these liberties are not, on the whole, respected, is free, whatever may be its form of government; and none is completely free in which they do not exist absolute and unqualified. The only freedom which deserves the name, is that of pursuing our own good in our own way, so long as we do not attempt to deprive others of theirs, or impede their efforts to obtain it. Each is the proper guardian of his own health, whether bodily, or mental and spiritual. Mankind are greater gainers by suffering each other to live as seems good to themselves, than by compelling each to live as seems good to the rest.

. . .

Apart from the peculiar tenets of individual thinkers, there is also in the world at large an increasing inclination to stretch unduly the powers of society over the individual, both by the force of opinion and even by that of legislation; and as the tendency of all the changes taking place in the world is to strengthen society, and diminish the power of the individual, this encroachment is not one of the evils which tend spontaneously to disappear, but, on the contrary, to grow more and more formidable. The disposition of mankind, whether as rulers or as fellow-citizens, to impose their own opinions and inclinations as a rule of conduct on others, is so energetically supported by some of the best and by some of the worst feelings incident to human nature, that it is hardly ever kept under restraint by anything but want of power; and as the power is not declining, but growing, unless a strong barrier of moral conviction can be raised against the mischief, we must expect, in the present circumstances of the world, to see it increase.

It will be convenient for the argument, if, instead of at once entering upon the general thesis, we confine ourselves in the first instance to a single branch of it, on which the principle here stated is, if not fully, yet to a certain point, recognized by the current opinions. This one branch is the Liberty of Thought: from which it is impossible to separate the cognate liberty of speaking and of writing. . . .

CHAPTER II
OF THE LIBERTY OF THOUGHT AND DISCUSSION

The time, it is to be hoped, is gone by, when any defence would be necessary of the "liberty of the press" as one of the securities against corrupt or tyrannical government. No argument, we may suppose, can now be needed, against permitting a legislature or an executive, not identified in interest with the people, to prescribe opinions to them, and determine what doctrines or what arguments they shall be allowed to hear. This aspect of the question, besides, has been so often and so triumphantly enforced by preceding writers, that it needs not be specially insisted on in this place. Though the law of England, on the subject of the press, is as servile to this day as it was in the time of the Tudors, there is little danger of its being actually put in force against political discussion, except during some temporary panic, when fear of insurrection drives ministers and judges from their propriety; and, speaking generally, it is not in constitutional countries to be apprehended that the government, whether completely responsible to the people or not, will often attempt to control the expression of opinion except when in doing so it makes itself the organ of the general intolerance of the public. Let us suppose, therefore, that the government is entirely at one with the people, and never thinks of exerting any power of coercion unless in agreement with what it conceives to be their voice. But I deny the right of the people to exercise such coercion, either by themselves or by their government. The power itself is illegitimate. The best government has no more title to it than the worst. It is as noxious, or more noxious, when exerted in accordance with public opinion, than when in opposition to it. If all mankind minus one, were of one opinion, and only one person were of the contrary opinion, mankind would be no more justified in silencing that one person, than he, if he had the power, would be justified in silencing mankind. Were an opinion a personal possession of no value except to the owner; if to be obstructed in the enjoyment of it were simply a private injury, it would make some difference whether the injury was inflicted only on a few persons or on many. But the peculiar evil of silencing the expression of an opinion is, that it is robbing the human race; posterity as well as the existing generation; those who dissent from the opinion, still more that those who hold it. If the opinion is right, they are deprived of the opportunity of exchanging error for truth; if wrong, they lose, what is almost as great a benefit, the clearer perception and livelier impression of truth, produced by its collision with error.

It is necessary to consider separately these two hypotheses, each of which has a distinct branch of the argument corresponding to it. We can never be sure that the opinion we are endeavouring to stifle is a false opinion; and if we were sure, stifling it would be an evil still.

First: the opinion which it is attempted to suppress by authority may possibly be true. Those who desire to suppress it, of course deny its truth; but they are not infallible. They have no authority to decide the question for all mankind, and exclude every other person from the means of judging. To refuse a hearing to an opinion, because they are sure that it is false, is to assume that *their* certainty is the same thing as *absolute* certainty. All silencing of discussion is an assumption of infallibility. Its condemnation may be allowed to rest on this common argument, not the worse for being common.

Unfortunately for the good sense of mankind, the fact of their fallibility is far from carrying the weight in their practical judgment, which is always allowed to it in theory; for while every one well knows himself to be fallible, few think it necessary to take any precautions against their own fallibility. . . .

. . .

Notes

For a contemporary elaboration of the concept of liberty, see Isaiah Berlin, *Two Concepts of Liberty*, in Liberalism and Its Critics (Michael J. Sandel, ed., 1984). Berlin distinguishes between liberty as freedom from restraint ("negative" freedom), and liberty as the capacity to be one's own master ("positive" freedom). Others have used the idea of "positive liberty" to support economic and social rights on the ground that "necessitous men are not freemen." See Franklin D. Roosevelt address, *infra* Part IV, Chapter 3(A).

B.   ALTERNATIVE WESTERN CONCEPTIONS OF THE GOOD SOCIETY

There were conceptions of "the good society," of justice and the just society, before the birth of the idea of rights, conceptions rooted in religion and in particular religious ideologies, in classical political theory, which appeared in what we now call the Middle East and in Europe, in China and other parts of Asia, doubtless also in societies and cultures elsewhere. Traditional ideas of the good society (without the idea of individual rights) did not disappear when the idea of rights appeared, and some maintained the traditional conceptions of the good society in opposition to the idea of rights. Later ideologies—notably variations on socialism—emerged afterwards, in deviation from, and even in opposition to, the idea of rights.

The idea of inherent universal rights which might "trump" the general interest met powerful critiques from within the natural rights movement, *e.g.*, by Rousseau, and later, by those in England who rejected the idea of natural rights—traditionalists such as Burke, and progressive, utilitarian positivists such as Bentham.

1.   "THE GENERAL WILL": JEAN–JACQUES ROUSSEAU

Jean–Jacques Rousseau is commonly associated with those who reject the idea of rights, but his place in the history of the idea is somewhat more complicated. Like John Locke, he posited the state of nature and a law of nature according to which man was free, had moral autonomy, and the right to enter into contracts; therefore he joined with others in a social contract. But whereas for Locke man retained natural rights in the society he contracted to establish, for Rousseau the social contract subjects each and all to the "the general will after the society is established." By the social contract, "each of us places his person and all his power in common under the supreme direction of the general will; and as one we receive each member as an indivisible part of the whole."

Jean–Jacques Rousseau, *On the Social Contract*

Book I, Chapters 5–8 (1762) in The Basic Political Writings (Donald Cress trans. 1987).*

CHAPTER V

That it is Always Necessary to Return to a First Convention

. . .

A people, says Grotius, can give itself to a king. According to Grotius, therefore, a people is a people before it gives itself to a king. This gift itself is a civil act; it presupposes a public deliberation. Thus, before examining the act whereby a people chooses a king, it would be well to examine the act whereby a people is a people. For since this act is necessarily prior to the other, it is the true foundation of society.

In fact, if there were no prior convention, then, unless the vote were unanimous, what would become of the minority's obligation to submit to the majority's choice, and where do one hundred who want a master get the right to vote for ten who do not? The law of majority rule is itself an established convention, and presupposes unanimity on at least one occasion.

* With permission of Hackett Publishing Company, Inc., Indianapolis and Cambridge. All rights reserved.

CHAPTER VI

On the Social Compact

I suppose that men have reached the point where obstacles that are harmful to their maintenance in the state of nature gain the upper hand by their resistance to the forces that each individual can bring to bear to maintain himself in that state. Such being the case, that original state cannot subsist any longer, and the human race would perish if it did not alter its mode of existence.

For since men cannot engender new forces, but merely unite and direct existing ones, they have no other means of maintaining themselves but to form by aggregation a sum of forces that could gain the upper hand over the resistance, so that their forces are directed by means of a single moving power and made to act in concert.

This sum of forces cannot come into being without the cooperation of many. But since each man's force and liberty are the primary instruments of his maintenance, how is he going to engage them without hurting himself and without neglecting the care that he owes himself? This difficulty, seen in terms of my subject, can be stated in the following terms:

"Find a form of association which defends and protects with all common forces the person and goods of each associate, and by means of which each one, while uniting with all, nevertheless obeys only himself and remains as free as before?" This is the fundamental problem for which the social contract provides the solution.

The clauses of this contract are so determined by the nature of the act that the least modification renders them vain and ineffectual, that, although perhaps they have never been formally promulgated, they are everywhere the same, everywhere tacitly accepted and acknowledged. Once the social compact is violated, each person then regains his first rights and resumes his natural liberty, while losing the conventional liberty for which he renounced it.

These clauses, properly understood, are all reducible to a single one, namely the total alienation of each associate, together with all of his rights, to the entire community. For first of all, since each person gives himself whole and entire, the condition is equal for everyone; and since the condition is equal for everyone, no one has an interest in making it burdensome for the others.

Moreover, since the alienation is made without reservation, the union is as perfect as possible, and no associate has anything further to demand. For if some rights remained with private individuals, in the absence of any common superior who could decide between them and the public, each person would eventually claim to be his own judge in all things, since he is on some point his own judge. The state of nature would subsist and the association would necessarily become tyrannical or hollow.

Finally, in giving himself to all, each person gives himself to no one. And since there is no associate over whom he does not acquire the same right that he would grant others over himself, he gains the equivalent of everything he loses, along with a greater amount of force to preserve what he has.

If, therefore, one eliminates from the social compact whatever is not essential to it, one will find that it is reducible to the following terms. *Each of us places his person and all his power in common under the supreme direction of the general will; and as one we receive each member as an indivisible part of the whole.*

. . .

CHAPTER VII
On the Sovereign

This formula shows that the act of association includes a reciprocal commitment between the public and private individuals, and that each individual, contracting, as it were, with himself, finds himself under a twofold commitment: namely as a member of the sovereign to private individuals, and as a member of the state toward the sovereign. But the maxim of civil law that no one is held to commitments made to himself cannot be applied here, for there is a considerable difference between being obligated to oneself, or to a whole of which one is a part.

It must be further noted that the public deliberation that can obligate all the subjects to the sovereign, owing to the two different relationships in which each of them is viewed, cannot, for the opposite reason, obligate the sovereign to itself, and that consequently it is contrary to the nature of the body politic that the sovereign impose upon itself a law it could not break. Since the sovereign can be considered under but one single relationship, it is then in the position of a private individual contracting with himself. Whence it is apparent that there neither is nor can be any type of fundamental law that is obligatory for the people as a body, not even the social contract. This does not mean that the whole body cannot perfectly well commit itself to another body with respect to things that do not infringe on this contract. For in regard to the foreigner, it becomes a simple being, an individual.

. . .

Thus, in order for the social compact to avoid being an empty formula, it tacitly entails the commitment—which alone can give force to the others—that whoever refuses to obey the general will will be forced to do so by the entire body. This means merely that he will be forced to be free. For this is the sort of condition that, by giving each citizen to the homeland, guarantees him against all personal dependence—a condition that produces the skill and the performance of the political machine, and which alone bestows legitimacy upon civil commitments. Without it such commitments would be absurd, tyrannical and subject to the worst abuses.

CHAPTER VIII
On the Civil State

. . .

Let us summarize this entire balance sheet so that the credits and debits are easily compared. What man loses through the social contract is his natural liberty and an unlimited right to everything that tempts him and that he can acquire. What he gains is civil liberty and the proprietary ownership of all he possess. So as not to be in error in these compensations, it is necessary to draw a careful distinction between natural liberty (which is limited solely by the force of the individual involved) and civil liberty (which is limited by the general will), and between possession (which is merely the effect of the force or the right of the first occupant) and proprietary ownership (which is based solely on a positive title).

To the preceding acquisitions could be added the acquisition in the civil state of moral liberty, which alone makes man truly the master of himself. For to be driven by appetite alone is slavery, and obedience to the law one has prescribed for oneself is liberty. But I have already said too much on this subject, and the philosophical meaning of the word *liberty* is not my subject here.

Notes

Are there echoes of Rousseau in various versions of socialism? Of communitarianism? See *infra* pp. 54, 92.

2.   Rights in the British Tradition: Edmund Burke

Burke rejected the ideology of the French Revolution including the Declaration of 1789, setting up instead the traditional liberties of Englishmen.

By implication as well as explicitly, Burke rejects any idea of natural rights or of universal rights. He finds the rights of English subjects in tradition, in heredity, in the (unwritten) Constitution dating back to *Magna Carta*, "a people inheriting privileges, franchises and liberties from a long line of ancestors." (References to "the Revolution" are to England's "Glorious Revolution" of 1688.) Compare Blackstone, *supra* Section B, who harks back to universal rights but suggests that, while others have abandoned them, England has maintained them through the Common Law. See p. 28.

Edmund Burke, *Reflections on the Revolution in France*

50–53, 88–90 (1790).

The third head of right ... namely, the "right to form a government for ourselves", has, at least, as little countenance from anything done at the Revolution, either in precedent or principle, as the two first of their claims. The Revolution was made to preserve our *ancient*, indisputable laws and liberties and the *ancient* constitution of government which is our only security for law and liberty. If you are desirous of knowing the spirit of our constitution and the policy which predominated in that great period which has secured it to this hour, pray look for both in our histories, in our records, in our acts of parliament, and journals of parliament, and not in . . . the after-dinner toasts of the Revolution Society. In the former you will find other ideas and another language. Such a claim is as ill-suited to our temper and wishes as it is unsupported by any appearance of authority. The very idea of the fabrication of a new government is enough to fill us with disgust and horror. We wished at the period of the Revolution, and do now wish, to derive all we possess *as an inheritance from our forefathers*. Upon that body and stock of inheritance we have taken care not to inoculate any scion alien to the nature of the original plant. All the reformations we have hitherto made have proceeded upon the principle of reverence to antiquity; and I hope, nay, I am persuaded, that all those which possibly may be made hereafter will be carefully formed upon analogical precedent, authority, and example.

Our oldest reformation is that of Magna Charta. You will see that Sir Edward Coke, that great oracle of our law, and indeed all the great men who follow him, to Blackstone, are industrious to prove the pedigree of our liberties. They endeavor to prove that the ancient charter, the Magna Charta of King John, was connected with another positive charter from Henry I, and that both the one and the other were nothing more than a reaffirmance of the still more ancient standing law of the kingdom. In the matter of fact, for the greater part these authors appear to be in the right; perhaps not always; but if the lawyers mistake in some particulars, it proves my position still the more strongly, because it demonstrates the powerful prepossession toward antiquity, with which the minds of all our lawyers and legislators, and of all the people whom they wish to influence, have been always filled, and the stationary policy of this kingdom in considering their most sacred rights and franchises as an *inheritance*.

In the famous law of the 3rd of Charles I, called the Petition of Right, the parliament says to the king, "Your subjects have *inherited* this freedom", claiming their franchises not on abstract principles "as the rights of men", but as the rights of Englishmen, and as a patrimony derived from their forefathers. Selden and the other profoundly learned men who drew this Petition of Right were as well acquainted, at least, with all the general theories concerning the "rights of men" as any of the discoursers in our pulpits or on your tribune; full as well as Dr. Price or as the Abbe Sieyes. But, for reasons worthy of that practical wisdom which superseded their theoretic science, they preferred this positive, recorded, *hereditary* title to all which can be dear to the man and the citizen, to that vague speculative right which exposed their sure inheritance to be scrambled for and torn to pieces by every wild, litigious spirit.

. . .

You will observe that from Magna Charta to the Declaration of Right it has been the uniform policy of our constitution to claim and assert our liberties as an *entailed inheritance* derived to us from our forefathers, and to be transmitted to our posterity—as an estate specially belonging to the people of this kingdom, without any reference whatever to any other more general or prior right. By this means our constitution preserves a unity in so great a diversity of its parts. We have an inheritable crown, an inheritable peerage, and a House of Commons and a people inheriting privileges, franchises, and liberties from a long line of ancestors.

. . .

Government is not made in virtue of natural rights, which may and do exist in total independence of it, and exist in much greater clearness and in a much greater degree of abstract perfection; but their abstract perfection is their practical defect. By having a right to everything they want everything. Government is a contrivance of human wisdom to provide for human *wants*. Men have a right that these wants should be provided for by this wisdom. Among these wants is to be reckoned the want, out of civil society, of a sufficient restraint upon their passions. Society requires not only that the passions of individuals should be subjected, but that even in the mass and body, as well as in the individuals, the inclinations of men should frequently be thwarted, their will controlled, and their passions brought into subjection. This can only be done *by a power out of themselves*, and not, in the exercise of its function, subject to that will and to those passions which it is its office to bridle and subdue. In this sense the restraints on men, as well as their liberties, are to be reckoned among their rights. But as the liberties and the restrictions vary with times and circumstances and admit to infinite modifications, they cannot be settled upon any abstract rule; and nothing is so foolish as to discuss them upon that principle.

3.   RIGHTS AS "ANARCHICAL FALLACY": JEREMY BENTHAM

A powerful voice against the idea of inherent rights was Jeremy Bentham's. Although originally an enthusiastic supporter of the French Revolution, he turned against it (and against the French Declaration of the Rights of Man). He declared that, for him, "natural rights is simple nonsense; natural and imprescriptible rights, rhetorical nonsense, nonsense upon stilts." For him it was an "anarchical fallacy": natural rights have included the divine right of kings, the natural inferiority of slaves and of women, the inherent right to property of the landed. Natural rights were an obstacle to economic and social progress. Rights depend on government and are established by law. Bentham saw the good society in terms of utilitarianism, dedicated to increasing the totality of happiness and maximizing the greatest good for the greatest number.

Bentham's attack on the French Declaration of the Rights of Man and of Citizens includes an article by article critique:

Jeremy Bentham, *Anarchical Fallacies*

Article II (1824).

The End in View of Every Political Association Is the Preservation of the Natural and Imprescriptible Rights of Man. These Rights Are Liberty, Property, Security, and Resistance to Oppression.

Sentence 1. The end in view of every political association, is the preservation of the natural and imprescriptible rights of man.

More confusion—more nonsense,—and the nonsense, as usual, dangerous nonsense. The words can scarcely be said to have a meaning; but if they have, or rather if they had a meaning, these would be the propositions either asserted or implied:

1. That there are such things as rights anterior to the establishment of governments: for natural, as applied to rights, if it mean anything, is meant to stand in opposition to *legal*, to such rights as are acknowledged to owe their existence to government, and are consequently posterior in their date to the establishment of government.

2. That these rights can *not* be abrogated by government: for can *not* is implied in the form of the word imprescriptible, and the sense it wears when so applied, is the cut-throat sense above explained.

3. That the governments that exist derive their origin from formal associations, or what are now called *conventions*: associations entered into by a partnership contract, with all the members for partners, entered into at a day prefixed, for a predetermined purpose, the formation of a new government where there was none before (for as to formal meetings holden under the controul of an existing government, they are evidently out of question here) in which it seems again to be implied in the way of inference, though a necessary and an unavoidable inference, that all governments (that is, self-called governments, knots of persons exercising the powers of government) that have had any other origin than an association of the above description, are illegal, that is, no governments at all; resistance to them, and subversion of them, lawful and commendable; and so on.

Such are the notions implied in this first part of the article. How stands the truth of things? That there are no such things as natural rights—no such things as rights anterior to the establishment of government—no such things as natural rights opposed to, in contradistinction to, legal: that the expression is merely figurative; that when used in the moment you attempt to give it a literal meaning it leads to error, and to that sort of error that leads to mischief—to the extremity of mischief.

We know what it is for men to live without government—and living without government, to live without rights: we know what it is for men to live without government, for we see instances of such a way of life—we see it in many savage nations, or rather races of mankind; for instance, among the savages of New South Wales, whose way of living is so well known to us: no habit of obedience, and thence no government—no government, and thence no laws—no laws, and thence no such things as rights—no security—no property:—liberty, as against regular controul, the controul of laws and government—perfect; but as against all irregular controul, the mandates of stronger individuals, none. In this state, at a time earlier than the commencement of history—in this same state, judging from analogy, we, the inhabitants of the part of the globe we call Europe, were;—no government, consequently no rights: no rights, consequently no property—no legal security—no legal liberty: security not more than belongs to beasts—

forecast and sense of insecurity keener—consequently in point of happiness below the level of the brutal race.

In proportion to the want of happiness resulting from the want of rights, a reason exists for wishing that there were such things as rights. But reasons for wishing there were such things as rights, are not rights;—a reason for wishing that a certain right were established, is not that right—want is not supply—hunger is not bread.

That which has no existence cannot be destroyed—that which cannot be destroyed cannot require anything to preserve it from destruction. *Natural rights* is simple nonsense: natural and imprescriptible rights, rhetorical nonsense,—nonsense upon stilts. But this rhetorical nonsense ends in the old strain of mischievous nonsense: for immediately a list of these pretended natural rights is given, and those are so expressed as to present to view legal rights. And of these rights, whatever they are, there is not, it seems, any one of which any government *can*, upon any occasion whatever, abrogate the smallest particle.

. . .

Notes

Earlier, Bentham had offered the "principle of utility," or the "greatest happiness principle."

Bentham's reaction to the French Declaration, after his initial support of it, reaffirmed his own commitment to utilitarianism as an alternative to rights. In the following excerpt, Bentham's utilitarianism is based on the supposition that "Nature has placed mankind under the governance of two sovereign masters, *pain* and *pleasure*," and that expecting anyone to follow an ethic not based on these two reference points is foolish.

Jeremy Bentham, *An Introduction to the Principles of Morals and Legislation*

Chapter 1 (1789).

CHAPTER I

OF THE PRINCIPLE OF UTILITY

1.   Nature has placed mankind under the governance of two sovereign masters, *pain* and *pleasure*. It is for them alone to point out what we ought to do, as well as to determine what we shall do. On the one hand the standard of right and wrong, on the other the chain of causes and effects, are fastened to their throne. They govern us in all we do, in all we say, in all we think: every effort we can make to throw off our subjection, will serve but to demonstrate and confirm it. In words a man may pretend to abjure their empire: but in reality he will remain subject to it all the while. The *principle of utility*[1] recognizes this subjection, and assumes it for the

---

1.   Note by the Author, July 1822. To this denomination has of late been added, or substituted, the *greatest happiness* or *greatest felicity* principle: this for shortness,

foundation of that system, the object of which is to rear the fabric of felicity by the hands of reason and of law. Systems which attempt to question it, deal in sounds instead of senses, in caprice instead of reason, in darkness instead of light.

But enough of metaphor and declamation: it is not by such means that moral science is to be improved.

2.   The principle of utility is the foundation of the present work: it will be proper therefore at the outset to give an explicit and determinate account of what is meant by it. By the principle of utility is meant that principle which approves or disapproves of every action whatsoever, according to the tendency which it appears to have to augment or diminish the happiness of the party whose interest is in question: or, what is the same thing in other words, to promote or to oppose that happiness. I say of every action whatsoever; and therefore not only of every action of a private individual, but of every measure of government.

3.   By utility is meant that property in any object, whereby it tends to produce benefit, advantage, pleasure, good, or happiness, (all this in the present case comes to the same thing) or (what comes again to the same thing) to prevent the happening of mischief, pain, evil, or unhappiness to the party whose interest is considered: if that party be the community in general, then the happiness of the community: if a particular individual, then the happiness of that individual.

4.   The interest of the community is one of the most general expressions that can occur in the phraseology of morals: no wonder that the meaning of it is often lost. When it has a meaning, it is this. The community is a fictitious *body*, composed of the individual persons who are considered as constituting as it were its *members*. The interest of the community then is, what?—the sum of the interests of the several members who compose it.

5.   It is in vain to talk of the interest of the community, without understanding what is the interest of the individual. A thing is said to promote the interest, or to be *for* the interest, of an individual, when it

instead of saying at length that principle which states the greatest happiness of all those whose interest is in question, as being the right and proper, and only right and proper and universally desirable, end of human action: of human action in every situation, and in particular in that of a functionary or set of functionaries exercising the powers of Government. The word *utility* does not so clearly point to the ideas of *pleasure* and *pain* as the words *happiness* and *felicity* do: nor does it lead us to the consideration of the *number*, of the interests affected; to the *number*, as being the circumstance, which contributes, in the largest proportion, to the formation of the standard here in question; the *standard of right and wrong*, by which alone the propriety of human conduct, in every situation, can with propriety be tried. This want of a sufficiently manifest connection between the ideas of *happiness* and *pleasure* on the one hand, and the idea of *utility* on the other, I have every now and then found operating, and with but too much efficiency, as a bar to the acceptance, that might otherwise have been given, to this principle.

tends to add to the sum total of his pleasures: or, what comes to the same thing, to diminish the sum total of his pains.

. . .

12.   Not that there is or ever has been that human creature breathing, however stupid or perverse, who has not on many, perhaps on most occasions of his life, deferred to it. By the natural constitution of the human frame, on most occasions of their lives men in general embrace this principle, without thinking of it: if not for the ordering of their own actions, yet for the trying of their own actions, as well as of those of other men. There have been, at the same time, not many, perhaps, even of the most intelligent, who have been disposed to embrace it purely and without reserve. There are even few who have not taken some occasion or other to quarrel with it, either on account of their not understanding always how to apply it, or on account of some prejudice or other which they were afraid to examine into, or could not bear to part with. For such is the stuff that man is made of: in principle and in practice, in a right track and in a wrong one, the rarest of all human qualities is consistency.

. . .

4.   RIGHTS AND SOCIALISM

Socialism, virtually by definition, rejected individual rights, as Karl Marx made clear in 1843. Individual rights implies a sense of individualism that is alien to the collectivist ideals of socialism. Any rights an individual would have are subordinated to the state, which expresses the interests of society as a whole. For Marx, individual rights in a capitalist society, even individual rights for the worker, were at best palliative and offered no escape from the evils of capitalism. In the socialist society, after the state has withered away, socialist man will not need or think in terms of individual rights. See generally Franciszek Przetacznik, *The Socialist Concept of Human Rights: Its Philosophical Background and Political Justification,* 13 Revue Belge de Droit International 239 (1977).

Marx was the principal voice for socialism in the Nineteenth Century. Together with Frederich Engels, he authored *The Communist Manifesto,* perhaps the most famous expression of socialism. Marx's best known attack on human rights appears in his essay, "On the Jewish Question."*

Socialism remained a powerful alternative to human rights virtually until its political demise with the end of the Soviet Empire and the fragmentation of the U.S.S.R. in 1987–90.

Karl Marx, On the Jewish Question (1843)

. . .

* The essay's title reflects its initial subject, debates over the civil and political emancipation of Jewish inhabitants in German states.

A distinction is made between the rights of man and the rights of the citizen. Who is this *man* distinct from the *citizen*? No one but the *member of civil society*. Why is the member of civil society called "man," simply man, and why are his rights called the "rights of man"? How is this fact to be explained? By the relation, between the political state and civil society, and by the nature of political emancipation.

Let us notice first of all that the so-called *rights of man*, as distinct from the *rights of the citizen*, are simply the rights of *a member of civil society*, that is, of egoistic man, of man separated from other men and from the community. The most radical constitution, that of 1793, says: *Declaration of the Rights of Man and of the Citizen*: Article 2. "These rights, etc. (the natural and imprescriptible rights) are: *equality, liberty, security, property*".

What constitutes liberty?

Article 6. "Liberty is the power which man has to do everything which does not harm the rights of others."

Liberty is, therefore, the right to do everything which does not harm others. The limits within which each individual can act without harming others are determined by law, just as the boundary between two fields is marked by a stake. It is a question of the liberty of man regarded as an isolated monad, withdrawn into himself. . . . But liberty as a right of man is not founded upon the relations between man and man, but rather upon the separation of man from man. It is the right of such separation. The right of the *circumscribed* individual, withdrawn into himself.

The practical application of the right of liberty is the right of private property. What constitutes the right of private property?

Article 16 (*Constitution* of 1793). "The right of *property* is that which belongs to every citizen of enjoying and disposing *as he will* of his goods and revenues, of the fruits of his work and industry."

The right of property is, therefore, the right to enjoy one's fortune and to dispose of it as one will; without regard for other men and independently of society. It is the right of self-interest. This individual liberty, and its application, form the basis of civil society. It leads every man to see in other men, not the *realization*, but rather the *limitation* of his own liberty. It declares above all the right "to enjoy and to dispose *as one will*, one's goods and revenues, the fruits of one's work and industry."

There remain the other rights of man, equality and security.

The term "equality" has here no political significance. It is only the equal right to liberty as defined above; namely that every man is equally regarded as a self-sufficient monad. The Constitution of 1795 defines the concept of [equality] in this sense.

Article 5 (Constitution of 1795). "Equality consists in the fact that the law is the same for all, whether it protects or punishes."

And security?

Article 8 (Constitution of 1793). "Security consists in the protection afforded by society to each of its members for the preservation of his person, his rights, and his property."

Security is the supreme social concept of civil society; the concept of the police. The whole society exists only in order to guarantee for each of its members the preservation of his person, his rights and his property. It is in this sense that Hegel calls civil society "the state of need and of reason."

The concept of security is not enough to raise civil society above its egoism. Security is, rather, the *assurance* of its egoism.

None of the supposed rights of man, therefore, go beyond the egoistic man, man as he is, as a member of civil society; that is, an individual separated from the community, withdrawn into himself, wholly preoccupied with his private interest and acting in accordance with his private caprice. Man is far from being considered, in the rights of man, as a species-being; on the contrary, species-life itself—society—appears as a system which is external to the individual and as a limitation of his original independence. The only bond between men is natural necessity, need and private interest, the preservation of their property and their egotistic persons.

It is difficult enough to understand that a nation which has just begun to liberate itself, to tear down all the barriers between different sections of the people and to establish a political community, should solemnly proclaim (*Declaration* of 1791) the rights of the egoistic man, separated from his fellow men and from the community, and should renew this proclamation at a moment when only the most heroic devotion can save the nation (and is, therefore, urgently called for), and when the sacrifice of all the interests of civil society is in question and egoism should be punished as a crime. (*Declaration of the Rights of Man, etc.* 1793). The matter becomes still more incomprehensible when we observe that the political liberators reduce citizenship, the *political community*, to a mere *means* for preserving these so-called rights of man; and consequently, that the citizen is declared to be the servant of egotistic "man," that the sphere in which man functions as a species-being is degraded to a level below the sphere where he functions as a partial being, and finally that it is man as a bourgeois and not man as a citizen who is considered the *true* and *authentic* man.

"The end of every *political association* is the preservation of the natural and imprescriptible rights of man." (*Declaration of the Rights of Man, etc.* 1791, Article 2.) "Government is instituted in order to guarantee man's enjoyment of his natural and imprescriptible rights." (*Declaration, etc.* 1793, Article 1.)

Thus, even in the period of its youthful enthusiasm, which is raised to fever pitch by the force of circumstances, political life declares itself to be only a *means*, whose end is the life of civil society. It is true that its revolutionary practice is in flagrant contradiction with its theory. While, for instance, security is declared to be one of the rights of man, the violation of the privacy of correspondence is openly considered. While the "unlimited freedom of the Press" (*Constitution* of 1793, Article 122), as a corollary of the right of individual liberty, is guaranteed, the freedom of the Press is completely destroyed, since "the freedom of the Press should not be permitted when it endangers public liberty." This amounts to saying: the right to liberty ceases to be a right as soon as it comes into conflict with *political* life, whereas in theory political life is no more than the guarantee of the rights of man—the rights of the individual man—and should, therefore, be suspended as soon as it comes into contradiction with its *end*, these rights of man. But practice is only the exception, while theory is the rule. Even if one decided to regard revolutionary practice as the correct expression of this relation, the problem would remain as to why it is that in the minds of political liberators the relation is inverted, so that the end appears as the means and the means as the end? This optical illusion of their consciousness would always remain a problem, though a psychological and theoretical one.

But the problem is easily solved.

Political emancipation is at the same time the *dissolution* of the old society, upon which the sovereign power, the alienated political life of the people, rests. Political revolution is a revolution of civil society. What was the nature of the old society? It can be characterized in one word: *feudalism*. The old society had a directly political character; that is, the elements of civil life such as property, the family, and types of occupation had been raised, in the form of lordship, caste and guilds, to elements of political life. They determined, in this form, the relation of the individual to the state as a whole; that is, his political situation, or in other words, his separation and exclusion from the other elements of society. For this organization of national life did not constitute property, and labour as social elements; it rather succeeded in *separating* them from the body of the state, and made them *distinct* societies within society. Nevertheless, at least in the feudal sense, the vital functions and conditions of civil society remained political. They excluded the individual from the body of the state, and *transformed* the particular relation which existed between his corporation and the state into a general relation between the individual and social life, just as they transformed his specific civil activity and situation into a general activity and situation. As a result of this organization, the state as a whole and its consciousness, will and activity—the general political power—also necessarily appeared as the *private* affair of a ruler and his servants, separated from the people.

The political revolution which overthrew this power of the ruler, which made state affairs the affairs of the people, and the political state a matter of *general* concern, i.e., a real state, necessarily shattered everything—estates, corporations, guilds, privileges—which expressed the separation of the people from community life. The political revolution therefore *abolished* the *political character of civil society*. It dissolved civil society into its basic elements, on the one hand *individuals*, and on the other hand the *material and cultural elements* which formed the life experience and the civil situation of these individuals. It set free the political spirit which had, so to speak, been dissolved, fragmented and lost in the various culs-de-sac of feudal society; it reassembled these scattered fragments, liberated the political spirit from its connection with civil life and made of it the community sphere, the *general* concern of the people, in principle independent of these particular elements of civil life. A *specific* activity and situation in life no longer had any but an individual significance. They no longer constituted the general relation between the individual and the state as a whole. Public affairs as such became the general affair of each individual, and political functions became general functions.

But the consummation of the idealism of the state was at the same time the consummation of the materialism of civil society. The bonds which had restrained the egoistic spirit of civil society were removed along with the political yoke. Political emancipation was at the same time an emancipation of civil society from politics and from even the *semblance* of a general content.

Feudal society was dissolved into its basic element, *man*; but into *egoistic* man who was its real foundation.

Man in this aspect, the member of civil society, is now the foundation and presupposition of the *political* state. He is recognized as such in the rights of man.

But the liberty of egoistic man, and the recognition of this liberty, is rather the recognition of the *frenzied* movement of the cultural and material elements which form the content of his life.

Thus man was not liberated from religion; he received religious liberty. He was not liberated from property; he received the liberty to own property. He was not liberated from the egoism of business; he received the liberty to engage in business.

The *formation of the political state*, and the dissolution of civil society into independent *individuals* whose relations are regulated by *law*, as the relations between men in the corporations and guilds were regulated by *privilege*, are accomplished by *one and the same act*. Man as a member of civil society—*non-political* man—necessarily appears as the *natural* man. The rights of man appear as natural rights because *conscious* activity is concentrated upon political *action*. *Egoistic* man is the *passive, given* result of the dissolution of society, an object of *direct apprehension* and consequently a *natural* object. The *political revolution* dissolves civil society into its elements without *revolutionizing* these elements themselves or subjecting them to criticism. This revolution regards civil society, the sphere of human needs, labour, private interests and civil law, as the *basis of its own existence*, as a self-subsistent *precondition*; and thus as its *natural basis*. Finally, man as a member of civil society is identified with *authentic man*, man as distinct from citizen, because he is man in his sensuous, individual and *immediate* existence, whereas *political* man is only abstract, artificial man, man as an *allegorical, moral person*. Thus man as he really is, is seen only in the form of *egoistic* man, and man in his *true* nature only in the form of the *abstract citizen*.

The abstract notion of political man is well formulated by Rousseau:

"Whoever dares undertake to establish a people's institutions must feel himself capable of *changing*, as it were, *human nature* itself, of *transforming* each individual who, in isolation, is a complete but solitary whole, into a *part* of something greater than himself, from which in a sense, he derives his life and his being; [of changing man's nature in order to strengthen it;] of substituting a limited and moral existence for the physical and independent life [with which all of us are endowed by nature]. His task, in short, is to take from *a man his own powers*, and to give him in exchange alien powers which he can only employ with the help of other men."

Every emancipation is a *restoration* of the human world and of human relationships to *man himself*.

Political emancipation is a reduction of man, on the one hand to a member of civil society, an *independent* and *egoistic* individual, and on the other hand, to a *citizen*, to a moral person.

Human emancipation will only be complete when the real, individual man has absorbed into himself the abstract citizen; when as an individual man, in his everyday life, in his work, and in his relationships, he has become a *species-being*; and when he has recognized and organized his own powers (*forces propres*) as *social* powers so that he no longer separates this social power from himself as *political* power.

. . .

Notes

1.   See also Louis Blanc, *Rights, Liberty, and Social Reform* (1847), in Human Rights in Western Civilization 1600–Present 51 (1994) :

Rights, considered in an abstract manner, are the mirage which, since 1789, has deluded the people. Rights are a dead, metaphysical protection which has replaced, for the people, the living protection owed to them. Rights, pompously and with no results proclaimed in charters, have served only to mask the injustice of a regime of individualism and the barbarism of the abandonment of the poor. It is because liberty has been defined with the word right that men have been called free who were slaves to hunger, slaves to cold, slaves to ignorance, slaves to chance. Let us then say once and for all: liberty consists not only in a RIGHT granted but in POWER given to a man to exercise, to develop his faculties under the empire of justice and under the safeguards of the law.

2.   After the Second World War, the U.S.S.R. formally accepted the idea of human rights in the UN Charter. Later, it committed itself to the principles of the Universal Declaration of Human Rights and it adhered to the international covenants and to a number of international human rights conventions. Individual rights were guaranteed in the U.S.S.R. constitution, *e.g.,* the Constitution of 1977, but by its terms rights depended on performance of duties and were trumped by the needs of socialism and the socialist state. See L. Henkin, *The Age of Rights* 167–72 (1990).

3.   Jeremy Waldron replies to the objections to rights by Bentham, Burke, and Marx, in *Nonsense upon Stilts?—A Reply*, in Nonsense Upon Stilts: Bentham, Burke and Marx on the Rights of Man (Waldron ed. 1987).

C.   HUMAN RIGHTS AND COMPETING IDEAS

Writing in The Age of Rights, Henkin sets forth the principal ideas he saw as competing with human rights in the second half of the Twentieth Century. Are the ideas he identified still competing with the idea of human rights at the end of the Twentieth Century? Is socialism still competing? See also the note on Human Rights and Religion, p. 71 below. Are there other competing ideas?

Louis Henkin, *The Age of Rights*
181–93 (1990).

To Americans, the idea of individual rights seems axiomatic, a "truth," "self-evident," Jefferson said. In fact, we know, the idea is modern and its wide acceptance only contemporary, since the Second World War. And though it is now, it appears, a universal "truth," universally self-evident, there are competing truths, and the idea of rights continues to arouse objection and resistance.*

Resistance to the idea of rights does not necessarily challenge the principal values enshrined in rights instruments. No one, no ideology surely, claims to favor arbitrary killing, or torture, or slavery, convicting the innocent or other forms of injustice, letting people starve or remain illiterate, or even lightly and carelessly invading privacy or denying freedom of speech or religion. What is sometimes resisted is the *idea* of rights, and its essential characteristics—the concentration on the individual and the exaltation of individual freedom and autonomy; the insistence that individuals have claims—by entitlement, as of right—upon their society; that society must mobilize itself to ensure these rights; that individuals can enforce their rights by judicial or other remedies; above all, that the individual's rights might frustrate the will of those in authority, and "trump" the public good as determined by them.

It should not be surprising that there is resistance to the idea of rights. For thousands of years there have been conceptions of the good, of the good life and the good society, without the idea of rights. There are today important ideologies, rooted in ancient traditions, that long antedate the

---

* I refer to alternatives or resistance to the idea of rights; I do not address here the sorry condition of human rights in various countries, the work of evil, corrupt, cruel, or blind men. To some extent, violations of rights may reflect resistance to the idea of rights or to some elements of it, but that is not always the case. In the United States, of whose record on rights Americans are justly proud, there are violations of human rights every day, as the courts continue to find; indeed, one might say, there are more formal, confirmed, recorded findings of violations here than anywhere else in the world. But that record is evidence not of rejection of the idea of rights but rather of commitment to it.

idea of rights and have not been adapted to assimilate or make room for rights. Most modern utopias (and not only the anarchic ones) have been based on the community not the individual, not on rights but on responsibilities. Indeed, for all of us in all societies, important relationships—love, family, friendship, neighborliness, community—have no need or even place for the idea of rights.

The bill of particulars against the idea of rights is long and weighty. From the perspective of some conceptions of the good society or the good life, the rights idea is selfish and promotes egoism. It is atomistic, disharmonious, confrontational, often litigious (as life in the United States shows daily). It is antisocial, permitting and encouraging the individual to set up selfish interests as he or she sees them against the common interest commonly determined. The idea of rights challenges democracy, negating popular sovereignty and frustrating the will of the majority. In principle as well as in detail, it may exalt individual autonomy over communality, egoism over *gemeinschaft*, freedom over order, adversariness over harmony. The idea of rights, it is argued, is inefficient, tending to weaken society and render it ungovernable. Exalting rights deemphasizes and breeds neglect of duties. It imposes an artificial and narrow view of the public good—of national security, emergency, public order, public morals—and takes critical decisions from those chosen to govern and the only ones capable of governing. In many societies and circumstances, the idea of rights helps immunize egotistic property interests and extravagant claims to autonomy and liberty, thereby entrenching reaction and preventing revolutionary social change.

Such objections, and others, have come from diverse ideas and ideologies. Some are variations on utilitarianism that claim to aim at maximizing total happiness and pursuing the good of society (or of some small collectivity) as a whole, but conflate human beings and do not take seriously the individual individually.* Prominent sources of objection today include unlikely bedfellows, those who look back and those who look ahead, religious and other traditional cultures as well as some forms of contemporary socialism and prophets of modernization and development.

RELIGION AND OTHER TRADITIONAL IDEOLOGIES

Perhaps it is necessary, especially in the United States, to justify citing religion as an alternative ideology, as a source of resistance to rights. Most

* Utilitarianism is commonly epitomized in formulae such as "the greatest good of the greatest number," or "the greatest total happiness." Neither formula attends to the happiness of the individual, and either goal could be achieved by total sacrifice of many individuals. The human rights idea concentrates on the individual, believes that every individual counts equally, and limits the extent to which the individual can be sacrificed to the good of the majority, for maximizing happiness, or for the common good.

The rights idea is sometimes challenged also by "communitarians" who insist that the individual is inevitably "situated" in a community, and see the emphasis on rights as divisive. Proponents of the rights idea agree that the individual does not exist in isolation but claim that respect for individual rights contributes to community and is essential especially as communities grow.

Americans see themselves committed to both rights and religion; they see freedom of religion as a basic right, and concern for that freedom as a main source of the idea of rights and of commitment to it. Americans (and Western Europeans and some others), moreover, generally live in essentially secular societies, and in the United States the Constitution insists on disestablishment of religion and stark separation of church and state. Our political ideology—including the idea of rights—seems largely distinct from, independent of, even unrelated or irrelevant to religion or religious ideology. Even the large majority of individuals in the United States who are described or who describe themselves as religious, do not seem to find in religion an all-embracing *Weltanschauung* that includes a complete political and moral ideology (that might not include rights). Or, perhaps, most Americans do not take religion seriously; perhaps they compartmentalize it, giving God only a little, and leaving very much for Caesar.

As a result, in the West, religion (and religions) generally appear to address rights only as the beneficiary of the freedom of religion; even when, occasionally, organized religious influence is exerted in the name of morality against some freedom—for example, against women's claim of a right to have an abortion, or against freedom to publish and read blasphemous, sacrilegious or obscene materials—the objections themselves may be couched in terms of competing rights. In other parts of the world, however, religion sometimes appears in opposition to individual rights, whether in parts of Islam where fundamentalism reigns (*e.g.,* Iran) or in countries where Christian churches have supported authoritarian repression, as at times in parts of Latin America, in South Africa, in Poland. Relations to political authority apart, major religions everywhere (including those prevalent in secular Western societies) have claimed to be complete ideologies, and the relation of religion, of religious thought, of the theology or doctrine of different religions, to the contemporary human rights idea, is itself an ideological question.

Religion is not a single or simple idea, and its relation to the idea of rights is neither single nor simple. The major religions can fairly claim ancestry to values central to human rights: right and wrong, good and evil; justice and injustice; legality and illegality; the essential equality of men; the equal protection of the laws. But the major religions have ancient roots and their theology and ideology were largely formed before the idea of rights was conceived. To ancient Judaism, Christianity, Islam—I think, too, to the older Eastern religions and to other traditional cultures—the idea of rights, surely of rights against society, was unknown. The Bible, for example, knew not rights but duties, and duties were to God; when by God's law one's duties to God related to one's neighbor, the neighbor was only what we would call a third-party-beneficiary. (Even love—"Thou shalt love thy neighbor as thyself"—was a command, a duty; my neighbor had no "right" to be loved and surely no remedy for my failure to love, except perhaps to complain to God.) Of course, ancient languages did not have a word for rights, and even our later English word suggests its derivation from what is "right," from a theory of good, of justice, without connotations of individual entitlement. The idea of human rights, moreover, is a political idea, addressing man's relation to political society, and ancient religions and other traditional cultures did not have a modern kind of political society to which an individual might have modern-style relationships, and upon which he or she might make claims.

The idea of rights reflects principles of interpersonal morality; the major religions reflected principles of interpersonal morality without an idea of rights. Justice was a divine command enforced by God and sometimes by his surrogates on earth. For some injustices the victim had remedies, on earth as well as in some heaven. The same principles of morality and justice applied between individual and authority—for example, the king—both governed equally by God's law. Witness the prophet's rebuke to David for taking Uriah's wife, to Ahab for murdering Naboth for his vineyard.* But claims against authority were limited, the victim's remedies for denial of such claims were not on earth, which markedly reduced the likelihood that he would enjoy the earthly benefits divinely ordained for him.

Traditional values, moreover, were not those identified with the modern rights idea: The traditional ideal was not individual autonomy,†† freedom, privacy—but conformity to God's will and to divine law. Early, and for thousands of years later, emphasis in religious thought was not upon the individual, but upon the community—the tribe, the people of Israel, the Church, Christendom, Islam—on God's will or the cosmic order. In the European medieval and feudal order, and in non-Christian societies in other parts of the world, the individual lived in a chain of hierarchical relations. The ideal was not individual freedom and autonomy, but conformity, compliance, cooperation, harmony, order. The guiding principle was not equality but concern for the hierarchies of the social order. Therefore, not contract, with its foundation in individual will and consent, but status, including responsibility to those lower in a hierarchical order as well as obligations to those higher up. Also, from a modern perspective, religions often achieved order at the cost of inequalities, of limitations on liberty, of suppressed individuality and of individual and social underdevelopment (and even spiritual underdevelopment), sometimes in association with ritual that included elements of cruelty.

Individual rights, constitutional rights, human rights, rights against political authority, were a later and radical idea. It came after Protestantism—combining with economic and social forces—brought a stronger sense of the individual, emphasized not only the nature of the cosmos but man's nature, and began to see man as autonomous, private, and equal to other men, rather than as a social atom in hierarchical relations to others in society. The idea of rights came after the Reformation sundered the single Christian church and helped breach the identity of church and state, after balance of political-military power led to the secular state and to the modern state system. Dissenters began to claim rights for individuals (and

---

* 2 Samuel 11–12; 1 Kings 21.

†† Doing what was right in one's own eyes was anarchy, depravity. Compare Judges 17:6, 21:24.

for their churches) against the established church and against the political authority aligned with it. In such circumstances, religion—those dissenting religions at least—were no longer content to rely on authority's sense of duty, a duty of tolerance, charity or love, and to see man as merely its beneficiary; rather, religion began to see man's needs—his religious needs, and then other needs—as matters of right, of entitlement under higher law.

In new and diverse political-societal contexts, religious thought has had to address the idea of rights, as part of a general development of a theory of God, man and society. Now religion itself—and every particular religion—has had to develop attitudes toward modern society and modern political authority, if only in self-defense: many religions are somewhere the established religion, allied with political authority, and have had to define an ideological attitude toward the human rights claims upon society of the country's inhabitants; every religion is somewhere a minority religion, and has had to adapt to minority status; every religion has had to respond to the needs of its members in large, impersonal, developed (or developing), urban industrial societies. Even Western religions, however, though they had had long experience with Caesar and the state, did not come ideologically prepared for the modern political-societal order. Their ideological attitudes to man's rights and duties vis-à-vis political authority have had an uncertain development and have taken different forms for different religions in different places and times. Often these attitudes depended on whether the religion was the state religion or a minority religion, whether political authority was theocratic, monarchic, republican or democratic, or, recently, totalitarian or authoritarian. To this day, religions have not developed a clear perspective on popular sovereignty and democracy, or on the idea of individual rights.

Today, religion and religious ideology embrace, indeed claim, the moral values underlying human rights. Religion and religious ideology espouse justice (including economic justice), reject torture and other inhuman treatment,*** now oppose slavery, are committed to fair trial, insist on freedom of religion (at least for themselves), support participation in government. Even some religions that did not in the past, may now accept toleration if not equality for the outsider, are reexamining hierarchy and caste, are widening the roles of women. But ideologically, religion, even today, remains uncomfortable with the idea of rights. There is resistance to putting the individual front and center; to the idea of individual entitlement; of claims against society (which may include religious society); of limitations on the public good, including the religious good, in the name of individualism; of the individual "trumping" authority; of only limited limitations on rights; of narrow conceptions of public order. Religion also resists rights as an independent, secular ideology, based on a nontheological view of the nature of man and of society. Although religion may respond with sympathy to claims of economic-social rights, corresponding to the duty of charity, it may see the emphasis on the individual and the

---

*** But some religions insist on, or accept, forms of punishment that are doubtless inhuman by international human rights standards.

apotheosis of autonomy and freedom as hubris if not idolatry, inclining to materialism and hedonism. When human rights proclaims freedom of conscience and religion, religion may welcome that in respect of its own as a matter of God's law or natural rights, but it may also see the claim to freedom of religion as implying the equality of all religions (as well as of nonreligions, of atheism and agnosticism), as rejecting the true religion, perhaps as trivializing all religion. Religion is also sensitive to the emergence of rights as, plausibly, a response to the inadequacies of religion in the modern world.

Slowly, however, religion, religions—principal comprehensive spokesmen for an alternative vision of the Good—have themselves come to see the need for rights in the modern world: as societies develop; where society is pluralistic; in urban society, where the individual is lonely but where some loneliness is perhaps essential for individual dignity. Once, in homogeneous, hermetic societies, religion had offered a complete, sufficient image of the Good, based in order, communality, harmony. Without an idea of rights, the principles of religious morality reflecting the Golden Rule and reciprocity, and buttressed by commanded love and charity, promised and sometimes produced respectable versions of the good society, perhaps even of the good life. Even then, from our modern perspective, ideologically and usually in practice, religion provided the good society for the believer, not for the infidel; for the resident, not the stranger; for men, not for women; for masters, not slaves. Now, religions—at least some religions—increasingly recognize that the idea of human rights is needed to move religions—at least some religions—to reexamine ancient practices that may be less a matter of theological doctrine or other enduring values than relics of the sociology of societies long gone.

Religion will continue to reject human rights as a total ideology. It sees that human rights—cold rights—do not provide warmth, belonging, fitting, significance, do not exclude need for love, friendship, family, charity, sympathy, devotion, sanctity, or for expiation, atonement, forgiveness. But if human rights may not be sufficient, they are at least necessary. If they do not bring kindness to the familiar, they bring—as religions have often failed to do—respect for the stranger. Human rights are not a complete, alternative ideology, but rights are a *floor*, necessary to make other values—including religion—flourish. Human rights not only protect religion, but have come to serve religious ethics in respects and contexts where religion itself has sometimes proved insufficient. Human rights are, at least, a supplemental "theology" for pluralistic, urban, secular societies.* There, religion can accept if not adopt the human rights idea as an affirmation of its own values, and can devote itself to the larger, deeper areas beyond the common denominator of human rights. Religion can provide, as the human rights idea does not adequately, for the tensions

---

* Religion has been adapting to eclectic, secular justifications of human rights (or to no justifications at all); it has also found religious justifications for human rights in human equality, in man created in the image of God, in the common human ancestor.

between rights and responsibilities, between individual and community, between the material and the spirit.

I have spoken of religion principally as represented by so-called Western religions. The idea of rights has had a not-dissimilar reception and experience vis-à-vis Eastern religions, and other traditional indigenous cultures. By them—or, more accurately, by Western commentators on their behalf—the human rights idea has been challenged as a foreign, undigestible, unnecessary, disruptive manifestation of Western cultural imperialism. I think they are mistaken. It may indeed be that the spread of the idea of human rights was made possible and accelerated by Western rule and example. That is not to say, however, that it is an idea that is congenial only to the West, likely to flourish only in Western climate and soil.[†] Western thinkers developed the idea of rights as a principle of political theory expressing the proper relation of individual to organized authority in political society, but the moral assumptions and values that underlie the idea are to be found in the East as in the West, in Confucianism or Buddhism as in Judaism, Christianity, or Islam. The hard core of human rights, surely—rights to physical and psychic integrity of the person, basic autonomy, freedom from torture, from slavery, from arbitrary detention, autonomy in personal matters and equality before the law—are as dear to Eastern as to Western man. Contact between the human rights idea and traditional ideology has brought not conflict but accommodation, and a mutual transformation, the superimposition of a secular ideology on ancient religious ones, resulting in a variety of human rights ideologies. Now traditions are being reinterpreted in the light of the human rights idea. The idea of rights, and its modest, essential content, not only respond to moral intuitions that are congenial to these cultures, but traditional societies have in fact been embracing them warmly. If not conclusive, it is surely relevant that the representatives of these societies—even official representatives who, as respondents to individual claims, have reason to resist the idea of rights—have uniformly and consistently espoused the idea and most of its content. Human rights have been enthusiastically received not only by earlier, Western-educated elites but by younger home-grown leaders, as, recently, in the Organization of African Unity. When spokesmen for these societies claim priority for economic and social rights, they do not reject the idea of rights, but embrace it; they do not reject its political-civil content but assert the essential interdependence of all the recognized rights. When they claim the needs of development (discussed *infra*) as a limitation on rights they are, of course, not invoking traditional values but a different set of imported, modern values.[*]

From reading I conclude that the idea of rights as presently understood was—is—unfamiliar as such to tribal societies as it was once—not long

---

† If Western thinkers gave the world the concept and vocabulary of rights, Western societies were as resistant to the idea as any others, and the worst violations of human rights in our day were committed in Western lands.

* Other contemporary political ideas—statehood, democracy, socialism—are also of Western origin, but are embraced by societies in all parts of the world.

ago—unfamiliar in Western cultures. Traditional societies, too, whether on religious or near-religious grounds, have had conceptions of the good that exalted not the individual but some larger unity—life, the generational chain, the village, the tribe, the cosmic order. Some traditions have deemphasized individual life as we understand it—presently living individuals between birth and death. They too have tended to exalt order not freedom, harmony not adverse claims, not equality but authority and sometimes hierarchy and caste with mutual responsibility. Despite apologist protestations, however, it appears that authoritarianism, caste, and hierarchy did not commonly bring harmony, mutual respect and responsibility (any more than was generally the case—as was sometimes claimed—for American slavery). In most such societies, also, it was principally men who insisted that women found dignity and fulfillment in their allotted subservient traditional role under traditional mores. But basic underlying values— freedom from arbitrary killing or from torture, from slavery or unwarranted detention, notions of justice, fair trial (in local context)—are not generally foreign to them. If some ancient practices, involving cruelty, slavery or inequality, still remain, it is the *Zeitgeist*, reflecting not only Western but also developing indigenous ideas, that rejects them.

In the village perhaps, without any idea of rights, community and sympathy provided dignity and fulfillment, and an unusual person might find some freedom and autonomy in the realm of the spirit, or by moving elsewhere. But tribal societies are evolving, if not disintegrating, and it is hardly individualism and the human rights idea that have undermined them. Like traditional Western cultures, modernizing, developing, industrializing, urbanizing, pluralistic national societies in Asia, Africa, and Latin America are apparently looking to human rights to help protect not only personal dignity but also traditional culture against modern political power, and are adapting local ideas and ideology to the human rights idea.

SOCIALISM

[Editors' Note: Henkin's essay, published in 1990, included discussion of socialism as an idea and an ideology competing with human rights. Since it was written, socialism ceased to exist as a significant political ideology (except perhaps in Cuba). Russia and the members of the former Soviet empire have embraced the human rights idea as part of a commitment to "constitutionalism," "democracy," and "the rule of law." They have adhered to the Covenants and to several human rights conventions, and some of them also to the European Convention.

In 1993, at the Vienna Conference on Human Rights, the People's Republic of China did not plead competing claims of socialism but invoked "cultural relativism" and—together with non-socialist states— "Asian values." See *infra* Part I, Chapter 2(C). In 1998, the People's Republic of China signed the International Covenant on Civil and Political Rights.

For the Twenty–First Century, socialism does not promise to be an ideology in significant competition with human rights. As a theoretical ideology, Henkin suggested in his original essay, socialism does not compete with human rights.]

Religion and tradition are old ideas that have been making their accommodation with the human rights idea; socialism is a modern ideology that is still developing its modus vivendi with human rights. Like some religions, it is sometimes seen as an exclusive ideology, and, by definition and hypothesis, one in which the individual is not central and individual rights are peripheral if not foreign.

There have been many socialisms and even more than one socialist idea; they have elements in common. Socialism worthy of the name would presumably include: a commitment to the welfare of the collective, to the interests of the society; to economic planning; to public ownership of "the means of production"; to a central concern for the laborer, the producer of goods; to limitations on the free market, on individual capital, on private economic enterprise, on accumulation of private property.

None of these commitments, I believe, is—or needs to be—inconsistent with the human rights idea. The commitment to the welfare of the collective need not preclude a hard core of respect for the individual; the human rights perspective—surely the contemporary international human rights perspective—accepts a right to own property and not be deprived of it arbitrarily, but does not preclude limitations on the kinds of property owned, on some uses of property, or on kinds of economic activity. Planning, some degree of societal intervention, I have suggested, is implied in the obligation of society to ensure rights, especially economic and social rights. Conflict between socialism and the idea of rights, then, is not inherent or inevitable, and some socialisms have combined socialist principles with deep attachment to individual rights.

. . .

DEVELOPMENT

There is another "idea" that sometimes competes with human rights: . . . I refer to development. . . .

"Development" is commonly intoned but rarely defined. It sometimes refers to individual, sometimes to societal, development. It sometimes means economic development, sometimes also political-social development. Sometimes it is the equivalent of modernization, industrialization. Development is properly not an idea, at least not a single idea, but a set of contemporary values. Lacking an ideology, it has sometimes attached itself to socialism, but it is preached as well by societies and governments that are and proclaim themselves to be vigorously antisocialist. Development has also appropriated and attached itself to the human rights idea, proclaiming itself one of a young "generation" of human rights. It has linked itself to the people's right to sovereignty over its own natural resources and to economic self-determination which, at the insistence of the less-developed majority of states, have been incorporated into and placed at the head of the principal human rights covenants. The attachment of development to the human rights idea is sometimes justified on the ground that it is "a people's right." In 1986, the United Nations General Assembly adopted a Declaration on the Right of Development (G.A. Res. 41/128) as "an inalienable human right" (Art. 1).

"Development" is shorthand for important plans, programs, and attitudes. Principally, it connotes economic "growth" to raise the gross national product, to improve trade balance and magnify per capita earnings. Sometimes—especially for new underdeveloped states—development includes social and political development, the establishment of national institutions and a political ethos, raising the level of education and of cultural and scientific activity. Sometimes it implies also eliminating archaic vestiges—slavery, caste disabilities, the subjugation of women. The effort to achieve such development may entail sacrificing other values, including traditional values associated with life in ancient, small, homogeneous, hermetic communities. By its character and in its historical context the drive to development is revolutionary, and like other revolutions it is in a hurry. Often it is single-minded and prepared to sacrifice other values to its needs, and the present to the future. Development, then, is not universally and indisputably seen as an unmixed virtue; but it may be a necessity in the world as it has become.

The drive for development is deeply intertwined with the idea of rights. Development is often justified as necessary to make it possible to respect and insure individual rights. Political development is essential to assure the human right to participate in self-government in one's own country. Economic development will enable a country better to guarantee the economic and social rights of its inhabitants, will increase the resources available for that purpose and help achieve it more expeditiously. Societal development is essential for individual development which is necessary to enable individuals to know their rights, to claim them, to realize and to enjoy them and the human dignity they promise.

Some paths to development, however, have a less supportive relation to individual rights. In some countries the needs of development have been invoked as grounds for authoritarian or single-party government, brooking no political opposition; for regimentation, imposing various degrees of forced labor and denying freedom to choose one's place of residence or work; for economic planning that entails sacrificing the rights, including the basic human needs, of people today for the sake of the nation or of future generations.

Development is surely important but its importance, and the homage, the compliment, implied in its appropriation of the rights terminology, should not confuse us as to its relation to the human rights idea. Individual development, the growth of human capabilities and human dignity, are indeed goals of the rights idea, and the development of a society may contribute to its ability to promote individual development and dignity. But, in itself, the economic development of a society—modernization, growth, GNP—is not an individual right; and immediately, at least, it does not necessarily improve the lot, even the economic and social lot, of human beings today, and may even divert energies and resources that might be devoted to their basic human needs. The development of a society is a public good, but, under the rights ideology, there is a minimum, a floor, below which one cannot reduce individual rights for a public good however worthy. The sacrifice of rights today for an uncertain future surely denies rights today, while the future remains uncertain; in any event, it is inherent in the idea of rights that there is a limit to sacrificing the present for the future; the rights of living persons for those of generations to come. Development needs are not a temporary public emergency permitting derogation of rights. They are not, like the needs of national security or public order, special, occasional needs permitting limitations on individual rights at the margin. Development is a comprehensive, pervasive, long-term program in which individual rights have to be integrated, not one that can be used as a basis for disregarding them.

Development—whether seen as a societal goal or as a right—cannot be allowed to swallow up the human rights of the Universal Declaration. Development should not be allowed to appear to be in opposition to human rights. In fact, the common assumption that one must choose between societal development and individual rights has not been proven, or even examined. Torturing people, killing them, making them disappear, detaining them without trial, or punishing them for what cannot (consistently with the human rights idea) be made a crime—none of these feeds or educates any individual, or builds factories and highways. But it has not been proven either that economic development generally requires regimentation, invasion of privacy and "personhood," suppression of political freedom, of rights of assembly and association, trade union rights. It is not proven, even, that economic development requires a society to deny individual basic human needs and other economic and social rights today. On the contrary, thoughtful leaders committed to development are of the view that development and human rights are symbiotic, not adversary. Development must be political and social as well as economic; it requires giving the villager as well as the city dweller a sense of personhood, worth, dignity; it requires more rather than less individualized rights. It is recognized that today there can be no freedom, no dignity without development; it is increasingly recognized that there can be no authentic development without freedom. . . .

Human rights may have become the idea of our time in part because ours is the age of development, industrialization, urbanization, which in many parts of the world have helped undermine what religion and tradition long offered the individual. In this modern, modernizing world, the human rights idea may sometimes appear as an ideology competing with religion, as a threat to traditional societies, as an obstacle to totalitarian socialism or to development in a hurry. But the idea of rights is not a complete, all embracing ideology, is not in fact in competition with other ideologies. Religion explains and comforts, tradition supports, socialism cares, development builds; the human rights idea does none of these. In today's world—and tomorrow's—there may be no less need for what religion and tradition have promised and provided . . . what development will bring; the idea of rights is not inconsistent, not in competition with any of them. Rather, religion, traditional societies ... developers, will find, I believe, that their values and goals, even along their particular path, depend on individual dignity and fulfillment, and in a modern world have to be firmly supported by the idea of human rights.

There is no agreement between the secular and the theological, or between traditional and modern perspectives, on man and the Universe. One cannot prove, or even persuade, whether a substantially free economy or substantial planning is more conducive to the good society or the good of individual man. But there is now a working consensus that every man and woman, between birth and death, counts, and has a claim to an irreducible core of integrity and dignity. In that consensus, in the world we have and are shaping, the idea of human rights is the essential idea.

Note: Human Rights and Religion at the Turn of the Century

1. Especially since the end of the Cold War, there has been growing interaction between the "world of religion" and the human rights movement. Representatives of the religious world have been actively affirming the affinity between religion and human rights. They have been stressing the origins of the human rights idea in religious sources: voices from the Judeo–Christian tradition, in particular, have been insisting that human equality and human dignity—the foundations of human rights—are rooted in the story of Adam, the single ancestor of all mankind and created in God's image. Religious authority has also claimed that the idea of justice, both criminal justice and distributive justice, implied in many elements of the human rights idea, is rooted in religious ideology.

Indeed, some religious voices have argued that only by basing human rights on religion can one provide them a solid foundation and lead to their implementation. See, *e.g.,* Stackhouse, *The Intellectual Crisis of a Good Idea*, 26 J. Religious Ethics 263 (1998); *but cf.* Henkin, *Religion, Religions, and Human Rights*, 26 J. Religious Ethics 229 (1998); Religion and Human Rights: Competing Claims? (C. Gustafson & P. Juviler eds., 1999); Michael Perry, The Idea of Human Rights: Four Inquiries (1998).

In the West, at the end of the Twentieth Century, relations between human rights and religion have also improved in fact. Religious representatives have been less likely to be allied with totalitarian governments, as they had been earlier in some countries. On the other hand, the rise of "fundamentalism," combined with notions of cultural relativism (Chapter 2(C) *infra*), has produced violations of human rights on religious grounds, such as religious authority as a limitation on representative government, on gender equality, on freedom of expression, and on religious freedom for religious dissidents or members of other religions. See John Witte, Jr., *Law, Religion, and Human Rights*, 28 Colum. Hum. Rts. L.Rev.1 (1996). For the relation of the human rights idea to Islam, see Abdullahi Ahmed An–Na'im, *Human Rights in the Muslim World: Socio–Political Conditions and Scriptural Imperatives*, 3 Harv. Hum. Rts. J.13 (1990).

See also Margaret E. Crahan, *Catholicism and Human Rights: the Case of Latin America,* in Presente y Futuro de los Derechos Humanos 341 (Lorena González Volio ed., 1998); Human Rights and the World's Religions (Leroy S. Rounder ed., reprinted 1994); Religious Diversity and Human Rights (Irene Bloom, J. Paul Martin, and Wayne L. Proudfoot eds., 1996); Religion and Human Rights: Basic Documents (Tad Stahnke and J. Paul Martin eds., 1998); Religious Human Rights in Global Perspective: Religious Perspectives (John Witte, Jr. and Johan D. van der Vyver eds., 1996). Compare also Confucianism and Human Rights (de Bary and Tu Weiming eds., 1997).

2. In the international law of human rights, the right to freedom of religion has been enshrined in several instruments, notably in the Universal Declaration of Human Rights (Article 18), and in the International Covenant on Civil and Political Rights (Article 18). But some states have rejected a right to change one's religion, and some have resisted a right to proselytize.

3. International instruments do not include a right to live in a society that does not have an establishment of religion. Compare the First Amendment to the U.S. Constitution. But the form and degrees of "Establishment" of religion, and—on the other hand—the regulation by the state of religious organizations (and their properties) may seriously interfere with the free exercise of religion.

4. In 1981, the General Assembly adopted the Declaration on the Elimination of All Forms of Intolerance and of Discrimination Based on Religion or Belief, U.N. Doc. A/RES/36/55 (1981), but there has been little movement toward translating these principles into a convention (comparable to the Convention on the Elimination of All Forms of Racial Discrimination). For a review of relevant state practices, see Implementation of the Declaration on the Elimination of All Forms of Intolerance and of Discrimination Based on Religion or Belief: Report Submitted by Abdelfattah Amor, Special Rapporteur, U.N. Doc. E/CN.4/1995/91 (1994).

5. In depositing their instruments of ratification, some states have entered reservations to the freedom of religion clauses in the International Covenant on Civil and Political Rights, and in particular to the Convention on the Elimination of All Forms of Discrimination Against Women.

CHAPTER 2

THE TRIUMPH OF HUMAN RIGHTS AFTER THE SECOND WORLD WAR

Until the late 1930's, the international political system, and international law, continued to maintain that how a state treated its own inhabitants was not a matter of legitimate international concern. With the advent of the Second World War, and with the mounting evidence of atrocities both within Germany and in the countries under its military occupation, how Nazi Germany treated those under its rule became a subject of acute international concern. The *Four Freedoms*, declared by President Franklin Roosevelt in 1941, became not only war aims of the Allies but part of the blueprint for the post-war world. See Part IV, Chapter 3(A). With victory, and as evidence of genocide and of the Holocaust became overwhelming and irrefutable, the Allies drafted the Nuremberg Charter which charged Nazi leaders not only with waging aggressive war and with violations of the laws of war ("war crimes") but also with *crimes against humanity,** the first formal assertion of an international law of human rights. Simultaneously, the Allies drafted and put into effect the Charter of the United Nations which declared the promotion of human rights to be a primary purpose of the new United Nations Organization. The Charter also projected a commission on human rights as an early activity of the new UN organization. As its first major activity, the UN Commission on Human Rights prepared the Universal Declaration of Human Rights, which was approved and proclaimed by the General Assembly in 1948. See Part III, Chapter 1.

The International Human Rights Movement was launched.

The Universal Declaration of Human Rights has come to represent the human rights idea in the Twentieth Century. The Declaration provides a catalog of rights in thirty articles, which has been universally accepted as an authoritative definition of human rights. The Declaration has inspired the incorporation of the human rights idea in constitutions around the world and formed the basis for covenants and conventions. The Declaration and the two covenants—the International Covenant on Civil and Political Rights and the International Covenant on Economic, Social and Cultural Rights—have earned the appellation "the International Bill of Rights." See Part III, Chapter 2(B).

---

* The phrase "crimes against humanity" appears to have entered the vocabulary of human rights from a letter written by George Washington Williams, a Baptist minister and journalist, to U.S. Secretary of State Blaine dated 15 Sept. 1890. Williams used the term in reference to the activities of King Leopold of Belgium in the Congo. See Adam Hochschild, *King Leopold's Ghost* 112, 317 n. 112 (1998).

A.   CONTEMPORARY JUSTIFICATIONS OF HUMAN RIGHTS

"Certainly there was, just a relatively few years ago, fairly general agreement that the doctrine of natural rights had been thoroughly and irretrievably discredited. Indeed this was sometimes looked upon as the paradigm case of the manner in which a moral and political doctrine could be both rhetorically influential and intellectually inadequate and unacceptable." R. Wasserstrom, *Rights, Human Rights, and Racial Discrimination,* 61 J. Phil. 628 (1964).

The rise of Nazism and the ascendance of Adolf Hitler began to shake the foundations of positivism, the view that "law was law" and that Hitler's racist laws had the character and quality of law as much as the benevolent law of any democracy.

With the birth of International Human Rights, using the language of rights usually associated with morality and with law, came the quest for legal and moral justifications. Traditional natural law and natural rights were revisited and revived, but with essential modifications. The utilitarianism of Bentham had to make room for safeguards against majorities prepared to sacrifice individuals and minorities to the "greatest good of the greatest number," as the majority saw it. See H.L.A. Hart *infra.* Rights had to be taken seriously. See Dworkin, *infra* p. 77. Philosophers prepared to accept the idea of rights, and in particular rights rooted in principles of liberty and equality, divided on the "rights-character" of welfare rights and other economic and social rights. The principal justifications for rights sought support in the idea of justice, with Rawls, *A Theory of Justice* as a principal vehicle for exploring that justification. (Rawls' difference principle has been invoked to justify economic and social rights as well as limitations on such rights.) Others have sought justifications for rights from other disciplines. See Shestack, *infra* Part I, p. 79.

1.   UTILITARIANISM AND RIGHTS

Professor H.L.A. Hart explains and perhaps justifies the "victory" of human rights over utilitarianism.

H.L.A. Hart, *Between Utility and Rights*
79 Colum. L. Rev. 828, 828–31 (1979).

I.

I do not think than anyone familiar with what has been published in the last ten years, in England and the United States, on the philosophy of government can doubt that this subject, which is the meeting point of moral, political and legal philosophy, is undergoing a major change. We are currently witnessing, I think, the progress of a transition from a once widely accepted old faith that some form of utilitarianism, if only we could discover the right form, *must* capture the essence of political morality. The new faith is that the truth must lie not with a doctrine that takes the maximisation of aggregate or average general welfare for its goal, but with a doctrine of basic human rights, protecting specific basic liberties and interests of individuals, if only we could find some sufficiently firm foundation for such rights to meet some long familiar objections. Whereas not so long ago great energy and much ingenuity of many philosophers were devoted to making some form of utilitarianism work, latterly such energies and ingenuity have been devoted to the articulation of theories of basic rights.

As often with such changes of faith or redirection of philosophical energies and attention, the new insights which are currently offered us seem to dazzle at least as much as they illuminate. Certainly, as I shall try to show by reference to the work of two now influential contemporary writers, the new faith has been presented in forms which are, in spite of much brilliance, in the end unconvincing. My two examples, both American, are taken respectively from the Conservative Right and the Liberal Left of the political spectrum; and while the former, the Conservative, builds a theory of rights on the moral importance of the *separateness* or *distinctness* of human persons which utilitarianism is said to ignore, the latter, the Liberal Left, seeks to erect such a theory on their moral title to equal concern and respect which, it is said, unreconstructed utilitarianism implicitly denies. So while the first theory is dominated by the duty of governments to respect the separateness of persons, the second is dominated by the duty of governments to treat their subjects as equals, with equal concern and respect.

II.

For a just appraisal of the first of these two theories it is necessary to gain a clear conception of what precisely is meant by the criticism, found in different forms in very many different modern writers, that unqualified utilitarianism fails to recognize or abstracts from the separateness of persons when, as a political philosophy, it calls on governments to maximise the total or the average net happiness or welfare of their subjects. Though this accusation of ignoring the separateness of persons can be seen as a version of the Kantian principle that human beings are ends in themselves it is nonetheless the distinctively modern criticism of utilitarianism. In England Bernard Williams and in America John Rawls have been the most eloquent expositors of this form of criticism; and John Rawls's claim that "Utilitarianism does not take seriously the distinction between persons" plays a very important role in his *A Theory of Justice*. Only faint hints of this particular criticism flickered through the many different attacks made in the past on utilitarian doctrine, ever since Jeremy Bentham in 1776 announced to the world that both government and the limits of government were to be justified by reference to the greatest happiness of the greatest number, and not by reference to any doctrine of natural rights: such doctrines he thought so much "bawling upon paper," and he first announced them in 1776 in a brief rude reply to the American Declaration of Independence.

What then does this distinctively modern criticism of utilitarianism, that it ignores the moral importance of the separateness of individuals, mean? I think its meaning is to be summed up in four main points, though not all the writers who make this criticism would endorse all of them.

The first point is this: In the perspective of classical maximising utilitarianism separate individuals are of no intrinsic importance but only important as the points at which fragments of what *is* important, *i.e.* the total aggregate of pleasure or happiness, are located. Individual persons for it are therefore merely the channels or locations where what is of value is to be found. It is for this reason that as long as the totals are thereby increased there is nothing, if no independent principles of distribution are introduced, to limit permissible trade-offs between the satisfactions of different persons. Hence one individual's happiness or pleasure, however innocent he may be, may be sacrificed to procure a greater happiness or pleasure located in other persons, and such replacements of one person by another are not only allowed but required by unqualified utilitarianism when unrestrained by distinct distributive principles.

Secondly, utilitarianism is not, as sometimes it is said to be, an individualistic and egalitarian doctrine, although in a sense it treats persons as equals, or of equal worth. For it does this only by in effect treating individual persons as of *no* worth; since not persons for the utilitarian but the experiences of pleasure or satisfaction or happiness which persons have are the sole items of worth or elements of value. It is of course true and very important that, according to the utilitarian maxim, "everybody [is] to count for one, nobody for more than one" in the sense that in any application of the greatest happiness calculus the equal pains or pleasures, satisfactions or dissatisfactions or preferences of different persons are given the same weight whether they be Brahmins or Untouchables, Jews or Christians, black or white. But since utilitarianism has no direct or intrinsic concern but only an instrumental concern with the relative levels of total well-being enjoyed by different persons, its form of equal concern and respect for persons embodied in the maxim "everybody to count for one, nobody for more than one" may license the grossest form of inequality in the actual treatment of individuals, if that is required in order to maximise aggregate or average welfare. So long as that condition is satisfied, the situation in which a few enjoy great happiness while many suffer is as good as one in which happiness is more equally distributed.

Of course in comparing the aggregate economic welfare produced by equal and unequal distribution of resources account must be taken of factors such as diminishing marginal utility and also envy. These factors favour an equal distribution of resources but by no means always favour it conclusively. For there are also factors pointing the other way, such as administrative and transaction costs, loss of incentives and failure of the standard assumption that all individuals are equally good pleasure or satisfaction machines, and derive the same utility from the same amount of wealth.

Thirdly, the modern critique of utilitarianism asserts that there is nothing self-evidently valuable or authoritative as a moral goal in the mere increase in totals of pleasure or happiness abstracted from all questions of distribution. The collective sum of different persons' pleasures, or the net balance of total happiness of different persons (supposing it makes sense to talk of adding them), is not in itself a pleasure or happiness which anybody experiences. Society is not an individual experiencing the aggregate collected pleasures or pains of its members; no person experiences such an aggregate.

Fourthly, according to this critique, maximising utilitarianism, if it is not restrained by distinct distributive principles, proceeds on a false analogy between the way in which it is rational for a single prudent individual to order his life and the way in which it is rational for a whole community to order its life through government. The analogy is this: it is rational for one man as a single individual to sacrifice a present satisfaction or pleasure for a greater satisfaction later, even if we discount somewhat the value of the later satisfaction because of its uncertainty. Such sacrifices are amongst the most elementary requirements of prudence and are commonly accepted as a virtue, and indeed a paradigm of practical rationality, and, of course, any form of saving is an example of this form of rationality. In its misleading analogy with an individual's prudence, maximising utilitarianism not merely treats one person's pleasure as replaceable by some greater pleasure of that same person, as prudence requires, but it also treats the pleasure or happiness of one individual as similarly replaceable without limit by the greater pleasure of other individuals. So in these ways it treats the division between persons as of no more moral significance than the division between times which separate one individual's earlier pleasure from his later pleasure, as if individuals were mere parts of a single persisting entity . . . .

2.   RIGHTS AS "TRUMPS": RONALD DWORKIN

Ronald Dworkin has been a leading contemporary exponent of the liberal theory of rights. For him

> Individual rights are political trumps held by individuals. Individuals have rights when, for some reason, a collective goal is not a sufficient justification for denying them what they wish, as individuals, to have or to do, or not a sufficient justification for imposing some loss or injury upon them.

Rights therefore impose significant obstacles to and burdens on governmental action. Taking rights seriously requires a powerful justification for such burdens:

> The institution of rights . . . is a complex and troublesome practice that makes the Government's job of securing the general benefit more difficult and more expensive, and it would be a frivolous and wrongful practice unless it served some point. Anyone who professes to take

rights seriously, and who praises our Government for respecting them, must have some sense of what that point is. He must accept, at the minimum, one or both of two important ideas. The first is the vague but powerful idea of human dignity. This idea, associated with Kant, but defended by philosophers of different schools, supposes that there are ways of treating a man that are inconsistent with recognizing him as a full member of the human community, and holds that such treatment is profoundly unjust.

The second is the more familiar idea of political equality. This supposes that the weaker members of a political community are entitled to the same concern and respect of their government as the more powerful members have secured for themselves, so that if some men have freedom of decision whatever the effect on the general good, then all men must have the same freedom. . . .

It makes sense to say that a man has a fundamental right against the Government, in the strong sense, like free speech, if that right is necessary to protect his dignity, or his standing as equally entitled to concern and respect, or some other personal value of like consequence. It does not make sense otherwise.

So if rights make sense at all, then the invasion of a relatively important right must be a very serious matter. It means treating a man as less than a man, or as less worthy of concern than other men. The institution of rights rests on the conviction that this is a grave injustice, and that it is worth paying the incremental cost in social policy or efficiency that is necessary to prevent it.

Ronald Dworkin, Taking Rights Seriously xi, 198–99 (1977).

3.   RIGHTS AND JUSTICE: JOHN RAWLS

John Rawls is perhaps the most influential moral and political philosopher of the second half of the Twentieth Century. *A Theory of Justice* (1971), as well as later works, are primarily concerned with justice rather than with rights *per se*, but Rawls has used the language of rights to articulate his two basic principles of justice. In particular, he has identified certain liberties that must be respected in a just society. As well, his second principle of justice, the "difference principle," implies that individuals have certain rights to economic equality, and that such rights are as fundamental as basic liberties.

[T]he two principles of justice read as follows:

> a.   Each person has an equal right to a fully adequate scheme of equal basic liberties which is compatible with a similar scheme of liberties for all.

> b.   Social and economic inequalities are to satisfy two conditions. First, they must be attached to offices and positions open to all under conditions of fair equality of opportunity; and second, they

must be to the greatest benefit of the least advantaged members of society.

. . .

[T]he equal basic liberties in the first principle of justice are specified by a list as follows: freedom of thought and liberty of conscience; the political liberties and freedom of association, as well as the freedoms specified by the liberty and integrity of the person; and finally, the rights and liberties covered by the rule of law. No priority is assigned to liberty as such, as if the exercise of something called "liberty" has a preeminent value and is the main if not the sole end of political and social justice. There is, to be sure, a general presumption against imposing legal and other restrictions on conduct without sufficient reason. But this presumption creates no special priority for any particular liberty. . . .

Throughout the history of democratic thought the focus has been on achieving certain specific liberties and constitutional guarantees, as found, for example, in various bills of rights and declarations of the rights of man. The account of the basic liberties follows this tradition.

John Rawls, Political Liberalism 291–92 (1993).

Notes

A survey of various philosophical foundations of human rights appears in Jerome Shestack, *The Philosophic Foundations of Human Rights*, 20 Hum. Rts. Q. 6 (1998), and in an earlier essay, *The Jurisprudence of Human Rights*, in Human Rights in International Law: Legal and Policy Issues 69 (T. Meron ed., 1984). Shestack describes "Modern Human Rights Theories" under the following headings: 1. Rights Based on Natural Rights: Core Rights; 2. Rights Based on the Value of Utility; 3. Rights Based on Justice; 4. Rights Based on Reaction to Injustice; 5. Rights Based on Dignity; and 6. Rights Based on Equality of Respect and Concern.

B.   HUMAN RIGHTS: THEORY AND CONTENT

In the Eighteenth Century, human rights were justified as "natural rights"; by the Twentieth Century, "natural rights" were thoroughly discredited. See p. 74 *supra*. The "triumph" of human rights after the Second World War required a new justification and a new theory; these have also shaped the content of human rights.

A theory and a justification of the contemporary idea of human rights are set forth in the Preamble to the Universal Declaration of Human Rights:

Whereas recognition of the inherent dignity and of the equal and inalienable rights of all members of the human family is the foundation of freedom, justice and peace in the world,

Whereas disregard and contempt for human rights have resulted in barbarous acts which have outraged the conscience of mankind, and the advent of a world in which human beings shall enjoy freedom of speech and belief and freedom from fear and want has been proclaimed as the highest aspiration of the common people,

Whereas it is essential, if man is not to be compelled to have recourse, as a last resort, to rebellion against tyranny and oppression, that human rights should be protected by the rule of law,

Whereas it is essential to promote the development of friendly relations between nations,

Whereas the peoples of the United Nations have in the Charter reaffirmed their faith in fundamental human rights, in the dignity and worth of the human person and in the equal rights of men and women and have determined to promote social progress and better standards of life in larger freedom,

. . .

Notes

1. The Universal Declaration of Human Rights can be seen as an expression of a common moral intuition, of the *Zeitgeist*, at the middle of the Twentieth Century, in the wake of the Holocaust and of Nuremberg. The Declaration asserts the idea of rights and the universality of rights. It declares rights to be "equal and inalienable" and links them to "the inherent dignity" of all human beings. Thereby, the Declaration, in effect helped establish "human dignity" as the "*ur*-principle"—the source and justification of human rights—and "human dignity" has served to define and determine the content of human rights as set forth in the Declaration.

The Preamble to the Declaration offers also teleological justifications for human rights: they are "the foundation of freedom, justice and peace"; they are the highest aspiration of the common people; protection for human rights will avoid recourse to rebellion; protection of human rights is essential to "friendly relations among nations."

Are these assertions subject to proof or only declarations of faith? Are they universally or widely shared?

2. The Universal Declaration of Human Rights is a declaration of *universal* human rights. During the Cold War, and then, prominently, at the Vienna Conference of Human Rights in 1993, the universality of human rights was challenged under the banner of "cultural relativism" and in particular of "Asian values." See Section C(3) infra.

1.   THE CONTENT OF HUMAN RIGHTS

References to human rights before and during the Second World War, at Dumbarton Oaks and in the UN Charter, did not define human rights or catalogue its contents. No doubt the human rights idea was assumed to refer to the human rights grossly violated by Nazi Germany. The UN Human Rights Commission, established pursuant to the UN Charter, early set about to define the idea and its contents. See Part III, p. 286.

The idea of human rights in the Western tradition (see *supra* Chapter 1(A)) was rooted in the natural rights of every individual in the state of nature, where every human being had moral rights to life, liberty, autonomy, property. For Locke, and for Jefferson, every individual sacrificed some of his/her autonomy and liberty by social contract, instituting government to secure these rights. The social contract assigned to government a limited *police power*, the individual retaining rights within (and against) government. Retained rights included rights of *personhood*: civil rights. Pursuant to the social contract, individuals also acquired political rights, as their part in popular sovereignty, and rights to establish and maintain representative government.

Every human being enjoyed such civil and political rights in the "minimal," liberal state. During the Nineteenth Century, states began to legislate and to spend for the general welfare, for public education, for some relief from poverty and unemployment, for other "welfare-state" entitlements, which come to be recognized as "economic, social or cultural rights."

Civil and Political Rights

The Universal Declaration did not categorize or characterize the rights it recognized and proclaimed. But Articles 1–21 recognize rights commonly seen and characterized as civil or political rights. They include equal rights to life, liberty and property familiar to Locke and Jefferson, rights in the Liberal State, "negative" rights, rights to freedom from governmental interference beyond what is required in the exercise of its "police power" for meeting the just requirements of morality, public order, and the general welfare in a democratic society. See Article 29(2).

For its catalogue of civil and political rights, the Universal Declaration drew upon the rights enshrined in liberal national constitutions, notably that of the United States, and upon European constitutions and laws. Later, the International Covenant on Civil and Political Rights (ICCPR) tracked closely the provisions of the Declaration. The Covenant also added provisions dealing with the rights of peoples to self-determination and to sovereignty over their natural wealth and resources. See Part III, Chapter 2(B); see also Part IV, Chapters 1 and 2.

Economic and Social Rights

1. Articles 22–28 of the Declaration recognize what have come to be called "economic and social rights", among them, rights to social security, to work with just compensation, to rest and leisure, to an adequate standard of living including food, clothing, housing, health care and social services, to education, to participation in cultural life. These economic and social rights were not designated as such in the Declaration, or distin-

guished in any way from the civil and political rights in Articles 1–21. See Part III, p. 321.

The Universal Declaration does not reflect the continuing controversy as to whether economic and social benefits are "rights." See notes 3 and 4 below. John Locke's conception of natural rights has been seen as supporting only "negative rights"–freedom from governmental interference with individual autonomy and freedoms beyond those subjected to government by the social contract for the exercise of "police power." Locke (and Jefferson) apparently did not contemplate that the social contract between the people and government might include an obligation on government to help the people meet their basic needs if they were unable to satisfy them from their own resources. (That was apparently seen as the responsibility of the church and of benevolent individuals through charity, not the responsibility of the political community.)

That conception of the limited role and responsibility of government changed. Building on views expressed by earlier philosophers, on various socialist ideologies, and on early manifestations of "the welfare state," the Twentieth Century saw the emergence of the idea of "positive rights"— individual entitlement, as a matter of right, to economic and social conditions that were deemed essential to human dignity and to making negative rights meaningful. Compare Kant, *supra* Chapter 1(B). (Earlier, Thomas Paine had suggested providing for the economic and social welfare of the poor as a matter not of charity but of right. See pp. 36–37.) In the United States—exceptionally—the right to an education blossomed in the States early in the Nineteenth Century. In 1848, John Stuart Mill wrote: "It may be regarded as irrevocably established that the fate of no member of the community need be abandoned to chance; that society can and therefore ought to insure every individual belonging to it against the extremes of want." (But Mill's conclusion was "under the proviso" that it be accompanied by restraints on the freedom to reproduce. See John Stuart Mill, Principles of Political Economy 366 and Chapter XIII, Book II (W. Ashley ed., 1961) (1848).)

2. The responsibility of government to promote and secure the welfare of the individual was recognized, and movement to the welfare state began, in Western Europe in the nineteenth century. That development was supported by various socialist ideologies, but realization of the idea, it has been said, is "not Marx' but Bismarck's," and had counterparts elsewhere in Europe. In the Twentieth Century, the welfare state ideology began to be realized in the United Kingdom (the "Beveridge Plan"), and in the United States (the New Deal) and a succinct and famous articulation of it was included in President Franklin Roosevelt's "Four Freedoms" address, which includes "freedom from want" as an essential freedom. In a later address, Roosevelt also said, "Necessitous men are not freemen."* See Part IV, Chapter 3(A).

---

* This statement appeared in President Roosevelt's Message on the State of the Un-   ion (January 11, 1944), see Part IV, Chapter 3(A) infra. It has been frequently attributed

In time, the Universal Declaration of Human Rights was converted into two covenants, a covenant on civil and political rights and another covenant on economic, social and cultural rights. United Nations bodies have continued to insist on economic and social entitlements as human rights equal in status to civil and political rights, though the character of state obligation in respect of the two covenants and the means for implementing them and to induce states to comply with them have differed. See Part III, Chapter 2(B) and Part IV, Chapter 3(C).

3. Most states have adhered to both covenants. See Part III, p. 321. But there have been recurrent expressions of skepticism as to whether economic and social benefits are and should be considered and treated as human rights. In the United States, for example, President Carter signed the Covenant on Economic, Social and Cultural Rights, as well as the Covenant on Civil and Political Rights, but whereas the United States ratified the latter, as of 1998 there has been no strong pressure on the U.S. Senate to consent to ratification of the other covenant, in part because of anticipated opposition by those who refuse to recognize economic and social benefits as "rights." See Part IV, Chapter 3(A).

4. Philosophers, too, have continued to divide as to whether economic and social benefits qualify as "rights." A principal voice in opposition was the English Professor Maurice Cranston, who wrote: "I believe that a philosophically respectable concept of human rights has been muddled, obscured and debilitated in recent years by attempts to incorporate into it specific rights of a different logical category." Maurice Cranston, What are Human Rights? 65 (1973). But see D.D. Raphael, *Human Rights, Old and New*, and the essay by Peter Schneider in Political Theory and the Rights of Man (D.D. Raphael ed., 1967). Compare James Nickel, Making Sense of Human Rights (1987), and Carl Wellman, Welfare Rights (1982).

Compare John Rawls's "difference principle": "Social and economic inequalities are to be arranged so that they are both: (a) to the greatest benefit of the least advantaged, consistent with the just savings principle, and (b) attached to offices and positions open to all under conditions of fair equality of opportunity." John Rawls, A Theory of Justice 302 (1971).

Might a contemporary conception of the social contract be seen as including agreement on establishing government that would not only protect inherent civil rights and derivative political rights, but would also meet basic human needs for those incapable of meeting them? See, for example, Wellman, Welfare Rights 174–181 (1982).

In particular, Jeremy Waldron has written:

It is no longer widely assumed that human rights must be pinned down to the protection of individual *freedom*. Humans have other needs as well, related to their health, survival, culture, education, and ability to work. We all know from our own case how important these

to Justice Oliver Wendell Holmes, Jr. An earlier version, "for necessitous men are not, truly speaking, free men," appears in an opinion of Lord Henley, Lord Chancellor of England, in *Vernon v. Bethell*, 28 Eng. Rep. 838 (1762).

needs are. Some theorists have made this concession through recognizing that the satisfaction of these needs is involved in any genuine concern about freedom. But whether one takes this "positive freedom" approach or not, it is now widely (though not universally) accepted that material needs generate moral imperatives which are as compelling as those related to democracy and civil liberty. If we want a catalogue of what people owe each other as a matter of moral priority, we should look not only to liberty but also to the elementary conditions of material well-being. . . .

Social thinkers like T.H. Green, J.A. Hobson and L.T. Hobhouse were able to convince many of their liberal colleagues that freedom was a mockery without the means for social security. A little later, the crisis of the 1930's convinced large sections of the population that the structure of the economy and the fundamental distribution of wealth and of power over the means of production could not be exempted from the sort of urgent moral scrutiny associated with a commitment to human rights. These concerns are reflected in many modern theories of social justice, where it is assumed that setting out a just order for society is not merely a matter of ordering its political institutions but also of determining, on the basis of rights to life and welfare, what structure the economy ought to have as well.

All this remains controversial. From the right there is still some insistence that individual rights to property and protection from aggression "leave no room" for rights to material security. And many deny that distributive justice is a legitimate political concern at all, let alone a proper subject for the idea of human rights. The politics of rights, they say, have been corrupted by the intrusion of these concerns. On the left, there is considerable apprehension that modern theories of rights do not go, or perhaps are incapable of going, far enough to accommodate social need. For one thing, these rights still proceed at an individual level: "Every*one* has a right to a standard of living adequate for the health and well-being of *himself and his family*" rather than (say) "The standard of life in a community is inseparably bound up with the health and well-being of its members". Thus rights are still seen as the *property* of man, the "isolated monad . . . withdrawn behind his private interests and whims and separated from the community" . . . For another thing, those socio-economic rights that are invoked are nearly always "welfarist" in character— focusing their concern on the *consumption* of material goods and services rather than on what socialists regard as "the real issue", namely power and class in control of the means of production. So though there has been this shift to accommodate new concerns, the theory of human rights has still not freed itself from the charge that it is, at bottom, just a bourgeois excrescence.

Waldron, Nonsense Upon Stilts 157–159 (1987).*

* Reprinted by permission, © 1987, Methuen & Co.

Waldron has also written that "a moral theory of individual dignity is plainly inadequate" if it regards "socioeconomic needs" as less important than civil and political rights:

> Instead of saying that economic security is necessary if *other* (first-generation) [civil and political] rights are to be taken seriously, we might insist bluntly that socioeconomic needs are as important as any other interests, and that a moral theory of individual dignity is plainly inadequate if it does not take them into account. The advantage of this more direct approach is that it concedes nothing in the way of priority to first-generation rights. Morally, it maintains that death, disease, malnutrition, and economic despair are as much matters of concern as any denials of political or civil liberty. Where these predicaments are plainly avoidable, a refusal to do anything to address them is evidently an insult to human dignity and a failure to take seriously the unconditional worth of each individual. Liberals sometimes express concern about the proliferation of rights claims: too many rights, they say, debase the currency of entitlement. But even if we are worried about this proliferation, it is by no means clear that rights based on economic need should be the ones to give way. The prevention or remedying of economic deprivation is not a luxury: on the contrary, it attends to the primal necessities and vulnerabilities of human life.
>
> · · ·
>
> [T]he liberal defense of welfare rights should root itself in the foundations of our theory of property, economy, and justice. It is not a luxurious accretion to liberal philosophy, in the way that talk of "*second*-generation" rights might suggest. Rights to decent subsistence . . . are fundamental to our conception of the dignity and the inherent claims of men and women, endowed with needs as well as with autonomy, in a world that contains the resources that might (if others let them) enable them to live.

Jeremy Waldron, Liberal Rights: Collected Papers 1981–1991, 10–11, 22 (1993).

For a different justification of economic and social rights, see Alan Gewirth, The Community of Rights (1996).

5. A common argument against recognizing economic and social rights is that they are not enforceable as political and civil rights are enforced, by judicial review in courts. Does the existence of a right depend on its being enforceable? Does it depend on its being enforced by a particular means? Does it depend on its being enforced by the courts? Are no economic and social rights judicially enforceable?

For the view that economic and social rights are in fact enforceable, whether through the courts or by other avenues, see Herman Schwartz, *Do Economic and Social Rights Belong in a Constitution?*, 10 Am. U. J. Int'l L. & Pol'y 1233 (1995). Some State courts have enforced some economic and social rights protected by the State constitution. See Part IV, Chapter 3, Sections C and D.

6. Recognition of economic and social rights as "rights" does not require that they be given constitutional status. Compare *Dandridge v. Williams*, 397 U.S. 471 (1970), *infra* Part IV, Chapter 3(C). The obligations of the Covenant on Economic, Social and Cultural Rights could be met by legislation, federal, state or municipal. Indeed, the obligations of the Covenant, it would seem, do not require that the state provide benefits, only that the state act as "guarantor" if basic human needs are not met by personal resources, by employment contract or other contracts, by insurance. See, *e.g.*, Henkin, *Economic and Social Rights as "Rights": A United States Perspective*, 2 Hum. Rts. L.J. 223 (1981).

7. Commitment to the welfare state does not require accepting economic and social benefits as "rights." Communitarians, for example—p. 92 below—might not recognize any "rights" to economic and social benefits, but may favor them for communitarian reasons. Michael Walzer writes:

> The right that members can legitimately claim is of a more general sort. It undoubtedly includes some version of the Hobbesian right to life, some claim on communal resources for bare subsistence. No community can allow its members to starve to death when there is food available to feed them; no government can stand passively by at such a time—not if it claims to be a government of or by or for the community. The indifference of Britain's rulers during the Irish potato famine in the 1840s is a sure sign that Ireland was a colony, a conquered land, no real part of Great Britain. This is not to justify the indifference—one has obligations to colonies and to conquered peoples—but only to suggest that the Irish would have been better served by a government, virtually any government, of their own. Perhaps Burke came closest to describing the fundamental right that is at stake here when he wrote: "Government is a contrivance of human wisdom to provide for human wants. Men have a right that these wants should be provided for by this wisdom." It only has to be said that the wisdom in question is the wisdom not of a ruling class, as Burke seems to have thought, but of the community as a whole. Only its culture, its character, its common understandings can define the "wants" that are to be provided for. But culture, character, and common understandings are not givens; they don't operate automatically; at any particular moment, the citizens must argue about the extent of mutual provision.

Michael Walzer, Spheres of Justice 79 (1983).

Note: Rights and Duties

The Universal Declaration is a declaration of human rights. Periodically, there has been criticism of the Declaration because it does not include human duties, and there have been suggestions that the Declaration be amended or supplemented by a declaration of duties or responsibilities.

It is hardly surprising that, during and after the Second World War, after Hitler and the Holocaust, the world saw the need to declare and protect human rights; that was the commitment at Dumbarton Oaks, at Nuremberg, and at San Francisco (in the UN Charter). There was hardly any perceived need to remind governments or citizens of every human being's duties or responsibilities to his/her fellow human beings and his/her society. And, in fact, the Universal Declaration of Human Rights explicitly declares: "Everyone has duties to the community in which alone the free and full development of his personality is possible." (Article 29(1)). And individual duties and responsibilities are clearly asserted in the following clause declaring that "everyone shall be subject ... to such limitations as are determined by law solely for the purpose of securing due recognition and respect for the rights and freedoms of others and of meeting the just requirements of morality, public order and the general welfare in a democratic society." (Article 29(2)). The International Covenants and conventions that derived from the Universal Declaration were designed to impose legal obligations on governments to respect and ensure the rights of their inhabitants; governments did not need to be reminded, or to assume obligations, to impose responsibilities and duties on their citizens. Occasional reminders of the duties of the individual appeared to serve governments as reasons to impose limitations on the enjoyment of individual rights.

Individual Rights and Collective (Group) Rights

The International Human Rights Movement, and the international law of human rights, have addressed the human rights of individual human beings; juristic persons and companies do not have human rights. But in some contexts such entities have been assimilated to natural persons for some purposes. For example, the First Protocol to the European Convention on Human Rights, Article 1, provides that "every natural *or legal person* is entitled to the peaceful enjoyment of his possessions." (Emphasis supplied). See Note 2 on p. 1126 infra.

The principal international human rights instruments do not address "collective rights" or "group rights." The Universal Declaration recognizes the rights of "everyone" to freedom of peaceful assembly and association, and no one may be compelled to belong to an association (Article 20), but the Declaration does not address the rights of the association. Article 18 of the Universal Declaration recognizes the freedom of every individual to manifest his religion "either alone or in community with others," but does not address the rights of religious communities. Exceptionally, the Covenant on Economic, Social and Cultural Rights recognizes "the right of trade unions to function freely" (subject to limitations). Article 21.

Increasingly, the literature of human rights has raised issues about "collective" or "group rights." Neither term has been used with precision or with an agreed definition. Sometimes the term "collective rights" is used to refer to the "rights" of the "community", as synonymous with "the public interest," as a limitation on rights. See Part III, Chapter 2(H)(2). There are increasing references to the rights of minorities, a subject of international concern (and international treaties) before and after the First

World War. Ethnic hostilities (and genocide) in the former Yugoslavia have revived interest in minority rights. See Part III, Chapter 2(H).

Self–Determination

A major invocation of "group rights" appears in Articles 1 and 2 of the two Covenants. Article 1 of each Covenant declares that "All peoples have the right of self-determination"; Article 2 of each Covenant declares that "All peoples may ... freely dispose of their natural wealth and resources." "Self-determination" was a political "right" proclaimed earlier in the century, and became a legal right after the Second World War, a right frequently proclaimed during the process of decolonization in the decades after the Second World War. It was included in the two Covenants over the objection of some states which insisted that self-determination was not a *human* right, and that the rights of peoples did not belong in the Covenants which addressed the claims of individuals against their own political society. But the contrary view prevailed.

There has been no authoritative definition of the right to self-determination, of the *peoples* which are entitled to that right, of the content of the right, or of the ways in which the right is to be exercised. It is accepted that the right to self-determination was enjoyed by the populations of the areas that had been subject to European colonialism, and that those populations were free to choose independence and statehood. (A few did not.) The right to self-determination has also been claimed by some entities asserting a right to secede from an existing state, *e.g.*, Biafra from Nigeria; and compare support for separation in Quebec. But that right has not been generally accepted. In the case of East Timor, the United Nations took action on the claim of the population to self-determination. See generally East Timor and the International Community: Basic Documents (Heike Krieger ed., 1997). (In 1999 there appeared signs of movement toward greater independence for East Timor.)

The right to self-determination was added to each of the Covenants after they had been essentially completed, and the right was not fully assimilated into the Covenants. It has not been clear who has the obligation to respect and ensure these rights, to what extent these rights are subject to the provisions of the Covenants declaring limitations on rights and permitting derogations from rights in emergency, or to the implementation provisions of the Covenants. See Part III, Chapter 2(B).

Does the "people" entitled to self-determination correspond to the "people" whose will "shall be the basis of the authority of government" (Universal Declaration, Article 21)? Compare "We the people" in the Preamble to the United States Constitution, and "the right of the people to be secure," in the Fourth Amendment to the Constitution. Compare the U.S. Supreme Court's decision in *Verdugo-Urquidez*, Part II, Chapter 1(F) below.

Claims to "group rights" were implicated in assertions of later generations of rights—the right to peace, to a healthful environment, to development. See Part III, Chapter 2(I).

2.   HUMAN RIGHTS AND DEMOCRACY

The Western rights tradition, as reflected in John Locke, in the American Declaration of Independence, and in the French Declaration of the Rights of Man and of the Citizen, derived natural rights from individual liberty in "the state of nature," then affirmed them within society on the basis of social contract and popular sovereignty. The American Declaration of Independence suggests that all human beings are endowed with rights, including the right to join in the social contract, and to institute government that shall represent them. And the French Declaration of 1789 provides:

> VI.   The law is an expression of the general will. All the citizens have a right to concur personally, or by their representatives, in its formation . . .

> XIV.   All the citizens have a right to determine the necessity of the public contribution, either in person or by their representatives, to consent freely thereto, to watch over its use, and to determine the amount, base, collection and duration thereof.

Beyond these, there was no commitment to any ideology that would be called "democracy" at the end of the Twentieth Century. The social contract included, or implied, government by the people's representatives, but it did not prescribe any particular form of representation, nor did it insist on government by institutions in which all the people were equally and fairly represented. Some early instruments speak of government with the consent of the governed, but they did not insist that all the governed had the right to be represented and had the right to vote for representatives. Limiting the right to vote to male citizens only, or to property owners only, was not uncommon.

The U.S. Constitution, like the early constitutions of the States of the United States, contains no reference to democracy or to democratic government. In fact, the framers of the Constitution were not "democrats," but "republicans." See Madison, Federalist Papers, No. 10. Nor was their commitment to popular sovereignty reflected in a commitment to fully representative government. State legislatures also combined chambers representing the people with chambers representing other interests.

In the U.S. Constitution, representation, even in the body intended to be (and described as) "representative," was not based on universal suffrage. The right to vote for members of the U.S. House of Representatives was open to those who had the right to vote in State representative bodies, which also limited suffrage. The Amendments to the U.S. Constitution since the Civil War extended suffrage by prohibiting denial of the vote on account of race (Amendment XV, 1870), on account of sex (Amendment XIX, 1920), on account of age (for those older than eighteen; Amendment XXVI, 1971). These Amendments prohibited discrimination in voting, but they did not grant anyone the right to vote.

England and other Western countries, too, did not exalt "democracy" and moved only slowly to fully representative government and universal suffrage. There too, until deep into the Twentieth Century, commitment to popular sovereignty did not include or imply commitment to fully representative government or universal suffrage. See Part IV, Chapter 2 *infra*.

Democracy and International Human Rights

The international human rights instruments developed in the second half of the Twentieth Century guarantee rights to suffrage and to representative government; they do not purport to guarantee "democracy." In the Universal Declaration of Human Rights and the Covenant on Civil and Political Rights, Part III, Chapter 2(B) *infra*, the concept of democracy appears to be distinct from, and independent of (though perhaps an element subsumed in), the human rights idea. In the Universal Declaration, the only explicit reference to democracy appears in Article 29, which declares rights and freedoms to be "subject only to such limitations as are determined by law solely for the purpose of ... meeting the just requirements of morality, public order and the general welfare in a democratic society." Some aspects of democracy appear by implication in Article 21 of the Universal Declaration, which establishes universal suffrage as a human right and the will of the people as the basis of the authority of government. Some may see implications of "a right to democracy" in the provision that "Everyone is entitled to a social and international order in which the rights and freedoms set forth in this Declaration can be fully realized" (Article 28).

In the International Covenant on Civil and Political Rights, the will of the people as the basis for the authority of government is not expressly stated, but may be inferred from the references to representative government. Article 25 provides:

"Every citizen shall have the right and the opportunity ...

a) To take part in the conduct of public affairs, directly or through freely chosen representatives;

b) To vote and to be elected at genuine periodic elections which shall be by universal and equal suffrage and shall be held by secret ballot, guaranteeing the free expression of the will of the electors;

c) To have access, on general terms of equality, to public service in his country."

Note that Article 25 affords those political rights to citizens only.

Democracy and Human Rights at the End of the Twentieth Century

With the end of the Cold War, "democracy" begins to appear explicitly in international instruments, not only as implied in the individual right to vote but as an overarching value in "constitutionalism" and the "rule of law."

After the Cold War, democracy emerged as an ideology deemed necessary to ensure the protection of human rights. For example, Boutros

Boutros–Ghali, then UN Secretary–General, stated at the opening of the World Conference on Human Rights in 1993, that the "process of democratization cannot be separated . . . from the protection of human rights." See the UN Secretary–General's speech "Human Rights: The Common Language of Humanity," at the World Conference on Human Rights, The Vienna Declaration and Programme of Action (1993).

In the regional human rights instruments, representative democracy and human rights were linked early. The Declaration of Santiago (1959) stated that "harmony among the American republics can be effective only insofar as human rights and fundamental freedoms and the exercise of representative democracy are a reality within each one of them." Declaration of Santiago, Final Act, Fifth Meeting of Consultation of Ministers of Foreign Affairs Res. I and VIII, at 4–6, OEA/Ser.C/II.5 (1959).

The "Helsinki Accords"—the Final Act of the Conference on Security and Cooperation in Europe (CSCE)—explicitly commits the parties to human rights, but democracy is not mentioned (perhaps because during the Cold War, East and West had different conceptions of democracy). After the Cold War, however, democracy emerged as a dominant element in a common world ideology. The Organization for Security and Cooperation in Europe (OSCE), successor to the Helsinki Conference on Security and Cooperation in Europe, committed its members to democracy and recognized the links between democracy and human rights.

In the 1989 Charter of Paris for a New Europe, members undertook "to build, consolidate and strengthen democracy as the only system of government of our nations." At Copenhagen, in 1990, participating states declared a commitment to the rule of law and to "justice based on the recognition and full acceptance of the supreme value of the human personality and guaranteed by institutions providing a framework for its fullest expression." In 1991, at the Moscow Meeting of the Conference on the Human Dimension of the CSCE, the participating states committed themselves to a new world order consisting of "human rights, fundamental freedoms, democracy and the rule of law." See, *e.g.*, Ernest S. Easterly, *The Rule of Law and the New World Order*, 22 S.U. L. Rev. 161 (1995).

For the United States, the end of the Cold War put an end to a policy of sometimes equating democracy with anti-communism and of accepting as democratic, autocratic governments that only obtained approval in occasional plebiscites.

For the former Communist states, the commitment to democracy after the Cold War involved a radical change. Although the Communist states had described themselves as "democratic," their system of government did not satisfy authentic representation and universal suffrage by Western standards or by those of the international human rights instruments. Communist constitutions promised respect for human rights but human rights were subordinated to duties and to the needs of socialism, and human rights were not respected and ensured in fact. The new post-communist constitutions have established democratic institutions and guarantees for individual rights in principle, though implementation has sometimes been chaotic. See generally Western Rights? Post–Communist Application (András Sajó ed., 1996).

For a discussion of democracy as an international legal human right, see, *e.g.,* Christina Cerna, *Universal Democracy: An International Legal Right or the Pipe Dream of the West?* 27 N.Y.U. J. Int'l L. & Pol. 289 (1995). Compare Makau Wa Mutua, *The Ideology of Human Rights*, 36 Va. J. Int'l L. 589 (1996).

C. CONTEMPORARY CRITIQUES OF HUMAN RIGHTS

The International Human Rights Movement and the international law of human rights are established, but criticism of the idea of human rights continues.

1. COMMUNITARIANISM

Communitarianism challenges an ideology of justice and rights as it is reflected in the writings of Kant and his twentieth century exponent John Rawls, and of Ronald Dworkin. A principal philosophical critic is Michael Sandel, in Liberalism and the Limits of Justice (1982). (A noted sociological proponent of "communitarianism" and critic of human rights is Amitai Etzioni. See, e.g., Etzioni, The Spirit of Community: Rights, Responsibilities, and the Communitarian Agenda (1993).)

Communitarians charge liberalism and its ideology of rights as seeing the individual as independent of, and "unencumbered" by, social context, and thus not defined by the "aims and attachments" of social life. Sandel argues instead that human beings are "situated" (rather than "unencumbered") and that our social roles are "partly constitutive of the person we are." This challenge to the liberal vision leads Communitarians to challenge the liberal idea of individual rights.

Communitarians have sometimes decried in particular the emphasis on human rights to the exclusion of duties, and some have suggested the need for a "Declaration of Human Duties." The human rights movement has responded that there is no need to declare and remind persons and governments of the duties of citizens since political authority is always quick to remind the citizenry of their duties and there are thousands of laws in every country to declare and enforce duties. Note also the reference to duties in Article 29(1) of the Universal Declaration, and the limitations clause in Article 29(2):

> In the exercise of his rights and freedoms, everyone shall be subject only to such limitations as are determined by law solely for the purpose of securing due recognition and respect for the rights and freedoms of others and of meeting the just requirements of morality, public order and the general welfare in a democratic society.

See Rights and Duties, p. 86 *supra.*

Michael Sandel, *Morality and the Liberal Ideal*

The New Republic 16, 17 (1984).

The [liberal] priority of the self over its ends means I am never defined by my aims and attachments, but always capable of standing back to survey and assess and possibly to revise them. This is what it means to be a free and independent self capable of choice. And this is the vision of the self that finds expression in the ideal of the state as a neutral framework. On the rights-based ethic, it is precisely because we are essentially separate, independent selves that we need a neutral framework, a framework of rights that refuses to choose among competing purposes and ends. If the self is prior to its ends, then the right must be prior to the good.

Communitarian critics of rights–based liberalism say we cannot conceive ourselves as independent in this way, as bearers of selves wholly detached from our aims and attachments. They say that certain of our roles are partly constitutive of the persons we are—as citizens of a country, or members of a movement, or partisans of a cause. But if we are partly defined by the communities we inhabit, then we must also be implicated in the purposes and ends characteristic of those communities.... Open–ended though it be, the story of my life is always embedded in the story of those communities from which I derive my identity—whether family or city, tribe or nation, party or cause. In the communitarian view, these stories make a moral difference, not only a psychological one. They situate us in the world and give our lives their moral particularity.

What is at stake for politics in the debate between unencumbered selves and situated ones? What are the practical differences between a politics of rights and politics of the common good? On some issues, the two theories may produce different arguments for similar policies. For example, the civil rights movement of the 1960s might be justified by liberals in the name of human dignity and respect for persons, and by communitarians in the name of recognizing the full membership of fellow citizens wrongly excluded from the common life of the nation. And where liberals might support public education in hopes of equipping students to become autonomous individuals, capable of choosing their own ends and pursuing them effectively, communitarians might support public education in hopes of equipping students to become good citizens, capable of contributing meaningfully to public deliberations and pursuits.

On other issues, the two ethics might lead to different policies. Communitarians would be more likely than liberals to allow a town to ban pornographic bookstores, on the grounds that pornography offends its way of life and the values that sustain it. But a politics of civic virtue does not always part company with liberalism in favor of conservative policies. For example, communitarians would be more willing than some rights–oriented liberals to see states enact laws regulating plant closings, to protect their communities from the disruptive effects of capital mobility and sudden industrial change. More generally, where the liberal regards the expansion of individual rights and entitlements as unqualified moral and political

progress, the communitarian is troubled by the tendency of liberal programs to displace politics from smaller forms of association to more
comprehensive ones. Where libertarian liberals defend the private economy
and egalitarian liberals defend the welfare state, communitarians worry
about the concentration of power in both the corporate economy and the
bureaucratic state, and the erosion of those intermediate forms of community that have at times sustained a more vital public life.

Notes

Neither "Virtue" nor "Communitarianism" necessarily contradicts
human rights. Communitarians and the human rights movement have
come to consider each other as alternative ideologies, but where lie their
differences? Communitarians, no doubt, would decry torture or slavery; the
human rights movement, for its part, accepts some limitations on rights in
the public interest and derogation from rights in public emergency. See
infra Part III, Chapter 2(B). Do their differences lie in their overall
conceptions of the good society? In the kinds of public interest that would
permit limitation of rights? Which public interests? Which rights? Which
limitations? Communitarians focus on community and see individual rights
as subsumed in that conception. The human rights ideology begins with a
core of individual rights and sees respect for rights as an important public
interest. They also see community interests as sometimes in tension with
individual rights. See Michael Sandel, Democracy's Discontent: America in
Search of a Public Philosophy (1996); Liberalism and its Critics (Michael
Sandel ed., 1984); compare Alasdair MacIntyre, After Virtue: A Study in
Moral Theory 66–70 (2d ed. 1984).

2.   CRITICAL LEGAL STUDIES AND HUMAN RIGHTS

Mark Tushnet represents views identified with the Critical Legal
Studies movement; his critique of human rights is both philosophical and
political.

Mark Tushnet, *An Essay on Rights**
62 Tex. L. Rev. 1363, 1363–65, 1370–75 (1984).

I.   The Critique of Rights

The liberal theory of rights forms a major part of the cultural capital
that capitalism's culture has given us. The radical critique of rights is a
Schumpeterian act of creative destruction that may help us build societies
that transcend the failures of capitalism. The first section of this Article
develops one version of the critique of rights. The second briefly explores
the epistemological basis of that critique.

Rights, most people believe, are "Good Things." In this Article I
develop four related critiques of rights discussed in contemporary American
legal circles. The critiques may be stated briefly as follows: (1) Once one

identifies what counts as a right in a specific setting, it invariably turns out that the right is unstable; significant but relatively small changes in the social setting can make it difficult to sustain the claim that a right remains implicated. (2) The claim that a right is implicated in some settings produces no determinate consequences. (3) The concept of rights falsely converts into an empty abstraction (reifies) real experiences that we ought to value for their own sake. (4) The use of rights in contemporary discourse impedes advances by progressive social forces, which I will call the "party of humanity."

Each of these critiques is bound up with a particular rejoinder to the general critique of rights. (1) The argument that rights are unstable responds to the "unions in Poland" or "freedom of choice in abortion matters" rejoinder: "Surely you on the Left have to think that workers in Poland have a right to form unions, and that women have a right to choose whether to bear children." (2) The argument that rights are indeterminate responds to the "rights structure discourse" rejoinder: "Surely the invocation of rights allows us to engage in rational arguments about what ought to be done." (3) The argument about reification responds to the "Stalinism" rejoinder: "Rights are what stand between us and the Gulag." (4) Finally, the argument about the pragmatic disutility of rights responds to the "working class" rejoinder: "The interests of the working class have always been, and will continue to be, advanced by the extension of rights."

A.   Instability

It does not advance understanding to speak of rights in the abstract. It matters only that some specific right is or is not recognized in some specific social setting. It is, for example, literally incoherent to claim that women in neolithic societies ought to have had the right to choose not to bear children. Such a claim would have been meaningless to them. Similarly, John Rawls restricts his analysis to societies that meet the circumstances of justice—moderate scarcity in material goods and pervasive differences among people over what constitutes the good for people. In this way, rights become identified with particular cultures and are relativized: to say that some specific right is (or ought to be) recognized in a specific culture is to say that the culture is what it is, ought to recognize what its deepest commitments are, or ought to be transformed into some other culture.

The immediate response to this relativization of rights is obvious. Rawls' "circumstances of justice" and other similar constraints on the coherence of rights-talk are themselves so broad that discussions of rights turn out to be coherent across large numbers of societies, all of which are similar enough to our own to make such discussions sensible. This is the "unions in Poland" rejoinder; given the Left's commitment to emancipation, it has to support the right of Polish workers to organize, because the circumstances of life in Poland are not so different from ours as to make incoherent the claim that Polish workers (ought to) have a right to organize. The "unions in Poland" argument tries to get at something important. It does not, however, undermine the basic claim that the recognition of specific rights is itself what constitutes specific cultures.

. . .

2.   The Generalization.—The inductive program whose first step I have just sketched would show that every specific right is just as contingent on social and technological facts as the right to reproductive choice. There is no reason to believe that the program cannot be executed. If it can, it will show that the set of rights recognized in any particular society is coextensive with that society. The conditions of the society define exactly what kind of rights-talk makes sense, and the sort of rights–talk that makes sense in turn defines what the society is. When someone objects to an act as a violation of a right, the ensuing dialogue either involves a claim that the challenged act is inconsistent with some "deeper" commitments that the actor has—and who is to resolve that claim?—or deals with what kind of society we ought to have. If both sides can identify enough openness in the existing structure of rights to make plausible arguments that a right is or is not involved—that the "deeper" commitments "really" mean something— they may talk as if they were debating about what kind of society actually exists. But as the next section shows, the indeterminacy of rights-claims means that the debate is always about what the society is and what it ought to be. In some social contexts, the party of humanity may be helped by the mutual illusion that the discussion is only about what is. Perhaps that is how observers in the capitalist heartland would like to construe the "unions in Poland" question. But I doubt that the members of Solidarity see it that way.

. . .

B.   Indeterminacy

I have argued that rights-talk often conceals a claim that things ought to be different within an argument that things are as the claimant contends. That masquerade is sometimes successful, at least until the claim is rejected by the courts or by the wider audience for the claim. It is successful because the language of rights is so open and indeterminate that opposing parties can use the same language to express their positions. Because rights-talk is indeterminate, it can provide only momentary advantages in ongoing political struggles.

. . .

. . . Fundamental indeterminacy.—I find it striking that in discussions about the critique of rights, people who think that there *are* rights take the high ground by identifying a highly abstract right as one whose existence cannot be challenged. And usually I don't challenge it. But fundamental indeterminacy makes it impossible to connect the abstract right—"autonomy" or "equal concern and respect" are the usual candidates—to any particular outcome without fully specifying a wide range of social arrangements that the proponents of the right take for granted but that another person who believes in "autonomy" might reject. Part of the argument for technical indeterminacy is that abstract rights get specified in particular legal contexts. The argument for fundamental indeterminacy is that abstract rights get specified in particular social contexts. Because both the legal and the social surroundings can readily be placed in question, the proponent of the abstract right gains nothing by eliciting agreement on the high ground.

· · ·

(b) The generalization.—Fundamental indeterminacy occurs because rights have a social context. When we try to specify a particularized right in some localized area, we discover that we have committed ourselves to a description of an entire social order.

· · ·

Even more generally, because rights have a social context, their realization as a fact of social life rather than their mere recognition in political and legal rhetoric requires that right-holders have the material and psychological resources that will allow them to exercise their rights. Yet liberal rights rhetoric ordinarily fails to consider that fundamental social changes are necessary to allow people to exercise their rights. As Fishkin puts it, liberalism "accepts background inequalities provided that certain process-related equalities are maintained." [San Antonio Independent School District v. Rodriguez] demonstrates this point also. Advocates of school finance equalization argued that it was required by the First Amendment, because children disadvantaged in the educational system—left functionally illiterate or ill-informed about public matters—would be disadvantaged in the political system as a result. The Court responded that it had "long afforded zealous protection against unjustifiable governmental interference with the individual's rights to speak and to vote. Yet we have never presumed to . . . guarantee to the citizenry the most *effective* speech or the most *informed* electoral choice." Similarly, a "volunteer" army in a class-divided society, which structures options so that some find it easier to choose to be soldiers than do others, illustrates the relation between one right and all the others.

Specifying a particular right is thus either an act of political rhetoric or a commitment to social transformation. In this way the indeterminacy critique recapitulates the instability argument.

· · ·

C. Reification

The language of rights is attractive in part because it seems to describe important aspects of human experience. We all fear, but also desire and need, the influence that other people have on our lives. Some rights, like the right to reproductive choice, protect us against the intrusions that others may seek to visit upon us. Other rights, like the rights to nutrition or education, secure from others some of the things we need to flourish. Thus, the language of rights captures the contradictory predicament of people as at once alone and together, independent and yet necessarily in solidarity with others, individuals whose lives have meaning only in society.

The language of rights attempts to describe how people can defend the interests they have by virtue of their humanity against efforts by others to suppress those interests or to live indifferent to the suffering caused by failing to recognize the interests of others.

I could not sensibly deny the importance of experiences of independence and solidarity. They are central parts of our humanity. But the reification critique claims that treating those experiences as instances of abstract rights mischaracterizes them. The experiences themselves are concrete confrontations in real circumstances, rich in detail and radiating in innumerable directions. When I march to oppose United States intervention in Central America, I am "exercising a right" to be sure, but I am also, and more importantly, being together with friends, affiliating myself with strangers, with some of whom I disagree profoundly, getting cold, feeling alone in a crowd, and so on. It is a form of alienation or reification to characterize this as a instance of "exercising my rights." The experiences become desiccated when described in that way. We must insist on preserving real experiences rather than abstracting general rights from those experiences. The language of rights should be abandoned to the very great extent that it takes as a goal the realization of the reified abstraction "rights" rather than the experiences of solidarity and individuality.

· · ·

D. Political Disutility

Conversations with people skeptical about the critique of rights lead me to suspect that much of what I have already said may be overkill. They usually agree with the indeterminacy critique rather quickly, and are willing to accept the instability critique for purposes of argument. But they say that the critique of rights ought to be rejected because the idea of rights is useful to the party of humanity. This section first will suggest some reasons to be skeptical of the claim that the idea of rights is politically useful and then will develop an argument that the idea of rights is affirmatively harmful to the party of humanity. I do not mean that the idea of rights is on balance actually harmful. Rather, my point is that the pragmatic argument to which defenders of rights retreat when pressed is much less powerful than they normally think.

1. Rights as Not Useful.—Initially, it seems difficult to reconcile the indeterminacy critique with the claim that rights are pragmatically useful. To say that rights are politically useful is to say that they *do* something, yet to say that rights are indeterminate is to say that one cannot know whether a claim of right will do anything. Perhaps on this level utility means that, although the indeterminacy critique is in some sense correct, enough relevant decisionmakers do not accept it that political advances can be achieved by making claims of right.

· · ·

If rights are only pragmatically useful, their defenders in foul times will abandon them when the weather changes. If a right to Y is only pragmatically useful as a means to X, Y will be abandoned as soon as some other means to X appears more promising. This consideration undermines at least this version of the argument that rights are pragmatically useful. Many civil libertarians who were attracted to the movement by its stand in favor of rights will feel betrayed when the defense of rights is relinquished. Some, perhaps, will stay on, having been persuaded that their civil libertarianism was false consciousness. But I suggest that the historical record does not stand strongly in favor of this version of the argument.

. . .

2. Rights as Harmful.—It is not just that rights-talk does not do much good. In the contemporary United States, it is positively harmful.

(a) An example: the first amendment.—In 1924, Felix Frankfurter wrote an article for the New Republic arguing that the due process clause of the fourteenth amendment should be repealed. On the negative side, he argued, the courts were using the clause to thwart the enforcement of socially beneficial programs adopted through the regular processes of democratic government. On the positive side, the American polity had reached the point at which regular democratic processes could be counted on to protect the interests in fairness with which the due process clause was properly concerned. The balance between harm and necessity tilted in favor of repealing the clause; the occasions for its proper use were rare enough to be outweighed by the opportunities for its abuse. I sketch here a parallel argument regarding the first amendment. Although I will concentrate on the negative side of the argument, its positive component, such as it is, should not be forgotten.

The first amendment has replaced the due process clause as the primary guarantor of the privileged. Indeed, it protects the privileged more perniciously than the due process clause ever did. Even in its heyday the due process cause stood in the way only of specific legislation designed to reduce the benefits of privilege. Today, in contrast, the first amendment stands as a general obstruction to all progressive legislative efforts. To protect their positions of privilege, the wealthy can make prudent investments either in political action or, more conventionally, in factories or stocks. But since the demise of substantive due process, their investments in factories and stocks can be regulated by legislatures. Under *Buckley v. Valeo* and *First National Bank v. Bellotti*, however, their investments in politics—or politicians—cannot be regulated significantly. Needless to say, careful investment in politics may prevent effective regulation of traditional investments.

The commercial speech cases similarly protect the privileged in the name of the less privileged....

. . .

(b) The generalization.—Part of the conventional wisdom about rights distinguishes between negative rights—to be free from interference—and positive rights to have various things. People sympathetic to the party of humanity usually agree that the present balance between negative and positive rights is askew and that we should strengthen or create positive rights while preserving most of our negative rights. Yet, viewed pragmatically, it may be impossible to carry out that program. In our culture, the image of negative rights overshadows that of positive ones and may obstruct the expansion of positive rights.

The distinction between negative and positive rights reflects and perhaps is based on a fundamental aspect of our social life. We fear that others with whom we live will act so as to crush our individuality, and thus we demand negative rights. But we also know that we need other people to create the conditions under which we can flourish as social beings, and thus we need positive rights. In our culture, the fear of being crushed by others so dominates the desire for sociality that our body of rights consists largely of negative ones. The language of negative rights supports a sharp distinction between the threatening public sphere and the comforting private one. The very idea of negative rights compels us to draw that distinction. But it is possible to see the public sphere as comforting and the private one as threatening. Indeed, the idea of positive rights compels us to blur the distinction. That means, however, that it will be difficult to develop a rhetoric of rights that both creates and denies the distinction between public and private, that justifies both negative and positive rights. The contemporary rhetoric of rights speaks primarily to negative ones. By abstracting from real experiences and reifying the idea of rights, it creates a sphere of autonomy stripped of any social context and counterposes to it a sphere of social life stripped of any content. Only by pretending that the abstract sphere of social life has content can we talk about positive rights.

Moreover, the predominance of negative rights creates an ideological barrier to the extension of positive rights in our culture. I find it striking that the rights actually recognized in contemporary constitutional law are almost all negative ones. To the extent that our society recognizes positive rights, it does so through statutory entitlement programs, which are subject to substantial political pressure and which receive almost no constitutional protection. . . .

. . .

Notes

1.   Criticism of the human rights idea has emerged also as a "Latino/a Critical (LatCrit) Theory." The LatCrit argument is that the U.S. Constitutional system, including the Equal Protection Clause and other measures aimed at addressing inequality, has implicitly established "a black-white binary" and serves as "a subordinating instrument and replicator of inequality for Latinos." See, *e.g.,* Richard Delgado, *Rodrigo's Fifteenth Chronicle: Racial Mixture, Latino–Critical Scholarship, and the Black–White Binary*, 75 Tex. L. Rev. 1181, 1200 (1997). LatCrits seek a legal system that acknowledges the needs and the importance of minorities. See generally, Colloquium, *International Law, Human Rights, and LatCrit Theory*, 28 U. Miami Inter–Am. L. Rev. 177 (1997); Symposium, *LatCrit Theory: Naming and Launching a New Discourse of Critical Legal Scholarship*, 2 Harv. Latino L. Rev. 1 (1997).

2.   Professor Patricia Williams responds to the Critical Legal Studies attack on rights, arguing that "rights-assertion and the benefits of rights have helped blacks, other minorities, and the poor."

Patricia Williams, *Alchemical Notes: Reconstructed Ideals from Deconstructed Rights*

22 Harv. C.R.–C. L. L. Rev. 401, 404–17 (1987).

The present paper is an attempt to detail my discomfort with that part of CLS which rejects rights-based theory, particularly that part of the debate and critique which applies to the black struggle for civil rights. There are many good reasons for abandoning a system of rights which are premised on inequality and helplessness; yet despite the acknowledged and compelling force of such reasons, most blacks have not turned away from the pursuit of rights even if what CLS scholars say about rights—that they are contradictory, indeterminate, reified and marginally decisive in social behavior—is so. I think this has happened because the so-called "governing narrative," or metalanguage, about the significance of rights is quite different for whites and blacks. For most whites, including the mostly-white elite of CLS, social relationships are colored by viewing achievement as the function of committed self-control, of self-possession. For blacks, including black lawyers, academics and clients, on the other hand, relationships are frequently dominated by historical patterns of physical and psychic dispossession. In a semantic, as well as a substantive sense, then, I think that CLS has ignored the degree to which rights-assertion and the benefits of rights have helped blacks, other minorities, and the poor.

I by no means want to idealize the importance of rights in a legal system in which rights are so often selectively invoked to draw boundaries, to isolate, and to limit. At the same time, it is very hard to watch the idealistic or symbolic importance of rights being diminished with reference to the disenfranchised, who experience and express their disempowerment as nothing more or less than the denial of rights. It is my belief that blacks and whites do differ in the degree in which rights-assertion is experienced as empowering or disempowering. The expression of these differing experiences creates a discourse boundary, reflecting complex and often contradictory societal understandings. The remainder of this article attempts to show how that opposition arises. It is my hope that in redescribing the historical alchemy of rights in black lives, the reader will experience some reconnection with that part of the self and of society whose story unfolds beyond the neatly-staked bounds of theoretical legal understanding.

II.   A Tale With Two Stories

A.   *Mini–Story (in Which Peter Gabel and I Set Out to Teach Contracts in the Same Boat While Rowing in Phenomenological Opposition)*

Some time ago, Peter Gabel and I taught a contracts class together. Both recent transplants from California to New York, each of us hunted for apartments in between preparing for class and ultimately found places within one week of each other. Inevitably, I suppose, we got into a discussion of trust and distrust as factors in bargain relations. It turned out that Peter had handed over a $900 deposit, in cash, with no lease, no exchange of keys and no receipt, to strangers with whom he had no ties other than a few moments of pleasant conversation. Peter said that he didn't need to sign a lease because it imposed too much formality. The handshake and the good vibes were for him indicators of trust more binding than a distancing form contract. At the time, I told Peter I thought he was stark raving mad, but his faith paid off. His sublessors showed up at the appointed time, keys in hand, to welcome him in. Needless to say, there was absolutely nothing in my experience to prepare me for such a happy ending.

I, meanwhile, had friends who found me an apartment in a building they owned. In my rush to show good faith and trustworthiness, I signed a detailed, lengthily-negotiated, finely-printed lease firmly establishing me as the ideal arm's length transactor.

As Peter and I discussed our experiences, I was struck by the similarity of what each of us was seeking, yet in such different terms, and with such polar approaches. We both wanted to establish enduring relationships with the people in whose houses we would be living; we both wanted to enhance trust of ourselves and to allow whatever closeness, whatever friendship, was possible. This similarity of desire, however, could not reconcile our very different relations to the world of law. Peter, for example, appeared to be extremely self-conscious of his power potential (either real or imagistic) as a white or male or lawyer authority figure. He therefore seemed to go to some lengths to overcome the wall which that image might impose. The logical ways of establishing some measure of trust between strangers were for him an avoidance of conventional expressions of power and a preference for informal processes generally.

I, on the other hand, was raised to be acutely conscious of the likelihood that, no matter what degree of professional or professor I became, people would greet and dismiss my black femaleness as unreliable, untrustworthy, hostile, angry, powerless, irrational and probably destitute. Futility and despair are very real parts of my response. Therefore it is helpful for me, even essential for me, to clarify boundary; to show that I can speak the language of lease is my way of enhancing trust of me in my business affairs. As a black, I have been given by this society a strong sense of myself as already too familiar, too personal, too subordinate to white people. I have only recently evolved from being treated as three-fifths of a human, a subpart of the white estate. I grew up in a neighborhood where landlords would not sign leases with their poor, black tenants, and demanded that rent be paid in cash; although superficially resembling Peter's transaction, such "informality" in most white-on-black situations signals distrust, not trust. Unlike Peter, I am still engaged in a struggle to set up transactions at arms' length, as legitimately commercial, and to portray myself as a bargainer of separate worth, distinct power, sufficient rights to manipulate commerce, rather than to be manipulated as the object of commerce.

Peter, I speculate, would say that a lease or any other formal mechanism would introduce distrust into his relationships and that he would suffer alienation, leading to the commodification of his being and the degradation of his person to property. In contrast, the lack of a formal relation to the other would leave me estranged. It would risk a figurative isolation from that creative commerce by which I may be recognized as whole, with which I may feed and clothe and shelter myself, by which I may be seen as equal—even if I am stranger. For me, stranger-stranger relations are better than stranger-chattel.

B. *Meta–Mini–Story in Which I Reflect Upon My Experiences With Peter, Climb to Celestial Heights While Juggling the Vocabulary of Rights Discourse, and Simultaneously Undo Not a Few Word–Combination Locks*

The unifying theme of Peter's and my experiences (assuming that my hypothesizing about Peter's end of things has any validity at all) is that one's sense of empowerment defines one's relation to the law, in terms of trust-distrust, formality-informality, or rights-no rights (or "needs"). In saying this I am acknowledging and affirming points central to CLS literature: that rights may be unstable and indeterminate. Despite this recognition, however, and despite a mutual struggle to reconcile freedom with alienation, and solidarity with oppression, Peter and I found the expression of our social disillusionment lodged on opposite sides of the rights/needs dichotomy.

On a semantic level, Peter's language of circumstantially-defined need—of informality, of solidarity, of overcoming distance—sounded dangerously like the language of oppression to someone like me who was looking for freedom through the establishment of identity, the formation of an autonomous social self. To Peter, I am sure, my insistence on the protective distance which rights provide seemed abstract and alienated.

Similarly, while the goals of CLS and of the direct victims of racism may be very much the same, what is too often missing from CLS works is the acknowledgment that our experiences of the same circumstances may be very, very different; the same symbol may mean different things to each of us. At this level, for example, the insistence of Mark Tushnet, Alan Freeman and others that the "needs" of the oppressed should be emphasized rather than their "rights" amounts to no more than a word game. It merely says that the choice has been made to put "needs" in the mouth of a rights discourse—thus transforming "need" into a new form of right. "Need" then joins "right" in the pantheon of reified representations of what it is that you, I and we want from ourselves and from society.

While rights may not be ends in themselves, it remains that rights rhetoric has been and continues to be an effective form of discourse for blacks. The vocabulary of rights speaks to an establishment that values the guise of stability, and from whom social change for the better must come (whether it is given, taken or smuggled). Change argued for in the sheep's clothing of stability (i.e., "rights") can be effective, even as it destabilizes certain other establishment values (i.e., segregation). The subtlety of rights' real instability thus does not render unusable their persona of stability.

. . .

The CLS disutility argument is premised on the assumption that rights' rigid systematizing may keep one at a permanent distance from situations which could profit from closeness and informality: "It is not just that rights-talk does not do much good. In the contemporary United States it is positively harmful." Furthermore, any marginal utility to be derived from rights discourse is perceived as being gained at the expense of larger issues; rights are pitted against, rather than asserted on behalf of, the agencies of social reform. This reasoning underlies much of the rationale for CLS' abandonment of rights discourse, and for its preference for informality—for restyling, for example, arguments about rights to shelter for the homeless into arguments about the "needs" of the homeless.

However, such statements about the relative utility of "needs" over "rights" discourse overlook that blacks have been describing their needs for generations. They overlook a long history of legislation against the self-described needs of black people, the legacy of which remains powerful today. While it is no longer against the law to teach black people to read, for example, there is still within the national psyche a deep, self-replicating strain of denial of the urgent need for a literate black population ("They're not intellectual;" "they can't . . ."). In housing, in employment, in public and in private life it is the same story: the undesired needs of black people transform them into undesirables or those-without-desire ("They're lazy;" "they don't want to . . . .").

For blacks, describing needs has been a dismal failure as political activity. It has succeeded only as a literary achievement. The history of our need is certainly moving enough to have been called poetry, oratory and epic entertainment—but it has never been treated by white institutions as a statement of political priority. Some of our greatest politicians have been forced to become ministers or blues singers. Even white descriptions of "the blues" tend to remove the day-to-day hunger and hurt from need and abstract it into a mood. And whoever would—how ever to—legislate against depression? Particularly something as rich, soulful and sonorously productive as black depression.

It may be different when someone white is describing need. Shorn of the hypnotic rhythmicity which blacks are said to bring to their woe, white statements of black needs suddenly acquire the sort of stark statistical authority which lawmakers can listen to and politicians hear. But from blacks, stark statistical statements of need are heard as "strident," "discordant" and "unharmonious"; heard not as political but only against the backdrop of their erstwhile musicality, they are again abstracted to mood and heard as angry sounds.

For blacks, therefore, the battle is not deconstructing rights, in a world of no rights; nor of constructing statements of need, in a world of abundantly apparent need. Rather, the goal is to find a political mechanism that can confront the denial of need. The argument that rights are disutile, even harmful, trivializes this aspect of black experience specifically, as well as that of any person or group whose genuine vulnerability has been protected by that measure of actual entitlement which rights provide.

For many white CLSers, the word "rights" seems to be overlaid with capitalist connotations of oppression, universalized alienation of the self, and excessive power of an external and distancing sort. The image of the angry bigot locked behind the gun-turreted, barbed wire walls of his white-only enclave, shouting "I have my rights!!" is indeed the rhetorical equivalent of apartheid. In the face of such a vision, "token bourgeoisification" of blacks is probably the best—and the worst—that can ever be imagined. From such a vantage point, the structure of rights is akin to that of racism in its power to constrict thought, to channel broad human experience into narrowly referenced and reified stereotypes. Breaking through such stereotypes would naturally entail some "unnaming" process.

For most blacks, on the other hand, running the risk—as well as having the power—of "stereo-typing" (a misuse of the naming process: a reduction of considered dimension rather than an expansion) is a lesser historical evil than having been unnamed altogether. The black experience of anonymity, the estrangement of being without a name, has been one of living in the oblivion of society's inverse, beyond the dimension of any consideration at all. Thus, the experience of rights-assertion has been one of both solidarity and freedom, of empowerment of an internal and very personal sort; it has been a process of finding the self.

These differences in experience between blacks and whites are not, I think, solely attributable to such divisions as positive/negative, bourgeois/proletariat; given our history, they are differences rooted firmly in race, and in the unconsciousness of racism. It is only in acknowledging this difference, however, that one can fully appreciate the underlying common ground of the radical left and the historically oppressed: the desire to heal a profound existential disillusionment. Wholesale rejection of rights does not allow for the expression of such essential difference.

. . .

For the historically disempowered, the conferring of rights is symbolic of all the denied aspects of humanity: rights imply a respect which places one within the referential range of self and others, which elevates one's status from human body to social being. For blacks, then, the attainment of rights signifies the due, the respectful behavior, the collective responsibility properly owed by a society to one of its own.

C. *Mega–Story (in Which, by Virtue of My Own Mortality, I Am Dragged From a Great Height in Order to Examine the Roots of My Existence)*

Another way of describing the dissonance between blacks and CLS is in terms of the degree of moral utopianism with which blacks regard rights. I remember, for example, going to a family funeral in Georgia, where, in the heat of summer and the small church, fans with pictures of Martin Luther King, Jr. on them were passed out—as they still are in many black churches around the country. This icon of King is a testament to the almost sacred attachment to the transformative promise of a black-conceived notion of rights, which exists, perhaps, somewhat apart from the day-to-day reality of their legal enforcement, but which gives rise to their power as a politically animating, socially cohesive force.

For blacks, the prospect of attaining full rights under the law has always been a fiercely motivational, almost religious, source of hope. It is an oversimplification to describe that hope as merely "compensation for . . . feelings of loss," rights being a way to "conceal those feelings. . . ." Black "loss" is not of the sort that can be "compensated" for or "concealed" by rights-assertion. It must be remembered that from the experiential perspective of blacks, there was and is no such thing as "slave law." The legal system did not provide blacks with structured expectations, promises, or reasonable reliances of any sort. If one views "rights" as emanating from either that body of "legal" history or from that of modern bourgeois legal structures, then of course rights would mean nothing because blacks have had virtually nothing under either. And if one envisions "rights" as economic advantages over others, one might well conclude that "because this sense of illegitimacy [of incomplete social relation] is always threatening to erupt into awareness, there is a need for 'the law.' " Where, however, one's experience is rooted not just in a "sense" of illegitimacy but in being illegitimate, in being raped, and in the fear of being murdered, then the black adherence to a scheme of negative rights—to the self, to the sanctity of one's personal boundaries—makes sense.

. . .

Note

See also Symposium, *Minority Critiques of the Critical Legal Studies Movement*, 22 Harv. C.R.—C.L.L. Rev. 297 (1987). On Critical Legal Studies generally, see *Critical Legal Studies Symposium*, 36 Stan. L. Rev. 1 (1984); *Symposium on Critical Legal Studies*, 6 Cardozo L. Rev. 691 (1985).

3.   CULTURAL RELATIVISM: ARE HUMAN RIGHTS UNIVERSAL?

The International Human Rights Movement, born during the Second World War, and the United Nations Charter, assumed the universality of the human rights idea, as implied in the very term. Human rights were the rights of all human beings. The Universal Declaration declared the human rights of all human beings, inherent in the human dignity of all human beings.

The Universal Declaration was adopted by the United Nations General Assembly without dissent, and even those who abstained did not express or necessarily imply dissent from the idea of human rights or challenge the universality of its definition and content. During the decades following the promulgation of the Declaration, no state, and few non-governmental representatives, questioned the Universal Declaration in principle or in detail. In the Helsinki Accord (1972), East and West accepted the idea of human rights and the principles of the Declaration. Time and again virtually unanimous international resolutions reaffirmed commitment to the universality of human rights.

Challenge to the universality of human rights began to appear on the world scene after the Cold War, principally in the guise of assertions of cultural relativism and of state sovereignty. At the Vienna Conference on Human Rights of 1993, several delegations, under Chinese leadership, without questioning the human rights idea, declared that human rights have to be seen in the context of particular cultures: some voiced in particular the independent authenticity of Asian values. (They also declared that interference in other states in the guise of monitoring the condition of human rights was a violation of the sovereign equality of states.) But the final Resolution of the Vienna Conference reaffirmed the universality of human rights, with the strong support of Asian delegates and Asian NGO's. See World Conference on Human Rights: The Vienna Declaration (1993).

Jack Donnelly, *Universal Human Rights in Theory and Practice*

109–114 (1989).

Cultural relativity is an undeniable fact; moral rules and social institutions evidence an astonishing cultural and historical variability. The doctrine of cultural relativism holds that at least some such variations cannot be legitimately criticized by outsiders. But if human rights are literally the rights everyone has simply as a human being, they would seem to be universal by definition. How should the competing claims of cultural relativism and universal human rights be reconciled? I defend an approach that maintains the fundamental universality of human rights while accommodating the historical and cultural particularity of human rights discussed above.

1.   DEFINING "CULTURAL RELATIVISM"

In its most extreme form, what we can call *radical cultural relativism* would hold that culture is the sole source of the validity of a moral right or rule. *Radical universalism* would hold that culture is irrelevant to the validity of moral rights and rules, which are universally valid. The body of the continuum defined by these ideal typical end–points—that is, those positions involving varying mixes of relativism and universalism—can be roughly divided into what we can call strong cultural realism and weak cultural relativism.

Strong cultural relativism holds that culture is the *principal* source of the validity of a moral right or rule. Universal human rights standards, however, serve as a check on potential excesses of relativism. At its furthest extreme, just short of radical relativism, strong cultural relativism would accept a few basic rights with virtually universal application, but allow such a wide range of variation for most rights that two entirely justifiable sets might overlap only slightly.[1]

Weak cultural relativism holds that culture may be an *important* source of the validity of a moral right or rule. Universality is initially presumed, but the relativity of human nature, communities, and rights serves as a check on potential excesses of universalism. At its furthest extreme, just short of radical universalism, weak cultural relativism would recognize a comprehensive set of prima facie universal human rights, but allow occasional and strictly limited local variations and exceptions.

We must be careful not to use merely quantitative measures of relativism; qualitative judgments of the significance of different cultural variations must also be incorporated. In a rough way, three hierarchical levels of variation can be distinguished, involving cultural relativity in the *substance* of lists of human rights, in the *interpretation* of individual rights, and in the *form* in which particular rights are implemented. As we move "down" the hierarchy, we are in effect further specifying and interpreting (in the ordinary sense of that term) the higher level, and the range of permissible variation at a given level is set by the next higher level. For example, "interpretations" of a right are logically limited by the substance of a right; even the range of variation in substance is set by the notions of human nature and dignity from which the list of rights derives. I shall ultimately defend a weak cultural relativist position that permits deviations from universal human rights standards[2] primarily at the level of form.

2.   RELATIVITY AND UNIVERSALITY: A NECESSARY TENSION

The dangers of the moral imperialism implied by radical universalism hardly need be emphasized. Radical universalism is subject to other moral objections as well. Moral rules, including human rights, function within a moral community. Radical universalism requires a rigid hierarchical ordering of the multiple moral communities to which individuals and groups belong. In order to preserve complete universality for human rights, the radical universalist must give absolute priority to the demands of the cosmopolitan moral community over all other ("lower") moral communities.

This complete denial of national and subnational ethical autonomy and self-determination is not acceptable. Even if the nation should prove to be a doomed, transitory stage in the development of human moral community, there is no inescapable logical or moral reason why peoples cannot accept or choose it as their principal form of social organization and the locus of important extrafamilial moral and political commitments. Similar argu-

1.   This is very similar to the argument from practical consensus for basic rights.

2.   Henceforth, I shall be concerned only with cultural relativist views as they apply to human rights, although my argument probably has broader applicability to other types of relativistic arguments as well.

ments might be made for other communities that do not encompass the entire human race.

Once we allow the moral validity of such commitments, we are bound to accept at least certain types of substantive moral variability, including variability in human rights practices. Such moral "nationalism" may be based on political reasons, such as an inability to agree on the structure of a supranational organization, or a fear of creating an instrument of universal tyranny. More directly moral reasons might also be advanced—for example, the advantages of international diversity provided by a strong commitment to national or local customs. Most important, it rests on the notion of self-determination. But however it is justified, at least certain choices of such moral communities demand respect from outsiders—not necessarily uncritical acceptance, let alone emulation, but, in some cases at least, tolerance.

If radical universalism cannot be justifiably maintained—at least with respect to any robust substantive list of human rights, such as that provided in the Universal Declaration and the Covenants—even a weak cultural relativist account of human rights seems on its face guilty of logical contradiction. If human rights are based in human nature, on the simple fact that one is a human being, then how can human rights be relative in any fundamental way?

The simple answer is that human nature is itself in some measure culturally relative. There is a sense in which this is true even biologically—for example, if marriage partners are chosen on the basis of cultural preferences concerning height, weight, hair color, skin tone, or other physical attributes, the gene pool in a community may be altered in ways that are equivalent to "natural" mechanisms of selection. More important, culture can significantly influence the presence and expression of many less easily quantified aspects of human nature—for example, by encouraging or discouraging the development or perpetuation of certain personality traits and types.

The effects of culture in shaping individuals are systematic and may lead to the predominance of distinctive social types in different cultures. For example, there are important, structurally determined differences between the modal "natures" of women in modern Western and traditional Islamic societies. In any particular case, "human nature"—the realized nature of real human beings—is a social as well as a "natural" product.

Whether we conceive of this process as involving cultural variation around an unalterable core or as cultural variation largely within a physio-logically fixed range, there is a social side to human nature that cannot be denied, at least insofar as that nature is expressed. "Human nature" is a range of possibilities varying, in part in response to culture, within certain psychobiological limits; it is as much a project and an individual and social discovery as it is a given. Even if all behavior should prove to be ultimately genetic, the expression of that genetic endowment in human behavior—which also merits being called "human nature"—is in considerable mea-sure culturally determined.

The cultural variability of human nature not only permits but requires significant allowance for cross-cultural variations in human rights.[3] But if all rights rested *solely* on culturally determined social rules, as radical cultural relativism holds, there could be no human rights, no rights one has simply as a human being. This denial of human rights is perfectly coherent and has been widely practiced. Nevertheless, it is morally indefensible today.

The strongest form of radical cultural relativism would hold that the concept "human being" is of no moral significance, that the mere fact that one is a human being is irrelevant to one's moral status. Many premodern societies have not even recognized "human being" as a descriptive category, but instead defined persons by social status or by group membership. For example, the very names of many cultures mean simply "the people" (*e.g.*, Hopi, Araphoe), and their origin myths may define them as separate from outsiders, who are somehow "not-human." Similarly, the ancient Greeks divided the world into Hellenes and barbarians.

This view, however, is almost universally rejected in the contemporary world. For example, chattel slavery and caste systems, which implicitly deny the existence of a morally significant common humanity, are almost universally condemned, even in the most rigid class societies. Likewise, moral distinctions between insiders and outsiders has been seriously eroded by greatly increased individual mobility and by an at least aspirational commitment to the idea of a universal human moral community. Even more striking is the apparent cross-cultural consensus on a few practices that cannot be justified by even the hoariest of traditions, and certainly not by any new custom. For example, the prohibition of torture and the requirement of procedural due process in imposing and executing legal punishments seem to be accepted as binding by virtually all cultures, despite profound differences in specifying the practical and substantive meanings of these notions. There is also a striking cross-cultural consensus on many of the values that today we seek to protect through human rights, especially when those values are expressed in relatively general terms. Life, social order, the family, protection from arbitrary rule, prohibition of inhuman and degrading treatment, the guarantee of a place in the life of the community, and access to an equitable share of the means of subsistence are central moral aspirations in nearly all cultures.

The radical relativist might respond that such consensus is irrelevant. Logically, this is correct; cross-cultural consensus does not necessarily entail any additional force for a moral rule. But most people do believe that such consensus adds force to the rule, so this kind of radical relativism, although logically impeccable, is in an important sense morally defective. In effect, a moral analogue to customary international law seems to operate. If a practice is nearly universal and generally perceived as obligatory, that practice is required of all members of the community. And if there is at least a weak cosmopolitan moral community, it would impose certain

---

3. I am arguing not that *all* such variations are morally justifiable but, quite the contrary, only that *some* variations *may* be justifiable.

substantive limitations on the range of permissible cultural moral variation.

Notice, however, that I contend only that there are at least a few cross-
culturally valid moral *values*. This still leaves open the possibility of a
radical cultural relativist denial of human *rights*. Such an argument would
hold that while there may be universal moral rules or values, human rights
in the strict and strong sense of the term (inalienable entitlements held
equally by all, grounding particularly strong claims that may be made
against the state and society) are but one of several defensible mechanisms
to protect human dignity, which in any case is largely a culturally determined notion.

Plausible arguments can be advanced to justify alternative mechanisms
to guarantee human dignity—for example, natural *law*, which imposes
transcultural moral obligations that are not correlative to rights. Few if any
states, however, actually advance such arguments. In the First, Second, and
Third Worlds alike, a strong commitment to human *rights* is almost
universally proclaimed, even where practice throws that commitment into
question. And even if such proclamations are mere rhetorical fashion, such
a widespread international moral "fashion" must have some substantive
basis.

That basis is the moral hazard presented by the modern state. Traditional rulers usually faced substantial moral limits on their political power,
customary limits that were entirely independent of human rights, and the
relative technological and administrative weakness of traditional states and
nonstate political institutions further restrained arbitrary abuses of power.
In such a world, inalienable entitlements of individuals held against state
and society might plausibly be held to be superfluous (because basic dignity
was being guaranteed by alternative mechanisms), if not positively dangerous to well-established practices that realized a cultural conception of
human dignity.

Such a world exists today only in a relatively small number of isolated
areas. And the modern state, particularly in the Third World, not only
operates relatively free of the moral constraints of custom but also has far
greater administrative and technological reach. It thus represents a serious
threat to basic human dignity, whether that dignity is defined in "traditional" terms or in "modern" terms. In such circumstances, at least certain
human rights seem necessary rather than optional. In contemporary circumstances, then, radical or unrestricted relativism is as inappropriate as
unrestricted universalism. Some kind of intermediate position is required.

3.   VARIETIES OF CULTURAL RELATIVISM

A.   *Internal Versus External Judgments*

What we can call an *internal judgment* asks whether the practice is
defensible within the fundamental value framework of that society. An
external judgment applies the standards of the evaluator (modified, as
appropriate, by relativistic arguments). Practices that are internally defen-

sible but unacceptable by external standards are the practices that are of interest in the discussion of cultural relativism and human rights.

This distinction between internal and external evaluations roughly corresponds to, and further elaborates, the distinction between strong and weak cultural relativism; the stronger one's relativism, the greater one's reliance on internal evaluations. It also helps to elucidate the dilemma we face in judging culturally specific practices, torn between the demands of relativism and universalism. . . .

. . .

Notes

1.   The claims of "cultural relativism" have been heard in particular in respect of the treatment of women. See Part III, Chapter 2(F). In recent years the issue has been raised in respect of "female circumcision," especially of children and juveniles. See Part III, Chapter 2(F), and see *Colloquium: Bridging Society, Culture, and Law: The Issue of Female Circumcision*, 47 Case W. Res. L. Rev. 263 (1997).

2.   As Donnelly notes, the international community since World War II has largely rejected strong versions of cultural relativism in favor of the view that all persons, regardless of culture, are entitled to core rights by virtue of their humanity. However, at the 1993 Vienna World Conference on Human Rights, China led a group of Asian nations in charging this view with cultural insensitivity. These charges reintroduced issues of cultural relativism to contemporary international human rights diplomacy.

The formal Asian position is laid out in the "Bangkok Declaration," which was issued by a regional Asian human rights meeting held in Bangkok in preparation for the full World Conference. Report of the Regional Meeting for Asia of the World Conference on Human Rights, UN Doc. A/CONF.157/ASRM/8—A/CONF.157/PC/59 (1993). The Declaration's preamble acknowledges "the universality, objectivity, and non-selectivity of all human rights." However, the Declaration argues, international human rights agreements unfairly focus on "one category of rights," i.e., civil and political rights, while ignoring the right to development and the rights of sovereign states to order their own affairs. In general, contends the Declaration, international human rights agreements fail to respect "the interdependence and indivisibility of economic, social, cultural, civil, and political rights, and the need to give equal emphasis to all categories of human rights." *Id.* § 10.

The Bangkok Declaration argues further that this failure is due to a "double standard" based on a lack of respect for the diversity of international cultures. "While human rights are universal in nature, they must be considered in the context of a dynamic and evolving process of international norm-setting, bearing in mind the significance of national and regional particularities and various historical, cultural, and religious backgrounds." *Id.* § 8.

In a speech at the Vienna World Conference, the head of the Chinese delegation expanded on this theme:

> The concept of human rights is a product of historical development. It is closely associated with specific social, political and economic conditions and the specific history, culture, and values of a particular country. Different historical development stages have different human rights requirements.... Thus, one should not and cannot think [of] the human rights standard and model of certain countries as the only proper ones and demand all other countries to comply with them....
>
> For the vast number of developing countries, to respect and protect human rights is first and foremost to ensure the full realization of the rights to subsistence and development ...
>
> To wantonly accuse another country of abuse of human rights and impose the human rights criteria of one's own country or region on other countries or regions are tantamount to an infringement upon the sovereignty of other countries and interference in the latter's internal affairs.... If the sovereignty of a state is not safeguarded, the human rights of its citizens are out of the question, like a castle in the air.

Speech by Liu Huaqiu, World Human Rights Conference, June 1993 (quoted in Michael C. Davis, *Human Rights in Asia: China and the Bangkok Declaration*, 2 Buff. J. Int'l L. 215, 226–27 (1996)).

The claim that human rights reflect "Western values" not necessarily appropriate to Asia elicited strong reactions, even within Asia. At the full World Conference on Human Rights in Vienna, Asian nongovernmental organizations (NGOs) spoke forcefully in support of the universality of human rights as defined in the Universal Declaration of Human Rights. This view was incorporated into the Vienna Declaration. See World Conference on Human Rights: The Vienna Declaration, UN Doc. DPI/1394 (1993).

Amartya Sen, *Human Rights and Asian Values*
The New Republic 33–40 (July 14, 1997).

A new class of arguments have emerged that deny the universal importance of these freedoms. The most prominent of these contentions is the claim that Asian values do not regard freedom to be important in the way that it is regarded in the West. Given this difference in value systems—the argument runs—Asia must be faithful to its own system of philosophical and political priorities.

Cultural differences and value differences between Asia and the West were stressed by several official delegations at the World Conference on Human Rights in Vienna in 1993. The foreign minister of Singapore warned that "universal recognition of the ideal of human rights can be harmful if universalism is used to deny or mask the reality of diversity." The Chinese delegation played a leading role in emphasizing the regional differences, and in making sure that the prescriptive framework adopted in the declarations made room for regional diversity. The Chinese foreign minister even put on record the proposition, apparently applicable in China and elsewhere, that "Individuals must put the states' rights before their own."

. . .

I now turn to the nature and the relevance of Asian values. This is not an easy exercise, for various reasons. The size of Asia is itself a problem. Asia is where about 60 percent of the world's population lives. What can we take to be the values of so vast a region, with so much diversity? It is important to state at the outset that there are no quintessential values that separate the Asians as a group from people in the rest of the world and which fit all parts of this immensely large and heterogeneous population. The temptation to see Asia as a single unit reveals a distinctly Eurocentric perspective.

. . .

The championing of order and discipline can be found in Western classics as well. Indeed, it is by no means clear to me that Confucius is more authoritarian than, say, Plato or Augustine. The real issue is not whether these non-freedom perspectives are present in Asian traditions, but whether the freedom-oriented perspectives are absent from them.

This is where the diversity of Asian value systems becomes quite central. An obvious example is the role of Buddhism as a form of thought. In Buddhist tradition, great importance is attached to freedom, and the traditions of earlier Indian thinking to which Buddhist thought relates allow much room for volition and free choice. Nobility of conduct has to be achieved in freedom, and even the ideas of liberation (such as *moksha*) include this feature. The presence of these elements in Buddhist thought does not obliterate the importance of the discipline emphasized by Confucianism, but it would be a mistake to take Confucianism to be the only tradition in Asia—or in China.

. . .

It is not my contention that Confucius was a democrat, or a great champion of freedom and dissent. Yet there is certainly good reason to question the monolithic image of the authoritarian Confucius that is championed by the contemporary advocates of Asian values.

. . .

It is important to recognize that many of these historical leaders in Asia not only emphasized the importance of freedom and tolerance, they also had clear theories as to why this is the appropriate thing to do.

. . .

Again, the championing of democracy and political freedom in the modern sense cannot be found in the pre-enlightenment tradition in any part of the world, West or East. What we have to investigate, instead, are the constituents, the components, of this compound idea. It is the powerful presence of some of these elements—in non-Western as well as Western societies—that I have been emphasizing. It is hard to make sense of the view that the basic ideas underlying freedom and rights in a tolerant society are "Western" notions, and somehow alien to Asia, though that view has been championed by Asian authoritarians and Western chauvinists.

. . .

To conclude, the so-called Asian values that are invoked to justify authoritarianism are not especially Asian in any significant sense. Nor is it easy to see how they could be made, by the mere force of rhetoric, into an Asian cause against the West. The people whose rights are being disputed are Asians, and, no matter what the West's guilt may be . . . the rights of Asians can scarcely be compromised on those grounds. The case for liberty and political rights turns ultimately on their basic importance and on their instrumental role. And this case is as strong in Asia as it is elsewhere.

There is a great deal that we can learn from studies of values in Asia and Europe, but they do not support or sustain the thesis of a grand dichotomy (or a "clash of civilizations"). Our ideas of political and personal rights have taken their particular form relatively recently, and it is hard to see them as "traditional" commitments of Western cultures. There are important antecedents of those commitments, but those antecedents can be found plentifully in Asian cultures as well as Western cultures.

The recognition of diversity within different cultures is extremely important in the contemporary world. . . . The authoritarian readings of Asian values that are increasingly championed in some quarters do not survive scrutiny. And the grand dichotomy between Asian and European values adds little to our understanding, and much to the confounding of the normative basis of freedom and democracy.

Notes

1.   See also Yash Ghai, *Human Rights and Asian Values*, 9 Public L. Rev. 168 (1998). Professor Ghai's article has been summarized:

Asian perceptions of human rights have been much discussed, particularly outside Asia, stimulated by the challenge to the international regime of rights by a few Asian governments in the name of Asian values. Placing the debate in the context of international developments since the Universal Declaration of Human Rights 50 years ago, this article argues that international discussions on human rights in Asia are sterile and misleading, obsessed as they are with Asian values. On the other hand, the debate within Asia is much richer, reflecting a wide variety of views, depending to a significant extent on the class, economic or political location of the proponents. Most governments have a statist view of rights, concerned to prevent the use of rights discourse to mobilise disadvantaged or marginal groups such as workers, peasants, or ethnic groups, or stifle criticisms and interventions from the international community. However, few of them subscribe to the crude versions of Asian values which are often taken abroad as representing some kind of Asian consensus. This article contrasts the views of governments with those of the non-governmental organisations (NGOs) who have provided a more coherent framework for the analysis of rights in the Asia context. They see rights as promoting international solidarity rather than divisions. Domestically, they see rights as a means of empowerment and central to the establishment of fair and just political, economic and social orders.

Id. at 168.

2. See also Yash Ghai, *Rights, Duties and Responsibilities,* in Asian Values, An Encounter With Diversity, (Josiane Cauquelin et al., eds. 1998); *The East Asian Challenge to Human Rights* (Joanne R. Bauer and Daniel A. Bell eds., forthcoming 1999). See generally, *Confucianism and Human Rights* (Wm. Theodore de Bary and Weiming Tu eds., 1998).

3. At the Vienna Conference, China and other states also raised an essentially different objection, that monitoring by others of the condition of human rights in any country was a violation of that state's sovereignty. Similar arguments had been made earlier by or on behalf of the Soviet Union. A Soviet author summarized them as follows:

> The Soviet Union and the other socialist countries seek to ensure that this cooperation should be directed towards the genuinely democratic development of rights and freedoms for all, without distinction as to race, nationality, sex and religion, on the basis of freely concluded equal agreements.

> They at the same time adhere to the position that international agreements must not contain clauses infringing the sovereign rights of States independently to define the rights and obligations of their citizens in accordance with their economic and social characteristics. Nor should agreements contain clauses establishing any supra-State agencies dealing with human rights and having legislative, administrative or judicial functions.

K.Y. Chizhov in International Law 137–8 (Institute of State and Law, Academy of Sciences of the U.S.S.R.) (quoted in Przetacznik, *The Socialist Concept of Protection of Human Rights*, 38 Soc. Res. 337, 340–341 (1971)). See generally, Socialist Concept of Human Rights (J. Halasz ed., Institute for Legal and Administrative Sciences, Hungarian Academy of Sciences, 1966).

Even before the end of the Cold War, the Soviet Union had accepted the universality of human rights, notably in the Final Act of the Conference on Security and Cooperation in Europe (the Helsinki Accord). See Part III, Chapter 2(D).

HUMAN RIGHTS IN NATIONAL LAW: THE UNITED STATES

Introduction: Human Rights, Legal Rights, Constitutional Rights

Human rights are claims—legitimate, valid, justified claims—by every human being upon his/her society, claims to guarantees and safeguards, to goods and benefits, that are essential to personal well-being and dignity. The society is required to respect and ensure these rights: they are to be respected by public authority and ensured against infringement by one's neighbors. In organized societies, human rights are generally safeguarded by rendering them legal rights, protected and promoted by law and institutions in the country's legal system. (But not all legal rights are seen as rising to the status of human rights.)

Human rights, then, are rights in national legal systems and are protected principally by national law. The study human rights and of the means of protecting them is primarily a study of rights in a national legal system. International human rights law and institutions aim to ensure that every national society, its legal system, and its institutions, safeguard the human rights of its inhabitants. See Preface and Part III, Chapter 2.

For students in the United States, the study of the law of human rights will permit meaningful comparison of an individual's rights under the U.S. legal system with their protection under international covenants and conventions (and under customary international law). Study of rights under U.S. law will help determine whether the condition of human rights in the United States measures up to international human rights standards in particular respects. It will provide guidance as to whether the inhabitants of the United States might enhance respect for their rights by invoking applicable international human rights norms. Citizens, students, lawyers, and judges will be able to determine the extent to which the national and state law of human rights in the United States has been modified by U.S. adherence to international covenants and conventions, and the significance of reservations, understandings, and declarations which the United States has attached to its ratification of international human rights treaties.

The legal system of every organized society in fact promotes and protects, in different measure, many human rights. Organized societies protect rights to life, physical security, some autonomy and liberty, and rights to property, and they do so by their civil law, principally law of torts and property, and by the criminal law; these laws may properly be seen as part of "human rights law." Generally, such laws protect against private infringement of rights, but to a large extent also against official violation. In many countries, rights recognized as of particular importance are also protected by a country's constitution and constitutional law, commonly at least against "state action," i.e., violation by public institutions and officials; in many countries there is also a constitutional requirement that there be civil and criminal law to safeguard rights against private infringement. At the end of the Twentieth Century, many states are welfare states and provide economic and social benefits pursuant to law, though such economic and social benefits, even when denominated rights, are not necessarily rights guaranteed by the constitution.

For any country, therefore, the study of its human rights law should, in principle, include the study of its tort and property law, its criminal law, its law of economic and social rights and entitlements, as well as its constitutional law. (It might also include understanding whether and how the constitutional system improves the protection of human rights by incorporating international human rights standards into domestic law. See Part III, Chapter 4.)

In the United States, too, the student (and the lawyer), looking for the law protecting human rights, turns to domestic law. In the United States (as elsewhere) the protection of life, liberty, property (and some pursuit of happiness) is perceived as a primary purpose of government, and the law that protects them is essentially, and may properly be regarded as, human rights law. Under the federal system in the United States, individual status, rights, relations, and responsibilities are governed primarily by the laws of the States; and the primary, perhaps the principal, safeguards for human rights in the United States are provided by the common law and its elaborations or modifications by State (and municipal) legislation—State and municipal law of tort and property (subject to, and supplemented by, State Constitutions). Additional protection for human rights and additional economic and social benefits are provided by federal law.

In the United States, however, the idea of human rights is commonly associated with the U.S. Constitution, and the protection and realization of human rights through State and federal law are supplemented by, and subsumed in, U.S. constitutional protections. The State legal system is subordinate to the U.S. constitutional system, and the protection of individual rights by State law is itself subordinated to constitutional doctrine, as embodied in some protections in the original Constitution, and others in the U.S. Bill of Rights, and in the later Constitutional Amendments. But constitutional rights in the United States also build on antecedent theory and history, and the rights protected by the Constitution stand substantially on rights at common law.

The U.S. Constitution is the supreme law of the land and the ultimate guardian of human rights in the United States. United States constitutional jurisprudence, moreover, has inspired, and served as a model for, numerous national constitutions and international (and regional) human rights norms.

Although the idea of human rights is commonly associated with the United States and with the United States Constitution, the idea of individual rights against political authority, we have seen, is much older than the United States. But the United States has the oldest continuing commitment to "constitutionalism," including a commitment to individual rights and to bills of rights as supreme constitutional law. It also has a long—perhaps the longest—history of constitutional government, including institutions to monitor and enforce respect for human rights. The international human rights movement, born during the Second World War, owes much to the example of the United States, and U.S. constitutional rights have been a principal source for international human rights law and a principal model for constitutional rights in the many new constitutions of old and new countries in the second half of the Twentieth Century.

In this Part we describe, briefly, the constitutional legal system governing human rights in the United States. Chapters 1 and 2 set forth the rights protected, and Chapter 3 explores remedies for violation of rights.*

* For some parallel studies, see e.g., International Law, Human Rights, Japanese Law: The Impact of International Law on Japanese Law (Yuji Iwasawa ed., 1998); Anne F. Bayefsky, *International Human Rights Law In Canada,* in Law, Policy, and International Justice: Essays in Honor of Maxwell Cohen (1993). And see Part IV.

CHAPTER 1

CONSTITUTIONAL RIGHTS: THEORY AND HISTORY

A. ANTECEDENTS: INDIVIDUAL RIGHTS BEFORE THE U.S. CONSTITUTION

Rights in the United States did not spring full-blown from the minds of the Framers of the U.S. Bill of Rights. The authors of the Constitution and of the Bill of Rights had read Locke and the European Encyclopedists, and were raised on Blackstone. Rights were in the political air. Before the U.S. Bill of Rights there were the Virginia Bill of Rights and bills of rights in other State constitutions. Behind them were the traditional rights of English subjects which had grown and spread since *Magna Carta*. (Behind them also were the Seventeenth Century English Constitutional instruments of the Glorious Revolution, including the Bill of Rights of 1688.)

But while England went the way of parliamentary government, leading to parliamentary supremacy, the American colonies went the way of individual rights. The framers of State bills of rights and of the U.S. Bill of Rights did not reject or deprecate the traditional rights of Englishmen enumerated in Blackstone; they wanted these rights for themselves too. But they also wanted safeguards for their natural, inherent rights, even against King and Parliament. The first words of the U.S. Bill of Rights reject parliamentary supremacy: "Congress shall make no law . . ."

Two early opinions by U.S. Supreme Court Justices suggested some willingness to resort to natural law to protect natural rights not mentioned in the Constitution. In *Calder v. Bull*, 3 U.S. (3 Dall.) 386 (1798), Justice Chase suggested that certain rights, including fairness in criminal proceedings and the right to private property, are inherent in the "social contract" that underlies a "free republican government," and may be derived from "general principles of law and reason"—quoted this Part, pp. 254–255 below. In *Fletcher v. Peck*, 10 U.S. (6 Cranch) 87 (1810)—the first Supreme Court opinion to use the term "human rights"—Chief Justice Marshall suggested that "general principles" as well as "particular provisions of the constitution" can provide a basis for judicial protection of rights. But in the end, Marshall did not rest his decision on "general principles" but found an alternative ground for his decision. Since then, the Court has not admitted to relying on natural law as a basis for invalidating legislation, not even to "fill in" the generalities of the Ninth Amendment (see *infra* p. 148). In a famous "debate" in 1947, Justice Black accused the majority of the Court of introducing natural law into "substantive due process," an accusation which Justice Frankfurter strongly denied. See *Adamson v. California*, 332 U.S. 46 (1947). Compare the resort to sources outside the Constitution to define "the privileges and immunities of citizens," in Article IV § 2. See *Corfield v. Coryell*, 6 F. Cas. 546 (C.C.E.D.Pa.1823).

1.   HUMAN RIGHTS AT COMMON LAW

The common law, the product of numerous judicial decisions and several acts of Parliament, has played two different roles in the development of human rights in the United States. The common-law tradition, as articulated by Blackstone, was a foundation for the bills of rights of the States and of the United States. The common law also continued to rule as law, and to evolve after the adoption of State constitutions and legislation.

Blackstone relates English rights both to *Magna Carta* and to natural rights, doubtless reflecting the intervening writings of John Locke. The three principal rights articulated by Blackstone are rights to life (integrity of the person), to liberty (including freedom of residence and the right to leave and return to one's country), and to property. These, too, reflect the writings of John Locke, and they are later cited in the Declaration of Independence and in the due process clause of the Fifth Amendment to the U.S. Constitution. Blackstone declares that rights are protected by Parliament, by "certain and notorious" limitations on the Executive, and by the availability of the courts. (Compare the later statement in the Declaration of Independence that governments are instituted to secure individual rights.)

Blackstone's fifth auxiliary right entitles English subjects to bear arms "suitable to their condition and degree, and such as are allowed by law," as the ultimate safeguard against tyranny. (Compare Blackstone's formulation of this right with the Second Amendment to the U.S. Constitution. And compare Blackstone's fourth auxiliary right to petition the king or Parliament with the First Amendment to the U.S. Constitution.)

William Blackstone, *Commentaries on the Laws of England*

Book 1, Chapter 1 (1769).

.   .   .

Thus much for the *declaration* of our rights and liberties. The rights themselves thus defined by these several statutes, consist in a number of private immunities; which will appear, from what has been premised, to be indeed no other, than either that *residuum* of natural liberty, which is not required by the laws of society to be sacrificed to public convenience; or else those civil privileges, which society hath engaged to provide, in lieu of the natural liberties so given up by individuals. These therefore were formerly, either by inheritance or purchase, the rights of all mankind; but, in most other countries of the world being now more or less debased and destroyed, they at present may be said to remain, in a peculiar and emphatical manner, the rights of the people of England. And these may be reduced to three principal or primary articles; the right of personal security, the right of personal liberty; and the right of private property: because as there is no other known method of compulsion, or of abridging man's natural free will, but by an infringement or diminution of one or other of these important rights, the preservation of these, inviolate, may justly be said to include the preservation of our civil immunities in their largest and most extensive sense.

I.   The right of personal security consists in a person's legal and uninterrupted enjoyment of his life, his limbs, his body, his health, and his reputation.

. . .

II.   Next to personal security, the law of England regards, asserts, and preserves the personal liberty of individuals. This personal liberty consists in the power of loco-motion, of changing situation, or removing one's person to whatsoever place one's own inclination may direct; without imprisonment or restraint, unless by due course of law. Concerning which we may make the same observations as upon the preceding article; that it is a right strictly natural; that the laws of England have never abridged it without sufficient cause; and, that in this kingdom it cannot ever be abridged at the mere discretion of the magistrate, without the explicit permission of the laws. Here again the language of the great charter is that no freeman shall be taken or imprisoned but by the lawful judgment of his equals, or by the law of the land.

. . .

III.   The third absolute right, inherent in every Englishman, is that of property: which consists in the free use, enjoyment, and disposal of all his acquisitions, without any control or diminution, save only by the law of the land.

. . .

In the three preceding articles we have taken a short view of the principal absolute rights which appertain to every Englishman. But in vain would these rights be declared, ascertained, and protected by the dead letter of the laws, if the constitution had provided no other method to secure their actual enjoyment. It has therefore established certain other auxiliary subordinate rights of the subject, which serve principally as barriers to protect and maintain inviolate the three great and primary rights, of personal security, personal liberty, and private property. These are,

1.   The constitution, powers, and privileges of parliament, of which I shall treat at large in the ensuing chapter . . . .

2.   The limitation of the king's prerogative, by bounds so certain and notorious, that it is impossible he should exceed them without the consent of the people . . . .

3.   A third subordinate right of every Englishman is that of applying to the courts of justice for redress of injuries....

4.   If there should happen any uncommon injury, or infringement of the rights beforementioned, which the ordinary course of law is too defective to reach, there still remains a fourth subordinate right appertaining to every individual, namely, the right of petitioning the king, or either house of parliament, for the redress of grievances....

5.   The fifth and last auxiliary right of the subject, that I shall at present mention, is that of having arms for their defense, suitable to their condition and degree, and such as are allowed by law....

. . .

In these several articles consist the rights, or, as they are frequently termed, the liberties of Englishmen: liberties more generally talked of than thoroughly understood; and yet highly necessary to be perfectly known and considered by every man of rank or property, lest his ignorance of the points whereon it is founded should hurry him into faction and licentiousness on the one hand, or a pusillanimous indifference and criminal submission on the other. And we have seen that these rights consist, primarily, in the free enjoyment of personal security, of personal liberty, and of private property. So long as these remain inviolate, the subject is perfectly free; for every species of compulsive tyranny and oppression must act in opposition to one or other of these rights, having no other object upon which it can possibly be employed. To preserve these from violation, it is necessary that the constitution of parliaments be supported in its full vigor; and limits certainly known, be set to the royal prerogative. And, lastly, to vindicate these rights, when actually violated or attacked, the subjects of England are entitled, in the first place, to the regular administration and free course of justice in the courts of law; next to the right of petitioning the king and parliament for redress of grievances; and lastly to the right of having and using arms for self-preservation and defence. And all these rights and liberties it is our birthright to enjoy entire; unless where the laws of our country have laid them under necessary restraints. Restraints in themselves so gentle and moderate, as will appear upon farther enquiry, that no man of sense or probity would wish to see them slackened. For all of us have it in our choice to do every thing that a good man would desire to do; and are restrained from nothing, but what would be pernicious either to ourselves or our fellow citizens. So that this review of our situation may fully justify the observation of a learned French author, who indeed generally both thought and wrote in the spirit of genuine freedom; and who hath not scrupled to profess, even in the very bosom of his native country, that the English is the only nation in the world, where political or civil liberty is the direct end of its constitution. Recommending therefore to the student in our laws a farther and more accurate search into this extensive and important title, I shall close my remarks upon it with the expiring wish of the famous father Paul to his country, "ESTO PERPETUA!"

Notes

The common law of torts and of property, originally summarized in Blackstone, has been restated by American authors and in the Restatements of the Law prepared by the American Law Institute. State courts continue to declare and update the common law of their state. As Justice Cooley stated:

> Every government must concern itself with the definition of rights and the providing of adequate security for their enjoyment. If a government is properly and justly administered, this will be its chief business; and this in its true sense constitutes civil liberty.

Thomas M. Cooley, A Treatise on the Law of Torts 4–5 (1879).

2. COMMON LAW ANTECEDENTS OF U.S. CONSTITUTIONAL RIGHTS

Most provisions of the U.S. Bill of Rights, and of the State Bills of Rights, did not create new rights; they guaranteed rights that were recognized at common law: "Congress shall make no law ... abridging *the* freedom of speech, or of the press" (Amendment I); "*The* right of people to be secure in their persons ..." (Amendment IV) (italics added). The common law generally provided remedies for violations of those rights; State law continues to provide such remedies through the State's common law as modified by state legislation.

The right of privacy, for example, is a noted instance of a human right developed by the common law, which became a right protected by the U.S. Constitution. At the end of the Nineteenth Century, a common law right of privacy was extended to include a right to be protected against additional invasions, e.g., the use of a person's photograph for commercial purposes without the subject's consent. Credit for the extension is commonly attributed to a famous article by Samuel Warren and Louis Brandeis, "The Right to Privacy," 4 Harv. L. Rev. 193 (1890). A Georgia court, adopting a dissenting opinion of a New York court, upheld the broader concept of privacy. *Pavesich v. New England Life Insurance Co.,* 122 Ga. 190 (1905), citing *Roberson v. Rochester Folding–Box Company,* 64 App.Div. 30 (N.Y. 1901). Other State courts have also recognized the common law right of privacy, e.g., *In re Farrell,* 529 A.2d 404, 410 (N.J. 1987) (substituting a common-law basis for privacy for the constitutional reasoning used in previous cases); *In re Estate of Longeway,* 549 N.E.2d 292, 297 (Ill.1989) (using a common-law basis for privacy when State and federal constitutions are unclear as to a particular application). In some states, the extended common law right of privacy was codified by legislation. See *e.g.,* N.Y. Civil Rights Law § 50.

A right of privacy, essentially as it was traditionally protected by the common law, acquired Constitutional protection against official violation ("state action") by the Fourth Amendment to the U.S. Constitution; it was later afforded protection by a "common law constitutional remedy." *Bivens v. Six Unknown Federal Narcotics Agents*, 403 U.S. 388 (1971).

That history of common law development of a right to privacy may have contributed to the recognition of a Constitutional right to "new privacy," in *Griswold v. Connecticut*, 381 U.S. 479 (1965), and *Roe v. Wade*, 410 U.S. 113 (1973). See Part IV, Chapter 1(B).

Common law rights other than the right of privacy have been identified by various State courts. See, *e.g.*, *Lloyd Corp. Ltd. v. Whiffen*, 773 P.2d 1294, 1297, 1299–1300 (Or.1989) (recognizing the right to circulate political petitions in privately-owned shopping malls); *State v. Shack*, 277 A.2d 369, 372–373 (N.J.1971) (right of migrant workers living on their employers' property to be visited by Legal Services lawyer). Such common law rights may have also found their place in State or U.S. Constitutional rights jurisprudence.

3. EARLY STATE BILLS OF RIGHTS

Individual rights came to the American continent with the English common law which was the law of the American Colonies and became the law of the States after American independence. With independence, the Colonies became independent States, later united into the United States by the Articles of Confederation and then by the U.S. Constitution. After the American Declaration of Independence, the newly independent American States ordained and established State constitutions, each with its own Bill of Rights.

The Virginia Bill of Rights antedated the American Declaration of Independence by days, and the two documents were to a large extent authored by the same people, under the leadership of Thomas Jefferson and George Mason. The Virginia Bill of Rights was an important influence on the U.S. Constitution, and later on the U.S. Bill of Rights. (And on the French Declaration of the Rights of Man and of the Citizen. See Part I, Chapter 1(A).) Differences between the Virginia Bill of Rights and the U.S. Bill of Rights largely reflect the fact that the Virginia Bill was part of, indeed appears at the head of, the Virginia Constitution, whereas the U.S. Constitution, as originally ordained and established, did not include a Bill of Rights; the U.S. Bill of Rights was appended by constitutional amendment after the U.S. Constitution was established. See *infra* pp. 156–161.

The early state bills of rights had much in common but also important differences. Compare, for example, the Virginia Bill of Rights, with the Massachusetts Constitution of 1780. Pennsylvania also had a bill of rights as part of its constitution (originally adopted in 1776). Note, in particular, provisions on freedom of religion.

The Virginia Bill of Rights (1776)

A declaration of rights made by the representatives of the good people of Virginia, assembled in full and free convention; which rights do pertain to them and their posterity, as the basis and foundation of government.

SEC. 1. That all men are by nature equally free and independent, and have certain inherent rights, of which, when they enter into a state of society, they cannot, by any compact, deprive or divest their posterity; namely, the enjoyment of life, and liberty, with the means of acquiring and possessing property, and pursuing and obtaining happiness and safety.

SEC. 2. That all power is vested in, and consequently derived from, the people; that magistrates are their trustees and servants, and at all times amenable to them.

SEC. 3. That government is, or ought to be, instituted for the common benefit, protection, and security of the people, nation, or community; of all the various modes and forms of government, that is best which is capable of producing the greatest degree of happiness and safety, and is most effectually secured against the danger of maladministration; and that, when any government shall be found inadequate or contrary to these purposes, a majority of the community hath an indubitable, inalienable, and indefeasible right to reform, alter, or abolish it, in such manner as shall be judged most conducive to the public weal.

SEC. 4. That no man, or set of men, are entitled to exclusive or separate emoluments or privileges from the community, but in consideration of public services; which, not being descendible, neither ought the offices of magistrate, legislator, or judge to be hereditary.

SEC. 5. That the legislative and executive powers of the State should be separate and distinct from the judiciary; and that the members of the two first may be restrained from oppression, by feeling and participating in the burdens of the people, they should, at fixed periods, be reduced to a private station, return into that body from which they were originally taken, and the vacancies be supplied by frequent, certain, and regular elections, in which all, or any part of the former members, to be again eligible, or ineligible, as the laws shall direct.

SEC. 6. That elections of members to serve as representatives of the people, in assembly, ought to be free; and that all men, having sufficient evidence of permanent common interest with, and attachment to, the community, have the right of suffrage, and cannot be taxed or deprived of their property for public uses, without their own consent, or that of their representatives so elected, nor bound by any law to which they have not, in like manner, assembled, for the public good.

SEC. 7. That all power of suspending laws, or the execution of laws, by any authority, without consent of the representatives of the people, is injurious to their rights, and ought not to be exercised.

SEC. 8. That in all capital or criminal prosecutions a man hath a right to demand the cause and nature of his accusation, to be confronted with the accusers and witnesses, to call for evidence in his favor, and to a speedy trial by an impartial jury of twelve men of his vicinage, without whose unanimous consent he cannot be found guilty; nor can he be compelled to give evidence against himself; that no man be deprived of his liberty, except by the law of the land or the judgment of his peers.

SEC. 9. That excessive bail ought not to be required, nor excessive fines imposed, nor cruel and unusual punishments inflicted.

SEC. 10. That general warrants, whereby an officer or messenger may be commanded to search suspected places without evidence of a fact committed, or to seize any person or persons not named, or whose offense is not particularly described and supported by evidence, are grievous and oppressive, and ought not to be granted.

SEC. 11. That in controversies respecting property, and in suits between man and man, the ancient trial by jury is preferable to any other, and ought to be held sacred.

SEC. 12. That the freedom of the press is one of the great bulwarks of liberty, and can never be restrained but by despotic governments.

SEC. 13. That a well-regulated militia, composed of the body of the people, trained to arms, is the proper, natural, and safe defence of a free State; that standing armies, in time of peace, should be avoided, as dangerous to liberty; and that in all cases the military should be under strict subordination to, and governed by, the civil power.

SEC. 14. That the people have a right to uniform government; and, therefore, that no government separate from, or independent of the government of Virginia, ought to be erected or established within the limits thereof.

SEC. 15. That no free government, or the blessings of liberty, can be preserved to any people, but by a firm adherence to justice, moderation, temperance, frugality, and virtue, and by frequent recurrence to fundamental principles.

SEC. 16. That a religion, or the duty which we owe to our Creator, and the manner of discharging it, can be directed only by reason and conviction, not by force or violence; and therefore all men are equally entitled to the free exercise of religion, according to the dictates of conscience; and that it is the mutual duty of all to practise Christian forbearance, love, and charity towards each other.

The Pennsylvania Constitution of 1776, Article II

Article II. That all men have a natural and unalienable right to worship Almighty God according to the dictates of their own consciences and understanding: and that no man ought or of right can be compelled to attend any religious worship, or erect or support any place of worship, or maintain any ministry, contrary to, or against, his own free will and consent: Nor can any man, who acknowledges the being of a God, be justly deprived or abridged of any civil right as a citizen, on account of his religious sentiments or peculiar mode of religious worship: And that no authority can or ought to be vested in, or assumed by any power whatever, that shall in any case interfere with, or in any manner control, the right of conscience in the free exercise of religious worship.

Notes

1. The Pennsylvania Constitution of 1776 was inspired also by the earlier Charter of Privileges for Pennsylvania of William Penn (1701). The Penn Charter included:

FIRST

BECAUSE no People can be truly happy, though under the greatest Enjoyment of Civil Liberties, if abridged of the Freedom of their Consciences, as to their Religious Profession and Worship: And Almighty God being the only Lord of Conscience, Father of Lights and Spirits; and the Author as well as Object of all divine Knowledge, Faith and Worship, who only doth enlighten the Minds and persuade and convince the Understandings of People, I do hereby grant and declare, That no Person or Persons, inhabiting in this Province of Territories, who shall confess and acknowledge *One* almighty God, the Creator, Upholder and Ruler of the World; and profess him or themselves obliged to live quietly under the Civil Government, shall be in any Case molested or prejudiced, in his or their Person or Estate, because of his or their conscientious Persuasion or Practice, nor be compelled to frequent or maintain any religious Worship, Place or Ministry, contrary to his or their Mind or to do or suffer any other Act or Thing, contrary to their religious Persuasion.

AND that all Persons who also profess to believe in *Jesus Christ*, the Saviour of the World, shall be capable (notwithstanding their other Persuasions and Practices in Point of Conscience and Religion) to serve this Government in any Capacity, both legislatively and executively, he or they solemnly promising, when lawfully required, Allegiance to the King as Sovereign, and Fidelity to the Proprietary and Governor, and taking the Attests as now established by the Law made at *New-Castle*, in the Year *One Thousand and Seven Hundred*, entitled, *An Act directing the Attests of several Officers and Ministers*, as now amended and confirmed this present Assembly.

In 1790, Pennsylvania adopted a second constitution. It revised its "free exercise" clause to apply to all actions, not only to acts of worship, and to permit all theists, even non-Christians, to hold office. Compare Article VI, clause 3 of the U.S. Constitution, and the religion clauses of the First Amendment.

2. Compare the Massachusetts Bill of Rights, which also appears at the head of its Constitution, with that of Virginia. The Massachusetts Constitution (1780), attributed largely to John Adams, is remarkable for its stress on virtue (Article XVIII) and on the need for an independent judiciary. It is especially notable, *inter alia*, for its explicit and elaborate expression of the principle of separation of powers which has been justified as a bulwark against tyranny and an important protection of rights. See Article XXX. According to Justice Brandeis, dissenting in *Myers v. United States*, 272 U.S. 52, 293 (1926):

The doctrine of the separation of powers was adopted by the Convention of 1787, not to promote efficiency but to preclude the exercise of arbitrary power. The purpose was, not to avoid friction, but by means of the inevitable friction incident to the distribution of the governmental powers among three departments, to save the people from autocracy.

The Massachusetts Constitution (1780)

PART THE FIRST

A Declaration of the Rights of the Inhabitants of the Commonwealth of Massachusetts.

ART. I. All men are born free and equal, and have certain natural, essential, and unalienable rights; among which may be reckoned the right of enjoying and defending their lives and liberties; that of acquiring, possessing, and protecting property; in fine, that of seeking and obtaining their safety and happiness.

ART. II. It is the right as well as the duty of all men in society, publicly and at stated seasons, to worship the Supreme Being, the great Creator and Preserver of the universe. And no subject shall be hurt, molested, or restrained, in his person, liberty, or estate, for worshiping God in the manner and season most agreeable to the dictates of his own conscience, or for his religious profession or sentiments, provided he doth not disturb the public peace or obstruct others in their religious worship.

ART. III. As the happiness of a people and the good order and preservation of civil government essentially depend upon piety, religion, and morality, and as these cannot be generally diffused through a community but by the institution of the public worship of God and of public instructions in piety, religion, and morality: Therefore, To promote their happiness and to secure the good order and preservation of their government, the people of this commonwealth have a right to invest their legislature with power to authorize and require, and the legislature shall, from time to time, authorize and require, the several towns, parishes, precincts, and other bodies-politic or religious societies to make suitable provision, at their own expense, for the institution of the public worship of God and for the support and maintenance of public Protestant teachers of piety, religion, and morality in all cases where such provision shall not be made voluntarily.

And the people of this commonwealth have also a right to, and do, invest their legislature with authority to enjoin upon all the subjects an attendance upon the instructions of the public teachers aforesaid, at stated times and seasons, if there be any on whose instructions they can conscientiously and conveniently attend.

Provided, notwithstanding, That the several towns, parishes, precincts, and other bodies-politic, or religious societies, shall at all times have the exclusive right of electing their public teachers and of contracting with them for their support and maintenance.

And all moneys paid by the subject to the support of public worship and of the public teachers aforesaid shall, if he require it, be uniformly applied to the support of the public teacher or teachers of his own religious sect or denomination, provided there be any on whose instructions he attends; otherwise it may be paid toward the support of the teacher or teachers of the parish or precinct in which the said moneys are raised.

And every denomination of Christians, demeaning themselves peaceably and as good subjects of the commonwealth, shall be equally under the protection of the law; and no subordination of any one sect or denomination to another shall ever be established by law.

ART. IV. The people of this commonwealth have the sole and exclusive right of governing themselves as a free, sovereign, and independent State, and do, and forever hereafter shall, exercise and enjoy every power, jurisdiction, and right which is not, or may not hereafter be, by them expressly delegated to the United States of America in Congress assembled.

ART. V. All power residing originally in the people, and being derived from them, the several magistrates and officers of government vested with authority, whether legislative, executive, or judicial, are their substitutes and agents, and are at all times accountable to them.

ART. VI. No man nor corporation or association of men have any other title to obtain advantages, or particular and exclusive privileges distinct from those of the community, than what arises from the consideration of services rendered to the public; and this title being in nature neither hereditary nor transmissible to children or descendants or relations by blood, the idea of a man born a magistrate, lawgiver, or judge is absurd and unnatural.

ART. VII. Government is instituted for the common good, for the protection, safety, prosperity, and happiness of the people, and not for the profit, honor, or private interest of any one man, family, or class of men; therefore the people alone have an incontestable, unalienable, and indefeasible right to institute government, and to reform, alter, or totally change the same when their protection, safety, prosperity, and happiness require it.

ART. VIII. In order to prevent those who are vested with authority from becoming oppressors, the people have a right at such periods and in such manner as they shall establish by their frame of government, to cause their public officers to return to private life; and to fill up vacant places by certain and regular elections and appointments.

ART. IX. All elections ought to be free; and all the inhabitants of this commonwealth, having such qualifications as they shall establish by their frame of government, have an equal right to elect officers, and to be elected, for public employments.

ART. X. Each individual of the society has a right to be protected by it in the enjoyment of his life, liberty, and property, according to standing laws. He is obliged, consequently, to contribute his share to the expense of this protection; to give his personal service, or an equivalent, when necessary; but no part of the property of any individual can, with justice, be taken from him, or applied to public uses, without his own consent, or that of the representative body of the people. In fine, the people of this commonwealth are not controllable by any other laws than those to which their constitutional representative body have given their consent. And whenever the public exigencies require that the property of any individual should be appropriated to public uses, he shall receive a reasonable compensation therefor.

ART. XI. Every subject of the commonwealth ought to find a certain remedy, by having recourse to the laws, for all injuries or wrongs which he may receive in his person, property, or character. He ought to obtain right and justice freely, and without being obliged to purchase it; completely, and without any denial; promptly, and without delay, conformably to the laws.

ART. XII. No subject shall be held to answer for any crime or offence until the same is fully and plainly, substantially and formally, described to him; or be compelled to accuse, or furnish evidence against himself; and every subject shall have a right to produce all proofs that may be favorable to him; to meet the witness against him face to face, and to be fully heard in his defense by himself, or his counsel at his election. And no subject shall be arrested, imprisoned, despoiled, or deprived of his property, immunities, or privileges, put out of the protection of the law, exiled or deprived of his life, liberty, or estate, but by the judgment of his peers, or the law of the land.

And the legislature shall not make any law that shall subject any person to a capital or infamous punishment, excepting for the government of the army and navy, without trial by jury.

ART. XIII. In criminal prosecutions, the verification of facts, in the vicinity where they happen, is one of the greatest securities of the life, liberty, and property of the citizen.

ART. XIV. Every subject has a right to be secure from all unreasonable searches and seizures of his person, his houses, his papers, and all his possessions. All warrants, therefore, are contrary to this right, if the cause or foundation of them be not previously supported by oath or affirmation, and if the order in the warrant to a civil officer, to make search in suspected places, or to arrest one or more suspected persons, or to seize their property, be not accompanied with a special designation of the persons or objects of search, arrest, or seizure; and no warrant ought to be issued but in cases, and with the formalities, prescribed by the laws.

ART. XV. In all controversies concerning property, and in all suits between two or more persons, except in cases in which it has heretofore been otherways used and practised, the parties have a right to a trial by jury; and this method of procedure shall be held sacred, unless, in causes arising on the high seas, and such as relate to mariners' wages, the legislature shall hereafter find it necessary to alter it.

ART. XVI. The liberty of the press is essential to the security of freedom in a State; it ought not, therefore, to be restrained in this commonwealth.

ART. XVII. The people have a right to keep and to bear arms for the common defence. And as, in time of peace, armies are dangerous to liberty, they ought not to be maintained without the consent of the legislature; and the military power shall always be held in an exact subordination to the civil authority and be governed by it.

ART. XVIII. A frequent recurrence to the fundamental principles of the constitution, and a constant adherence to those of piety, justice, moderation, temperance, industry, and frugality, are absolutely necessary to preserve the advantages of liberty and to maintain a free government. The people ought, consequently, to have a particular attention to all those principles, in the choice of their officers and representatives; and they have a right to require of their lawgivers and magistrates an exact and constant observance of them, in the formation and execution of the laws necessary for the good administration of the commonwealth.

ART. XIX. The people have a right, in an orderly and peaceable manner, to assemble to consult upon the common good; give instructions to their representatives, and to request of the legislative body, by the way of addresses, petitions, or remonstrances, redress of the wrongs done them, and of the grievances they suffer.

ART. XX. The power of suspending the laws, or the execution of the laws, ought never to be exercised but by the legislature, or by authority derived from it, to be exercised in such particular cases only as the legislature shall expressly provide for.

ART. XXI. The freedom of deliberation, speech, and debate, in either house of the legislature, is so essential to the rights of the people, that it cannot be the foundation of any accusation or prosecution, action or complaint, in any other court or place whatsoever.

ART. XXII. The legislature ought frequently to assemble for the redress of grievances, for correcting, strengthening, and confirming the laws, and for making new laws, as the common good may require.

ART. XXIII. No subsidy, charge, tax, impost, or duties, ought to be established, fixed, laid or levied, under any pretext whatsoever, without the consent of the people, or their representatives in the legislature.

ART. XXIV. Laws made to punish for actions done before the existence of such laws, and which have not been declared crimes by preceding laws, are unjust, oppressive, and inconsistent with the fundamental principles of a free government.

ART. XXV. No subject ought, in any case, or in any time, to be declared guilty of treason or felony by the legislature.

ART. XXVI. No magistrate or court of law shall demand excessive bail or sureties, impose excessive fines, or inflict cruel or unusual punishments.

ART. XXVII. In time of peace, no soldier ought to be quartered in any house without the consent of the owner; and in time of war, such quarters ought not to be made but by the civil magistrate, in a manner ordained by the legislature.

ART. XXVIII. No person can in any case be subjected to law-martial, or to any penalties or pains, by virtue of that law, except those employed in the army or navy, and except the militia in actual service, but by authority of the legislature.

ART. XXIX. It is essential to the preservation of the rights of every individual, his life, liberty, property, and character, that there be an impartial interpretation of the laws, and administration of justice. It is the right of every citizen to be tried by judges as free, impartial, and independent as the lot of humanity will admit. It is, therefore, not only the best policy, but for the security of the rights of the people, and of every citizen, that the judges of the supreme judicial court should hold their offices as long as they behave themselves well, and that they should have honorable salaries ascertained and established by standing laws.

ART. XXX. In the government of this commonwealth, the legislative department shall never exercise the executive and judicial powers, or either of them; the executive shall never exercise the legislative and judicial powers, or either of them; the judicial shall never exercise the legislative and executive powers, or either of them; to the end it may be a government of laws, and not of men.

Notes

Early State bills of rights, the U.S. Constitution, and the U.S. Bill of Rights, were the works of a single generation, generally of similar education and culture and ideological commitment. Are there significant differences among these instruments as regards the theory of individual rights or as to the rights protected?

The bills of rights of the States were placed at the front of the State constitutions and formed part of it. The U.S. Bill of Rights was added to a Constitution already ordained, and was put into effect by the process of amendment prescribed by the Constitution. (The supporters of the U.S. Constitution had successfully resisted proposals that a Bill of Rights be incorporated in the draft of the Constitution before it was ratified.) Might that explain a less-developed, more limited, articulation of rights in the U.S. Bill of Rights? Might State bills of rights be properly referred to in the interpretation and application of the U.S. Bill of Rights?

In the Twentieth Century, the interpretation of the U.S. Bill of Rights by the Supreme Court has clearly influenced the interpretation of State bills of rights, and the independence of State bills of rights became an issue in the jurisprudence of judicial review of State judgments by the Supreme Court of the United States. See p. 239.

B.   THEORY OF CONSTITUTIONAL RIGHTS IN THE UNITED STATES

The U.S. Constitution does not declare its underlying political theory; the U.S. Bill of Rights does not set forth explicitly a theory of rights. Presumably, the theory underlying both the Constitution and the Bill of Rights is that set forth in the Declaration of Independence, in the Virginia Bill of Rights, and in other early State bills of rights.

The Declaration of Independence and the Constitution

The Declaration of Independence declares as "self evident" that men are endowed by their creator with certain unalienable rights; that governments are instituted to secure those rights, and that governments govern with the consent of the governed. The theory of the United States Constitution as rooted in popular sovereignty is reflected lightly in the Preamble and in the Tenth Amendment; the theory of individual rights is reflected in the Ninth Amendment.

Preamble [1787]

> We the People of the United States, in Order to form a more perfect Union, establish Justice, ensure domestic Tranquility, provide for the common defence, promote the general Welfare, and secure the Blessings of Liberty to ourselves and our Posterity, do ordain and establish this Constitution for the United States of America.

. . .

Amendment IX [1791]

> The enumeration in the Constitution, of certain rights, shall not be construed to deny or disparage others retained by the people.

Amendment X [1791]

> The powers not delegated to the United States by the Constitution, nor prohibited by it to the States, are reserved to the States respectively, or to the people.

The Preamble to the U.S. Constitution, with its references to justice, liberty, and the general welfare, has sometimes been invoked to support the idea of rights, and even as a basis for invalidating particular violations of rights. The Supreme Court dismissed that use of the Preamble in *Jacobson v. Massachusetts*, 197 U.S. 11, 22 (1905). See p. 199 below. The Court there declared that the United States does not derive any of its substantive powers from the Preamble of the Constitution, and that the United States cannot exercise any power to secure the declared objects of the Constitution unless, apart from the Preamble, such power be found in, or can properly be inferred from, some express delegation in the Constitution.

Strictly, justice, liberty, and the general welfare are not declared to be aims and purposes to guide the institutions being established by the Constitution, but appear to be the purposes and anticipated consequences of the "more perfect Union" which was being established by the new Constitution.

Theory has not played a large role in the interpretation of constitutional rights in the United States, and on one occasion the Supreme Court explicitly eschewed reliance on theory. See the 1850 opinion of the Court in *Piqua Branch of the State Bank of Ohio v. Knopp*, 57 U.S. (16 How.) 369, (1850) quoted p. 141 below.

Louis Henkin, *The Idea of Rights and the United States Constitution*

in The Age of Rights 83–97 (1990).

Individual rights under the Constitution are the stuff of innumerable judicial decisions and of a luxuriant jurisprudence but these ... hardly address the idea of rights or the political and moral principles that inspire that idea. Doubtless as the result of judicial neglect, law schools teach constitutional law as though the Constitution has no theory, and some students of the law may be surprised to learn—and some may deny—that it has one.

. . .

THE THEORY OF CONSTITUTIONAL RIGHTS

In the United States, we tend to see rights as constitutional protections, established by the framers or added later by formal constitutional amendment. We know that constitutional rights have been shaped and defined by construction and interpretation, by Congress, by the President, as well as by the judiciary, but all of them have based what they have done on the Constitution and have disclaimed any authority to add, subtract or modify rights on any basis not supported by the Constitution.

Our rights, then, are noted in the Constitution and are respected because they are there, or deemed to be there. The Constitution is positive law, a higher positive law, "the supreme law of the land" (Article VI). That the Constitution is the source and the protector of individual rights, that it is binding and must be accepted as higher law is assumed, not justified, not explained. For the explanation and the justification I turn to Thomas Jefferson.

That may be surprising. We acclaim Jefferson as the author of the Declaration of Independence, as the dominant spirit of 1776, but he was not in Philadelphia that second time (1787), and has not been considered one of the constitutional fathers. Indeed, it has long been commonplace to stress the differences in tone and ideology between the Declaration of Independence and the Constitution, and some have suggested that some of those differences are due to the dominance of Jefferson at Philadelphia I and his absence from Philadelphia II.

These suggestions, I believe, are misleading if not mistaken. There are indeed differences between a declaration of independence with its rhetoric of revolution, and a constitutional blueprint designed for the sobrieties of governing. But Jefferson based his bill of particular grievances justifying revolution on a theory of government. That theory was in the intellectual and political air of the day—it was "self-evident"—and it animated the constitutional framers. The ideas declared by Jefferson in 1776 constitute, I believe, the theory of American constitutionalism. Those ideas, however, found their early realization principally in the state constitutions, which were the direct descendants of the Declaration and were concerned with the principles of government. In Virginia, in Massachusetts, and elsewhere, our political ancestors wrote state constitutions according to their political faith as proclaimed by Jefferson.

The United States Constitution came later and had a limited purpose, "to form a more perfect union," and those who framed that constitution did not feel required to "reaffirm or even address that faith."* But the United States Constitution was conceived in the same faith and reflected the same principles as did the state constitutions. "The Constitution," the Supreme Court has said, "was conceived in largest part in the spirit of the Declaration of Independence." It does not depreciate the importance of economic, social, and political forces in the shaping of the Constitution, it does not require overlooking the important respects in which the Constitution deviated from theory and principle, to recognize that the United States Constitution reflects the political philosophythat found its most famous articulation in the Declaration of Independence. I propose, therefore, to take Jefferson seriously, and explore some of the implications of doing so for constitutional jurisprudence.

Consider the words we all know:

> We hold these truths to be self-evident, that all men are created equal, that they are endowed by their Creator with certain unalienable Rights, that among these are Life, Liberty, and the pursuit of Happiness. That to secure these rights, Governments are instituted among Men, deriving their just powers from the consent of the governed. That whenever any form of Government becomes destructive of these ends, it is the Right of the People to alter or to abolish it, and to institute new Governments, laying its foundation on such principles and organizing its powers in such form, as to them shall seem most likely to effect their Safety and Happiness.

Jefferson's truths are rhetoric, "self-evident," not analytically derived, but their antecedents and underpinnings, I think, can be discerned and some of their implications can be readily developed. Jefferson played

---

* That may be an explanation and a small excuse for the later neglect of its theory.

variations on a theme by John Locke. He took "natural rights" and made them secular, rational, universal, individualist, democratic, and radical. For Jefferson, the rights of man are not (or not necessarily) divinely conceived and ordained; they are God's gift in that they result from his creation. They are natural in the sense that nature (and nature's God) created and inspired man's reason and judgment; they are natural also in a different sense, in that they are man's in the "state of nature," and he brings them with him when, by contract—a social contract—he joins with others to form a political society and establish a government. The individual was autonomous, sovereign, before society was established, and he and other individuals taken together—"the people"—remain sovereign in any society and under any government they form, for their sovereignty is inalienable, and government is only by consent of the governed.* Sovereignty of the people implies self-government by the people, directly or through chosen representatives. But every individual retains some of his or her original autonomy as "rights" that are protected even against the people and their representatives.[†]

American constitutionalism, then, has two elements: representative government and individual rights. Both are confirmed by constitutional compact. The Constitution is a contract among all the people to create a political society and to establish and to submit to representative government. The contract among the people to form a polity implies, it would seem, ancillary contracts: every individual agrees to respect the rights of every other individual within the polity; the people, and every individual as a member of the people, agree that, through elected representatives, they will respect individual rights and maintain laws and institutions to protect them. The Constitution serves also as a contract between the people and their representatives, or better, as a bill of instructions by the people to their representatives, prescribing the terms and conditions of government. And high among these conditions is that government is responsible to the people and must respect individual rights. The government's responsibility to the people, and its respect for individual rights, are the condition of the people's consent to be governed and the basis of the government's legitimacy.

Individual rights, then, are "natural," inherent. They cannot be taken away or even suspended. They are not a gift from society or from any government. They are not merely concessions extracted from, and limitations imposed on, preexisting established government, in the tradition of Magna Carta and subsequent English bills; rather, they are freedoms and entitlements of all men, everywhere, antecedent and superior to government. They do not derive from any constitution; they antecede all constitu-

---

* The leap from autonomy of the individual to the sovereignty of the people and majority rule was not commonly noted or explained; presumably that was agreed upon or deemed implicit in the social compact.

† Contrast Rousseau: By his social contract, "the surrender [of the individual to the community] is made without reserve." J. J. Rousseau, *The Social Contract* Book I, Chapter VI in *The Essential Rousseau* (L. Blair trans., 1974).

tions. When, after 1776, the American people adopted state constitutions creating new governments, when in 1789 they ordained the United States Constitution, they retained substantial autonomy and freedoms, for themselves and for their descendants, as individual rights against government. Their "right" to rights was axiomatic, an *a priori* entitlement; the right to retain rights vis-à-vis their government, and the content of the rights they retained, were fixed by the contract.

The rights retained on entering society reflect conceptions of the good society, of justice, and of other values accepted as self-evident. Every human being is a person, entitled to the political, social and legal implications of personhood. The family is the natural unit. The individual is essentially autonomous, free to pursue his or her happiness. The good society is the liberal society in which individuals enjoy their antecedent freedoms—religion, speech, press, assembly, general autonomy—giving up only a little to the needs of society. They are entitled to property acquired honestly by labor, exchange or inheritance. An individual accused of crime is entitled to a fair trial because it is unjust—obviously—to punish him, to deprive him of his liberty, without due process of law.

Neither the Declaration of Independence nor the early state constitutions describe fully the rights the people retained. The Declaration lists among the unalienable rights "life, liberty and the pursuit of happiness," but that was an elegant distillation, hardly intended to be an exhaustive list.* The Virginia Bill, other early state bills of rights, as well as the United States Bill of Rights, go on to enumerate important freedoms government must respect—political and religious liberty, privacy, procedural justice especially in respect of government's criminal process. They all refer, in addition and separately, to "liberty" generally, and the Bill of Rights that soon became part of the United States Constitution provides expressly that other rights not enumerated in the Constitution are also "retained by the people" (Amendment IX).

Of course, what the people retained is determined also by what they agreed to give up in creating a political society and establishing a government. Individuals pooled some of their autonomy when they formed "the people," subjecting themselves to majority rule; the people also gave up some of their autonomy to their government, retaining the rest as individual rights and freedoms under government.[**] The people gave to their representatives the authority they needed for governing, and gave up such rights, and submitted other rights to such limitations, as the purposes of

---

* Much has been made of the fact that in that triad "the pursuit of happiness" is substituted for "property" in John Locke's earlier enumeration, but, for present purposes at least, I would not exaggerate the significance of that change. Jefferson would surely have agreed that his formulation includes what was in his less-eloquent model, the Virginia Bill of Rights, which expressly included "the means of acquiring and possessing property," as well as "pursuing and obtaining happiness and safety."

[**] Thomas Paine distinguished "that class of natural rights which man retains after entering into society, and those which he throws into the common stock as a member of society" because he cannot execute them himself (*The Rights of Man*, pp. 88–90).

government required. The authority granted to government was not particularized either, but its scope is defined by the purposes for which governments were formed, purposes commonly understood.

By implication, the purposes of government were central to the ancestral conception of rights that Jefferson articulated. Governments, he said, are instituted "to secure these rights," the rights of every individual to life, liberty and the pursuit of happiness, and the other rights they implied. Later, President Thomas Jefferson, in his First Inaugural Address, described the purposes of government as follows:

> Still one thing more, fellow-citizens—a wise and frugal Government, which shall restrain men from injuring one another; shall leave them otherwise free to regulate their own pursuits of industry and improvement; and shall not take from the mouth of labor the bread it has earned. This is the sum of good government, and this is necessary to close the circle of our felicities.

Government was to be a watchman, a policeman protecting every person's rights against violation by others. That would safeguard every individual's life and liberty and leave the individual free to pursue his or her happiness. Government, it was doubtless assumed, should also serve safety, health, and morals. Government itself, of course, should let people alone; inter alia, it should not tax them more than was essential.[†]

For the founders' generation the social contract was not a myth or a hypothetical construct; it was a real compact. The parties to the contract— the people—sought to assure that it would be carried out by building in safeguards: the separation and balance of powers of government to prevent corruption and abuse of authority, and periodic elections to review the performance of the people's agents and maintain the consent of the governed. In some respects, perhaps, this contract, like contracts generally, could be enforced in court, if the courts were independent of the political branches. The people could also revise their contract to change their government, replace their representatives, reconsider the authority they delegated. Ultimately, the people—not any few individuals—could terminate the contract and reconstitute themselves in a new political society by a new compact.[††]

Like Locke's, Jefferson's political principles derived from and depended on individual consent. Societies are properly formed, and governments properly created, only by consent of the participants, and they owe their legitimacy and authority to that consent. Consent derives its effectiveness, its justificatory power, from the fact that all men are born equally free and autonomous, competent and responsible moral agents; they can therefore consent and make binding contracts. Responding voluntarily to perceived

[†] For Jefferson, I believe, it was not the business of the government to provide the people with the benefits of what the twentieth century was to call the "welfare state"; government was to leave the individual free to pursue his livelihood himself.

[††] The individual, presumably, could leave society (if his obligations were paid) and seek admission to another society, or live outside society.

needs, men agree to form societies and consent to government and law, persuaded that the benefits of society are worth its costs and its risks. But the people do not, cannot, alienate their fundamental responsibility as moral agents, the right to govern themselves. They do not, perhaps cannot, delegate all their moral authority, give up all their autonomy or freedom, but only as much as is necessary for the limited purposes of government.

For Jefferson, I deduce, there were moral rights and obligations between men before there were political societies and governments. Because there was a moral community there could be a political community. . . .

. . .

JEFFERSONIAN PRINCIPLES AND CONSTITUTIONAL JURISPRUDENCE

I have attempted to distill the political theory of the constitutional fathers, and the moral assumptions that seem to underlie their idea of rights. Though we think of the Constitution as Madisonian (and in important respects Hamiltonian), our idea of rights is Jeffersonian: The idea of rights articulated in the Declaration of Independence is reflected in constitutional text. But the jurisprudence we have spun out of that text has lagged behind and diverged from Jeffersonian principles. In the growth of that jurisprudence, text and canonical exegesis have dominated, but theory has been at best assumed, often neglected or abandoned. The reasons for the divergence of doctrine from theory are complex. I cite two: We became committed to constitutional text and to the judicial remedy for monitoring it; and, as regards rights, the text was—is—deficient.

It is not necessary to repeat what we owe to John Marshall. In establishing judicial review he helped make the courts what they are today, the final arbiters of what the Constitution means, and the rock and the redeemer of our rights. But Marshall achieved his success by establishing the Constitution as law, the thing of courts and lawyers. His justification for judicial review was that the Constitution was written law, and the courts had the unique responsibility and talent to expound law. Since Marshall, the courts, concerned to establish judicial supremacy, and mindful of their political weakness and the delicacy of their function, grounded their authority in the constitutional text ordained by the people and sought to reassure those who feared "government by judiciary" by promising to cling to that text. The text became all: what was written is the effective Constitution. The Justices continued to proclaim that "it is a *constitution* we are expounding," but they felt constrained to look only into the text; what was not there was excluded.* And among the elements missing from the Constitution was its theory. And so, the Supreme Court said in 1850:

---

* In time, the ascendancy of philosophical positivism in the nineteenth century also tended to impel judges to treat the Constitution as positive law and to eschew external sources that had the smell of natural law.

... [W]e have not felt ourselves at liberty to indulge in general remarks on the theory of our government. That is a subject which belongs to a convention for the formation of a constitution; and, in a limited view, to the law-making power. Theories depend so much on the qualities of the human mind, and these are so diversified by education and habit as to constitute an unsafe rule for judicial action. Our prosperity, individually and nationally, depends upon a close adherence to the settled rules of law, and especially to the great fundamental law of the Union.

Dogma and method that had developed perhaps to help justify judicial review shaped constitutional history for political purposes as well—when Congress and the President determined their own authority and responsibility, or when the people considered their social compact. We were condemned to be textualists, "interpretivists"; other parts of our hagiography—notably the Declaration of Independence—were excluded from the jurisprudential canon; ancestral theory might sneak in, but only occasionally, and in the guise of construction of the constitutional text.*

Since our constitutional jurisprudence is limited to and by the text, it is shaped by the fact that, by Jeffersonian standards, the text is deficient, one might say "congenitally defective." As written, the Constitution was not designed for the purposes it has come to serve. It was supposed to support a small, supplemental, superstructure of government, imposed on powerful, self-sufficient state governments subject essentially to their own constitutions; it has become, without significant amendment in respects here relevant, the constitution of a powerful national government largely subordinating state governments and itself governing the people. The United States Constitution was designed for minimal government for a small population and a pre-industrial economy; it now supports the complex government of a nuclear superpower, urban, highly industrial, and a welfare state. Among the weaknesses of the Constitution for its aggrandized function, I suggest, are respects in which it does not conform to essential principles of Jefferson's constitutionalism: a constitution as social compact, retained rights, government for agreed-upon purposes.

---

* Through Marshall, too, the courts came to judicial review as part of their daily business of deciding cases and controversies. See *Marbury v. Madison.* Unlike twentieth century counterparts in Western Europe, the Supreme Court is not a constitutional court with unique powers and wielding unique remedies. It decides constitutional issues while acting as a court of law in the British tradition. It has therefore limited itself by an entire code of reasons for not deciding issues; and its quiver contains only the traditional remedies of English common law and equity courts, subject to inherent as well as self-imposed limitations. For example, the courts will enjoin officials not to give effect to an act of Congress that violates the Constitution; they do not command Congress to adopt a different law or to appropriate money to carry out a constitutional obligation, even if such an obligation could be found in the Constitution.

Despite their commitment to the text, the courts felt obligated to conclude that the Constitution is not complete in that it does not include all the powers of the United States inherent in its nationhood and international sovereignty, such as powers over foreign affairs and immigration. See *U.S. v. Curtiss–Wright Export Corp.*, 299 U.S. 304 (1936).

THE CONSTITUTION AS SOCIAL COMPACT

The founding generation, I think, saw the Constitution as their social compact. The United States Constitution declares itself to be a social compact: Such, I believe, is the purpose and purport of the preamble, in which "[W]e the people ... ordain and establish this Constitution." But was it an authentic social compact? And is it our social compact?

"We the people" who ordained the Constitution were not all the inhabitants. It has been estimated that "the people" who voted for the delegates to the state conventions that ratified the Constitution constituted some 5 percent of the inhabitants.* "We the people" did not include slaves, for they were property, not persons, not part of the political society being established; in some states even free blacks could not vote. The people did not include women.† The people included only property owners, those (I quote from the Virginia Bill of Rights) "having sufficient evidence of permanent common interest with, and attachment to, the community." Was a constitution so ordained a proper social contract?

More troubling, is the Constitution of the framing generation properly our constitution, is their social compact our social compact? It is difficult to justify that conclusion by Jefferson's principles. The people of 1789 may have deemed their values eternal and their rights timeless, valid for their children's children as for themselves. But in principle, surely, the autonomy and sovereignty of the people of two hundred years ago did not include the right to impose their values on their descendants; their moral principles are not necessarily ours; their consent does not justify coercive authority over us. Later generations might decide that their ancestors improperly alienated rights that were unalienable; or, to the contrary, they might decide it wise to delegate to their government new kinds of authority for new purposes, and retain less autonomy for themselves. We are as autonomous as they were, equally endowed with unalienable rights. Their principles would warrant us in writing our own social contract and substituting our own terms with each other and with government, terms that would reflect our views of the proper purpose of government and that would retain the rights and liberties that we consider inalienable or that we do not wish to alienate.

Thomas Jefferson indeed may have sensed that difficulty when he suggested that a constitution expires automatically after nineteen years. But nineteen years after 1789, President Thomas Jefferson did not act as though the Constitution had expired; rather, he felt bound by his oath to preserve, protect and defend it, and to take care that it be faithfully executed. Perhaps Jefferson would have said that the consent of every new generation may be presumed, and the original contract remains valid and effective, unless the people reconstituted themselves in a new polity by a

---

* In half the states almost half the delegates voted against ratification, and in some states the authenticity of the successful vote might not pass scrutiny. See generally R. Schuyler, *The Constitution of the United States* (New York: Macmillan, 1923), ch. 4, esp. p. 138.

† In theory, perhaps, some of them were represented by family males.

new compact. But is that consent authentic, is our acquiescence in the original social compact properly presumed? Do the people today prescribe to the same terms, wish to retain the same rights, accept the same purposes of government, share eighteenth century moral principles and intuitions—except in so far as we mobilize ourselves to reconstitute our society anew, or succeed in amending the ancestral compact by the difficult procedure imposed on us by the founders?

Perhaps it was this difficulty that early caused neglect of the character of the Constitution as social compact, and led instead to a jurisprudence that treated the Constitution as positive law, even if positive law of a higher order. Like other positive law, it controls unless superseded by later law of equal authority properly adopted, and what is in the Constitution can be superseded only by new constitutional provision ordained according to the prescribed process of amendment. At the same time, however, some abiding commitment to the Constitution as social compact among the people of every generation may have shaped some of that constitutional jurisprudence. Some have suggested that the people of every generation do indeed acquiesce in the original compact, but they tacitly update that continuing, self-renewing social contract; every generation, therefore, has felt entitled to read some rights reserved and some delegations to government in the constitutional text as adjustable to time and context. It has been suggested also that the people have effectively delegated to the courts authority to calibrate, reinterpret and reshape the text to reflect the contemporary social compact, the original compact as the contemporary people have tacitly revised it. That, however, is not what the courts generally admit they are doing, or think they are doing. That view of our jurisprudence, moreover, would require the courts to find and articulate some way of determining what changes in the original social compact the people of the United States at a given time have tacitly adopted—what new purposes the people today assign to their government, what new authority is being delegated, what rights are now being subjected to that authority and which are being retained.*

There is a different set of difficulties with treating the United States Constitution as our contemporary social compact. For the Constitution was born without principal ingredients of a social compact, and age has not cured and has even aggravated those defects. A direct and immediate descendant of the Articles of Confederation, "a more perfect union" of the states, the Constitution was declared to be ordained by "We the people" as had been the constitutions of the several states, but the compact implied in that preambular phrase was largely rhetorical and symbolic. The small federal superstructure which the framers projected was not, and was not expected to become, a significant government with significant relations to

---

* In our federal system, there is yet another difficulty. In ordaining the original Constitution, the people decided how much governmental authority was to be delegated to the new federal government, how much was being left to the states. Are the people in every generation tacitly deciding also a new redistribution of responsibility between states and federal government?

the people, implicating their rights. The real social compact remained the state constitution, the polity that the people had contracted for was the state polity, the government instituted to secure their rights was the state government; the United States Constitution was only a small "codicil" to state social compacts.

Some four score and seven years later, after civil war, the Constitution was amended, and the country was on the way to being what it is today. The federal government became a real government, the dominant government, supervising—and soon in substantial measure superseding—the states in responsibility for the rights of the individual. But the Constitution was not changed to reflect that transformation. Although the Preamble permanently proclaims the Constitution to be the social compact of every succeeding generation, the body of the Constitution has remained essentially the compact of 1787 of the people of 1787 to create the government of 1787. Major, radical amendments followed as the peace treaty of the Civil War, but there was no attempt then, or since, to make the Constitution a complete compact for the complete government that the federal government has become. Never supplied were the elements essential to a Jeffersonian compact—those found in the ancestral state constitutions: articulation of and commitment to the theory of constitutional government, undertakings of the people to each other, reaffirmation of popular sovereignty, a statement of the purposes of government, a list of the rights the people retained and of the powers delegated, directions to and empowerment of government to do that for which Jefferson said government was instituted—"to secure these rights." Commitment to text discouraged any effort to supply those missing elements from outside the Constitution, perhaps by invoking the Declaration of Independence as the implicit theoretical foundation of the Constitution.

The consequences of these defects have troubled our polity since the beginning, surely since the United States government became *the* government of the United States. The limited conception of the government of the United States, and the limited conception of "We the people," have continued to maintain largely indirect elections for national office, and state control of qualifications for voting. Even the constitutional amendments addressed to suffrage did not take suffrage from state control, nor did they recognize the right of the people, all of the people, to vote.* Only some twenty-five years ago did the Supreme Court, by constitutional constructions that are hardly obvious and that some consider dubious, put together a constitutional right for all to vote and to vote equally, and thus found in the Constitution authentic popular sovereignty and the consent of

---

* A state cannot deny the right to vote on account of race (Amendment XV), or sex (Amendment XIX), or age (Amendment XXVI), but in principle those Amendments did not assure anyone a right to vote: they assured only that if the state gave the right to vote it could not deny it to anyone on account of race, gender, or age. Note that—on the face of the text—religious and other invidious discriminations remain not forbidden. Not until 1964 was the Constitution amended to remove a property requirement—the poll tax—as an obstacle to voting (Amendment XXIV).

all the governed—which by Jeffersonian principles is the only basis for legitimate government.

For Jefferson, all men were created equal, therefore autonomous, therefore able to make contracts—including the social contract—and to create political society and government. It is incredible today, but the word "equality" was not in the original Constitution, nor in the Bill of Rights. We have not to this day filled that historic—and embarrassing—lacuna. Since the Fourteenth Amendment (1868), there is in the Constitution a requirement that states not deny the equal protection of the laws; on the face of the Constitution, there is still no commitment by "We the people of the United States" to equality, no contract with, no command to, the government of the United States that we shall all be equal in its eyes, nothing to prevent Congress, or the President, or the federal courts from discriminating on account of race, religion, or gender. It has taken some intellectually and historically dubious constitutional construction by the Supreme Court in the second half of the twentieth century to remedy that defect in fact.

For Jefferson, I have suggested, the social compact was a contract among all persons constituting the people, and between each person and the people, to respect each other's rights and to create institutions to secure those rights; the compact also includes the conditions that govern the government to assure that it respects our rights. But only the last part of that compact is in the United States Constitution and in constitutional law: Only that aspect of the social compact that imposes conditions on government is constitutional law; one member of the people cannot enforce the compact against another individual, or against the people. As law, notably, the Fourteenth and Fifteenth Amendments protect only against "state action," against violation by government, not against private invasion of rights; and the power that the amendments gave Congress to secure rights is limited by the same conception. Then, having hung that doctrine on a literal reading of the Fourteenth Amendment—"no State shall"*—we have read the state action requirement also into the Bill of Rights, although in largest part the text does not compel it, and might have been read to include protection of rights against violation by individuals, in accordance with a Jeffersonian compact. A complete Jeffersonian constitution would have included an agreement among the people to respect each other's rights, including their equality; an agreement that the government to be created would respect those rights, including equality; an agreement that not only authorizes but requires government to protect every person from

---

* The words chosen reflect perhaps the immediate concerns of the authors of those Amendments to prevent official political subjugation of blacks; it is not obvious that they intended to continue to deny constitutional protection against private violation of rights. Only the—perhaps fortuitous—absence of a reference to the state in the Thirteenth Amendment gave warrant to reading in it direct constitutional protection of one person against enslavement by another. That fortunate omission later created an opportunity for a jurisprudence that freedom from slavery implies protection against private discrimination on account of race as a badge of slavery.

actions by his or her neighbor as well as from official actions that deny individual rights, including equality.

Ironically, despite our commitment to text, our jurisprudence has excluded even the small amount of political theory that is in our text, in the Preamble. John Marshall invoked the Preamble in a leading case, but the Preamble has not been law, and nothing has been permitted to hang on it. One might suggest that, as the Preamble sets forth the basis of our polity, it is relevant for the interpretation of the text as amended, including the Bill of Rights. Since the Preamble affirms the character of the Constitution as a social compact, the Constitution might have been read as though the compact were spelled out, as though it included what it was intended to contain, what would have been included had it been foreseen that we were establishing a national political society with a real national political government. It might be instructive to speculate as to what our constitutional law would have been if the Constitution had incorporated the Declaration of Independence, if only by reference.* Or, if it had included, from John Adams' Massachusetts Constitution of 1780:

> The body politic is ... a social compact, by which the whole people covenants with each citizen, and each citizen with the whole people, that all shall be governed by certain laws for the common good.

> Each individual of the society has a right to be protected by it in the enjoyment of his life, liberty and property according to standing laws.

> Every subject ... ought to find a certain remedy, by having recourse to the laws, for all injuries or wrongs which he may receive in his person, property, or character. He ought to obtain right and justice freely, and without being obliged to purchase it.

With such text, might the courts have proceeded to articulate the terms of the compact between citizens, and between the citizen and the people, and given them constitutional effect and remedy? Might they have enforced the obligation of society to provide laws and remedies, even perhaps by mandamus to the legislature? Might the courts—when the federal government effectively became supreme to the states in respect of the individual's relation to society—have upheld civil rights acts without regard to interstate commerce, without limitation to state action? If so, can all or some of that be read as implied in the social compact implied in the Preamble?

RETAINED RIGHTS

We have done better by Jefferson in respect of retained rights. The original Constitution contained little reference to rights. The federal government being designed as only marginally a government, it was not seen as implicating rights, or having any significant concern with them. Propos-

---

* Compare the reference to the French Declaration of the Rights of Man and of the Citizen in the recent constitutions of France, and the consequences for French constitutional jurisprudence.

als at the constitutional Convention to include a bill of rights did not carry. From an abundance of caution—and prescience—the Bill of Rights became a condition of ratification and was added by constitutional amendment.

Except in that it omits any reference to equality, the Bill of Rights is Jeffersonian, reflecting the principles of the Declaration. The Bill of Rights does not grant rights; it only recognizes and guarantees them. For example, Congress shall make no law abridging "the freedom" of speech, press, assembly, and "[t]he right of the people to be secure"—these are not grants of rights, they refer to and incorporate pre-existing rights. Because rights do not derive from the Constitution, the framers of the Bill of Rights were not impelled to enumerate them all. They enumerated, I believe, the rights they were most concerned to protect in light of their recent history, corresponding to those contemplated by Jefferson and enumerated in early state constitutions.* They include the freedoms specified in the First Amendment, protection for property, and the inherent rights to privacy and personal freedom subject to the legitimate needs of government in the criminal process. Basic civil rights went without saying. The Ninth Amendment—affirming that there are other rights retained by the people—was, I believe, not merely a residual clause from abundance of caution; it represented and articulated the basic principle that the individual has rights before and without the Constitution, only some of which it seemed desirable to mention in the Constitution. The Ninth Amendment, therefore, would seem to provide a firm basis in constitutional text for identifying other rights, by determining what rights the people had originally, naturally, then subtracting what they delegated to government. Identifying a right as retained within the purport of the Ninth Amendment would be legitimate constitutional construction, not a daring usurpation.

In fact, we have not used the Ninth Amendment. Constitutional jurisprudence built instead on express rights provisions and to that extent, at least, text (or textualism) triumphed over theory. The explanation, I believe, lies in our history. Before the Civil War, rights hardly figured in constitutional jurisprudence, since the federal government impinged on individuals only minimally; rights of individuals in respect of the states were not governed by the federal Constitution (and the federal social compact), and the Bill of Rights, including the Ninth Amendment, did not apply to the states. The Civil War amendments, notably the Fourteenth, subjected individual rights vis-à-vis the states to federal scrutiny but as an ad hoc addition. Those Amendments were not integrated into the Bill of Rights and subsumed under its Jeffersonian theory including the Ninth Amendment; the jurisprudence of the Civil War amendments was based wholly on interpretation of their text. Slowly, the Fourteenth Amendment, and its due process clause in particular, became the "rights compact" in relation to the states. Later, much later, when rights became significant in respect of the federal government, the jurisprudence that was developed for

---

* Even the state constitutions did not purport to include a complete catalogue of rights.

purposes of the Fourteenth Amendment and the states came to control federal rights as well, and due process in the Fifth Amendment became a textual basis for additional retained rights against the federal government. The Ninth Amendment remained unused.

But the triumph of text over theory, and the demise of the Ninth Amendment, have not been complete. In the development of due process jurisprudence, theory and moral intuitions have echoed strongly and continue to do so: the due process clause became the receptacle of that theory, "the Ninth Amendment" of the states (and secondarily, derivatively, of the federal government). In that development, theory has struggled continuously with text. Powerful voices have feared the uncertain, theological, "natural rights" overtones that the due process clause came to reflect, especially after that clause was abused by the judiciary.

. . .

Notes

1.   Henkin wrote that "the Bill of Rights does not grant rights; it only recognizes and guarantees them." Is that true of the Second and Third Amendments?

2.   The essay was re-published in 1990 (and had been written earlier). Does it require modification in light of the winds of change in Supreme Court jurisprudence in the intervening years? Has the Court moved closer to "textualism," to original intent? Does a reassertion by the Court of some "States' rights" promise reexamination of some of the Court's rights jurisprudence? How far towards original intent can the Court go in view of intervening interpretations deviating from the original intent and the commitment to *stare decisis*?

3.   As this essay suggests, although the Constitution does not articulate a theory, it apparently had one, consisting of inherent rights, social compact, and retained rights. For the influence of this theory on constitutions of other countries and on the international human rights movement, see Part III, Chapter 1.

Note: The Ninth Amendment

Laurence Tribe, *Beyond Incorporation: The Ninth Amendment and the "Rational Continuum"*

in American Constitutional Law § 11–3 (2d Ed. 1988).

Justice Harlan's dissenting opinion in *Poe v. Ullman* stated the thesis best: "[T]he full scope of the liberty guaranteed by the Due Process Clause cannot be found in or limited by the precise terms of the specific guarantees elsewhere provided in the Constitution. This 'liberty' is not a series of isolated points picked out in terms of the taking of property; the freedom of speech, press, and religion; the right to keep and bear arms; the freedom from unreasonable searches and seizures; and so on. It is a rational continuum which, broadly speaking, includes a freedom from all substantial arbitrary impositions and purposeless restraints, ... and which also recognizes, ... that certain interests require particularly careful scrutiny of the state needs asserted to justify their abridgement." The history of the framing and ratification of the Constitution and of the Bill of Rights leaves little doubt about the correctness of Justice Harlan's proposition. Indeed, James Madison introduced the ninth amendment in specific response to the arguments of Hamilton and others that enactment of a Bill of Rights might dangerously suggest "that those rights which were not singled out, were intended to be assigned into the hands of the General Government, and were consequently insecure." The ninth amendment, which provides that "[t]he enumeration in the Constitution, of certain rights, shall not be construed to deny or disparage others retained by the people," therefore *at least* states a rule of construction pointing away from the reverse incorporation view that only the interests secured by the Bill of Rights are encompassed within the fourteenth amendment, and *at most* provides a positive source of law for fundamental but unmentioned rights. In either case, the "Bill of Rights presumes the existence of a substantial body of rights not specifically enumerated but easily perceived in the broad concept of liberty and so numerous and so obvious as to preclude listing them." The line of cases protecting, as unenumerated aspects of liberty, the right to teach one's child a foreign language, the right to send one's child to a private school, the right to procreate, the right to be free of certain bodily intrusions, and the right to travel abroad, had set the stage for the most important substantive due process decision of the modern period, *Griswold v. Connecticut.* That case presented the question whether a married couple could be sent to jail by the State of Connecticut for using birth control. Professor Charles Black wrote of *Griswold* that it was "not so much a case that the law tests as a case that tests the law." He continued: "If our constitutional law could permit such a thing to happen, then we might almost as well not have any law of constitutional limitations, partly because the thing is so outrageous in itself, and partly because a constitutional law inadequate to deal with such an outrage would be too feeble, in method and doctrine, to deal with a very great amount of equally outrageous material. Virtually all the intimacies, privacies and autonomies of life would be regulable by the legislature—not necessarily by the legislature of this year or last year, but, it might be, by the legislature of a hundred years ago, or even by an administrative board in due form thereunto authorized by a recent or long-dead legislature." The Court held that Connecticut's law was unconstitutional. Justice Douglas' opinion for the Court relied on "the zone of privacy created by several fundamental constitutional guarantees," explaining that "specific guarantees in the Bill of Rights"—he was referring to the first, third, fourth, fifth, and ninth—"have penumbras, formed by emanations from those guarantees that help give them life and substance."

Justice Goldberg, concurring in an opinion joined by Chief Justice Warren and Justice Brennan, agreed that the unmentioned right to privacy resolved the case but was more unabashed about locating the right, with the help of the ninth amendment as a rule of construction,[14] in "the concept of liberty," and had no hesitation in concluding that there existed no sufficiently compelling justification for the state's drastic infringement of the right. Justice Harlan concurred in the judgment but on the still broader ground that the law violated "basic values 'implicit in the concept of ordered liberty' " whether or not it could be "found to violate some right assured by the letter or penumbra of the Bill of Rights." Finding the " '[s]pecific' provisions of the Constitution" no more precise or determinate than "due process," Justice Harlan urged replacing the illusory certitude of reliance on the "specifics" with "continual insistence upon the teachings of history, solid recognition of the basic values that underlie our society, and wise appreciation of the great roles that the doctrines of federalism and separation of powers have played in establishing and preserving American freedoms." Justice White, also concurring in the judgment, agreed that the law was a substantial denial of liberty, especially for the "disadvantaged citizens of Connecticut"; but for him the crucial fact was that this denial could not significantly advance any of the purposes the state claimed for it. Justices Black and Stewart both dissented, claiming that the majority was usurping a legislative function. By 1973, however, Justice Stewart had "accepted" *Griswold* "as one in a long line of . . . cases decided under the doctrine of substantive due process," and indeed all nine of the Justices as of 1973 had accepted the Court's role in giving the fourteenth amendment due process clause substantive content beyond the Bill of Rights, despite significant disagreements over exactly how the role should be performed. . . . Where, beyond the Bill of Rights, is the "substance" in substantive due process to come from?

Note on Individual Rights, Democracy, and Representative Government

1.   The U.S. Constitution, like the early State constitutions, contains no reference to "democracy" or to democratic government. The Framers of the U.S. Constitution, and their generation, were not "democrats," but "republicans." They defined democracy as direct (rather than representative) government and tended to decry such democracy as dangerous to the public weal. See *The Federalist Papers* No. 10 (Madison). In the Framers' conception, good government was republican government, government by the elite, by the virtuous, for the public good.

---

14. It is a common error, but an error nonetheless, to talk of "ninth amendment rights." The ninth amendment is *not* a source of rights as such; it is simply a rule about how to read the Constitution. But it is a vital rule—one without which the Bill of Rights might have been more threatening than reassuring and one without which, therefore, the 1787 Constitution might not have lasted. . . . To the extent the ninth amendment is deemed a "repositor[y] for an external schedule of rights," an argument is available that this "list" was "closed as of 1791 or 1868." But if, as seems plain, the ninth amendment is not a "repository" at all but a prohibition against certain forms of argument by negative implication, then the "closed set" position loses most of its plausibility.

Republican government was representative government, but although all the governed were to be represented in principle, in fact not all of the institutions of government are representative, of "the people," not even in conception. Only the "House of Representatives" was characterized as "representative." The Senate was to represent states, not people. The President, as is indicated by the method of his election, was apparently not to be directly representative of the people.

Moreover, although in principle the House of Representatives represented all the people, and its members were to be chosen according to the population, not all the inhabitants were counted, and not all people had the right to vote for their representatives. See Article I, section 2. The right to vote for Representatives is available only to those who had the right to vote in State representative bodies ("the Electors of the most numerous Branches of the State Legislature," Article 1, section 2), which also were chosen by limited suffrage. Senators were chosen by State legislatures.

Direct election of Senators finally came in 1913 with the Seventeenth Amendment, but in a large sense the Senate has remained representative of States, not of people. (Each State elects two Senators, regardless of differences in population.) The President continues to be chosen by "the Electoral College," which was not intended to be elected by popular vote nor to be representative of people according to population.

2. "Universal suffrage"—commonly understood as the right of all adult citizens to vote for the principal elective institutions of government—came to the United States in stages. The U.S. Bill of Rights did not include a right to vote for any office. Later Amendments extended suffrage, in effect, by prohibiting the denial of the right to vote on account of race (Amendment XV), on account of sex (Amendment XIX), on account of age (for those older than eighteen; Amendment XXVI), but these Amendments only prohibited discrimination in voting, they did not grant anyone the right to vote, for any office. Finally, the United States came to universal suffrage not from a commitment to popular sovereignty and democracy, but from commitment to equal, individual rights. If any one votes, all must be accorded the right to vote and all have an equal vote. *Reynolds v. Sims*, 377 U.S. 533 (1964).

The Framers' limited conception of representation, as reflected notably in the U.S. Senate and in the Presidency, continues to prevail. But, within that limited conception of representation, the United States has achieved universal suffrage through the principle of equality and the equal protection of the laws.

3. The Constitution of the United States is not violated if a State limits voting to citizens, or if it deprives a citizen of the right to vote if he/she has been convicted of a felony. See *Richardson v. Ramirez*, 418 U.S. 24 (1974). See also Gerald Neuman, *"We Are the People": Alien Suffrage in German and American Perspective*, 13 Mich. J. Int'l L. 259 (1991). Such limitations may be considered also as within the meaning of "universal suffrage" in the international instruments. See pp. 1091–1092 infra.

4.   In popular elections, as in voting in representative bodies, majority rule was assumed (except where a special majority was expressly provided, as, for example, in the provision requiring the approval of Constitutional Amendments by two-thirds of both Houses of Congress). Compare Rousseau, *supra* Part I, Chapter 1(C). Since our republican democracy is committed to government by majority, individual rights, protected even against legislative encroachment, are sometimes described as "anti-majoritarian." The United States, then, may be characterized as a modified, republican, representative democracy, subject to individual rights.

The right to vote is included as a human right in the Universal Declaration of Human Rights and in the International Covenant of Civil and Political Rights (as "universal and equal suffrage" in Article 25 of the ICCPR). The Universal Declaration refers to the right as applicable to every person "in his country"; the International Covenant, Article 25, declares this to be a right of "Every citizen. . . . ". See Part IV, Chapter 2.

Note: Rights and Remedies

The idea of rights in the United States is commonly seen as implying the availability of remedies to prevent, deter, terminate, compensate for, their violation. But the Constitution does not expressly provide remedies for violation of constitutional rights. The prominent "remedy," judicial review and invalidation, was developed early. *Marbury v. Madison,* 5 U.S. (1 Cranch) 137 (1803). In special contexts the courts have inferred a remedy for violation of rights. See *Bivens v. Six Unknown Federal Narcotics Agents*, 403 U.S. 388 (1971) (inferring such authority from the Fourth Amendment). In general, however, remedies have been provided by legislation. See *infra* Chapter 3.

Constitutional Rights as Rights Against Government: Notes on "State Action"

1.   The history and theory of U.S. constitutionalism suggests a social contract consisting of two contracts. The first is a contract among the people to respect each other's rights and to join in establishing a government to secure those rights. By a second contract, the people consent to be governed, and the governors agree to respect the rights of the people and to abide by their mandate. See p. 145 above. Only the second contract has entered U.S. constitutional jurisprudence.

That, in general, the Constitution protects individual rights only against "state action" was established in the *Civil Rights Cases*:

> [C]ivil rights, such as are guaranteed by the Constitution against state aggression, cannot be impaired by the wrongful acts of individuals, unsupported by State authority in the shape of laws, customs, or judicial or executive proceedings. The wrongful act of an individual, unsupported by any such authority, is simply a private wrong, or a crime of that individual; an invasion of the rights of the injured party, it is true, whether they affect his person, his property, or his reputa-

tion; but if not sanctioned in some way by the State or not done under State authority, his rights remain in full force, and may presumably be vindicated by resort to the laws of the State for redress. An individual cannot deprive a man of his right to vote, to hold property, to buy and sell, to sue in the courts, or to be a witness or juror; he may, by force or fraud, interfere with the enjoyment of the right in a particular case; he may commit an assault against the person, or commit murder, or use ruffian violence at the polls, or slander the good name of a fellow citizen; but, unless protected in these wrongful acts by some shield of State law or State authority, he cannot destroy or injure the right; he will only render himself amenable to satisfaction and punishment and amenable therefor to the laws of the State were the wrongful acts are committed.

109 U.S. 3, 17 (1883).

2. The U.S. Supreme Court established the "state action" requirement in refusing to apply the equal protection clause of the Fourteenth Amendment to discrimination by private persons. The Fourteenth Amendment provides: "Nor shall any State ... deny to any person the equal protection of the laws." The Court may have derived the requirement of "state action" from a strict reading of the words "Nor shall any *State* ..." (Italics added). But the Court seemed also to be articulating a theory as to the character of a constitution, drawing an "inherent" distinction between a constitution and laws: private wrongs are declared and governed by laws; a constitution governs official action. Is that distinction inherent, inevitable, indisputable? Note that, with the exception of the First Amendment, the provisions of the Bill of Rights are not addressed to government, but arguably declare guaranties against violations from any source, private or public. But compare the Thirteenth Amendment discussed below, Note 8.

3. The "state action" requirement has been justified as required by constitutional text, by the constitutional commitment to individual autonomy, and to pluralism.

4. Professor Stone has written:

Might one look to principles concerning the appropriate scope of individual autonomy to give content to the state action requirement?

... Without some sort of state action doctrine, private autonomy would be subject to the same limitations as government autonomy. Instead of *protecting* individual rights from *legislative* interference, the Constitution might *subject* them to *judicial* interference.... Newspapers might be prohibited from exclusively promoting a particular point of view. Private home owners might be precluded from choosing their guests on racial or political grounds. Even marriage and divorce decisions might be judicially reviewable for improper motivation.

... Consider in this regard *Columbia Broad. System v. Democratic National Committee*, 412 U.S. 94 (1973). Respondents claimed that the refusal of broadcasters to accept their editorial advertisements violated the First Amendment. The Federal Communications Commission rejected this contention and refused to require that broadcasters accept such advertisements. The Court agreed with the Commission.

. . .

The result in *CBS* maximizes the journalistic freedom of broadcasters, who need not account to a court or government agency for their editorial decisions. But it arguably does so at the expense of the freedom of those wishing to present editorial advertisements, who may be prevented from securing a forum. . . .

. . . [w]hen is the goal of individual autonomy advanced by reading the Constitution to give private entities coercive power that is withheld from government? It is not obvious, for example, that individual freedom is maximized by giving large newspapers and television networks unfettered control over what opinions and information they disseminate.

Geoffrey Stone et al., *Constitutional Law* 1699–1700 (3rd ed., 1996). See also Henkin, Shelley v. Kraemer, *Notes for a Revised Opinion,* 110 U. Pa. L. Rev. 473 (1962); Henkin, *Some Reflections on Current Constitutional Controversies,* 109 U. Pa. L. Rev. 637 (1961).

5.   The "state action" doctrine has also been defended as furthering the value of pluralism:

[P]ublic governmental institutions—there being only one government—cannot adopt at one and the same time values that conflict with one another . . .

. . .

The Constitution binds the public monopoly of government to the public values expressed in the Constitution. But there exist many other conflicting values. Private "persons" are also many. The pluralist case for the state action doctrine is that there should be no constitutional bar to diverse persons pursuing diverse values—values that conflict, yet values that are all good in the eyes of at least some of the people some of the time.

Maimon Schwarzschild, *Value Pluralism and the Constitution: In Defense of the State Action Doctrine,* 1988 Sup. Ct. Rev. 129, 137–38 (1988).

If individual autonomy and pluralism are the values underlying the "state action" doctrine, does that make it easier to determine when "state action" is present? Consider the following situations:

a.   An all-white private club, holding a liquor license issued by the state, refuses to serve a member's guest because the guest is black. Cf. *Moose Lodge No. 107 v. Irvis,* 407 U.S. 163 (1972).

b.   A regulated public utility, privately owned, cuts off power to a residence for alleged nonpayment of utility bills; it has provided neither prior notice nor opportunity to be heard. Is the utility subject to the Constitution and its requirement of due process of law? Cf. *Jackson v. Metro. Edison Co.,* 419 U.S. 345 (1974).

6. The "state action" requirement has not been seriously challenged, but its scope has ebbed and flowed within broad limits. The Supreme Court has found "state action," of course, in State (and federal) legislation, official acts, as well as the actions of the courts. See *Shelley v. Kraemer*, 334 U.S. 1 (1948). It has found "state action" in state encouragement of private actions, even in community custom; in state delegation of traditional public functions to private bodies; and in other forms of official entanglement, e.g., private activities on state-owned property. See *Evans v. Newton*, 382 U.S. 296 (1966); *Reitman v. Mulkey*, 387 U.S. 369 (1967); *Burton v. Wilmington Parking Auth.*, 365 U.S. 715 (1961).

7. The Supreme Court found no state responsibility in *DeShaney v. Winnebago County Dept. of Social Services,* 489 U.S. 189 (1989). County social workers had received several reports that a father was physically abusing his 4 year old child who was living with him. The county social workers investigated but took no steps to protect the child or to remove him from the father's custody. Later, the father beat the child so that he suffered permanent brain damage and had to be institutionalized for life. The Supreme Court stressed that the child was not in state custody when he was beaten. The Court ruled that the due process clause does not require the State to protect a child's life or liberty against private action. "While the State may have been aware of the dangers that Joshua faced in the free world, it played no part in their creation." Justice Brennan dissenting, insisted that "inaction can be every bit as abusive of power as action, that oppression can result when a state undertakes a vital duty and then ignores it."

8. The presence or absence of "state action" has figured prominently in decisions as to whether the state has denied equal protection of the laws by racial discrimination. The courts have sometimes found, but sometimes have refused to find, "state action" also in deprivations of liberty by private entities engaged in particular activities of near-public character. See, for example, *Marsh v. Alabama*, 326 U.S. 501 (1946); *Amalgamated Food Employees Union v. Logan Valley Plaza, Inc.*, 391 U.S. 308 (1968); *Hudgens v. NLRB*, 424 U.S. 507 (1976); *Jackson v. Metropolitan Edison Co.*, 419 U.S. 345 (1974).

The Supreme Court has held that, unlike the Fourteenth Amendment, the Thirteenth Amendment (which contains no reference to the State) applies even in the absence of "state action," and that Congress and the States may legislate against private acts that constitute slavery or "badges of slavery." *Jones v. Alfred H. Mayer Co.*, 392 U.S. 409 (1968); *Reitman v. Mulkey*, 387 U.S. 369 (1967).

9. It has been suggested, supra p. 137, that the Declaration of Independence appears to require government to protect an individual's rights against his or her neighbor (as well as against the government). Presumably, the "state action" requirement does not necessarily deny that obligation of government; it may imply that the Framers left such protection to the common law and to legislation (State and federal), but did not intend to provide constitutional protection. (Or perhaps the Constitution

only refrains from providing the protections of judicial review for private action.) Compare the provisions in Article 2 of the International Covenant on Civil and Political Rights, in which states party to the Covenant undertake to respect "and ensure" the rights recognized in that Covenant. See Part III, pp. 316–317.

Many, perhaps all, of the rights protected by the law of torts and property would raise constitutional issues if invaded by law or by official action. But in relation to private violations of such rights, the individual enjoys protection only as to such remedies as the law provides, and the law is subject to change by legislation. Of course, legislation changing the law of tort or property would constitute "state action" and may constitute a deprivation of property or liberty in violation of the due process clause of the Fifth or of the Fourteenth Amendment. Compare *Truax v. Corrigan*, 257 U.S. 312 (1921); *Pennsylvania Coal Co. v. Mahon*, 260 U.S. 393 (1922).

10.   The U.S. Constitution, generally, does not provide protection against private violation of rights, but Congress can provide such protection under its enumerated powers, notably the Commerce Power, as well as under its power conferred by the Enabling Clause of the Thirteenth Amendment. See Note 8 above.

C.   RIGHTS PROTECTED BY THE U.S. CONSTITUTION

1.   RIGHTS IN THE ORIGINAL CONSTITUTION

The original Constitution contained no Bill of Rights and during the debates on ratification, the supporters of the Constitution felt obliged to explain and justify that omission.

Absence of a Bill of Rights

The Federalist No. 84 (1788) (A. Hamilton)

The most considerable of the remaining objections is, that the plan of the convention contains no bill of rights. Among other answers given to this, it has been upon different occasions remarked, that the constitutions of several of the states are in a similar predicament. I add, that New York is of the number. And yet the persons who in this state oppose the new system, while they profess an unlimited admiration for our particular constitution, are among the most intemperate partisans of a bill of rights. To justify their zeal in this matter they allege two things: one is, that though the constitution of New York has no bill of rights prefixed to it, yet it contains, in the body of it, various provisions in favour of particular privileges and rights, which, in substance, amount to the same thing; the other is, that the constitution adopts, in their full extent, the common and statute law of Great Britain, by which many other rights, not expressed, are equally secured.

To the first I answer, that the constitution offered by the convention contains, as well as the constitution of this state, a number of such provisions.

Independent of those which relate to the structure of the government, we find the following: Article I, section 3, clause 7. "Judgment in cases of impeachment shall not extend further than to removal from office, and disqualification to hold and enjoy any office of honour, trust, or profit under the United States; but the party convicted shall, nevertheless, be liable and subject to indictment, trial, judgment, and punishment, according to law." Section 9 of the same article, clause 2. "The privilege of the writ of *habeas corpus* shall not be suspended, unless when in cases of rebellion or invasion the public safety may require it." Clause 3. "No bill of attainder or *ex post facto* law shall be passed." Clause 7. "No title of nobility shall be granted by the United States; and no person holding any office of profit or trust under them, shall, without the consent of the congress, accept of any present, emolument, office, or title, of any kind whatever, from any king, prince, or foreign state." Article III, section 2, clause 3. "The trial of all crimes, except in cases of impeachment, shall be by jury; and such trial shall be held in the state where the said crimes shall have been committed; but when not committed within any state, the trial shall be at such place or places as the congress may by law have directed." Section 3 of the same article, "Treason against the United States shall consist only in levying war against them, or in adhering to their enemies, giving them aid and comfort. No person shall be convicted of treason, unless on the testimony of two witnesses to the same overt act, or on confession in open court." And clause 3 of the same section, "The congress shall have power to declare the punishment of treason; but no attainder of treason shall work corruption of blood, or forfeiture, except during the life of the person attainted."

. . .

It has been several times truly remarked, that bills of rights are, in their origin, stipulations between kings and their subjects, abridgements of prerogative in favour of privilege, reservations of rights not surrendered to the prince. Such was MAGNA CHARTA, obtained by the Barons, sword in hand, from king John. Such were the subsequent confirmations of that charter by succeeding princes. Such was the *petition of right* assented to by Charles the First, in the beginning of his reign. Such also, was the declaration of right presented by the lords and commons to the Prince of Orange in 1688, and afterwards thrown into the form of an act of parliament, called the bill of rights. It is evident, therefore, that according to their primitive signification, they have no application to constitutions professedly founded upon the power of the people, and executed by their immediate representatives and servants. Here, in strictness, the people surrender nothing; and as they retain everything, they have no need of particular reservations. "WE THE PEOPLE of the United States, to secure the blessings of liberty to ourselves and our posterity do *ordain* and *establish* this constitution for the United States of America:" This is a better recognition of popular rights, than volumes of those aphorisms, which make the principal figure in several of our state bills of rights, and which would sound much better in a treatise of ethics, than in a constitution of government.

But a minute detail of particular rights is certainly far less applicable to a constitution like that under consideration, which is merely intended to regulate the general political interests of the nation, than to one which has the regulation of every species of personal and private concerns. If therefore the loud clamours against the plan of the convention, on this score, are well founded, no epithets of reprobation will be too strong for the constitution of this state. But the truth is, that both of them contain all which, in relation to their objects, is reasonably to be desired.

I go further, and affirm, that bills of rights, in the sense and to the extent they are contended for, are not only unnecessary in the proposed constitution, but would even be dangerous. They would contain various exceptions to powers not granted; and on this very account would afford a colourable pretext to claim more than were granted. For why declare that things shall not be done which there is no power to do? Why, for instance, should it be said, that the liberty of the press shall not be restrained, when no power is given by which restrictions may be imposed? . . . .

Notes

1. Is Hamilton persuasive? Might our constitutional jurisprudence have been different had the original Constitution included a Bill of Rights? To what extent are the safeguards for rights which Hamilton invoked to justify the absence of a Bill of Rights operative today? Do we still find some protection for rights in enumeration of limited powers and in the separation of powers?

2. If the original Constitution was not to have a Bill of Rights, why were a few rights included? Why those?

3. Article IV, section 2 provides that "The Citizens of each State shall be entitled to all Privileges and Immunities of Citizens in the several States." It has been described as a bill of rights for citizens of one State when in the territory of another State. Why does the Constitution guarantee rights for out-of-state citizens but not for local citizens, or for non-citizens?

Are the "Privileges and Immunities of Citizens" the equivalent of "rights"? Does Article IV, section 2 in effect constitute a bill of rights though guaranteed only for out-of-state residents? Can Article IV, section 2 serve to define the conception and content of rights held by the Framers? Does it matter that they are described as Privileges and Immunities of Citizens, rather than of persons? Compare the more general articulation of some rights, not defined as rights of citizens and not limited to citizens, in other clauses of the original Constitution or later in the Bill of Rights, e.g., the right to a jury trial.

What are the privileges and immunities of citizens? In 1823, interpreting the phrase "Privileges and Immunities" in Article IV, section 2, Justice Bushrod Washington wrote:

The inquiry is, what are the privileges and immunities of citizens of the several States? We feel no hesitation in confining these expressions to those privileges and immunities which are *fundamental*, which belong of right to the citizens of all free governments, and which have at all times been enjoyed by citizens of the several States which compose this Union, from the time of their becoming free, independent and sovereign. What these fundamental principles are, it would be more tedious than difficult to enumerate. They may all, however, be comprehended under the following general heads: protection by the government, with the right to acquire and possess property of every kind, and to pursue and obtain happiness and safety, subject, nevertheless, to such restraints as the government may prescribe for the general good of the whole.

Corfield v. Coryell, 6 F. Cas. 546, 551 (C.C.E.D.Pa.1823).

Compare the definition of "privileges or immunities of citizens of the United States" protected by the Fourteenth Amendment against violation by the States, in *Slaughter–House Cases*, 83 U.S. (16 Wall.) 36 (1873), discussed *infra* p. 194.

Justice Washington seems to have misquoted Article IV, section 2. Does the Article mean the same thing if read as "privileges and immunities of citizens *of* the several States," rather than "privileges and immunities of citizens *in* the several States"? Does Article IV, Section 2 guarantee to citizens of other States "the equal protection of the laws"?

2. RIGHTS ADDED BY CONSTITUTIONAL AMENDMENT

The United States Bill of Rights (Amendments I–X)

Amendment I.[1]

Congress shall make no law respecting an establishment of religion, or prohibiting the free exercise thereof; or abridging the freedom of speech, or of the press; or the right of the people peaceably to assemble, and to petition the Government for a redress of grievances.

Amendment II.

A well regulated Militia, being necessary to the security of a free State, the right of the people to keep and bear Arms, shall not be infringed.

Amendment III.

No Soldier shall, in time of peace be quartered in any house, without the consent of the Owner, nor in time of war, but in a manner to be prescribed by law.

---

1. The first ten Amendments were ratified by the State legislatures effective December 15, 1791.

Amendment IV.

The right of the people to be secure in their persons, houses, papers, and effects, against unreasonable searches and seizures, shall not be violated, and no Warrants shall issue, but upon probable cause, supported by Oath or affirmation, and particularly describing the place to be searched, and the persons or things to be seized.

Amendment V.

No person shall be held to answer for a capital, or otherwise infamous crime, unless on a presentment or indictment of a Grand Jury, except in cases arising in the land or naval forces, or in the Militia, when in actual service in time of War or public danger; nor shall any person be subject for the same offence to be twice put in jeopardy of life or limb; nor shall be compelled in any criminal case to be a witness against himself, nor be deprived of life, liberty, or property, without due process of law; nor shall private property be taken for public use, without just compensation.

Amendment VI.

In all criminal prosecutions, the accused shall enjoy the right to a speedy and public trial, by an impartial jury of the State and district wherein the crime shall have been committed, which district shall have been previously ascertained by law, and to be informed of the nature and cause of the accusation; to be confronted with the witnesses against him; to have compulsory process for obtaining witnesses in his favor, and to have the Assistance of Counsel for his defence.

Amendment VII.

In Suits at common law, where the value in controversy shall exceed twenty dollars, the right of trial by jury shall be preserved, and no fact tried by a jury, shall be otherwise re-examined in any Court of the United States, than according to the rules of the common law.

Amendment VIII.

Excessive bail shall not be required, nor excessive fines imposed, nor cruel and unusual punishments inflicted.

Amendment IX.

The enumeration in the Constitution, of certain rights, shall not be construed to deny or disparage others retained by the people.

Amendment X.

The powers not delegated to the United States by the Constitution, nor prohibited by it to the States, are reserved to the States respectively, or to the people.

Notes

1. The Bill of Rights is the appellation commonly given to the first ten Amendments to the U.S. Constitution. The Amendments fulfilled the commitment given to those who were reluctant to ratify the Constitution because it contained no bill of rights. The decision to have a bill or rights added by amendment after the Constitution was ratified, rather than by reopening the text of the Constitution and inserting a Bill of Rights prior to ratification, no doubt avoided long delays in bringing the Constitution into effect. It may also help explain why the Constitution does not include any theory of rights and no articles designated "Bill of Rights," and why the U.S. Bill of Rights (Amendments 1 to 10) seems to lack unity and consists of 10 discrete provisions. Compare the Virginia Bill of Rights, Section A above.

2. The Ninth and Tenth Amendments are commonly considered part of the Bill of Rights, although, unlike the first eight Amendments, they do not guarantee particular rights. The reference in the Ninth Amendment to rights "retained" by the people reflects the Framers' theory that the people come endowed with rights, give some up to government for the purposes of government, but retain the rest. See Section B above. The Ninth Amendment has not been invoked by the courts to protect rights not enumerated in the Constitution, and even individual Justices have hardly relied on it. See, e.g., the majority and concurring opinions in *Griswold v. Connecticut*, 381 U.S. 479 (1965). Compare the discussion of "substantive due process," below.

The Tenth Amendment reserves to the people (or to the States) "powers" not delegated to the federal government. Does that clause reserve "rights" (as well as powers), thus justifying the inclusion of the Tenth Amendment, along with the Ninth Amendment, within the "Bill of Rights"? In fact, the Tenth Amendment has not served to protect unenumerated rights, but the "vertical" separation of powers implied in federalism (which the Tenth Amendment exemplifies) has served to limit the exercise of federal governmental authority. The Tenth Amendment was depreciated as "stating but a truism." *United States v. Darby*, 312 U.S. 100, 124 (1941); it has had a rebirth towards the end of the Twentieth Century. Compare *New York v. United States*, 505 U.S. 144 (1992), and *United States v. Lopez*, 514 U.S. 549 (1995), but it has not provided protection for additional rights as powers "reserved . . . to the people."

3. Though appended by constitutional amendment, the Bill of Rights may be seen as part of the "original package." The Constitution has hardly been amended since then, but a few of the subsequent amendments, notably the Civil War Amendments, added importantly to the jurisprudence of rights. The Thirteenth Amendment abolished slavery, the Fourteenth Amendment "nationalized" rights and added a right to equal protection of the laws, and the Fifteenth Amendment forbade racial discrimination in voting. (Later, the Nineteenth Amendment prohibited discrimination in voting on grounds of sex, and the Twenty–Sixth Amendment forbids age discrimination in voting for those above eighteen years of age.) Some see

the Sixteenth Amendment permitting a graduated income tax as a major step towards establishing economic and social rights in the United States. See generally Part IV, Chapter 3.

4. Beyond doubt, the most important Amendment to the Constitution since the Bill of Rights was the Fourteenth Amendment, sometimes referred to as our Second Constitution. The Fourteenth Amendment defined and guaranteed citizenship, and it "nationalized rights," protecting rights against violation by the States; it added a provision that no State shall deny to any person the equal protection of the laws. (The Fourteenth Amendment also prohibited the States from abridging the privileges or immunities of citizens of the United States, but that provision was read narrowly and has had little effect. *Slaughter–House Cases*, 83 U.S. (16 Wall.) 36 (1873)). See p. 194 below. The Fourteenth Amendment also gave Congress power to implement the Amendment, thus conferring on Congress an additional legislative power of particular importance for the jurisprudence of rights.

Subsequent Constitutional Amendments Safeguarding Rights

Amendment XIII.[1]

Section 1. Neither slavery nor involuntary servitude, except as a punishment for crime whereof the party shall have been duly convicted, shall exist within the United States, or any place subject to their jurisdiction.

Section 2. Congress shall have power to enforce this article by appropriate legislation.

Amendment XIV.[2]

Section 1. All persons born or naturalized in the United States and subject to the jurisdiction thereof, are citizens of the United States and of the State wherein they reside. No State shall make or enforce any law which shall abridge the privileges or immunities of citizens of the United States; nor shall any State deprive any person of life, liberty, or property, without due process of law; nor deny to any person within its jurisdiction the equal protection of the laws.

. . .

Section 5. The Congress shall have power to enforce, by appropriate legislation, the provisions of this article.

Amendment XV.[3]

Section 1. The right of citizens of the United States to vote shall not be denied or abridged by the United States or by any State on account of race, color, or previous condition of servitude.

1. Ratified December 6, 1865.
2. Ratified July 9, 1868.
3. Ratified February 3, 1870.

Section 2.   The Congress shall have power to enforce this article by appropriate legislation.

Amendment XIX.[4]

The right of citizens of the United States to vote shall not be denied or abridged by the United States or by any State on account of sex.

Congress shall have power to enforce this article by appropriate legislation

Amendment XXIV.[5]

Section 1.   The right of citizens of the United States to vote in any primary or other election for President or Vice President, for electors for President or Vice President, or for Senator or Representative in Congress, shall not be denied or abridged by the United States or any State by reason of failure to pay any poll tax or other tax.

Section 2.   The Congress shall have power to enforce this article by appropriate legislation.

Amendment XXVI.[6]

Section 1.   The right of citizens of the United States, who are eighteen years of age or older, to vote shall not be denied or abridged by the United States or by any State on account of age.

Section 2.   The Congress shall have power to enforce this article by appropriate legislation.

3.   EXPANDING RIGHTS BY INTERPRETATION

One reason why the U.S. Constitution has had few amendments may be that the amendment process is difficult, and that the courts, in performing the function of judicial review (see Chapter 3), have effectively exercised authority to "update" and "calibrate" the Constitution by interpretation. Nearly every provision of the Bill of Rights has been construed by the Supreme Court and some of them have been the subjects of major jurisprudential elaboration, e.g., the protections of the First Amendment and the Amendments addressing the Criminal Process. By interpretation, the courts have added constitutional protections perhaps not intended by the Framers of the Constitution or of the Amendments, e.g., the expanded conception of "liberty" protected by the Fifth and Fourteenth Amendments, the extension of "due process of law" in those amendments to provide substantive protections ("substantive due process"), and the incorporation of almost all of the provisions of the Bill of Rights into the Fourteenth Amendment to render them applicable to the States. The courts have also found "reverse incorporation" of the provision in the Fourteenth Amendment requiring the equal protection of the laws into the Due Process

4. Ratified August 18, 1920.   **6.** Ratified July 1, 1971.
5. Ratified January 23, 1964.

clause of the Fifth Amendment, to render it applicable to the federal government. See *infra* p. 192.

Theories of Interpretation: Justices Brennan, Scalia, Rehnquist

The principal contemporary exponent of "The Living Constitution" was Justice Brennan:

> To remain faithful to the content of the Constitution, therefore, an approach to interpreting the text must account for the existence of these substantive value choices and must accept the ambiguity inherent in the effort to apply them to modern circumstances. The Framers discerned fundamental principles through struggles against particular malefactions of the Crown; the struggle shapes the particular contours of the articulated principles. But our acceptance of the fundamental principles has not and should not bind us to those precise, at times anachronistic, contours. Successive generations of Americans have continued to respect these fundamental choices and adopt them as their own guide to evaluating quite different historical practices. Each generation has the choice to overrule or add to the fundamental principles enunciated by the Framers; the Constitution can be amended or it can be ignored. Yet with respect to its fundamental principles, the text has suffered neither fate. Thus, if I may borrow the words of an esteemed predecessor, Justice Robert Jackson, the burden of judicial interpretation is to translate "the majestic generalities of the Bill of Rights, conceived as part of the pattern of liberal government in the eighteenth century, into concrete restraints on officials dealing with the problems of the twentieth century ..."

> Current Justices read the Constitution in the only way that we can: as twentieth-century Americans. We look to the history of the time of framing and to the intervening history of interpretation. But the ultimate question must be: What do the words of the text mean in our time? For the genius of the Constitution rests not in any static meaning it might have had in a world that is dead and gone, but in the adaptability of its great principles to cope with current problems and current needs. What the constitutional fundamentals meant to the wisdom of other times cannot be the measure to the vision of our time. Similarly, what those fundamentals mean for us, our descendants will learn, cannot be the measure to the vision of their time. This realization is not a novel one of my own creation ...

> Interpretation must account for the transformative purpose of the text. Our Constitution was not intended to preserve a preexisting society but to make a new one, to put in place new principles that the prior political community had not sufficiently recognized. Thus, for example, when we interpret the Civil War amendments—abolishing slavery, guaranteeing blacks equality under law, and guaranteeing blacks the right to vote—we must remember that those who put them

in place had no desire to enshrine the status quo. Their goal was to make over their world, to eliminate all vestige of the slave caste.

William Brennan, *The Constitution of the United States: Contemporary Ratification,* 27 S. Tex. L. Rev. 433, 437–438 (1986).

Updating the Constitution by judicial "interpretation" has not been unanimously acclaimed. In challenging the legitimacy of the Supreme Court's authority to expand rights by interpretation, Justice Scalia has written:

> It certainly cannot be said that a constitution naturally suggests changeability; to the contrary, its whole purpose is to prevent change— to embed certain rights in such a manner that future generations cannot readily take them away. A society that adopts a bill of rights is skeptical that "evolving standards of decency" always "mark progress," and that societies always "mature," as opposed to rot. Neither the text of such a document nor the intent of its framers (whichever you choose) can possibly lead to the conclusion that its only effect is to take the power of changing rights away from the legislature and give it to the courts. . . .

> Perhaps the most glaring defect of Living Constitutionalism, next to its incompatibility with the whole antievolutionary purpose of a constitution, is that there is no agreement, and no chance of agreement, upon what is to be the guiding principle of the evolution. *Panta rei* is not a sufficiently informative principle of constitutional interpretation. What is it that the judge must consult to determine when, and in what direction, evolution has occurred? Is it the will of the majority, discerned from newspapers, radio talk shows, public opinion polls, and chats at the country club? Is it the philosophy of Hume, or of John Rawls, or of John Stuart Mill, or of Aristotle? As soon as the discussion goes beyond the issue of whether the Constitution is static, the evolutionists divide into as many camps as there are individual views of the good, the true, and the beautiful. I think that is inevitably so, which means that evolutionism is simply not a practicable constitutional philosophy.

> I do not suggest, mind you, that originalists always agree upon their answer. There is plenty of room for disagreement as to what original meaning was, and even more as to how that original meaning applies to the situation before the court. But the originalist at least knows what he is looking for: the original meaning of the text . . .

> If the courts are free to write the Constitution anew, they will, by God, write it the way the majority wants; the appointment and confirmation process will see to that. This, of course, is the end of the Bill of Rights, whose meaning will be committed to the very body it was meant to protect against: the majority. By trying to make the Constitution do everything that needs doing from age to age, we shall have caused it to do nothing at all.

Antonin Scalia, A Matter of Interpretation 37–47 (1997). See also Scalia, *Originalism: The Lesser Evil,* 57 U. Cin. L. Rev. 849 (1989).

Chief Justice Rehnquist tends to agree with Justice Scalia:

[T]he living Constitution, in the last analysis, is a formula for an end run around popular government. To the extent that it makes possible an individual's persuading one or more appointed federal judges to impose on other individuals a rule of conduct that the popularly elected branches of government would not have enacted and the voters have not and would not have embodied in the Constitution. . . . the living Constitution is genuinely corrosive of the fundamental values of our democratic society.

William Rehnquist, *The Notion of a Living Constitution,* in Views from the Bench 135–36 (Mark Cannon and David O'Brien eds., 1985).

But, if only from commitment to the principles of *stare decisis,* there has been no apparent disposition to reconsider many established interpretations, including the expansive interpretations detailed below.

D. CONSTITUTIONAL RIGHTS—TWO HUNDRED YEARS LATER

Louis Henkin, *The Age of Rights*
118–26 (1990).

The rapid growth of human rights in the United States came with the New Deal (1933–1939), and accelerated after World War II. Perhaps under the influence of world events that transformed the United States in many respects, and of a new *Zeitgeist* including the international human rights movement, constitutional rights in the United States were radically modified both in gross and in detail.

Rights in the United States are large and complex, but the Constitution still has the same words with which the United States began, the Bill of Rights has not been formally amended, and even the Fourteenth Amendment seemed to promise only a little. It is easy today to overlook the limited conception of individual rights held by the Framers—of 1787 as well as 1868—and the radical transformation in that conception in the latter half of this century.*

Originally, the rights declared in the Bill of Rights were essentially political, protecting, it has been said, not the rights of man but the rights of gentlemen. The freedoms put in first place—speech, press, assembly—were seen primarily as political liberties with political purposes; it is open to question whether they sought to safeguard individual "self-expression," or even radical political heresy. Even the guarantee of the free exercise of religion may have reflected a desire to avoid religious hostility more than concern for individual conscience. The "right of the people to be secure . . .

---

* In this section I draw on my book *The Rights of Man Today* (1978), chapter 2.

against unreasonable searches and seizures," the guarantee of "due process of law," the protection of property against confiscation, the catalogue of safeguards for those who might be accused of crime, were couched as rights of every person, but they seem to have reflected a desire to safeguard the established, respectable citizenry against various known forms of repression by tyrannical governments, rather than tenderness and respect for any individual, even the least worthy. The Civil War amendments, too, were probably not designed to realize radical advances in human rights generally, but only to abolish slavery (as some of the states and other countries had done earlier), establish the citizenship of the former slaves, and remove disabilities and other "badges" of slavery for black citizens.

Today, the conception of rights and the constitutional jurisprudence of rights ring very differently. By radical reinterpretation, the Supreme Court held that the Fourteenth Amendment had effectively incorporated, and rendered applicable to the states, the principal provisions of the Bill of Rights[†]—freedom of speech, press, assembly, religion, the security of the home and the person, and virtually every safeguard for persons accused of crime. Now, every state law impinging on important freedoms, and every state criminal trial, is subject to scrutiny by the federal courts. And Congress has the power to protect rights against violation and provide remedies for violations by state legislatures, by state or federal courts or officials.

Even more radical, perhaps, was the expansion of eighteenth-century rights in conception and content. Without formal amendment, the Constitution has been read to protect new rights and old rights newly conceived. The Constitution has been opened to every man and woman, to the least and the worst of them. Constitutional protection has moved beyond political rights to civil and personal rights, rooted in conceptions of the essential dignity and worth of the individual. The Constitution safeguards not only political freedom but, in principle, also social, sexual, and other personal freedoms, and individual privacy, autonomy, idiosyncrasy. Notably:

- Freedom of speech and press now protects advocacy even of radical ideas or expressions that are deeply disturbing or offensive, as long as expressions do not incite to violence or other unlawful action; it protects not only political and religious expression but also economic speech and publication, e.g., labor picketing and commercial advertising, as well as "self-expression" even if it approaches "obscenity." Speech is protected even when it is "symbolic," as in wearing an arm band to protest a war; one's money, too, may talk, without ready limits, as by contributions to political campaigns. The press enjoys freedom far beyond its relevance to the political process. The freedom to publish is now associated with the reader's "right to know";

---

† Incorporation also "homogenized" rights against the federal and state governments, rendering the rights essentially the same in every state as they were against the increasingly interventionist federal government. In a separate development the Court in effect held that the equal protection of the laws was required of the federal government as of the states.

prior restraint on publication as by censorship, requirement of license, or by injunction is virtually excluded.* The right to publish and the right to know may outweigh also the right of an official or of another "public" person to be free from libel, or the privacy rights of even private persons. Freedom of speech and press includes a right of access to a public forum. It includes also the freedom *not* to speak or publish, to speak and publish anonymously, to be free of governmental inquiry into what one thinks and says. Out of these rights and right of assembly, the courts have made a right of association, of anonymous association, of nonassociation.

- Freedom of religion means not only that there must be no state interference with, but also no burden on, the free exercise of religion. The prohibition on establishing religion requires a wall of separation between church and state. Neither the federal nor the state governments may give financial aid to religious institutions or permit Bible reading or prayer in public schools. Government must not advance or inhibit religion or be excessively entangled with religion.

- Freedom from unreasonable search and seizure applies—though perhaps differently—not only to the home but also to the office and the automobile; not only to physical but also to technological intrusion, e.g., wiretapping; not only to incursions by the police, but also to visits by health and fire inspectors.

- Perhaps the greatest expansion has been in the rights of those accused of crime. The Bill of Rights—its principal provisions applicable also to the states—protects not only the respectable and innocent against the governmental oppressor; even criminals have rights to a fair trial (without improperly obtained evidence), to counsel (provided by the government if the defendant cannot provide his own), to freedom from self-incrimination and from comment on one's failure to testify.

- The equal protection of the laws has also acquired new ramifications. By new interpretation of the due process clause of the Fifth Amendment, the Constitution now effectively requires of the federal government the same equal protection of the laws that the Fourteenth Amendment expressly commanded to the states. All racial classifications—by state or federal government—are suspect, and invidious discrimination on account of race, "whether accomplished ingeniously or ingenuously," is readily rejected. Official separation of the races, even "separate but equal," is outlawed.

- There has been a fundamental and, I believe, irreversible transformation in the constitutional status of women. Discriminations

---

* *The New York Times* could not be enjoined from publishing confidential official documents relating to the Vietnam War because the Government could not persuade the Supreme Court that there was a compelling need for such prior restraint on publication. See *New York Times v. United States*, 403 U.S. 713 (1971).

against women on the basis of generalizations reflecting stereotyped and outdated sociological assumptions no longer seem "natural" and inevitable, and are invalid. And the new equality of the genders entitles males also to freedom from unwarranted discrimination.

- The poor, too, have some rights to equal protection. A state that offers for pay benefits that only the state provides—a criminal appeal, a divorce—must make them available gratis to those who cannot pay.

- Other once-axiomatic inequalities are no longer acceptable. The states cannot deny to aliens welfare benefits, public employment, or admission to the professions; they cannot maintain irrelevant distinctions between legitimate and illegitimate children. Other once-excluded categories are now included: prisoners have rights, as do military personnel, mental patients, pupils in the schools; children have rights independently of and even against their parents.

- In the Constitution now are new rights, for example a right to travel, abroad as well as interstate; a local residence requirement as a condition of enjoying rights or benefits is invalid because it burdens the right to travel.

- In what can be seen as a reversion to the eighteenth-century principle of antecedent natural rights to individual autonomy and liberty, the courts have found an area of fundamental individual autonomy ("privacy"). Hence, the state may not forbid the use of contraceptives, or the resort to abortion in the first trimester of pregnancy, or indulging oneself with obscene materials in private. Parents may send their children to private schools; they may even refuse to send their children to high school at all when to do so would offend their religious scruples.

- Finally, the United States has become a democracy. The indirect election of the President through an electoral college remains in the Constitution (Article II, section 2; Amendment XII) but has been largely reduced to a formality, and the Presidency is now generally responsive to popular suffrage. The Constitution seemed to leave voting qualifications to the states, but later Amendments forbidding the denial of the vote on invidious grounds (race, sex, age, poverty) have supported voting rights legislation that has rendered suffrage virtually universal in fact. In effect, the Supreme Court has built a constitutional right to vote, and a right to a vote of equal weight, out of a few straws, including the right to the equal protection of the laws.

The explosion of rights I have described confirms the essentially open character of the Constitution, and constitutional rights as the fruit of a continuing synthesis of immutable principle with contemporary values both homegrown and imported. Old assumptions are reexamined, stereotypes are penetrated, and rights are accepted today that were not conceived a few decades ago.*

Perhaps the inevitable consequence of expanding and proliferating rights was the clear emergence of the principle of "balancing" individual liberty and public interest to determine the limits of each. The courts do not now attend seriously to objections that economic and social regulation limits individual autonomy or liberty, but in principle all governmental action must justify itself as a means rationally linked to some public purpose. Rights are not absolute, however, and virtually every right might, in some times and circumstances, give way to some other public good. Some individual rights and freedoms, however—speech, press, assembly, religion, old and new privacy, freedom from racial discrimination—are fundamental, preferred; invasions are suspect, will be sharply scrutinized, and will be sustained only for a compelling state interest.†

In the second half of the twentieth century, one constitutional blessing is noteworthy: the constitutional theory of the framers, the institutions they established, the availability of the judiciary to adapt and develop the general principles of the Constitution and to arbitrate political controversy—as well, no doubt, as great good fortune—have saved the United States from extraconstitutional government. There have been no emergency suspensions of the Constitution or of particular rights, such as have bedeviled constitutional government and human rights in other countries. The Constitution does not provide for its own suspension, and that has never been attempted, even in time of war. Habeas corpus was suspended during the Civil War and on two or three other occasions; other rights have been curtailed during war: the relocation of Americans of Japanese ancestry during World War II was an inglorious chapter, held by the courts at the time to be constitutionally permissible. But there have not otherwise been mass detentions or other major derogations from rights.

I have been discussing constitutional rights—the rights Americans enjoy as higher law, regardless of the will of majorities and of their representatives and officials. But, by interpreting the constitutional powers of Congress broadly, the courts have unleashed and encouraged Congress to expand individual rights. The extension of federal power, notably the Commerce Power, has enabled Congress to legislate against private discriminations (e.g., on account of race) and other private infringements. Expansive interpretations of the Civil War amendments have permitted sophisticated legislation to protect the right to vote and to safeguard the exercise of some other rights from official or private interference. Imaginative lawyers and sympathetic courts have found that old civil rights acts give protections against invasions of newly conceived rights,[**] prohibiting,

---

* On the horizon may be rights un-dreamed of—a right to be born and a right to die, and rights for the dead and the unborn.

† The Supreme Court has not done well in justifying the weight it gives to particular rights and has done virtually nothing to ex-plain the weights assigned to different public interests.

[**] Congress has also created the "right to know" by freedom of information acts. It has extended the right of conscientious objec-tion to military service. It has created rights

for example, private discrimination in the sale or rental of housing or in admission to private school.

By contemporary human rights standards, perhaps the most significant legislative extension of rights has been that which, beginning some fifty years ago, brought economic and social "rights" to the inhabitants of the United States. These rights did not come easily. Except for public education provided by the states early, the welfare state began slowly. The United States has become a welfare state not by constitutional imperative or encouragement but, indeed, over strong constitutional resistance. Welfare programs had to overcome resistance to governmental intervention and "activism," resistance that flew the flag of individual autonomy and limited conceptions of government; resistance to various economic regulations, flying the flag of economic liberty; resistance to strong federal government, flying the flag of states' rights; resistance to massive governmental spending based on heavy progressive taxation, flying flags of property, liberty and equality; the Sixteenth Amendment was required to permit a federal progressive income tax, on which the welfare state depends. Only after deep economic depression did traditional fear of government begin to give way to demands upon government—for intensive regulation of business and labor relations, for minimum wages and maximum hours, social security, expanding government employment and government work programs—with constitutional reinterpretations to make them acceptable.

A second world war, decades of technological, political, and social change, and ideas and examples from abroad proliferated welfare programs and magnified them manifold. Economic and social benefits have effectively established equal entitlement as regards minimum basic needs; they have even moved United States society a few steps from equal opportunity to somewhat less inequality in fact. But not being constitutional rights, economic and social entitlements are subject to political and budgetary restraints, sometimes also to recurrent ideological resistance. In the 1980s, the drive for lower taxes and higher defense expenditures, some ideological commitment to "market forces," and some resistance to the welfare state in principle, significantly weakened economic-social "rights" in the United States. But the United States remains a welfare state and welfare programs are likely to increase again.

The 1980s have also seen some regression in constitutional rights. Since the scope and content of rights are ultimately decided by the Supreme Court, they will fluctuate with changes in judicial interpretation. After the luxuriant growth I have described, the Supreme Court entered a period of consolidation and retrenchment, perhaps of reaction. In the 1980s there have been more restrained readings of the Constitution, greater reluctance to increase individual protection, a tendency to give greater scope and weight to public authority, particularly in the criminal process. There are suggestions of greater judicial toleration of state "accommodation" rather than "neutrality" in its relations to religion; the right of

to a more healthful environment. Federal example has encouraged emulation by the states, and some states have taken such rights further.

privacy has been held not to include the right of adults to engage in private homosexual activity. Some fear that the case upholding the right of a woman to have an abortion may be restricted if not overruled. New fears— increasing crime, spreading AIDS—bring proposals that would threaten established constitutional guarantees, and some of these proposals may be upheld. But whatever the years ahead bring in detail they are not likely to weaken the commitment to individual rights now more than two hundred years old.

The rights of man in the United States, it need hardly be said, are far from perfect. Past sins are grievous and notorious: genocide and lesser violations of the Indian; slavery, racial segregation, and other badges of slavery for blacks; other racial, ethnic, and religious discriminations, including relocations and concentrations of citizens of Japanese ancestry in time of war; Chinese exclusion and other racist immigration laws; postwar anti-Communist hunts, which also "chilled" political freedoms of others; and many more.

If these are for the largest part happily past, there are still racial discriminations and inequalities, at least de facto, and debatable acceptance of instances of private discrimination. Valued freedoms are sometimes empty for those unable or afraid to exercise them, or who are denied access to media that will make them effective or competitive. There is poverty, unemployment (which falls particularly heavily on blacks and other minorities), inadequate housing and health care, even hunger, and there are wider economic inequities and inequalities. Immigration, exclusion, and deportation laws are built on outdated conceptions, such as the absolute right of Congress to exclude and deport. Some object to balancing away rights in principle or to the balance struck in particular instances, say, the preference for the right to know over the right of privacy. Some see violations of rights in laws against obscenity, in other limitations on newspapers and newspapermen, in regulation of other communications media; some have objected to constitutional tolerance of laws against group libel. Some see retrogression in "affirmative action" discrimination in favor of the once-oppressed to the disadvantage of others. Some see failures of rights in excessive toleration, in respecting freedom for those who abuse it, in too much "legalism" at the expense of order, in failing generally to provide freedom from fear. Even where principles are unexceptionable, there are ever-present instances where practice deviates from principle and is not readily remedied; at various times, in various places, there have been accusations and some evidence of "political justice"—denial of due process and equal protection to "leftists," to blacks, to "long hairs," to the deviant, or the stranger. Police abuses are too frequent and notorious, and new technology available to government threatens essential privacy.

But in all, I conclude human rights—civil-political as well as economic-social rights—are alive and reasonably well in the United States.

THE ENFORCEMENT OF RIGHTS: CONGRESS AND THE COURTS

The framers of the Constitution, including those who appended the Bill of Rights, expected that tyranny and oppression would be avoided by preventing the concentration of political authority. Individual rights would be safeguarded by federalism—by dividing authority between the federal government and the states—and by separation of powers and checks and balances among the branches of the federal government. Secondarily, perhaps, the framers expected that Congress might have power to enact some laws against some abuses of rights, and that the courts would monitor governmental respect for rights in some measure and by some means.

It is difficult to determine to what extent the original expectations have in fact been realized, and how much United States constitutionalism has moved beyond all expectations. Federalism and the separation of powers, though transformed during two hundred years, doubtless continue to prevent the concentration of power and some of the abuses that concentrated power brings. But today, constitutional guarantees rather than institutional arrangements are perceived as the principal safeguards of rights, and the courts are seen as their primary guardians, with Congress in a supporting role. During the eighty years before the Civil War, Congress enacted little that could be characterized as civil rights legislation, perhaps because Congress did not seem to have the power to do so. In the wake of the Civil War, under new powers granted to Congress by the Civil War Amendments, Congressional civil rights acts loomed large, but they were largely nullified by the courts, and Congress did not enact significant civil rights legislation again for a hundred years, until the 1960s.

Today, civil rights laws are important safeguards against executive and police violations. But only the courts can protect against violations by Congress, and the courts monitor and enforce constitutional rights also—indeed principally—against violation by the states, including state legislatures, state executives, state courts. It is not incorrect to conclude that against the bureaucracy, whether state or federal, against state legislation, and to a lesser extent against acts of Congress, individual rights are safeguarded in the United States by an alert, independent judiciary, activated by individuals, public-interest groups and energetic legal professionals.

In enforcing constitutional rights, the courts have also determined their scope and content. In deciding that the Fourteenth Amendment incorporated most of the Bill of Rights, the Supreme Court gave the courts a major role in monitoring the state criminal process as well as state regulation of religion, expression and assembly. The courts read the due process clauses as including substantive as well as procedural limitations, and the rise and fall—and rise—of substantive due process have determined the ebb and flow of judicial enforcement. Periodically, judicial activism encouraged legislative activism, and new—as well as old—civil rights acts in turn gave the courts new opportunities to determine the limits of rights by (or in the guise of) statutory interpretation. Congress has rarely "corrected" judicial interpretation.

Judicial supremacy is established in constitutional jurisprudence and is commonly seen as the hallmark of—and the linchpin of—United States constitutionalism. But to credit the courts with the radical growth of rights in the United States is too simple. Often the courts have merely acquiesced in and legitimated what political authority (both state and federal) had done. The influence of the courts, moreover, has not been constant and linear. During the course of United States history, courts have sometimes construed constitutional safeguards narrowly, reducing the scope of constitutional protection of rights or denying to state or federal legislatures the power to safeguard or promote rights. At different periods, courts have been more activist or more self-restrained, more liberal or more conservative, in their reading and application of the Constitution. But, after two hundred years, the principle of judicial review, and the central part of the courts in the protection of rights, are deeply entrenched. The United States has become a democracy with universal suffrage, but a democracy subject to individual rights; and the courts determine the scope and content of those rights and calibrate the balance between representative government and individual rights.

In the United States, the judicial role in rights enforcement has often been, and in the 1980s is again, a focus of controversy. At the beginning of the twentieth century the Supreme Court earned condemnation for developing substantive due process and equating it with *laissez-faire*, for frustrating representative government and becoming a superlegislature. Retreat during the 1930s was followed after the Second World War by resurgent activism in support of political freedom, self-expression, separation of church and state, safeguards for those accused of crime, racial desegregation, a new zone of autonomy in personal matters such as the freedom of women to seek abortion. In the last decade of the second century under the Constitution, voices are again heard to challenge "government by judiciary," this time voices of a different ideology—the voices of "law and order," and "traditional" values.

The United States is sometimes described as a rights-ridden society. Surely, even as its democracy has improved, the rights of the individual have increased. The mix of democratic-republicanism and individualism are not universally commended or understood. But it remains, I think, an important if idiosyncratic expression by the United States of eighteenth-century ideas adapted to this country's place in the twentieth century. The United States regime of rights is envied and emulated, not always with success, as our idiosyncrasies flourish less well in less-hospitable cultures, in less-fortunate, less-stable societies.

The United States—with France—can lay claim to having launched the idea of rights and helped to give it political expression in national constitutions and in international instruments. The use of courts to monitor the tensions between individual autonomy and public good has been emulated in unlikely places: several European countries have established constitutional courts; France has something like it; the United Kingdom is seriously talking of a bill of rights to be given effect by the courts. International human rights courts and near-courts flourish. The eighteenth-century authors of the Declaration of Independence and the framers of the Constitution, and Thomas Paine, and even John Locke, might not recognize their offspring but they would not be uncomfortable at this two hundredth birthday celebration.

Notes

1. There have been few serious efforts to add to the Bill of Rights by constitutional amendment. One reason is the difficult amendment process prescribed in Article V.

Six Constitutional amendments have been adopted since World War II. During that period, Congress proposed amending the Constitution by an Equal Rights Amendment, but though the amendment received the necessary support in Congress, it failed to be ratified by the Legislatures of three-fourths of the States. The proposed ERA would have, in effect, amended the Fourteenth Amendment to ensure that the "equal protection of the laws" extended to individuals regardless of their sex, and would have prohibited gender distinctions unless they served a very important, perhaps a compelling, public interest. The Establishment Clause in the First Amendment has also been the subject of proposals for modification, principally to permit prayer in the classroom.

Some proposals for Constitutional amendment might be seen as designed to *limit* rights, for example the proposal to permit Congress to outlaw desecration of the U.S. flag. The proposed amendment received the votes of a majority of both Houses of Congress but not the necessary two-thirds.

In some cases, proposals for constitutional amendment might be seen as enhancing rights for some while limiting rights for others. For example, proposals to overrule *Roe v. Wade,* 410 U.S. 113 (1973), would claim to expand the rights of the fetus while limiting the rights of women. See Part IV, Chapter 1(B).

2. Since 1990 when this essay was published, there appears to have been no major expansion of rights by constitutional interpretation. Human rights continue to be a staple of constitutional jurisprudence in the United States, but the end of the Twentieth Century has brought adaptations, not radical change. Notable examples and trends include the Supreme Court's conclusion that the protection for freedom of religion in the First Amendment does not exempt religious practice from otherwise-valid laws of general applicability. See *Employment Div., Dep't of Human Resources of Oregon v. Smith*, 494 U.S. 872, 890 (1990) (concluding that Oregon may apply laws regulating drug use to those who use drugs in religious ritual). Congressional legislation to overturn *Smith* and to provide a statutory basis for the extension of the freedom of religion which the Court had not found in the Constitution, the Religious Freedom Restoration Act of 1993 (RFRA), was declared invalid as an unconstitutional attempt by Congress to impose its interpretation of the Constitution. *City of Boerne v. Flores,* 521 U.S. 507 (1997). See pp. 218–219 below.

There has been adaptation also in the jurisprudence of the Establishment Clause. Compare *Everson v. Board of Education*, 330 U.S. 1 (1947), and *Lemon v. Kurtzman*, 397 U.S. 1034 (1970), with *Agostini v. Felton*, 521 U.S. 203 (1997). Is non-establishment of religion required by the human rights idea and by the principal international human rights instruments? See Part III, Chapter 2(B), and Note 2 on pp. 1205–1206 infra.

The Supreme Court has also been extending the reach of the "takings" clause in the Fifth Amendment as applied to the States through the protections afforded to property by substantive due process of law. Economic regulations that the modern Court accepts as rational, not arbitrary, under *Nebbia v. New York*, 291 U.S. 502 (1934), may nonetheless constitute a taking of property requiring compensation. See, e.g., *Pennsylvania Coal Co. v. Mahon*, 260 U.S. 393 (1922); *First English Evangelical Lutheran Church of Glendale v. County of Los Angeles*, 482 U.S. 304 (1987); *Nollan v. California Coastal Comm'n*, 483 U.S. 825 (1987); *Dolan v. City of Tigard*, 512 U.S. 374 (1994); also *Lucas v. South Carolina Coastal Council*, 505 U.S. 1003 (1992). In 1998, a plurality of the Court decided that retroactive legislation regulating the coal industry constituted an unconstitutional taking because it "improperly place[d] a severe, disproportionate, and extremely retroactive burden." *Eastern Enters. v. Apfel*, 524 U.S. 498 (1998). See Part IV, Chapter 3(B).

4.   The Supreme Court has not revisited the declaration in the Second Amendment of the right to bear arms, or addressed its relevance for "gun control." See *United States v. Miller*, 307 U.S. 174 (1939). Is the right to bear arms a human right?

5.   A footnote in Henkin's essay mentions "rights on the horizon." The debate on the "right to die" continues. The Court's decision in *Cruzan v. Director, Mo. Dep't of Health*, 497 U.S. 261 (1990), which held that a State can require proof of a patient's wishes before allowing discontinuation of life support, was thought to imply the right of a competent person to refuse life support, in other words some measure of a "right to die." But, in *Washington v. Glucksberg*, 521 U.S. 702 (1997), the Court upheld a State's prohibition of doctor-assisted suicide.

The Court has not addressed the "rights of the unborn" or the "right to be born" as such, but developments in the jurisprudence following *Roe v. Wade* recognized the authority of the State to impose important limitations on the right to have an abortion. *Planned Parenthood v. Casey*, 505 U.S. 833 (1992). See Part IV, Chapter 1 (B).

1.   CONSTITUTIONAL PROTECTION FOR LIBERTY, AUTONOMY, AND PROPERTY

Liberty: The Scope of Constitutionally Protected "Liberty"

The interpretation of "liberty" in the Due Process clause of the Fourteenth Amendment as meaning essentially individual autonomy was suggested by Justice Field in his dissent in *Munn v. Illinois*, 94 U.S. 113

(1876), immediately following, and was not disowned there by the majority of the Court in *Munn,*. An expansive definition of "liberty" was restated twenty years later by Justice Peckham in *Allgeyer v. Louisiana, infra* p. 181, and was confirmed and applied in *Lochner v. New York,* 198 U.S. 45 (1905). Although *Lochner* was later overruled, the *Allgeyer* definition has remained the established meaning of "liberty" in the Due Process clauses of both the Fifth and Fourteenth Amendments. Controversy, and difference of opinion about the Due Process clauses, have swirled not about the broad definition of liberty but about the meaning in that clause of "due process of law." Distinctions between different zones of liberty surfaced when the Supreme Court addressed freedoms explicitly guaranteed in the Bill of Rights, and suggested preference for the freedoms guaranteed in the First Amendment. See *infra* p. 220.

Substantive Due Process

The importance of interpreting "liberty" as equivalent to "autonomy" was much enhanced by the interpretation of the requirement of "due process of law" as providing substantive protection for life, for liberty (autonomy), and for property, against arbitrary action by government. The Supreme Court had conceived of substantive due process in the notorious *Dred Scott* case, in invalidating an act of Congress because it took the owner's property in his slave without "due process of law." *Scott v. Sanford,* 60 U.S. (19 How.) 393, 450 (1857). Substantive due process reappeared after the Civil War in challenges to economic regulation, principally regulation by the States.

Munn v. Illinois

94 U.S. 113 (1877).

■ Mr. Chief Justice Waite delivered the opinion of the Court.

The question to be determined in this case is whether the general assembly of Illinois can, under the limitations upon the legislative power of the States imposed by the Constitution of the United States, fix by law the maximum of charges for the storage of grain in warehouses at Chicago and other places in the State having not less than one hundred thousand inhabitants, "in which grain is stored in bulk, and in which the grain of different owners is mixed together, or in which grain is stored in such a manner that the identity of different lots or parcels cannot be accurately preserved."

It is claimed that such a law is repugnant . . .

. . .

[t]o that part of amendment 14 which ordains that no State shall "deprive any person of life, liberty, or property, without due process of law,

nor deny to any person within its jurisdiction the equal protection of the laws.''

. . .

While this provision of the amendment is new in the Constitution of the United States, as a limitation upon the powers of the States, it is old as a principle of civilized government. It is found in Magna Charta, and, in substance if not in form, in nearly or quite all the constitutions that have been from time to time adopted by the several States of the Union. By the Fifth Amendment, it was introduced into the Constitution of the United States as a limitation upon the powers of the national government, and by the Fourteenth, as a guaranty against any encroachment upon an acknowledged right of citizenship by the legislatures of the States.

When the people of the United Colonies separated from Great Britain they changed the form, but not the substance, of their government. They retained for the purposes of government all the powers of the British Parliament, and through their State constitutions, or other forms of social compact, undertook to give practical effect to such as they deemed necessary for the common good and the security of life and property. All the powers which they retained they committed to their respective States, unless in express terms or by implication reserved to themselves. Subsequently, when it was found necessary to establish a national government for national purposes, a part of the powers of the States and of the people of the States was granted to the United States and the people of the United States. This grant operated as a further limitation upon the powers of the States, so that now the governments of the States possess all the powers of the Parliament of England, except such as have been delegated to the United States or reserved by the people. The reservations by the people are shown in the prohibitions of the constitutions.

When one becomes a member of society, he necessarily parts with some rights or privileges which, as an individual not affected by his relations to others, he might retain. ''A body politic,'' as aptly defined in the preamble of the Constitution of Massachusetts, ''is a social compact by which the whole people covenants with each citizen, and each citizen with the whole people, that all shall be governed by certain laws for the common good.'' This does not confer power upon the whole people to control rights which are purely and exclusively private ...; but it does authorize the establishment of laws requiring each citizen to so conduct himself, and so use his own property, as not unnecessarily to injure another. This is the very essence of government, and has found expression in the maxim *sic utere tuo ut alienum non lædas*. From this source come the police powers, which, as was said by Mr. Chief Justice Taney in *The License Cases*, 46 U.S. (5 How.) 504, 583 (1847), ''are nothing more or less than the powers of government inherent in every sovereignty, ... that is to say, ... the power to govern men and things.'' Under these powers the government regulates the conduct of its citizens one towards another, and the manner in which each shall use his own property, when such regulation becomes necessary for the public good. In their exercise it has been customary in England from time immemorial, and in this country from its first colonization, to regulate ferries, common carriers, hackmen, bakers, millers, wharfingers, innkeepers, & c., and in so doing to fix a maximum of charge to be made for services rendered, accommodations furnished, and articles sold. To this day, statutes are to be found in many of the States upon some or all these subjects; and we think it has never yet been successfully contended that such legislation came within any of the constitutional prohibitions against interference with private property. With the Fifth Amendment in force, Congress, in 1820, conferred power upon the city of Washington "to regulate ... the rates of wharfage at private wharves, ... the sweeping of chimneys, and to fix the rates of fees therefor, ... and the weight and quality of bread," 3 Stat. 587, sect. 7; and, in 1848, "to make all necessary regulations respecting hackney carriages and the rates of fare of the same, and the rates of hauling by cartmen, wagoners, carmen, and draymen, and the rates of commission of auctioneers," 9 *id.* 224, sect. 2.

From this it is apparent that, down to the time of the adoption of the Fourteenth Amendment, it was not supposed that statutes regulating the use, or even the price of the use, of private property necessarily deprived an owner of his property without due process of law. Under some circumstances they may, but not under all. The amendment does not change the law in this particular: it simply prevents the States from doing that which will operate as such a deprivation.

This brings us to inquire as to the principles upon which this power of regulation rests, in order that we may determine what is within and what without its operative effect. Looking, then, to the common law, from whence came the right which the Constitution protects, we find that when private property is "affected with a public interest, it ceases to be *juris privati* only." This was said by Lord Chief Justice Hale more than two hundred years ago, in his treatise *De Portibus Maris*, 1 Harg. Law Tracts, 78, and has been accepted without objection as an essential element in the law of property ever since. Property does become clothed with a public interest when used in a manner to make it of public consequence, and affect the community at large. When, therefore, one devotes his property to a use in which the public has an interest, he, in effect, grants to the public an interest in that use, and must submit to be controlled by the public for the common good, to the extent of the interest he has thus created. He may withdraw his grant by discontinuing the use; but, so long as he maintains the use, he must submit to the control....

. . .

We know that this is a power which may be abused; but that is no argument against its existence. For protection against abuses by legislatures the people must resort to the polls, not to the courts....

. . .

■ MR. JUSTICE FIELD. I am compelled to dissent from the decision of the court in this case, and from the reasons upon which that decision is founded. The principle upon which the opinion of the majority proceeds is, in my judgment, subversive of the rights of private property, heretofore believed to be protected by constitutional guaranties against legislative interference, and is in conflict with the authorities cited in its support. . . .

The question presented, therefore, is one of the greatest importance,— whether it is within the competency of a State to fix the compensation which an individual may receive for the use of his own property in his private business, and for his services in connection with it

. . .

If this be sound law, if there be no protection, either in the principles upon which our republican government is founded, or in the prohibitions of the Constitution against such invasion of private rights, all property and all business in the State are held at the mercy of a majority of its legislature. The public has no greater interest in the use of buildings for the storage of grain than it has in the use of buildings for the residences of families, nor, indeed, any thing like so great an interest; and, according to the doctrine announced, the legislature may fix the rent of all tenements used for residences, without reference to the cost of their erection. If the owner does not like the rates prescribed, he may cease renting his houses. He has granted to the public, says the court, an interest in the use of the buildings, and "he may withdraw his grant by discontinuing the use; but, so long as he maintains the use, he must submit to the control." The public is interested in the manufacture of cotton, woollen, and silken fabrics, in the printing and publication of books and periodicals, and in the making of utensils of every variety, useful and ornamental; indeed, there is hardly an enterprise or business engaging the attention and labor of any considerable portion of the community, in which the public has not an interest in the sense in which that term is used by the court in its opinion; and the doctrine which allows the legislature to interfere with and regulate the charges which the owners of property thus employed shall make for its use, that is, the rates at which all these different kinds of business shall be carried on, has never before been asserted, so far as I am aware, by any judicial tribunal in the United States.

. . .

No State "shall deprive any person of life, liberty, or property without due process of law," says the Fourteenth Amendment to the Constitution. By the term "life," as here used, something more is meant than mere animal existence. The inhibition against its deprivation extends to all those limbs and faculties by which life is enjoyed. The provision equally prohibits the mutilation of the body by the amputation of an arm or leg, or the putting out of an eye, or the destruction of any other organ of the body through which the soul communicates with the other world. The deprivation not only of life, but of whatever God has given to every one with life, for its growth and enjoyment, is prohibited by the provision in question if its efficacy be not frittered away by judicial decision.

By the term "liberty," as used in the provision, something more is meant than mere freedom from physical restraint or the bounds of a prison. It means freedom to go where one may choose, and to act in such manner, not inconsistent with the equal rights of others, as his judgment may dictate for the promotion of his happiness; that is, to pursue such callings and avocations as may be most suitable to develop his capacities, and give to them their highest enjoyment.

The same liberal construction which is required for the protection of life and liberty, in all particulars in which life and liberty are of any value, should be applied to the protection of private property. If the legislature of a State, under pretense of providing for the public good, or for any other reason, can determine, against the consent of the owner, the uses to which private property shall be devoted, or the prices which the owner shall receive for its uses, it can deprive him of the property as completely as by a special act for its confiscation or destruction. If, for instance, the owner is prohibited from using his building for the purposes for which it was designed, it is of little consequence that he is permitted to retain the title and possession; or, if he is compelled to take as compensation for its use less than the expenses to which he is subjected by its ownership, he is, for all practical purposes, deprived of the property, as effectually as if the legislature had ordered his forcible dispossession. If it be admitted that the legislature has any control over the compensation, the extent of that compensation becomes a mere matter of legislative discretion. The amount fixed will operate as a partial destruction of the value of the property, if it fall below the amount which the owner would obtain by contract, and, practically, as a complete destruction, if it be less than the cost of retaining its possession. There is, indeed, no protection of any value under the constitutional provision, which does not extend to the use and income of the property, as well as to its title and possession.

· · ·

Notes

The interpretation of the Due Process clause as guaranteeing not merely fair legal procedure, but as providing protection against arbitrary regulation of life, liberty or property, is clear and explicit in Justice Field's dissent, but it is implied also in Chief Justice Waite's majority opinion. *Munn v. Illinois* relied on the fact that the grain warehouses were "affected with a public interest." In *Nebbia v. New York*, 291 U.S. 502 (1934), the Supreme Court abandoned that requirement, but did not question the concept of substantive due process.

Substantive due process has had its most luxurious growth as a limitation on regulations of "liberty," as expansively defined in *Allgeyer v. Louisiana*, 165 U.S. 578, 589 (1897). Echoing Justice Field's dissent in *Munn*, Justice Peckham wrote:

The liberty mentioned in that amendment means not only the right of the citizen to be free from the mere physical restraint of his person, as by incarceration, but the term is deemed to embrace the right of the citizen to be free in the enjoyment of all his faculties; to be free to use them in all lawful ways; to live and work where he will; to earn his livelihood by any lawful calling; to pursue any livelihood or avocation, and for that purpose to enter into all contracts which may be proper, necessary and essential to his carrying out to a successful conclusion the purposes above mentioned.

Henkin, in his article above, traces the vagaries of the history of substantive due process as regards regulation of economic liberty, from *Lochner* to *Nebbia* and its near demise since *West Coast Hotel Co. v. Parrish*, 300 U.S. 379 (1937). In the 1960's, in *Roe v. Wade,* the Court identified an area of individual liberty, denominated a right of privacy—"new privacy"—as to which substantive due process requires greater deference by lawmakers and a more important public interest to support regulation. See below.

Substantive Due Process, Liberty and the "New Privacy"

The near-demise of substantive due process as a limitation on the regulation of economic liberty, and "selective"—near total—incorporation of the Bill of Rights into the Fourteenth Amendment, rendering the incorporated provisions applicable to the States, sharply reduced resort to substantive due process as protection for "liberty." Substantive due process has retained some small use to protect against invasions of "ordered liberty" not covered by any of the Bill of Rights, such as the right to travel abroad (*Aptheker v. Secretary of State*, 378 U.S. 500 (1964)), the right to educate one's children (*Meyer v. Nebraska*, 262 U.S. 390 (1923); *Pierce v. Society of Sisters*, 268 U.S. 510 (1925)), and protection against governmental action that shocks the conscience (*Rochin v. California*, 342 U.S. 165 (1952)). See *Palko v. Connecticut*, p. 191 below. That substantive due process bars official conduct that "shocks the conscience" was confirmed in *County of Sacramento v. Lewis*, 118 S. Ct. 1708 (1998).

Since the 1960s, however, important rights not explicitly guaranteed by the Bill of Rights have found protection as "liberty" and its guarantees by substantive due process: notably, a zone of "privacy"—the "new privacy"—has been recognized as a "fundamental" liberty, deserving extraordinary scrutiny and extraordinary protection by the courts, and their violation—whether by State or federal government—to be justified only by an extra-ordinary public interest.

In *Roe v. Wade*, 410 U.S. 113, 152 (1973), Justice Blackmun stated:

> The Constitution does not explicitly mention any right of privacy. In a line of decisions, however ... the Court has recognized that a right of personal privacy, or a guarantee of certain areas or zones of privacy, does exist under the Constitution.... These decisions make it clear that only personal rights that can be deemed "fundamental" or "implicit in the concept of ordered liberty," *Palko v. Connecticut*, 302 U.S. 319 (1937), are included in this guarantee of personal privacy....

The Court concluded that the right of privacy was "founded in the Fourteenth Amendment's concept of personal liberty." The Court concluded "that the right of personal privacy includes the abortion decision, but that this right is not unqualified and must be considered against important state interests in regulation."

Justice Stewart concurring also placed the new privacy concept within "liberty" in the Fourteenth Amendment:

> The Constitution nowhere mentions a specific right of personal choice in matters of marriage and family life, but the "liberty" protected by the Due Process Clause of the Fourteenth Amendment covers more than those freedoms explicitly named in the Bill of Rights....
>
> Several decisions of this Court make clear that freedom of personal choice in matters of marriage and family life is one of the liberties protected by the Due Process Clause of the Fourteenth Amendment. *Loving v. Virginia*, 388 U.S. 1; *Griswold v. Connecticut,* supra; *Pierce v. Society of Sisters*, supra; *Meyer v. Nebraska*, supra.

Id. at 168.

For a fuller discussion and comparative treatment of the right to an abortion, see Part IV, Chapter 1(B).

Substantive Due Process and Property

Substantive due process protects private property, as it does liberty, against "arbitrary" deprivation by "state action." Like economic liberty, private property is subject to regulation for the public welfare, for example by laws for abatement of "nuisances," and by zoning. See subsection E(2) below. Like regulations of economic liberty, the regulations of the uses of property is subject only to light judicial scrutiny. See Part IV, Chapter 3(B).

Substantive due process does not preclude the exercise of eminent domain; taking for a public use is explicitly authorized to the federal government, subject to just compensation (Amendment V). And substantive due process in the Fourteenth Amendment has been interpreted to apply the same right of eminent domain to the States, subject to the same limitations (public use, just compensation). Taking for private use, or a failure to provide just compensation, would render the taking a deprivation of property in violation of substantive due process. See *Hawaii Housing Authority v. Midkiff*, 467 U.S. 229 (1984); compare *Cities Serv. Co. v. McGrath*, 342 U.S. 330 (1952).

Like regulations of the uses of property, the exercise of eminent domain has been subject to little judicial scrutiny. In no case has the Supreme Court found a taking to be not for a public use. Compare *Berman v. Parker*, 348 U.S. 26 (1954), and *Hawaii Hous. Auth. v. Midkiff*, p. 204 below. But see the plurality opinion in *Eastern Enters. v. Apfel,* 524 U.S. 498 (1998).

In *Pennsylvania Coal Co. v. Mahon,* 260 U.S. 393, the Supreme Court held a regulation of the use of property to constitute a taking requiring just compensation. In recent years, the Court has been increasingly disposed to find regulations of the use of property to constitute "takings" requiring just compensation. See p. 176 *supra*.

For comparative discussion of the right to property, see Part IV, Chapter 3 (B).

2.   THE U.S. BILL OF RIGHTS AND THE STATES

The Original Construction

Judicial interpretation effected another major change in jurisprudence when the Court held that the Fourteenth Amendment incorporated most provisions of the Bill of Rights, rendering them applicable to the States.

Was the Bill of Rights, when adopted in 1791, intended to protect the rights indicated against violation by the States? The First Amendment is explicitly addressed to Congress; the later provisions of the Bill of Rights are not addressed to anyone.

In *Barron*, decided in 1833, Chief Justice Marshall found the question, "of great importance, but not of much difficulty."

Barron v. Mayor of Baltimore

32 U.S. (7 Pet.) 243 (1833)

■ MARSHALL, CH. J., delivered the opinion of the Court. . . .

The plaintiff in error contends, that it comes within that clause in the fifth amendment to the constitution, which inhibits the taking of private property for public use, without just compensation. He insists, that this amendment being in favor of the liberty of the citizen, ought to be so construed as to restrain the legislative power of a state, as well as that of the United States. . . .

The question thus presented is, we think, of great importance, but not of much difficulty.

The constitution was ordained and established by the people of the United States for themselves, for their own government, and not for the government of the individual states. Each state established a constitution for itself, and in that constitution, provided such limitations and restrictions on the powers of its particular government, as its judgment dictated. The people of the United States framed such a government for the United States as they supposed best adapted to their situation and best calculated to promote their interests. The powers they conferred on this government were to be exercised by itself; and the limitations on power, if expressed in general terms, are naturally, and, we think, necessarily, applicable to the government created by the instrument. They are limitations of power granted in the instrument itself; not of distinct governments, framed by different persons and for different purposes.

If these propositions be correct, the fifth amendment must be understood as restraining the power of the general government, not as applicable to the states. In their several constitutions, they have imposed such restrictions on their respective governments, as their own wisdom suggested; such as they deemed most proper for themselves. It is a subject on which they judge exclusively, and with which others interfere no further than they are supposed to have a common interest.

The counsel for the plaintiff in error insists, that the constitution was intended to secure the people of the several states against the undue exercise of power by their respective state governments; as well as against that which might be attempted by their general government. In support of this argument he relies on the inhibitions contained in the tenth section of the first article.

We think, that section affords a strong, if not a conclusive, argument in support of the opinion already indicated by the court.

The preceding section contains restrictions which are obviously intended for the exclusive purpose of restraining the exercise of power by the departments of the general government. Some of them use language applicable only to congress; others are expressed in general terms. The third clause, for example, declares, that "no bill of attainder or ex post facto law shall be passed." No language can be more general; yet the demonstration is complete, that it applies solely to the government of the United States. In addition to the general arguments furnished by the instrument itself, some of which have been already suggested, the succeeding section, the avowed purpose of which is to restrain state legislation, contains in terms the very prohibition. It declares, that "no state shall pass any bill of attainder or ex post facto law." This provision, then, of the ninth section, however comprehensive its language, contains no restriction on State legislation.

. . .

Had the people of the several states, or any of them, required changes in their constitutions; had they required additional safe-guards to liberty from the apprehended encroachments of their particular governments; the remedy was in their own hands, and could have been applied by themselves. A convention could have been assembled by the discontented state, and the required improvements could have been made by itself. The unwieldy and cumbrous machinery of procuring a recommendation from two-thirds of congress, and the assent of three-fourths of their sister states, could never have occurred to any human being, as a mode of doing that which might be effected by the state itself. Had the framers of these amendments intended them to be limitations on the powers of the state governments, they would have imitated the framers of the original constitution, and have expressed that intention. Had congress engaged in the extraordinary occupation of improving the constitutions of the several states, by affording the people additional protection from the exercise of power by their own governments, in matters which concerned themselves alone, they would have declared this purpose in plain and intelligible language.

. . .

We are of the opinion that the provision in the fifth amendment to the Constitution, declaring that private property shall not be taken for public use without just compensation, is intended solely as a limitation on the exercise of power by the government of the United States, and is not applicable to the legislation of the States. . . .

Homogenizing State and Federal Rights: "Selective Incorporation"

Did the Fourteenth Amendment "overrule" *Barron v. Baltimore* and render the provisions of the Bill of Rights applicable to the States? Four justices of the Supreme Court so argued in *Adamson v. California*, 332 U.S. 46 (1947), but that view did not prevail.

In *Palko v. Connecticut*, Justice Cardozo had written:

> We have said that in appellant's view the Fourteenth Amendment is to be taken as embodying the prohibitions of the Fifth. His thesis is even broader. Whatever would be a violation of the original bill of rights (Amendments 1 to 8) if done by the federal government is now equally unlawful by force of the Fourteenth Amendment if done by a state. There is no such general rule.

302 U.S. 319, 323 (1937).

Instead, Cardozo reaffirmed a line of cases that had held that "liberty" in the Fourteenth Amendment, protected by substantive due process, guarantees what Cardozo characterized as "the very essence of a scheme of ordered liberty" against violation by the States, which often—but not always—may approximate what particular provisions of the Bill of Rights prohibit to the federal government. These protections of substantive due process apply as well to the federal government under the Fifth Amendment and thereby add protections against the federal government to those expressed in other provisions of the Bill of Rights. Cardozo concluded, however, that some select provisions of the Bill of Rights, notably those in the First Amendment, had been "absorbed" in the protection afforded to "liberty" by substantive due process. *Id.* at 326. See Note: *Palko v. Connecticut* and Selective Incorporation, p. 191.

In the 1960's, the Supreme Court in effect adopted "selective incorporation," reading the Fourteenth Amendment, in successive cases, as incorporating most (not all) of the provisions of the Bill of Rights and rendering them applicable to the States. Over some dissent, the Court concluded that incorporated provisions apply to the States exactly ("jot for jot" and "bag and baggage") as they apply to the federal government. But some differences between the scope of federal protection and state protection persist. See *Apodaca*, p. 190 below.

Duncan v. Louisiana

391 U.S. 145 (1968)

■ MR. JUSTICE WHITE delivered the opinion of the Court.

Appellant, Gary Duncan, was convicted of simple battery in the Twenty-fifth Judicial District Court of Louisiana. Under Louisiana law simple battery is a misdemeanor, punishable by a maximum of two years' imprisonment and a $300 fine. Appellant sought trial by jury, but because the Louisiana Constitution grants jury trials only in cases in which capital punishment or imprisonment at hard labor may be imposed, the trial judge denied the request. Appellant was convicted and sentenced to serve 60 days in the parish prison and pay a fine of $150. Appellant sought review in the Supreme Court of Louisiana, asserting that the denial of jury trial violated rights guaranteed to him by the United States Constitution. The Supreme Court, finding "[n]o error of law in the ruling complained of," denied appellant a writ of certiorari. Pursuant to 28 U.S.C. § 1257(2) appellant sought review in this Court, alleging that the Sixth and Fourteenth Amendments to the United States Constitution secure the right to jury trial in state criminal prosecutions where a sentence as long as two years may be imposed. . . .

· · ·

I.

The Fourteenth Amendment denies the States the power to "deprive any person of life, liberty, or property, without due process of law." In resolving conflicting claims concerning the meaning of this spacious language, the Court has looked increasingly to the Bill of Rights for guidance; many of the rights guaranteed by the first eight Amendments to the Constitution have been held to be protected against state action by the Due Process clause of the Fourteenth Amendment. That clause now protects the right to compensation for property taken by the State; the rights of speech, press, and religion covered by the First Amendment; the Fourth Amendment rights to be free from unreasonable searches and seizures and to have excluded from criminal trials any evidence illegally seized; the right guaranteed by the Fifth Amendment to be free of compelled self-incrimination; and the Sixth Amendment rights to counsel, to a speedy and public trial, to confrontation of opposing witnesses, and to compulsory process for obtaining witnesses.

The test for determining whether a right extended by the Fifth and Sixth Amendments with respect to federal criminal proceedings is also protected against state action by the Fourteenth Amendment has been phrased in a variety of ways in the opinions of this Court. The question has been asked whether a right is among those "fundamental principles of liberty and justice which lie at the base of all our civil and political institutions," *Powell v. State of Alabama*, 287 U.S. 45, 67 (1932); whether it is "basic in our system of jurisprudence," *In re Oliver*, 333 U.S. 257, 273 (1948); and whether it is "a fundamental right, essential to a fair trial,"

Gideon v. Wainwright, 372 U.S. 335, 343—344 (1963); *Malloy v. Hogan*, 378 U.S. 1, 6 (1964); *Pointer v. State of Texas*, 380 U.S. 400, 403 (1965). The claim before us is that the right to trial by jury guaranteed by the Sixth Amendment meets these tests. The position of Louisiana, on the other hand, is that the Constitution imposes upon the States no duty to give a jury trial in any criminal case, regardless of the seriousness of the crime or the size of the punishment which may be imposed. Because we believe that trial by jury in criminal cases is fundamental to the American scheme of justice, we hold that the Fourteenth Amendment guarantees a right of jury trial in all criminal cases which—were they to be tried in a federal court—would come within the Sixth Amendment's guarantee.[14] Since we consider the appeal before us to be such a case, we hold that the Constitution was violated when appellant's demand for jury trial was refused.

. . .

14. In one sense recent cases applying provisions of the first eight Amendments to the States represent a new approach to the "incorporation" debate. Earlier the Court can be seen as having asked, when inquiring into whether some particular procedural safeguard was required of a State, if a civilized system could be imagined that would not accord the particular protection. For example, *Palko v. State of Connecticut*, 302 U.S. 319 (1937), stated: "The right to trial by jury and the immunity from prosecution except as the result of an indictment may have value and importance. Even so, they are not of the very essence of a scheme of ordered liberty. * * * Few would be so narrow or provincial as to maintain that a fair and enlightened system of justice would be impossible without them." The recent cases, on the other hand, have proceeded upon the valid assumption that state criminal processes are not imaginary and theoretical schemes but actual systems bearing virtually every characteristic of the common-law system that has been developing contemporaneously in England and in this country. The question thus is whether given this kind of system a particular procedure is fundamental—whether, that is, a procedure is necessary to an Anglo–American regime of ordered liberty. It is this sort of inquiry that can justify the conclusions that state courts must exclude evidence seized in violation of the Fourth Amendment; that state prosecutors may not comment on a defendant's failure to testify; and that criminal punishment may not be imposed for the status of narcotics addiction. Of immediate relevance for this case are the Court's holdings that the States must comply with certain provisions of the Sixth Amendment, specifically that the States may not refuse a speedy trial, confrontation of witnesses, and the assistance, at state expense if necessary, of counsel. . . . Of each of these determinations that a constitutional provision originally written to bind the Federal Government should bind the States as well it might be said that the limitation in question is not necessarily fundamental to fairness in every criminal system that might be imagined but is fundamental in the context of the criminal processes maintained by the American States.

When the inquiry is approached in this way the question whether the States can impose criminal punishment without granting a jury trial appears quite different from the way it appeared in the older cases opining that States might abolish jury trial. A criminal process which was fair and equitable but used no juries is easy to imagine. It would make use of alternative guarantees and protections which would serve the purposes that the jury serves in the English and American systems. Yet no American State has undertaken to construct such a system. Instead, every American State, including Louisiana, uses the jury extensively, and imposes very serious punishments only after a trial at which the defendant has a right to a jury's verdict. In every State, including Louisiana, the structure and style of the criminal process—the supporting framework and the subsidiary procedures—are of the sort that naturally complement jury trial, and have developed in connection with and in reliance upon jury trial.

The guarantees of jury trial in the Federal and State Constitutions reflect a profound judgment about the way in which law should be enforced and justice administered. A right to jury trial is granted to criminal defendants in order to prevent oppression by the Government. Those who wrote our constitutions knew from history and experience that it was necessary to protect against unfounded criminal charges brought to eliminate enemies and against judges too responsive to the voice of higher authority. The framers of the constitutions strove to create an independent judiciary but insisted upon further protection against arbitrary action. Providing an accused with the right to be tried by a jury of his peers gave him an inestimable safeguard against the corrupt or overzealous prosecutor and against the compliant, biased, or eccentric judge. If the defendant preferred the common-sense judgment of a jury to the more tutored but perhaps less sympathetic reaction of the single judge, he was to have it. Beyond this, the jury trial provisions in the Federal and State Constitutions reflect a fundamental decision about the exercise of official power—a reluctance to entrust plenary powers over the life and liberty of the citizen to one judge or to a group of judges. Fear of unchecked power, so typical of our State and Federal Governments in other respects, found expression in the criminal law in this insistence upon community participation in the determination of guilt or innocence. The deep commitment of the Nation to the right of jury trial in serious criminal cases as a defense against arbitrary law enforcement qualifies for protection under the Due Process clause of the Fourteenth Amendment, and must therefore be respected by the States.

. . .

MR. JUSTICE BLACK, with whom MR. JUSTICE DOUGLAS joins, concurring [opinion omitted].

■ MR. JUSTICE FORTAS, concurring.

I join the judgments and opinions of the Court in these cases because I agree that the Due Process Clause of the Fourteenth Amendment requires that the States accord the right to jury trial in prosecutions for offenses that are not petty.

. . .

But although I agree with the decision of the Court, I cannot agree with the implication ... that the tail must go with the hide: that when we hold, influenced by the Sixth Amendment, that "due process" requires that the States accord the right of jury trial for all but petty offenses, we automatically import all of the ancillary rules which have been or may hereafter be developed incidental to the right to jury trial in the federal courts. I see no reason whatever, for example, to assume that our decision today should require us to impose federal requirements such as unanimous verdicts or a jury of 12 upon the States. We may well conclude that these and other features of federal jury practice are by no means fundamental—

that they are not essential to due process of law—and that they are not obligatory on the States.

. . .

This Court has heretofore held that various provisions of the Bill of Rights such as the freedom of speech and religion guarantees of the First Amendment, the prohibition of unreasonable searches and seizures in the Fourth Amendment, the privilege against self-incrimination of the Fifth Amendment, and the right to counsel and to confrontation under the Sixth Amendment "are all to be enforced against the States under the Four-teenth Amendment according to the same standards that protect those personal rights against federal encroachment." *Malloy v. Hogan*, 378 U.S. 1, 10 (1964); *Pointer v. State of Texas*, 380 U.S. 400, 406 (1965); *Miranda v. State of Arizona*, 384 U.S. 436, 464 (1966). I need not quarrel with the specific conclusion in those specific instances. But unless one adheres slavishly to the incorporation theory, body and substance, the same conclu-sion need not be superimposed upon the jury trial right. I respectfully but urgently suggest that it should not be. Jury trial is more than a principle of justice applicable to individual cases. It is a system of administration of the business of the State. While we may believe (and I do believe) that the right of jury trial is fundamental, it does not follow that the particulars of according that right must be uniform. We should be ready to welcome state variations which do not impair—indeed, which may advance—the theory and purpose of trial by jury.

MR. JUSTICE HARLAN, whom MR. JUSTICE STEWART joins, dissenting [opinion omitted].

Notes

1. If a provision of the Bill of Rights is "incorporated" and rendered applicable to the States, is incorporation complete, "tail with hide," "bag and baggage," so that the protection against the States is identical with that against the federal government, "jot for jot"? *Duncan v. Louisiana* appeared to imply that requirement, but some of the justices demurred.

The Supreme Court's apparent insistence that "incorporation" implies identity—that every provision that is incorporated applies to the States exactly as to the federal government—may have led to an interpretation that some saw as diluting the Constitution's guarantee in order to render it less onerous on the States. Thus, after *Duncan*, the Court held that the jury trial required by the Sixth Amendment, as incorporated into the Fourteenth Amendment, does not require a state to provide a jury of twelve persons or to require an unanimous jury verdict. *Williams v. Florida*, 399 U.S. 78, 99 (1970); *Apodaca v. Oregon*, 406 U.S. 404, 406 (1972). In *Apodaca*, as a result of a "swing vote" by Justice Powell, the Court held that the States did not have to insist on unanimous jury verdict. Justice Powell wrote that trial by jury was "fundamental" (and is required of the States) but a unanimous jury verdict, though established as a requirement in federal trial, was not a fundamental requirement and therefore not required of the States. Has the Court reconsidered "jot for jot" as general principle? Or has it found that a 12 person jury and a unanimous verdict are required in the federal courts by virtue of other provisions in the Constitution or of history and precedent, which are beyond the scope of "incorporation?"

2. The Supreme Court's opinion in *Duncan* lists the provisions of the Bill of Rights that (as of 1968) had been held to be incorporated and applicable to the States. Since *Duncan*, the Court has held "that the double jeopardy prohibition of the Fifth Amendment represents a fundamental ideal in our Constitutional heritage," and therefore applies to the States. *Benton v. Maryland*, 395 U.S. 784, 794 (1969). Whether the "excessive bail" provision of the Eighth Amendment has been incorporated has not been definitively determined. It is commonly assumed that, except the requirement of a presentment or indictment by a grand jury (Fifth Amendment) and jury trial in civil cases (Seventh Amendment), all other provisions of the Bill of Rights are incorporated. Is the Second Amendment incorporated? Is the Third Amendment? Does the provision of Article I, section 9 (not part of the Bill of Rights), limiting the suspension of the writ of *habeas corpus*, apply to the States? See, e.g., Jordan Steiker, *Incorporating the Suspension Clause: Is There a Constitutional Right to Federal Habeas Corpus for State Prisoners?*, 92 Mich. L. Rev. 862 (1994).

Note: Palko v. Connecticut and Selective Incorporation

Palko v. Connecticut is frequently cited as the case launching selective incorporation; but the case seems to reflect a more complex view of the Fourteenth Amendment. The Court begins by rejecting total incorporation. See p. 186 above. Then the Court reaffirmed that important rights (whether or not they are in the Bill of Rights) are protected under the concept of "ordered liberty" as implied in substantive due process in the Fourteenth Amendment. *Ibid.* Finally, Cardozo suggested that some of the substantive provisions of the Bill of Rights, notably those in the First Amendment, were of particular importance and therefore were "absorbed" in the "liberty" protected by the Due Process clause, and perhaps protected to the same extent as those rights are safeguarded against the federal government by the provisions in the Bill of Rights. See the discussion of "preferred rights," p. 220 below. Cardozo said:

> [W]e reach a different plane of social and moral values when we pass to the privileges and immunities that have been taken over from the earlier articles of the Federal Bill of Rights and brought within the Fourteenth Amendment by a process of absorption. These in their origin were effective against the federal government alone. If the Fourteenth Amendment has absorbed them, the process of absorption has had its source in the belief that neither liberty nor justice would exist if they were sacrificed. *Twining v. New Jersey*, supra, 211 U.S. 78,

at page 99.[4] This is true, for illustration, of freedom of thought and speech. Of that freedom one may say that it is the matrix, the indispensable condition, of nearly every other form of freedom. With rare aberrations a pervasive recognition of that truth can be traced in our history, political and legal. So it has come about that the domain of liberty, withdrawn by the Fourteenth Amendment from encroachment by the states, has been enlarged by latter-day judgments to include liberty of the mind as well as liberty of action. The extension became, indeed, a logical imperative when once it was recognized, as long ago it was, that liberty is something more than exemption from physical restraint, and that even in the field of substantive rights and duties the legislative judgment, if oppressive and arbitrary, may be overridden by the courts.

Cardozo appears to have retained his primary allegiance to "due process" as "ordered liberty," and seems to have limited "incorporation" to "absorbing" first amendment freedoms into his conception of "liberty" and giving it great weight. The Court's later doctrine of "selective incorporation" examined each provision of the Bill of Rights (notably the procedural safeguards in the criminal process) for potential incorporation; for the later court "ordered liberty" survives as a distinctly secondary source of protection.

"Reverse Incorporation"

"Selective incorporation" has rendered most of the Bill of Rights applicable to the States. By a kind of "reverse incorporation," the Court has rendered some Constitutional safeguards against the States applicable also to the federal government, notably the equal protection of the laws. On the day the Court decided *Brown v. Board of Education*, 347 U.S. 483 (1954), prohibiting school segregation as a violation of the equal protection clause of the Fourteenth Amendment, it decided *Bolling v. Sharpe*.

Bolling v. Sharpe

347 U.S. 497 (1954).

■ Mr. Chief Justice Warren delivered the opinion of the Court.

We have this day held that the Equal Protection Clause of the Fourteenth Amendment prohibits the states from maintaining racially segregated public schools. The legal problem in the District of Columbia is somewhat different, however. The Fifth Amendment, which is applicable in the District of Columbia, does not contain an equal protection clause as

---

4. "It is possible that some of the personal rights safeguarded by the first eight Amendments against national action may also be safeguarded against state action, because a denial of them would be a denial of due process of law. *Chicago, Burlington &* *Quincy Railroad Co. v. Chicago*, 166 U.S. 226. If this is so, it is not because those rights are enumerated in the first eight Amendments, but because they are of such a nature that they are included in the conception of due process of law."

does the Fourteenth Amendment which applies only to the states. But the concepts of equal protection and due process, both stemming from our American ideal of fairness, are not mutually exclusive. The "equal protection of the laws" is a more explicit safeguard of prohibited unfairness than "due process of law," and, therefore, we do not imply that the two are always interchangeable phrases. But, as this Court has recognized, discrimination may be so unjustifiable as to be violative of due process.

Classifications based solely upon race must be scrutinized with particular care, since they are contrary to our traditions and hence constitutionally suspect.[3] As long ago as 1896, this Court declared the principle "that the Constitution of the United States, in its present form, forbids, so far as civil and political rights are concerned, discrimination by the General Government, or by the States, against any citizen because of his race." And in *Buchanan v. Warley*, 245 U.S. 60, the Court held that a statute which limited the right of a property owner to convey his property to a person of another race was, as an unreasonable discrimination, a denial of due process of law.

Although the Court has not assumed to define "liberty" with any great precision, that term is not confined to mere freedom from bodily restraint. Liberty under law extends to the full range of conduct which the individual is free to pursue, and it cannot be restricted except for a proper governmental objective. Segregation in public education is not reasonably related to any proper governmental objective, and thus it imposes on Negro children of the District of Columbia a burden that constitutes an arbitrary deprivation of their liberty in violation of the Due Process Clause.

In view of our decision that the Constitution prohibits the states from maintaining racially segregated public schools, it would be unthinkable that the same Constitution would impose a lesser duty on the Federal Government. We hold that racial segregation in the public schools of the District of Columbia is a denial of the due process of law guaranteed by the Fifth Amendment to the Constitution.

Notes

1. Does *Bolling v. Sharpe* rule that the equal protection of the laws, found to be implied in the due process clause of the Fifth Amendment, applies to the federal government "jot for jot, bag and baggage"—the same principles that govern the States under the explicit equal protection clause in the Fourteenth Amendment? (Before *Bolling v. Sharpe*, the Supreme Court had sometimes relied on the lack of an explicit equal protection clause in the Fifth Amendment to reject objections to discrimination by the federal government.)

3. *Korematsu v. United States*, 323 U.S.   U.S. 81, 100.
214, 216; *Hirabayashi v. United States*, 320

The Supreme Court held that under the authority of Congress to implement the Fourteenth Amendment (Amendment XIV, § 5), Congress could authorize "affirmative action" programs that might be prohibited to the States in the absence of Congressional legislation. In *Adarand Constructors, Inc. v. Pena*, 515 U.S. 200 (1995), however, the Court concluded that federal "affirmative action" programs authorized by Congress were subject to the same "scrutiny," and could be justified only by a compelling public interest as required of the states.

2. Distinctions between citizens and aliens, which may be suspect when made by the States, are not necessarily so when made by the federal government. Compare *Graham v. Richardson*, 403 U.S. 365 (1971), with *Mathews v. Diaz*, 426 U.S. 67 (1976).

3. Does "reverse incorporation" suggest that other constitutional provisions applicable to the States might also apply to the federal government through the due process clause of the Fifth Amendment? For example, the Clause prohibiting the states to impair obligation of contract? Some found support for that result in an earlier case, *Lynch v. United States*, 292 U.S. 571 (1934), but even after *Bolling v. Sharpe* the Supreme Court rejected that view in *Pension Benefit Guaranty Corp. v. R. A. Gray and Co.*, 467 U.S. 717 (1984).

Does Article IV, section 2, in effect forbidding discrimination between citizens of different States in respect of "the Privileges and Immunities of Citizens," apply to the federal government through the Due Process clause of the Fifth Amendment?

Some guarantees are explicitly applied to both the federal government and the States, e.g., the prohibition on bills of attainder and *ex post facto* laws.

4. The provision in the Fourteenth Amendment prohibiting the States to deny the privileges and immunities of citizenship has been held to protect only the privileges and immunities of national citizenship. *Slaughter-House Cases*, 83 U.S. (16 Wall.) 36 (1873). Does that provision apply as well to the federal government? Or are "the privileges and immunities" of U.S. citizenship, by implication, protected by other clauses of the Constitution?

5. The "citizenship clause" of the Fourteenth Amendment (Amendment XIV, § 1) is not addressed to either the States or the federal government and presumably is binding equally on both.

E. LIMITATIONS ON RIGHTS

1. INDIVIDUAL RIGHTS AND THE PUBLIC INTEREST

The power of the courts to expand rights by interpretation is, of course, a consequence of their authority to exercise "judicial review," itself, some think, a product of judicial interpretation, if not judicial usurpation. *Marbury v. Madison*; see Chapter 3 below. In other respects too, the

Supreme Court's conception of the judicial function has shaped the jurisprudence of rights under the Constitution, determined the relation of individual rights to other aspects of Constitutional government, and the role of the courts in monitoring respect for rights in the U.S. Constitutional system.

A large part of the jurisprudence of Constitutional rights derives from the need to determine the scope of particular rights and their relation to other values and interests in a constitutional polity. Compare Article 29(2) of the Universal Declaration of Human Rights, Part III, p. 324.

The authors of the U.S. Constitution and of the U.S. Bill of Rights apparently saw rights as "natural" and apparently considered them to be "absolute," qualified only by the competing rights of others. Rights in society pursuant to the social contract also were apparently seen as absolute, subject however to the powers delegated to government for its proper purposes, generally subsumed in "the police power." But "the police power" is itself constrained by the obligation to respect rights: rights often "trump" and limit even bona fide exercises of the police power deemed by law-makers to be in the public's interest.

The U.S. Bill of Rights appears to declare absolute rights. For example, the First Amendment provides that "Congress shall make no law ... abridging the freedom of speech or of the press," and Justice Hugo Black was known to have insisted that "no law" means *no law*. But the Supreme Court—and even Justice Black—sometimes escaped the rigor of an absolute reading of that Amendment by interpreting the protected freedoms narrowly, or by construing the word "abridging" narrowly. In time, the Supreme Court drew lines and developed categories: prohibition as distinguished from lesser regulation; regulation of the content of expression as distinguished from time, place or manner of expression. Later, the Court concluded that some subjects of expression, e.g., commercial speech, deserved less protection than other subjects, such as political expression.

Some rights in the Constitution are limited by the terms used to declare them. Bills of attainder or *ex post facto* laws are prohibited both to the States and to the federal government (U.S. Constitution Article 1, §§ 9, 10), but both rights are limited by their traditional definitions. The right to a "speedy" and "public" trial also requires definition. Some of the provisions in the Bill of Rights have qualifications built into them—e.g. "The right of the people to be secure ... against *unreasonable* searches and seizures" (Amendment IV); "*Excessive* bail ... and ... *cruel* and *unusual* punishment" (Amendment VIII) (emphasis added). On the other hand, the right to a jury trial appears to be absolute (though it is limited by its historic character; for example, by history the right to trial by jury is subject to an exception for petty offenses). Compare *Duncan v. Louisiana*, p. 187 above.

The need to accommodate rights to the police power (and to exercises of recognized, legitimate governmental authority generally) has been largely addressed through the Due Process clauses. Limitations on rights were built into the right to "liberty" subject to "substantive due process."

Cardozo's conception of "ordered liberty," in *Palko*, p. 186 above, may be an elegant, eloquent (perhaps oxymoronic) conception, but it is not self-defining. It is particularly in respect of that right that constitutional jurisprudence has developed the conception and the art of "balancing," balancing the right against the public interest, attributing greater weight to some rights and to some public interests than to others, and scrutinizing—with different degrees of intensity—both the weights and the act of balancing. Similarly, the right not to be denied the equal protection of the laws permits distinctions in law corresponding to differences in fact, but some differences—e.g., classifications or distinctions based on race—are suspect: alleged justifications will be sharply scrutinized, and only compelling public interests will be accepted as justifying the discrimination. Similarly, distinctions in respect of the enjoyment of a fundamental right or interest will be subject to strict scrutiny and will be justified only by an important, weighty, sometimes even a compelling public interest.

The Constitution does not appear to have anticipated that there may be conflict between rights. Are choice and accommodation between rights to be determined by the courts as a matter of constitutional interpretation, however uncertain the basis for such construction? Or is authority to choose between or to accommodate conflicting constitutional rights lodged in Congress (or the State legislatures) as an aspect of the police power? The Supreme Court has decided between some competing rights—between a right to privacy, or the protection of reputation, and the freedom of the press; between freedom of the press and the right to a fair trial. But the Court has not articulated a general principle or "methodology" for resolving such conflicts, or even a compelling justification for a particular choice between particular rights.

Implicit in the idea of rights is its potentially "anti-democratic" character. Rights are retained, and protected, not only against tyrants and other evil agents of government; they are limitations even on the benevolent decisions "in the public interest" of majorities and democratically elected representatives.

2.   THE POLICE POWER: SAFETY, MORALS, HEALTH, AND PUBLIC WELFARE

Theory and Principles of Application

Rights are subject to limitation by proper use of the police power, as contemplated by the social contract. But the police power is in turn limited by the obligation on government to respect constitutional rights.

The police power is not self-defining. The term is sometimes used to describe all the powers of government, whether traditional municipal powers or State powers, or the special powers delegated by the Constitution to the federal government, e.g., to regulate commerce, or provide for the common defense. A broad definition was provided by Chief Justice Taney, in the *License Cases*:

But what are the police powers of the State? They are nothing more or less than the powers of government inherent in every sovereignty to the extent of its dominions. And whether a State passes a quarantine law, or a law to punish offences, or to establish courts of justice, or requiring certain instruments to be recorded, or to regulate commerce within its own limits, in every case it exercises the same powers: that is to say, the power of sovereignty, the power to govern men and things within the limits of its dominion.

The License Cases, 46 U.S. (5 How.) 504, 583 (1847).

However, the courts have sometimes distinguished certain powers of government as coming within a narrower, undisputed conception of the police power. Blackstone defined the scope of the police power in England, and its limitations by individual rights at common law. See *supra* Section A. An American exposition was provided early in the Twentieth Century by Professor Ernst Freund in *The Police Power* (1904). Freund identifies "the great objects of government: the maintenance of national existence; the maintenance of right or justice; and the public welfare"; and the "primary social interests as safety, order and morals." *Id*. §§ 4, 10. Compare the "definitions" in contemporary international instruments, e.g., The Universal Declaration of Human Rights Art. 29(2), and the International Covenant on Civil and Political Rights Art. 12(3), 18(3), 19(3).

National security as a legitimate concern of the police power may be seen as a special case of "public safety"; but it has made its way into the definitions of permissible limitations on rights and has indeed achieved primacy. See *Haig v. Agee*, below.

The police power warrants also invasion of rights to property. The right to the free enjoyment of one's property was limited at common law by the law of nuisance and the U.S. Supreme Court, interpreting the Constitution, sustained that limitation; the Court accepted also the validity in principle of zoning laws. *Village of Euclid v. Ambler Realty*, p. 202 below. Property is subject also to the power of eminent domain, the taking of property for public use subject to just compensation. Public use includes land redistribution (*Hawaii Housing Authority v. Midkiff*, p. 204 below), and warrants limitations on private property for aesthetic purposes as for other public "uses." *Penn Central Transp. Co. v. New York City*, p. 204 below.

In U.S. constitutional jurisprudence, limitations on rights by exercises of the police power have been modified by "limitations on limitations": all rights may be subject to limitations in the public interest but some rights are "preferred"; and police power invasions of such rights are subject to particular scrutiny and may be justified only by an important or even compelling public interest. Important versus compelling public interest may be required to justify deviations from equal protection of the law of as in *Korematsu*. "Preferred rights" and "compelling public interests" were introduced into U.S. constitutional jurisprudence earlier in the Twentieth Century in cases such as *Palko v. Connecticut*, p. 220 infra, and *United States v. Carolene Products Co.*. The suggestion that the courts might balance differently certain rights and certain public interests was the subject of what is perhaps the most famous footnote in constitutional jurisprudence, footnote 4 in *Carolene Products*. See p. 221 below.

Safety

By any account, the police power includes the power to promote "safety"—the public safety as well as the safety of individuals. That principle is not in doubt, and there have been few significant challenges to the authority of government to regulate liberty and property for this purpose.

In *Barbier v. Connolly*, 113 U.S. 27 (1884), the Supreme Court upheld a San Francisco ordinance regulating the establishment of laundries, limiting their location and their hours of operation, and requiring inspection and certification by a health official and a fire warden.

> [T]he board of supervisors of the city and county of San Francisco . . . passed an ordinance reciting that the indiscriminate establishment of public laundries and wash-houses, where clothes and other articles were cleansed for hire, endangered the public health and the public safety, prejudiced the well-being and comfort of the community, and depreciated the value of property in their neighborhood; and then ordaining, . . . that . . . it should be unlawful for any person to establish, maintain, or carry on the business of a public laundry or of a public wash-house within certain designated limits of the city and county without first having obtained a certificate, signed by the health officer of the municipality, that the premises were properly and sufficiently drained, and that all proper arrangements were made to carry on the business without injury to the sanitary condition of the neighborhood; also a certificate, signed by the board of fire-wardens of the municipality, that the stoves, washing and drying apparatus, and the appliances for heating smoothing-irons were in good condition, and that their use was not dangerous to the surrounding property from fire, and that all proper precautions were taken to comply with the provisions of the ordinance defining the fire limits of the city and county, and making regulations concerning the erection and use of buildings therein.
>
> The ordinance requires the health officer and board of fire-wardens, upon application of anyone to open or conduct the business of a public laundry, to inspect the premises in which it is proposed to carry on the business, in order to ascertain whether they are provided with proper drainage and sanitary appliances, and whether the provisions of the fire ordinance have been compiled with; and, if found satisfactory in all respects, to issue to the applicant the required certificates without charge for the services rendered. Its fourth section declares that no person owning or employed in a public laundry or a public wash-house, within the prescribed limits, shall wash or iron clothes

between the hours of 10 in the evening and 6 in the morning, or upon any portion of Sunday; . . .

. . . .

. . . The provision is purely a police regulation within the competency of any municipality possessed of the ordinary powers belonging to such bodies . . . It may be a necessary measure to precaution in a city composed largely of wooden buildings like San Francisco, that occupations, in which fires are constantly required, should cease after certain hours at night until the following morning; and of the necessity of such regulations the municipal bodies are the exclusive judges; at least, any correction of their action in such matters can come only from state legislation or state tribunals. . . . The specification of the limits within which the business cannot be carried on without the certificates of the health officer and board of fire-wardens is merely a designation of the portion of the city in which the precautionary measures against fire and to secure proper drainage must be taken for the public health and safety.

There have been questions as to whether the police power includes authority to protect an individual from endangering himself. Such regulations can generally be justified in that acts that are dangerous to oneself also often involve danger to others, as well as other public costs. Speed limits, safety inspections, seat-belt and helmet laws, and similar regulations have not been challenged successfully. But individuals, courts have held, have the right to refuse medical treatment, although not to deny it to minors for whom they are responsible, even on religious grounds. See *Jehovah's Witnesses v. King County Hosp.*, 278 F.Supp. 488 (W.D.Wash. 1967); *People v. Labrenz*, 104 N.E.2d 769, 771 (Ill.1952), *cert. denied*, 344 U.S. 824. Laws against attempted suicide are now uncommon and the decision of the Supreme Court in *Cruzan v. Missouri Dept. of Health,* 497 U.S. 261 (1990), has been characterized as recognizing "a right to die"; but the Supreme Court has unanimously upheld the constitutionality of laws criminalizing physician-assisted suicide. See *Washington v. Glucksberg,* 521 U.S. 702 (1997); *Vacco v. Quill,* 521 U.S. 793 (1997).

Compare Article IV in the French Declaration of the Rights of Man and of the Citizen establishing the principle that "Liberty consists in the power of doing whatever does not injure another", *supra* p. 32. This "harm principle" has been commonly associated with John Stuart Mill. See Joseph Raz, *The Morality of Freedom* 412–20 (1986).

Health

The regulation in *Barbier v. Connolly,* above, was characterized as promoting health as well as safety. The Court focused on health in *Jacobson v. Commonwealth of Massachusetts,* 197 U.S. 11 (1905), which upheld the authority of the States to require vaccination as legitimate public welfare legislation to safeguard health, though it entailed an important invasion of the person and a deprivation of liberty.

The Court said:

> According to settled principles, the police power of a state must be held to embrace, at least, such reasonable regulations established directly by legislative enactment.... We are not prepared to hold that a minority, residing or remaining in any city or town where smallpox is prevalent, and enjoying the general protection afforded by an organized local government, may thus defy the will of its constituted authorities, acting in good faith for all, under the legislative sanction of the state.... We are unwilling to hold it to be an element in the liberty secured by the Constitution of the United States that one person, or a minority of persons, residing in any community and enjoying the benefits of its local government, should have the power thus to dominate the majority when supported in their action by the authority of the state.

Morals

Definitions of the police power have commonly recognized the authority of government to take measures to protect "morality." But "morality" has not been authoritatively defined, or persuasively distinguished from offensiveness, indecency, obscenity, nuisance, and other disturbances of "public order." (See the reference to the "just requirements of morality, public order and the general welfare in a democratic society" as permissible limitations on human rights, in the Universal Declaration, Article 29; also the references to morals in the International Covenant on Civil and Political Rights, Articles 12(3), 19(3)(b), 21, 22. See *infra* Part IV, Chapter 1(B).)

The U.S. Supreme Court has not squarely addressed the meaning and scope of "morality," as a permissible purpose of the police power and a permissible limitation on individual rights; but it upheld limitations on liberty for the preservation of public standards of morality in *Bowers v. Hardwick*, 478 U.S. 186 (1986); compare *Roth v. United States*, 354 U.S. 476 (1957), and *Miller v. California*, 413 U.S. 15 (1973) (obscenity), *Bethel School Dist. No. 403 v. Fraser*, 478 U.S. 675 (1986), and *Federal Communications Commission v. Pacific Foundation*, 438 U.S. 726 (1978) (indecency). And see Henkin, *Morals and the Constitution: the Sin of Obscenity*, 63 Colum. L. Rev. 301 (1963).

In *Bowers v. Hardwick,* 478 U.S. 186, 196 (1986), the Court said:

> Even if the conduct at issue here is not a fundamental right, respondent asserts that there must be a rational basis for the law and that there is none in this case other than the presumed belief of a majority of the electorate in Georgia that homosexual sodomy is immoral and unacceptable. This is said to be an inadequate rationale to support the law. The law, however, is constantly based on notions of morality, and if all laws representing essentially moral choices are to be invalidated under the Due Process Clause, the courts will be very busy indeed. Even respondent makes no such claim, but insists that

majority sentiments about the morality of homosexuality should be declared inadequate. We do not agree, and are unpersuaded that the sodomy laws of some 25 States should be invalidated on this basis.

But Justice Blackmun stated for the dissent:

> Nor can § 16–6–2 be justified as a "morally neutral" exercise of Georgia's power to "protect the public environment." ...Certainly, some private behavior can affect the fabric of society as a whole. Reasonable people may differ about whether particular sexual acts are moral or immoral, but "we have ample evidence for believing that people will not abandon morality, will not think any better of murder, cruelty and dishonesty, merely because some private sexual practice which they abominate is not punished by the law." H.L.A. Hart, Immorality and Treason, reprinted in The Law as Literature 220, 225 (L. Blom–Cooper ed. 1961). Petitioner and the Court fail to see the difference between laws that protect public sensibilities and those that enforce private morality. Statutes banning public sexual activity are entirely consistent with protecting the individual's liberty interest in decisions concerning sexual relations: the same recognition that those decisions are intensely private which justifies protecting them from governmental interference can justify protecting individuals from unwilling exposure to the sexual activities of others. But the mere fact that intimate behavior may be punished when it takes place in public cannot dictate how States can regulate intimate behavior that occurs in intimate places.

Id. at 212.

Bowers v. Hardwick is discussed and compared in Part IV, Chapter 1 (B).

Public Welfare

Formulations of the police power generally include the authority to regulate for the "public welfare." The scope and context of that power have hardly been defined. It has been held to support zoning laws and landmark preservation (see below), but it might include much else. The regulation in *Jacobson* requiring vaccination was characterized by the Court as legitimate public welfare legislation to safeguard health.

In a special category, historically, is regulation of the economy for the public welfare. The scope of the police power became particularly controversial in *Lochner v. New York*, 198 U.S. 45 (1905). Reading the Due Process clause of the Fourteenth Amendment as protecting "liberty" broadly conceived, the majority of the Court accepted that "liberty" was subject to regulation by the police power for public health, safety, morals, but construed the power narrowly: in particular, the majority took a limited view of the power of the government to adopt economic regulations for the general welfare, and effectively *laissez-faire* became a premise of the American constitutional system. (An exception recognized by the Court during that period permitted regulation designed to keep the market free as by antitrust laws; limitations on free enterprise for the protection of health and safety, as well as safeguards against fraud, were also upheld as within the police power even as narrowly conceived.)

That *Lochner* view was abandoned in 1937. The demise of *Lochner* began with *Nebbia v. New York*, 291 U.S. 502 (1934), and was completed in *West Coast Hotel Co. v. Parrish*, 300 U.S. 379 (1937), which sustained a State's minimum wage law for women. *Nebbia* established a presumption of constitutionality for governmental regulation of private enterprise, even of enterprise that was not a public utility or otherwise "affected with the public interest." It accepted a broad view of the police power to regulate for the general welfare, and reduced judicial scrutiny to a determination that regulation had "a reasonable relation to a proper legislative purpose and [is] neither arbitrary nor discriminatory." See *Nebbia, infra* p. 1138. With *West Coast Hotel*, the Supreme Court effectively ceased to scrutinize economic regulation as a denial of liberty without due process of law. See, *e.g.*, *Williamson v. Lee Optical of Oklahoma*, 348 U.S. 483, 487–88 (1955). In some instances, however, the Court found that some regulations constitute "takings" requiring "just compensation." See *Penn Central infra* p. 204. On the other hand, the Supreme Court identified some freedoms as having extraordinary weight, deserving higher protection, and their infringement required sharper scrutiny and a more weighty public interest. See Justice Cardozo in *Palko*, p. 220 below.

Police Power Limitations on Property Rights

In *Village of Euclid v. Ambler Realty Co.*, 272 U.S. 365 (1926), the Supreme Court upheld "zoning." The Court said:

> There is no serious difference of opinion in respect of the validity of laws and regulations fixing the height of buildings within reasonable limits, the character of materials and methods of construction, and the adjoining area which must be left open, in order to minimize the danger of fire or collapse, the evils of overcrowding and the like, and excluding from residential sections offensive trades, industries and structures likely to create nuisances.

The Supreme Court of Illinois, in *City of Aurora v. Burns,* in sustaining a comprehensive building zone ordinance dividing the city into eight districts, including exclusive residential districts for one and two family dwellings, churches, educational institutions, and schools, said:

> "The constantly increasing density of our urban populations, the multiplying forms of industry and the growing complexity of our civilization make it necessary for the state, either directly or through some public agency by its sanction, to limit individual activities to a greater extent than formerly. With the growth and development of the state the police power necessarily develops, within reasonable bounds, to meet the changing conditions.

. . .

"[T]he harmless may sometimes be brought within the regulation or prohibition in order to abate or destroy the harmful. The segregation of industries, commercial pursuits, and dwellings to particular districts in a city, when exercised reasonably, may bear a rational relation to the health, morals, safety, and general welfare of the community. The establishment of such districts or zones may, among other things, prevent congestion of population, secure quiet residence districts, expedite local transportation, and facilitate the suppression of disorder, the extinguishment of fires, and the enforcement of traffic and sanitary regulations. The danger of fire and contagion are often lessened by the exclusion of stores and factories from areas devoted to residences, and, in consequence, the safety and health of the community may be promoted. . . .

"[T]he exclusion of places of business from residential districts is not a declaration that such places are nuisances or that they are to be suppressed as such, but it is a part of the general plan by which the city's territory is allotted to different uses, in order to prevent, or at least to reduce, the congestion, disorder, and dangers which often inhere in unregulated municipal development."

The Supreme Court of Louisiana, in *State v. City of New Orleans*, said: "In the first place, the exclusion of business establishments from residence districts might enable the municipal government to give better police protection. Patrolmen's beats are larger, and therefore fewer, in residence neighborhoods than in business neighborhoods . . ."

. . .

The matter of zoning has received much attention at the hands of commissions and experts, and the results of their investigations have been set forth in comprehensive reports. These reports which bear every evidence of painstaking consideration, concur in the view that the segregation of residential, business and industrial buildings will make it easier to provide fire apparatus suitable for the character and intensity of the development in each section; that it will increase the safety and security of home life, greatly tend to prevent street accidents, especially to children, by reducing the traffic and resulting confusion in residential sections, decrease noise and other conditions which produce or intensify nervous disorders, preserve a more favorable environment in which to rear children, etc. . . .

"Racial Zoning." In *Buchanan v. Warley*, 245 U.S. 60 (1917), the Supreme Court invalidated an ordinance that sought to achieve "racial zoning". The Court held that, by denying a property owner the right to alienate his property to a person of his choice because of that person's race, the municipality deprived the owner of property without due process of law; the ordinance could not be justified as an exercise of the police power.

Taking for Public Use

After declaring that no person may be deprived of property without due process of law, see *supra* p. 183, the Fifth Amendment provides: "nor shall any person's property be taken for public use without just compensation." Under the Constitution, then, the right to property is limited in that it is subject to eminent domain. The scope of the power of eminent domain and the Constitutional limitations to which it is subject, including the meaning of "taking" and the requirement of just compensation, continues to be the subject of a rich jurisprudence. See *Penn Central* following and Part IV, Chapter 3(B).

The requirement that taking be for "public use" has not proved to be a significant limitation. In *Hawaii Housing Authority v. Midkiff*, 467 U.S. 229, 240 (1984), Justice O'Connor said:

> The "public use" requirement is thus coterminous with the scope of a sovereign's police powers. . . . But where the exercise of the eminent domain power is rationally related to a conceivable public purpose, the Court has never held a compensated taking to be proscribed by the Public Use Clause . . . On this basis, we have no trouble concluding that the Hawaii Act is constitutional. . . . When the legislature's purpose is legitimate and its means are not irrational, our cases make clear that empirical debates over the wisdom of takings—no less than debates over the wisdom of other kinds of socioeconomic legislation—are not to be carried out in the federal courts. . . . The mere fact that property taken outright by eminent domain is transferred in the first instance to private beneficiaries does not condemn that taking as having only a private purpose.

Public use for purposes of eminent domain has been held to include takings for aesthetic "uses."

Penn Central Transportation Co. v. City of New York,

438 U.S. 104 (1978).

■ MR. JUSTICE BRENNAN delivered the opinion of the Court.

. . .

This case involves the application of New York City's Landmarks Preservation Law to Grand Central Terminal (Terminal). The Terminal, which is owned by the Penn Central Transportation Co. and its affiliates (Penn Central), is one of New York City's most famous buildings. Opened in 1913, it is regarded not only as providing an ingenious engineering solution to the problems presented by urban railroad stations, but also as a magnificent example of the French beaux-arts style.

. . .

II

The issues presented by appellants are (1) whether the restrictions imposed by New York City's law upon appellants' exploitation of the

Terminal site effect a "taking" of appellants' property for a public use within the meaning of the Fifth Amendment, which of course is made applicable to the States through the Fourteenth Amendment, and, (2), if so, whether the transferable development rights afforded appellants constitute "just compensation" within the meaning of the Fifth Amendment. We need only address the question whether a "taking" has occurred.

. . .

Pennsylvania Coal Co. v. Mahon, 260 U.S. 393 (1922), is the leading case for the proposition that a state statute that substantially furthers important public policies may so frustrate distinct investment-backed expectations as to amount to a "taking." There the claimant had sold the surface rights to particular parcels of property, but expressly reserved the right to remove the coal thereunder. A Pennsylvania statute, enacted after the transactions, forbade any mining of coal that caused the subsidence of any house, unless the house was the property of the owner of the underlying coal and was more than 150 feet from the improved property of another. Because the statute made it commercially impracticable to mine the coal, *id.* at 414, and thus had nearly the same effect as the complete destruction of rights claimant had reserved from the owners of the surface land, see *id.* at 414–415, the Court held that the statute was invalid as effecting a "taking" without just compensation. . . .

In contending that the New York City law has "taken" their property in violation of the Fifth and Fourteenth Amendments, appellants make a series of arguments, which, while tailored to the facts of this case, essentially urge that any substantial restriction imposed pursuant to a landmark law must be accompanied by just compensation if it is to be constitutional.

. . .

... We now must consider whether the interference with appellants' property is of such a magnitude that "there must be an exercise of eminent domain and compensation to sustain [it]." *Pennsylvania Coal Co. v. Mahon*, 260 U.S. at 413. That inquiry may be narrowed to the question of the severity of the impact of the law on appellants' parcel, and its resolution in turn requires a careful assessment of the impact of the regulation on the Terminal site.

Unlike the governmental acts in [earlier cases cited], the New York City law does not interfere in any way with the present uses of the Terminal. Its designation as a landmark not only permits but contemplates that appellants may continue to use the property precisely as it has been used for the past 65 years: as a railroad terminal containing office space and concessions. So the law does not interfere with what must be regarded as Penn Central's primary expectation concerning the use of the parcel. More importantly, on this record, we must regard the New York City law as permitting Penn Central not only to profit from the Terminal but also to obtain a "reasonable return" on its investment.

On this record, we conclude that the application of New York City's Landmarks Law has not effected a "taking of appellants' property". The restrictions imposed are substantially related to the promotion of the general welfare and not only permit reasonable beneficial use of the landmark site but also afford appellants opportunities further to enhance not only the Terminal site proper but also other properties.

MR. JUSTICE REHNQUIST, with whom THE CHIEF JUSTICE and MR. JUSTICE STEVENS join, dissenting. [Opinion omitted]

3. NATIONAL SECURITY

"National security" has often not been included in definitions of the police power, perhaps because the police power was seen as addressing internal affairs generally within the authority of local government, whereas national security was the concern of the Crown, and, in the United States, of the federal government. (One might see national security as a special case of "public safety," above.) But no one has doubted the authority of government to take measures for national security, and contemporary statements of the police power explicitly include it. See p. 197 above.

Limitations on individual rights for national security create issues of accommodation (and drawing lines) generally similar to those involved in accommodation or limitation of individual rights by local police powers. But few regulations declared to be required for national security have been invalidated though they involved important invasions of individual rights.

In *Haig v. Agee*, below, the Court upheld the denial of a passport, and thereby, effectively, the right (liberty) to travel abroad, on grounds of national security. And in *Korematsu v. United States*, 323 U.S. 214 (1944), the Court upheld the authority of the military authorities in time of war to interfere with the freedom of residence and movement, relocating and "concentrating" citizens of Japanese ancestry. On the other hand, in the *Pentagon Papers Case*, infra p. 208, the Court refused to enjoin the publication of "classified documents" despite claims that publication would jeopardize national security, concluding that the Government had not met the heavy burden of justifying "prior restraint" on the freedom of the press.

Haig v. Agee

453 U.S. 280 (1981).

■ CHIEF JUSTICE BURGER delivered the opinion of the Court.

The question presented is whether the President, acting through the Secretary of State, has authority to revoke a passport on the ground that the holder's activities in foreign countries are causing or are likely to cause serious damage to the national security or foreign policy of the United States.

Philip Agee, an American citizen, currently resides in West Germany. From 1957 to 1968, he was employed by the Central Intelligence Agency. He held key positions in the division of the Agency that is responsible for covert intelligence gathering in foreign countries. In the course of his duties at the Agency, Agee received training in clandestine operations, including the methods used to protect the identities of intelligence employees and sources of the United States overseas. He served in the undercover assignments abroad and came to know many Government employees and other persons supplying information to the United States. The relationships of many of these people to our Government are highly confidential; many are still engaged in intelligence gathering.

· · ·

III

Agee also attacks the Secretary's action on three constitutional grounds: first, that the revocation of his passport impermissibly burdens his freedom to travel; second, that the action was intended to penalize his exercise of free speech and deter his criticism of Government policies and practices; and third, that failure to accord him a pre-revocation hearing violated his Fifth Amendment right to procedural due process.

In light of the express language of the passport regulations, which permits their application only in cases involving likelihood of "serious damage" to national security or foreign policy, these claims are without merit.

· · ·

Revocation of a passport undeniably curtails travel, but the freedom to travel abroad with a "letter of introduction" in the form of a passport issued by the sovereign is subordinate to national security and foreign policy considerations; as such, it is subject to reasonable governmental regulation. The Court has made it plain that the *freedom* to travel outside the United States must be distinguished from the *right* to travel within the United States. . . .

· · ·

It is "obvious and unarguable" that no governmental interest is more compelling than the security of the Nation. *Aptheker v. Secretary of State,* [378 U.S. 500, 509 (1964)]; accord *Cole v. Young,* 351 U.S. 536, 546 (1956); see *Zemel* [*v. Rusk,* 381 U.S. 1, 13–17 (1965)]. Protection of the foreign policy of the United States is a governmental interest of great importance, since foreign policy and national security considerations cannot neatly be compartmentalized.

· · ·

JUSTICE BRENNAN, with whom JUSTICE MARSHALL joins, dissenting [opinion omitted].

Notes

1. The Court links national security and "foreign policy", and asserts that foreign policy and national security considerations "cannot neatly be compartmentalized." But can they be distinguished? Are all national security considerations of equal significance? Are all foreign policy considerations of equal significance? Are courts in a position to weigh them and to balance them against individual rights?

2. The Court distinguishing "a right" from "a freedom." Is that a constitutional distinction? Where did the Court find it?

New York Times Co. v. United States [The Pentagon Papers Case]

403 U.S. 713 (1971).

■ PER CURIAM

We granted certiorari in these cases in which the United States seeks to enjoin the New York Times and the Washington Post from publishing the contents of a classified study entitled "History of U.S. Decision–Making Process on Viet Nam Policy." "Any system of prior restraints of expression comes to this Court bearing a heavy presumption against its constitutional validity." *Bantam Books, Inc. v. Sullivan*, 372 U.S. 58, 70 (1963); see also *Near v. Minnesota*, 283 U.S. 697 (1931). The Government "thus carries a heavy burden of showing justification for the imposition of such a restraint." *Organization for a Better Austin v. Keefe*, 402 U.S. 415, 419 (1971). The District Court for the Southern District of New York in the New York Times case and the District Court for the District of Columbia and the Court of Appeals for the District of Columbia Circuit in the Washington Post case held that the Government had not met that burden. We agree.

. . .

[Opinions of individual Justices omitted.]

Notes

Why the particular resistance to "prior restraint?" Is it consistently and rationally applied? Compare the decision on "prior restraint" in *Nebraska Press Association v. Stuart*, p. 213 below.

4. CONFLICTING RIGHTS

In *New York Times Co. v. Sullivan*, following, the Supreme Court overturned a libel judgment against the New York Times. In *Time, Inc. v. Hill*, p. 212 below, the Court overturned an award of damages against a periodical that falsely reported that a stage play portrayed an experience suffered by the plaintiffs. In these cases, the Court ruled that the First

Amendment does not preclude suits for libel or for invasion of privacy, but that such laws can allow recovery only if the false publication was published with "malice."

Conflict between freedom of the press and a right to a fair trial was resolved in *Nebraska Press Association v. Stuart,* p. 213 below, in favor of the press, overturning a judge's order restricting publication of facts about the trial.

Reputation and Freedom of the Press

New York Times Co. v. Sullivan

376 U.S. 254 (1964).

■ MR. JUSTICE BRENNAN delivered the opinion of the Court.

We are required in this case to determine for the first time the extent to which the constitutional protections for speech and press limit a State's power to award damages in a libel action brought by a public official against critics of his official conduct.

. . .

Under Alabama law as applied in this case, a publication is "libelous per se" if the words "tend to injure a person * * * in his reputation" or to "bring [him] into public contempt".... Once "libel per se" has been established, the defendant has no defense as to stated facts unless he can persuade the jury that they were true in all their particulars. His privilege of "fair comment" for expressions of opinion depends on the truth of the facts upon which the comment is based. Unless he can discharge the burden of proving truth, general damages are presumed, and may be awarded without proof of pecuniary injury. A showing of actual malice is apparently a prerequisite to recovery of punitive damages, and the defendant may in any event forestall a punitive award by a retraction meeting the statutory requirements. Good motives and belief in truth do not negate an inference of malice, but are relevant only in mitigation of punitive damages if the jury chooses to accord them weight.

. . .

The question before us is whether this rule of liability, as applied to an action brought by a public official against critics of his official conduct, abridges the freedom of speech and of the press that is guaranteed by the First and Fourteenth Amendments.

Respondent relies heavily, as did the Alabama courts, on statements of this Court to the effect that the Constitution does not protect libelous publications. Those statements do not foreclose our inquiry here. None of the cases sustained the use of libel laws to impose sanctions upon expression critical of the official conduct of public officials.... Like insurrection, contempt, advocacy of unlawful acts, breach of the peace, obscenity, solicitation of legal business, and the various other formulae for the repression of expression that have been challenged in this Court, libel can claim no talismanic immunity from constitutional limitations. It must be measured by standards that satisfy the First Amendment.

. . .

Thus we consider this case against the background of a profound national commitment to the principle that debate on public issues should be uninhibited, robust, and wide-open, and that it may well include vehement, caustic, and sometimes unpleasantly sharp attacks on government and public officials. The present advertisement, as an expression of grievance and protest on one of the major public issues of our time, would seem clearly to qualify for the constitutional protection. The question is whether it forfeits that protection by the falsity of some of its factual statements and by its alleged defamation of respondent.

Authoritative interpretations of the First Amendment guarantees have consistently refused to recognize an exception for any test of truth—whether administered by judges, juries, or administrative officials—and especially one that puts the burden of proving truth on the speaker.... The constitutional protection does not turn upon "the truth, popularity, or social utility of the ideas and beliefs which are offered." ...

... [E]rroneous statement is inevitable in free debate, and ... it must be protected if the freedoms of expression are to have the "breathing space" that they "need ... to survive"....

Injury to official reputation affords no more warrant for repressing speech that would otherwise be free than does factual error. Where judicial officers are involved, this Court has held that concern for the dignity and reputation of the courts does not justify the punishment as criminal contempt of criticism of the judge or his decision. This is true even though the utterance contains "half-truths" and "misinformation." Such repression can be justified, if at all, only by a clear and present danger of the obstruction of justice. If judges are to be treated as "men of fortitude, able to thrive in a hardy climate," surely the same must be true of other government officials, such as elected city commissioners. Criticism of their official conduct does not lose its constitutional protection merely because it is effective criticism and hence diminishes their official reputations.

If neither factual error nor defamatory content suffices to remove the constitutional shield from criticism of official conduct, the combination of the two elements is no less inadequate. This is the lesson to be drawn from the great controversy over the Sedition Act of 1798, which first crystallized a national awareness of the central meaning of the First Amendment. That statute made it a crime, punishable by a $5,000 fine and five years in prison, "if any person shall write, print, utter or publish ... any false, scandalous and malicious writing or writings against the government of the United States, or either house of the Congress ..., or the President ..., with intent to defame ... or to bring them, or either of them, into contempt or disrepute; or to excite against them, or either or any of them, the hatred of the good people of the United States." The Act allowed the defendant the defense of truth, and provided that the jury were to be judges both of the law and the facts. Despite these qualifications, the Act was vigorously condemned as unconstitutional in an attack joined in by Jefferson and Madison. . . .

Although the Sedition Act was never tested in this Court, the attack upon its validity has carried the day in the court of history. Fines levied in its prosecution were repaid by Act of Congress on the ground that it was unconstitutional . . . Jefferson, as President, pardoned those who had been convicted and sentenced under the Act and remitted their fines, stating: "I discharged every person under punishment or prosecution under the sedition law, because I considered, and now consider, that law to be a nullity, as absolute and as palpable as if Congress had ordered us to fall down and worship a golden image." The invalidity of the Act has also been assumed by Justices of this Court. These views reflect a broad consensus that the Act, because of the restraint it imposed upon criticism of government and public officials, was inconsistent with the First Amendment.

. . .

The constitutional guarantees require, we think, a federal rule that prohibits a public official from recovering damages for a defamatory falsehood relating to his official conduct unless he proves that the statement was made with "actual malice"—that is, with knowledge that it was false or with reckless disregard of whether it was false or not. . .

Such a privilege for criticism of official conduct is appropriately analogous to the protection accorded a public official when he is sued for libel by a private citizen. In *Barr v. Matteo*, 360 U.S. 564, 575, this Court held the utterance of a federal official to be absolutely privileged if made "within the outer perimeter" of his duties. The States accord the same immunity to statements of their highest officers, although some differentiate their lesser officials and qualify the privilege they enjoy. But all hold that all officials are protected unless actual malice can be proved. The reason for the official privilege is said to be that the threat of damage suits would otherwise "inhibit the fearless, vigorous, and effective administration of policies of government" and "dampen the ardor of all but the most resolute, or the most irresponsible, in the unflinching discharge of their duties." Analogous considerations support the privilege for the citizen-critic of government. It is as much his duty to criticize as it is the official's duty to administer.

. . .

. . . [W]e consider that the proof presented to show actual malice lacks the convincing clarity which the constitutional standard demands, and hence that it would not constitutionally sustain the judgment for respondent under the proper rule of law. The case of the individual petitioners requires little discussion. Even assuming that they could constitutionally be found to have authorized the use of their names on the advertisement, there was no evidence whatever that they were aware of any erroneous statements or were in any way reckless in that regard. The judgment against them is thus without constitutional support.

■ Mr. Justice Black, with whom Mr. Justice Douglas joins, concurring.

. . . [I] base my vote to reverse on the belief that the First and Fourteenth Amendments not merely "delimit" a State's power to award damages to "public officials against critics of their official conduct" but completely prohibit a State from exercising such a power. The Court goes on to hold that a State can subject such critics to damages if "actual malice" can be proved against them. "Malice," even as defined by the Court, is an elusive, abstract concept, hard to prove and hard to disprove. The requirement that malice be proved provides at best an evanescent protection for the right critically to discuss public affairs and certainly does not measure up to the sturdy safeguard embodied in the First Amendment. Unlike the Court, therefore, I vote to reverse exclusively on the ground that the Times and the individual defendants had an absolute, unconditional constitutional right to publish in the Times advertisement their criticisms of the Montgomery agencies and officials.

Mr. Justice Goldberg, with whom Mr. Justice Douglas joins (concurring in the result) [opinion omitted].

Freedom of the Press and Privacy

In *Time Inc. v. Hill*, 385 U.S. 374 (1967), Justice Brennan, in an opinion for the Court, wrote:

> The question in this case is whether appellant, publisher of Life Magazine, was denied constitutional protections of speech and press by the application by the New York courts of §§ 50–51 of the New York Civil Rights Law . . . to award appellee damages on allegations that Life falsely reported that a new play portrayed an experience suffered by appellee and his family.

> . . .

> Appellant's defense was that the article was "a subject of legitimate news interest," "a subject of general interest and of value and concern to the public" at the time of publication, and that it was "published in good faith without any malice whatsoever. . . ."

> We hold that the constitutional protections for speech and press preclude the application of the New York statute to redress false reports of matters of public interest in the absence of proof that the defendant published the report with knowledge of its falsity or in reckless disregard of the truth.

> . . .

> In this context, sanctions against either innocent or negligent misstatement would present a grave hazard of discouraging the press from exercising the constitutional guarantees. Those guarantees are not for the benefit of the press so much as for the benefit of all of us. A broadly defined freedom of the press assures the maintenance of our political system and an open society. Fear of large verdicts in damage

suits for innocent or merely negligent misstatement, even fear of the expense involved in their defense, must inevitably cause publishers to "steer ... wider of the unlawful zone". . . .

But the constitutional guarantees can tolerate sanctions against calculated falsehood without significant impairment of their essential function. We held in *New York Times* that calculated falsehood enjoyed no immunity in the case of alleged defamation of a public official concerning his official conduct. Similarly, calculated falsehood should enjoy no immunity in the situation here presented us. . . .

Compare the decisions addressing the relevance of *Sullivan* to libel of "public figures" or of private persons. See *Curtis Publ'g Co. v. Butts*, 388 U.S. 130 (1967) ("public figures"); and *Gertz v. Robert Welch, Inc.*, 418 U.S. 323 (1974) (private persons).

Freedom of the Press and Prior Restraint to Protect Fair Trial

Nebraska Press Association v. Stuart

427 U.S. 539 (1976).

■ MR. CHIEF JUSTICE BURGER delivered the opinion of the Court.

The respondent State District Judge entered an order restraining the petitioners from publishing or broadcasting accounts of confessions or admissions made by the accused or facts "strongly implicative" of the accused in a widely reported murder of six persons. . . .

. . .

The Nebraska Supreme Court ... modified the District Court's order to accommodate the defendant's right to a fair trial and the petitioners' interest in reporting pretrial events. The order as modified prohibited reporting of only three matters: (a) the existence and nature of any confessions or admissions made by the defendant to law enforcement officers, (b) any confessions or admissions made to any third parties, except members of the press, and (c) other facts "strongly implicative" of the accused. The Nebraska Supreme Court did not rely on the Nebraska Bar–Press Guidelines. After construing Nebraska law to permit closure in certain circumstances, the court remanded the case to the District Judge for reconsideration of the issue whether pretrial hearings should be closed to the press and public.

. . .

III

The problems presented by this case are almost as old as the Republic. Neither in the Constitution nor in contemporaneous writings do we find that the conflict between these two important rights was anticipated, yet it is inconceivable that the authors of the Constitution were unaware of the potential conflicts between the right to an unbiased jury and the guarantee of freedom of the press. The unusually able lawyers who helped write the Constitution and later drafted the Bill of Rights were familiar with the historic episode in which John Adams defended British soldiers charged with homicide for firing into a crowd of Boston demonstrators; they were intimately familiar with the clash of the adversary system and the part that passions of the populace sometimes play in influencing potential jurors. They did not address themselves directly to the situation presented by this case; their chief concern was the need for freedom of expression in the political arena and the dialogue in ideas. But they recognized that there were risks to private rights from an unfettered press.

. . .

IV

The Sixth Amendment in terms guarantees "trial, by an impartial jury ..." in federal criminal prosecutions. Because "trial by jury in criminal cases is fundamental to the American scheme of justice," the Due Process Clause of the Fourteenth Amendment guarantees the same right in state criminal prosecutions. *Duncan v. Louisiana*, 391 U.S. 145, 149 (1968).

> "In essence, the right to jury trial guarantees to the criminally accused a fair trial by a panel of impartial, 'indifferent' jurors.... 'A fair trial in a fair tribunal is a basic requirement of due process.' *In re Murchison*, 349 U.S. 133, 136. In the ultimate analysis, only the jury can strip a man of his liberty or his life. In the language of Lord Coke, a juror must be as 'indifferent as he stands unsworne.' *Co.Litt.* 155b. His verdict must be based upon the evidence developed at the trial." *Irvin v. Dowd*, 366 U.S. 717, 722 (1961)....

Taken together, these cases demonstrate that pretrial publicity, even pervasive, adverse publicity, does not inevitably lead to an unfair trial. The capacity of the jury eventually impaneled to decide the case fairly is influenced by the tone and extent of the publicity, which is in part, and often in large part, shaped by what attorneys, police, and other officials do to precipitate news coverage. The trial judge has a major responsibility. What the judge says about a case, in or out of the courtroom, is likely to appear in newspapers and broadcasts. More important, the measures a judge takes or fails to take to mitigate the effects of pretrial publicity—the measures described in *Sheppard* [*v. Maxwell,* 384 U.S. 333 (1966)]—may well determine whether the defendant receives a trial consistent with the requirements of due process. That this responsibility has not always been properly discharged is apparent from the decisions just reviewed.

The costs of failure to afford a fair trial are high. In the most extreme cases, like *Sheppard* and *Estes*, the risk of injustice was avoided when the convictions were reversed. But a reversal means that justice has been delayed for both the defendant and the State; in some cases, because of lapse of time retrial is impossible or further prosecution is gravely handicapped. Moreover, in borderline cases in which the conviction is not reversed, there is some possibility of an injustice unredressed. The "strong measures" outlined in *Sheppard v. Maxwell* are means by which a trial judge can try to avoid exacting these costs from society or from the accused.

. . .

V

The First Amendment provides that "Congress shall make no law . . . abridging the freedom . . . of the press," and it is "no longer open to doubt that the liberty of the press and of speech, is within the liberty safeguarded by the due process clause of the Fourteenth Amendment from invasion by state action." *Near v. Minnesota*, 283 U.S. 697, 707 (1931). See also *Grosjean v. American Press Co.*, 297 U.S. 233, 244 (1936). The Court has interpreted these guarantees to afford special protection against orders that prohibit the publication or broadcast of particular information or commentary—orders that impose a "previous" or "prior" restraint on speech. None of our decided cases on prior restraint involved restrictive orders entered to protect a defendant's right to a fair and impartial jury, but the opinions on prior restraint have a common thread relevant to this case.

. . .

The thread running through all these cases is that prior restraints on speech and publication are the most serious and the least tolerable infringement on First Amendment rights. A criminal penalty or a judgment in a defamation case is subject to the whole panoply of protections afforded by deferring the impact of the judgment until all avenues of appellate review have been exhausted. Only after judgment has become final, correct or otherwise, does the law's sanction become fully operative.

A prior restraint, by contrast and by definition, has an immediate and irreversible sanction. If it can be said that a threat of criminal or civil sanctions after publication "chills" speech, prior restraint "freezes" it at least for the time.

The damage can be particularly great when the prior restraint falls upon the communication of news and commentary on current events. Truthful reports of public judicial proceedings have been afforded special protection against subsequent punishment. See *Cox Broadcasting Corp. v. Cohn*, 420 U.S. 469, 492–493 (1975); see also *Craig v. Harney*, 331 U.S. 367, 374 (1947). For the same reasons the protection against prior restraint should have particular force as applied to reporting of criminal proceedings, whether the crime in question is a single isolated act or a pattern of criminal conduct.

"A responsible press has always been regarded as the handmaiden of effective judicial administration, especially in the criminal field. Its function in this regard is documented by an impressive record of service over several centuries. The press does not simply publish information about trials but guards against the miscarriage of justice by subjecting the police, prosecutors, and judicial processes to extensive public scrutiny and criticism." *Sheppard v. Maxwell*, 384 U.S. at 350.

The extraordinary protections afforded by the First Amendment carry with them something in the nature of a fiduciary duty to exercise the protected rights responsibly—a duty widely acknowledged but not always observed by editors and publishers. It is not asking too much to suggest that those who exercise First Amendment rights in newspapers or broadcasting enterprises direct some effort to protect the rights of an accused to a fair trial by unbiased jurors.

. . .

The authors of the Bill of Rights did not undertake to assign priorities as between First Amendment and Sixth Amendment rights, ranking one as superior to the other. In this case, the petitioners would have us declare the right of an accused subordinate to their right to publish in all circumstances. But if the authors of these guarantees, fully aware of the potential conflicts between them, were unwilling or unable to resolve the issue by assigning to one priority over the other, it is not for us to rewrite the Constitution by undertaking what they declined to do. It is unnecessary, after nearly two centuries, to establish a priority applicable in all circumstances. Yet it is nonetheless clear that the barriers to prior restraint remain high unless we are to abandon what the Court has said for nearly a quarter of our national existence and implied throughout all of it. The history of even wartime suspension of categorical guarantees, such as habeas corpus or the right to trial by civilian courts, see *Ex parte Milligan*, 4 Wall. 2 (1867), cautions against suspending explicit guarantees.

. . .

Our analysis ends as it began, with a confrontation between prior restraint imposed to protect one vital constitutional guarantee and the explicit command of another that the freedom to speak and publish shall not be abridged. We reaffirm that the guarantees of freedom of expression are not an absolute prohibition under all circumstances, but the barriers to prior restraint remain high and the presumption against its use continues intact. We hold that, with respect to the order entered in this case prohibiting reporting or commentary on judicial proceedings held in public, the barriers have not been overcome; to the extent that this order restrained publication of such material, it is clearly invalid. To the extent that it prohibited publication based on information gained from other sources, we conclude that the heavy burden imposed as a condition to securing a prior restraint was not met and the judgment of the Nebraska Supreme Court is therefore

Reversed.

[Some concurring opinions omitted]

■ JUSTICE STEVENS, concurring in the judgment.

. . . I agree that the judiciary is capable of protecting the defendant's right to a fair trial without enjoining the press from publishing information in the public domain, and that it may not do so. Whether the same absolute protection would apply no matter how shabby or illegal the means by which the information is obtained, no matter how serious an intrusion on privacy might be involved, no matter how demonstrably false the information might be, no matter how prejudicial it might be to the interests of innocent persons, and no matter how perverse the motivation for publishing, it, is a question I would not answer without further argument. . . .

Other Conflicting Rights

Freedom of Expression and Property Rights

In *Hudgen v. National Labor Relations Board*, 424 U.S. 507 (1976), a group of labor union members who engaged in peaceful primary picketing within the confines of a privately owned shopping center were threatened by an agent of the owner with arrest for criminal trespass if they did not depart.

The Supreme Court ruled:

> If a large self-contained shopping center is the functional equivalent of a municipality, . . . then the First and Fourteenth Amendments would not permit control of speech within such a center to depend upon the speech's content. For while a municipality may constitutionally impose reasonable time, place, and manner regulations on the use of its streets and sidewalks for First Amendment purposes, and may even forbid altogether such use of some of its facilities, what a municipality may not do under the First and Fourteenth Amendments is to discriminate in the regulation of expression on the basis of the content of that expression. "[A]bove all else, the First Amendment means that government has no power to restrict expression because of its message, its ideas, its subject matter, or its content." It conversely follows, therefore, that if the respondents in [*Lloyd Corp. v. Tanner*, 407 U.S. 551 (1972),] did not have a First Amendment right to enter that shopping center to distribute handbills concerning Vietnam, then the pickets in the present case did not have a First Amendment right to enter this shopping center for the purpose of advertising their strike against the Butler Shoe Co.

> We conclude, in short, that under the present state of the law the constitutional guarantee of free expression has no part to play in a case such as this. . . .

[Concurring and dissenting opinions omitted.]

Freedom of Religion and the Rights of Others

Choice between competing rights involves particular complexities in respect of freedom of religion. Constitutional jurisprudence mediates between the free exercise of religion and the provision that the state may not establish religion. The free exercise of religion sometimes claims exception from general rules, including some rules that protect the rights of others.

In *Paul v. Watchtower Bible and Tract Society of New York, Inc.*, 819 F.2d 875 (9th Cir. 1987), the federal court decided:

A religious organization has a defense of constitutional privilege to claims that it has caused intangible harms—in most, if not all, circumstances. As the United States Supreme Court has observed, "the values underlying these two provisions [of the first amendment] relating to religion have been zealously protected, sometimes even at the expense of other interests." [*Wisconsin v. Yoder*, 406 U.S. 205, 214 (1972).]

Providing the Church with a defense to tort is particularly appropriate here because Paul is a former Church member. Courts generally do not scrutinize closely the relationship among members (or former members) of a church. Churches are afforded great latitude when they impose discipline on members or former members. We agree with Justice Jackson's view that "religious activities which concern only members of the faith are and ought to be free—as nearly absolutely free as anything can be." *Prince v. Massachusetts*, 321 U.S. 158, 177 (1944) (concurring).

The members of the Church Paul decided to abandon have concluded that they no longer want to associate with her. We hold that they are free to make that choice. The Jehovah's Witnesses' practice of shunning is protected under the first amendment of the United States Constitution and therefore under the provisions of the Washington state constitution.

In *Prince v. Massachusetts*, 321 U.S. 158 (1944), the Supreme Court upheld the application of child labor restrictions as a regulation in the public interest, in the face of an asserted right to the free exercise of religion:

The case brings for review another episode in the conflict between Jehovah's Witnesses and the state authority. This time Sarah Prince appeals from convictions for violating Massachusetts' child labor laws, by acts said to be a rightful exercise of her religious convictions.

. . .

Justice Jackson concurred:

My own view may be shortly put: I think the limits begin to operate whenever activities begin to affect or collide with liberties of others or of the public. Religious activities which concern only members of the faith are and ought to be free—as nearly absolutely free as anything can be. But beyond these, many religious denominations or sects engage in collateral and secular activities intended to obtain means from unbelievers to sustain the worshippers and their leaders.

Prince is commonly seen as a regulation by the State for the health and welfare of children, but it may also be seen as a choice between conflicting rights: the rights of the parent and the rights of the child.

Does *Paul* survive *Employment Div., Dep't of Human Resources of Oregon v. Smith*, 494 U.S. 872 (1990)? In that case, the Supreme Court upheld the denial of unemployment benefits to a member of the Native American Church who was fired from his job for using peyote. Smith had ingested the peyote as part of a supervised sacramental ritual which church members consider a central form of religious worship. Unlike some states, Oregon's statute criminalizing peyote use did not, at the time, contain an exception for use as part of religious observance.

Justice Scalia, writing for the majority, rejected the application of the "compelling government interest" test which the Court had used in *Sherbert v. Verner*, 374 U.S. 398 (1963). Under that test, a generally applicable statute that "burdened" religious observance would be held unconstitutional unless it served a "compelling government interest" and "no alternative forms of regulation would [satisfy that interest] without infringing First Amendment rights." Id. at 407. Justice Scalia wrote that the right of free exercise does not relieve an individual of obligations to comply with neutral laws of general applicability on grounds that the law proscribes or requires conduct that is contrary to the individual's religious beliefs or practice. *Smith*, 494 U.S. at 879. Four justices (three in dissent and Justice O'Connor concurring in the judgment) urged that the compelling government interest test articulated in *Sherbert* be retained.

In 1991, Oregon revised its criminal statutes to make religious use a defense to the crime of peyote use. See Or. Rev. Stat. § 475.992 (1997).

In 1993, Congress adopted the Religious Freedom Restoration Act (RFRA), 42 U.S.C. § 2000bb (1994), with the express purpose of overruling *Smith* and restoring "the compelling interest test as set forth in *Sherbert v. Verner*." The Supreme Court held the Act unconstitutional as an attempt by Congress to expand the protections afforded by the First and Fourteenth Amendments, and beyond the power of Congress under Section 5 of the Fourteenth Amendment. See *City of Boerne v. Flores*, 521 U.S. 507 (1997).

The "New Privacy" and the Rights of Others

In recognizing the right of a woman to have an abortion, as an aspect of her "privacy" inherent in her "liberty" and enjoying special constitutional protection, the Supreme Court addressed competing claims by others. In *Roe v. Wade*, 410 U.S. 113 (1973), the Court dismissed claims on behalf of the fetus, at least in the early stages of pregnancy, but allowed the State to protect the fetus later in pregnancy. In *Planned Parenthood of Southeastern Pennsylvania v. Casey*, 505 U.S. 833 (1992), the Court accepted the authority of the State to give effect to some competing interests and values later in pregnancy but not to allow the interests of the husband to interfere with the woman's right to an abortion. The cases are discussed (and compared with the jurisprudence of other countries) in Part IV.

5. ADJUDICATING ACCOMMODATION BETWEEN RIGHTS AND PUBLIC INTERESTS

A judicial role in the accommodation of individual rights and the public interest is implied in the constitutional articulation of some rights, for example, the Fourth Amendment safeguards against unreasonable searches and seizures and contemplation of a warrant. The courts also decide the scope of particular rights, e.g., the freedom of speech and the limitations to which that right may be subject (though no limitation is explicit).

Limitations on Limitations: Preferred Rights and Extraordinary Public Interests

In U.S. Constitutional jurisprudence, limitations or individual rights through exercise of the police power have themselves been modified by what may be characterized as "limitations on limitations". In principle, all rights may be subject to limitation in the public interest. Compare *Nebbia*, p. 202 above and p. 1138 infra. But some rights are preferred, and invasions of such rights are subject to particular scrutiny and may be justified only by important, sometimes only by a compelling public interest. Deviations from equal treatment and the equal protection of the laws, too, may sometimes be justified only by an important or even a compelling public interest. See *Korematsu* below.

In the process of balancing individual rights and public interests, the Supreme Court has not only weighed particular public interests but has also graded different rights, and has applied differing levels of scrutiny depending on the importance of the right in question. In *Palko v. Connecticut*, p. 191 above, Justice Cardozo noted the particular weight to be given to the freedoms guaranteed by the First Amendment, as deserving special protection, as "the matrix, the indispensable condition, of nearly every other form of [freedom]." 302 U.S. at 326. The role of the courts in the accommodation of constitutional rights to the public interest was addressed and developed in a footnote in *United States v. Carolene Products*, 304 U.S. 144 (1938), following. Stone was attempting to resolve tension between judicial review and judicial self-restraint. The Court, while moving away from intensive judicial review in economic cases, suggested special judicial scrutiny of legislation that impinges on rights enumerated in the Bill of Rights, or that restricts the political process. Justice Stone's *Carolene* footnote also singled out for judicial scrutiny legislation directed at "discrete and insular minorities" that limits their full political participation.

The Warren Court further developed the jurisprudence of balancing and scrutiny. Strict scrutiny was applied to "suspect classifications," e.g., race. Intermediate scrutiny is applied to other classifications under the equal protection clause, e.g., gender. Deferential review, requiring only that the government demonstrate a "rational basis" for its actions, was applied to cases of economic regulation. Distinctions and classifications are scrutinized sharply if they impinge on fundamental interests such as voting, see *Reynolds v. Sims*, 377 U.S. 533 (1964), or possibly if they effectively deny a child all access to education, see *Plyler v. Doe*, 457 U.S. 202 (1982). And see Part IV, Chapter 3(D).

"Suspect classifications" as requiring justification by a compelling public interest was first announced in *Korematsu v. United States*, 323 U.S. 214 (1944). In upholding a military order to relocate Americans of Japanese ancestry during the Second World War, the Court said:

[All] legal restrictions which curtail the civil rights of single racial group are immediately suspect. That is not to say that all such restrictions are unconstitutional. It is to say that courts must subject them to the most rigid scrutiny. Pressing public necessity may sometimes justify the existence of such restrictions; racial antagonism never can.

Ironically the requirement of a compelling public interest was deemed satisfied in *Korematsu*. But later invocations of the need for a compelling public interest were commonly deemed not satisfied, and scrutiny strict in name was usually fatal in fact. In *Adarand Constructors, Inc. v. Pena*, 515 U.S. 200, 237 (1995), however, the Court troubled to insist that "strict scrutiny" and the requirement of a compelling public interest are not necessarily fatal in fact.

Note: The Carolene Products footnote

In *United States v. Carolene Products Co.*, 304 U.S. 144, 153 n. 4 (1938), Justice Stone dropped a famous footnote:

There may be narrower scope for operation of the presumption of constitutionality when legislation appears on its face to be within a specific prohibition of the Constitution, such as those of the first ten Amendments, which are deemed equally specific when held to be embraced within the Fourteenth.

It is unnecessary to consider now whether legislation which restricts those political processes which can ordinarily be expected to bring about repeal of undesirable legislation, is to be subjected to more exacting judicial scrutiny under the general prohibitions of the Fourteenth Amendment than are most other types of legislation. On restrictions upon the right to vote, see *Nixon v. Herndon*, 273 U.S. 536; *Nixon v. Condon*, 286 U.S. 73; on restraints upon the dissemination of information, see *Near v. Minnesota*, 283 U.S. 697, 713–714, 718–720, 722; *Grosjean v. American Press Co.*, 297 U.S. 233; *Lovell v. Griffin*, supra; on interferences with political organizations, see *Stromberg v. California*, supra, 369; *Fiske v. Kansas*, 274 U.S. 380; *Whitney v. California*, 274 U.S. 357, 373–378; *Herndon v. Lowry*, 301 U.S. 242; and see Holmes, J., in *Gitlow v. New York*, 268 U.S. 652, 673; as to prohibition of peaceable assembly, see *De Jonge v. Oregon*, 299 U.S. 353, 365.

Nor need we enquire whether similar considerations enter into the review of statutes directed at particular religious, *Pierce v. Society of Sisters*, 268 U.S. 510, or national, *Meyer v. Nebraska*, 262 U.S. 390; *Bartels v. Iowa*, 262 U.S. 404; *Farrington v. Tokushige*, 273 U.S. 284, or racial minorities, *Nixon v. Herndon*, supra; *Nixon v. Condon*, supra; whether prejudice against discrete and insular minorities may be a special condition, which tends seriously to curtail the operation of those political processes ordinarily to be relied upon to protect minorities, and which may call for a correspondingly more searching judicial inquiry. Compare *McCulloch v. Maryland*, 4 Wheat. 316, 428; *South Carolina v. Barnwell Bros.*, 303 U.S. 177, 184, n. 2, and cases cited.

Balancing Constitutional Rights and the Public Interest

American jurisprudence has sought to refine the accommodation of individual rights to public interest by doctrines of "balancing" and "drawing lines"; by according different values to different individual rights and different weights to different public interests; and by prescribing different levels of judicial scrutiny to resolve the uncertainties of balancing and accommodation. The degree of scrutiny will often determine the outcome.

T. Alexander Aleinikoff, *Constitutional Law in the Age of Balancing*

96 Yale L. J. 943, 945–61 (1987).

The metaphor of balancing refers to theories of constitutional interpretation that are based on the identification, valuation, and comparison of competing interests. By a "balancing opinion," I mean a judicial opinion that analyzes a constitutional question by identifying interests implicated by the case and reaches a decision or constructs a rule of constitutional law by explicitly or implicitly assigning values to the identified interests....

[B]alancing, as I define it, differs from methods of adjudication that look at a variety of factors in reaching a decision. These would include some of the familiar multi-pronged tests and "totality of the circumstances" approaches. These standards ask questions about how one ought to characterize particular events. Was the confession voluntary or involuntary? Did the government action constitute a "taking"? In answering such questions, one starts with some conception of what constitutes voluntariness and involuntariness and then asks whether the particular situation shares more of the voluntary elements or the involuntary elements. Or one begins with a checklist of factors that have been used in the past to determine whether a "taking" has occurred. The reasoning is thus primarily analogical. Balancing represents a different kind of thinking. The focus is directly on the interests or factors themselves. Each interest seeks recognition on its own and forces a head-to-head comparison with competing interests....

The balancing metaphor takes two distinct forms. Sometimes the Court talks about one interest outweighing another. Under this view, the Court places the interests on a set of scales and rules the way the scales tip. For example, in *New York v. Ferber*, the court upheld a statute criminalizing the distribution of child pornography because "the evil ... restricted [by the statute] so overwhelmingly outweighs the expressive interests, if any, at stake." Constitutional standards requiring "compelling" or "important" state interests also exemplify this form of the balancing metaphor.

The Court employs a different version of balancing when it speaks of "striking a balance" between or among competing interests. The image is one of balanced scales with constitutional doctrine calibrated according to the relative weights of the interests. One interest does not override another; each survives and is given its due.... What unites these two types of balancing—and the reason they will be considered together—is their shared conception of constitutional law as a battleground of competing interests and their claimed ability to identify and place a value on those interests....

Balancing is not nearly as old as the Constitution. As an explicit method of constitutional interpretation, it first appears in majority opinions in the late 1930's and early 1940's. No Justice explained why such a methodology was a proper form of constitutional construction, nor did any purport to be doing anything novel or controversial. Yet balancing was a major break with the past, responding to the collapse of nineteenth century conceptualism and formalism as well as to half a century of intellectual and social change....

The great constitutional opinions of the nineteenth century and early twentieth century did not employ balancing as a method of constitutional argument or justification.... To be sure, early Justices such as Marshall, Story, and Taney recognized great clashes of interest: federal versus state, public versus private, executive versus legislative, free versus slave. But they resolved these disputes in a categorical fashion. Supreme Court opinions generally recognized differences in kind, not degree: The power to tax was the power to destroy; states could exercise police power but could not regulate commerce; legislatures could impair contractual remedies but not obligations....

[But, by the 1930's,] many of John Marshall's tunes simply wouldn't play any more. Categories designed to create and protect an ideal structure of federalism and individual rights in the nineteenth century seemed out of place in a country that had grown in ways wholly unforeseeable by the Framers and early Justices. The poor fit between doctrine and the real world led some members of the Court to question earlier constitutional truths, and they did so with an eye more to social facts than to abstract categories.

Holmes, Brandeis, and Stone led the early charge in constitutional law. To Holmes, the absolutes of the past had to yield to experience and the social facts of the day. Dissenting in a case in 1928 that woodenly applied the prevailing intergovernmental immunity doctrine, he wrote: "In [Marshall's] days it was not recognized as it is today that most of the distinctions of the law are distinctions of degree.... The power to tax is not the power to destroy while this Court sits."

Along with balancing's respectable intellectual pedigree, several other factors enhanced its attraction as a method of constitutional adjudication. On the most practical level, balancing facilitated doctrinal change in times of social flux. The law could grow because balancing focused on interests in the real world; changes in society would provoke corresponding developments in constitutional doctrine. But balancing did not necessarily commit the Court to a liberal or conservative agenda. Changes could occur in either direction. As the First Amendment cases of the 1950's and 1960's showed, balancing could provide for an expansion or a restriction of rights. Nor did balancing commit the Court to an overall theory of a constitutional provision. The old conceptualization could be discarded and a balancing approach could temporarily fill the theoretical void while the Court groped towards a conception more attuned to the times. . . .

Notes

1. See also Henkin, *Infallibility Under Law: Constitutional Balancing,* 78 Colum. L. Rev. 1022 (1978).

2. The principle of balancing rights and public interest, and choice between individual rights, is implied in international instruments. See the Universal Declaration of Human Rights, Article 29 (2); International Covenant on Civil and Political Rights, e.g., Articles 12, 19. But the international jurisprudence of accommodating rights and the public interest is comparatively primitive, reflecting not only its brief history but the absence of a single, authoritative institution to perform the balancing.

Balancing is increasingly reflected in General Comments by the Human Rights Committee under the International Covenant on Civil and Political Rights and in the views expressed by that Committee in considering private complaints of violations pursuant to the First Optional Protocol to the Covenant. It has become prominent in the jurisprudence of the regional human rights institutions, notably the European Commission and the European Court of Human Rights, and to a lesser extent in the jurisprudence of the Inter–American Court of Human Rights. See Part III.

Drawing Lines

The need to define particular rights, to accommodate conflicting rights, and to resolve tensions between individual rights and public interest, led the Court towards principles of interpretation and resolution, often by "balancing." It also declared the need and the legitimacy of drawing lines. Writing in a negligence case, Justice Oliver Wendell Holmes, said:

> I do not think we need trouble ourselves with the thought that my view depends upon differences of degree. The whole law does so as soon as it is civilized. Negligence is all degree–that of the defendant here degree of the nicest sort; and between the variations according to distance that I suppose to exist and the simple universality of the rules in the Twelve Tables or the *Leges Barbarorum,* there lies the culture of two thousand years.

Leroy Fibre Co. v. Chicago, Milwaukee & St. Paul Ry., 232 U.S. 340, 354 (1914). See generally Henkin, *The Supreme Court, 1967 Term. Foreword: On Drawing Lines,* 82 Harv. L. Rev. 63 (1968).

F.   RIGHTS BEYOND NATIONAL BORDERS

1.   THE CONSTITUTION ABROAD

Where and to whom do the provisions of the U.S. Constitution protecting individual rights apply? These questions have received varying answers over the two centuries of U.S. constitutional history. Even today, the answers are not settled. The availability of U.S. constitutional protections to aliens outside the United States, and the impact of constitutional rights on government regulation of immigration, continue in dispute. This section briefly examines those contested issues.

From the beginning, it has been understood that U.S. citizens within the borders of the states are fully protected by the Bill of Rights. The Supreme Court has also held for over a century that aliens within the United States are persons entitled to constitutional protection. See *Yick Wo v. Hopkins*, 118 U.S. 356 (1886). That includes aliens who are unlawfully present. See *Plyler v. Doe*, 457 U.S. 202 (1982); *Wong Wing v. United States*, 163 U.S. 228 (1896). Moreover, the Court has also held that aliens not present in the United States are entitled to constitutional protection with regard to actions taken within the United States against their property rights in the United States. See *Asahi Metal Indus. Co. v. Superior Court*, 480 U.S. 102 (1987); *Russian Volunteer Fleet v. United States*, 282 U.S. 481 (1931).

The history of constitutional limits on extraterritorial government action has been more complicated. In the nineteenth century, the Supreme Court generally maintained that government action outside the borders of the *nation* was not constrained by anyone's constitutional rights. See, e.g., *Ross v. McIntyre*, 140 U.S. 453 (1891) (no constitutional rights in trial for a capital offense before an American consul in Japan). In a series of decisions known as the Insular Cases, the Supreme Court held that the Constitution does not necessarily "follow the flag," that is, the United States may acquire sovereignty of "unincorporated" possessions where it will be bound only by those provisions of the Constitution that the Court deems "fundamental." See *Downes v. Bidwell*, 182 U.S. 244 (1901); *Torres v. Puerto Rico*, 442 U.S. 465 (1979).

In 1957, however, in *Reid v. Covert*, 354 U.S. 1 (1957), the Supreme Court held that even in foreign countries, the requirements of trial by jury and indictment by grand jury must be afforded when United States authorities prosecute U.S. citizen civilians for capital crimes. Justice Black's plurality opinion included: "The United States is entirely a creature of the Constitution. Its power and authority have no other source. It can only act in accordance with all the limitations imposed by the Constitution."

Black wrote in case involving a U.S. citizen abroad. Might it apply as well to someone not a citizen? In the years that followed, some courts interpreted *Reid v. Covert* as implying that all provisions of the Bill of Rights apply equally outside the borders of the United States, and some courts interpreted it as implying that extraterritorial constitutional rights apply equally to citizens and aliens.

The Supreme Court transformed the terms of the debate in the following 1990 decision, in which it held that the Warrant Clause of the Fourth Amendment placed no restrictions on searches of property in a foreign country belonging to a foreign national not resident in the United States.

United States v. Verdugo–Urquidez

494 U.S. 259 (1990).

[Verdugo–Urquidez, a citizen and resident of Mexico, was accused of leading a violent narcotics-smuggling organization, and of directing the torture and murder of a U.S. narcotics agent. He was arrested in Mexico and delivered to the United States. Shortly thereafter, U.S. agents and Mexican police searched Verdugo–Urquidez's Mexican residence and found evidence relating to the smuggling operation. In the resulting prosecution, the lower courts granted Verdugo–Urquidez's motion to suppress that evidence on the ground that it had been obtained without a U.S. warrant, in violation of his Fourth Amendment rights.]

■ CHIEF JUSTICE REHNQUIST delivered the opinion of the Court.

The question presented by this case is whether the Fourth Amendment applies to the search and seizure by United States agents of property that is owned by a nonresident alien and located in a foreign country. We hold that it does not.

. . .

The Fourth Amendment provides:

> The right of the people to be secure in their persons, houses, papers, and effects, against unreasonable searches and seizures, shall not be violated, and no Warrants shall issue, but upon probable cause, supported by Oath or affirmation, and particularly describing the place to be searched, and the persons or things to be seized.

That text, by contrast with the Fifth and Sixth Amendments, extends its reach only to "the people." "[T]he people" seems to have been a term of art employed in select parts of the Constitution. ... While this textual exegesis is by no means conclusive, it suggests that "the people" protected by the Fourth Amendment, and by the First and Second Amendments, and to whom rights and powers are reserved in the Ninth and Tenth Amendments, refers to a class of persons who are part of a national community or who have otherwise developed sufficient connection with this country to be considered part of that community.... The language of these Amendments contrasts with the words "person" and "accused" used in the Fifth and Sixth Amendments regulating procedure in criminal cases.

What we know of the history of the drafting of the Fourth Amendment also suggests that its purpose was to restrict searches and seizures which might be conducted by the United States in domestic matters....

. . .

The global view taken by the Court of Appeals of the application of the Constitution is also contrary to this Court's decisions in the Insular Cases, which held that not every constitutional provision applies to governmental activity even where the United States has sovereign power. . . . If that is true with respect to territories ultimately governed by Congress, respondent's claim that the protections of the Fourth Amendment extend to aliens in foreign nations is even weaker. And certainly, it is not open to us in light of the Insular Cases to endorse the view that every constitutional provision applies wherever the United States Government exercises its power.

Indeed, we have rejected the claim that aliens are entitled to Fifth Amendment rights outside the sovereign territory of the United States. In *Johnson v. Eisentrager,* 339 U.S. 763 (1950), the Court held that enemy aliens arrested in China and imprisoned in Germany after World War II could not obtain writs of habeas corpus in our federal courts on the ground that their convictions for war crimes had violated the Fifth Amendment and other constitutional provisions. The *Eisentrager* opinion acknowledged that in some cases constitutional provisions extend beyond the citizenry; "[t]he alien . . . has been accorded a generous and ascending scale of rights as he increases his identity with our society." But our rejection of extraterritorial application of the Fifth Amendment was emphatic. . . .

. . .

To support his all-encompassing view of the Fourth Amendment, respondent points to language from the plurality opinion in *Reid v. Covert,* 354 U.S. 1 (1957). . . . Four Justices "reject[ed] the idea that when the United States acts against citizens abroad it can do so free of the Bill of Rights." The plurality went on to say:

> The United States is entirely a creature of the Constitution. Its power and authority have no other source. It can only act in accordance with all the limitations imposed by the Constitution. When the Government reaches out to punish a citizen who is abroad, the shield which the Bill of Rights and other parts of the Constitution provide to protect his life and liberty should not be stripped away just because he happens to be in another land.

Respondent urges that we interpret this discussion to mean that federal officials are constrained by the Fourth Amendment wherever and against whomever they act. But the holding of *Reid* stands for no such sweeping proposition: it decided that United States citizens stationed abroad could invoke the protection of the Fifth and Sixth Amendments. The concurrences by Justices Frankfurter and Harlan in *Reid* resolved the case on much narrower grounds than the plurality and declined even to hold that United States citizens were entitled to the full range of constitutional protections in all overseas criminal prosecutions. . . . See id., at 75 (Harlan, J., concurring in result) ("I agree with my brother FRANKFURTER that . . . we have before us a question analogous, ultimately, to issues of due process; one can say, in fact, that the question of which specific safeguards of the Constitution are appropriately to be applied in a particular context overseas can be reduced to the issue of what process is 'due' a defendant in the particular circumstances of a particular case"). Since respondent is not a United States citizen, he can derive no comfort from the *Reid* holding.

Verdugo–Urquidez also relies on a series of cases in which we have held that aliens enjoy certain constitutional rights.... These cases, however, establish only that aliens receive constitutional protections when they have come within the territory of the United States and developed substantial connections with this country.... Respondent is an alien who has had no previous significant voluntary connection with the United States, so these cases avail him not.

. . .

... [T]he result of accepting his claim would have significant and deleterious consequences for the United States in conducting activities beyond its boundaries. The rule adopted by the Court of Appeals would apply not only to law enforcement operations abroad, but also to other foreign policy operations which might result in "searches or seizures." The United States frequently employs Armed Forces outside this country—over 200 times in our history—for the protection of American citizens or national security. Application of the Fourth Amendment to those circumstances could significantly disrupt the ability of the political branches to respond to foreign situations involving our national interest. Were respondent to prevail, aliens with no attachment to this country might well bring actions for damages to remedy claimed violations of the Fourth Amendment in foreign countries or in international waters.... The Members of the Executive and Legislative Branches are sworn to uphold the Constitution, and they presumably desire to follow its commands. But the Court of Appeals' global view of its applicability would plunge them into a sea of uncertainty as to what might be reasonable in the way of searches and seizures conducted abroad. . . .

. . .

For better or for worse, we live in a world of nation-states in which our Government must be able to "functio[n] effectively in the company of sovereign nations." Some who violate our laws may live outside our borders under a regime quite different from that which obtains in this country. Situations threatening to important American interests may arise half-way around the globe, situations which in the view of the political branches of our Government require an American response with armed force. If there are to be restrictions on searches and seizures which occur incident to such American action, they must be imposed by the political branches through diplomatic understanding, treaty, or legislation.

The judgment of the Court of Appeals is accordingly

Reversed.

■ J<small>USTICE</small> K<small>ENNEDY</small>, concurring....

... Though it must be beyond dispute that persons outside the United States did not and could not assent to the Constitution, that is quite irrelevant to any construction of the powers conferred or the limitations imposed by it. As Justice Story explained in his Commentaries:

> A government may originate in the voluntary compact or assent of the people of several states, or of a people never before united, and yet when adopted and ratified by them, be no longer a matter resting in compact; but become an executed government or constitution, a fundamental law, and not a mere league....

... For somewhat similar reasons, I cannot place any weight on the reference to "the people" in the Fourth Amendment as a source of restricting its protections....

... The question before us then becomes what constitutional standards apply when the Government acts, in reference to an alien, within its sphere of foreign operations. ... Justice Harlan made this observation in his opinion concurring in the judgment in *Reid v. Covert*:

> I cannot agree with the suggestion that every provision of the Constitution must always be deemed automatically applicable to American citizens in every part of the world. ... [T]here are provisions in the Constitution which do not necessarily apply in all circumstances in every foreign place. In other words, it seems to me that the basic teaching of *Ross* and the Insular Cases is that there is no rigid and abstract rule that Congress, as a condition precedent to exercising power over Americans overseas, must exercise it subject to all the guarantees of the Constitution, no matter what the conditions and considerations are that would make adherence to a specific guarantee altogether impracticable and anomalous.

The conditions and considerations of this case would make adherence to the Fourth Amendment's warrant requirement impracticable and anomalous. ... The absence of local judges or magistrates available to issue warrants, the differing and perhaps unascertainable conceptions of reasonableness and privacy that prevail abroad, and the need to cooperate with foreign officials all indicate that the Fourth Amendment's warrant requirement should not apply in Mexico as it does in this country. For this reason, in addition to the other persuasive justifications stated by the Court, I agree that no violation of the Fourth Amendment has occurred in the case before us. The rights of a citizen, as to whom the United States has continuing obligations, are not presented by this case.

· · ·

[Justice Stevens concurred in the judgment, on the ground that the challenged search was not "unreasonable," and that the Warrant Clause does not apply extraterritorially because American magistrates have no power to authorize extraterritorial searches.]

■ JUSTICE BRENNAN, with whom JUSTICE MARSHALL joins, dissenting ... The Court today creates an antilogy: the Constitution authorizes our Government to enforce our criminal laws abroad, but when Government agents exercise this authority, the Fourth Amendment does not travel with them.

This cannot be. At the very least, the Fourth Amendment is an unavoidable correlative of the Government's power to enforce the criminal law.

. . .

By concluding that respondent is not one of "the people" protected by the Fourth Amendment, the majority disregards basic notions of mutuality. If we expect aliens to obey our laws, aliens should be able to expect that we will obey our Constitution when we investigate, prosecute, and punish them. We have recognized this fundamental principle of mutuality since the time of the Framers. James Madison, universally recognized as the primary architect of the Bill of Rights, emphasized the importance of mutuality when he spoke out against the Alien and Sedition Acts less than a decade after the adoption of the Fourth Amendment:

> [I]t does not follow, because aliens are not parties to the Constitution, as citizens are parties to it, that, whilst they actually conform to it, they have no right to its protection. Aliens are no more parties to the laws than they are parties to the Constitution; yet it will not be disputed that, as they owe, on one hand, a temporary obedience, they are entitled, in return, to their protection and advantage.

Madison's Report on the Virginia Resolutions (1800), reprinted in 4 Elliot's Debates 556 (2d ed. 1836).

. . . [T]he Framers of the Bill of Rights did not purport to "create" rights. Rather, they designed the Bill of Rights to prohibit our Government from infringing rights and liberties presumed to be pre-existing. . . . Bestowing rights and delineating protected groups would have been inconsistent with the Drafters' fundamental conception of a Bill of Rights as a limitation on the Government's conduct with respect to all whom it seeks to govern. . . .

[Dissenting opinion of Justice Blackmun omitted.]

Notes

1. Different passages in the *Verdugo-Urquidez* opinions suggest support for a variety of propositions concerning the constitutional rights of aliens. Among others:

> (i) nonresident aliens, unlike resident aliens, are not included in "the people," and have no Fourth Amendment rights against searches and seizures of their property outside the borders of the United States;

> (ii) no aliens have any constitutional rights whatsoever with regard to United States government action outside the borders of the United States;

> (iii) the extent of an alien's constitutional rights against U.S. governmental action outside the borders of the United States is determined by a "due process" analysis, and does not include rights whose application would be "impracticable and anomalous";

(iv) aliens are protected by constitutional rights in accordance with their terms whenever and wherever the United States exercises sovereignty over them.

What normative arguments could justify each of those propositions?

2. Despite the fact that the first opinion is designated the Opinion of the Court, and Justice Kennedy states that he concurs in it, the reasons he gives for his crucial fifth vote are so different that arguably his "due process" analysis provides the narrowest explanation for the holding.

3. Consider the following perspective on the proper scope of constitutional rights:

> ... [N]either the Declaration of Independence nor the early state constitutions articulated the character of the social compact. The Declaration of Independence declared that "to secure these rights, Governments are instituted among Men." Was the Constitution only a compact establishing a government to secure the individual rights of the people creating it? Or, since they believed that all men, everywhere, "are endowed by their Creator with certain unalienable Rights," did the framers intend to create a government that would secure and respect the unalienable rights of all human beings, including those in their midst not party to the contract, and human beings in other societies upon whom their new government might impinge? ...

> The social compact ... is not merely an arrangement for mutual protection; it is a compact to establish a "community of righteousness." It declares that a government instituted to secure rights must respect those rights. The United States must secure and respect not only the rights of the people who were party to the compact, but also of all others who come within its jurisdiction. If, in a world of states, the United States is not in a position to secure the rights of all individuals everywhere, it is always in a position to respect them. Our federal government must not invade the individual rights of any human being. The choice in the Bill of Rights of the word "person" rather than "citizen" was not fortuitous; nor was the absence of a geographical limitation. Both reflect a commitment to respect the individual rights of all human beings.

> The compact recognizes the rights of all men and women everywhere and creates a government that must respect these rights. The United States may not deprive a person, whether a citizen or foreign national, of his life, liberty, or property without due process of law. Our government may not take anyone's property without just compensation—citizen or alien, abroad or at home. I do not suggest that the Constitution "applies" throughout the world or that it gives "rights" to all human beings everywhere. The Constitution does not give rights, not even to us. Our rights and the rights of people everywhere, do not derive from the Constitution; they antecede it. The effect of the Constitution, however, is to require the United States government to

respect these human rights, with which all men and women are endowed equally.

Louis Henkin, *The Constitution as Compact and as Conscience: Individual Rights Abroad and at Our Gates*, 27 Wm. & Mary L. Rev. 11, 31–32 (1985). For the articulation of an alternative "mutuality of obligation" approach to determining the scope of constitutional rights, similar to that reflected in portions of the dissenting opinions in *Verdugo*, see Gerald L. Neuman, Strangers to the Constitution: Immigrants, Borders, and Fundamental Law (1996).

2. IMMIGRATION LAW AND THE U.S. CONSTITUTION

The constitutional limits on the power of Congress to control immigration into the United States (and related matters) have also been the subject of continuing controversy. The seminal case on the subject of federal immigration power was the so-called *Chinese Exclusion Case*, decided shortly after the federal government had begun to restrict immigration to the United States.

The Chinese Exclusion Case

(Chae Chan Ping v. United States)
130 U.S. 581 (1889).

■ FIELD, J. . . .

The appeal involves a consideration of the validity of the act of congress of October 1, 1888, prohibiting Chinese laborers from entering the United States who had departed before its passage, having a certificate issued under the act of 1882 as amended by the act of 1884, granting them permission to return. The validity of the act is assailed as being in effect an expulsion from the country of Chinese laborers, in violation of existing treaties between the United States and the government of China, and of rights vested in them under the laws of congress. . . .

The discovery of gold in California in 1848, as is well known, was followed by a large immigration thither from all parts of the world, attracted not only by the hope of gain from the mines, but from the great prices paid for all kinds of labor. The news of the discovery penetrated China, and laborers came from there in great numbers, a few with their own means, but by far the greater number under contract with employers, for whose benefit they worked. These laborers readily secured employment, and, as domestic servants, and in various kinds of outdoor work, proved to be exceedingly useful. For some years little opposition was made to them, except when they sought to work in the mines, but, as their numbers increased, they began to engage in various mechanical pursuits and trades, and thus came in competition with our artisans and mechanics, as well as our laborers in the field. . . . As they grew in numbers each year the people of the coast saw, or believed they saw, in the facility of immigration, and in the crowded millions of China, where population presses upon the means of subsistence, great danger that at no distant day that portion of our country would be overrun by them, unless prompt action was taken to restrict their immigration. The people there accordingly petitioned earnestly for protective legislation. . . .

. . .

. . . That the government of the United States, through the action of the legislative department, can exclude aliens from its territory is a proposition which we do not think open to controversy. Jurisdiction over its own territory to that extent is an incident of every independent nation. It is a part of its independence. If it could not exclude aliens it would be to that extent subject to the control of another power. . . .

While under our constitution and form of government the great mass of local matters is controlled by local authorities, the United States, in their relation to foreign countries and their subjects or citizens, are one nation, invested with powers which belong to independent nations, the exercise of which can be invoked for the maintenance of its absolute independence and security throughout its entire territory. The powers to declare war, make treaties, suppress insurrection, repel invasion, regulate foreign commerce, secure republican governments to the states, and admit subjects of other nations to citizenship, are all sovereign powers, restricted in their exercise only by the constitution itself and considerations of public policy and justice which control, more or less, the conduct of all civilized nations. . . .

The control of local matters being left to local authorities, and national matters being intrusted to the government of the Union, the problem of free institutions existing over a widely extended country, having different climates and varied interests, has been happily solved. For local interests the several states of the Union exist, but for national purposes, embracing our relations with foreign nations, we are but one people, one nation, one power. To preserve its independence, and give security against foreign aggression and encroachment, is the highest duty of every nation, and to attain these ends nearly all other considerations are to be subordinated. It matters not in what form such aggression and encroachment come, whether from the foreign nation acting in its national character, or from vast hordes of its people crowding in upon us. The government, possessing the powers which are to be exercised for protection and security, is clothed with authority to determine the occasion on which the powers shall be called forth; and its determinations, so far as the subjects affected are concerned, are necessarily conclusive upon all its departments and officers. If, therefore, the government of the United States, through its legislative department, considers the presence of foreigners of a different race in this country, who will not assimilate with us, to be dangerous to its peace and security, their exclusion is not to be stayed because at the time there are no actual hostilities with the nation of which the foreigners are subjects. The existence of war would render the necessity of the proceeding only more obvious and pressing. The same necessity, in a less pressing degree, may arise when war does not exist, and the same authority which adjudges the necessity in one case must also determine it in the other. In both cases its determination is conclusive upon the judiciary. If the government of the country of which the foreigners excluded are subjects is dissatisfied with this action, it can make complaint to the executive head of our government, or resort to any other measure which, in its judgment, its interests or dignity may demand; and there lies its only remedy. . . .

Notes

1.   Does *the Chinese Exclusion Case* imply that the federal immigration power is not subject to constitutional limitations? That the courts should refrain from enforcing whatever constitutional limitations might exist? Is its holding an example of the political question doctrine? Compare *United States v. Curtiss–Wright Export Corp.*, 299 U.S. 304 (1936); Henkin, Foreign Affairs and the U.S. Constitution ch. 1 (2d ed. 1996).

2.   As the case law has developed, the applicability of constitutional limitations to the immigration process has depended on a variety of factors, including distinctions between exclusion and deportation, and distinctions between procedure and substance. In *Fong Yue Ting v. United States*, 149 U.S. 698 (1893), the Supreme Court extended the deferential approach of the *Chinese Exclusion Case* from the exclusion of arriving passengers to deportation of resident aliens from within the United States. In *Yamataya v. Fisher*, 189 U.S. 86 (1903), however, the Supreme Court distinguished between the substantive criteria for deportation of aliens and the procedures by which aliens are deported, and held that deportation procedures must be measured against the requirements of the Due Process Clause of the Fifth Amendment. Subsequently, in *United States ex rel. Knauff v. Shaughnessy*, 338 U.S. 537 (1950), the Supreme Court held that an arriving nonresident alien is not entitled to procedural due process when the government seeks to exclude her. The Court further held that neither procedural due process nor substantive due process limits the federal government's power to detain indefinitely an alien who is excludable but whom other countries are unwilling to receive. *Shaughnessy v. United States ex rel. Mezei*, 345 U.S. 206 (1953).

3.   Since the 1970's, the Supreme Court has opened the door to some limited degree of judicial review of substantive immigration criteria. In *Fiallo v. Bell*, 430 U.S. 787 (1977), the Court confronted claims of gender discrimination and discrimination on grounds of illegitimacy in the rules under which citizens and resident aliens could obtain immigration visas for their parents or children. Although the majority upheld the challenged statutes, it observed that "Our cases reflect acceptance of a limited judicial responsibility under the Constitution even with respect to the power of Congress to regulate the admission and exclusion of aliens, and there is no occasion to consider in this case whether there may be actions of the Congress with respect to aliens that are so essentially political in character as to be nonjusticiable." At the same time, the Court declined to apply the usual standards of review for gender discrimination or illegitimacy discrimination under equal protection doctrine. So long as the statutory rule was

supported by a "facially legitimate and bona fide reason," the Court would not look behind that reason, nor balance it against the constitutional interests of the persons affected (citing *Kleindienst v. Mandel*, 408 U.S. 753 (1972)). The Court explained that "[s]ince decisions in these matters may implicate our relations with foreign powers, and since a wide variety of classifications must be defined in the light of changing political and economic circumstances, such decisions are frequently of a character more appropriate to either the Legislature or the Executive than to the Judiciary."

Lower court decisions have understood *Fiallo* as applying the "rational basis" test to substantive criteria for the admission or exclusion of aliens.

4.   Since aliens in the United States enjoy constitutional rights to freedom of speech and to equal protection of the laws, do not these rights place constraints on congressional power to exclude or deport? If Congress cannot impose criminal sanctions on an alien's exercise of free speech rights, can Congress nonetheless exclude or deport the alien for that very reason? Might affording rational basis review, instead of no judicial review at all, help eliminate the anomaly?

CHAPTER 2

RIGHTS UNDER FEDERAL LAW AND UNDER STATE CONSTITUTIONS

A. RIGHTS UNDER FEDERAL LAW

Human rights are commonly equated with constitutional rights, but society's undertakings to respect and ensure rights do not require that they be given constitutional character. (Compare Article 2 of the Covenant on Civil and Political Rights, Part III, p. 315). Society's commitment to realize "economic and social rights" in particular is commonly not written into constitutions. (See Part IV, Chapter 3.) Even civil and political rights, however, are not always and completely "constitutionalized," and important guarantees for individual rights are set forth in national or local legislation. Since constitutions generally protect only against "state action," see p. 152 above, insuring rights against private violation depends on legislation or on the common law.

In the United States, in addition to rights recognized and protected by the U.S. Constitution, individuals enjoy rights granted by Congress acting under its powers to implement the Thirteenth, Fourteenth, and other amendments, or under its general legislative powers. In particular, the power of Congress to regulate interstate and foreign commerce, and the "spending power" ("to provide for the general welfare"), have provided federal sources of authority for legislation to protect, ensure and enhance individual rights.

Congress enacted civil rights laws during the years immediately following the Civil War. Some of them were held to be beyond the power of Congress because they sought to protect rights against private (not state) action. See p. 152 above. Congress enacted another series of Civil Rights Acts in the 1960's. See below Professor Monaghan has observed that since *Roe v. Wade*, all new fundamental rights have been essentially statutory. Henry Monaghan, *The Age of Statutory Fundamental Rights,* 14 Tocqueville Rev. 139 (1993).

Congress has provided both criminal punishment for, and civil remedies against, those who violate individual rights, in particular against denials of the equal protection of the laws. Congress has provided for civil action by the victim of discrimination and made provision for investigation of complaints by a special body, the Community Relations Service of the Department of Justice. 42 U.S.C. §§ 2000a–2000h (1994). Congress has also granted authority to the U.S. Attorney–General to institute civil actions against violators.

Civil Rights Legislation

The Declaration of Independence declared that all men are created equal, and implies that all (equally) are endowed with (equal) inalienable rights, but there was no reference to "equality," to equal rights, or to the equal protection of the laws in the original United States Constitution. The right to equal protection of the laws was added by the Fourteenth Amendment; it was made applicable to the federal government by interpretation in *Bolling v. Sharpe*, p. 192 above.

The Constitution and especially the Bill of Rights recognize equality in rights in that the rights protected are guaranteed to all persons: the freedom of speech and religion, the right to a jury trial, the elements of due process of law, are enjoyed by all persons, equally and without discrimination. In addition to equality in rights, the Constitution now provides equal protection of the laws for all, although law may distinguish and may provide differently for persons differently situated.

The commitment to equality is reflected in the various civil rights acts adopted immediately after the Civil War and again in the 1960's. All the civil rights acts were designed primarily to give remedies against invidious discrimination in the enjoyment of basic rights. For example, 42 U.S.C. § 1981(a), which derives from the Civil Rights Act of 1866, provides: "All persons within the jurisdiction of the United States shall have the same right in every State and Territory to make and enforce contracts, to sue, be parties, give evidence, and to the full and equal benefit of all laws and proceedings for the security of persons and property as is enjoyed by white citizens, and shall be subject to like punishment, pains, penalties, taxes, licenses, and exactions of every kind, and to no other."*

The civil rights acts and their focus on non-discrimination have engendered a major area of United States constitutional law, which includes the idea of "suspect classifications" and various levels of judicial scrutiny, leading to a requirement of extraordinary, or even compelling, public interests to justify certain distinctions or classifications. See p. 220 above.

Congress enacted a series of civil rights acts beginning in 1957, the comprehensive Civil Rights Act of 1964 and occasional smaller acts thereafter. In the 1964 Act, Title II provides injunctive relief and other remedies against discrimination in places of public accommodation "if its operations affect commerce, or if discrimination or segregation by it is supported by State action." 42 U.S.C. § 2000a. Title VII prohibits discrimination in employment because of race, color, religion, sex or national origin. See 42 U.S.C. § 2000e–2.

U.S. Civil Rights acts are directed at two different targets. In substantial part, they are designed to provide remedies for violations of constitutional rights pursuant to the powers of Congress to enforce the Fourteenth

---

* In 1991, Congress enacted the Civil Rights Act of 1991 in order to "strengthen and improve Federal civil rights laws." Pub. L. 102–166 (1991). The Act amended § 1981 and added a new § 1981a. Section 1981a provides for monetary damages (not including backpay) in cases of *intentional* employment discrimination by private employers.

Amendment (or other amendments). The Civil Rights Acts also provide remedies for violations of statutory rights, by authority of the regulatory powers of Congress. See Chapter 3(c) below.

The two aspects of the Civil Rights Acts have been blurred because of doubt about the reach of the different legislative powers of Congress. Under its authority to enforce the Fourteenth Amendment, Congress can address violations by "state actors." See "State action," p. 152 above. Under its power to regulate interstate commerce, Congress can also address violations by individuals (or companies), but only if they derive from activities that are in or that substantially affect interstate commerce.

The application of the Civil Rights Acts has also engendered judicial interpretation of Congressional legislation: the courts have clarified vague and open-ended phrases, applied laws to unanticipated situations, reconciled inconsistencies, filled in unintended (or deliberate) ambiguities. In a noted instance in 1998, for example, the Court in effect rewrote (or wrote) the law of sexual harassment in the workplace in Title VII of the Civil Rights Act of 1964. See *Faragher v. City of Boca Raton,* 524 U.S. 775 (1998), and *Burlington Industries, Inc. v. Ellerth,* 524 U.S. 742 (1998).

Note: The Voting Rights Act of 1965

The right to vote is hardly indicated in the U.S. Constitution (see p. 150 above) and legislation to promote or protect a right to vote has focused primarily on the elimination of racial discrimination in voting, prohibited explicitly by the Fifteenth Amendment, as well as by the requirement of the equal protection of the laws in the Fourteenth Amendment.

The Voting Rights Act of 1965, current version codified at 42 U.S.C. §§ 1973 et seq., was a comprehensive attempt to assure against racial discrimination in voting, involving radical departures from accepted principles of federalism and transforming relations between federal and State authority in respect of voting. The Court upheld the Voting Rights Act of 1965 in principle and in its key applications, in *South Carolina v. Katzenbach,* 383 U.S. 301 (1966).

The implications of equal protection in respect of voting were elaborated by the Supreme Court in *Reynolds v. Sims,* 377 U.S. 533 (1964), and *Wesberry v. Sanders,* 376 U.S. 1 (1964). For a series of cases struggling with the problems of racial gerrymandering, see Note 7 on p. 1080.

B.   RIGHTS UNDER STATE CONSTITUTIONS

Individual rights in the United States are protected by the U.S. Constitution and by U.S. laws. But the United States is a federal system of delegated powers and many individual rights are governed and protected in the first instance by the laws and constitutions of the States. Individual rights are protected against violation by State authorities, as well as by private actors, through the State's legal system, including its common and statutory law of torts and property. Rights are protected against inadequacies in State law by State constitutions, and are commonly addressed as such before they become a matter of concern for U.S. constitutional jurisprudence.

Some State constitutions had bills of rights before the U.S. Bill of Rights was adopted. See p. 125 above. Today, all State constitutions have bills of rights, and rights under State constitutions largely parallel and duplicate rights enjoyed under the U.S. Constitution. The adoption of bills of rights in State constitutions did not replace or render unimportant the protection of individual rights under State legislation or common law. The individual continues to enjoy his or her rights under the common law, unless abrogated or modified by legislation. State legislatures are free to abridge common law rights unless doing so would violate the State constitution or the Constitution of the United States.

Some State constitutions recognize and protect rights in addition to those guaranteed by the U.S. Constitution. Moreover, even when a State constitution recognizes the same rights and even uses language identical to that of the U.S. Constitution, State courts have sometimes construed that language to provide more expansive protection than the federal courts have found to be available under the U.S. Constitution.

In *Michigan v. Long*, 463 U.S. 1032, 1041–42 (1983), the majority of the Court concluded that unless the highest State court, in deciding a case under both the federal and State constitutions, indicates "clearly and expressly" that its decision is based on a "separate, adequate and independent state ground," the Supreme Court will treat this decision as based on the federal constitution and therefore within the Supreme Court's authority to review.

In some respects, State constitutions have gone beyond the federal constitution. Whereas the U.S. Constitution has hardly been amended since the Bill of Rights and the Civil War Amendments, State constitutions are comparatively easy to amend in response to contemporary political concerns. Early, States developed a right to public education. In several instances, State courts have departed from the Supreme Court's decision upholding methods of public school financing under the Federal Constitution, finding that such methods of financing violate State constitutional provisions. See Part IV, Chapter 3 (D). Constitutions of particular States have responded to claims for "social welfare rights" which have not made it into the federal constitution. See Part IV, Chapter 3 (C). State constitutions have sometimes been interpreted to prevent the erosion of common law protections, or to add protection where an analogous provision in the federal Constitution was deemed inapplicable or insufficient. In *Arcara v. Cloud Books, Inc.*, p. 244 below, for example, the State Constitution was interpreted to afford protection for speech beyond that afforded by the U.S. Constitution as interpreted by the U.S. Supreme Court. In *Saylor v. Hall*, p. 246 below, the Kentucky court held that the State legislature may not destroy a common law right of action for negligence by terminating the period of limitations before the injury occurs. In *Ravin v. State*, p. 249

below, the Supreme Court of Alaska found in its Constitution a right of privacy that includes a right to ingest marijuana in the privacy of one's home. State courts have sometimes interpreted their constitutions as requiring different balancing of rights and public interest, or as rejecting distinctions and classifications that have been found acceptable under the Fourteenth Amendment of the U.S. Constitution. For further examples, see Part IV, Chapters 1(B)(2), 3(C) and 3(D).

For a discussion of the relationship between common law and State constitutional rights, see Judith Kaye, *Foreword: The Common Law and State Constitutional Law as Full Partners in the Protection of Individual Rights,* 23 Rutgers L.J. 727 (1992). For a general text on state constitutional law, see Robert F. Williams, State Constitutional Law: Cases and Materials. (3d ed. 1999).

Some law reviews have annual issues on state constitutional law, and others have devoted specific issues to state constitutionalism. See, e.g., *Annual Issue on New York State Constitutional Law,* 14 Touro L. Rev. 560 (Spring 1998); *Fifth Annual Issue on State Constitutional Law,* 26 Rutgers L.J. 907 (1995); *The Idaho Constitution Symposium Edition,* 31 Idaho L. Rev. 387 (1995); *The Law of the Land: Tennessee Constitutional Law,* 61 Tenn. L. Rev. 405 (1994); *Symposium, State Constitutional History: In Search of a Usable Past,* 53 Alb. L. Rev. 255 (1989); *Symposium, The Emergence of State Constitutional Law,* 63 Tex. L. Rev. 959 (1985).

William Brennan, Jr., *The Bill of Rights and the States: The Revival of State Constitutions as Guardians of Individual Rights*

61 N.Y.U. L. Rev. 535, 537–552 (1986).

Prior to the passage of [the Fourteenth] Amendment, the Supreme Court had made it plain that the Bill of Rights was applicable only to the federal government. . . .

Only after the Civil War did the demand arise for the national protection of individual rights against abuses of state power. The war exposed a serious flaw in the notion that states could be trusted to nurture individual rights: the assumption of "an identity of interests between the states, as the level of government closest to the people, and the primary corpus of civil rights and liberties of the people themselves—an identity incomplete from the start and . . . impossible to maintain after the great battle over slavery had been fought." In fact, the primary impetus to the adoption of the Fourteenth Amendment was the fear that the former Confederate states would deny newly freed persons the protection of life, liberty, and property formally provided by the state constitutions. But the majestic goals of the Fourteenth Amendment were framed in terms of more general application. . . .

. . .

The issue of application of the Bill of Rights to the states involved two separate questions: whether the guarantee in question should apply to the states, and what its content should be when applied. For several years now, there has been an unmistakable trend in the Court to read the guarantees of individual liberty restrictively, which means that the content of the rights applied to the states is likewise diminished.

. . .

This trend is not visible solely in the enfeebled protection of individual rights under the Federal Bill and the Fourteenth Amendment. The venerable remedy of *habeas corpus* has been sharply limited in the name of federalism, the Equal Protection Clause has been denied its full reach, and a series of decisions shaping the doctrines of justiciability, jurisdiction, and remedy "increasingly bar the federal courthouse door in the absence of showings probably impossible to make."

For a decade now, I have felt certain that the Court's contraction of federal rights and remedies on grounds of federalism should be interpreted as a plain invitation to state courts to step into the breach. In the 1960's, the "understandable enthusiasm that championed the application of the Bill of Rights to the states . . . contribute[d] to the disparagement of other rights retained by the people, namely state constitutional rights." Busy interpreting the onslaught of federal constitutional rulings in state criminal cases, the state courts fell silent on the subject of their own constitutions. Now, the diminution of federal scrutiny and protection out of purported deference to the states mandates the assumption of a more responsible state court role. And state courts have taken seriously their obligation as coequal guardians of civil rights and liberties.

As is well known, federal preservation of civil liberties is a minimum, which the states may surpass so long as there is no clash with federal law. Between 1970 and 1984, state courts, increasingly reluctant to follow the federal lead, have handed down over 250 published opinions holding that the constitutional minimums set by the United States Supreme Court were insufficient to satisfy the more stringent requirements of state constitutional law. When the United States Supreme Court cut back the reach of First Amendment protections, the California Supreme Court responded by interpreting its state constitution to protect freedom of speech in shopping centers and malls. The Massachusetts, Pennsylvania, and Washington courts responded in kind when confronted with similar questions involving freedom of expression. Under the federal Constitution, a motorist stopped by a police officer for a simple traffic violation may be subject to a full body search and a search of his vehicle. Such police conduct offends state constitutional provisions in California and Hawaii, unless the officer has articulable reasons to suspect other illegal conduct. South Dakota has rejected the inventory search rule announced in *South Dakota v. Opperman*. Other examples abound. Truly, the state courts have responded with marvelous enthusiasm to many not-so-subtle invitations to fill the constitutional gaps left by the decisions of the Supreme Court majority.

As Professor Sager has so convincingly argued, the institutional position of the national Supreme Court may cause it to "underenforce"
constitutional rules. The national Court must remain highly sensitive to
concerns of state and local autonomy, obviously less of a problem for state
courts, which are local, accountable decisionmakers. It must further be
remembered that the Federal Bill was enacted to place limits on the federal
government while state bills are widely perceived as granting affirmative
rights to citizens.

In addition, the Supreme Court formulates a national standard which,
some suggest, must represent the common denominator to allow for diversity and local experimentation. In the Warren era, federalism was unsuccessfully invoked to support the view of the anti-incorporationists that the
rights granted in federal courts need not apply with the same breadth or
scope in state courts. Dissenting Justices extolled the virtues of allowing
the States to serve as "laboratories" and objected to incorporation as
"press[ing] the States into a procrustean federal mold." Justice Harlan and
others felt that the phenomenon of incorporation complicated the federal
situation, creating a kind of "constitutional schizophrenia" as the Court
attempted both to recognize diversity and faithfully to enforce the Bill of
Rights. In order to make room for such diversity, Justice Harlan felt that
the Bill should not apply to the states exactly as it applied to the federal
government.

As is well known, however, I believe that the Fourteenth Amendment
fully applied the provisions of the Federal Bill of Rights to the states,
thereby creating a federal floor of protection and that the Constitution and
the Fourteenth Amendment allow diversity only above and beyond this
federal constitutional floor. Experimentation which endangers the continued existence of our national rights and liberties cannot be permitted; a call
for that brand of diversity is, in my view, antithetical to the requirements
of the Fourteenth Amendment. While state experimentation may flourish
in the space above this floor, we have made a national commitment to this
minimum level of protection through enactment of the Fourteenth Amendment. This reconciliation of local autonomy and guaranteed individual
rights is the only one consistent with our constitutional structure. And the
growing dialogue between the Supreme Court and the state courts on the
topic of fundamental rights enables all courts to discern more rapidly the
"evolving standards of decency that mark the progress of a maturing
society."

. . .

State experimentation cannot be excoriated simply because the experiments provide more rather than less protection for civil liberties and
individual rights. While the Fourteenth Amendment does not permit a
state to fall below a common national standard, above this level, our
federalism permits diversity. As tempting as it may be to harmonize results
under state and national constitutions, our federalism permits state courts
to provide greater protection to individual civil rights and liberties if they
wish to do so. The Supreme Court has no conceivable justification for

interfering in a case plainly decided on independent and adequate state grounds.

Finally, those who regard judicial review as inconsistent with our democratic system—a view I do not share—should find constitutional interpretation by the state judiciary far less objectionable than activist intervention by their federal counterparts. It cannot be denied that state court judges are often more immediately "subject to majoritarian pressures than federal courts, and are correspondingly less independent than their federal counterparts." Federal judges are guaranteed a salary and lifetime tenure; in contrast, state judges often are elected, or, at the least, must succeed in retention elections. The relatively greater degree of political accountability of state courts militates in favor of continued absolute deference to their interpretations of their own constitutions. Moreover, state constitutions are often relatively easy to amend; in many states the process is open to citizen initiative. Prudential considerations requiring a cautious use of the power of judicial review, though not insignificant, should "weigh less heavily upon elected state judges than on tenured federal judges."

Some critics fear that the Supreme Court will become increasingly hostile to state courts' protection of individual rights and will meddle in those cases, refusing to find that a decision is based on independent and adequate state grounds. I am not so pessimistic. Despite the recent tendency of the Court to give gratuitous advice to state citizens to amend their constitutions, I believe that the Court has set appropriate "ground rules" for federalism with its recent decision in *Michigan v. Long*. If a state court plainly states that its judgment rests on its analysis of state law, the United States Supreme Court will honor that statement and will not review the state court decision. So long as the Court adheres strictly to this rule, state courts may shield state constitutional law from federal interference and insure that its growth is not stunted by national decisionmakers. I join Justice Mosk of the California Supreme Court in his most apt observation: "I detect a phoenix-like resurrection of federalism, or, if you prefer, states' rights, evidenced by state courts' reliance upon provisions of state constitutions."

This said, I must conclude on a warning note. Federal courts remain an indispensable safeguard of individual rights against governmental abuse. The revitalization of state constitutional law is no excuse for the weakening of federal protections and prohibitions. Slashing away at federal rights and remedies undermines our federal system. The strength of our system is that it "provides a double source of protection for the rights of our citizens. Federalism is not served when the federal half of that protection is crippled."

Federalism does not require that one level of government take a back seat to the other when the question involved is one of individual civil and political rights; federalism is not an excuse for one court system to abdicate responsibility to another. Indeed, federal courts have been delegated a special responsibility for the definition and enforcement of the guarantees of the Bill of Rights and the Fourteenth Amendment. . . .

Freedom of Expression Under the New York Constitution.

Arcara v. Cloud Books, Inc.

503 N.E.2d 492 (N.Y.1986).

■ WACHTLER, CHIEF JUDGE.

. . . Briefly the case reaches us in the following posture. Cloud Books operates a store where it sells adult books and shows movies which are sexually explicit but not obscene. Certain patrons have used the premises for indecent and illegal sexual acts. The owner is aware of the activities but has done nothing to prevent them; however, there is no contention that the owner is criminally responsible.

A divided [U.S.] Supreme Court held that the bookstore's First Amendment rights were not affected because they were not sought to be affected. The majority in that court held that the object of the order [to close the bookstore] is the customers' illegal sexual activity which, it noted, "manifests absolutely no element of protected expression" (106 S.Ct. at p. 3177). To the extent the order might have an effect on the defendant's legitimate bookselling activities, it was deemed to be too remote to implicate First Amendment concerns. The "least restrictive means test" was held to be applicable only when the government's action was triggered by and directly aimed at curtailing "conduct that has an expressive element". . . .

We, of course, are bound by Supreme Court decisions defining and limiting Federal constitutional rights but "in determining the scope and effect of the guarantees of fundamental rights of the individual in the Constitution of the State of New York, this court is bound to exercise its independent judgment and is not bound by a decision of the Supreme Court of the United States limiting the scope of similar guarantees in the Constitution of the United States." The Supreme Court's role in construing the Federal Bill of Rights is to establish minimal standards for individual rights applicable throughout the Nation. The function of the comparable provisions of the State Constitution, if they are not to be considered purely redundant, is to supplement those rights to meet the needs and expectations of the particular State.

Freedom of expression in books, movies and the arts, generally, is one of those areas in which there is great diversity among the States. Thus it is an area in which the Supreme Court has displayed great reluctance to expand Federal constitutional protections, holding instead that this is a matter essentially governed by community standards (*Miller v. California*, 413 U.S. 15). However, New York has a long history and tradition of fostering freedom of expression, often tolerating and supporting works which in other States would be found offensive to the community. Thus, the minimal national standard established by the Supreme Court for First

Amendment rights cannot be considered dispositive in determining the scope of this State's constitutional guarantee of freedom of expression.

It is established in this State that the government may not impose a prior restraint on freedom of expression to silence an unpopular view, absent a showing on the record that such expression will immediately and irreparably create public injury. It is also settled that when government regulation designed to carry out a legitimate and important State objective would incidentally burden free expression, the government's action cannot be sustained unless the State can prove that it is no broader than needed to achieve its purpose. Although these holdings were based essentially on First Amendment principles, they are equally applicable under the State Constitution, since "at the very least, the guarantee of freedom of expression set forth in our State Constitution is of no lesser vitality than that set forth in the Federal Constitution".

The only remaining question is whether the State constitutional guarantee of freedom of expression is implicated by an order closing the defendant's bookstore to prevent illegal acts by patrons. There can be no doubt that bookselling is a constitutionally protected activity or that closing a bookstore for a year may have a substantial impact on that activity. The prosecutor urges that this impact may be constitutionally ignored when, as here, the State's purpose is not to interfere with the store's legitimate bookselling activities but is aimed at preventing patrons from committing illegal acts having no expressive content. That, however, is just another way of saying that the impact of the State's action is not direct but only incidental. Actions of this type are subject to lesser scrutiny than those directed at restraining free expression, but they cannot be said to have absolutely no constitutional implications. The crucial factor in determining whether State action affects freedom of expression is the impact of the action on the protected activity and not the nature of the activity which prompted the government to act. The test, in traditional terms, is not who is aimed at but who is hit.

Of course a bookstore cannot claim an exemption from statutes of general operation aimed at preventing nuisances or hazards to the public health and safety. It is, however, entitled to special protection, and no undue burden is placed on the State by requiring it to prove that in seeking to close the store it has chosen a course no broader than necessary to accomplish its purpose. If other sanctions, such as arresting the offenders, or injunctive relief prove unavailing, then its burden would be met.

Finally, we note that not every government regulation of general application, having some impact on free expression, implicates constitutional guarantees. Arresting a newspaper reporter for a traffic violation is one example where the impact would not be constitutionally cognizable, as Justice O'Connor noted in her concurring opinion at the Supreme Court. But closing a bookstore for a year, as is required by this statute, cannot be said to have such a slight and indirect impact on free expression as to have no significance constitutionally.

Accordingly, on reargument following remand from the United States Supreme Court, the order of the Appellate Division should be modified to grant defendant partial summary judgment dismissing those portions of the second cause of action seeking an order directing the closing of the premises in question.

Constitutionalization of Common Law Remedies in Kentucky

Saylor v. Hall

497 S.W.2d 218 (Ky.1973).

■ REED, JUSTICE

The operative facts are: In May 1955, the defendant, E.H. Hall, a builder, completed construction of a house on a lot he owned. Shortly thereafter, he sold the house and lot to the defendants, Thomas and Kathryn Johnson, who thereafter owned and controlled the property. The house was originally occupied in June 1955, when the improvements had been substantially completed. In July 1969, James Saylor and his wife rented the property from the Johnsons and moved in. The Saylors had two children, Jimmy, then age 6, and Marvin, then age 4. Four months later, while the Saylor children were sitting on the floor watching television, a stone fireplace and mantel located in the room collapsed; Jimmy was crushed to death, and Marvin was severely injured.

In July 1970, within one year of the date of the accident, James Saylor as personal representative of his dead son, Jimmy, and Marvin, through his father, James, as next friend, instituted this lawsuit against the Johnsons and Hall. The suit alleged that Jimmy's death and Marvin's personal injuries were caused by the negligence of Hall, the builder, and by the negligence of the Johnsons who had leased the property to the Saylors. The trial judge did not reach the merits concerning the triability of the lawsuit. He decided that action against Hall, the builder, was barred by limitations because of the provisions of KRS 413.120(14) and KRS 413.135. From this order of dismissal of the builder, the plaintiffs appealed, after meeting the procedural requisites for such action.

In 1964, the General Assembly carved out for different treatment from other actions for personal injuries, those where the claim was against "the builder of a home or other improvements." KRS 413.120(14). This statute provides that such an action must be commenced with five years after the cause of action accrues, and [the] "cause of action shall be deemed to accrue at the time of original occupancy of the improvements which the builder caused to be erected." *Ibid.*

The builder's potential liability was again the subject of legislative concern in 1966 when a more expansive statute, KRS 413.135, was enacted. It provided in part that no tort action for *personal injuries or for wrongful death arising out of "deficiency"* in construction of any improvement to real property could be brought against the builder after the expiration of five years following the "substantial completion of such improvement." Both of these statutes were expressed as parts of the general chapter on limitations of actions.

The plaintiffs argue that the application of these two statutes to bar their claims violates the Constitution of the United States and particularly the Due Process and Equal Protection Clauses of the Fourteenth Amendment. They also assert application of the questioned statutes to their causes of action is prohibited by numerous sections of the Constitution of Kentucky. We find it necessary, however, to consider only the effect of sections 14, 54, and 241 of the Kentucky Constitution as they have been judicially construed.

The defendant points out that substantially similar statutes have been adopted in 31 other states, and have been held valid by each state court of last resort that has considered them except in one instance. The defendant's arguments are: that the legislature may abolish old common law rights of action or create new ones; that it may enact statutes of "ultimate repose"; and that it may reasonably and rationally classify legal areas to be protected in order to achieve a permissible legislative objective in the manner provided by the concerned statutes. Nevertheless, the defendant concedes, tacitly if not explicitly, the Kentucky legislature has no constitutional power to extinguish common-law rights of action for negligence, but counters with the assertion that no such right of action for negligence against a builder existed at the time the questioned statutes were enacted, and, therefore, the legislature was free to act. Here, in our judgment, lies the heart of the issue to be decided. If the defendant is wrong in his assertion of the nonexistence of a right of action for negligence against the builder under the circumstances present when the statutes were passed, then the application of these statutes to the plaintiff's claim is constitutionally impermissible in this state. . . .

Section 14 of the Constitution of Kentucky states:

> All courts shall be open and every person, for an *injury* done him in his lands, goods, *person* or reputation, shall have remedy by due course of law, and right and justice administered without sale, denial or delay. (italics supplied)

This section was held to apply to the legislative branch of government as well as to the judicial in *Commonwealth v. Werner, Ky.*, 280 S.W.2d 214 (1955). Section 54 of the same Constitution states:

> The General Assembly shall have no power to limit the amount to be recovered for *injuries resulting in death, or for injuries to person* or property. (italics supplied).

The Kentucky Constitution in Section 241 states:

> Whenever the death of a person shall result *from an injury inflicted by negligence* or wrongful act, then, *in every such case,* damages may be recovered for such death from the corporations and persons so causing the same. Until otherwise provided by law, the action to recover such damages shall in all cases be prosecuted

by the personal representative of the deceased person. The General Assembly may provide how the recovery shall go and to whom it belongs; and until such provision is made the same shall form part of the personal estate of the deceased person. (italics supplied).

This court construed section 241 in 1911 to mean that "... it is not within the power of the legislature to deny this right of action. The section is as comprehensive as language can make it. The words 'negligence' and 'wrongful act' are sufficiently broad to embrace every degree of tort that can be committed against the person...." *Britton's Adm'r v. Samuels*, 143 Ky. 129, 136 S.W. 143.

Kentucky has no guest-passenger automobile statute, not because of legislative inaction, but because such a statute was voided as violative of our state Constitution. In the decision, section 54 played a prominent part. In *Ludwig v. Johnson et al*, 243 Ky. 533, 49 S.W.2d 347 (1932), this court struck down a statute that prohibited recovery by a guest passenger in an automobile against the owner or host driver for personal injuries or death resulting from the driver's negligence. Recovery was permitted by the statute only in the instance of intentional conduct. The court's holding was: "The [automobile guest-passenger] statute under consideration violates the spirit of our Constitution as well as its letter as found in sections 14, 54 and 241. It was the manifest purpose of the framers of that instrument to preserve and perpetuate the common law right of a citizen injured by the negligent act of another to sue to recover damages for his injury."

The defendant builder concedes that our legislature cannot abolish a common-law right of action for negligence. It is his contention, however, that at the time the questioned statutes were enacted, there was no existing right of action for negligence in this state where the plaintiff was a third party and the defendant was a builder whose work had been completed and accepted by the owner with whom he had contracted....

. . .

The legislature's power to enact statutes of limitation governing the time in which a cause of action must be asserted by suit is, of course, unquestioned. In this state, however, it is equally well settled that the legislature may not abolish an existing common-law right of action for personal injuries or wrongful death caused by negligence. KRS 413.120(14) provides that an action for personal injuries caused by the negligence of the builder of a home must be brought within five years, and the "cause of action shall be deemed to accrue at the time of original occupancy of the improvements which the builder caused to be erected." KRS 413.135(1) provides, in part, that no action "sounding in tort" resulting from "deficiency" in the construction of any improvement to real property or "for injury to the person or for wrongful death arising out of any such deficiency," shall be brought against the builder after the expiration of five years following "the substantial completion of such improvement." In our view the application of these statutory expressions to the claims here asserted destroys, *pro tanto*, a common-law right of action for negligence that proximately causes personal injury or death, which existed at the times the statutes were enacted. The statutory expressions as they related to actions based on negligence perform an abortion on the right of action, not in the first trimester, but before conception.

The right of action for negligence proximately causing injury or death, which is constitutionally protected in this state, requires more than mere conduct before recovery can be attempted. Recovery is not possible until a cause of action exists. A cause of action does not exist until the conduct causes injury that produces loss or damage. The action for negligence evolved chiefly out the old common-law form of action on the case, and it has always retained the rule of that action, that proof of damage was an essential part of the plaintiff's case. See Prosser, Handbook of the Law of Torts, section 30, page 143 (4th Edition 1971). Indeed, the Supreme Court of New Jersey realized the relevance of this consideration in the recent case cited by the defendant builder in support of his argument on another phase of the case. See *Rosenberg v. Town of North Bergen*, 61 N.J. 190, 293 A.2d 662, 666 (1972).

"It is not within the power of the legislature, under the guise of a limitation provision, to cut off an existing remedy entirely, since this would amount to a denial of justice, and, manifestly, an existing right of action cannot be taken away by legislation which shortens the period of limitation to a time that has already run." 51 Am.Jur.2d, Limitations of Actions, section 28, page 613. Surely then, the application of purported limitation statutes in such manner as to destroy a cause of action before it legally exists cannot be permissible if it accomplishes destruction of a constitutionally protected right of action. . . .

Privacy in Alaska

Ravin v. State

537 P.2d 494, 503–04 (Alaska 1975).

■ RABINOWITZ, CHIEF JUSTICE

· · ·

In Alaska we have also recognized the distinctive nature of the home as a place where the individual's privacy receives special protection. This court has consistently recognized that the home is constitutionally protected from unreasonable searches and seizures, reasoning that the home itself retains a protected status under the Fourth Amendment and Alaska's constitution distinct from that of the occupant's person. The privacy amendment to the Alaska Constitution was intended to give recognition and protection to the home. Such a reading is consonant with the character of life in Alaska. Our territory and now state has traditionally been the home of people who prize their individuality and who have chosen to settle or to continue living here in order to achieve a measure of control over their own lifestyles which is now virtually unattainable in many of our sister states.

The home, then, carries with it associations and meanings which make it particularly important as the situs of privacy. Privacy in the home is a fundamental right, under both the federal and Alaska constitutions. We do not mean by this that a person may do anything at anytime as long as the activity takes place within a person's home. There are two important limitations on this facet of the right to privacy. First, we agree with the Supreme Court of the United States, which has strictly limited the *Stanley* guarantee to possession for purely private, noncommercial use in the home. And secondly, we think this right must yield when it interferes in a serious manner with the health, safety, rights and privileges of others or with the public welfare. No one has an absolute right to do things in the privacy of his own home which will affect himself or others adversely. Indeed, one aspect of a private matter is that it is private, that is, that it does not adversely affect persons beyond the actor, and hence is none of their business. When a matter does affect the public, directly or indirectly, it loses its wholly private character, and can be made to yield when an appropriate public need is demonstrated.

Thus, we concluded that citizens of the State of Alaska have a basic right to privacy in their homes under Alaska's constitution. This right to privacy would encompass the possession and ingestion of substances such as marijuana in a purely personal, non-commercial context in the home unless the state can meet its substantial burden and show that proscription of possession of marijuana in the home is supportable by achievement of a legitimate state interest....

Notes

In November 1990, 54% of Alaskans voted, in an initiative, to amend the criminal laws on the possession of marijuana. The proposition took effect in March 1991 and makes it illegal to possess up to four ounces of marijuana, even in a private place. As of July 1999, the Alaska Supreme Court has not reconsidered the *Ravin* decision in light of this initiative.

CHAPTER 3

REMEDIES UNDER U.S. LAW FOR VIOLATIONS OF RIGHTS

A. RIGHTS AND REMEDIES: GENERAL PRINCIPLES

The Bill of Rights is couched in terms of prohibitions: "Congress shall make no law . . ." (Amendment I), "The right of the people to be secure . . . shall not be violated . . ." (Amendment IV). But the prohibitions of the Amendments recognize rights, rights of individuals, and the Bill of Rights is a bill of *rights*, rights of individuals. The Declaration of Independence declared that men (and women) are endowed with rights.

The Constitution, then, does not merely impose prohibitions and limitations on government; it recognizes and protects rights. Designating the limitations on governments as rights moves the focus to the individual rights-holder, and it is not a major step to infer that the rights-holder ought to have remedies.

> The very essence of civil liberty certainly consists in the right of every individual to claim the protection of the laws, whenever he receives an injury. One of the first duties of government is to afford that protection. [The] government of the United States has been emphatically termed a government of laws, and not of men. It will certainly cease to deserve this high appellation, if the laws furnish no remedy for the violation of a vested legal right.

Marbury v. Madison, 5 U.S. (1 Cranch) 137, 163 (1803).

In the United States, at least, the idea of rights is commonly seen as implying the availability of remedies. Formal remedies generally include compensation for past violations or injunctions or declaratory judgments against future violations. Remedies for violations of rights available to private individuals include actions at common law or under State tort statutes, as well as under federal or State civil rights legislation. Principles of sovereign immunity preclude suit against the United States, or against a State, without its consent, but both the United States and the States have consented to be sued in particular categories of cases, such as personal injury claims under the Federal Tort Claims Act. Suits against officials are often provided and regulated by law.

The U.S. Constitution does not explicitly provide remedies for violation of constitutional rights and until the Civil War Amendments it was not easy to find constitutional authority empowering Congress to provide remedies for violations of constitutional rights. It is established that, in an appropriate proceeding, courts will hear challenges to the constitutionality of legislation or official action and will not give effect to laws or actions that violate constitutional rights ("judicial review"). In appropriate proceedings, courts will enjoin, or issue a declaratory judgment against, continuing or future violations of constitutional rights. Even if the State (or the United States) has not consented to be sued, a suit will lie against an official to enjoin his action or to declare it unlawful, on the ground that the law under which he/she acted was unconstitutional. See *Ex parte Young*, 209 U.S. 123 (1908).

Under its powers to enforce the Thirteenth, Fourteenth, and Fifteenth Amendments, Congress has provided civil remedies for violations of constitutional rights by officials or others acting under color of law. Acting under its general regulatory powers, notably the Commerce Power (and to some extent under the Thirteenth Amendment which does not imply a "state action" requirement), Congress has provided some remedies also for violations by individuals and private entities. The courts, on their own authority, have provided a remedy in damages against an official who had violated the plaintiff's rights under the Fourth Amendment. See *Bivens v. Six Unknown Federal Narcotics Agents*, infra.

Judicial remedies are limited by constitutional requirements of "case or controversy" and by prudential considerations supporting requirements of standing, ripeness, non-mootness and related elements governing justiciability and procedures of adjudication. The courts have also developed a doctrine under which certain issues are seen to be "political questions" and are not justiciable.

Bivens v. Six Unknown Named Agents of Federal Bureau of Narcotics

403 U.S. 388 (1971).

■ Mr. Justice Brennan delivered the opinion of the Court.

The Fourth Amendment provides that:

> "The right of the people to be secure in their persons, houses, papers, and effects, against unreasonable searches and seizures, shall not be violated . . . ."

In *Bell v. Hood*, 327 U.S. 678 (1946), we reserved the question whether violation of that command by a federal agent acting under color of his authority gives rise to a cause of action for damages consequent upon his unconstitutional conduct. Today we hold that it does.

This case has its origin in an arrest and search carried out on the morning of November 26, 1965. Petitioner's complaint alleged that on that day respondents, agents of the Federal Bureau of Narcotics acting under claim of federal authority, entered his apartment and arrested him for alleged narcotics violations. The agents manacled petitioner in front of his wife and children, and threatened to arrest the entire family. They searched the apartment from stem to stern. Thereafter, petitioner was taken to the federal courthouse in Brooklyn, where he was interrogated, booked, and subjected to a visual strip search. . . .

I

Respondents do not argue that petitioner should be entirely without remedy for an unconstitutional invasion of his rights by federal agents. In respondents' view, however, the rights that petitioner asserts—primarily rights of privacy—are creations of state and not of federal law. Accordingly, they argue, petitioner may obtain money damages to redress invasion of these rights only by an action in tort, under state law, in the state courts. In this scheme the Fourth Amendment would serve merely to limit the extent to which the agents could defend the state law tort suit by asserting that their actions were a valid exercise of federal power: if the agents were shown to have violated the Fourth Amendment, such a defense would be lost to them and they would stand before the state law merely as private individuals.

. . .

We think that respondents' thesis rests upon an unduly restrictive view of the Fourth Amendment's protection against unreasonable searches and seizures by federal agents, a view that has consistently been rejected by this Court. Respondents seek to treat the relationship between a citizen and a federal agent unconstitutionally exercising his authority as no different from the relationship between two private citizens. In so doing, they ignore the fact that power, once granted, does not disappear like a magic gift when it is wrongfully used. An agent acting—albeit unconstitutionally—in the name of the United States possesses a far greater capacity for harm than an individual trespasser exercising no authority other than his own. . . . Accordingly, as our cases make clear, the Fourth Amendment operates as a limitation upon the exercise of federal power regardless of whether the State in whose jurisdiction that power is exercised would prohibit or penalize the identical act if engaged in by a private citizen. It guarantees to citizens of the United States the absolute right to be free from unreasonable searches and seizures carried out by virtue of federal authority. And "where federally protected rights have been invaded, it has been the rule from the beginning that courts will be alert to adjust their remedies so as to grant the necessary relief." *Bell v. Hood*, 327 U.S. at 684 (footnote omitted); see *Bemis Bros. Bag Co. v. United States*, 289 U.S. 28, 36 (1933) (Cardozo, J.); *The Western Maid*, 257 U.S. 419, 433 (1922) (Holmes, J.).

. . .

Second. The interests protected by state laws regulating trespass and the invasion of privacy, and those protected by the Fourth Amendment's guarantee against unreasonable searches and seizures, may be inconsistent or even hostile. Thus, we may bar the door against an unwelcome private intruder, or call the police if he persists in seeking entrance. The availability of such alternative means for the protection of privacy may lead the State to restrict imposition of liability for any consequent trespass. A private citizen, asserting no authority other than his own, will not normally be liable in trespass if he demands, and is granted, admission to another's house. *See* W. Prosser, *The Law of Torts* 109—110 (3d ed. 1964); 1 F. Harper & F. James, *The Law of Torts* s 1.11 (1956). But one who demands admission under a claim of federal authority stands in a far different position. *Cf. Amos v. United States*, 255 U.S. 313, 317 (1921). The mere invocation of federal power by a federal law enforcement official will normally render futile any attempt to resist an unlawful entry or arrest by resort to the local police; and a claim of authority to enter is likely to unlock the door as well.

. . .

[Concurring and dissenting opinions omitted.]

Notes

1.   See Al Katz, *The Jurisprudence of Remedies; Constitutional Legality and the Law of Tort in Bell v. Hood*, 117 U. Pa. L. Rev. 1 (1968).

2.   The Supreme Court upheld remedies for violation of the Fifth Amendment in *Davis v. Passman*, 442 U.S. 228 (1979), and for violation of the Eighth Amendment in *Carlson v. Green*, 446 U.S. 14 (1980), but not in other cases, such as *Chappell v. Wallace*, 462 U.S. 296 (1983); *Bush v. Lucas*, 462 U.S. 367 (1983), and *Schweiker v. Chilicky*, 487 U.S. 412 (1988).

In *Carlson*, the Court declared as a general principle the right to recover damages, which could be defeated if the defendants demonstrate special factors counseling hesitation, or if Congress has provided an alternative remedy.

Remedies for violation of "natural rights"

Early in U.S. history, individual Justices, including John Marshall, suggested that the courts might provide a remedy on their own authority to invalidate governmental acts that violate "general principles," i.e., natural law. In *Calder v. Bull*, 3 U.S. (3 Dall.) 386 (1798), the Supreme Court upheld a state statute that set aside a judicial decree and ordered a new trial. Justice Chase wrote:

I cannot subscribe to the omnipotence of a State Legislature, or that it is absolute and without control; although its authority should not be expressly restrained by the Constitution, or fundamental law, of the State. The people of the United States erected their Constitutions, or forms of government, to establish justice, to promote the general welfare, to secure the blessings of liberty; and to protect their persons and property from violence. The purposes for which men enter into society will determine the nature and terms of the social compact; and as they are the foundation of the legislative power, they will decide what are the proper objects of it: The nature, and ends of legislative power will limit the exercise of it. This fundamental principle flows from the very nature of our free Republican governments, that no man should be compelled to do what the laws do not require; nor to refrain from acts which the laws permit. There are acts which the Federal, or State, Legislature cannot do, without exceeding their authority. There are certain vital principles in our free Republican governments, which will determine and over-rule an apparent and flagrant abuse of legislative power; as to authorize manifest injustice by positive law; or to take away that security for personal liberty, or private property, for the protection whereof the government was established. An ACT of the Legislature (for I cannot call it a law) contrary to the great first principles of the social compact, cannot be considered a rightful exercise of legislative authority. The obligation of a law in governments established on express compact, and on republican principles, must be determined by the nature of the power, on which it is founded. A few instances will suffice to explain what I mean. A law that punished a citizen for an innocent action, or, in other words, for an act, which, when done, was in violation of no existing law; a law that destroys, or impairs, the lawful private contracts of citizens; a law that makes a man a Judge in his own cause; or a law that takes property from A and gives it to B: It is against all reason and justice, for a people to entrust a Legislature with SUCH powers; and, therefore, it cannot be presumed that they have done it. The genius, the nature, and the spirit, of our State Governments, amount to a prohibition of such acts of legislation; and the general principles of law and reason forbid them. The Legislature may enjoin, permit, forbid, and punish; they may declare new crimes; and establish rules of conduct for all its citizens in future cases; they may command what is right, and prohibit what is wrong; but they cannot change innocence into guilt; or punish innocence as a crime; or violate the right of an antecedent lawful private contract; or the right of private property. To maintain that our Federal, or State, Legislature possesses such powers, if they had not been expressly restrained, would, in my opinion, be a political heresy, altogether inadmissible in our free republican governments.

Id. at 387–89. Justice Iredell, however, argued in the same case that the courts were not given authority to apply and enforce "natural law."

In *Fletcher v. Peck,* 10 U.S. (6 Cranch) 87 (1810), Chief Justice Marshall also suggested that the Federal Judiciary should not give effect to legislation that violated "general principles," but in the end held the state law invalid because it violated a Constitutional provision.

B.   ENFORCEMENT AND REMEDIES: JUDICIAL REVIEW AND ITS LIMITATIONS

The principal remedy for violations of constitutional rights has not been money damages for the victim, but judicial review, with a declaration of unconstitutionality and a declaratory judgment or an injunction against future violation.

Judicial Review

It is emphatically the province and duty of the judicial department to say what the law is. Those who apply the rule to particular cases, must of necessity expound and interpret that rule. If two laws conflict with each other, the courts must decide on the operation of each.

So if a law be in opposition to the constitution; if both the law and the constitution apply to a particular case, so that the court must either decide that case conformably to the law, disregarding the constitution; or conformably to the constitution, disregarding the law; the court must determine which of these conflicting rules governs the case. This is the very essence of judicial duty.

Marbury v. Madison, 5 U.S. (1 Cranch) 137, 177 (1803).

Judicial review is a hallmark of American constitutional jurisprudence. Though it has not escaped controversy, it is no longer subject to challenge and is the principal "remedy" for violation of individual rights in the United States. In fact, judicial review is an incomplete remedy: in itself it does not undo human rights violations or compensate the victim, but it can terminate continuing violations and prevent future violations. Remedies for past violations were provided by the common law and by legislation, both State and federal. See Section C, below. Legislation is designed to indemnify victims of violations of rights and to punish those responsible for violations; both indemnification and punishment also serve to deter violations in the future.

A classic justification of judicial review to be exercised by an independent judiciary was provided by Alexander Hamilton.

The Federalist No. 78 (Alexander Hamilton)

. . .

The complete independence of the courts of justice is peculiarly essential in a limited constitution. By a limited constitution, I understand one which contains certain specified exceptions to the legislative authority; such, for instance, as that it shall pass no bills of attainder, no *ex post facto* laws, and the like. Limitations of this kind can be preserved in practice no other way than through the medium of the courts of justice; whose duty it must be to declare all acts contrary to the manifest tenor of the constitution void. Without this, all the reservations of particular rights or privileges would amount to nothing.

Some perplexity respecting the right of the courts to pronounce legislative acts void, because contrary to the constitution, has arisen from an imagination that the doctrine would imply a superiority of the judiciary to the legislative power. It is urged that the authority which can declare the acts of another void, must necessarily be superior to the one whose acts may be declared void. As this doctrine is of great importance in all the American constitutions, a brief discussion of the grounds on which it rests cannot be unacceptable.

There is no position which depends on clearer principles than that every act of a delegated authority, contrary to the tenor of the commission under which it is exercised, is void. No legislative act, therefore, contrary to the constitution, can be valid. To deny this would be to affirm, that the deputy is greater than his principal; that the servant is above his master; that the representatives of the people are superior to the people themselves; that men, acting by virtue of powers, may do not only what their powers do not authorize, but what they forbid.

If it be said that the legislative body are themselves the constitutional judges of their own powers, and that the construction they put upon them is conclusive upon the other departments, it may be answered, that this cannot be the natural presumption, where it is not to be collected from any particular provisions in the constitution. It is not otherwise to be supposed that the constitution could intend to enable the representatives of the people to substitute their *will* to that of their constituents. It is far more rational to suppose that the courts were designed to be an intermediate body between the people and the legislature, in order, among other things, to keep the latter within the limits assigned to their authority. The interpretation of the laws is the proper and peculiar province of the courts. A constitution is, in fact, and must be, regarded by the judges as a fundamental law. It must therefore belong to them to ascertain its meaning, as well as the meaning of any particular act proceeding from the legislative body. If there should happen to be an irreconcilable variance between the two, that which has the superior obligation and validity ought, of course, to be preferred; in other words, the constitution ought to be preferred to the statute, the intention of the people to the intention of their agents.

. . .

If then the courts of justice are to be considered as the bulwarks of a limited constitution, against legislative encroachments, this consideration will afford a strong argument for the permanent tenure of judicial offices, since nothing will contribute so much as this to that independent spirit in the judges, which must be essential to the faithful performance of so arduous a duty.

But it is not with a view to infractions of the constitution only, that the independence of the judges may be an essential safeguard against the effects of occasional ill-humours in the society. These sometimes extend no farther than to the injury of the private rights of particular classes of citizens, by unjust and partial laws. Here also the firmness of the judicial magistracy is of vast importance in mitigating the severity, and confining the operation of such laws. It not only serves to moderate the immediate mischiefs of those which may have been passed, but it operates as a check upon the legislative body in passing them; who, perceiving that obstacles to the success of an iniquitous intention are to be expected from the scruples of the courts, are in a manner compelled by the very motives of the injustice they meditate, to qualify their attempts.... That inflexible and uniform adherence to the rights of the constitution, and of individuals, which we perceive to be indispensable in the courts of justice, can certainly not be expected from judges who hold their offices by a temporary commission. Periodical appointments, however regulated, or by whomsoever made, would, in some way or other, be fatal to their necessary independence. If the power of making them was committed either to the executive or legislature, there would be danger of an improper complaisance to the branch which possessed it: if to both, there would be an unwillingness to hazard the displeasure of either; if to the people, or to persons chosen by them for the special purpose, there would be too great a disposition to consult popularity, to justify a reliance that nothing would be consulted but the constitution and the laws.

There is yet a further and a weighty reason for the permanency of judicial offices; which is deducible from the nature of the qualifications they require. It has been frequently remarked, with great propriety, that a voluminous code of laws is one of the inconveniences necessarily connected with the advantages of a free government. To avoid an arbitrary discretion in the courts, it is indispensable that they should be bound down by strict rules and precedents, which serve to define and point out their duty in every particular case that comes before them; and it will readily be conceived, from the variety of controversies which grow out of the folly and wickedness of mankind, that the records of those precedents must unavoidably swell to a very considerable bulk, and must demand long and laborious study to acquire a competent knowledge of them. Hence it is, that there can be but few men in the society, who will have sufficient skill in the laws to qualify them for the stations of judges. And making the proper deductions for the ordinary depravity of human nature, the number must be still smaller, of those who unite the requisite integrity with the requisite knowledge. These considerations apprize us, that the government can have no great option between fit characters; and that a temporary duration in office, which would naturally discourage such characters from quitting a lucrative line of practice to accept a seat on the bench, would have a tendency to throw the administration of justice into hands less able, and less well qualified, to conduct it with utility and dignity. In the present circumstances of this country, and in those in which it is likely to be for a long time to come, the disadvantages on this score would be greater than they may at first sight appear; but it must be confessed, that they are far inferior to those which present themselves under the other aspects of the subject.

Upon the whole, there can be no room to doubt, that the convention acted wisely in copying from the models of those constitutions which have established *good behaviour* as the tenure of judicial offices, in point of duration; and that, so far from being blameable on this account, their plan would have been inexcusably defective, if it had wanted this important feature of good government. The experience of Great Britain affords an illustrious comment on the excellence of the institution.

Notes

1. Reviewing the continuing debates as to whether judicial review was intended by the Framers of the Constitution, Professor Leonard Levy concludes that "long acquiescence by the people and their representatives has legitimated judicial review.... Judicial review would never have flourished had the people been opposed to it.... Judicial review, in fact, exists by the tacit consent of the governed." Leonard Levy, *Judicial Review, History and Democracy,* in Judicial Review and the Supreme Court 1–2 (Levy ed. 1967).

The "tacit consent of the governed" applies not only to the institution of judicial review but to the particular form it has taken in the United States. There has been no significant move to modify the aspects of judicial review which Hamilton praised—review by a court of law, with judges having life tenure and assured compensation.

2. Constitutional review in some form has been adopted by virtually all countries, including the new constitutional systems established in the second half of the 20th Century. But many have opted for review by special constitutional courts (rather than for the US model of judicial review in the course of adjudication of cases or controversies). And judicial life tenure as in the United States is highly exceptional.

France has established constitutional review not by a judicial body but by a constitutional council ("conseil constitutionnel"), reviewing proposed legislation before it goes into effect, and not at the behest of an aggrieved person with standing but of a number of members of Parliament or by the heads of the Parliamentary Chambers (or of the President of the Republic).

See generally, Constitutionalism and Rights—The Influence of the United States Constitution Abroad (L. Henkin and Albert J. Rosenthal, eds. 1990), and Louis Favoreu, *Constitutional Review in Europe, id.* at 38.

Limitations on Judicial Review

In the United States, judicial review is exercised by the ordinary courts in the exercise of their general jurisdiction (not by a special Constitutional Court). The federal courts can exercise "the judicial power" of the United States, only in "cases or controversies." Article III, section 2. "Case or controversy" has been held to require an adversary proceeding initiated by persons having "standing," against officials responsible for the alleged violation; and the case must be "ripe," but not moot. Ordinarily, a person may not raise constitutional claims of third parties. The courts have also refused to adjudicate "political questions," where the Constitution has been interpreted to bar judicial review of particular issues or where for other prudential reasons the question is deemed not justiciable. See *Baker v. Carr*, 369 U.S. 186 (1962), quoted at p. 262 below.

The jurisdiction of the federal courts is only that prescribed by Congress, but constitutional questions may also be decided by State courts, subject to review by the U.S. Supreme Court.

Requirements of "cases or controversies," and prudential reasons for not hearing a case (or for not addressing a constitutional question), lead to the result that many constitutional questions are not addressed and constitutional violations remain without judicial remedy. In *United States v. Richardson*, 418 U.S. 166, 179 (1974), Chief Justice Burger said: "It can be argued that if respondent is not permitted to litigate this issue, no one can do so. In a very real sense, the absence of any particular individual or class to litigate these claims gives support to the argument that the subject matter is committed to the surveillance of Congress, and ultimately to the political process." In *Schlesinger v. Reservists Committee to Stop the War*, 418 U.S. 208, 227 (1974), Chief Justice Burger concluded, "Our system of government leaves many crucial decisions to the political processes." Compare also *Laird v. Tatum*, 408 U.S. 1 (1972); *Gilligan v. Morgan*, 413 U.S. 1 (1973).

In *Gilligan v. Morgan,* 413 U.S. 1 (1973), the Court said:

It would be difficult to think of a clearer example of the type of governmental action that was intended by the Constitution to be left to the political branches directly responsible—as the Judicial Branch is not—to the electoral process. Moreover, it is difficult to conceive of an area of governmental activity in which the courts have less competence. The complex, subtle, and professional decisions as to the composition, training, equipping, and control of a military force are essentially professional military judgments, subject *always* to civilian control of the Legislative and Executive Branches. The ultimate responsibility for these decisions is appropriately vested in branches of the government which are periodically subject to electoral accountability. It is this power of oversight and control of military force by elected representatives and officials which underlies our entire constitutional system. . . .

Compare Justice Powell, concurring, in *United States v. Richardson*, 418 U.S. 166, 188–92 (1974). In that case the Court denied a citizen and taxpayer standing to challenge provisions of the Central International Agency Act of 1949 that forbade making certain expenditures public, on the ground that the provision violated the "Statement and Account requirement of Article 1, Section 9, of the Constitution". Justice Powell wrote more broadly:

. . .

Relaxation of standing requirements is directly related to the expansion of judicial power.[7] It seems to me inescapable that allowing

---

7. One commentator predicted this phenomenon and its possible implications at the outset of the past decade of dramatic changes in standing doctrine: "[Judicial] power expands as the requirements of standing are relaxed. . . . [If] the so-called public action . . . were allowed with respect to constitutional challenges to legislation, then the halls of

unrestricted taxpayer or citizen standing would significantly alter the allocation of power at the national level, with a shift away from a democratic form of government. I also believe that repeated and essentially head-on confrontations between the life-tenured branch and the representative branches of government will not, in the long run, be beneficial to either. The public confidence essential to the former and the vitality critical to the latter may well erode if we do not exercise self-restraint in the utilization of our power to negative the actions of the other branches. We would be ever mindful of the contradictions that would arise if a democracy were to permit general oversight of the elected branches of government by a nonrepresentative, and in large measure insulated, judicial branch. Moreover, the argument that the Court should allow unrestricted taxpayer or citizen standing underestimates the ability of the representative branches of the Federal Government to respond to the citizen pressure that has been responsible in large measure for the current drift toward expanded standing. Indeed, taxpayer or citizen advocacy, given its potentially broad base, is precisely the type of leverage that in a democracy ought to be employed against the branches that were intended to be responsive to public attitudes about the appropriate operation of government. "We must as judges recall that, as Mr. Justice Homes wisely observed, the other branches of the Government 'are ultimate guardians of the liberties and welfare of the people in quite as great a degree as the courts.' *Missouri, Kansas & Texas R. Co. v. May*, 194 U.S. 267, 270." *Flast v. Cohen*, 392 U.S., at 131 (Harlan, J., dissenting).

Unrestrained standing in federal taxpayer or citizen suits would create a remarkably illogical system of judicial supervision of the coordinate branches of the Federal Government. Randolph's proposed Council of Revision, which was repeatedly rejected by the Framers, at least had the virtue of being systematic; every law passed by the legislature automatically would have been previewed by the Judiciary before the law could take effect. On the other hand, since the Judiciary cannot select the taxpayers or citizens who bring suit or the nature of the suits, the allowance of public actions would produce uneven and sporadic view, the quality of which would be influenced by the resources and skill of the particular plaintiff. And issues would be presented in abstract form, contrary to the Court's recognition that "judicial review is effective largely because it is not available simply at the behest of a partisan faction, but is exercised only to remedy a particular, concrete injury." *Sierra Club v. Morton*, 405 U.S. 727, 740–741, n. 16 (1972).

The power recognized in *Marbury v. Madison*, 1 Cranch 137 (1803), is a potent one. Its prudent use seems to me incompatible with unlimited notions of taxpayer and citizen standing. Were we to utilize

Congress and of the state legislatures would become with regularity only Act I of any contest to enact legislation involving public officials in its enforcement or application. Act II would, with the usual brief interlude, follow in the courts...."

this power as indiscriminately as is now being urged, we may witness efforts by the representative branches drastically to curb its use. Due to what many have regarded as the unresponsiveness of the Federal Government to recognized needs or serious inequities in our society, recourse to the federal courts has attained an unprecedented popularity in recent decades. Those courts have often acted as a major instrument of social reform. But this has not always been the case, as experiences under the New Deal illustrate. The public reaction to the substantive due process holdings of the federal courts during that period requires no elaboration, and it is not unusual for history to repeat itself.

Quite apart from this possibility, we risk a progressive impairment of the effectiveness of the federal courts if their limited resources are diverted increasingly from their historic role to the resolution of public-interest suits brought by litigants who cannot distinguish themselves from all taxpayers or all citizens. The irreplaceable value of the power articulated by Mr. Chief Justice Marshall lies in the protection it has afforded the constitutional rights and liberties of individual citizens and minority groups against oppressive or discriminatory government, that has maintained public esteem for the federal courts and has permitted the peaceful coexistence of the countermajoritarian implications of judicial review and the democratic principles upon which our Federal Government in the final analysis rests.

.   .   .

Note

The Supreme Court has generally denied the standing of a U.S. taxpayer to challenge the validity of a spending of federal funds, with small exceptions; i.e., *Flast v. Cohen*, 392 U.S. 83 (1968). The *Flast* requirements for standing were reaffirmed in *Valley Forge Christian College v. Americans United*, 454 U.S. 464 (1982).

"Political questions" and Baker v. Carr

That there is a "political question doctrine" was in effect accepted by the Supreme Court in *Baker v. Carr*, 369 U.S. 186 (1962). Justice Brennan expressed the doctrine as follows:

Prominent on the surface of any case held to involve a political question is found a textually demonstrable constitutional commitment of the issue to a coordinate political department; or a lack of judicially discoverable and manageable standards for resolving it; or the impossibility of deciding without an initial policy determination of a kind clearly for nonjudicial discretion; or the impossibility of a court's undertaking independent resolution without expressing lack of the respect due coordinate branches of government; or an unusual need for unquestioning adherence to a political decision already made; or the potentiality of embarrassment from multifarious pronouncements by various departments on one question. Unless one of these formulations is inextricable from the case at bar, there should be no dismissal for nonjusticiability on the ground of a political question's presence. The doctrine of which we treat is one of "political questions," not one of "political cases."

But the Court found that the issue in the case of *Baker v. Carr* itself was not a political question, was justiciable, and proceeded to adjudicate it. There have in fact been hardly any issues held to be non-justiciable, but the courts assume the doctrine and apply *Baker v. Carr* as the standard. The Court seems to have found a non-justiciable political question in *Gilligan v. Morgan*, supra.

In *Nixon v. United States*, 506 U.S. 224, 241 (1993), the Court held that the provision in the Constitution that provides that the "Senate shall have the sole Power to try all Impeachments" (Article I, § 3), implied that the courts had no jurisdiction to consider complaints about the conduct of the Senate trial following the impeachment of Judge Walter Nixon. Compare *Powell v. McCormack*, 395 U.S. 486 (1969), and the different opinions in *Goldwater v. Carter*, 444 U.S. 996 (1979).

Louis Henkin, *Is There a "Political Question" Doctrine?*

85 Yale L. J. 597, 605–06 (1976).

If any clauses in the Constitution are properly interpreted as conferring power not subject to judicial review, so be it (though there might be too few of such bricks and it might be otherwise misleading to build a "political question doctrine"). If the cases have established that courts must, or should, or may, abstain from judicial review of constitutionality because of one or more of the considerations distilled by Justice Brennan or from Bickel's undifferentiated "prudence," so be that too (although Professor Wechsler is surely entitled to ask where the Court found authority for such abstention). I am not satisfied, however, that the older cases called for extra-ordinary judicial abstention in the sense of the pure "political question doctrine"; the considerations distilled from them by Justice Brennan seem rather to be elements of the ordinary respect which the courts show to the substantive decisions of the political branches. Different (perhaps only clearer) opinions might have been written in the leading cases that would justify and explain their result without even using the words "political question," and without suggesting a doctrine that would also be deemed to support an exception to our commitment to judicial review.

The Court, I suggest, was following (or might have followed) one of several established jurisprudential lines which are sometimes confused with the "political question doctrine" but which essentially have nothing to do with it:

1. The act complained of was within the power conferred upon the political branches of the federal government by the Constitution, and their action was law binding on the courts.

2. Contrary to petitioner's assertion, the act complained of fell within the enumerated powers conferred upon the political branches by the Constitution (or within the inherent powers of the state) and was not prohibited to them explicitly or by any warranted inference from the Constitution; nor did it violate any right reserved to the petitioner by the Constitution.

3. Although a legal claim existed, indeed although a constitutional violation may have been committed, the remedy sought was an equitable remedy and would not be granted in the circumstances by a court of equity in the exercise of sound discretion.

The first two are commonplace: courts have held one or the other of these in innumerable cases. In such cases, I stress, the court does not refuse judicial review; it exercises it. It is not dismissing the case or the issue as nonjusticiable; it adjudicates it. It is not refusing to pass on the power of the political branches; it passes upon it, only to affirm that they had the power which had been challenged and that nothing in the Constitution prohibited the particular exercise of it.

Denial of a particular, or any, equitable remedy is also not an exception to judicial review. The court may indeed review, find a violation, and still deny the remedy; or it may deny some remedy, say, an injunction, but grant other relief, *e.g.*, a declaratory judgment.

C. CIVIL AND CRIMINAL ENFORCEMENT OF RIGHTS UNDER U.S. LAW

Remedies for past violations of human rights, and proceedings for the prevention of some anticipated violations, are provided by federal and State law. The principal federal remedies specifically designed for the vindication of constitutional rights were enacted by Congress in the Civil Rights Acts following the Civil War and during the 1960s. See p. 237 above. (Congress had also enacted legislation to implement rights under international instruments, e.g., the Convention Against Torture.) U.S. implementation of international human rights obligations is discussed in Part III, Chapter 4. Under State law, the traditional common law of torts, and the general criminal law, provide some remedies for human rights violations, and States have supplemented these with additional human rights legislation.

Civil Enforcement

State common law originally provided a variety of tort remedies by which individuals could seek redress for invasions of their rights by private or public actors. In addition, Congress has created federal remedies, affording a judicial forum in which individuals may enforce their constitutional or federal statutory rights. Choice of the proper remedy and the proper court is sometimes difficult, and particular defendants may be shielded by doctrines of sovereign immunity or official immunity. The following major federal remedial procedures deserve mention:

1. *State violations.* A provision of the Civil Rights Act of 1871, currently codified as 42 U.S.C. § 1983, affords a remedy against persons responsible for the violation of federal rights under color of State law. Section 1983 does not create new substantive rights, but provides a remedy for the violation of existing rights under the Constitution and federal laws. See *Maine v. Thiboutot*, 448 U.S. 1 (1980); *Wright v. Roanoke Redevelopment & Housing Authority*, 479 U.S. 418 (1987). Depending on the circumstances, the court may award declaratory or injunctive relief, or compensatory or punitive damages. Potential defendants include State officials, private individuals acting under color of State law, and municipalities, but not a State itself or a government agency regarded as an arm of the State. *Will v. Michigan Dept. of State Police*, 491 U.S. 58 (1989). Prospective relief against ongoing or future constitutional violations by the State may be achieved by a suit against the responsible State officials, under the fiction that they are the wrongful acts of the individual officials and not acts of the State, a doctrine associated with the case *Ex parte Young*, 209 U.S. 123 (1908).

2. *Federal violations.* One remedy for federal constitutional violations, discussed above, is the *Bivens* action inferred directly from the Constitution. *Bivens* actions are a remedy of last resort; more common statutory remedies include the following:

a. *Habeas Corpus.* The one remedy expressly guaranteed by the Constitution is the writ of habeas corpus, whose suspension is prohibited, except in time of "Rebellion or Invasion," by Article I, section 9. The writ of habeas corpus provides a judicial remedy for unlawful detention. Statutory jurisdiction to issue the writ on behalf of federal prisoners is provided by 28 U.S.C. § 2241.

b. *The Administrative Procedure Act (APA).* Building on earlier traditions of administrative law, the APA provides a general authorization for judicial review of unlawful acts of federal administrative agencies. Where regulatory statutes do not supply a specific statutory remedy, the APA creates a presumption of reviewability of final agency action. See 5 U.S.C. § 702. The APA does not provide a remedy in damages for past violations of rights, but rather creates a vehicle for invalidation of administrative orders that would infringe rights, with the possibility of an injunction against future violations if necessary. The APA excludes a limited number of governmental functions from its scope, and also contemplates congressional power to exempt particular classes of decisions from review.

c. *The Federal Tort Claims Act (FTCA).* The FTCA authorizes suit against the federal government for compensatory damages to redress misconduct that would have been tortious if engaged in by a private actor. See 28 U.S.C. §§ 2671–2680. FTCA cases most frequently involve negligence, although some categories of intentional torts are also covered. In the cases within its scope, the FTCA requires a plaintiff to sue the federal government, and not the responsible officer as an individual.

d. *The Tucker Act.* The Tucker Act authorizes suit against the federal government for certain monetary claims not sounding in tort, particularly actions based on contracts, and actions to receive just compensation for an intentional taking of private property. See 28 U.S.C. §§ 1346(a)(1), 1491(a)(1).

Criminal Enforcement

Congress has also enacted criminal legislation to deter and punish violations of rights as necessary and proper to implement laws enacted under general powers of Congress such as the commerce power, or under its authority to implement the Fourteenth Amendment. Criminalization by Congress of civil rights violations often parallels and duplicates State criminal laws, as in *United States v. Guest* and *Screws v. United States,* below.

Principal federal laws imposing criminal sanctions for violation of civil rights include the following:

18 U.S.C. § 241. *Conspiracy against rights of citizens.* If two or more persons conspire to injure, oppress, threaten, or intimidate any citizen in the free exercise or enjoyment of any right or privilege secured to him by the Constitution or laws of the United States, or because of his having so exercised the same; or

If two or more persons go in disguise on the highway, or on the premises of another, with intent to prevent or hinder his free exercise or enjoyment of any right or privilege so secured—

They shall be fined not more than $10,000 or imprisoned not more than ten years, or both; and if death results, they shall be subject to imprisonment for any term of years or for life.

18 U.S.C. § 242. *Deprivation of rights under color of law.* Whoever, under color of any law, statute, ordinance, regulation, or custom, willfully subjects any inhabitant of any State, Territory, or District to the deprivation of any rights, privileges, or immunities secured or protected by the [Constitution or laws], or to different punishments, pain or penalties, on account of such inhabitant being an alien, or by reason of his color, or race, than are prescribed for the punishment of citizens, shall be fined not more than $1,000 or imprisoned not more than one year, or both; and if death results shall be subject to imprisonment for any term of years or for life.

18 U.S.C. § 245. *Federally protected activities.*

. . .

(b) Whoever, whether or not acting under color of law, by force or threat of force willfully injures, intimidates or interferes with, or attempts to injure, intimidate or interfere with—

(1) any person because he is or has been, or in order to intimidate such person or any other person or any class of persons from—

(A) voting or qualifying to vote, qualifying or campaigning as a candidate for elective office, or qualifying or acting as a poll watcher, or any legally authorized election official, in any primary, special, or general election;

(B) participating in or enjoying any benefit, service, privilege, program, facility, or activity provided or administered by the United States;

(C) applying for or enjoying employment, or any perquisite thereof, by any agency of the United States;

(D) serving, or attending upon any court in connection with possible service, as a grand or petit juror in any court of the United States;

(E) participating in or enjoying the benefits of any program or activity receiving Federal financial assistance; or

(2) any person because of his race, color, religion or national origin and because he is or has been—

(A) enrolling in or attending any public school or public college;

(B) participating in or enjoying any benefit, service, privilege, program, facility or activity provided or administered by any State or subdivision thereof;

(C) applying for or enjoying employment, or any perquisite thereof, by any private employer or any agency of any State or subdivision thereof, or joining or using the services or advantages of any labor organization, hiring hall, or employment agency;

(D) serving, or attending upon any court of any State in connection with possible service, as a grand or petit juror,

(E) traveling in or using any facility of interstate commerce, or using any vehicle, terminal, or facility of any common carrier by motor, rail, water, or air;

(F) enjoying the goods, services, facilities, privileges, advantages, or accommodations of any inn, hotel, motel, or other establishment which provides lodging to transient guests, or of any restaurant, cafeteria, lunchroom, lunch counter, soda fountain, or other facility which serves the public and which is principally engaged in selling food or beverages for consumption on the premises, or of any gasoline station, or of any motion picture house, theater, concert hall, sports arena, stadium, or any other place of exhibition or entertainment which serves the public, or of any other establishment which serves the public and (i) which is located within the premises of any of the aforesaid establishments or within the premises of which is physically located any of the aforesaid establishments, and (ii) which holds itself out as serving patrons of such establishments; ...

. . .

shall be fined under this title, or imprisoned not more than one year, or both; and if bodily injury results from the acts committed in violation of this section or if such acts include the use, attempted use, or threatened use of a dangerous weapon, explosives, or fire shall be fined under this title, or imprisoned not more than ten years, or both; and if death results from the acts committed in violation of this section or if such acts include kidnapping or an attempt to kidnap, aggravated sexual abuse or an attempt to commit aggravated sexual abuse, or an attempt to kill, shall be fined under this title or imprisoned for any term of years or for life, or both, or may be sentenced to death. . . .

Notes

1. Note that 18 U.S.C. § 241 applies to conspiracies to injure any citizen in the exercise of any right or privilege secured to him by the Constitution or laws of the United States.

18 U.S.C. § 242 would punish only those who act "under color of any law, etc."

18 U.S.C. § 245 would punish those "whether or not acting under color of law" who interfere with federally protected activities (including voting).

2. Criminal enforcement of constitutional rights has raised two important sets of issues. The first involves the application of federal criminal law to acts by State officials that violate the State's criminal law. There have also been issues of fairness and due process for those who violate the federal statute.

In *Screws v. United States*, 325 U.S. 91 (1945), a Georgia country sheriff and two other policemen severely beat a young black man whom they had arrested; he died shortly thereafter. Federal authorities prosecuted the Georgia officers for violation of § 20 of the Criminal Code (the predecessor of 18 U.S.C. § 242 above). Defendants argued that their action violated the State's criminal law, and that Congress had not made it a federal offense for a state official to violate State law.

In finding against the defendants the Court said:

> Some of the arguments which have been advanced in support of the contrary conclusion suggested that the question under § 20 is whether Congress has made it a federal offense for a state officer to violate the law of his state. But there is no warrant for treating the question in state law terms. The problem is not whether state law has been violated but whether an inhabitant of a State has been deprived of a federal right by one who acts under "color of any law." He who acts under "color" of law may be a federal officer or a state officer. He may act under "color" of federal law or of state law. The statute does not come into play merely because the federal law or the state law under which the officer purports to act is violated. It is applicable when and only when some one is deprived of a federal right by that action. The fact that it is also a violation of state law does not make it any less

a federal offense punishable as such. Nor does punishment by federal authority encroach on state authority or relieve the state from its responsibility for punishing state offenses.[10]

Three Justices dissented: They argued:

> ... By holding, in this case, that State officials who violate State law nevertheless act "under color of" State law, and by establishing as federal crimes violations of the vast, undisclosed range of the Fourteenth Amendment, this Court now creates new delicate and complicated problems for the enforcement of the criminal law. The answers given to these problems, in view of the tremendous scope of potential offenses against the Fourteenth Amendment, are bound to produce a confusion detrimental to the administration of criminal justice.

> . . .

> The complicated and subtle problems for law enforcement raised by the Court's decision emphasize the conclusion that § 20 was never designed for the use to which it has now been fashioned. The Government admits that it is appropriate to leave the punishment of such crimes as this to local authorities. Regard for this wisdom in federal-State relations was not left by Congress to executive discretion. It is, we are convinced, embodied in the statute itself. . . .

3. The Supreme Court revisited the issue of Congressional power under the Fourteenth Amendment in *United States v. Guest*, 383 U.S. 745 (1966). In *Guest*, the Court found that, under the Fourteenth Amendment, Congress could reach a range of private, racially discriminatory conduct.

The defendants in *Guest*, all private individuals, were prosecuted for criminal conspiracy under 18 U.S.C. § 241. The indictment alleged a conspiracy by the defendants to deprive black citizens of the free exercise and enjoyment of specified rights secured by the Constitution and laws of the United States, including the right to use State-owned facilities and the right to travel in interstate commerce.

The Court essentially avoided deciding whether § 241 could constitutionally be applied to racially discriminatory, but purely private, interference with the use of public facilities. But Congress could reach purely private interference with the federally-guaranteed right of interstate travel, a right fundamental to the federal union.

> The constitutional right to travel from one State to another, and necessarily to use the highways and other instrumentalities of interstate commerce in doing so, occupies a position fundamental to the concept of our Federal Union. It is a right that has been firmly

---

10. The petitioners may be guilty of manslaughter or murder under Georgia law and at the same time liable for the federal offense proscribed by § 20. The instances where "an act denounced as a crime by both national and state sovereignties" may be punished by each without violation of the double jeopardy provision of the Fifth Amendment are common. *United States v. Lanza*, 260 U.S. 377, 382; Herbert Louisiana, 272 U.S. 312.

established and repeatedly recognized. In *Crandall v. Nevada*, 6 Wall. 35, invalidating a Nevada tax on every person leaving the State by common carrier, the Court took as its guide the statement of Chief Justice Taney in the *Passenger Cases*, 7 How. 283, 492:

> "For all the great purposes for which the Federal government was formed, we are one people, with one common country. We are all citizens of the United States; and, as members of the same community, must have the right to pass and repass through every part of it without interruption, as freely as in our own States."

Although there have been recurring differences in emphasis within the Court as to the source of the constitutional right of interstate travel. . . . All have agreed that the right exists. Its explicit recognition as one of the federal rights protected by what is now 18 U.S.C. § 241 goes back at least as far as 1904. *United States v. Moore.*

4. Due process for the criminal defendant was raised in a number of cases, most importantly in *Screws* and *United States v. Lanier*, 520 U.S. 259 (1997).

In 1945, in *Screws v. United States*, the Supreme Court held that § 242 was not unconstitutionally vague. The defendants, who were charged with depriving Hall of his constitutionally protected rights in violation of the predecessor of § 242, challenged its constitutionality, arguing that the statute lacked the specificity necessary for criminal statutes to give notice to potential violators. Although the Court acknowledged the danger that a vague criminal statute poses, the Court emphasized that the word "willful" in a criminal statute denotes an act done intentionally and with a malign purpose. The Court reasoned that the specific intent required by the statute is the intent to deprive a person of a right that has been "made specific either by the express terms of the Constitution or laws of the United States or by decisions interpreting them." This definition of rights "made specific" provides adequate notice to potential violators that they are criminally liable. Thus, the Supreme Court held that the requirement of specific intent to deprive a person of a federal right saves the statute from being unconstitutionally vague.

> It is said, however, that this construction of the Act will not save it from the infirmity of vagueness since neither a law enforcement official nor a trial judge can know with sufficient definiteness the range of rights that are constitutional. But that criticism is wide of the mark. For the specific intent required by the Act is an intent to deprive a person of a right which has been made specific either by the express terms of the Constitution or laws of the United States or by decisions interpreting them. . . . If those acts are done willfully, how can the officer possibly claim that he had not fair warning that his act was prohibited by the statute? He violates the statute not merely because he has a bad purpose but because he acts in defiance of announced rules of law. He who defies a decision interpreting the Constitution knows precisely what he is doing. If sane, he hardly maybe heard to say that he knew not what he did. Of course, willful conduct cannot make

definite that which is undefined. But willful violators of constitutional requirements, which have been defined, certainly are in no position to say that they had no adequate advance notice that they would be visited with punishment. When they act willfully in the sense in which we use the word, they act in open defiance or in reckless disregard of a constitutional requirement which has been made specific and definite. When they are convicted for so acting, they are not punished for violating an unknowable something.

The right to fair warning was revisited in *United States v, Lanier*, 520 U.S. 259 (1997), where the Court considered whether criminal prosecution required that the constitutional rights in issue had been previously identified as such by the Supreme Court.

David Lainier was convicted under 18 U.S.C. § 242 of criminally violating the constitutional rights of five women by assaulting them sexually while Lainier served as a state judge. The court of appeals had reversed his convictions on the ground that the constitutional right in issue had not previously been identified by the Supreme Court in a case with fundamentally similar facts. The Supreme Court, however, held that that standard of notice is higher than the Constitution requires. Any concern over the due process requirement of notice is satisfied if potential defendants have "fair warning" of what constitutes constitutionally impermissible conduct such that they are not "held criminally responsible for conduct which [they] could not reasonably understand to be proscribed." The touchstone is whether "the statute, [either] standing alone or as construed, made it reasonably clear at the relevant time that the defendant's conduct was criminal."

> We applied this standard in Screws v. United States, 325 U.S. 91 (1945).... [T]he Court majority "recognized that this constitutional difficulty does not arise when the accused is charged with violating a 'right which has been made specific either by the express terms of the Constitution or laws of the United States or by decisions interpreting them.'" Id., at 104. When broad constitutional requirements have been "made specific" by the text or settled interpretations, willful violators "certainly are in no position to say that they had no adequate advance notice that they would be visited with punishment.... [T]hey are not punished for violating an unknowable something." Id., at 105. Accordingly, Screws limited the statute's coverage to rights fairly warned of, having been "made specific" by the time of the charged conduct.

D.   The United States as a Constitutional Rights System

The United States was conceived in the idea of rights, and individual rights were and remain a sturdy pillar of US constitutionalism. Original, "genetic" defects in U.S. constitutionalism and rights—notably, abiding slavery, gender distinctions and other inequalities, and less than representative government—were slowly cured after the Civil War. And constitutional amendments—principally the 14th Amendment—have nationalized individual rights and made them the special "responsibility" of Congress and of the courts.

United States rights jurisprudence has inspired some emulation (and some deviation) in the spreading constitutionalism around the world and in the international law of human rights. The U.S. example has promoted rights to liberty, principally the freedoms of expression, press, religion and association, and liberty as individual autonomy as in the new "privacy," and in the United States has been strong in its commitment to fair procedures in the criminal process. Rights to education flourished early in the United States through State constitutions. But, whereas others have abolished capital punishment, the United States has retained and indeed extended capital punishment. And the United States, though a welfare state in some measure for more than a half-century, has not given economic and social rights constitutional dimension and leaves them to the mercies of budget-politics and "compassion fatigue."

Rights in the United States have been shaped by its history and its geography—its English origins, its struggle with slavery, its Civil War and its chronic race problems, and its federal system. Its chief contribution to universal human rights, one might say, has been its commitment to the idea of rights enshrined in a written Constitution and a written Bill of Rights, and its emphasis on liberty. Above all, perhaps, it has contributed judicial review, adopted and adapted in constitutional systems throughout the world and supporting the spread of international and regional judicial and quasi-judicial bodies to monitor human rights.

PART III

INTERNATIONAL HUMAN RIGHTS

Introduction

In Part I, we discussed the idea of human rights and alternative visions of the good society in the Western political tradition. In Part II, we saw how the human rights idea has played out in the life of the United States, a principal exponent of the human rights idea and the principal exemplar of a constitutional system committed to that idea.

In Part III, we address the "universalization" and the "internationalization" of human rights: how the international political system has attempted to make the human rights idea and its realization "universal," i.e., applicable to all human beings in all countries; as well as "international," i.e., a subject of international politics and international law. Chapter 1 describes the Human Rights "Movement," its antecedents, its history, and its theoretical basis. Chapter 2 highlights, prominently though briefly, the Universal Declaration of Human Rights, the principal expression and definition of the idea of human rights, an instrument for universalizing the idea and the foundation for the international law of human rights. We then consider the international law of human rights, its character and sources and its principal content, incorporating by reference the principal international legal instruments, both universal and regional. In Section F of Chapter 2, we single out for special attention the human rights of women. We give special consideration also to the human rights of refugees, to group rights, and to other "generations" of rights. Chapter 3 addresses the implementation and enforcement of the international law of human rights, and remedies, both national and international, designed to promote respect for human rights, to prevent, terminate or deter violations, and to compensate the victims of violations. Chapter 4 addresses briefly the international human rights obligations of the United States and their enforcement.

CHAPTER 1

The International Human Rights Movement

From Constitutional Rights to International Human Rights

Until the Second World War, the idea of rights was a domestic constitutional idea, recognized in a few—very few—countries; and the United States Constitution was the principal—almost exclusive—embodiment of that idea.* The French Declaration of the Rights of Man and of the Citizen, *supra* Part I, had been shelved and fallen into desuetude. (The Constitution of the French Third Republic did not mention rights.) In the United Kingdom, a tradition of rights, traced to *Magna Carta* and supported by the common law, *supra* Part I, benefited the inhabitants of the United Kingdom, but even their rights were subject to parliamentary supremacy. Among political philosophers, natural law and natural rights had fallen into disrepute, giving way to positivism and positivist theories of state sovereignty. Throughout the world, human rights were a matter of domestic, not international, concern: How a nation treated its own inhabitants was its own affair, not a subject of international politics, surely not of international law.

All that changed with the Second World War, with the realization of the enormities of Hitler and the shock of the Holocaust. The idea of human rights was heralded in President Franklin Roosevelt's famous "Four Freedoms" speech as rights of all people everywhere (Part IV, Chapter 3(A)), and achieving respect for human rights became a principal war-aim of the Allies fighting Hitler.** The plans for a new international organization developed at Dumbarton Oaks in 1944 projected that the purposes of the organization will include the promotion of respect for human rights.*** The Allies imposed a commitment to respect human rights in early peace treaties with Italy and Central European powers, and later the Allies included protection for human rights in the laws they imposed in occupied

---

* Even in the United States, rights were still a secondary concern of constitutional jurisprudence (second to federalism and to separation of powers), and the Bill of Rights had not yet been incorporated into the Fourteenth Amendment and applied to the States. See Part II.

** For the historical role of Roosevelt's "Four Freedoms," see Louis B. Sohn, "The Human Rights Movement: From Roosevelt's Four Freedoms to the Interdependence of Peace, Development, and Human Rights," Edward A. Smith Lecture, Harvard Law School Human Rights Program, 1995.

*** On Dumbarton Oaks, see Louis Henkin, Human Rights from Dumbarton Oaks, in The Dumbarton Oaks Conversations and the United Nations 1944–1994 at 97 (May and Laiver eds., 1998).

Germany and Japan. At Nuremberg, Nazi leaders were tried not only for "war crimes," i.e., violations of the international law of war, but also for "crimes against humanity," the first reference to a customary law of human rights in a major international instrument.

The internationalization of human rights was confirmed in the United Nations Charter. The Charter declared that promoting respect for human rights was a principal purpose of the United Nations Organization, and states party to the Charter pledged themselves to cooperate in promoting that purpose. In 1946, the General Assembly of the United Nations established a Commission on Human Rights. (During that year the General Assembly also affirmed the principles of the Nuremberg Charter.) By 1948, the Human Rights Commission had produced, and the General Assembly had adopted, the Universal Declaration of Human Rights, as well as the Convention on the Prevention and Punishment of the Crime of Genocide, the first post-war human rights convention.

In its conception as well as in its realization, the "International Human Rights Movement" has not sought to supplant national protection of human rights, but to make the protection of human rights more effective within national systems. The international human rights movement sought to "universalize" human rights, to have the idea of human rights recognized and rights given protection in the constitutions and constitutional systems of all countries. International human rights norms set forth an agreed minimum of rights to be guaranteed by every state through its own national legal-political system. International remedies are designed to supplement national remedies to make them more effective so that human rights are ensured in fact, everywhere.

Human rights are no longer a matter of the domestic jurisdiction of a state, either for international law or for international politics. But the traditional attitude that how a state treats its own inhabitants is its own affair dies hard. It is reflected in reluctance to raise the minimum international standard of rights and unwillingness to reduce the permissible limitations on rights that may be imposed in the name of the public interest; in reluctance to adhere to covenants or conventions and a tendency to attach reservations to adherence; in resistance to external scrutiny, to effective monitoring or judgment by independent, impartial judicial or "quasi-judicial" bodies. The traditional attitude also helps explain the reluctance of states to scrutinize others and to call them to account when they fail to live up to their human rights undertakings.

And yet, international human rights are established in law and politics, and have had major achievements, *e.g.*, the burgeoning of democracy in formerly totalitarian societies, the death of apartheid in South Africa. Perhaps the idea's greatest achievements are incommensurable: the acceptance of the idea of human rights, and its universalization in the ideology of "constitutionalism" and in constitutions around the world; its influence in shaping laws and institutions, and its ability to permeate national and international cultures in ways that help "mobilize shame" so as to deter or terminate gross violations.

A.   THE INTERNATIONALIZATION OF HUMAN RIGHTS: ANTECEDENTS, HISTORY, AND THEORY

International human rights may fairly be dated from the Second World War and its aftermath, but the international political system, and international law, in fact addressed some human rights in special contexts much earlier. For example, international law early developed principles of "justice" which governed every state in its treatment of foreign nationals within its territory. Long before the Second World War, there were Treaties on religious and ethnic toleration, for the abolition of the slave trade, as well as the early development of humanitarian law to govern the conduct of war.

The contemporary international human rights movement began with the Second World War and its declared war-aims, with the Nuremberg Charter and the United Nations Charter, and the United Nations Organization. The Nuremberg Charter recognized "crimes against humanity" as a violation of international law; the Nuremberg principles were later ratified by the General Assembly. See p. 618 below. The promises of the UN Charter were developed between 1945 and 1948 by the Human Rights Commission and the General Assembly, leading to the adoption of the Genocide Convention and the Universal Declaration of Human Rights on successive days, December 9 and 10, 1948. The Universal Declaration was converted into two covenants, adopted by the General Assembly in 1966.

International human rights have no theory formally or authoritatively expressed. But international human rights have adopted as an "ur-value" the concept of "human dignity," to justify the idea of rights, and to define and give it content. At bottom, the idea and ideology of human rights may reflect a contemporary political morality, a conception of the purposes of government, political principles governing the relation of the individual to political authority, and beneath them moral principles governing relations between human beings. See p. 281 below.

Louis Henkin, *The Age of Rights*

13–20 (1990).

The internationalization of human rights, the transformation of the idea of constitutional rights in a few countries to a universal conception and a staple of international politics and law, is a phenomenon of the middle of our century. But it did not spring full-blown.

Historically, how a state treated persons in its territory was indeed its own affair, implicit in its territorial sovereignty. International law developed one early exception when it recognized that how a country treats a national of another state is the proper concern of that state. That exception might be seen as essentially political, not humanitarian, in motivation: if a citizen of the United States is abused elsewhere, the United States is offended. It was widely accepted, therefore, that injustice to a stateless person was not a violation of international law since no state was offended thereby; surely, there was no state that could invoke a remedy for such injustice. But assuming that the doctrine developed because the offended state was concerned for its own rather than for human dignity, it is significant that governments were offended by violations of the "human rights" of their nationals.

In order to determine whether a state could properly claim that its national had been denied "justice," international law developed an international standard of justice. There was no accepted philosophical foundation for such a standard, and no agreed definition of its content; doubtless, it was redolent of "natural rights" and tantamount to a notion of "fairness." Whatever its underpinnings, whatever its substance, the standard for the treatment of foreign nationals that was invoked by their governments and acquiesced in by host governments was often higher than that—if any— applied by these countries to their own citizens at home. The international standard, then, was not a universal human standard, and governments that invoked or accepted it did not suggest that it applied also to how governments treated their own citizens. The treatment accorded by a state to its own citizens was not the concern of international law or the business of other governments, and in fact governments rarely concerned themselves with domestic injustice elsewhere. The few major-power intercessions—for example, that of the United States in the nineteenth century in response to Russian pogroms—did not invoke international law and occurred only when violations were egregious and dramatic. This was usually the case when there was a demand for intercession by a domestic constituency with special affinity for the victims in the other country (as in the United States, for example, the Irish, the Jews, and others).

International political considerations inspired other exceptions to the principle that how a government acts toward individuals at home is a matter of domestic concern only. Beginning in the seventeenth century, Catholic and Protestant princes (and others) concluded agreements according freedom of worship and wider toleration to each other's coreligionists. Later, governments assumed international obligations to respect freedoms for ethnic minorities, even those who as a matter of law were nationals of the country in which they lived; in the late nineteenth and early twentieth century, such minority treaties were virtually imposed by the major powers on smaller ones in Central and Eastern Europe because it was believed that violation of minority rights led to intervention by countries that identified with them, and thus to war. Again, the basis for international concern in these cases was some special affinity on the part of some government for some inhabitants of other countries, and concern for international peace, not concern by governments generally for the basic dignity of all human beings, including their own inhabitants. . . .

The International Labor Organization was an early and noteworthy contributor to international human rights. The ILO was organized after

World War I to promote common basic standards of labor and social welfare. In the intervening seventy years, the ILO has promulgated more than a hundred international conventions, which have been widely adhered to and fairly well observed. Again, some might find political-economic rather than humanitarian motivations for what the ILO achieved. The ILO, it is said, was the West's fearful answer to socialism, which had gained its first bridgehead in the USSR; perhaps the conventions reflected also a desire by developed states to reduce "unfair competition" from countries with substandard labor conditions.

A less ambiguous example of early international concern for human rights was the movement in the nineteenth century, after major powers abolished slavery in their countries, to outlaw slavery and slave trade by international agreement. Perhaps slavery was sufficiently egregious that no state could be allowed to claim to contain it within its domestic jurisdiction. Moreover, the products of slave labor were sold abroad at a competitive advantage with goods produced by societies that had abolished slavery. Slave trade, surely, was not an internal matter only, involving as it did international trade and colonial competition.

In all, international relations before our time were not impervious to the human condition inside countries, but concern for individual welfare was framed and confined within the state system. That concern could not spill over state borders except in ways and by means that were consistent with the assumptions of that system, that is, when a state identified with inhabitants of other states on recognized grounds, and that identification threatened international order; when the condition of individuals inside a country impinged on the economic interests of other countries. Whatever the reasons, primitive human rights provisions appeared in international instruments, and the seeds of international human rights were planted.

THE INTERNATIONAL HUMAN RIGHTS MOVEMENT

"International human rights" is a term used with varying degrees of precision (or imprecision) and with different connotations in different contexts. In wide usage it corresponds to the "international human rights movement," born during the Second World War out of a spreading conviction that how human beings are treated anywhere concerns everyone, everywhere. That attitude itself perhaps blended several different "statements": an assertion of fact about human psychology and emotion, that human beings cannot close their minds and hearts to mistreatment or suffering of other human beings; a moral statement that mistreatment or suffering of human beings violates a common morality (perhaps also natural law or divine law) and that all human beings are morally obligated to do something about such mistreatment or suffering, both individually and through their political and social institutions; an international political statement that governments will attend to such mistreatment or suffering in other countries through international institutions and will take account of them also in their relations with other states. These three kinds of statements combined to support a concept of "human rights" and a program to promote their enjoyment, as implied in declarations like President Franklin Roosevelt's Four Freedoms message, in various articulations of the war aims of the Allies in the Second World War, and in their plans for the postwar world.

The end of the war saw wide acceptance of human rights reflected in two forms. Human rights appeared in the constitutions and laws of virtually all states. Victors in the war, for instance, the United States, wrote human rights into law for occupied countries, as for Germany and Japan. Later, departing colonial powers sometimes required a commitment to human rights of newborn states as part of the price of independence; many new states wrote them into their constitutions as their own commitment. Older states, responding to the Zeitgeist, also emphasized human rights in new constitutions and other national documents.

The human rights movement also took a second transnational form. Human rights were prominent in the new postwar international order: in treaties imposed upon vanquished nations, for example, Italy and Rumania; in the Nuremberg Charter and the UN Charter; in numerous resolutions and declarations of the new international institutions, notably, the United Nations, and of regional institutions in Latin America and Europe and, later, in Africa. In the United Nations, human rights were on every agenda, and the dedicated efforts of individuals and of some governments resulted in important international political and legal instruments, beginning with the Universal Declaration of Human Rights and the Convention on the Prevention and Punishment of the Crime of Genocide, both adopted without dissent in 1948.* There followed a series of other resolutions and declarations and an impressive array of other international covenants and conventions, principally the International Covenant on Civil and Political Rights and the International Covenant on Economic, Social and Cultural Rights, both completed in 1966 and in force since 1976. Europe and Latin America also developed important regional human rights laws and institutions. The African Charter on Human and Peoples' Rights came into effect in 1987. At Helsinki, in 1975, in the Final Act of the Conference on Security and Cooperation in Europe, 35 countries from Eastern and Western Europe, as well as the United States and Canada, made an important political bargain in which Western states accepted the political status quo in Europe and the Communist states committed themselves to respect human rights.[**]

---

* When the Universal Declaration was adopted, "the Communist bloc" (then including Yugoslavia, but not China) abstained, as did Saudi Arabia and South Africa. The European communist states have since accepted the Declaration in various ways, formally by explicit reference in the Final Act of the Conference on Security and Cooperation in Europe, Helsinki 1975. Spokesmen for the People's Republic of China have also invoked the Declaration in the United Nations.

** These are undertakings that the parties agreed would not have binding legal character but are nonetheless important "political obligations." See generally Thomas Buergenthal, ed., *Human Rights, International Law, and the Helsinki Accord* (Montclair, N.J.: Allanheld, Osmun, 1977).

I stress—and distinguish—those two different manifestations of general, worldwide concern with human rights. "Universalization" has brought acceptance, at least in principle and rhetoric, of the concept of individual human rights by all societies and governments and is reflected in national constitutions and law. "Internationalization" has brought agreement, at least in political-legal principle and in rhetoric, that individual human rights are of "international concern" and a proper subject for diplomacy, international institutions, and international law.

Strictly, "international human rights," that is, human rights as a subject of international law and politics, are to be distinguished from individual rights in national societies under national legal systems, but the two are not unrelated in law or in politics. The international movement accepts human rights as rights that, according to agreed-upon moral principles, the individual should enjoy under the constitutional-legal system for his or her society. But national protections for accepted human rights are often deficient; international human rights were designed to induce states to remedy those deficiencies. That would be done by establishing a common international standard by which to judge national rights systems, and by inducing states to undertake international obligations to abide by those standards and to submit to international "machinery" that would monitor compliance. The law, politics, and institutions of international human rights, then, do not replace national laws and institutions; they provide additional international protections for rights under national law. The international law of human rights is implemented largely by national law and institutions; it is satisfied when national laws and institutions are sufficient.

. . .

An important change took place during the process by which the idea of rights became universal as well as international. Individual human rights as a political idea derives both conceptually and historically from Euro–American ideas, rooted in individual autonomy and supported by conceptions of popular sovereignty and social contract. The rights implied in those ideas were rights of autonomy and freedom, limitations on government, immunities from undue, unreasonable exercises of authority. But in the nineteenth century there began to grow another sense of right, rooted not in individual autonomy but in community, adding to liberty and equality the implications of fraternity. The various socialisms and the burgeoning welfare-state ideology began to accept a broader view of the obligations of society and the purposes of government—not only to maintain security and protect life, liberty, and property, but also to guarantee and if necessary provide basic human needs. What began in Europe crossed the Atlantic during the New Deal. In his Four Freedoms message, Franklin Roosevelt articulated the new conception, wrapped—perhaps disguised—in the language of freedom, when he added freedom from want to eighteenth-century liberties. When, in the postwar years, individual rights became universal and international, they did so in their broader conception. The Universal Declaration of Human Rights contains not only rights to life, liberty, and property, but also rights to social security, declaring that everyone is entitled to the realization "of economic, social and cultural rights indispensable for his dignity and the free development of his personality" (Art. 22). Specified, in addition, are the right to work, to rest and leisure, to a standard of living adequate for health and well being, and to education.

.   .   .

The international law of human rights derives principally from contemporary international agreements in which states undertake to recognize, respect, and ensure specific rights for the inhabitants of their own countries. The older obligations in international law not to "deny justice" to nationals of other states are extended and supplemented—not superseded—by the new human rights law that applies to nationals and aliens alike. The older international agreements devoted to specific conditions—the anti-slavery conventions, the ILO conventions on labor and social conditions—continue in effect, and give special and strong emphasis to particular rights, but the benefit they brought to individuals are now subsumed in larger conceptions. Antislavery, for example, is not only state policy reflected in a willingness to assume international obligations to abolish the practice. Freedom from slavery is a right, an entitlement for every individual, one of an array of individual rights that in their sum reflect a conception of the minimum implications and needs of human dignity that states have come to recognize and to which they are obliged to give effect.

.   .   .

Notes

The international law of human rights is contained principally in the Nuremberg and the UN Charters, the International Covenants, several universal conventions, and a growing customary law of human rights. Rights have been further elaborated and protected in regional arrangements. See *infra* Chapter 2, Sections B, C, D and E.

Political and Moral Underpinnings

Louis Henkin, *The Age of Rights*
6–10 (1990).

The idea of rights here distilled from contemporary international instruments responds, I believe, to common moral intuitions and accepted political principles. Those intuitions and principles have not been authoritatively articulated. Developed during the decades following the Second World War, international human rights are not the work of philosophers, but of politicians and citizens, and philosophers have only begun to try to build conceptual justifications for them. The international expressions of rights themselves claim no philosophical foundation, nor do they reflect any clear philosophical assumptions; they articulate no particular moral principles or any single, comprehensive theory of the relation of the individual to society. That there are "fundamental human rights" was a declared article of faith, "reaffirmed" by "the peoples of the United Nations" in the United Nations Charter. The Universal Declaration of Human Rights, striving for a pronouncement that would appeal to diverse political systems governing diverse peoples, built on that faith and shunned philosophical exploration. Because of that faith—and of political and ideological forces—governments accepted the concept of human rights, agreed that they were properly matters for international concern, cooperated to define them, assumed international obligations to respect them, and submitted to some international scrutiny as to their compliance with these obligations.

International human rights derive from natural rights theories and systems, harking back through English, American, and French constitutionalism to John Locke et al., and earlier natural rights and natural law theory. In its American version, that constitutionalism included concepts of original individual autonomy translated into popular sovereignty; of a social compact providing for continued self-government through accountable representatives; of limited government for limited purposes; and retained, inalienable, individual rights (...). But the profound influence of that constitutionalism on international acceptance of human rights did not depend on, or take with it, commitment to all the underlying theory. International human rights reflect no comprehensive political theory of the relation of individual to society, only what is implied in the idea of individual rights against society. Human rights are "inherent" but not necessarily "retained" from any hypothetical state of nature anteceding government. There is a nod to popular sovereignty, but nothing of social compact or of continuing consent of the governed. Retained rights are not the condition of government, and violating them does not necessarily give rise to a right to undo government by revolution. Inevitably, international human rights also implicate the purposes for which governments are created, but they surely do not imply a commitment to government for limited purposes only. Born after various forms of socialism were established and spreading, and commitment to welfare economics and the welfare state was nearly universal, international human rights implied rather a conception of government as designed for all purposes and seasons. The rights deemed to be fundamental included not only limitations precluding government from invading civil and political rights, but positive obligations for government to promote economic and social well-being, implying government that is activist, intervening, planning, committed to economic-social programs for the society that would translate into economic-social rights for the individual (...)

Those who built international human rights perhaps saw these rights as "natural," but in a contemporary sense; human rights correspond to the nature of human beings and of human society, to *his* or *her* psychology and *its* sociology. Rights (to quote from the principal international instruments) "derive from the inherent dignity of the human person." "Recognition ... of the equal and inalienable rights of all members of the human family is the foundation of freedom, justice and peace in the world." Respect for, and observance of, human rights will help create "conditions of stability and well-being which are necessary for peaceful and friendly relations among nations." We are not told what theory justifies "human dignity" as the source of rights, or how human dignity is defined or its needs determined. We are not told what conception of justice is reflected in human rights, or how preserving human rights will promote peace in the world.

Necessarily, however, the idea of rights reflected in the instruments, the particular rights recognized, and the consequent responsibilities for political societies, imply particular political ideas and moral principles. International human rights does not hint at any theory of social contract, but it is committed to popular sovereignty. "The will of the people shall be the basis of the authority of government" and is to "be expressed in periodic and genuine elections which shall be by universal and equal suffrage." It is not required that government based on the will of the people take any particular form. Presumably, Western-style presidential or parliamentary systems and communist "democratic centralism" might both be equally consistent with the international standard—provided the people in fact have control over how they are governed, provided they have the freedom and the means to inform their governors of their wishes, provided the governors are accountable in fact and the people can replace them at frequent, regular intervals. In any system, government by bureaucracy is presumably not government by the people if, although political authority is conceived and couched in legal forms and decorated with occasional formal votes, arbitrary power in fact prevails, without meaningful accountability and meaningful opportunity for the people to terminate or control the exercise of such power. The will of the people is not the basis of the authority of government if the people are not free to change their form of government or their political and economic system, for instance, to move toward—or away from—socialism or a market economy.*

International human rights has no commitment to any particular economic system, and a society is free to choose between a market economy and socialism and among the various gradations and combinations of each. Some of the human rights recognized, however, imply commitment to some political-economic principles. Every person has a right to own property and not to be arbitrarily deprived of it; the right to work and be free to choose employment; to enjoy trade union protection against a powerful employer, private or public; and to be protected against unemployment or its consequences.

International human rights imply a broad conception of the purposes and responsibilities of government. The obligation of society to ensure rights may require government to plan, to regulate, to tax and to spend. Perhaps civil and political rights can be respected—in a fortunate society— by a civilized citizenry, and a minimal, honest, and benign officialdom, without any special societal interventions. But if citizen civility and official

---

* Of course, even the will of the people does not justify government in violating the rights of individuals or minority groups.

self-restraint are insufficient, the society must intervene, by civil rights acts and other laws, by institutions and remedies governing the behavior of citizen and official. Economic and social rights (food, shelter, work, health, and education) can perhaps be secured—in a fortunate society—by private initiative and means, by market forces, by employment contracts, by private insurance. But society must ensure these rights, must act as "insurer" for them; it must do what is necessary to see that such rights are in fact enjoyed, whether by improving the performance of private agencies or by supplementing or replacing these efforts by official programs.

Beneath the responsibilities of government for individual rights are political principles governing the relation of the individual to political authority, and beneath those political principles appear to be moral principles governing relations between individual human beings. If government responds to the will of the governed, the undertaking by governments to respect and ensure individual rights implies that the governed recognize these rights for each of them, and assume responsibility for these rights even when other interests, including other common interests, compete. The individual must recognize the obligation, both as an individual and as a member of the sovereign people (the majority), to respect and ensure those rights, to support the laws and institutions and the costs necessary to make the agreed-upon rights secure.

Political-moral principles are implied both in the idea of rights and in the particular rights recognized. Of course, a commitment to fair trial in the criminal process reflects a common sense of justice requiring that a person—not only I, but any other person—not be found guilty and deprived of freedom if he or she is innocent. Political-moral principles are implied in the fact that individuals not only demand for themselves, but also recognize for others equally, the autonomy, the physical integrity and freedom, the rights to due process, to property, to privacy, to "personhood," to liberties, as well as to basic human needs and other economic and social rights.

Less obvious are the moral assumptions underlying the other dispositions of the idea of rights. In general, what government may not do are those things we may not do to each other, and the reason why officials may not do them—say, deprive us of our life, liberty, privacy, or property—is because ordinarily no individual may do that to another. Human dignity requires respect from my neighbor as well as from the state. Under the international instruments the state is required not only to respect but to ensure rights, that is, ensure respect for them by private persons. By what moral calculus, then, are officials permitted to do to an individual what his neighbor may not?

Implicit political-moral principles accept limitations on individual rights for the common good—to protect society against external enemies and internal disorder, or to regulate individual activity for the benefit of others and for the common welfare. Therefore, the state is permitted to take away my freedom through the criminal law, at least when imprisonment is designed to prevent and rehabilitate, probably also if it aims to deter, and perhaps even when the purpose is to express moral judgment by societal retribution. It is permissible to take away my property through taxation in order to provide for the common defense and the public welfare. From some perspectives at least, it may be assumed that these limitations on the individual are acceptable because the individual consents to them, or consented to them, in principle and in advance, by living in society, and thereby submitting to government by democratic process. Individuals consent *a priori*, it can be argued, even to the possibility that they might be sent to their deaths for the common cause, on the assumption, or hope, that the need will not arise, and the sacrifice not prove necessary; that if someone will have to be sacrificed it will be someone else; that others submit to the same risk for one's own welfare, and that the selection will be by lot or chance or at least according to some rational, neutral principle. Whether such consent to the sacrifice of one's rights is authentic, whether an individual is really free to leave society so that his or her continuing consent can be assumed, is debatable and may differ from society to society, time to time, context to context, individual to individual. Or, perhaps—without insisting on consent and contract as the basis for rights and for limitations on rights—limitations on individual liberty or property are to be justified on notions of equity and practicability and some uncertain blend of the rights idea with utilitarian dedication to the "general welfare" or to maximum total happiness.*

The commitment in the human rights idea to the welfare society may imply other political-moral principles or assumptions. It implies, I think, that the basic human needs of those unable to provide for themselves are the responsibility of all, and that it is permissible if not obligatory to take from those who have (as by taxation) to provide for those who have not. Such moral obligation has been supported on various grounds:

- In the twentieth century, societies and political institutions are created and maintained for broad purposes; not only for security against one's neighbor and against external aggression, but to assure the welfare of all and each. The social contract includes agreement to create a welfare state.

- In a society with a complex, integrated economy, the economically disadvantaged—for example, the unemployed—are victims of deficiencies in the economic system, often of policies that purposefully maintain such disadvantages for systemic ends. Those who benefit from the system are therefore morally obligated to help those who suffer from it, at least to the extent of assuring their basic human needs.

- We are all members of a community that benefits all. Community and communality imply obligations, and high among them is the obligation to assure basic human needs for those who cannot satisfy their own.

---

* The rights idea, however, rejects the extreme utilitarian position that would justify even the complete sacrifice of individuals if it would increase total happiness.

- We have moved away from the moral intuitions of the Anglo–Saxon tradition which saw the Good Samaritan as acting from charity, not from moral obligation. Today, we are coming to believe, one is morally obligated to save a person in danger, at least if it can be done without undue risk or cost to oneself. There is, then, a moral obligation, for one who can, to save another from death or serious injury, as by starvation. If, in the case of the hungry in the community, that obligation is indeterminate in that the moral obligation to save any one person does not ordinarily attach to any other particular person, it attaches to all members of the community collectively. The collective obligation can be met by any collective action but effectively falls on the political authorities of society to meet by public action with public funds.

The moral foundations for human rights within society apply to all societies, and perhaps also between societies, as economies and polities become interdependent and community and communality expand. The idea of human rights, born in the West, has spread and, nominally at least, been universally accepted. Sovereign states continue to resist, but the implementation of the human rights idea has been "internationalized," and become the concern of the international community of states.

B. THE UNIVERSAL DECLARATION OF HUMAN RIGHTS

The Universal Declaration of Human Rights is the fundamental document of international human rights, and has claim to be one of the most important international instruments of the Twentieth Century.

At its creation, the Universal Declaration was seen as but a "second best." Nongovernmental organizations, and some smaller governments, had urged attaching to the UN Charter a legally binding Bill of Rights; instead, producing such a bill of rights was deferred, and was assigned to the new Commission on Human Rights established under the authority of the new UN General Assembly. In the Commission, there was also some desire to draft an international agreement to which states would adhere and which would be legally binding; instead, the Commission drafted, and the UN General Assembly proclaimed, the Universal Declaration of Human Rights.

The Universal Declaration converted an Eighteenth Century political idea of natural rights largely discredited in the Nineteenth and early Twentieth Centuries into a reigning ideology, an essential element in "constitutionalism," "the rule of law," "democracy." It transformed a colloquial, loosely used phrase—"human rights"—into a detailed definition, a remarkable synthesis of civil-political rights identified with the "Liberal State" and economic-social benefits of a "Welfare State," which became the accepted standard, an authoritative code. It took an idea constitutionalized in a few countries and rendered it universal for all political societies. It took a strictly domestic idea and ideology applicable to national political societies and internationalized it, rendering it of international political concern at the highest level, and the subject of international treaties and of customary international law.

Before the Commission on Human Rights began the work that produced the Declaration, UNESCO commissioned a study by selected philosophers of diverse cultural and jurisprudential origin.* Among materials available to those who produced the Universal Declaration was also a 1945 "Statement of Essential Human Rights," "drafted by a committee representing principal cultures of the world, appointed by the American Law Institute." The Statement set forth "Eighteen Articles of Essential Human Rights" and includes what later came to be called "economic and social" as well as "civil and political" rights.**

The Universal Declaration was adopted and proclaimed by the UN General Assembly on December 10, 1948, the day after the Assembly approved the first treaty of the modern human rights movement, the Genocide Convention. Together, the Declaration and the Genocide Convention formalized and solemnized the international human rights movement.

The content of the Universal Declaration of Human Rights and its status in international law are discussed *infra* pp. 321–323.

Universal Declaration of Human Rights

G.A. Res. 217A, U.N. Doc. A/810, at 71 (1948).

PREAMBLE

Whereas recognition of the inherent dignity and of the equal and inalienable rights of all members of the human family is the foundation of freedom, justice and peace in the world,

Whereas disregard and contempt for human rights have resulted in barbarous acts which have outraged the conscience of mankind, and the advent of a world in which human beings shall enjoy freedom of speech and belief and freedom from fear and want has been proclaimed as the highest aspiration of the common people,

Whereas it is essential, if man is not to be compelled to have recourse, as a last resort, to rebellion against tyranny and oppression, that human rights should be protected by the rule of law,

Whereas it is essential to promote the development of friendly relations between nations,

Whereas the peoples of the United Nations have in the Charter reaffirmed their faith in fundamental human rights, in the dignity and worth of the human person and in the equal rights of men and women and

---

* Later published as Human Rights, edited by Jacques Maritain (1948).

** See *Statement of Essential Human Rights*, 243 Annals Am. Acad. Pol. & Soc. Sci. 18 (January 1946), reprinted in The American Law Institute, Seventy-fifth Anniversary 1923–1998, at 261–95 (1998).

have determined to promote social progress and better standards of life in larger freedom,

Whereas Member States have pledged themselves to achieve, in cooperation with the United Nations, the promotion of universal respect for and observance of human rights and fundamental freedoms,

Whereas a common understanding of these rights and freedoms is of the greatest importance for the full realization of this pledge,

Now, therefore,

The General Assembly

Proclaims this Universal Declaration of Human Rights as a common standard of achievement for all peoples and all nations, to the end that every individual and every organ of society, keeping this Declaration constantly in mind, shall strive by teaching and education to promote respect for these rights and freedoms and by progressive measures, national and international, to secure their universal and effective recognition and observance, both among the peoples of Member States themselves and among the peoples of territories under their jurisdiction.

Article 1

All human beings are born free and equal in dignity and rights. They are endowed with reason and conscience and should act towards one another in a spirit of brotherhood.

Article 2

Everyone is entitled to all the rights and freedoms set forth in this Declaration, without distinction of any kind, such as race, colour, sex, language, religion, political or other opinion, national or social origin, property, birth or other status.

Furthermore, no distinction shall be made on the basis of the political, jurisdictional or international status of the country or territory to which a person belongs, whether it be independent, trust, non-self-governing or under any other limitation of sovereignty.

Article 3

Everyone has the right to life, liberty and security of person.

Article 4

No one shall be held in slavery or servitude; slavery and the slave trade shall be prohibited in all their forms.

Article 5

No one shall be subjected to torture or to cruel, inhuman or degrading treatment or punishment.

Article 6

Everyone has the right to recognition everywhere as a person before the law.

Article 7

All are equal before the law and are entitled without any discrimination to equal protection of the law. All are entitled to equal protection against any discrimination in violation of this Declaration and against any incitement to such discrimination.

Article 8

Everyone has the right to an effective remedy by the competent national tribunals for acts violating the fundamental rights granted him by the constitution or by law.

Article 9

No one shall be subjected to arbitrary arrest, detention or exile.

Article 10

Everyone is entitled to full equality to a fair and public hearing by an independent and impartial tribunal, in the determination of his rights and obligations and of any criminal charge against him.

Article 11

1. Everyone charged with a penal offense has the right to be presumed innocent until proved guilty according to law in a public trial at which he has had all the guarantees necessary for his defence.

2. No one shall be held guilty of any penal offence on account of any act or omission which did not constitute a penal offence, under national or international law, at the time when it was committed. Nor shall a heavier penalty be imposed than the one that was applicable at the time the penal offence was committed.

Article 12

No one shall be subjected to arbitrary interference with his privacy, family, home or correspondence, nor to attacks upon his honour and reputation. Everyone has the right to the protection of the law against such interference or attacks.

Article 13

1. Everyone has the right to freedom of movement and residence within the borders of each State.

2. Everyone has the right to leave any country, including his own, and to return to his country.

Article 14

1. Everyone has the right to seek and to enjoy in other countries asylum from persecution.

2. This right may not be invoked in the case of prosecutions genuinely arising from non-political crimes or from acts contrary to the purposes and principles of the United Nations.

Article 15

1. Everyone has the right to a nationality.

2. No one shall be arbitrarily deprived of his nationality nor denied the right to change his nationality.

Article 16

1. Men and women of full age, without any limitation due to race, nationality or religion, have the right to marry and to found a family. They are entitled to equal rights as to marriage, during marriage and at its dissolution.

2. Marriage shall be entered into only with the free and full consent of the intending spouses.

3. The family is the natural and fundamental group unit of society and is entitled to protection by society and the State.

Article 17

1. Everyone has the right own property alone as well as in association with others.

2. No one shall be arbitrarily deprived of his property.

Article 18

Everyone has the right to freedom of thought, conscience and religion; this right includes freedom to change his religion or belief, and freedom, either alone or in community with others and in public or private, to manifest his religion or belief in teaching, practice, worship and observance.

Article 19

Everyone has the right to freedom of opinion and expression; this right includes freedom to hold opinions without interference and to seek, receive and impart information and ideas through any media and regardless of frontiers.

Article 20

1. Everyone has the right to freedom of peaceful assembly and association.

2. No one may be compelled to belong to an association.

Article 21

1. Everyone has the right to take part in the government of his country, directly or through freely chosen representatives.

2. Everyone has the right of equal access to public service in his country.

3. The will of the people shall be the basis of the authority of government; this will shall be expressed in periodic and genuine elections which shall be by universal and equal suffrage and shall be held by secret vote or by equivalent free voting procedures.

Article 22

Everyone, as a member of society, has the right to social security and is entitled to realization, through national effort and international cooperation and in accordance with the organization and resources of each State, of the economic, social and cultural rights indispensable for his dignity and the free development of his personality.

Article 23

1. Everyone has the right to work, to free choice of employment, to just and favourable conditions of work and to protection against unemployment.

2. Everyone, without any discrimination, has the right to equal pay for equal work.

3. Everyone who works has the right to just and favourable remuneration ensuring for himself and his family an existence worthy of human dignity, and supplemented, if necessary, by other means of social protection.

4. Everyone has the right to form and to join trade unions for protection of his interests.

Article 24

Everyone has the right to rest and leisure, including reasonable limitation of working hours and periodic holidays with pay.

Article 25

1. Everyone has the right to a standard of living adequate for the health and well-being of himself and of his family, including food, clothing, housing and medical care and necessary social services, and the right to security in the event of unemployment, sickness, disability, widowhood, old age or other lack of livelihood in circumstances beyond his control.

2. Motherhood and childhood are entitled to special care and assistance. All children, whether born in or out of wedlock, shall enjoy the same social protection.

Article 26

1. Everyone has the right to education. Education shall be free, at least in the elementary and fundamental stages. Elementary education shall be compulsory. Technical and professional education shall be made generally available and higher education shall be equally accessible to all on the basis of merit.

2. Education shall be directed to the full development of the human personality and to the strengthening of respect for human rights and fundamental freedoms. It shall promote understanding, tolerance and friendship among all nations, racial or religious groups, and shall further the activities of the United Nations for the maintenance of peace.

3. Parents have a prior right to choose the kind of education that shall be given to their children.

Article 27

1. Everyone has the right freely to participate in the cultural life of the community, to enjoy the arts and to share in scientific advancement and its benefits.

2.   Everyone has the right to the protection of the moral and material interests resulting from any scientific, literary or artistic production of which he is the author.

Article 28

Everyone is entitled to a social and international order in which the rights and freedoms set forth in this Declaration can be fully realized.

Article 29

1.   Everyone has duties to the community in which alone the free and full development of his personality is possible.

2.   In the exercise of his rights and freedoms, everyone shall be subject only to such limitations as are determined by law solely for the purpose of securing due recognition and respect for the rights and freedoms of others and of meeting the just requirements of morality, public order and the general welfare in a democratic society.

3.   These rights and freedoms may in no case be exercised contrary to the purposes and principles of the United Nations.

Article 30

Nothing in this Declaration may be interpreted as implying for any State, group or person any right to engage in any activity or to perform any act aimed at the destruction of any of the rights and freedoms set forth herein.

Note: "Authorship" of the Universal Declaration

John Humphrey, the first and thereafter a long-serving director of the Human Rights Division of the United Nations Secretariat, played a major role in drafting the Universal Declaration. See John P. Humphrey, Human Rights and the United Nations: A Great Adventure 31–33, 42–43 (1984), and *The Universal Declaration of Human Rights: Its History, Impact and Juridical Character*, in Thirty Years of Human Rights at the United Nations 21–37 (1979), which contains a fuller discussion of the drafting process. A major contribution has been attributed to others, including René Cassin of France, Eleanor Roosevelt, Charles Malik of Lebanon.

Other non-governmental organizations, scholarly conferences, and individual scholars and publicists pursued the idea of an international Bill of Rights, and prepared draft bills or declarations of rights, among them: the Institut de Droit International (1929); H. G. Wells (1940); a World Citizen Association Conference (in a report by Prof. Quincy Wright); the Universities Committee on Post–War International Problems (1944); the highly influential work by Prof. Hersch Lauterpacht, An International Bill of the Rights of Man (1945); and the Committee on Human Rights of the Commission to Study the Organization of the Peace (1946). See W. Michael Reisman, *Private International Declaration Initiatives*, in La Déclaration Universelle des Droits de l'Homme, 1948–98: Avenir d'un Idéal Commun 79 (1999). See also Johannes Morsink, The Universal Declaration of Human Rights: Origins, Drafting, and Intent 1–35 (1999).

Note: Human Rights and Humanitarian Law

The materials in this Part do not include substantial treatment of international "humanitarian law," the law that governs the conduct of war. A body of humanitarian law—including limitations on the use of certain weapons, regulations for the treatment of prisoners of war, the sick and the wounded, and rules safeguarding civilian populations—was established in the Nineteenth Century, was developed and updated after the First World War, and again in recent decades. Humanitarian law is contained largely in a series of Geneva Conventions and Protocols, and it is monitored principally by the International Committee of the Red Cross, a non-governmental body with headquarters in Geneva, and by national Red Cross Societies. Virtually all states are parties to the principal conventions comprising humanitarian law. The United States is party to some of the humanitarian conventions but not to all, though it has promised to abide by the major provisions.

Humanitarian law has not been superseded by or subsumed in the international law of human rights. Until recently, the two bodies of international law remained largely separate, embracing different norms, contained in different international agreements, monitored by different enforcement "machinery," and addressed in different bodies of legal literature. Considerations of time and space require that, in general, we maintain that division and exclude humanitarian law from these materials (and from the course for which these materials are designed).

In the 1990's, however, human rights law and humanitarian law converged in particular, grave, and dramatic circumstances. Human rights violations of genocidal proportions, committed during war or in war-like contexts, provoked new international initiatives which engendered new international institutions and law at the frontiers between human rights law and humanitarian law. The United Nations Security Council established a criminal tribunal for the former Yugoslavia and a parallel one for Rwanda; the Statutes of these *ad hoc* tribunals conferred upon them jurisdiction over "war crimes" (aspects of humanitarian law), but also over "genocide" and other gross human rights violations. See *infra* Chapter 3(C). In 1993, the UN International Law Commission adopted a Statute for a permanent International Criminal Court, and in July 1998 a plenipotentiary conference in Rome adopted and opened for signature a statute for a permanent court. If and when established, the ICC will have jurisdiction over some violations of humanitarian law, i.e., grave breaches of the Geneva Conventions and violations of the laws and customs of war, as well as over major violations of human rights law, i.e., genocide and enumerated crimes against humanity, with special attention to crimes of sexual violence.

Writings on humanitarian law include J.S. Pictet, Humanitarian Law and the Protection of War Victims (1975); The Geneva Conventions of 12 August 1949: Commentary (1952–1960); Development and Principles of International Humanitarian Law (1985); and G. Draper, The Red Cross Conventions (1958). For a list of the principal humanitarian conventions and a discussion of the scope of humanitarian law, see Partsch, *Humanitarian Law and Armed Conflict*, 3 Encyclop. of Public Int'l Law 215 (R. Bernhardt ed., 1982).

Writers increasingly explore the relation between humanitarian law and international human rights law. See, *e.g.,* T. Meron, Human Rights and Humanitarian Norms as Customary Law (1989); Meyrowitz, Le Droit de la guerre et les droits de l'homme, 88 Rev. Droit Public & Science Politique en France & à l'Étranger 1059 (1972); Draper, *Humanitarian Law and Human Rights*, 1979 Acta Juridica 193; Robertson, *Human Rights as the Basis of International Humanitarian Law*, in Proceedings of the International Conference on Humanitarian Law 55 (1970).

The legal literature on the *ad hoc* tribunals for the former Yugoslavia and for Rwanda, and on the proposed permanent International Criminal Court, also continues to grow. See, for example, The Statute of the International Tribunal for the Prosecution of Persons Responsible for Serious Violations of International Humanitarian Law Committed in the Territory of the Former Yugoslavia since 1991, UN Doc. S/25704 (1993), reprinted in 32 ILM 1159; Virginia Morris and Michael P. Scharf, An Insider's Guide to the International Criminal Tribunal for the Former Yugoslavia: a Documentary Analysis (1995); M. Cherif Bassiouni and Peter Manikas, The Law of the International Criminal Tribunal for the Former Yugoslavia (1996); and International Criminal Law (M.C. Bassiouni ed., 2d ed. 1999). On the International Criminal Court, see Report of the International Law Commission on the work of its forty-sixth session, U.N. GAOR, 49th Sess., Supp. No. 10, at 382, 383, U.N. Doc. A/49/10 (1994); the proposed Statute of the International Criminal Court, adopted, by the UN Diplomatic Conference of Plenipotentiaries on the Establishment of an International Criminal Court, A/CONF.183/9 (July 1998); and *Developments in International Criminal Law*, 93 Am. J. Int'l L. 1-123 (1999).

CHAPTER 2

THE INTERNATIONAL LAW OF HUMAN RIGHTS

Universalization of the ideology of human rights rendered it applicable to all human beings in all political societies. The internationalization of human rights rendered the condition of human rights in every society a subject of international political concern, and led to the gradual growth of an international law of human rights, of international legal undertakings and obligations by states to respect and to ensure the human rights of persons subject to their jurisdiction.

A. INTRODUCTION: INTERNATIONAL LAW IN GENERAL: CHARACTER AND SOURCES

The international law of human rights is part of international law generally, and partakes of its essential character, its values, principles, and institutions. Like international law generally, the international law of human rights is the law of "the international community of states," made principally by treaty and by customary law, and supplemented, secondarily, by "general principles" that have been absorbed from national legal systems. Unlike international law generally, the international law of human rights did not begin with a deeply-rooted basis in customary law; it has been established primarily by treaty. But human rights treaties—and the Universal Declaration—have also contributed to the growth and acceptance of a core of important customary human rights norms.

It is useful to recall and review here the fundamentals of international law generally. The character and sources of international law are summarized in the Restatement of Foreign Relations Law.

Restatement (Third) of the Foreign Relations Law of the United States

Introductory Note to Chapter One, §§ 101–102, and Comments (1987).

Introductory Note:

International law is the law of the international community of states. It deals with the conduct of nation-states and their relations with other states, and to some extent also with their relations with individuals, business organizations, and other legal entities. See § 101. In its conceptions, its specific norms and standards, and largely in practice, international law functions between states, as represented by their governments. Its implementation and the remedies for its violation are also largely intergovernmental. . . .

The international community of states. The principal entities of the international political system are states. The system includes also international (intergovernmental) organizations with independent status and character, for example, the United Nations, the International Monetary Fund, the Organization of American States. Nongovernmental organizations, juridical persons (*e.g.,* national and "multinational" companies), and individuals are not primary actors in the system but may influence it and are affected by it. . . .

The international political system is loose and decentralized. Its principal components—"sovereign" states—retain their essential autonomy. There is no "world government" as the term "government" is commonly understood. There is no central legislature with general law-making authority; the General Assembly and other organs of the United Nations influence the development of international law but only when their product is accepted by states. See § 103, Comment *c* and Reporters' Note 2. There is no executive institution to enforce law; the United Nations Security Council has limited executive power to enforce the provisions of the Charter and to maintain international peace and security, but it has no authority to enforce international law generally; within its jurisdiction, moreover, the Council is subject to the veto power of its five permanent members, *viz.* People's Republic of China, France, the U.S.S.R., the United Kingdom, and the United States. There is no international judiciary with general, comprehensive and compulsory jurisdiction; the International Court of Justice decides cases submitted to it and renders advisory opinions but has only limited compulsory jurisdiction. See § 903.

Law, however, is essential to the system. International law has the character and qualities of law, and serves the functions and purposes of law, providing restraints against arbitrary state action and guidance in international relations.

International law as law. The absence of central legislative and executive institutions had led to skepticism about the legal quality of international law. Many observers consider international law to be only a series of precepts of morality or etiquette, of cautions and admonitions lacking in both specificity and binding quality. Governments, it is sometimes assumed, commonly disregard international law and observe it only when they deem it to be in their interest to do so.

These impressions are mistaken. International law is law like other law, promoting order, guiding, restraining, regulating behavior. States, the principal addressees of international law, treat it as law, consider themselves bound by it, attend to it with a sense of legal obligation and with concern for the consequences of violation. Some states refer to international law in their constitutions; many incorporate it into their domestic legal systems; all take account of it in their governmental institutional arrangements and in their international relations. There is reference to the "Law of Nations" in the Constitution of the United States (Article I, Section 8). It is part of the law of the United States, respected by Presidents and Congresses, and by the States, and given effect by the courts.

International law based on acceptance. While there have been relations between "states" since early human history, and some law governing those relations, modern international law is commonly dated from the Peace of Westphalia (1648) and the rise of the secular state. There have been major changes in that law, but its basic concepts and general outlines have remained essentially intact, even in our times when ideological conflict has polarized the international political system, and when many states—newly independent, non-Western, less-developed—were disposed to reexamine the international system into which they came.

Modern international law is rooted in acceptance by states which constitute the system. Specific rules of law also depend on state acceptance. Particular agreements create binding obligations for the particular parties, but general law depends on general acceptance. Law cannot be made by the majority for all, although states may be bound by a rule of customary law that they did not participate in making if they did not clearly dissociate themselves from it during the process of its development. See § 102, Comment *d*. There has been a growing practice in international organizations and at law-making conferences of seeking agreement by "consensus" (rather than by vote), a practice that also discourages dissent and puts pressure on dissidents to acquiesce. In principle, law that has been generally accepted cannot be later modified unilaterally by any state (see previous Restatement § 1), but particular states and groups of states can contribute to the process of developing (and modifying) law by their actions as well as by organized attempts to achieve formal change.

Custom and international agreement. International law is made in two principal ways—by the practice of states ("customary law") and by purposeful agreement among states (sometimes called "conventional law," *i.e.*, law by convention, by agreement). See § 102. Until recently, international law was essentially customary law: agreements made particular arrangements between particular parties, but were not ordinarily used for general law-making for states. In our day, treaties have become the principal vehicle for making law for the international system; more and more of established customary law is being codified by general agreements. To this day, however, many rules about status, property, and international delicts are still customary law, not yet codified. The law of international agreements itself has recently been codified (in the Vienna Convention on the Law of Treaties, see this Restatement, Part III), but the basic principle that makes international agreements (including the Vienna Convention itself) binding is the principle of customary law that agreements must be observed. Indeed, codification itself assumes the essential validity of the customary law that is being codified and the authenticity of its substantive content. Even after codification, moreover, custom maintains its authority, particularly as regards states that do not adhere to the codifying treaty. See

§ 102, Comment *i*. Customary law, then, remains an important element of international law and its rules and principles are included in this Restatement.

Customary international law has developed slowly and unevenly, out of action and reaction in practice, rather than systematically or by major leaps. National courts required to determine questions of international law must do so by imprecise methods out of uncertain materials, and they must look at a process that is worldwide and includes the actions and determinations of foreign actors (including foreign courts). Determinations by United States courts are also part of the process. A determination of international law by the Supreme Court of the United States resolves the matter for purposes of the law of the United States; it is not conclusive as to what international law is for other states, and perhaps not even as to what it is for the United States in its relations with other countries. See § 112, Comments *a* and Reporters' Note 1.

. . .

Content of international law. International law is made by states, but the law so created deals not only with the conduct of states and international organizations and with relations among them, but increasingly also with relations of states with juridical and natural persons, including those in the state's own territory. See Part VII. International law includes norms, standards and principles, not different in character (and sometimes in complexity) from those in developed national law. Much international law is specific, for example the rules of diplomatic intercourse and immunity. Some international law mandates essentially a rule of reason, which leaves much room for disagreement, but such rules are not much more uncertain than, say, principles such as "unreasonable" search and seizure, "cruel and unusual" punishments, or "due process of law," in United States constitutional law. That in the international system there is no mandatory, authoritative process for deciding what the law is and where lines shall be drawn makes an important difference, but, in general, even broadly stated rules and principles of international law are respected and observed.

International law includes the basic, classic concepts of law in national legal systems—status and property, obligation and delict. It includes substantive law, process and procedure, remedies. International law is still often described as "primitive" but increasing complexity in international relations has brought increasingly complex international law. A law that not long ago was almost wholly customary is now overlaid by an elaborate network of treaties. At one time, international law dealt largely with rules of "abstention" by states *inter se*; now it includes a growing law of cooperation through a web of international organizations and other multilateral arrangements, law addressing the activities of giant "juridical persons" (multinational companies), and the human rights of individuals in their own national societies.

International law does not address all conduct of states or international organizations, or all of their relations. International law does not address some matters because they are not of sufficient international concern, and it is accepted that they are and should remain essentially "domestic." Some matters clearly of international concern are not regulated because the international community has not addressed them or has not been able to agree on how to deal with them.

.   .   .

§ 101.   International Law Defined

International law, as used in this Restatement, consists of rules and principles of general application dealing with the conduct of states and of international organizations and with their relations *inter se,* as well as with some of their relations with persons, whether natural or juridical.

.   .   .

§ 102.   Sources of International Law

(1) A rule of international law is one that has been accepted as such by the international community of states

(a) in the form of customary law;

(b) by international agreement; or

(c) by derivation from general principles common to the major legal systems of the world.

(2) Customary international law results from a general and consistent practice of states followed by them from a sense of legal obligation.

(3) International agreements create law for the states parties thereto and may lead to the creation of customary international law when such agreements are intended for adherence by states generally and are in fact widely accepted.

(4) General principles common to the major legal systems, even if not incorporated or reflected in customary law or international agreement, may be invoked as supplementary rules of international law where appropriate.

Comment:

.   .   .

b. Practice as customary law. "Practice of states," Subsection (2), includes diplomatic acts and instructions as well as public measures and other governmental acts and official statements of policy, whether they are unilateral or undertaken in cooperation with other states, for example in organizations such as the Organization for Economic Cooperation and Development (OECD). Inaction may constitute state practice, as when a state acquiesces in acts of another state that affect its legal rights. The practice necessary to create customary law may be of comparatively short duration, but under Subsection (2) it must be "general and consistent." A practice can be general even if it is not universally followed; there is no precise formula to indicate how widespread a practice must be, but it should reflect wide acceptance among the states particularly involved in the relevant activity. Failure of a significant number of important states to adopt a practice can prevent a principle from becoming general customary law though it might become "particular customary law" for the participating states. See Comment *e*. A principle of customary law is not binding on a state that declares its dissent from the principle during its development. See Comment d.

c.   *Opinio juris*. For a practice of states to become a rule of customary international law it must appear that the states follow the practice from a sense of legal obligation (*opinio juris sive necessitatis*); a practice that is generally followed but which states feel legally free to disregard does not contribute to customary law. A practice initially followed by states as a matter of courtesy or habit may become law when states generally come to believe that they are under a legal obligation to comply with it. It is often difficult to determine when that transformation into law has taken place. Explicit evidence of a sense of legal obligation (*e.g.,* by official statements) is not necessary; *opinio juris* may be inferred from acts or omissions.

d.   *Dissenting views and new states*. Although customary law may be built by the acquiescence as well as by the actions of states (Comment *b*) and become generally binding on all states, in principle a state that indicates its dissent from a practice while the law is still in the process of development is not bound by that rule even after it matures. Historically, such dissent and consequent exemption from a principle that became general customary law has been rare. See Reporters' Note 2. As to the possibility of dissent from peremptory norms (*jus cogens*), see Comment *k*. A state that enters the international system after a practice has ripened into a rule of international law is bound by that rule.

.   .   .

f.   *International agreement as source of law*. An international agreement creates obligations binding between the parties under international law. See § 321. Ordinarily, an agreement between states is a source of law only in the sense that a private contract may be said to make law for the parties under the domestic law of contracts. Multilateral agreements open to all states, however, are increasingly used for general legislation, whether to make new law, as in human rights (Introduction to Part VII), or for codifying and developing customary law, as in the Vienna Convention on the Law of Treaties. For the law of international agreements, see Part III. "International agreement" is defined in § 301(1). International agreements may contribute to customary law. See Comment *i*.

g.   *Binding resolutions of international organizations*. Some international agreements that are constitutions or charters of international organizations confer power on those organizations to impose binding obligations on their members by resolution, usually by qualified majorities. Such obligations derive their authority from the international agreement constituting the organization, and resolutions so adopted by the organization can be seen as "secondary sources" of international law for its members. For example, the International Monetary Fund may prescribe rules concerning maintenance or change of exchange rates or depreciation of currencies. See § 821. The International Civil Aviation Organization may set binding standards for navigation or qualifications for flight crews in aviation over the high seas.

For resolutions of international organizations that are not binding but purport to state the international law on a particular subject, see § 103, Comment *c*.

h.   The United Nations Charter. The Charter of the United Nations has been adhered to by virtually all states. Even the few remaining non-member states have acquiesced in the principles it established. The Charter provisions prohibiting the use of force have become rules of international law binding on all states. Compare Article 2(6). See § 905, Comment *g*.

Article 103 of the Charter provides:

> In the event of a conflict between the obligations of the Members of the United Nations under the present Charter and their obligations under any other international agreement, their obligations under the present Charter shall prevail.

Members seem to have read this article as barring them from making agreements inconsistent with the Charter, and have refrained from making such agreements. See, *e.g.,* Article 7 of the North Atlantic Treaty, 1949, 63 Stat. 2241, T.I.A.S. No. 1964, 34 U.N.T.S. 243; Article 102 of the Charter of the Organization of American States, 1948, 2 U.S.T. 2394, T.I.A.S. No. 2361, 119 U.N.T.S. 3. And see Comment *k*.

. . .

k.   Peremptory norms of international law (jus cogens). Some rules of international law are recognized by the international community of states as peremptory, permitting no derogation. These rules prevail over and invalidate international agreements and other rules of international law in conflict with them. Such a peremptory norm is subject to modification only by a subsequent norm of international law having the same character. It is generally accepted that the principles of the United Nations Charter prohibiting the use of force (Comment *h*) have the character of *jus cogens*. See § 331(2) and Comment *e* to that section.

l.   General principles as secondary source of law. Much of international law, whether customary or constituted by agreement, reflects principles analogous to those found in the major legal systems of the world, and historically may derive from them or from a more remote common origin. See Introductory Note to Chapter 1 of this Part and Reporters' Note 1 to this section. General principles common to systems of national law may be resorted to as an independent source of law. That source of law may be important when there has not been practice by states sufficient to give the particular principle status as customary law and the principle has not been legislated by general international agreement.

General principles are a secondary source of international law, resorted to for developing international law interstitially in special circumstances. For example, the passage of time as a defense to an international claim by a state on behalf of a national may not have had sufficient application in practice to be accepted as a rule of customary law. Nonetheless, it may be invoked as a rule of international law, at least in claims based on injury to persons (Part VII), because it is a general principle common to the major legal systems of the world and is not inappropriate for international claims. Other rules that have been drawn from general principles include rules relating to the administration of justice, such as the rule that no one may be judge in his own cause; *res judicata*; and rules of fair procedure generally. General principles may also provide "rules of reason" of a general character, such as acquiescence and estoppel, the principle that rights must not be abused, and the obligation to repair a wrong. International practice may sometimes convert such a principle into a rule of customary law.

Treaties and Customary Law of Human Rights

Louis Henkin, *Introduction*
in The International Bill of Rights:
The Covenant on Civil and Political Rights, 13–16 (Henkin ed., 1981).

Human Rights as International Law

Human rights are rights which the individual has, or should have, in his society. If societies respected these rights adequately, there would be no need for international law and institutions to help protect them. International human rights law and institutions are designed to induce states to remedy the inadequacies of their national laws and institutions so that human rights will be respected and vindicated. The individual must pursue his rights through his own laws and institutions. Even when these fail him, international law and institutions cannot provide those rights; they can only press the state to provide them. International human rights obligations are met when, and only when, national laws and institutions meet the minimum international standards and give effect to the minimum of human rights.

International human rights agreements are international agreements like all others. They create rights and duties between states parties to the agreement; they may create also rights in third parties, whether states or individuals. Failure to honor these undertakings brings the same consequences as for other international agreements; other parties can demand compliance and seek reparations, and may resort to any tribunal which has jurisdiction over such claims between these parties. Some agreements also provide for special remedies before particular bodies.

International Human Rights and Domestic Jurisdiction

The United Nations Charter made human rights a legitimate subject for discussion and recommendation by the [UN General] Assembly and its sub-organs. Human rights may also properly come into the ken of the

Security Council when it implicates peace and security, *e.g.*, in South Africa. By discussing human rights the General Assembly does not intervene in matters "which are essentially within the domestic jurisdiction of any state" (Article 2(a)). Intervention, strictly, means dictatorial interference by force, and there have been no UN military interventions in support of human rights; discussion and recommendation are not intervention. Human rights, moreover, are a matter of international concern, not essentially within any state's domestic jurisdiction. Enforcement measures by the Security Council are in any event exempted from Article 2(7).

Article 2(7) speaks only to intervention by the UN, not by member states, but most challenges to activities by states on behalf of human rights as "intervention" are equally unfounded. Peaceful objections by states to human rights violations by other states are not interventions. Generally, human rights are no longer within a state's domestic jurisdiction. That which is governed by international law or agreement is ipso facto and by definition a matter of international concern, not a matter of any state's domestic jurisdiction. Certainly, any state that adheres to an international human rights agreement has made the subject of that agreement a matter of international concern. It has submitted its performance to scrutiny and to appropriate, peaceful reaction by other parties, and to any special procedures or machinery provided by the agreement for its implementation.

Human Rights and International Legal Rights

The international instruments speak of human rights, but they do not purport to create them; they recognize their preexistence in some other moral or legal order. They confirm the concept of human rights and give it status and value in the international system. Like other international agreements, the international human rights agreements create rights and obligations among the states parties to the agreement: every party is obligated to every other state to carry out its undertakings; every other state has the right to have the obligation carried out. But these are the legal rights of states, not the human rights of the individual.

If states are the promisors and promisees, however, the authentic beneficiaries are the individual inhabitants whose "human rights" the state promises to respect. Whether the international agreements also create international legal rights for the individual is debated. Some have strongly denied it. Others argue that as third-party beneficiaries, and the true beneficiaries, individuals have rights under international law, even when they have no direct remedy but must rely on states and international bodies to vindicate their rights. And some instruments—for example the Optional Protocol to the International Covenant on Civil and Political Rights, the Convention on the Elimination of All Forms of Racial Discrimination, and the European and the American Conventions on Human Rights—also provide some remedy for the individual to pursue his international legal rights by international legal remedies.

National and International Enforcement

Human rights are rights to be enjoyed by individuals in their own societies and implemented and enforced under their laws and institutions.

International undertakings are designed to help assure that national societies in fact respect the human rights of their inhabitants. International instruments require states to enact legislation and otherwise ensure that the rights are respected. In some legal systems international human rights obligations may be "self-executing" and will be given effect by officials and courts without domestic legislation.

The international system also provides "enforcement machinery." Such international instrumentalities, however, do not operate directly to grant the individual his rights; they work on the state and are designed to induce the state to carry out its obligations. Even when the individual is given some kind of an international remedy, for example, the right to "communicate" to the Human Rights Committee pursuant to the Optional Protocol to the Covenant, the communication does not produce an international mandate conferring the right; it serves only to trigger an international process to induce the state to desist from violation or to provide a remedy for past violations.

.   .   .

Notes

Customary law has had a smaller part in human rights law than in many other areas of international law. Because human rights were not a substantial subject of international relations before the Second World War, there was little state practice of respect for human rights with a sense of international legal obligation. See the discussion of sources of international law, *supra* pp. 299–300. Also, with an active movement developing a law of human rights by treaty, there was less room, or need, for developing law by custom. But treaties are binding only on states parties and, of course, states will not adhere to treaties that outlaw practices they were determined to continue. The impetus for developing and identifying a customary law of human rights came in particular from a near-universal desire to outlaw some practices by one or two states, notably *apartheid* in South Africa. It was possible to identify and develop a customary law of human rights also in regard to practices that no state was prepared to claim the right to practice, *e.g.*, torture. See *Filartiga v. Pena–Irala*, *infra* p. 856. Ambiguity of definition, and the absence of special bodies to monitor compliance, may also have lessened resistance to identifying some norms as customary law.

Restatement (Third) of the Foreign Relations Law of the United States

§ 701 Comments and Notes (1987).

§ 701.   Obligation to Respect Human Rights

A State is obligated to respect the human rights of persons subject to its jurisdiction

(a) that it has undertaken to respect by international agreement;

(b) that states generally are bound to respect as a matter of customary international law (§ 702); and

(c) that it is required to respect under general principles of law common to the major legal systems of the world.

Comment:

. . .

b. Human rights and sources of international law. The international law of human rights has strong antecedents in natural law, in contemporary moral values, and in the constitutional law of states. Human rights principles come into international law by the same means and from the same sources as other international law, *viz.*, as customary law, by international agreement, or from general principles of law common to the major legal systems of the world. This chapter specifies human rights obligations deriving from customary law or international agreement; some obligations deriving from those sources may also be regarded as having been absorbed into international law as general principles common to the major legal systems. As of 1986, it has not been authoritatively determined whether any obligations to observe human rights, in addition to those included in clauses (a) and (b), have been absorbed into international law as general principles common to the major legal systems.

c. Human rights law as obligations between states. Like international agreements generally, international human rights agreements create legal obligations between the states parties, although the agreements are for the benefit of individuals, including nationals, residents, and others subject to the jurisdiction of the promisor state. Human rights obligations in customary international law generally are obligations to all other states. Remedies for violations of human rights obligations are generally state to state (see § 703 and § 902(2)), but some international agreements also provide remedies to individuals whose human rights have been violated, or to individuals or nongovernmental bodies acting on their behalf.

d. Human rights obligations under United Nations Charter. Almost all states are parties to the United Nations Charter, which contains human rights obligations. There has been no authoritative determination of the full content of those obligations, but it is increasingly accepted that states parties to the Charter are legally obligated to respect some of the rights recognized in the Universal Declaration. A violation of the rights protected by customary law, § 702, also may be seen as a violation of the Charter.

Notes

1.   Like other international law, human rights law is made principally by treaty or by customary law. Human rights treaties include two principal covenants, and a growing number of conventions; the UN Charter, an

international treaty, also includes several undertakings related to human rights. See *infra*.

2.   The international law of treaties does not distinguish among international agreements on the basis of what they are called. Whether an international agreement is called a covenant, a convention, a protocol, or by one of several other appellations, it is equally binding as a matter of law. Different terms may reflect political and rhetorical preference: *e.g.,* "covenant" is used usually to suggest importance and to enhance the influence of the particular agreement. The UN Charter, by its terms, Article 103, accords superiority to the obligations of states under the Charter over obligations under other international agreements. See Restatement of Foreign Relations Law § 102, comment *h*, above.

3.   International human rights law includes also a small but growing body of customary law. See Section E(1) below.

4.   On "humanitarian intervention," see Chapter 3, Section E(2)(c) below. In the 1990's the UN Security Council authorized intervention in several instances where it found a threat to international peace and security.

Note: The UN Charter and the Nuremberg Charter

The birth of the international law of human rights is sometimes dated from the recognition in the Nuremberg Charter of the concept of "crimes against humanity." By charging Nazi leaders with such crimes, notably genocide, the Allies in effect decided that international law had developed a principle of customary law rendering it a violation of international law for states to commit such atrocities even against their own population. The Nuremberg Charter determined also that these were crimes for which individuals could be held personally responsible, and if found guilty could be severely punished. (At Nuremberg, Nazi leaders were found guilty of crimes against humanity but none of them was hanged for such crimes alone).

The principles of the Nuremberg Charter were unanimously approved by the United Nations General Assembly, see G.A. Res. 95, U.N. Doc. A/236 (1946), and their status as international law is not in doubt.

The Nuremberg Charter and the United Nations Charter have been described as twin offspring of the Allied agreements for the post-war world order. See Telford Taylor, *Nuremberg and Vietnam: An American Tragedy,* 78–79 (1970). *Inter alia*, the UN Charter established that human rights were a matter of legitimate and appropriate international concern, and declared it to be a purpose of the United Nations to promote universal respect and observance of human rights. Whether the Charter also establishes legally-binding norms rendering violation of human rights a violation of international law is still debated, but clearly the Charter, and the Genocide Convention, and the Universal Declaration, contributed to principles of customary law of human rights.

1. HUMAN RIGHTS AGREEMENTS UNDER INTERNATIONAL LAW

International human rights covenants and conventions are international treaties and governed by the international law of treaties, including the law as to their formation and termination, the locus of commitment and responsibility for compliance, the interpretation of the treaty. But the special character of human rights undertakings and obligations has inspired some exceptional doctrines and practices, for example in respect of reservations to human rights agreements, the interpretation of human rights agreements, the entity making the commitment and responsible for compliance.

a. HUMAN RIGHTS AGREEMENTS AND THE LAW OF TREATIES

Like other treaties, human rights agreements are governed by the international law of treaties, which has long been customary international law but was codified in the Vienna Convention on the Law of Treaties. See U.N. Doc. A/CONF. 39/27 (1969). The United States has not ratified the Vienna Convention, but it has accepted the provisions of the Convention as accurately reflecting the customary law of treaties.

Reservations to Treaties: In General

Reservations to treaties are governed by the Vienna Convention on the Law of Treaties, Articles 19–22. The Restatement of Foreign Relations Law restates the law as to reservations in § 313:

(1) A state may enter a reservation to a multilateral international agreement unless

(a) reservations are prohibited by the agreement,

(b) the agreement provides that only specified reservations not including the reservation in question may be made, or

(c) the reservation is incompatible with the object and purpose of the agreement.

(2) A reservation to a multilateral agreement entered in accordance with Subsection (1) is subject to acceptance by the other contracting states as follows:

(a) a reservation expressly authorized by the agreement does not require subsequent acceptance by the other contracting states;

(b) where application of the agreement in its entirety among the parties is an essential condition to their consent, a reservation requires acceptance by all the parties;

(c) where a reservation is neither authorized nor prohibited, expressly or by implication,

(i) acceptance of a reservation by another contracting state constitutes the reserving state a party to the agreement in relation to the accepting state as soon as the agreement is in force for those states;

(ii) objection to a reservation by another contracting state does not preclude entry into force of the agreement between the reserving and accepting states unless a contrary intention is expressed by the objecting state.

. . .

Comment:

a.   Reservation defined. A reservation is defined in the Vienna Convention, Article 2(1)(d), as a unilateral statement made by a state when signing, ratifying, accepting, approving, or acceding to an international agreement, whereby it purports to exclude or modify the legal effect of certain provisions of that agreement in their application to that state....

. . .

g.   Declarations and understandings. When signing or adhering to an international agreement, a state may make a unilateral declaration that does not purport to be a reservation. Whatever it is called, it constitutes a reservation in fact if it purports to exclude, limit, or modify that state's legal obligation. Sometimes, however, a declaration purports to be an "understanding," an interpretation of the agreement in a particular respect. Such an interpretive declaration is not a reservation if it reflects the accepted view of the agreement. But another contracting party may challenge the expressed understanding, treating it as a reservation which it is not prepared to accept.

Reservations to Human Rights Agreements

In principle, the law as to reservations applies to human rights agreements as to treaties generally. However, in its Advisory Opinion on Reservations to the Convention on the Prevention and Punishment of the Crime of Genocide, 1951 I.C.J. 15 (May 28, 1951), the International Court of Justice said:

It is well established that in its treaty relations a State cannot be bound without its consent, and that consequently no reservation can be effective against any State without its agreement thereto. It is also a generally recognized principle that a multilateral convention is the result of an agreement freely concluded upon its clauses and that consequently none of the contracting parties is entitled to frustrate or impair, by means of multilateral decisions or particular agreements, the purpose and *raison d'être* of the convention. To this principle was linked the notion of the integrity of the convention as adopted, a notion which in its traditional concept involved the proposition that no reservation was valid unless it was accepted by all the contracting parties without exception, as would have been the case if it had been stated during the negotiations.

This concept, which is directly inspired by the notion of contract, is of undisputed value as a principle. However, as regards the Genocide Convention, it is proper to refer to a variety of circumstances which would lead to a more flexible application of this principle. Among these circumstances may be noted the clearly universal character of the United Nations under whose auspices the Convention was concluded, and the very wide degree of participation envisaged by Article XI of the Convention. Extensive participation in conventions of this type has already given rise to greater flexibility in the international practice concerning multilateral conventions. More general resort to reservations, very great allowance made for tacit assent to reservations, the existence of practices which go so far as to admit that the author of reservations which have been rejected by certain contracting parties is nevertheless to be regarded as a party to the convention in relation to those contracting parties that have accepted the reservations—all these factors are manifestations of a new need for flexibility in the operation of multilateral conventions.

It must also be pointed out that although the Genocide Convention was finally approved unanimously, it is nevertheless the result of a series of majority votes. The majority principle, while facilitating the conclusion of multilateral conventions, may also make it necessary for certain States to make reservations. This observation is confirmed by the great number of reservations which have been made of recent years to multilateral conventions.

.   .   .

[T]he Genocide Convention was ... intended by the General Assembly and by the contracting parties to be definitely universal in scope. It was in fact approved on December 9th, 1948, by a resolution which was unanimously adopted by fifty-six States.

The objects of such a convention must also be considered. The Convention was manifestly adopted for a purely humanitarian and civilizing purpose. It is indeed difficult to imagine a convention that might have this dual character to a greater degree, since its object on the one hand is to safeguard the very existence of certain human groups and on the other to confirm and endorse the most elementary principles of morality. In such a convention the contracting States do not have any interests of their own; they merely have, one and all, a common interest, namely, the accomplishment of those high purposes which are the *raison d'être* of the convention. Consequently, in a convention of this type one cannot speak of individual advantages or disadvantages to States, or of the maintenance of a perfect contractual balance between rights and duties. The high ideals which inspired the Convention provide, by virtue of the common will of the parties, the foundation and measure of all its provisions.

.   .   .

The object and purpose of the Genocide Convention imply that it was the intention of the General Assembly and of the States which adopted it that as many States as possible should participate. The complete exclusion from the Convention of one or more States would not only restrict the scope of its application, but would detract from the authority of the moral and humanitarian principles which are its basis. It is inconceivable that the contracting parties readily contemplated that an objection to a minor reservation should produce such a result. But even less could the contracting parties have intended to sacrifice the very object of the Convention in favour of a vain desire to secure as many participants as possible. The object and purpose of the Convention thus limit both freedom of making reservations and that of objecting to them. It follows that it is the compatibility of a reservation with the object and purpose of the Convention that must furnish the criterion for the attitude of a State in making the reservation on accession as well as for the appraisal by a State in objecting to the reservation.

. . .

Notes

1.   Does the Advisory Opinion on Reservations to the Genocide Convention apply as well to human rights agreements generally? Is it persuasive today? Compare the U.S. reservations to the International Covenant on Civil and Political Rights and to other human rights conventions, and the observations of the Human Rights Committee, *infra* Chapter 4(B).

2.   Reservations to multilateral treaties on human rights are common and have become a feature of the human rights treaty systems. Is such a permissive, flexible system desirable? See Anne F. Bayefsky, *Making the Human Rights Treaties Work*, in Human Rights: An Agenda for the Next Century 229 (Louis Henkin & John Lawrence Hargrove eds. 1994); Liesbeth Lijnzaad, Reservations to UN Human Rights Treaties: Ratify or Ruin? (1995), and compare the Advisory Opinion of the Inter–American Court of Human Rights, *infra* note 5. Is it desirable to exclude incompatible reservations to human rights treaties by special provision, for example by providing for the rejection of a reservation if two-thirds of the contracting states object to the reservation? A clause to this effect is included in Article 20(2) of the International Convention on the Elimination of All Forms of Racial Discrimination, entered into force January 4, 1969, 660 U.N.T.S. 195.

3.   Is a reservation or group of reservations designed to reduce the obligations of a state to the level of its existing domestic law compatible with the object of a human rights convention, that its obligations be observed by all parties? See Oscar Schachter, *The Obligation of the Parties to Give Effect to the Covenant on Civil and Political Rights*, 73 Am. J. Int'l L. 462, 464–65 (1979). Compare the U.S. reservations to the International Covenant on Civil and Political Rights and the observation of the Human Rights Committee, Chapter 4, Section B below.

4.   The UN International Law Commission* has played a significant role in the formulation of law in respect of "reservations to treaties" since

* The International Law Commission was established by the UN General Assembly in 1947 to promote the codification and progressive development of international law.

receiving its mandate by G.A. Res. 478 (V) of 16 November 1950. In its early reports, the Commission stated that the measure of compatibility of a reservation with the "object and purpose" of a treaty or convention—a standard applied by the International Court of Justice in its Advisory Opinion above—would not be suitable for application to multilateral conventions in general. The Commission also urged that clauses on reservations should be incorporated into future conventions. See in this regard the Report of the International Law Commission, 6 GAOR Supp. 9, U.N. Doc. A/1858, ch. II, paras. 12–34 (1951).

At its forty-fifth session, in 1993, the ILC decided to include in its agenda the subject "The law and practice related to the law of treaties." The Commission has since decided that it would not call into question the provisions of the Vienna Convention on reservations and would attempt only to clarify obscurities. In addition, the Commission determined that the work of the ILC would culminate in the preparation of a "Guide to Practice," a set of guidelines that could be attached onto existing provisions. For "the text of the draft guidelines on reservations to treaties provisionally adopted by the Commission on first reading," including commentary, see Report of the International Law Commission on the work of its fiftieth session, U.N. GAOR, 53d Sess., Supp. No. 10, at 194, U.N. Doc. A/53/10 (1998). For a response by the ILC to comments on reservations to the ICCPR, see Chapter 4, Section B, infra.

5. In its Advisory Opinion on Restrictions to the Death Penalty, the Inter–American Court on Human Rights considered whether a reservation made by Guatemala to Article 4(4) of the American Convention on Human Rights ("inasmuch as the Constitution of the Republic of Guatemala only excludes from the application of the death penalty political crimes but not common crimes related to political crimes") could be invoked to justify the application of the death penalty to common crimes connected with political crimes to which that penalty did not previously apply. Restrictions to the Death Penalty, Advisory Opinion OC–3/83, 3 Inter–Am. Ct.H.R. (ser. A) (1983). The Court concluded that "Article 4(2) contains an absolute prohibition on the extension of the death penalty." As the reservation was restricted by its own wording to Article 4(4), Guatemala was not allowed by subsequent legislation to extend the death penalty to crimes to which that penalty was not previously applied.

Interpretation of Treaties: In General

On the interpretation of international agreements, the Restatement of Foreign Relations Law § 325 states:

(1) An international agreement is to be interpreted in good faith in accordance with the ordinary meaning to be given to its terms in their context and in the light of its object and purpose.

The Commission meets annually and is composed of 24 members elected by the General Assembly for five-year terms. The Commission principally develops draft conventions on subjects in international law.

(2) Any subsequent agreement between the parties regarding the interpretation of the agreement, and subsequent practice between the parties in the application of the agreement, are to be taken into account in its interpretation.

Comment:

a. Customary international law of interpretation. Customary international law has not developed rules and modes of interpretation having the definiteness and precision to which this section aspires. Therefore, unless the Vienna Convention comes into force for the United States, this section does not strictly govern interpretation by the United States or by courts in the United States. But it represents generally accepted principles and the United States has also appeared willing to accept them despite differences of nuance and emphasis. See Comment *g* as to United States practice.

. . .

d. Interpretation of different types of agreements. Different types of agreements may call for different interpretative approaches. Agreements creating international organizations have a constitutional quality, and are subject to the observation in *McCulloch v. Maryland*, 17 U.S. (4 Wheat.) 316, 407, 4 L.Ed. 579 (1819), that "we must never forget that it is *a constitution* that we are expounding." Treaties that lay down rules to be enforced by the parties through their internal courts or administrative agencies should be construed so as to achieve uniformity of result despite differences between national legal systems. Agreements involving a single transaction between governments, such as a transfer of territory or a grant of economic assistance should be construed like similar private contracts between private parties. Different approaches to interpretation have developed for particular categories of agreements such as extradition treaties, tax treaties, etc.

. . .

e. Recourse to travaux préparatoires. The Vienna Convention, in Article 32, requires the interpreting body to conclude that the "ordinary meaning" of the text is either obscure or unreasonable before it can look to "supplementary means." Some interpreting bodies are more willing to come to that conclusion than others ... Article 32 of the Vienna Convention reflects reluctance to permit the use of materials constituting the development and negotiation of an agreement (*travaux préparatoires*) as a guide to the interpretation of the agreement. The Convention's inhospitality to *travaux* is not wholly consistent with the attitude of the International Court of Justice and not at all with that of United States courts.

Interpretation of Human Rights Agreements

Why and in what respects might human rights agreements be interpreted differently from other treaties? Compare Restatement § 325 Comment *d*. In view of the subject matter, should a human rights agreement be interpreted, where fairly possible, to enlarge the scope of the right and enhance the protection guaranteed? See the suggestion, *infra* p. 328, that human rights treaties should be interpreted as not permitting unilateral withdrawal.

Professor Rudolf Bernhardt (who served on the European Court of Human Rights) has written:

[A]ccording to the settled case-law of the European Court of Human Rights, States have a certain "margin of appreciation" in the implementation of the Human Rights Convention....

The international institution does not and cannot leave the States unfettered discretion, but rather has the right and the duty to fix the limits of national discretion and appreciation, and must therefore draw the borderline between the national margin of appreciation and international supervision. Since this borderline cannot be drawn in the abstract, but only in the individual case, it is inevitable that opinions should often differ as to whether it has been drawn correctly.

Our next point concerns the question whether human-rights treaties require a more "subjective" or a more "objective" interpretation. In traditional international law, the intentions of the parties to a treaty and the *travaux préparatoires* as evidence of those intentions were of considerable importance and even decisive whenever they showed a clear common understanding on the part of the drafters of a treaty provision (which is not very often the case). In modern international law and under the rules of the Vienna Convention on the Law of Treaties, the preparatory work has lost much of its relevance and is recognized only as a subsidiary means of interpretation in case of remaining doubts. In the human-rights field, this limited relevance seems to be further restricted, as stated by the Inter–American Court of Human Rights in the following terms:

"In the case of human rights treaties, moreover, objective criteria of interpretation that look to the texts themselves are more appropriate than subjective criteria that seek to ascertain only the intent of the Parties. This is so because human rights treaties, as the Court has already noted, 'are not multilateral treaties of the traditional type concluded to accomplish the reciprocal exchange of rights for the mutual benefit of the contracting States'; rather 'their object and purpose is the protection of the basic rights of individual human beings, irrespective of their nationality, both against the State of their nationality and all other contracting States....' "

There are good reasons for this statement, which is obviously shared in substance by the European Court of Human Rights.

In a considerable number of decisions, the European Court has stressed that the Convention must be interpreted and applied in accordance with present-day conditions in law and society, not with past convictions. This "dynamic" interpretation dispenses with consideration of the preparatory work and the intentions of the drafters of the treaty at least to the extent to which modern convictions and conditions have been substituted for those which existed in law and society at the time of the conclusion of the treaty.

. . .

With regard to traditional rules of treaty interpretation, human-rights conventions pose several other problems. According to an old (and now outdated) maxim, treaties should, in case of doubt, be interpreted in favor of the freedom of the States concerned, i.e. in favor of State sovereignty. If this principle were applied to human-rights treaties, the rights guaranteed to individuals would have to be construed restrictively. But such a rule would be in plain contradiction to another maxim, occasionally relied on by the European Court of Human Rights, namely that individual liberties need a broad interpretation, whereas restrictions on these liberties require a restrictive interpretation. There are, in the author's view, good reasons for doubting whether either of these principles is entirely correct. Human-rights conventions are designed to protect individual liberties, and such protection should be effective; at the same time, modern States also have the task of protecting the community and its members against abuse of privileges. The "fair balance" which must be struck between the rights of the individual and community interests cannot be found by applying technical rules (interpretation in favour of State sovereignty on the one hand or unrestricted individual liberty on the other), but rather through a process in which civil liberties and community interests must be weighed against each other.

Summing up, we may conclude from our observations that the general rules of treaty interpretation are in principle also applicable to human-rights treaties, but the object and purpose of these treaties are different and, therefore, the traditional rules need some adjustment. The notions contained in human-rights conventions have an autonomous international meaning; however, such meaning must be determined by a comparative analysis of the legal situation in the participating States. To the extent that this analysis shows considerable differences and disparities among the States, a national "margin of appreciation" is and must be recognized. Human-rights treaties must be interpreted in an objective and dynamic manner, by taking into account social conditions and developments; the ideas and conditions prevailing at the time when the treaties were drafted retain hardly any continuing validity. Nevertheless, treaty interpretation must not amount to treaty revision. Interpretation must therefore respect the text of the treaty concerned.

Rudolf Bernhardt, "Thoughts on the Interpretation of Human–Rights Treaties," in *Protecting Human Rights: the European Dimension: Studies in Honor of Gérard J. Wiarda* 67–71 (1988).

b. RESPONSIBILITY UNDER HUMAN RIGHTS TREATIES

State Responsibility

Like all international law, the international law of human rights is generally made by states and generally governs the behavior of states.

International human rights agreements are agreements among states by which states parties assume obligations to other states parties. In human rights treaties, however, the obligations to other parties are undertakings to respect the rights of individuals, generally the rights of individuals subject to the promisor state's jurisdiction, and to provide them remedies for violation. International human rights agreements generally also include undertakings by states parties to submit to international human rights remedies, for example, to report to an international "treaty body" such as the Human Rights Committee established by the International Covenant on Civil and Political Rights, or the Committee Against Torture established by the Torture Convention, or to accept the jurisdiction of a regional commission or court.

Human rights treaties and the customary law of human rights ordinarily create obligations for states, and states are responsible for carrying out those obligations. A state commits a violation if it fails to respect and to ensure the rights recognized by a covenant or convention to which the state is party, or if it fails to provide remedies it is required to provide. A state also commits a violation of international law if, as a matter of state policy, it violates recognized principles of the customary international law of human rights. See p. 349 below. A private person or entity may be guilty of a violation of human rights law if the obligation to respect international human rights norms was imposed on that person by treaty, or by customary law, or by the law of a state that has jurisdiction over that person. See pp. 316.

Where a state is obligated, by treaty or customary law, to respect the human rights of an individual, the state is responsible for acts or omissions by any of its officials or by others acting "under color of law"; in a federal system the state is responsible as well for acts or omissions of the constituent units, their officials and others acting "under color of" their law. But under some human rights agreements, the state's obligation is not only to *respect* the rights of individuals but also to "ensure" them. For example, ICCPR, Article 2, has been interpreted to mean that the State Party undertakes to see to it that the rights of its inhabitants are not violated by others—by other states, or by any private person or entity subject to the state's jurisdiction or authority.

Under international treaties generally, and under customary law, a state is responsible for violations of rights of persons "subject to its jurisdiction." See, *e.g.,* the European Convention on Human Rights, Art. 1. Does a person become subject to a state's jurisdiction if the state acts against the person outside its territory? Compare, for example, the official acts involved in *United States v. Alvarez–Machain,* 504 U.S. 655 (1992); *Sale v. Haitian Centers Council, Inc.,* 509 U.S. 155 (1993), infra pp. 809, 421. (On the interpretation of Article 2 of ICCPR, see p. 323 below).

In practical effect, the responsibility of the state to respect and ensure the rights of persons subject to its jurisdiction, and to provide remedies for violations, runs to the person whose rights are violated or to his or her representative. See, for example, the Optional Protocol to the ICCPR, and provisions under regional conventions for private complaint to regional bodies. See Chapter 3, Sections A and B. Strictly, however, international legal obligations run to the other states parties to the covenant or the convention, with the individual concerned, in effect, a third party beneficiary. Thus, for example, under Article 41 of the ICCPR, a state may complain to the Human Rights Committee of a violation of individual rights by another state. That is also the implication of the provision in some human rights conventions that a state can bring a claim before the International Court of Justice to raise issues as to the interpretation and implementation of the treaty. See, *e.g.,* the Genocide Convention, Article IX, and the Convention Relating to the Status of Refugees, Article 38.

Human rights obligations under customary international law are obligations *"erga omnes"*—to all states—and, in principle, any state may pursue remedies against a violating state. States, it has been urged also, have responsibility in respect of violations by other states; they have an obligation to monitor and take measures to prevent, deter, or terminate violations by other states.

The International Law Commission has been engaged in the elaboration of a Code of Offenses against the Peace and Security of Mankind, later denominated the Draft Code of Crimes. At one time the Commission addressed crimes by states as well as by individuals, but the Commission abandoned the notion of a criminal law applicable to states and has pursued a criminal code governing individuals only. The Code has been long in preparation, slowed, no doubt, by the Cold War and other political forces. The Commission completed draft articles for the Code in 1996, and the General Assembly requested governments to submit comments on the Draft Code by the end of 1998. See G.A. Res. 51/160, U.N. GAOR, 51st Sess., Supp. No. 49, at 333–34, U.N. Doc. A/51/49 (1996). Approval of the Draft Code by the UN General Assembly, and its development into a treaty, are anticipated for about the end of the Century.

Responsibility of Individuals and Other Private Entities

International agreements ordinarily create obligations for states, not for private persons, but there is nothing to prevent states, by agreement, from establishing norms to govern the behavior of natural or juridical persons. By treaty (or by customary law) states may impose obligations to respect human rights on private persons or entities, and such individuals or entities may then be guilty of international human rights violations. See Andrew Clapham, Human Rights in the Private Sphere (1993). Compare the development of "international crimes" in and since the Nuremberg Charter, the "code of offenses" developed by the International Law Commission, and the growth of international criminal tribunals with jurisdiction over crimes against humanity, as well as genocide and war crimes. See *infra* Chapter 3(C).

The International Covenant on Civil and Political Rights does not address its norms to private persons, but the obligations of states "to respect and to ensure" the rights recognized in the Covenant appears to create an obligation on States Parties to ensure that private persons, subject to their jurisdiction or authority, also respect the rights recognized in the Covenant. Compare *A. v. United Kingdom* 1998–VI Eur. Ct. H.R. 2692 (1998), in which the European Court of Human Rights ruled that a state had a duty to protect children against physical abuse by parents (or step-parents).

The Restatement of U.S. Foreign Relations Law declares that a state violates customary international law if, as a matter of state policy, it "practices, encourages or condones" defined gross violations of human rights. See p. 349, *infra*. Does a state violate customary international law if, as a matter of policy, it fails to prohibit and punish such violations by persons subject to its jurisdiction? Does it thereby "condone" them?

Note: *Globalization and Responsibility for Human Rights*

At the end of the Twentieth Century, transformations in the world's economic-political-communications structures have brought important consequences for human rights. The sweep of privatization after the demise of state socialism, the dominance of "the world market" supported by the instant communication of cyberspace, have steadily enhanced the growth of large transnational or multinational companies and reduced the significance of state sovereignty and territorial boundaries, with important implications for international law and politics. Large companies determine policy and take actions independently of governments, or in complicity with governments and international financial institutions (the World Bank, the International Monetary Fund), which affect the living conditions of millions of human beings, raising issues of slave and child labor, wage levels, the scope and quality of economic and social conditions. Large development programs sometimes involve massive relocations of human beings and environmental degradation; sometimes such programs have induced oppressive police and military practices for the benefit of multinational companies, sometimes with their cooperation.

Human rights law (and politics) have not yet effectively taken account of these developments. In principle, states governments are responsible for the activities of multinational companies; the policies and activities of a multinational company are subject to regulation by the state of nationality of the parent company and by the state of its principal headquarters, as well as by states in which its activities take place. "The market" is subject to regulation by one or more states and by international bodies pursuant to international law and agreement. Governments are sometimes unwilling, and often unable, to regulate the activities of multinational companies, or "the market," to protect human rights; international law and agreement have generally not been directed to nongovernmental activity. But there is movement in that direction. If international law does not impose human rights responsibility directly on companies as a matter of law, it does require states "to respect and ensure" the human rights of persons subject to their jurisdiction. Under some existing agreements, *e.g.*, the ICCPR, and under treaties that might be developed, governments can be made responsible for the activities of multinationals, and the companies themselves can be rendered responsible. Compare, *Doe v. Unocal Corp.*, 963 F.Supp. 880 (C.D.Cal.1997), in which the court held that a multinational company may be liable for violating or conspiring with state actors to violate customary human rights norms. See *infra* p. 880.

With increasing globalization and privatization, international norms and sanctions may be interpreted as governing the acts and omissions of multinational companies, or as establishing the responsibility of states to ensure the rights of persons who are subject to acts and omissions of multinational companies, for example in respect of child labor or prison or other coerced labor, or environmental degradation, or complicity with repressive regimes.

Whether out of increasing sensitivity and concern, or as a result of pressure from non-governmental organizations, from shareholders and consumers, some multinational corporations have agreed to follow corporate "codes of conduct" to police their own activities. The most prominent example was the "Sullivan Principles" for multinational corporations conducting business in South Africa under apartheid.

Are voluntary corporate codes of conduct an effective and appropriate means of enforcing human rights? What role should states play in developing or monitoring compliance with corporate codes of conduct? See U.S. Dep't of Labor, Bureau of Int'l Labor Affairs, The Apparel Industry and Codes of Conduct: A Solution to the International Child Labor Problem? (1996); Barbara A. Frey, *The Legal and Ethical Responsibilities of Transnational Corporations in the Protection of International Human Rights*, 6 Minn. J. Global Trade 153 (1997); Doug Cassel, *Corporate Initiatives: A Second Human Rights Revolution?* 9 Fordham Int'l L.J. 1963 (1996).

Some U.S. States and local governments have attempted to impose economic sanctions on companies that they regard as implicated in human rights abuses. The extent of state and local power to impose such sanctions within U.S. federalism is disputed. See Note on p. 841 infra.

On globalization and human rights generally, see Debora L. Spar, *The Spotlight and the Bottom Line: How Multinationals Export Human Rights*, 77(2) Foreign Aff. 7 (1998); Brian A. Langille, "Eight Ways to Think About Labour Standards and Globalization," Occasional Paper, Program for the Study of International Organizations (March 1997).

2. CUSTOMARY INTERNATIONAL LAW: CREATING CUSTOMARY LAW OF HUMAN RIGHTS

In principle, customary international law of human rights, like customary international law generally, "results from a general and consistent practice of states followed by them from a sense of legal obligation." See Restatement of Foreign Relations Law, § 102(2), *supra* p. 299. In respect of customary law of human rights, however, the practice of states that creates customary law may take unusual forms. The Reporters of the Restatement of Foreign Relations Law, § 701, Reporters' Note 2, wrote:

> *Practice creating customary human rights law.* International human rights law governs relations between a state and its own inhabitants. Other states are only occasionally involved in monitoring such law through ordinary diplomatic practice. Therefore, the practice of states that is accepted as building customary international law of human rights includes some forms of conduct different from those that build customary international law generally. See § 102, Comment *b*. Practice accepted as building customary human rights law includes: virtually universal adherence to the United Nations Charter and its human rights provisions, and virtually universal and frequently reiterated acceptance of the Universal Declaration of Human Rights even if only in principle; virtually universal participation of states in the preparation and adoption of international agreements recognizing human rights principles generally, or particular rights; the adoption of human rights principles by states in regional organizations in Europe, Latin America, and Africa (see Introductory Note to this Part); general support by states for United Nations resolutions declaring, recognizing, invoking, and applying international human rights principles as international law; action by states to conform their national law or practice to standards or principles declared by international bodies, and the incorporation of human rights provisions, directly or by reference, in national constitutions and laws; invocation of human rights principles in national policy, in diplomatic practice, in international organization activities and actions; and other diplomatic communications or action by states reflecting the view that certain practices violate international human rights law, including condemnation and other adverse state reactions to violations by other states. The International Court of Justice and the International Law Commission have recognized the existence of customary human rights law. [citations omitted] Some of these practices may also support the conclusion that particular human rights have been absorbed into international law as general principles common to the major state legal systems. See § 702, Reporters' Note 1.

For the development of customary international law generally, see Restatement § 102, Reporters' Note 2.

Notes

Skepticism as to the legal character of the international law of human rights has largely dissipated, but doubts persist as to the effectiveness of human rights law to determine or shape the behavior of governments. Skepticism and doubts are no doubt aggravated by reports of terrible human rights violations, some of them of genocidal character, as in Bosnia and Rwanda, and of political repression in a number of other countries. Is the legal character of international human rights law more apparent in some countries or regions than in others, as to some human rights norms than to others? Which regions? Which norms? Why? And see generally Henkin, How Nations Behave: Law and Foreign Policy (2d ed. 1979), Part I and Chapter 12; Henkin, International Law: Politics and Values (1995), Chapters III and XII. And see "Rhetoric and Reality," p. 1209 below.

B. PRINCIPAL INTERNATIONAL HUMAN RIGHTS AGREEMENTS AND INSTRUMENTS

1. THE UN CHARTER AS HUMAN RIGHTS LAW

The United Nations Charter, a multilateral treaty to which virtually all states are parties, declares it to be a purpose of the United Nations "[t]o achieve international co-operation ... in promoting and encouraging respect for human rights and for fundamental freedoms for all without distinction as to race, sex, language, or religion" (Article 1). Under Article 56, "All Members pledge themselves to take joint and separate action in cooperation with the Organization for the achievement of the purposes" of the United Nations, purposes which include the promotion of "universal respect for, and observance of, human rights and fundamental freedoms for all without distinction as to race, sex, language or religion" (Article 55).

Human rights are not defined in the Charter, and there have been continuing debates as to whether the pledge of a member state in Article 56 creates legal obligations not to commit gross violations of widely-accepted human rights, perhaps also not to violate any of the human rights later recognized in the Universal Declaration. (Another argument sees the Charter's pledge and the Universal Declaration together as contributing to obligations under customary law.)

With the elaboration and wide acceptance of human rights covenants and conventions, it became less important to find human rights norms in the Charter. But in regard to a state not party to a relevant covenant or convention, the Charter is available as an additional source of human rights law. During the apartheid era, for example, the UN General Assembly declared apartheid to be a violation of the principles of the Charter. See G.A. Res. 32/42, U.N. GAOR, 32d Sess., at 498, U.N. Doc. A/32/L.36 and Add. 1 (1977).

2. "THE INTERNATIONAL BILL OF RIGHTS"*

There is no single document entitled the "International Bill of Rights," but that title is now commonly bestowed upon three instruments taken together—the Universal Declaration of Human Rights, the International Covenant on Civil and Political Rights, and the International Covenant on Economic, Social, and Cultural Rights.

* This section draws on Louis Henkin, International Law: Politics and Values ch. 11 (1995).

The appellation "International Bill of Rights" was doubtless intended to echo and parallel national bills of rights, notably the U.S. Bill of Rights, and the French Declaration of the Rights of Man and of the Citizen. But the term "International Bill of Rights" also sums up and subsumes the early history and development of human rights law. Calls for an "International Bill of Rights" were heard frequently towards the end of the Second World War when the Allies were planning the post-war world order. Some smaller governments and non-governmental organizations proposed that an International Bill of Rights be part of, or appended to, the United Nations Charter. A draft International Bill of Rights was expected from the new UN Human Rights Commission when it began its work in 1946. But the members of the Commission early concluded that drafting a binding international human rights agreement would be an extended undertaking, and that it would be wise to produce more quickly a declaration of rights while proceeding simultaneously to prepare a binding covenant.

The Universal Declaration was proclaimed on December 10, 1948; the Covenants took eighteen years to complete (1966), and another ten years to come into effect (1976). During those nearly thirty years, the Universal Declaration stood alone as the voice of international human rights. The Declaration, moreover, did not require ratification, and its influence reached all states, including the many new states born after 1948, and even states that had abstained in the vote to proclaim it in 1948.

The Universal Declaration of Human Rights includes what came to be called "civil and political rights" as well as what came to be called "economic and social rights" (Compare Articles 3–16, 18–21 with Articles 22–28; Article 17 (property) may fall in either category.) Neither group of rights is characterized as such, nor does the Declaration distinguish between them in any way. But it was recognized from the beginning that rights might be seen as falling into one or the other of these categories, that the two categories of rights may have different theoretical justifications, and that each may require different normative elaboration and different articulation of the obligation to respect such rights, and different remedies for their violation. Some indeed questioned whether economic and social benefits are "rights." (Compare the discussion of U.S. constitutional rights in Part II, keeping in mind that international covenants do not require that rights be "constitutionalized," only that they be respected and realized.)

After the General Assembly proclaimed the Universal Declaration, states began the task of creating a legally-binding covenant that would implement the rights proclaimed in it. On the initiative of Western states, the proposed covenant was bifurcated into two covenants, the International Covenant on Civil and Political Rights (ICCPR) and the International Covenant on Economic, Social, and Cultural Rights (ICESCR). Contrary to early expectation, most states have become party to both covenants. (As of January 1, 1999, 141 states are party to the ICESCR and 144 states are party to the ICCPR.)

The Covenants have important similarities as well as important differences. Compare the articulation of a State Party's obligation in Article 2 of each Covenant; compare also the different procedures for their implementation (elaborated *infra*, Chapter 3). The two Covenants have come to reflect a political and ideological divide between developed and developing states (formerly called the "First World" and the "Third World"), but UN resolutions have repeatedly reaffirmed the equal value of both categories of rights. See, for example, the General Assembly Declaration on the Right to Development, *infra* p. 481 which declares that "all human rights and fundamental freedoms are indivisible and interdependent; equal attention and urgent consideration should be given to the implementation, promotion, and protection of civil, political, economic, social and cultural rights." In any event, both Covenants are legally binding instruments that create legal obligations.

a. THE UNIVERSAL DECLARATION OF HUMAN RIGHTS: THE RIGHTS RECOGNIZED

The Universal Declaration has been acclaimed as one of the most important instruments of the Twentieth Century. There have been no serious suggestions that it be reexamined or amended, despite the fact that it was the product of the Cold War years and that the world has changed during the fifty years of its existence. Its greatest importance may be its influence on the development of constitutionalism and the establishment of human rights in the one hundred (and more) constitutions that have been ordained in the second half of the century.

The status of the Universal Declaration in international law remains somewhat controversial. It is commonly accepted that, when proclaimed, it had no clear normative character, though some saw it as an articulation and elaboration of the inchoate human rights obligations in the UN Charter. See p. 321 above. It is also commonly accepted that at least some of the provisions of the Declaration were, or may have become, obligations under customary law. That, of course, would be particularly significant in respect of provisions in the Declaration that are not included in the Covenants, notably the right to property (Article 17), and the ambiguous provision in respect of asylum (Article 14). The conclusion that a provision of the Declaration had achieved the status of customary law would be important also in respect of states that have not ratified the Covenants or have done so with significant reservations.

The Universal Declaration of Human Rights is a remarkable synthesis of political-civil and economic-social rights, with equality and freedom from discrimination as principal themes. It declared the rights to life, liberty, and security of person, to fair criminal process, to freedom of conscience, thought, expression, association, and privacy; the right to seek and enjoy asylum, to leave one's country and return to it, rights to marriage and family, and rights of property. The Declaration declared the will of the people to be the basis of the authority of government, and called for universal suffrage and bona fide elections. It speaks of the right to work and to leisure, to health care and education. (Because the Declaration was designed to be universal, it included provisions that some national constitutions assumed and took for granted, or did not consider necessary or "constitution-worthy," for example, the fundamentality of the family [Article 16(3)].)

Are there individual human rights that are not included in this list?

On other "generations" of human rights, see Section H(2) below. On group rights, see Section H(1) below.

b.   THE INTERNATIONAL COVENANT ON CIVIL AND POLITICAL RIGHTS

The International Covenant on Civil and Political Rights is set forth in 999 U.N.T.S. 171, and in virtually every collection of human rights documents.

Whose Rights?

Article 2(1) of the ICCPR provides:

> Each State Party to the present covenant undertakes to respect and to ensure to all individuals within its territory and subject to its jurisdiction the rights recognized in the present covenant. . . .

The Covenant recognizes rights of individuals, not of juridical persons. But compare the European Convention, p. 339 below.

The Covenant obligates the state to respect and ensure rights of all individuals "within its territory and subject to its jurisdiction." It is commonly accepted that "within its territory and subject to its jurisdiction" was intended to mean "those within its territory and *those otherwise* subject to its jurisdiction." See Buergenthal, *To Respect and to Ensure: State Obligations and Permissible Derogations,* in The International Bill of Rights, 73–75 (L. Henkin ed. 1981). The State is obligated to respect the rights of persons not within its territory but nevertheless subject to the State's jurisdiction, whether because they are nationals of the State, or residents temporarily outside the territory, or even generally, perhaps because the State Party reaches out beyond its territory to exercise jurisdiction over them.

Principal Rights Protected

The civil and political rights declared in Articles 1–21 of the Universal Declaration were included in the International Covenant on Civil and Political Rights, generally with only minor differences. One important right included in the Universal Declaration but not in either of the two Covenants is the right to own and not to be arbitrarily deprived of property (Article 17), which was the victim of ideological conflict and of an extended controversy over the principles of international law governing investments and other properties of foreign nationals. That controversy prevented agreement on the scope and articulation of a right to property in the Covenant, though no state denied that an individual has a human right to own and not be arbitrarily deprived of some property.

Civil and political rights are often described as negative rights: they are freedoms, immunities, which a state can respect by abstention, by leaving the individual alone. In fact, to describe all civil and political rights as negative is misleading; a number of the rights articulated apply in the criminal process, by which a state may legitimately take liberty and property (or even life) in punishment, but in those cases the state is required not merely to leave the individual alone but "positively" to organize itself, by institutions and laws, to assure against arbitrary detention, and to provide due process, fair trial, and humane punishment. Moreover, the obligation to "ensure" some rights has been interpreted as requiring the state to take steps to protect them against private infringement.

The Covenant on Civil and Political Rights is supplemented by two optional protocols. The first provides for individual complaints. See *infra* p. 498. The second provides for the abolition of the death penalty; promulgated in 1989, it entered into force in 1991 and has thirty-seven ratifications as of July 1999.

Limitations on and Derogations From Rights

Under the international law of human rights (as under the Constitution of the United States and other constitutions), civil and political rights are not absolute. One person's rights may conflict with another's, and one right may have to be sacrificed to another right; or, individual rights may impinge heavily on other "goods," on societal values and public interests. The Universal Declaration recognizes that one person's human rights may conflict with those of another person but it provides no principle or guidelines for determining priority or preference between conflicting rights. The Covenant in effect chooses between two rights when it permits a state to restrict freedom of expression by law if necessary "for respect of the rights or reputations of others" (Article 19(3)(a)), or when it permits a state to exclude the press and the public from a criminal trial "when the interest of the private lives of the parties so requires" (Article 14(1)). But other conflicts between rights are possible and do occur. Is a state free to choose between them as it will?

Both the Universal Declaration and the Covenant recognize that a state may limit rights when necessary to protect certain public interests. The Universal Declaration (Art. 29(2)) provides:

> "In the exercise of his rights and freedoms, everyone shall be subject *only* to such limitations *as are determined by law solely* for the purpose of securing due recognition and respect for the rights and freedoms of others and of meeting the *just* requirements of *morality, public order* and the *general welfare* in a *democratic society*."

(Emphasis added.) The words emphasized appear to imply that limitations are limited; and the articulated purposes of limitations are themselves to be strictly construed. Some of the terms have historic meaning and scope in national constitutional jurisprudence. Compare Part II, p. 196. It was deemed necessary to emphasize the special character that "ordre public" had in French jurisprudence which was not fully captured by the words "public order." But what is included in "the general welfare?" By the term "in a democratic society"? Most (but not all) of these terms are used in the limitation clauses of the ICCPR and have been interpreted in that context.

See generally, A. C. Kiss, *Permissible Limitations on Rights*, in The International Bill of Rights (L. Henkin ed. 1981). The Declaration may imply that there may be limitations on any rights. The Covenant on Civil and Political Rights makes permissible limitations explicit only in regard to particular rights (and in terms somewhat different from those in the Declaration). For example, as regards the freedom of movement and residence, and the right to leave a country and to return to one's own country, Article 12(3) of the ICCPR permits restrictions:

> which are provided by law, are necessary to protect national security, public order *(ordre public),* public health or morals or the rights and freedoms of others, and are consistent with the other rights recognized in the present Covenant.

Such clauses are included in similar language in other provisions; some provisions indicate permissible limitations in other terms but to the same general effect. Most articles recognizing particular rights, however, do not mention limitations. Does failure to mention limitations suggest that those rights are absolute and do not permit of limitations? Is "general welfare" in the Universal Declaration broader—or narrower—than the specific grounds listed as permissible grounds for limitation in particular articles of the Covenant?

A principal "loophole," which has sometimes tempted some states virtually to swallow up human rights, is the state's authority to derogate from rights in an emergency.

Article 4 of the Covenant provides:

> 1. In time of public emergency which threatens the life of the nation and the existence of which is officially proclaimed, the States Parties to the present Covenant may take measures derogating from their obligations under the present Covenant to the extent strictly required by the exigencies of the situation, provided that such measures are not inconsistent with their other obligations under international law and do not involve discrimination solely on the ground of race, colour, sex, language, religion or social origin.

. . .

Derogation in public emergency is to be distinguished from limitations on rights. Limitations are not restricted to time of emergency but are permitted at all times under the state's police power for such reasons as "national security, public order, public health or morals or the rights and freedoms of others," see, *e.g.,* ICCPR Articles 12(3), 14(1), 18(3), 19(3)(b); and see Article 17(1) which prohibits "arbitrary or unlawful interference," thus accepting interference that is lawful and not arbitrary. Compare *Limitations on Rights supra* Part II, Chapter 1(E).

Derogation in emergency was not expressly authorized or addressed in the Universal Declaration of Human Rights. But Article 29(2) of the Declaration permits limitations for the purpose, *inter alia*, "of meeting the just requirements of . . . public order and the general welfare in a democratic society," and presumably would permit derogations from rights to the extent strictly required by the exigencies of the situation in time of public emergency.

Article 4 of the ICCPR is limited, by its terms, to proclaimed public emergencies "which threaten the life of the nation," not merely the life of a particular system of government, of a particular regime or of a particular party or head of state. The threat to the life of the nation might come from the outside, as by aggression by another state, but conceivably a public emergency might be due to a threat to the life of the nation from major natural disaster, or even from widespread internal disorder.

Article 4(1) permits derogation "to the extent strictly required by the exigencies of the situation." Inevitably, perhaps, the State Party would enjoy "a margin of appreciation"* in deciding whether a particular derogation is strictly required, but that question, in an international agreement, and permitting derogation from international treaty obligations, involves interpretation and application of the agreement, and is a question of international law. The State Party that would derogate may decide that question in the first instance, but other parties to the ICCPR may disagree, and an appropriate international body may have the final say, *e.g.*, the Human Rights Committee under Article 41 or under the Optional Protocol to ICCPR, or even the International Court of Justice if it has jurisdiction (or in an appropriate advisory opinion). See generally, Buergenthal, *To Respect and to Ensure: State Obligations and Permissible Derogations*, in The International Bill of Rights (L. Henkin ed. 1981).

Article 4(2) excludes several articles as not subject to derogation under Article 4(1). This provision bars derogation from rights which the state parties considered too fundamental to be "derogated" even in time of emergency, *e.g.*, the prohibitions on racial, religious, and other discrimination in Article 4(1); the prohibitions on genocide and the limitations on capital punishment in Article 6; the prohibition on torture or other cruel, inhuman or degrading treatment or punishment (Art. 7) or slavery (Art. 8); or the right to personhood (Art. 16). But Article 4(2) bars derogation also from other rights which do not seem to be required, or relevant, or appropriate for derogation even in time of public emergency, *e.g.*, the right not to be imprisoned for debt (Art. 11), or the right to freedom of thought (conscience and religion, (Art. 18)), and the prohibition of ex post facto laws (Art. 15).

---

* This term entered human rights law through the jurisprudence of the European Court of Human Rights. See Ronald St. John Macdonald, "The Margin of Appreciation in the Jurisprudence of the European Court of Human Rights," infra p. 564.

In its General Comment on Article 4 of the ICCPR, the Human Rights Committee indicated that an alleged emergency will justify a derogation under that article only if the relevant circumstances are of an exceptional and temporary nature:

3. The Committee holds the view that measures taken under article 4 are of an exceptional and temporary nature and may only last as long as the life of the nation concerned is threatened and that, in times of emergency, the protection of human rights becomes all the more important, particularly those rights from which no derogations can be made. The Committee also considers that it is equally important for States parties, in times of public emergency, to inform the other States parties of the nature and extent of the derogations they have made and of the reasons therefor and, further, to fulfill their reporting obligations under article 40 of the Covenant by indicating the nature and extent of each right derogated from together with the relevant documentation.

General Comment 5, in Report of the Human Rights Committee, U.N. GAOR Human Rights Comm., 36th Sess., Annex VII, U.N. Doc. A/36/40 at 110 (1981).

For the suggestion that rights not subject to derogation may not be subject to reservation and that a reservation to such clauses may be inconsistent with the object and purpose of the treaty, see General Comment 24 discussed in Chapter 4(B) below.

Derogation in public emergency sometimes takes the form of suspension of democratic institutions, for example, the suspension of parliament, or of judicial bodies. Such derogations are not explicitly addressed in Article 4 but may be included by implication in clauses addressing derogation from particular rights, *e.g.*, those protecting freedom from arbitrary arrest or requiring fair public trial, ICCPR, Articles 14, 15, or providing for elections, Article 25.*

* In 1994, the Human Rights Committee decided not to draft a third optional protocol to the International Covenant on Civil and Political Rights that would have added the right to prompt and fair trial (Articles 9, 14) to the list of rights that cannot be derogated under Article 4. See Annual Report of the Human Rights Committee, U.N. GAOR, 49th Sess., Supp. No. 40, at 120, U.N. Doc. a/49/40 (1994).

The US Constitution does not provide for the suspension of any institutions or laws, even in public emergency. Only the privilege of the writ of habeas corpus may be suspended, and only in time of insurrection or invasion. See, *e.g.*, *Ex parte Milligan*, 71 U.S. (4 Wall.) 2 (1866); *Ex parte Merryman*, 17 F.Cas. 114 (C.C.D.Md.1861). But rights may in effect be derogated from or suspended in the United States under general powers of Congress or of the President, and in many circumstances their acts, valid under the Constitution, may "trump" individual rights. Notably, during war declared by Congress, the war powers of the President were held to include the authority to provide for trial by court martial, *Ex parte Quirin*, 317 U.S. 1 (1942); to impose martial law in occupied territory, *Madsen v. Kinsella*, 343 U.S. 341 (1952); *Duncan v. Kahanamoku*, 327 U.S. 304 (1946); to intern or relocate persons of Japanese ancestry, *Korematsu v. United States*, 323 U.S. 214 (1944). See Part II, p. 220 supra.

On derogation in public emergency, see generally Joan Fitzpatrick, Human Rights in Crisis: The International System for Protecting Rights During States of Emergency (1994); Jaime Oraa, Human Rights in States of Emergency in International Law (1992); Subrata Roy Chowdhury, Rule of Law in a State of Emergency: The Paris Minimum Standards of Human Rights Norms in a State of Emergency (1989); International Commission of Jurists, States of Emergency: Their Impact on Human Rights (1983).

National and International Implementation

The Covenant creates international obligations for state parties "to respect and ensure" the rights that it recognizes. The Covenant expressly obligates states to take specific measures to that end and to provide specific remedies in case of violations. The Covenant also established international measures to implement these obligations, principally through reporting to and scrutiny by the Human Rights Committee which the Covenant established, and through optional procedures for placing complaints before the Committee. See *infra* Chapter 3(A)(1).

Withdrawal or Termination

Can a State Party to the Covenant unilaterally denounce the Covenant and terminate its obligations? In its General Comment No. 26, U.N. Doc. CCPR/C/21/Rev.1/Add.9 (1997), the Human Rights Committee declared that a state may not do so. The Committee noted that the Covenant contains no provision permitting termination or withdrawal. In the absence of such a provision, the Covenant should be interpreted in the light of the Vienna Convention on the Law of Treaties, which allows withdrawal only if the treaty has an explicit provision for withdrawal or if it implies a right to terminate. The Committee observed that the absence of any withdrawal provision was not an oversight, but was a deliberate decision; that the Covenant expressly permits withdrawal of consent to the procedure under Article 41, and to the Optional Protocol. The Committee noted that there were explicit provisions per million withdrawal noted in other documents negotiated at the same time. Also, the nature of the Covenant implies that there is no right to denounce: the Covenant codifies universal human rights enshrined in the Universal Declaration of Human Rights; these rights belong to the inhabitants of state parties, not to the states themselves; no action by the state, including a change of government or disintegration, can destroy those rights.

Note: Interpretation of the ICCPR

A multi-author volume interpreting the various provisions of the Covenant, in the light if its travaux préparatoires, was published as The International Bill of Rights: The Covenant on Civil and Political Rights (Louis Henkin, ed. 1981). See also studies of particular rights, e.g., Lawyers Committee for Human Rights, What is a Fair Trial: A Basic Guide to Legal Standards and Practice (1995), providing an interpretation of the ICCPR provisions relating to fair trial.

And see generally, Manfred Nowak, CCPR Commentary (1993), and Dominick McGoldrick, The Human Rights Committee (1994).

c.   THE INTERNATIONAL COVENANT ON ECONOMIC, SOCIAL, AND CULTURAL RIGHTS

The International Covenant on Economic, Social, and Cultural Rights is set forth in 993 U.N.T.S. 3 and is in every collection of human rights documents.

With the bifurcation of the Universal Declaration into two covenants, differences between the two categories emerged—as to the character and limits of the undertakings of state parties, the permissible limitations on rights that may be imposed in the public interest (whether in "normal times" or in public emergency), and the procedures for monitoring compliance and implementation.

Division into two categories of rights requires definition and characterization, and the principle of allocation to one category or the other is not always obvious. Some rights might have appeared in the other category; some might well appear in both categories. For example, the right to work (Art. 6) might be a civil right; the right to join a trade union (Art. 8) may be also a right of association protected by the Covenant on Civil and Political Rights.

Principal Rights Protected

The obligations of States Parties to the ICESCR are set forth in Article 2:

> Each State Party to the present Covenant undertakes to take steps, individually and through international assistance and cooperation, especially economic and technical, to the maximum of its available resources, with a view to achieving progressively the full realization of the rights recognized in the present Covenant by all appropriate means, including particularly the adoption of legislative measures.

The rights recognized in the Covenant include among others: the right to work; to social security; to an adequate standard of living, including food, clothing and housing; to the highest attainable standard of health; the right to education; the right to take part in cultural life.

Despite what some might describe as the "softness" of the undertakings in the ICESCR ("to the maximum of its available resources," "to achieving progressively") they were designed to establish, and did establish, legally binding obligations. The law of economic-social rights has some ambiguities, but not many more than are found in the Covenant on Civil and Political Rights. Some ambiguities were probably purposeful, papering over ideological differences as to certain human values, such as the right to work (Art. 6): does the Covenant recognize a freedom to seek work of one's choice (as the West claimed), or also a right to have a job, which the state must provide if none is available on the labor market (as Socialist states insisted)? Is the right to work satisfied if a society maintains or tolerates unemployment but provides adequate unemployment insurance and other welfare benefits?

The international law of economic and social rights covers over tensions between state values and human values. States insisted on autonomy as to their economic-social systems: the Covenant was drafted so as to be acceptable to Socialist as well as to liberal "free-market" states. Some states resisted what many states desired—commitments by the wealthy states to provide economic assistance to poorer states so as to help them meet their economic-social obligations to their inhabitants. The issue was compromised through ambiguity: state parties are obligated to realize rights under the Covenant "individually and through international assistance and co-operation."

For a discussion of the enforcement and monitoring of the ICESCR, see *infra* Chapter 3(A)(2).

Notes

1. For a brief history of the ICESCR and an annotated list of its key provisions, see United Nations Centre for Human Rights, Human Rights Fact Sheet No. 16 (Rev. 1), The Committee on Economic, Social and Cultural Rights (1996). For interpretive principles to guide the implementation of the ICESCR, prepared by unofficial "experts," see "The Limburg Principles on the Implementation of the International Covenant on Economic, Social, and Cultural Rights," U.N. Doc. No. E/CN.4/1987/17, Annex, *reprinted in* 9 Hum. Rts. Q. 122 (1987), and the Maastricht Guidelines on Violations of Economic, Social and Cultural Rights reprinted in 20 Hum. Rts. Q. 691 (1998).

2. Determining the edges of "the envelope" of guaranteed economic, social, and cultural rights remains a task fraught with political peril as well as theoretical difficulty. On particular economic and social rights, see, *e.g.,* The Right to Adequate Housing: Second Progress Report Submitted by Mr. Rajindar Sachar, Special Rapporteur, U.N. ESCOR, Commission on Human Rights, Sub–Commission on Prevention of Discrimination and Protection of Minorities, 46th Sess., U.N. Doc. E/CN.4/Sub.2/1994/20 (1994); United Nations Centre for Human Rights, "Forced Evictions and Human Rights," Fact Sheet No. 25 (1996); Asbjorn Eide, Right to Adequate Food as a Human Right, United Nations Centre for Human Rights Study Series No. 1 (1989).

C. SELECTED INTERNATIONAL CONVENTIONS*

Beginning with the Genocide Convention (1948), the United Nations has sponsored a growing number of conventions on specified human rights

---

* Conventions open for accession by all states (as distinguished from those limited to particular regions). See Section D below.

subjects. Such conventions are generally designed to establish international obligations on a particular subject, for states that may not be prepared to assume all the obligations provided in the principal covenants; or to elaborate and enhance obligations on the particular subject beyond those in the covenants; or to establish procedures and provide remedies that states might be willing to assume in respect of a particular subject though not for all the subjects included in the principal covenants.

The special conventions developed under the auspices of the United Nations address civil and political rights which are covered generally by the International Covenant on Civil and Political Rights, *e.g.*, compare the Convention against Torture with the International Covenant on Civil and Political Rights, Article 7. Some conventions, notably the Convention on the Elimination of all Forms of Racial Discrimination, and the Convention on the Elimination of all Forms of Discrimination against Women, enhance obligations and increase remedies beyond those provided in the two covenants. With time, states, previously hesitant, adhered to international human rights agreements in increasing numbers, although often with important reservations. States were particularly reluctant to appear indifferent to particular rights, hence the large number of adherents to the Genocide Convention, the Convention on the Elimination of All Forms of Racial Discrimination, the Convention on the Elimination of all Forms of Discrimination against Women, and the Convention against Torture. In 1989, the UN General Assembly, by overwhelming vote, adopted the Convention on the Rights of the Child (G.A. Res. 44/25).

The United Nations Economic Social and Cultural Organization (UNESCO), a specialized agency of the United Nations, has sponsored a Convention on the Elimination of Discrimination in Education.

Of particular note are the conventions elaborated by the International Labor Organization (ILO), continuing the program begun shortly after the First World War by its predecessor organization, the International Labor Office. As of 1999, the ILO has sponsored more than 100 human rights conventions, many of them widely adhered to. (The United States, however, is party to very few, dealing with the labor conditions of seamen on U.S. vessels.)

In addition to the covenants and conventions open for adherence by all states, conventions have been adopted by regional organizations for adherence by their members, *e.g.*, the European Convention for the Protection of Human Rights and Fundamental Freedoms, the American Convention on Human Rights, and the African Charter on Human and Peoples' Rights. See *infra* Section D.

International human rights agreements prior to the establishment of the United Nations include the Treaty of Paris (1856), the Treaty of Berlin (1878), the Slavery Convention (1926), "minorities treaties" protecting the rights of particular national minorities in particular countries, and several accords sponsored by the International Labor Organization, p. 335 below. See also the Humanitarian Law conventions, p. 293 above.

Of the numerous special conventions sponsored by the United Nations, several have particular importance.*

1. THE GENOCIDE CONVENTION

The Convention on the Prevention and Punishment of the Crime of Genocide, set forth in 78 U.N.T.S. 277, was the first post-war human rights agreement, a memorial to the Holocaust. States generally have not "dared" to refrain from adhering to this convention; as of January 1, 1999, 127 states are party to it.

The Genocide Convention recognizes a right of group identity and the need to protect that right. By Article I, the parties to the convention confirm that genocide is a crime under international law which they undertake to prevent and to punish. Article II defines genocide in comprehensive terms. The Convention obligates States Parties to try and to punish genocide, as well as conspiracy, incitement, or attempt to commit genocide, either in a national court or by an international tribunal that might be established.

Genocide is one of the crimes within the jurisdiction of the Tribunals established by the UN Security Council for the former Yugoslavia and Rwanda. It is also one of the crimes within the jurisdiction of the International Criminal Court launched in 1998. See generally Chapter 3(C) infra.

2. THE CONVENTION ON RACIAL DISCRIMINATION

The Convention on the Elimination of all Forms of Racial Discrimination has been ratified by the large majority of states (152 as of January 1, 1999). It elaborates the commitment of the Human Rights Movement to equality and non-discrimination; in particular at represents the determination of the international system to eliminate racial discrimination and its special manifestation as *apartheid* in South Africa. States were willing to assume obligations and to accept scrutiny in respect of these rights which they were not prepared to accept for rights under the Covenants generally. States Parties "undertake to prohibit and to eliminate racial discrimination in all its forms" (Article 5), but also to take affirmative action (Art. 2(2)) as temporary measures until their objectives have been achieved; see Part IV, Chapter 1(D) infra. And see, *e.g.*, Article 11, providing for interstate complaints; under the Covenant on Civil and Political Rights, submission to such complaint is optional (ICCPR, Article 41).

3. THE CONVENTION ON DISCRIMINATION AGAINST WOMEN

The Convention on the Elimination of all Forms of Discrimination Against Women was modeled in many respects on the Race Convention.

---

* There is substantial material also on other specific international human rights conventions; *e.g.*, for the International Convention on the Protection of the Rights of All Migrant Workers and Members of Their Families (1990), see United Nations Center for Human Rights, "The Rights of Migrant Workers," Fact Sheet No. 24 (1996).

But the commitment to eliminate discrimination against women has not been universally shared, and has faced historic obstacles, many deeply rooted in culture and tradition.

The Women's Convention is discussed in greater detail in Section F below, in the context of the human rights of women generally.

4.   THE CONVENTION AGAINST TORTURE

Article 7 of the ICCPR provides: "No one shall be subjected to torture or to cruel, inhuman or degrading treatment or punishment. In particular, no one shall be subjected without his free consent to medical or scientific experimentation."

In 1975 the UN General Assembly adopted a Declaration on the protection of all persons from being subjected to torture and other cruel, inhuman or degrading treatment or punishment. In 1984 the UN General Assembly adopted the Convention against Torture and other Cruel, Inhuman, or Degrading Treatment or Punishment (A./Res./39/51). Proponents of the Convention sought to engage states which were not party to the ICCPR but which might not be comfortable abstaining from a convention against torture. States were persuaded to elaborate and accept obligations in respect of the right not to be tortured (by officials and others acting under color of law) which they were not prepared to assume in respect of the full array of civil and political rights, or even of cruel and inhuman and degrading treatment or punishment that did not reach the level of torture. And states were prepared to assume obligations not to expel, return ("refouler") or extradite a person to another country where there are substantial grounds for believing that he would be in danger of being subjected to torture. In addition, states accepted implementation provisions more intrusive (and likely to be more effective) than those they had been prepared to accept for the ICCPR.

5.   THE CONVENTION ON THE RIGHTS OF THE CHILD

Like other specialized conventions, the Convention on the Rights of the Child elaborates rights already protected by the principal covenants. See, for example, ICCPR Articles 23(4), 24. ICESCR requires special measures for the health and education of children, in particular in Articles 10(3), 12(2), and 13. Other international documents also declared that childhood is entitled to special care and assistance and sought protection for children in the context of family. See the preamble to the Convention on the Rights of the Child. In November 1990, the UN General Assembly adopted a comprehensive Convention on the Rights of the Child that recognizes the rights of the child independently of his/her family, even within and against the family. As of January 1, 1999, 191 states were parties to the Convention.

Table of International Human Rights Instruments
As of January 1, 1999

	Date	No. of Parties	U.S. a Party?	Citation
The Covenants and their Protocols				
International Covenant on Economic, Social and Cultural Rights	12/16/66	139	No	993 UNTS 3
International Covenant on Civil and Political Rights	12/16/66	141	Yes	999 UNTS 171
Optional Protocol on Civil and Political Rights	12/16/66	95	No	999 UNTS 171
Second Optional Protocol on Civil and Political Rights (death penalty)	12/15/89	35	No	A/Res./44/128
Genocide, War Crimes, Crimes Against Humanity				
Convention on the Prevention and Punishment of the Crime of Genocide	12/9/48	127	Yes	78 UNTS 277
Convention on the Non–Applicability of Statutory Limitations to War Crimes Against Humanity	11/26/68	43	No	754 UNTS 73
Slavery and Forced Labor				
Slavery Convention of 1926, as amended by 1953 Protocol	9/25/26 amended 12/7/53	94	Yes	182 UNTS 51; 212 UNTS 17
Supplementary Convention on the Abolition of Slavery	9/7/56	117	Yes	266 UNTS 3
Convention for the Suppression of Traffic in Persons and of the Exploitation of the Prostitution of Others	3/21/50	72	No	96 UNTS 271
ILO Convention on the Abolition of Forced Labor	6/25/57	133	Yes	320 UNTS 291
Refugees and Stateless Persons				
Convention Relating to the Status of Refugees	7/28/51	132	No	189 UNTS 137
Protocol Relating to the Status of Refugees	1/31/67	132	Yes	606 UNTS 267
Convention Relating to the Status of Stateless Persons	9/28/54	44	No	360 UNTS 131
Racial Discrimination				
International Convention on the Elimination of All Forms of Racial Discrimination	12/21/65	152	Yes	660 UNTS 195
International Convention on the Suppression and Punishment of the Crime of Apartheid	11/30/73	101	No	1015 UNTS 243
Rights of Women and Children				
Convention on the Political Rights of Women	12/20/52	111	Yes	193 UNTS 135
Convention on the Nationality of Married Women	2/20/57	66	No	309 UNTS 65
Convention on the Elimination of All Forms of Discrimination Against Women	12/18/79	163	No	G.A.Res. 34/180
Convention on the Rights of the Child	11/20/89	191	No	G.A. Res. 44/25
Other				
Geneva Conventions [Conduct of War]	8/12/49	188	Yes	77 UNTS 31, 85, 135, 287
Convention Against Torture and Other Cruel, Inhuman or Degrading Punishment	12/10/84	110	Yes	G.A. Res. 39/46
Convention Against Discrimination in Education	12/14/60	85	No	429 UNTS 93
Convention on the International Right of Correction	3/31/53	14	No	439 UNTS 191

	Date	No. of Parties	U.S. a Party?	Citation
International Convention on the Protection of the Rights of All Migrant Workers	12/18/90	10	No	G.A. Res. 45/158

Note: The ILO and Its Conventions

The ILO seeks to improve labor and social conditions by preparing and promoting conventions and recommendations. It is governed by a General Conference of Representatives of member states, including representatives of governments, of employers, and of labor. The ILO has promoted more than 100 conventions which have been widely accepted. See International Labour Organization, International Labour Conventions and Recommendations 1919–1981 (1982) and supplements. See generally International Labour Office, Handbook for Procedures relating to International Labour Conventions and Recommendations (1995); N. Valticos and G. von Potobsky, International Labour Law (2d ed., 1995).

International Labour Organization (ILO)

in International Law: Cases and Materials
1488–91 (Henkin et al. eds., 3d. ed. 1993).*

1. History

The ILO antedates most of the other specialized agencies by twenty-five years, the original constitution being embodied in the peace treaties concluding World War I (Part XIII of the Treaty of Versailles of June 28, 1919, of the Treaty of Saint Germain of Sept. 10, 1919, and of the Treaty of Trianon of June 4, 1920, and Part XII of the Treaty of Neuilly of Nov. 27, 1919). During the first twenty-five years, the ILO functioned as an official intergovernmental organization, autonomously associated with the League. The bulk of its work consisted of elaborating international conventions regulating such conditions as working hours, female labor, industrial injury, and unemployment compensation, and of providing advice on labor questions.

. . .

The dissolution of the League necessitated articulation of a new relationship with the U.N. through the adoption of instruments of amendment in 1945 and 1946. The ILO became the first international organization to be linked to the U.N. as a "special agency" through a Special Agreement between the U.N. and ILO, effective Dec. 16, 1946.

. . .

2. Organization

STRUCTURE

In 1919, the European countries wanted a labor organization which would develop rules regulating working conditions and persuade governments to adopt these, while the United States pushed for an organization

* Reprinted from Henkin, Pugh, Schachter, and Smit, eds., International Law: Cases and Materials, 3d ed., @ 1993, with permission of the West Group.

that would aid the development of independent labor movements. The compromise reached established a structure unique to the ILO: a tripartite system of representation. Each member was given the right to send four delegates to a Conference, two of them government representatives and one delegate each representing workers' and employers' organizations (Art. 3(5)). The latter delegates were to speak and vote independently, being elected by the most "representative organizations" of workers and employers in each country. Difficult questions have arisen in the implementation of these provisions. For example, how are delegates to be selected when there are no organizations in a member country of the prescribed categories? What criteria determine whether the organizations are "most representative"? If not by numbers, are they to be subjectively chosen in terms of "ruling groups"? See Beguin, ILO and the Tripartite System, International Conciliation 523 (1959). So that the importance of labor representation would not undercut the ultimate responsibility of governments to enforce the adopted legislation, the ratio of two government delegates for every worker and employer delegate was established.

The principal organ of the ILO is the International Labour Conference, which meets annually. Workers' and employers' representatives have an equal voice with those of governments. The ILO's Governing Body is its executive body. It now has 56 regular members. Of the 28 government representatives, ten hold non-elective seats representing members states of "chief industrial importance" and 18 represent members elected by the conference. In 1986, the conference adopted amendments to the constitution relating to the membership of the Governing Body. Under the new provisions, the regular membership will be increased to 56 government members and 28 employers' and workers' members respectively. The category of states of "chief industrial importance" will disappear. The amendments will not come into force, however, until instruments of acceptance have been deposited by two-thirds of member states, including five of the ten states of chief industrial importance.

LEGISLATION

Conventions and Recommendations which set international labor standards are adopted at meetings of the International Labor Conference which are held annually (Art. 19). Conventions, ratified by member states, create binding obligations, while Recommendations are guidelines on policy, legislation, and practice.

Between 1919 and 1990, 169 Conventions and 176 Recommendations were adopted, covering a range of matters such as certain basic human rights (freedom of association, abolition of forced labor, elimination of discrimination in employment), labor administration, industrial relations, employment policy, working conditions, social security, occupational safety and health, and employment of women and children and special categories of workers (migrants and seafarers). The body of basic principles thus developed was compiled into an International Labor Code issued in 1939 and 1951. For the 1951 Code, see International Labour Office, The International Labour Code, 1951 (1952).

Each member state is required to submit all Conventions and Recommendations adopted by the Conference to its competent national authority in order to give effect to the provisions. The procedure of adoption at Conferences, established instead of the more conventional method of signing by plenipotentiaries, gives the Conventions their hybrid nature of legal and contractual characteristics.

A supervisory procedure has been established to monitor the implementation and application of Conventions by ratifying states. Each member must submit reports every two years (Arts. 19, 22), and copies of these reports must be sent to the member's, workers' and employers' organizations (Art. 23). A committee of independent experts evaluate these reports and tripartite bodies examine individual cases of compliance.

The enforcement of obligations can be achieved through contentious proceedings as well. Individual associations of workers and employers may submit reports to the International Labour Office on the failure of their government to observe a Convention (Art. 24). Members who have ratified a Convention and are dissatisfied with the adherence of other ratifying members may file a complaint. A Commission of Inquiry investigates the charges and files a report with findings of facts and recommendations on steps to be taken. The members can accept the report or refer the matter to the ICJ, whose decision is final (Arts. 26–29, 31–34). Complaints have been infrequent, and thus far all members have accepted the Commission's suggestions.

3.   *Problems in a Changing World*

The ILO was created at a time when its constituency of democratic countries were at the same stage of development. Its two goals of universal membership and pure tripartite representation posed no conflicts. The emergence of communist and socialist countries, as well as the increased degree of governmental control over employer and worker groups in both democratic and developing countries, has put a strain upon adherence to the organization's original ideals.

. . .

In 1970, the United States cut off its ILO assessments, comprising 21% of all contributions to the ILO fund, in order to exert pressure against the appointment of a Soviet delegate as assistant Director–General and to indicate dissatisfaction with the use of the ILO by members as a forum for political issues. ... On November 5, 1975, the United States gave notice of its intent to withdraw from the ILO (14 ILM 1582–4 (1975)). Four reasons were given: (1) the system of tripartite representation had eroded due to the admission of nondemocratic members, (2) the usual procedures for prosecuting member violations of obligations had been bypassed in recent years, as Conferences passed resolutions on member states' actions without prior referral to the appropriate investigating commission, (3) the organization ignored the alleged violation of rights in all but a handful of states, thus expressing only a selective concern for human rights, and (4) the organization had become increasingly politicized and heedless of its goal of promoting social welfare.

Before a member's withdrawal is effective, two years notice must be given and all financial obligations must be met (Art. 1(5)). The United States did not pay its financial obligations, but permitted the two years to elapse and declared its membership in the ILO terminated. United States withdrawal did not affect practice in the United States, since 6 out of the 7 Conventions it has ratified pertain to technical maritime matters.

In February, 1980, President Carter issued a statement to the effect that a majority of the members of the ILO had successfully joined together to return the ILO to its original purposes and that "[I] have decided, therefore, that the United States should now rejoin the ILO. * * * " 80 State Dep't Bull. No. 2037, p. 65 (1980).

· · ·

Notes

1.   The ILO Constitution emphasizes the necessity of cooperation between federal and state governments in the enforcement of Conventions that relate to matters falling within the domain of a constituent state. Federalist countries must report on the laws of their constituent states as well as those of the federal government. Ratification of Conventions is more difficult in federations but the United States' record is worse than that of Canada, Australia or Switzerland; it has ratified only 7 of 143 Conventions, declaring the remainder to be within the domain of its states.

2.   The ILO does not allow reservations to Conventions to be made when member states ratify them, since this would hamper the goal of a uniform system of obligations, which must be reciprocally assumed. Other methods ... allow ratifying developing countries some flexibility in the assumption of obligations. See Gormley, "Modification of Multilateral Conventions by 'Negotiating Reservations' and Alternatives: Comparative Study of the ILO and the Council of Europe," 39 Fordham L.Rev. 59 (1970).

· · ·

D.   REGIONAL HUMAN RIGHTS ARRANGEMENTS

After the Second World War, while the international system produced international (inter-governmental) organizations open for membership to all states, particular areas of the world developed regional organizations. The Pan American Union, notably, long antedated the United Nations, and the American states sought to maintain their regional character after the United Nations was established. The UN Charter recognizes and contemplates a role for regional organizations (see UN Charter, Chapter VIII). With the advent of the Cold War, there grew also regional collective defense organizations, *e.g.,* NATO and the Warsaw Pact. Western Europe also developed economic organizations, the Coal and Steel Community leading to the European Economic Community and then the European Union, and political bodies such as the Council of Europe.

Regional bodies early developed human rights programs, adopted human rights conventions, and established human rights institutions.

For the implementation and enforcement of regional human rights agreements, see *infra* Chapter 3(B).

1. THE EUROPEAN CONVENTION AND THE EUROPEAN SOCIAL CHARTER

The European Human Rights System

In International Law: Cases and Materials 657–63
(Henkin et al. eds., 3d. ed. 1993).*

The European Convention for the Protection of Human Rights and Fundamental Freedoms, 213 U.N.T.S. 221 (1950), entered into force on September 3, 1953. It was drafted under sponsorship of the Council of Europe, and open to accession by all members of the Council. By early 1993 it had been ratified by all twenty-one Council members, but not all members have ratified the various protocols to the Convention. See Chart Showing Signature and Ratifications of Council of Europe Conventions and Agreements (Council of Europe Legal Affairs, May 1993).

Although France was one of the original signatories to the Convention, it did not ratify the Convention until May 3, 1974. The instrument of ratification was accompanied by two reservations relating to Articles 5, 6 and 75(1), and a declaration of interpretation relating to Articles 10 and 63. After the Cold War, some former members of the Soviet bloc ... moved to join the Council of Europe and become parties to the European Convention.

1. The Rights and Freedoms Protected

While there are sometimes significant differences in their formulation, the substantive provisions of the European Convention are comparable to those in the International Covenant on Civil and Political Rights. They include: the right to life; freedom from torture and inhuman or degrading treatment; freedom from slavery, servitude or forced labor; liberty and security of person, and detention only in accordance with procedures prescribed by law; the right to a fair and public hearing in determining civil rights and obligations, or criminal charges; respect for privacy and family life; freedom of thought, conscience and religion; freedom of expression, peaceful assembly and association; the right to marry and found a family; freedom from invidious discrimination. Everyone whose rights are violated shall have a remedy. Subsequent protocols added protection for property;**

---

* Reprinted from Henkin, Pugh, Schachter, and Smit, eds., International Law: Cases and Materials, 3d ed., © 1993, with permission of the West Group.

** [The First Protocol protects the property rights of "Every natural *or legal* person" (emphasis added).—Editors' Note.]

the right to an education; a provision for free elections; no deprivation of liberty for inability to fulfill a contractual obligation; freedom of movement and residence and the right to leave the country; the right to enter the territory of the state of which one is a national; freedom from expulsion from the country of one's nationality, and no collective expulsion of aliens. Unlike the International Covenant, the European Convention contains no reference to a right of peoples to self-determination and to "economic self-determination" (International Covenant, Article 1); to the rights of persons belonging to ethnic, religious or linguistic minorities (Article 27); the right to recognition everywhere as a person before the law (Article 16); and the right to equality before the law and the equal protection of the law (Article 26; but cf. European Convention Article 14, forbidding discrimination on grounds of sex, race, color etc. in the enjoyment of rights). There is also no European counterpart to the International Covenant's prohibition on war propaganda or advocacy of national, racial or religious hatred that constitutes incitement to discrimination (Article 20). And there is no mention of rights of the child (International Covenant, Article 24). Unlike the International Covenant, the European Convention protects property. The Convention also provides that no one shall be deprived of the right to enter his own country, while the Covenant provides that no one shall be *arbitrarily* deprived of that right (Article 12(4)). The Convention provides explicitly that no one may be expelled from the territory of the state of which he is a national (Protocol 4, Article 3).

In 1985, the adherence of a seventh member brought into force Protocol 6 prohibiting capital punishment in time of peace. Protocol 7 gives additional substantive protections—restrictions on expulsion of aliens, the right to review of a conviction by a higher tribunal, the right of a victim of a miscarriage of justice to be compensated, freedom from double jeopardy, and the equality of spouses in respect of marriage. Protocol 7 entered into force in 1988 and had 12 adherents as of January 1, 1993.*

. . .

THE EUROPEAN SOCIAL CHARTER

In 1961, the countries of Western Europe adopted the European Social Charter, 529 U.N.T.S. 89; it came into force on 26 February 1965. The following states have become parties: Austria, Belgium, Cyprus, Denmark, Finland, France, Germany, Greece, Iceland, Ireland, Italy, Luxembourg, Malta, The Netherlands, Norway, Portugal, Sweden, Spain, Turkey, and the United Kingdom. The Charter expresses the resolution of the parties "to make every effort in common to improve the standard of living and to promote the social well-being of both their urban and rural populations by means of appropriate institutions and action." In Part I, the parties "accept as the aim of their policy, to be pursued by all appropriate means,

---

* [Protocols 8–10 effected procedural changes, later copied and subsumed in Protocol 11, which made major structural changes in the institutions for implementation and enforcement of the Convention. See *infra.* pp. 552–553.—Editors' Note.]

both national and international in character, the attainment of conditions in which the following rights and principles may be effectively realized." Part II lists undertakings in various categories, *e.g.,* the right to work, the right to a fair remuneration, the right to bargain collectively, the rights of children, the right of employed women to protection, the right to Social Security, the right to social and medical assistance.

Notes

1.   The European Social Charter was revised in 1996, see ETS No. 163; the parties recognizing "the advantage of embodying in a Revised Charter, designed progressively to take the place of the European Social Charter, the rights guaranteed by the Charter the rights guaranteed by the Charter as amended, the rights guarantees by the Additional Protocol of 1988 and to add new rights." The Revised Charter follows and elaborates on the scheme of the original Charter: In the revision, the parties consider themselves bound by at least six (instead of five, as in the original Charter) of nine articles (instead of seven, articles as in the original Charter), and a party undertakes to consider itself bound "by an additional number of articles or numbered paragraphs of Part II of the Charter which it may select, provided that the total number of Articles or numbered paragraphs by which it is bound is not less than sixteen articles on sixty-three numbered paragraphs" (10 articles or 45 numbered paragraphs in the original Charter).

2.   For the implementation of the European human rights system, see *infra* Chapter 3(B)(2). For more information on European regional human rights arrangements, see *Agenda of the Comité des Sages and Final Project Report,* in Leading by Example: A Human Rights Agenda for the European Union for the Year 2000 (European University Institute, 1998); D.J. Harris, M. O'Boyle, C. Warbrick, Law of the European Convention on Human Rights (1995); Mark W. Janis, Richard Kay & Anthony Bradley, European Human Rights Law: Text and Materials (2d ed. 1995); The European System for the Protection of Human Rights (R. St. J. Macdonald, F. Matscher, and H. Petzold eds., 1993); Jochen A. Frowein, *The European Convention on Human Rights as the Public Order of Europe*, 1 Collected Courses of the Academy of European Law, bk. 2, 267–358 (1992); David Harris, The European Social Charter (1984).

3.   European human rights treaties on specific topics include: European Convention for the Prevention of Torture and Inhuman or Degrading Treatment or Punishment, European Treaty Series [ETS] 126 (1987); European Agreement on the Abolition of Visas for Refugees, ETS 107 (1959); European Agreement on the Transfer of Responsibility for Refugees, ETS 107 (1980); European Convention on the Legal Status of Migrant Workers, ETS 93 (1977); Convention for the Protection of Individuals with Regard to the Automatic Processing of Personal Data, ETS 108 (1981); European Convention on Social Security, ETS 78 (1972); European Convention on the Exercise of Children's Rights, ETS 160 (1996); European

Framework Convention for the Protection of National Minorities, ETS 157 (1995), described *infra* p. 474.

2.   THE AMERICAN CONVENTION

The Inter–American Human Rights System

in International Law: Cases and Materials
666–67 (Henkin et al. eds., 3d. ed. 1993).*

Organizations of the states in the Western Hemisphere have been concerned with human rights since the Second World War. The Charter of the Organization of American States includes the provision: "Each State has the right to develop its cultural, political and economic life freely and naturally. In this free development the State shall respect the rights of the individual and the principles of universal morality" (originally Chapter III, Art. 13; now Chapter IV, Art. 16). These have been deemed to be words of legal obligation. Thomas & Thomas, The Organization of American States 223 (1963).

The American Declaration on the Rights and Duties of Man was adopted in 1948, seven months before the Universal Declaration was approved. It is generally accepted that the American Declaration was not intended to have legally binding character.... See LeBlanc, The OAS and the Promotion and Protection of Human Rights 13 (1977).**

In 1959, the Fifth Meeting of Consultation of Ministers of Foreign Affairs resolved that the Inter–American Council of Jurists should prepare a Convention on Human Rights, and also one to create an Inter–American Court for the Protection of Human Rights. The Meeting decided also to organize an Inter–American Commission on Human Rights. The American Convention on Human Rights was signed in San Jose, Costa Rica on 22 November 1969, and came into force in June 1978. As of 1986, 19 states have ratified the Convention. Elections to the Inter–American Court of Human Rights created by the Convention first took place in May 1979. Terms are for six years and are staggered. Article 52 of the Convention permits nationals of all member states of the O.A.S. to serve on the Court, whether or not the member state is a party to the Convention. (Thomas Buergenthal of the United States—which is not a party to the Convention—has served on the Court.)

1.   *The Rights and Freedoms Protected*

Substantively, the American Declaration and the American Convention parallel the Universal Declaration and the International Covenant on Civil and Political Rights. The American Declaration, however, is entitled the American Declaration of Rights *and Duties* of Man and includes a chapter containing 10 articles setting forth the individual's duties (Compare Article

* Reprinted from Henkin, Pugh, Schachter, and Smit, eds., International Law: Cases and Materials, 3d ed., © 1993, with permission of the West Group.

** [But see Notes following this Selection, p. 343 below.—Editors' Note.]

29(1) of the Universal Declaration). The American Convention protects the accepted political-civil rights, although some in terms significantly different from those in the International Covenant on Civil and Political Rights. In the American Convention, for example, the right to life "shall be protected by law and, in general, from the moment of conception" (Art. 4(1)). The protected rights include: the right to life, freedom from torture and inhuman treatment, freedom from slavery and servitude, the right to liberty and security, the right to a fair trial, freedom from retroactivity of the criminal law, the right to respect for private and family life, freedom of conscience and religion, freedom of thought and expression, freedom of assembly, freedom of association, freedom to marry and found a family, the right to property, freedom of movement, freedom from exile, prohibition of the collective expulsion of aliens, the right to participate in free elections, the right to an effective remedy if one's rights are violated, the right to recognition as a person before the law, the right to compensation for miscarriage of justice, the right of reply, the right to a name, the rights of the child, the right to a nationality, the right to equality before the law, the right of asylum. Like the European Convention but unlike the International Covenant, the American Convention includes protection for property, and freedom from exile and collective expulsion for aliens. Unlike both the International Covenant and the European Convention, the American Convention recognizes a right of reply (to anyone injured by inaccurate or offensive statements or ideas) and a right to seek and be granted asylum. But the American Convention does not include the right to an education or other economic-social rights. It commits the states parties, in Article 26, to work to achieve progressively "by legislation or other appropriate means, the full realization of the rights implicit in the economic, social, educational, scientific, and cultural standards set forth in the Charter of the Organization of American States. * * *"

. . .

Notes

1. It may no longer be accurate to conclude that American states not party to the American Convention (e.g., the United States, as of 1999) are not subject to any human rights obligations in the American system. In an Advisory Opinion in 1989 the Inter–American Court noted that the American Declaration is an authoritative interpretation of the OAS Charter (a treaty to which the United States is party), and may also have contributed to customary law. The Inter–American Human Rights Commission has considered several complaints against the United States. See Chapter 3, Section B(1) *infra*.

2. The Additional Protocol to the American Convention on Human Rights in the Area of Economic, Social and Cultural Rights, OAS Treaty Series No. 69, reprinted at 28 I.L.M. 156 (1989), enacted at San Salvador in November 1988, is the progeny of Article 26 of the original Convention. In the Additional Protocol, the States Parties to the American Convention

reaffirm the close relationship between economic, social, and cultural rights, and civil and political rights, and the requirement that all be protected and promoted. Member States who have ratified the Additional Protocol undertake to guarantee the rights set forth by legislation or other domestic provisions. The "new" protected rights include: the right to work including just, equitable, and satisfactory conditions of work, trade union rights, the right to social security, the right to health and a healthy environment, the right to food, the right to education, the right to the benefits of culture, the right to the formation and protection of families, rights of children, and the protection of the elderly and the handicapped. The Additional Protocol requires eleven deposited instruments of ratification or accession for it to enter into force. As of July 1999, ten States Parties have committed to the development and protection of economic, social and cultural rights in the Inter–American system.

3. For the regional implementation of the Inter-American human rights system, see *infra* Chapter 3(B)(1).

Specific Inter-American human rights instruments include: the Inter–American Convention to Prevent and Punish Torture, OAS Treaty Series 67 (1985); OAS Convention on Asylum, OAS Treaty Series 34 (1928); OAS Convention on Diplomatic Asylum, OAS Treaty Series 18 (1954); Inter–American Convention on the Granting of Political Rights to Women, OAS Treaty Series 3 (1948); Inter–American Convention on the Granting of Civil Rights to Women, OAS Treaty Series 23 (1948); Inter–American Convention on the Prevention, Punishment and Eradication of Violence Against Women (1994).

3. THE AFRICAN CHARTER

Thomas Buergenthal, *The African System of Human and Peoples' Rights*
in International Human Rights in a Nutshell 228 (2d ed. 1995).*

I. INTRODUCTION

The African Charter on Human and Peoples' Rights entered into force on October 21, 1986. Nowak, "The African Charter of Human and Peoples' Rights," 7 Hum. Rts. L.J. 399 (1986). The Charter was adopted by the Organization of African Unity in 1981 and has to date been ratified by 49 states. For the drafting history of the Charter, *see* Mbaye, "Introduction to the African Charter on Human and Peoples' Rights," in International Commission of Jurists, *Human and Peoples' Rights in Africa and the African Charter* 19 (1985); Gittleman, "The African Charter on Human and Peoples' Rights: A Legal Analysis," 22 Va. J. Int'l L. 667 (1982); Ramcharan, "The Travaux Préparatoires of the African Convention or Human and Peoples' Rights," 13 Human Rights L. J. 307 (1992).

The African Charter establishes a system for the protection and promotion of human rights that is designed to function within the institutional framework of the OAU. The OAU is a regional intergovernmental

* Reprinted from Thomas Buergenthal, International Human Rights in a Nutshell, 2d ed., © 1995, with permission of the West Group.

organization which came into being in 1963 and has a membership of 53 states. It operates through a permanent Secretariat, various Ministerial Conferences, a Council of Ministers and the Assembly of Heads of State and Government. The Assembly meets once a year and is the highest policy-making body of the OAU. *See generally* Bello, "Organization of African Unity," in *Encyclopedia of Public International Law, Instalment 6*, at 270 (R. Bernhardt, ed. 1983).

II. RIGHTS AND DUTIES

§ 5-1. Introduction

The African Charter differs from the European and American Conventions on Human Rights in a number of respects. *See generally*, Okere, "The Protection of Human Rights in Africa and the African Charter on Human and Peoples' Rights: Comparative Analysis with the European and American Systems," 6 Hum. Rights Q. 141 (1984). First, the African Charter proclaims not only rights but also duties. Second, it codifies individual as well as peoples' rights. Third, in addition to guaranteeing civil and political rights, it protects economic, social and cultural rights. Fourth, the treaty is drafted in a form that permits the States Parties to impose very extensive restrictions and limitations on the exercise of rights it proclaims. *See* Weston, Lukes & Hnatt, "Regional Human Rights Regimes: A Comparison and Appraisal," 20 Vand. J. Transnat'l L. 585, 608–14 (1987); Flinterman & Ankumah, "The African Charter on Human and Peoples' Rights," in Hannum (ed.) Guide to International Human Rights Practice 159 (2d ed. 1992).

The provisions of the Charter reflect the influence of UN human rights instruments and African traditions. Thus, it bears a stronger resemblance to the International Covenants of Human Rights than to the two other regional human rights treaties. *See* van Boven, "The Relations between Peoples' Rights and Human Rights in the African Charter," 7 Hum. Rts. L.J. 183, 186–90 (1986). The emphasis the Charter places on African tradition finds expression in its preamble as well as in the form in which many of its rights and duties are articulated. Mbaye, *supra*, at 26. The preamble speaks of "the virtues of [African] historical tradition and the values of African civilization which should inspire and characterize their reflection on the concept of human and peoples' rights." Other principles that inform the African Charter are referred to in the following provision of the preamble:

> *Convinced* that it is henceforth essential to pay a particular attention to the right to development and that civil and political rights cannot be dissociated from economic, social and cultural rights in their conception as well as universality and that the satisfaction of economic, social and cultural rights is a guarantee for the enjoyment of civil and political rights.

The emphasis on the right to development, which is a peoples' right, and the linking together of different categories of individual rights has its conceptual source in the standard-setting practice of the UN.

§ 5–2.   Individual rights

The Charter contains a broad non-discrimination clause and an equal protection clause. It guarantees the right to life and it prohibits slavery as well as torture, cruel, inhuman or degrading treatment and punishment. It bars arbitrary arrest and detention as well as *ex post facto* criminal legislation and punishment. The Charter contains provisions designed to ensure due process of law and fair hearings. It guarantees freedom of religion, the right to receive information, to express one's opinions, freedom of association and assembly. In addition to recognizing the right to freedom of movement, the Charter prohibits mass expulsions of non-nationals "aimed at national, racial, ethnic or religious groups." (Art. 12.)

The Charter guarantees the right to property, to work, to equal remuneration for equal work, to the enjoyment of "the best attainable state of physical and mental health" (Art. 16(1)), and the right to education. The provision, which proclaims the right to education and the right to take part in the cultural life of one's community also declares that "the promotion and protection of morals and traditional values recognized by the community shall be the duty of the State." (Art. 17(3)). A similar concept finds expression in Article 18, which characterizes the family as "the natural unit and basis of society" and declares, *inter alia*, that "the State shall have the duty to assist the family which is the custodian of morals and traditional values recognized by the community." Besides providing that "the aged and the disabled shall ... have the right to special measures of protection in keeping with their physical and moral needs," Article 18 also contains the following provisions:

> The State shall ensure the elimination of every discrimination against women and also ensure the protection of the rights of the woman and the child as stipulated in international declarations and conventions. (Art. 18(3).)

Very few, if any, human rights treaties resort to this extremely liberal form of incorporation by reference of other international instruments. On the utility of this approach as far as the rights of women are concerned, see Welch, "Human Rights and African Women: A Comparison of Protection Under Two Major Treaties," 15 Hum. Rts. Q. 548 (1993); Butegwa, "Using the African Charter on Human and Peoples' Rights to Secure Women's Access to Land in Africa," in R. Cook (ed.), *Human Rights of Women: National and International Perspectives* 495 (1994). See also Beyani, "Toward a More Effective Guarantee of Women's Rights in the African Human Rights System," in Cook, *supra*, at 285.

Although the aforementioned catalog of individual rights is very extensive, some of the rights are phrased in language that seems designed to deprive the guarantee of much meaning. See Flinterman & Ankumah, supra at 165–66. Article 8, for example which proclaims "freedom of conscience, the profession and free practice of religion," declares that "no one may, *subject to law and order*, be submitted to measures restricting the exercise of these freedoms." (Emphasis added.) And Article 10(1) provides that "every individual shall have the right to free association *provided that*

he abides by the law." (Emphasis added.) Similarly, Article 9(2) articulates
the right to freedom of expression by declaring that "every individual shall
have the right to express and disseminate his opinions *within the law*."
(Emphasis added.) It should be noted, however, that other rights, particularly those which concern the physical integrity of the individual and due
process, do not authorize the restrictions that are permitted with regard to
the rights applicable to the exercise of political freedoms. Noteworthy, too,
is the fact that the African Charter does not contain a general derogation
clause permitting the States Parties to suspend the enjoyment of certain
rights during national emergencies. Whether the existence of this power
may be implied or whether it is incorporated by reference through the
language of Article 60 of the Charter, which refers to other human rights
instruments, remains to be seen. On this subject, see Gittleman, supra at
704. For an analysis of Article 60, see § 5–7 *infra*. Some commentators
suggest that the many "clawback" clauses found in the African Charter
make a general derogation clause unnecessary for states wishing to impose
restrictions during national emergencies. Flinterman & Ankumah, *supra*
166.

§ 5–3. Peoples' rights

It has become fashionable in the human rights field to speak of
"generations" of rights. Civil and political rights are characterized as "first
generation" rights, whereas economic, social and cultural rights are classified as "second generation" rights. Most of the freedoms which the African
Charter denominates as peoples' rights are sometimes described as "third
generation" rights. *See generally*, Marie, "Relations between Peoples'
Rights and Human Rights: Semantic and Methodological Distinctions," 7
Hum. Rts. L.J. 195 (1986); Kiwanuka, "The Meaning of 'People' in the
African Charter on Human and Peoples' Rights," 82 Am. J. Int'l L. 80
(1988); Swanson, "The Emergence of New Rights in the African Charter,"
12 N.Y.L. Sch. J. Int'l & Comp. L. 307 (1991). Among these are the right of
peoples to self-determination and to full sovereignty over their natural
resources. Also on the list are the right to development, the right to peace,
and "the right to a general satisfactory environment favourable to their
development." (Art. 24.) The right to development, which has already been
mentioned, is formulated as follows: "All peoples shall have the right to
their economic, social and cultural development with due regard to their
freedom and identity and in the equal enjoyment of the common heritage of
mankind." (Art. 22(1).) This and similar language found in the African
Charter reinforces the OAU's political agenda in the UN by giving it treaty
status. A few of these rights do, of course, already enjoy that status. *See,
e.g.*, Common Article 1 of the International Covenants on Human Rights.
See generally, van Boven *supra*, at 189–90; Kiss, "The Peoples' Right to
Self–Determination," 7 Hum. Rights. L.J. 165 (1986). On the right to
development in the Charter, see Bello, "Article 22 of the African Charter
on Human and People's Rights," in E. Bello & B. Ajibola (eds.), *Essays in
Honor of Judge Taslim Olawale Elias*, vol. I, at 447 (1991).

§ 5–4.   Duties

A distinguished African jurist and former vice president of the International Court of Justice, who played an important role in drafting the African Charter, points out that "in Africa, laws and duties are regarded as being two facets of the same reality: two inseparable realities." Mbaye, *supra*, at 27. See also Umozurike, "Autochthony in the African Charter on Human and People's Rights," in E. Bello & B. Ajibola (eds.), *Essays in Honour of Judge Taslim Olawale Elias*, Vol. I, at 475 (1992). Mbaye suggests that it should therefore come as no surprise to anyone that the African Charter proclaims duties as well as rights. Here it is worth recalling that the American Declaration on the Rights and Duties of Man adopted the same approach, but that the drafters of the American Convention did not follow the same course.

The duties that the African Charter proclaims fall into two broad categories. In the first group are duties which can be characterized as correlatives of rights. The other category might be described as restrictions on the enjoyment of rights disguised as duties. Article 27(2), for example, which declares that "the rights and freedoms of each individual shall be exercised with due regard to the rights of others, collective security, morality and common interest," appears to codify both categories of duties. Here, it is evident that the scope of these duties or their impact on the rights guaranteed in the Charter would differ significantly depending upon whether an individual's rights were to be limited by the rights of others or by considerations of collective security; the latter type of duties appear to be dangerously vague. The contrast between these different types of duties is even more striking in Article 29, which imposes on the individual the duty "to respect his parents at all times, to maintain them in case of need" and "to preserve and strengthen social and national solidarity, particularly when the latter is threatened." (Arts. 29(1) and 29(4).) The first two duties differ very considerably from the third, which is an invitation to the imposition of unlimited restrictions on the enjoyment of rights.

Other types of duties reflect the African values which the Charter seeks to advance. Article 29(7) imposes the duty "to preserve and strengthen positive African cultural values in relation with other members of the society, in the spirit of tolerance, dialogue and consultation and, in general, to contribute to the promotion of the moral well-being of society." Whether the inclusion of these duties and those set out in Chapter II of the Charter will adversely affect the enjoyment of the rights that the treaty guarantees remains to be seen. It cannot be doubted, however, that the catalog of duties which the Charter proclaims carries with it a serious risk of governmental abuse. Umozurike, "The African Charter on Human and Peoples' Rights," 77 Am. J. Int'l L. 902, 911 (1983). The seriousness of this risk will depend, in part at least, on the pace and success of the process of democratization in Africa. On this subject, see Aidoo, "Africa: Democracy Without Human Rights?" 15 Hum. Rts. Q. 703 (1993); Mutua, "Human Rights and Politics in Africa," 1 E. Afr. J. Peace & Hum. Rts. 250 (1993).

. . .

Notes

Specific African human rights instruments include: African Charter on the Rights and Welfare of the Child, OAU Doc. CAB/LEG/24.9/49 (1990); OAU Convention Regarding the Specific Aspects of Refugee Problems in Africa (1969). On legal and institutional development in Africa, see Towards the Renaissance of Constitutionalism in Africa (Babacar Kanté and Marlies E. Pietermaat–Kros eds., 1998); and *The Evolving African Constitutionalism*, 60 Rev. Int'l Comm'n Jurists (June 1998) (Special Issue), which appends texts of various African declarations, the African Charter of Human and Peoples' Rights, and the Protocol on the Establishment of an African Court on Human and Peoples' Rights. The Protocol was drafted and signed in 1998 and will go into effect upon ratification or accession by fifteen member states.

For the implementation of the African human rights system, see *infra* Chapter 3(B)(3).

E.   CUSTOMARY LAW OF HUMAN RIGHTS AND NONBINDING HUMAN RIGHTS REGIMES

1.   CUSTOMARY LAW OF HUMAN RIGHTS

Restatement (Third) of the Foreign Relations Law of United States

§ 702 and Comments (1987).

§ 702.   Customary International Law of Human Rights

A state violates international law if, as a matter of state policy, it practices, encourages, or condones

(a) genocide,

(b) slavery or slave trade,

(c) the murder or causing the disappearance of individuals,

(d) torture or other cruel, inhuman, or degrading treatment or punishment,

(e) prolonged arbitrary detention,

(f) systematic racial discrimination, or

(g) a consistent pattern of gross violations of internationally recognized human rights.

Comment:

a.   Scope of customary law of human rights. This section includes as customary law only those human rights whose status as customary law is generally accepted (as of 1987) and whose scope and content are generally agreed. See § 701, Reporters' Note 6. The list is not necessarily complete, and is not closed: human rights not listed in this section may have achieved the status of customary law, and some rights might achieve that status in the future. See Comments *j*, *k*, and *l*.

b.   State policy as violation of customary law. In general, a state is responsible for acts of officials or official bodies, national or local, even if the acts were not authorized by or known to the responsible national authorities, indeed even if expressly forbidden by law, decree or instruction. The violations of human rights cited in this section, however, are violations of customary international law only if practiced, encouraged, or condoned by the government of a state as official policy. A state is not responsible under this section for a violation of human rights by an official that was not authorized, encouraged, or condoned by the responsible governmental authorities of the state. (Compare the different rule as to state responsibility for official injuries to nationals of another state, § 711, Comment *a* and § 207, Comment *d*.)

A government may be presumed to have encouraged or condoned acts prohibited by this section if such acts, especially by its officials, have been repeated or notorious and no steps have been taken to prevent them or to punish the perpetrators. That state law prohibits the violation and provides generally effective remedies is strong evidence that the violation is not state policy. A state is not ordinarily responsible under this section for violations of human rights by individuals, such as individual acts of torture or of racial discrimination. A state would be responsible if, as a matter of state policy, it required, encouraged, or condoned such private violations, but mere failure to enact laws prohibiting private violations would not ordinarily constitute encouragement or condonation. International law requires a state to outlaw genocide, slavery, and the slave trade, and the state would be responsible under this section if it failed to prohibit them or to enforce the prohibition.

Even when a state is not responsible under this section because a violation is not state policy, the state may be responsible under some international agreement that requires the state to prevent the violation. For example, under the Covenant on Civil and Political Rights, a state party is guilty of a violation if any of the acts listed in this section is perpetrated by officials, persons acting under color of law, or other persons for whose acts the state is responsible under § 207, even when their acts are contrary to state law or policy. See also § 207, Comment *a*. And see Reporters' Note 2 to this section.

c.   Customary law of human rights as United States law. The customary law of human rights is part of the law of the United States to be applied as such by State as well as federal courts.

d.   Genocide. Genocide is defined in Article II of the Convention on the Prevention and Punishment of the Crime of Genocide as

> any of the following acts committed with intent to destroy, in whole or in part, a national, ethnical, racial or religious group, as such:

> (a) Killing members of the group;

(b) Causing serious bodily or mental harm to members of the group;

(c) Deliberately inflicting on the group conditions of life calculated to bring about its physical destruction in whole or in part;

(d) Imposing measures intended to prevent births within the group;

(e) Forcibly transferring children of the group to another group.

That definition is generally accepted for purposes of customary law under this section.

A state violates customary law if it practices or encourages genocide, fails to make genocide a crime or to punish persons guilty of it, or otherwise condones genocide. Parties to the Genocide Convention are bound also by the provisions requiring states to punish persons guilty of conspiracy, direct and public incitement, or attempt to commit genocide, or complicity in genocide, and to extradite persons accused of genocide. [The United States ratified the Convention in 1988.]

e. Slavery and slave trade. Many states, including the United States, are parties to conventions outlawing slavery and slave trade, but states not parties to any such conventions are bound by essentially the same obligations as a matter of customary law. Slavery is outlawed by the Constitution and laws of the United States and by the law of states generally.

f. Murder as state policy and capital punishment. Under this section, it is a violation of international law for a state to kill an individual other than as lawful punishment pursuant to conviction in accordance with due process of law, or as necessary under exigent circumstances, for example by police officials in line of duty in defense of themselves or of other innocent persons, or to prevent serious crime.

Capital punishment, imposed pursuant to conviction in accordance with due process of law, has not been recognized as a violation of the customary law of human rights. It may, however, constitute cruel or inhuman punishment under clause (d) if grossly disproportionate to the crime. Compare Article 6 of the Covenant on Civil and Political Rights, which provides that capital punishment may be imposed "only for the most serious crimes in accordance with law in force at the time of the commission of the crime." See also *Coker v. Georgia*, 433 U.S. 584 (1977), where the plurality opinion barred capital punishment for rape of an adult, and would permit such punishment only for unjustified taking of human life.

g. Torture and other cruel, inhuman, or degrading treatment or punishment. Torture has been defined as "any act by which severe pain or suffering, whether physical or mental, is intentionally inflicted by or at the instigation of a public official on a person for such purposes as obtaining from him or a third person information or confession, punishing him for an act he has committed or is suspected of having committed, or intimidating him or other persons. It does not include pain or suffering arising only from, inherent in, or incidental to, lawful sanctions to the extent consistent with the Standard Minimum Rules for the Treatment of Prisoners." Declaration on the Protection of All Persons from Being Subjected to Torture and Other Cruel, Inhuman or Degrading Treatment or Punishment, Article 1(1), G.A. Res. 3452, 30 U.N. GAOR Supp. No. 34, at 91. Article 1(2) of the Declaration provides: "Torture constitutes an aggravated and deliberate form of cruel, inhuman or degrading treatment or punishment." See also the Convention Against Torture and other Cruel, Inhuman or Degrading Punishment.

h. Prolonged arbitrary detention. Detention is arbitrary if it is not pursuant to law; it may be arbitrary also if "it is incompatible with the principles of justice or with the dignity of the human person." Statement of U.S. Delegation, 13 GAOR, U.N.Doc. A/C.3/SR.863 at 137 (1958). Detention is arbitrary if it is supported only by a general warrant, or is not accompanied by notice of charges; if the person detained is not given early opportunity to communicate with family or to consult counsel; or is not brought to trial within a reasonable time. Customary international law probably does not require a state to provide for release on bail pending trial so long as trial is not unreasonably delayed. However, Article 9(3) of the Covenant on Civil and Political Rights provides: "It shall not be the general rule that persons awaiting trial shall be detained in custody, but release may be subject to guarantees to appear for trial, at any other stage of the judicial proceedings, and should occasion arise, for execution of the judgment." A single, brief, arbitrary detention by an official of a state party to one of the principal international agreements might violate that agreement; arbitrary detention violates customary law if it is prolonged and practiced as state policy.

i. Systematic racial discrimination. Discrimination on account of race is prohibited by all the comprehensive international human rights instruments, and is the subject of the Convention on the Elimination of All Forms of Racial Discrimination and of the Convention on the Suppression and Punishment of the Crime of *Apartheid.* It is forbidden also by the constitutions or laws of many states. Racial discrimination is a violation of customary law when it is practiced systematically as a matter of state policy, *e.g., apartheid* in the Republic of South Africa. Occasional official practices of racial discrimination would not violate this section but such acts of discrimination would violate numerous provisions in international covenants or conventions if practiced by officials of states parties.

As to systematic discrimination on account of religion, see Comment *j*; on account of gender, see Comment *l*.

j. Systematic religious discrimination. The United Nations Charter (Articles 1, 13, 55) links religious discrimination with racial discrimination and treats them alike; to the extent that racial discrimination violates the Charter religious discrimination does also. Religious discrimination is also treated identically with racial discrimination in the principal covenants and in the constitutions and laws of many states. There is as yet no convention on the elimination of religious discrimination, and there has been no concerted attack on such discrimination comparable to that on *apartheid,* but there is a strong case that systematic discrimination on grounds of religion as a matter of state policy is also a violation of customary law.

k. Right to property. The Universal Declaration of Human Rights includes the right to own and not to be arbitrarily deprived of property. There is, however, wide disagreement among states as to the scope and content of that right, which weighs against the conclusion that a human right to property generally has become a principle of customary law. All states have accepted a limited core of rights to private property, and violation of such rights, as state policy, may already be a violation of customary law. Invasions of rights in private property that have not achieved the status of customary law may nonetheless violate a particular international agreement or, where the victim is a foreign national, the principles of customary law governing state responsibility to foreign nationals.

l. Gender discrimination. The United Nations Charter (Article 1(3)) and the Universal Declaration of Human Rights (Article 2) prohibit discrimination in respect of human rights on various grounds, including sex. Discrimination on the basis of sex in respect of recognized rights is prohibited by a number of international agreements, including the Covenant on Civil and Political Rights, the Covenant on Economic, Social and Cultural Rights, and more generally by the Convention on the Elimination of All Forms of Discrimination Against Women, which, as of 1987, had been ratified by 91 states and signed by a number of others. The United States had signed the Convention but had not yet ratified it. The domestic laws of a number of states, including those of the United States, mandate equality for, or prohibit discrimination against, women generally or in various respects. Gender-based discrimination is still practiced in many states in varying degrees, but freedom from gender discrimination as state policy, in many matters, may already be a principle of customary international law. Discrimination by a state that does not constitute a violation of customary law may violate a particular international agreement if practiced by a state party.

m. Consistent pattern of gross violations of human rights. The acts enumerated in clauses (a) to (f) are violations of customary law even if the practice is not consistent, or not part of a "pattern," and those acts are inherently "gross" violations of human rights. Clause (g) includes other infringements of recognized human rights that are not violations of customary law when committed singly or sporadically (although they may be forbidden to states parties to the International Covenants or other particular agreements); they become violations of customary law if the state is guilty of a "consistent pattern of gross violations" as state policy. A violation is gross if it is particularly shocking because of the importance of the right or the gravity of the violation. All the rights proclaimed in the Universal Declaration and protected by the principal International Covenants are internationally recognized human rights, but some rights are fundamental and intrinsic to human dignity. Consistent patterns of violation of such rights as state policy may be deemed "gross" *ipso facto.* These include, for example, systematic harassment, invasions of the privacy of the home, arbitrary arrest and detention (even if not prolonged); denial of fair trial in criminal cases; grossly disproportionate punishment; denial of freedom to leave a country; denial of the right to return to one's country; mass uprooting of a country's population; denial of freedom of conscience and religion; denial of personality before the law; denial of basic privacy such as the right to marry and raise a family; and invidious racial or religious discrimination. A state party to the Covenant on Civil and Political Rights is responsible even for a single, isolated violation of any of these rights; any state is liable under customary law for a consistent pattern of violations of any such right as state policy.

  n. Customary law of human rights and jus cogens. Not all human rights norms are peremptory norms (*jus cogens*), but those in clauses (a) to (f) of this section are, and an international agreement that violates them is void.

  o. Responsibility to all states (erga omnes). Violations of the rules stated in this section are violations of obligations to all other states and any state may invoke the ordinary remedies available to a state when its rights under customary law are violated.

Notes

  1. In addition to treaty and custom, Article 38 of the ICJ Statute recognizes a third, independent source of international law, "general principles of law." But with the proliferation of human rights conventions and the development of customary law of human rights, general principles have not proven to be a fertile source of human rights law. But compare Bruno Simma and Philip Alston, *The Sources of Human Rights Law: Custom, Jus Cogens, and General Principles*, 12 Australian Yb. Int'l L. 82 (1992), and Bin Cheng, General Principles of Law: As Applied by International Courts and Tribunals (1993).

  2. Although the Universal Declaration of Human Rights was originally not intended to be law, there has been an increasing tendency to attribute legal character to many of its provisions. Virtually universal and frequently reiterated acceptance of the Declaration has led some to argue that these provisions have the force of customary law. See Hurst Hannum, *The Status of the Universal Declaration of Human Rights in National and International Law*, 25 Ga. J. Int'l & Comp. L. 287 (1995–96). Hannum also discusses reference to the Universal Declaration by national courts. See also Louis Henkin, International Law: Politics and Values 180–81 (1995).

  3. "The rights specified in the Covenant on Civil and Political Rights are binding on states parties to the Covenant. It is now accepted that respect for a number of the rights protected by the Covenant has become an international obligation by customary law, for all states, and such obligations are *erga omnes*, obligations to all states. At a minimum, 'a state violates international law if, as a matter of state policy, it practices, encourages, or condones' any of the following: genocide; slavery or slave

trade; murder or causing the disappearance of a person; torture or cruel, inhuman or degrading treatment or punishment; prolonged arbitrary detention; systematic racial discrimination; or any consistent pattern of gross violations of other human rights. No government has challenged the existence of a customary law of human rights, or this minimum list (except, presumably, South Africa [at that earlier time], as regards racial discrimination)." Henkin, International Law: Politics and Values, at 189–90.

4. A limited number of international human rights norms have the status of *jus cogens*, peremptory norms that have the character of supreme law and that cannot be modified by treaty or ordinary customary law, and which do not depend on state practice or consent to be binding.

2. NON-BINDING INTERNATIONAL HUMAN RIGHTS INSTRUMENTS

The international political system and the history of diplomacy have known "agreements" that were not legally binding but which had important influence, some of them with virtually the political force of law, including, *e.g.,* several "gentlemen's agreements." Some arrangements set forth in written, even formal instruments, though not denominated "agreements," have also had virtually the force of law. See Oscar Schachter, *the Twilight Existence of Nonbinding International Agreements,* 77 Am.J.Int'l L. 296 (1977).

A notable example in recent history was the "Helsinki Accord," formally known as the Final Act of the Conference on Security and Cooperation in Europe. In that instrument, Western powers in effect agreed to accept post-war borders (and not seek to roll back Soviet authority there); in exchange, the U.S.S.R. and its satellites made commitments to respect human rights, accepted the Universal Declaration, and promised to abide by human rights treaties. The participants were content with the non-binding character of the accord; for the United States it also obviated the need to seek consent of the U.S. Senate. Cf. Chapter 4(B) infra; see Henkin, International Law: Politics and Values 181 (1995). Though not legally binding, the Accord was an important human rights instrument during the Cold War, and laid the groundwork for the growth of constitutionalism in the former Soviet Union and in Eastern and Central Europe. (In 1994, the name was changed to "Organization for Security and Cooperation in Europe.")

Conference on Security and Co-operation in Europe: Final Act, Helsinki 1975

Article VII.

Respect for human rights and fundamental freedoms, including the freedom of thought, conscience, religion or belief.

49 The participating States will respect human rights and fundamental freedoms, including the freedom of thought, conscience, religion or belief, for all without distinction as to race, sex, language or religion.

50   They will promote and encourage the effective exercise of civil, political, economic, social, cultural and other rights and freedoms all of which derive from the inherent dignity of the human person and are essential for his free and full development.

51   Within this framework the participating States will recognize and respect the freedom of the individual to profess and practise, alone or in community with others, religion or belief acting in accordance with the dictates of his own conscience.

52   The participating States on whose territory national minorities exist will respect the right of persons belonging to such minorities to equality before the law, will afford them the full opportunity for the actual enjoyment of human rights and fundamental freedoms and will, in this manner, protect their legitimate interests in this sphere.

53   The participating States recognize the universal significance of human rights and fundamental freedoms, respect for which is an essential factor for the peace, justice and well-being necessary to ensure the development of friendly relations and co-operation among themselves as among all States.

54   They will constantly respect these rights and freedoms in their mutual relations and will endeavour jointly and separately, including in co-operation with the United Nations, to promote universal and effective respect for them.

55   They will confirm the right of the individual to know and act upon his rights and duties in this field.

56   In the field of human rights and fundamental freedoms, the participating States will act in conformity with the purposes and principles of the Charter of the United Nations and with the Universal Declaration of Human Rights. They will also fulfil their obligations as set forth in the international declarations and agreements in this field, including inter alia the International Covenants on Human Rights, by which they may be bound.

Notes

1.   Paragraph 55 laid the foundation for NGO monitoring, the first explicit recognition of a right to know and act upon one's rights. See Vratislav Pechota, The Right to Know One's Human Rights: A Road Toward Individual Freedom (1983).

2.   Other international human rights instruments that, strictly speaking, have no legal character, have had important weight. Most important, of course, was the Universal Declaration: a *declaration*, not an agreement. General Assembly resolutions generally are not legally binding but they contribute to the law-making process; some resolutions of the General Assembly are denominated "Declarations," and have extraordinary weight. In addition to the Universal Declaration (followed by the covenants), there

have been declarations leading to conventions on racial discrimination. Important declarations that have not (or not yet as of 1999), resulted in agreements include, *e.g.,* the Declaration on the Elimination of All Forms of Intolerance and of Discrimination Based on Religion or Belief (1981) and the Declaration on the Right to Development (1986).

Resolutions of the UN General Assembly (or of other intergovernmental organizations such as UNESCO, WHO, and other specialized agencies of the United Nations) sometimes purport to declare a principle of international law. That such a resolution is adopted unanimously is seen as evidence that it represents an accurate statement of law. See Oscar Schachter, *International Law in Theory and Practice*, 178 Rec. Des Cours 114–21 (1982–V).

Can UN resolutions contribute to the evolution of the customary law of human rights? Can UN resolutions serve as evidence that a state has been guilty of "a consistent pattern of gross violations of internationally recognized human rights"? See p. 349 above.

Restatement of Foreign Relations Law, § 103, Reporters' Note 2 reads in part:

> *Declaratory resolutions of international organizations . . . .* Given the universal character of many [international] organizations and the forum they provide for the expression by states of their views regarding legal principles, such resolutions sometimes provide important evidence of law. A resolution purporting to state the law on a subject is some evidence of what the states voting for the resolution regard the law to be, although what states do is more weighty evidence than their declarations or the resolutions they vote for. The evidentiary value of such a resolution is high if it is adopted by consensus or by virtually unanimous vote of an organization of universal membership such as the United Nations or its Specialized Agencies. On the other hand, majorities may be tempted to declare as existing law what they would like the law to be, and less weight must be given to such a resolution when it declares law in the interest of the majority and against the interest of a strongly dissenting minority. See, e.g., the General Assembly resolution declaring that the use of nuclear weapons is a violation of international law (G.A. Res. 1653, U.N. GAOR, Supp. No. 17 at 4) . . . [which was] challenged by the United States. . . . Even a unanimous resolution may be questioned when the record shows that those voting for it considered it merely a recommendation or a political expression, or that serious consideration was not given to its legal basis. A resolution is entitled to little weight if it is contradicted by state practice . . . or is rejected by international courts or tribunals. On the other hand, a declaratory resolution that was less than unanimous may be evidence of customary law if it is supported by thorough study by the International Law Commission or other serious legal examination. See, for example, the reliance on one United Nations General Assembly resolution but deprecation of another resolution by the

arbitrator in Texas Overseas Petroleum Co. v. Libyan Arab Republic (1977), 17 Int'l Leg. Mat. 1 (1978).

Resolutions by a principal organ of an organization interpreting the charter of the organization may be entitled to greater weight. In some instances, such an interpretation may, by the terms of the charter, be binding on the parties.... Declarations interpreting a charter are entitled to considerable weight if they are unanimous or nearly unanimous and have the support of all the principal members.

. . .

F. THE HUMAN RIGHTS OF WOMEN

In the final decade of the twentieth century the human rights of women emerged as a major focus of international advocacy efforts. These efforts have had a significant impact on institutional responses to violations of women's human rights: The subject received prominent attention in the Declaration and Programme of Action adopted at the United Nations' World Conference on Human Rights in Vienna in 1993, the following year the UN Commission on Human Rights appointed a Special Rapporteur on Violence Against Women, and in 1995 the United Nations sponsored a World Conference on Women, in Beijing. During this same period various treaty bodies and international criminal tribunals issued key decisions clarifying gender-specific human rights protections.

While the human rights of women received unprecedented attention in the 1990s, international human rights law has, from the outset, applied to men and women equally. The Universal Declaration of Human Rights declares that all human beings are equal in dignity and rights (Article 1). The rights set forth in the Declaration are held to be rights of everyone, "without distinction of any kind, such as ... sex ..." (Article 2).

The Universal Declaration expressed the equal human rights of men and women in the plainest possible terms. So, too, did the two Covenants, as well as the United Nations Charter, whose enumeration of Purposes of the Organization includes the following: "To achieve international co-operation in solving international problems of an economic, social, cultural, or humanitarian character, and in promoting and encouraging respect for human rights and for fundamental freedoms for all without distinction as to ... sex...." (Article 1(3).) Like the UN Covenants, each of the comprehensive regional human rights treaties guarantees enjoyment of protected rights without discrimination on the basis of sex.

The customary law of human rights protects women and men equally, and it may also be a violation of customary law for any state, as a matter of state policy, to practice, encourage or condone systematic gender discrimination. See Restatement, Third, Foreign Relations Law of the United States, § 702, comment (*l*) (p. 353 supra).

Yet despite these legal guarantees, women have long experienced gross inequalities in the enjoyment of fundamental rights. In many societies women remain subordinate in the home, in the family, in political processes, in social-sexual relations, in the enjoyment of property rights, in matters of employment and in the marketplace. In some countries, these inequalities are enshrined in law; in others, they reflect social, cultural and political resistance to legally-mandated assurances of equality.

Just as in the case of racial discrimination, it was thought necessary to adopt a special treaty dealing specifically with gender-based discrimination. In 1979, the UN General Assembly adopted the Convention on the Elimination of All Forms of Discrimination Against Women ("Women's Convention"), GA Res. 34/180, which entered into force two years later. But unlike the Convention on the Elimination of All Forms of Racial Discrimination, the Women's Convention has attracted numerous reservations, reflecting deeply ingrained historical, cultural and religious attitudes. (For the proposed reservations of the United States, see below).

Resistance to international protection of women's human rights is reflected also in the comparatively weak powers and procedures of the Committee on the Elimination of Discrimination Against Women (CEDAW), the treaty body that monitors States Parties' compliance with the Women's Convention.* In larger perspective, until relatively recently the human rights of women scarcely figured in international efforts to secure compliance with established standards. Instead, as many have noted, women's human rights were substantially ignored or marginalized in the principal international fora where human rights are promoted.

In this chapter we examine the Women's Convention, the most important human rights treaty concerned specifically with the human rights of women, as well as several important developments in international law concerned with women's human rights. We also consider various factors that may have contributed to the longstanding neglect or marginalization of women's human rights, including challenges emanating from cultural justifications for subordination of women and girls.

1. CONVENTION ON DISCRIMINATION AGAINST WOMEN

As its name implies, the central aim of the Women's Convention is to eliminate all forms of discrimination against women, which Article 1 defines as "any distinction, exclusion or restriction made on the basis of sex which has the effect or purpose of impairing or nullifying the recognition, enjoyment or exercise by women, irrespective of their marital status, on a basis of equality of men and women, of human rights and fundamental freedoms in the political, economic, social, cultural, civil or any other field."

While the convention's overall thrust is to ensure the enjoyment of rights in every sphere on a basis of equality between men and women, it

---

* As noted below, in 1999 the UN Commission on the Status of Women adopted an Optional Protocol to the Women's Convention. The protocol will expand CEDAW's supervisory powers when and if it enters into force.

also requires States Parties to take all appropriate measures "to ensure the full development and advancement of women." (Article 3.) Although this requirement is, to be sure, aimed at assuring the exercise and enjoyment of rights "on a basis of equality with men," it also conveys the distinct and important idea that the full development of women is a goal to be pursued in its own right.

Several other aspects of this convention are noteworthy. First, discrimination against women, which States Parties undertake to eliminate (Article 2), is defined in terms of distinctions, exclusions or restrictions that have the effect *or* purpose of impairing the enjoyment of rights on a basis of equality between men and women. Thus, even when it is not possible to establish discriminatory intent, a State Party might be responsible for a breach of the Women's Convention by virtue of practices that have a discriminatory effect. Second, the Women's Convention authorizes States Parties to undertake "temporary special measures"—measures that would be termed "affirmative action" programs in a United States context—to accelerate the achievement of de facto equality between men and women. (Article 4.)

One of the most distinctive features of the Women's Convention is its requirement that States Parties undertake affirmative steps to modify cultural patterns that impair the enjoyment of rights on a basis of equality of men and women. Article 5(a) requires States Parties "[t]o modify the social and cultural patterns of conduct of men and women, with a view to achieving the elimination of prejudices and customary and all other practices which are based on the idea of the inferiority or the superiority of either of the sexes or on stereotyped roles for men and women." Similarly, Article 10(c) requires States Parties to eliminate discrimination against women in the field of education by, *inter alia*, eliminating "any stereotyped concept of the roles of men and women at all levels and in all forms of education by encouraging coeducation and other types of education which will help to achieve this aim and, in particular, by the revision of textbooks and school programmes and the adaptation of teaching methods."

Finally, perhaps more than any other human rights treaty, the Women's Convention embodies a vision of human rights in which the enjoyment of civil and political rights is indivisible from realization of economic, social and cultural rights. For example, Article 13 requires States Parties to take all appropriate measures to eliminate discrimination against women in the areas of economic and social life. To this end, States Parties must take measures to ensure that women enjoy the right to acquire bank loans, mortgages and other forms of financial credit on a basis of equality with men.

Notably, the Women's Convention is textually silent about violence against women, except in its requirement that States Parties take measures to suppress trafficking in women (Article 6). Nonetheless, CEDAW has interpreted the convention to prohibit violence against women and to require States Parties to take affirmative steps to prevent and punish such violence. In 1992, CEDAW adopted the following General Recommendation on Violence Against Women:

CEDAW Committee, General Recommendation No. 19, Violence Against Women

U.N. Doc. A/47/38 at 1 (1992).

1.   Gender-based violence is a form of discrimination that seriously inhibits women's ability to enjoy rights and freedoms on a basis of equality with men.

. . .

4.   . . . The full implementation of the Convention require[s] States to take positive measures to eliminate all forms of violence against women.

. . .

6.   The Convention in article 1 defines discrimination against women. The definition of discrimination includes gender-based violence, that is, violence that is directed against a woman because she is a woman or that affects women disproportionately. It includes acts that inflict physical, mental or sexual harm or suffering, threats of such acts, coercion and other deprivations of liberty. Gender-based violence may breach specific provisions of the Convention, regardless of whether those provisions expressly mention violence.

7.   Gender-based violence, which impairs or nullifies the enjoyment by women of human rights and fundamental freedoms under general international law or under human rights conventions, is discrimination within the meaning of article 1 of the Convention. These rights and freedoms include:

(a) The right to life;

(b) The right not to be subject to torture or to cruel, inhuman or degrading treatment or punishment;

(c) The right to equal protection according to humanitarian norms in time of international or internal armed conflict;

(d) The right to liberty and security of person;

(e) The right to equal protection under the law;

(f) The right to equality in the family;

(g) The right to the highest standard attainable of physical and mental health;

(h) The right to just and favourable conditions of work.

8.   The Convention applies to violence perpetrated by public authorities. Such acts of violence may breach that State's obligations under general international human rights law and under other conventions, in addition to breaching this Convention.

9. It is emphasized, however, that discrimination under the Convention is not restricted to action by or on behalf of Governments.... For example, under article 2(e) the Convention calls on States parties to take all appropriate measures to eliminate discrimination against women by any person, organization or enterprise. Under general international law and specific human rights covenants, States may also be responsible for private acts if they fail to act with due diligence to prevent violations of rights or to investigate and punish acts of violence, and for providing compensation.

. . .

11. Traditional attitudes by which women are regarded as subordinate to men or as having stereotyped roles perpetuate widespread practices involving violence or coercion, such as family violence and abuse, forced marriage, dowry deaths, acid attacks and female circumcision. Such prejudices and practices may justify gender-based violence as a form of protection or control of women. The effect of such violence on the physical and mental integrity of women is to deprive them of the equal enjoyment, exercise and knowledge of human rights and fundamental freedoms. While this comment addresses mainly actual or threatened violence the underlying consequences of these forms of gender-based violence help to maintain women in subordinate roles and contribute to their low level of political participation and to their lower level of education, skills and work opportunities.

12. These attitudes also contribute to the propagation of pornography and the depiction and other commercial exploitation of women as sexual objects, rather than as individuals. This in turn contributes to gender-based violence.

. . .

Reservations to CEDAW

As of April 1999, the Women's Convention had been ratified by 163 countries. But adherence to this convention has been highly selective; among UN human rights treaties, the Women's Convention "has attracted the greatest number of reservations with the potential to modify or exclude most, if not all, of the terms of the treaty." Belinda Clark, *The Vienna Convention Reservations Regime and the Convention on Discrimination Against Women*, 85 Am. J. Int'l L. 281, 317 (1991).

Article 19(c) of the Vienna Convention on the Law of Treaties does not permit states, when ratifying a treaty, to enter a reservation if it "is incompatible with the object and purpose of the treaty." Similarly, Article 28(2) of CEDAW provides: "A reservation incompatible with the object and purpose of the present Convention shall not be permitted."

Consider whether the following reservations to CEDAW violate these provisions:

Reservation Entered by Algeria

The Government of the People's Democratic Republic of Algeria declares that it is prepared to apply the provisions of [Article 2] on condition that they do not conflict with the provisions of the Algerian Family Code.

Reservation Entered by Egypt

The Arab Republic of Egypt is willing to comply with the content of [Article 2], provided that such compliance does not run counter to the Islamic Sharia.

Reservation Entered by Iraq

Approval of and accession to this Convention shall not mean that the Republic of Iraq is bound by the provisions of article 2, sub-paragraphs (f) and (g), of article 9, paragraphs 1 and 2, nor of article 16 of the Convention. The reservation to this last-mentioned article shall be without prejudice to the provisions of the Islamic Shariah according women rights equivalent to the rights of their spouses so as to ensure a just balance between them....

Reservation Entered by Kuwait

The Government of Kuwait enters a reservation regarding article 7 (a), inasmuch as the provision contained in that paragraph conflicts with the Kuwaiti Electoral Act, under which the right to be eligible for election and to vote is restricted to males.

Reservation Entered by Maldives*

The Government of the Republic of Maldives reserves its right to apply article 16 of the Convention concerning the equality of men and women in all matters relating to marriage and family relations without prejudice to Islamic Sharia, which govern all marital and family relations of the 100 percent Muslim population of the Maldives.

Reservation Entered by Singapore

In the context of Singapore's multi-racial and multi-religious society and the need to respect the freedom of minorities to practise their religious and personal laws, the Republic of Singapore reserves the right not to apply the provisions of articles 2 and 16 where compliance with these provisions would be contrary to their religious or personal laws.

Article 2 of the Women's Convention, to which several of the above-quoted reservations refer, sets forth the convention's core obligation to eliminate all forms of discrimination against women. A number of states have entered objections to other states' reservations to Article 2 and to

---

* [This text reflects a modification in 1999 of the reservation entered by the Government of Maldives upon accession.—Editors' Note.]

several other provisions of the Women's Convention, on the ground that the reservations are incompatible with the object and purpose of the Convention.

The large number of reservations to the Women's Convention, as well as the broad reach of some reservations, prompted States Parties in 1986 to adopt a decision urging full respect for Article 28(2) of the Women's Convention and to request the Secretary–General of the United Nations to seek States Parties' views on reservations that would be considered to come within the scope of that provision. Among the submissions of States Parties pursuant to this initiative were several expressing the view that the Women's Convention "should be afforded a lesser status than other treaties because its subject matter was culturally sensitive." Clark, supra, at 285. Consideration of this subject by the General Assembly's Third Committee was contentious, with several Islamic countries accusing Western states of cultural insensitivity.

At its next session, CEDAW requested the UN "to promote or undertake studies on the status of women under Islamic laws and customs and in particular on the status and equality of women in the family ... taking into consideration the principle of El Ijtihad in Islam." Bangladesh and Egypt accused the committee of cultural imperialism and religious intolerance, and the General Assembly decided to take no action on the committee's request. CEDAW has, however, continued to express to States Parties its concerns about reservations to the Women's Convention. See William A. Schabas, *Reservations to the Convention on the Elimination of All Forms of Discrimination Against Women and the Convention on the Rights of the Child*, 3 Wm. & Mary J. of Women & L. 79, 94–95 (1997). The Vienna Declaration and Programme of Action, adopted at the conclusion of the 1993 World Conference on Human Rights, included the following statement: "Ways and means of addressing the particularly large number of reservations to the [Women's] Convention should be encouraged.... States are urged to withdraw reservations that are contrary to the object and purpose of the Convention...." Report of the World Conference on Human Rights, U.N. GAOR, at 37, U.N. Doc. A/CONF.157/24 (1993) (Part III, Vienna Declaration and Programme of Action).

Although the United States has not yet ratified the Women's Convention, it signed the convention in 1980 and has proposed a number of reservations, understandings and declarations:

Proposed U.S. Reservations, Understandings, and Declarations to the Convention on the Elimination of All Forms of Discrimination Against Women

140 Cong. Rec. S13927–04 (1994).

Mr. PELL, from the COMMITTEE on FOREIGN RELATIONS, submitted the following report (No. 103–38) Convention on the Elimination of

All Forms of Discrimination Against Women to accompany Executive Report 96–2:

The Committee on Foreign Relations to which was referred the Convention on the Elimination of All Forms of Discrimination Against Women, adopted by the United Nations General Assembly on December 18, 1979, and signed on behalf of the United States of America on July 17, 1980, having considered the same, reports favorably thereon and recommends that the Senate give its advice and consent to ratification thereof subject to 4 reservations, 4 understandings, and 2 declarations as [s]et forth in this report and the accompanying resolution of ratification.

Resolved, (two-thirds of the Senators present concurring therein), That the Senate advise and consent to the ratification of the Convention on the Elimination of All Forms of Discrimination Against Women, adopted by the United Nations General Assembly on December 18, 1979, and signed on behalf of the United States of America on July 17, 1980, (Executive R), subject to the following Reservations, Understandings and Declarations:

I.   The Senate's advice and consent is subject to the following reservations:

(1) That the Constitution and laws of the United States establish extensive protections against discrimination, reaching all forms of governmental activity as well as significant areas of non-governmental activity. However, individual privacy and freedom from governmental interference in private conduct are also recognized as among the fundamental values of our free and democratic society. The United States understands that by its terms the Convention requires broad regulation of private conduct, in particular under Articles 2, 3 and 5. The United States does not accept any obligation under the Convention to enact legislation or to take any other action with respect to private conduct except as mandated by the Constitution and laws of the United States.

(2) That under current U.S. law and practice, women are permitted to volunteer for military service without restriction, and women in fact serve in all U.S. armed services, including in combat positions. However, the United States does not accept an obligation under the Convention to assign women to all military units and positions which may require engagement in direct combat.

(3) That U.S. law provides strong protections against gender discrimination in the area of remuneration, including the right to equal pay for equal work in jobs that are substantially similar. However, the United States does not accept any obligation under this Convention to enact legislation establishing the doctrine of comparable worth as that term is understood in U.S. practice.

(4) That current U.S. law contains substantial provisions for maternity leave in many employment situations but does not require paid maternity leave. Therefore, the United States does not accept any obligation under Article 11(2)(b) to introduce maternity leave with pay or with comparable

social benefits without loss of former employment, seniority or social allowances.

II.   The Senate's advice and consent is subject to the following understandings:

(1) That the United States understands that this Convention shall be implemented by the Federal Government to the extent that it exercises jurisdiction over the matters covered therein, and otherwise by the state and local governments. To the extent that state and local governments exercise jurisdiction over such matters, the Federal Government shall, as necessary, take appropriate measures to ensure the fulfillment of this Convention.

(2) That the Constitution and laws of the United States contain extensive protections of individual freedom of speech, expression and association. Accordingly, the United States does not accept any obligation under this Convention, in particular under Articles 5, 7, 8 and 13, to restrict those rights, through the adoption of legislation or any other measures, to the extent that they are protected by the Constitution and laws of the United States.

(3) That the United States understands that Article 12 permits States Parties to determine which health care services are appropriate in connection with family planning, pregnancy, confinement and the post-natal period, as well as when the provision of free services is necessary, and does not mandate the provision of particular services on a cost-free basis.

(4) That nothing in this Convention shall be construed to reflect or create any right to abortion and in no case should abortion be promoted as a method of family planning.

III.   The Senate's advice and consent is subject to the following declarations:

(1) That the United States declares that, for purposes of its domestic law, the provisions of the Convention are non-self-executing.

(2) That with reference to Article 29(2), the United States declares that it does not consider itself bound by the provisions of Article 29(1). The specific consent of the United States to the jurisdiction of the International Court of Justice concerning disputes over the interpretation or application of this Convention is required on a case-by-case basis.

Notes

1.   As noted earlier, the Committee on the Elimination of Discrimination against Women (CEDAW) is the supervisory body established by the Women's Convention. CEDAW's principal means of supervising compliance is through consideration of reports that States Parties are required to submit on a periodic basis. Pursuant to Article 18(a) of the Convention, these reports should describe "the legislative, judicial, administrative or other measures" that States Parties have adopted "to give effect to the provisions of the Convention and on the progress made in this respect."

The Committee's "general recommendations," adopted pursuant to Article 21 of the Convention, have emerged as a principal vehicle for interpretations of its obligations.

On March 10, 1999, the UN Commission on the Status of Women adopted the text of an Optional Protocol to the Women's Convention. The Protocol provides for two procedures. Articles 2–7 establish a procedure enabling the Committee to consider communications submitted by individuals or groups of individuals under the jurisdiction of a State Party who claim to be victims of a violation of any of the rights set forth in the Convention by that State Party. Article 8 establishes a procedure enabling the Committee to initiate inquiries into situations of grave or systematic violations of women's rights. Both procedures will be available only with respect to states that have ratified the Protocol. For the text of this Protocol, see UN Doc. E/CN.6/1999/WG/L.2.

2.   The Women's Convention defines discrimination against women as "any distinction, exclusion or restriction made on the basis of sex which has the effect or purpose of impairing or nullifying the recognition, enjoyment or exercise by women, irrespective of their marital status, on a basis of equality of men and women, of human rights and fundamental freedoms in the political, economic, social, cultural, civil or any other field." Many advocates of women's human rights consider this language regrettable because, in their view, the benchmark of women's rights should not be what they regard as a male-based standard. In contrast, the Inter–American Convention on the Prevention, Punishment and Eradication of Violence Against Women, OAS/Ser.L.V/II.92, doc. 31 rev. 3, May 3, 1996, frames the rights that it protects without reference to men. For example, Article 4 begins: "Every woman has the right to the recognition, enjoyment, exercise and protection of all human rights and freedoms embodied in regional and international human rights instruments." Article 5 provides in full:

> Every woman is entitled to the free and full exercise of her civil, political, economic, social and cultural rights, and may rely on the full protection of those rights as embodied in regional and international instruments on human rights. The States Parties recognize that violence against women prevents and nullifies the exercise of those rights.

Compare also Article 6 of the Inter–American Convention on the Prevention, Punishment and Eradication of Violence Against Women with CEDAW's General Recommendation 19. While the latter interprets the Women's Convention's basic prohibition of discrimination against women to encompass a prohibition on violence against women, the former takes an inverse approach, providing:

> The right of every woman to be free from violence includes, among others:
>
> a.   The right of women to be free from all forms of discrimination; and
>
> b.   The right of women to be valued and educated free of stereotyped patterns of behavior and social and cultural practices based on concepts of inferiority or subordination.

Is the approach embodied in this provision merely a different means of stating the same basic principles recognized in General Recommendation 19? Does Article 6 of the Inter–American Convention prohibit all forms of conduct described in paragraphs a and b, or would the Convention be violated only if a link could be established between such conduct and a particular experience of violence? Consider in this regard the following provisions of the convention:

Article 1

For the purposes of this Convention, violence against women shall be understood as any act or conduct, based on gender, which causes death or physical, sexual or psychological harm or suffering to women, whether in the public or private sphere.

Article 2

Violence against women shall be understood to include physical, sexual and psychological violence:

a.   that occurs within the family or domestic unit or within any other interpersonal relationship, whether or not the perpetrator shares or has shared the same residence with the woman, including, among others, rape battery and sexual abuse;

b.   that occurs in the community and is perpetrated by any person, including, among others, rape sexual abuse, torture, trafficking in persons, forced prostitution, kidnapping and sexual harassment in the workplace, as well as in educational institutions, health facilities or any other place; and

c.   that is perpetrated or condoned by the state or its agents regardless of where it occurs.

Article 7

The States Parties condemn all forms of violence against women and agree to pursue, by all appropriate means and without delay, policies to prevent, punish and eradicate such violence and undertake to:

. . .

e.   take all appropriate measures, including legislative measures, . . . to modify legal or customary practices which sustain the persistence and tolerance of violence against women . . .

3.   The material on reservations to the Women's Convention raises substantial questions about the extent to which reservations relating to religious law and to culture are compatible with the object and purpose of the convention. While the states that have objected to these reservations and the CEDAW Committee take the view that religious observance and culture cannot be invoked to defeat the core goals of the Women's Convention, others have suggested that the larger problem is the "cultural insensitivity" of the convention. See., e.g., Bharathi Anandhi Venkatraman, *Islamic States and the United Nations Convention on the Elimination of All*

Forms of Discrimination Against Women: Are the Shari'a and the Convention Compatible?, 44 Am. U.L. Rev. 1949 (1995). Consider, in this regard, Article 10(c) of the Convention, which requires States Parties to take appropriate measures to eliminate "any stereotyped concept of the roles of men and women at all levels and in all forms of education by encouraging coeducation ..." One writer has suggested that "[t]his objective does not take into account the possibility that compulsory coeducation could have an undesirable effect on the goal of women's equality by motivating some parents, especially in milieus where strict purdah (separation of the sexes and veiling of women) is observed, to pull their daughters out of school to enforce gender separation. The coeducation recommendation illustrates that neglecting the varying cultural and religious circumstances of women may be a self-defeating feature of the Convention." Id. at 2004. Does the Convention itself provide a plausible response to this critique?

4.   Several states have withdrawn or modified earlier reservations. For example on October 24, 1991 the government of Malawi notified the Secretary General of the UN of its decision to withdraw the reservations entered upon Malawi's accession to the convention. Its previous reservations included the following:

> Owing to the deep-rooted nature of some traditional customs and practices of Malawians, the Government of the Republic of Malawi shall not, for the time being, consider itself bound by such of the provisions of the Convention as require immediate eradication of such traditional customs and practices.

On July 5, 1995, the Libyan government notified the Secretary–General of its new formulation of reservations to the Women's Convention, which replaced its earlier formulation. The previous formulation provided that accession "is subject to the general reservation that such accession cannot conflict with the laws on personal status derived from the Islamic Shariah." The new formulation provided:

> 1.   Article 2 of the Convention shall be implemented with due regard for the peremptory norms of the Islamic Shariah relating to determination of the inheritance portions of the estate of a deceased person, whether female or male.

> 2.   The implementation of article 16 paragraphs 1 (c) and (d) of the Convention shall be without prejudice to any of the rights guaranteed to women by the Islamic Shariah.

5.   For more on U.S. reservations, understandings and declarations to international human rights agreements, see below, Part III, Chapter 4, Section B. For a discussion of the concept of non-self-executing treaties, see also Part III, Chapter 4, Section A.

6.   As of July 1999, final U.S. action on the Women's Convention has yet to occur.

2.   DEFINING "THE HUMAN RIGHTS OF WOMEN"

Many activists have long advocated for recognition that "women's rights are human rights," eschewing treatment of the human rights of women as a special category of "women's rights." What then, does the phrase "the human rights of women" mean?

One way of approaching this question is to attempt to identify practices that constitute violations of women's human rights. Consider the following possibilities:

- *Human rights violations that are peculiar to women*, such as forced pregnancy. Forced pregnancy might violate a number of basic rights, such as the rights to physical integrity, family life, and privacy—*and* it is a type of violation of these rights that is peculiar to women.

- *Human rights violations to which women are especially—but not exclusively—vulnerable by virtue of their gender*, such as domestic violence.

- *Human rights violations that are gender-specific in the sense that they are committed or directed against women at least in part because they are women*, such as sexual violence. Unlike forced sterilization, sexual violence is not a violation of physical integrity that only women can experience. Neither, however, is gender beside the point in respect of this offence. Similarly, both boys and girls are potentially subject to genital mutilation, but no one would question that when girls are made to undergo this procedure in cultures where it is commonly practiced, they are subjected to it because they are female.

CEDAW has defined "gender-based violence" in a manner that combines elements of the last two definitions. In its General Recommendation on Violence Against Women, CEDAW defined "gender-based violence" to include "violence that is directed against a woman because she is a woman or that affects women disproportionately." (See p. 361 above.)

In 1994 the UN Commission on Human Rights invited its Special Rapporteur on Torture, Professor Nigel Rodley, "to examine questions concerning torture directed disproportionately or primarily against women and conditions conducive to such torture, and to make appropriate recommendations concerning prevention of gender-specific forms of torture." In response, Professor Rodley included the following conclusions in his 1995 report to the Commission:

Report of the Special Rapporteur, Mr. Nigel S. Rodley, Submitted Pursuant to Commission on Human Rights Resolution 1992/32

U.N. Doc. E/CN.4/1995/34 (1995).

. . .

16.   Methods of torture involving sexual abuse may be characterized as essentially gender-based.

. . .

18.   In certain countries, rape and other forms of sexual assault were reported to be common means of torture. It was alleged in the case of one country that 85 per cent of women held in police custody were subjected to some form of sexual abuse, including rape. Although allegations of sexual abuse were occasionally received wherein men were the target, the vast majority of such allegations concerned women. When sexual abuse occurred in the context of custodial detention, interrogators were said to have used rape as a means of extracting confessions or information, to punish, or to humiliate detainees. In some instances, the gender of an individual constituted at least part of the very motive for the torture itself, such as in those where women were raped allegedly for their participation in political and social activism.

19.   In addition to being an especially traumatic form of torture for the victim, rape may have insidious correlative consequences. In many situations a woman may be reluctant to seek redress by reporting a rape because of the severe social repercussions that may flow therefrom. The stigma attached in many communities to a woman who has been raped may result in particularly dire consequences for the private and public life of the woman. In addition to social stigma, some victims may be subjected to direct reprisals from relatives. In a few countries, where severe legal sanctions have been adopted against adultery and where the evidentiary requirements to demonstrate rape are stringent, a woman reporting a rape may risk holding herself open to prosecution. Consequently, when rape or sexual assault against a woman constitutes a torture method, the chances of the torturer acting with impunity would appear disproportionately higher than with other torture methods.

. . .

21.   Pregnant women are particularly vulnerable to torture. A woman facing torture risks miscarriage and other health risks, as well as damage to the foetus.

22.   Torture may also be used as a means to punish an exclusively or predominantly gender-based crime. In one country, for example, flogging is prescribed for women who fail to conform to strict Islamic dress laws. Flogging and death by stoning of women for adultery are also prescribed in some penal provisions.

23.   Finally, women are sometimes tortured as surrogates for the real target, who may be the victim's spouse or family member or friend. Such an attack may be conducted in order to induce a suspect to come out of hiding, to provide a confession or information if the suspect is already in custody or to inflict punishment.

Notes

1.   Suppose that you worked for an NGO whose mandate is to promote protection of women's human rights. If a woman were arrested and

detained arbitrarily because her husband was a political dissident, would you include her case in a report that your organization planned to publish on gender-specific human rights violations? Suppose instead that your organization planned to issue a report on gender-specific violence in circumstances of detention. Would you include in your report accounts of female political detainees who were tortured in the same manner as male political detainees but who happened to be pregnant at the time they were tortured? These and similar questions have formed the pith of "mandate" discussions in the board rooms of NGOs as they have undertaken advocacy efforts on behalf of women's human rights.

2.   How did the Special Rapporteur on Torture resolve these questions in the excerpted passages of his 1995 report to the UN Commission on Human Rights? More generally, what conceptions of "gender-specific violations of human rights" were implicit in his report?

3.   RAPE AND OTHER FORMS OF SEXUAL VIOLENCE

Major advances in the recognition and protection of human rights have often resulted from sustained advocacy efforts. For example, NGO campaigns to eradicate torture and disappearances, respectively, played a key role in the development of specialized instruments on those two human rights violations. In similar fashion, significant advances in international protections of women's human rights have been the product of concerted advocacy efforts. In this section, we examine two examples: recognition of rape as a form of torture, and recognition of rape as a war crime.

a.   RAPE AS TORTURE

As advocates for women's human rights coalesced into a global movement, a key priority for many—particularly Western activists—was to secure recognition of rape as a form of torture. One of the first major breakthroughs came in 1986, when the Special Rapporteur on Torture of the UN Commission on Human Rights, at that time Professor (now Judge) Pieter Kooijmans, included rape in an enumeration of "methods of physical torture" in his first report to the Commission. Report by the Special Rapporteur, Mr. P. Kooijmans, appointed pursuant to Commission on Human Rights resolution 1985/33, UN Doc. E/CN.4/1986/15, p. 29 (1986).

In his oral introduction to his 1992 report to the Commission, Professor Kooijmans noted: "Since it was clear that rape or other forms of sexual assault against women in detention were a particularly ignominious violation of the inherent dignity and the right to physical integrity of the human being, they accordingly constituted an act of torture." UN Doc. E/CN.4/1992/SR.21, para. 35. As the previously-quoted excerpt from the 1995 report of the Special Rapporteur on Torture reflects, Professor Kooijmans' recognition of rape as a form of torture has been reaffirmed by his successor, Nigel Rodley.

Advocates for women's human rights sought to build on this development not only in the United Nations system, but also in regional human rights regimes. By the mid–1990s, their efforts resulted in significant milestones in the Inter–American and European Human rights systems.

i.   The Inter–American System

Article 5 of the American Convention on Human Rights is entitled ''Right to Humane Treatment,'' and provides in pertinent part:

1.   Everyone has the right to have his physical, mental, and moral integrity respected.

2.   No one shall be subjected to torture or to cruel, inhuman, or degrading punishment or treatment. All persons deprived of their liberty shall be treated with respect for the inherent dignity of the human person.

In several reports issued between 1982 and 1994, the Inter–American Commission on Human Rights found that rapes attributable to government forces constituted violations of the right to humane treatment assured by Article 5, without specifying whether the breaches amounted to torture or other forms of inhumane treatment. See, e.g., *Mining Community of Caracoles v. Bolivia*, Case 7481, Inter–Am. Comm'n H.R. 36, OEA/Ser.L/V/II.57, doc. 6, rev. 1 (1982); *Ita Ford et al. v. El Salvador*, Case 7575, Inter–Am. Comm'n H.R. 53, OEA/Ser.L/V/II.61, doc. 22, rev. 1 (1983). The distinction is significant because international law regards torture as a severe or aggravated form of cruel, inhuman or degrading treatment or punishment. Cf. UN Declaration on the Protection of all Persons from being Subjected to Torture and Other Cruel, Inhuman or Degrading Treatment or Punishment, G.A. Res. 3452 (XXX), art. 1(2), U.N. Doc. A/RES/3452 (XXX) (1976).

Since 1995, however, the Commission has forthrightly determined rape to constitute torture in violation of Article 5(2) of the American Convention. In its 1995 *Report on the Situation of Human Rights in Haiti*, OEA/Ser.L/V/II.88, Doc. 10 rev. 9 (1995), the Commission concluded that ''rape represents not only inhumane treatment that infringes upon physical and moral integrity under Article 5 of the Convention, but also a form of torture in the sense of Article 5(2) of that instrument,'' and reasoned:

Consistent with the definitions elaborated in the Inter–American Convention to Prevent, Punish and Eradicate Torture, which Haiti has signed, and the United Nations's Convention Against Torture and Other Cruel, Inhuman or Degrading Treatment or Punishment, the Commission considers that the rape and other sexual abuse of Haitian women inflicted physical and mental pain and suffering in order to punish women for their militancy and/or their association with militant family members and to intimidate or destroy their capacity to resist the regime and sustain the civil society particularly in the poor communities. Rape and the threat of rape against women also qualifies as torture in that it represents a brutal expression of discrimination against them as women. From the testimonies and expert opinions provided in the documentation to the Commission, it is clear that in the experience of torture victims, rape and sexual abuse are forms of

torture which produce some of the most severe and long-lasting traumatic effects.

The Commission further elaborated its jurisprudence on rape as a form
of torture in the case of *Fernando Mejía Egocheaga and Raquel Martin de
Mejía v. Peru,* Case 10.970, Inter–Am. Comm'n H.R. 157, OEA/Ser. L/V/
II.91, doc. 7 rev. (1996). Noting that Article 5(2) of the Convention
prohibits "torture" without defining the term, the Commission invoked the
definition set forth in the Inter–American Convention to Prevent and
Punish Torture and concluded that, "for torture to exist three elements
have to be combined":

1) it must be an intentional act through which physical and
mental pain and suffering is inflicted on a person;

2) it must be committed with a purpose;

3) it must be committed by a public official or by a private person
acting at the instigation of the former.

With respect to the first element, the Commission stated its view "that
rape is a physical and mental abuse that is perpetrated as a result of an act
of violence." The Commission also noted that rape is considered to be a
method of psychological torture "because its objective, in many cases, is not
just to humiliate the victim but also her family or community." It concluded:

Rape causes physical and mental suffering in the victim. In addition to
the violence suffered at the time it is committed, the victims are
commonly hurt or, in some cases, are even made pregnant. The fact of
being made the subject of abuse of this nature also causes a psychological trauma that results, on the one hand, from having been humiliated
and victimized, and on the other, from suffering the condemnation of
the members of their community if they report what has been done to
them.

The Commission observed that "[t]he second element establishes that
for an act to be torture it must have been committed intentionally, i.e. to
produce a certain result in the victim," and that such purposes include
"personal punishment and intimidation."

ii.   The European System

Comparatively few of the cases decided by the European Court and
Commission of Human Rights have involved allegations of sexual violence.
For many years, when these bodies had occasion to consider such allegations they tended to characterize rape as a form of "inhuman treatment"
or a breach of the right to private life.

Exemplifying the first approach is the Commission's findings in a case
arising out of Turkey's 1974 invasion of Cyprus. In *Cyprus v. Turkey,* App.
Nos. 6780/74 and 6950/75 (10 July 1976), 4 E.H.R.R. 482 (1982), the
Commission made the following factual findings:

373. The evidence shows that rapes were committed by Turkish soldiers and at least in two cases even by Turkish officers, and this not only in some isolated cases of indiscipline. It has not been shown that the Turkish authorities took adequate measures to prevent this happening or that they generally took any disciplinary measures following such incidents. The Commission therefore considers that the non-prevention of the said acts is imputable to Turkey under the Convention.

Based on these factual findings, the Commission concluded by a vote of 12 to 1 that "the incidents of rape described in the above cases and regarded as established constitute 'inhuman treatment' in the sense of Article 3 of the Convention, which is imputable to Turkey." (Paragraph 374.)

Another case involving sexual assault arose out of an incident in which a mentally disabled 16–year old girl, "Miss Y," was assaulted and sexually abused in a privately-run home for mentally-handicapped children. The girl's father, "X," unsuccessfully sought to compel the prosecutor to open proceedings against the perpetrator; his appeal of the prosecutor's decision not to do so was dismissed in part because Dutch law did not make any provision for another person to institute a complaint on behalf of such a victim. In a complaint to the European Commission, the father claimed that

> his daughter had been subject to inhuman and degrading treatment, within the meaning of Article 3 of the Convention, and that the right of both his daughter and himself to respect for their private life, guaranteed by Article 8, had been infringed. He further maintained that the right to respect for family life, also guaranteed by the same Article, meant that parents must be able to have recourse to remedies in the event of their children being the victims of sexual abuse, particularly if the children were minors and if the father was their legal representative.

X and Y v. Netherlands, 91 Eur. Ct. H.R. (ser. A), para. 18, 8 E.H.R.R. 235 (1985). By a vote of 15 to 1, the Commission found a violation of Article 8 but not of Article 3. With respect to Article 3, the Commission reasoned:

> 93. The Commission has no reason to doubt, and the Government have not contested this allegation, that [Miss Y], as a result of the events, was subject to mental suffering. It is true that, according to the *jurisprudence constante* of the Commission and the Court, mental suffering leading to acute psychiatric disturbances falls into the category of treatment prohibited by Art. 3 of the Convention....

> 94. However, the Commission does not consider it necessary to establish whether the mental suffering inflicted on [Miss Y] was of such a nature and had reached such a degree of intensity as to bring it within the scope of the above provision, since in any event the preliminary question whether the Netherlands Government could be held responsible for such treatment must be answered in the negative.

95. In reaching this conclusion, the Commission found it necessary in the present case to distinguish the issue under Art. 3 clearly from the issue under Art. 8. In the latter, it has held that the failure by the Dutch legislator to include a particular category of especially vulnerable persons in an otherwise comprehensive system of criminal legal protection of the sexual integrity of vulnerable persons constituted a violation of the Convention. However, sexual abuse and inhuman or degrading treatment—even though they may overlap in individual cases—are by no means congruent concepts. The gap in the law relating to the protection of the sexual integrity of vulnerable persons cannot therefore be assimilated to a gap in the protection of persons against inhuman or degrading treatment.

X and Y v. Netherlands, App. No. 8978/80, 6 E.H.R.R. 311 (Eur. Comm'n H.R. 1983). The case was referred to the European Court of Human Rights, which, finding that Article 8 of the Convention had been breached, did "not consider that it ha[d] also to examine the case under Article 3." *X and Y v. Netherlands*, 91 Eur. Ct. H.R. (ser. A), para. 34, 8 E.H.R.R. 235 (1985).

In 1996, the European Commission finally found that the rape of a female detainee constituted torture within the meaning of Article 3 of the European Convention. The case that gave rise to this finding, *Aydin v. Turkey*, resulted in a determination by the European Court of Human Rights that the "especially cruel act of rape" to which the applicant had been subjected "amounted to torture in breach of Article 3 of the [European] Convention."

Aydin v. Turkey

European Court of Human Rights, 1997.
1997–VI Eur. Ct. H.R. 1866, 25 E.H.R.R. 251.

AS TO THE FACTS

1. The Applicant

13. The applicant, Mrs Sükran Aydin, is a Turkish citizen of Kurdish origin. . . . At the time of the events at issue she was 17 years old and living with her parents in the village of Tasit, which is about ten kilometres from the town of Derik where the district gendarmerie headquarters are located. The applicant had never travelled beyond her village before the events which led to her application to the Commission.

2. The Situation in the South–East of Turkey

14. Since approximately 1985, serious disturbances have raged in the South–East of Turkey between the security forces and the members of the PKK (Workers' Party of Kurdistan). This confrontation has so far, according to the Government, claimed the lives of 4,036 civilians and 3,884 members of the security forces.

At the time of the Court's consideration of the case, ten of the eleven provinces of south-eastern Turkey had since 1987 been subjected to emergency rule.

. . .

I.   PARTICULAR CIRCUMSTANCES OF THE CASE

. . .

F.   The Commission's evaluation of the evidence and findings of fact

. . .

40.   The Commission's findings can be summarised as follows:

. . .

4.   Having regard to her evidence and her demeanour before the Delegates, and having given due consideration in particular to the medical reports drawn up by Dr Akkus, Dr Çetin and the doctor from the Diyarbakir Maternity Hospital, the Commission found it established that during her custody in the Derik gendarmerie station:

> ". . . the applicant was blindfolded, beaten, stripped, placed inside a tyre and sprayed with high pressure water, and raped. It would appear probable that the applicant was subjected to such treatment on the basis of suspicion of collaboration by herself or members of her family with members of the PKK, the purpose being to gain information and/or to deter her family and other villagers from becoming implicated in terrorist activities."

. . .

AS TO THE LAW

. . .

II.   ALLEGED VIOLATION OF ARTICLE 3 OF THE CONVENTION

. . .

C.   The Court's assessment of the evidence and the facts established by the Commission

. . .

73.   The Court considers that it should accept the facts as established by the Commission. . . .

2.   The Court's Assessment

. . .

81.   As it has observed on many occasions, Article 3 of the Convention enshrines one of the fundamental values of democratic societies and as such it prohibits in absolute terms torture or inhuman or degrading treatment or punishment. . . .

82. In order to determine whether any particular form of ill-treatment should be qualified as torture, regard must be had to the distinction drawn in Article 3 between this notion and that of inhuman treatment or degrading treatment. This distinction would appear to have been embodied in the Convention to allow the special stigma of "torture" to attach only to deliberate inhuman treatment causing very serious and cruel suffering.

83. While being held in detention the applicant was raped by a person whose identity has still to be determined. Rape of a detainee by an official of the State must be considered to be an especially grave and abhorrent form of ill-treatment given the ease with which the offender can exploit the vulnerability and weakened resistance of his victim. Furthermore, rape leaves deep psychological scars on the victim which do not respond to the passage of time as quickly as other forms of physical and mental violence. The applicant also experienced the acute physical pain of forced pen-etration, which must have left her feeling debased and violated both physically and emotionally.

84. The applicant was also subjected to a series of particularly terrifying and humiliating experiences while in custody at the hands of the security forces at Derik gendarmerie headquarters having regard to her sex and youth and the circumstances under which she was held. She was detained over a period of three days during which she must have been bewildered and disoriented by being kept blindfolded, and in a constant state of physical pain and mental anguish brought on by the beatings administered to her during questioning and by the apprehension of what would happen to her next. She was also paraded naked in humiliating circumstances thus adding to her overall sense of vulnerability and on one occasion she was pummelled with high pressure water while being spun around in a tyre.

85. The applicant and her family must have been taken from their village and brought to Derik gendarmerie headquarters for a purpose, which can only be explained on account of the security situation in the region ... and the need of the security forces to elicit information. The suffering inflicted on the applicant during the period of her detention must also be seen as calculated to serve the same or related purposes.

86. Against this background the Court is satisfied that the accumulation of acts of physical and mental violence inflicted on the applicant and the especially cruel act of rape to which she was subjected amounted to torture in breach of Article 3 of the Convention. Indeed the Court would have reached this conclusion on either of these grounds taken separately.

87. In conclusion, there has been a violation of Article 3 of the Conven-tion.

Notes

1. What was the basis of the distinction drawn by the European Commis-sion in *X and Y v. Netherlands* between the Dutch government's responsi-bility for a possible breach of Article 3 and its responsibility for a breach of

Article 8 of the European Convention? Does its analysis imply a value judgment in respect of the gravity of the injury suffered by Miss Y? Consider in particular the observation of the Commission that "sexual abuse and inhuman or degrading treatment—even though they may overlap in individual cases—are by no means congruent concepts." Does this observation imply that sexual abuse is not invariably degrading? Or was the Commission's conclusion based on other considerations?

2.   Consider also the approach taken by the European Court in *X and Y v. Netherlands*. Recall that, having found that Article 8 of the Convention had been breached, the Court did "not consider that it ha[d] also to examine the case under Article 3." Violations of Article 3 would generally be considered more serious than breaches of Article 8. In light of this, was it appropriate for the Court to avoid ruling on the more serious alleged breach because it established state responsibility for a lesser breach?

3.   Compare the reasoning of the Commission in *X and Y v. Netherlands* with the approach taken by the Court in the case of *A. v. United Kingdom* (Chapter 3, Section B(2), below). In the latter case, the Court found that the British government was responsible for a breach of Article 3 because of a substantive gap in British law that allowed the stepfather of the applicant to escape prosecution for corporal punishment. The Court reasoned:

> The Court considers that the obligation on the High Contracting Parties under Article 1 of the Convention to secure to everyone within their jurisdiction the rights and freedoms defined in the Convention, taken together with Article 3, requires States to take measures designed to ensure that individuals within their jurisdiction are not subjected to torture or inhuman or degrading treatment or punishment, including such ill-treatment administered by private individuals.... Children and other vulnerable individuals, in particular, are entitled to State protection, in the form of effective deterrence, against such serious breaches of personal integrity....

A. v. United Kingdom, 1998–VI Eur. Ct. H.R. 2692 (1998). If the same facts that gave rise to *X and Y v. Netherlands* were presented to the European Court following its judgment in *A. v. United Kingdom*, would it reach the same decision that it reached in 1986?

4.   What was the legal relevance of the European Court's conclusion in paragraph 85 of the *Aydin* case that "The applicant and her family must have been taken from their village and brought to Derik gendarmerie headquarters for a purpose, which can only be explained on account of the security situation in the region ... and the need of the security forces to elicit information. The suffering inflicted on the applicant during the period of her detention must also be seen as calculated to serve the same or related purposes." Compare the conclusion of the Trial Chamber of the International Criminal Tribunal for the former Yugoslavia in its verdict in the *Čelebiči* case (see 381 below).

b. RAPE AS A WAR CRIME

In 1992–93, reports of mass rapes committed during the conflict in Bosnia and Herzegovina galvanized global public opinion. When the UN Security Council decided in 1993 to establish a tribunal to prosecute those responsible for the most serious abuses committed since 1991 in the territory of the former Yugoslavia, including Bosnia, there was considerable public pressure to ensure that rapes were prosecuted as war crimes.

The statute of the International Criminal Tribunal for the former Yugoslavia (ICTY), adopted by the Security Council, confers subject matter jurisdiction over two categories of war crimes, as well as over genocide and crimes against humanity. The war crimes categories comprise (1) grave breaches of the Geneva Conventions of 1949, and (2) other violations of the laws or customs of war. Neither of the provisions of the tribunal's statute conferring jurisdiction over these categories explicitly mentions rape.

One and one-half years after the Security Council established the ICTY, it created a similar tribunal with jurisdiction over crimes relating to the 1994 genocide in Rwanda, the International Criminal Tribunal for Rwanda (ICTR). As already noted, the statutes of both tribunals establish subject-matter jurisdiction over certain categories of war crimes, as well as over genocide and crimes against humanity.

In contrast to the statute of the ICTY, which did not include the word "rape" in its enumeration of war crimes, the provision of the ICTR Statute establishing jurisdiction over war crimes explicitly mentions rape:

Article 4

Violations of Common Article 3 and of Protocol II

The International Tribunal for Rwanda shall have the power to prosecute persons committing or ordering to be committed serious violations of Article 3 common to the Geneva Conventions of 12 August 1949 for the Protection of Victims of War, and of Additional Protocol II thereto of 8 June 1977. These violations shall include, but not be limited to:

. . .

(e) Outrages upon personal dignity, in particular humiliating and degrading treatment, rape, enforced prostitution and any form of indecent assault. . . .

Although advocates for women's human rights had lobbied for explicit recognition of "rape" as a war crime, the formulation used in Article 4, which tracked Article 4(e) of Additional Protocol II, was controversial. Many activists had worked hard to de-link rape and other forms of sexual violence from the concept, reflected in Article 4(3) of Additional Protocol II and in Article 27 of the Fourth Geneva Convention of 1949, of violations of honor and dignity.

The jurisprudence that has emerged from early cases before the ICTY and ICTR has made clear that rape is a war crime and can also constitute a crime against humanity and an act of genocide when other elements of these crimes are established. In its verdict in the *Čelebići* case, a Trial Chamber of the ICTY held in the plainest terms: "There can be no doubt that rape and other forms of sexual assault are expressly prohibited under international humanitarian law." *Prosecutor v. Zejnil Delalić et al.*, Case No. IT–96–21–T, Judgment, para. 476 (Nov. 16, 1998). When other elements of the war crime of torture—such as state action—are established, the Trial Chamber found, rape constitutes the specific war crime of torture. See id. paras. 495–96. These conclusions were affirmed in a subsequent judgment rendered by Trial Chamber II in the *Furundžija* case. *Prosecutor v. Anto Furundžija*, Case No. IT–95–17/1–T, Judgment (Dec. 10, 1998).

The *Čelebići* judgment made an important contribution to the broader jurisprudence of rape as a form of torture. Of particular importance is the Trial Chamber's analysis in respect of the "purposive" element of torture. The Trial Chamber drew upon the definition of torture set forth in Article 1 of the 1984 Convention Against Torture and Other Cruel, Inhuman or Degrading Treatment or Punishment ("Torture Convention") for guidance in establishing the elements of "torture" under the law of armed conflict. Article 1 of the Torture Convention provides that

> the term "torture" means any act by which severe pain or suffering, whether physical or mental, is intentionally inflicted on a person for such purposes as obtaining from him or a third person information or a confession, punishing him for an act he or a third person has committed or is suspected of having committed, or intimidating or coercing him or a third person, or for any reason based on discrimination of any kind, when such pain or suffering is inflicted by or at the instigation of or with the consent or acquiescence of a public official or other person acting in an official capacity.

Some analysts have expressed concern about the possibility that the "purposive" element of this definition could present an obstacle to the recognition of rape as a form of torture when the assault is not committed for such purposes as eliciting a confession. Addressing this issue, the Trial Chamber that presided over the *Čelebiči* case noted that,

> in a recent report, the United Nations Special Rapporteur on Contemporary Forms of Slavery, Systematic Rape, Sexual Slavery and Slavery-like Practices during Armed Conflict, has considered the issue of rape as torture with particular regard to the prohibited purpose of discrimination. The United Nations Special Rapporteur referred to the fact that the Committee on the Elimination of Discrimination against Women has recognised that violence directed against a woman because she is a woman, including acts that inflict physical, mental or sexual harm or suffering, represent a form of discrimination that seriously inhibits the ability of women to enjoy human rights and freedoms. Upon this basis, the United Nations Special Rapporteur opined that, "in many cases the discrimination prong of the definition of torture in the Torture Convention provides an additional basis for prosecuting

rape and sexual violence as torture.''[509]

Prosecutor v. Zejnil Delalić et al., Case No. IT–96–21–T, Judgment, para. 493 (Nov. 16, 1998). Significantly, in rendering convictions on specific charges of rape, the Trial Chamber cited the defendants' discriminatory intent as one among several bases for its conclusion that the purposive element of torture had been established.*

Verdicts rendered by Trial Chambers of the ICTR and ICTY have also endeavored to define "rape" itself under international law, thereby filling a major gap in the law. A Trial Chamber of the ICTR defined rape as "a physical invasion of a sexual nature, committed on a person under circumstances which are coercive. Sexual violence which includes rape, is considered to be any act of a sexual nature which is committed on a person under circumstances which are coercive." *Prosecutor v. Jean–Paul Akayesu,* Case No. ICTR–96–4–T, Trial Chamber I, Judgment, para. 598 (Sept. 2, 1998). While this definition was adopted in the context of the Trial Chamber's consideration of crimes against humanity charges, a Trial Chamber of the ICTY followed the ICTR Chamber's definition of "rape" in its analysis of the war crimes charge of "torture".**

Notes

1.   In the portion of its verdict in the *Čelebići* case addressing the purposive element of torture, did the ICTY Trial Chamber imply that this element is always satisfied in cases of rape? That it is always satisfied when the victim is a woman? Under the Chamber's analysis, would the purposive element be satisfied if the perpetrator and victim of rape were the same sex?

2.   The statute for a permanent International Criminal Court (ICC) adopted in Rome in July 1998 (see Chapter 3, Section C(1)) explicitly includes rape and other forms of sexual violence in its enumeration of war crimes that can be prosecuted before the ICC. See Article 8(2)(b)(xxii) and (c)(vi) (enumerating, in addition to the war crime of rape, "sexual slavery, enforced prostitution, forced pregnancy . . . , [and] enforced sterilization"). In view of the jurisprudence of the ICTY and ICTR Trial Chambers noted above, is it significant that rape is explicitly enumerated as a war crime? In addressing this question, consider both the goals of advocates for women's

---

509. "Contemporary Forms of Slavery: Systematic Rape, Sexual Slavery and Slavery-like Practices during Armed Conflict"; Final Report submitted by Ms. Gay J. McDougall, Special Rapporteur, E/CN.4/Sub.2/1998/13, 22 June 1998, para. 55.

* See, e.g., id., para. 329 (noting that, in addition to other bases for the Tribunal's conclusion that the purposive element had been established in respect of a particular instance of rape, the violence suffered by the victim was inflicted by the defendant because

the victim "is a woman" and stating that, "[a]s discussed above, this represents a form of discrimination which constitutes a prohibited purpose for the offence of torture"). See also id., para. 963.

** *Prosecutor v. Zejnil Delalić et al.,* Case No. IT–96–21–T, Judgment, paras. 478–479 (Nov. 16, 1998). Compare the definition adopted by Trial Chamber II in its verdict in the *Furundžija* case, supra, at paras. 185–186.

human rights and due process concerns from the perspective of a defendant who might face prosecution on charges of rape in violation of relevant provisions of international criminal law.

3. For an overview of the gender-related jurisprudence of the ICTY and ICTR, see Kelly D. Askin, *Sexual Violence in Decisions and Indictments of the Yugoslav and Rwandan Tribunals: Current Status*, 93 Am. J. Int'l L. 97 (1999), and Patricia Viseur–Sellers, *Emerging Jurisprudence on Crimes of Sexual Violence*, in *Symposium: War Crimes Tribunals: The Record and the Prospects*, 13 Am. U. Int'l L. Rev. 1523 (1998). For a broader historical treatment of gender-specific war crimes, see Kelly Dawn Askin, War Crimes Against Women: Prosecution in International War Crimes Tribunals (1997); Theodor Meron, *Rape as a Crime under International Humanitarian Law*, 87 Am. J. Int'l L. 424 (1993).

4. WOMEN'S HUMAN RIGHTS IN PERSPECTIVE

The preceding sections have noted important advances in international legal protections of women's human rights. Notably, these can generally be dated to the final decade of the twentieth century. Until the 1990s, this area of human rights received comparatively scant attention by the leading human rights advocacy organizations and inadequate attention by the principal inter-governmental bodies that promote states' compliance with international human rights standards. Consider the following:

- Women's human rights scarcely figured in the work of the leading international human rights NGOs until the 1990s. Two major programs in this area, the Women's Rights Project of Human Rights Watch and the Women's Rights Advocacy Program of the International Human Rights Law Group, were established in 1990 and 1992, respectively.

- Similarly, the U.S. Department of State, which has produced an annual report on human rights worldwide since the late 1970s, did not include a section on women's human rights until 1993.

- The United Nations Commission on Human Rights did not appoint a Special Rapporteur on Violence Against Women until 1994. The Commission had long before established thematic mechanisms to address other human rights issues. Its first thematic mechanism, a Working Group on Disappearances, was established in 1980. In the ensuing years, the Commission appointed Special Rapporteurs or Working Groups to address torture, extrajudicial executions, and other concerns.

What factors account for the belated attention to women's human rights suggested by these benchmarks? The materials set forth below propound several explanations. Some emphasize institutional and structural factors, such as the under-representation of women in national governments and in international organizations, while other explanations focus on the nature of international law in general and human rights law in particular.

a.   THE PUBLIC/PRIVATE DISTINCTION IN INTERNATIONAL LAW

Hilary Charlesworth, Christine Chinkin and Shelley Wright, *Feminist Approaches to International Law*

85 Am. J. Int'l L. 613, 625–29 (1991).*

. . .

The normative structure of international law has allowed issues of particular concern to women to be either ignored or undermined. For example, modern international law rests on and reproduces various dichotomies between the public and private spheres, and the "public" sphere is regarded as the province of international law. . . .

. . . One explanation feminist scholars offer for the dominance of men and the male voice in all areas of power and authority in the western liberal tradition is that a dichotomy is drawn between the public sphere and the private or domestic one. The public realm of the work place, the law, economics, politics and intellectual and cultural life, where power and authority are exercised, is regarded as the natural province of men; while the private world of the home, the hearth and children is seen as the appropriate domain of women. The public/private distinction has a normative, as well as a descriptive, dimension. Traditionally, the two spheres are accorded asymmetrical value: greater significance is attached to the public, male world than to the private, female one. The distinction drawn between the public and the private thus vindicates and makes natural the division of labor and allocation of rewards between the sexes. Its reproduction and acceptance in all areas of knowledge have conferred primacy on the male world and supported the dominance of men.

. . .

What force does the feminist critique of the public/private dichotomy in the foundation of domestic legal systems have for the international legal order? Traditionally, of course, international law was regarded as operating only in the most public of public spheres: the relations between nation-states. We argue, however, that the definition of certain principles of international law rests on and reproduces the public/private distinction. It thus privileges the male world view and supports male dominance in the international legal order.

The grip that the public/private distinction has on international law, and the consequent banishment of women's voices and concerns from the discipline, can be seen in the international prohibition on torture. The right to freedom from torture and other forms of cruel, inhuman or degrading treatment is generally accepted as a paradigmatic civil and political right. It is included in all international catalogs of civil and political rights and is the focus of specialized United Nations and regional treaties. The right to be free from torture is also regarded as a norm of customary international law—indeed, like the prohibition on slavery, as a norm of jus cogens.

. . . Behavior constituting torture is defined in the Convention against Torture as any act by which severe pain or suffering, whether physical or mental, is intentionally inflicted on a person for such purposes as obtaining from him or a third person information or a confession, punishing him for an act he or a third person has committed or is suspected of having committed, or intimidating or coercing him or a third person, or for any reason based on discrimination of any kind, when such pain or suffering is inflicted by or at the instigation of or with the consent or acquiescence of a public official or other person acting in an official capacity.

... [T]he description of the prohibited conduct relies on a distinction between public and private actions that obscures injuries to their dignity typically sustained by women. The traditional canon of human rights law does not deal in categories that fit the experiences of women. It is cast in terms of discrete violations of rights and offers little redress in cases where there is a pervasive, structural denial of rights.

. . .

States are held responsible for torture only when their designated agents have direct responsibility for such acts and that responsibility is imputed to the state. States are not considered responsible if they have maintained a legal and social system in which violations of physical and mental integrity are endemic.... A feminist perspective on human rights would require a rethinking of the notions of imputability and state responsibility and in this sense would challenge the most basic assumptions of international law. If violence against women were considered by the international legal system to be as shocking as violence against people for their political ideas, women would have considerable support in their struggle.

The assumption that underlies all law, including international human rights law, is that the public/private distinction is real: human society, human lives can be separated into two distinct spheres. This division, however, is an ideological construct rationalizing the exclusion of women from the sources of power.

Karen Engle, *After the Collapse of the Public/Private Distinction: Strategizing Women's Rights*

in Reconceiving Reality: Women and International Law 143, 146, 148–50 (Dorinda Dallmeyer ed., 1993).

. . .

Concentrating too much on the public/private distinction excludes important parts of women's experiences. Not only does such a focus often omit those parts of women's lives that figure into the "public," however that gets defined, it also assumes that "private" is bad for women. It fails to recognize that the "private" is a place where many have tried to be (such as those involved in the market), and that it might ultimately afford protection to (at least some) women.

. . .

[Critiques of the public/private dichotomy] make us think of the unregulated private as something that is necessarily bad for women. We rarely look at the ways in which privacy (even if only because it seems the best available paradigm) is seen by at least some women to offer them protection. A number of examples immediately come to mind, each of which centers on women's bodies and, not surprisingly, on women's sexuality. The language of privacy, and sketching out zones of privacy, many would argue, is our best shot at legally theorizing women's sexuality. . . .

Examples of where "the private" is sometimes seen to have liberating potential for women are abortion (which is most obvious to us in the United States); battering; the protection of "alternative" sexual lifestyles; prostitution; right to wear the veil as protection from sexual harassment; right to participate in *or be free of* clitoridectomies, sati, breast implants, the wearing of spike-heeled shoes. Failure to focus on these issues affecting women's relationships to our bodies obscures the way that many women see their lives.

. . .

[On a related point], many have seen the European Court of Human Rights as having recognized protection for women in the legal concept of privacy. Beginning with the *Airey*[29] case, the court has acknowledged that Article 8 of the European Convention for the Protection of Human Rights and Fundamental Freedoms might require state interference to ensure that an Irish woman could get the legal services necessary to legally separate from her abusive husband. Privacy, then, is an indeterminate concept; in itself it neither creates nor requires a space outside of the state's protection or regulation.

[Further,] the critiques often cause us to think of the private as bad in general. The private comes to represent the marginal; the problem with the exclusion of the private sphere, we often say, is that it makes women marginal to international law. International law, we assume, is where the powerful spend their lives. The discipline of international trade, though, suggests otherwise. Constantly attempting to distinguish itself from public international law, trade tries to stay on the margins, where transactions are presumed to be engaged in freely. . . . The point I am making . . . is that some, particularly some who have a lot of power, see being outside the grip of public international law as positive and liberating. . . .

Notes

1.   Charlesworth et al. argue that, under the international law definition of torture, "severe pain and suffering that is inflicted outside the most public context of the state—for example, within the home or by private persons, which is the most pervasive and significant violence sustained by women—does not qualify as torture despite its impact on the inherent

29. Airey v. Ireland, 2 Eur. Ct. H.R. (ser. A) (1979).

dignity of the human person." Is this view still persuasive in light of recent jurisprudence by human rights treaty bodies? In the *Velásquez Rodríguez* case, excerpts of which appear in Part III, Chapter 3, Section B, the Inter–American Court of Human Rights stated: "An illegal act which violates human rights and which is initially not directly imputable to a State (for example because it is the act of a private person . . .) can lead to international responsibility of the State, not because of the act itself, but because of the lack of due diligence to prevent the violation or to respond to it as required. . . ." Although this judgment construed the American Convention on Human Rights, it is generally considered to be one of the leading international law decisions on state responsibility for human rights violations. Like the Inter–American Court, the Human Rights Committee and the European Court of Human Rights have interpreted the human rights conventions with respect to which they have supervisory authority to impose affirmative obligations on States Parties to ensure that private parties do not violate rights protected by those conventions. See pp. 902, 576–579, infra.

2. The Women's Convention takes an unambiguous position on various dimensions of the public/private distinction addressed in the selection by Charlesworth et al. Article 2 requires States Parties not only to ensure that public authorities refrain from any act of discrimination, but also to "take all appropriate measures to eliminate discrimination against women by any person, organization or enterprise." Other provisions require States Parties to take measures to eradicate cultural practices, including those many would characterize as belonging to the "private" sphere, that account for endemic disparities between men and women in their enjoyment of rights. Article 2 requires States Parties to "take all appropriate measures . . . to modify or abolish existing laws, regulations, customs and practices which constitute discrimination against women." Article 5 requires States Parties to "take all appropriate measures: (a) To modify the social and cultural patterns of conduct of men and women, with a view to achieving the elimination of prejudices and customary and all other practices which are based on the idea of the inferiority or the superiority of either of the sexes or on stereotyped roles for men and women." See also Inter–American Convention on the Prevention, Punishment and Eradication of Violence Against Women, OAS/Ser. L. V/II. 92 doc. 31 rev. 3, May 3, 1996, arts. 1 & 2.

3. To the extent that critiques of international law's public/private distinction are persuasive, is the principal problem that international law utilizes this distinction or that the public dimension of abuses against women has not been adequately recognized?

b. STRUCTURAL EXPLANATIONS

Hilary Charlesworth, Christine Chinkin and Shelley Wright, *Feminist Approaches to International Law*

85 Am. J. Int'l L. 613 (1991).*

. . .

* Reproduced with permission from 85 AJIL 613 (1991) © The American Society of International Law.

The Organizational Structure of International Law

The structure of the international legal order reflects a male perspective and ensures its continued dominance. The primary subjects of international law are states and, increasingly, international organizations. In both states and international organizations the invisibility of women is striking. Power structures within governments are overwhelmingly masculine: women have significant positions of power in very few states, and in those where they do, their numbers are minuscule.[56] Women are either unrepresented or underrepresented in the national and global decision-making processes.

· · ·

International organizations are functional extensions of states that allow them to act collectively to achieve their objectives. Not surprisingly, their structures replicate those of states, restricting women to insignificant and subordinate roles. Thus, in the United Nations itself, where the achievement of nearly universal membership is regarded as a major success of the international community, this universality does not apply to women.

... The Group on Equal Rights for Women in the United Nations has observed that "gender racism" is practiced in UN personnel policies "every week, every month, every year."

Women are excluded from all major decision making by international institutions on global policies and guidelines, despite the often disparate impact of those decisions on women. Since 1985, there has been some improvement in the representation of women in the United Nations and its specialized agencies.[61] It has been estimated, however, that "at the present rate of change it will take almost 4 more decades (until 2021) to reach equality (i.e.: 50% of professional jobs held by women)." This situation was recently described as "grotesque."[63]

56. In March 1991, women headed their country's government in 4 of the 159 member states of the United Nations. In mid–1989, at cabinet level only 3.5% of the ministries in 155 countries were held by women, and 99 nations had no women ministers.... States are slow to make women permanent representatives to the United Nations: in March 1990, 4 out of 149 were women. ...

61. In 1985 the Secretary–General appointed a Co-ordinator for the Improvement of the Status of Women to a term of 12 months. This period was subsequently extended. The Secretary–General's report, Review and Appraisal of the Implementation of the Nairobi Forward–Looking Strategies for the Advancement of Women, ... [hereinafter Nairobi Review], indicates that between 1984 and 1988 the total increase in the representation of women in professional and management positions in the United Nations was 3.6%, to a total of 21% of the professional staff. At the senior management level in 1988, however, only 4% of the staff were women.... In March 1990 the figure for women in posts subject to geographical distribution was 27.7%. UN Rev., August 1990, at 4. Although by the mid-eighties over 40% of the Secretariat staff were women, they were mainly in lower-status secretarial and clerical positions.... The important and prestigious positions of Under–Secretary–General and Assistant Secretary–General are almost entirely held by men. In 1990 two women held the position of Under–Secretary–General and no women were Assistant Secretaries–General.

63. B. Urquhart & E. Childers, A World in Need of Leadership: Tomorrow's United Nations 29 (1990); *see also id.* at 61.

The silence and invisibility of women also characterizes those bodies with special functions regarding the creation and progressive development of international law. Only one woman has sat as a judge on the International Court of Justice[64] and no woman has ever been a member of the International Law Commission. Critics have frequently pointed out that the distribution of judges on the Court does not reflect the makeup of the international community, a concern that peaked after the decision in the *South West Africa* cases in 1966. Steps have since been taken to improve "the representation of the main forms of civilization and of the principal legal systems of the world"[66] on the Court, but not in the direction of representing women, half of the world's population.

Despite the common acceptance of human rights as an area in which attention can be directed toward women, they are still vastly under represented on UN human rights bodies. The one committee that has all women members, the Committee on the Elimination of Discrimination against Women (CEDAW Committee), the monitoring body for the Convention on the Elimination of All Forms of Discrimination against Women (Women's Convention), has been criticized for its "disproportionate" representation of women by the United Nations Economic and Social Council (ECOSOC)....[70]

Why is it significant that all the major institutions of the international legal order are peopled by men? Long-term domination of all bodies wielding political power nationally and internationally means that issues traditionally of concern to men become seen as general human concerns, while "women's concerns" are relegated to a special, limited category. Because men generally are not the victims of sex discrimination, domestic violence, and sexual degradation and violence, for example, these matters can be consigned to a separate sphere and tend to be ignored....

Notes

1. The preceding selections cite the low representation of women in international organizations and on most human rights treaty bodies as a

---

64. Mme. Suzanne Bastid was a judge ad hoc in Application for Revision and Interpretation of the Judgment of 24 February 1982 in the Case concerning the Continental Shelf (Tunisia/Libyan Arab Jamahiriya) (Tunisia v. Libya), 1985 ICJ Rep. 192 (Judgment of Dec. 10). [Editors' Note: In 1995, Judge Rosalyn Higgins became the first full-time female member of the 15–judge International Court of Justice.]

66. Statute of the International Court of Justice, Art. 9. . . .

70. . . . Another reflection of the low status of women's concerns within the United Nations system is the apparently low priority the Women's Convention is given on the human rights agenda. At its seventh session in 1987, the CEDAW Committee claimed to have been provided with far worse working conditions than other human rights committees. [Andrew] Byrnes has observed:

> The fact that CEDAW has been given less time than other comparable bodies while covering economic and social rights as well as civil and political rights is perhaps the reflection of a less than full commitment to the pursuit of the goals of the Convention or at least a serious underestimate of the extent of the work to be done.

. . .

factor contributing to the downgrading of women's human rights that long characterized the work of international organizations and the jurisprudence of treaty bodies. As of August 1998, two of the eleven members of the African Commission on Human and Peoples' Rights were women. As of November 1998, when the European Commission on Human Rights and the previous European Court of Human Rights were replaced by a single, full-time court, only three out of thirty-two members of the Commission were women, and only one of the thirty-six members of the Court was a woman. The first panel of judges appointed to the new European Court had forty members, of whom eight were women. As of February 1999, no member of either the Inter–American Court or Commission of Human Rights was a woman. Four of the eighteen members of the Human Rights Committee, which monitors States Parties' compliance with the ICCPR, were women.

2.   Recent instruments have sought to address this pattern. For example, the Protocol to the African Charter on Human and Peoples' Rights on the Establishment of an African Court on Human and Peoples' Rights, adopted in June 1998, explicitly calls for adequate gender representation in the nomination and election of judges. Similarly, Article 8(a)(iii) of the Rome Statute of the International Criminal Court, UN Doc. A/CONF.183/9 (1998), provides that, in selecting judges, States Parties shall take into account the need for a "fair representation of female and male judges." The United Nations has also acted to increase the percentage of women in professional and decision-making positions within the UN system, with discernible impact. See The United Nations and the Advancement of Women 1945–1995, UN Blue Books Series, vol. VI, paras. 243–245 (1995).

5.   HUMAN RIGHTS OF WOMEN AND THE CHALLENGE OF CULTURAL RELATIVISM

In preceding sections we have noted recent milestones in the advancement of women's human rights. In the words of one writer, those advances have resulted above all from the emergence of a vibrant women's-rights advocacy movement—"the coalescence of women as a global presence." Rhonda Copelon, *Introduction: Bringing Beijing Home*, 21 Brooklyn J. Int'l L. 599 (1996).

Yet, during the same period when concern for women's human rights moved into the foreground of international attention and concern, other trends presented serious challenges to the core claims of women's human rights advocates. Most importantly, the 1990s saw claims of cultural relativism take on renewed force. These were, for example, asserted by several governments at the 1993 Vienna Conference on Human Rights. Although these claims have been pressed most prominently by several Asian political leaders, issues of cultural relativism have significant implications across the globe, notably—but by no means exclusively—in Islamic countries.

While the cultural-relativism challenge has profound implications for virtually the entire spectrum of human rights protected by international law, it presents a particularly acute challenge in respect of women's human rights since many denials of those rights are justified in terms of social and/or religious custom, sometimes enacted into law. Efforts to combat culturally-rooted practices that violate universal human rights standards also raise complex issues relating to the appropriateness and efficacy of global advocacy approaches. As several of the following materials reflect, efforts to combat culturally-derived practices have at times drawn charges of cultural imperialism—often from advocates who are themselves working to eradicate the challenged practices.

Seble Dawit and Salem Mekuria, *The West Just Doesn't Get It*

The New York Times, Dec. 7, 1993, p. A27.

We are African women who have been working to abolish the ancient practice of female genital mutilation: the removal of all or part of a girl's external genitalia, usually to insure virginity or control sexuality.

Some of us are survivors of the practice, others are not. Along with other African professional women living in the United States . . . , we oppose it and call for its eradication.

But we take great exception to the recent Western focus on female genital mutilation in Africa, most notably by the novelist Alice Walker.

Ms. Walker's new film "Warrior Marks" portrays an African village where women and children are without personality, dancing and gazing blankly through some stranger's script of their lives. The respected elder women of the village's Secret Society turn into slit-eyed murderers wielding rusted weapons with which to butcher children.

As is common in Western depictions of Africa, Ms. Walker and her collaborator, Prathiba Parmar, portray the continent as a monolith. African women and children are the props, and the village the background against which Alice Walker, heroine-savior, comes to articulate their pain and condemn those who inflict it.

Like Ms. Walker's novel "Possessing the Secret of Joy," this film is emblematic of the Western feminist tendency to see female genital mutilation as the gender oppression to end all oppressions. Instead of being an issue worthy of attention in itself, it has become a powerfully emotive lens through which to view personal pain—a gauge by which to measure distance between the West and the rest of humanity.

The implications go far beyond Ms. Walker's work. Consider that the State Department's human rights reports now require African countries to report on the incidence of genital mutilation. Influential lawmakers and commentators have called for discontinuing financial assistance to governments that do not address this issue in the manner dictated by the West.

We do not believe that force changes traditional habits and practices. Superior Western attitudes do not enhance dialogue or equal exchange of ideas. Genital mutilation does not exist in a vacuum but as part of the social fabric, stemming from the power imbalance in relations between the sexes, from the levels of education and the low economic and social status of most women. All eradication efforts must begin and proceed from these basic premises.

Five countries—Sudan, Kenya, Egypt, Ivory Coast and Burkina Faso— have taken legal or policy measures against genital mutilation, and there are groups working on it in almost every country where it is practiced. Some are working with ministries of health and education. Others work in villages to move traditional circumcisers away from their trade and teach villagers about the physical and psychological harm of the practice. Still others work with doctors and other health-care providers to make them more responsive to the women's needs and work with powerful religious leaders and village elders to make them advocates against the practice.

A media campaign in the West will not stop genital mutilation. Westerners and those of us living in the West who wish to work on this issue must forge partnerships with the hundreds of African women on the continent who are working to eradicate the practice. Neither Alice Walker nor any of us here can speak for them; but if we have the power and the resources, we can create the room for them to speak, and to speak with us as well.

Hope Lewis, *Between* Irua *and "Female Genital Mutilation": Feminist Human Rights Discourse and the Cultural Divide*

8 Harv. Hum. Rts. J. 1, 1–2, 20–24 (1995).

. . .

"Irua,"[3] or traditional female genital surgery ("FGS"), implicates the most private aspects of individual female physical and cultural identity. Accordingly, African women who have undergone FGS have the most significant stake in determining whether and how the practice is treated in public international law. However, the serious public and private health consequences of FGS have aroused concern in cultures in which FGS is not traditionally practiced. Some Western feminists, for example, have placed FGS on the international human rights agenda, posing a challenge to traditional distinctions between "public" and "private" spheres of international legal obligation.

. . .

3. "Irua" is a Kikuyu word for traditional initiation ceremonies associated with the clitoridectomy of girls and the circumci- sion of boys within that Kenyan ethnic group. See Jomo Kenyatta, Facing Mt. Kenya 129 (1965). . . .

To address FGS as a human rights violation, Western feminists have had to face both the gender politics of international human rights and the tension between universalism and cultural relativism. In doing so, the discourse has argued first, that the cultural bases for the practice are misguided or based in ignorance; second, that FGS somehow falls outside the domain of "culture"; or third, that "culture" itself is a patriarchal construction vulnerable to challenge. To sustain these arguments, Western feminists have had to examine the origins of FGS and the modern justifications for its continued practice.

There is no single explanation for the practice of the many forms of traditional FGS. Different ethnic groups identify different motivations or point to a mixture of rationales. Female genital surgery is most prevalent in predominantly Islamic countries in Africa, but it is also found among groups that practice Christian, Jewish, and African religions. While a few Muslim religious leaders continue to promote the practice of FGS on religious grounds, historians suggest that FGS pre-dates Islam, and that its origins in other religious traditions are unclear.

. . .

The most controversial segment of the discourse on Western feminist involvement in the eradication campaign is whether FGS is based on the sexual subordination of women by men. Some Western feminists argue that "cultural" justifications, such as initiation into adulthood, merely serve to perpetuate male control over women's physical and intellectual autonomy. Among many practicing groups, women who have not been subjected to FGS are viewed as "unclean" and may be considered unsuitable for marriage and thus excluded from a vital source of socioeconomic support. The fact that women perform the operations in the traditional context, or that some girls look forward to initiation is largely attributed to false consciousness, or to social pressure. Several Western feminist texts have pointed out that many justifications for FGS explicitly relate to modifying the behavior of women: eliminating "promiscuity," ensuring virginity at marriage, making rape more difficult for an assailant, increasing the sexual pleasure of the husband, increasing the sexual pleasure of the wife, and making it easier to maintain celibacy for contraceptive reasons.

Western feminists who hope to "enlighten" African women risk replacing patriarchal oppression with Western cultural oppression. In an effort to avoid this trap, Western feminist rights discourse often draws analogies between traditional FGS and oppressive practices that have occurred in the West. . . .

. . .

Some Western feminist literature cites the explicit focus on sexual control of women in nineteenth-and early twentieth-century Western versions of FGS as evidence that similar motivations perpetuate the practice in Africa. Several Western feminist scholars also analogize traditional FGS to modern elective cosmetic surgery or to the high incidence of medically unnecessary radical hysterectomies performed in the United States.

. . .

Eugenie Anne Gifford, *"The Courage to Blaspheme"*: *Confronting Barriers to Resisting Female Genital Mutilation*
4 UCLA Women's L.J. 329, 334–36 (1994).

. . .

. . . Professor [Isabelle R.] Gunning prescribes a three-part methodology of "world-travelling":

> One has to be clear about the cultural influences and pressures that are inextricably involved in one's own sense of self. This requires understanding oneself in one's own historical context with an emphasis on the overlap, influences and conditions which one is observing in the "other." Recognizing interconnectedness requires two additional approaches. The first is to understand one's historical relationship to the "other" and to approach that understanding from the "other's" perspective, i.e., to see the self as the "other" might see you. Second, one must see the "other" in her own cultural context as she sees herself. This prong requires both an in-depth look at one's own complex cultural context in search of analogues to culturally challenging practices in the "other's" culture, as well as an in-depth look at the rich cultural context of the other woman's life.[25]

. . .

There are . . . pitfalls to the world-travelling approach. The most obvious lies in ensuring that the technique does what it says it does: allows us to theorize about "culturally challenging" practices—without engaging in cultural imperialism—by visualizing our interconnectedness with the members of that "other" culture. Gunning urges us to approach the task with " 'playfulness' . . . an openness in travelling, an attitude that rejects rules and structure and a willingness to engage in a reconstruction of self without a concern for competence."[29] But surely our identified "other" would beg us to be cautious while "playing" with their lives. In fact, is it not the very essence of cultural imperialism itself that leads us to believe we have the right to play with others in the first place?

If the first challenge of world-travelling is ensuring our caution, the second lies in making sure that we are not *over* cautious. That is, that we do not let our well-meaning concern for avoiding cultural imperialism and racism coax us into accepting too willingly practices and justifications that

25. [Isabelle R. Gunning, *Arrogant Perception, World–Travelling and Multicultural Feminism: The Case of Female Genital Surgeries*, 23 Colum. Hum. Rts. L. Rev. 189, 204–05 (1992).]

29. [*Id.*] at 204.

simply do not comport with what we know or suspect to be true. A passage
in Gunning's article describing the possible appeal of genital mutilation to
its young victims is instructive:

> The surgeries are performed by women, largely midwives[,] and
> are part of the creation of a special and exclusive "women's space." A
> young girl often has the surgery performed along with other young-
> sters, her sisters or other girls in the area of the same age group. She is
> never alone during the ceremony. In addition to other young partici-
> pants, her female relatives will go through the pain with her; keeping
> her secure during the operation, but also supporting and soothing her
> during and afterwards. Whatever pain is endured by the girl has to
> mingle with the joy of being like the other women, becoming clean and
> experiencing the "most important day of a girl's life."[30]

Not a single sentence of this portrayal rings true in light of the numerous
first-hand accounts in which survivors speak of an indescribable pain,
imprinted permanently upon their memories, obliterating all but the consciousness of agony. By avoiding racism, Gunning has herself become
complicit in genocide—and gynocide—in the guise of political correctness.
. . . We must guard against the charge of racism when it becomes just one
more way of silencing women's voices when they are raised to help each
other.

. . .

———

Notes

1.   What is the pith of Ms. Dawit's and Ms. Mekuria's criticism of Western
feminists' approach to the practice that they term "female genital mutilation," or "FGM"? Consider the following characterization of their argument: "These writers' critique is not so much one of cultural relativism as
cultural imperialism." Do you agree? Suppose that Alice Walker's portrait
of African women who practice FGM more nearly resembled that evoked by
Isabelle Gunning in the passage quoted—and critiqued—by Eugenie Anne
Gifford. Would this approach address Ms. Dawit's and Ms. Mekuria's
concerns?

2.   Are the critiques of Western feminists' campaign against FGM/S principally based upon strategic calculations or substantive principles—or both?
To the extent that these critiques reflect strategic concerns, what advocacy
approach on the part of "outsiders" would be most effective in eradicating
FGM/S in countries where it is practiced? What prescription do Ms. Dawit
and Ms. Mekuria offer?

3.   In recent years, one approach that has gained widespread support
emphasizes education—that is, educating both men and women in the
communities where FGM/S is practiced about the deleterious health and

---

30. *Id.* at 219 (footnotes omitted).

other long-term consequences for those who undergo different forms of procedure. In the view of those who have participated in such programs, they are more effective than "lecturing" by outsiders. If this insight is well-founded, what implications does it have for the universalist/cultural relativist dichotomy in relation to the practice of FGM/S?

6. CONFLICTS BETWEEN WOMEN'S HUMAN RIGHTS AND OTHER INTERNATIONALLY-PROTECTED HUMAN RIGHTS

An issue that overlaps with but is distinct from questions of cultural relativism concerns the question of how conflicts between rights that are protected by international law should be resolved. As the following excerpt by Professor An–Na'im suggests, some abridgements of women's human rights are justified in terms of religious doctrine mandating separate roles for men and women. In these circumstances, there may be a direct clash between the internationally-protected right to manifest one's religious beliefs in community with others and the right not to be subjected to discrimination on the basis of sex. Even if one accepts in principle the claim that human rights are universal, this situation raises the question of how to resolve conflicts between and among rights each of which is internationally-protected.

Article 18(3) of the ICCPR provides that "[f]reedom to manifest one's religion or beliefs may be subject only to such limitations as are prescribed by law and are necessary to protect public safety, order, health, or morals or the fundamental rights and freedoms of others." Presumably, then, the Covenant permits some restrictions on religious practice if *necessary* to protect women's fundamental human rights and if those restrictions are prescribed by law. Still, this does not tell us how to determine whether particular forms of religious practice may—or must—be curbed to protect women's human rights. The following selections by Professors Abdullahi A. An–Na'im and Donna J. Sullivan offer two perspectives on these issues.

Abdullahi A. An–Na'im, *Islamic Law, International Relations, and Human Rights: Challenge and Response*

20 Cornell Int'l L. J. 317, 328–34 (1987).

Under *Shari'a* rule, some basic human rights are at serious risk. Had Muslims not temporarily abandoned public *Shari'a* during secular rule, there would have been massive violations of the most basic human rights.[61] Recent attempts to re-introduce public *Shari'a* in Iran and Pakistan provide horrific examples of persecution of religious minorities and violation of individual civil liberties. . . .

---

61. For example, it should be noted that slavery has been abolished in the Muslim world as a matter of secular law and not through the reform of the relevant rules of *Shari'a*. Despite the call to formally abolish slavery as a matter of *Shari'a* law . . ., abolition was achieved only through secular law. . . .

... *Shari'a* classifies all the subjects of an Islamic state in terms of gender and religion. At the top of the hierarchy are Muslim men, who enjoy the highest level of civil and political rights, followed by Muslim women and "tolerated" non-Muslim minorities.

... *Shari'a* treats women as the wards of men. As such, women lack the capacity to hold high-ranking general executive or judicial office. While *Shari'a* achieved significant advances over contemporary practice in improving the status of women, it generally inhibits women's participation in public life.

. . .

It must be emphasized that the object of critically noting all these limitations on the basic civil rights of Muslim men, women and non-Muslims is not to doubt the validity of such limitations in their proper historical context. *Shari'a*'s view of civil liberties compared favorably with civil rights under Roman and Persian law prevailing at the time. Rather, criticism and strong objection must be raised to any attempt to reintroduce historical public *Shari'a* today because it is inconsistent with prevailing human rights standards.

... Claims of cultural relativism, including allegiance to a religious legal system such as *Shari'a*, are limited by minimum standards of universal human rights. For example, slavery and torture cannot be justified with reference to any set of prevailing social norms or traditional cultural standards....

Discrimination on grounds of gender or religion is as objectionable as discrimination on grounds of race. ...[A] modern Islamic state cannot justify discrimination among its own citizens on grounds of gender or religion.

. . .

A legitimate and lasting constitutional and legal order that can address modern international relations and domestic human rights must develop from within Islam. Although Muslims presently live with superficial patterns of western-style government, Muslim belief precludes a purely secular approach to law and state.

. . .

The best solution to the current Muslim dilemma of legitimizing peaceful coexistence and basic human rights from within Islam is based on the work of the late Sudanese Muslim reformer *Ustadh* Mahmoud Mohamed Taha. According to Taha, public *Shari'a* did not enact the whole of Islam. ...[T]he jurists' understanding of the sources were bound to their historical context. One may find the modern model of an Islamic state in the broad principles of justice and equality contained in the *Qur'an* and *Sunna* of the earlier stage of Mecca....

Taha's approach provides a framework for the discovery of solutions from within Islam. Such a model would emphasize that Islam suits *all* ages and places, not just its early historical context. Muslims must recall that the Prophet was a man of his time and for all times. In delivering the whole of the *Qur'an* and living up to its values, the Prophet faithfully executed his role as the Prophet of the universal and eternal message of Islam. Working out of the totality of Islam, the Prophet then constructed the best workable model and left the rest for the Muslims to develop and implement in light of their own needs and experience. Thus, Islam suits all ages and places by providing a flexible framework from which the right answers may be developed according to the demands of the times.

. . .

Donna J. Sullivan, *Gender Equality and Religious Freedom: Toward a Framework For Conflict Resolution*

24 N.Y.U. J. Int'l L. & Politics 795, 810–11, 817, 821–23 (1992).

. . .

In practice, restrictions on the freedom of religion for the purpose of protecting the human rights of others are readily conceded to be justified where the moral and political authority accorded to a particular human right, or set of rights, is generally acknowledged. . . .

Certain rights central to the protection of human dignity, notably the peremptory norms prohibiting extralegal killings, genocide, slavery, torture and systematic racial discrimination, clearly must prevail in all situations of conflict with the right to manifest religion or belief.

. . .

. . . Gender-specific violations of . . . peremptory norms clearly fall within the category of practices subject to absolute prohibition. For example, *sati*, the practice of burning a Hindu widow to death on her husband's funeral pyre, demands blanket prohibition as a violation of the right to life.

. . .

Many conflicts between women's human rights and religious freedom involve norms that have not as yet been accorded overriding significance by the international community. . . . In such situations of conflict, a balancing approach that takes into account particularized facts concerning the impact of the rights involved on one another, and on the underlying principles of gender equality and religious freedom, can provide a framework for conflict resolution.

One of the primary factors to be considered is the relationship between the specific equality right at issue and the overarching goal of gender equality.[64] A second factor, conversely, is the importance of the religious

---

64. For example, a bar on women's accession to the throne in constitutional monarchies, although clearly a violation of article 7 of the Women's Convention, has a less widespread impact on women's equality than restrictions on their right to vote in "free and fair" elections. . . .

law or practice to the right of religious freedom upon which it is premised. Assessments of the significance of a religious practice should proceed from the significance accorded that practice by the religion or belief itself. A third factor to be analyzed is the degree to which each practice infringes the other or the underlying rights and interests. In other words, does the conflict result in only a slight degree of interference, or is either of the practices totally barred and the exercise of the underlying rights extensively restricted or foreclosed? A fourth factor to be considered is whether other human rights are implicated. For example, if the religion in question is one practiced by a minority group, the impact of the proposed restrictions on the rights of minorities under article 27 of the Political Covenant must be taken into account.[66] Fifth, if religious law imposes a series of limitations on women's rights, their cumulative effect on women's status should be weighed, as should the effect of multiple restrictions of religious practice on the religion concerned. Finally, where the state has determined that restriction of a religious law or practice is necessary for the purpose of ensuring women's rights under the Women's Convention or general guarantees of gender equality, the proportionality of the restriction must be assessed.

.   .   .

———

A communication filed by Sandra Lovelace with the Human Rights Committee, the body that monitors States Parties' compliance with the ICCPR, presented a situation in which Ms. Lovelace's right of non-discrimination on the basis of sex conflicted with the cultural rights of members of her tribe, both of which are protected by the Covenant.

Lovelace v. Canada

Human Rights Committee, 1981.
U.N. Doc. CCPR/C/OP/1 at 83.

Views under Article 5(4) of the Optional Protocol

1. The author of the communication ... is a 32–year-old woman, living in Canada. She was born and registered as "Maliseet Indian" but has lost her rights and status as an Indian in accordance with section 12(1)(*b*) of the Indian Act, after having married a non-Indian on 23 May 1970. Pointing out that an Indian man who marries a non-Indian woman does not lose his Indian status, she claims that the Act is discriminatory on the grounds of sex and contrary to articles 2(1), 3, 23(1) and (4), 26 and 27 of the Covenant. . . .

.   .   .

66. Article 27 protects the right of ethnic, religious or linguistic minorities to "enjoy their own culture, to profess and practice their own religion, or to use their own language." . . .

5. In its submission under article 4(2) of the Optional Protocol concerning the merits of the case, ..., the State party recognized that "many of the provisions of the ... Indian Act, including section 12(1)(*b*), require serious reconsideration and reform". The Government further referred to an earlier public declaration to the effect that it intended to put a reform bill before the Canadian Parliament. It none the less stressed the necessity of the Indian Act as an instrument designed to protect the Indian minority in accordance with article 27 of the Covenant. A definition of the Indian was inevitable in view of the special privileges granted to the Indian communities, in particular their right to occupy reserve lands. Traditionally, patrilineal family relationships were taken into account for determining legal claims. Since, additionally, in the farming societies of the nineteenth century, reserve land was felt to be more threatened by non-Indian men than by non-Indian women, legal enactments as from 1869 provided that an Indian woman who married a non-Indian man would lose her status as an Indian. These reasons were still valid. A change in the law could only be sought in consultation with the Indians themselves who, however, were divided on the issue of equal rights. The Indian community should not be endangered by legislative changes. Therefore, although the Government was in principle committed to amending section 12(1)(*b*) of the Indian Act, no quick and immediate legislative action could be expected.

6. The author of the communication ... disputes the contention that legal relationships within Indian families were traditionally patrilineal in nature....

. . .

7.2 [In an interim decision the] Human Rights Committee recognized that the relevant provision of the Indian Act, although not legally restricting the right to marry as laid down in article 23(2) of the Covenant, entails serious disadvantages on the part of the Indian woman who wants to marry a non-Indian man and may in fact cause her to live with her fiancé in an unmarried relationship. There is thus a question as to whether the obligation of the State party under article 23 of the Covenant with regard to the protection of the family is complied with. Moreover, since only Indian women and not Indian men are subject to these disadvantages under the Act, the question arises whether Canada complies with its commitment under articles 2 and 3 to secure the rights under the Covenant without discrimination as to sex. On the other hand, article 27 of the Covenant requires States parties to accord protection to ethnic and linguistic minorities and the Committee must give due weight to this obligation....

. . .

7.4 ... The Human Rights Committee has been informed that persons in [Ms. Lovelace's] situation are denied the right to live on an Indian reserve with resultant separation from the Indian community and members of their families. Such prohibition may affect rights which the Covenant guarantees in articles 12(1), 17, 23(1), 24 and 27....

. . .

9.3   As to the legal basis of a prohibition to live on a reserve, the State party offers the following explanations:

Section 14 of the Indian Act provides that "(an Indian) woman who is a member of a band ceases to be a member of that band if she marries a person who is not a member of that band".[3] As such, she loses the right to the use and benefits, in common with other members of the band, of the land allotted to the band. It should, however, be noted that "when (an Indian woman) marries a member of another band, she thereupon becomes a member of the band of which her husband is a member". As such, she is entitled to the use and benefit of lands allotted to her husband's band.

An Indian (including a woman) who ceases to be a member of a band ceases to be entitled to reside by right on a reserve. None the less it is possible for an individual to reside on a reserve if his or her presence thereon is tolerated by a band or its members. It should be noted that under section 30 of the Indian Act, any person who trespasses on a reserve is guilty of an offence. . . .

.   .   .

9.6   As to Ms. Lovelace's place of abode prior to her marriage both parties confirm that she was at that time living on the Tobique Reserve with her parents. Sandra Lovelace adds that as a result of her marriage, she was denied the right to live on an Indian reserve. As to her abode since then the State party observes:

Since her marriage and following her divorce, Mrs. Lovelace has, from time to time, lived on the reserve in the home of her parents, and the Band Council has made no move to prevent her from doing so. However, Mrs. Lovelace wishes to live permanently on the reserve and to obtain a new house. To do so, she has to apply to the Band Council. Housing on reserves is provided with money set aside by Parliament for the benefit of registered Indians. The Council has not agreed to provide Mrs. Lovelace with a new house. It considers that in the provision of such housing priority is to be given to registered Indians.

9.7   In this connection the following additional information has been submitted on behalf of Mrs. Lovelace:

At the present time, Sandra Lovelace is living on the Tobique Indian Reserve, although she has no right to remain there. She has returned to the Reserve, with her children because her marriage has broken up and she has no other place to reside. She is able to remain on the reserve in violation of the law of the local Band Council because dissident members of the tribe who support her cause have threatened to resort to physical violence in her defence should the authorities attempt to remove her.

[The Committee found that Mrs. Lovelace's loss of status as a Maliseet Indian by operation of the Indian Act upon her marriage to a non-Indian

---

3.   Mrs. Lovelace married a non-Indian. As such, she ceased to be a member of the Tobique band. In addition, by the application of sub-paragraph 12(1), (b) of the Indian Act, she lost her Indian status.

did not constitute a violation of the ICCPR since her marriage preceded the entry into force of the Covenant for Canada on August 19, 1976. It did, however, consider the effects of the Indian Act that continued after August 19, 1976.]

12. The Committee first observes that from 19 August 1976 Canada had undertaken under article 2(1) and (2) of the Covenant to respect and ensure to all individuals within its territory and subject to its jurisdiction, the rights recognized in the Covenant without distinction of any kind such as sex, and to adopt the necessary measures to give effect to these rights. Further, under article 3, Canada undertook to ensure the equal right of men and women to the enjoyment of these rights. These undertakings apply also to the position of Sandra Lovelace. The Committee considers, however, that it is not necessary for the purposes of her communication to decide their extent in all respects. The full scope of the obligation of Canada to remove the effects or inequalities caused by the application of existing laws to past events, in particular as regards such matters as civil or personal status, does not have to be examined in the present case, for the reasons set out below.

13.1 The Committee considers that the essence of the present complaint concerns the continuing effect of the Indian Act, in denying Sandra Lovelace legal status as an Indian, in particular because she cannot for this reason claim a legal right to reside where she wishes to, on the Tobique Reserve. This fact persists after the entry into force of the Covenant, and its effects have to be examined, ... [T]he significant matter is her ... claim ... that "the major loss to a person ceasing to be an Indian is the loss of the cultural benefits of living in an Indian community, the emotional ties to home, family, friends and neighbours, and the loss of identity".

13.2 Although a number of provisions of the Covenant have been invoked by Sandra Lovelace, the Committee considers that the one which is most directly applicable to this complaint is article 27, which reads as follows:

> In those States in which ethnic, religious or linguistic minorities exist, persons belonging to such minorities shall not be denied the right, in community with the other members of their group, to enjoy their own culture, to profess and practise their own religion, or to use their own language.

. . .

14. The rights under article 27 of the Covenant have to be secured to "persons belonging" to the minority. At present Sandra Lovelace does not qualify as an Indian under Canadian legislation.... Persons who are born and brought up on a reserve, who have kept ties with their community and wish to maintain these ties must normally be considered as belonging to that minority within the meaning of the Covenant. Since Sandra Lovelace is ethnically a Maliseet Indian and has only been absent from her home reserve for a few years during the existence of her marriage, she is, in the opinion of the Committee, entitled to be regarded as "belonging" to this

minority and to claim the benefits of article 27 of the Covenant. The question whether these benefits have been denied to her, depends on how far they extend.

15. The right to live on a reserve is not as such guaranteed by article 27 of the Covenant. Moreover, the Indian Act does not interfere directly with the functions which are expressly mentioned in that article. However, in the opinion of the Committee the right of Sandra Lovelace to access to her native culture and language "in community with the other members" of her group, has in fact been, and continues to be interfered with, because there is no place outside the Tobique Reserve where such a community exists....

16. [T]he Committee is of the view that statutory restrictions affecting the right to residence on a reserve of a person belonging to the minority concerned, must have both a reasonable and objective justification and be consistent with the other provisions of the Covenant, read as a whole. Article 27 must be construed and applied in the light of the other provisions mentioned above ..., and also the provisions against discrimination, such as articles 2, 3 and 26 ... It is not necessary, however, to determine in any general manner which restrictions may be justified under the Covenant, in particular as a result of marriage, because the circumstances are special in the present case.

17. The case of Sandra Lovelace should be considered in light of the fact that her marriage to a non-Indian has broken up. It is natural that in such a situation she wishes to return to the environment in which she was born, particularly as after the dissolution of her marriage her main cultural attachment again was to the Maliseet band. Whatever may be the merits of the Indian Act in other respects, it does not seem to the Committee that to deny Sandra Lovelace the right to reside on the reserve is reasonable, or necessary to preserve the identity of the tribe. The Committee therefore concludes that to prevent her recognition as belonging to the band is an unjustifiable denial of her rights under article 27 of the Covenant, read in the context of the other provisions referred to.

18. In view of this finding, the Committee does not consider it necessary to examine whether the same facts also show separate breaches of the other rights invoked [including the right to non-discrimination].

Notes

1. The Human Rights Committee resolved Ms. Lovelace's claim in a manner that enabled it to avoid squarely confronting the question of how to balance her right not to be subjected to discrimination on the basis of sex and the cultural rights of other members of the Maliseet band. Had the Committee reached this question, how should it have resolved the conflict? Suppose that Ms. Lovelace were still married to her husband. How should the Human Rights Committee resolve her claim in this circumstance?

2.   Consider the application of Islamic law by a *salish*—a village council in Bangladesh—described in a 1993 report by Amnesty International. The report recounts the case of Shefali, a fourteen year-old girl who had been raped by a village elder. A *salish* comprising village elders and clergy was convened when Shefali became pregnant. The participating clergy decided that since there had been no witness to the intercourse, the elder could not be held responsible since, under Islamic law, four adult male Muslim witnesses of good repute need to have witnessed illicit intercourse to permit conviction for rape or adultery. While her rapist escaped punishment, Shefali, unable to prove that her pregnancy resulted from rape, was sentenced to 100 lashes in public for adultery. Her mother was given the same sentence for having accused the village elder of rape. See Amnesty International, Bangladesh, Taking the Law in Their Own Hands: The Village Salish, AI Index: ASA 13/12/93. If the practices of this *salish* were challenged as a breach of universal human rights, a strong version of cultural relativism would defend them as rooted in cultural values, while a strong version of universalism would condemn them as a violation of internationally-protected human rights. Does the approach advocated by Professor An–Na'im address this clash between the beliefs and practices of Shefali's community and the rights guaranteed by international law, and if so, how? How would this situation be assessed under the framework offered by Professor Sullivan?

3.   In the article excerpted at p. 392 above, Hope Lewis observes: "While a few Muslim religious leaders continue to promote the practice of FGS on religious grounds, historians suggest that FGS pre-dates Islam, and that its origins in other religious traditions are unclear." What weight, if any, should this observation be given if Professor Sullivan's balancing test were applied to evaluate a challenge to FGM/S in a country where the practice is justified in religious terms by Muslim leaders?

4.   In some circumstances, women's right to freedom from discrimination on the basis of sex might conflict with the internationally-protected right to freedom of expression. Radhika Coomaraswamy, the United Nations' Special Rapporteur on Violence Against Women, has taken the position that pornography has the endemic effect of perpetuating women's subordination. CEDAW's General Recommendation No. 19 similarly suggested that "the propagation of pornography and the depiction and other commercial exploitation of women as sexual objects, rather than as individuals ... contributes to gender-based violence." In this view, the law assuring women's human rights justifies at least some restrictions—if not outright suppression—of pornography. Yet such restrictions might conflict with the internationally-protected right to freedom of expression. How should this conflict be resolved? Would the answer to this question be different under the ICCPR and the European Convention? Cf. Part IV, Chapter 1, Section C.

5.   Traditional Jewish law (the halakha) apparently prohibits a husband from divorcing his wife without her consent, except perhaps in special circumstances, e.g., if she has committed adultery. In those special circumstances, the husband may even be required to divorce his wife, whether or not she consents. However, a woman has no corresponding right, because

sexual relations by the husband with a woman other than his wife were not prohibited in ancient Jewish law, which accepted bigamy for men (but not for women).

If a husband should proceed to divorce his wife because of her adultery as required by the halakha, he would presumably claim that this action is justified as an aspect of his "freedom, either individually or in community with others and in public or private, to manifest his religion or belief in worship, observance, practice or teaching." International Covenant on Civil and Political Rights, article 18(1). If, in parallel circumstances, a woman were denied the right to divorce her husband, would that be consistent with "the equal right of men and women to the enjoyment of all civil and political rights set forth in the present Covenant" (Article 3)?

6.   For a comprehensive treatment of issues relating to women's internationally-recognized human rights, see the four-volume Women and International Human Rights Law (Kelly D. Askin ed., 1999).

G.   HUMAN RIGHTS OF PERSONS BETWEEN STATES: INTERNATIONAL INSTRUMENTS RELATING TO REFUGEES

The two Covenants do not address a major problem of the second half of this century: the plight of refugees and internally displaced persons. The Universal Declaration recognizes the right of any individual "to leave any country, including his own," and the right "to seek and to enjoy in other countries asylum from persecution." UDHR arts. 13(2), 14(1). The Covenant on Civil and Political Rights restates the former right, but not the latter. ICCPR art. 12(2). States have been reluctant to assume obligations to grant residence rights to aliens, even those fleeing persecution.

As of 31 December 1998, the world had some 13 million refugees, and an estimated 17 million more persons "internally displaced" within their own country. U.S. Committee for Refugees, World Refugee Survey 1998 at 3, 6 (1999). Their condition is grave, and the condition of women refugees (the majority) especially so. Important measures for the sustenance, protection, and sometimes resettlement of refugees are carried on under the aegis of the UN High Commissioner for Refugees and non-governmental organizations.

Nearly half a century ago, the United Nations prepared a Convention Relating to the Status of Refugees. The Refugee Convention accorded important protections and economic-social benefits but only to refugees as narrowly defined and only in a State Party to the Convention to which the refugee was lawfully admitted. A refugee not lawfully admitted has one principal safeguard under the Convention, the right of *non-refoulement*, not to be expelled or returned to a territory where his or her life or freedom would be threatened (Art. 33). That has proved to be a crucial right, creating effectively a limited right of refuge, but it does not guarantee permanent asylum, and does not ensure the reluctantly tolerated refugee full enjoyment of the array of rights recognized by the Declaration and the Covenants.

The following cases illustrate the implementation of international refugee law in the United States. As the *Cardoza–Fonseca* decision explains, since 1968 the United States has been a party to the 1967 Protocol Relating to the Status of Refugees. The Protocol incorporates the substantive provisions of the 1951 Refugee Convention, but drops the geographical and temporal limitations in the definition of "refugee" in the Convention, which focused on postwar refugees in Europe. The Protocol does not, however, incorporate Article 38 of the Refugee Convention, which provides for resolution by the International Court of Justice of disputes between states over the interpretation or application of the Convention. Nor does either the Convention or the Protocol create a specialized international body with authority to give binding interpretations of its provisions.

This section turns first to the statutory framework of refugee law in the United States, including the difference between discretionary grants of asylum and mandatory compliance with the obligation of *non-refoulement*, and the accompanying variations in the burden of proof under U.S. law. Next, the section explores more deeply the governing definition of "refugee," including the requirement that what the refugee flees must be persecution on account of one of the five grounds enumerated in the Refugee Convention: race, religion, nationality, membership in a particular social group, or political opinion. As the *Kasinga* case illustrates, the failure of the Convention to expressly address gender-based persecution has complicated the interpretation of the "particular social group" category in recent years. Finally, the section turns to an area in which U.S. practice prompted international criticism in the 1990s, the extraterritorial applicability of the *non-refoulement* prohibition.

To clarify the administrative context of the cases that follow, it should be mentioned that most of the authority for enforcing the immigration laws in the United States is vested by statute in the Attorney General as head of the Department of Justice. Much of the enforcement is performed by the Immigration and Naturalization Service (INS), an agency within the Department of Justice, which has both prosecutorial and adjudicatory responsibilities. In addition, formal adjudicatory hearings are held by Immigration Judges, executive decisionmakers within the Department whose decisions may be appealed to the Board of Immigration Appeals (BIA), an appellate administrative tribunal. The decisions of the BIA may in turn be subject to judicial review in the federal courts in accordance with typical administrative law procedures.

Well–Founded Fear of Persecution and the Obligation on Non–Refoulement

Immigration and Naturalization Service v. Cardoza–Fonseca

Supreme Court of the United States, 1987.
480 U.S. 421.

■ JUSTICE STEVENS delivered the opinion of the Court.

Since 1980, the Immigration and Nationality Act has provided two methods through which an otherwise deportable alien who claims that he will be persecuted if deported can seek relief. Section 243(h) of the Act, 8 U.S.C. § 1253(h),* requires the Attorney General to withhold deportation of an alien who demonstrates that his "life or freedom would be threatened" on account of one of the listed factors if he is deported. In INS v. Stevic, 467 U.S. 407 (1984), we held that to qualify for this entitlement to withholding of deportation, an alien must demonstrate that "it is more likely than not that the alien would be subject to persecution" in the country to which he would be returned. The Refugee Act of 1980 also established a second type of broader relief. Section 208(a) of the Act, 8 U.S.C. § 1158(a), authorizes the Attorney General, in his discretion, to grant asylum to an alien who is unable or unwilling to return to his home country "because of persecution or a well-founded fear of persecution on account of race, religion, nationality, membership in a particular social group, or political opinion." § 101(a)(42), 8 U.S.C. § 1101(a)(42).

In *Stevic*, we rejected an alien's contention that the § 208(a) "well-founded fear" standard governs applications for withholding of deportation under § 243(h). Similarly, today we reject the Government's contention that the § 243(h) standard, which requires an alien to show that he is more likely than not to be subject to persecution, governs applications for asylum under § 208(a). Congress used different, broader language to define the term "refugee" as used in § 208(a) than it used to describe the class of aliens who have a right to withholding of deportation under § 243(h). The Act's establishment of a broad class of refugees who are eligible for a discretionary grant of asylum, and a narrower class of aliens who are given a statutory right not to be deported to the country where they are in danger, mirrors the provisions of the United Nations Protocol Relating to the Status of Refugees, which provided the motivation for the enactment of the Refugee Act of 1980. In addition, the legislative history of the 1980 Act makes it perfectly clear that Congress did not intend the class of aliens who qualify as refugees to be coextensive with the class who qualify for § 243(h) relief.

I

Respondent is a 38-year-old Nicaraguan citizen who entered the United States in 1979 as a visitor. After she remained in the United States longer than permitted, and failed to take advantage of the Immigration and Naturalization Service's (INS) offer of voluntary departure, the INS commenced deportation proceedings against her. Respondent conceded that she was in the country illegally, but requested withholding of deportation pursuant to § 243(h) and asylum as a refugee pursuant to § 208(a).

To support her request under § 243(h), respondent attempted to show that if she were returned to Nicaragua her "life or freedom would be

---

* [This provision has subsequently been recodified as section 241(b)(3) of the Act, 8 U.S.C. § 1231(b)(3).—Editors' note.]

threatened" on account of her political views; to support her request under § 208(a), she attempted to show that she had a "well-founded fear of persecution" upon her return. The evidence supporting both claims related primarily to the activities of respondent's brother who had been tortured and imprisoned because of his political activities in Nicaragua. Both respondent and her brother testified that they believed the Sandinistas knew that the two of them had fled Nicaragua together and that even though she had not been active politically herself, she would be interrogated about her brother's whereabouts and activities. Respondent also testified that because of her brother's status, her own political opposition to the Sandinistas would be brought to that government's attention. Based on these facts, respondent claimed that she would be tortured if forced to return.

The Immigration Judge applied the same standard in evaluating respondent's claim for withholding of deportation under § 243(h) as he did in evaluating her application for asylum under § 208(a). He found that she had not established "a clear probability of persecution" and therefore was not entitled to either form of relief. . . .

II

The Refugee Act of 1980 established a new statutory procedure for granting asylum to refugees. The 1980 Act added a new § 208(a) to the Immigration and Nationality Act of 1952, reading as follows:

> The Attorney General shall establish a procedure for an alien physically present in the United States or at a land border or port of entry, irrespective of such alien's status, to apply for asylum, and the alien may be granted asylum in the discretion of the Attorney General if the Attorney General determines that such alien is a refugee within the meaning of section 1101(a)(42)(A) of this title.

Under this section, eligibility for asylum depends entirely on the Attorney General's determination that an alien is a "refugee," as that term is defined in § 101(a)(42), which was also added to the Act in 1980. That section provides:

> The term "refugee" means (A) any person who is outside any country of such person's nationality or, in the case of a person having no nationality, is outside any country in which such person last habitually resided, and who is unable or unwilling to return to, and is unable or unwilling to avail himself or herself of the protection of, that country because of persecution or a well-founded fear of persecution on account of race, religion, nationality, membership in a particular social group, or political opinion. . . .

Thus, the "persecution or well-founded fear of persecution" standard governs the Attorney General's determination whether an alien is eligible for asylum.

In addition to establishing a statutory asylum process, the 1980 Act amended the withholding of deportation provision,[6] § 243(h). Prior to 1968, the Attorney General had discretion whether to grant withholding of deportation to aliens under § 243(h). In 1968, however, the United States agreed to comply with the substantive provisions of Articles 2 through 34 of the 1951 United Nations Convention Relating to the Status of Refugees. Article 33.1 of the Convention, which is the counterpart of § 243(h) of our statute, imposed a mandatory duty on contracting States not to return an alien to a country where his "life or freedom would be threatened" on account of one of the enumerated reasons.[7] Thus, although § 243(h) itself did not constrain the Attorney General's discretion after 1968, presumably he honored the dictates of the United Nations Convention.[8] In any event, the 1980 Act removed the Attorney General's discretion in § 243(h) proceedings....

[T]he language Congress used to describe the two standards conveys very different meanings. The "would be threatened" language of § 243(h) has no subjective component, but instead requires the alien to establish by objective evidence that it is more likely than not that he or she will be subject to persecution upon deportation. In contrast, the reference to "fear" in the § 208(a) standard obviously makes the eligibility determination turn to some extent on the subjective mental state of the alien....

That the fear must be "well-founded" does not alter the obvious focus on the individual's subjective beliefs, nor does it transform the standard into a "more likely than not" one. One can certainly have a well-founded fear of an event happening when there is less than a 50% chance of the occurrence taking place. As one leading authority has pointed out:

> Let us . . . presume that it is known that in the applicant's country of origin every tenth adult male person is either put to death or sent to some remote labor camp. . . . In such a case it would be only too apparent that anyone who has managed to escape from the country in

---

6. Asylum and withholding of deportation are two distinct forms of relief. First, as we have mentioned, there is no entitlement to asylum; it is only granted to eligible refugees pursuant to the Attorney General's discretion. Once granted, however, asylum affords broader benefits. As the BIA explained in the context of an applicant from Afghanistan who was granted § 243(h) relief but was denied asylum:

> Section 243(h) relief is "country specific" and accordingly, the applicant here would be presently protected from deportation to Afghanistan pursuant to section 243(h). But that section would not prevent his exclusion and deportation to Pakistan or any other hospitable country under section 237(a) if that country will accept him. In contrast, asylum is a greater form of relief. When granted asylum the alien may be eligible for adjust-

ment of status to that of a lawful permanent resident pursuant to section 209 of the Act, after residing here one year, subject to numerical limitations and the applicable regulations.

7. Article 33.1 of the Convention provides: "No Contracting State shall expel or return ('refouler') a refugee in any manner whatsoever to the frontiers of territories where his life or freedom would be threatened on account of his race, religion, nationality, membership of a particular social group or political opinion."

8. While the Protocol constrained the Attorney General with respect to § 243(h) between 1968 and 1980, the Protocol does not *require* the granting of asylum to anyone, and hence does not subject the Attorney General to a similar constraint with respect to his discretion under § 208(a).

question will have "well-founded fear of being persecuted" upon his eventual return.

1 A. Grahl–Madsen, The Status of Refugees in International Law 180 (1966).

. . .

III

The message conveyed by the plain language of the Act is confirmed by an examination of its history. . . .

. . . Adoption of the INS's argument that the term "well-founded fear" requires a showing of clear probability of persecution would clearly do violence to Congress' intent that the standard for admission under § 207 be no different than the one previously applied under § 203(a)(7).

If one thing is clear from the legislative history of the new definition of "refugee," and indeed the entire 1980 Act, it is that one of Congress' primary purposes was to bring United States refugee law into conformance with the 1967 United Nations Protocol Relating to the Status of Refugees, to which the United States acceded in 1968. Indeed, the definition of "refugee" that Congress adopted, is virtually identical to the one prescribed by Article 1(2) of the Convention . . .

The origin of the Protocol's definition of "refugee" is found in the 1946 Constitution of the International Refugee Organization (IRO). The IRO defined a "refugee" as a person who had a "valid objection" to returning to his country of nationality, and specified that "fear, based on reasonable grounds of persecution because of race, religion, nationality, or political opinions . . ." constituted a valid objection. The term was then incorporated in the United Nations Convention Relating to the Status of Refugees. The Committee that drafted the provision explained that "[t]he expression 'well-founded fear of being the victim of persecution . . .' means that a person has either been actually a victim of persecution or can show good reason why he fears persecution." The 1967 Protocol incorporated the "well-founded fear" test, without modification. The standard, as it has been consistently understood by those who drafted it, as well as those drafting the documents that adopted it, certainly does not require an alien to show that it is more likely than not that he will be persecuted in order to be classified as a "refugee."[21]

In interpreting the Protocol's definition of "refugee" we are further guided by the analysis set forth in the Office of the United Nations High Commissioner for Refugees, Handbook on Procedures and Criteria for Determining Refugee Status (Geneva, 1979).[22] The Handbook explains that "[i]n general, the applicant's fear should be considered well-founded if he can establish, to a reasonable degree, that his continued stay in his country of origin has become intolerable to him for the reasons stated in the

---

21. Although the United States has never been party to the 1951 Convention, it is a party to the Protocol, which incorporates the Convention's definition in relevant part.

22. We do not suggest, of course, that the explanation in the U.N. Handbook has the force of law or in any way binds the INS with reference to the asylum provisions of

definition, or would for the same reasons be intolerable if he returned there." . . .

In *Stevic*, we dealt with the issue of withholding of deportation, or nonrefoulement, under § 243(h). This provision corresponds to Article 33.1 of the Convention. Significantly though, Article 33.1 does not extend this right to everyone who meets the definition of "refugee." Rather, it provides that "[n]o Contracting State shall expel or return ('refouler') a refugee in any manner whatsoever to the frontiers or territories where his life or freedom would be threatened on account of his race, religion, nationality, membership or a particular social group or political opinion." Thus, Article 33.1 requires that an applicant satisfy two burdens: first, that he or she be a "refugee," i.e., prove at least a "well-founded fear of persecution"; second, that the "refugee" show that his or her life or freedom "would be threatened" if deported. Section 243(h)'s imposition of a "would be threatened" requirement is entirely consistent with the United States' obligations under the Protocol.

Section 208(a), by contrast, is a discretionary mechanism which gives the Attorney General the *authority* to grant the broader relief of asylum to refugees. As such, it does not correspond to Article 33 of the Convention, but instead corresponds to Article 34. That Article provides that the contracting States "shall as far as possible facilitate the assimilation and naturalization of refugees. . . ." Like § 208(a), the provision is precatory; it does not require the implementing authority actually to grant asylum to all those who are eligible. Also like § 208(a), an alien must only show that he or she is a "refugee" to establish eligibility for relief. No further showing that he or she "would be" persecuted is required.

Thus, as made binding on the United States through the Protocol, Article 34 provides for a precatory, or discretionary, benefit for the entire class of persons who qualify as "refugees," whereas Article 33.1 provides an entitlement for the subcategory that "would be threatened" with persecution upon their return. This precise distinction between the broad class of refugees and the subcategory entitled to § 243(h) relief is plainly revealed in the 1980 Act. . . .

[Concurring and dissenting opinions omitted.]

The Concept of "Persecution"

Immigration and Naturalization Service v. Elias–Zacarias

Supreme Court of the United States, 1992.
502 U.S. 478.

■ JUSTICE SCALIA delivered the opinion of the Court.

§ 208(a). Indeed, the Handbook itself disclaims such force, explaining that "the determination of refugee status under the 1951 Convention and the 1967 Protocol . . . is incumbent upon the Contracting State in whose territory the refugee finds himself."

Nonetheless, the Handbook provides significant guidance in construing the Protocol, to which Congress sought to conform. It has been widely considered useful in giving content to the obligations that the Protocol establishes.

The principal question presented by this case is whether a guerrilla organization's attempt to coerce a person into performing military service *necessarily* constitutes "persecution on account of ... political opinion" under § 101(a)(42) of the Immigration and Nationality Act.

I

Respondent Elias–Zacarias, a native of Guatemala, was apprehended in July 1987 for entering the United States without inspection. In deportation proceedings brought by petitioner Immigration and Naturalization Service (INS), Elias–Zacarias conceded his deportability but requested asylum and withholding of deportation.

The Immigration Judge summarized Elias–Zacarias' testimony as follows:

> [A]round the end of January in 1987 [when Elias–Zacarias was 18], two armed, uniformed guerrillas with handkerchiefs covering part of their faces came to his home. Only he and his parents were there.... [T]he guerrillas asked his parents and himself to join with them, but they all refused. The guerrillas asked them why and told them that they would be back, and that they should think it over about joining them.

> [Elias–Zacarias] did not want to join the guerrillas because the guerrillas are against the government and he was afraid that the government would retaliate against him and his family if he did join the guerrillas. [H]e left Guatemala at the end of March [1987] ... because he was afraid that the guerrillas would return.

The Immigration Judge understood from this testimony that Elias–Zacarias' request for asylum and for withholding of deportation was "based on this one attempted recruitment by the guerrillas." She concluded that Elias–Zacarias had failed to demonstrate persecution or a well-founded fear of persecution on account of race, religion, nationality, membership in a particular social group, or political opinion, and was not eligible for asylum. She further concluded that he did not qualify for withholding of deportation....

II

Section 208(a) of the Immigration and Nationality Act, authorizes the Attorney General, in his discretion, to grant asylum to an alien who is a "refugee" as defined in the Act, i.e., an alien who is unable or unwilling to return to his home country "because of persecution or a well-founded fear of persecution on account of race, religion, nationality, membership in a particular social group, or political opinion." The BIA's determination that Elias–Zacarias was not eligible for asylum must be upheld if "supported by reasonable, substantial, and probative evidence on the record considered as a whole." 8 U.S.C. § 1105a(a)(4). It can be reversed only if the evidence presented by Elias–Zacarias was such that a reasonable factfinder would have to conclude that the requisite fear of persecution existed.[1]

The Court of Appeals found reversal warranted. In its view, a guerrilla organization's attempt to conscript a person into its military forces necessarily constitutes "persecution on account of ... political opinion," because "the person resisting forced recruitment is expressing a political opinion hostile to the persecutor and because the persecutors' motive in carrying out the kidnapping is political." The first half of this seems to us untrue, and the second half irrelevant.

Even a person who supports a guerrilla movement might resist recruitment for a variety of reasons—fear of combat, a desire to remain with one's family and friends, a desire to earn a better living in civilian life, to mention only a few. The record in the present case not only failed to show a political motive on Elias–Zacarias' part; it showed the opposite. He testified that he refused to join the guerrillas because he was afraid that the government would retaliate against him and his family if he did so. Nor is there any indication (assuming, *arguendo*, it would suffice) that the guerrillas erroneously *believed* that Elias–Zacarias' refusal was politically based.

As for the Court of Appeals' conclusion that the guerrillas' "motive in carrying out the kidnapping is political": It apparently meant by this that the guerrillas seek to fill their ranks in order to carry on their war against the government and pursue their political goals. But that does not render the forced recruitment "persecution on account of ... political opinion." In construing statutes, "we must, of course, start with the assumption that the legislative purpose is expressed by the ordinary meaning of the words used." The ordinary meaning of the phrase "persecution on account of ... political opinion" in § 101(a)(42) is persecution on account of the victim's political opinion, not the persecutor's. If a Nazi regime persecutes Jews, it is not, within the ordinary meaning of language, engaging in persecution on account of political opinion; and if a fundamentalist Moslem regime persecutes democrats, it is not engaging in persecution on account of religion. Thus, the mere existence of a generalized "political" motive underlying the guerrillas' forced recruitment is inadequate to establish (and, indeed, goes far to refute) the proposition that Elias–Zacarias fears persecution *on account of* political opinion, as § 101(a)(42) requires.

Elias–Zacarias appears to argue that not taking sides with any political faction is itself the affirmative expression of a political opinion. That seems to us not ordinarily so, since we do not agree with the dissent that only a "narrow, grudging construction of the concept of 'political opinion,'" would distinguish it from such quite different concepts as indifference,

---

1. Quite beside the point, therefore, is the dissent's assertion that "the record in this case is more than adequate to *support the conclusion* that this respondent's refusal [to join the guerrillas] was a form of expressive conduct that constituted the statement of a 'political opinion.'" To reverse the BIA finding we must find that the evidence not only *supports* that conclusion, but *compels* it—and also compels the further conclusion that Elias–Zacarias had a well-founded fear that the guerrillas would persecute him *because* of that political opinion.

indecisiveness and risk-averseness. But we need not decide whether the evidence compels the conclusion that Elias–Zacarias held a political opinion. Even if it does, Elias–Zacarias still has to establish that the record also compels the conclusion that he has a "well-founded fear" that the guerrillas will persecute him *because of* that political opinion, rather than because of his refusal to fight with them. He has not done so with the degree of clarity necessary to permit reversal of a BIA finding to the contrary; indeed, he has not done so at all.[2]

Elias–Zacarias objects that he cannot be expected to provide direct proof of his persecutors' motives. We do not require that. But since the statute makes motive critical, he must provide *some* evidence of it, direct or circumstantial. And if he seeks to obtain judicial reversal of the BIA's determination, he must show that the evidence he presented was so compelling that no reasonable factfinder could fail to find the requisite fear of persecution. That he has not done.

The BIA's determination should therefore have been upheld in all respects, and we reverse the Court of Appeals' judgment to the contrary.

It is so ordered.

■ JUSTICE STEVENS, with whom JUSTICE BLACKMUN and JUSTICE O'CONNOR join, dissenting.

. . . It is undisputed that respondent has a well-founded fear that he will be harmed, if not killed, if he returns to Guatemala. It is also undisputed that the cause of that harm, if it should occur, is the guerrilla organization's displeasure with his refusal to join them in their armed insurrection against the government. The question of law that the case presents is whether respondent's well-founded fear is a "fear of persecution on account of . . . political opinion" within the meaning of § 101(a)(42) of the Immigration and Nationality Act. . . .

Today the Court holds that respondent's fear of persecution is not "on account of . . . political opinion" for two reasons. First, he failed to prove that his refusal to join the guerrillas was politically motivated; indeed, he testified that he was at least in part motivated by a fear that government forces would retaliate against him or his family if he joined the guerrillas. Second, he failed to prove that his persecutors' motives were political. In

---

2. The dissent misdescribes the record on this point in several respects. For example, it exaggerates the "well-foundedness" of whatever fear Elias–Zacarias possesses, by progressively transforming his testimony that he was afraid the guerrillas would " 'take me or kill me,' " into, first, "the guerrillas' *implied threat* to 'take' him or to 'kill' him," and, then, into the flat assertion that the guerrillas "*responded by threatening* to 'take' or to 'kill' him." The dissent also erroneously describes it as "undisputed" that the cause of the harm Elias–Zacarias fears, if that harm should occur, will be "the guerrilla organization's displeasure with his refusal to join them in their armed insurrection against the government." The record shows no such concession by the INS, and all Elias–Zacarias said on the point was that he feared being taken or killed by the guerrillas. It is quite plausible, indeed likely, that the taking would be engaged in by the guerrillas in order to augment their troops rather than show their displeasure; and the killing he feared might well be a killing in the course of resisting being taken.

particular, the Court holds that the persecutors' implicit threat to retaliate against respondent "because of his refusal to fight with them," is not persecution on account of political opinion. I disagree with both parts of the Court's reasoning....

A political opinion can be expressed negatively as well as affirmatively. A refusal to support a cause—by staying home on election day, by refusing to take an oath of allegiance, or by refusing to step forward at an induction center—can express a political opinion as effectively as an affirmative statement or affirmative conduct. Even if the refusal is motivated by nothing more than a simple desire to continue living an ordinary life with one's family, it is the kind of political expression that the asylum provisions of the statute were intended to protect....

[The decisionmaking process] should resolve any doubts concerning the political character of an alien's refusal to take arms against a legitimate government in favor of the alien. In my opinion, the record in this case is more than adequate to support the conclusion that this respondent's refusal was a form of expressive conduct that constituted the statement of a "political opinion" within the meaning of § 208(a).[5] ...

It follows as night follows day that the guerrillas' implied threat to "take" him or to "kill" him if he did not change his position constituted threatened persecution "on account of" that political opinion.... [T]he statute does not require that an applicant for asylum prove exactly why his persecutors would act against him; it only requires him to show that he has a "well-founded fear of persecution on account of ... political opinion." As we recognized in INS v. Cardoza Fonseca, the applicant meets this burden if he shows that there is a " 'reasonable possibility' " that he will be persecuted on account of his political opinion. Because respondent expressed a political opinion by refusing to join the guerrillas, and they responded by threatening to "take" or to "kill" him if he did not change his mind, his fear that the guerrillas will persecute him on account of his political opinion is well founded.

In re Kasinga

Board of Immigration Appeals, U.S. Department of Justice (1996).
1996 WL 379826 (Int. Dec. 3278).

■ SCHMIDT, CHAIRMAN:

... A fundamental issue before us is whether the practice of female genital mutilation ("FGM") can be the basis for a grant of asylum.... We

---

5. Here, respondent not only engaged in expressive conduct by refusing to join the guerrilla organization but also explained that he did so "[b]ecause they see very well, that if you join the guerrillas ... then you are against the government. You are against the government and if you join them then it is to die there. And, then the government is against you and against your family." Respondent thus expressed the political view that he was for the government and against the guerrillas. The statute speaks simply in terms of a political opinion and does not require that the view be well developed or elegantly expressed.

find that FGM can be a basis for asylum.... In deciding this case, we decline to speculate on, or establish rules for, cases that are not before us....

The applicant is a 19–year old native and citizen of Togo. She attended 2 years of high school. She is a member of the Tchamba–Kunsuntu Tribe of northern Togo. She testified that young women of her tribe normally undergo FGM at age 15. However, she did not because she initially was protected from FGM by her influential, but now deceased, father.

The applicant stated that upon her father's death in 1993, under tribal custom her aunt, her father's sister, became the primary authority figure in the family. The applicant's mother was driven from the family home, left Togo, and went to live with her family in Benin....

The applicant further testified that her aunt forced her into a polygamous marriage in October 1994, when she was 17. The husband selected by her aunt was 45 years old and had three other wives at the time of marriage. The applicant testified that, under tribal custom, her aunt and her husband planned to force her to submit to FGM before the marriage was consummated.

The applicant testified that she feared imminent mutilation. With the help of her older sister, she fled Togo....

· · ·

... [U]pon arrival at Newark International Airport on December 17, 1994, she immediately requested asylum. She remained in detention by the Immigration and Naturalization Service ("INS") until April 1996....

· · ·

The applicant testified that she could not find protection anywhere in Togo. She stated that Togo is a very small country and her husband and aunt, with the help of the police, could locate her anywhere she went. She also stated that her husband is well known in Togo and is a friend of the police....

Description of FGM

According to the applicants testimony, the FGM practiced by her tribe, the Tchamba–Kunsuntu, is of an extreme type involving cutting the genitalia with knives, extensive bleeding, and a 40–day recovery period. The background materials confirm that the FGM practiced in some African countries, such as Togo, is of an extreme nature causing permanent damage, and not just a minor form of genital ritual. See, e.g., Nahid Toubia, Female Genital Mutilation: A Call for Global Action 9, 24–25 (Gloria Jacobs ed., Women Ink. 1993).

The record material establishes that FGM in its extreme forms is a practice in which portions of the female genitalia are cut away. In some cases, the vagina is sutured partially closed. This practice clearly inflicts harm or suffering upon the girl or woman who undergoes it.

FGM is extremely painful and at least temporarily incapacitating. It permanently disfigures the female genitalia. FGM exposes the girl or woman to the risk of serious, potentially life-threatening complications. These include, among others, bleeding, infection, urine retention, stress, shock, psychological trauma, and damage to the urethra and anus. It can result in permanent loss of genital sensation and can adversely affect sexual and erotic functions.

The *FGM Alert*, compiled and distributed by the INS Resource Information Center, notes that "few African countries have officially condemned female genital mutilation and still fewer have enacted legislation against the practice." Further, according to the *FGM Alert*, even in those few African countries where legislative efforts have been made, they are usually ineffective to protect women against FGM. The *FGM Alert* notes that "it remains practically true that [African] women have little legal recourse and may face threats to their freedom, threats or acts of physical violence, or social ostracization for refusing to undergo this harmful traditional practice or attempting to protect their female children." Togo is not listed in the *FGM Alert* as among the African countries that have made even minimal efforts to protect women from FGM....

FGM as Persecution

... While a number of descriptions of persecution have been formulated in our past decisions, we have recognized that persecution can consist of the infliction of harm or suffering by a government, or persons a government is unwilling or able to control, to overcome a characteristic of the victim. See *Matter of Acosta*, 19 I & N Dec. 211, 222–23 (BIA 1985), *modified on other grounds*, *Matter of Mogharrabi*, 19 I & N Dec. 439 (BIA 1987). The "seeking to overcome" formulation has its antecedents in concepts of persecution that predate the Refugee Act of 1980 [which incorporates the language of the Refugee Convention].

As observed by the INS, many of our past cases involved actors who had a subjective intent to punish their victims. However, this subjective "punitive" or "malignant" intent is not required for harm to constitute persecution.

Our characterization of FGM as persecution is consistent with our past definitions of that term. We therefore reach the conclusion that FGM can be persecution....

Social Group

To be a basis for a grant of asylum, persecution must relate to one of five categories described in section 101(a)(42)(A) of the Act. The parties agree that the relevant category in this case is "particular social group." Each party has advanced several formulations of the "particular social group" at issue in this case. However, each party urges the Board to adopt only that definition of social group necessary to decide this individual case.

In the context of this case, we find the particular group to be the following: Young women of the Tchamba–Kunsuntu Tribe who have not had FGM, as practiced by that tribe, and who oppose the practice. . . .

. . .

In accordance with *Acosta*, the particular social group is defined by common characteristics that members of the group either cannot change, or should not be required to change because such characteristics are fundamental to their individual identities. The characteristics of being a "young woman" and a "member of the Tchamba–Kunsuntu Tribe" cannot be changed. The characteristic of having intact genitalia is one that is so fundamental to the individual identity of a young woman that she should not be required to change it. . . .

"On Account of"

To be eligible for asylum, the applicant must establish that her well-founded fear of persecution is "on account of" one of the five grounds specified in the Act, here her membership in a "particular social group."

Both parties have advanced, and the background materials support, the proposition that there is no legitimate reason for FGM. Group Exhibit 4 contains materials showing that the practice has been condemned by such groups as the United Nations, the International Federation of Gynecology and Obstetrics, the Council on Scientific Affairs, the World Health Organization, the International Medical Association, and the American Medical Association.

Record materials state that FGM "has been used to control woman's sexuality," *FGM Alert*, supra, at 4. It is also characterized as a form of "sexual oppression" that is "based on the manipulation of women's sexuality in order to assure male dominance and exploitation." During oral argument before us, the INS General Counsel agreed with the latter characterization. He also stated that the practice is a "severe bodily invasion" that should be regarded as meeting the asylum standard even if done with "subjectively benign intent."

We agree with the parties that, as described and documented in this record, FGM is practiced, at least in some significant part, to overcome sexual characteristics of young women of the tribe who have not been, and do not wish to be, subjected to FGM. We therefore find that the persecution the applicant fears in Togo is "on account of" her status as a member of the defined social group.

. . .

The applicant has a well-founded fear of persecution in the form of FGM if returned to Togo. The persecution she fears is on account of her membership in a particular social group consisting of young women of the Tchamba–Kunsuntu tribe who [have not had] FGM, as practiced by that tribe, and who oppose the practice. Her fear of persecution is country-wide. We exercise our discretion in her favor, and we grant her asylum. . . .

■ FILPPU, BOARD MEMBER, concurring:

... The Service points out that it is "estimated that over eighty million females have been subjected to FGM." It further notes that there is "no indication" that "Congress considered application of [the asylum laws] to broad cultural practices of the type involved here." The Service proceeds to argue that the "underlying purposes of the asylum system ... are unavoidably in tension" in both providing protection for those seriously in jeopardy and in maintaining broad overall governmental control over immigration. The Service further argues that "the Board's interpretation in this case must assure protection for those most at risk of the harms covered by the statute, but it cannot simply grant asylum to all who might be subjected to a practice deemed objectionable or a violation of a person's human rights." It is from these underpinnings that the Service argues that the class of FGM victims who may be eligible for asylum "does not consist of all women who come from the parts of the world where FGM is practiced, nor of all who have been subjected to it in the past." ...

The Board certainly is not oblivious to immigration policy considerations in the disposition of cases falling within our jurisdiction.... The Service should not, however, expect the Board to endorse a significant new framework for assessing asylum claims in the context of a single novel case, especially when that framework seems intended primarily to address cases that are not in fact before the Board yet.

■ ROSENBERG, BOARD MEMBER, concurring:

... There is nothing about a social group definition based upon gender that requires us to treat it as either an aberration, or as an unanticipated development requiring a new standard....

Unlike requests for asylum premised upon political opinion, social group claims, like those involving race, ethnicity, or religion, are status based and do not necessarily require a showing of the presence of an individual's opinions or activities which spurs the persecutor's wrath or otherwise motivates the harm or persecution.... Consequently, while not inaccurate, it is surplusage to define the social group in this case as including as an element the applicant's opposition to the practice of female genital mutilation....

The only distinguishing characteristic about this case that I can perceive to set it apart from others we have already decided is that it involves a woman. Reliance upon such a distinction to support a separate category for treatment of women's asylum claims, to my mind, would be impermissible. Here, the applicant is a member of a group—girls and women of a given tribe, some perhaps of marriageable age, whose members are routinely subjected to the harm which the majority finds to constitute persecution. The applicant's opposition (which happens to be present in this case) or the lack of it, is neither determinative, nor necessary to define the social group in accordance with the statutory language....

Notes

1. The Universal Declaration proclaims the right to seek and to enjoy asylum from persecution. The Refugee Convention, as modified by its 1967

Protocol, defines refugees as those persons unable or unwilling to return to their country because of persecution or a well-founded fear of persecution on account of race, religion, nationality, membership in a particular social group, or political opinion. Does this list include all the conceivable types of persecution from which someone might seek asylum? Does the language of the Refugee Convention definition capture the common understanding of the term refugee?

The Refugee Convention definition also requires the refugee to be a person who "is outside the country of his nationality ... or who, not having a nationality [is] outside the country of his former habitual residence." As a result, this definition excludes "internally displaced persons" who have been forced to flee within their own country but have not crossed an international border. The services of the UN High Commissioner for Refugees have also been extended to internally displaced persons, but their protection raises additional problems because they remain in the territory of the state that is unwilling or unable to protect them. See, e.g., Guy S. Goodwin–Gill, The Refugee in International Law 264–68 (2d ed. 1996).

2.   Did the Supreme Court hold that Elias–Zacarias was not a refugee, or only that the administrative agency did not act unreasonably in concluding that Elias–Zacarias had not proven that he was a refugee? What further evidence could he have provided that would have carried his burden of proof? Testimony of the guerrilla leaders? Internal documents of the guerrilla organization? Evidence about more fully articulated threats made against others? Reports of human rights organizations, or of the U.S. State Department?

Assuming that Elias–Zacarias is not a refugee within the meaning of the Refugee Convention, but merely someone facing death at the hands of one or both factions in a civil war, is he less in need of protection than an actual refugee?

3.   The *Kasinga* decision of the Board of Immigration Appeals reflects an important trend in the 1990s toward increased protection for women refugees. That trend includes greater sensitivity to forms of persecution directed against women on account of race, religion, nationality or political opinion. It also includes recognition of some forms of gender-based persecution under the rubric of persecution on account of membership in a particular social group.

Why does the BIA conclude that female genital mutilation constitutes "persecution"? Why is the relevant social group so narrowly defined? Given that narrow definition, in what sense does the mistreatment from which Ms. Kasinga fled constitute persecution "on account of" her membership in that social group?

Does the Refugee Convention entitle every woman in Africa who objects to being subjected to FGM to come to the United States? To remain in the United States if she can somehow get there?

4.   The Refugee Convention is not the only human rights treaty imposing *non-refoulement* obligations. For example, Article 22(8) of the American

Convention on Human Rights prohibits *refoulement* in terms similar to those of the Refugee Convention. Article 3 of the Convention against Torture and Other Cruel, Inhuman or Degrading Treatment or Punishment expressly provides that "No State Party shall expel, return ('refouler') or extradite a person to another State where there are substantial grounds for believing that he would be in danger of being subjected to torture." Moreover, some provisions of some other human rights treaties have been interpreted as including implied prohibitions against *refoulement*. See, e.g., *Soering v. United Kingdom*, (construing art. 3 of the European Convention for the Protection of Human Rights and Fundamental Freedoms), infra Part IV, Chapter 1(A); *Kindler v. Canada*, (construing art. 7 of the ICCPR), infra p. 913. The Organization of African Unity sponsored the 1969 Convention on the Specific Aspects of Refugee Problems in Africa, 1000 U.N.T.S. 46, which includes a *non-refoulement* guarantee for refugees who are threatened not only on one of the five Refugee Convention grounds, but also as a result of "external aggression, occupation, foreign domination or events seriously disturbing public order."

5.   The U.S. Supreme Court has never perceived the obligation of *non-refoulement* as constitutionally mandated. One contributing factor to the absence of case law imposing a constitutional requirement of *non-refoulement* is the Supreme Court's extraordinary deference to congressional power over immigration, discussed in Part II, pp. 232–235 supra. Should Congress interpret the Due Process Clause as prohibiting the return of refugees to a country where their lives or freedom is threatened?

6.   Suggestions for further reading. On international refugee law generally, see Guy S. Goodwin–Gill, The Refugee in International Law (2d ed. 1996); James C. Hathaway, The Law of Refugee Status (1991). On United States refugee law, see Thomas Alexander Aleinikoff, David A. Martin and Hiroshi Motomura, Immigration and Citizenship: Process and Policy (4th ed. 1998); Deborah E. Anker, The Law of Asylum in the United States (4th ed. 1998); Stephen H. Legomsky, Immigration and Refugee Law and Policy (2d ed. 1997); Karen Musalo, Jennifer Moore and Richard Boswell, Refugee Law and Policy (1997). On women refugees, see *Special Issue: UNHCR Symposium on Gender–Based Persecution*, 9 Int'l J. Refugee L. 1 (Autumn 1997); Deborah Anker, Lauren Gilbert and Nancy Kelly, *Women Whose Governments Are Unable or Unwilling to Provide Reasonable Protection from Domestic Violence May Qualify as Refugees Under United States Asylum Law*, 11 Geo. Immig. L. J. 709 (1997); Audrey Macklin, *Refugee Women and the Imperative of Categories*, 17 Hum. Rts. Q. 214 (1995).

The Territorial Scope of the Non–Refoulement Obligation

Sale v. Haitian Centers Council, Inc.

Supreme Court of the United States, 1993.
509 U.S. 155.

■ JUSTICE STEVENS delivered the opinion of the Court.

The President has directed the Coast Guard to intercept vessels illegally transporting passengers from Haiti to the United States and to return those passengers to Haiti without first determining whether they may qualify as refugees. The question presented in this case is whether such forced repatriation, "authorized to be undertaken only beyond the territorial sea of the United States," violates § 243(h)(1) of the Immigration and Nationality Act of 1952 (INA or Act). We hold that neither § 243(h) nor Article 33 of the United Nations Protocol Relating to the Status of Refugees applies to action taken by the Coast Guard on the high seas.

. . .

On September 23, 1981, the United States and the Republic of Haiti entered into an agreement authorizing the United States Coast Guard to intercept vessels engaged in the illegal transportation of undocumented aliens to our shores. While the parties agreed to prosecute "illegal traffickers," the Haitian Government also guaranteed that its repatriated citizens would not be punished for their illegal departure. The agreement also established that the United States Government would not return any passengers "whom the United States authorities determine[d] to qualify for refugee status."

. . .

On September 30, 1991, a group of military leaders displaced the government of Jean Bertrand Aristide, the first democratically elected president in Haitian history. As the District Court stated in an uncontested finding of fact, since the military coup "hundreds of Haitians have been killed, tortured, detained without a warrant, or subjected to violence and the destruction of their property because of their political beliefs. Thousands have been forced into hiding." Following the coup the Coast Guard suspended repatriations for a period of several weeks, and the United States imposed economic sanctions on Haiti.

On November 18, 1991, the Coast Guard announced that it would resume the program of interdiction and forced repatriation.... During the six months after October 1991, the Coast Guard interdicted over 34,000 Haitians. [T]he Department of Defense established temporary facilities at the United States Naval Base in Guantanamo, Cuba, to accommodate them during the screening process.... On May 22, 1992, the United States Navy determined that no additional migrants could safely be accommodated at Guantanamo.

[The Government] had to choose between allowing Haitians into the United States for the screening process or repatriating them without giving them any opportunity to establish their qualifications as refugees. In the judgment of the President's advisors, the first choice not only would have defeated the original purpose of the program (controlling illegal immigration), but also would have impeded diplomatic efforts to restore democratic government in Haiti and would have posed a life-threatening danger to thousands of persons embarking on long voyages in dangerous craft. The second choice would have advanced those policies but deprived the fleeing Haitians of any screening process at a time when a significant minority of them were being screened in.

On May 23, 1992, President Bush adopted the second choice. We must decide ... whether Executive Order No. 12807, 57 Fed.Reg. 23133 (1992), which reflects and implements [that choice], is consistent with § 243(h) of the INA ...

. . .

Both parties argue that the plain language of § 243(h)(1) is dispositive. It reads as follows:

> "The Attorney General shall not deport or return any alien (other than an alien described in section 1251(a)(4)(D) of this title) to a country if the Attorney General determines that such alien's life or freedom would be threatened in such country on account of race, religion, nationality, membership in a particular social group, or political opinion."

Respondents emphasize the words "any alien" and "return"; neither term is limited to aliens within the United States. . . . Respondents also contend that the 1980 amendment deleting the words "within the United States" from the prior text of § 243(h), ..., obviously gave the statute an extraterritorial effect. This change, they further argue, was required in order to conform the statute to the text of Article 33.1 of the Convention, which they find as unambiguous as the present statutory text.

Petitioners' response is that a fair reading of the INA as a whole demonstrates that § 243(h) does not apply to actions taken by the President or Coast Guard outside the United States; that the legislative history of the 1980 amendment supports their reading; and that both the text and the negotiating history of Article 33 of the Convention indicate that it was not intended to have any extraterritorial effect.

We shall first review the text and structure of the statute and its 1980 amendment, and then consider the text and negotiating history of the Convention. . . .

The reference to the Attorney General in the statutory text is significant not only because that term cannot reasonably be construed to describe either the President or the Coast Guard, but also because it suggests that it applies only to the Attorney General's normal responsibilities under the INA. The most relevant of those responsibilities for our purposes is her conduct of the deportation and exclusion hearings in which requests for asylum or for withholding of deportation under § 243(h) are ordinarily advanced. Since there is no provision in the statute for the conduct of such proceedings outside the United States, and since Part V and other provisions of the INA obviously contemplate that such proceedings would be held in the country, we cannot reasonably construe § 243(h) to limit the Attorney General's actions in geographic areas where she has not been authorized to conduct such proceedings. Part V of the INA contains no reference to a possible extraterritorial application.

Even if Part V of the Act were not limited to strictly domestic procedures, the presumption that Acts of Congress do not ordinarily apply outside our borders would support an interpretation of § 243(h) as applying only within United States territory. . . .

. . . Both Congress and the Executive Branch gave extensive consideration to the Protocol before ratifying it in 1968; in all of their published consideration of it there appears no mention of the possibility that the United States was assuming any extraterritorial obligations. Nevertheless, because the history of the 1980 Act does disclose a general intent to conform our law to Article 33 of the Convention, it might be argued that the extraterritorial obligations imposed by Article 33 were so clear that Congress, in acceding to the Protocol, and then in amending the statute to harmonize the two, meant to give the latter a correspondingly extraterritorial effect. Or, just as the statute might have imposed an extraterritorial obligation that the Convention does not (the argument we have just rejected), the Convention might have established an extraterritorial obligation which the statute does not; under the Supremacy Clause, that broader treaty obligation might then provide the controlling rule of law. With those possibilities in mind we shall consider both the text and negotiating history of the Convention itself.

Like the text and the history of § 243(h), the text and negotiating history of Article 33 of the United Nations Convention are both completely silent with respect to the Article's possible application to actions taken by a country outside its own borders. Respondents argue that the Protocol's broad remedial goals require that a nation be prevented from repatriating refugees to their potential oppressors whether or not the refugees are within that nation's borders. In spite of the moral weight of that argument, both the text and negotiating history of Article 33 affirmatively indicate that it was not intended to have extraterritorial effect.

. . .

The drafters of the Convention and the parties to the Protocol—like the drafters of § 243(h)—may not have contemplated that any nation would gather fleeing refugees and return them to the one country they had desperately sought to escape; such actions may even violate the spirit of Article 33; but a treaty cannot impose uncontemplated extraterritorial obligations on those who ratify it through no more than its general humanitarian intent. Because the text of Article 33 cannot reasonably be read to say anything at all about a nation's actions toward aliens outside its own territory, it does not prohibit such actions.

. . . Whether the President's chosen method of preventing the "attempted mass migration" of thousands of Haitians . . . poses a greater risk of harm to Haitians who might otherwise face a long and dangerous return voyage, is irrelevant to the scope of his authority to take action that neither the Convention nor the statute clearly prohibits. As we have already noted, Acts of Congress normally do not have extraterritorial application unless such an intent is clearly manifested. That presumption has special force when we are construing treaty and statutory provisions that may involve foreign and military affairs for which the President has unique responsibility. We therefore find ourselves in agreement with the conclusion expressed in Judge Edwards' concurring opinion in [Haitian Refugee Center v. Gracey, 809 F.2d 794, 841 (1987)]:

> "This case presents a painfully common situation in which desperate people, convinced that they can no longer remain in their homeland, take desperate measures to escape. Although the human crisis is compelling, there is no solution to be found in a judicial remedy."

The judgment of the Court of Appeals is reversed.

■ JUSTICE BLACKMUN, dissenting. . . .

I believe that the duty of nonreturn expressed in both the Protocol and the statute is clear. The majority finds it "extraordinary," . . . that Congress would have intended the ban on returning "any alien" to apply to aliens at sea. That Congress would have meant what it said is not remarkable. What is extraordinary in this case is that the Executive, in disregard of the law, would take to the seas to intercept fleeing refugees and force them back to their persecutors—and that the Court would strain to sanction that conduct. . . .

Article 33.1 is clear not only in what it says, but also in what it does not say: it does not include any geographical limitation. It limits only where a refugee may be sent "to", not where he may be sent from. This is not surprising, given that the aim of the provision is to protect refugees against persecution. . . . .

The judicially created canon of statutory construction against extraterritorial application of United States law has no role here. . . .

. . .

In this case we deal with a statute that regulates a distinctively international subject matter: immigration, nationalities, and refugees. Whatever force the presumption may have with regard to a primarily domestic statute evaporates in this context. There is no danger that the Congress that enacted the Refugee Act was blind to the fact that the laws it was crafting had implications beyond this Nation's borders. The "common-sense notion" that Congress was looking inwards—perfectly valid in a case involving the Federal Tort Claims Act, such as *Smith*,—cannot be reasonably applied to the Refugee Act of 1980. . . .

The refugees attempting to escape from Haiti do not claim a right of admission to this country. They do not even argue that the Government has no right to intercept their boats. They demand only that the United States, land of refugees and guardian of freedom, cease forcibly driving them back to detention, abuse, and death. That is a modest plea, vindicated by the Treaty and the statute. We should not close our ears to it.

Notes

1. Is the Supreme Court's interpretation of the Refugee Convention's prohibition on *refoulement* in *Sale*, as applying only within the territory of the United States, persuasive? Why would the drafters of the Convention

provide that a state could not engage in *refoulement* from within its territory, but permit the state to reach outside its territory to capture refugees and return them to persecution? Does the Supreme Court's opinion reflect an assumption that human rights guarantees do not apply outside a state's territory? That aliens outside a state's territory have no rights against the state? (Cf. *United States v. Verdugo–Urquidez*, supra at p. 226.

2. The UN High Commissioner for Refugees issued a statement critical of the *Sale* decision, expressing the view that the *non-refoulement* obligation of Article 33 also applied outside a state's own borders. See *UN High Commissioner for Refugees Responds to U.S. Supreme Court Decision in Sale v. Haitian Centers Council*, 32 I.L.M. 1215 (1993). The Inter–American Commission on Human Rights later expressed its conclusion that the interdiction program upheld in *Sale* violated Article 33 of the Refugee Convention, and also entailed violations of several provisions of the American Declaration of the Rights and Duties of Man. See *Haitian Centre for Human Rights v. United States*, Case 10.675, Inter–Am. Comm'n H.R. 550, OEA/Ser.L/V/II.95 doc. 7 rev. (1997). The United States government has continued to maintain that Article 33 does not apply extraterritorially.

In 1998, however, Congress enacted an appropriations rider forbidding the use of appropriated funds for extraterritorial *refoulement* of refugees, and also establishing the policy of applying the *non-refoulement* requirement of the Torture Convention (see note 4 on p. 420 supra) without regard to geographical location. See Pub. L. No. 105–277, §§ 2241, 2242, 112 Stat.2681–821 (1998) (22 U.S.C. § 1231 note).

3. For comparison, observe that the International Covenant on Civil and Political Rights requires parties to respect and to ensure "to all individuals within its territory and subject to its jurisdiction" the enumerated rights. That phrasing has often been interpreted as including responsibilities to individuals who are outside the state's territory but subject to its jurisdiction. See Theodor Meron, *Extraterritoriality of Human Rights Treaties*, 89 Am. J. Int'l L. 78 (1995); Gerald L. Neuman, *Extraterritorial Violation of Human Rights by the United States*, 9 Amer. U. J. Int'l L. & Pol. 213 (1994). The European Convention for the Protection of Human Rights and Fundamental Freedoms requires parties to secure the enumerated rights "to everyone within their jurisdiction"; the European Court of Human Rights has held, confirming earlier case law of the European Commission on Human Rights, that this obligation is not limited to the national territory. See *Drozd and Janousek v. France and Spain*, 240 Eur. Ct. H.R. (ser. A), 14 E.H.R.R. 745 (1992); *Loizidou v. Turkey*, 1996–VI Eur. Ct. H.R. 2216, 23 E.H.R.R. 513 (1996).

H. BEYOND INDIVIDUAL RIGHTS

1. GROUP RIGHTS

With few exceptions, the rights set forth in the principal postwar human rights instruments are framed in terms of individual rights. The

Universal Declaration of Human Rights provides that "everyone" is entitled to the rights set forth therein (Article 2) and, with one notable exception (Article 1), the International Covenant on Civil and Political Rights (ICCPR) defines protected rights in similar terms. Moreover, apart from its assurance of rights "without distinction of any kind" (Article 2), the Declaration does not include any provision specifically protecting the rights of individuals belonging to minority groups as such. Such a provision does appear in Article 27 of the ICCPR, but the rights that it seeks to secure are defined in reference to individuals belonging to certain minorities (specifically, ethnic, religious and linguistic minorities), and not the groups themselves.

This general approach is noteworthy, not least because the principal impetus behind adoption of the postwar human rights instruments was the experience of Nazi persecution of victims targeted because of their membership in such minority groups as Jews, homosexuals, and Roma and Sinti communities. In light of this experience, one might have expected to find a special emphasis on minority rights in the postwar instruments. Indeed, Hitler's crimes provided the impetus for one postwar treaty concerned specifically with atrocities against groups—the 1948 Convention on the Prevention and Punishment of the Crime of Genocide, which aims at preventing the destruction of "national, ethnical, racial or religious groups."

But the prevailing sentiment in the aftermath of World War II was to eschew a special concern with rights of minorities, affirming instead the rights of everyone to enjoy fundamental rights on a basis of equality. Key considerations underlying this preference were expressed during the drafting of the Universal Declaration: The UN Secretariat and some states proposed including in the Declaration a provision that would protect the rights of a "minority to use its own language and to maintain schools and other cultural institutions." But other states believed that vulnerable groups could be adequately protected by assuring every person a core set of human rights and explicitly assuring that each person was entitled to enjoy those rights without discrimination on such grounds as national origin, race, religion, or sex. In addition,

> It was even said that the very concept of "minorities" is inconsistent with the principle of absolute equality enshrined in the Charter of the United Nations and in many national constitutions, as the term "national minority" signifies "a category of citizens whose political, economic, and social status was inferior to that of citizens belonging to the majority."

>   . . .

Some thought an article on minorities was not only unnecessary but undesirable. The Universal Declaration should not deal with rights which did not have universal applicability, did not apply to all human beings, and did not apply in all countries in the same way. Some thought that it was undesirable to perpetuate protections for minorities because it would discourage their assimilation. Others thought it might result in cutting them off from the mainstream of national life, frustrating their emancipation and full development, and denying them equal opportunity.

Louis B. Sohn, *The Rights of Minorities*, in The International Bill of Rights 270, 272 (L. Henkin ed. 1981).

The postwar approach was in part a reaction against the regime of minority rights treaties that had been imposed on various states in Central and Eastern Europe as part of the settlement of World War I. Whatever its salutary effects may have been, the interwar regime was widely judged a failure, not least because of the barbaric ends for which the Nazis invoked the rhetoric of minority rights. The delegates who drafted the postwar instruments had recent memories of Hitler invoking the banner of minority rights to justify Germany's annexation of Czechoslovakia in 1938 and its invasion of Poland in 1939, purportedly to protect German minorities in those countries. Further, World War II had amply demonstrated the dangers attending the elevation of collectivities over the fundamental unit of moral concern—individual persons.

But if a special focus on minorities and other groups is largely absent from treaties drafted in the aftermath of the Second World War, an explicit focus on minority rights is more common in recently adopted instruments. The latter include the Declaration on the Rights of Persons Belonging to National or Ethnic, Religious and Linguistic Minorities, which was adopted by the UN General Assembly in 1992; the European Framework Convention on the Protection of National Minorities, which was adopted in 1994 and entered into force in 1998; and the European Charter for Regional or Minority Languages, which was adopted in 1992 and entered into force in 1998.

In view of the special concern with minority rights reflected in recently drafted instruments, the rich jurisprudence of the interwar period has acquired renewed relevance. Accordingly, this section includes material on the interwar minority rights regime as well as on postwar human rights law. Before turning to relevant law, we explore preliminary issues relating to the adequacy and appropriateness of the individual rights framework that dominates postwar human rights protections, as well as critiques of "collective rights."

a.   GROUP RIGHTS AND INDIVIDUAL RIGHTS

The term "group rights" can be ambiguous and misleading. Literally, the term seems to refer to—and often is intended to connote—rights that vest in a collectivity, such as the "peoples" who are entitled to exercise the right of self-determination recognized in common Article 1 of the ICCPR and the ICESCR. Often, the term is used more imprecisely to refer to rights that are framed in terms of individuals who "belong to" certain groups. Article 27 of the ICCPR exemplifies the latter type of right:

In those States in which ethnic, religious or linguistic minorities exist, persons belonging to such minorities shall not be denied the right, in community with the other members of their group, to enjoy their own culture, to profess and practise their own religion, or to use their own language.

In the terminology of international law, it would be more accurate to say that Article 27 recognizes "minority rights" than "group rights." As the following article makes clear, there has been considerable debate concerning the conceptual coherence of "group rights," as well as the desirability of recognizing rights that vest in groups themselves.

In reading the following materials, consider why the distinction between "group rights" and rights of individuals belonging to certain groups has been thought consequential.

Adeno Addis, *Individualism, Communitarianism, and the Rights of Ethnic Minorities*
66 Notre Dame L. Rev. 1219 (1991).*

. . .

This Article . . . argues that the only plausible way to understand the notion of ethnic rights is to conceive of it as being a right of a group.

. . .

The dominant perspective, "the individualist perspective" as I shall refer to it, holds that the notion of ethnic rights, if it is not meant to refer to secession, can ultimately be understood only as individual rights. The individualist seeks to persuade us of the conceptual plausibility . . . of this position [with an argument], which for convenience sake we might refer to as "methodological individualism," [which] contends that, since the individual is the ultimate agent of action, it is only to that agent a moral right could attach. Groups here are merely seen as simple collections of individual agents, aggregations of the constituent parts. To the methodological individualist, the concept of group rights is "a metaphysical absurdity." Only individuals can have rights, for only they can be treated justly or unjustly.

. . .

But is the individualist correct? . . .

Let me first make the point that the individualist might, in fact, recognize group rights more than he thinks he does. Take, for example, secession. . . . If the individualist supports secession as one institutional manifestation of ethnic rights, . . . then his support is informed not by the rights of individuals, but by the right of the group. Presumably, even if there are some individuals who do not support the idea of seceding from the larger political unit, the individualist will feel justified in supporting the wish of the majority to establish itself as a new political unit.

. . .

In any case, on the conceptual level, the individualist's claim that there can never be circumstances in which the appropriate unit of agency is the

* Volume 66, Number 5, the *Notre Dame Law Review* (1996) 1219–1280. Reprinted with permission, © by *Notre Dame Law Re-*view, University of Notre Dame. The Editors of this book bear resposibility for any errors which have occured in reprinting or editing.

community (or the group) to which the individual belongs seems to be incorrect. There are circumstances in which simple aggregation of the activities and functions of individual members will not tell us the whole story about the community or the group to which the individuals belong.

. . .

Consider, for instance, the example Ronald Dworkin gives to highlight the importance of community as a point of departure, the orchestra. Individual members of an orchestra are

> exhilarated, in the way personal triumph exhilarates, not by the quality and brilliance of their individual contributions, but by the performance of the orchestra as a whole. It is the orchestra that succeeds or fails, and the success or failure of that community is the success or failure of each of its members.[96]

In Dworkin's example, one could legitimately talk about the group, the orchestra, being a unit of agency. To say that the community or the group is the unit of agency is to make the claim that the lives of the members of the group or of the community "are bound in their communal life, and that there can be no private accounting of the critical success or failure of their individual lives one by one."[97] Accordingly, one cannot understand the success of the enterprise in terms of the statistical summary of the success or failure of individual members.

If groups can be units of agency, then they can be units of our moral concern in the same way individuals are or can be. Groups as units of agency can be treated justly or unjustly; conversely, they can treat others justly or unjustly. Since rights are conferred, and duties imposed, on individuals precisely for those reasons, as the individualist is quick to remind us, it seems logical to insist that once the capacity of groups to be units of agency is admitted, then it must be accepted that it is not metaphysical nonsense to talk about the rights of groups.

[Having countered the argument that the idea of "group rights" is conceptually incoherent, Addis proceeds to advance a strategic argument for his vision of "group rights."]

... The individualist claims that her objective is to treat individuals equally, and that she does so by treating them as abstract individuals rather than as members of a group. In reality, for members of minority ethnic groups, having equal treatment turns out to be merely the right to be turned into some version of the members of the dominant culture. One can treat individuals equally only if one is comparing them from a given point of view. That point of view is not the abstract individual, for there is not such a creature, but rather the individual who is located in and circumscribed by the dominant culture and tradition.

In addition, the individualist argument that to treat individuals equally is to simply allow them to associate with whomever they want has,

---

96. Dworkin, *Liberal Community*, 77   **97.** *Id.* at 494.
Calif. L. Rev. 479, 493 (1989).

although seemingly neutral in relation to each individual and each cultural group, a greatly disproportionate negative impact on ethnic minorities. [W]hat this apparent neutrality masks is the fact that minority cultures, unlike the dominant culture, are vulnerable to the decisions of non-minority groups. Dominant majority groups are able to outvote and outbid the minority groups regarding the resources crucial to the survival of the latter's cultures. This is a threat that the dominant group does not face.

Take, for example, the Aboriginal people of Australia, a people which was, and has been, subjected to one of the most brutal treatments of an indigenous people by a colonizing power. What does it mean to say that Aboriginal people enjoy the same right as European Australians for their culture to compete in the marketplace of cultural values? It is a hollow right. Aboriginal people number slightly more than one percent of the population. In the past, their culture was systematically undermined by the government. Under such circumstances, to claim that the Aboriginal people can place their cultural practices in the marketplace of cultures is to be oblivious to two crucial facts. First, the government has had an important role in undermining the competitive capacity of the Aboriginal culture. Secondly, the Aboriginal people will be outvoted and outbid by European Australians in relation to the resources needed for the survival and the flourishing of their culture. The majority will determine the fate of the culture that it has always seen as the Other.

[In the following passage, Addis argues against one prevailing approach to group differences, which he terms "paternalistic pluralism," and argues that "critical pluralism" is better able to address the concerns outlined in the preceding passage.]

[One of the three common responses of dominant groups to ethnic minorities], which I have referred to as pluralism, holds that differences are to be celebrated rather than feared.... Actually, there are two kinds of pluralism. The first could be referred to as paternalistic ... pluralism....

Paternalistic pluralism "protects" the culture of minorities as the Other. Here, the toleration of the culture of ethnic minorities is motivated by a desire to save a particular group and its cultural practices from the majority's own actions which threaten to annihilate the minority. Under this model, the minority group cannot engage, and is not regarded as capable of engaging, the majority in a creative and constant dialogue. And the structure and resources that will enable such a dialogue are denied this group. What governments have done to indigenous peoples in Australia, Canada, New Zealand and the United States is a good example of this. Indigenous peoples in these countries are treated in the same way one would treat a "vanishing species of nonhuman fauna...."[13] They are to be preserved as Another, rather than to be engaged as partners in the creation and recreation of the social world that both inhabit. Pluralism of the paternalistic kind is as dehumanizing as negation itself, for it is based on

---

13. Van den Bergh, *Protection of Ethnic Minorities: A Critical Appraisal*, in Protec- tion of Minorities: Comparative Perspectives 343 (R. Wirising ed. 1981).

the assumption that the minority has little to impart to the majority and cannot therefore be regarded as a partner in dialogue.

What I have elected to refer to as "critical pluralism" does more than "protect" the minority. In fact, it is not even comfortable with the notion of protection. Rather, it is committed to doing two things. First, it actively intervenes to provide the resources that will enable the minority culture to flourish. But that alone is not sufficient. It is also committed to developing institutional structures that will enable the majority to open itself up to the minority, to accept the minority as a dialogue partner. Put simply, critical pluralism will adhere simultaneously to the politics of difference and dialogue. When the dominant group engages the oppressed in a dialogue it is acknowledging two things. First, it assumes that the dialogue partner cannot be understood either as an imitation of or deviation from the dominant culture. One does not engage a deviant in a dialogue. Rather, one seeks to heal the deviant, either medically or with divine guidance. Healing, by its very nature, is one-directional. Second, the dominant group sees its experience and culture not as universal and neutral, but as specific and located in the same way it sees the marginal cultures to be.

. . .

[C]ritical pluralism argues against what Jean–Francois Lyotard calls the "great story," the grand narratives within which all of us are supposed to find ourselves and through which each of us is to be inscribed. It argues that both descriptively and normatively it is better to think of societies as contests of narratives, "struggle[s] for the privilege of recounting the past."[89] Unlike paternalistic pluralism, which defines ethnic minorities as the "Other," critical pluralism starts with the proposition that the right of ethnic minorities is not merely one to be preserved from the cultural threat of the majority, but also to have the institutional capacity to interrogate the majority. . . .

Critical pluralism is pluralist in the sense that its objective is to provide the necessary resources and institutional structures for the cultures of the minorities to flourish. It believes in multiplicity. In its vision, the good society does not eliminate (or transcend) group differences. On the other hand, unlike paternalistic pluralism, where multiplicity is accompanied by the attitude of the Other, critical pluralism sees society as a constant and desirable mutual interrogation of various narratives. As such, critical pluralism is concerned not only with providing resources for minorities so as to enable them to maintain and develop their culture, to produce and tell their stories, but it seeks also to develop institutional structures that will enable the minority cultures to engage the dominant culture in a dialogue. . . .

Why is institutional dialogue an important aspect of critical pluralism? First, if it is true, as I have argued it is, that groups are contingent rather

---

89. Luban, *Difference Made Legal: The Court and Dr. King*, 87 Mich. L. Rev. 2152 (1989).

than essential, and that their very meaning can be rearranged and recast, then dialogic engagement becomes the means by which this recasting takes place. Second, it is through the process of dialogue, where different cultural groups are recognized as dialogue partners rather than as either negations or imitations of the dominant groups, that dominant groups might cease to see their norms as neutral and universal. When the traditions of ethnic groups are positively affirmed, the dominant group will slowly discover its own specificity. This feeling of specificity is the most important condition for the respect and celebration of difference. When, for example, African Americans' culture is positively affirmed, European Americans will realize that their cultures and attributes are not neutrally American and universal, but specific, perhaps European.

Third, institutional dialogue among cultural groups will serve the same function Roberto Unger saw being served when theoretical insights are considered along with their institutional realizations: there will be necessary mutual correction. Dialogue among cultural groups is likely to lead to mutually corrective engagement.... The process of mutual correction might be understood to be the recasting and reconceptualizing of groups, a process that is the result of the contingency of groups.

Fourth, it is in the process of dialogue, where social groups attempt to accommodate in their "own normative world the objective reality of the other,"[92] that the dominant group will come to understand how it feels to be oppressed.

Robert Cullen, *Human Rights Quandary*
71 Foreign Affairs 79–88 (Winter 1992/93).*

. . .

Around the globe the assertion of collective rights by one or another national group roils the status quo. Francophone residents of Quebec agitate for distinct status within, or perhaps secession from, Canada. In Asia Tibetans seek independence from China, and Tamils want to partition Sri Lanka. In Africa a civil war tears apart Ethiopia. In the Middle East Kurds wish to carve their own country out of Iraq, Iran and Turkey, and Palestinians demand the right to create a state in the West Bank and Gaza Strip territories occupied by Israel—itself the product of one of this century's more successful campaigns for the collective right of self-determination.

. . .

Yugoslavia most dramatically demonstrates the disastrous potential of the assertion of collective rights in the postcommunist era. The Yugoslavs, as constituted from 1918 to 1991, were divided by nationality, religion and

---

92. Cover, *The Supreme Court Term, 1982–Forward: Nomos and Narrative,* 97 Harv. L. Rev. 4, 28–29 (1983), *cited in* Singer, *Property and Coercion in Federal Indian Law: The Conflict Between Critical and Com-* *placent Pragmatism*, 63 S. Cal. L. Rev. 1821, 1837 (1990).

* Reprinted by permission, © 1993, Council on Foreign Relations, Inc.

history. Repression by the communist government and the personal authority of Josip Broz Tito held this unlikely amalgam together for 35 years after World War II. But Tito's death in 1980 inaugurated a process of disintegration. . . .

Yugoslavia's war [in the early 1990s], as well as others in the former Soviet republics, demonstrates several sobering realities. . . .

[One is that] conflicting assertions of collective rights cannot be resolved by simply endorsing the right to political self-determination via referendum in a given geographic area. Populations are not cleanly divided. There are too many areas with two, three or four claimants. . . . Finally, in the absence of countervailing factors there is more than enough suffering and injustice in the history of virtually any national group to prompt it toward vindictiveness and vengeance against its neighbors.

. . .

Collective rights . . . span a spectrum from simple freedom of association to a variety of special remedies and protections. The ultimate collective right, of course, is the right to create an independent state. Short of that, groups may assert the right to their own schools and to make their language the official language in a given area. They may seek to block the entrance of other nationalities into their homeland. They may seek special political rights.

. . .

For both philosophical and pragmatic reasons . . . Americans have good reason to be troubled by the assertion of collective rights. The United States was founded on the idea that citizenship and political rights cannot be based on ethnic or religious identity. The idea that within a given European, Asian or African country groups of people cannot coexist because of their religious or ethnic differences is fundamentally alien to American values. The [expanding definition of the cultural and linguistic rights of minorities by the Conference on the Security and Cooperation in Europe] has already reached the point where it begins to challenge the American ideal engraved on U.S. coins, e pluribus unum. And from a practical standpoint the tendency for the assertion of collective rights to be accompanied by violent conflict has been adequately demonstrated.

Yet, as Yugoslavia showed, an American policy that opposes national independence movements whose time has come runs the risk of being overwhelmed by tides of nationalist passion.

. . .

The cornerstone of the solution to this dilemma is a human rights policy focused firmly on individual, rather than collective, rights. The demise of communism has not ended assaults on individual rights. In some areas of the world communism's disappearance has only increased the number of actors . . . bent on depriving individuals of their rights to free speech, to security from torture, to travel and to all the rights enumerated in the 1948 U.N. Universal Declaration of Human Rights. . . .

At the same time the United States should resist the trend toward expanding collective rights. A policy based on American support for collective rights, including political self-determination, will inevitably fail. First, it would tend to put the United States increasingly in the position of arbiter among conflicting claims to a particular homeland. These claims are generally rooted in assertions about ancient history that are difficult to prove one way or another. No one is likely ever to know with certainty, for instance, whether Romanians or Hungarians were the original inhabitants of Transylvania. Second, it would inevitably be applied selectively. The United States could conceivably support the right of Iraq's Kurds to self-determination, but it is never going to support the right of Scots, for instance, to secede from an unwilling Great Britain. A human rights policy applied selectively deservedly loses much of its moral authority. Third, the expansion of internationally recognized collective rights could lead to conflict with American domestic policies. The United States cannot, without a fatal measure of hypocrisy, demand that foreign governments grant minority languages equal status and simultaneously insist on the dominant role of English within its own borders.

The appropriate American attitude toward collective rights is a skeptical neutrality.... If American policy concerns itself with whether governments afford their people, as individuals, the full spectrum of political rights—the right to speak out and publish, the right to form associations, the right to worship, the right to call for change without fear of repression—then the issue of collective rights will in many cases take care of itself.

Minorities that are treated properly by their governments, as individuals, will probably be less likely to join separatist movements.

Notes

1. Addis argues that "groups can be units of agency," and that therefore "they can be units of our moral concern" and rights can appropriately be conferred upon them. Does this imply that groups can possess rights independent of the interests of their members, or even contrary to the interests of all their members? Even if, as Ronald Dworkin suggests, the good of the orchestra is not reducible to the statistical average of the good of its members, does it follow that there are things that are good for the orchestra and which should be supported for that reason even if they are bad for its members? One historical form of individualism has insisted on "the supreme intrinsic value, or dignity, of the individual human being," in contrast to the organic conception of society under which "the individual did not exist for his own sake, but for the sake of the whole society." See Steven Lukes, Individualism 45–51 (1973). Can this vision of human dignity, expressed in the Universal Declaration, be reconciled with the attribution of rights to groups as such? Does it imply limits on the kinds of rights that can be properly attributed to groups as such?

2.   Invoking the example of secession, Addis suggests that "the individualist might, in fact, recognize group rights more than he thinks he does." Consider in this regard whether the body of international law concerning genocide supports his claim. The term "genocide" was coined by Raphael Lemkin, who introduced the concept of genocide in his 1944 book *Axis Rule in Occupied Europe*:

> New conceptions require new terms. By "genocide" we mean the destruction of a nation or of an ethnic group. This new word, coined by the author to denote an old practice in its modern development, is made from the ancient Greek word *genos* (race, tribe) and the Latin *cide* (killing), thus corresponding in its formation to such word as tyrannicide, homicide, infanticide, etc. Generally speaking, genocide does not necessarily mean the immediate destruction of a nation, except when accomplished by mass killings of all members of a nation. It is intended rather to signify a coordinated plan of different actions aiming at the destruction of essential foundations of the life of national groups, with the aim of annihilating the groups themselves. The objectives of such a plan would be disintegration of the political and social institutions, of culture, language, national feelings, religion, and the economic existence of national groups, and the destruction of the personal security, liberty, health, dignity, and even the lives of the individuals belonging to such groups. Genocide is directed against the national group as an entity, and the actions involved are directed against individuals, not in their individual capacity, but as members of the national group.

Raphael Lemkin, Axis Rule in Occupied Europe 79 (1944). Consider also whether rights relating to political participation provide an example of internationally-protected rights that cannot be understood solely in terms of the rights of individuals. Article 25 of the ICCPR provides:

> Every citizen shall have the right and the opportunity . . . :
>
> > (a) To take part in the conduct of public affairs, directly or through freely chosen representatives;
> >
> > (b) To vote and to be elected at genuine periodic elections which shall be by universal and equal suffrage and shall be held by secret ballot, guaranteeing the free expression of the will of the electors;
> >
> > (c) To have access, on general terms of equality, to public services in his country.

Note that the basic political rights recognized in this provision are framed in terms of individuals' rights ("every citizen"). But Article 25(b) speaks of elections that guarantee "the free expression of the will of the electors." In what sense does this provision use the term "will of the electors"? Does this phrase connote a collective will?

Compare Article 3 of Protocol No. 1 to the European Convention for the Protection of Human Rights and Fundamental Freedoms, 213 U.N.T.S. 262 (entered into force May 18, 1954), which provides:

The High Contracting Parties undertake to hold free elections at reasonable intervals by secret ballot, under conditions which will ensure the free expression of the opinion of the people in the choice of the legislature.

By assuring the "free expression of the opinion of the people in the choice of the legislature," does this provision implicitly recognize that a collective will, as expressed through secret voting, should be the basis of election results? The 1990 Document of the Copenhagen Meeting of the Conference on the Human Dimension of the Conference on Security and Co-operation in Europe similarly declares that "the will of the people, freely and fairly expressed through periodic and genuine elections, is the basis of the authority and legitimacy of all government."

3.   Article 27 of the ICCPR recognizes rights of "persons belonging to" certain minorities rather than rights of minority groups themselves. In contrast, Article 1 is framed in terms of a collective right, providing that all "peoples have the right of self-determination." Alleged violations of this right cannot, however, be challenged through the individual complaint procedure established by the Optional Protocol to the Covenant. In the view of the Human Rights Committee, the Optional Protocol "provides a procedure under which individuals can claim that their individual rights have been violated," and not a procedure for challenging alleged breaches of the collective rights recognized in Article 1. See *Bernard Ominayak, Chief of the Lubicon Lake Band v. Canada*, U.N. Doc. A/45/40, vol. II, 27, para. 32.1 (1990). Still, the Committee has arguably recognized not only the rights of individuals belonging to groups, but also collective rights of minorities themselves. Consider, for example, the Committee's views in the *Lubicon Lake Band* case, which included the conclusion that "[h]istorical inequities ... and certain more recent developments threaten the way of life and culture of the Lubicon Lake Band, and constitute a violation of article 27 so long as they continue." Id., para. 33.

4.   Why, in Addis's view, is it desirable for "minority cultures to engage the dominant culture in dialogue"? What are the ultimate objectives of such a process, and why, in Addis's view, are they desirable?

5.   Cullen argues for the United States to base its human rights policy "firmly on individual, rather than collective rights" and suggests that if U.S. policy "concerns itself with whether governments afford their people, as individuals, the full spectrum of political rights—the right to speak out and publish, the right to form associations, the right to worship, the right to call for change without fear of repression—then the issue of collective rights will in many cases take care of itself." This prescription assumes that the rights enumerated are properly conceived as individual rights. Earlier, however, Cullen suggests that "collective rights span a spectrum" that includes "simple freedom of association." If Cullen's principal concern relates to what he terms "the ultimate collective right," does it matter whether other rights that, in his view, merit support, such as that of freedom of association, are termed "individual" or "collective" rights?

6. Does Addis's critique of "the individualist perspective" address the concerns set forth in Cullen's analysis? Does Cullen's critique of group rights address Addis's arguments?

b.   MINORITY RIGHTS

i.   *The Interwar Regime*

Oscar Janowsky, *Nationalities and National Minorities*
110–15 (1945).

The Western statesmen [at the Paris Peace Conference convened in the aftermath of World War I] recognized the inescapable need of protecting minorities and took vigorous steps to render such protection effective. But for them, the minorities would have been left to their fate, and millions of human beings, certainly in Poland, Rumania, Hungary and Jugoslavia, would have suffered oppression and forcible denationalization, similar in aim and method to the Prussianization and Russification of the preceding decades.

It must be reiterated that never before in the history of peacemaking was so much attention given to the principle of nationality. The attempt was made to draw frontiers along "ethnic" or nationality lines, and where conflicting claims were encountered, the plebiscite was freely resorted to. Yet, because of the composite character of the population, national minorities remained in every new or enlarged state of east-central Europe, and in not a few in alarming numbers.... In numerous states it proved utterly impossible to disentangle mixed populations, while in a number of instances economic and strategic considerations were allowed to determine the final territorial decision.

Once they were convinced that minorities would remain, the leaders of the Paris Peace Conference proceeded to draft the minimum guarantees necessary for their protection. With the exception of Czechoslovakia, ... the states containing minorities resisted vigorously. But the "Big Three" stood their ground, overriding all opposition and compelling every new and enlarged state—except Italy—to assume international obligations to protect minorities. Poland, Czechoslovakia, Rumania, Jugoslavia and Greece, each was obliged to sign a special Minorities Treaty; appropriate articles were incorporated in the general treaties with the defeated states, except Germany; and the Baltic States, as also Albania, made Declarations accepting League [of Nations] supervision of their treatment of minorities.

· · ·

The provisions for the protection of minorities are best studied by examining the Polish Minorities Treaty, the first to be drafted and the model for all subsequent engagements.

(1) *Human rights.* Life, liberty and religious freedom were guaranteed to all inhabitants of the country ...; and equal civil and political rights,

equality before the law in particular, were assured to all citizens, including members of minorities who differed from the majority in "race, language or religion." It was reiterated that members of minorities were to "enjoy the same treatment and security in law and in fact" as the other citizens of the country. . . .

(2) *Citizenship.* There was grave danger that persons belonging to weak or unpopular minorities might be excluded from citizenship in their native land. It was well known that Rumania had pursued such a policy before the First World War. Although bound by the Treaty of Berlin (1878) to accord equality to religious minorities, the Rumanian Government had successfully evaded its international obligation by declaring its Jewish inhabitants—even those born and habitually resident in the country— "foreigners who are not subject to another power." To prevent such perversion of justice in the future, the Polish Minorities Treaty—and the other minorities treaties as well—included carefully worded and tightly drawn provisions for the naturalization of persons born or habitually resident in the state. However, those who did not wish to become citizens of the new state were permitted to "opt for any other nationality," provided they migrated within a specified period to the state for which they had opted. . . .

(3) *Language rights.* Members of minorities whose mother tongue differed from that of the majority were protected against any such suppression of their language as had been attempted by the Prussian and Czarist Russian governments. The state obliged to sign the Minorities Treaty— Poland, for example—undertook to impose no restriction upon "the free use by any Polish national of any language in private intercourse, in commerce, in religion, in the press or in publications of any kind, or at private meetings." Moreover, regardless of the probable establishment of Polish as the official language, "adequate facilities" must be accorded "to Polish nationals of non-Polish speech for the use of their language, either orally or in writing, before the courts." In like manner, members of minorities were authorized to establish and control, at their own expense, charitable, educational, religious and social institutions, "with the right to use their own language . . . freely therein." . . .

(4) *Scholastic rights.* In a country containing linguistic and cultural minorities, the schools are likely to become a battleground for the youth of the land. If the language, literature, history and national ideals of the majority could be imposed on all children, the denationalization of minorities would, in time, become inevitable. Fully conscious minorities would naturally resist, and strife would be unavoidable. Therefore, the state was obligated to provide, in towns and districts with "a considerable proportion" of minorities, primary schools in which the children of minorities would be instructed "through the medium of their own language." The state, however, was not prohibited from requiring the teaching of the majority language as an obligatory subject in the minority schools.

It was likewise evident that the scholastic guarantees might be nullified by withholding state funds from minority schools. The Minorities

Treaties, therefore, imposed upon the Government the duty of assuring minorities "an equitable share in the enjoyment and application" of public funds which might be allotted "for educational, religious or charitable purposes." . . .

. . .

(6) *The guarantee of the rights of minorities.* The provisions respecting citizenship and human and linguistic rights were to be recognized as fundamental law taking precedence over any other law, regulation or official action. . . . Moreover, the League of Nations was charged with the duty of supervising the enforcement of the treaties.

The stipulations "so far as they affect persons belonging to racial, religious or linguistic minorities" were declared "obligations of international concern" and placed under the guarantee of the League of Nations. They were not to be modified without the approval of a majority of the League Council. Any member of the Council was authorized "to bring to the attention of the Council any infraction, or any danger of infraction" of the obligations; and the Council was empowered to "take such action and give such direction as it may deem proper and effective in the circumstances."

Finally, any difference of opinion "as to questions of law or fact" between a state and any one of the Principal Allied and Associated Powers, or a member of the League Council, was to be recognized as a dispute "of an international character" and referred to the Permanent Court of International Justice on the demand of a member of the League Council or one of the Principal Allied and Associated Powers.

ii. Postwar Law

Hurst Hannum, *Minorities, Indigenous Peoples, and Self–Determination*

in Human Rights: An Agenda for the Next Century 1, 2–8
(Louis Henkin & John Lawrence Hargrove, eds., 1994).*

. . .

B. Protection of Human Rights of Groups: 1945–1989

With few exceptions, post–1945 human rights instruments have dealt almost exclusively with the rights of *individuals*, not groups. While certain classes of particularly vulnerable individuals have been singled out for special protection—such as refugees, women, children, migrant workers, and members of racial and religious minorities—the assumption of most human rights advocates has been that effective guarantees of equality within a democratic system would be sufficient to respond to legitimate interests of individuals and groups within society.

Nevertheless, the need to pay special attention to groups under some circumstances was recognized as early as 1948, when the UN General

Assembly adopted the Convention on the Prevention and Punishment of the Crime of Genocide. . . .

This initiative was paralleled by creation of a subsidiary body to the UN Commission on Human Rights: the Sub–Commission on Prevention of Discrimination and Protection of Minorities. As the Sub–Commission's name suggests, the rights of minorities were considered to be closely linked to the issue of nondiscrimination, although concern with minority rights *per se* was not as evident in the United Nations as it was during the brief existence of the League of Nations and the so-called "Minorities Treaties" that were imposed on several states after World War I. However, early Sub–Commission initiatives concerning minorities were rebuffed or ignored by its parent bodies, and it soon became clear that the United Nations was much more interested in formal equality than in the politically more sensitive issue of the rights of minorities.

There were a few exceptions to this general UN attitude. The International Labor Organization early in its life addressed the problems faced by indigenous or tribal laborers, and, in 1957, it adopted Convention No. 107 Concerning the Protection and Integration of Indigenous and Other Tribal and Semi–Tribal Populations in Independent Countries. Despite its broadly assimilationist approach, Convention No. 107 recognized that special protection for indigenous peoples was necessary and recognized, inter alia, the right of collective indigenous land ownership, the relevance of indigenous customary laws, and the right to be compensated for land taken by the state. The needs of minorities also were recognized in provisions designed to protect the interests of particular minority communities contained in the peace treaty with Italy (concerning the German-speaking residents of South Tyrol) and the treaty recognizing the full political independence of Austria (concerning the rights of the Croat and Slovene minorities).

But at the same time that it was largely ignoring the rights of minorities and indigenous peoples, the United Nations was engaged in one of its most successful attempts at lawmaking: the ending of colonialism, through the invocation and gradual expansion of the "principle of equal rights and self-determination of peoples" mentioned in the [UN] Charter. The most significant resolutions adopted during this process were the 1960 Declaration on the Granting of Independence to Colonial Countries and Peoples and the comprehensive 1970 Declaration on Principles of International Law Concerning Friendly Relations and Co-operation among States in accordance with the Charter of the United Nations. The latter is widely considered to restate customary international law, and it provides that "all peoples have the right freely to determine, without external interference, their political status and to pursue their economic, social and cultural development." . . .

The General Assembly directed that an article on the right of self-determination be included in the human rights covenants being drafted by the Commission on Human Rights during the 1950s and 1960s, and each covenant contains an identical first article:

1. All peoples have the right of self-determination. By virtue of that right they freely determine their political status and freely pursue their economic, social and cultural development.

2. All peoples may, for their own ends, freely dispose of their natural wealth and resources without prejudice to any obligations arising out of international economic co-operation, based upon the principle of mutual benefit, and international law. In no case may a people be deprived of its own means of subsistence.

3. The States Parties to the present Covenant, including those having responsibility for the administration of Non–Self–Governing and Trust Territories, shall promote the realization of the right of self-determination, and shall respect that right, in conformity with the provisions of the Charter of the United Nations.

The Covenant on Civil and Political Rights also contains what was (in 1966) the only clear provision specifically directed to the issue of the rights of minorities. Article 27 of the Covenant states, in full:

In those States in which ethnic, religious or linguistic minorities exist, persons belonging to such minorities shall not be denied the right, in community with the other members of their group, to enjoy their own culture, to profess and practise their own religion, or to use their own language.

This minimalist and individually oriented text (note that "persons belonging to" protected minorities are the possessors of rights) reflected the prevalent view of the 1950s and 1960s that issues of ethnicity, religion, and language would gradually diminish in importance as marginal or less developed population groups were integrated or assimilated into a democratic, non-discriminatory society. So long as members of minority groups were not forced to assimilate and were treated on a basis of equality, it was not felt necessary or desirable to emphasize differences by highlighting special minority rights.

This expectation that societies would gradually become more homogeneous fit nicely with the individualistic orientation of the United States and other Western countries, which believed that "group" rights were a vague, primarily Marxist-inspired concept that could undermine the much more important personal freedoms of the individual. Nor were group rights favored by the newly independent African and Asian states, most of whom faced a colonial legacy of extraordinary ethnic, religious, and linguistic diversity within their borders. The concern of these states was "nation-building," which it was thought could be best accomplished by ignoring ethnic and other divisions and creating a new national (that is, "state") identity. Recognition of minority rights could only interfere with this process.

Thus, development of norms for protecting minorities and indigenous communities as such were halting, at best. The only widely accepted group right was the right of self-determination, but self-determination in the era of decolonization was based primarily on territory, not human beings.

Despite frequent proclamations that all "peoples" had the right to self-determination, it was colonial territories that were granted independence, not their peoples. . . .

Although it is only recently that events in the former Soviet Union and Yugoslavia have put the issues of minority rights on the front pages of the Western press, it has been evident for decades that the assumption made by the West and developing countries alike that minorities would gradually disappear or become less relevant to individuals' sense of identity was false. . . .

C.   Protection of Human Rights of Groups: Contemporary Norms

The growing recognition that the mere protection of individual human rights may not always be sufficient to guarantee legitimate values of group identity or demands for more effective participation in the larger society led to adoption of a plethora of new international instruments in the late 1980s and 1990s. Whether phrased in the technical terms of individual rights ("persons belonging to" minorities) or more broadly, these instruments constitute an explicit recognition of the fact that true democracy may require more than one-person, one-vote, and that the self-determination of states may not be sufficient to respond to demands by peoples for self-government.

These recent instruments include:

- ILO Convention No. 169 Concerning Indigenous and Tribal Peoples in Independent Countries, adopted in 1989;

  . . .

- a Proposed European Convention for the Protection of Minorities, prepared by the European Commission for Democracy through Law, submitted to (although not formally adopted by) the Council of Europe in 1991;*

- the European Charter for Regional or Minority Languages, opened for signature in 1992; and

- the Declaration on the Rights of Persons belonging to National or Ethnic, Religious or Linguistic Minorities, adopted by the UN General Assembly in 1992.

In addition, the participating states in the Conference on Security and Cooperation in Europe [now the Organization for Security and Cooperation in Europe] created the position of High Commissioner [on] National Minorities in June 1992, and the Working Group on Indigenous Populations of the UN Sub–Commission on Prevention of Discrimination and Protection of Minorities completed a draft of a Declaration on the Rights of Indigenous Peoples in August 1993. . . .

---

* [Editors' Note: As noted earlier, in 1994 the Council of Europe adopted the Framework Convention on the Protection of National Minorities, which entered into force in 1998.]

Notes

1. What accounts for the fundamentally different approach to rights of persons belonging to minorities under the interwar regime described by Janowsky and the postwar approach summarized by Hannum? Do the different approaches respond to fundamentally different historical experiences? Which of the two approaches—the minority rights regime of the interwar period or the postwar emphasis on individual rights assured on a basis of equality—is more likely to secure effective equality? Consider in this regard the analysis of Adeno Addis in sub-section 1, above.

2. As the preceding materials reflect, a range of different international instruments include provisions that afford special protections to particular categories of minorities. For example, Article 27 of the ICCPR recognizes certain rights in respect of persons belonging to "ethnic, religious or linguistic minorities." The 1948 Genocide Convention protects "national, ethnical, racial, or religious" groups from campaigns to destroy them, in whole or in part. Groups protected by the interwar treaty that was the subject of a case examined in the following sub-section were racial, linguistic and religious minorities. These provisions raise a number of fundamental questions: How should drafters of international instruments determine which groups ought to be given special recognition and protection? Why, for example, weren't racial groups explicitly included in Article 27? Should Article 27's reference to "ethnic" groups be interpreted to include "racial" groups? Do different kinds of groups raise different concerns?

Beyond the question of which categories should be identified in instruments protecting persons belonging to specified minorities, such provisions raise fundamental issues of interpretation. Is membership in an "ethnic" or "racial" group an "objective" question? Does it entail a subjective element? To what extent do seemingly objective concepts such as "race" in fact reflect social constructs?

iii. "Belonging to" a Minority Group: Who Decides?

As the preceding materials suggest, issues surrounding international law's special concern with minority groups have been complex and challenging. Among the more difficult and important issues raised by special provisions for persons belonging to minorities is the question of how—and by whom—membership in a protected group should be determined when membership is contested.

This last issue was at the heart of a dispute that arose under the interwar regime described in the excerpt by Oscar Janowsky, which led to a case before the Permanent Court of International Justice (PCIJ), *Rights of Minorities in Upper Silesia Case (Minority Schools)*. Briefly, the background to this case is as follows: President Woodrow Wilson's postwar aims included the goal of incorporating into the new Polish state "territories inhabited by indisputably Polish populations."* In light of this aim, during the peace conference Germany argued that non-Germans in Upper Silesia

* This was the thirteenth of President Wilson's Fourteen Points, which outlined Allied aims for the peace settlement concluding World War I. Woodrow Wilson, An Address to

spoke a Polish dialect rather than High Polish and that "this dialect is not a sign of nationality, especially not a contradiction to the consciousness of German nationality."**

Although Upper Silesia was eventually partitioned between Poland and Germany, for fifteen years it was governed by an interim regime, established by an internationally-supervised convention between Germany and Poland, which maintained the temporary unity of the region under the shared sovereignty of the two states. The German–Polish Convention concerning Upper Silesia included minority rights provisions modeled on the Minority Protection Treaty imposed upon Poland. Persons belonging to linguistic minorities were entitled, inter alia, to send their children to state schools that would provide instruction in their language. Minority schools were to be established upon the demand of at least forty children belonging to a linguistic minority. Article 131(1) of the German–Polish Convention provided:

> In order to determine the language of a pupil or child, account shall be taken of the verbal or written statement of the person legally responsible for the education of the pupil or child. This statement may not be verified or disputed by the authorities.

Article 74 of the convention more generally prohibited authorities from verifying or disputing "[t]he question whether a person does or does not belong to a racial, linguistic or religious minority."

The dispute that gave rise to the case before the PCIJ arose when Polish authorities undertook an investigation to establish the authenticity of applications for admission to minority schools; as a result of this inquiry, several thousand students enrolled in German minority schools in Polish Upper Silesia were not allowed to continue attending those schools. Although the children's parents had claimed they belonged to a German linguistic minority, Polish authorities rejected those claims, asserting that the question whether children belonged to a linguistic minority was an objective one. Germany brought a case against Poland in the PCIJ, arguing inter alia that relevant provisions of the German–Polish Convention "establish the unfettered liberty of an individual to declare according to his own conscience and on his own personal responsibility that he himself does or does not belong to" a minority group and did not permit state verification of such declarations.

Rights of Minorities in Upper Silesia (Minority Schools)

Permanent Court of International Justice, 1928.
1928 P.C.I.J. (ser. A) No. 12 (Apr. 26).

. . .

a Joint Session of Congress (Fourteen Points Address) (1918), *in* 45 The Papers of Woodrow Wilson 534 (Arthur S. Link ed. 1984).

** 2 H.W.V. Temperley, History of the Peace Conference 287, *quoted in* Nathaniel

Berman, *Nationalism Legal and Linguistic: The Teachings of European Jurisprudence,* 24 N.Y.U.J. Int'l L. & Politics 1515, 1538 (1992).

The Court is of opinion that Poland is justified in construing the Minorities Treaty* (the provisions of which, subject to slight modifications of no importance in this connection, are embodied as such [in the German–Polish] Convention) as meaning that the question whether a person does or does not belong to a racial, linguistic or religious minority, and consequently is entitled to claim the advantages arising under the provisions which the Treaty comprises with regard to the protection of minorities, is a question of fact and not solely one of intention. The Treaty became directly operative over the whole of the territories which the Treaty of Versailles transferred from Germany to Poland. Although the Minorities Treaty does not specifically state what persons belong to a minority, it must not, therefore, be inferred that there exists a gap which must necessarily be filled by subsequent stipulations. The Treaty would fail in its purposes if it were not to be considered as an established fact that persons who belonged *de facto* to such a minority must enjoy the protection which had been stipulated.

[I]t does not, however, follow that the contracting Parties were unable validly to agree to extend the rights provided as regards minorities also to persons who do not in the normal course come within the conception of a minority.... But on the other hand, such an extension cannot be presumed....

Among those of the articles of the Convention adduced by the German Government in support of its contention, Article 74 alone refers in general to the question whether a person does or does not belong to a racial, linguistic or religious minority....

Article 74 runs as follows:

"The question whether a person does or does not belong to a racial, linguistic or religious minority may not be verified or disputed by the authorities."

Does this stipulation provide a sufficient basis for the construction attributed thereto by the German Government and according to which it is a question of intention alone (the "subjective principle")? The Court does not think so.

In the first place it should be observed that the article does not state in specific terms that it is a declaration by a person which is decisive as to whether such person belongs to a minority, nor that such declaration must be a declaration of intention alone and not a declaration determining what such person considers to be the *de facto* situation in the particular case. The prohibition as regards verification or dispute which is comprised in the article can be quite easily understood even if the construction placed upon it by Germany be rejected.

* [This reference is to the Minorities   land.—Editors' Note.]
Treaty imposed by the Allied Powers on Po-

There is reason to believe that, in the conditions which exist in Upper Silesia, a multitude of cases occur in which the question whether a person belongs to a minority particularly of race or language does not clearly appear from the facts. Such an uncertainty might for example exist, as regards language, where either a person does not speak literary German or literary Polish, or where he knows and makes use of several languages, and, as regards race, in the case of mixed marriages. If the authorities wish to verify or dispute the substance of a declaration by a person, it is very unlikely that in such cases they would be able to reach a result more nearly corresponding to the actual state of facts. Such a proceeding on the part of the authorities would, moreover, very easily assume in public opinion the aspect of a vexatious measure which would inflame political passions and would counteract the aims of pacification which are also at the basis of the stipulations concerning the protection of minorities.

In the opinion of the Court, the prohibition of verification and dispute has as its object not the substitution of a new principle for that which in the nature of things and according to the provisions of the Minorities Treaty determines membership of a racial, linguistic or religious minority, but solely the avoidance of the disadvantages—particularly great in Upper Silesia—which would arise from a verification or dispute on the part of the authorities as regards such membership. . . .

It must be admitted that the prohibition of any verification or dispute on the part of the authorities may lead to certain persons who, in fact, do not belong to a minority, having to be treated as though they belonged thereto. That, in the opinion of the Court, is a consequence which the contracting Parties accepted in order to avoid the much greater disadvantages which would arise from verification or dispute by the authorities. If, according to what has been stated above, a declaration which clearly does not conform to the facts is to be considered as not in conformity with the [German–Polish] Convention, it does not follow, as the Polish Government appears to maintain, that the prohibition to verify or dispute ceases to be applicable in such a case. The prohibition which is expressed in unqualified terms cannot be subject to any restriction. But it must not be inferred from this that the construction given above, according to which the declaration must on principle be in conformity with the facts, is therefore of no value. It is indeed of some importance to establish what is the situation at law.

. . .

As regards the point whether Article 131 contemplates a declaration which ascertains a fact and not an expression of an intention or of a wish, the Court adopts the construction put upon it by the Polish Government. . . . The Court does not find in the text of the Convention any grounds for construing Article 131 as does the German Government, as solely contemplating a declaration of intention or of a wish that the instruction of a child or pupil should be given in the minority language. . . .

. . .

But although the conclusion drawn by the Court from the terms of the Convention is that Article 131 contemplates a declaration which on principle must refer to the existence of a fact and not express an intention or a wish, that does not exclude the possibility, when appreciating those facts, of properly taking into account a subjective element. Indeed, what is to be understood as a person's tongue is not always clear and beyond doubt; particularly when a child reaching the school age is concerned, it is no doubt proper not exclusively to take into account the language which the child generally employs if the parents employ another language to satisfy their cultural requirements and if it is that language which they by preference consider as their own....

. . .

If a declaration has been made, it must always be respected. With regard to Article 131, as well as to Article 74, the Court holds that the prohibition as regards any verification or dispute does not cease to apply in cases where it appears that the declaration is not in accordance with the facts.

Notes

1. Did the majority of the PCIJ endorse an objective or subjective approach to the question of linguistic identity in the *Rights of Minorities in Upper Silesia Case (Minority Schools)*? Or did it recognize that self-identity, which by its nature entails subjective perceptions, is the best guide to "the actual state of facts"? Why, in the majority's view, did the Minorities Treaty at issue prohibit verification of claimed membership in a racial, linguistic or religious minority? To what extent did this prohibition reflect a recognition of the inherent ambiguity of group identity? To what extent did it reflect other considerations?

Although the Court endorsed the Polish claim that the issue whether one belongs to a linguistic minority is "a question of fact and not solely one of intention," a dissenting judge argued that the court had effectively adopted a subjective interpretation because a "declaration which cannot be disputed or verified ... cannot be limited by the rules of law." Responding to this observation, Professor Nathaniel Berman argues that, "rather than a clumsy obfuscation, the court's decision should be understood as articulating a novel conception of the effect of a supranational regime on both sovereign power and linguistic identity, as well as on their interrelationship." He explains:

> The court directed its analysis at determining the appropriate *locus of legal authority* over the intrinsically indeterminate, "non-objective," issue of linguistic identity. It decided that that locus resided in the "conscience" *vested with legal stature*. The court declared that the parents or guardians were uniquely qualified to accomplish the necessarily "discretionary" evaluation of the "true position" concerning the children's identity. The court thus held that international law mandated a *decentralization*, rather than an abdication, of legal authority; this

decentralization was required by the distinctive nature of the issue in question. Only such a decentralized locus of decision-making could "establish what is the situation at law."

Nathaniel Berman, *Nationalism Legal and Linguistic: The Teachings of European Jurisprudence*, 24 N.Y.U.J. Int'l L. & Politics 1515, 1543 (1992).

2.   The *Rights of Minorities in Upper Silesia (Minority Schools)* case raised the question whether governmental authorities should be able to challenge individuals' claims to membership in a particular group whose members enjoy special rights. In these circumstances, the relevant international treaty provided that individuals' self-identification with such a group could not be subjected to verification by state authorities. Should individuals' claims to membership in such groups similarly be decisive when those claims are challenged by other members of the group in question? Does the answer to this question depend upon the specific rights that are claimed? Consider in this regard the provisions of a Hungarian law, Act LXXVII of 1993 on the Rights of National Ethnic Minorities, concerning education and minority self-government. The Act's provisions relating to minority education include the following:

Article 43

(2) In accordance with the decision of the parents or guardian, children belonging to a minority will be and may be educated in their mother tongue, "bilingually" (in their mother tongue and in Hungarian), or in Hungarian.

. . .

(4) At the request of the parents or legal representatives of eight students belonging to the same minority group, it is compulsory to establish and run a minority class or group.

Article 48

(1) Those who do not belong to the minority concerned may only study in educational institutions for minorities if the institutions still have places available after satisfying the needs of the minority.

Whether a person is to be acknowledged as belonging to an ethnic or national minority and thus entitled to claim rights established by Act LXXVII "is the exclusive and inalienable right of the individual." Suppose that a German minority in Hungary established an educational institution for its children and that a parent whom members of the German minority regard as Croatian claimed that her child is German and therefore entitled to attend the school. Suppose also that the school does not have sufficient resources to admit non-Germans. Could members of the German minority who established the school challenge the applicant's claim under Act LXXVII? *Should* the parents who established the school be allowed to challenge the applicant's claim? If so, what criteria would be relevant and valid? Is ascription of Croatian identity essentially a matter of national origin? Language? Culture?

Act LXXVII also establishes a system of minority self-government, which operates on both local and national levels. Pursuant to procedures elaborated in the Act, minorities may establish a minority self-government, a council that in most instances operates alongside the regular council, at both the national and local levels. Minority self-governments have the right to establish minority schools and other institutions, and their consent must be obtained with respect to certain official decisions regarding language use and other matters that affect minorities. (Articles 27 and 29.) Because the determination of membership in a minority group is left to each individual, anyone can declare himself a member of a minority with respect to which a minority self-government is established and may stand for election to that body without the possibility of his claim being challenged. Further, members of a minority self-government potentially can be elected by all voting citizens of the electoral district in which the self-government is established, including members of the majority. Thus in principle—and sometimes in practice—voters can elect to a self-government of a particular minority individuals who, by an "objective" test, do not belong to that minority. Should members of the minority group that is represented by such a body be able to challenge the authenticity of a candidate's claim to membership in the group? For an assessment of the Hungarian law's application to Gypsy minorities,* see Timothy William Waters and Rachel Guglielmo, *"Two Souls to Struggle With . . .": The Failing Implementation of Hungary's New Minorities Law and Discrimination Against Gypsies*, 9 Harv. Hum Rts. J. 297 (1996).

3. On the interplay between objective and subjective factors in determining membership in a minority, consider the following attempt by a United Nations expert to define "minorities" covered by Article 27 of the ICCPR:

> 7. In discussions on the definition of the term "minorities" two sorts of criteria have in fact been proposed: criteria described as objective and a criterion described as subjective.
>
> 8. The first of the criteria described as objective to which general reference is made is the existence, within a State's population, of distinct groups possessing stable ethnic, religious or linguistic characteristics that differ sharply from those of the rest of the population. The inclusion of such a component in the definition of the term "minority" is not controversial; as the Permanent Court of International Justice pointed out, the existence of such groups is a question of fact. It is therefore essential that it should be regarded as a basic element in any definition. A second objective criterion concerns the numerical size of such groups: they must in principle be numerically inferior to the rest of the population. . . .
>
> 9. As to the subjective criterion, it has generally been defined as a will on the part of the members of the groups in question to preserve their

---

* Many members of this minority eschew the term "Gypsy," which has a pejorative connotation, and prefer the designation "Roma." In Hungary, however, a majority of members of this minority still refer to themselves as "Cigany," the Hungarian word for "Gypsy."

own characteristics. If the existence of such a will had to be formally established before applying article 27, there would be reason to fear that any State wishing to evade the rule might justify its refusal by claiming that the groups themselves did not intend to preserve their individuality. Apart from this point, however, it must be said that the will in question generally emerges from the fact that a given group has kept its distinctive characteristics over a period of time. Once the existence of a group or particular community having its own identity (ethnic, religious or linguistic) in relation to the population as a whole is established, this identity implies solidarity between the members of the group, and consequently a common will on their part to contribute to the preservation of their distinctive characteristics. Bearing these observations in mind, it can be said that the subjective factor is implicit in the basic objective element, or at all events in the behaviour of the members of the group. It is possible to bring these considerations together in a tentative definition of the term "minority".

10.   The Special Rapporteur wishes to emphasize that the definition he proposes is limited in its objective. It is drawn up solely with the application of article 27 of the Covenant in mind. In that precise context, the term "minority" may be taken to refer to: "A group numerically inferior to the rest of the population of a State, in a non-dominant position, whose members—being nationals of the State—possess ethnic, religious or linguistic characteristics differing from those of the rest of the population and show, if only implicitly, a sense of solidarity, directed toward preserving their culture, traditions, religion or language."

Francesco Capotorti, *Study of the Rights of Persons Belonging to Ethnic, Religious and Linguistic Minorities*, UN Doc. E/CN.4/Sub.2/384/Add.5 (1977).

In contrast to the issues presented to the PCIJ in the *Rights of Minorities in Upper Silesia (Minority Schools)* case, several cases considered by the Human Rights Committee, the body that monitors States Parties' compliance with the ICCPR, have raised the difficult question of how to resolve claims of group membership when there is a dispute between an individual claiming membership in a protected group and an authoritative body representing the group. These issues were raised in the case of *Lovelace v. Canada*, excerpts of which are set forth in Section F(6) of this Chapter (p. 399, supra), which you may wish to re-read at this point.

Similar issues are raised by the case of *Kitok v. Sweden*, excerpts of which are set forth below. As you read the Committee's views in this case, note the multiple layers of actors who play a part in resolving contested claims of membership in a group that enjoys the rights recognized in Article 27. These actors include the individual claiming that he "belongs to'' the group; the group ''itself''; the State Party that may be in breach of its obligations under Article 27; and the Human Rights Committee.

Kitok v. Sweden

Human Rights Committee, 1988.
UN Doc. A/43/40 at 221.

. . .

1.   The author of the communication . . . is Ivan Kitok, a Swedish citizen of Sami ethnic origin, born in 1926. . . . He claims to be the victim of violations by the Government of Sweden of articles 1 and 27 of the Covenant.

2.1   It is stated that Ivan Kitok belongs to a Sami family which has been active in reindeer breeding for over 100 years. On this basis, the author claims that he has inherited the ''civil right'' to reindeer breeding from his forefathers as well as the rights to land and water in Sörkaitum Sami Village. It appears that the author has been denied the exercise of these rights because he is said to have lost his membership in the Sami village (''*sameby*'', formerly ''*lappby*''), which under a 1971 Swedish statute is like a trade union with a ''closed shop'' rule. A non-member cannot exercise Sami rights to land and water.

2.2   In an attempt to reduce the number of reindeer breeders, the Swedish Crown and the Lap bailiff have insisted that, if a Sami engages in any other profession for a period of three years, he loses his status and his name is removed from the rolls of the *lappby*, which he cannot re-enter except with special permission. Thus it is claimed that the Crown arbitrarily denies the immemorial rights of the Sami minority and that Ivan Kitok is the victim of such denial of rights.

. . .

4.2   With respect to an alleged violation of article 27, the State party [observed as follows:]

> ''The reindeer grazing legislation had the effect of dividing the Sami population of Sweden into reindeer-herding and non-reindeer-herding Sami, a distinction which is still very important. Reindeer herding is reserved for Sami who are members of a Sami village (*sameby*). . . . These Sami [today number] about 2,500. . . . Other Sami, however—the great majority, since the Sami population in Sweden today numbers some 15,000 to 20,000—have no special rights under the present law. These other Sami have found it more difficult to maintain their Sami identity and many of them are today assimilated in Swedish society. . . .
>
> ''The rules applicable on reindeer grazing are laid down in the 1971 Reindeer Husbandry Act [hereinafter the 'Act']. The *ratio legis* for this legislation is to improve the living conditions for the Sami who

have reindeer husbandry as their primary income, and to make the existence of reindeer husbandry safe for the future. There had been problems in achieving an income large enough to support a family living on reindeer husbandry. From the legislative history it appears that it was considered a matter of general importance that reindeer husbandry be made more profitable. Reindeer husbandry was considered necessary to protect and preserve the whole culture of the Sami . . .

". . . [T]he area available for reindeer grazing limits the total number of reindeer to about 300,000. No more than 2,500 Sami can support themselves on the basis of these reindeer and additional incomes.

. . .

". . . Under the present legislation, membership in a Sami village is granted by the members of the Sami village themselves.

"A person who has been denied membership in a Sami village can appeal against such a decision to [certain administrative bodies].

"An appeal against a decision of a Sami community to refuse membership may, however, be granted only if there are special reasons for allowing such membership. . . .

. . .

[The State party also argued that, although Ivan Kitok has been denied membership in the Sami community of Sörkaitum, that community had allowed him limited rights relating to reindeer husbandry.] "Thus, it cannot be said that he has been prevented from 'enjoying his own culture'. For that reason the Government maintains that the complaint should be declared inadmissible as being incompatible with the Covenant."

4.3   Should the Committee arrive at another opinion, the State party submits that:

"As is evident from the legislation, the Reindeer Husbandry Act aims at protecting and preserving the Sami culture and reindeer husbandry as such. The conflict that has occurred in this case is not so much a conflict between Ivan Kitok as a Sami and the State, but rather between Kitok and other Sami. As in every society where conflicts occur, a choice has to be made between what is considered to be in the general interest on the one hand and the interests of the individual on the other. A special circumstance here is that reindeer husbandry is so closely connected to the Sami culture that it must be considered part of the Sami culture itself.

"In this case the legislation can be said to favour the Sami community in order to make reindeer husbandry economically viable now and in the future. The pasture areas for reindeer husbandry are limited, and it is simply not possible to let all Sami exercise reindeer husbandry without jeopardizing this objective and running the risk of endangering the existence of reindeer husbandry as such.

"In this case it should be noted that it is for the Sami community to decide whether a person is to be allowed membership or not. It is only when the community denies membership that the matter can become a case for the courts.

. . .

"Article 27 guarantees the right of persons belonging to minority groups to enjoy their own culture. However, although not explicitly provided for in the text itself, such restrictions on the exercise of this right ... must be considered justified to the extent that they are necessary in a democratic society in view of public interests of vital importance or for the protection of the rights and freedoms of others. In view of the interests underlying the reindeer husbandry legislation and its very limited impact on Ivan Kitok's possibility of 'enjoying his culture', the Government submits that under all the circumstances the present case does not indicate the existence of a violation of article 27."

. . .

5.3 With respect to article 27 of the Covenant, [Ivan Kitok] states:

... Sweden has tried hard ... to promote industrial solidarity among the Swedish Sami and to divide them into full Sami and half-Sami ... It is characteristic that the 1964 Royal Committee wanted to ... make the *renby* an entirely economic association with increasing voting power for the big reindeer owners. This has also been achieved in the present *sameby*, where members get a new vote for every extra 100 reindeer. It is because of this organization of the voting power that Ivan Kitok was not admitted into his fatherland Sörkaitum Lappby.

. . .

9.1 The main question before the Committee is whether the author of the communication is the victim of a violation of article 27 of the Covenant because, as he alleges, he is arbitrarily denied immemorial rights granted to the Sami community, in particular, the right to membership of the Sami community and the right to carry out reindeer husbandry. In deciding whether [there has been a violation of article 27], the Committee bases its findings on the following considerations.

9.2 The regulation of an economic activity is normally a matter for the State alone. However, where that activity is an essential element in the culture of an ethnic community, its application to an individual may fall under article 27 of the Covenant ...

. . .

9.4 With regard to the State party's argument that the conflict in the present case is not so much a conflict between the author as a Sami and the State party, but rather between the author and the Sami community (see para. 4.3 above), the Committee observes that the State party's responsibility has been engaged, by virtue of the adoption of the Reindeer Husbandry

Act of 1971, and that it is therefore State action that has been challenged. As the State party itself points out, an appeal against a decision of the Sami community to refuse membership can only be granted if there are special reasons for allowing such membership; furthermore, the State party acknowledges that the right of the Ländsstyrelsen to grant such an appeal should be exercised very restrictively.

9.5   . . . Both parties agree that effective measures are required to ensure the future of reindeer breeding and the livelihood of those for whom reindeer farming is the primary source of income. The method selected by the State party to secure these objectives is the limitation of the right to engage in reindeer breeding to members of the Sami villages. The Committee is of the opinion that all these objectives and measures are reasonable and consistent with article 27 of the Covenant.

9.6   The Committee has none the less had grave doubts as to whether certain provisions of the Reindeer Husbandry Act, and their application to the author, are compatible with article 27 of the Covenant. Section 11 of the Reindeer Husbandry Act provides that:

"A member of a Sami community is:

"1.   A person entitled to engage in reindeer husbandry who participates in reindeer husbandry within the pasture area of the community.

"2.   A person entitled to engage in reindeer husbandry who has participated in reindeer husbandry within the pasture area of the village and who has had this as his permanent occupation and has not gone over to any other main economic activity."

. . .

9.7   It can thus be seen that the Act provides certain criteria for participation in the life of an ethnic minority whereby a person who is ethnically a Sami can be held not to be a Sami for the purposes of the Act. The Committee has been concerned that the ignoring of objective ethnic criteria in determining membership of a minority, and the application to Mr. Kitok of the designated rules, may have been disproportionate to the legitimate ends sought by the legislation. It has further noted that Mr. Kitok has always retained some links with the Sami community, always living on Sami lands and seeking to return to full-time reindeer farming as soon as it became financially possible, in his particular circumstances, for him to do so.

9.8   In resolving this problem, in which there is an apparent conflict between the legislation, which seems to protect the rights of the minority as a whole, and its application to a single member of that minority, the Committee has been guided by the *ratio decidendi* in the Lovelace case . . . , namely, that a restriction upon the right of an individual member of a minority must be shown to have a reasonable and objective justification and to be necessary for the continued viability and welfare of the minority as a whole. After a careful review of all the elements involved in this case, the Committee is of the view that there is no violation of article 27 by the

State party. In this context, the Committee notes that Mr. Kitok is permitted, albeit not as of right, to graze and farm his reindeer, to hunt and to fish.

Notes

1. Does the approach taken by the PCIJ in the *Rights of Minorities in Upper Silesia (Minority Schools)* case provide any guidance in resolving the type of dispute presented to the Human Rights Committee in the *Lovelace* and *Kitok* cases? (For the former, see Section F(6) *supra*.) In both cases, the state law that was challenged purported to enforce a protected minority group's right to make its own determination of membership. And in both cases, a determination by an authoritative body of the group in question—a determination given effect by state law, thereby potentially engaging state responsibility for a breach of the Covenant—was challenged by an individual who believed he or she had been wrongly excluded from full membership.

2. In the *Kitok* case, the Human Rights Committee observed that, under Swedish law, ethnic Samis such as Ivan Kitok were denied full Sami status when they engaged in a profession other than reindeer breeding for three years (see para. 2.2). Mr. Kitok sought "to return to full-time reindeer farming as soon as it became financially possible, in his particular circumstances, for him to do so" (para. 9.7). Under these circumstances, was it appropriate for the Committee to accept Swedish law's exclusion of Mr. Kitok from enjoying full Sami status—and with it the right to engage in reindeer husbandry? Does this depend upon whether the contested Swedish legislation, which had the effect of distinguishing between two categories of Sami members, was enacted with the support or at the behest of the Sami community? Does the answer depend upon the motives of the Sami body that denied membership rights to Mr. Kitok? Consider in this regard paragraph 5.3, in which Mr. Kitok seems to suggest that the system established by Swedish legislation had the effect of giving members of the community in which he sought full membership a vested economic interest in excluding him.

3. More generally, did the Human Rights Committee reach the right result in resolving the disputes presented by the *Kitok* and *Lovelace* cases? How should one characterize the conflicts between rights that were at issue in those cases? Consider the following proposition: "In both cases, the Human Rights Committee had to resolve a conflict between group rights and individual rights." Is this statement correct? What, precisely, was the rationale supporting the Swedish legislation that provided a basis for Mr. Kitok's exclusion? See in this regard paras. 4.2 and 4.3 of the Committee's views. Did the Swedish government—and the HRC—justify the exclusion of Mr. Kitok from full Sami membership on the ground that, in order for any Samis to enjoy their distinct culture fully, only a finite number could do so? Is this persuasive? If so, are the criteria used to distinguish "full Samis" from "half Samis" appropriate?

4.   The phrasing of Article 27 (persons belonging to minority groups "shall not be denied the right") of the ICCPR suggests that States Parties' duties vis-a-vis minorities are essentially negative. Professor Louis B. Sohn has written that, when Article 27 was being drafted, a key difference emerged "between those who favored an article requiring the state only to respect the cultural rights and freedoms of the minority, and those who sought also an obligation for the state to supply or support minority institutions from public funds." Louis B. Sohn, *The Rights of Minorities*, in The International Bill of Rights 270, 283–84 (L. Henkin ed. 1981). Although the drafting history suggests that the former prevailed, the Human Rights Committee has interpreted Article 27 to impose some affirmative obligations on States Parties. In 1994 the Committee adopted a "general comment" on Article 27 that included the following observations:

> 6.1   Although article 27 is expressed in negative terms, that article, nevertheless, does recognize the existence of a "right" and requires that it shall not be denied. Consequently, a State party is under an obligation to ensure that the existence and the exercise of this right are protected against their denial or violation. Positive measures of protection are, therefore, required not only against the acts of the State party itself, whether through its legislative, judicial or administrative authorities, but also against the acts of other persons within [the jurisdiction of] the State party.

> 6.2.   Although the rights protected under article 27 are individual rights, they depend in turn on the ability of the minority group to maintain its culture, language or religion. Accordingly, positive measures by States may also be necessary to protect the identity of a minority and the rights of its members to enjoy and develop their culture and language and to practice their religion, in community with the other members of the group....

> 7.   With regard to the exercise of the cultural rights protected under article 27, the Committee observes that culture manifests itself in many forms, including a particular way of life associated with the use of land resources, specially in the case of indigenous peoples. That right may include such traditional activities as fishing or hunting and the right to live in reserves protected by law. The enjoyment of those rights may require positive legal measures or protection and measures to ensure the effective participation of members of minority communities in decisions which affect them.

General Comment 23, U.N. Doc. CCPR/C/21/Rev.1/Add.5 (1994). Does the Committee's approach to Article 27 address the principal concerns addressed by Adeno Addis in the selection excerpted above?

c.   SELF–DETERMINATION

As the excerpt by Professor Hannum suggests, the two principal articles in the ICCPR that address rights relating to groups or members of groups are Article 1, which recognizes the right of "peoples" to self-determination, and Article 27, which recognizes rights of persons belonging to certain minority groups. The latter provision presumes that the groups whose members are protected by Article 27 are part of an established state. The meaning of Article 1 is more ambiguous. As the following material makes clear, the accepted understanding of "self-determination"—formerly a principle and later a right—has undergone several transformations.

Diane F. Orentlicher, *Separation Anxiety: International Responses To Ethno–Separatist Claims*

23 Yale J. Int'l L. 1, 21, 32, 39–43 (1998).

. . .

III.   The Nation–State in International Law

. . . [I]ssues of national identity remained largely—though not wholly—irrelevant to determinations of statehood under international law until 1919, when the "principle of national self-determination" became the touchstone for peacemakers at Versailles.

Pursuant to that principle, the boundaries of new and reconfigured states in Central and Eastern Europe would, to the extent possible, be drawn along national lines. . . .

[U.S. President Woodrow] Wilson hoped to universalize the principle applied in the postwar settlements by incorporating it into the Covenant of the League of Nations, an integral part of the Treaty of Versailles. . . . But the proposal encountered powerful opposition, not least among some of Wilson's own advisors, and was defeated.

. . .

D.   Self–Determination: Decolonization

. . .

. . . In many respects, international law experienced a fundamental disruption with the onset of World War II, and the principle of self-determination might have seemed a leading candidate for entombment as a manifest failure of the interwar system. Yet it was impossible to contain the concept's mobilizing power in the ensuing years and decades. The principle (later "right") reappeared across decades in a raft of international instruments, the legitimacy of its inclusion no longer subject to serious challenge—but its meaning periodically subject to renewed contention.

The Charter of the United Nations gave a prominent place to the "principle of self-determination," yet the sponsoring countries could not agree on the meaning of this conveniently ambiguous phrase. The U.N. Charter enshrines the principle in its first article: "The Purposes of the United Nations are . . . [t]o develop friendly relations among nations based on respect for the principle of equal rights and self-determination of peoples. . . ." Different views about the meaning of this provision emerged when it was first proposed by the Soviet Union at the San Francisco Conference, and states approved the language without resolving their differences.... Other Charter provisions addressed the administration of dependent territories in terms that supported progress toward self-government but did not, on their face, establish an absolute right to independence.

How the principle of self-determination became a right and acquired a distinctive meaning in the postwar period ... can be briefly summarized here. The "principle of self-determination of peoples" was a natural banner for the decolonization movement that swept the globe in the early decades of the United Nations' life and it took little time for the principle, previously associated with the right of subject nationalities to form their own state, to metamorphose into a right of colonial territories to break free of the metropolitan state.

In 1950, the General Assembly adopted the first of what would be many resolutions recognizing "the right of peoples and nations to self-determination" as fundamental. Among later resolutions reaffirming that right, two stand out for their normative importance. The first, the 1960 Declaration on the Granting of Independence to Colonial Countries and Peoples ("Declaration on Colonial Countries"),[220] linked the right unambiguously to a decolonization context, equating self-determination to freedom from "alien subjugation" and requiring that "[i]mmediate steps" be taken to secure the independence of "Trust and Non–Self–Governing Territories or all other territories which have not yet attained independence." In 1970, the General Assembly adopted the Declaration on Principles of International Law Concerning Friendly Relations and Co-operation Among States in Accordance with the Charter of the United Nations,[223] which reaffirmed that the "right of self-determination of peoples" was to be understood as a right to decolonization. Again, the "people" entitled to self-determination was "the people of the [territory of a] colony or non-self-governing territory...." States, in turn, had a duty to assist the United Nations in "bring[ing] about a speedy end to colonialism, having due regard to the freely expressed will of the peoples concerned."

. . .

While supporting colonial territories' right to free themselves from metropolitan rule, U.N. instruments affirming "peoples' right to self-determination" simultaneously affirmed states' right to territorial integrity.[228] A resolution adopted by the General Assembly the day after it adopted the 1960 Declaration on Colonial Countries left little doubt that

---

220. G.A. Res. 1514, U.N. GAOR, 15th Sess., Supp. No. 16, at 66, 67, U.N. Doc. A/4684 (1960) [hereinafter G.A.Res. 1514].

223. G.A. Res. 2625, U.N. GAOR, 25th Sess., Supp. No. 28, at 121, U.N. Doc. A/8018 (1970) [hereinafter G.A. Res. 2625].

228. The 1960 Declaration, for example, proclaimed that "[a]ny attempt aimed at the partial or total disruption of the national unity and the territorial integrity of a country is incompatible with the purposes and principles of the Charter of the United Nations," G.A. Res. 1514, *supra* note 220, para. 6, and the 1970 Declaration contained similar language. See G.A. Res. 2625, *supra* note 222, Annex, at 122.

the solidifying "right of self-determination" was limited to a colonial context. Establishing the so-called "salt-water" test, the resolution implied that the "peoples" entitled to independence were limited to inhabitants of discontiguous territories governed by European states.[229] The "peoples" entitled to self-determination were defined as the inhabitants of a colony, but not as ethnically distinct groups *within* those territories or established states.

It was not just established states that were eager narrowly to define the right of self-determination as a right to end colonial status. The newly independent states of Africa were keen to erect a breakwater against the spread of secessionist proclivities to subgroups in their territories. And so, with the dawning of decolonization in its continent, the Organization of African Unity adhered to the principle of *uti possidetis*, developed a century earlier when Latin American states acquired independence from Spain.[231] That principle "upgraded former administrative delimitations, established during the colonial period, to international frontiers,"[232] thereby assuring their sanctity as state borders.[233] It also provided a bright line test for assessing claims to self-determination—one that could be rationalized more readily in terms of international stability concerns than of political philosophy.

The postwar interpretation of self-determination recognized one possible exception to *uti possidetis*.... [The] Declaration on Friendly Relations hinted at the possibility that established states might forfeit their right to territorial integrity if they abused the rights of [racial or religious] minorities:

> Nothing in the foregoing paragraphs shall be construed as authorizing or encouraging any action which would dismember or impair, totally or in part, the territorial integrity or political unity of sovereign and independent States conducting themselves in compliance with the principle of equal rights and self-determination of peoples as described above and thus *possessed of a government representing the whole people belonging to the territory without distinction as to race, creed or colour.*[235]

In the postwar era, then, ... self-determination ... [finally acquired the status of] a rule of international law....

---

229. The resolution, which sets forth principles relevant to non-self-governing territories governed by Chapter XI of the U.N. Charter, asserts that a territory is presumed to be non-self-governing if it is geographically separate and ethnically or culturally distinct. *See* G.A. Res. 1541, U.N. GAOR, 15th Sess., Supp., No. 16, at 29, U.N. Doc. A/4651 (1960).

231. *See Resolution on the Intangibility of Frontiers*, Organization of African Unity,

AGH/Res. 16(1) (1964), *reprinted in* Documents of the Organization of African Unity 49 (Gino J. Naldi ed., 1992)....

232. Frontier Dispute (Burk. Faso v. Mali), 1986 I.C.J. 554, 566, paras. 23–24 (Dec. 22).

233. *Id.*, paras. 23–24.

235. G.A. Res. 2625, *supra* note 223, at 340 (emphasis added)....

But [by coupling self-determination with the principle of *uti possidetis*, postwar law severely contracted the meaning of the former. By] defining the "self" entitled to exercise the right in strictly territorial terms, the postwar rendering of self-determination drained the principle of its rich interwar meaning. Self-determination thus was transformed from a principle for state-making into a corrective to the historical injustice of alien subjugation. Through this legal alchemy, international law could claim to preserve a principle that had acquired a potent symbolic power while simultaneously depriving that principle of its power to threaten established states' territorial boundaries.

. . .

Katangese Peoples' Congress v. Zaire

African Commission on Human and Peoples' Rights, 1995.
Communication 75/92, Eighth Annual Activity Report of the Commission on Human and Peoples' Rights, 1994–95, 31st Sess. (1995).

THE FACTS

1. The communication was submitted in 1992 by Mr. Gerald Moke, President of the Katangese Peoples' Congress requesting the African Commission on Human and Peoples' Rights to:

> -recognize the Katangese Peoples' Congress as a liberation movement entitled to support in the achievement of independence for Katanga;
>
> -recognize the independence of Katanga;
>
> -help secure the evacuation of Zaire from Katanga

2. The claim is brought under Article 20(1) of the African Charter on Human and Peoples' Rights. There are no allegations of specific breaches of other human rights apart from the claim of the denial of self-determination.

3. All peoples have a right to self-determination. There may however be controversy as to the definition of peoples and the content of the right. The issue in the case is not self-determination for all Zaireans as a people but specifically for the Katangese. Whether the Katangese consist of one or more ethnic groups is, for this purpose immaterial and no evidence has been adduced to that effect.

4. The Commission believes that self-determination may be exercised in any of the following [ways:] independence, self-government, local government, federalism, confederalism, unitarism or any other form of relations that accords with the wishes of the people but fully cognizant of other recognized principles such as sovereignty and territorial integrity.

5. The Commission is obliged to uphold the sovereignty and territorial integrity of Zaire, a member of the OAU and a party to the African Charter on Human and Peoples' Rights.

6.   In the absence of concrete evidence of violations of human rights to the point that the territorial integrity of Zaire should be called to question and in the absence of evidence that the people of Katanga are denied the right to participate in Government as guaranteed by Article 13(1) of the African Charter, the Commission holds the view that Katanga is obliged to exercise a variant of self-determination that is compatible with the sovereignty and territorial integrity of Zaire.

FOR THE ABOVE REASONS, THE COMMISSION

declares that the case holds no evidence of violations of any rights under the African Charter. The request for independence for Katanga therefore has no merit under the African Charter on Human and Peoples' Rights.

Notes

1.   In paragraph 6 of its decision in the Katangese Peoples' Congress case, the African Commission seems to imply that either "violations of human rights" that reach a certain level or the denial of a people's right to participate in government might justify an exception to the general rule that only colonial peoples are entitled to claim independence from their existing sovereign. What might be the basis for such an exception?

Reports by two League of Nations bodies involved in addressing a dispute over the status of the Aaland Islands (which were and remain subject to Finnish sovereignty) during the interwar period similarly hinted that, although distinct groups within an established country are not generally entitled to secede merely because a majority of their members may wish to do so, the situation might be different if the government with sovereignty over these groups violates their basic rights. One of these bodies, a Commission of Jurists, proclaimed the "sovereign rights of a State" not to be threatened with secession, but implied that the League might have jurisdiction to consider the status of a minority group in the event of "a manifest and continued abuse of sovereign power, to the detriment of a section of the population of a State." *Report of the International Committee of Jurists Entrusted by the Council of the League of Nations with the Task of Giving an Advisory Opinion upon the Legal aspects of the Aaland Islands Question*, League of Nations O.J. Spec. Supp. 3, at 5 (1920). The second body, a Commission of Rapporteurs, suggested that secession might be available as a "last resort when the State lacks either the will or the power to enact and apply just and effective guarantees" of minority rights. The Aaland Islands Question: Report Submitted to the Council of the League of Nations by the Commission of Rapporteurs, League of Nations Doc. B7.21/68/106, at 28 (1921).

In a similar vein, the 1970 Declaration on Principles of International Law Concerning Friendly Relations and Cooperation Among States in Accordance with the Charter of the United Nations, G.A. Res. 2625, UN GAOR, 25th Sess., Supp. No. 28, at 121, UN Doc. A/8018 (1970), made clear that the right of peoples to self-determination was to be understood as a right to decolonization, but then hinted at the possibility that established states might forfeit their right to territorial integrity if they excluded groups from full political participation based upon their race or "creed":

> Nothing in the foregoing paragraphs shall be construed as authorizing or encouraging any action which would dismember or impair, totally or in part, the territorial integrity or political unity of sovereign and independent States conducting themselves in compliance with the principle of equal rights and self-determination of peoples as described above and thus *possessed of a government representing the whole people belonging to the territory without distinction as to race, creed or colour.*

(Emphasis added). The following analysis suggests that the Declaration contemplates secession in only a narrow set of circumstances:

> [T]he right of internal self-determination[*] embodied in the 1970 Declaration is a right conferred only on *racial* or *religious* groups living in a sovereign State which are denied access to the political decision-making process; *linguistic* or *national* groups *do not* have a concomitant right....

> By limiting self-determination to racial and religious groups, the draftsmen made it clear that self-determination was not considered a right held by *the entire people* of an authoritarian state. The existence of a government which tramples upon its citizens' basic rights and fundamental freedoms does not give rise to a right of internal self-determination. However, even those groups that *are* afforded rights under the Declaration are not as well off as one might expect, for it is *equal access to government* to which they are entitled, not *equal rights*. The Declaration does not require States to grant racial and religious groups a menu of rights, nor does it prohibit the imposition of invidious measures. It simply demands that States allow racial and religious groups to have access to government institutions....

> . . .

> Although secession is implicitly authorized by the Declaration, it must however be strictly construed, as with all exceptions. It can therefore be suggested that the following conditions might warrant secession: when the central authorities of a sovereign State persistently refuse to grant participatory rights to a religious or racial group, grossly and systematically trample upon their fundamental rights, and deny the possibility of reaching a peaceful settlement within the framework of the State structure. Thus, denial of the basic right of representation does not give rise *per se* to the right of secession. In addition, there must be gross breaches of fundamental human rights, and, what is more, the exclusion of any likelihood for a possible peaceful solution within the existing State structure.

* [The term "internal self-determination" generally is used to refer to self-government within defined political boundaries, while the phrase "external self-determination" refers to the determination by a people of the international political status of its territory.—Editors' Note.]

If this reasoning is correct, the contention could be made that the Declaration on Friendly Relations *links external self-determination to internal self-determination in exceptional circumstances.* A racial or religious group may attempt secession, a form of external self-determination, when it is apparent that internal self-determination is absolutely beyond reach. Extreme and unremitting persecution and the lack of any reasonable prospect for peaceful challenge may make secession legitimate. A racial or religious group may secede—thus exercising the most radical form of external self-determination—once it is clear that all attempts to achieve internal self-determination have failed or are destined to fail.

Antonio Cassese, Self–Determination of Peoples: A Legal Reappraisal 114–115 & 119–120 (1995).

Is Judge Cassese's view that the 1970 Declaration does not entitle racial and religious groups to "equal rights", but rather to "equal access to government", persuasive? What underlying theory or theories supports secession by groups that are denied certain fundamental rights? What is the rationale for limiting such a right of secession to the grounds identified in the various instruments and decisions noted above?

2. In late March 1999, as the North Atlantic Treaty Organization (NATO) attacked Yugoslav forces in an effort to bring an end to their atrocities against ethnic Albanians in the Yugoslav province of Kosovo, leaders of NATO member states began to suggest that the systematic and brutal repression of Kosovar Albanians by Yugoslav authorities might have the consequence that Yugoslavia had "forfeited" its sovereignty over the province. Are these statements evidence of state practice in support of the views of the two Commissions that examined the Aaland Islands case?

———

In its postwar incarnation, the principle of self-determination has now largely accomplished its assigned task—emancipating colonial territories. In this setting, a significant measure of scholarly support has begun to coalesce around the view that self-determination should once again be invested with new meaning, this time emphasizing its internal dimension—democratic governance.

Gregory H. Fox, *Self–Determination in the Post–Cold War Era: A New Internal Focus?*

16 Mich. J. Int'l L. 733, 733–36, 752–55 (1995).

Self-determination . . . is now generally understood as a binding principle of international law, drawing its normative force primarily from treaties but also from important sources of customary law. At the same time, with the effective end of decolonization and the virtually unanimous refusal of states to recognize a right of secession, the legal norm appears to have been deprived of much of its content. . . .

. . .

Commentators and legal actors have [devised] a number of strategies to avoid one of two equally unsettling conclusions . . .: either that self-determination as a legal norm was relevant only to the specific historical period of decolonization or that its ascent into law was misguided from the start. Primary among these strategies has been to view the right as operating solely within the territorial confines of existing states, manifesting itself not in the relations between colonies and metropolitan powers or states and self-defined "peoples" but in the structure of domestic political institutions. These institutions may include minority protection regimes, democratic political processes, safeguards for cultural rights, and various forms of federative autonomy. Viewing self-determination as an "internal" right may require a substantial reordering of a state's domestic law . . . ; it would not, however, require the redrawing of its boundaries.

. . . [A]n internal conception of self-determination is slowly gaining acceptance. . . .

. . .

Internal self-determination takes as an important premise the view that struggles for autonomy often find their roots in the failure of national political institutions to address the interests of minority groups. . . . Internal self-determination attempts to ameliorate such histories of exclusion by creating inclusive political processes through which, collectively, the entire population may chart its own destiny. It "enables the people of a country to choose their political system, their political, economic and social institutions and their political leaders, or to make important constitutional political decisions."[95] In cases of decolonization the people of the territory are consulted only once; where the self is a sovereign state, however, consultation is ongoing, bolstered by the legal assurances of participation that an institutionalized democratic institution entails.

In recent years, the international community has begun describing three aspects of such an inclusive political process as manifestations of the right of self-determination. The first . . . is democratic elections, which are the primary form of consultation required by the right. . . .

The second element is the protection of minority rights, which traces its pedigree to the minority regimes of the interwar period but is also the subject of more recent legal instruments. Even where elections are free and fair, minority groups may by definition find few of their views reflected in national policy, particularly if a state does not follow a proportional representation electoral system. Groups effectively excluded from meaningful participation in this fashion, or through outright discrimination, are increasingly granted protections that focus on their group status. These

---

95. [Yves Beigbeder, International Monitoring of Plebiscites, Referenda and National Elections: Self–Determination and Transition to Democracy 18 (1994)].

rights include not only those of a political nature but also certain protections of groups' cultural integrity. In contrast to rights concerned solely with political participation, minority rights more closely approximate the collective nature of the right to self-determination. . . .

Third, international organizations are beginning to involve themselves in the construction of autonomy regimes within states. . . .

. . . As these three categories of rights suggest, an internal right functions not so much as an independent source of entitlements but as an analytical organizing principle. Its own unique contribution consists mainly of refocussing autonomy claims from the expectation of independence brought on by the success of decolonization to modes of participation in the domestic political arena. . . . The particular legal guarantees represented by an internal right draw on the jurisprudence of other human rights concerned more specifically with pluralism and nondiscrimination in domestic politics. . . . In short, internal self-determination functions as an omnibus interpretive tool, weaving together a variety of more particular rights in order to demonstrate that a principled co-existence is possible between claims to group autonomy and the maintenance of states' territorial integrity.

. . .

Diane F. Orentlicher, *Separatism and the Democratic Entitlement*

92 ASIL Proc. 131 (1998).*

. . .

. . . While international law does not generally support the claims of state-seeking groups, contemporary developments may lend some secessionists a new source of legitimacy and have significant—if complex—implications for the resolution of many separatist claims.

The developments I have in mind were chronicled by Thomas Franck in an important article published six years ago in the *American Journal of International Law*. In that article Franck identified an emerging "democratic entitlement" and described the nascent law this way: "Democracy is on the way to becoming a global entitlement, one that increasingly will be promoted and protected by collective international processes."[1] Although Franck did not suggest that this emerging law has substantial implications for separatist movements, I believe that principles underlying the "democratic entitlement" are scarcely irrelevant to the legitimacy of their claims.

Before I develop this point, it may be helpful first to make clear what I am *not* claiming. It is not my view that the emerging right to self-

---

* Reproduced with permission from 92 ASIL Prac. 131 (1998) © The American Society of International Law.

1. Thomas M. Franck, *The Emerging Right to Democratic Governance*, 86 Am. J. Int'l L. 46, 46 (1992).

government *generally* privileges separatist claims. On the contrary, considerations relating to democratic theory may point in much the opposite direction. I do, however, disagree with the view that democratic theory is largely, if not wholly, irrelevant to the resolution of separatist claims.

This view is, in fact, commonplace among political theorists.[2] Whether the issue is how to identify nations that are entitled to their own state or local populations entitled to home rule, many writers claim that "there is no theory for determining when one ... polity ought to end and another begin."[3] ...

These scholars are surely correct in claiming that a right to democratic government does not automatically or generally entitle separatists to achieve their aims. Still, it does not follow that the democratic entitlement is irrelevant to separatist claims.

An appeal to common-sense intuition may help make this clear. Suppose that, instead of opposing Quebec's bid to secede, the rest of Canada voted in support of the separatists' claim. Suppose at the same time that residents of Quebec, including all of its significant minority populations, overwhelmingly voted in favor of secession. If, with Franck, we believe that an emerging body of international law "requires democracy to validate governance,"[5] I suspect that most of us would conclude that the mutual desire of Canada's citizens to divide should—perhaps must—be honored. To do otherwise would manifestly subject Canada's citizens to government without their consent. And as [Jamin] Raskin has written, "the very heart of the democratic idea" is "that governmental legitimacy depends upon the affirmative consent of those who are governed."[6]

The position I have suggested is not as novel as it may seem. For some eighteenth-century nationalists—the intellectual progenitors of Franck's democratic entitlement—it seemed axiomatic that the right to self-government implies the right to choose one's fellow citizens. The point seemed equally plain to John Stuart Mill:

> Where the sentiment of nationality exists in any force, there is a *prima facie* case for uniting all the members of the nationality under the same government, and a government to themselves apart. *This is merely saying that the question of government ought to be decided by the governed. One hardly knows what any division of the human race*

---

2. *See, e.g.,* Frederick G. Whelan, *Prologue: Democratic Theory and the Boundary Problem,* in Liberal Democracy, 25 NOMOS 13, 16 (J. Roland Pennock & John W. Chapman eds. 1983) (asserting that "[b]oundaries comprise a problem ... that is insoluble within the framework of democratic theory...."); Richard Briffault, *Voting Rights, Home Rule, and Metropolitan Governance: The Secession of Staten Island as a Case Study in the Dilemmas of Local Self–Determination,* 92 Colum. L. Rev. 775, 800 (1992)

(observing that "the concept of self-government says nothing about who is the 'self' that does the governing").

3. Briffault, *supra* note 2, at 801.

5. [Franck, *supra* note 1,] at 47.

6. Jamin B. Raskin, *Legal Aliens, Local Citizens: The Historical, Constitutional and Theoretical Meanings of Alien Suffrage,* 141 U. Pa. L. Rev. 1391, 1444 (1993).

should be free to do, if not to determine with which of the various-collective bodies of human beings they choose to associate themselves.[7]

The argument is elegant in its simplicity: Since democracy is, by definition, government with the consent of the governed, the boundaries of political commitment should be determined in accordance with the principle of consent.

This argument need not imply that the boundaries of states are perennially up for popular reconsideration; the continuing consent of states' citizens can generally be assumed, and indeed this assumption is indispensable to the daily practice of democracy. But if consent is manifestly withdrawn by a significant portion of a state's population, the legitimacy of that state's sovereignty over the rebel population is surely placed in doubt.

Again, let me appeal to common-sense intuition to make this point. It is now established doctrine that alien states may not lawfully impose their rule upon unconsenting peoples. Put differently, international law no longer abides colonization or forcible annexation. But if these forms of non-consensual rule are incompatible with accepted principles of self-determination, surely those same principles are at least challenged by a state's continued assertion of sovereignty over a defined population that has unambiguously and irrevocably rejected its sovereignty.

I have tried to make the point that Franck's democratic entitlement may have significant implications for separatist claims by invoking the proverbial easy case—a hypothetical situation in which all affected citizens support a separatist claim. But few cases are easy; most separatist claims are contested. When the will of the affected polity is divided, democratic theories are not readily dispositive of contested separatist claims. Even so, theories of democratic government may point to considerations that are relevant to the legitimacy and resolution of such claims, principally because some resolutions may better promote values relating to democratic governance than others. By way of illustration, I would like to explore the implications for separatist claims of two different strands of democratic theory—utilitarianism and republicanism.

A utilitarian justification for democracy claims that self-government is more likely than its alternatives to secure the interests of the greatest number of persons subject to governmental authority. For eighteenth-century utilitarians like Jeremy Bentham and James Mill, democracy was not an end in itself but a means for maximizing the realization of individuals' interests through aggregation of private preferences. But this justification may begin to fray if a polity is too diverse, at least if its diversity entails significant differences in political choices.

When individuals define their political interests in terms of the well-being of the national group to which they belong, nationalism and utilitari-

---

7. John Stuart Mill, Considerations on Representative Government (1861), *in* Utilitarianism, On Liberty, Considerations on Representative Government 392 (Everyman's ed. 1993) (emphasis added).

an justifications for democracy may converge to support national separatist movements. . . .

        . . .

Thus far I have offered examples of how democratic theories might support separatist claims. But other considerations, also derived from justifications for self-government or considerations relating to its successful practice, may point in the opposite direction. As President Lincoln argued, if a secessionist movement opposed by most of a country's citizens prevailed, its success would vitiate the principle of majority rule. Further, even the possibility of secession may thwart democratic deliberations by diminishing incentives for opposing groups to reach accommodative solutions. When secession is known to be possible, political minorities within a democracy can distort the outcome of political processes by threatening to secede if their views do not prevail.

Further, a counterpoint to the claim that too much diversity may impair democratic deliberations is the argument that ethno-national states by their nature tend toward authoritarian social arrangements. . . . If, with John Locke, we believe that the principle of self-government follows from the intrinsic and equal worth of all people, it is plain that the authoritarian arrangements associated with ethno-national states imperil the core values justifying democratic government itself.

        . . .

        ———

In the Matter of Section 53 of the Supreme Court Act (Reference Re Secession of Quebec)

Supreme Court of Canada, 1998.
[1998] 2 S.C.R. 217.

[The following decision was rendered pursuant to the reference jurisdiction of the Canadian Supreme Court, which enables that Court to render advisory opinions on questions referred by the Governor in Council.]

I.   *Introduction*

This Reference requires us to consider momentous questions that go to the heart of our system of constitutional government. . . .

        . . .

III.   *Reference Questions*

A.   *Question 1*

Under the Constitution of Canada, can the National Assembly, legislature or government of Quebec effect the secession of Quebec from Canada unilaterally?

(1) *Introduction*

... [Although the constitutional texts] have a primary place in determining constitutional rules, they are not exhaustive. The Constitution also "embraces unwritten, as well as written rules", [including]

> the global system of rules and principles which govern the exercise of constitutional authority in the whole and in every part of the Canadian state.

... Such principles and rules emerge from an understanding of the constitutional text itself, the historical context, and previous judicial interpretations of constitutional meaning. In our view, there are four fundamental and organizing principles of the Constitution which are relevant in addressing the question before us (although this enumeration is by no means exhaustive): federalism; democracy; constitutionalism and the rule of law; and respect for minorities.

· · ·

(b) *Federalism*

It is undisputed that Canada is a federal state....

In a federal system of government such as ours, political power is shared by two orders of government: the federal government on the one hand, and the provinces on the other....

The principle of federalism recognizes the diversity of the component parts of Confederation, and the autonomy of provincial governments to develop their societies within their respective spheres of jurisdiction. The federal structure of our country also facilitates democratic participation by distributing power to the government thought to be most suited to achieving the particular societal objective having regard to this diversity....

The principle of federalism facilitates the pursuit of collective goals by cultural and linguistic minorities which form the majority within a particular province. This is the case in Quebec, where the majority of the population is French-speaking, and which possesses a distinct culture....

(c) *Democracy*

Democracy is a fundamental value in our constitutional law and political culture. While it has both an institutional and an individual aspect, the democratic principle was also argued before us in the sense of the supremacy of the sovereign will of a people, in this case potentially to be expressed by Quebecers in support of unilateral secession....

The principle of democracy has always informed the design of our constitutional structure, and continues to act as an essential interpretive consideration to this day....

· · ·

Democracy ... is fundamentally connected to substantive goals, most importantly, the promotion of self-government. Democracy accommodates cultural and group identities ...

· · ·

It is, of course, true that democracy expresses the sovereign will of the people. Yet this expression ... must be taken in the context of the other institutional values we have identified as pertinent to this Reference. The relationship between democracy and federalism means, for example, that in Canada there may be different and equally legitimate majorities in different provinces and territories and at the federal level. No one majority is more or less "legitimate" than the others as an expression of democratic opinion, although, of course, the consequences will vary with the subject matter. A federal system of government enables different provinces to pursue policies responsive to the particular concerns and interests of people in that province. At the same time, Canada as a whole is also a democratic community in which citizens construct and achieve goals on a national scale through a federal government acting within the limits of its jurisdiction. The function of federalism is to enable citizens to participate concurrently in different collectivities and to pursue goals at both a provincial and federal level.

. . .

Finally, we highlight that a functioning democracy requires a continuous process of discussion. The Constitution mandates government by democratic legislatures, and an executive accountable to them, "resting ultimately on public opinion reached by discussion and the interplay of ideas" ... At both the federal and provincial level, by its very nature, the need to build majorities necessitates compromise, negotiation, and deliberation. No one has a monopoly on truth, and our system is predicated on the faith that in the marketplace of ideas, the best solutions to public problems will rise to the top. Inevitably, there will be dissenting voices. A democratic system of government is committed to considering those dissenting voices, and seeking to acknowledge and address those voices in the laws by which all in the community must live.

The *Constitution Act, 1982* gives expression to this principle, by conferring a right to initiate constitutional change on each participant in Confederation. In our view, the existence of this right imposes a corresponding duty on the participants in Confederation to engage in constitutional discussions in order to acknowledge and address democratic expressions of a desire for change in other provinces. This duty is inherent in the democratic principle which is a fundamental predicate of our system of governance.

. . .

(4) *The Operation of the Constitutional Principles in the Secessionist Context*

. . .

[The Court observed that, although the Canadian Constitution is silent on secession, an act of secession would alter the country's constitutional arrangements.]

The Constitution is the expression of the sovereignty of the people of Canada. It lies within the power of the people of Canada, acting through their various governments duly elected and recognized under the Constitution, to effect whatever constitutional arrangements are desired within Canadian territory, including should it be so desired, the secession of Quebec from Canada. As this Court [has previously held], "The Constitution of a country is a statement of the will of the people to be governed in accordance with certain principles held as fundamental and certain prescriptions restrictive of the powers of the legislature and government". The manner in which such a political will could be formed and mobilized is a somewhat speculative exercise, though we are asked to assume the existence of such a political will for the purpose of answering the question before us. By the terms of this Reference, we have been asked to consider whether it would be constitutional in such a circumstance for the National Assembly, legislature or government of Quebec to effect the secession of Quebec from Canada *unilaterally*.

The "unilateral" nature of the act is of cardinal importance and we must be clear as to what is understood by this term. In one sense, any step towards a constitutional amendment initiated by a single actor on the constitutional stage is "unilateral". We do not believe that this is the meaning contemplated by Question 1, nor is this the sense in which the term has been used in argument before us. Rather, what is claimed by a right to secede "unilaterally" is the right to effectuate secession without prior negotiations with the other provinces and the federal government. At issue is not the legality of the first step but the legality of the final act of purported unilateral secession. The supposed juridical basis for such an act is said to be a clear expression of democratic will in a referendum in the province of Quebec. . . .

. . . [A] referendum undoubtedly may provide a democratic method of ascertaining the views of the electorate on important political questions on a particular occasion. The democratic principle identified above would demand that considerable weight be given to a clear expression by the people of Quebec of their will to secede from Canada, even though a referendum, in itself and without more, has no direct legal effect, and could not in itself bring about unilateral secession. Our political institutions are premised on the democratic principle, and so an expression of the democratic will of the people of a province carries weight, in that it would confer legitimacy on the efforts of the government of Quebec to initiate the Constitution's amendment process in order to secede by constitutional means. In this context, we refer to a "clear" majority as a qualitative evaluation. The referendum result, if it is to be taken as an expression of the democratic will, must be free of ambiguity both in terms of the question asked and in terms of the support it achieves.

The federalism principle, in conjunction with the democratic principle, dictates that the clear repudiation of the existing constitutional order and the clear expression of the desire to pursue secession by the population of a province would give rise to a reciprocal obligation on all parties to Confederation to negotiate constitutional changes to respond to that desire. . . . The corollary of a legitimate attempt by one participant in Confederation to seek an amendment to the Constitution is an obligation on all parties to come to the negotiating table. The clear repudiation by the people of Quebec of the existing constitutional order would confer legitimacy on demands for secession, and place an obligation on the other provinces and the federal government to acknowledge and respect that expression of democratic will by entering into negotiations and conducting them in accordance with the underlying constitutional principles already discussed.

What is the content of this obligation to negotiate? . . .

The conduct of the parties in such negotiations would be governed by the same constitutional principles which give rise to the duty to negotiate: federalism, democracy, constitutionalism and the rule of law, and the protection of minorities. Those principles lead us to reject two absolutist propositions. One of those propositions is that there would be a legal obligation on the other provinces and federal government to accede to the secession of a province, subject only to negotiation of the logistical details of secession. . . .

For both theoretical and practical reasons, we cannot accept this view. We hold that Quebec could not purport to invoke a right of self-determination such as to dictate the terms of a proposed secession to the other parties: that would not be a negotiation at all. . . . The democracy principle . . . cannot be invoked to trump . . . the operation of democracy in the other provinces or in Canada as a whole.

However, we are equally unable to accept the reverse proposition, that a clear expression of self-determination by the people of Quebec would impose *no* obligations upon the other provinces or the federal government. The continued existence and operation of the Canadian constitutional order cannot remain indifferent to the clear expression of a clear majority of Quebecers that they no longer wish to remain in Canada. This would amount to the assertion that other constitutionally recognized principles necessarily trump the clearly expressed democratic will of the people of Quebec. . . . The rights of other provinces and the federal government cannot deny the right of the government of Quebec to pursue secession, should a clear majority of the people of Quebec choose that goal, so long as in doing so, Quebec respects the rights of others.

· · ·

[In considering whether Quebec is entitled under international law to secede unilaterally, the Court found that international law indisputably entitles a population to choose independence at *its* will only in cases of colonial domination. Noting that some commentators believe that international law also entitles a population to secede unilaterally if it is systematically denied equal representation in its country's political system, the court concluded that "the current Quebec context cannot be said to approach such a threshold."]

Notes

1.   The resurgence of ethnic assertion in Europe during the final decade of the twentieth century has prompted some scholars and regional organiza-

tions to support autonomy regimes and other forms of decentralization as means of promoting the "self-determination" of ethnic communities within established states. Traces of this approach are evident in the Canadian Supreme Court's discussion of federalism in the Reference concerning Quebec. A number of documents adopted by the Commission (now Organization) for Security and Cooperation in Europe (CSCE) in the early 1990s affirm regional autonomy regimes as one appropriate means of assuring effective participation of minorities in public affairs. These include the Document of the Copenhagen Meeting of the Conference on the Human Dimension of the CSCE, para. 35 (1990) and the CSCE Charter of Paris for a New Europe (1990). The latter cites, as one approach that has achieved "positive results ... in an appropriate democratic manner," "local and autonomous administration, as well as autonomy on a territorial basis, including the existence of consultative, legislative and executive bodies chosen through free and periodic elections."

The 1994 European Framework Convention on the Protection of National Minorities reflects similar support for efforts to vest greater responsibility for self-governance in minority communities. Article 15 of the Convention provides that Parties "shall create the conditions necessary for the effective participation of persons belonging to national minorities in cultural, social and economic life and in public affairs, in particular those affecting them." An explanatory report accompanying the convention cites "decentralised or local forms of government" as one measure through which States Parties could promote "the necessary conditions for such participation." For an analysis of the compatibility of various autonomy regimes with international human rights law, see David Wippman, *Practical and Legal Constraints on Internal Power Sharing, in* International Law and Ethnic Conflict 211 (David Wippman ed., 1998).

2.   Efforts to apply democratic principles to resolve contested separatist claims raise a number of vexing issues, including the questions of who should be entitled to vote in a plebiscite concerning secession, and how mixed polling results should be evaluated. Suppose, for example, a referendum on secession by Quebec were held throughout Canada. Suppose further that a majority of Quebecers voted to secede, but that Quebec's indigenous communities, along with the majority of Canadians outside Quebec, voted overwhelmingly against secession. How should such dilemmas be resolved? Does the Canadian Supreme Court address this issue— either explicitly or implicitly—in its advisory opinion on Quebec's right to secede unilaterally? If so, how does the Court address this dilemma? Does its approach reflect a particular vision of democracy?

3.   In its advisory opinion on Quebec secession, the Canadian Supreme Court observed that "[t]he corollary of a legitimate attempt by one participant in Confederation to seek an amendment to the Constitution is an obligation on all parties to come to the negotiating table." Suppose, however, that the rest of Canada were unwilling to negotiate. Does the Court's opinion provide any guidance as to whether Quebec would be entitled to secede in such a situation?

2.   OTHER "GENERATIONS" OF RIGHTS

The Universal Declaration, the Covenants, and the particular conventions (including regional conventions), generally address civil and political rights, the "first generation" of rights identified with U.S. and other Western constitutional rights, and a "second generation" of economic and social rights associated with the "welfare state." Except for the addition of the right to "self-determination" in the two Covenants, there has been no serious move to append to these instruments, or to adopt new conventions to protect additional kinds of rights (thus giving them the mantle of international human rights). But there have been proposals to recognize additional "generations" of rights—a right to peace, to a healthful environment, to permanent sovereignty over natural resources, to development. A right to development has been recognized by a General Assembly declaration, *infra* p. 481. And there has been a comprehensive effort to develop laws and institutions to protect the world environment, some of which use the language of rights. In general, these additional generations of rights are claimed not for individuals but for societies or other groups, or for individuals as members of those societies or groups.

Louis Henkin, *Other "Generations" of Rights*

in International Law: Politics and Values 196–202 (1995).

. . .

The Universal Declaration is a noble instrument but there was no suggestion that it was exhaustive. The human values of human rights have been so politically appealing, and the human rights mantle so attractive, they have inspired moves to add new rights to those identified as in the first two generations, and to promote additional "generations" of rights.

In general, the new rights that have been added, or proposed for addition, to those listed in the Universal Declaration have been "collective" rather than individual rights. Of course, all human rights are collective in that they are universal: all human beings are entitled to them. They are collective in that rights are enjoyed in society and society is required to organize itself to realize them for all. They are collective in that, according to the human rights ideology, respect for the rights of each inures to the benefit of all and is essential to the good society. But in essence, the rights in the first two generations are rights of individuals; in a later development the mantle of human rights has been claimed also by groups of varying dimension, invoked even by the society and by the state as a whole.

It is useful to distinguish individual rights from group rights, and both from communal, societal goods, as well as from what I have called state values. For example, the right not to be a victim of genocide is both a right of the group threatened and of each individual member of the group. But the group threatened may constitute only a small minority in the state. The right not to be a victim of genocide is clearly a human value, not directly the "right" or the "good" of the society as a whole, or a reflection of values of state autonomy. As with other individual rights, the claim to freedom from genocide is a claim upon the state, and the state—the government—is required itself to refrain from genocide and to ensure that the right is protected against violation by others. The minorities treaties, too, protected rights of the ethnic group, as well as the rights of their members, against the majority and against the society as a whole. Similarly, the rights of cultural and religious groups, or of trade unions and other voluntary associations, also assert individual human values for their members as against the interests of the majority, or against alleged goods for the society as a whole. Such group rights are rights within a society, are claims by an aggregation of individuals upon society, and the state is required to respect and ensure them.

Other "collective rights," however, are not "constitutional" limitations on society, or claims upon the society for the benefit of individuals or small groups; they are really values asserted by the society as a whole to override individual or minority claims. A state may assert the needs of national security or public order as limitations on individual rights; it is not entitled to dress these values in the garb of human rights and individual human dignity. States have many rights under international law, but they are not human rights.

Self–Determination

Both International Covenants include the right of every people to self-determination and to sovereignty over its natural resources ("economic self-determination"). Those provisions were added over opposition that insisted that these are not individual rights, and that they were not in fact being integrated (and could not be integrated) into the scheme of obligations and implementation of the rest of the Covenant. At bottom, the objection to including the right of self-determination was not that it was a collective or group right (a right of a "people"), but that, unlike the other rights in the Covenants, it was not a continuing claim by some elements in society against the society, but ordinarily a one-time claim by a "people" to leave a society. The right of a people to sovereignty over its resources, too, seems not to be a claim against the state by persons or groups subject to its jurisdiction.

It is not clear what has been added to human rights law by declaring these principles to be human rights, or how states parties to the Covenants are to respect and ensure them. Their inclusion in the Covenants, however, confirms their legal character at least for states parties to those Covenants, and has helped them become principles of customary law. Controversy as to the scope, content and implications of these principles has not been resolved. There is no agreement as to what (or who) is a people or what the right of self-determination implies. It is accepted that self-determination outlaws traditional colonialism over unwilling peoples; apparently it does not include a right of secession from an existing state for a "people" or for the inhabitants of part of the territory of a state. There is even less agreement as to the consequences of the provision that a people has sovereignty over its resources.* Those who have invested in these resources (with the consent of the state) have insisted that state sovereignty over its resources does not justify or legitimate expropriation of foreign investments, or breach of concession contracts with foreign nationals, without just compensation.

The Right to Development

Some have claimed the human rights mantle for third, fourth, fifth and even more generations of rights, principally rights to development, peace, a healthful environment. There has been no resistance in the political system to recognizing and accepting these values, but much resistance to denominating them human rights and giving them legally binding character.

There has been strongest support for—and least resistance to—a human right to development. Efforts to establish its character as a human right have been frustrated by lack of definition of the right and of the obligations it may imply. There has been particular uncertainty as to whether the right addresses political, social or economic development, and whether it speaks to individual or societal development.

It is arguable that the right to development, both individual and societal, and the obligation of a state (and perhaps of the international system) to contribute to such development, are already provided or at least prefigured in the Universal Declaration. In a large sense, the right to development is the sum, or the aim, of all the rights in the Declaration, especially the right to an education and of other economic and social rights, but also of civil and political rights. The Declaration also includes specific references that point to development: "Everyone is entitled to a social and international order in which the rights and freedoms set forth in this Declaration can be fully realized" (Art. 28). "Everyone has duties to the community in which alone the free and full development of his personality is possible" (Art. 29 (1)).

In 1986, the United Nations General Assembly capped many debates by adopting the Declaration on the Right to Development. The Assembly declared it to be an "inalienable human right" of every human person and all people to participate in, contribute to, and enjoy economic, social, cultural and political development. The right declared is a skillful blend of individual rights and individual responsibility, of individual rights as well as people's rights, and of various opinions and values. It attempts to declare the relation to development of the first and second generations of rights.

---

* Perhaps individuals or groups within a state, claiming to represent the people, can argue that the state violates the provision if it alienates the people's "patrimony" in its resources by corrupt or unwise concessions to foreign bodies. A claim of this kind was advanced in 1992 before the International Court of Justice. Nauru claimed that Australia breached "the obligation to respect the right of the Nauruan people to permanent sovereignty over their natural wealth and resources" by exploiting certain phosphate lands before Nauru's independence, at a time when Australia was an Administering Authority for Nauru under the Trusteeship System provided for by Chapter XII of the U.N. Charter. See Case Concerning Certain Phosphate Lands in Nauru (Nauru v. Australia) (Preliminary Objections), 1992 I.C.J. 240, 243.

The Preamble affirms that failure to respect human rights (civil-political as well as economic-social-cultural) is a serious obstacle to development and that there must be equal attention to civil-political and to economic-social-cultural rights. The Declaration calls for disarmament and for devoting resources released thereby to development, especially for developing countries. Efforts to promote human rights should be accompanied by efforts to establish a new economic order "based on sovereign equality, interdependence, mutual interest and cooperation among all States."

The Declaration on the Right to Development is a declaration, not a convention, and its significance for the international law of human rights is uncertain. But it is interesting as a political reflection on human rights generally, and as interpretation of the international law of human rights. The General Assembly does not declare the right to development to be a new generation of rights, perhaps not even an independent human right, but it links development with established human rights as cause and effect. The Declaration is notable for its reaffirmation that all human rights are indivisible and interdependent; that respect for some rights does not justify violation of others; and that the right to development itself cannot serve as reason (or pretext) for violating any of the rights in either of the first generations of rights.

A Human Right to Peace

Peace between states is a primary value of the inter-state system, the objective of the law of the United Nations Charter. Every state can be said to have a right to peace. Assertions of a human right to peace have generally been dismissed as yet another exercise in rhetoric: states generally have seen no need to establish obligations for states in this regard beyond those already assumed in the United Nations Charter.

Yet, conceptually at least, an individual human right to peace cannot be dismissed out of hand. The state's right to peace under international law is designed not merely to safeguard state autonomy but to secure the deepest values of its society and of each of its inhabitants. Surely, human dignity requires that the individual not be subject to the horrors of war. But is peace a human right like those listed in the Universal Declaration and legislated in the Covenants?

An individual human right to peace is perhaps implied in Article 28 of the Universal Declaration: "Everyone is entitled to a social and international order in which the rights and freedoms set forth in this Declaration can be fully realized." That Article, however, has not been converted by the Covenants into specific legal rights which the state must recognize, respect, ensure and strive to realize.

As with the individual's share in a people's right to self-determination or in a society's right to development, it would not be easy to integrate a human right to peace in the scheme of the existing covenants or to make it the subject of a new meaningful convention. An explicit human right to peace would surely be resisted if it were seen as binding a state to prefer individual rights over "national security" or other "reasons of state" and to give human values dominance over sate values to a degree greater than the international system is accustomed to or is likely to accommodate. Without any new conventions or provisions, however, it is plausible to insist that if a state launches war, courts war, or engages in policies likely to lead to war, any one of its inhabitants might claim a violation of one or more established human rights: war would invade or jeopardize rights to life, liberty and property, and would lead to derogations from other rights under Article IV of the Covenant on Civil and Political Rights. The individual could claim also that unnecessary resort to war diverts resources that should be available to realize economic-social rights, in violation of the Covenant on Economic, Social and Cultural Rights. Whether such arguments would be heard, whether they would contribute directly to either the cause of peace or the cause of human rights is open to debate, but they illuminate the intimate links between the values of peace and the values of human rights.

A Right to a Healthful Environment

A right to a healthful environment also requires special conceptualization if it is to fit comfortably within the framework of established human rights law. Obviously, the healthful environment is a "good" which states should pursue. Obviously, it is related to individual health and well-being. As such, it can be argued, a state party to the Covenant on Economic, Social and Cultural Rights is required to pursue a healthful environment progressively to the extent of available resources as part of its obligations to realize the specific rights recognized in the Covenant. A right to a healthful environment can perhaps be linked also to civil-political rights, since purposeful, knowing, or even negligent assaults on the environment amount to inhuman treatment by a state of its inhabitants, in violation of Article 7 of the Covenant on Civil and Political Rights. If so, as with other civil-political rights, the state (the government) itself must respect that right and must ensure respect for it by private persons subject to its jurisdiction. Some will suggest also an obligation to respect the environment of other states, to seek respect for it by other states, and to co-operate with other states to protect the common environment—a form of commonage.

All these new generations suggested have several things in common. They are accepted "goods" seeking the mantle of human rights for political-rhetorical uses. They are not "individuated" individual rights like the traditional civil-political rights or even like those in the economic-social generation, but rather claims for the whole society that are of vital concern to every individual member of society. They cannot be readily couched in normative terms and incorporated into the international law of human rights we now have, if only because they cut across state lines and challenge the basic assumptions of the state system. At bottom, efforts to declare these to be human rights are pleas for international co-operation to address major problems facing the human race.

Human rights are not the only "good," and some "goods" may be even more important than many human rights. In fact, the proposed generations may have already been recognized as individual rights in Article 28 of the

Universal Declaration and may be implied in the existing Covenants. To make them explicit in new provisions or new conventions might be redundant, but that is not a compelling objection: the international system has developed special conventions on numerous human rights clearly covered by the Covenants—on genocide, racial discrimination, apartheid, torture, women's rights, children's rights. There is little harm, and some potential benefit, in recognizing additional goods as human rights, and in developing human rights already recognized, if to do so would serve human values significantly, so long as it is clear (as the Declaration on the Right to Development makes clear) that pursuit of these newer rights does not justify easy sacrifice of the older rights.**

The proposed new generations may lead us along paths further removed from the state-oriented values and methods of the international political system we have known. Additional commitment to human values may require further derogations from state values, additional penetrations of state societies, additional interference with the free market, perhaps even additional deviations from the consent principle. The system still resists these even when they are required to ensure respect for the two accepted generations of rights.

The end of the Cold War has not produced, and does not promise, major change in the international law of human rights. Additional conventions can be expected, especially on the rights of minorities. Whether by interpretation or by new agreement, some of the lacunae in existing law may be filled—recognition of the right to property, and of economic liberties (in addition to economic welfare rights), perhaps the elimination of all forms of religious discrimination (by a convention, analogous to the Convention on the Elimination of All Forms of Racial Discrimination). Without formal amendment, "cold-war" ambiguities in some provisions, notably in the Covenant on Economic and Social Rights, will lose significance. Additional rights may be recognized as customary law. The right to development will continue to rally support from the developing states. A right to a healthful environment will probably gain adherents, but the environment will be less a human rights concern than a global issue with a focus for tension between environmental rights and obligations, and economic development and international trade.

Declaration on the Right of Peoples to Peace

G.A.Res. 39/11, annex, 39 U.N. GAOR Supp. (No. 51) at 22, U.N. Doc. A/39/51 (1984)

The General Assembly,

Reaffirming that the principal aim of the United Nations is the maintenance of international peace and security,

---

** Without recognizing peace or a healthful environment as a human right, states may be entitled to claim them as considerations of "public order" or "general welfare" warranting some limitations on human rights. Compare Article 20 of the Covenant on Civil and Political Rights requiring a state to prohibit propaganda for war.

Bearing in mind the fundamental principles of international law set forth in the Charter of the United Nations,

Expressing the will and the aspirations of all peoples to eradicate war from the life of mankind and, above all, to avert a world-wide nuclear catastrophe,

Convinced that life without war serves as the primary international prerequisite for the material well-being, development and progress of countries, and for the full implementation of the rights and fundamental human freedoms proclaimed by the United Nations,

Aware that in the nuclear age the establishment of a lasting peace on Earth represents the primary condition for the preservation of human civilization and the survival of mankind,

Recognizing that the maintenance of a peaceful life for peoples is the sacred duty of each State,

1. *Solemnly proclaims* that the peoples of our planet have a sacred right to peace;

2. *Solemnly declares* that the preservation of the right of peoples to peace and the promotion of its implementation constitute a fundamental obligation of each State;

3. *Emphasizes* that ensuring the exercise of the right of peoples to peace demands that the policies of States be directed towards the elimination of the threat of war, particularly nuclear war, the renunciation of the use of force in international relations and the settlement of international disputes by peaceful means on the basis of the Charter of the United Nations;

4. *Appeals* to all States and international organizations to do their utmost to assist in implementing the right of peoples to peace through the adoption of appropriate measures at both the national and the international level.

Declaration on the Right to Development

G.A.Res. 41/128, annex, 41 U.N. GAOR Supp. (No. 53) at 186, U.N. Doc. A/41/53 (1986)

The General Assembly,

Bearing in mind the purposes and principles of the Charter of the United Nations relating to the achievement of international co-operation in solving international problems of an economic, social, cultural or humanitarian nature, and in promoting and encouraging respect for human rights and fundamental freedoms for all without distinction as to race, sex, language or religion,

Recognizing that development is a comprehensive economic, social, cultural and political process, which aims at the constant improvement of the well-being of the entire population and of all individuals on the basis of their active, free and meaningful participation in development and in the fair distribution of benefits resulting therefrom,

Considering that under the provisions of the Universal Declaration of Human Rights everyone is entitled to a social and international order in which the rights and freedoms set forth in that Declaration can be fully realized,

Recalling the provisions of the International Covenant on Economic, Social and Cultural Rights and of the International Covenant on Civil and Political Rights,

Recalling further the relevant agreements, conventions, resolutions, recommendations and other instruments of the United Nations and its specialized agencies concerning the integral development of the human being, economic and social progress and development of all peoples, including those instruments concerning decolonization, the prevention of discrimination, respect for and observance of, human rights and fundamental freedoms, the maintenance of international peace and security and the further promotion of friendly relations and co-operation among States in accordance with the Charter,

Recalling the right of peoples to self-determination, by virtue of which they have the right freely to determine their political status and to pursue their economic, social and cultural development,

Recalling also the right of peoples to exercise, subject to the relevant provisions of both International Covenants on Human Rights, full and complete sovereignty over all their natural wealth and resources,

Mindful of the obligation of States under the Charter to promote universal respect for and observance of human rights and fundamental freedoms for all without distinction of any kind such as race, colour, sex, language, religion, political or other opinion, national or social origin, property, birth or other status,

Considering that the elimination of the massive and flagrant violations of the human rights of the peoples and individuals affected by situations such as those resulting from colonialism, neo-colonialism, *apartheid*, all forms of racism and racial discrimination, foreign domination and occupation, aggression and threats against national sovereignty, national unity and territorial integrity and threats of war would contribute to the establishment of circumstances propitious to the development of a great part of mankind,

Concerned at the existence of serious obstacles to development, as well as to the complete fulfilment of human beings and of peoples constituted, *inter alia*, by the denial of civil, political, economic, social and cultural rights, and considering that all human rights and fundamental freedoms are indivisible and interdependent and that, in order to promote development, equal attention and urgent consideration should be given to the implementation, promotion and protection of civil, political, economic, social and cultural rights and that, accordingly, the promotion of, respect for and enjoyment of certain human rights and fundamental freedoms cannot justify the denial of other human rights and fundamental freedoms,

Considering that international peace and security are essential elements for the realization of the right to development,

Reaffirming that there is a close relationship between disarmament and development and that progress in the field of disarmament would considerably promote progress in the field of development and that resources released through disarmament measures should be devoted to the economic and social development and well-being of all peoples and, in particular, those of the developing countries,

Recognizing that the human person is the central subject of the development process and that development policy should therefore make the human being the main participant and beneficiary of development,

Recognizing that the creation of conditions favourable to the development of peoples and individuals is the primary responsibility of their States,

Aware that efforts at the international level to promote and protect human rights should be accompanied by efforts to establish a new international economic order,

Confirming that the right to development is an inalienable human right and that equality of opportunity for development is a prerogative both of nations and of individuals who make up nations,

Proclaims the following Declaration on the Right to Development:

Article 1

1.   The right to development is an inalienable human right by virtue of which every human person and all peoples are entitled to participate in, contribute to, and enjoy economic, social, cultural and political development, in which all human rights and fundamental freedoms can be fully realized.

2.   The human right to development also implies the full realization of the right of peoples to self-determination, which includes, subject to the relevant provisions of both International Covenants on Human Rights, the exercise of their inalienable right to full sovereignty over all their natural wealth and resources.

Article 2

1.   The human person is the central subject of development and should be the active participant and beneficiary of the right to development.

2.   All human beings have a responsibility for development, individually and collectively, taking into account the need for full respect for their human rights and fundamental freedoms as well as their duties to community, which alone can ensure the free and complete fulfilment of the human being, and they should therefore promote and protect an appropriate political, social and economic order for development.

3.   States have the right and the duty to formulate appropriate national development policies that aim at the constant improvement of the well-being of the entire population and of all individuals, on the basis of their active, free and meaningful participation in development and in the fair distribution of the benefits resulting therefrom.

Article 3

1.   States have the primary responsibility for the creation of national and international conditions favourable to the realization of the right to development.

2.   The realization of the right to development requires full respect for the principles of international law concerning friendly relations and co-operation among States in accordance with the Charter of the United Nations.

3.   States have the duty to co-operate with each other in ensuring development and eliminating obstacles to development. States should realize their rights and fulfil their duties in such a manner as to promote a new international economic order based on sovereign equality, interdependence, mutual interest and co-operation among all States, as well as to encourage the observance and realization of human rights.

Article 4

1.   States have the duty to take steps, individually and collectively, to formulate international development policies with a view to facilitating the full realization of the right to development.

2.   Sustained action is required to promote more rapid development of developing countries. As a complement to the efforts of developing countries, effective international co-operation is essential in providing these countries with appropriate means and facilities to foster their comprehensive development.

Article 5

States shall take resolute steps to eliminate the massive and flagrant violations of the human rights of peoples and human beings affected by situations such as those resulting from *apartheid*, all forms of racism and racial discrimination, colonialism, foreign domination and occupation, aggression, foreign interference and threats against national sovereignty, national unity and territorial integrity, threats of war and refusal to recognize the fundamental right of peoples to self-determination.

Article 6

1.   All States should co-operate with a view to promoting, encouraging and strengthening universal respect for and observance of all human rights and fundamental freedoms for all without any distinction as to race, sex, language or religion.

2.   All human rights and fundamental freedoms are indivisible and interdependent; equal attention and urgent consideration should be given

to the implementation, promotion and protection of civil, political, economic, social and cultural rights.

3.   States should take steps to eliminate obstacles to development resulting from failure to observe civil and political rights, as well as economic, social and cultural rights.

Article 7

All States should promote the establishment, maintenance and strengthening of international peace and security and, to that end, should do their utmost to achieve general and complete disarmament under effective international control, as well as to ensure that the resources released by effective disarmament measures are used for comprehensive development, in particular that of the developing countries.

Article 8

1.   States should undertake, at the national level, all necessary measures for the realization of the right to development and shall ensure, *inter alia*, equality of opportunity for all in their access to basic resources, education, health services, food, housing, employment and the fair distribution of income. Effective measures should be undertaken to ensure that women have an active role in the development process. Appropriate economic and social reforms should be carried out with a view to eradicating all social injustices.

2.   States should encourage popular participation in all spheres as an important factor in development and in the full realization of all human rights.

Article 9

1.   All the aspects of the right to development set forth in the present Declaration are indivisible and interdependent and each of them should be considered in the context of the whole.

2.   Nothing in the present Declaration shall be construed as being contrary to the purposes and principles of the United Nations, or as implying that any State, group or person has a right to engage in any activity or to perform any act aimed at the violation of the rights set forth in the Universal Declaration of Human Rights and in the International Covenants on Human Rights.

Article 10

Steps should be taken to ensure the full exercise and progressive enhancement of the right to development, including the formulation, adoption and implementation of policy, legislative and other measures at the national and international levels.

"Permanent Sovereignty Over Natural Resources"

In the early 1960's, after decolonization and the emergence of "The Third World," the U.N. General Assembly adopted measures to promote "economic self-determination." During those years, the Third World was engaged in an effort to modify the principles of international law governing foreign investment, as they were understood by the developed countries, so as to remove (or reduce) the obligation of developing states to pay "just compensation" for nationalized foreign properties and investments. The U.N. General Assembly adopted Resolution 1803 (XVII) printed below. The General Assembly also approved Article 1(2) for inclusion in the Human Rights Covenants. Later, the Assembly adopted other resolutions including a second resolution on "Permanent Sovereignty over Natural Resources" (XXVIII) 1973; a Declaration on Establishment of a New International Economic Order, G.A. Res. 3 201 (S–VI 1974); and a Charter of Economic Rights and Duties of State (XXIX) 1974.

G.A. Resolution 1803 (XVII) 1962

G.A. Res. 1803 (XVII), 17 U.N. GAOR Supp. No. 17 at 15, U.N. Doc. A/5217 (1962)

The General Assembly,

. . .

Bearing in mind its resolution 1515 (XV) of 15 December 1960, in which it recommended that the sovereign right of every State to dispose of its wealth and its natural resources should be respected,

Considering that any measure in this respect must be based on the recognition of the inalienable right of all States freely to dispose of their natural wealth and resources in accordance with their national interests, and on respect for the economic independence of States,

. . .

Noting that the subject of succession of States and Governments is being examined as a matter of priority by the International Law Commission,

Considering that it is desirable to promote international co-operation for the economic development of developing countries, and that economic and financial agreements between the developed and the developing countries must be based on the principles of equality and of the right of peoples and nations to self-determination,

Considering that the provision of economic and technical assistance, loans and increased foreign investment must not be subject to conditions which conflict with the interests of the recipient State,

Considering the benefits to be derived from exchanges of technical and scientific information likely to promote the development and use of such resources and wealth, and the important part which the United Nations and other international organizations are called upon to play in that connection,

Attaching particular importance to the question of promoting the economic development of developing countries and securing their economic independence,

Noting that the creation and strengthening of the inalienable sovereignty of States over their natural wealth and resources reinforces their economic independence,

Desiring that there should be further consideration by the United Nations of the subject of permanent sovereignty over natural resources in the spirit of international co-operation in the field of economic development, particularly that of the developing countries,

Declares That:

1. The right of peoples and nations to permanent sovereignty over their natural wealth and resources must be exercised in the interest of their national development and of the well-being of the people of the State concerned.

2. The exploration, development and disposition of such resources, as well as the import of the foreign capital required for these purposes, should be in conformity with the rules and conditions which the peoples and nations freely consider to be necessary or desirable with regard to the authorization, restriction or prohibition of such activities.

3. In cases where authorization is granted, the capital imported and the earnings on that capital shall be governed by the terms thereof, by the national legislation in force, and by international law. The profits derived must be shared in the proportions freely agreed upon, in each case, between the investors and the recipient State, due care being taken to ensure that there is no impairment, for any reason, of that State's sovereignty over its natural wealth and resources.

4. Nationalization, expropriation or requisitioning shall be based on grounds or reasons of public utility, security or the national interest which are recognized as overriding purely individual or private interests, both domestic and foreign. In such cases the owner shall be paid appropriate compensation, in accordance with the rules in force in the State taking such measures in the exercise of its sovereignty and in accordance with international law. In any case where the question of compensation gives rise to a controversy, the national jurisdiction of the State taking such measures shall be exhausted. However, upon agreement by sovereign States and other parties concerned, settlement of the dispute should be made through arbitration or international adjudication.

5. The free and beneficial exercise of the sovereignty of peoples and nations over their natural resources must be furthered by the mutual respect of States based on their sovereign equality.

6. International co-operation for the economic development of developing countries, whether in the form of public or private capital investments, exchange of goods and services, technical assistance, or exchange of scientific information, shall be such as to further their independent national development and shall be based upon respect for their sovereignty over their natural wealth and resources.

7. Violation of the rights of peoples and nations to sovereignty over their natural wealth and resources is contrary to the spirit and principles of the Charter of the United Nations and hinders the development of international co-operation and the maintenance of peace.

8. Foreign investment agreements freely entered into by or between sovereign States shall be observed in good faith; States and international organizations shall strictly and conscientiously respect the sovereignty of peoples and nations over their natural wealth and resources in accordance with the Charter and the principles set forth in the present resolution.

Notes

1. The issues underlying the Resolution on Permanent Sovereignty over natural resources have largely abated. Developing states have not abandoned their doctrinal position on "economic self-determination," but many developing countries moved to encourage foreign investment. They have concluded hundreds of bilateral treaties for the protection of foreign investments and have adhered to the Convention on the Settlement of Investment Disputes between States and Nationals of other States (ICSID). Some developing countries have themselves invested in less-developed countries and have sought protection for their investments, playing down the "economic self-determination" of the investment-receiving countries.

2. Do some of the "Other Generations" have better claims to the human rights mantle than do others?

3. The other generations of rights have not attracted the strong support of the human rights movement and of the principal human rights NGO's, and indeed these have tended to depreciate these other generations and even to resist their claims. Why? Neither have the other generations attracted resistance from the political and other forces that tend to resist claims to individual human rights. Why?

4. Philip Alston warned of the undesirability of proliferating new rights and suggested a procedure to ensure "quality control." See Alston, Conjuring Up Human Rights: A Proposal for Quality Control, 78 Am. J. Int'l L. 607 (1984).

CHAPTER 3

IMPLEMENTATION OF HUMAN RIGHTS

Rights, it is commonly assumed, imply remedies. If human rights are claims upon society, society is required to provide means to realize them, to assure that they are respected, and to provide compensation to victims whose rights are violated.

International human rights conventions typically require States Parties not only to respect the rights recognized in the treaties, but also to ensure that those rights are protected through national law. For example, Article 2(1) of the International Covenant on Civil and Political Rights (ICCPR) provides:

1. Each State Party to the present Covenant undertakes to respect and to ensure to all individuals within its territory and subject to its jurisdiction the rights recognized in the present Covenant, without distinction of any kind. . . .

As the materials in this Chapter concerning international and regional human rights systems make clear, this and similar language in regional conventions have been interpreted to require States Parties not only to refrain from committing human rights violations, as implied in the word "respect," but also to undertake affirmative measures to "ensure" that individuals subject to their jurisdiction enjoy enumerated rights.

The ICCPR makes clear in Article 2(2) and 2(3) that these affirmative obligations require States Parties to organize their national legal systems in such a manner as to ensure protection of rights and provide an effective remedy:

2. Where not already provided for by existing legislative or other measures, each State Party to the present Covenant undertakes to take the necessary steps, in accordance with its constitutional processes and with the provisions of the present Covenant, to adopt such legislative or other measures as may be necessary to give effect to the rights recognized in the present Covenant.

3. Each State Party to the present Covenant undertakes:

a. To ensure that any person whose rights or freedoms as herein recognized are violated shall have an effective remedy, notwithstanding that the violation has been committed by persons acting in an official capacity;

b.   To ensure that any person claiming such a remedy shall have his right thereto determined by competent judicial, administrative or legislative authorities, or by any other competent authority provided for by the legal system of the State, and to develop the possibilities of judicial remedy;

c.   To ensure that the competent authorities shall enforce such remedies when granted.

While the ICCPR and its regional counterparts contemplate enforcement and implementation principally through domestic legal systems, they also provide for the establishment and operation of treaty bodies to monitor compliance by States Parties. The ICCPR provides for oversight by a Human Rights Committee, whose members are nominated by States Parties to the Covenant; compliance with the American Convention on Human Rights is supervised by both a Commission and a Court. Until recently, compliance with the European Convention for the Protection of Human Rights and Fundamental Freedoms was supervised by both a European Commission and Court. Pursuant to Protocol No. 11, these two bodies were replaced in November 1998 with a single, full-time Court.

Although the powers of these bodies vary, none of them is intended to replace national legal systems. The machinery established by human rights conventions is designed above all to secure compliance by States Parties with their treaty obligations through the effective operation of national law and procedures, and to supplement national remedies when necessary. The material included in this Chapter highlights the overarching relationship between oversight mechanisms established by those conventions and national law and remedies.

A number of international human rights bodies and mechanisms have been established through means other than the provisions of human rights treaties. These include, in particular, the Commission on Human Rights of the United Nations, which meets annually in Geneva, and various mechanisms established by that body and by the United Nations Secretary General.

These mechanisms, like the treaty systems examined in Sections A and B of this Chapter, are concerned with the conduct of states in ensuring that individuals subject to their authority enjoy internationally-protected human rights. Ordinarily, when violations of international human rights obligations have been established, the responsible actor is the state that failed to meet its obligations.

But international law also imposes some human rights obligations directly on individuals, making them liable to criminal punishment. The principle of individual responsibility was recognized and enforced during the period immediately following World War II, when Allied countries established tribunals in Nuremberg and Tokyo to prosecute major war criminals from Germany and Japan, respectively.

The work of these tribunals provided a foundation for two international tribunals established by the UN Security Council in the 1990s. In 1993 the Security Council created an hoc criminal tribunal with jurisdiction over human rights crimes committed during the ethnic conflicts in the former Yugoslavia that began in 1991, and in 1994 it established a second tribunal with jurisdiction over international crimes committed in Rwanda during 1994. Building on the precedents and momentum created by these two tribunals, a Diplomatic Conference was convened in Rome in 1998 to finalize the text of a statute for a permanent International Criminal Court (ICC). The statute was adopted with the affirmative votes of 120 states; seven countries, including the United States, voted against it. The ICC will come into existence when 60 states have ratified the statute adopted in Rome.

A. IMPLEMENTATION OF INTERNATIONAL COVENANTS AND CONVENTIONS BY TREATY BODIES

1. INTERNATIONAL COVENANT ON CIVIL AND POLITICAL RIGHTS

Together with the Universal Declaration of Human Rights and the International Covenant on Economic, Social, and Cultural Rights, the ICCPR is considered an integral component of the International Bill of Rights.* As noted in the introduction to this Chapter, the Covenant requires States Parties to respect and to ensure to individuals in its territory and subject to its jurisdiction a comprehensive range of civil and political rights through an effective system of domestic remedies. Pursuant to Article 28 of the Covenant, a Human Rights Committee (HRC) was established in 1976 to monitor States Parties' compliance with these obligations. The HRC held its first meeting in 1977.

Torkel Opsahl, *The Human Rights Committee*

in The United Nations and Human Rights: A Critical Appraisal 369.
(Philip Alston, ed. 1992).**

. . .

Technically speaking, the Human Rights Committee is a body of 'experts' working part-time, and assisted by the UN Secretariat. Its functions are defined and limited by the International Covenant on Civil and Political Rights ..., as well as by the Optional Protocol to that Covenant....

... In brief, it may be described as the guardian of the Covenant, with responsibility for monitoring its implementation.[4]

---

* Adopted by the United Nations General Assembly in 1966, the ICCPR entered into force in 1976. As of April 1999, 144 States were parties to the Covenant. The United States signed the Covenant in 1977 and ratified it in 1992.

** Reprinted by permission, © 1992 Oxford University Press.

4. No description of the Committee's functions is entirely neutral. 'Monitoring' is preferred here over more controversial terms such as 'supervising', 'enforcing', or 'protecting' rights.

Its two main functions . . . are to consider *reports* from, and *complaints* against, the States Parties. The former is obligatory for all States Parties, while the latter is optional and exists in two forms: interstate 'communications' under the Covenant, as well as individual 'communications' under the Optional Protocol.

The basic obligation of States Parties is to implement the rights provided for in Parts I and III of the Covenant.[5] . . .

. . .

B. *The Reporting System*

All States Parties have undertaken to submit reports for consideration by the Committee on the measures they have taken to implement the Covenant. . . . [Pursuant to Article 40 of the ICCPR, these reports are due one year after the Covenant enters into force for the State Party concerned and periodically thereafter as requested by the Committee. The Committee has, subject to certain qualifications, requested follow-up reports at five-year intervals.*]

. . .

. . . States Parties are required to submit reports 'on measures they have adopted' which give effect to the rights recognized in the Covenant, and 'on the progress made in the enjoyment of those rights'.[137] To these terms is added: 'Reports shall indicate the factors and difficulties, if any, affecting the implementation of the present Covenant.'[138] . . .

. . .

The main importance of State reports is to provide a basis for an active examination of the situation by the Committee through a process of direct co-operation with representatives of the reporting States. . . . The competence and duties of the Committee follow from Article 40(4), which states only that the Committee '*shall* study' States' reports, and '*shall* transmit its reports, and such general comments as it *may* consider appropriate, to the States Parties' (emphasis added). For many years the proper role of the Committee in the light of this provision 'proved to be the most controversial issue of all'.[150] . . .

. . .

5. They are laid down in Arts. 6–27 (Part III), International Covenant, and concern mainly the rights to life, integrity, personal freedom, humane treatment, movement, fair trial, legal personality, privacy, freedom of conscience and religion, expression, assembly, association, family, children, political rights, non-discrimination, and certain rights of persons belonging to minorities, all of which must be read together with Article 1 (Part I) on the right of all peoples to self-determination and Arts. 2–5 (Part II) which contain a number of general provisions affecting the substance of the rights and freedoms enshrined in the Covenant.

* [The Committee has occasionally requested states parties on an urgent basis to submit information about situations that entail a substantial risk to fundamental rights.—Editors' Note.]

137. Art. 40(1), International Covenant.

138. Ibid. Art. 40(2).

150. Avery, 'The Human Rights Committee after Six Years[: Thirty Operational

... [F]or initial reports, 'study' by the Committee became an examination by its members in public meetings, commenting one by one—favourably or critically—and questioning. They often went into the details and employed legalistic terms, usually in light of what they knew about the specific human rights situation in a particular country. That information did not necessarily come from the government.

. . .

The examination of each State report extends over several meetings and sometimes includes hundreds of questions.... An observer once wrote that it was 'unlikely' that the delegates drafting the Covenant 'knew what they were letting their governments in for' when they provided for the Committee and its role in the reporting system; 'in fact, it is hard to imagine where else top government officials would find themselves being so closely questioned about their country's law and policies, and needing to justify them.'

. . .

Even when States Parties submit elaborate reports, additional information is crucial for the examination process. Members of the Committee have been particularly concerned about obtaining more facts and examining existing limitations on rights and their justifications. Quite often they raise particular events, not referred to by the State, or indicate problems and situations which require further study and answers. Members have sometimes openly disagreed concerning the degree to which such material, from academic studies to newspaper articles, could be brought into their comments and questions and how to refer to it.

The restrictive attitude advocated by some, in particular the Eastern European members*, was partly based on considerations of principle. It was argued, notably, that under Article 40 the Committee is not an investigatory body for allegations made against a State Party of violations of the Covenant. It is true that an accusatory or condemning approach by the Committee would be contrary to the purpose of the reporting system, but an inquisitive role of individual members in matters of implementation is different and legitimate under Article 40.... However, part-time members cannot do all the work required for the study of the reports together with other material between sessions. In the absence of Secretariat support, the role of the non-governmental organizations has become of paramount importance, but at the same time controversial.

From the beginning, non-governmental organizations sent documents to members on an individual basis and their representatives met informally with members during sessions. Gradually a few of them have approached the work of the Committee more systematically, providing information, comments, and 'critiques' of State reports. Some members have actively

Issues]' [unpub. MS (Columbia University School of Law, 1982)], 15.

 * [Before the collapse of the Soviet bloc, the Human Rights Committee's operation was profoundly affected by East–West divisions. The author's observation refers to the Cold War period of the Committee's history.—Editors' Note.]

solicited such help, and others have gratefully accepted it, while still others have considered the information tainted. It is generally accepted by the non-governmental organizations that they have to be tactful and not seek visibility during Committee sessions. Amnesty International, the International Commission of Jurists, and the International League for Human Rights in particular have provided useful information without which many members would have felt rather helpless.

Members do not, of course, lightly accept or present such material as evidence of violations of the Covenant, although this is usually the thrust of it and members may individually point this out. Most of them use the material as a basis for their own comments or questions; they thus avoid limiting the examination process to an inquiry into a State report which in many cases bears little resemblance to reality.

[The preceding excerpt focuses on one portion of the reporting process established by Article 40 of the ICCPR—direct questioning of state representatives by members of the Human Rights Committee. Despite its obvious limitations as a means of monitoring and promoting compliance with the Covenant, the review process has the advantage of ensuring that the Committee scrutinizes the compliance record of every State Party, and not just that of states that are the subject of communications alleging violations under the Optional Protocol.

Beyond their impact on the States Parties whose reports are reviewed, the review sessions offer insights into how the Human Rights Committee interprets the Covenant. Although they are not authoritative sources of interpretation, the Summary Records of these sessions have often been examined and cited for the insights they provide into Committee members' views concerning the Covenant's requirements.

A more important source of interpretation is the Committee's "general comments," which are based on its review of States Parties' compliance reports. The treaty basis and historical evolution of these comments are described in the following portion of Opsahl's analysis.]

[The HRC's annual report for 1980, published shortly after a major debate about the proper role of the Committee,] pointed out that many members were of the view that individual questioning was not sufficient, and that 'the Committee had not yet, collectively as a Committee "studied" the reports.' The problem was defined in terms of Article 40 as follows:

> Since States Parties, by the submission of their reports under article 40(1) and (2) of the Covenant, and the Secretary–General, by the transmission of those reports under article 40(3) of the Covenant, had fulfilled their obligations, it was incumbent on the Committee to fulfill its obligations under article 40(4) of the Covenant which requires the Committee as such to 'study the reports' and 'transmit its reports, and such general comments as it may consider appropriate, to the States Parties.' The Committee should, therefore, as a Committee and as distinct from its individual members, now continue and complete its work in relation to the reports of States Parties which it had examined.

However, opinions differed as to what the end result should be, and as to whether reports and comments by the Committee should be made to States Parties individually or to all the States Parties as a whole.... [The] majority opinion [expressed the view that the Committee's 'study' of states' reports]

> should lead to the adoption of separate reports by the Committee on each State Party's report. The exercise would, however, be conducted in such a way as not to turn the reporting procedure into contentious or inquisitory proceedings, but rather to provide valuable assistance to the State Party concerned in the better implementation of the provisions of the Covenant.

General comments would highlight matters of common interest to the States Parties.

Despite these concessions, the minority clearly feared that the reporting procedure might be abused, and no agreement could be reached on the main points. The minority held that the Committee's role was limited to the exchange of information and promotion of co-operation among States and to the maintenance of a dialogue with them; 'the study did not have in it any element of assessment or evaluation' which would go 'far beyond the wording of the Covenant'. The term 'its reports' in Article 40(4) was seen as a reference to the annual reports of the Committee to the General Assembly under Article 45....

Facing this disagreement, the Committee reported in July 1980 that there was 'a convergence of opinion on the need for the Committee, at the very least, to make general comments' and that it wished to proceed to that task 'pending a decision on further work, if any, under Article 40 of the Covenant.'

. . .

The agreed framework implies that comments shall be 'addressed to the States Parties' which so far has been applied to them collectively, not individually. Comments should summarize the Committee's experience with reports and promote certain obvious goals such as co-operation between States Parties, improvement of reporting, and Covenant implementation. [While the first two "general comments" adopted by the Committee provided guidance in respect of States Parties' reporting obligations, most of them have sought to elucidate substantive provisions of the ICCPR.]

———

Following the end of the Cold War, the Human Rights Committee was able to make progress in resolving the earlier division among its members concerning the appropriateness of making collective comments about specific states' compliance reports. The Committee revisited this issue in 1992, and decided that

> comments would be adopted reflecting the views of the Committee as a whole at the end of the consideration of each State party report. That

would be in addition to, and would not replace, comments made by members, at the end of the consideration of each State party report. . . . Such comments were to be embodied in a written text and . . . were to provide a general evaluation of the State party report and of the dialogue with the delegation and to underline positive developments . . ., factors and difficulties affecting the implementation of the Covenant, as well as specific issues of concern regarding the application of the provisions of the Covenant. Comments were also to include suggestions and recommendations formulated by the Committee. . . .

Report of the Human Rights Committee, U.N. Doc. A/47/40 (1992), at 18, para. 45.

Since 1992, the Committee's comments on States Parties' reports have often included expressions of serious concern about particular practices and very specific suggestions and recommendations. Consider, for example, the following excerpts from the Committee's 1996 preliminary observations on the report of Peru.

Preliminary Observations of the Human Rights Committee: Peru

U.N. Doc. CCPR/C/79/Add.67 (1996).

· · ·

A.   Introduction

2.   The Committee welcomes the third periodic report submitted by the State party and welcomes the delegation's willingness to engage in a dialogue with the Committee. The Committee regrets, however, that although the report and the additional written and oral information provided by the delegation of Peru in answer to the questions raised by the Committee provided information on general legislative norms in Peru, it largely failed to deal with the actual state of implementation of the Covenant in practice and the difficulties encountered in the course of implementation. . . .

· · ·

D.   Principal subjects of concern

8.   The Committee deplores that its suggestions and recommendations contained in the Concluding Observations adopted at the end of the consideration of Peru's second periodic report and supplementary reports . . . have not been implemented.

9.   The Committee is deeply concerned that the amnesty granted by Decree Law 26,479 on 14 June 1995 absolves from criminal responsibility and, as a consequence, from all forms of accountability, all military, police and civilian agents of the State who are accused, investigated, charged, processed or convicted for common and military crimes for acts occasioned

by the "war against terrorism" from May 1980 until June 1995. It also makes it practically impossible for victims of human rights violations to institute successful legal action for compensation. Such an amnesty prevents appropriate investigation and punishment of perpetrators of past human rights violations, undermines efforts to establish respect for human rights, contributes to an atmosphere of impunity among perpetrators of human rights violations, and constitutes a very serious impediment to efforts undertaken to consolidate democracy and promote respect for human rights and is thus in violation of article 2 of the Covenant. In this connection, the Committee reiterates its view, as expressed in its General Comment 20 (44), that this type of amnesty is incompatible with the duty of States to investigate human rights violations, to guarantee freedom from such acts within their jurisdiction, and to ensure that they do not occur in the future.

10.   In addition, the Committee expresses serious concern in relation to the adoption of Decree Law 26,492 and Decree Law 26,6181, which purport to divest individuals of the right to have the legality of the amnesty law reviewed in courts. With regard to article 1 of this law, declaring that the Amnesty Law does not undermine the international human rights obligations of the State, the Committee stresses that domestic legislation cannot modify a State party's international obligations under the Covenant.

. . .

16.   The Committee expresses its deepest concern with respect to cases of disappearances, summary executions, torture, ill-treatment, and arbitrary arrest and detention by members of the army and security forces, and by the government's failure to investigate fully these cases, to prosecute alleged offences, to [punish] those found guilty and provide compensation to the victims and their families. The Committee is particularly concerned at the failure to resolve the high number of cases of past disappearances.

. . .

E.   Suggestions and recommendations

20.   The Committee recommends that necessary steps be taken to restore the authority of the judiciary, give effect to the right to effective remedy under article 2 of the Covenant and thus overcome the prevailing atmosphere of impunity. In view of the fact that the Committee considers that the Amnesty laws violate the Covenant, it recommends that the Government of Peru review and repeal these laws to the extent of such violations. In particular, it urges the government to remedy the unacceptable consequences of these laws by, inter alia, establishing an effective system of compensation for the victims of human rights violations and by taking the necessary steps to ensure that the perpetrators of these violations do not continue to hold government positions.

. . .

22.   The Committee urges the State party to take effective measures to investigate allegations of summary executions, disappearances, cases of torture and ill-treatment, and arbitrary arrest and detention, to bring the perpetrators to justice, to punish them and to compensate victims. If allegations of such crimes have been made against members of the security forces, whether military or civilian, the investigations should be carried out by an impartial body that does not belong to the organization of the security forces themselves. Persons convicted of such crimes should be dismissed and, pending the outcome of the investigation, be suspended from office.

Notes

1.   In its observations concerning Peru's third periodic report, the Human Rights Committee expressed its "deepest concern with respect to cases of disappearances, summary executions, torture, ill-treatment, and arbitrary arrest and detention by members of the army and security forces...." Should the Committee make findings of fact of this nature when it is reviewing States Parties' compliance reports? Does the appropriateness of such conclusions depend on whether government representatives have acknowledged the relevant facts?

2.   Note that the Committee expressed its view that Peru's amnesty law is incompatible with the ICCPR (see paras. 9, 20) and also suggested that members of security forces who are convicted of serious violations of rights relating to physical integrity be dismissed. What is the textual basis in the Covenant for this legal conclusion and recommendation?

3.   In addition to the HRC's decision in 1992 to adopt collective comments on States Parties' reports, the early 1990s brought another change in the Committee's general practice. Since 1991, it has occasionally requested states to submit "emergency" reports when "recent or current events [indicated] that the enjoyment of [Covenant] rights [had] been seriously affected" in the state. For discussion of this practice, see Sarah Joseph, *New Procedures Concerning the Human Rights Committee's Examination of State Reports*, 13 Netherlands Q. Hum. Rts. 5, 13–23 (1995). What accounts for the HRC's more robust interpretation of its mandate? Writing of both reforms, Ms. Joseph refers to its "more adventurous post-Cold War spirit," *id*. at 23, implying that the end of the Cold War freed the Committee's members to undertake an approach that had, perhaps, long been warranted.

––––––––

In addition to its role in reviewing States Parties' compliance reports under Article 40 of the Covenant, the HRC is authorized to receive and consider both inter-state and individual communications alleging that a State Party has breached its obligations under the ICCPR. Pursuant to Article 41, States Parties can recognize the Committee's competence to consider complaints filed by one State Party alleging that another State Party has failed to comply with its obligations under the Covenant. The Committee's competence extends only to communications submitted by and against States Parties that have recognized its competence under Article 41. As of January 1999, no State Party had ever utilized this procedure.

The Committee can also receive and consider communications "from individuals claiming to be victims of violations of any of the rights set forth in the Covenant" with respect to States Parties that have ratified the first Optional Protocol, which was adopted in 1966 and entered into force in 1976. (A second Optional Protocol, which was adopted in 1989 and entered into force in 1991, aims at abolishing the death penalty.) Although the Committee acts in a quasi-judicial fashion when it considers individual communications, the Optional Protocol does not explicitly vest the Committee with the power to render legally binding decisions. It merely authorizes the Committee to "forward its views to the State Party concerned and to the individual" that has filed the communication alleging a breach of the Covenant. (Optional Protocol, Article 5(4).) The following article analyzes the effectiveness of this procedure.

Laurence R. Helfer & Anne–Marie Slaughter, *Toward a Theory of Effective Supranational Adjudication*

107 Yale L.J. 273 (1997).

. . .

3. *The Petition System*

[In addition to its role in relation to reports by states parties, the] Committee's other major jurisprudential function is the consideration of written "communications" from individuals under the First Optional Protocol to the ICCPR.[295] . . .

The Committee cannot perform these functions for all of the states party to the Covenant, . . . since it is only authorized to consider complaints against states that have ratified the Optional Protocol. To date, only 86 of the 132 states parties have ratified that agreement.* This creates a "double standard of adherence to covenant rights" in which states that have ratified the Optional Protocol are subject to a far greater level of scrutiny of their compliance with the ICCPR than states that have refrained from ratification.

. . .

---

295. See Optional Protocol, [art. 2] ("Individuals who claim that any of their rights enumerated in the Covenant have been violated . . . may submit a written communication to the Committee for consideration.") . . . .

* [As of April 1999, 95 countries had ratified the Optional Protocol.—Editors' Note.]

[If the Committee finds a petition admissible,] it receives written submissions by both the aggrieved individual and the state party. The Committee cannot engage in factfinding and it does not take testimony or hear oral arguments from the parties.[306] After reviewing the written submissions, the Committee determines in a private meeting whether the facts presented disclose a violation of the Covenant.

The Committee then authors an opinion, ambiguously referred to in the Optional Protocol as the "views" of the Committee.[307] These views, which "follow a judicial pattern and are effectively decisions on the merits,"[308] set forth the allegations of the author, the responses of the state party, the decision on admissibility, and any interim measures, followed by the facts upon which the Committee bases its decision. The views also list certain "considerations" upon which the Committee has based its decision. These include a state party's degree of cooperation with the Committee in resolving the case, the burden of proof, a reference to one or more general comments or to prior case law, and an interpretation of the substantive requirements of the treaty. Finally, the decisions contain a statement of "the view of the [Committee] on the 'obligation' of the State party in light of [its] findings."[310]

From the inception of the petition procedure in 1977 through October 1996, the Committee had registered 716 communications concerning fifty-one states parties. Of these, 239 had been concluded with the adoption of views on the merits.[312] Of the remaining communications, 224 had been declared inadmissible, 115 had been discontinued or withdrawn by the author, and 96 were pending as of October 1996 at the pre-or post-admissibility stage.

B. *Toward an Increasingly Judicial Approach to the Petition System*

[I]t is the consideration of communications under the Optional Protocol that has recently brought the most attention to the Committee and its work. In addition, the increasing number of states that have ratified the Optional Protocol over the last decade,[314] together with the widening audience of litigants, attorneys, activists, and scholars who follow the Committee's activities, has made the petition system an ever more important part of its work. With greater visibility has come a concomitant rise in

---

306. . . . McGoldrick notes that the Optional Protocol does not preclude the Committee from hearing oral argument. See [Dominic McGoldrick, The Human Rights Committee 144–45 (1991)].

307. See Optional Protocol, [art. 5(4)].

308. McGoldrick, supra note [306], at 151.

310. Id. at 152. Once adopted, the Committee forwards its views to both parties and publishes them, along with selected admissi-bility decisions, in its annual report to the General Assembly. See Optional Protocol, [art. 5(4)].

312. . . . As of October 1995, the Committee had found treaty violations in 154 of the 208 decisions on the merits. . . .

314. As of 1991, only 55 States had ratified the Optional Protocol. . . . As of late 1995, 86 States had done so. . . .

the number of communications filed with the Committee and an increase in their complexity.[315]

The Committee's response to these developments reveals a trend of remarkable importance: In numerous and diverse ways, the Committee is behaving more and more like a judicial arbiter of human rights disputes, even when granted only limited powers by states parties. Although lacking many of the institutional characteristics possessed by supranational tribunals such as the [European Court of Human Rights, the European Court of Justice], and the European Commission of Human Rights, the Committee has, within the limits of its authority and sometimes arguably beyond it, followed an increasingly court-like method of operation. Particularly striking ... are the Committee's efforts to improve compliance with its decisions.

Since 1990, the Committee has become quite outspoken in its view that defending states are under an obligation to comply with unfavorable decisions against them.[316] Further, it has taken concrete steps to monitor compliance, appointing one of its members as a special rapporteur to record states' responses.[317] As of October 1995, the rapporteur had received information in 81 of 154 views in which the Committee found a treaty violation. Of the responses received, the Committee considered only about thirty percent to be "satisfactory," meaning "that they displayed a willingness on the part of the State party concerned to implement the Committee's Views or to offer the applicant an appropriate remedy."[319] In light of this lukewarm response by states parties, the Committee has taken steps to increase adherence to its decisions. Specifically, it has begun to publish the compliance information it collects and to identify publicly each state that refuses to implement its views.[320]

. . .

315. Although the Committee's early case law generally concerned gross violations of human rights or situations that required only a cursory legal analysis, more recently the Committee has begun to consider cases that require "more subtle legal reasoning." [Torkal Opsahl, *The Human Rights Committee*, *in* The United Nations and Human Rights at 428, 429 (Philip Alston ed. 1992)].

316. Although the Committee's early decisions failed to announce whether states were obliged to inform the Committee of their responses to its views, in 1990 the Committee began concluding its decisions with the statement that it "would welcome information on any relevant measures taken by the State party in respect of the Committee's views." ... The Committee's current practice is to ask for a response from the defending state within 90 days in each case in which it determines that a violation of the ICCPR has occurred....

317. Prior to 1990, a dispute among the members over the legal basis for initiating any follow-up procedures prevented the Committee from assessing the extent of compliance.... In that year, however, the Committee resolved this internal debate and appointed the special rapporteur....

319. ... The remaining responses

either explicitly challenged the Committee's findings on factual or legal grounds (nine replies), indicated that the State party would not, for one reason or another, give effect to the Committee's recommendations (nine replies), promised an investigation of the matter considered by the Committee or constituted much belated submissions on the merits of the case.

... On the whole, the Committee characterized these statistics as "encouraging" but "not fully satisfactory." ...

320. In 1995, the Committee published what it termed a "separate and highly visible chapter on follow-up activities under the

The early days under the Optional Protocol brought disappointingly few communications to the Committee. During the 1980s, the Committee reached only five to ten decisions on the merits each year. More recently, however, the Committee's case load has begun to increase "markedly": Between October 1993 and July 1994, the Committee adopted thirty-two "views" on the merits and declared thirty cases to be inadmissible; another fifteen views and thirteen admissibility decisions were reached during the next year. During this period, the number of communications filed with the Committee also increased.

Although the Committee's workload is burgeoning and must be regarded as respectable for a fledgling supranational tribunal in the first twenty years of its existence, it is still quite modest given the large number of states party to the Optional Protocol (at eighty-six more than twice the number of signatories to the European Convention on Human Rights) and the vast number of human rights violations occurring every year around the world. Two related factors help explain the relative paucity of cases: the inadequate resources provided to the Committee and the lack of knowledge on the part of potential plaintiffs of the Optional Protocol's function or existence.

The material and financial support necessary to create the physical and personal infrastructure for rendering decisions is a critical factor in the Committee's ability to enhance its effectiveness.[339] Members of the Committee are chronically starved for resources. They must follow all proceedings while simultaneously preparing interventions and responding to or commenting on state reports covering complex issues of law and fact. Most observers conclude that members of the Committee do more than can reasonably be expected, making it impossible for the Committee to assume added work or to work between sessions without substantial additional resources. The Committee has repeatedly requested such resources from the United Nations, most recently stressing that it could "no longer examine communications expeditiously" in light of its increasing workload and "highlight[ing] the urgent need to reinforce the Secretariat staff." ...

. . .

c. *Independent Factfinding Capacity*

Unlike other supranational courts, the Committee has no authority to conduct independent factfinding or to require states parties to supply

Optional Protocol." ... This chapter includes a list identifying those states that cooperated with the Committee's follow-up procedures and those that did not.... The Committee has also resolved to give "every form of publicity" to its follow-up procedures, including issuing separate press communiques "highlight[ing] both positive and negative developments," meeting with gov-ernment representatives, and urging nongovernmental organizations to submit information on compliance....

339. Pursuant to Article 36 of the Covenant, "[t]he Secretary–General of the United Nations shall provide the necessary staff and resources for the effective performance of the functions of the Committee under the present Covenant." ...

information concerning an alleged treaty violation. Nor may it compel the parties or their representatives to appear before it in person to assess their credibility, query their proof, or evaluate their legal arguments. Instead, the Committee must merely consider the communications it receives "in light of all written information made available to it by the individual and the State Party concerned."[350]

. . .

Although hobbled by its limited textual mandate, the Committee has attempted to compensate for its limited powers by spelling out in detail what is expected of states parties when it brings a communication to their attention. In particular, the Committee has emphasized that a state "should make available to [it] all the information at its disposal," including "copies of the relevant decisions of the courts and findings of any investigations which have taken place into the validity of the complaints made." The state must also "investigate in good faith all the allegations of violations of the Covenant against it and its authorities and furnish the Committee with detailed information about the measures, if any, taken to remedy the situation."

Notwithstanding these procedural requirements, in numerous cases the Committee has received either insufficient or no cooperation from the state involved. To prevent the truculent attitude on the part of such states from vitiating the Optional Protocol procedures, the Committee has developed a default judgment jurisprudence under which the author's plausible and substantiated allegations form the basis for its findings of fact and legal conclusion that the Covenant has been violated. Although attractive to individuals seeking to hold such states accountable for human rights abuses, this body of decisions nevertheless may be seen as crediting factual assertions that have not been fully substantiated or skirting difficult legal issues for want of any meaningful adversarial process. . . .

d. *Formal Authority or Status as Law*

The domestic legal status of the Covenant and Optional Protocol, like that of other multilateral treaties including . . . the European Convention on Human Rights, is a function not of international law but rather of the domestic constitutional and legislative regimes established by the states party to the treaty. In one major respect, however, the ICCPR differs significantly from the European treaty regimes: The "views" of the Committee are not binding under international law on the parties to the dispute before it. The Committee itself considers this fact "a major shortcoming in the implementation machinery established by the Covenant."

The ultimate power to make the Committee's decisions legally binding rests with the states party to the Covenant. . . . The Committee has not permitted states parties to control this issue entirely, however. To the contrary, the Committee has taken steps toward imbuing its views with a tone that suggests they are de facto legally binding in character. These

---

350. Optional Protocol, [art. 5(1)].

steps include articulating in its case law and general comments an interpretation of the ICCPR strongly suggesting that its views must be obeyed[362] and urging states parties to amend the Optional Protocol to make the Committee's views legally binding.

. . .

Notes

1. Professors Helfer and Slaughter assert that "[t]he 'views' of the Committee are not binding under international law on the parties to the dispute before it" and note that the "Committee itself considers this fact 'a major shortcoming in the implementation machinery established by the Covenant.' " Is it clear that the Committee's views are not legally binding? As the authors note, the Committee has in recent years begun to assert that States Parties are legally required to act in accordance with the Committee's views. In this regard, see Helfer and Slaughter, supra, at note 362 (discussing the Committee's views in *Bradshaw v. Barbados*). Some years ago, a member of the Committee suggested an interpretation that is more in line with the Committee's views in *Bradshaw* than with what had long been the prevailing position concerning the legal authority of the Committee's "views":

> Since in the preamble to the Optional Protocol, this international instrument is defined as a means of implementation of the Covenant, the States parties, it may be assumed, are under an obligation to cooperate with the Committee when a violation is brought before it. Such cooperation cannot be considered as confined to the procedure leading to the adoption of the views of the Committee, but must logically include the views themselves.

362. In Bradshaw v. Barbados, No. 489/1992, U.N. GAOR, Hum. Rts. Comm., 49th Sess., Supp. No. 40, Annex X, at 305, 307, U.N. Doc. A/49/40 (1994), the Court of Appeal of Barbados had rejected the argument of a death row inmate that "the provisions enabling written representations to the Human Rights Committee, and the procedural and other provisions thereunder," are part of the law of Barbados. As a result, the defendant had no "legitimate expectation that the State would not carry out the sentence of death before his rights under the Covenant and the Optional Protocol had been considered by the Committee...." Id. The Committee criticized this rejection of its powers in no uncertain terms:

> By ratifying the Covenant and the Optional Protocol, Barbados has undertaken to fulfil its obligations thereunder and

has recognized the Committee's competence to receive and consider communications from individuals.... While the Covenant is not part of the domestic law of Barbados which can be applied directly by the courts, the State party has nevertheless accepted the legal obligation to make the provisions of the Covenant effective. To this extent, it is an obligation for the State party to adopt appropriate measures to give legal effect to the views of the Committee as to the interpretation and application of the Covenant in particular cases arising under the Optional Protocol. This includes the Committee's views ... on the desirability of interim measures of protection to avoid irreparable damage to the victim of the alleged violation.

Id. at 309....

Fausto Pocar, *Legal Value of the Human Rights Committee's Views*, 1991–92 Canadian Hum. Rts. Y.B. 119. Is this interpretation of the legal status of the HRC's "views" persuasive?

2.   Professors Helfer and Slaughter observe: "Unlike other supranational courts, the [Human Rights] Committee has no authority to conduct independent factfinding or to require states parties to supply information concerning an alleged treaty violation." Is it clear that the Committee "has no authority" to conduct independent factfinding (as distinguished from lacking sufficient resources to do so)? Compare the Committee's authority under the Optional Protocol with the authority of the Committee on Economic, Social and Cultural Rights to review periodic reports of States Parties to the International Covenant on Economic, Social, and Cultural Rights. As noted below, the latter Committee has on at least two occasions asked States Parties that had failed to respond to requests for information from that Committee to receive a mission comprising one or two Committee members. Could the Human Rights Committee exercise similar innovation in interpreting its authority under the Optional Protocol procedure? Should it?

Human Rights Committee Views Under the Optional Protocol

The preceding material evaluates the Human Rights Committee in light of a range of criteria, including its fact-finding capacity and the quality of its legal reasoning. In reading the following "views" of the Committee in Optional Protocol cases, consider how well the Committee performed in light of these and other criteria that ought to be invoked when evaluating the effectiveness of supranational human rights bodies.

All three decisions excerpted below address the issue of "forced disappearances," which are not proscribed as such in the ICCPR. The term "forced disappearance" is generally used to describe a situation in which an individual has been abducted by persons acting on behalf of or with the acquiescence of the state, followed by a complete denial of information or other forms of accountability by state authorities. By their nature, disappearances present unique challenges to bodies that seek to establish relevant facts. In light of the denial of accountability that is their hallmark, disappearances also present special jurisprudential challenges in respect of efforts to determine state responsibility.

In subsequent sections, we include excerpts of leading cases on disappearances by supranational courts established pursuant to the American Convention on Human Rights and the European Convention for the Protection of Human Rights and Fundamental Freedoms, respectively. When reading the three treaty bodies' decisions, note the similarities as well as differences in their jurisprudential analysis and in their approach to issues of fact.

Bleier v. Uruguay

Human Rights Committee, 1982.
U.N. Doc. A/37/40 at 130 (1982).

. . .

1. The author of the original communication . . . is Irene Bleier Lewenhoff. . . . She is the daughter of the alleged victim. Her information was supplemented by further letters . . . from Rosa Valino de Bleier, . . . who is the alleged victim's wife.

2.1 In her letter of 23 May 1978, the author, Irene Bleier Lewenhoff, states the following:

2.2 Her father, Eduardo Bleier, was arrested without a court order in Montevideo, Uruguay, at the end of October 1975. The authorities did not acknowledge his arrest and he was held incommunicado at an unknown place of detention. Her father's detention was, however, indirectly confirmed because his name was on a list of prisoners read out once a week at an army unit in Montevideo where his family delivered clothing for him and received his dirty clothing. His name appeared on that list for several months until the middle of 1976. On 11 August 1976, "Communique No. 1334 of the Armed Forces Press Office" was printed in all the Montevideo newspapers requesting the general public to co-operate in the capture of 14 persons, among whom Eduardo Bleier was listed, "known to be associated with the banned Communist Party, who had not presented themselves when summoned before the military courts". The author also alleges that her father was subjected to particularly cruel treatment and torture because of his Jewish origin.

2.3 A number of detainees who were held, together with the author's father, and who were later allowed to communicate with their families or were released, gave independent but similar accounts of the cruel torture to which Eduardo Bleier was subjected. They generally agreed that he was singled out for especially cruel treatment because he was a Jew. Thus, on one occasion, the other prisoners were forced to bury him, covering his whole body with earth, and to walk over him. As a result of this treatment inflicted upon him, he was in a very bad state and towards December 1975 had to be interned in the Military Hospital.

. . .

2.6 [The author] further states that the authorities never answered the numerous letters addressed to them by various personalities, institutions or organizations, asking for information about her father's situation. . . .

. . .

[The Committee's views summarize written testimonies submitted by the authors. These included testimonies of former detainees who had seen Eduardo Bleier in military detention. One witness, who had known Eduardo Bleier for more than twenty years, saw him "being subjected to savage torture" while he himself was being tortured.]

9.   In its submission of 9 October 1980, the State party repeated what it had stated in its brief submission of 29 December 1978, namely, that a warrant was still out for the arrest of Eduardo Bleier, whose whereabouts were still unknown. No information, explanations or observations were offered with regard to the various submissions from the authors concerning Mr. Bleier's detention.

[In response to further testimonies by former detainees, the State party "reiterated its position that it did not know the whereabouts of Eduardo Bleier."]

.   .   .

13.2   The Committee notes that the State party has ignored the Committee's repeated requests for a thorough inquiry into the authors' allegations.

13.3   With regard to the burden of proof, this cannot rest alone on the author of the communication, especially considering that the author and the State party do not always have equal access to the evidence and that frequently the State party alone has access to relevant information. It is implicit in article 4 (2) of the Optional Protocol* that the State party has the duty to investigate in good faith all allegations of violation of the Covenant made against it and its authorities, especially when such allegations are corroborated by evidence submitted by the author of the communication, and to furnish to the Committee the information available to it. In cases where the author has submitted to the Committee allegations supported by substantial witness testimony, as in this case, and where further clarification of the case depends on information exclusively in the hands of the State party, the Committee may consider such allegations as substantiated in the absence of satisfactory evidence and explanations to the contrary submitted by the State party.

13.4   The Committee finds that the disappearance of Eduardo Bleier in October 1975 does not alone establish that he was arrested by Uruguayan authorities. But, the allegation that he was so arrested and detained is confirmed (i) by the information, unexplained and substantially unrefuted by the State party, that Eduardo Bleier's name was on a list of prisoners read out once a week at an army unit in Montevideo where his family delivered clothing for him and received his dirty clothing until the summer of 1976, and (ii) by the testimony of other prisoners that they saw him in Uruguayan detention centres. Also there are the reports of several eyewitnesses that Eduardo Bleier was subjected to severe torture while in detention.

14.   It is therefore the Committee's view that the information before it reveals breaches of articles 7, 9 and 10 (1) of the International Covenant on

---

* [Article 4(2) of the Optional Protocol provides:

2.   Within six months [of receiving from the Committee a communication alleging that it has breached the ICCPR], the receiving State shall submit to the Committee written explanations or statements clarifying the matter and the remedy, if any, that may have been taken by that State.

(Editors' Note.)]

Civil and Political Rights and that there are serious reasons to believe that the ultimate violation of article 6 has been perpetrated by the Uruguayan authorities.*

15.   As regards the latter point the Human Rights Committee urges the Uruguayan Government to reconsider its position in this case and to take effective steps (i) to establish what has happened to Eduardo Bleier since October 1975; to bring to justice any persons found to be responsible for his death, disappearance or ill-treatment; and to pay compensation to him or his family for any injury which he has suffered; and (ii) to ensure that similar violations do not occur in the future.

. . .

Quinteros v. Uruguay

Human Rights Committee, 1983.
U.N. Doc. A/38/40 at 216.

. . .

1.1   The author of the communication . . . is a Uruguayan national, residing at present in Sweden. She submitted the communication on behalf of her daughter, Elena Quinteros Almeida, and on her own behalf.

1.2   The author describes the relevant facts as follows:

"My daughter (born on 9 September 1945) was arrested at her home in the city of Montevideo on 24 June 1976. Four days later, while she was being held completely incommunicado, she was taken by military personnel to a particular spot in the city near the Embassy of Venezuela. My daughter would appear to have told her captors that she had a rendezvous at that place with another person whom they wished to arrest. Once she was in front of a house adjoining the Embassy of Venezuela, my daughter succeeded in getting away from the persons accompanying her, jumped over a wall and landed inside the Embassy grounds. At the same time, she shouted out her name so as to alert passers-by to what was happening in case she was recaptured. The military personnel accompanying her then entered the diplomatic mission and, after striking the Secretary of the Embassy and other members of its staff, dragged my daughter off the premises."

. . .

1.4   The author claims that since that day (28 June 1976) she could never obtain from the authorities any official information about her daughter's

---

* [Article 7 provides, in pertinent part: "No one shall be subjected to torture or to cruel, inhuman or degrading treatment or punishment." Article 9 establishes the right to "liberty and security of person," and enumerates safeguards against arbitrary arrest and detention. Article 10(1) provides: "All persons deprived of their liberty shall be treated with humanity and with respect for the inherent dignity of the human person." Article 6 assures the right to life.—Editors' Note.]

whereabouts, nor was her detention officially admitted.... The author, in addition, encloses [a document which noted] that on 2 March 1979, the Ambassador and Representative of Uruguay to the United Nations Commission on Human Rights at Geneva, who was at that time Director of Foreign Policy of the Ministry of Foreign Affairs, told the author that her daughter was alive, that she had been taken from the Venezuelan Embassy by members of the Uruguayan police and army, that she was being kept a prisoner and that efforts were being made to clarify responsibilities.

[The author of the communication submitted testimonies of two witnesses, one of whom had seen Elena Quinteros Almeida in military detention and another of whom had seen a police officer arrest Ms. Quinteros on the grounds of the Venezuelan Embassy in Montevideo.]

. . .

1.9 The author claims that the following articles of the Covenant have been violated with respect to her daughter: 7, 9, 10, 12, 14, 17 and 19. She adds that she is herself a victim of violations of article 7 (psychological torture because she does not know where her daughter is) and of article 17 of the Covenant, because of interference with her private and family life.

. . .

6. In its submission under article 4 (2) of the Optional Protocol, dated 13 August 1982, the State party referred to the contents of an earlier note, dated 14 June 1982, which appeared to be a late submission under rule 91 of the provisional rules of procedure. The text of this earlier note read as follows:

"The Uruguayan Government wishes to inform that the person in question (Elena Quinteros) has been sought throughout Uruguay since 8 May 1975. The assertions contained in this communication are therefore rejected as unfounded, since the Government had no part in the episode described."

. . .

7.3 Addressing the question raised by the Committee whether she comes within the jurisdiction of Uruguay as to the violations alleged in her own behalf, the author states . . .

". . . Since the continued violation of my daughter's human rights constitutes the crucial factor of the violation of my own rights, the Government cannot, in my view, in any way evade its responsibility towards me. I continue to suffer day and night because of the lack of information on my dear daughter, and I therefore believe that, from the moment when my daughter was arrested, I was, and I continue to be, the victim of a violation of articles 7 and 17 of the Covenant."

[In an interim decision, the Committee concluded that information thus far submitted by the State party "is insufficient to comply with the requirements of article 4(2) of the Optional Protocol" and urged it to conduct a thorough inquiry into the allegations and to inform the Committee of the outcome of that inquiry. In response, the State party sent a note asserting the following: "The Government of Uruguay wishes to reiterate what it said to the Committee in its reply to the note of 4 December 1981 on this case".]

. . .

10.6 The author refers to the position the Committee has taken, in previous cases, that in the face of specific and detailed complaints, it was not sufficient for the State party to refute these allegations in general terms but that "it should have investigated the allegations". . . .

. . .

11.   In accordance with its mandate under article 5 (1) of the Optional Protocol, the Committee has considered the communication in the light of the information made available to it by the author of the communication and by the State party concerned. In this connection, the Committee has adhered strictly to the principle *audiatur et altera pars* and has given the State party every opportunity to furnish information to refute the evidence presented by the author. The State party appears to have ignored the Committee's request for a thorough inquiry into the author's allegations. The Committee reiterates that it is implicit in article 4 (2) of the Optional Protocol that the State party has the duty to investigate in good faith all allegations of violation of the Covenant made against it and its authorities, especially when such allegations are corroborated by evidence submitted by the author of the communication, and to furnish to the Committee the information available to it. In cases where the author has submitted to the Committee allegations supported by substantial witness testimony, as in this case, and where further clarification of the case depends on information exclusively in the hands of the State party, the Committee may consider such allegations as substantiated in the absence of satisfactory evidence and explanations to the contrary submitted by the State party.

12.1 With regard to the identity of the alleged victim, the Committee on the basis of (a) the detailed information submitted by the author, including an eyewitness testimony, and (b) the statement made to the Working Group on Enforced or Involuntary Disappearance by the representative of Uruguay to the Commission on Human Rights, on 1 December 1981,* has no doubt that the woman who was able to go inside the Embassy of Venezuela at Montevideo, on 28 June 1976, requesting asylum and who was forcibly removed from the Embassy grounds, put in a car and taken away, was Elena Quinteros.

12.2 In addition, the Committee cannot but give appropriate weight [to the eyewitness testimony submitted by the author of the communication].

. . .

---

* [This representative acknowledged the forcible abduction of Ms. Quinteros from the entrance of the Venezuelan Embassy, saying that it had occurred "[b]efore she was able to go inside and before she could initiate the procedure for applying for asylum . . . ."—Editors' Note, quoting from para. 10.7 of Committee's views.]

12.3   The Human Rights Committee, accordingly, finds that, on 28 June 1976, Elena Quinteros was arrested on the grounds of the Embassy of Venezuela at Montevideo by at least one member of the Uruguayan police force and that in August 1976 she was held in a military detention centre in Uruguay where she was subjected to torture.

13.   It is, therefore, the Committee's view that the information before it reveals breaches of articles 7, 9 and 10 (1) of the International Covenant on Civil and Political Rights.

14.   With regard to the violations alleged by the author on her own behalf, the Committee notes that, the statement of the author that she was in Uruguay at the time of the incident regarding her daughter, was not contradicted by the State party. The Committee understands the anguish and stress caused to the mother by the disappearance of her daughter and by the continuing uncertainty concerning her fate and whereabouts. The author has the right to know what has happened to her daughter. In these respects, she too is a victim of the violations of the Covenant suffered by her daughter in particular, of article 7.

15.   The Human Rights Committee reiterates that the Government of Uruguay has a duty to conduct a full investigation into the matter. There is no evidence that this has been done.

16.   The Human Rights Committee, acting under article 5 (4) of the Optional Protocol to the International Covenant on Civil and Political Rights, therefore concludes that responsibility for the disappearance of Elena Quinteros falls on the authorities of Uruguay and that, consequently, the Government of Uruguay should take immediate and effective steps (a) to establish what has happened to Elena Quinteros since 28 June 1976, and secure her release; (b) to bring to justice any persons found to be responsible for her disappearance and ill-treatment; (c) to pay compensation for the wrongs suffered; and (d) to ensure that similar violations do not occur in the future.

. . .

Mojica v. Dominican Republic

Human Rights Committee, 1994.
U.N. Doc. CCPR/C/51/D/449/1991.

. . .

1.   The author of the communication is Barbarín Mojica, a citizen of the Dominican Republic and labour leader residing in Santo Domingo, Dominican Republic. He submits the communication on behalf of his son Rafael Mojica, a Dominican citizen born in 1959, who disappeared in May 1990. The author claims violations by the State party of articles 6, 7, 9, paragraph 1, and 10, paragraph 1, of the Covenant in respect of his son.

The facts as submitted by the author:

2.1 The author is a well-known labour leader. His son, Rafael Mojica, a dock worker in the port of Santo Domingo, was last seen by his family in the evening of 5 May 1990. Between 8 p.m. and 1 a.m., he was seen by others at the restaurant "El Aplauso" in the neighbourhood of the Arrimo Portuario union, with which he was associated. Witnesses affirm that he then boarded a taxi in which other, unidentified, men were travelling.

2.2 The author contends that during the weeks prior to his son's disappearance, Rafael Mojica had received death threats from some military officers of the Dirección de Bienes Nacionales, in particular from Captain Manuel de Jesus Morel and two of the latter's assistants, known under their sobriquets of "Martin" and "Brinquito". They allegedly threatened him because of his presumed communist inclinations.

2.3 On 31 May 1990, the author, his family and friends requested the opening of an investigation into the disappearance of Rafael Mojica.... One month after Rafael Mojica's disappearance, two decapitated and mutilated bodies were found in another part of the capital, close to the industrial zone of Haina and the beach of Haina. Fearing that one of the bodies might be that of his son, the author requested an autopsy, which was performed on 22 June 1990. While the autopsy could not establish the identity of the victims, it was certain that Rafael Mojica was not one of them, as his skin, unlike that of the victims, was dark....

2.4 On 16 July 1990, the author, through a lawyer, requested the Principal Public Prosecutor in Santo Domingo to investigate the presumed involvement of Captain Morel and his assistants in the disappearance of his son. The author does not specify whether the request received any follow-up between 23 July 1990, date of the communication to the Human Rights Committee, and the beginning of 1994.

. . .

The complaint:

3. It is submitted that the above facts reveal violations by the State party of articles 6, 7, 9, paragraph 1, and 10, paragraph 1, of the Covenant.

The Committee's admissibility decision:

4.1 During its 47th session, the Committee considered the admissibility of the communication. It noted with concern the absence of cooperation on the part of the State party and observed that the author's contention that there were no effective domestic remedies to exhaust for cases of disappearances of individuals had remained uncontested. In the circumstances, the Committee was satisfied that the requirements of article 5, paragraph 2(b), of the Optional Protocol had been met.

. . .

4.3 Concerning the author's claims under articles 6, 7 and 9, paragraph 1, the Committee considered them to be substantiated, for purposes of admissibility.... The State party was requested ... to provide information about the results of the investigation into Mr. Mojica's disappearance and to forward copies of all relevant documentation in the case.

Examination of the merits:

5.1 ... No submission on the merits has been received from the State party, in spite of a reminder addressed to it on 2 May 1994.

5.2 The Committee has noted with regret and concern the absence of cooperation on the part of the State party, in respect of both the admissibility and the merits of the communication. It is implicit in article 4, paragraph 2, of the Optional Protocol and in rule 91 of the rules of procedure that a State party investigate thoroughly, in good faith and within the imparted deadlines, all the allegations of violations of the Covenant made against it, and to make available to the Committee all the information at its disposal. This the State party has failed to do. Accordingly, due weight must be given to the author's allegations, to the extent that they have been substantiated.

5.3 The author has alleged a violation of article 9, paragraph 1, of the Covenant. Although there is no evidence that Rafael Mojica was actually arrested or detained on or after 5 May 1990, the Committee recalls that under the terms of the decision on admissibility, the State party was requested to clarify these issues; it has not done so. The Committee further notes the allegation that Rafael Mojica had received death threats from some military officers of the Dirección de Bienes Nacionales in the weeks prior to his disappearance; this information, again, has not been refuted by the State party.

5.4 The first sentence of article 9, paragraph 1, guarantees to everyone the right to liberty and security of person. In its prior jurisprudence, the Committee has held that this right may be invoked not only in the context of arrest and detention, and that an interpretation which would allow States parties to tolerate, condone or ignore threats made by persons in authority to the personal liberty and security of non-detained individuals within the State party's jurisdiction would render ineffective the guarantees of the Covenant. . . . In the circumstances of the case, the Committee concludes that the State party has failed to ensure Rafael Mojica's right to liberty and security of the person, in violation of article 9, paragraph 1, of the Covenant.

5.5 In respect of the alleged violation of article 6, paragraph 1, the Committee recalls its General Comment 6 on article 6, which states, inter alia, that States parties should take specific and effective measures to prevent the disappearance of individuals and establish effective facilities and procedures to investigate thoroughly, by an appropriate impartial body, cases of missing and disappeared persons in circumstances that may involve a violation of the right to life.

5.6 The Committee observes that the State party has not denied that Rafael Mojica (a) has in fact disappeared and remains unaccounted for since the evening of 5 May 1990, and (b) that his disappearance was caused by individuals belonging to the Government's security forces. In the circumstances, the Committee finds that the right to life enshrined in article 6 has not been effectively protected by the Dominican Republic, especially considering that this is a case where the victim's life had previously been threatened by military officers.

5.7   The circumstances surrounding Rafael Mojica's disappearance, including the threats made against him, give rise to a strong inference that he was tortured or subjected to cruel and inhuman treatment. Nothing has been submitted to the Committee by the State party to dispel or counter this inference. Aware of the nature of enforced or involuntary disappearances in many countries, the Committee feels confident to conclude that the disappearance of persons is inseparably linked to treatment that amounts to a violation of article 7.

6.   The Human Rights Committee, acting under article 5, paragraph 4, of the Optional Protocol to the International Covenant on Civil and Political Rights, is of the view that the facts as found by the Committee reveal a violation by the State party of articles 6, paragraph 1, 7 and 9, paragraph 1, of the Covenant. Under article 2, paragraph 3, of the Covenant, the State party is under an obligation to provide the author with an effective remedy. The Committee urges the State party to investigate thoroughly the disappearance of Rafael Mojica, to bring to justice those responsible for his disappearance, and to pay appropriate compensation to his family.

. . .

Notes

1.   Professors Helfer and Slaughter observe that "the [Human Rights] Committee has developed a default judgment jurisprudence under which the author's plausible and substantiated allegations form the basis for its findings of fact and legal conclusion that the Covenant has been violated" in situations where States Parties have failed to provide detailed responses to allegations submitted under the Optional Protocol procedure. This observation seems especially relevant in explaining the Committee's factual conclusions in the *Bleier* and *Quinteros* cases. In both of those cases, the authors of the communications submitted detailed testimonies by eyewitnesses, to which the State Party concerned provided highly general responses. Is the explanation of the Committee's practice offered by Professors Helfer and Slaughter equally applicable in respect to the *Mojica* case?

Note that, in contrast to the testimonies submitted in the *Bleier* and *Quinteros* cases, the author of the *Mojica* communication apparently did not provide testimony of eyewitnesses who observed the victim in the custody of state officials. Did the author provide sufficient evidence to justify the Committee's legal conclusions? Recall that "default" jurisprudence generally assumes, in light of the respondent's failure to participate in the proceedings, that the petitioner's allegations are true. Even assuming that all of the facts alleged by the author of the *Mojica* communication are true, do they establish a breach of Articles 6, 7 and 9(1) of the ICCPR? In particular, is the Committee's reasoning in paragraphs 5.6 and 5.7 persuasive? What evidence formed the basis of the Committee's conclusion that "[t]he circumstances surrounding Rafael Mojica's disappearance . . .

give rise to a strong inference that he was tortured or subjected to cruel and inhuman treatment" in violation of Article 7? What evidence supported its conclusions that Mojica's "disappearance was caused by individuals belonging to the Government's security forces" and that "the right to life enshrined in article 6 has not been effectively protected by the Dominican Republic"?

2.   As noted above, the authors of the communications in the *Bleier* and *Quinteros* cases submitted detailed eyewitness testimonies. Is it appropriate for the Committee to base its findings on written statements when it has not had the opportunity to observe the demeanor of the witnesses? Does the appropriateness depend upon whether the State Party concerned has cooperated with the Committee pursuant to its obligations under the Optional Protocol? Does the fact that the Committee is "starved" of resources justify shifting the burden of proof to the State once compelling allegations have been lodged against it? Do other considerations justify this approach?

3.   In paragraph 13.3 of the *Bleier* case, the HRC stated that Uruguay has a duty to investigate in good faith allegations of violations of the Covenant made against it and its authorities. In paragraph 15, it urged the Uruguayan government to take effective steps to establish the fate of Eduardo Bleier, the subject of the communication. Both the statement in paragraph 13.3 and the recommendation in paragraph 15 entail investigation by Uruguayan authorities. Was the Committee invoking two distinct legal grounds for Uruguay's duty to investigate? What are the legal bases for the Committee's observations in this regard? Compare the observations of the HRC in paragraphs 11, 15 and 16 of the *Quinteros* case, and in paragraphs 5.2 and 6 of the *Mojica* case.

2.   THE INTERNATIONAL COVENANT ON ECONOMIC, SOCIAL, AND CULTURAL RIGHTS

Supervisory Mechanisms: The Committee on Economic, Social and Cultural Rights

In contrast to the ICCPR, the International Covenant on Economic, Social, and Cultural Rights (ICESCR) did not provide for the establishment of a special treaty body to supervise States Parties' compliance. The principal mechanism of supervision envisaged in the Covenant is a requirement of reporting to the Economic and Social Council (ECOSOC):

Article 16

1.   The States Parties to the present Covenant undertake to submit in conformity with this part of the Covenant reports on the measures which they have adopted and the progress made in achieving the observance of the rights recognized herein.

The Covenant specifies that these reports should be submitted to the UN Secretary–General, who in turn would transmit copies to the Economic and Social Council "for consideration in accordance with the provisions of the present Covenant" (Article 16(2) (a)) and to relevant specialized agencies (Article 16(2)(b)). At first, states' reports were reviewed by ECOSOC's Sessional Working Group on the Implementation of the International Covenant on Economic, Social and Cultural Rights, which reported its general findings to ECOSOC and several other UN bodies and specialized agencies.

Pursuant to a 1985 ECOSOC resolution, a "treaty body" was finally established to provide supervision in respect of the ICESCR. In the terms of ECOSOC Res. 1985/17, the Sessional Working Group was "renamed" the "Committee on Economic, Social and Cultural Rights," comprising 18 experts elected by ECOSOC to serve in their personal capacity. The Committee, which held its first meeting in 1987, was given the following authority:

> The Committee shall submit to the Council a report on its activities, including a summary of its consideration of the reports submitted by States parties to the Covenant, and shall make suggestions and recommendations of a general nature on the basis of its consideration of those reports and of the reports submitted by the specialized agencies, in order to assist the Council to fulfil, in particular its responsibilities under articles 21 and 22 of the Covenant[.]

ECOSOC Res. 1985/17, para.(f).

Reviewing States Parties' reports is the central supervisory role provided by the Committee. As the Committee has observed, the review sessions are similar to those undertaken by the Human Rights Committee and other UN human rights treaty bodies:

> 33.   In accordance with the established practice of each of the United Nations human rights treaty monitoring bodies, representatives of the reporting States are entitled, and indeed are strongly encouraged, to be present at the meetings of the Committee when their reports are examined. The following procedure is generally followed. The representative of the State party is invited to introduce the report by making brief introductory comments and introducing any written replies to the list of issues drawn up by the pre-sessional working group. The Committee then considers the report on an article-by-article basis, taking particular account of the replies furnished in response to the list of issues. During this period, representatives of relevant specialized agencies and other international bodies are also able to contribute to the dialogue. The representatives of the State party are invited to reply immediately to questions that do not require further reflection or research. Other questions remaining to be answered are taken up at a subsequent meeting. Members of the Committee are free to pursue specific issues in the light of the replies thus provided. Questions which cannot adequately be dealt with in this manner may be the subject of additional information provided to the Committee in writing.

> 34.   The final phase of the Committee's examination of the report consists of the drafting and adoption of its concluding observations.

For this purpose, the Committee usually sets aside a brief period, in closed session, to enable its members to express their preliminary views. The country rapporteur then prepares, with the assistance of the Secretariat, a draft set of concluding observations for consideration by the Committee. The agreed structure of the concluding observations is as follows: introduction; positive aspects; factors and difficulties impeding the implementation of the Covenant; principal subjects of concern; and suggestions and recommendations. At a later stage, the Committee then discusses the draft, again in private session, with a view to adopting it by consensus.

35.   The concluding observations are formally adopted in public session on the final day of the session. As soon as this occurs they are considered to have been made public and are available to all interested parties. They are forwarded as soon as possible to the State party concerned and included in the Committee's report. If it so wishes, the State party may address any of the Committee's concluding observations in the context of any additional information which it provides to the Committee.

Committee on Economic, Social and Cultural Rights, Report on the Sixteenth and Seventeenth Sessions (Sessional/Annual Report of Committee), U.N. Doc. E/1998/22.

The Committee at times requests additional information "to enable it to continue its dialogue with the State party concerned." Id., para. 38. When its requests for information have not enabled it to obtain the information it requires, the Committee has on at least two occasions asked the State Party concerned to receive a mission comprising one or two Committee members. Id., para. 39.

Like other UN human rights treaty bodies, the Committee on Economic, Social and Cultural Rights has faced the problem of chronic failures by States Parties to satisfy their reporting obligations. In the Committee's words, "a situation of persistent non-reporting by States parties risks bringing the entire supervisory procedure into disrepute, thereby undermining one of the foundations of the Covenant." Id., para. 42. To address this problem, the Committee decided that it would begin scheduling "very much overdue" reports to be considered at future sessions and would notify the States Parties concerned. If that state failed to provide a report, the Committee would proceed, in the absence of a report, "to consider the status of economic, social and cultural rights in the light of all available information". Id., para. 44.

Following the practice of the Human Rights Committee, the Committee on Economic, Social and Cultural Rights has developed the practice of adopting "general comments." In the Committee's words, the aim of these comments is

> to make the experience gained so far through the examination of States' reports available for the benefit of all States parties in order to assist and promote their further implementation of the Covenant; to

draw the attention of the States parties to insufficiencies disclosed by a large number of reports; to suggest improvements in the reporting procedures; and to stimulate the activities of the States parties, international organizations and the specialized agencies concerned in achieving progressively and effectively the full realization of the rights recognized in the Covenant.

Id., para. 51.

By July 1999, the Committee had adopted the following general comments: General Comment No. 1 (1989) on reporting by States parties; General Comment No. 2 (1990) on international technical assistance measures; General Comment No. 3 (1990) on the nature of States parties' obligations; General Comment No. 4 (1991) on the right to adequate housing; General Comment No. 5 (1994) on the rights of persons with disabilities; General Comment No. 6 (1995) on the economic, social and cultural rights of older persons; General Comment No. 7 (1997) on forced evictions; General Comment No. 8 (1997) on economic sanctions; General Comment No. 9 (1998) on the domestic application of the Covenant; General Comment No. 10 (1998) on national human rights institutions; General Comment No. 11 (1999) on plans of action for primary education; and General Comment No. 12 (1999) on the right to adequate food.

Since 1990, the Committee on Economic, Social and Cultural Rights has been considering developing an optional protocol to the ICESCR, modeled after the first Optional Protocol to the ICCPR. In 1996 the Committee adopted a report proposing adoption of a draft optional protocol. Pursuant to the proposed protocol, States Parties would recognize the competence of the Committee to receive and examine communications from individuals or groups subject to the state's jurisdiction who claim to be victims of a violation of the Covenant. See Annual Report of the Committee on Economic, Social and Cultural Rights on its 14th and 15th Sessions, U.N. Doc. E/1997/22, Annex IV.

Monitoring State Implementation of the ICESCR

As noted in Part III, Chapter 2, Section B, the nature of the obligations undertaken by States Parties to the ICESCR is fundamentally different from the obligations assumed under the ICCPR. While States Parties to the latter undertake to "respect and ensure" enumerated rights to individuals within their territory and subject to their jurisdiction, the basic obligation of States Parties to the ICESCR is "to take steps, individually and through international assistance and co-operation, especially economic and technical, to the maximum of its available resources, with a view to achieving progressively the full realization of the rights recognized in the present Covenant by all appropriate means, including particularly the adoption of legislative measures." (Article 2(1)).

The qualified language ("take steps", "to the maximum of its available resources," "with a view to achieving progressively . . .") has led many to doubt whether one can meaningfully speak of obligations imposed on States

Parties to the ICESCR. In similar vein, skeptics have wondered whether it is appropriate to contemplate supranational supervisory procedures—in particular, the type of complaint procedure contemplated in the proposed optional protocol—if it is not possible to agree on whether a state's practices constitute compliance or a breach of the ICESCR. In this setting, the Committee on Economic, Social and Cultural Rights has used its "general comments" to provide clarity and a fuller understanding of the obligations undertaken by States Parties to the ICESCR. Its third general comment, adopted in 1990, addressed the nature of States Parties obligations under Article 2(1) of the Covenant. That general comment, as well as other aspects of the ICESCR's jurisprudence, are examined in Part IV, Chapter 3, Section C.

3. OTHER HUMAN RIGHTS TREATY MECHANISMS

In addition to the comprehensive conventions examined in the preceding sections, the United Nations has adopted a number of conventions that are concerned with specific rights. These include the Convention on the Elimination of All Forms of Racial Discrimination, the Convention on the Elimination of All Forms of Discrimination Against Women, both of which are addressed in greater depth in other sections, the Convention on the Rights of the Child and the Convention Against Torture and Other Cruel, Inhuman or Degrading Treatment or Punishment.

Numerous specialized conventions have also been adopted by regional organizations. Both the Council of Europe and the Organization of American States (OAS) have adopted conventions on torture. Some conventions adopted under regional auspices reflect concerns of particular salience for the region in question. For example, the OAS, whose member states have been especially afflicted with the scourge of enforced disappearance, adopted the Inter–American Convention on Forced Disappearance of Persons. The Council of Europe, many of whose member states are struggling with human rights challenges relating to ethnic, national, racial and religious minorities, adopted both the European Charter for Regional or Minority Languages and the Framework Convention for the Protection of National Minorities in the 1990s.

With variations among them, each of these conventions provides for oversight by a treaty body. The Inter–American Convention on Forced Disappearance of Persons contemplates utilization of the petition machinery established under the American Convention on Human Rights (Article XIII) as well as an additional "urgent action" role for the American Commission (Article XIV). Each of the other specialized conventions mentioned in the preceding paragraph establishes its own monitoring or enforcement machinery.

In fact, the hallmark of the European Convention for the Prevention of Torture is its monitoring procedure. Pursuant to the convention, the European Committee for the Prevention of Torture and Inhuman or Degrading Treatment or Punishment (CPT) is entitled to visit any place within the jurisdiction of States Parties where individuals are held by public authorities. (Compare Article 20 of the UN Convention Against Torture.) As of July 21, 1998, the CPT had carried out 75 visits in 35 countries. See Council of Europe, NGOs and the Human Rights Work of the Council of Europe: Opportunities for Co-operation, Council of Europe Doc. H (98) 12, p. 24 (1998).

The following report addresses some of the problems associated with the multiplication of treaties and treaty bodies within the United Nations system, while also providing a broader perspective on the effectiveness of UN human rights treaty systems.

Final Report on Enhancing the Long–term Effectiveness of the United Nations Human Rights Treaty System

U.N. Doc. E/CN.4/1997/74.

. . .

1. This report is submitted by the independent expert, Mr Philip Alston, appointed by the Secretary–General. . . .

. . .

7. (d) The number of overdue reports has increased by 34 per cent [since 1993] and the delays experienced by States parties between the submission and examination of their reports have increased to the point where some States will wait almost three years before their reports are examined;

(e) The number of communications being processed under the various complaints procedures has greatly increased and existing backlogs are unacceptably high. At the same time, there is a clear need to create additional complaints systems in order to ensure that due attention is paid to economic, social and cultural rights and to the full range of women's rights. Specific proposals in relation to both the Convention on the Elimination of All Forms of Discrimination against Women and the International Covenant on Economic, Social and Cultural Rights are currently under consideration;

(f) The resources available to service this sizeable expansion in the system have actually contracted rather than expanded and there have been consistent calls, escalating in volume and intensity, . . . for increased resources and improved servicing to be made available;

. . .

8. The extent of the shortcomings inherent in the treaty monitoring system has led some observers to propose radical solutions. Thus, for example, in 1994 one commentator proposed, *inter alia*, that States which do not satisfy a set of minimum requirements drawn from the relevant treaties should be expelled from the treaty regime; the system of State reporting should be discontinued; the treaty bodies should undertake on-site fact-finding in every State party; and acceptance of a right to petition

under all six treaties should be made mandatory.[3] Writing in August 1996, in a report for the International Law Association, the same commentator considered there to be an "implementation crisis . . . of dangerous proportions".[4] In her view, "the treaty regime has been depreciated by chronic levels of non-compliance, both with the substantive terms of the treaties, and with existing enforcement mechanisms".[5] . . .

. . .

9.   The present report is based upon several premises. The first is that the basic assumptions of the treaty supervisory system are sound and remain entirely valid. In other words, the principle of holding States accountable for non-compliance with their treaty obligations by means of an objective and constructive dialogue, on the basis of comprehensive information and inputs from all interested parties, has been vindicated in practice and has the potential to be an important and effective means by which to promote respect for human rights. . . .

10.   The fourth premise is that the present system is unsustainable and that significant reforms will be required if the overall regime is to achieve its objectives.

. . .

37.   Most of the committees continue to express concern over the consequences of the large number of significantly overdue reports. . . .

38.   In its 1996 annual report . . . the Committee against Torture noted . . . that there were 96 States parties and . . . that there were 55 States with overdue reports [some of which were more than four years late]. . . . The Committee took two measures in response. The first was to issue a separate document listing overdue reports. The second was to give wide publicity to the list at its end of session press conferences.

39.   In its 1996 annual report . . . the Human Rights Committee expressed "its serious concern" that "more than two thirds of all States parties . . . were in arrears with their reports". . . .

. . .

41.   . . . [R]esponses might include an easing of the reporting requirements under certain circumstances. . . . The Human Rights Committee decided in 1996 that, "under very exceptional circumstances", when a report is overdue "because of material difficulties", the State party could be invited to send a delegation to discuss those difficulties or be asked to submit a provisional report dealing only with certain aspects of the Covenant. . . .

---

3. Bayefsky, "Making the Human Rights Treaties Work", in L. Henkin and J.L. Hargrove (eds.), *Human Rights: An Agenda for the Next Century*, Studies in Transnational Legal Policy No. 26 (Washington D.C., American Society of International Law, 1994) p. 229 at p. 264.

4. Bayefsky, "Report on the UN Human Rights Treaties: Facing the Implementation Crisis", in *First Report of the Committee on International Law and Practice*, International Law Association, Helsinki Conference (1996), p. 11.

5. Ibid., p. 12.

42. Another approach ... would be to eliminate the obligation to provide comprehensive periodic reports....

· · ·

45. The key question ... is what types of measures designed to raise the costs of non-compliance [with reporting obligations] might be appropriate, potentially productive in terms of upholding the integrity of the system, consistent with the legal framework of the relevant treaty, and politically and otherwise acceptable. Various palliatives are available.... They include: the elimination of reporting and its replacement by detailed questions to which answers must be given; the preparation of a single consolidated report to satisfy several different requirements; and the much wider use of a more professional advisory services programme designed to assist in the preparation of reports. Ultimately, however, none of these might make a difference in hard-core cases. Under those circumstances the only viable option open to the treaty bodies is to proceed with an examination of the situation in a State party in the absence of a report. This has been done for a number of years by the Committee on Economic, Social and Cultural Rights and the Committee on the Elimination of Racial Discrimination has adopted a very similar approach....

· · ·

47. In implementing such an approach, the experience of the Committee on Economic, Social and Cultural Rights is instructive. Ample notice has been given to the States concerned and, in a majority of the cases taken up so far, reports which had been dramatically overdue have suddenly materialized. For the rest, it is particularly important that the Committee is in a position to undertake detailed research work and to be able to base its examination upon a wide range of sources of information....

48. The present supervisory system can function only because of the large-scale delinquency of States which either do not report at all, or report long after the due date....

49. ... [I]f every State party with a report overdue under either of the Covenants were to submit that report tomorrow, the last to be received could not be considered, on the basis of existing arrangements, before the year 2003. At that point, the relevant committee would be considering an eight-year-old report and would have a huge backlog of subsequent reports pending.

· · ·

90. [One possible option for addressing the reporting backlog is] the preparation of a single consolidated report by each State party, which would then be submitted in satisfaction of the requirements under each of the treaties to which the State is a party....

· · ·

91. Another proposal ... would be to eliminate the requirement that States parties' periodic reports should be comprehensive. Such an approach would clearly not be appropriate in relation to initial reports....

· · ·

[The report also recommends the convening of an expert group to consider the consolidation (reduction) of the number of treaty bodies.]

. . .

Notes

1.   While the preceding report considers only treaty bodies established to monitor conventions adopted under UN auspices, it touches upon issues that are equally relevant to regional treaties. The submission and review of reports by states parties is the principal monitoring mechanism contemplated by the Framework Convention for the Protection of National Minorities, and is also an important part of the supervisory machinery for the African Charter on Human and Peoples' Rights. The reporting requirements imposed by these regional treaties, which may overlap with states' obligations under UN conventions, further compound the problems identified by Professor Alston.

2.   Professor Alston's report notes a range of proposals that have been put forth to address the chronic delays by states parties in meeting their reporting obligations under UN human rights conventions. Which of these—and other possible reforms—merit support? For an analysis of the effectiveness of human rights treaty regimes, see, in addition to citations provided in notes 3 and 4 of the preceding excerpt, *The UN Human Rights Regime: Is It Effective?*, 1997 ASIL Proc. 460–484.

B.   REGIONAL ARRANGEMENTS

1.   AMERICAN CONVENTION ON HUMAN RIGHTS

The American Convention on Human Rights, informally known as the Pact of San José, was adopted by the Organization of American States (OAS) in San José, Costa Rica in 1969 and entered into force in 1978. Like the ICCPR and the European Convention, the American Convention requires States Parties to respect and ensure a comprehensive range of civil and political rights; it also includes provisions relating to property rights (Article 21) and economic, social and cultural rights (Article 26). See Chapter 2(D)(2) supra.

The Convention provides for supervision by two organs. One, the Inter–American Commission of Human Rights, existed as a human rights organ of the OAS before the American Convention was adopted and acquired additional powers as a treaty organ. Created in 1959 to "further respect" for human rights among OAS member states, the Commission was granted authority in 1965 to examine communications alleging violations of human rights. The resolution establishing this function authorized the Commission to request information from the relevant government, to make appropriate recommendations and to publish observations on matters covered in the communications in its annual report. Resolution XXII, "Expanded Functions of the Inter–American Commission on Human Rights," Final Act of the Second Special Inter–American Conference, OAS/ ser.E./XIII.1, at 45–46 (1965).

Pursuant to its statute, the Commission can examine communications alleging violations of the American Convention in relation to States Parties, and to rights set forth in the American Declaration of the Rights and Duties of Man, which was adopted when the OAS itself was established in 1948, with respect to other OAS member states. It is the latter provision that has enabled the Commission to receive and consider communications alleging human rights violations by the United States, which signed the Convention in 1977 but has not yet ratified it.

The Commission can receive communications alleging violations of the American Convention from either individuals or States Parties. Its competence to receive individual petitions is automatic under the American Convention (Article 44), while it can receive communications from a State Party alleging a breach by another State Party only when both the petitioner and respondent states have made declarations recognizing this competence (Article 45). The seven-member Commission meets in Washington, D.C. at the headquarters of the OAS.

The second supervisory body, the Inter–American Court on Human Rights, was created pursuant to the American Convention. The seven-member Court is based in San Jose, Costa Rica. Although a treaty organ, the Court's members can include nationals of any OAS member state whether or not it has ratified the American Convention.

Like the International Court of Justice, the Inter–American Court exercises both advisory and contentious jurisdiction. Its advisory jurisdiction is established in Article 64 of the American Convention, which provides:

Article 64

1.   The member states of the Organization may consult the Court regarding the interpretation of this Convention or of other treaties concerning the protection of human rights in the American states. Within their spheres of competence, the organs listed in Chapter X of the Charter of the Organization of American States, as amended by the Protocol of Buenos Aires, may in like manner consult the Court.

2.   The Court, at the request of a member state of the Organization, may provide that state with opinions regarding the compatibility of any of its domestic laws with the aforesaid international instruments.

Note that the Court's advisory jurisdiction is not confined to interpreting the American Convention. It can also render opinions on "other treaties concerning the protection of human rights in the American states."

The Court's contentious jurisdiction, established by Article 62, extends to cases between States Parties that have accepted this jurisdiction, either through a prospective declaration or by special agreement. Pursuant to

Article 68 of the American Convention, States Parties undertake to comply with the judgment of the Court in any case to which they are parties. Contentious cases may be submitted to the Court by States and by the Commission. (Article 61.) The Commission can refer contentious cases only after it has first itself admitted the case for investigation and only with respect to States Parties that have accepted the Court's jurisdiction.

For many years, the Commission declined to refer cases to the Court and rarely submitted requests for advisory opinions. In a 1985 Advisory Opinion that had been referred to the Court by Costa Rica after a divided Commission failed to do so, the Court admonished the Commission for failing to act upon its "special duty to consider the advisability of coming to the Court." *Compulsory Membership in an Association Prescribed by Law for the Practice of Journalism (Arts. 13 and 19 of the American Convention on Human Rights)*, Advisory Opinion OC–5/85, 5 Inter–Am. Ct. H.R. (ser. A) 145 (1985). In view of states' disinclination to bring cases before the Court, the Commission's reluctance to refer cases to the Court meant that the latter had scant work during its early years. This finally began to change in 1986, when the Commission referred three contentious cases involving disappearances in Honduras during the period 1981–84.

The Court's judgment in the principal case, *Velásquez Rodríguez*, is a landmark decision on the subject of state responsibility for human rights violations. The judgment, excerpted below, also provides an important case study in how a supranational human rights system responds to systemic and gross violations of human rights—a phenomenon that the supervisory mechanisms established under the American Convention have had to confront more often than their European counterparts. Particularly noteworthy is the Court's approach to the phenomenon of "disappearances," the signature human rights violation of many Latin American military governments during the 1970s and '80s. Like the ICCPR, the American Convention does not proscribe disappearances as such. Nevertheless, the Court found that the enforced disappearance of Manfredo Velásquez Rodríguez entailed multiple violations of Honduras's duties under the Convention.

Velásquez Rodríguez Case

Inter–American Court of Human Rights, 1988.
4 Inter–Am. Ct. H.R. (ser. C).

. . .

3. According to the petition filed with the Commission, and the supplementary information received subsequently, Manfredo Velásquez, a student at the National Autonomous University of Honduras, "was violently detained without a warrant for his arrest by members of the National Office of Investigations (DNI) and G–2 of the Armed Forces of Honduras." The detention took place in Tegucigalpa on the afternoon of September 12, 1981. According to the petitioners, several eyewitnesses reported that Manfredo Velásquez and others were detained and taken to the cells of

Public Security Forces Station No. 2 located in the Barrio El Manchén of Tegucigalpa, where he was "accused of alleged political crimes and subjected to harsh interrogation and cruel torture." The petition added that on September 17, 1981, Manfredo Velásquez was moved to the First Infantry Battalion, where the interrogation continued, but that the police and security forces denied that he had been detained.

.   .   .

56.   The Court will first consider the legal arguments relevant to the question of exhaustion of domestic remedies and then apply them to the case.

57.   Article 46(1)(a) of the Convention provides that, in order for a petition or communication lodged with the Commission in accordance with Articles 44 or 45 to be admissible, it is necessary "that the remedies under domestic law have been pursued and exhausted in accordance with generally recognized principles of international law."

58.   The same article, in the second paragraph, provides that this requirement shall not be applicable when

"a.   the domestic legislation of the state concerned does not afford due process of law for the protection of the right or rights that have allegedly been violated;

b.   the party alleging violation of his rights has been denied access to the remedies under domestic law or has been prevented from exhausting them; or

c.   there has been unwarranted delay in rendering a final judgment under the aforementioned remedies."

.   .   .

61.   The rule of prior exhaustion of domestic remedies allows the State to resolve the problem under its internal law before being confronted with an international proceeding. This is particularly true in the international jurisdiction of human rights, because the latter reinforces or complements the domestic jurisdiction (American Convention, Preamble).

62.   It is a legal duty of the States to provide such remedies, as this Court indicated in its Judgment of June 26, 1987, when it stated:

"The rule of prior exhaustion of domestic remedies under the international law of human rights has certain implications that are present in the Convention. Under the Convention, States Parties have an obligation to provide effective judicial remedies to victims of human rights violations (Art. 25), remedies that must be substantiated in accordance with the rules of due process of law (Art. 8(1)), all in keeping with the general obligation of such States to guarantee the free and full exercise of the rights recognized by the Convention to all persons subject to their jurisdiction (Art. 1). (Velásquez Rodríguez Case, Preliminary Objections, supra 23, para. 91)."

63. Article 46(1)(a) of the Convention speaks of "generally recognized principles of international law." Those principles refer not only to the formal existence of such remedies, but also to their adequacy and effectiveness, as shown by the exceptions set out in Article 46(2).

64. Adequate domestic remedies are those which are suitable to address an infringement of a legal right.... If a remedy is not adequate in a specific case, it obviously need not be exhausted....

65. Of the remedies cited by the Government, habeas corpus would be the normal means of finding a person presumably detained by the authorities, of ascertaining whether he is legally detained and, given the case, of obtaining his liberty.... If, however, as the Government has stated, the writ of habeas corpus requires the identification of the place of detention and the authority ordering the detention, it would not be adequate for finding a person clandestinely held by State officials, since in such cases there is only hearsay evidence of the detention, and the whereabouts of the victim is unknown.

66. A remedy must also be effective—that is, capable of producing the result for which it was designed. Procedural requirements can make the remedy of habeas corpus ineffective: if it is powerless to compel the authorities; if it presents a danger to those who invoke it; or if it is not impartially applied.

67. On the other hand, contrary to the Commission's argument, the mere fact that a domestic remedy does not produce a result favorable to the petitioner does not in and of itself demonstrate the [non]existence or exhaustion of all effective domestic remedies. For example, the petitioner may not have invoked the appropriate remedy in a timely fashion.

68. It is a different matter, however, when it is shown that remedies are denied for trivial reasons or without an examination of the merits, or if there is proof of the existence of a practice or policy ordered or tolerated by the government, the effect of which is to impede certain persons from invoking internal remedies that would normally be available to others. In such cases, resort to those remedies becomes a senseless formality. The exceptions of Article 46(2) would be fully applicable in those situations and would discharge the obligation to exhaust internal remedies since they cannot fulfill their objective in that case.

· · ·

74. The record before the Court shows that the following remedies were pursued on behalf of Manfredo Velásquez: [Habeas corpus petitions were filed on three occasions, all without result. Criminal complaints were filed by relatives of Manfredo Velásquez on two occasions. The first brought no result; in response to the second complaint, the proceedings were dismissed except with respect to one defendant, against whom the complaint was left open because he was absent.]

· · ·

76.   The record ... contains testimony of members of the Legislative Assembly of Honduras, Honduran lawyers, persons who were at one time disappeared, and relatives of disappeared persons, which purports to show that in the period in which the events took place, the legal remedies in Honduras were ineffective in obtaining the liberty of victims of a practice of enforced or involuntary disappearances (hereinafter "disappearance" or "disappearances"), ordered or tolerated by the Government. The record also contains dozens of newspaper clippings which allude to the same practice. According to that evidence, from 1981 to 1984 more than one hundred persons were illegally detained, many of whom never reappeared, and, in general, the legal remedies which the Government claimed were available to the victims were ineffective.

· · ·

78.   The evidence offered shows that lawyers who filed writs of habeas corpus were intimidated, that those who were responsible for executing the writs were frequently prevented from entering or inspecting the places of detention, and that occasional criminal complaints against military or police officials were ineffective, either because certain procedural steps were not taken or because the complaints were dismissed without further proceedings.

· · ·

80.   The testimony and other evidence received and not refuted leads to the conclusion that, during the period under consideration, although there may have been legal remedies in Honduras that theoretically allowed a person detained by the authorities to be found, those remedies were ineffective in cases of disappearances because the imprisonment was clandestine; formal requirements made them inapplicable in practice; the authorities against whom they were brought simply ignored them, or because attorneys and judges were threatened and intimidated by those authorities.

81.   ... The evidence offered by the Commission ... is sufficient to reject the Government's preliminary objection that the case is inadmissible because domestic remedies were not exhausted.

82.   The Commission presented testimony and documentary evidence to show that there were many kidnappings and disappearances in Honduras from 1981 to 1984 and that those acts were attributable to the Armed Forces of Honduras (hereinafter "Armed Forces"), which was able to rely at least on the tolerance of the Government. Three officers of the Armed Forces testified on this subject at the request of the Court.

· · ·

107.   According to the testimony of his sister, eyewitnesses to the kidnapping of Manfredo Velásquez told her that he was detained on September 12, 1981, between 4:30 and 5:00 p.m., in a parking lot in downtown Tegucigalpa by seven heavily-armed men dressed in civilian clothes (one of them

being First Sgt. José Isaías Vilorio), who used a white Ford without license plates. . . .

. . .

113. The former member of the Armed Forces who claimed to have belonged to the group that carried out kidnappings told the Court that, although he did not take part in the kidnapping of Manfredo Velásquez, Lt. Flores Murillo had told him what had happened. According to this testimony, Manfredo Velásquez was kidnapped in downtown Tegucigalpa in an operation in which Sgt. José Isaías Vilorio, men using the pseudonyms Ezequiel and Titanio, and Lt. Flores Murillo himself, took part. The Lieutenant told him that during the struggle Ezequiel's gun went off and wounded Manfredo in the leg. They took the victim to INDUMIL (Military Industries) where they tortured him. They then turned him over to those in charge of carrying out executions who, at the orders of General Alvarez, Chief of the Armed Forces, took him out of Tegucigalpa and killed him with a knife and machete. They dismembered his body and buried the remains in different places. . . .

. . .

115. One witness testified that he was taken prisoner on September 29, 1981 by five or six persons who identified themselves as members of the Armed Forces and took him to the offices of DNI. They blindfolded him and took him in a car to an unknown place, where they tortured him. On October 1, 1981, while he was being held, he heard a moaning and pained voice through a hole in the door to an adjoining room. The person identified himself as Manfredo Velásquez and asked for help. According to the testimony of the witness, at that moment Lt. Ramón Mejía came in and hit him because he found him standing up, although the witness told the Lieutenant that he had gotten up because he was tired. He added that, subsequently, Sgt. Carlos Alfredo Martínez, whom he had met at the bar where he worked, told him they had turned Manfredo Velásquez over to members of Battalion 316. . . .

[The Court reviewed evidence concerning the ineffectiveness of domestic remedies in Honduras during the period in question.]

122. Before weighing the evidence, the Court must address some questions regarding the burden of proof and the general criteria considered in its evaluation and finding of the facts in the instant proceeding.

123. Because the Commission is accusing the Government of the disappearance of Manfredo Velásquez, it, in principle, should bear the burden of proving the facts underlying its petition.

124. The Commission's argument relies upon the proposition that the policy of disappearances, supported or tolerated by the Government, is designed to conceal and destroy evidence of disappearances. When the existence of such a policy or practice has been shown, the disappearance of a particular individual may be proved through circumstantial or indirect

evidence or by logical inference. Otherwise, it would be impossible to prove that an individual has been disappeared.

. . .

126. The Court finds no reason to consider the Commission's argument inadmissible. If it can be shown that there was an official practice of disappearances in Honduras, carried out by the Government or at least tolerated by it, and if the disappearance of Manfredo Velásquez can be linked to that practice, the Commission's allegations will have been proven to the Court's satisfaction, so long as the evidence presented on both points meets the standard of proof required in cases such as this.

. . .

130. The practice of international and domestic courts shows that direct evidence, whether testimonial or documentary, is not the only type of evidence that may be legitimately considered in reaching a decision. Circumstantial evidence, indicia, and presumptions may be considered, so long as they lead to conclusions consistent with the facts.

131. Circumstantial or presumptive evidence is especially important in allegations of disappearances, because this type of repression is characterized by an attempt to suppress all information about the kidnapping or the whereabouts and fate of the victim.

. . .

147. The Court now turns to the relevant facts that it finds to have been proven. They are as follows:

"a. During the period 1981 to 1984, 100 to 150 persons disappeared in the Republic of Honduras, and many were never heard from again. . . .

b. Those disappearances followed a similar pattern, beginning with the kidnapping of the victims by force, often in broad daylight and in public places, by armed men in civilian clothes and disguises, who acted with apparent impunity and who used vehicles without any official identification, with tinted windows and with false license plates or no plates. . . .

c. It was public and notorious knowledge in Honduras that the kidnappings were carried out by military personnel or the police, or persons acting under their orders. . . .

d. The disappearances were carried out in a systematic manner, regarding which the Court considers the following circumstances particularly relevant:

i. The victims were usually persons whom Honduran officials considered dangerous to State security. . . . In addition, the victims had usually been under surveillance for long periods of time . . . ;

ii. The arms employed were reserved for the official use of the military and police, and the vehicles used had tinted glass, which requires special official authorization. In some cases, Government agents carried out the detentions openly and without any pretense or disguise; in others, government agents had cleared the areas where the kidnappings were to take place and, on at least one occasion, when government agents stopped the kidnappers they were allowed to continue freely on their way after showing their identification . . . ;

    iii. The kidnappers blindfolded the victims, took them to secret, unofficial detention centers and moved them from one center to another. They interrogated the victims and subjected them to cruel and humiliating treatment and torture. Some were ultimately murdered and their bodies were buried in clandestine cemeteries . . . ;

    iv. When queried by relatives, lawyers and persons or entities interested in the protection of human rights, or by judges charged with executing writs of habeas corpus, the authorities systematically denied any knowledge of the detentions or the whereabouts or fate of the victims. That attitude was seen even in the cases of persons who later reappeared in the hands of the same authorities who had systematically denied holding them or knowing their fate . . . ;

    v. Military and police officials as well as those from the Executive and Judicial Branches either denied the disappearances or were incapable of preventing or investigating them, punishing those responsible, or helping those interested discover the whereabouts and fate of the victims or the location of their remains. The investigative committees created by the Government and the Armed Forces did not produce any results. The judicial proceedings brought were processed slowly with a clear lack of interest and some were ultimately dismissed . . . ;

e. On September 12, 1981, between 4:30 and 5:00 p.m., several heavily-armed men in civilian clothes driving a white Ford without license plates kidnapped Manfredo Velásquez from a parking lot in downtown Tegucigalpa. Today, nearly seven years later, he remains disappeared, which creates a reasonable presumption that he is dead. . . .

f. Persons connected with the Armed Forces or under its direction carried out that kidnapping. . . .

g. The kidnapping and disappearance of Manfredo Velásquez falls within the systematic practice of disappearances referred to by the facts deemed proved in paragraphs a-d. To wit:

    i. Manfredo Velásquez was a student who was involved in activities the authorities considered "dangerous" to national security. . . .

    ii. The kidnapping of Manfredo Velásquez was carried out in broad daylight by men in civilian clothes who used a vehicle without license plates.

    iii. In the case of Manfredo Velásquez, there were the same type of denials by his captors and the Armed Forces, the same omissions of the latter and of the Government in investigating and revealing his whereabouts, and the same ineffectiveness of the courts where three writs of habeas corpus and two criminal complaints were brought. . . . ["]

. . .

148.   Based upon the above, the Court finds that the following facts have been proven in this proceeding: (1) a practice of disappearances carried out or tolerated by Honduran officials existed between 1981 and 1984; (2) Manfredo Velásquez disappeared at the hands of or with the acquiescence of those officials within the framework of that practice; and (3) the Government of Honduras failed to guarantee the human rights affected by that practice.

149.   Disappearances are not new in the history of human rights violations. However, their systematic and repeated nature and their use not only for causing certain individuals to disappear, either briefly or permanently, but also as a means of creating a general state of anguish, insecurity and fear, is a recent phenomenon. Although this practice exists virtually worldwide, it has occurred with exceptional intensity in Latin America in the last few years.

150.   The phenomenon of disappearances is a complex form of human rights violation . . . .

. . .

155.   The forced disappearance of human beings is a multiple and continuous violation of many rights under the Convention that the States Parties are obligated to respect and guarantee. The kidnapping of a person is an arbitrary deprivation of liberty, an infringement of a detainee's right to be taken without delay before a judge and to invoke the appropriate procedures to review the legality of the arrest, all in violation of Article 7 of the Convention which recognizes the right to personal liberty . . . .

156.   Moreover, prolonged isolation and deprivation of communication are in themselves cruel and inhuman treatment, harmful to the psychological and moral integrity of the person and a violation of the right of any detainee to respect for his inherent dignity as a human being. Such treatment, therefore, violates Article 5 of the Convention, which recognizes the right to the integrity of the person . . . .

In addition, investigations into the practice of disappearances and the testimony of victims who have regained their liberty show that those who are disappeared are often subjected to merciless treatment, including all types of indignities, torture and other cruel, inhuman and degrading treatment, in violation of the right to physical integrity recognized in Article 5 of the Convention.

157.   The practice of disappearances often involves secret execution without trial, followed by concealment of the body to eliminate any material evidence of the crime and to ensure the impunity of those responsible. This is a flagrant violation of the right to life, recognized in Article 4 of the Convention . . . .

158.   The [existence of the] practice of disappearances . . . evinces a disregard of the duty to organize the State in such a manner as to guarantee the rights recognized in the Convention, as set out below.

. . .

161. Article 1(1) of the Convention provides:

. . .

1. The States Parties to this Convention undertake to respect the rights and freedoms recognized herein and to ensure to all persons subject to their jurisdiction the free and full exercise of those rights and freedoms, without any discrimination for reasons of race, color, sex, language, religion, political or other opinion, national or social origin, economic status, birth, or any other social condition.

. . .

164. Article 1(1) is essential in determining whether a violation of the human rights recognized by the Convention can be imputed to a State Party. In effect, that article charges the States Parties with the fundamental duty to respect and guarantee the rights recognized in the Convention. Any impairment of those rights which can be attributed under the rules of international law to the action or omission of any public authority constitutes an act imputable to the State, which assumes responsibility in the terms provided by the Convention.

165. The first obligation assumed by the States Parties under Article 1(1) is "to respect the rights and freedoms" recognized by the Convention. . . .

166. The second obligation of the States Parties is to "ensure" the free and full exercise of the rights recognized by the Convention to every person subject to its jurisdiction. This obligation implies the duty of the States Parties to organize the governmental apparatus and, in general, all the structures through which public power is exercised, so that they are capable of juridically ensuring the free and full enjoyment of human rights. As a consequence of this obligation, the States must prevent, investigate and punish any violation of the rights recognized by the Convention and, moreover, if possible attempt to restore the right violated and provide compensation as warranted for damages resulting from the violation.

. . .

169. According to Article 1(1), any exercise of public power that violates the rights recognized by the Convention is illegal. Whenever a State organ, official or public entity violates one of those rights, this constitutes a failure of the duty to respect the rights and freedoms set forth in the Convention.

170. This conclusion is independent of whether the organ or official has contravened provisions of internal law or overstepped the limits of his authority: under international law a State is responsible for the acts of its agents undertaken in their official capacity and for their omissions, even when those agents act outside the sphere of their authority or violate internal law.

. . .

172. Thus, in principle, any violation of rights recognized by the Convention carried out by an act of public authority or by persons who use their position of authority is imputable to the State. However, this does not define all the circumstances in which a State is obligated to prevent,

investigate and punish human rights violations, nor all the cases in which the State might be found responsible for an infringement of those rights. An illegal act which violates human rights and which is initially not directly imputable to a State (for example, because it is the act of a private person or because the person responsible has not been identified) can lead to international responsibility of the State, not because of the act itself, but because of the lack of due diligence to prevent the violation or to respond to it as required by the Convention.

173. ... What is decisive is whether a violation of the rights recognized by the Convention has occurred with the support or the acquiescence of the government, or whether the State has allowed the act to take place without taking measures to prevent it or to punish those responsible....

174. The State has a legal duty to take reasonable steps to prevent human rights violations and to use the means at its disposal to carry out a serious investigation of violations committed within its jurisdiction, to identify those responsible, to impose the appropriate punishment and to ensure the victim adequate compensation.

175. This duty to prevent includes all those means of a legal, political, administrative and cultural nature that promote the protection of human rights and ensure that any violations are considered and treated as illegal acts, which, as such, may lead to the punishment of those responsible and the obligation to indemnify the victims for damages.... Of course, while the State is obligated to prevent human rights abuses, the existence of a particular violation does not, in itself, prove the failure to take preventive measures. On the other hand, subjecting a person to official, repressive bodies that practice torture and assassination with impunity is itself a breach of the duty to prevent violations of the rights to life and physical integrity of the person, even if that particular person is not tortured or assassinated, or if those facts cannot be proven in a concrete case.

176. The State is obligated to investigate every situation involving a violation of the rights protected by the Convention. If the State apparatus acts in such a way that the violation goes unpunished and the victim's full enjoyment of such rights is not restored as soon as possible, the State has failed to comply with its duty to ensure the free and full exercise of those rights to the persons within its jurisdiction. The same is true when the State allows private persons or groups to act freely and with impunity to the detriment of the rights recognized by the Convention.

177. In certain circumstances, it may be difficult to investigate acts that violate an individual's rights. The duty to investigate, like the duty to prevent, is not breached merely because the investigation does not produce a satisfactory result. Nevertheless, it must be undertaken in a serious manner and not as a mere formality preordained to be ineffective. An investigation must have an objective and be assumed by the State as its own legal duty, not as a step taken by private interests that depends upon the initiative of the victim or his family or upon their offer of proof, without an effective search for the truth by the government. This is true regardless of what agent is eventually found responsible for the violation.

Where the acts of private parties that violate the Convention are not seriously investigated, those parties are aided in a sense by the government, thereby making the State responsible on the international plane.

178.   In the instant case, the evidence shows a complete inability of the procedures of the State of Honduras, which were theoretically adequate, to carry out an investigation into the disappearance of Manfredo Velásquez, and of the fulfillment of its duties to pay compensation and punish those responsible, as set out in Article 1(1) of the Convention.

179.   As the Court has verified above, the failure of the judicial system to act upon the writs brought before various tribunals in the instant case has been proven. Not one writ of habeas corpus was processed. No judge had access to the places where Manfredo Velásquez might have been detained. The criminal complaint was dismissed.

180.   Nor did the organs of the Executive Branch carry out a serious investigation to establish the fate of Manfredo Velásquez. There was no investigation of public allegations of a practice of disappearances nor a determination of whether Manfredo Velásquez had been a victim of that practice. The Commission's requests for information were ignored to the point that the Commission had to presume, under Article 42 of its Regulations, that the allegations were true. The offer of an investigation in accord with Resolution 30/83 of the Commission resulted in an investigation by the Armed Forces, the same body accused of direct responsibility for the disappearances. This raises grave questions regarding the seriousness of the investigation. . . . No proceeding was initiated to establish responsibility for the disappearance of Manfredo Velásquez and apply punishment under internal law. All of the above leads to the conclusion that the Honduran authorities did not take effective action to ensure respect for human rights within the jurisdiction of that State as required by Article 1(1) of the Convention.

181.   The duty to investigate facts of this type continues as long as there is uncertainty about the fate of the person who has disappeared. Even in the hypothetical case that those individually responsible for crimes of this type cannot be legally punished under certain circumstances, the State is obligated to use the means at its disposal to inform the relatives of the fate of the victims and, if they have been killed, the location of their remains.

182.   The Court is convinced, and has so found, that the disappearance of Manfredo Velásquez was carried out by agents who acted under cover of public authority. However, even had that fact not been proven, the failure of the State apparatus to act, which is clearly proven, is a failure on the part of Honduras to fulfill the duties it assumed under Article 1(1) of the Convention, which obligated it to ensure Manfredo Velásquez the free and full exercise of his human rights.

. . .

184.   According to the principle of the continuity of the State in international law, responsibility exists both independently of changes of government over a period of time and continuously from the time of the act that

creates responsibility to the time when the act is declared illegal. The foregoing is also valid in the area of human rights although, from an ethical or political point of view, the attitude of the new government may be much more respectful of those rights than that of the government in power when the violations occurred.

185.   The Court, therefore, concludes that the facts found in this proceeding show that the State of Honduras is responsible for the involuntary disappearance of Angel Manfredo Velásquez Rodríguez. Thus, Honduras has violated Articles 7, 5 and 4 of the Convention.

186.   As a result of the disappearance, Manfredo Velásquez was the victim of an arbitrary detention, which deprived him of his physical liberty without legal cause and without a determination of the lawfulness of his detention by a judge or competent tribunal. Those acts directly violate the right to personal liberty recognized by Article 7 of the Convention (supra 155) and are a violation imputable to Honduras of the duties to respect and ensure that right under Article 1(1).

187.   The disappearance of Manfredo Velásquez violates the right to personal integrity recognized by Article 5 of the Convention (supra 156). First, the mere subjection of an individual to prolonged isolation and deprivation of communication is in itself cruel and inhuman treatment which harms the psychological and moral integrity of the person, and violates the right of every detainee under Article 5(1) and 5(2) to treatment respectful of his dignity. Second, although it has not been directly shown that Manfredo Velásquez was physically tortured, his kidnapping and imprisonment by governmental authorities, who have been shown to subject detainees to indignities, cruelty and torture, constitute a failure of Honduras to fulfill the duty imposed by Article 1(1) to ensure the rights under Article 5(1) and 5(2) of the Convention. The guarantee of physical integrity and the right of detainees to treatment respectful of their human dignity require States Parties to take reasonable steps to prevent situations which are truly harmful to the rights protected.

188.   The above reasoning is applicable to the right to life recognized by Article 4 of the Convention (supra 157). The context in which the disappearance of Manfredo Velásquez occurred and the lack of knowledge seven years later about his fate create a reasonable presumption that he was killed. Even if there is a minimal margin of doubt in this respect, it must be presumed that his fate was decided by authorities who systematically executed detainees without trial and concealed their bodies in order to avoid punishment. This, together with the failure to investigate, is a violation by Honduras of a legal duty under Article 1(1) of the Convention to ensure the rights recognized by Article 4(1). That duty is to ensure to every person subject to its jurisdiction the inviolability of the right to life and the right not to have one's life taken arbitrarily. These rights imply an obligation on the part of States Parties to take reasonable steps to prevent situations that could result in the violation of that right.

. . .

Notes

1.   At several points in the *Velásquez Rodríguez* case the Inter–American Court noted that more than one hundred individuals disappeared in Honduras from 1981 to 1984. Why was this legally relevant to the issue before the Court—whether Manfredo Velásquez disappeared under circumstances that give rise to state responsibility?

2.   The Court accepted the validity of circumstantial evidence in the proceeding before it (see paragraphs 130–31). In what way did circumstantial evidence prove important in establishing key conclusions in the *Velásquez Rodríguez* judgment? How persuasive is the Court's analysis of the evidence compared to the evidentiary analysis of the Human Rights Committee in the *Bleier*, *Quinteros*, and *Mojica* cases (see Section A, supra)? Did the Court and Committee employ similar or different evidentiary presumptions to reach their respective conclusions in these cases?

3.   In paragraph 164, the Inter–American Court asserts that Article 1(1) of the American Convention, which imposes on States Parties a duty to "respect" and "ensure" the rights and freedoms set forth in the Convention, is essential in determining whether a violation of those rights can be imputed to a State Party. In the case of Manfredo Velásquez, it found that Honduras had violated Articles 4, 5 and 7 read in conjunction with Article 1(1). For each of these violations, which Article 1(1) obligation did Honduras breach—the duty to "respect" or to "ensure" the relevant right(s), or both? What reasoning did the Court employ to reach the conclusion that Honduras violated Article 4 (right to life), read in conjunction with Article 1(1), in respect of Manfredo Velásquez, whose death was not conclusively established?

4.   At paragraphs 74–80, the Inter–American Court reviewed evidence establishing the ineffectiveness of domestic remedies in Honduras in respect of disappearances in general, and in respect of the case of Manfredo Velásquez in particular. Later (see, e.g., paras. 147; 178–80), the Court again reached conclusions regarding the ineffectiveness of legal process in Honduras in respect of Manfredo Velásquez. Its discussion in these separate sections of its judgment may seem redundant, but in fact the Court was addressing two distinct legal issues—the procedural requirement of exhaustion of domestic remedies and the substantive issue of state responsibility. How were the same facts relevant in establishing two distinct legal conclusions—ineffectiveness of domestic remedies and state responsibility for conduct that may not necessarily have been carried out by state agents? That is, what was the legal relevance of those facts in respect of each distinct legal issue?

5.   At several points in its discussion of principles of state responsibility under the American Convention, the Inter–American Court implied that States Parties must investigate and punish "any" violation of the rights recognized in the Convention. See, e.g., para. 166. Does this mean that even relatively minor violations, such as a State Party's interference with property rights in breach of Article 21, require punishment of those responsible? Does the Court's analysis leave any room for amnesty laws that prevent further punishment of those responsible for past human rights

violations as a measure of national reconciliation? Do paragraphs 181 and 184 of the *Velásquez Rodríguez* judgment shed any light on the latter question? For analysis of these issues, see Diane F. Orentlicher, *Settling Accounts: The Duty to Prosecute Human Rights Violations of a Prior Regime*, 100 Yale L. J. 2537, 2599–2603 (1991). See also Section C(2), below. For an analysis of the *Velásquez Rodríguez* case by two attorneys who participated in the litigation, see Juan Méndez and José Miguel Vivanco, *Disappearances and the Inter–American Court: Reflections on a Litigation Experience*, 13 Hamline L. Rev. 507 (1990).

Remedial Powers of the Court

Pursuant to Article 63(1) of the American Convention, the Court can order remedies, including compensation, for violations of the Convention:

> 1. If the Court finds that there has been a violation of a right or freedom protected by this Convention, the Court shall rule that the injured party be ensured the enjoyment of the right or freedom that was violated. It shall also rule, if appropriate, that the consequences of the measure or situation that constituted the breach of such right or freedom be remedied and that fair compensation be paid to the injured party.

In the *Velásquez Rodríguez* case, the Inter–American Court awarded approximately $165,000 for lost income and $80,000 in moral damages. Judgment of July 21, 1989 (Compensation), 7 Inter–Am. Ct. H.R. (ser. C), paras. 49–52 (1989).

A subsequent case, *Aloeboetoe*, provided the occasion for further development of the Court's jurisprudence concerning reparations. The Court's judgment on reparations arose out of a contentious case filed by the Inter–American Commission against the government of Suriname for violations committed by government soldiers against a group of "Bushnegroes (Maroons)".* As a result of an attack against the group in 1987, seven men were killed after enduring physical and emotional abuse. The government of Suriname eventually admitted responsibility after first contesting it. In September 1993, the Inter–American Court issued a judgment ordering the government to provide various forms of reparation to the victims. The judgment, excerpted below, is noteworthy not only for its general articulation of principles governing reparations, but for its effort to shape reparations to the peculiar circumstances of the victims in the *Aloeboetoe* case.

Aloeboetoe et al. Case (Reparations)
Inter–American Court of Human Rights, 1993.
15 Inter–Am. Ct. H.R. (ser. C).

43. [Article 63(1)] codifies a rule of customary law which, moreover, is one of the fundamental principles of current international law....

* Reparations Judgment of September   2 (1994).
10, 1993, 15 Inter–Am. Ct. H.R. (ser. C) para.

44. The obligation contained in Article 63(1) of the Convention is governed by international law in all of its aspects, such as, for example, its scope, characteristics, beneficiaries, etc. Consequently, this judgment must be understood to impose international legal obligations....

. . .

50. ... [I]nsofar as the right to life is concerned, it is impossible to reinstate the enjoyment of that right to the victims. In such cases, reparation must take other, alternative forms, such as pecuniary compensation....

This compensation refers primarily to actual damages suffered. According to arbitral case law, it is a general principle of law that such damages comprise both indirect damages and loss of earnings.... Compensation shall furthermore include the moral damages suffered by the victims....

51. In the instant case, the victims who died at Tjongalangapassi suffered moral damages when they were abused by an armed band which deprived them of their liberty and later killed them. The beatings received, the pain of knowing they were condemned to die for no reason whatsoever, the torture of having to dig their own graves are all part of the moral damages suffered by the victims. In addition, the person who did not die outright had to bear the pain of his wounds being infested by maggots and of seeing the bodies of his companions being devoured by vultures.

52. In the Court's opinion, it is clear that the victims suffered moral damages, for it is characteristic of human nature that anybody subjected to the aggression and abuse described above will experience moral suffering. The Court considers that no evidence is required to arrive at this conclusion; the acknowledgment of responsibility by Suriname suffices.

. . .

54. The damages suffered by the victims up to the time of their death entitle them to compensation. That right to compensation is transmitted to their heirs by succession.

... With respect to [successors], it is assumed that the death of the victim has caused them actual and moral damages and the burden of proof is on the other party to show that such damages do not exist. Claimants who are not successors, however, must provide specific proof justifying their right to damages....

55. In the instant case, there is some difference of opinion between the parties as to who the successors of the victims are. The Commission urges that this decision be made with reference to the customs of the Saramaka tribe, whereas Suriname requests that its civil law be applied.

The Court earlier stated that the obligation to make reparation provided in Article 63(1) of the American Convention is governed by international law, which also applies to the determination of the manner of compensation and the beneficiaries thereof.... Nevertheless, it is useful to refer to the national family law in force, for certain aspects of it may be relevant.

56.   The Saramakas are a tribe that lives in Surinamese territory and was formed by African slaves fleeing from their Dutch owners. . . .

58.   . . . [T]he evidence offered leads to the conclusion that Surinamese family law is not effective insofar as the Saramakas are concerned. The members of the tribe are unaware of it and adhere to their own rules. . . . It should be pointed out that, in the instant case, Suriname recognized the existence of a Saramaka customary law.

. . .

59.   The Commission has produced information on the social structure of the Saramakas indicating that the tribe displays a strongly matriarchal(*) familial configuration where polygamy occurs frequently. The principal group of relatives appears to be the "bêè", composed of all the descendants of one single woman. This group assumes responsibility for the actions of any of its members who, in theory, are each in turn responsible to the group as a whole. This means that the compensation payable to one person would be given to the "bêè", whose representative would distribute it among its members.

. . .

61.   [U]nder international law there is no conventional or customary rule that would indicate who the successors of a person are. Consequently, the Court has no alternative but to apply general principles of law (Art. 38(1)(c) of the Statute of the International Court of Justice).

62.   It is a norm common to most legal systems that a person's successors are his or her children. It is also generally accepted that the spouse has a share in the assets acquired during a marriage; some legal systems also grant the spouse inheritance rights along with the children. If there is no spouse or children, private common law recognizes the ascendants as heirs. It is the Court's opinion that these rules, generally accepted by the community of nations, should be applied in the instant case, in order to determine the victims' successors for purposes of compensation.

These general legal principles refer to children, "spouse," and "ascendants." Such terms shall be interpreted according to local law. As already stated (supra, para. 58), here local law is not Surinamese law, for the latter is not effective in the region insofar as family law is concerned. It is necessary, then, to take Saramaka custom into account. That custom will be the basis for the interpretation of those terms, to the degree that it does not contradict the American Convention. Hence, in referring to "ascendants," the Court shall make no distinction as to sex, even if that might be contrary to Saramaka custom.

. . .

76.   Listed among the so-called dependents of the victims are their parents. . . . [I]n this particular case, it can be presumed that the parents have

---

* Probably a more precise anthropologi-   original.]
cal term would be matrilineal. [Footnote in

suffered morally as a result of the cruel death of their offspring, for it is essentially human for all persons to feel pain at the torment of their child.

77.   For these reasons, the Court deems it only appropriate that those victims' parents who have not been declared successors also participate in the distribution of the compensation for moral damages.

. . .

81.   The Commission asks the Court to order Suriname to pay the Saramaka tribe compensation for moral damages and to make certain, non-pecuniary reparations.

. . .

83.   In its brief, the Commission explains that, in traditional Maroon society, a person is a member not only of his or her own family group, but also of his or her own village community and tribal group. According to the Commission, the villagers make up a family in the broad sense. This is why damages caused to one of its members also represent damages to the community, which would have to be indemnified.

As for the argument linking the claim for moral damages to the unique social structure of the Saramakas who were generally harmed by the killings, the Court believes that all persons, in addition to being members of their own families and citizens of a State, also generally belong to intermediate communities. In practice, the obligation to pay moral compensation does not extend to such communities, nor to the State in which the victim participated; these are redressed by the enforcement of the system of laws. If in some exceptional case such compensation has ever been granted, it would have been to a community that suffered direct damages.

. . .

96.   The compensation fixed for the victims' heirs includes an amount that will enable the minor children to continue their education until they reach a certain age. Nevertheless, these goals will not be met merely by granting compensatory damages; it is also essential that the children be offered a school where they can receive adequate education and basic medical attention. At the present time, this is not available in several of the Saramaka villages.

Most of the children of the victims live in Gujaba, where the school and the medical dispensary have both been shut down. The Court believes that, as part of the compensation due, Suriname is under the obligation to reopen the school at Gujaba and staff it with teaching and administrative personnel to enable it to function on a permanent basis as of 1994. In addition, the necessary steps shall be taken for the medical dispensary already in place there to be made operational and reopen that same year.

. . .

97.   As regards the distribution of the amounts fixed for the various types of compensation, the Court considers that it would be fair to apply the following criteria:

"a. Of the reparations for material damages caused to each victim, one third is assigned to their wives. If there is more than one wife, this amount shall be divided among them in equal parts. Two thirds shall go to the children, who shall also divide their portion equally among themselves if there is more than one child.

b.   The reparations for moral damages caused to each victim shall be divided as follows: one half is allocated to the children, one quarter to the wives and the remaining quarter to the parents. If there is more than one beneficiary in any of these categories, the amount shall be divided among them in equal parts . . . ."

Notes

1.   One of the notable aspects of the *Aloeboetoe* Judgment is the interplay between relevant principles of international law and the customary law of the Saramakas. The Inter–American Court applied international law to establish basic principles concerning compensation, and turned to general principles of national law to establish that spouses, children and "ascendants" are commonly considered successors to persons who have died (see paras. 61–62). It then turned to the customary law of the Saramakas to determine who should be considered "spouses" and "ascendants" of the victims in the *Aloeboetoe* case itself.

In light of the fact that the customary law of the Saramakas sanctioned polygamy, the Court awarded damages to all of the spouses of the men killed by Surinamese forces. (See paras. 59 and 97.) Yet the Court was not willing to defer unreservedly to Saramaka custom, saying that it would "make no distinction as to sex, even if that might be contrary to Saramaka custom" (para. 62), in determining who qualified as ascendants of the victims. Was the Court's willingness to recognize the customary practice of polygamy consistent with its determination not to respect customs that are discriminatory on the basis of sex?

2.   For reasons not made altogether clear in the Court's judgment, the Inter–American Commission had argued that "the Saramakas enjoy internal autonomy by virtue of a treaty dated September 19, 1762, which granted them permission to be governed by their own laws" and that "these people 'acquired their rights on the basis of a treaty entered into with the Netherlands, which recognizes, among other things, the local authority of the Saramaka (sic) over their own territory.'" *Aloeboetoe*, supra, para. 56. The Commission's brief argued that the obligations undertaken pursuant to that treaty "are applicable, by succession, to the state of Suriname." See id. In response, the Court wrote:

57.   The Court does not deem it necessary to investigate whether or not that agreement is an international treaty. Suffice it to say that even if that were the case, the treaty would today be null and void because it contradicts the norms of jus cogens superveniens. In point of fact, under that treaty the Saramakas undertake to, among other things, capture any slaves that have deserted, take them prisoner and

return them to the Governor of Suriname, who will pay from 10 to 50 florins per slave, depending on the distance of the place where they were apprehended. Another article empowers the Saramakas to sell to the Dutch any other prisoners they might take, as slaves. No treaty of that nature may be invoked before an international human rights tribunal.

This aspect of the Court's judgment gives effect to the principle recognized in Articles 53 and 64 of the Vienna Convention on the Law of Treaties, which provide:

Article 53

A treaty is void if, at the time of its conclusion, it conflicts with a peremptory norm of general international law. For the purposes of the present Convention, a peremptory norm of general international law is a norm accepted and recognized by the international community of States as a whole as a norm from which no derogation is permitted and which can be modified only by a subsequent norm of general international law having the same character.

Article 64

If a new peremptory norm of general international law emerges, any existing treaty which is in conflict with that norm becomes void and terminates.

Article 44 of the Vienna Convention sets forth conditions in which grounds for invalidity may be invoked with respect to particular provisions rather than the treaty as a whole. Paragraph 5 of Article 44 makes clear that a treaty that is governed by Article 53 is invalid in its entirety: "In cases falling under articles 51, 52 and 53, no separation of the provisions of the treaty is permitted." Note that Article 44(5) does not mention "cases falling under" Article 64. Should this be considered an oversight, or is it possible that Article 64 might allow for separation of the provision that conflicts with a peremptory norm? Is it, in any case, clear which of these two provisions was the basis of the Inter–American Court's ruling in the *Aloeboetoe* Case?

————

During substantial parts of its history, the Inter–American Commission of Human Rights has had to confront widespread and grave violations of human rights by military governments. The Commission thus has faced extraordinary challenges in carrying out its mandate of promoting human rights in OAS member states; governments that commit gross violations on a wide scale are unlikely to respect the authority of a supranational human rights body.

In these circumstances, the Commission has often relied upon a technique that is commonly associated with non-governmental organizations—publishing comprehensive reports on country situations based upon on-site investigations. The Commission began carrying out on-site visits in 1961. As of 1997, it had carried out 69 visits to 23 states. In that same period, the Commission had published 44 special country reports based upon its on-site visits.

Today, however, the greater portion of the Commission's resources is devoted to its consideration of individual petitions. (As of January 1999, the Commission had never received an inter-state petition pursuant to Article 45.) Although the Commission still publishes country reports when warranted by serious human rights conditions in an OAS member state, such reports have become less central to the Commission's activities as democracy has been restored throughout most of Latin America.

The Commission has received thousands of petitions since 1965, when it first received authority to consider them. The Commission's final reports on cases initiated by these petitions are published in the Annual Reports of the Commission.

As already noted, the Commission's charter authorizes it to receive petitions alleging violations of the American Convention with respect to States Parties, and of the American Declaration of the Rights and Duties of Man with respect to other OAS member states. But in an important case decided in 1997, *Abella v. Argentina*, the Commission interpreted and applied international humanitarian law—that is, the law governing the conduct of armed conflict. On what basis could the Commission invoke this body of law? The following excerpt of the Commission's report on the *Abella* case reflects its reasoning.

Abella v. Argentina

Inter–American Commission on Human Rights, 1997.
Case 11.137, Inter–Am. Comm'n H. R. 271, OEA/ser.L/V/II.98, doc. 7 rev. (1997).

1.   This case concerns events that took place on January 23 and 24, 1989, at the barracks of the General Belgrano Mechanized Infantry Regiment No. 3 (RIM 3), located at La Tablada, Buenos Aires province, and the consequences ensuing from those events for 49 persons on whose behalf a complaint was filed with the Inter–American Commission on Human Rights (hereinafter called the Commission). On January 23, 1989, 42 armed persons [who were members of the Movimiento Todos por la Patria (MTP)] launched an attack on the aforementioned barracks. The attack precipitated a combat of approximately 30 hours duration between the attackers and Argentine military personnel which resulted in the deaths of 29 of the attackers and several State agents. . . .

· · ·

3.   In their complaint, the petitioners allege that, after the fighting at the base had ceased, State agents participated in the summary execution of four of the captured attackers, the disappearance of six others, and the torture of a number of other captured attackers, which occurred both in the barracks and in police facilities. Following the attack, five MTP members

were arrested in an area near the barracks, and two others turned themselves in voluntarily to the authorities who detained them. According to the petition, these seven persons were tortured physically and psychologically. [The complaint also alleges violations relating to legal proceedings in Argentina that grew out of the events described above.]

. . .

147.   In their complaint, petitioners invoke various rules of International Humanitarian Law, i.e. the law of armed conflict, in support of their allegations that State agents used excessive force and illegal means in their efforts to recapture the La Tablada military base. For its part, the Argentine State, while rejecting the applicability of interstate armed conflict rules to the events in question, nonetheless have in their submissions to the Commission characterized the decision to retake the La Tablada base by force as a "military operation".... Both the Argentine State and petitioners are in agreement that on the 23 and 24 of January 1989 an armed confrontation took place at the La Tablada base between attackers and Argentine armed forces for approximately 30 hours.

148.   The Commission believes that before it can properly evaluate the merits of the petitioner's claims concerning the recapture of the La Tablada base by the Argentine military, it must first determine whether the armed confrontation at the base was merely an example of an "internal disturbance or tensions" or whether it constituted a non-international or internal armed conflict within the meaning of Article 3 common to the four 1949 Geneva conventions ("Common Article 3")....

. . .

156.   [For reasons omitted here, the Commission concludes] that, despite its brief duration, the violent clash between the attackers and members of the Argentine armed forces triggered application of the provisions of Common Article 3, as well as other rules relevant to the conduct of internal hostilities.

    iv.   The Commission's competence to apply international humanitarian law

157.   Before addressing petitioner's specific claims, the Commission thinks it useful to clarify the reasons why it has deemed it necessary at times to apply directly rules of international humanitarian law or to inform its interpretations of relevant provisions of the American Convention by reference to these rules. A basic understanding of the interrelationship of these two branches of international law—human rights and humanitarian law—is instructive in this regard.

158.   The American Convention, as well as other universal and regional human rights instruments, and the 1949 Geneva Conventions share a common nucleus of non-derogable rights and a common purpose of protecting human life and dignity. These human rights treaties apply both in peacetime, and during situations of armed conflict. Although one of their purposes is to prevent warfare, none of these human rights instruments

was designed to regulate such situations and, thus, they contain no rules governing the means and methods of warfare.

159.   In contrast, international humanitarian law generally does not apply in peacetime, and its fundamental purpose is to place restraints on the conduct of warfare in order to diminish the effects of hostilities. It is understandable therefore that the provisions of conventional and customary humanitarian law generally afford victims of armed conflicts greater or more specific protections than do the more generally phrased guarantees in the American Convention and other human rights instruments.

160.   It is, moreover, during situations of internal armed conflict that these two branches of international law most converge and reinforce each other. . . .

161.   For example, both Common Article 3 [of the 1949 Geneva Conventions] and Article 4 of the American Convention protect the right to life and, thus, prohibit, inter alia, summary executions in all circumstances. Claims alleging arbitrary deprivations of the right to life attributable to State agents are clearly within the Commission's jurisdiction. But the Commission's ability to resolve claimed violations of this non-derogable right arising out of an armed conflict may not be possible in many cases by reference to Article 4 of the American Convention alone. This is because the American Convention contains no rules that either define or distinguish civilians from combatants and other military targets, much less, specify when a civilian can be lawfully attacked or when civilian casualties are a lawful consequence of military operations. Therefore, the Commission must necessarily look to and apply definitional standards and relevant rules of humanitarian law as sources of authoritative guidance in its resolution of this and other kinds of claims alleging violations of the American Convention in combat situations. To do otherwise would mean that the Commission would have to decline to exercise its jurisdiction in many cases involving indiscriminate attacks by State agents resulting in a considerable number of civilian casualties. Such a result would be manifestly absurd in light of the underlying object and purposes of both the American Convention and humanitarian law treaties.

162.   Apart from these considerations, the Commission's competence to apply humanitarian law rules is supported by the text of the American Convention, by its own case law, as well as the jurisprudence of the Inter–American Court of Human Rights. Virtually every OAS member State that is a State Party to the American Convention has also ratified one or more of the 1949 Geneva Conventions and/or other humanitarian law instruments. As States Parties to the Geneva Conventions, they are obliged as a matter of customary international law to observe these treaties in good faith and to bring their domestic law into compliance with these instruments. Moreover, they have assumed a solemn duty "to respect and to ensure respect" of these Conventions in all circumstances, most particularly, during situations of interstate or internal hostilities.

163.   In addition, as States Parties to the American Convention, these same states are also expressly required under Article 25 of the American

Convention to provide an internal legal remedy to persons for violations by State agents of their fundamental rights "recognized by *the constitution or laws* of the state concerned or by this Convention" (emphasis supplied). Thus, when the claimed violation is not redressed on the domestic level and the source of the right is a guarantee set forth in the Geneva Conventions, which the State Party concerned has made operative as domestic law, a complaint asserting such a violation, can be lodged with and decided by the Commission under Article 44 of the American Convention. Thus, the American Convention itself authorizes the Commission to address questions of humanitarian law in cases involving alleged violations of Article 25.

164.   The Commission believes that in those situations where the American Convention and humanitarian law instruments apply concurrently, Article 29(b) of the American Convention necessarily require[s] the Commission to take due notice of and, where appropriate, give legal effect to applicable humanitarian law rules. Article 29(b)—the so-called "most-favorable-to-the-individual-clause"—provides that no provision of the American Convention shall be interpreted as "restricting the enforcement or exercise of any right or freedom recognized by virtue of the laws of any State Party of another convention which one of the said states is a party."

165.   The purpose of this Article is to prevent States Parties from relying on the American Convention as a ground for limiting more favorable or less restrictive rights to which an individual is otherwise entitled under either national or international law. Thus, where there are differences between legal standards governing the same or comparable rights in the American Convention and a humanitarian law instrument, the Commission is duty bound to give legal effort to the provision(s) of that treaty with the higher standard(s) applicable to the right(s) or freedom(s) in question. If that higher standard is a rule of humanitarian law, the Commission should apply it.

166.   Properly viewed, the close interrelationship between human rights law and humanitarian law also supports the Commission's authority under Article 29(b) to apply humanitarian law, where it is relevant. In this regard, the authors of the New Rules make the following pertinent point regarding the reciprocal relationship between Protocol II and the Covenant on Civil and Political Rights:

> Protocol II should not be interpreted as remaining behind the basic standard established in the Covenant. On the contrary, when Protocol II in its more detailed provisions establishes a higher standard than the Covenant, this higher standard prevails, on the basis of the fact that the Protocol is "lex specialis" in relation to the Covenant. On the other hand, provisions of the Covenant which have not been reproduced in the Protocol which provide for a higher standard of protection than the protocol should be regarded as applicable irrespective of the relative times at which the two instruments came into force for the respective State. It is a general rule for the application of concurrent instruments of Human Rights—and Part II "Humane Treatment" [of

Protocol II] is such an instrument—that they implement and complete each other instead of forming a basis for limitations.

167.   Their point is equally valid concerning the mutual relationship between the American Convention and Protocol II and other relevant sources of humanitarian law, such as Common Article 3.

168.   In addition, the Commission believes that a proper understanding of the relationship between applicable humanitarian law treaties and Article 27(1), the derogation clause of the American Convention, is relevant to this discussion. This Article permits a State Party to the American Convention to temporarily derogate, i.e., suspend, certain Convention based guarantees during genuine emergency situations. But, Article 27(1) requires that any suspension of guarantees not be "inconsistent with that State's other obligations under international law". Thus, while it cannot be interpreted as incorporating by reference into the American Convention all of a State's other international legal obligations, Article 27(1) does prevent a State from adopting derogation measures that would violate its other obligations under conventional or customary international law.

. . .

170.   ... [W]hen reviewing the legality of derogation measures taken by a State Party to the American Convention by virtue of the existence of an armed conflict to which both the American Convention and humanitarian law treaties apply, the Commission should not resolve this question solely by reference to the text of Article 27 of the American Convention. Rather, it must also determine whether the rights affected by these measures are similarly guaranteed under applicable humanitarian law treaties. If it finds that the rights in question are not subject to suspension under these humanitarian law instruments, the Commission should conclude that these derogation measures are in violation of the State Parties obligations under both the American Convention and the humanitarian law treaties concerned.

[The Commission analyzed the events that were the basis of the petition in light of relevant principles of humanitarian law. Its conclusions concerning whether Argentine forces breached those principles guided the Commission's conclusions about whether there had been a breach of the American Convention. For example, it stated, "Because of the lack of sufficient evidence establishing that State agents used illegal methods and means of combat, the Commission must conclude that the killing or wounding of the attackers which occurred prior to the cessation of combat on January 24, 1989 were legitimately combat related and, thus, did not constitute violations of the American Convention or applicable humanitarian law rules." (Paragraph 188.)]

Notes

1.   That the Inter–American Commission interpreted and applied international humanitarian law in order to determine whether a State Party had

breached the American Convention is notable in itself, but the *Abella* report is especially noteworthy in light of its important contribution to the development of humanitarian law. In a portion of its opinion that is not reproduced above, the Commission concluded that the armed confrontation at La Tablada triggered application of the rules of humanitarian law governing internal armed conflicts even though the entire confrontation lasted approximately 30 hours. Many experts in humanitarian law have assumed that an armed conflict must be protracted in order to meet the threshold for application of Common Article 3 of the 1949 Geneva Conventions.

2. Following the jurisprudence of the European Commission of Human Rights, the Inter–American Commission has invoked and applied what it terms the "fourth instance formula" in its determinations of admissibility. In the *Abella* case, it summarized the doctrine as follows:

> 141. ... The basic premise of this formula is that the Commission cannot review the judgments issued by the domestic courts acting within their competence and with due judicial guarantees, unless it considers that a possible violation of the Convention is involved.

> 142. The Commission is competent to declare a petition admissible and rule on its merits when it portrays a claim that a domestic legal decision constitutes a disregard of the right to a fair trial, or if it appears to violate any other right guaranteed by the American Convention. However, if it contains nothing but the allegation that the decision was wrong or unjust in itself, the petition must be dismissed under this formula. The Commission's task is to ensure the observance of the obligations undertaken by the States parties to the American Convention, but it cannot serve as an appellate court to examine alleged errors of internal law or fact that may have been committed by the domestic courts acting within their jurisdiction. Such examination would be in order only insofar as the mistakes entailed a possible violation of any of the rights set forth in the American Convention.

One of the Commission's leading cases on the "fourth instance formula" is *Marzioni v. Argentina*, Case 11.673, Inter–Am.C.H.R. 76, OEA/ser.L/V/II.95 doc. 7 rev. (1997).

3. The United States has been the respondent in a number of petitions filed with the Inter–American Commission alleging violations of the American Declaration of the Rights and Duties of Man. For example, in *White and Potter v. United States*, Case 2141, Inter–Am. Comm'n H.R. 25, OEA/ser.L/V/II.54, doc. 9 rev. 1 (1980–81), the commission held that U.S. laws permitting abortion did not violate the right to life declared in the American Declaration. See Part IV, Chapter 1(B) infra.

In *Roach and Pinkerton v. United States*, Case 9647, Inter–Am. Comm'n H.R. 147, OEA/ser.L/V/II.71, doc. 9 rev. 1 (1986–87), the Commission considered a petition challenging the use of capital punishment in the United States in respect of persons who were under 18 years of age when they committed the crime. Unlike the American Convention, which specifies that persons who were under the age of 18 when they committed a capital offense should not be executed (Article 4(5)), the Declaration merely provides: "Every human being has the right to life, liberty and the security of his person."

Although the Commission concluded that there was a general norm among OAS states prohibiting execution of children, it agreed with the United States that "there does not now exist a norm of customary international law establishing 18 to be the minimum age for imposition of the death penalty." Nevertheless, the Commission concluded that the United States had violated Article I (right to life) of the American Declaration by virtue of the execution of two men who were both 17 when they committed capital offenses, reasoning:

> 62.   The Commission finds that the diversity of state practice in the U.S.—reflected in the fact that some states have abolished the death penalty, while others allow a potential threshold limit of applicability as low as 10 years of age—results in very different sentences for the commission of the same crime. The deprivation by the State of an offender's life should not be made subject to the fortuitous element of where the crime took place. . . .

> 63.   For the federal Government of the United States to leave the issue of the application of the death penalty to juveniles to the discretion of State officials results in a patchwork scheme of legislation which makes the severity of the punishment dependent, not, primarily on the nature of the crime committed, but on the location where it was committed. Ceding to state legislatures the determination of whether a juvenile may be executed is not of the same category as granting states the discretion to determine the age of majority for purposes of purchasing alcoholic beverages or consenting to matrimony. The failure of the federal government to preempt the states as regards this most fundamental right—the right to life—results in a pattern of legislative arbitrariness throughout the United States which results in the arbitrary deprivation of life and inequality before the law, contrary to Articles I and II [(right to equality before the law)] of the American Declaration of the Rights and Duties of Man, respectively.

How persuasive is the Commission's reasoning? If none of the federal states' legislation concerning the minimum age of execution violated Inter–American standards, why should the disparity among their laws amount to a breach?

In 1997, in response to a petition by several groups of Haitian refugees, the Commission found that, by interdicting Haitian "boat people" on the high seas and repatriating them to Haiti, the United States had violated the right to life, the right to liberty, the right to equality before the law, and the right to seek and receive asylum, as provided in the American Declaration. *Haitian Center for Human Rights v. United States*, Case 10.675, Inter–Am. Comm'n H.R. 550, OEA/ser.L./V/II.95, doc. 7 rev. (1997); compare *Sale v. Haitian Centers Council* in Chapter 2, part G *supra*.

4. Until recently, the jurisprudence of the Inter–American human rights system had not been systematically compiled. The Inter–American Human Rights Digest Project, based at American University's Washington College of Law, is preparing a repertoire of that jurisprudence. The first two volumes of the Digest, published in 1998, cover the jurisprudence of the Inter–American Court on Human Rights from 1980 through 1997. The Digest includes excerpts selected primarily from decisions, reports, and resolutions of the Inter–American Commission and Court. The excerpts are indexed and analyzed according to the terms of the American Convention on Human Rights and the American Declaration of the Rights and Duties of Man. The project's database is available at http://www.wcl.american.edu/pub/humright/digest/.

2. EUROPEAN CONVENTION FOR THE PROTECTION OF HUMAN RIGHTS AND FUNDAMENTAL FREEDOMS

The European Convention for the Protection of Human Rights and Fundamental Freedoms,* (European Convention), drafted in the wake of the Second World War, establishes the most advanced and effective human rights treaty system. Since the Convention entered into effect in 1953, the principal treaty bodies charged with supervising compliance have received and acted upon tens of thousands of applications alleging breaches by States Parties. In the course of considering these applications, the Convention's supervisory bodies have addressed an extraordinary range of issues traditionally considered matters of domestic jurisdiction and have produced an extensive body of substantive human rights jurisprudence.

The Convention is open to adherence by states that are members of the Council of Europe, a regional organization for co-operation among the governments and parliaments of Europe with headquarters in Strasbourg, France. Membership in the Council of Europe is restricted to European states that "accept the principles of the rule of law and of the enjoyment by all persons within [their] jurisdiction of human rights and fundamental freedoms." Statute of the Council of Europe, art. 3. For most of its history the Council's membership—and, correspondingly, the states constituting High Contracting Parties to the European Convention—consisted of Western European states. Since the end of the Cold War, the Council's membership has expanded to include most of the states that had previously belonged to the Soviet bloc. As of June 1999, all forty–one members of the Council of Europe were parties to the European Convention.**

* 213 U.N.T.S. 221, E.T.S. 5 (1953), signed at Rome Nov. 4, 1950; entered into force Sept. 3, 1953.

** The membership of the Council of Europe includes Albania, Andorra, Austria, Belgium, Bulgaria, Croatia, Cyprus, Czech Republic, Denmark, Estonia, Finland, France, Georgia, Germany, Greece, Hungary, Iceland, Ireland, Italy, Latvia, Liechtenstein, Lithuania, Luxembourg, Malta, Moldova, the Netherlands, Norway, Poland, Portugal, Romania, the Russian Federation, San Marino, Slovakia, Slovenia, Spain, Sweden, Switzerland, "the former Yugoslav Republic of Macedonia," Turkey, Ukraine and the United Kingdom of Great Britain and Northern Ireland.

For more than four decades, compliance by the High Contracting Parties with the European Convention was supervised by two bodies, the European Commission of Human Rights and the European Court of Human Rights. Pursuant to Protocol No. 11, this machinery was replaced in November 1998 with a single full-time Court. See Protocol No. 11 to the Convention for the Protection of Human Rights and Fundamental Freedoms, Restructuring the Control Machinery Established Thereby, E.T.S. No. 155.

Like other human rights treaty organs, the previous European Court had no police powers to compel compliance with its judgments (nor does the new Court). Nevertheless, the record of compliance with its final judgments has been impressive. Judgments finding States Parties in breach of their obligations under the European Convention and its Protocols have prompted losing parties not only to provide compensation to victims, but also to enact significant legislative measures to assure full compliance with their treaty obligations as elucidated by the Court's judgments.

Like other human rights treaty machinery, the European system is designed above all to ensure effective protection of Convention rights through national law and procedures, while providing an international remedy in the event internal law falls short. A central aspect of the relationship between States Parties and the supervisory organs established by the European Convention is captured in the principle of "subsidiarity," a term more widely associated with the supranational system established by the Treaty of Rome and related treaties of the European Union but also relevant to the supranational regime established by the European Convention. A senior officer of the European Court's Registry has described the meaning of "subsidiarity" in relation to the latter in the following terms:

> The object and purpose of the [European] Convention is to achieve the "collective enforcement"—to use the words of the Preamble—of those fundamental freedoms which are enshrined in the Convention itself and in its additional Protocols. Their normative and procedural rules were in no way intended to take the place of national human-rights provisions and machinery, but were clearly designed to add a supplementary and ultimate remedy to those safeguards which the internal law of the Convention States afford to the individual. National protection of human rights and European protection form a couple; they go hand in hand. This is the basic philosophy underlying the Convention. . . .

Herbert Petzold, *The Convention and the Principle of Subsidiarity, in* The European System for the Protection of Human Rights 41, 43 (R. St. J. McDonald et al. eds., 1993).

Approximately half of the Contracting States incorporate the European Convention into their domestic law, making the treaty's norms directly enforceable in national courts. The others have given effect to judgments by the European Court of Human Rights through such national measures as amending legislation, reopening judicial proceedings, providing administrative remedies and paying compensation to individuals whose rights were violated. See Laurence R. Helfer and Anne–Marie Slaughter, *Toward a Theory of Effective Supranational Adjudication*, 107 Yale L.J. 273, 295 (1997).

a. SUPERVISORY ORGANS AND PROCEDURES

The European Commission and the earlier European Court of Human Rights produced a rich and substantial body of jurisprudence. Although the two bodies were replaced by a single Court in November 1998,* a basic understanding of their competence is an important foundation for exploring the Convention's jurisprudence and for appreciating the reasons underlying the reforms that became effective in November 1998.

The European Convention authorized the Commission to receive both individual petitions (Article 25**) and inter-state referrals (Article 24) alleging violations of the Convention by Contracting Parties. Although Contracting States were not required to recognize the Commission's competence to receive individual petitions, eventually all High Contracting Parties accepted this procedure.

After the Commission determined that an application alleging a breach was admissible, it attempted a friendly settlement of the dispute. (Article 28.) When the Commission was unable to achieve a friendly settlement, it prepared a detailed report setting forth its findings of fact and its opinions as to whether there had been a breach of the Convention. (Article 31(1).)

Within three months of the transmittal of these reports to the parties concerned and to the Committee of Ministers of the Council of Europe, either government-parties or the Commission could refer the case to the European Court of Human Rights. (Article 48.) Under the Convention itself, individuals had no right of appeal, but an optional protocol adopted in 1990 allowed individuals and groups to appeal a decision of the Commission to a three-judge panel of the Court. (Protocol No. 9, art. 5, para. 2, E.T.S. No. 140.) If the Court determined that it had jurisdiction over the case, it would then determine whether there had been a breach of the Convention. These judgments were final and binding. (Articles 52 & 53.) If there was no recourse to the Court, the case was referred to the Committee of Ministers of the Council of Europe, which then rendered a final and binding decision on the case. (Article 32.)

The following excerpt explores the legacy of these two bodies and the reasons underlying their replacement with a single full-time court.

* Article 5(3) of Protocol No. 11 made provision for the continued operation of the Commission in a limited capacity for a one year transition period: "Applications which have been declared admissible at the date of entry into force of this Protocol shall continue to be dealt with by members of the Commission within a period of one year thereafter. Any applications the examination of which has not been completed within the aforesaid period shall be transmitted to the Court which shall examine them as admissible cases in accordance with the provisions of this Protocol."

** These citations refer to articles of the European Convention prior to its amendment by Protocol No. 11.

Nicolas Bratza and Michael O'Boyle, *The Legacy of the Commission to the New Court under the Eleventh Protocol*

in The Birth of European Human Rights Law: Studies in Honor of Carl Aage NØrgaard 377. (Michele de Salvia & Mark E. Villiger, eds. 1998).*

. . .

The steadily increasing workload of the European Commission and Court of Human Rights over the years and the resulting problem of the length of Convention proceedings gave rise to reflection towards the end of the 1980s as to how the Convention's enforcement machinery could be streamlined. With the dramatic increase in the number of High Contracting Parties due to developments in eastern and central Europe, reform of the Convention, as a means of preserving and building upon its achievements, became an urgent priority of the Council of Europe in the early 1990s.

Discussion centered on whether adjustments and improvements should be made to the existing system or whether the existing Commission and Court should be merged to form a single Court of Human Rights. The proposal of a single Court was finally endorsed by a meeting of the Council of Europe's Heads of State and Government in the Vienna Declaration of 9 October 1993 and was given form by Protocol No. 11 to the Convention which was opened for signature on 11 May 1994.

Overview of Protocol No. 11

Protocol No. 11 provides for the establishment of a full-time single Court to replace the Convention's present enforcement machinery. . . .

Other important changes brought about by the Protocol are as follows: (1) the right of individual petition is now mandatory and the Court will have jurisdiction over all inter-State cases;[3] (2) the . . . role [of the Council of Ministers] will henceforth be limited to supervising the execution of the Court's judgments. All allegations of a violation of a Convention right will thus be adjudicated only by the Court. . . .

. . . The new Court, in its various case-handling compositions, will have responsibility for determining all aspects of the admissibility and merits of registered applications.

. . . Once an application is registered, a Judge Rapporteur will be assigned to it by a Chamber. The Rapporteur may consider that the case should be considered by a Committee of three judges. This Committee may by a unanimous vote, declare individual cases inadmissible or strike cases off the list. If no such decision is taken by a Committee, the application will be referred to a Chamber which will decide on the admissibility and merits of the case. As under the present system, once a case has been declared admissible the Court will have the dual function of establishing the facts and placing itself at the disposal of the parties with a view to securing a

---

3. Article 34. However, the optional character of the right of individual petition has been retained in respect of overseas territories. . . .

friendly settlement. All inter-State cases must be decided upon by a Chamber.... The criteria of admissibility remain unchanged.

Where a case raises a serious question affecting the interpretation of the Convention or the Protocols or where the resolution of an issue before a Chamber might have a result inconsistent with a judgment previously delivered by the Court, the Chamber may relinquish jurisdiction to the Grand Chamber. However relinquishment cannot take place if one of the parties to the case objects. The Protocol also provides for the possibility of a re-hearing of the case before the Grand Chamber in exceptional cases at the request of any party within a period of three months from the date of judgment of the Chamber. This request shall be considered by a panel of five judges of the grand Chamber and accepted "if the case raises a serious question affecting the interpretation or application of the Convention or Protocols thereto, or a serious issue of general importance". The judgment of a Chamber thus becomes final: (a) when the parties declare that they will not request that the case be referred to the Grand Chamber; or (b) three months after the date of the judgment if referral has not been requested; or (c) when the panel of five judges rejects a referral request.

Problems of Transition to the New System

The fundamental purpose of Protocol No. 11 ... is to bring about an improvement in the Convention's enforcement machinery which will lead to the examination of human rights complaints by a single [Court] within a reasonable time. With the removal of the duplication of procedures that characterises the existing machinery, encompassing both the Commission and Court, there ought to be a significant reduction in the amount of time it takes to process the large volume of complaints registered by the single Court....

. . .

In the course of the reform debate it seemed correct to describe the notions of merger and fusion as misnomers. After all the proposal was not to merge or fuse existing institutions but to create a new body. But now that the new Court is a reality and thought is being given as to how it will function in practice the concepts of "merger" and "fusion" appear particularly apt to describe how the new institution will come into being. The text of Protocol No. 11 already reflects a judicious blend of features drawn from each of the existing institutions, interwoven to define the salient characteristics of the new body, but bearing the unmistakable imprint of its provenance.... While every effort will be made to find ways of dealing with the large number of cases on its docket ..., the single Court will carry on in continuous succession to the existing organs. In a real sense therefore neither the Commission nor the Court will become extinct. They will merely merge their identities to form the single European Court of Human Rights....

Both bodies are distinctive fora in their own right: the strengths and experience of the present [i.e., former] Court lie in adjudication and the drafting of carefully reasoned binding judgments in both official languages.

Its practice in these areas and as regards the award of compensation and costs under Article 50 and in permitting interventions by *amici curiae* . . . will form an important part of the *acquis conventionnel*. The Commission, on the other hand, has a more multi-faceted Convention role than the Court comprising, at the same time, quasi-judicial (the determination of admissibility and the drawing up of legal opinions), investigative, conciliation, representative and advisory functions. The transfer of most of the above functions to a single Court provides an appropriate moment to highlight aspects of the specific legacy of the Commission to the new arrangements.

Case-handling

The Commission is at the frontline of the Strasbourg system of human rights protection. It is responsible under the Convention for examining the admissibility of thousands of cases each year. . . . [I]n 1997 the Secretariat opened 12,469 provisional files and registered 4,750 individual applications. In the same year the Commission declared inadmissible 3,073 cases. It also adopted 468 Article 31 reports. Faced with such an onslaught of complaints it is hardly surprising that its backlog on 31 December 1997 amounted to 6,447 cases of which 4,146 were still awaiting a first examination by the Commission. By contrast, however, the Court was seised of 165 in 1996 and 119 in 1997 (including 68 and 38 referrals under Protocol 9 respectively). Its caseload—in itself remarkably high for an international Court—represents, in a sense the distillation of the fruits of the Commission's labours. The statistical contrast between the two institutions demonstrates that the single Court will not only inherit a large backlog of cases from the Commission and Court but will be called upon to handle a constantly increasing number of complaints. . . .

. . .

Friendly Settlements

The Commission has every reason to be satisfied with the procedures it has developed over the years to facilitate the wishes of the parties to reach a friendly settlement. In the 1990's settlement efforts have become increasingly successful. Thus, for example, between 1992 and 1997 there were 242 settlements as opposed to 15 between 1980 and 1984. Compared with the total number of Article 31 reports (2,792) since the inception of the Commission in 1955 (until the end of 1997), the number of settlements (369) during the same period (13%) is a high settlement rate by any standards. The Commission is, of course, attached to settlements because it brings about a consensual Convention result involving individual and sometimes general measures in a non-triumphalist manner. The applicant is similarly satisfied because, often after a lengthy procedure, he achieves vindication without being required to run the gauntlet before the Court for a further 16–18 months with no guaranteed prospect of winning his case. The Government, like the applicant, having been told the Commission's provisional opinion on the merits (and knowing that this is unlikely to change), is content to cut its losses in the context of a private arrangement which usually attracts little publicity even where it includes an undertaking to introduce new legislation or to change an administrative practice. It is really not surprising that experience has taught Governments to adopt a less combative approach in cases where it can be reasonably predicted that continued resistance to an inevitable result may be financially, legally and politically costly.

The Commission's experience in brokering friendly settlements shows that three features are central to reaching the desired result: First, the Commission's practice of communicating to both sides, in confidence, its provisional view of the merits of the complaint. Why should a Government be motivated to take settlement procedures seriously if it thought that it still had a good chance of successfully defending its case? Second, the willingness of the parties to pursue a settlement purposefully by formulating realistic proposals which satisfy the Commission's requirements. The initial written proposals forwarded by post to the Secretary of the Commission often provide a clear indication of the likelihood of success or failure. Third, the informality of the procedure. The process involves a written stage where the Secretary acts as a mail box for both sides and, where it appears that settlement may be possible, an informal series of separate or joint meetings between the Secretary (usually accompanied by the Secretariat lawyer handling the case) and the parties. While the Commission will be kept informed of the progress (or lack of it) that has been made during the negotiations, it is the exception rather than the rule that members of the Commission actually take part in such meetings.

Although in the course of the reform discussions there was much debate about whether the Commission's friendly settlement procedure could be inherited by the new Court, the Explanatory Report to Protocol No. 11 envisages that the settlement practice should continue. This is clearly in harmony with the desires of Contracting Parties which have appreciated its utility in the past. Wisely, the report passes over in silence the contentious issue as to whether it would be proper for a court to intimate a provisional opinion to the parties in confidence. This is obviously a matter for the new Court to decide. However the new Article 38 § 2 by providing that "proceedings conducted under paragraph 1.b [friendly settlement] shall be confidential"—an almost unnecessary and self-evident provision when one considers the Commission's present practice—provides a suggestion that this practice could continue. Of course it would be unusual, for some, and perhaps out-of-keeping with traditional conceptions of the judicial role for a court to intimate a provisional opinion to the parties. On the other hand, it should be remembered that this practice was already unusual for the Commission; that the new Court, with provision made for the possibility of an internal appeal, is already a singular institution which does not fit easily into the traditional mould; and, more importantly, that the experience of the Commission in winning its 369 settlements demonstrates that the effective protection of human rights may require the triumph of pragmatism over principle. The Commission's experience amply demonstrates that parties tend to respect confidences when settlement is in the air and that the practice of intimating a provisional opinion could be carried over to the new system without damage to judicial integrity and with clear benefits for the valuable institution of friendly settlement....

· · ·

The Commission's case-law

· · ·

Since its inception in 1955 the Commission has registered more than 39,000 cases and has rendered decisions in more than 33,000 applications. The Commission's case-law legacy rests primarily in its admissibility decisions. The new Article 35 of the Convention, introduced by Protocol No. 11, lays down substantially the same criteria for admissibility as those in the current Articles 26 and 27 of the Convention and the Commission's numerous admissibility decisions are likely to prove a valuable repository of learning and guidance for the new body. On many questions of admissibility the Commission's decision will provide the only source of guidance, since the rejection of applications by the Commission at the admissibility stage has meant that numerous issues have never been addressed by the present Court.

· · ·

Extensive case-law has also been developed by the Commission on the question of compatibility of complaints with the Convention....

· · ·

Notes

1. Some critics believe that the aims of Protocol No. 11 would have been better served by streamlining the existing system of supervision, thereby preserving the efficiencies and expertise of established institutions, than by establishing a new system. At the very time that it would have to establish its basic institutional framework, they noted, the new Court would inherit a formidable backlog of cases from the Commission and previous Court while also responding to new challenges occasioned by the recent accession of States Parties from the former Soviet bloc.

In the view of some analysts, the reforms effected by Protocol No. 11 were made necessary not so much by the burgeoning case load of the Commission and Court, but by the expansion of the Council of Europe to include former Soviet bloc countries following the end of the Cold War. Pursuant to Article 20 of the Convention, the Commission comprised "a number of members equal to that of the High Contracting Parties" and no two members could be nationals of the same state. While there is no guarantee that the new system will be more efficient than the one it replaced, it has been noted, the expansion of the Council of Europe "without reform would mean a great many part-time or full-time commissioners or judges." The task of coordinating as many as 80 commissioners would be seen as too unwieldy, whatever reforms were instituted. Mark W.

Janis, Richard S. Kay & Anthony W. Bradley, European Human Rights Law: Text and Materials 117 (1995).

For further analysis of Protocol No. 11, see Karel de Vey Mestdagh, *Reform of the European Convention on Human Rights in a Changing Europe, in* The Dynamics of the Protection of Human Rights in Europe 337 (Rick Lawson & Matthijs de Blois eds., 1994); Yvonne Klerk, *Protocol No. 11 to the European Convention for Human Rights: A Drastic Revision of the Supervisory Mechanism under the ECHR,* Netherlands Q. Hum. Rts. 35 (1996); Andrew Drzemczewski & Jens Meyer–Ladewig, *Principal Characteristics of the New ECHR Control Mechanism, as Established by Protocol No. 11, Signed on 11 May, 1994,* 15 Hum. Rts. L.J. 81 (1994); Henry G. Schermers, *The Eleventh Protocol to the European Convention on Human Rights,* 19 Eur. L. Rev. 367 (1994).

2.   Under the two-body supervisory system that was replaced by Protocol No. 11, the European Commission had primary responsibility for establishing facts. Although the Court was not bound by the Commission's findings of fact, its policy was to exercise its freedom to reach different conclusions only in "exceptional circumstances." A notable aspect of this system was that the Commission frequently undertook on-site inquiries, in the course of which it interviewed witnesses and conducted site inspections. Article 28 of the European Convention established the textual basis for this approach. Paragraph (a) provided that if the Commission accepted a petition, "it shall, with a view to ascertaining the facts, undertake together with the representatives of the parties an examination of the petition and, if need be, an investigation, for the effective conduct of which the States concerned shall furnish all necessary facilities...." Article 38(1) (a) of the amended Convention similarly provides that, if the Court declares an application admissible, it shall "pursue the examination of the case, together with the representatives of the parties, and if need be, undertake an investigation, for the effective conduct of which the States concerned shall furnish all necessary facilities." Although the Court thus appears to have fact-finding powers that are identical to those formerly possessed by the Commission, will it be as free to conduct on-site inquiries? Or is it more appropriate for judges to confine their fact-finding to that which is possible within a Strasbourg courtroom?

3.   As the excerpt by Judge Bratza and Mr. O'Boyle indicates, the vast caseload of the European Commission and Court of Human Rights was generated principally by individual petitions rather than referrals by states. Some commentators regard the inter-state complaint system of the European Convention to be a failure, noting that there have been only a handful of such complaints in the history of the Convention system and that the complaints which have been filed have generally (although not always) reflected unfriendly relations between the complaining and respondent states. States' reticence to utilize this procedure has been explained as follows: "[T]he contracting States have not been willing to expose situations in other States if no interest of their own is involved. Such a step generally runs counter to their own interest in that a charge of violation of

the Convention will be considered an unfriendly act by the other party, with all the political consequences that may be involved." P. van Dijk & G.J.H. van Hoof, Theory and Practice of the European Convention on Human Rights 33 (1984). Others have observed that settlements reached in inter-state cases are more likely to compromise the interests of individual rights than those reached in respect of petitions filed by individuals. See, e.g., A.H. Robertson & J.G. Merrills, Human Rights in Europe 284–85 (3d ed. 1993).

Yet compared to other supra-national systems examined in this chapter, the European Convention system is notable for the fact that states have at times utilized the inter-state complaint process in response to serious violations of the Convention. As noted in our discussion of the International Covenant on Civil and Political Rights, the American Convention on Human Rights, and the African Charter on Human and Peoples' Rights, the inter-state complaint procedures established by those treaties had never been utilized as of early 1999.

When inter-state cases are instituted, how should one judge the effectiveness of the procedure? Consider the following analysis of the significance and impact of an interstate complaint brought against Greece in 1967, which alleged serious violations of the European Convention following a military coup:

The Greek military's coup d'état on 21 April 1967 was quickly followed ... by a debate in the Consultative Assembly of the Council of Europe protesting infringements by the new Greek government of the [Convention]. The four state complaints leading to the proceedings against Greece were lodged in response to a resolution of the Standing Committee of the Consultative Assembly of the Council of Europe [calling on Contracting Parties to the Convention to refer the Greek case to the Commission]. Before then, states bringing suit against other states ... had had some sort of ethnic or religious link with the injured individuals.... Denmark, Norway, Sweden and the Netherlands had no such ethnic or religious ties to the Greek population. Rather, it seems that the four countries complained to the Commission because they felt they had a moral duty to do so. There was a sentiment ... that if European human rights law was not employed against the Greek Colonels' military regime, the whole Strasbourg system would be endangered and the experiment in international human rights machinery defeated.

. . .

[Although the Commission's report prompted the Greek government to terminate its participation in the European Convention and the Council of Europe, one commentator] believed that the Commission's fact-finding, its Report and the Council's Resolution [affirming the Commission's Report and finding that Greece's denunciation of the Convention did not have retroactive effect] nonetheless constituted a significant restraint on the behaviour of the Greek authorities. Though it is difficult to demonstrate, it is most probable that fewer Greeks were tortured than otherwise might have been. The negotiations over a friendly settlement pushed the government to sign an agreement with the International Red Cross that imposed further restraints. Because of the Commission and international pressure the Greek government did not carry out serious reprisals against witnesses who testified before the Commission in Greece, and because these people testified, the truth was known abroad. The *Greek Case* cannot be considered a success in terms of protecting the human rights of Greeks, but it probably had something of a positive effect.

Mark W. Janis, Richard S. Kay & Anthony W. Bradley, European Human Rights Law: Text and Materials 62–63 (1995).

On July 23, 1974, a new civilian government under Constantine Karamanlis assumed power. His government moved quickly to restore democracy, holding elections on November 17, 1974. A number of senior military officials of the military regime were prosecuted. One set of proceedings related to the April 21, 1967 seizure of power. Other charges related to human rights violations, including the violent repression of students at the Athens Polytechnic and torture committed by the military police. For an analysis of the role of these prosecutions in consolidating Greece's transition to democracy, see Nicos C. Alivizatos and P. Nikiforos Diamandouros, *Politics and the Judiciary in the Greek Transition to Democracy,* in Transitional Justice and the Rule of Law in New Democracies (A. James McAdams, ed. 1997).

b. DOCTRINES AIDING INTERNATIONAL SUPERVISION

Several jurisprudential doctrines are central to understanding the basic structure of supranational supervision established by the European Convention. These doctrines include the "margin of appreciation," the exhaustion of remedies requirement applied by the Commission and the Court, and their elucidation of the conditions in which conduct that infringes rights give rise to state responsibility.

Margin of Appreciation

Handyside v. United Kingdom
European Court of Human Rights, 1976.
24 Eur. Ct. H.R. (ser. A), 1 E.H.R.R. 737.

[The applicant, Mr. Richard Handyside, had been convicted of violating the United Kingdom's Obscene Publications Act for publishing *The Little Red Schoolbook*, which was deemed obscene under that statute. Applying Article 10 of the European Convention, the Court concluded that the various measures taken against the applicant, including his criminal conviction, clearly constituted "interferences by a public authority" in the exercise of his freedom of expression. It then considered whether those measures were "necessary in a democratic society ... for the protection of ... morals," which, under the terms of Article 10, would justify the interference.]

46. ... [T]he Court first finds that the 1959/1964 Acts have an aim that is legitimate under Article 10 § 2, namely, the protection of morals in a democratic society....

47. ... The Commission's report and the subsequent hearings before the Court ... brought to light clear-cut differences of opinion on a crucial problem, namely, how to determine whether the actual "restrictions" and "penalties" complained of by the applicant were "necessary in a democratic society", "for the protection of morals". According to the Government and the majority of the Commission, the Court has only to ensure that the English courts acted reasonably, in good faith and within the limits of the margin of appreciation left to the Contracting States by Article 10 § 2. On the other hand, the minority of the Commission sees the Court's task as being not to review the Inner London Quarter Sessions judgment but to examine the Schoolbook directly in the light of the Convention and of nothing but the Convention.

48. The Court points out that the machinery of protection established by the Convention is subsidiary to the national systems safeguarding human rights.... The Convention leaves to each Contracting State, in the first place, the task of securing the rights and freedoms it enshrines. The institutions created by it make their own contribution to this task but they become involved only through contentious proceedings and once all domestic remedies have been exhausted (Article 26).

These observations apply, notably, to Article 10 § 2. In particular, it is not possible to find in the domestic law of the various Contracting States a uniform European conception of morals. The view taken by their respective laws of the requirements of morals varies from time to time and from place to place, especially in our era which is characterised by a rapid and far-reaching evolution of opinions on the subject. By reason of their direct and continuous contact with the vital forces of their countries, State authorities are in principle in a better position than the international judge to give an opinion on the exact content of these requirements as well as on the "necessity" of a "restriction" or "penalty" intended to meet them. The Court notes at this juncture that, whilst the adjective "necessary", within the meaning of Article 10 § 2, is not synonymous with "indispensable" ..., neither has it the flexibility of such expressions as "admissible", "ordinary" ..., "reasonable" ... or "desirable". Nevertheless, it is for the national authorities to make the initial assessment of the reality of the pressing social need implied by the notion of "necessity" in this context.

Consequently, Article 10 § 2 leaves to the Contracting States a margin of appreciation. This margin is given both to the domestic legislator ("prescribed by law") and to the bodies, judicial amongst others, that are called upon to interpret and apply the laws in force.

49. Nevertheless, Article 10 § 2 does not give the Contracting States an unlimited power of appreciation. The Court, which, with the Commission, is responsible for ensuring the observance of those States' engagements (Article 19), is empowered to give the final ruling on whether a "restriction" or "penalty" is reconcilable with freedom of expression as protected

by Article 10. The domestic margin of appreciation thus goes hand in hand with a European supervision. Such supervision concerns both the aim of the measure challenged and its "necessity"; it covers not only the basic legislation but also the decision applying it, even one given by an independent court. . . .

The Court's supervisory functions oblige it to pay the utmost attention to the principles characterising a "democratic society". Freedom of expression constitutes one of the essential foundations of such a society, one of the basic conditions for its progress and for the development of every man. Subject to paragraph 2 of Article 10, it is applicable not only to "information" or "ideas" that are favourably received or regarded as inoffensive or as a matter of indifference, but also to those that offend, shock or disturb the State or any sector of the population. Such are the demands of that pluralism, tolerance and broadmindedness without which there is no "democratic society". . . .

50. It follows from this that it is in no way the Court's task to take the place of the competent national courts but rather to review under Article 10 the decisions they delivered in the exercise of their power of appreciation. . . .

52. The Court attaches particular importance to a factor to which the [British court] judgment ... did not fail to draw attention, that is, the intended readership of the Schoolbook [which was aimed at children and adolescents between twelve and eighteen.] ... In these circumstances, despite the variety of views on ethics and education, the competent English judges were entitled, in the exercise of their discretion, to think at the relevant time that the Schoolbook would have pernicious effects on the morals of many of the children and adolescents who would read it. . . .

57. The applicant and the minority of the Commission laid stress on the further point that, in addition to the original Danish edition, translations of the "Little Book" appeared and circulated freely in the majority of the member states of the Council of Europe.

Here again, the national margin of appreciation and the optional nature of the "restrictions" and "penalties" referred to in Article 10 § 2 prevent the Court from accepting the argument. The Contracting States have each fashioned their approach in the light of the situation obtaining in their respective territories; they have had regard, *inter alia*, to the different views prevailing there about the demands of the protection of morals in a democratic society. The fact that most of them decided to allow the work to be distributed does not mean that the contrary decision of the Inner London Quarter Sessions was a breach of Article 10. . . .

59. On the strength of the data before it, the Court thus reaches the conclusion that no breach of the requirements of Article 10 has been established. . . .

———

R. St. J. Macdonald, *The Margin of Appreciation*

in The European System for the Protection of Human Rights 83.
(R. St. J. Macdonald et al.eds., 1993).

The doctrine of margin of appreciation illustrates the general approach of the European Court of Human Rights to the delicate task of balancing the sovereignty of Contracting Parties with their obligations under the Convention. The dilemma facing the Court, evident in recent cases on the margin of appreciation, is how to remain true to its responsibility to develop a reasonably comprehensive set of review principles appropriate for application across the entire Convention, while at the same time recognizing the diversity of political, economic, cultural and social situations in the societies of the Contracting Parties. The doctrine introduces an element of relativity into the uniform interpretation of the Convention, resulting in differences in scope and emphasis depending on the circumstances of the case.

. . .

. . . The judgment in *Handyside* (1976) remains the basis of the Court's application of the margin of appreciation.[3] However, it is apparent that the Court is endeavouring to develop a more rigorous application of its guidelines, with the result that there has probably been a narrowing of an originally expansive concept of the margin of appreciation. . . . The fact is that variations in the width of the margin of appreciation are inevitable: the Court must deal with different rights, different claims in respect of the same right by applicants in different situations, and with different justifications advanced by States at different times.

The principles governing the width of the margin of appreciation are linked to the notion of European standards. Although the margin of appreciation is probably wider in the absence of applicable European standards, the Court has not yet had an opportunity to fully develop its method of ascertaining, accepting or rejecting a minimum European standard. . . .

In many ways, the margin of appreciation can be seen as a label about the appropriate scope of supervisory review. A court can be said to exercise a supervisory jurisdiction when its task is to review public decisions for their conformity to certain standards and to grant a remedy if it finds that there has been an unjustifiable breach of those standards. The scope of review refers to the intensity of judicial scrutiny of a challenged decision in order to see if it amounts to an unjustifiable breach of those standards. The intensity of scrutiny is a function of the appropriateness of judicial intervention in a particular case.

. . .

The Court has never set out a universal and general formula to identify certain Articles suitable for the application of the margin of appreciation, although it has given reasons for the application of the

---

3. Handyside judgment of 7 December 1976, Series A no. 24.

margin of appreciation in particular contexts. It has used the margin of appreciation to incorporate some discretion in the text or where difficult issues of economic and social policy or technology are involved, or where the justifiability of an act of discrimination is at stake, or simply where the Court thinks the national judge is in a better position than the international judge to make a decision.

Nevertheless, it is difficult to see the common denominator among these various situations, and it is probable that there is indeed no common denominator. The margin of appreciation has played the role of lubricant in the working of the Convention and has enabled the Court to deal with the different situations and needs which could not have been envisaged at the time of the drafting of the Convention but which in its work daily confront it.

Above all, the margin of appreciation has given the Court great flexibility in dealing with the myriad problems of everyday life within the Contracting States that have come before it. Since the Contracting Parties adhere to diverse and often contradictory conceptions of human rights, attributable to differences in political, economic, social and cultural traditions, the task of the Court is to reconcile this lack of homogeneity in the audience at large with the recognition and development of an effective and reasonably uniform standard of protection for Convention rights within the jurisdiction of each of the High Contracting Parties. The margin of appreciation, which is more a principle of justification than interpretation, aims to help the Court show the proper degree of respect for the objectives that a Contracting Party may wish to pursue, and the trade-offs that it wants to make, while at the same time preventing unnecessary restrictions on the fullness of the protection which the Convention can provide.

This flexibility has enabled the Court to avoid any damaging dispute with Contracting States over the respective areas of authority of the Court and the margin of appreciation has also helped the Court strike a proper balance between the application of the Convention by national organs and the central institutions of the Court and Commission. Practices within States vary. In one State a law viewed in the abstract outside other national circumstances might be seen as violating the Convention, but viewed in the light of some other national matter or practice it may not. The intention of the drafters of the Convention was not that each Contracting State would have uniform laws but that there would be a European standard which, if violated, would give redress to the Members of the Contracting State. The margin of appreciation has very much assisted in this task.

The justification of the margin of appreciation is usually a pragmatic one. The argument is that the margin of appreciation is a useful tool in the eventual realization of a European-wide system of human-rights protection, in which a uniform standard of protection is secured. Progress towards that goal must be gradual, since the entire legal framework rests on the fragile foundations of the consent of the Contracting Parties. The margin of appreciation gives the flexibility needed to avoid damaging confrontations between the Court and Contracting States over their respective spheres of authority and enables the Court to balance the sovereignty of Contracting Parties with their obligations under the Convention.

The recommendation that the scope of the margin of appreciation be narrowed by the recognition of "common European standards" is best understood as part of this pragmatic gradualist project. On this view, the gradual refining of an originally expansive margin of appreciation reflects the increasing legitimacy of the Convention organs in the European legal order....

Buckley v. United Kingdom

European Court of Human Rights, 1996.
1996–IV Eur. Ct. H.R. 1271, 23 E.H.R.R. 101.

. . .

7.   The applicant is a British citizen and a Gypsy. She lives with her three children in caravans parked on land owned by her off Meadow Drove, Willingham, South Cambridgeshire, England....

. . .

12.   Her land is now part of a group of six adjacent sites which are occupied by Gypsies. One plot has received permanent planning permission for the residential use of three caravans.... The remaining three sites have been occupied without planning permission and the occupants have been subject to enforcement proceedings (see paragraph 32 below)....

. . .

14.   On 4 December 1989 the applicant applied retrospectively to South Cambridgeshire District Council for planning permission for the three caravans on her site.

She was refused on 8 March 1990 on the grounds that (1) adequate provision had been made for Gypsy caravans elsewhere in the South Cambridgeshire area, which had in the Council's opinion reached "saturation point" for Gypsy accommodation; (2) the planned use of the land would detract from the rural and open quality of the landscape, contrary to the aim of the local development plan which was to protect the countryside from all but essential development ...; and (3) Meadow Drove was an agricultural drove road which was too narrow to allow two vehicles to pass in safety.

15.   On 9 April 1990 the Council issued an enforcement notice requiring the caravans to be removed within a month.

The applicant appealed against the enforcement notice to the Secretary of State for the Environment....

16.   An inspector was appointed by the Secretary of State to report on the appeal.... The inspector visited the site and considered written representations submitted by the applicant and the District Council.

[The principal findings of this inspector, the Secretary of State, and a second inspector are summarized in portions of the Court's analysis excerpted below. In addition to the facts summarized therein, the following findings by the second inspector are pertinent in evaluating the Court's conclusions.]

22.   ...

The inspector considered, first, whether the continued use of the land as a Gypsy caravan site would detract from the rural nature of the area, and, secondly, if so, whether there were any special circumstances sufficient to outweigh this objection. She found that the road safety objection, which had been one of the grounds of refusal in April 1991 ..., no longer applied.

With regard to the first question, the inspector found [that although the applicant's caravans were hidden from the road by an agricultural engineering business],

"... the continued use of the rear plots considerably extends the depth of development south of the road. This intensification of use in itself inevitably detracts from the rural appearance and generally open character of the area, contrary to the objectives of national and local countryside policy. I must therefore conclude that the continued occupation of the land as gypsy caravan sites is harmful to the character and appearance of the countryside."

With regard to the special circumstances of the case, in particular the applicant's Gypsy status, the inspector ... described the applicant's site as "clean, spacious and well-ordered". By contrast, the council-run site on Meadow Drove ... was "isolated, exposed and somewhat uncared for". Nevertheless, it was

"a relevant consideration that there is available alternative accommodation close by, which would enable the appellants to stay in the Willingham area and their children to continue at the local schools".

·   ·   ·

The inspector considered the impact of [government] Circular 1/94 on the applicant's case, but concluded that, although it placed greater emphasis on the provision of sites by Gypsies themselves, it was government policy that proposals for Gypsy sites should continue to be determined solely in relation to land-use factors.

II.   Alleged Violation of Article 8 of the Convention

51.   The applicant submitted that since she was prevented from living in caravans on her own land with her family and from following a travelling life there had been, and continued to be, a violation of her right to respect for her private life and her home. She relied on Article 8 of the Convention, which provides as follows:

"1.   Everyone has the right to respect for his private and family life, his home and his correspondence.

2. There shall be no interference by a public authority with the exercise of this right except such as is in accordance with the law and is necessary in a democratic society in the interests of national security, public safety or the economic well-being of the country, for the prevention of disorder or crime, for the protection of health or morals, or for the protection of the rights and freedoms of others.''

. . .

[The Court concluded that the case ''concerns the applicant's right to respect for her 'home'.'' Therefore, it found it unnecessary to consider whether the case also concerns the applicant's right to respect for her ''private life'' and ''family life.'' It also found that the denial of permission to live in the caravans on her property constituted ''interference by a public authority'' with the applicant's exercise of her right to respect for her home. Since it was not contested that the measures in question were ''in accordance with the law,'' the Court next considered whether they were taken in pursuit of a legitimate aim in accordance with Article 8 of the Convention.]

62. According to the Government, the measures in question were taken in the enforcement of planning controls aimed at furthering highway safety, the preservation of the environment and public health. The legitimate aims pursued were therefore public safety, the economic well-being of the country, the protection of health and the protection of the rights of others.

. . .

63. On the facts of the case the Court sees no reason to doubt that the measures in question pursued the legitimate aims stated by the Government.

[The remaining issue under Article 8 was whether the measures taken were ''necessary in a democratic society.'']

74. As is well established in the Court's case-law, it is for the national authorities to make the initial assessment of the ''necessity'' for an interference. . . . Although a margin of appreciation is thereby left to the national authorities, their decision remains subject to review by the Court for conformity with the requirements of the Convention.

The scope of this margin of appreciation is not identical in each case but will vary according to the context. . . . Relevant factors include the nature of the Convention right in issue, its importance for the individual and the nature of the activities concerned.

75. The Court has already had occasion to note that town and country planning schemes involve the exercise of discretionary judgment in the implementation of policies adopted in the interest of the community . . . . It is not for the Court to substitute its own view of what would be the best policy in the planning sphere or the most appropriate individual measure in planning cases. . . . By reason of their direct and continuous contact with the vital forces of their countries, the national authorities are in principle better placed than an international court to evaluate local needs and

conditions. In so far as the exercise of discretion involving a multitude of local factors is inherent in the choice and implementation of planning policies, the national authorities in principle enjoy a wide margin of appreciation.

76. The Court cannot ignore, however, that in the instant case the interests of the community are to be balanced against the applicant's right to respect for her "home," a right which is pertinent to her and her children's personal security and well being.... The importance of that right for the applicant and her family must also be taken into account in determining the scope of the margin of appreciation allowed to the respondent State.

Whenever discretion capable of interfering with the enjoyment of a Convention right such as the one in issue in the present case is conferred on national authorities, the procedural safeguards available to the individual will be especially material in determining whether the respondent State has, when fixing the regulatory framework, remained within its margin of appreciation. Indeed it is settled case-law that, whilst Article 8 contains no explicit procedural requirements, the decision-making process leading to measures of interference must be fair and such as to afford due respect to the interests safeguarded to the individual by Article 8....

[Reviewing the procedures available to challenge and obtain review of the enforcement notice, the Court was "satisfied that the procedural safeguards provided for in the regulatory framework were ... such as to afford due respect to the applicant's interests under Article 8...."]

80. In the instant case, an investigation was carried out by the inspector.... In conformity with government policy ..., the special needs of the applicant as a Gypsy following a traditional lifestyle were taken into account. The inspector and later the Secretary of State had regard to the shortage of Gypsy caravan sites in the area and weighed the applicant's interest in being allowed to continue living on her land in caravans against the general interest of conforming to planning policy.... They found the latter interest to have greater weight given the particular circumstances pertaining to the area in question.

Thus, in her report the inspector stated:

"... [the applicant's caravan site] extends development further from the road than that permitted. It thus intrudes into the open countryside, contrary to the aim of the Structure Plan to protect the countryside from all but essential development."

And:

"It is ... clear in my mind that a need exists for more authorised spaces.... Nevertheless, I consider it important to keep concentrations of sites for gypsies small, because in this way they are more readily accepted by the local community.... [T]he concentration of gypsy sites in Willingham has reached the desirable maximum and I do not consider that the overall need for sites should, in this case, outweigh the planning objections."

The Secretary of State's reasoning in his decision included the following:

> "The decisive issue in regard to the planning merits of your appeals is considered to be whether the undisputed need for additional gypsies' caravan site provision, in the administrative areas of the District Council, and of the County Council, is so pressing that it should be permitted to override the objections on planning policy and highway safety grounds to the retention of the use of the appeal site as a residential caravan site for gypsies. On this approach, the view is taken that the objections to the continued use of the appeal site as a residential gypsy caravan site are so strong, on planning policy and highway safety grounds, that a grant of planning permission could not be justified, either on a temporary or personal basis. In reaching this conclusion, full consideration has been given to policy advice in the Department's Circular 28/77, giving guidance to councils on the need to provide adequate accommodation in the form of caravan sites, for gypsies residing in or resorting to their area."

81.   The applicant was offered the opportunity . . . to apply for a pitch on the official caravan site situated about 700 metres from the land which she currently occupies. . . . Evidence has been adduced which tends to show that the alternative accommodation available at this location was not as satisfactory as the dwelling which she had established in contravention of the legal requirements. . . . [The Court referred to an earlier paragraph citing high levels of violence and disorder in the officially-sanctioned caravan site.] However, Article 8 does not necessarily go so far as to allow individuals' preferences as to their place of residence to override the general interest.

82.   It is also true that . . . in her report of July 1995, the second inspector found that the applicant's caravans could have been adequately screened from view by planting hedges; this would have hidden them from view but, so the inspector concluded, would not have reduced their intrusion into open countryside in a way which national and local planning policy sought to prevent. . . .

. . .

84.   In the light of the foregoing, the Court considers that proper regard was had to the applicant's predicament both under the terms of the regulatory framework, which contained adequate procedural safeguards protecting her interest under Article 8, and by the responsible planning authorities when exercising their discretion in relation to the circumstances of her case. . . . [T]he means employed to achieve the legitimate aims pursued cannot be regarded as disproportionate. In sum, the Court does not find that in the present case the national authorities exceeded their margin of appreciation.

. . .

85.   In conclusion, there has been no violation of Article 8.

. . .

■ Partly Dissenting Opinion of JUDGE REPIK

. . .

The concept of necessity implies a pressing social need; in particular, the measure taken must be proportionate to the legitimate aim pursued. It has to be determined whether a fair balance has been struck between the aim pursued and the right concerned, regard being had to the latter's importance and to the seriousness of the infringement. . . .

In the present case the national authorities did not properly assess whether the aim pursued was proportionate to the applicant's right to respect for her home and to the seriousness of the infringement of that right. At no stage during the domestic proceedings was the problem before the authorities considered in terms of a right of the applicant protected by the Convention. . . . The applicant's interests, confronted with the requirements of the protection of the countryside, were only taken into account in abstract, general terms, such as "the undisputed need for additional gypsies' caravan site provision" . . . or "the applicant's Gypsy status". . . . There was never any mention of the applicant's right to respect for her home or the importance of that right to her given her financial and family situation. Nor was any account taken of the possible consequences for the applicant and her children were she to be evicted from her land.

In these circumstances the Court, in order to fulfil its supervisory role, ought itself to have considered whether the interference was proportionate to the right in issue and to its importance to the applicant, all the more so as where a fundamental right of a member of a minority is concerned, especially a minority as vulnerable as the Gypsies, as the Court has an obligation to subject any such interference to particularly close scrutiny.

Respect for planning policy, in particular protection of the countryside, has been placed on one side of the scales. The Court has not taken into account that the weight of that interest is considerably reduced by the fact . . . that the applicant did not park her caravans either on land under special protection or in unspoilt open countryside. There are in fact already a number of buildings on neighbouring land . . . and the applicant's caravans could have been adequately screened from view by planting hedges. . . .

Much importance was attached to the fact that the applicant could have moved to a different site. The Commission considered that it was not reasonably open to the applicant to move to a private site and that the official Meadow Drove site was not suitable for her . . . . The Court underestimates the cogency of the arguments advanced by the Commission, which reported in detail on the condition of the Meadow Drove site and the numerous incidents which have occurred there. The safety of the applicant's family is not guaranteed there and it is an unsuitable place for bringing up her children. The applicant did not, therefore, refuse to move there out of sheer capriciousness.

. . .

■ Dissenting Opinion of JUDGE PETTITI

. . .

The Government's reliance on the lawful aim pursued was not justi-fied, because the grounds of public safety, economic well-being of the country and protection of health and of the rights of others were not established and should not therefore have been accepted [by the majority].

. . .

The Court, which rightly recalls that it cannot act as an appeal court, nonetheless states its conviction that the authority's grounds were rele-vant, a statement that may appear to be contradictory. But the grounds could not be relevant under the Convention as the Government's approach is to give priority to protection of the landscape over respect for family life. The ranking of fundamental rights under Article 8 and Protocol No. 1 (concerning the use of property) . . . is thereby reversed. . . .

. . .

The Court uses the notion of margin of appreciation in formulations (see paragraph 84 of the judgment) which appear to me to extend that concept too far when compared with the Court's previous case-law and without laying down any precise criteria. The practice established under the Court's case-law has been to restrict the States' margin of appreciation by making it subject to review by the Court by reference to the criteria which the Court has laid down by virtue of its autonomous power to interpret the Convention. . . .

In the present case, moreover, there was no necessity for the measures in a democratic State (on the contrary) and the interference was, at the very least, disproportionate.

. . .

Notes

1. In the *Handyside* case, the European Court upheld restraints imposed upon publication of *The Little Red Book* in the United Kingdom despite the fact that the book had "circulated freely in the majority of the member states of the Council of Europe." Invoking the margin of appreciation, the Court observed that "Contracting States have each fashioned their ap-proach in the light of the situation obtaining in their respective territories; they have had regard, *inter alia*, to the different views prevailing there about the demands of the protection of morals in a democratic society." Yet in its 1981 judgment in the *Dudgeon* case, see Part IV, Chapter 1(B)(2), which found a law criminalizing homosexual conduct in Northern Ireland to be incompatible with Article 8 of the European Convention, the Court said that it "cannot overlook" the fact that a majority of member states of the Council of Europe no longer considered it appropriate to criminalize homosexual conduct. In light of this European consensus, the divergent approach taken by the United Kingdom was found inconsistent with the

European Convention. Can these decisions be reconciled—or otherwise explained?

2.   Professors Helfer and Slaughter explain the European Court's application of the margin of appreciation in light of the "consensus principle" on pragmatic grounds:

> In striking the balance between deference and independent judicial review, the [European Court of Human Rights (ECHR)] looks to the degree of consensus or harmony among the national laws of signatory states in deciding how wide or narrow a margin to afford the respondent state in the case before it. This approach allows the court to narrow the margin of discretion allotted to national governments in an incremental fashion, finding against state respondents according to the underlying treatment of the right at issue within other European nations. As a result, the ECHR is able to identify potentially problematic practices for the contracting states before they actually become violations, thereby permitting the states to anticipate that their laws may one day be called into question. In the meantime, a state government lagging behind in the protection of a certain right is allowed to maintain its national policy but is forced to bear a heavier burden of proof before the ECHR—whose future opinions will turn in part on its own conception of how far the "trends" in European domestic law have evolved. The conjunction of the margin of appreciation doctrine and the consensus inquiry thus permits the ECHR to link its decisions to the pace of change of domestic law, acknowledging the political sovereignty of respondent states while legitimizing its own decisions against them.

Helfer & Slaughter, supra, at 316–317. Is the approach suggested by the authors legitimate? That is, if the European Court believed that a High Contracting Party's practices skirted the margins of permissible choice, should it validate those practices under the rubric of the "margin of appreciation" even for a limited period? Principled considerations aside, is this approach strategically sound? Is it possible that, by applying the "margin of appreciation," the Court might lead states to believe that their practices are within the permissible range rather than at the margins of permissible discretion?

3.   Is the margin of appreciation doctrine based principally on pragmatic or principled considerations—or a combination of both? How would one justify the doctrine on principled grounds? One justification that has been put forth relates to the principle of subsidiarity underlying the European Convention:

> ... Article 1 of the Convention makes it clear that the primary responsibility for securing the guaranteed rights and freedoms within the domestic legal order lies with the national authorities of the Contracting States.... Because the Convention lays down standards of conduct rather than detailed rules, there will be a spectrum of choices available to the national authorities for fulfilling their duty of implementation.... In other words, the primary responsibility vested by

Article 1 in the national authorities carries with it a variable degree of discretion . . . as to the appropriate means of implementation.

Paul Mahoney, *Marvelous Richness of Diversity or Invidious Cultural Relativism?, in Symposium: The Doctrine of the Margin of Appreciation under the European Convention on Human Rights: Its Legitimacy in Theory and Application in Practice*, 19 Hum. Rts. L.J. 1, 2 (1998). Another rationale relates to the commitment to democratic principles that infuses the European Convention and in light of which the Convention is to be interpreted. In light of this guiding principle, "the power of the Convention institutions to sit in final and binding judgment on national measures, whether adopted by the legislative, executive or judicial ranch of government, must give due recognition to the democratic processes of the many and varied countries making up the Convention's legal community." Id.

4.   To the extent that the doctrine reflects a pragmatic calculation that the long-term aim of achieving "a uniform standard of protection" within Europe is likely to be secured most effectively through a "gradualist approach," how will this process be affected by the expanded membership of the Council of Europe? Now that the European Convention system has established its authority, is it necessary for the new Court to accommodate diverging approaches under the convention or is it in a better position than its predecessor institutions to assert a uniform standard—notwithstanding the growing diversity of Contracting States?

5.   The scope of the margin of appreciation accorded to respondent states has varied depending on the nature of the alleged violation. As the Court observed in *Buckley v. United Kingdom*, "the scope of [states'] margin of appreciation is not identical in each case [; r]elevant factors include the nature of the Convention right in issue, its importance for the individual and the nature of the activities concerned." (Para. 74.) Is the Court's application of the margin of appreciation in *Buckley* itself consistent with this general rule? Or does the *Buckley* judgment support the following critique?:

> The concept of the "margin of appreciation" has become as slippery and elusive as an eel. Again and again the Court now appears to use the margin of appreciation as a substitute for coherent legal analysis of the issues at stake. . . . The danger of continuing to use the standardless doctrine of the margin of appreciation is that . . . it will become the source of a pernicious "variable geometry" of human rights, . . . giving undue deference to local conditions, traditions and practices.

Lord Lester of Herne Hill, QC, *The European Convention on Human Rights in the New Architecture of Europe: General Report*, Proceedings of the 8th International Colloquy on the European Convention on Human Rights (Council of Europe) 227, 236–37 (1995), quoted in Mahoney, supra, at 1 n.2.

6.   In paragraph 76 of its judgment in *Buckley v. United Kingdom*, the European Court observed: "Whenever discretion capable of interfering with the enjoyment of a Convention right such as the one in issue in the present case is conferred on national authorities, the procedural safeguards avail-

able to the individual will be especially material in determining whether the respondent State has, when fixing the regulatory framework, remained within its margin of appreciation." Applying this consideration to the case at hand, the Court concluded that the procedural safeguards available to Mrs. Buckley were adequate (paras. 79 and 84) and that the authorities that reviewed her case had "proper regard ... to the applicant's predicament ... when exercising their discretion in relation to the particular circumstances of her case" (para. 84). Consider the following proposition: "The Court's review demonstrates that, principally by virtue of the fact that British authorities acknowledged the merits of Mrs. Buckley's position, their decisions were able to survive scrutiny by the European Court." Is this conclusion warranted?

7. For further discussion of the margin of appreciation doctrine, see Howard Charles Yourow, The Margin of Appreciation Doctrine in the Dynamics of European Human Rights Jurisprudence (1996); *Symposium: The Doctrine of the Margin of Appreciation under the European Convention on Human Rights: Its Legitimacy in Theory and Application in Practice*, 19 Human Rights Law Journal 1–36 (1998).

Exhaustion of Domestic Remedies and State Responsibility

Like other supra-national human rights supervisory bodies, the European Commission could consider applications alleging that a Contracting Party had breached the European Convention only if domestic remedies had been exhausted. (Article 26.) The exhaustion rule has been carried over into the supervisory machinery established by Protocol No. 11. (Article 35.)

Under some circumstances, the same facts that excuse a petitioner from further recourse to domestic remedies may also help establish state responsibility for a breach of the European Convention. The following cases highlight the somewhat overlapping concerns of these two distinct legal doctrines.

Ireland v. United Kingdom

European Court of Human Rights, 1978.
25 Eur. Ct. H.R. (ser. A), 2 E.H.R.R. 25.

[This case originated in an application by the Government of Ireland against the Government of the United Kingdom of Great Britain lodged with the European Commission on December 16, 1971. After the Commission adopted a report finding the respondent government in breach of the European Convention, the Government of Ireland lodged an application with the Court asking it, inter alia, to confirm the opinion of the Commission that the respondent state had breached the Convention.

The allegations concerned the exercise by authorities in Northern Ireland of various emergency measures to combat what the respondent government described as "the longest and most violent terrorist campaign witnessed in either part of the island of Ireland.'' Those measures, in effect from 1971 to 1975, entailed extrajudicial arrest and internment, as well as the use of ''five techniques'' of interrogation alleged to be incompatible with Article 3 of the European Convention.]

. . .

158.   . . . [T]he Irish Government indicated . . . that they were asking the Court to hold that there had been in Northern Ireland, from 1971 to 1974, a practice or practices in breach of Article 3 (art. 3) and to specify, if need be, where they had occurred. . . .

159.   A practice incompatible with the Convention consists of an accumulation of identical or analogous breaches which are sufficiently numerous and inter-connected to amount not merely to isolated incidents or exceptions but to a pattern or system; a practice does not of itself constitute a violation separate from such breaches.

It is inconceivable that the higher authorities of a State should be, or at least should be entitled to be, unaware of the existence of such a practice. Furthermore, under the Convention those authorities are strictly liable for the conduct of their subordinates; they are under a duty to impose their will on subordinates and cannot shelter behind their inability to ensure that it is respected.

The concept of practice is of particular importance for the operation of the rule of exhaustion of domestic remedies. This rule, as embodied in Article 26 of the Convention, applies to State applications (Article 24), in the same way as it does to ''individual'' applications (Article 25) . . . . On the other hand and in principle, the rule does not apply where the applicant State complains of a practice as such, with the aim of preventing its continuation or recurrence, but does not ask the Commission or the Court to give a decision on each of the cases put forward as proof or illustrations of that practice. The Court agrees with the opinion which the Commission, following its earlier case-law, expressed on the subject in its decision of 1 October 1972 on the admissibility of the Irish Government's original application. Moreover, the Court notes that that decision is not contested by the respondent Government.

———

A. v. United Kingdom

European Court of Human Rights, 1998.
1998–VI Eur. Ct. H.R. 2692.

. . .

7.   The applicant is a British citizen, born in 1984.

In May 1990 he and his brother were placed on the local Child Protection Register because of ''known physical abuse''. The co-habitant of the boys' mother was given a police caution after he admitted hitting A. with a cane. Both boys were removed from the Child Protection Register in November

1991. The co-habitant subsequently married the applicant's mother and became his stepfather.

8. In February 1993, the head teacher at A.'s school reported to the local Social Services Department that A.'s brother had disclosed that A. was being hit with a stick by his stepfather. The stepfather was arrested on 5 February 1993 and released on bail the next day.

9. On 5 February 1993 the applicant was examined by a consultant paediatrician, who found the following marks on his body, inter alia: (1) a fresh red linear bruise on the back of the right thigh, consistent with a blow from a garden cane, probably within the preceding twenty-four hours; (2) a double linear bruise on the back of the left calf, consistent with two separate blows given some time before the first injury; (3) two lines on the back of the left thigh, probably caused by two blows inflicted one or two days previously; (4) three linear bruises on the right bottom, consistent with three blows, possibly given at different times and up to one week old; (5) a fading linear bruise, probably several days old.

The paediatrician considered that the bruising was consistent with the use of a garden cane, applied with considerable force, on more than one occasion.

10. The stepfather was charged with assault occasioning actual bodily harm and tried in February 1994. It was not disputed by the defence that the stepfather had caned the boy on a number of occasions, but it was argued that this had been necessary and reasonable since A. was a difficult boy who did not respond to parental or school discipline.

In summing-up, the judge advised the jury on the law as follows:

> "... What is it the prosecution must prove? If a man deliberately and unjustifiably hits another and causes some bodily injury, bruising or swelling will do, he is guilty of actual bodily harm. What does unjustifiably mean in the context of this case? It is a perfectly good defence that the alleged assault was merely the correcting of a child by its parent, in this case the stepfather, provided that the correction be moderate in the manner, the instrument and the quantity of it. Or, put another way, reasonable. It is not for the defendant to prove it was lawful correction. It is for the prosecution to prove it was not.
>
> This case is not about whether you should punish a very difficult boy. It is about whether what was done here was reasonable or not and you must judge that...."

11. The jury found by a majority verdict that the applicant's stepfather was not guilty of assault occasioning actual bodily harm.

II. RELEVANT DOMESTIC LAW

A. Criminal sanctions against the assault of children

12. The applicant's stepfather was charged with "assault occasioning actual bodily harm" contrary to section 47 of the Offences against the Person Act 1861, as amended ....

13. In addition, it is an offence under section 1(1) of the Children and Young Persons Act 1933 to assault or ill-treat a child in a manner likely to cause him unnecessary suffering or injury to health. The maximum penalty on conviction is ten years' imprisonment.

14. In criminal proceedings for the assault of a child, the burden of proof is on the prosecution to satisfy the jury, beyond a reasonable doubt, inter alia that the assault did not constitute lawful punishment.

Parents or other persons in loco parentis are protected by the law if they administer punishment which is moderate and reasonable in the circumstances. The concept of "reasonableness" permits the courts to apply standards prevailing in contemporary society with regard to the physical punishment of children.

. . .

AS TO THE LAW

I. ALLEGED VIOLATION OF ARTICLE 3 OF THE CONVENTION

19. The applicant asked the Court to find a violation of Article 3 of the Convention, which provides:

> "No one shall be subjected to torture or to inhuman or degrading treatment or punishment."

. . .

20. The Court recalls that ill-treatment must attain a minimum level of severity if it is to fall within the scope of Article 3. The assessment of this minimum is relative: it depends on all the circumstances of the case, such as the nature and context of the treatment, its duration, its physical and mental effects and, in some instances, the sex, age and state of health of the victim (see the Costello–Roberts v. the United Kingdom judgment of 25 March 1993, Series A no. 247–C, p. 59 § 30).

21. The Court recalls that the applicant, who was then nine years old, was found by the consultant paediatrician who examined him to have been beaten with a garden cane which had been applied with considerable force on more than one occasion (see paragraph 9 above).

The Court considers that treatment of this kind reaches the level of severity prohibited by Article 3.

22. It remains to be determined whether the State should be held responsible, under Article 3, for the beating of the applicant by his stepfather.

The Court considers that the obligation on the High Contracting Parties under Article 1 of the Convention to secure to everyone within their jurisdiction the rights and freedoms defined in the Convention, taken together with Article 3, requires States to take measures designed to ensure that individuals within their jurisdiction are not subjected to torture or inhuman or degrading treatment or punishment, including such ill-treatment administered by private individuals (see, mutatis mutandis, the H.L.R. v. France judgment of 29 April 1997, Reports 1997–III, p. 758, § 40). Children and other vulnerable individuals, in particular, are entitled to State protection, in the form of effective deterrence, against such serious breaches of personal integrity....

23.   The Court recalls that under English law it is a defence to a charge of assault on a child that the treatment in question amounted to "reasonable chastisement" (see paragraph 14 above). The burden of proof is on the prosecution to establish beyond reasonable doubt that the assault went beyond the limits of lawful punishment. In the present case, despite the fact that the applicant had been subjected to treatment of sufficient severity to fall within the scope of Article 3, the jury acquitted his stepfather, who had administered the treatment (see paragraphs 10–11 above).

24.   In the Court's view, the law did not provide adequate protection to the applicant against treatment or punishment contrary to Article 3. Indeed, the Government have accepted that this law currently fails to provide adequate protection to children and should be amended.

In the circumstances of the present case, the failure to provide adequate protection constitutes a violation of Article 3 of the Convention.

. . .

Notes

1.   The "administrative practice" exception to the exhaustion requirement was applied by the Commission as well as the Court, and has been applied in cases initiated by both states and individuals. The Commission explained the rationale of this exception in the *Greek* case, 12 Yb. Eur. Conv. H. R. 196 (Eur. Comm. H.R. 1969):

> Where ... there is a practice of non-observance of certain Convention provisions, the remedies prescribed will of necessity be side-stepped or rendered inadequate. Thus, if there was an administrative practice of torture or ill-treatment, judicial remedies prescribed would tend to be rendered ineffective by the difficulty of securing probative evidence, and administrative inquiries would either be not instituted, or, if they were, would be likely to be half-hearted and incomplete....

2.   On what basis did the Court find that the respondent state had breached its obligation to ensure A.'s right to freedom from ill-treatment? Would the state have been found responsible for the conduct of A.'s stepfather if the jury had convicted the defendant? Would the Court have found the respondent state in breach if it had not admitted that its law failed to provide adequate protection to children (see para. 24)? Following the judgment in *A. v. United Kingdom*, the respondent state announced that it would amend national law to remove the provision allowing "reasonable chastisement" by parents and those in loco parentis.

3.   Although the supra-national system for enforcing the European Convention is not meant to replace national institutions, in some respects the Convention and its enforcement machinery supplement domestic institutions. Pursuant to Article 41 of the Convention as amended by Protocol No.

11, for example, the European Court can afford "just satisfaction to the injured party" if it has found a High Contracting Party in breach of the Convention and "the internal law of the High Contracting Party concerned allows only partial reparation to be made." (A similar provision formerly appeared in Article 50 of the Convention.) In the case of *A. v. United Kingdom*, the Court awarded the applicant compensation in the amount of 10,000 pounds sterling for non-pecuniary damages, and also awarded twice that amount for costs and expenses. For discussion of the jurisprudence under Article 50, see Montserrat Enrich Mas, *Right to Compensation under Article 50, in* The European System for the Protection of Human Rights 775 (R. St. J. Macdonald et al. eds., 1993).

---

c. ADJUDICATING DISAPPEARANCES UNDER THE EUROPEAN CONVENTION

In contrast to the Human Rights Committee and the Inter–American Commission and Court, the European Commission and the previous European Court had few occasions to address the practice of "enforced disappearances." As noted earlier, this practice has been more common in Latin America, particularly during recent periods of military rule, than in Europe. The European Commission and Court have, however, been presented with allegations of such a practice in Turkey. Compare the Court's approach to evidentiary issues in the following case to that of the Inter–American Court in the *Velásquez Rodríguez* case.

Kurt v. Turkey

European Court of Human Rights, May 25, 1998.
1998–III Eur. Ct. H.R. 1152, 27 E.H.R.R. 91.

. . .

8.   The applicant[, Mrs Koçeri Kurt,] is a Turkish citizen who was born in 1927 and is at present living in Bismil in south-east Turkey. At the time of the events giving rise to her application to the Commission she was living in the nearby village of Agilli. Her application to the Commission was brought on her own behalf and on behalf of her son, Üzeyir Kurt, who, she alleges, has disappeared in circumstances engaging the responsibility of the respondent State.

. . .

9.   The facts surrounding the disappearance of the applicant's son are disputed.

. . .

13.   The Commission, with a view to establishing the facts in the light of the dispute over the circumstances surrounding the disappearance of the applicant's son, conducted its own investigation pursuant to Article 28

§ 1(a) of the Convention. To this end, the Commission examined a series of documents submitted by both the applicant and the Government in support of their respective assertions and appointed three delegates to take evidence of witnesses at a hearing conducted in Ankara on 8 and 9 February 1996....

. . .

[According to the applicant, her son, Üzeyir, was taken into custody by Turkish security forces during an operation in the village of Agilli which took place from November 23 through 25, 1993. By her account, on November 24, 1993 soldiers went to the home of Üzeyir's aunt, where Üzeyir had spent the previous night, and took him from that house. Üzeyir spent the next two nights with soldiers in the house of Hasan Kiliç.]

15. ... On the morning of 25 November 1993, the applicant received a message from a child that Üzeyir wanted some cigarettes. The applicant took cigarettes and found Üzeyir in front of Hasan Kiliç's house surrounded by about ten soldiers and five to six village guards. She saw bruises and swelling on his face as though he had been beaten. Üzeyir told her that he was cold. She returned with his jacket and socks. The soldiers did not allow her to stay so she left. This was the last time she saw Üzeyir. The applicant maintains that there is no evidence that he was seen elsewhere after this time.

[In response to the applicant's efforts to obtain information about her son, public authorities replied that they believed he had been kidnapped by the Kurdish Workers' Party (PKK).

In its account, the Turkish government denied that Üzeyir Kurt had been taken into custody by security forces and submitted that "there are strong grounds for believing that [he] has in fact joined or been kidnapped by the PKK." The government also challenged the credibility of the applicant, citing certain discrepancies among various accounts of the events of November 23–25 provided by the applicant. The government placed particular emphasis as well on the fact that, in his statement to the gendarmes of December 7, 1994, Hasan Kiliç stated that, after spending the night at Kiliç's home, Üzeyir Kurt had departed on the morning of November 25 with his mother, and not with soldiers.

In addition to documentary evidence submitted by the applicant and the respondent state in support of their factual claims, the Commission took oral testimony from six witnesses during a two-day hearing in Ankara, Turkey.

Faced with the contradictory evidence of the two parties, the Commission accepted the applicant's testimony that she had seen her son surrounded by soldiers and village guards outside the home of Hasan Kiliç on the morning of November 25, 1993. It also found that this was the last time that Üzeyir Kurt had been seen by any member of his family or any other person from the village.]

. . .

84.   The applicant requested the Court to find on the basis of the facts established by the Commission that the disappearance of her son engaged the responsibility of the respondent State under Articles 2, 3 and 5 of the Convention and that each of those Articles had been violated. She urged the Court, in line with the approach adopted by the Inter–American Court of Human Rights under the American Convention on Human Rights and by the United Nations Human Rights Committee under the International Covenant on Civil and Political Rights . . . to the phenomenon of disappearances, not to confine its consideration of her son's plight to the issues raised under Article 5 of the Convention but to have regard also to those raised under Articles 2 and 3.

. . .

86.   The Commission concluded, for its part, that the respondent State had committed a particularly serious and flagrant violation of Article 5 of the Convention taken as a whole and for that reason had not found it necessary to examine separately the applicant's complaints under Articles 2 and 3.

. . .

99.   . . . [T]he Court is not persuaded that there exist any exceptional circumstances which would compel it to reach a conclusion different from that of the Commission [concerning the latter body's findings of fact]. It considers that there is a sufficient factual and evidentiary basis on which the Commission could properly conclude, beyond reasonable doubt, that the applicant did see her son outside Hasan Kiliç's house on the morning of 25 November 1993, that he was surrounded by soldiers and village guards at the time and that he has not been seen since.

B.   Article 2

100.   The applicant maintained that a number of factors militated in favour of a finding that her son was the victim of violations of Article 2 of the Convention, which [assures the right to life].

101.   The applicant stressed that her son's disappearance occurred in a context which was life-threatening. She requested the Court to base itself on the approach taken by the Inter–American Court of Human Rights in the Velásquez Rodríguez v. Honduras case (judgment of 29 July 1988) as well as by the United Nations Human Rights Committee in the Mojica v. Dominican Republic case (decision of 15 July 1994) to the issue of enforced disappearances . . . and to find the respondent State in breach of its positive obligation under Article 2 to protect her son's life. Such a finding could be reached, she maintained, even though there may not exist specific evidence that her son had died at the hands of the authorities of the respondent State.

102.   In an alternative submission, the applicant asserted that there existed a well-documented high incidence of torture, unexplained deaths in custody as well as of "disappearances" in south-east Turkey which not only gave rise to a reasonable presumption that the authorities were in breach of their obligation to protect her son's life under Article 2 but, in addition,

constituted compelling evidence of a practice of "disappearances" such as to ground a claim that her son was also the victim of an aggravated violation of that provision. She contended that the Inter–American Court in the above-mentioned Velásquez Rodríguez v. Honduras judgment of 29 July 1988 was prepared to draw the conclusion that the respondent State in that case had violated the right to life provision of the American Convention on Human Rights on the existence of either sort of evidence.

. . .

105.   The Commission found that in the absence of any evidence as to the fate of Üzeyir Kurt subsequent to his detention in the village, it would be inappropriate to draw the conclusion that he had been a victim of a violation of Article 2. It disagreed with the applicant's argument that it could be inferred that her son had been killed either from the life-threatening context she described or from an alleged administrative practice of disappearances in the respondent State. In the Commission's opinion, the applicant's allegation as to the apparent forced disappearance of her son and the alleged failure of the authorities to take reasonable steps to safeguard him against the risks to his life attendant on his disappearance fell to be considered under Article 5 of the Convention.

106.   The Court recalls at the outset that it has accepted the Commission's findings of fact in respect of the detention of the applicant's son by soldiers and village guards on 25 November 1993. Almost four and a half years have passed without information as to his subsequent whereabouts or fate. In such circumstances the applicant's fears that her son may have died in unacknowledged custody at the hands of his captors cannot be said to be without foundation. She has contended that there are compelling grounds for drawing the conclusion that he has in fact been killed.

107.   However, like the Commission, the Court must carefully scrutinise whether there does in fact exist concrete evidence which would lead it to conclude that her son was, beyond reasonable doubt, killed by the authorities either while in detention in the village or at some subsequent stage. It also notes in this respect that in those cases where it has found that a Contracting State had a positive obligation under Article 2 to conduct an effective investigation into the circumstances surrounding an alleged unlawful killing by the agents of that State, there existed concrete evidence of a fatal shooting which could bring that obligation into play . . . .

108.   It is to be observed in this regard that the applicant's case rests entirely on presumptions deduced from the circumstances of her son's initial detention bolstered by more general analyses of an alleged officially tolerated practice of disappearances and associated ill-treatment and extrajudicial killing of detainees in the respondent State. The Court for its part considers that these arguments are not in themselves sufficient to compensate for the absence of more persuasive indications that her son did in fact meet his death in custody. As to the applicant's argument that there exists a practice of violation of, inter alia, Article 2, the Court considers that the evidence which she has adduced does not substantiate that claim.

109.   Having regard to the above considerations, the Court is of the opinion that the applicant's assertions that the respondent State failed in its obligation to protect her son's life in the circumstances described fall to be assessed from the standpoint of Article 5 of the Convention.

C.   Article 3 in respect of the applicant's son

110.   The applicant, consonant with her approach to her complaints under Article 2, further alleged that her son had been the victim of breaches by the respondent State of Article 3 of the Convention, which stipulates:

> "No one shall be subjected to torture or to inhuman or degrading treatment or punishment."

111.   Relying, *mutatis mutandis*, on the arguments used to support her complaints under Article 2, she reasoned that the respondent State was in breach of Article 3 of the Convention since the very fact of her son's disappearance in a context devoid of the most basic judicial safeguards must have exposed him to acute psychological torture. In addition, she had seen with her own eyes that he had been beaten by the security forces and this in itself gave rise to a presumption that he was physically tortured subsequent to his detention outside Hasan Kiliç's house.

112.   The applicant maintained that this presumption must be considered even more compelling in view of the existence of a high incidence of torture of detainees in the respondent State. With reference to the materials relied on by her to ground her allegation of a practice of violation of Article 2, she requested the Court to conclude also that her son was the victim of an aggravated violation of Article 3 on account of the existence of an officially tolerated practice of disappearances and ill-treatment of detainees.

113.   She submitted further that the failure of the authorities to provide any satisfactory explanation for her son's disappearance also constituted a violation of Article 3, and that the absence of any adequate investigation into her complaint resulted in a separate breach of that provision.

114.   The Government repudiated the factual basis of the applicant's allegation under Article 3.

115.   Before the Court, the Delegate explained that in the absence of any evidence as to the ill-treatment to which Üzeyir Kurt may have been subjected while in custody the Commission did not find it appropriate to find a violation of that provision. It considered that the applicant's complaints in respect of her son under Article 3 fell, like the Article 2 complaints, to be examined in the context of Article 5 of the Convention.

116.   The Court agrees with the conclusion reached by the Commission on this complaint and refers in this respect to the reasons which have led it to reject the applicant's arguments alleging a violation of Article 2 (see paragraphs 107–09 above). In particular, the applicant has not presented any specific evidence that her son was indeed the victim of ill-treatment in breach of Article 3; nor has she adduced any evidence to substantiate her claim that an officially tolerated practice of disappearances and associated ill-treatment of detainees exists in the respondent State.

117. The Court, like the Commission, considers that the applicant's complaints concerning the alleged violations by the respondent State of Article 3 in respect of her son should, like the Article 2 complaints, be dealt with from the angle of Article 5 of the Convention.

Article 5

118. The applicant submitted that the disappearance of her son gave rise to multiple violations of Article 5 of the Convention, which, to the extent relevant, provides:

"1. Everyone has the right to liberty and security of person. No one shall be deprived of his liberty save in the following cases and in accordance with a procedure prescribed by law:

(a) the lawful detention of a person after conviction by a competent court;

(b) the lawful arrest or detention of a person for non-compliance with the lawful order of a court or in order to secure the fulfilment of any obligation prescribed by law;

(c) the lawful arrest or detention of a person effected for the purpose of bringing him before the competent legal authority on reasonable suspicion of having committed an offence or when it is reasonably considered necessary to prevent his committing an offence or fleeing after having done so;

. . .

2. Everyone who is arrested shall be informed promptly, in a language which he understands, of the reasons for his arrest and of any charge against him.

3. Everyone arrested or detained in accordance with the provisions of paragraph 1(c) of this Article shall be brought promptly before a judge or other officer authorised by law to exercise judicial power and shall be entitled to trial within a reasonable time or to release pending trial. Release may be conditioned by guarantees to appear for trial.

4. Everyone who is deprived of his liberty by arrest or detention shall be entitled to take proceedings by which the lawfulness of his detention shall be decided speedily by a court and his release ordered if the detention is not lawful.

5. Everyone who has been the victim of arrest or detention in contravention of the provisions of this Article shall have an enforceable right to compensation."

. . .

121. The Commission considered that the disappearance of the applicant's son raised fundamental and grave issues under Article 5 having regard to the importance of the guarantees offered by the provision for securing respect for the rights guaranteed by Articles 2 and 3. Having established that Üzeyir Kurt was in the custody of the security forces on 25 November 1993, the Commission reasoned that this finding gave rise to a presumption

of responsibility on the part of the authorities to account for his subsequent fate. The authorities could only rebut this presumption by offering a credible and substantiated explanation for his disappearance and by demonstrating that they had taken effective steps to inquire into his disappearance and ascertain his fate. The Commission concluded that neither of these requirements was satisfied in the circumstances. For these reasons in particular, the Commission found that the unacknowledged detention and subsequent disappearance of Üzeyir Kurt involved a flagrant disregard of the guarantees of Article 5.

122. The Court notes at the outset the fundamental importance of the guarantees contained in Article 5 for securing the right of individuals in a democracy to be free from arbitrary detention at the hands of the authorities. It is precisely for that reason that the Court has repeatedly stressed in its case-law that any deprivation of liberty must not only have been effected in conformity with the substantive and procedural rules of national law but must equally be in keeping with the very purpose of Article 5, namely to protect the individual from arbitrariness.... This insistence on the protection of the individual against any abuse of power is illustrated by the fact that Article 5 § 1 circumscribes the circumstances in which individuals may be lawfully deprived of their liberty, it being stressed that these circumstances must be given a narrow interpretation having regard to the fact that they constitute exceptions to a most basic guarantee of individual freedom....

123. It must also be stressed that the authors of the Convention reinforced the individual's protection against arbitrary deprivation of his or her liberty by guaranteeing a corpus of substantive rights which are intended to minimise the risks of arbitrariness by allowing the act of deprivation of liberty to be amenable to independent judicial scrutiny and by securing the accountability of the authorities for that act. The requirements of Article 5 §§ 3 and 4 with their emphasis on promptitude and judicial control assume particular importance in this context. Prompt judicial intervention may lead to the detection and prevention of life-threatening measures or serious ill-treatment which violate the fundamental guarantees contained in Articles 2 and 3 of the Convention.... What is at stake is both the protection of the physical liberty of individuals as well as their personal security in a context which, in the absence of safeguards, could result in a subversion of the rule of law and place detainees beyond the reach of the most rudimentary forms of legal protection.

124. The Court emphasises in this respect that the unacknowledged detention of an individual is a complete negation of these guarantees and a most grave violation of Article 5. Having assumed control over that individual it is incumbent on the authorities to account for his or her whereabouts. For this reason, Article 5 must be seen as requiring the authorities to take effective measures to safeguard against the risk of disappearance and to conduct a prompt effective investigation into an arguable claim that a person has been taken into custody and has not been seen since.

125. Against that background, the Court recalls that it has accepted the Commission's finding that Üzeyir Kurt was held by soldiers and village guards on the morning of 25 November 1993. His detention at that time was not logged and there exists no official trace of his subsequent whereabouts or fate. That fact in itself must be considered a most serious failing since it enables those responsible for the act of deprivation of liberty to conceal their involvement in a crime, to cover their tracks and to escape accountability for the fate of the detainee. In the view of the Court, the absence of holding data recording such matters as the date, time and location of detention, the name of the detainee as well as the reasons for the detention and the name of the person effecting it must be seen as incompatible with the very purpose of Article 5 of the Convention.

126. Furthermore, the Court considers that having regard to the applicant's insistence that her son was detained in the village the public prosecutor should have been alert to the need to investigate more thoroughly her claim. . . .

. . .

128. Having regard to these considerations, the Court concludes that the authorities have failed to offer any credible and substantiated explanation for the whereabouts and fate of the applicant's son after he was detained in the village and that no meaningful investigation was conducted into the applicant's insistence that he was in detention and that she was concerned for his life. They have failed to discharge their responsibility to account for him and it must be accepted that he has been held in unacknowledged detention in the complete absence of the safeguards contained in Article 5.

129. The Court, accordingly, like the Commission, finds that there has been a particularly grave violation of the right to liberty and security of person guaranteed under Article 5 raising serious concerns about the welfare of Üzeyir Kurt.

IV. Alleged violation of article 3 of the convention in respect of the applicant herself

130. The applicant contended that she herself was the victim of inhuman and degrading treatment on account of her son's disappearance at the hands of the authorities. She requested the Court to find, like the Commission, that the suffering which she has endured engages the responsibility of the respondent State under Article 3 of the Convention.

She invoked in support of her argument the decision of the United Nations Human Rights Committee in the case of Quinteros v. Uruguay of 21 July 1983 . . . affirming that the next-of-kin of disappeared persons must also be considered victims of, inter alia, ill-treatment.

. . .

133. The Court notes that ill-treatment must attain a minimum level of severity if it is to fall within the scope of Article 3. . . . It recalls in this respect that the applicant approached the public prosecutor in the days following her son's disappearance in the definite belief that he had been

taken into custody. She had witnessed his detention in the village with her own eyes and his non-appearance since that last sighting made her fear for his safety, as shown by her petitions of 30 November and 15 December 1993.... However, the public prosecutor gave no serious consideration to her complaint, preferring instead to take at face value the gendarmes' supposition that her son had been kidnapped by the PKK. As a result, she has been left with the anguish of knowing that her son had been detained and that there is a complete absence of official information as to his subsequent fate. This anguish has endured over a prolonged period of time.

134.   Having regard to the circumstances described above as well as to the fact that the complainant was the mother of the victim of a human rights violation and herself the victim of the authorities' complacency in the face of her anguish and distress, the Court finds that the respondent State is in breach of Article 3 in respect of the applicant.

V.   Alleged violation of article 13 of the convention

135.   The applicant, with whom the Commission agreed, asserted that the failure of the authorities to conduct an effective investigation into her son's disappearance gave rise to a breach of Article 13 of the Convention. The Government challenged this contention.

Article 13 provides:

"Everyone whose rights and freedoms as set forth in [the] Convention are violated shall have an effective remedy before a national authority notwithstanding that the violation has been committed by persons acting in an official capacity."

. . .

139.   ... The scope of the obligation under Article 13 varies depending on the nature of the applicant's complaint under the Convention. Nevertheless, the remedy required by Article 13 must be "effective" in practice as well as in law, in particular in the sense that its exercise must not be unjustifiably hindered by the acts or the omissions of the authorities of the respondent State

140.   In the instant case the applicant is complaining that she has been denied an "effective" remedy which would have shed light on the whereabouts of her son. She asserted in her petitions to the public prosecutor that he had been taken into custody and that she was concerned for his life since he had not been seen since 25 November 1993. In the view of the Court, where the relatives of a person have an arguable claim that the latter has disappeared at the hands of the authorities, the notion of an effective remedy for the purposes of Article 13 entails, in addition to the payment of compensation where appropriate, a thorough and effective investigation capable of leading to the identification and punishment of those responsible and including effective access for the relatives to the investigatory procedure.... Seen in these terms, the requirements of Article 13 are broader than a Contracting State's obligation under Article 5 to conduct an effective investigation into the disappearance of a person who

has been shown to be under their control and for whose welfare they are accordingly responsible.

141. For the reasons given earlier (see paragraphs 124 and 126 above), Mrs Kurt can be considered to have had an arguable complaint that her son had been taken into custody. That complaint was never the subject of any serious investigation, being discounted in favour of an unsubstantiated and hastily reached explanation that he had been kidnapped by the PKK. The public prosecutor had a duty under Turkish law to carry out an investigation of allegations of unlawful deprivation of liberty (see paragraph 58 above). The superficial approach which he took to the applicant's insistence that her son had not been seen since being taken into custody cannot be said to be compatible with that duty and was tantamount to undermining the effectiveness of any other remedies that may have existed (see paragraphs 56–61 above).

142. Accordingly, in view in particular of the lack of any meaningful investigation, the Court finds that the applicant was denied an effective remedy in respect of her complaint that her son had disappeared in circumstances engaging the responsibility of the authorities.

There has therefore been a violation of Article 13.

. . .

IX. Alleged administrative practice of violations of the Convention

166. The applicant requested the Court to find that there was a practice of "disappearances" in south-east Turkey which gave rise to aggravated violations of Articles 2, 3 and 5 of the Convention. She highlighted in this regard the reports produced by the United Nations Working Group on Enforced and Involuntary Disappearances, in particular its 1994 report which indicated that the highest number of alleged cases of disappearances reported in 1994 was in Turkey. The applicant further maintained that there was an officially tolerated practice of ineffective remedies in south-east Turkey, in aggravated violation of Article 13 of the Convention. She referred in support of her contention to the fact that there was convincing evidence of a policy of denial of incidents of extra-judicial killing, torture of detainees and disappearances and of a systematic refusal or failure of the prosecuting authorities to conduct investigations into victim's grievances. Having regard to the centrality of the public prosecutor's role in the operation of the system of remedies as a whole it could only be concluded that remedies were wholly ineffective in south-east Turkey and that this result was condoned by the authorities.

. . .

168. The Commission, for its part, found that it was unnecessary to decide whether or not there was a practice of unacknowledged detention in the respondent State as maintained by the applicant. As to the alleged practice of ineffective remedies, the Delegate informed the Court that the Commission had also found it unnecessary to examine this complaint in reaching its admissibility decision.

169.   The Court recalls that it has rejected the applicant's complaints that there exists a practice of violation of Articles 2 and 3 of the Convention, being of the view that she had not substantiated her allegations (see paragraphs 108 and 116 above). It is not persuaded either that the evidence which she has adduced substantiates her allegations as to the existence of a practice of violation of either Article 5 or Article 13 of the Convention.

. . .

■ Partly Dissenting Opinion of JUDGE MATSCHER

While I am conscious of the difficulties which the Commission faces in cases of this type, I consider that in the present case the manner in which it established the facts, which were accepted by the Court, was so superficial and insufficient and the analysis of those facts so clearly unsatisfactory that, in my view, neither provides a sufficiently sound basis for a finding of a violation. Furthermore, a careful study of the summary of the Commission's findings (see paragraphs 45–53 of the judgment) confirms that view, without it being necessary for me to go into detail.

None of the many witnesses heard by the local authorities or by the delegates of the Commission were able to say that the applicant's son had been taken away by the soldiers; the mere fact that the applicant "genuinely and honestly believed" (see paragraph 53) that such was the case does not amount to proof, especially as most of the witnesses said the opposite or declared that they had no personal direct knowledge of what, in this connection, is the crucial issue in the case.

Ultimately, . . . the applicant failed by a large margin to prove the truth of her allegations beyond all reasonable doubt.

. . .

Notes

1.   The applicant in *Kurt v. Turkey* unsuccessfully sought to have the European Court hold that the facts found to have been established constituted violations of Articles 2 and 3 of the European Convention. In view of the fact that the Court found Turkey in breach of Articles 5 and 13, were human rights considerations disserved by the Court's refusal to find a breach of Articles 2 and 3? Were Articles 2 and 3 irrelevant to the Court's conclusions in respect of Article 5? See in particular paras. 121 and 123 of its judgment.

2.   Invoking the approach taken by the Inter–American Court of Human Rights in the *Velásquez Rodríguez* case as well as that of the Human Rights Committee in the case of *Mojica v. Dominican Republic*, the applicant asked the Court to find that Turkey had breached its "positive obligation under Article 2 to protect her son's life." (Para. 101). Did the Court find that Article 2 can never be breached unless the victim's death is established, or that the applicant did not provide sufficient evidence enabling it to conclude that Turkey had breached its affirmative obligation to ensure the right to life?

3. What accounts for the fact that the European Court did not find a breach of Article 2 (right to life) of the European Convention in *Kurt v. Turkey,* while the Inter–American Court found a breach of Article 4 (right to life) of the American Convention in the *Velásquez Rodríguez* case? Did the two Courts apply different substantive legal standards? Different evidentiary standards? Were there differences in the persuasiveness of the evidence marshaled by the applicants in the two cases? If so, does that difference fully account for the different legal conclusions reached by the European and Inter–American courts?

4. Affirming the conclusion of the Commission, the Court found that the applicant had not presented "any specific evidence that her son was indeed the victim of ill-treatment in breach of Article 3" (para. 116). Do you agree? Recall that the applicant testified that she observed the face of Üzeyir Kurt to be bruised and swollen after he had spent one night in the custody of Turkish soldiers. Under these circumstances, is it appropriate to require the applicant to provide further evidence concerning the manner in which the bruises were sustained?

Compare the Court's approach in *Kurt* with its judgment in the case of *Assenov and Others v. Bulgaria*, No. 90/1997/874/1086 (28 Oct. 1998). One of the applicants in the latter case, Mr. Anton Assenov, had suffered injuries while briefly in the custody of Bulgarian police, but the circumstances in which they had been sustained were in dispute. Mr. Assenov had been arrested by an off-duty police officer and taken to a nearby bus station. The parents of Mr. Assenov, who was then 14 years old, came to the station and asked for their son's release. To demonstrate "that he would administer any necessary punishment," Mr. Assenov's father "took a strip of plywood and hit his son." Id., para. 9. According to the applicants, two other police officers who subsequently arrived at the bus station hit Mr. Assenov with truncheons. Mr. Assenov was then taken, along with his father, to the police station where the two were detained for two hours. Mr. Assenov alleges that he was "beaten with a toy pistol and with truncheons and pummelled in the stomach by officers at the police station." Id., para. 9. A forensic medical expert examined Mr. Assenov the following day and issued a certificate stating that he had a "band-like haematoma about 5 cm long and 1 cm wide on the upper outer side of his right arm; three band-like haematomae ... on the right side of his chest; another bruise ... on the left scapula; a haematoma 2 cm. in diameter on the back of the head; and five grazes each about 5 cm long on the right chest." Id., para. 11. Bulgarian authorities maintained that these injuries had been sustained as a result of the beating by Mr. Assenov's father.

The Court found it "impossible to establish on the basis of the evidence before it whether or not the applicant's injuries were caused by the police as he alleged." Id., para. 100. It nonetheless found that Bulgaria was in breach of Article 3 of the European Convention, reasoning "that the medical evidence, Mr Assenov's testimony, the fact that he was detained for two hours at the police station, and the lack of any account from any witness of Mr Ivanov beating his son with sufficient severity to cause the reported bruising, together raise a reasonable suspicion that these injuries may have been caused by the police." Id., para. 101. Following its established case law, the Court concluded:

> 102.   The Court considers that, in these circumstances, where an individual raises an arguable claim that he has been seriously ill-treated by the police or other such agents of the State unlawfully and in breach of Article 3, that provision, read in conjunction with the State's general duty under Article 1 of the Convention to "secure to everyone within their jurisdiction the rights and freedoms in [the] Convention", requires by implication that there should be an effective official investigation. This obligation ... should be capable of leading to the identification and punishment of those responsible. . . .

> 103.   The Court notes that following [the complaint by Mr. Assenov's mother], the State authorities did carry out some investigation into the applicant's allegations. It is not, however, persuaded that this investigation was sufficiently thorough and effective to meet the above requirements of Article 3. . . .

>   . . .

> 106.   Against this background, in view of the lack of a thorough and effective investigation into the applicant's arguable claim that he had been beaten by police officers, the Court finds that here has been a violation of Article 3 of the Convention.

Was the Court's conclusion in *Kurt* consistent with the foregoing analysis? Does this depend upon whether the applicant in *Kurt* reported to Turkish authorities the apparent mistreatment of her son while in military custody? Do other differences, such as the fact that forensic medical evidence was presented by the applicants in the *Assenov* case but not by the applicant in *Kurt,* account for—or justify—the different conclusions reached by the Court with respect to alleged violations of Article 3?

5.   In rejecting the applicant's claim that the Turkish government had breached Article 2 of the European Convention, the European Court stated that, "like the Commission, [it] must carefully scrutinise whether there does in fact exist concrete evidence which would lead it to conclude that [the applicant's] son was, beyond reasonable doubt, killed by the authorities either while in detention in the village or at some subsequent stage." (Paragraph 107.) Is "beyond a reasonable doubt" the appropriate burden of proof for establishing state responsibility before a supranational human rights court? Consider the observation by Judge Pettiti in his dissent: "The majority looked at the case as though it were an international criminal court trying a person suspected of a serious crime (crime) while using the personal conviction ... standard applied in French and Belgian criminal courts. But that type of textbook example concerns the trial of an individual, whose evidence is weighed against that of all the witnesses."

The following analysis places the Court's approach in *Kurt v. Turkey* in a broader perspective:

The [European] Court has ... steered clear of the concept of the burden of proof. In *Ireland v. UK*[17] it indicated that its approach was rather to examine "all the material before it, whether originating from the Commission, the parties or other sources" and, if necessary, to obtain material *proprio motu*. It subsequently refused to accept submissions that the burden of proof should be borne by one or other of the two governments concerned. Accordingly at this stage of the proceedings the applicant does not have the burden of proving the factual basis underlying the admissible complaints. This will have been done to some extent at the Commission stage....

The position is different, however, with injuries sustained during detention.... In effect, where injuries are sustained during a period of police custody, the burden of proving that they were not inflicted by the police shifts to the state.

It has also adopted a flexible approach to the question of standard of proof, preferring, in most cases, to carry out a global assessment of the evidence without reference to any particular standard. In *Ireland v. UK*,[20] however, it accepted that allegations of ill-treatment should be established "beyond reasonable doubt" but added, in response to an argument that the standard was too high, that:

> "Such proof may follow from the coexistence of sufficiently strong, clear and concordant inferences or of similar unrebutted presumptions of fact. In this context, the conduct of the parties when evidence is obtained had to be taken into account."

· · ·

Finally the Court has made it clear that it will rely, as a general rule, on the findings of fact by domestic courts. It has stated that it will not substitute its own assessment of the facts for that of the local courts which have had the benefit of hearing and observing the witness at first hand. Nevertheless it retains a general power to reach its own conclusions where, for example, the assessment of evidence is arbitrary or where the evidence was improperly obtained.

D.J. Harris, M. O'Boyle & C. Warbrick, Law of the European Convention on Human Rights 679–680 (1995). Compare the approach to evidentiary burdens taken by the European Court in *Kurt v. Turkey* with that of the Inter–American Court in the *Velásquez Rodríguez* judgment. Discussing the appropriate standard of proof, the Inter–American Court observed:

> 129.   The Court cannot ignore the special seriousness of finding that a State Party to the [American] Convention has carried out or has tolerated a practice of disappearances in its territory. This requires the Court to apply a standard of proof which considers the seriousness of the charge and which, notwithstanding what has already been said, is

---

17. A 25 para 160 (1978).   **20.** A 25 para 161 (1978).

capable of establishing the truth of the allegations in a convincing manner.

. . .

134.   The international protection of human rights should not be confused with criminal justice. States do not appear before the Court as defendants in a criminal action. The objective of international human rights law is not to punish those individuals who are guilty of violations, but rather to protect the victims and to provide for the reparation of damages resulting from the acts of the States responsible.

135.   In contrast to domestic criminal law, in proceedings to determine human rights violations the State cannot rely on the defense that the complainant has failed to present evidence when it cannot be obtained without the State's cooperation.

In light of its observations in paragraphs 134 and 135, what did the Inter-American Court seem to mean by its observation in paragraph 129 that it "cannot ignore the special seriousness of finding that a State Party . . . has carried out or has tolerated a practice of disappearances"? Did it, like its European counterpart, believe that a comparatively high standard of proof should be applied in respect of the most serious allegations?

6.   What was the legal significance of Kurt's effort, summarized in paragraph 166, to persuade the Court to find that there was a practice of "disappearances" in south-east Turkey?

7.   Some of the European Commission's key factual conclusions in the *Kurt* case, which were affirmed by the European Court, apparently turned in significant measure on the demeanor of the applicant. In light of the importance that the Commission attached to its assessment of her credibility, does the practice of the Human Rights Committee, which relies on written evidence submitted by authors of communications and States Parties, seem an adequate basis for reaching factual conclusions? Does the Committee's comparative dearth of resources justify its relying on written submissions?

8.   The Digest of Strasbourg Case–Law, established by the Netherlands Institute of Human Rights (SIM) in cooperation with the Directorate of Human Rights of the Council of Europe, provides a complete compilation of the Strasbourg organs' case-law, analyzed according to the text of the European Convention on Human Rights and its Protocols. There is also a substantial body of secondary literature on the European Convention and its supervisory machinery. In addition to sources cited above, see, e.g., Francis G. Jacobs and Robin C.A. White, The European Convention on Human Rights (2d ed. 1996); D.J. Harris, M. O'Boyle & C. Warbrick, Law of the European Convention on Human Rights (1995); A.H. Robertson & J.G. Merrills, Human Rights in Europe (3d ed. 1993); Henry G. Schermers, *The European Court of Human Rights After the Merger*, 18 Eur. L. Rev. 493 (1993).

An Estimate of the Impact of the European Convention

D. J. Harris, M. O'Boyle and C. Warbrick, *Law of the European Convention on Human Rights*

29–32 (1995)*

Impact on the protection of human rights in Europe

a. Influence Upon National Law

The Convention has had a considerable effect upon the national law of the contracting parties. It has served as a catalyst for legal change that has furthered the protection of human rights and has, in so doing, assisted in the process of harmonising law in Europe. So far, it has been as an agent of law reform in the context of particular breaches of human rights rather than a means of controlling human rights violations on a grand scale that the Convention has made its mark. Changes in the law have occurred mostly following judgments or decisions in cases to which the state amending its law has been a party. Insofar as a judgment or decision involves a determination that a national law or administrative practice is inconsistent with the Convention, the defendant state is required by international law to change its law or practice in order to comply with its treaty obligation in Article 1 of the Convention to 'secure' the rights and freedoms guaranteed. In compliance with this obligation, the parties to the Convention as a whole have made many changes in their laws and practice following decisions or judgments against them. In a number of cases, a Strasbourg judgment or decision has provided a government with a lever to help overcome local opposition to law reform, as with the change in the law on homosexuality in Northern Ireland following *Dudgeon v UK*. Sometimes, however, it is uncertain whether the steps taken by the defendant state go far enough.[19] In other cases, a state may be slow in putting the necessary measures in place. Thus it took fifteen years before the Isle of Man Tynwald legislated to abolish judicial corporal punishment, thereby bringing the United Kingdom fully into line with its obligations under Article 3 following the *Tyrer* case.[1] Prior to the 1993 legislation, in the context of the special constitutional position of the Isle of Man,[2] the UK government had informed the Manx government after the *Tyrer* case that judicial corporal punishment

---

* Reprinted by permission, © 1995, Reed Elsevier (UK) Ltd.

19. As Churchill and Young, 62 BYIL 283 at 346 (1992) point out, it may be unclear what steps are required by a judgment or decision or whether legislation read *in abstracto* goes far enough.... Legislation intended to comply with a judgment or decision should clearly be interpreted by national courts so as to comply with this objective if possible.

1. [26 Eur. Ct. H.R. (ser. A) (1978).] Belgium took nearly eight years to amend its law to comply with *Marckx v Belgium* [31 Eur. Ct. H.R. (ser. A) (1979).] In *Vermeire v Belgium* [214–C Eur. Ct. H.R. (ser. A) (1991)], it was held that the fact that law reform to comply with *Marckx* was pending was not a defence to an application that arose in the interim challenging the same law. See also Mahoney and Prebensen, *European Supervision*, Ch 26 at p 636.

2. The Isle of Man in a Crown possession that by convention is not subject to the legislative powers of Westminster on most internal matters.

would be contrary to the Convention and the case was brought to the attention of the local courts by the Manx authorities. Although this was considered sufficient by the Committee of Ministers, acting under Article 54, to comply with the *Tyrer* judgment,[3] it would appear that the United Kingdom's obligation to 'secure' the rights and freedoms in the Convention required that it go further and for the relevant law to be amended. The only clear case in which a state has refused point blank to change its law or practice to comply with a judgment or decision is *Brogan v UK*. There the UK informed the Committee of Ministers that it did not feel able to change the prevention of terrorism legislation that had been held to be contrary to Article 5 of the Convention and would make an Article 15 declaration instead. In a number of cases, states have acted to amend their law or practice to bring it into line with the Convention following decisions in cases to which they have not been a party.[6] For example, the Netherlands amended its legislation on children born out of wedlock as a consequence of *Marckx v Belgium*.[7] There have also been instances of a state changing its law in order to comply with the Convention or a Protocol before becoming a party. The Convention's influence upon the law of states that are not parties to a case illustrates the following general point. The real achievement of the Convention system can be said to go beyond the statistical tally of cases and the provision of remedies for individuals. It resides in the deterrent effect of an operational system. States, confronted with a system that works, must keep their law and administrative practices under review. As happens in Whitehall, new legislation must, as far as foreseeable, be 'Strasbourg proofed.' In this way the Convention radiates a constant pressure for the maintenance of human rights standards and for change throughout the new Europe. A judgment of the Court in a case brought by one person may have an impact on 30 or so national jurisdictions. Finally, it may be noted that the Convention has also influenced national law outside of Europe. Its text is echoed in the bills of rights of a number of states that were formerly colonies and the jurisprudence of the Convention organs has been relied upon or cited in the national courts or non-European states.

3.   CM Res DH (78) 39. There was no case in which a sentence of judicial corporal punishment was executed prior to its abolition in 1993. In *Teare v O'Callaghan*, 4 EHRR 232 (1981) a post-*Tyrer* sentence of corporal punishment was quashed by the Isle of Man High Court on the ground that it was contrary to Isle of Man international obligations and should be imposed only if other forms of punishment are unsuitable.

6.   Although, as non-parties, they are not legally bound by the judgment or decision, they are bound to 'secure' the rights protected by the Convention.

7.   [31 Eur. Ct. H.R. (ser. A) (1979).] The Netherlands also amended its laws con-

cerning the time-limit within which a suspect must be brought before a court in the light of the *Brogan* case; see Myjer, NCJM–Bulletin 1989, p 459. The Danish laws on the closed shop was amended following *Young, James and Webster v UK* [44 Eur. Ct. H.R. (ser. A) (1981)]; see Bernhardt, European System, Ch 3 at p. 39, n. 41. France amended its law on interpretation costs because of *Luedicke, Belkacem and Koç v FRG* [29 Eur. Ct. H.R. (ser. A) (1978)]; see French decree no 87–634 of 4 August 1987. For other examples, see Polakiewicz and Jacob–Foltzer, 12 HRLJ 125 (1991).

b. A Remedy for Individuals

As far as individuals who claim to be victims of human rights violations are concerned, the primary effect of the Convention has been to provide a remedy before an international court of justice when all national remedies have failed. 'We will now take our case to Strasbourg' is a familiar refrain that may mean more than just blowing off steam.

One measure of the undoubted value of the Convention remedy from the individual's point of view is the large number of admitted applications that have led to a favourable outcome for the applicant before the Court or the Committee on Ministers or by way of a friendly settlement.[12] Another is the wide variety of cases in which breaches have been found. Most violations have concerned the right to a fair trial. Cases under Article 6 have brought to light many delays in the hearing of cases in breach of the right to 'trial within a reasonable time'. Other common infringements have concerned the rights to an independent and impartial tribunal, to judicial review of executive action, to due process in disciplinary proceedings and to legal aid. The next most problematic guarantee for states has been that of freedom of the person. Many breaches of Article 5 have concerned various aspects of defendants' rights, such as the information required upon arrest, the right to bail, the length of detention on remand and the practice concerning discretionary life sentences. Other cases have involved the preventive detention of terrorists and the detention of the mentally disordered, vagrants, children and deportees. Claims relying upon the right to respect for family life, privacy, etc, in Article 8 have been almost equally successful. It is in this context that the Court has made most use of its 'dynamic' approach to the interpretation of the Convention and the idea that there may be positive obligations upon states, requiring them, for example, to legislate so as to respect the rights of homosexuals and children born out of wedlock in accordance with current social values. Cases under Article 10 have confirmed the fundamental importance attached to freedom of expression, particularly freedom of the press. Several violations of Article 3 have been found, in such diverse areas as the ill-treatment of persons in detention, judicial corporal punishment and extradition to face the death row phenomenon. At the other extreme, the guarantees of freedom from slavery and forced labour (Article 4), the right to free elections (Article 3, First Protocol) and all of the rights in the Fourth and Seventh Protocols have yet to lead to an adverse ruling.

Analysing the Strasbourg case-law from another perspective, the blind-spots revealed by the Convention have varied from one state to another. For example, in the United Kingdom the Convention has thrown a spotlight on prisons, causing an antiquated system of prison administration to be brought up to date. It has also provided checks upon state conduct in such diverse contexts as the Northern Ireland emergency and discretionary

---

12. To date, a breach of at least one article of the Convention has been found by the Court in over two-thirds of the cases that it has decided on the merits.... Note, however, that only 9% of registered applications for which decisions as to admissibility had been taken by the end of 1994 had been declared admissible.

life sentences. In the Netherlands and Sweden, the Convention has high-lighted the absence of judicial control over executive action in such areas as the licensing of commercial activities. In Italy, as well as in a number of other civil law jurisdictions, it has uncovered repeated delays in the administration of justice.

Note: Implementation and Enforcement of the European Social Charter

States Parties implement the European Social Charter (see p. 340 supra) by domestic legislation where the matter is not one "normally left to agreements between employers or employers' organizations and workers' organizations." Article 33. The Charter also provides for international monitoring of compliance by the Contracting Parties (Articles 21 to 29). While Parties undertake to consider themselves bound only by a selected number of the rights enumerated in Part II of the Charter, Member States are required to submit reports responding to detailed questionnaires in relation to both accepted and non-accepted provisions. These responses are initially reviewed by a Committee of Experts, independent specialists on social questions, joined by a representative from the International Labor Organization. The Committee reaches conclusions as to the domestic imple-mentation of accepted Part II provisions, and comments also on those terms that are non-binding in respect of the particular Contracting Party. The Committee then submits its conclusions to the Governmental Commit-tee of the Council of Europe, which presents its findings to the Committee of Ministers. The enforcement procedure, passing through several stages, often results in general recommendations directed at all states rather than criticism of individual states by the Committee of Ministers. This process has been characterized as leading to a "tug of war" between the Committee of Experts, backed by the Parliamentary Assembly, and the Committee of Ministers, "with the former urging the latter to demand more effective compliance by various governments." Thomas Buergenthal, International Human Rights in a Nutshell 156 (1995).

The Revised European Social Charter (1996) takes important steps toward streamlining the Charter's supervisory mechanism. The most im-portant changes strengthen the role and independence of the Committee of Experts by conferring on it, *inter alia*, the power to "assess from a legal standpoint the compliance of national law and practice with the obligations arising from the Charter for the Contracting Parties concerned." Protocol Amending the European Social Charter, Article 2. The Revised Charter also enlarges the Committee of Experts, gives greater powers to the Parliamen-tary Assembly, and makes the entire review process more transparent. The Additional Protocol to the European Social Charter, opened for signature in 1995, provides for collective complaints against alleged violations of the Charter and aims to reduce reliance on information from governments under the system of state reporting. The Additional Protocol also encour-ages the active participation of the Council's social partners as well as certain NGOs by allowing them to report Charter violations directly to the

Committee of Experts in the form of a complaint. These developments have resulted in part from the limited efficacy of the Charter in its original form, from plans of the European Union to create a Social Charter of its own, and from the expansion of the Council of Europe to Eastern European Members. See generally, Wolfgang Strasser, *European Social Charter*, in Encyclopedia of Public International Law, 291–295 (Rudolf Bernhardt ed. 1995).

Note: The European Court of Justice as a Human Rights Tribunal

The Court of Justice of the European Communities (ECJ), sitting in Luxembourg, should not be confused with the European Court of Human Rights, sitting in Strasbourg. The ECJ is the highest judicial organ of the European Union (EU), and the authoritative interpreter of its European Community law. The EU is a supranational system of regional economic and political cooperation whose membership includes 15 Member States (as of July 1, 1999). All the EU Member States are also members of the much larger Council of Europe, under whose auspices the European Court of Human Rights operates. Although all EU Member States are parties to the European Convention, the EU itself is not a party, and the actions of EU institutions are not subject to challenge before the European Court of Human Rights.*

Among its other tasks, the ECJ decides upon the validity of actions taken by other EU institutions, and decides whether actions taken by Member States conflict with Community law. The treaties that form the basis of the EU contain a few express provisions that have a human rights character, such as those regarding freedom of movement of persons, non-discrimination, and voting rights. Although decisions interpreting these provisions represent a small proportion of the ECJ's case law, they have generated substantial jurisprudence in select areas. See, e.g., Case C–379/87, *Groener v. Minister for Educ.*, 1989 E.C.R. I–3967, [1990] 1 C.M.L.R. 401 (1989) (finding that, because promoting Irish as the national language is a legitimate public policy objective, Irish government's requirement that full-time lecturers have proficiency in Irish language does not breach EEC Treaty provision prohibiting national measures that significantly limit number of non-nationals who can qualify for certain posts or related Regulation, even when the proficiency requirement is applied to instructor whose courses would be taught in English).

In response to criticism of the paucity of express human rights protections, the ECJ developed a jurisprudence that restricts the powers of EU institutions and the powers of Member States acting within the sphere of Community law, in order to ensure respect for additional fundamental human rights. "[F]undamental rights form an integral part of the general principles of the law, the observance of which [the ECJ] ensures." Case

---

* The ECJ held in 1996 that the treaty creating the European Community does not confer the power to accede to the European Convention. See *In re the Accession of the* *Community to the European Human Rights Convention*, Opinion 2/94, 1996 E.C.R. I–1759, [1996] 2 C.M.L.R. 265 (1996).

44/79, *Hauer v. Land Rheinland Pfalz*, 1979 E.C.R. 3727, 3744, [1980] 3 C.M.L.R. 42, 64 (1979). Those rights include rights protected by the European Human Rights Convention and other rights derived from the constitutional traditions common to the Member States.

The ECJ has had occasion to recognize such rights as the right to fair hearing, the right to privacy, the right to equality, freedom of religion, freedom of expression, and nonretroactivity of penal laws, as well as economic rights such as the right to property and the right to pursue a trade. Because the ECJ has the authority to interpret Community norms, it is sometimes able to construe a measure narrowly in order to avoid a potential human rights violation. In other cases its invocation of human rights has resulted in the invalidation of an action of an EU institution or a Member State. See, e.g., Case C–49/88, *Al-Jubail Fertilizer Co. v. Council*, 1991 E.C.R. I–3236, [1991] 3 C.M.L.R. 377 (1991) (invalidating regulation imposing antidumping duty without fair hearing); Case 5/88, *Wachauf v. Bundesamt für Ernährung und Forstwirtschaft*, 1989 E.C.R. 2609, [1991] 1 C.M.L.R. 328 (1989) (regulations governing milk production quotas must be implemented in manner that guarantees lessee compensation for value created by his labor upon termination of lease); cf. Case C–260/89, *Elliniki Radiophonia Tileorassi AE v. Dimotiki Etairia Piliroforissis*, 1991 E.C.R. I–2925, [1994] 4 C.M.L.R. 540 (1991) (Community law restricting broadcast monopoly cannot accommodate national policies that violate freedom of expression). And see The European Union and Human Rights (Nanette A. Neuwahl & Allan Rosas eds. 1995); J.H.H. Weiler & Nicolas J.S. Lockhart, *"Taking Rights Seriously" Seriously: The European Court and Its Fundamental Rights Jurisprudence (Parts I & II)*, 32 Comm. Mkt. L. Rev. 51, 579 (1995).

3.   AFRICAN CHARTER ON HUMAN AND PEOPLES' RIGHTS

The African Charter on Human and Peoples' Rights, commonly known as the "Banjul Charter," was adopted in 1981 by the Organization of African Unity (OAU) and entered into force on October 21, 1986. Like the ICCPR, the African Charter provides for only one supervisory body, the African Commission on Human and Peoples' Rights ("African Commission"). In June 1998, the OAU Assembly adopted a Protocol to the Charter on the Establishment of an African Court on Human and Peoples' Rights. The Court will come into existence when 15 states have ratified the Protocol.

The African Commission, which was established in 1987, is an 11-member body whose basic mandate is to "promote human and peoples' rights and ensure their protection in" Africa (Article 30). Pursuant to Article 45 of the Banjul Charter, the Commission's functions are:

1.   To promote Human and Peoples' Rights and in particular;

   a) to collect documents, undertake studies and researches on African problems in the field of human and peoples' rights, organize seminars, symposia and conferences, disseminate information, encourage national and local institutions concerned with human and peoples' rights and, should the case arise, give its views or make recommendations to Governments.

b) to formulate and lay down, principles and rules aimed at solving legal problems relating to human and peoples' rights under conditions laid down by the present Charter.

c) co-operate with other African and international institutions concerned with the promotion and protection of human and peoples' rights.

2.   Ensure the protection of human and peoples' rights under conditions laid down by the present Charter.

3.   Interpret all the provisions of the present Charter at the request of a State party, an institution of the OAU or an African Organization recognized by the OAU.

4.   Perform any other tasks which may be entrusted to it by the Assembly of Heads of State and Government.

Other provisions of the Charter provide for an inter-state complaint procedure (Articles 47–54) and consideration by the Commission of "other communications" (Articles 55–58). Pursuant to Article 58(1), "[w]hen it appears after deliberations of the Commission that one or more communications apparently relate to special cases which reveal the existence of a series of serious or massive violations of human and peoples' rights, the Commission shall draw the attention of the Assembly of Heads of State and Governments to these special cases."

Article 62 requires States Parties to "submit"—presumably to the Commission—biannual reports "on the legislative or other measures taken with a view to giving effect to the rights and freedoms recognized and guaranteed by the present Charter," but does not specify any review process by the Commission. All of the measures taken pursuant to the Charter are to remain confidential "until such a time as the Assembly of Heads of State and Government shall decide otherwise." (Article 59.)

For a variety of reasons, some of which are explored in the following materials, the African Commission has been less visible and, at least until recently, more reluctant to challenge governments than the treaty bodies examined in previous sections. Beginning in the early 1990s, however, it became increasingly active and accessible.

Evelyn A. Ankumah, *The African Commission on Human and Peoples' Rights: Practice and Procedures*

4–9, 23–25, 79 (1996).

. . .

Serious discussions regarding the adoption of a human rights treaty for Africa began as early as in 1961. But it was not until 1979, after many

Africans had suffered at the hands of ruthless rulers that the drafting of the African Charter on Human and Peoples' Rights began. Prior to the adoption of the African Charter there existed and still exists the Charter of the OAU . . ., an inter-governmental organization established for the purposes of bringing together governments of African States so as to provide a better life for the people of Africa. The OAU Charter makes references to the protection of human rights as well as general statements regarding the welfare and well being of Africans. Having been adopted in 1963 in the wake of decolonization, the OAU Charter was definitely concerned with the eradication of colonialism and the dismantling of apartheid. In spite of its expressions on human rights, the OAU Charter did not proclaim individual rights for African people. In practice, the OAU's preoccupation has been political unity, non interference in the internal affairs of OAU Member States, and the liberation of other African territories which were under foreign domination. Thus, the OAU and its Member States have been reluctant to criticize massive and notorious breaches of human rights in specific African States with the notable exception of South Africa and Namibia. . . . Despite strong pressure from NGOs and the international community, the OAU failed to condemn the massacres which occurred in Uganda, the Central African Republic, Equatorial Guinea, [Eritrea], Burundi and Angola to cite only a few examples.

The OAU and its Member States justified their silence by relying on the domestic jurisdiction principle. African leaders adopted a restrictive interpretation of the Universal Declaration and the International Covenants. In their view, the human rights instruments were for the purpose of promoting peaceful and positive international cooperation. . . .

The protection of human rights in post-independent Africa is a controversial subject. Having fought very hard to acquire their independence from colonial powers, African States were preoccupied with maintaining their political sovereignty and territorial integrity. . . .

Notwithstanding the genuine concern of African leaders to maintain their national sovereignty and territorial integrity, the African public, NGOs and the international community were justifiably outraged by the OAU's inaction if not indifference to massive human rights violations in Africa. [Severe criticism of the OAU in Africa and abroad] led to the adoption of Decision 115 . . . at the OAU's 16th Ordinary Session in 1979. Under Decision 115, the OAU Secretary General was entrusted to organize a restricted meeting of highly qualified experts to prepare a preliminary draft of an African Charter on Human and Peoples' Rights. . . .

· · ·

[A first draft was prepared in 1979 in Dakar, Senegal.] The second draft . . . was prepared in Banjul, the Gambia in June 1980 and in January 1981. The second draft was different in some important respects from the first draft. In particular, the preamble . . . no longer refers to co-operation with non African States. Rather it mentions the virtues of African tradition and the values of African civilization. The changes emphasize the regional character of the document. In addition, the Banjul draft stresses the interdependence of civil and political rights and economic, social and cultural rights. Furthermore, the Banjul draft addresses more forcefully the right to development, the elimination of colonialism, neo-colonialism, apartheid, Zionism and of "aggressive foreign military bases."

Another important difference ... relates to the Charter's enforcement. Article 56(3) of the Dakar draft empowered the Chairperson of the Assembly of Heads of States and government to take action in urgent cases in order to protect human and peoples' rights. This power was deleted in the Banjul draft making the decisions of the Assembly non-binding to States Parties. Furthermore, the publicity element, an effective tool in the promotion of human rights, is watered down in the Banjul draft. The Dakar draft provided that the Assembly could publicize reports on violations of human rights upon a decision of one third of its members. However, a decision of a simple majority is now required....

... On June 27, 1981, ... the [Charter] was approved by the OAU Heads of State without amendments....

The African Charter seeks to combine African values with international norms. In other words, it has important similarities with but also significant differences from other international human rights instruments. The Charter guarantees Civil and Political rights. The rights to life, liberty and freedom from torture are recognized by the Charter. Slavery, cruel and inhuman treatment are prohibited.... The civil and political rights guaranteed by the Charter include, equal protection of laws, the right to due process and the freedom from ex post facto laws. The freedoms of conscience, religion, expression, association, assembly and the right to participate in government are enshrined in the Charter. The treaty recognizes the right to asylum and prohibits the mass expulsion of non nationals.

Furthermore, the treaty guarantees economic, social and cultural rights by guaranteeing the right to property, the right to work, the right to equal remuneration for equal work, the right to enjoyment of physical and mental health and the right to education.

Noteworthy too, is the fact that the African Charter departs from recognized international norms and proclaims collective rights and individual duties. The treaty guarantees the rights of people to self determination and to full sovereignty over their natural resources. The list includes the right to peace and the right to a satisfactory environment favourable to a peoples' development. The treaty imposes a duty on individuals towards their family, community and State.

Also, unlike other human rights treaties, the African Charter does not contain a general derogation clause which would permit States to suspend a limited number of rights in times of national crises. Instead, many of the individual rights guaranteed by the Charter contain "clawback" clauses which restrict rights in a very broad sense. For example, Article 9 of the Charter provides that the right to express and disseminate opinions is subject to law and order.

The only enforcement or rather supervisory institution of the Charter is the African Commission on Human and Peoples' Rights. States, individuals and others can submit petitions to the Commission for acts by member States which are in violation of the Charter's provisions. Unlike the European and Inter–American systems, the African Charter does not establish a court not even in an optional protocol. The idea to establish a court was considered by the drafters of the treaty and rejected. The reason being that Africans prefer to settle disputes through negotiation and conciliation rather than the adversarial open confrontation approach. Another reason for rejecting a court is the fear that African States would not want to be subjected to the jurisdiction of a supra-national body. It is important to note that under Article 66, special protocols or agreements may supplement the Charter. These could be used to remedy the omission of a Court.*

The non inclusion of a court coupled with the weaknesses in the substantive and procedural provisions of the Charter discussed below have caused commentators to question whether the African Charter can be used to promote and protect human rights. Perhaps the most pessimistic view is expressed by Makau Wa Mutua. He states: "We cannot and should not, continue to delude ourselves that we have a human rights system. What we have is a facade, a yoke that African States have put around our necks. We must cast it off and reconstruct a system that we can proudly proclaim as ours." In spite of the weaknesses mentioned above, most commentators, including the present author, are more optimistic and believe that the African Commission has potential to become an effective protector of human rights. The potentials are examined throughout the study.

. . .

Inter-state Communications

The procedures for State complaints are covered by Articles 47 through 54 of the African Charter. Under the procedure, if a State has reasonable grounds to believe that another State party has breached its obligations under the charter, the complainant State may write to the respondent State regarding the matter. A copy of the correspondence should be submitted to the Secretary General of the OAU and the Chairperson of the African Commission. This first attempt to settle the dispute between the member States is an effort to resolve disputes through dialogue and negotiation rather than through confrontation. This amicable settlement of disputes is in conformity with international norms which are also consistent with African tradition. In traditional Africa, disputes are resolved with a view to getting at the truth and attaining harmony. Under this approach there are no winners or losers as there would have been in an adversarial system.

---

* [As noted above, in June 1998, the OAU Assembly adopted a Protocol to the Charter that will establish an African Court of Human and Peoples' Rights once 15 states have ratified the Protocol.—Editors' Note.]

If within three months the matter is not resolved satisfactorily by the States involved, either State may submit the matter to the African Commission. Notwithstanding the above procedures, a State party which has reason to believe that another State party has breached any of the principles set forth in the African Charter may bring the matter directly to the attention of the Commission. But even then, the Commission should use all appropriate means to resolve the dispute amicably. The Commission is entrusted to investigate the matter by using any appropriate means. The Commission's ultimate power to address interstate complaints is to prepare a report to the [Assembly of Heads of State and Government (AHSG)] within a reasonable period from the date the Commission is seized of the matter. The report may be accompanied by recommendations from the Commission.

The Commission's powers under the interstate communications procedure are less than those of a judicial body as the Commission cannot enforce its decisions against States....

To date, the Commission has not received communications submitted by a State against another. This is hardly strange, inter-state complaint procedures are hardly used (just as in the European and Inter–American systems) as a mechanism for human rights protection. Therefore one is left with the individual and NGO complaint procedure as the major mechanism for human rights protection....

Individual and NGO Complaints

The African Commission is also mandated to consider other communications. This is the individual and NGO complaint procedure governed by Articles 55 through 59 of the Charter. Under the procedure, individuals and NGOs are entitled to submit a written complaint to the Commission of actions by states parties which are in violation of the principles set forth in the African Charter.... Once a complaint is declared admissible, the Commission is required under the Charter to bring the complaint to the knowledge of the State concerned prior to any substantive consideration.

... Like in the area of inter-State complaints, the Commission does not have the authority to bind States to its decisions. The Commission's findings and recommendations must be sent to the AHSG. In other words, the decisions of the Commission are subject to the approval of the OAU, a political body. This undermines the effectiveness of the Commission. Notwithstanding these limitations, ... the Commission can use its powers of examining complaints to develop an African human rights jurisprudence which can enhance the protection of human rights.

The Charter provides in Article 59(1) that all measures taken by the Commission in the examination of complaints should remain confidential until the AHSG decides otherwise. Article 59(2) provides that the Chairperson of the Commission is entitled to publish the activities of the Commission after it has been considered by the AHSG. The African Commission has so far interpreted the concept of confidentiality restrictively. This is problematic as publicity can have a major deterrent effect in preventing future human rights abuses. However, ... some important developments have been made in the area of publicity....

The State Reporting Procedure

. . .

Article 62 of the African Charter calls upon States parties to submit every two years a report on the legislative or other measures they have taken to give effect to the rights and freedoms recognized by the Charter. The Charter however does not specify where States should submit their reports. The mandate of the African Commission ... does not authorize the Commission to examine State reports. However, as the body entrusted to supervise the implementation of the African Charter, it would seem that it is the Commission's task to examine State reports. To fill the lacuna, the Commission, at its third session sought and later received authorization from the OAU General Assembly to examine State reports.

. . .

The reporting procedure is a non adversarial proceeding. It is an effort to persuade States to implement their human rights obligations. While the Sate reporting procedure is not a mechanism for examining and remedying specific violations of human rights, it provides a forum for constructive dialogue between the African Commission and States parties, and enables a treaty body to monitor States' implementation of a human rights convention.

. . .

Examination of the reports takes place in a public forum in the presence of NGOs and members of the African civil society and can have a tremendous impact on the protection of human rights. The Commission examines reports of States that send their representatives to discuss their reports with the Commission. While only members of the Commission may put questions to the State representative who presents the report, the fact that the examination occurs in a public rather than a private forum subjects the State under review to public scrutiny and could effect some positive changes....

Notes

1. Limitations on the authority and powers of the African Commission were a major factor inspiring efforts to establish an African Court. Consider the following criticism of the Commission:

> The secrecy and bureaucratic procedures provided for under Articles 58 and 59 of the Charter [are] a complete negation of the expectations of victims. These provisions do not mandate the Commission to take any action nor provide for interim measures to protect victims. Even in cases of emergency, what is required is that a report be made by the Commission to the Assembly of Heads of State and Government. The latter may then request an in-depth study to be conducted. Assuming

the Commission had adequate funding for such studies, an in-depth study takes considerable time and effort. Almost all Commissioners have full-time jobs and they can hardly devote time for such studies. Furthermore, the matter seems to end with the in-depth study.

Dr. Philip K.A. Amoah, *The African Charter on Human and Peoples' Rights: A Decade of Achievement in Securing Human Rights for Africans?*, Africa Legal Aid Q. 21, 23–24 (July–Sept. 1996).

2. As noted in the Ankumah excerpt and reflected in the preceding note, human rights activists have long been critical of the confidentiality mandated by Article 59 of the African Charter. In recent years, the Commission has taken steps to overcome these constraints:

> In the past, the Commission has interpreted "confidentiality" to mean secrecy and lack of transparency. Recently, a remarkable inroad has been made into the principle of confidentiality. In its 7th and 8th Annual Activity Reports, the Commission has started publishing its decisions regarding the over 150 individual communications that have been submitted to it.

Amoah, supra, at 24.

3. In the view of Amnesty International (AI), "a significant draw-back to the effectiveness and credibility of the African Commission is the perceived lack of independence and impartiality of some of its members." In the past, "there have been two instances when Commissioners have also held the posts of Attorney General and Minister of the Interior respectively, at the same time as serving on the African commission." Amnesty International, Organization of African Unity: Making Human Rights a Reality for Africans, AI Index: IOR 63/01/98, p. 6 (August 1998).

4. Like other human rights treaty bodies, the African Commission has encountered chronic failures by States Parties to meet their reporting obligations in a timely fashion. As noted earlier, States Parties are supposed to submit reports on the legislative and other measures taken to give effect to the Charter every two years. As of June 1998, 200 reports were overdue. Eighteen states had not yet submitted their first reports, which were due eleven years earlier. Some states have failed to attend sessions at which they were scheduled to present their reports to the Commission. See Amnesty International, Organization of African Unity: Making Human Rights a Reality for Africans, AI Index: IOR 63/01/98, p. 12 and n.34 (August 1998).

5. As the preceding materials reflect, a principal weakness in the supervisory machinery established by the African Charter is the subordination of the Commission to the Assembly of Heads of State and Government. This aspect of the Charter is not unique among human rights treaties. Implementation of the Framework Convention for the Protection of National Minorities, which was adopted by the Council of Europe in 1994 and entered into force in 1998, is monitored by the Council's Committee of Ministers (Article 24(1)). The Committee of Ministers comprises the Ministers of Foreign Affairs of the member states of the Council of Europe. The

Committee of Ministers is assisted by an Advisory Committee of experts (Article 26(1)), but the latter is subordinate to the former. The Advisory Committee considers reports submitted by States Parties and transmits its opinions to the Committee of Ministers. The Advisory Committee's "opinion ... concerning the report of a Party" is to be made public only when the Committee of Ministers publishes its own conclusions and recommendations (if any) in respect of the State Party concerned "unless in a specific case the Committee of Ministers decides otherwise." Resolution (97) 10, Rules Adopted by the Committee of Ministers on the Monitoring Arrangements under Articles 24 to 27 of the Framework Convention for the Protection of National Minorities, Rules 24 and 26.

C. INTERNATIONAL CRIMINAL LAW

As the preceding materials in Part III reflect, postwar human rights law establishes obligations that are, for the most part, imposed upon and borne by states. We have seen, for example, that when a supervisory body concludes that a treaty obligation has been violated, it has established *state* responsibility for that breach. This is true even when the principal act that infringed a protected right was committed by a private person acting in his individual capacity. Recall, for example, the case of *A. v. United Kingdom*, which involved physical punishment of a child by his stepfather. (See Section B(2) above.) Although the injury suffered by A. was inflicted by a non-state actor, it was the United Kingdom that was found in breach of the European Convention on the Protection of Human Rights and Fundamental Freedoms by virtue of deficiencies in British law.

But while international law typically imposes human rights responsibilities upon states, it also imposes some obligations directly upon individuals, making them liable to criminal punishment. This principle of "individual responsibility" was recognized and enforced in the Trial of Major War Criminals at Nuremberg and in other postwar prosecutions. More recently, two international criminal tribunals established by the UN Security Council have conducted trials of individuals alleged to be responsible for serious violations of international humanitarian law committed in the former Yugoslavia and Rwanda, respectively. Building on the momentum generated by these two tribunals, a Diplomatic Conference in Rome adopted a statute for a permanent international criminal court in July 1998.

The following section explores core concepts underlying the jurisdiction of and substantive law enforced by these tribunals. The materials set forth below emphasize one of the central issues raised by direct enforcement of international criminal law (as distinguished from enforcement of national criminal law enacted in compliance or in conformity with international law)—whether, or under what circumstances, such efforts breach the prohibition of retroactive punishment.

We next consider enforcement of international criminal law by national courts. In sub-section 2, we examine two distinct aspects of national enforcement. First, we consider emerging standards of international law that require states, under some circumstances, to investigate, prosecute and punish those responsible for certain human rights violations. These materials focus on one of the most pressing human rights policy debates of our time: In light of these emerging standards, may states adopt amnesty laws covering past atrocities as a means of consolidating a transition to democracy or promoting national reconciliation? If so, under what conditions?

Second, we consider international law governing prosecutions by national courts of human rights abuses committed in the territory of another state. Rarely used in the past, universal jurisdiction is increasingly invoked by national courts to prosecute such crimes as genocide, war crimes and crimes against humanity.

1. INTERNATIONAL CRIMINAL TRIBUNALS

Nuremberg

Even before World War II came to an end, the Allied Powers made plans for prosecuting the leading Nazi war criminals. In October 1943, the Allies established the United Nations Commission for the Investigation of War Crimes. Later that month the United Kingdom, the United States and the Soviet Union issued the Moscow Declaration, which stated that German war criminals should be judged and punished in the countries in which their crimes were committed except that "the major criminals, whose offences have no particular geographical localization," would be punished "by the joint decision of the Governments of the Allies." Meeting in London in August 1945, representatives of the United States, the United Kingdom, France and the Soviet Union concluded an agreement providing for the establishment of the International Military Tribunal ("IMT") in Nuremberg to try the leading Nazi war criminals. The Charter of the IMT was annexed to the London Agreement, to which nineteen other governments expressed their adherence.

Charter of the International Military Tribunal

. . .

Article 1. In pursuance of the Agreement signed on 8 August 1945, . . . there shall be established an International Military Tribunal (hereinafter called "the Tribunal") for the just and prompt trial and punishment of the major war criminals of the European Axis.

. . .

Art. 6. The Tribunal established by the Agreement referred to in Article 1 hereof for the trial and punishment of the major war criminals of the European Axis countries shall have the power to try and punish persons who, acting in the interests of the European Axis countries, whether as individuals or as members of organizations, committed any of the following crimes.

The following acts, or any of them, are crimes coming within the jurisdiction of the Tribunal for which there shall be individual responsibility:

(a) *Crimes against peace:* namely, planning, preparation, initiation or waging of a war of aggression, or a war in violation of international treaties, agreements or assurances, or participation in a common plan or conspiracy for the accomplishment of any of the foregoing;

(b) *War crimes:* namely, violations of the laws or customs of war. Such violations shall include, but not be limited to, murder, ill-treatment or deportation to slave labour or for any other purpose of civilian population of or in occupied territory, murder or ill-treatment of prisoners of war or persons on the seas, killing of hostages, plunder of public or private property, wanton destruction of cities, towns or villages, or devastation not justified by military necessity;

(c) *Crimes against humanity:* namely, murder, extermination, enslavement, deportation, and other inhumane acts committed against any civilian population, before or during the war, or persecutions on political, racial or religious grounds in execution of or in connection with any crime within the jurisdiction of the Tribunal, whether or not in violation of the domestic law of the country where perpetrated.

Leaders, organizers, instigators and accomplices participating in the formulation or execution of a common plan or conspiracy to commit any of the foregoing crimes are responsible for all acts performed by any persons in execution of such plan.

Art. 7.   The official position of defendants, whether as Heads of State or responsible officials in Government Departments, shall not be considered as freeing them from responsibility or mitigating punishment.

Art. 8.   The fact that the Defendant acted pursuant to order of his Government or a superior shall not free him from responsibility, but may be considered in mitigation of punishment if the Tribunal determines that justice so requires.

. . .

Diane F. Orentlicher, *Genocide and Crimes Against Humanity: The Legal Regime*

(1998).

. . .

Article 6 of the Charter gave the Nuremberg Tribunal jurisdiction over ... crimes against peace—in essence the crime of aggressive war; war crimes, that is serious violations of the laws or customs of war; and crimes against humanity. Each of these categories presented its own issues of retroactivity, but neither of the first two categories—crimes against peace and war crimes—challenged international law's bedrock principle of state sovereignty in the way that crimes against humanity did. The first two crimes by definition concerned interstate relations—specifically, war between states. In contrast, the category of crimes against humanity included atrocities committed by Nazis against Germans, notably including German Jews, who would not be covered by the humanitarian protections of the laws of war.

To the extent that crimes against humanity included conduct by Germans against other Germans within Germany, they represented a radical innovation in international law. How a government treated its own citizens was, with some exceptions, considered by international law to be a matter of sovereign prerogative and surely not the business of other states.

How, then, did the Allies justify this encroachment on state sovereignty? The answer has two parts: The first addresses the political impetus behind the Allies' decision to criminalize atrocities even when they were committed by state authorities against their own nationals. The second concerns the way the Allies legally rationalized their decision to do so.

The political impetus was essentially a moral impulse. In the course of the second World War it became clear that some of the worst atrocities of Hitler's Germany did not fall within the province of classical war crimes. Yet as the Allies turned their thoughts to the question of how to punish Nazi criminals once the war was over, it soon became plain that it would be intolerable not to address these atrocities. In 1944 Henry Stimson, the United States Secretary of War, asked Colonel Murray Bernays, then head of the Special Projects Office of the Defense Department, to prepare a memorandum on how to punish Nazi criminals once the war was over. In his memorandum, Bernays observed that many of the worst Nazi practices could not be classified as war crimes, and remarked that "to let these brutalities go unpunished will leave millions of persons frustrated and disillusioned." Further, he observed, both the United States and United Kingdom were under pressure . . . to ensure that [these atrocities] should be punished.

.   .   .

By 1945 the Allies resolved to establish a new category of crimes. . . .

Several aspects of [Article 6(c) of the Nuremberg Charter] represented a profound rupture with international law's longstanding deference to what had been regarded the province of sovereign prerogative. First, the phrase "against any civilian population" would include Germans who suffered inhumane acts at the hands of German authorities. Further, the phrase "before or during the war" seemed to signify that the Nuremberg tribunal could concern itself with a government's treatment of its own citizens even in peacetime, at least in some circumstances. That it could do so "whether or not" the conduct was "in violation of the domestic law of the country where perpetrated" represented yet another major encroachment on sovereign authority. It seemed as though international society had been so deeply shaken by Hitler's atrocities that it could no longer bear to respect the principles of law that it had shaped long before.

And yet. At least with respect to the Trial of Major War Criminals ..., the Allied states were not yet prepared to endorse so radical a reversal of established doctrine.... Article 6(c) of the Nuremberg Charter gave the Tribunal power to punish crimes against humanity only when they were committed "in execution of or in connection with any crime within the jurisdiction of the Tribunal"—that is, when linked to either war crimes or crimes against peace.

This nexus requirement provided the principal legal rationalization for what would otherwise be an extreme assault on the citadel of state sovereignty. The Tribunal took this limitation very seriously indeed; in fact, most of the conduct supporting convictions on the charge of crimes against humanity also constituted conventional war crimes. In the view of legal experts writing shortly after the Nuremberg trials, the Tribunal treated crimes against humanity largely as "a subsidiary or accessory to the traditional types of war crimes,"[11] applicable mainly where a crime was not specifically covered by what was then the most important codified source of humanitarian law, the Hague Regulations of 1907.

. . .

———

As the preceding selection notes, by including crimes against humanity in the jurisdiction of the IMT the Nuremberg Charter departed from international law's longstanding approach to violations of individual rights within sovereign states: With few exceptions, they had been considered a matter of "domestic jurisdiction" and therefore outside the domain of international regulation. An even greater innovation was the Charter's claim that individuals could be criminally prosecuted under the authority of international law for conduct set forth in Article 6. In a trial lasting nine and one-half months, 22 leading Nazi figures were prosecuted before the IMT. Nineteen were convicted on charges under the Tribunal's jurisdiction; twelve were sentenced to death.

This central feature of the Nuremberg prosecution—the principle of individual responsibility—inevitably raised issues of retroactivity. In the following excerpt of the IMT's Judgment, consider whether the Tribunal effectively addressed this charge, particularly with respect to its jurisdiction over crimes against humanity.

Nazi Conspiracy and Aggression, Opinion and Judgment

Nuremberg Tribunal, 1946.
Reprinted in 41 Am. J. Int'l L. 172 (1947).

. . .

11. Egon Schwelb, *Crimes Against Humanity*, 23 Brit. Y.B. Int'l L. 178, 207 (1946).

(E) The Law of the Charter

The jurisdiction of the Tribunal is defined in the Agreement and Charter, and the crimes coming within the jurisdiction of the Tribunal, for which there shall be individual responsibility, are set out in Article 6. The law of the Charter is decisive, and binding on the Tribunal.

. . . The Charter is not an arbitrary exercise of power on the part of the victorious nations, but in the view of the Tribunal, . . . it is the expression of international law existing at the time of its creation; and to that extent is itself a contribution to international law.

. . .

The Charter makes the planning or waging of a war of aggression or a war in violation of international treaties a crime; and it is therefore not strictly necessary to consider whether and to what extent aggressive war was a crime before the execution of the London Agreement. But in view of the great importance of the questions of law involved, the Tribunal has heard full argument from the prosecution and the defense, and will express its view on the matter.

It was urged on behalf of the defendants that a fundamental principle of law—international and domestic—is that there can be no punishment of crime without a preexisting law. *"Nullum crimen sine lege, nulla poena sine lege."* It was submitted that *ex post facto* punishment is abhorrent to the law of all civilized nations, that no sovereign power had made aggressive war a crime at the time the alleged criminal acts were committed, that no statute had defined aggressive war, that no penalty had been fixed for its commission, and no court had been created to try and punish offenders.

In the first place, it is to be observed that the maxim *nullum crimen sine lege* is not a limitation on sovereignty, but is in general a principle of justice. To assert that it is unjust to punish those who in defiance of treaties and assurances have attacked neighboring states without warning is obviously untrue, for in such circumstances the attacker must know that he is doing wrong, and so far from it being unjust to punish him, it would be unjust if his wrong were allowed to go unpunished. Occupying the positions they did in the government of German, the defendants, or at least some of them must have known of the treaties signed by Germany, outlawing recourse to war for the settlement of international disputes; they must have known that they were acting in defiance of all international law when in complete deliberation they carried out their designs of invasion and aggression. On this view of the case alone, it would appear that the maxim has no application to the present facts.

[The Tribunal then considered the "state of international law in 1939, so far as aggressive war is concerned," focusing on the Kellogg–Briand Pact of 1928, to which German was a party.]

The question is, what was the legal effect of this pact? The nations who signed the pact or adhered to it unconditionally condemned recourse to war for the future as an instrument of policy, and expressly renounced it. After the signing of the pact, any nation resorting to war as an instrument of national policy breaks the pact. In the opinion of the Tribunal, the solemn renunciation of war as an instrument of national policy necessarily involves the proposition that such a war is illegal in international law; and that those who plan and wage such a war, with its inevitable and terrible consequences, are committing a crime in so doing. . . .

But it is argued that the pact does not expressly enact that such wars are crimes, or set up courts to try those who make such wars. To that extent the same is true with regard to the laws of war contained in the Hague Convention. The Hague Convention of 1907 prohibited resort to certain methods of waging war. These included the inhumane treatment of prisoners, the employment of poisoned weapons, the improper use of flags of truce, and similar matters. Many of these prohibitions had been enforced long before the date of the Convention; but since 1907 they have certainly been crimes, punishable as offenses against the laws of war; yet the Hague Convention nowhere designates such practices as criminal, nor is any sentence prescribed, nor any mention made of a court to try and punish offenders. For many years past, however, military tribunals have tried and punished individuals guilty of violating the rules of land warfare laid down by this Convention. In the opinion of the Tribunal, those who wage aggressive war are doing that which is equally illegal, and of much greater moment than a breach of one of the rules of the Hague Convention. In interpreting the words of the pact, it must be remembered that international law is not the product of an international legislature, and that such international agreements as the Pact of Paris have to deal with general principles of law, and not with administrative matters of procedure. The law of war is to be found not only in treaties, but in the customs and practices of states which gradually obtained universal recognition, and from the general principles of justice applied by jurists and practiced by military courts. This law is not static, but by continual adaptation follows the needs of a changing world. Indeed, in many cases treaties do no more than express and define for more accurate reference the principles of law already existing.

The view which the Tribunal takes of the true interpretation of the pact is supported by the international history which preceded it. [The Tribunal then reviewed various instruments condemning aggressive war as an international crime; the instruments cited were either declarations, draft treaties or treaties that were not ratified.]

All these expressions of opinion . . ., so solemnly made, reinforce the construction which the Tribunal placed upon the Pact of Paris, that resort to a war of aggression is not merely illegal, but is criminal. . . .

It is also important to remember that Article 227 of the Treaty of Versailles provided for the constitution of a special tribunal, composed of representatives of five of the Allied and Associated Powers which had been belligerents in the First World War opposed to Germany, to try the former German Emperor "for a supreme offence against international morality and the sanctity of treaties." The purpose of this trial was expressed to be "to vindicate the solemn obligations of international undertakings, and the validity of international morality." In Article 228 of the Treaty, the German Government expressly recognized the right of the Allied Powers "to bring before military tribunals persons accused of having committed acts in violation of the laws and customs of war."

It was submitted that international law is concerned with the actions of sovereign States, and provides no punishment for individuals; and further, that where the act in question is an act of State, those who carry it out are not personally responsible, but are protected by the doctrine of the sovereignty of the State. In the opinion of the Tribunal, both these submissions must be rejected. That international law imposes duties and liabilities upon individuals as well as upon states has long been recognized. In the recent case of Ex parte Quirin (1942 317 U.S. 1), before the Supreme Court of the United States, persons were charged during the war with landing in the United States for purposes of spying and sabotage. The late Chief Justice Stone, speaking for the court, said:

> "From the very beginning of its history this Court has applied the law of war as including that part of the law of nations which prescribes for the conduct of war, the status, rights, and duties of enemy nations as well as enemy individuals."

He went on to give a list of cases tried by the courts, where individual offenders were charged with offences against the laws of nations, and particularly the laws of war. Many other authorities could be cited, but enough has been said to show that individuals can be punished for violations of international law. Crimes against international law are committed by men, not by abstract entities, and only by punishing individuals who commit such crimes can the provisions of international law be enforced.

. . .

(F) The Law Relating to War Crimes and Crimes Against Humanity

. . .

The Tribunal is of course bound by the Charter, in the definition which it gives both of war crimes and crimes against humanity. . . .

. . .

With regard to crimes against humanity, there is no doubt whatever that political opponents were murdered in Germany before the war, and that many of them were kept in concentration camps in circumstances of great horror and cruelty. The policy of terror was certainly carried out on a vast scale, and in many cases was organized and systematic. The policy of persecution, repression, and murder of civilians in Germany before the war of 1939, who were likely to be hostile to the Government, was most ruthlessly carried out. The persecution of Jews during the same period is established beyond all doubt. To constitute crimes against humanity, the acts relied on before the outbreak of war must have been in execution of, or in connection with, any crime within the jurisdiction of the Tribunal. The Tribunal is of the opinion that revolting and horrible as many of these crimes were, it has not been satisfactorily proved that they were done in execution of, or in connection with, any such crime. The Tribunal therefore cannot make a general declaration that the acts before 1939 were crimes against humanity within the meaning of the Charter, but from the beginning of the war in 1939 war crimes were committed on a vast scale, which were also crimes against humanity; and insofar as the inhuman acts charged in the indictment, and committed after the beginning of the war, did not constitute war crimes, they were all committed in execution of, or in connection with, the aggressive war, and therefore constituted crimes against humanity.

. . .

Notes

1. At the outset of its response to the charge of retroactivity, the IMT observed: "In the first place, it is to be observed that the maxim *nullum crimen sine lege* is not a limitation on sovereignty, but is in general a principle of justice." What did the Tribunal mean by this?

2. How effectively did the Tribunal counter charges that, in prosecuting defendants for crimes against peace, the Allies violated the "fundamental principle . . . that there can be no punishment of crime without a preexisting law"? Note that the statement of this principle set forth in Article 15(1) of the ICCPR, which is the most important contemporary human rights norm concerning retroactivity, makes clear that the "preexisting law" must be *criminal law*. Article 15 provides in pertinent part:

> 1. No one shall be held guilty of any criminal offense on account of any act or omission which did not constitute a criminal offence, under national or international law, at the time when it was committed. . . .
>
> 2. Nothing in this article shall prejudice the trial and punishment of any person for any act or omission which, at the time when it was committed, was criminal according to the general principles of law recognized by the community of nations.

If the standard embodied in Article 15 of the ICCPR had governed the IMT proceedings, would the following observation by the Tribunal be a satisfactory response to the charge of retroactivity?:

> In the opinion of the Tribunal, the solemn renunciation of war as an instrument of national policy necessarily involves the proposition that such a war is illegal in international law; and that those who plan and wage such a war . . . are committing a crime in so doing.

How did the Tribunal respond to the defendants' claim that the Kellogg–Briand Pact, pursuant to which Germany and other states renounced recourse to war as an instrument of policy, did "not expressly enact that such wars are crimes"? Was its response persuasive? How much of the Tribunal's analysis turns on the fact that the defendants prosecuted before it were senior officials? Is the IMT's reasoning equally relevant to soldiers?

3. How effectively did the Tribunal justify its conclusion that war crimes charges did not violate the *nullum crimen* principle? Does the fact that states had prosecuted violations of the 1907 Hague Regulations *before national courts* by itself mean that those same breaches constituted crimes under *international law*? Would this fact be relevant in applying the standard set forth in Article 15 of the ICCPR (see Note 2, above)?

4. The IMT's response to charges of retroactivity focused in particular on the crime of waging aggressive war and also addressed war crimes charges. Does the Tribunal's analysis shed light on the question whether prosecuting defendants for crimes against humanity violated the principle of *nullum crimen sine lege*, or did the Tribunal simply fail to address the issue?

5. In addition to the IMT, a tribunal was established in Tokyo to prosecute senior Japanese officials. Its charter was based upon but not identical to the Nuremberg Charter. See Charter of the International Military Tribunal for the Far East, Special Proclamation by the Supreme Commander for the Allied Powers at Tokyo, Charter dated Jan. 19, 1946, amended Charter dated Apr. 26, 1946, T.I.A.S. 1589, 4 Bevans 20. The Tokyo Tribunal was established by an executive order of General Douglas MacArthur, the Supreme Allied Commander for Japan following the war, rather than through a multilateral treaty. General MacArthur also personally selected the Tokyo Tribunal's judges and prosecutor.

Other postwar prosecutions in German were undertaken pursuant to Control Council Law No. 10, which was adopted by the Allied Powers on December 20, 1945. This law delegated to each power occupying vanquished Germany the right to arrest suspected war criminals and initiate prosecutions in its respective zone of occupation. Pursuant to this law, U.S. Military Tribunals in Nuremberg tried 185 defendants in twelve trials. The defendants had held important positions in the German High Command, government ministries, private industry, the Gestapo, the SS or other organizations. Additional postwar prosecutions were undertaken before courts of various countries that had been occupied by German forces during the war and, eventually, before national courts in Germany.

6. A much-debated issue relating to crimes against humanity is whether the requirement of a nexus to war crimes or crimes against peace was an element of the crime as it was defined in customary international law during World War II, or merely a jurisdictional limitation imposed by the Nuremberg Charter. Does the IMT Judgment shed any light on this question?

The jurisdictional provisions of Control Council Law No. 10 (see note 5, supra) were modeled on Article 6 of the Nuremberg Charter, but there was no explicit nexus requirement in its definition of crimes against humanity. Article II(1)(c) of Control Council Law No. 10 defined crimes against humanity as:

> Atrocities and offences, including but not limited to murder, extermination, enslavement, deportation, imprisonment, torture, rape or other inhumane acts committed against any civilian population, or persecu-

tions on political, racial or religious grounds whether or not in violation of the domestic laws of the country where perpetrated.

This phrasing suggests that crimes against humanity could be proved
under Control Council Law No. 10 regardless of whether they were connected to crimes against peace or war crimes, and the judgments in two
cases prosecuted before U.S. Military Tribunals supported this interpretation. But two other U.S. Military Tribunals concluded that they had no
jurisdiction over conduct charged as crimes against humanity that occurred
before the war. One basis for this interpretation was that Article I of
Control Council Law No. 10 provided that the Nuremberg Charter was an
integral part of that law. See Diane F. Orentlicher, *Settling Accounts: The
Duty to Prosecute Human Rights Violations of a Prior Regime*, 100 Yale L.J.
2537, 2589 & n. 231 (1991).

Contemporary International Tribunals

Many of the individuals involved in the Nuremberg prosecution hoped
that it would lay the foundation for a permanent international criminal
court. Although there was significant interest in pursuing this possibility in
the immediate aftermath of World War II, the political will to establish
such a court dissipated as Cold War tensions set in. Half a century would
pass before states would once again cooperate to create a tribunal with
jurisdiction over international crimes.

In the meantime, the Nuremberg precedent—in particular, its recognition and punishment of crimes against humanity—provided the foundation
for much of the postwar law of human rights. Further, in the immediate
aftermath of the Nuremberg trial the United Nations took steps to affirm
the law generated by Nuremberg. On December 11, 1946, the UN General
Assembly unanimously adopted a resolution affirming "the principles of
international law recognized by the Charter of the Nürnberg Tribunal and
the judgment of the Tribunal" and directing the Committee on the codification of international law to treat as a matter of primary importance plans
for the formulation of those principles. G.A. Res. 95(I), U.N. Doc. A/64/
Add.1, at 188 (1946). Pursuant to this resolution, the International Law
Commission adopted its formulation of the Nuremberg Principles in 1950.
See Report of the International Law Commission to the General Assembly,
5 U.N. GAOR Supp. (No. 12) at 11–14, U.N. Doc. A/1316 (1950). Thus, if
the Nuremberg prosecution raised questions of retroactivity, future prosecutions based squarely upon the Nuremberg precedent would be founded
on established law.

Beyond these measures, several conventions were drafted to codify and
further develop Nuremberg's substantive law. Notably, these treaties reflected Nuremberg's central premise that crimes against the basic code of
humanity warrant criminal punishment. The four Geneva Conventions of
1949, which further develop the law of armed conflict encompassed in
Article 6(b) of the Nuremberg Charter, identify certain violations as "grave
breaches." These include such acts as "wilful killing, torture or inhuman
treatment, including biological experiments, wilfully causing great suffering

or serious injury to body or health, unlawful deportation or transfer or unlawful confinement. . . ." Geneva Convention Relative to the Protection of Civilian Persons in Time of War, adopted Aug. 12, 1949, art. 147, 6 U.S.T. 3516, T.I.A.S. No. 3365, 75 U.N.T.S. 287. All four Geneva Conventions require High Contracting Parties to "enact any legislation necessary to provide effective penal sanctions for persons committing, or ordering to be committed, any of the grave breaches" of those conventions, e.g., id., art. 146, and further provide:

> Each High Contracting Party shall be under the obligation to search for persons alleged to have committed, or to have ordered to be committed, such grave breaches, and shall bring such persons, regardless of their nationality, before its own courts. It may also, if it prefers, . . . hand such persons over for trial to another High Contracting Party concerned, provided such High Contracting Party has made out a *prima facie* case.

Id. According to the Commentary to the Geneva Conventions prepared under the auspices of the International Committee of the Red Cross, these provisions do "not exclude handing over the accused to an international criminal court whose competence has been recognized by the Contracting Parties." Commentary to Geneva Convention IV 593 (Jean S. Pictet, ed. 1958).

While the Geneva Conventions of 1949 developed the law of armed conflict, the Genocide Convention of 1948 developed an important part of the law of crimes against humanity. The role of criminal punishment figures prominently in this convention. In Article I, Contracting Parties "confirm that genocide . . . is a crime under international law which they undertake to prevent and punish," while Article IV provides that persons "committing genocide . . . shall be punished, whether they are constitutionally responsible rulers, public officials or private individuals." Article VI identifies the courts that should try cases of genocide:

> Persons charged with genocide [or other forms of criminal participation in genocide] shall be tried by a competent tribunal of the State in the territory of which the act was committed, or by such international penal tribunal as may have jurisdiction with respect to those Contracting Parties which shall have accepted its jurisdiction.

Although this provision contemplated the creation of an "international penal tribunal," another half century passed before an international criminal court with jurisdiction over genocide and other international crimes was established. Atrocities committed during successive conflicts in the former Yugoslavia beginning in 1991 provided the impetus for the Security Council to establish the International Criminal Tribunal for the Prosecution of Persons Responsible for Serious Violations of International Humanitarian Law Committed in the Territory of the former Yugoslavia since 1991 (the International Criminal Tribunal for the former Yugoslavia, or ICTY). In May 1993, the Council adopted the Secretary–General's proposed statute in a resolution establishing the ICTY, S.C. Res. 827 (1993).

This resolution invoked Chapter VII of the UN Charter. Accordingly, the Council's action in establishing the ICTY was a measure to restore and maintain international peace and was backed by the Security Council's coercive authority. Among other things, this meant that any objection that the Tribunal infringed state sovereignty would be overcome by the Council's Chapter VII authority. (See Section E(2), below.)

Still, there remained the question whether provisions of the ICTY Statute defining the Tribunal's substantive jurisdiction might breach the international legal prohibition of retroactive punishment. Mindful of this issue, the Secretary–General asserted in his report proposing the ICTY Statute:

> 33. According to paragraph 1 of resolution 808 (1993), the international tribunal shall prosecute persons responsible for serious violations of international humanitarian law committed in the territory of the former Yugoslavia since 1991. This body of law exists in the form of both conventional law and customary law. While there is international customary law which is not laid down in conventions, some of the major conventional humanitarian law has become part of customary international law.

> 34. In the view of the Secretary–General, the application of the principle *nullum crimen sine lege* requires that the international tribunal should apply rules of international humanitarian law which are beyond doubt part of customary law so that the problem of adherence of some but not all States to specific conventions does not arise. This would appear to be particularly important in the context of an international tribunal prosecuting persons responsible for serious violations of international humanitarian law.

> 35. The part of conventional international humanitarian law which has beyond doubt become part of international customary law is the law applicable in armed conflict as embodied in: the Geneva Conventions of 12 August 1949 for the Protection of War Victims; the Hague Convention (IV) Respecting the Laws and Customs of War on Land and the Regulations annexed thereto of 18 October 1907; the Convention on the Prevention and Punishment of the Crime of Genocide of 9 December 1948; and the Charter of the International Military Tribunal of 8 August 1945.

Report of the Secretary–General pursuant to paragraph 2 of Security Council Resolution 808 (1993), U.N. Doc. S/25704.

As the Secretary–General's report suggests, the Nuremberg precedent and the treaties enacted in its aftermath seemed to provide a firm foundation for the substantive jurisdiction of the ICTY. Yet the contextual backdrop to the crimes that could be prosecuted before the ICTY left it unclear whether the well-established principles of law cited by the Secretary–General would cover all of the atrocities committed during those conflicts.

Consider, for example, crimes against humanity. Recall that the Nuremberg Tribunal could convict defendants of this crime only when the acts charged were committed in execution of or in connection with crimes against peace or war crimes. Under international law at the time of Nuremberg, the concept of "war crimes" applied only to interstate armed conflict, while crimes against peace by definition entailed aggression by one state against another. If the "nexus" requirement set forth in the Nuremberg Charter represented an element of crimes against humanity under international law rather than a limitation on the IMT's jurisdiction, and still remained an element of the crime in the 1990s, atrocities committed either in peacetime or in the context of a civil war would not constitute crimes against humanity as defined in customary international law.

In the context of the crimes prosecuted before the ICTY, this ambiguity had significant implications. Most of the crimes prosecuted before the ICTY were allegedly committed in the context of what appeared to be a civil war that had international elements. For example, the first defendant prosecuted before the ICTY, Duško Tadić, was a Bosnian Serb charged with criminal responsibility for atrocities committed against Bosnian Muslims. Yet Bosnian Serb forces received substantial support from Yugoslav forces. In the view of some commentators, the involvement of the latter effectively internationalized the conflict in Bosnia.

Against this backdrop, the report of the Secretary–General proposing the ICTY Statute set forth the following interpretation of contemporary law concerning crimes against humanity:

> Crimes against humanity were first recognized in the Charter and Judgement of the Nürnberg Tribunal, as well as in Law No. 10 of the Control Council for Germany. Crimes against humanity are aimed at any civilian population and are prohibited *regardless of whether they are committed in an armed conflict, international or internal in character.*

Report of the Secretary General, U.N. Doc. S/25704, para. 47 (emphasis added).

But while the Secretary–General thus expressed his view that crimes against humanity do not require a nexus to armed conflict of any kind, he proposed the following provision defining the ICTY's jurisdiction over this category of crime:

Article 5

Crimes against humanity

> The International Tribunal shall have the power to prosecute persons responsible for the following crimes *when committed in armed conflict, whether international or internal in character*, and directed against any civilian population: [specific acts, such as extermination, torture and rape enumerated].

Id. para. 9 (emphasis added).

Along with the rest of the statute proposed by the Secretary–General, this provision was adopted by the Security Council in S.C. Resolution 827 (1993). The ambiguities presented by this provision were addressed by an ICTY Trial Chamber in the case of *Prosecutor v. Duško Tadić*.

Prosecutor v. Duško Tadić

ICTY Trial Chamber, 1995. Case No. IT–94–1–T.
Decision on the Defence Motion on Jurisdiction (Aug. 10, 1995)

. . .

77.   The Defence claims that "the Tribunal only has jurisdiction under Article 5 of the Statute if it involves crimes that have been committed in the execution of or in connection with an international armed conflict." It purports to find authority for this proposition requiring the existence of an armed conflict of an *international* nature in the Nuremberg Charter which, in its definition of crimes against humanity, spoke of inhumane acts committed "in execution of or in connection with any crime within the jurisdiction of the Tribunal ..." and in the affirmation given to the principles of international law recognised by the Charter of the Nuremberg Tribunal and Judgement of the Tribunal in General Assembly resolution 95(1) of 194[6]. The Defence further contends that the broadening of the scope of Article 5 to crimes when committed in armed conflicts of an *internal* character offends the *nullum crimen* principle.

78.   The Trial Chamber does not agree. The nexus in the Nuremberg Charter between crimes against humanity and the other two categories, crimes against peace and war crimes, was peculiar to the context of the Nuremberg Tribunal established specifically "for the just and prompt trial and punishment of the major war criminals of the European Axis countries." *(Nuremberg Charter*, Article 1). As some of the crimes perpetrated by Nazi Germany were of such a heinous nature as to shock the conscience of mankind, it was decided to include crimes against humanity in order to enable the International Military Tribunal to try the major war criminals for the barbarous acts committed against German Jews, amongst others, who, as German nationals, were outside the protection of the laws of warfare which only prohibited violations involving the adversary or enemy population. . . .

79.   That no nexus is required in customary international law between crimes against humanity and crimes against peace or war crimes is strongly evidenced by subsequent case law. The military tribunal established under Control Council Law No. 10 stated in the *Einsatzgruppen* case that:

> Crimes against humanity are acts committed in the course of wholesale and systematic violation of life and liberty ... The International Military Tribunal, operating under the London Charter, declared that the Charter's provisions limited the Tribunal to consider only those crimes against humanity which were committed in the execution of or in connection with crimes against peace and war crimes. The Allied

Control Council, in its Law No. 10, removed this limitation so that the present Tribunal has jurisdiction to try all crimes against humanity as long known and understood under the general principles of criminal law. (4 Trials of War Criminals 499).

80.   Further, the Special Rapporteur of the International Law Commission had this to say:

First linked to a state of belligerency . . . the concept of crimes against humanity gradually came to be viewed as autonomous and is today quite separate from that of war crimes . . . Crimes against humanity may be committed in time of war or in time of peace; war crimes can only be committed in time of war. (Seventh Report on the Draft Code of Crimes Against the Peace and Security of Mankind, [1989] 2 Yearbook of ILC, U.N. Doc., A/N/CN.4/SER.A/1986 (Add.1)).

81.   Finally, this view that crimes against humanity are autonomous is confirmed by the opus classicus on international law, Oppenheim's International Law, where special reference is made to the fact that crimes against humanity "are now generally regarded as a self-contained category, without the need for any formal link with war crimes . . ." (R. Jennings and A. Watts, *Oppenheim's International Law* 966 (1992)).

. . .

83.   In conclusion, the Trial Chamber emphasises that the definition of Article 5 is in fact more restrictive than the general definition of crimes against humanity recognised by customary international law. The inclusion of the nexus with armed conflict in the article imposes a limitation on the jurisdiction of the International Tribunal from trying the crimes enumerated therein. Because the language of Article 5 is clear, the crimes against humanity to be tried in the International Tribunal must have a nexus with an armed conflict, be it international or internal. . . .

Notes

1.   Did the Trial Chamber's judgment shed light on the question whether the nexus requirement included in the Nuremberg Charter reflected the definition of customary international law at the time the Nazi crimes were committed (as distinguished from a jurisdictional limitation imposed on the Nuremberg Tribunal)? In this regard, what did the Chamber mean when it asserted: "The nexus in the Nuremberg Charter between crimes against humanity and the other two categories, crimes against peace and war crimes, was peculiar to the context of the Nuremberg Tribunal established specifically 'for the just and prompt trial and punishment of the major war criminals of the European Axis countries' "?

2.   How persuasive are the authorities cited by the Trial Chamber for its conclusion that there is no (longer a) nexus requirement in the definition of crimes against humanity under customary international law?

3.   Duško Tadić appealed various aspects of the Trial Chamber's decision on jurisdiction. Although he did not appeal the portion of the decision

quoted above, the ICTY Appeals Chamber decided to "comment briefly" on the nexus question "in view of the importance of the matter." Decision on the Defence Motion for Interlocutory Appeal on Jurisdiction, *The Prosecutor v. Duško Tadić*, Case No. IT–94–1–AR72, para. 139 (Oct. 2, 1995). It observed:

> 140.   . . . Although the nexus requirement in the Nuremberg Charter was carried over to the 194[6] General Assembly resolution affirming the Nuremberg principles, there is no logical or legal basis for this requirement and it has been abandoned in subsequent State practice with respect to crimes against humanity. Most notably, the nexus requirement was eliminated from the definition of crimes against humanity contained in Article II(1)(c) of Control Council Law No. 10 of 20 December 1945. . . . The obsolescence of the nexus requirement is evidenced by international conventions regarding genocide and apartheid, both of which prohibit particular types of crimes against humanity regardless of any connection to armed conflict. . . .

> 141.   It is by now a settled rule of customary international law that crimes against humanity do not require a connection to international armed conflict. Indeed, as the Prosecutor points out, customary international law may not require a connection between crimes against humanity and any conflict at all. Thus, by requiring that crimes against humanity be committed in either internal or international armed conflict, the Security Council may have defined the crime in Article 5 more narrowly than necessary under customary international law. There is no question, however, that the definition of crimes against humanity adopted by the Security Council in Article 5 comports with the principle of *nullum crimen sine lege*.

The Appeals Chamber's conclusion regarding abandonment of the nexus requirement was based in part on "subsequent State practice"—that is, state practice since the Nuremberg Charter. What "State practice" did the Chamber have in mind? Are the authorities cited persuasive on this point? Elsewhere in the same decision the Appeals Chamber observed that "customary international law *no longer* requires any nexus between crimes against humanity and armed conflict" (para. 78, emphasis added), citing to the paragraphs quoted above. When, in the view of the Appeals Chamber, did the law change in this regard?

Some aspects of the Appeals Chamber's observations seem to take a more conservative approach than that of the Trial Chamber. For example, the Appeals Chamber seems to equivocate on whether there is still a nexus requirement of some sort, even though it finds that a nexus to *interstate* armed conflict is not required. On what basis could it conclude that crimes against humanity do not have to be linked to interstate armed conflict while leaving open the possibility that a nexus to some kind of armed conflict may be necessary?

4. In 1998 and 1999, the United States and United Nations initiated efforts to establish an international tribunal to prosecute senior leaders of the Khmer Rouge for atrocities committed when they ruled Cambodia in

the 1970s. (Some one and one-half million Cambodians are estimated to have died as a result of Khmer Rouge policies and practices.) Crimes against humanity would be one of the principal charges against the Khmer Rouge defendants if such a tribunal were established. Based upon the jurisprudence examined above, is it clear whether prosecutors would have to establish a nexus to armed conflict—interstate or internal—in order to convict the defendants?

5. The nexus requirement was omitted entirely from the statute of the International Criminal Tribunal for Rwanda (ICTR), which was adopted by the U.N. Security Council in November 1994. See S.C. Res. 955, Annex (1994). The ICTR has the "power to prosecute persons responsible for [enumerated] crimes when committed as part of a widespread or systematic attack against any civilian population on national, political, ethnic, racial or religious grounds ..." Id., art. 3. The requirement was also abandoned in the Statute of the International Criminal Court, adopted in Rome in July 1998. Article 7 of the Rome Statute defines crimes against humanity subject to the Court's jurisdiction in the following terms:

Article 7

Crimes against humanity

1. For the purpose of this Statute, "crime against humanity" means any of the following acts when committed as part of a widespread or systematic attack directed against any civilian population, with knowledge of the attack:

(a) Murder;

(b) Extermination;

(c) Enslavement;

(d) Deportation or forcible transfer of population;

(e) Imprisonment or other severe deprivation of physical liberty in violation of fundamental rules of international law;

(f) Torture;

(g) Rape, sexual slavery, enforced prostitution, forced pregnancy, enforced sterilization, or any other form of sexual violence of comparable gravity;

(h) Persecution against any identifiable group or collectivity on political, racial, national, ethnic, cultural, religious, gender as defined in paragraph 3, or other grounds that are universally recognized as impermissible under international law, in connection with any act referred to in this paragraph or any crime within the jurisdiction of the Court;

(i) Enforced disappearance of persons;

(j) The crime of apartheid;

(k) Other inhumane acts of a similar character intentionally causing great suffering, or serious injury to body or to mental or physical health.

2.   For the purpose of paragraph 1:

(a) "Attack directed against any civilian population" means a course of conduct involving the multiple commission of acts referred to in paragraph 1 against any civilian population, pursuant to or in further-ance of a State or organizational policy to commit such attack;

(b) "Extermination" includes the intentional infliction of conditions of life, inter alia the deprivation of access to food and medicine, calculated to bring about the destruction of part of a population;

(c) "Enslavement" means the exercise of any or all of the powers attaching to the right of ownership over a person and includes the exercise of such power in the course of trafficking in persons, in particular women and children;

(d) "Deportation or forcible transfer of population" means forced displacement of the persons concerned by expulsion or other coercive acts from the area in which they are lawfully present, without grounds permitted under international law;

(e) "Torture" means the intentional infliction of severe pain or suffer-ing, whether physical or mental, upon a person in the custody or under the control of the accused; except that torture shall not include pain or suffering arising only from, inherent in or incidental to, lawful sanc-tions;

(f) "Forced pregnancy" means the unlawful confinement, of a woman forcibly made pregnant, with the intent of affecting the ethnic composi-tion of any population or carrying out other grave violations of interna-tional law. This definition shall not in any way be interpreted as affecting national laws relating to pregnancy;

(g) "Persecution" means the intentional and severe deprivation of fundamental rights contrary to international law by reason of the identity of the group or collectivity;

(h) "The crime of apartheid" means inhumane acts of a character similar to those referred to in paragraph 1, committed in the context of an institutionalized regime of systematic oppression and domination by one racial group over any other racial group or groups and committed with the intention of maintaining that regime;

(i) "Enforced disappearance of persons" means the arrest, detention or abduction of persons by, or with the authorization, support or acquies-cence of, a State or a political organization, followed by a refusal to acknowledge that deprivation of freedom or to give information on the fate or whereabouts of those persons, with the intention of removing them from the protection of the law for a prolonged period of time.

3.   For the purpose of this Statute, it is understood that the term "gender" refers to the two sexes, male and female, within the context of society. The term "gender" does not indicate any meaning different from the above.

———

Note on the Relationship Between Human Rights and Humanitarian Law

A notable aspect of the jurisprudence that has been developed by the ICTY concerns the relationship between human rights law and the law of armed conflict. As we have seen, in the Nuremberg Charter the principal relationship between those two bodies of law was that crimes against humanity, which included atrocities committed by a government against individuals subject to its territorial jurisdiction, could be prosecuted by the IMT only if they were committed in connection with violations of the laws of war or crimes against peace.

The Appeals Chamber of the ICTY has elucidated a fundamentally different and more complex relationship between the law of armed conflict and postwar human rights law. As elaborated in the excerpt that follows, the Chamber has concluded that the development of human rights law in this century has had a profound effect on the very structure and scope of international humanitarian law.

In the case of *The Prosecutor v. Duško Tadić*, the ICTY had to determine whether Article 3 of its Statute, which establishes jurisdiction over violations of "the laws or customs of war," encompasses breaches of the sub-set of humanitarian law governing internal armed conflicts. Before this issue was resolved by the ICTY Appeals Chamber, most commentators had assumed that, while customary international law now prohibits certain conduct during internal armed conflicts, breaches of those norms did not yet constitute international crimes.

As noted earlier, the Four Geneva Conventions of 1949 identify certain violations as "grave breaches," which must be prosecuted by High Contracting Parties. Most of the substantive provisions of these conventions apply only in interstate armed conflicts and it is widely believed that the "grave breaches" provisions apply only in that context. Article 3, which is identical in all four conventions, establishes standards governing internal armed conflicts, but makes no mention of criminal punishment for violations of those standards.

Nonetheless, the Appeals Chamber concluded that serious violations of Common Article 3 not only violate customary international law and the Geneva Conventions, but also give rise to individual responsibility under customary law. The following excerpt reflects how, in the Appeals Chamber's view, the development of human rights law in this century contributed to this important development.

Prosecutor v. Duško Tadić

ICTY Appeals Chamber, 1995.Case No. IT–94–1–AR72 (Oct. 2, 1995).
Decision on the Defence Motion for Interlocutory Appeal on Jurisdiction

. . .

95.   The Appeals Chamber deems it necessary to consider now two of the requirements set out above [governing the ICTY's jurisdiction under Article 3 of its Statute], namely: (i) the existence of customary international rules governing internal strife: and (ii) the question of whether the violation of such rules may entail individual criminal responsibility. The Appeals Chamber focuses on these two requirements because before the Trial Chamber the Defence argued that they had not been met in the case at issue. This examination is also appropriate because of the paucity of authoritative judicial pronouncements and legal literature on this matter.

(iii) *Customary Rules of International Humanitarian Law Governing Internal Armed Conflicts*

a. *General*

96.   Whenever armed violence erupted in the international community, in traditional international law the legal response was based on a stark dichotomy: belligerency or insurgency. The former category applied to armed conflicts between sovereign States (unless there was recognition of belligerency in a civil war), while the latter applied to armed violence breaking out in the territory of a sovereign State. Correspondingly, international law treated the two classes of conflict in a markedly different way: interstate wars were regulated by a whole body of international legal rules, governing both the conduct of hostilities and the protection of persons not participating (or no longer participating) in armed violence (civilians, the wounded, the sick, shipwrecked, prisoners of war). By contrast, there were very few international rules governing civil commotion, for States preferred to regard internal strife as rebellion, mutiny and treason coming within the purview of national criminal law and, by the same token, to exclude any possible intrusion by other States into their own domestic jurisdiction. This dichotomy was clearly sovereignty-oriented and reflected the traditional configuration of the international community, based on the coexistence of sovereign States more inclined to look after their own interests than community concerns or humanitarian demands.

97.   Since the 1930s, however, the aforementioned distinction has gradually become more and more blurred, and international legal rules have increasingly emerged or have been agreed upon to regulate internal armed conflict. There exist various reasons for this development. First, civil wars have become more frequent, not only because technological progress has made it easier for groups of individuals to have access to weaponry but also on account of increasing tension, whether ideological, inter-ethnic or economic; as a consequence the international community can no longer turn a blind eye to the legal regime of such wars. Secondly, internal armed conflicts have become more and more cruel and protracted, involving the whole population of the State where they occur: the all-out resort to armed violence has taken on such a magnitude that the difference with international wars has increasingly dwindled (suffice to think of the Spanish civil war, in 1936–39, of the civil war in the Congo, in 1960–1968, the Biafran conflict in Nigeria, 1967–70, the civil strife in Nicaragua, in 1981–1990 or

El Salvador, 1980–1993). Thirdly, the large-scale nature of civil strife, coupled with the increasing interdependence of States in the world community, has made it more and more difficult for third States to remain aloof: the economic, political and ideological interests of third States have brought about direct or indirect involvement of third States in this category of conflict, thereby requiring that international law take greater account of their legal regime in order to prevent, as much as possible, adverse spillover effects. Fourthly, the impetuous development and propagation in the international community of human rights doctrines, particularly after the adoption of the Universal Declaration of Human Rights in 1948, has brought about significant changes in international law, notably in the approach to problems besetting the world community. A State-sovereignty-oriented approach has been gradually supplanted by a human-being-oriented approach. Gradually the maxim of Roman law hominem causa omne jus constitutum est (all law is created for the benefit of human beings) has gained a firm foothold in the international community as well. It follows that in the area of armed conflict the distinction between interstate wars and civil wars is losing its value as far as human beings are concerned. Why protect civilians from belligerent violence, or ban rape, torture or the wanton destruction of hospitals, churches, museums or private property, as well as proscribe weapons causing unnecessary suffering when two sovereign States are engaged in war, and yet refrain from enacting the same bans or providing the same protection when armed violence has erupted "only" within the territory of a sovereign State? If international law, while of course duly safeguarding the legitimate interests of States, must gradually turn to the protection of human beings, it is only natural that the aforementioned dichotomy should gradually lose its weight.

. . .

2. NATIONAL PROSECUTIONS, AMNESTIES AND TRUTH COMMISSIONS

Efforts to establish a permanent international criminal court preceded the Nuremberg prosecution by some decades, and gained momentum in its aftermath. But support quickly dissipated as Cold War tensions set in. Proposals to establish a permanent court languished for nearly half a century.

Even so, criminal law has occupied a significant place in postwar human rights law, particularly and increasingly since the 1980s. Some treaties, including the 1948 Convention on the Prevention and Punishment of the Crime of Genocide and the 1984 Convention Against Torture and Other Cruel, Inhuman or Degrading Treatment or Punishment, explicitly require States Parties to criminalize certain conduct and to institute criminal proceedings under specified circumstances. Although comprehensive treaties such as the ICCPR and the American Convention do not explicitly impose obligations of this nature, the bodies that supervise compliance with these conventions have found that criminal punishment plays a necessary part in States Parties' fulfilment of their conventional obligations.

For example, when considering communications pursuant to the Optional Protocol (see Section A, above) involving allegations of torture, enforced disappearance and extra-judicial execution, the Human Rights Committee has repeatedly expressed its view that, in addition to compensating victims, States Parties to the ICCPR should investigate the violations and bring to justice those who are responsible. In the landmark *Velásquez Rodríguez* case, the Inter–American Court of Human Rights found the Honduran government responsible for multiple violations of the American Convention on Human Rights in relation to the 1981 disappearance of Manfredo Velásquez Rodríguez. Analyzing the duty of States Parties, set forth in Article 1, to "ensure" the rights elaborated in the Convention, the Court reasoned:

> This obligation implies the duty of the States Parties to organize the governmental apparatus and, in general, all the structures through which public power is exercised, so that they are capable of juridically ensuring the free and full enjoyment of human rights. As a consequence of this obligation, the States must prevent, investigate and punish any violation of the rights recognized by the Convention....

Velásquez Rodríguez Case, 4 Inter–Am. Ct. H.R. (ser. C), para. 166 (1988) (Judgment). (More extensive excerpts of this decision are included in Section B, above.)

The Restatement (Third) of the Foreign Relations Law of the United States takes the position that a complete failure to punish repeated or notorious violations of rights protected by customary international law generates state responsibility for a breach of that law. Declaring that a state violates customary law "if, as a matter of state policy, it practices, encourages or condones" torture, murder, disappearances and several other acts, the Restatement suggests that "[a] government may be presumed to have encouraged or condoned [these] acts ... if such acts, especially by its officials, have been repeated or notorious and no steps have been taken to prevent them or to punish the perpetrators." Restatement, § 702 and Comment *b*.

The Dilemmas of Transitional Justice: Amnesties and Truth Commissions

In contrast to the law of Nuremberg and Tokyo, the obligations enunciated in the aforementioned decisions by human rights treaty bodies and in the Restatement are generally to be discharged by national courts.*

---

* In addition to national prosecutions in the state where proscribed conduct occurs, the Genocide Convention contemplates the possibility of prosecution before an international tribunal. Article VI provides:

Persons charged with genocide [or certain related acts] shall be tried by a competent tribunal of the State in the territory of which the act was committed, or by such international penal tribunal as may have jurisdiction with respect to those Contracting Parties which shall have accepted its jurisdiction.

In the reasoning of the Human Rights Committee and the Inter–American Court of Human Rights, bringing to justice those responsible for human rights violations plays a necessary part in the duty *of States Parties* to "ensure" the enjoyment of rights protected by the ICCPR and the American Convention. Conversely, the Restatement suggests, a state's wholesale failure to punish repeated or notorious violations of basic rights condones such violations and serves to encourage them.

But what if a government has systematically failed to meet its obligations in this regard, as happened in numerous countries ruled by military juntas in the 1970s and '80s: Must the successor government punish all of those who bear criminal responsibility for the prior regime's violations? Must it prosecute *any* of those crimes? Suppose that the outgoing regime insists upon amnesty as a condition to relinquishing power and thereby enabling a society recently scourged by mass atrocity to begin the difficult transition toward constitutional democracy. Or suppose that, as a matter of national policy, a society emerging from a period of wholesale violations of human dignity decides that it can better come to terms with its past through a process of "truth-telling" (see below) than through criminal prosecutions. Does international law circumscribe the society's choices in this regard? Do the answers to these questions depend upon whether:

- an amnesty covering abuses of the past has been affirmed by a democratic process;

- the fledgling democracy that has emerged in the wake of repressive governance faces a serious threat of destabilizing force if it attempts to prosecute human rights crimes committed during the recent past; or

- the successor democracy, while honoring an amnesty that precludes criminal prosecution, has provided alternative forms of accountability for abuses of the past, such as establishing an officially-sanctioned record of past abuses and providing compensation to victims?

Consider how these questions are addressed in the two decisions of the Human Rights Committee and the Inter–American Commission excerpted below. Before turning to those decisions, and as a foundation for exploring them, we consider a non-judicial form of "transitional justice" that has been used in a growing roster of countries emerging from protracted periods of systemic abuse—"truth commissions."

Truth Commissions: An Alternative or Complement to Criminal Prosecutions?

"Truth commissions" have been established in some twenty countries in the past fifteen years, in three instances pursuant to UN-brokered peace accords. Typically established during a period of political transition following a period of mass atrocity, these bodies investigate, report upon and acknowledge the truth about past abuses. Although several commissions have been widely judged to have been ineffective, the contributions of others have given the institution a pride of place in the evolving repertoire of responses to mass atrocity.

Although truth commissions have been established in various regions, their contemporary manifestation emerged in Latin America as numerous countries in the region emerged from protracted periods of military governance. These bodies seemed peculiarly appropriate in countries such as Argentina and Chile, where the paradigmatic crime of the prior regime was that of "disappearance"—a crime whose essence is the state's denial of information and responsibility about the victim's fate. But in recent years, truth commissions have been proposed or created in an ever-widening set of circumstances and regions. The following excerpt addresses their unique role in countries emerging from mass atrocity.

Lawrence Weschler, *A Miracle, a Universe: Settling Accounts With Torturers*

3, 4–5 (2d ed. 1998)

In the fall of 1988, a group of academics and lawyers and clerics and activists ... gathered at the Aspen Institute's Wye Woods Conference Center to try to puzzle through one of the most complicated issues facing polities all over the world as they try to move from dictatorial to democratic systems of governance—the question of what to do with former torturers still in their midst. In many cases, the receding security and military apparatuses, which were responsible for the preponderance of human-rights abuses during the previous regime, retain tremendous power—and they will not abide any settling of accounts. They demand blanket amnesties covering all violations committed during their tenure, amnesties designed to enforce a total amnesia regarding those crimes. The fledgling democracies thus face a harrowing challenge to a bulwark of their authority—the very principle of equality before the law—just as they are attempting to consolidate their rule.

Over and over again, the same sorts of issues get played out, and over and over again, ... the same two imperatives seem to rise to the fore—the intertwined demands for justice and for truth. The security forces, of course, will abide neither, but if anything the desire for truth is often more urgently felt by the victims of torture than the desire for justice. People don't necessarily insist that the former torturers go to jail—there's been enough of jail—but they do want to see the truth established. Fragile, tentative democracies time and again hurl themselves toward an abyss, struggling over this issue of truth. It's a mysteriously powerful, almost magical notion, because often everyone already knows the truth—everyone knows who the torturers were and what they did, the torturers know that everyone knows, and everyone knows that they know. Why, then, this need to risk everything to render the knowledge explicit?

The participants at the ... conference worried this question around the table several times—the distinctions here seemed particularly slippery and elusive—until Thomas Nagel, a professor of philosophy and law at New York University, almost stumbled upon an answer. "It's the difference," Nagel said haltingly, "between knowledge and *acknowledgment*. It's what happens and can only happen to knowledge when it becomes officially sanctioned, when it is made part of the public cognitive scene." Yes, several of the panelists agreed. And that transformation, offered another participant, is sacramental.

. . .

True forgiveness is achieved in community; it is something people do for each other and with each other and at a certain point for free. It is history working itself out as grace, but it can only be accomplished in truth. That truth is not merely knowledge: it is, as we have seen, *acknowledgment*, it is a coming-to-terms-with, and it is a labor. Ironically, in places where former antagonists refuse to acknowledge the horror of their past depredations, even truth-tellings may not be enough. Full-scale trials—the painstaking laying out and proving of guilt, under exacting conditions of due process—may be both necessary and salutary before any forgiveness can be extended. And, of course, forgiveness makes sense only in the context of starting anew—something that cannot be done if the prior malefactors retain their positions of authority, immune and unaccountable.

Such forgiveness, in any case, is never done once and for all: the past is kept alive, is continuously revisited, but in the mode of supercession, of moving on....

. . .

———

In South Africa, the post-apartheid government headed by Nelson Mandela established a Commission on Truth and Reconciliation (TRC) with several roles, including a truth-finding function and the power to confer amnesty on an individual basis. The law establishing the TRC and setting forth the conditions in which amnesty could be conferred was adopted following a wide-ranging public debate. Although the policy embodied in that law enjoyed substantial public support, its provisions on amnesty were strongly criticized by others. Some individuals challenged the amnesty before South Africa's Constitutional Court. Portions of its decision upholding the law are set forth below.

Azanian Peoples Organization v. The President of the Republic of South Africa

Constitutional Court of South Africa, 1996.
1996 (4) South Africa Law Reports 637

■ MAHOMED DP:

[1] For decades South African history has been dominated by a deep conflict between a minority which reserved for itself all control over the

political instruments of the state and a majority who sought to resist that domination. Fundamental human rights became a major casualty of this conflict as the resistance of those punished by their denial was met by laws designed to counter the effectiveness of such resistance. . . .

[2]   During the eighties it became manifest to all that our country . . . was on a disaster course unless that conflict was reversed. It was this realisation which mercifully rescued us in the early nineties as those who controlled the levers of state power began to negotiate a different future with those who had been imprisoned, silenced, or driven into exile in consequence of their resistance to that control and its consequences. Those negotiations resulted in an interim Constitution committed to a transition towards a more just, defensible and democratic political order based on the protection of fundamental human rights. It was wisely appreciated by those involved in the preceding negotiations that the task of building such a new democratic order was a very difficult task because of the previous history and the deep emotions and indefensible inequities it had generated; and that this could not be achieved without a firm and generous commitment to reconciliation and national unity. It was realised that much of the unjust consequences of the past could not ever be fully reversed. It might be necessary in crucial areas to close the book on that past.

[3]   This fundamental philosophy is eloquently expressed in the epilogue to the Constitution which reads as follows:

"National Unity and Reconciliation

This Constitution provides a historic bridge between the past of a deeply divided society characterised by strife, conflict, untold suffering and injustice, and a future founded on the recognition of human rights, democracy and peaceful co-existence . . .

. . .

The adoption of this Constitution lays the secure foundation for the people of South Africa to transcend the divisions and strife of the past, which generated gross violations of human rights, the transgression of humanitarian principles in violent conflicts and a legacy of hatred, fear, guilt and revenge.

These can now be addressed on the basis that there is a need for understanding but not for vengeance, a need for reparation but not for retaliation, a need for ubuntu but not for victimisation.

In order to advance such reconciliation and reconstruction, amnesty shall be granted in respect of acts, omissions and offences associated with political objectives and committed in the course of the conflicts of the past. To this end, Parliament under this Constitution shall adopt a law . . . providing for the mechanisms, criteria and procedures, including tribunals, if any, through which such amnesty shall be dealt with at any time after the law has been passed.

With this Constitution and these commitments we, the people of South Africa, open a new chapter in the history of our country."

Pursuant to the provisions of the epilogue, Parliament enacted during 1995 what is colloquially referred to as the Truth and Reconciliation Act. Its proper name is the Promotion of National Unity and Reconciliation Act 34 of 1995 ("the Act").

[4] The Act establishes a Truth and Reconciliation Commission.... Its main objective is to "promote national unity and reconciliation in a spirit of understanding which transcends the conflicts and divisions of the past". It is enjoined to pursue that objective by "establishing as complete a picture as possible of the causes, nature and extent of the gross violations of human rights" committed during the period commencing 1 March 1960 to the "cut-off date"....

The Commission is further entrusted with the duty to establish and to make known "the fate or whereabouts of victims" and of "restoring the human and civil dignity of such victims" by affording them an opportunity to relate their own accounts of the violations and by recommending "reparation measures" in respect of such violations and finally to compile a comprehensive report in respect of its functions, including the recommendation of measures to prevent the violation of human rights.

[5] Three committees are established for the purpose of achieving the objectives of the Commission.... The third and the most directly relevant committee for the purposes of the present dispute is the Committee on Amnesty.... The Committee has the power to grant amnesty in respect of any act, omission or offence to which the particular application for amnesty relates, provided that the applicant concerned has made a full disclosure of all relevant facts and provided further that the relevant act, omission or offence is associated with a political objective committed in the course of the conflicts of the past....

· · ·

[6] ... [S]ection 20(7) (the constitutionality of which is impugned in these proceedings) provides as follows:

"(7)(a) No person who has been granted amnesty in respect of an act, omission or offence shall be criminally or civilly liable in respect of such act, omission or offence and no body or organisation or the State shall be liable, and no person shall be vicariously liable, for any such act, omission or offence.["]

· · ·

[8] The applicants sought in this court to attack the constitutionality of section 20(7) on the grounds that its consequences are not authorised by the Constitution. They aver that various agents of the state, acting within the scope and in the course of their employment, have unlawfully murdered and maimed leading activists during the conflict against the racial policies of the previous administration and that the applicants have a clear right to insist that such wrongdoers should properly be prosecuted and punished,

that they should be ordered by the ordinary courts of the land to pay adequate civil compensation to the victims or dependants of the victims and further to require the state to make good to such victims or dependants the serious losses which they have suffered in consequence of the criminal and delictual acts of the employees of the state. In support of that attack [counsel for the applicants] contended that section 20(7) was inconsistent with section 22 of the Constitution which provides that

"[e]very person shall have the right to have justiciable disputes settled by a court of law or, where appropriate, another independent or impartial forum."

He submitted that the Amnesty Committee was neither "a court of law" nor an "independent or impartial forum" and that in any event the Committee was not authorised to settle "justiciable disputes". All it was simply required to decide was whether amnesty should be granted in respect of a particular act, omission or offence.

[9]   The effect of an amnesty undoubtedly impacts upon very fundamental rights. All persons are entitled to the protection of the law against unlawful invasions of their right to life, their right to respect for and protection of dignity and their right not to be subject to torture of any kind. When those rights are invaded those aggrieved by such invasion have the right to obtain redress in the ordinary courts of law and those guilty of perpetrating such violations are answerable before such courts, both civilly and criminally. An amnesty to the wrongdoer effectively obliterates such rights.

[10]   There would therefore be very considerable force in the submission that [the amnesty provisions] of the Act constitute[ ] a violation of section 22 of the Constitution, if there was nothing in the Constitution itself which permitted or authorised such violation. The crucial issue, therefore, which needs to be determined, is whether the Constitution, indeed, permits such a course. [The Court found that the epilogue to the Constitution not only authorizes Parliament to enact a law providing for amnesty in certain circumstances, but obliges it to do so.]

. . .

[17]   Every decent human being must feel grave discomfort in living with a consequence which might allow the perpetrators of evil acts to walk the streets of this land with impunity, protected in their freedom by an amnesty immune from constitutional attack, but the circumstances in support of this course require carefully to be appreciated. Most of the acts of brutality and torture which have taken place have occurred during an era in which neither the laws which permitted the incarceration of persons or the investigation of crimes, nor the methods and the culture which informed such investigations, were easily open to public investigation, verification and correction. Much of what transpired in this shameful period is shrouded in secrecy and not easily capable of objective demonstration and proof. Loved ones have disappeared, sometimes mysteriously and most of them no longer survive to tell their tales. Others have had their freedom invaded, their dignity assaulted or their reputations tarnished by

grossly unfair imputations hurled in the fire and the cross-fire of a deep and wounding conflict. The wicked and the innocent have often both been victims. Secrecy and authoritarianism have concealed the truth in little crevices of obscurity in our history. Records are not easily accessible, witnesses are often unknown, dead, unavailable or unwilling. All that often effectively remains is the truth of wounded memories of loved ones sharing instinctive suspicions, deep and traumatising to the survivors but otherwise incapable of translating themselves into objective and corroborative evidence which could survive the rigours of the law. The Act seeks to address this massive problem by encouraging these survivors and the dependants of the tortured and the wounded, the maimed and the dead to unburden their grief publicly, to receive the collective recognition of a new nation that they were wronged, and crucially, to help them to discover what did in truth happen to their loved ones, where and under what circumstances it did happen, and who was responsible. That truth, which the victims of repression seek so desperately to know is, in the circumstances, much more likely to be forthcoming if those responsible for such monstrous misdeeds are encouraged to disclose the whole truth with the incentive that they will not receive the punishment which they undoubtedly deserve if they do. Without that incentive there is nothing to encourage such persons to make the disclosures and to reveal the truth which persons in the positions of the applicants so desperately desire. With that incentive, what might unfold are objectives fundamental to the ethos of a new constitutional order. The families of those unlawfully tortured, maimed or traumatised become more empowered to discover the truth, the perpetrators become exposed to opportunities to obtain relief from the burden of a guilt or an anxiety they might be living with for many long years, the country begins the long and necessary process of healing the wounds of the past, transforming anger and grief into a mature understanding and creating the emotional and structural climate essential for the "reconciliation and reconstruction" which informs the very difficult and sometimes painful objectives of the amnesty articulated in the epilogue.

[18] The alternative to the grant of immunity from criminal prosecution of offenders is to keep intact the abstract right to such a prosecution for particular persons without the evidence to sustain the prosecution successfully, to continue to keep the dependants of such victims in many cases substantially ignorant about what precisely happened to their loved ones, to leave their yearning for the truth effectively unassuaged, to perpetuate their legitimate sense of resentment and grief and correspondingly to allow the culprits of such deeds to remain perhaps physically free but inhibited in their capacity to become active, full and creative members of the new order by a menacing combination of confused fear, guilt, uncertainty and sometimes even trepidation. Both the victims and the culprits who walk on the "historic bridge" described by the epilogue will hobble more than walk to the future with heavy and dragged steps delaying and impeding a rapid and enthusiastic transition to the new society at the end of the bridge, which is the vision which informs the epilogue.

[19] Even more crucially, but for a mechanism providing for amnesty, the "historic bridge" itself might never have been erected. For a successfully negotiated transition, the terms of the transition required not only the agreement of those victimized by abuse but also those threatened by the transition to a "democratic society based on freedom and equality". If the Constitution kept alive the prospect of continuous retaliation and revenge, the agreement of those threatened by its implementation might never have been forthcoming, and if it had, the bridge itself would have remained wobbly and insecure, threatened by fear from some and anger from others. It was for this reason that those who negotiated the Constitution made a deliberate choice, preferring understanding over vengeance, reparation over retaliation, ubuntu over victimisation.

. . .

[24] What emerges from the experience of [Argentina, Chile, El Salvador] and other countries that have ended periods of authoritarian and abusive rule, is that there is no single or uniform international practice in relation to amnesty. Decisions of states in transition, taken with a view to assisting such transition, are quite different from acts of a state covering up its own crimes by granting itself immunity. In the former case, it is not a question of the governmental agents responsible for the violations indemnifying themselves, but rather, one of a constitutional compact begin entered into by all sides, with former victims being well-represented, as part of an ongoing process to develop constitutional democracy and prevent a repetition of abuses.

[Counsel for the applicants argued that the amnesty was inconsistent with South Africa's obligations under international law, citing the duty to prosecute "grave breaches" of the four Geneva Conventions of 1949. The Court expressed doubt whether these provisions, which apply in situations of interstate armed conflict, "apply at all to the situation in which this country found itself" during the period in question.]

[30] [In addition,] whatever be the proper ambit and technical meaning of these Conventions and Protocols, the international literature in any event clearly appreciates the distinction between the position of perpetrators of acts of violence in the course of war (or other conflicts between states or armed conflicts between liberation movements seeking self-determination against colonial and alien domination of their countries), on the one hand, and their position in respect of violent acts perpetrated during other conflicts which take place within the territory of a sovereign state in consequence of a struggle between the armed forces of that state and other dissident armed forces operating under responsible command, within such a state on the other. In respect of the latter category, there is no obligation on the part of a contracting state to ensure the prosecution of those who might have performed acts of violence or other acts which would ordinarily be characterised as serious invasions of human rights. On the contrary, article 6(5) of Protocol II to the Geneva Conventions of 1949 provides that

"[a]t the end of hostilities, the authorities in power shall endeavour to grant the broadest possible amnesty to persons who participated in the armed conflict, or those deprived of their liberty for reasons related to the armed conflict, whether they are interned or detained."

[31]   The need for this distinction is obvious. It is one thing to allow the officers of a hostile power which has invaded a foreign state to remain unpunished for gross violations of human rights perpetrated against others during the course of such conflict. It is another thing to compel such punishment in circumstances where such violations have substantially occurred in consequence of conflict between different formations within the same state in respect of the permissible political direction which that state should take with regard to the structures of the state and the parameters of its political policies and where it becomes necessary after the cessation of such conflict for the society traumatised by such a conflict to reconstruct itself. The erstwhile adversaries of such a conflict inhabit the same sovereign territory. They have to live with each other and work with each other and the state concerned is best equipped to determine what measures may be most conducive for the facilitation of such reconciliation and reconstruction. That is a difficult exercise which the nation within such a state has to perform by having regard to its own peculiar history, its complexities, even its contradictions and its emotional and institutional traditions. What role punishment should play in respect of erstwhile acts of criminality in such a situation is part of the complexity. . . .

. . .

[32]   . . . I am not persuaded that there is anything in the Act . . . which can properly be said to be a breach of the obligations of this country in terms of the instruments of public international law relied on by [plaintiffs' counsel.] The amnesty contemplated is not a blanket amnesty against criminal prosecution for all and sundry, granted automatically as a uniform act of compulsory statutory amnesia. It is specifically authorised for the purposes of effecting a constructive transition towards a democratic order. It is available only where there is a full disclosure of all facts to the Amnesty Committee and where it is clear that the particular transgression was perpetrated during the prescribed period and with a political objective committed in the course of the conflicts of the past. That objective has to be evaluated having regard to the careful criteria listed in section 20(3) of the Act, including the very important relationship which the act perpetrated bears in proportion to the object pursued.

. . .

Order

[51]   In the result, the attack on the constitutionality of section 20(7) of the Promotion of National Unity and Reconciliation Act 34 of 1995 must fail. That was the only attack which was pursued on behalf of the applicants in this Court. It accordingly follows that the application must be, and is, refused.

Antonio Cassese, *Reflections on International Criminal Justice**

61 Mod. L. Rev. 1, 3–6 (1998).

. . .

. . . In a recent case in the South African Constitutional Court, many of the legal and moral quandaries of granting amnesties in exchange for a full confession of political crimes are discussed. In *Azanian Peoples Organization v. President of the Republic of South Africa* (25 July 1996), the plaintiffs challenged the constitutionality of South Africa's Promotion of National Unity and Reconciliation Act, specifically its granting of amnesty to apartheid-era human rights abusers. The Court upheld the Act on a number of grounds.

Four important points deserve to be made in relation to this ruling. First, as the Decision recognised, the Truth Commission solution is suitable for a nation which is freeing itself from a regime of terror and undergoing a transition to democracy, and is thus appropriate to the needs of South Africa, El Salvador, Guatemala or Chile. When we turn, however, to the former Yugoslavia, and in particular to Bosnia and Herzegovina, the inappropriateness of this paradigm soon becomes apparent. Here one is concerned not with emergence from an authoritarian State apparatus to a pluralistic democracy, but rather the reverse: the transition, by means of "ethnic cleansing", from a peaceful, multi-dimensional State, ie the Socialist Federal Republic of Yugoslavia and its constituent republics, to several ethnically-based mini-States and entities, ... which, far from wishing to be reconciled, seem to prefer to remain antagonistic to, and separate from, each other.

Second, the South African solution was predicated on the impossibility, or at least extreme difficulty of conducting prosecutions, given the secrecy and deadly efficiency of the anti-apartheid abuses. . . .

. . . [T]he premise underlying the new South Africa [is] that the apartheid-era is now over, that everyone was, in a sense, the victim of that regime and that the chief object ahead is to build a new and better society. Again, this medicine is inappropriate for a society which is still riven by, and built on, ethnic divisions and where the perpetrators of atrocities still preach the gospel of ethnic separation (think of the former Yugoslavia), or for a society such as that of Rwanda where ethnic hatred still persists and the victims of genocide, or their relatives, demand that the culprits be duly punished.

Third, it should be borne in mind that amnesty, under the terms of the South African Truth and Reconciliation Act, is by no means automatic. For one thing, it is extended only for what are political crimes under the Act's

* [This article was originally delivered as a lecture in June 1997. At that time, Judge Cassese, a member of the Appeals Chamber of the International Criminal Tribunal for the former Yugoslavia and of its sister tribunal for Rwanda, served as President of the Yugoslavia Tribunal.—Editors' Note.]

strict criteria and, for another, it is only available for those who "make *full disclosure* of all the relevant facts relating to acts associated with a political objective".

Fourth, as a general comment, the notion of domestic prosecutions is sometimes dismissed in favour of amnesty and truth commissions when the society in question is too fragile to survive the destabilising effects of politically charged trials. As a US State Department official observed, "There is a need to empty wounds of all the old infection before healing can start. But in some countries, like Angola and Mozambique, I'm not sure you'd have anything left if you cleaned out all the infection." In those countries, however, this consideration would only operate as a bar to domestic tribunals—an international tribunal, by contrast, could conduct the work at a distance—both physical and political—from the destabilising national forces. This is a reason for preferring international tribunals to national courts, in certain circumstances. . . .

Thus in my view, the best option is to bring to court alleged culprits and to dispense justice, as is happening both in the former Yugoslavia and in Rwanda, given that (a) they have been the scene of appalling atrocities which are beyond amnesty, (b) they are still riven by the violent national-isms or ethnic hatred over which the wars were fought, and (c) they are not yet willing to be reconciled. I should add that arguably, under international law, an amnesty for genocide would anyway be precluded by *jus cogens*. It may be concluded that the general principles of customary international law *prohibiting* genocide and *imposing* the obligation to punish the authors of genocide may not be derogated from through international agreements; *a fortiori* they may not be set aside by national legislation.

Turning now to criminal *justice*, as opposed to revenge, forgetting and amnesty. . . .

. . .

. . . [B]ringing culprits to justice has some notable merits that can be briefly enumerated as follows:

- trials establish *individual responsibility* over *collective* assignation of guilt, ie, they establish that not all Germans were responsible for the Holocaust, nor all Turks for the Armenian genocide, nor all Serbs, Muslims, Croats or Hutus but individual perpetrators—although, of course, there may be a great number of perpetrators;

- *justice dissipates the call for revenge*, because when the Court metes out to the perpetrator his just deserts, then the victims' calls for retribution are met;

- by dint of dispensation of justice, victims are prepared to be *reconciled* with the erstwhile tormentors, because they know that the latter have now paid for their crimes;

- a fully reliable *record* is established of atrocities so that *future generations* can remember and be made fully cognisant of what happened.

. . .

Notes

1.   A number of writers have identified an emerging "right to the truth"—a concept affirmed in the revised final report of a United Nations expert, Louis Joinet, on the "Question of the Impunity of Perpetrators of Human Rights Violations (Civil and Political)" in terms of the "victims' right to know." As elucidated in Joinet's report, this right "is not simply the right of any individual victim or closely related persons to know what happened," but is also "a collective right, drawing upon history to prevent violations from recurring in the future." U.N. Doc. E/CN.4/Sub.2/1992/20/Rev.1, para. 17. See also the report of the Inter-American Commission on Human Rights in respect of communications challenging a Chilean amnesty law, portions of which are set forth below. Some proponents, including Joinet, characterize the "right to the truth" as an emerging principle, not yet crystallized as an obligatory norm of customary law.

With many other proponents of a right to the truth, Mr. Joinet advocates the establishment of truth commissions as a complement to, and not a substitute for, the operation of the criminal justice system. Do you agree? When, if ever, should truth commissions serve as an alternative to criminal prosecutions? What insights into this question are provided by Judge Cassese and by the South African Constitutional Court? Does the opinion of the South African Constitutional Court imply that prosecutions are essentially a form of "retaliation and revenge" (see paragraph 19)? Does that opinion imply that, at least under the circumstances prevailing in South Africa, a truth commission was more likely than trials to fulfil the key functions that would have been served by prosecutions if they had been a viable prospect? (See in this regard paragraph 17.) What precisely, did the Court consider the most important function to be served by South Africa's post-apartheid accountability process? What additional rationales did the Court offer in support of South Africa's Truth and Reconciliation Act? How much of the Court's reasoning turns on its doubts about the ability of South Africa's courts to dispense justice? To what extent was the Court swayed by the claim that some form of amnesty was a precondition to the end of apartheid itself? (See paragraph 19.) How much weight did the Court attach to what it seemed to regard as the TRC's ability to perform a sort of national therapy—a role that trials, presumably, would not serve?

2.   Does the validity of an amnesty program depend in part upon whether the democratic opposition to a repressive regime has judged acceptance of an amnesty to be a necessary precondition to the prior regime's readiness to cede power? Should a national majority be able to approve amnesty in respect of specific crimes whose victims do not accept the majority decision?

3.   Does the selection by Judge Cassese suggest that trials may not be necessary or appropriate in societies that have already overcome the divisions that formed the context of atrocities? If this is a relevant consideration, how would one determine whether trials are necessary? How, for example, would one assess the risk that racial or ethnic prejudices underly-

ing past atrocities might remain latent until a new provocation revives them?

4.   Judge Cassese suggests that international tribunals may play an important role in respect of countries where "the society . . . is too fragile to survive the destabilising effects of politically charged trials." Should international tribunals also be able to prosecute individuals who benefit from amnesties adopted in societies that seem to have largely overcome divisions of the past and which have decided to emphasize policies of reconciliation?

5.   Judge Cassese concludes that the best course is to prosecute those responsible for atrocities under certain circumstances, of which the first is that the crimes entailed "atrocities which are beyond amnesty." Although the issue has never been squarely presented for resolution by an authoritative tribunal, some legal experts believe that crimes against humanity fall into this category. Notably, South Africa's TRC concluded that crimes committed during the apartheid era constituted crimes against humanity, and indeed apartheid itself has long been recognized as a crime against humanity. In light of this, if someone who received an amnesty in South Africa could be prosecuted in another country's courts or before an international court, should the latter courts decline to prosecute?

6.   Judge Cassese observed that, under South Africa's Promotion of National Unity and Reconciliation Act, amnesty "is only available for those who 'make *full disclosure* of all the relevant facts relating to acts associated with a political objective'." Why might this factor be legally or morally relevant to whether an amnesty should be deemed legitimate?

7.   Are the views of the South African Constitutional Court expressed in paragraph 31 of its opinion in the *Azanian Peoples Organization (AZAPO)* case consistent with the position expressed in the excerpt from the ICTY Appeals Chamber's decision on jurisdiction in the *Tadić* case excerpted in sub-section 1, supra?

8.   There is a burgeoning literature on issues of accountability for human rights atrocities, some of which focuses on mechanisms of "transitional justice." For further reading on these subjects, see War Crimes: The Legacy of Nuremberg (Belinda Cooper, ed. 1999); Lawrence Weschler, A Miracle, A Universe: Settling Accounts with Torturers (2d ed. 1998); Martha Minow, Between Vengeance and Forgiveness: Facing History After Genocide and Mass Violence (1998); Aryeh Neier, War Crimes: Brutality, Genocide, Terror, and the Struggle for Justice (1998); Transitional Justice and the Rule of Law in New Democracies (A. James McAdams, ed. 1997); Steven R. Ratner and Jason S. Abrams, Accountability for Human Rights Atrocities in International Law: Beyond the Nuremberg Legacy (1997); *Symposium: Accountability for International Crimes and Serious Violations of Fundamental Human Rights*, 59 Law & Contemp. Prob. 1–347 (1996); I–III Transitional Justice: How Emerging Democracies Reckon with Former Regimes (Neil Kritz, ed. 1995); Impunity and Human Rights in International Law and Practice (Naomi Roht–Arriaza, ed. 1995); Mark J. Osiel, Mass Atrocity, Collective Memory, and the Law (1997); State Crimes: Punishment or Pardon? (Alice Henkin, ed. 1989); Priscilla Hayner, *Fifteen*

Truth Commissions—1974 to 1994: A Comparative Study, 16 Hum. Rts. Q. 598 (1994).

————

Although the most extensive jurisprudence on amnesties is to be found in decisions of the Inter–American Commission, the Human Rights Committee was the first human rights treaty body to address formally the validity of amnesties. In 1992, the Committee replaced an earlier general comment on Article 7 of the ICCPR, which prohibits torture, with a revised text. The latter included the following observation:

> The Committee has noted that some States have granted amnesty in respect of acts of torture. Amnesties are generally incompatible with the duty of States to investigate such acts; to guarantee freedom from such acts within their jurisdiction; and to ensure that they do not occur in the future.

General Comment No. 20 (on article 7), in Compilation of General Comments and General Recommendations Adopted by Human Rights Treaty Bodies, U.N. Doc. HRI/GEN/1/Rev. 1 at 30 (1994).

The HRC's views on amnesties grew out of its views in a number of Optional Protocol cases involving serious violations of physical integrity, such as extra-judicial killings, torture and disappearances. As noted earlier, the Committee had repeatedly concluded that the government responsible for those violations should conduct an investigation, bring to justice those responsible, and provide compensation to the victims.

A challenge to Uruguay's amnesty law presented the first opportunity for the Committee to consider the validity of a specific amnesty law under its Optional Protocol procedure. Invoking its 1992 general comment, the Committee concluded that Uruguay's amnesty was incompatible with its obligations under the ICCPR.

Rodriguez v. Uruguay

Human Rights Committee, 1994.
U.N. Doc. CCPR/C/51/D/322/1988, Annex (1994).

[The author of the communication, Hugo Rodriguez, asserted that he and his wife were arrested by Uruguayan police in June 1983. Mr. Rodriguez, an Uruguayan citizen, asserted that he had endured various forms of torture while detained. He further stated that he was unable to initiate a judicial investigation until 1985, when constitutional guarantees were re-introduced following the transition from military to civilian rule in Uruguay. But efforts to secure a judicial investigation were blocked by Law No. 15,848, the Limitations Act or Law of Expiry (Ley de Caducidad), enacted by Uruguay's Parliament in December 1986. This law effectively provided for the immediate end of judicial investigation into crimes such as those of which the author complained and made impossible the pursuit of this category of crimes committed during the years of military rule.]

The complaint

3. The author denounces the acts of torture to which he was subjected as a violation of article 7 of the Covenant and contends that he and others have been denied appropriate redress in the form of investigation of the abuses allegedly committed by the military authorities, punishment of those held responsible and compensation to the victims. In this context, he notes that the State party has systematically instructed judges to apply Law No. 15,848 uniformly and close pending investigations; the President of the Republic himself allegedly advised that this procedure should be applied without exception. The author further contends that the State party cannot, by simple legislative act, violate its international commitments and thus deny justice to all the victims of human rights abuses committed under the previous military regime.

The State party's information and observations and the author's comments thereon

. . .

4.2 The State party ... explains that there are other remedies, judicial and non-judicial, which were not exhausted in the case: first, "the only thing which Law No. 15,848 does not permit ... is criminal prosecution of the offenders; it does not leave the victims of the alleged offences without a remedy". Thus, victims of torture may file claims for compensation....

4.3 Subsidiarily, it is submitted that Law No. 15,848 is consistent with the State party's international legal obligations. The State party explains that the law "did establish an amnesty of a special kind and subject to certain conditions for military and police personnel alleged to have been engaged in violations of human rights during the period of the previous ... regime.... The object of these legal normative measures was, and still is, to consolidate the institution of democracy and to ensure the social peace necessary for the establishment of a solid foundation of respect of human rights." ... In short, an amnesty or abstention from criminal prosecution should be considered not only as a valid form of legal action but also the most appropriate means of ensuring that situations endangering the respect for human rights do not occur in the future....

. . .

8.2 The State party emphasizes that Law No. 15,848 on the lapsing of State prosecutions was endorsed in 1989 by referendum, "an exemplary expression of direct democracy on the part of the Uruguayan people". Moreover, by a decision of 2 May 1988, the Supreme Court declared the law to be constitutional. It maintains that the law constituted a sovereign act of clemency that is fully in accord and harmony with the international instruments on human rights.

8.3   It is argued that notions of democracy and reconciliation ought to be taken into account when considering laws on amnesty and on the lapsing of prosecutions. . . .

8.4   With regard to the right to judicial safeguards and the obligation to investigate, the State party asserts that Law No. 15,848 in no way restricts the system of judicial remedies established in article 2, paragraph 3, of the Covenant. Pursuant to this law, only the State's right to bring criminal charges lapsed. The law did not eliminate the legal effects of offences in areas outside the sphere of criminal law. . . .

8.5   In this connection, the State party contends that "to investigate past events . . . is tantamount to reviving the confrontation between persons and groups. This certainly will not contribute to reconciliation, pacification and the strengthening of democratic institutions . . . . The State can, subject to the law and in certain circumstances, refrain from making available to the person concerned the means of establishing the truth formally and officially in a criminal court, which is governed by public, not private interest. This, of course, does not prevent or limit the free exercise by such a person of his individual rights, such as the right to information, which in many cases in themselves lead to the discovery of the truth, even if it is not the public authorities themselves that concern themselves with the matter."

8.6   With regard to the author's contention that Law No. 15,848 "frustrates any attempt to obtain compensation, as the enforcement of the law bars an official investigation of his allegations" the State party asserts that there have been many cases in which claims similar to that of the author have succeeded in civil actions and that payment has been obtained.

. . .

The Committee's views on the merits

. . .

12.1   With regard to the merits of the communication, the Committee notes that the State party has not disputed the author's allegations that he was subjected to torture by the authorities of the then military regime in Uruguay. Bearing in mind that the author's allegations are substantiated, the Committee finds that the facts as submitted sustain a finding that the military regime in Uruguay violated article 7 of the Covenant. . . .

12.2   As to the appropriate remedy that the author may claim pursuant to article 2, paragraph 3, of the Covenant, the Committee finds that the adoption of Law No. 15,848 and subsequent practice in Uruguay have rendered the realization of the author's right to an adequate remedy extremely difficult.

12.3   The Committee cannot agree with the State party that it has no obligation to investigate violations of Covenant rights by a prior regime, especially when these include crimes as serious as torture. Article 2, paragraph 3 (a) of the Covenant clearly stipulates that each State party undertakes "to ensure that any person whose rights or freedoms as herein recognized are violated shall have an effective remedy, notwithstanding that the violation has been committed by persons acting in an official capacity". In this context, the Committee refers to its general comment No. 20 (44) on article 7, which provides that allegations of torture must be fully investigated by the State:

"Article 7 should be read in conjunction with article 2, paragraph 3.... The right to lodge complaints against maltreatment prohibited by article 7 must be recognized in the domestic law. Complaints must be investigated promptly and impartially by competent authorities so as to make the remedy effective....

"The Committee has noted that some States have granted amnesty in respect of acts of torture. Amnesties are generally incompatible with the duty of States to investigate such acts; to guarantee freedom from such acts within their jurisdiction; and to ensure that they do not occur in the future. States may not deprive individuals of the right to an effective remedy, including compensation and such full rehabilitation as may be possible."

The State party has suggested that the author may still conduct private investigations into his torture. The Committee finds that the responsibility for investigations falls under the State party's obligation to grant an effective remedy. Having examined the specific circumstances of this case, the Committee finds that the author has not had an effective remedy.

12.4 The Committee moreover reaffirms its position that amnesties for gross violations of human rights and legislation such as Law No. 15,848 ... are incompatible with the obligations of the State party under the Covenant. The Committee notes with deep concern that the adoption of this law effectively excludes in a number of cases the possibility of investigation into past human rights abuses and thereby prevents the State party from discharging its responsibility to provide effective remedies to the victims of those abuses. Moreover, the Committee is concerned that, in adopting this law, the State party has contributed to an atmosphere of impunity which may undermine the democratic order and give rise to further grave human rights violations.

13. The Human Rights Committee ... is of the view that the facts before it disclose a violation of article 7, in connection with article 2, paragraph 3, of the Covenant.

14. The Committee is of the view that Mr. Hugo Rodríguez is entitled, under article 2, paragraph 3 (a), of the Covenant, to an effective remedy. It urges the State party to take effective measures (a) to carry out an official investigation into the author's allegations of torture, in order to identify the persons responsible for torture and ill-treatment and to enable the author to seek civil redress; (b) to grant appropriate compensation to Mr. Rodríguez; and (c) to ensure that similar violations do not occur in the future.

. . .

Chanfeau Orayce and Others v. Chile

Inter–American Commission on Human Rights, 1998.
Cases 11.505 et al., Inter–Am. Comm'n H.R. 512, OEA/ser.L/V/II.98, doc. 7 rev. (1997)

. . .

I. BACKGROUND

1.   The Inter–American Commission on Human Rights has continued to receive complaints against the State of Chile based on the continued effective application in that country of the amnesty law—Decree Law 2191 promulgated on March 10, 1978 under the regime of General Augusto Pinochet. It is alleged in these complaints that the very existence of the amnesty law ... causes numerous acts of violation of the right to justice.... The complaints allege that under this law, crimes committed between 1973 and 1978 are pardoned; the investigation and punishment of such crimes are hindered, and the perpetrators of crimes of atrocity are unpunished....

. . .

VI. ALLEGATIONS PRESENTED BY THE STATE OF CHILE

12.   The State of Chile ... requests that the Commission, in considering these cases, take into account the historical context surrounding the events and the special situation of the return of the country to a democratic regime which obliged the new government to accept the rules imposed by the de facto military regime, which could only be modified in accordance with the law and the Constitution.

13.   The Government has sought to have the Decree Law repealed, but the relevant constitutional provision requires that any initiatives concerning matters of amnesty be tabled from the Senate (Article 62 (2) of the Constitution), where a majority in favor does not exist because of the number of persons in that Chamber who were not elected by popular vote.*

. . .

15.   Law 19.123 passed at the initiative of the democratic government grants to the family members of the victims a life-long pension in an amount no less than the average income of a family in Chile; provides a special procedure for the declaration of presumed death; grants special attention from the state in matters of health, education and housing; writes off any educational, housing and tax debts as well as other debts to state enterprises, and exempts the children of the victims from obligatory military service.

. . .

---

* [The 1980 Constitution, adopted when General Pinochet was still President of Chile, provides for a substantial number of appointed members of both chambers of Congress. It also contains provisions making amendment of the Constitution quite difficult.—Editors' Note.]

VII. OBSERVATIONS OF THE COMMISSION ON THE ALLEGATIONS OF THE PARTIES

. . .

33. The democratic government denied all responsibility for the acts perpetrated by the military dictatorship but recognized its obligation to investigate past human rights violations and established a Truth Commission to ascertain the facts and publish its findings.** As a gesture to the families of the victims, ex-President Aylwin sought their forgiveness on behalf of the State of Chile. In addition, the ex-President publicly protested the decision of the Supreme Court that the Amnesty Decree Law should be applied in a manner which would suspend all investigations into the facts. The Democratic Government, citing its inability to change or repeal the Amnesty Decree–Law and its obligation to respect the decisions of the Judiciary, maintained that the measure already adopted would be sufficiently effective to fulfill Chile's obligations under the Convention, and that any further steps were thereby rendered unnecessary.

. . .

42. The Commission has repeatedly noted that the application of amnesties renders ineffective or invalid the international obligation of States parties imposed by Article 1.1 of the Convention. Consequently they constitute a violation of said Article and they eliminate the most effective measure for the exercise of those rights—the trial and punishment of the responsible individuals.

43. As the petitioners have clearly stated, their claims do not concern human rights violations resulting from the illegal detention and disappearance of the persons mentioned in their claims, acts which had been perpetrated by agents of the State of Chile during the former military regime, but rather the fact that Amnesty Decree Law 2191, which was enacted by the military government, has not been repealed and has consequently remained in effect under the democratic government, even after Chile has ratified the American Convention and acceded to its conditions. Their claims concern the fact that there has been neither trial nor identification of those responsible nor punishments meted out against the perpetrators of these acts and that this situation which began during the military regime still prevails under the rule of the democratic and constitutional government.

44. The democratic Government of Chile recognizes the close relationship existing in these cases between amnesty and impunity, and for that reason it enacted law No. 19.123, which compensated the relatives of the victims of human rights violations. . . .

. . .

** [This "commission" was appointed by the first democratically-elected government, headed by President Patricio Alwyn, following the 17–year Pinochet regime.—Editors' Note.]

46. The Commission has taken into account that the democratic government went to the Supreme Court in March 1991, urging that it consider that the amnesty in effect should not and could not legally be an obstacle to the investigation and the identification of those responsible and that it has vetoed a law which could have lent further support to the Amnesty.

47. The Commission recognizes and advocates the importance of the creation of the National Commission for Truth and Reconciliation and also the work which the latter has carried out in gathering antecedents on prior cases on human rights violations and detainees who disappeared, out of which came a report identifying individual victims—and among them cases of persons named in the claims—tried to establish their whereabouts and measures of compensation and redress for each one. It recognized that the cases of these persons constitute serious violations of fundamental rights on the part of State agents. . . .

48. Law No. 19.123, an initiative of the Democratic Government, [described in paragraph 15, supra,] deserves equal recognition.

· · ·

50. These measures, however, are not sufficient to guarantee the human rights of the petitioners, in keeping with the terms set forth in Articles 1.1 and 2 of the American Convention on Human Rights, for as long as they continue to be denied the right to justice.

b) The denial of justice

51. In such cases, the violation of the right to justice and the consequent impunity that it generates represent, as has been established, a confluence of events which begin when the military government issues for its own benefit or for the benefit of the agents of the state who committed violations of human rights, a series of regulations designed to create a complex juridical web of impunity. These developments began formally in 1978, when the military government adopted Decree Law 2191 on amnesty.

· · ·

53. Consequently, the Chilean State, through its Legislature, is liable for the failure to amend or repeal Decree Law 2191 of 19–4–78, which is a violation of the obligations assumed by this State to ensure conformity of their laws with the precepts of the Convention, pursuant to Articles 1.1 and 2.

· · ·

d) The violation of the right to judicial protection (Article 25)

60. The complaint alleges that the victims and their families were deprived of the right to effective recourse, as provided for in Article 25 of the Convention, which confers protection from any acts which violate their rights.

· · ·

64. The amnesty decree law gave rise to juridical inefficacy with respect to crimes; the victims and their families were left with no legal recourse by

which perpetrators of human rights violations committed under the military dictatorship could be identified and the corresponding punishment imposed.

65. By promulgating and ensuring compliance of de facto Decree Law 2191, the Chilean State ceased to guarantee the rights to legal protection provided for under Article 25 of the Convention.

e) Non-compliance with the obligation to investigate

66. In its interpretation of Article 1.1 of the American Convention on Human Rights, the Inter–American Court stipulates that "The second obligation of the States Parties is to 'ensure' the free and full exercise of the rights recognized by the Convention to every person subject to its jurisdiction. ... As a consequence of this obligation, the States must prevent, investigate and punish any violation of the rights recognized by the Convention ..." ...

67. The National Truth and Reconciliation Commission established by the democratic Government to investigate human rights violations committed in the past, examined most of the total number of cases and granted reparation to the victims and their families. Nevertheless, the investigation carried out by the Commission into cases involving the violation of the victims' right to life as well as the victims of other violations provided no legal recourse or any other type of compensation.

68. Moreover, the National Truth and Reconciliation Commission was not a judicial organ and its work was restricted to establishing the identity of victims of the violation of the right to life. By the very nature of its mandate, that Commission was not authorized to publish the names of persons who had committed the crimes nor impose any type of sanction. For this reason, despite the important role it played in establishing the facts and granting compensation, the Truth Commission cannot be seen as a viable alternative to judicial process.

. . .

70. The admission of responsibility by the Government, a partial investigation of the facts and the subsequent payment of compensation are not, in themselves, sufficient to fulfill the obligations provided for in the Convention. In accordance with the provisions of Article 1.1 of the Convention, the state has the obligation to investigate violations committed within its jurisdiction, in order to identify those responsible, to impose the necessary sanctions and ensure adequate reparation to the victim.

71. By authorizing de facto Decree Law 2191 on amnesty, the State of Chile failed to comply fully with the obligation stipulated in Convention Article 1.1, and thus violated, to the detriment of the claimants, the human rights recognized by the American Convention.

f) The international responsibility of the State

. . .

76. Amnesty Law 2191 and its legal effects are part of a general policy of human rights violations by the military regime that governed Chile from

September 1973 to March 1990. Although this law was enacted under the regime of General Augusto Pinochet, it is still applied each time a complaint of human rights violation is brought against the military government or its agents in Chilean courts. The continued application of the amnesty law by a democratic government even after the end of the military regime which enacted this law, has legal implications which are incompatible with the provisions of the American Convention on Human Rights.

. . .

80. The non-compliance by the State of Chile with the provision of Articles 1 and 2 of the Convention is demonstrated by the fact that Decree Law 2191 enacted under the military dictatorship which took power between 1973 and 1990 has not been derogated by the present Legislative, but has remained in force; that the domestic legislation of Chile has not been adapted to comply with the norms of the Convention; and that as was stated by the present judicial organ, such domestic legislation prevails for ongoing judicial processes.

. . .

The Right to Know the Truth

85. Pursuant to the American Convention, the State has the duty to ensure the right of the victims' families and of society as a whole, to know the truth of the facts connected with the serious violations to human rights which occurred in Chile, as well as the identity of those who committed them. Such an obligation is primarily established in Articles 1.1, 8, 25 and 13 of the Convention.

86. According to Article 1.1, States Parties must "respect" the rights enshrined in the American Convention as well as "ensure" their free and full exercise. Such a duty, as explained by the Inter–American Court, involves the true "obligation to do something" in order to effectively guarantee such rights. Pursuant to this obligation, the Chilean State is in a position where it has the legal obligation to reasonably prevent human rights violations. It must also, according to the means at its disposal, investigate the violations committed within its jurisdiction, identify those responsible and impose the pertinent sanctions on them, as well as ensure the adequate reparation of the consequences suffered by the victim.

87. The interpretation of the generic obligations established in Article 1.1 made by the Court in [past] cases ... allows for the conclusion that the "right to truth" is a basic and indispensable consequence for every State Party. The disregard for the facts connected with the violations is translated into a system of protection which, in practice, cannot guarantee the identification and eventual punishment of those responsible. In the specific case of forced disappearances, we are concerned with violations of a continuous nature. The Court has interpreted that in such cases the duty to investigate the facts extends for as long as the uncertainty over the final fate of the disappeared person exists.

88. The right to truth constitutes both a right of a collective nature which allows society as a whole to have access to essential information on the

development of the democratic system, and an individual right which allows the families of the victims to have access to some kind of reparation in those cases in which amnesty laws are in force. The American Convention protects the rights to access and receive information in the case of disappearances. In such cases both the Court and the Commission have established that the State has the obligation to determine the whereabouts of the individuals "disappeared". The Court has noted that "the duty to investigate facts of this type continues as long as there is uncertainty about the fate of the person who has disappeared ... the State is obligated to use the means at its disposal to inform the relatives of the fate of the victims and, if they have been killed, the location of their remains". The Court has also said that "the State has a legal duty to ... use the means at its disposal to carry out a serious investigation of violations committed within its jurisdiction, to identify those responsible, to impose the appropriate punishment and to ensure the victim adequate compensation".

89. The right to truth is also related to Article 25 of the Convention, which provides for the right to a simple and prompt remedy to protect the rights therein enshrined. The mere existence of factual or legal impediments (such as an amnesty law) to access relevant information connected to the facts and circumstances where the violation of a fundamental right has occurred, constitutes an open violation to Article 25 of the American Convention; apart from the fact that such impediments prevent the availability of domestic remedies allowing for the judicial protection of the fundamental rights established in the Convention, the Constitution and the statutes.

. . .

92. The Commission has ... said that "Every society has the inalienable right to know the truth about past events, as well as the motives and circumstances in which aberrant crimes came to be committed, in order to prevent repetitions of such acts in the future. Moreover, the family members of the victims are entitled to information on what happened to their relatives. Such access to truth presupposes freedom of speech; the establishment of investigating committees whose membership and authority must be determined in accordance with the internal legislation of each country, or the provision of the necessary resources so that the judiciary itself may undertake whatever investigation may be necessary".

. . .

95. Both the right of every person and the right of society to know the whole truth on the facts, the circumstances and the participants in a human rights violation is part of the reparation owed as a satisfaction and a commitment not to repeat the violation in the future. The right of society to know about its past does not only constitute a reparation and a way to shed light on the facts which have occurred, but also serves the purpose of preventing future violations.

96. States which have resorted to the enactment of amnesty legislation while in search of mechanisms for national pacification and reconciliation,

have abandoned the very part of the their population which includes many of the innocent victims of violence. They have abandoned the victims who are denied the right to justice when claiming against those who have committed excesses and abhorrent acts of violence against them. In situations such as this, the international obligation established in Article 1.1 of the Convention is left inoperative and worthless. It constitutes a clear case of disregard of the obligation to effectively redress the rights that have been violated.

97.   In the particular case of Chile, the Truth and Reconciliation Commission carried out a commendable task, by gathering information on human rights violations and on the situation of those "disappeared", with a view to establishing their whereabouts, as well as the corresponding measures to redress their rights and clear their name. However, neither the investigation of the crimes committed by State agents nor their identification and punishment was allowed. Through the amnesty decree, the Chilean State impeded the realization of the right of the survivors and the families of the victims to know the truth.

. . .

X. RECOMMENDATIONS

108.   In light of the foregoing, the Inter–American Commission on Human Rights, based on its analysis of the facts and in accordance with the international provisions invoked,

AGREES:

109.   To recommend that the State of Chile adjust its domestic legislation by derogating Decree–Law 2191 enacted in 1978, in order to comply with the provisions of the American Convention on Human Rights, in order that the human rights violations of the military de facto government may be investigated and the perpetrators may be identified, their responsibility established and that they may be effectively punished, thus guaranteeing for the victims and their families the right to justice.

110.   To recommend that the State of Chile make it possible for the families of the victims mentioned in this case to receive fair and effective compensation for the damages incurred.

. . .

Notes

1.   According to Uruguay, the principal legal effect of the law that was found incompatible with the ICCPR in the case of *Rodriguez v. Uruguay* was that the law foreclosed criminal prosecution (para. 4.2). Yet the analysis of the Human Rights Committee emphasized the victim's right to redress as the principal basis for its conclusion that the amnesty was incompatible with the Covenant. In what sense does foreclosure of criminal prosecution violate an individual's right of redress? What other legal

theories seemed to support the Committee's conclusion that the Ley de Caducidad violated Uruguay's obligations under the ICCPR?

2.   Note that, in its views in the *Rodriguez* case, the Human Rights Committee did not urge the government of Uruguay to prosecute those responsible for torturing the applicant, nor did it suggest that the government should repeal the amnesty law. Why did it stop short of making these recommendations?

3.   Uruguay argued that its amnesty law was the most appropriate means of ensuring that abuses like those committed in the recent past do not recur (see paras. 4.3 and 8.5). The Human Rights Committee, in contrast, expressed concern that the amnesty may contribute to "an atmosphere of impunity which may undermine the democratic order and give rise to further grave human rights violations." (Para. 12.4.) Given the speculative nature of this issue, which view should prevail? Is this the type of situation in which a supervisory body should accord states a "margin of appreciation" to determine the most appropriate means of satisfying their treaty obligations? What are the principal arguments against deferring to states on this type of calculation?

4.   What was the legal basis for the Inter–American Commission's conclusion that States Parties to the American Convention have "the duty to ensure the right of the victims' families and of society as a whole, to know the truth of the facts connected with the serious violations to human rights" (para. 85)? Is the right to the truth based upon the importance of information in leading to criminal punishment, as the Commission seems to suggest in paragraph 87? If so, is it appropriate to recognize a right to the truth as a distinct right rather than to maintain that states must take all necessary steps to ensure punishment of those responsible for human rights violations? Or is the right to the truth based upon the right of relatives to know the fate of their loved ones? (See in this regard the Commission's analysis in paragraph 88.) To the extent that the latter rationale supports the Commission's general conclusion that there is a "right to know the truth," would this rationale support the right of "society as a whole" to have access to information (as distinguished from individuals whose loved ones have disappeared) (see para. 88)? Or is society's right to know the truth based on other considerations (see in this respect paras. 88, 92 and 95)? In its discussion of society's "right to know the truth," did the Commission implicitly recognize a form of "collective right" under the American Convention?

5.   Did the Commission find that the "right to know the truth" was breached notwithstanding the operation of Chile's truth commission? What was its reasoning? Is it persuasive?

6.   In its report assessing Chile's amnesty law, the Inter–American Commission observed: "Moreover, the National Truth and Reconciliation Commission was not a judicial organ and its work was restricted to establishing the identity of victims of the violation of the right to life. By the very nature of its mandate, that Commission was not authorized to publish the names of persons who had committed the crimes nor impose any type of

sanction. For this reason, despite the important role it played in establishing the facts and granting compensation, the Truth Commission cannot be seen as a viable alternative to judicial process." (Para. 68.) Does this suggest that, if the National Truth and Reconciliation Commission had been able to "name names" of perpetrators, its work would have been an acceptable alternative to criminal prosecutions? Do other portions of the Inter–American Commission's report shed light on this question?

7. In light of the Inter–American Commission's analysis of Chile's amnesty law, when, if ever, might an amnesty law survive scrutiny by the Commission? Would the South African amnesty scheme, which provides for individual rather than blanket amnesties and makes those amnesties contingent upon full disclosure of the truth by applicants, survive scrutiny under the standards elucidated by the Commission?

8. For analysis of the legal issues raised by amnesty laws, see Impunity and Human Rights in International Law and Practice, chs. 3 & 4 (Naomi Roht Arriaza, ed. 1995); Douglass Cassel, *Lessons from the Americas: Guidelines for International Response to Amnesties for Atrocities*, 59 Law and Contemp. Probs. 197 (1996); Diane F. Orentlicher, *Addressing Gross Human Rights Abuses: Punishment and Victim Compensation*, in Human Rights: An Agenda for the Next Century 425 (Louis Henkin and John Lawrence Hargrove, eds., 1994); and Diane F. Orentlicher, *Settling Accounts: The Duty to Prosecute Human Rights Violations of a Prior Regime*, 100 Yale L.J. 2537 (1991).

Universal Jurisdiction

The preceding section focused on the obligations of states to investigate certain human rights violations committed in their own territory and to bring the perpetrators to justice in their own courts, but states have sometimes also prosecuted serious violations of human rights committed outside their territory. For example, in the early 1960s the government of Israel prosecuted Adolf Eichmann for crimes relating to his role in executing Hitler's Final Solution, after abducting Eichmann from Argentina. Eichmann was prosecuted under a law enacted in 1950 that enabled Israeli courts to try persons who committed an act constituting a crime against the Jewish people, a crime against humanity, or a war crime during the period of the Nazi regime.

Prosecutions of this nature potentially raise several issues of international law. Among them, questions concerning jurisdictional authority may be raised. As the following section of the Restatement of Foreign Relations Law reflects, several distinct aspects of jurisdictional authority may be implicated in a prosecution such as that of Adolf Eichmann.

§ 401. CATEGORIES OF JURISDICTION

Under international law, a state is subject to limitations on

(a) jurisdiction to prescribe, i.e., to make its law applicable to the activities, relations, or status of persons, or the interests of persons in things, whether by legislation, by executive act or order, by administrative rule or regulation, or by determination of a court;

(b) jurisdiction to adjudicate, i.e., to subject persons or things to the process of its courts or administrative tribunals, whether in civil or in criminal proceedings, whether or not the state is a party to the proceedings;

(c) jurisdiction to enforce, i.e., to induce or compel compliance or to punish noncompliance with its laws or regulations, whether through the courts or by use of executive, administrative, police, or other nonjudicial action.

In the materials that follow, we are concerned principally with questions concerning states' jurisdiction to prescribe.

International law recognizes several bases for prescriptive jurisdiction. The most well established and generally accepted basis is territorial jurisdiction. In the words of the Restatement, "a state has jurisdiction to prescribe law with respect to ... conduct that, wholly or in substantial part, takes place within its territory." Restatement, § 402(1)(a). It is also widely accepted that states may apply their law to their nationals, even when the latter are abroad. See id., para. 2. With respect to a narrow category of crimes, including certain acts of terrorism, states may rely upon "passive personality" jurisdiction—that is, they may assert jurisdiction over extra-territorial crimes committed against their nationals even when committed by non-nationals. In exceptional cases, states may apply their law to acts committed outside their territory by non-nationals whose victims also were not their nationals, pursuant to the principle of "universal jurisdiction":

§ 404. UNIVERSAL JURISDICTION TO DEFINE AND PUNISH CERTAIN OFFENSES

A state has jurisdiction to define and prescribe punishment for certain offenses recognized by the community of nations as of universal concern, such as piracy, slave trade, attacks on or hijacking of aircraft, genocide, war crimes, and perhaps certain acts of terrorism, even where none of the bases of jurisdiction indicated in § 402 is present.

Israel's prosecution of Nazi official Adolf Eichmann in 1961 relied in part on this ground of jurisdiction. The Jerusalem District Court upheld Israel's jurisdiction to try Eichmann, reasoning:

The abhorrent crimes defined in this Law are not crimes under Israel [sic] law alone. These crimes, which struck at the whole of mankind and shocked the conscience of nations, are grave offences against the law of nations itself.... Therefore, so far from international law negating or limiting the jurisdiction of countries with respect to such crimes, international law is, in the absence of an International Court, in need of the judicial and legislative organs of every country to give effect to its criminal interdictions and to bring the criminals to trial. The jurisdiction to try crimes under international law is *universal*.

Attorney General of Israel v. Eichmann, reprinted in 36 I.L.R. 18, 26 (Isr. Dist. Ct.—Jerusalem 1961), aff'd, 36 I.L.R. 277 (Isr. Sup. Ct. 1962). The Israeli Supreme Court affirmed this holding, concluding that "[i]t is the peculiarly universal character of [the crimes with which Eichmann was charged] that vests in every State the authority to try and punish anyone who participated in their commission." *Attorney General of Israel v. Eichmann*, reprinted in 36 I.L.R. 277, 287 (Isr. Sup. Ct. 1962).

The 1990s saw increased use of universal jurisdiction for crimes entailing grave violations of human rights. The operation of the two ad hoc international tribunals apparently spurred several states in Western Europe to prosecute persons suspected of criminal responsibility for atrocities committed in the former Yugoslavia and Rwanda. In September 1997, a German court convicted a Bosnian Serb of genocide—the first person convicted of this crime in Germany outside the context of World War II prosecutions. See Alan Cowell, *German Court Sentences Serb to Life for Genocide in Bosnia*, Sept. 27, 1997.

The defendants in many of these national prosecutions have been relatively low-level soldiers. But in October 1998, British authorities arrested a former Chilean head of state, General Augusto Pinochet, at the request of a Spanish magistrate, Judge Baltasar Garzón. For more than two years Judge Garzón and another Spanish magistrate had been investigating various alleged crimes committed in Argentina during its "dirty war," in which as many as 30,000 persons may have been murdered or "disappeared," and in Chile during the period of General Pinochet's rule. The judicial process that led to General Pinochet's arrest was triggered by a criminal complaint filed by the Association of Progressive Prosecutors of Spain acting in its capacity as a private complainant. The Association's complaint set the criminal process in motion, and was joined by other private organizations and individuals. (Under a procedure in Spanish criminal law known as an *acción popular*, any Spanish citizen can initiate and participate in criminal investigations as a private prosecutor.) The investigations in Spain were based upon two principal grounds of prescriptive jurisdiction, passive personality (some victims of the alleged crimes were Spanish nationals) and universal jurisdiction. Spanish criminal law provides for the exercise of universal jurisdiction with respect to several crimes, including genocide, terrorism and torture.

While General Pinochet was in London on a private visit, Judge Garzón issued an international arrest warrant and asked British authorities to detain the former President so that he could be questioned in connection with "crimes of genocide and terrorism that include murder." In mid-October 1998, British police arrested General Pinochet. Soon thereafter, Judge Garzón expanded the charges against the former Chilean president, and the government of Spain formally sought his extradition on November 4, 1998.

Head of State Immunity

The proceedings against General Pinochet raised several complex legal and policy issues. The most important legal question presented at the outset of the proceedings in the United Kingdom was whether General Pinochet enjoyed immunity from legal process by virtue of his status as a former head of state. The British courts' approach to this issue is noteworthy, not least for the significance attached at various phases of the domestic proceedings to the fact that the crimes with which General Pinochet had been charged were proscribed as criminal under international law.

Although the international law governing head of state immunity is not as well defined as that relating to diplomatic immunity, current heads of state on official visits abroad are generally accorded the same immunities as those enjoyed by diplomats. It is less clear, however, to what extent former heads of state enjoy immunity from legal process for acts committed while they were in office. Further, international law derived from Nuremberg denies immunity even to current heads of state under certain circumstances. The Nuremberg Principles, adopted in 1950 pursuant to an earlier UN General Assembly resolution affirming principles of international law recognized in the Nuremberg Charter and the judgment of the Nuremberg Tribunal, include the following:

Principle III

The fact that a person who committed an act which constitutes a crime under international law acted as Head of State or responsible Government official does not relieve him from responsibility under international law.

This principle has been incorporated into the statutes of the Yugoslavia and Rwanda Tribunals (Articles 7 and 6, respectively),* as well as the Rome Statute for a permanent international criminal court (Article 27).

In the British extradition proceedings, General Pinochet's claim of head of state immunity was governed by a domestic law, the State Immunity Act 1978. Interpreting this law, a British Divisional Court ruled on October 28, 1998 that General Pinochet was entitled to immunity as a former sovereign from the criminal and civil process of English courts. The portion of this decision relating to General Pinochet's claim of immunity was immediately reviewed on appeal by a judicial panel of the House of Lords, the highest court in the United Kingdom. By a vote of 3 to 2, the Law Lords panel overturned the lower court's ruling. All five members of the panel believed that General Pinochet would have been entitled to head of state immunity were he still President of Chile, but they divided on whether the immunity conferred by the State Immunity Act was available to a former head of state charged with the crimes alleged against General Pinochet.

---

* On May 24, 1999, a judge of a Trial Chamber of the Yugoslavia Tribunal confirmed an indictment submitted two days earlier charging Yugoslav President Slobodan Milošević and four other senior leaders with crimes against humanity and war crimes. *Prosecutor v. Slobodan Milošević et al.*, Case No. IT–99–37–I, Decision on Review of Indictment and Application for Consequential Orders (May 24, 1999). The Rwanda Tribunal had previously convicted a former Prime Minister of Rwanda of genocide based upon the defendant's guilty plea.

Under the 1978 law, the key issue was whether the acts charged should be deemed to have been official acts committed in the exercise of then President Pinochet's functions as head of state. Interpreting the State Immunity Act in light of international law, three judges concluded that General Pinochet was not immune from judicial process in respect of the charges on which his extradition was sought. In the words of Lord Nicholls, "torture of his own subjects, or of aliens, would not be regarded by international law as a function of a head of state"; "international law has made plain that certain types of conduct, including torture and hostage-taking, are not acceptable conduct on the part of anyone." In an opinion joined by Lord Hoffman, Lord Steyn similarly reasoned that

> the development of international law since the second world war justifies the conclusion that by the time of the 1973 coup d'etat [by General Pinochet], and certainly ever since, international law condemned genocide, torture, hostage-taking and crimes against humanity (during an armed conflict or in peace time) as international crimes deserving of punishment. Given this state of international law, it seems to me difficult to maintain that the commission of such high crimes may amount to acts performed in the exercise of the functions of a head of state.

Regina v. Bow Street Metropolitan Stipendiary Magistrate ex parte Pinochet Ugarte, [1998] 3 W. L. R. 1456, 1506 (1998) (Opinion of Lord Steyn).

This decision was subsequently vacated by another panel of the Law Lords because Lord Hoffman, one of the three Lords who voted to deny General Pinochet former head of state immunity, had failed to disclose that he had worked as a volunteer fund-raiser for Amnesty International. (That London-based non-governmental organization had been granted special leave to intervene in the proceedings against General Pinochet.) The appeal was reargued before a seven-member panel of Law Lords.

On March 24, 1999, that panel ruled, by a majority vote of six, that General Pinochet was not entitled to head of state immunity. *Regina v. Bow Street Metropolitan Stipendiary Magistrate ex parte Pinochet Ugarte (No. 3)*, [1999] 2 W. L. R. 827 (1999). The legal consequences of the Torture Convention, to which the United Kingdom, Spain and Chile are parties, loomed large in the opinions of several Lords constituting the majority on this issue.

In reasoning similar to that of the majority of the earlier panel whose judgment had been vacated, Lord Browne–Wilkinson, the senior Law Lord, judged that, as a former head of state, General Pinochet "enjoys immunity ratione materiae in relation to acts done by him as head of state as part of his official functions as head of state." Having also found that the crime of torture is a peremptory norm with respect to which universal jurisdiction exists, Lord Browne–Wilkinson continued:

> Can it be said that the commission of a crime which is an international crime against humanity and jus cogens is an act done in an official capacity on behalf of the state? I believe there to be strong ground for

saying that the implementation of torture as defined by the Torture Convention cannot be a state function.

Even so, Lord Browne–Wilkinson expressed

> doubts whether, before the coming into force of the Torture Convention, the existence of the international crime of torture as jus cogens was enough to justify the conclusion that the organisation of state torture could not rank for immunity purposes as performance of an official function. At that stage there was no international tribunal to punish torture and no general jurisdiction to permit or require its punishment in domestic courts. Not until there was some form of universal jurisdiction for the punishment of the crime of torture could it really be talked about as a fully constituted international crime. But in my judgment the Torture Convention did provide what was missing: a worldwide universal jurisdiction.

As this observation indicates, the Torture Convention establishes a form of universal jurisdiction. Article 5 requires States Parties to take necessary measures to establish their jurisdiction over torture in certain specified circumstances, including when "the alleged offender is present in any territory under its jurisdiction and it does not extradite him." Article 7(1) provides that a State Party "in the territory under whose jurisdiction a person alleged to have committed [torture] is found shall in the cases contemplated in article 5, if it does not extradite him, submit the case to its competent authorities for the purpose of prosecution."

The opinions of several other Lords cited the status of torture under customary international law as well as the Torture Convention in support of their determination to deny General Pinochet absolute head of state immunity. One of the seven jurists, Lord Goff of Chieveley, would have granted Pinochet complete immunity.

While the Torture Convention played a significant part in the majority's decision to deny absolute immunity with respect to torture-related charges, the date of the United Kingdom's adherence served to exclude all but a handful of the charges that had already been submitted from being considered a lawful basis for extradition. Like the extradition law of many countries, the relevant British law includes a "dual criminality" requirement—it allows British authorities to extradite suspects only with respect to conduct that would constitute a criminal offense if committed in the United Kingdom—and also requires that such conduct be punishable by at least one year's imprisonment. In the view of a majority of Lords sitting on the seven-member panel, torture *committed outside the United Kingdom's territorial jurisdiction* did not constitute a crime under British law until September 29, 1988. On that date, Section 134 of the Criminal Justice Act 1988, which gave effect to Britain's obligations under the Torture Convention, entered into force. Before that date, British law did not treat *extraterritorial* torture as a crime. Further, a majority of Lords ruled that the conduct for which extradition was sought had to have been criminal under United Kingdom law at the time it was committed; it is not sufficient that the conduct would have been criminal under British law at the time extradition is sought.

The result was that General Pinochet could be extradited only with respect to alleged acts of torture occurring after September 29, 1988. But as Lord Browne–Wilkinson acknowledged, "The result of this decision is to eliminate the majority of the charges leveled against Senator Pinochet by the Government of Spain and relied upon as the basis for extraditing him"; the vast majority of charges filed by Judge Garzón at that time involved crimes alleged to have occurred in the 1970s. Warren Hoge, *Pinochet Arrest Upheld, but Most Charges Are Discarded,* N.Y. Times, Mar. 25, 1999.

In view of the radically narrowed scope of charges for which extradition was possible, many of the Lords constituting the majority suggested that British Home Secretary Jack Straw, who had earlier issued an authority to proceed with the extradition process, reconsider his decision. In mid-April 1999, Secretary Straw once again authorized the extradition proceedings against General Pinochet to go forward.

Notes

1. Lord Browne–Wilkinson expressed doubt whether, "before the coming into force of the Torture Convention, the existence of the international crime of torture as jus cogens was enough to justify the conclusion that the organisation of state torture could not rank for immunity purposes as performance of an official function." On what basis does Lord Browne–Wilkinson conclude that "the existence of the international crime of torture as jus cogens" is insufficient in itself to justify denial of head of state immunity for torture? Why should the entry into force of the Torture Convention make a decisive difference?

2. Another Lord joining the majority in the March 24, 1999 decision, Lord Hope of Craighead, doubted whether even the terms of the Torture Convention "were sufficient to remove the immunity from prosecution [that former heads of state generally enjoy under customary law] for all acts of torture. The jus cogens character of the immunity enjoyed by serving heads of state ratione personae suggests that, on any view, that immunity was not intended to be affected by the Convention." He reasoned:

> There is no requirement [in the Torture Convention] that [torture] should have been perpetrated on such a scale as to constitute an international crime . . ., that is to say a crime which offends against the public order of the international community. A single act of torture by an official against a national of his state within that state's borders will do. . . .
>
> Nevertheless there remains the question whether the immunity can survive Chile's agreement to the Torture Convention if the torture which is alleged was of such a kind or on such a scale as to amount to an international crime.

Citing instruments that define torture as a crime against humanity when committed as part of a widespread or systematic attack against any civilian population, he noted that the allegations made against General Pinochet by Spanish authorities "fall into that category":

> We are dealing with the remnants of an allegation that he is guilty of what would now, without doubt, be regarded by customary international law as an *international* crime. This is because he is said to have been involved in acts of torture which were committed in pursuance of a policy to commit systematic torture within Chile and elsewhere as an instrument of government. . . .
>
> . . . In my opinion, once the machinery which [the Torture Convention] provides was put in place to enable jurisdiction over such crimes to be exercised in the courts of a foreign state, it was no longer open to any state which was a signatory to the Convention to invoke the immunity ratione materiae in the event of allegations of systematic or widespread torture committed after that date being made in the courts of that state against its officials or any other person acting in an official capacity.

Rejecting the possibility that the Torture Convention contains an implied term abrogating the immunity of former heads of state with respect to all acts of torture, he continued:

> It is just that the obligations which were recognised by customary international law in the case of such serious international crimes by the date when Chile ratified the Convention are so strong as to override any objection by it on the ground of immunity ratione materiae to the exercise of the jurisdiction over crimes committed after that date which the United Kingdom had made available.
>
> I consider that the date as from which the immunity ratione materiae was lost was . . . the date when Chile's ratification of the Torture Convention . . . took effect. . . . But I am prepared to accept the view of . . . Lord Saville of Newdigate that Senator Pinochet continued to have immunity until 8 December 1988 when the United Kingdom ratified the Convention.

If, as Lord Hope's analysis suggests, it is the customary international law governing systematic torture that removed General Pinochet's immunity ratione materiae, why should Chile's ratification of the Torture Convention be relevant to the question of Pinochet's immunity? Is Lord Hope's analysis persuasive?

3. Consider also Lord Hope's assertion that "The jus cogens character of the immunity enjoyed by serving heads of state ratione personae suggests that, on any view, that immunity was not intended to be affected by the Convention." Recall that, if a norm has the status of jus cogens, no treaty may derogate from that norm. In light of this, is Lord Hope correct in characterizing the immunity of current heads of state as a peremptory norm? Article 27 of the Rome Statute for a permanent international criminal court, which is an international treaty, provides:

1.   This Statute shall apply equally to all persons without any distinction based on official capacity. In particular, official capacity as a head of state or Government, a member of a Government or parliament, an elected representative or a government official shall in no case exempt a person from criminal responsibility under this Statute, nor shall it, in and of itself, constitute a ground for reduction of sentence.

2.   Immunities or special procedural rules which may attach to the official capacity of a person, whether under national or international law, shall not bar the court from exercising its jurisdiction over such a person.

Can this provision be reconciled with Lord Hope's position?

4.   The March 24, 1999 judgment of the Law Lords affirmed the principle of universal jurisdiction over torture. In the words of Lord Browne–Wilkinson:

> Apart from the law of piracy, the concept of personal liability under international law for international crimes is of comparatively modern growth. The traditional subjects of international law are states not human beings. But consequent upon the war crime trials after the 1939–1945 World War, the international community came to recognise that there could be criminal liability under international law for a class of crimes such as war crimes and crimes against humanity. . . . In the early years state torture was one of the elements of a war crime. In consequence torture, and various other crimes against humanity, were linked to war or at least to hostilities of some kind. But in the course of time this linkage with war fell away and torture, divorced from war or hostilities, became an international crime on its own. . . . Ever since 1945, torture on a large scale has featured as one of the crimes against humanity. . . .

> . . .

> The jus cogens nature of the international crime of torture justifies states in taking universal jurisdiction over torture wherever committed. International law provides that offences jus cogens may be punished by any state because the offenders are "common enemies of all mankind and all nations have an equal interest in their apprehension and prosecution": *Demjanjuk v. Petrovsky*, [776 F.2d 571 (6th Cir. 1985).]

The U.S. decision cited by Lord Browne–Wilkinson recognized that universal jurisdiction existed over certain crimes and relied upon this in support of a decision to extradite the plaintiff to Israel. In general, however, the United States has been reluctant to enact legislation establishing universal jurisdiction over international human rights crimes or war crimes. One exception is 18 U.S.C. § 2340(3)(b), which enables U.S. courts to exercise universal jurisdiction with respect to torture. This law was enacted to implement the Torture Convention, which the United States ratified in 1994. See p. 784 infra.

D. IMPLEMENTATION BY INTERNATIONAL ADJUDICATION: THE INTERNATIONAL COURT OF JUSTICE

The International Court of Justice (ICJ), widely known as the "World Court," has had relatively few occasions to apply or interpret international human rights law. Two of its most important decisions concerning human rights, which we examine in this section, have involved the 1948 Convention on the Prevention and Punishment of the Crime of Genocide ("Genocide Convention"). The Court and individual judges have also rendered important pronouncements on racial discrimination in the context of decisions relating to South West Africa (Namibia). See Part IV, Chapter 1, Section D(1).

Established as the "principal judicial organ of the United Nations" (UN Charter, Article 92), the ICJ has two types of jurisdiction—advisory and contentious. Pursuant to Article 65(1) of its Statute, the Court can render an advisory opinion "on any legal question at the request of whatever body may be authorized by or in accordance with the Charter of the United Nations to make such a request." Article 96 of the Charter empowers the General Assembly and the Security Council to request an advisory opinion "on any legal question" and empowers other UN organs and specialized agencies that have been so authorized by the General Assembly to request advisory opinions "on legal questions arising within the scope of their activities."

The ICJ's contentious jurisdiction extends only to disputes between states that have consented to its jurisdiction. (ICJ Statute, Articles 34–36.) States can provide such consent in various ways, e.g., by agreement with respect to a particular dispute (id., Article 36(1)), through a clause in a treaty by which states parties agree to submit disputes arising under the treaty to the ICJ (id.), or by making a declaration under the so-called "optional clause" prospectively recognizing the Court's jurisdiction (id., Article 36(2)). An example of a treaty clause providing for submission of disputes to the ICJ, known as a compromissory clause, is Article IX of the Genocide Convention:

> Disputes between the Contracting Parties relating to the interpretation, application or fulfilment of the present Convention, including those relating to the responsibility of a State for genocide or for any of the other acts enumerated in article III, shall be submitted to the International Court of Justice at the request of any of the parties to the dispute.

See also Note on ICJ Clauses, infra p. 683.

1. RESERVATIONS TO THE GENOCIDE CONVENTION

The Genocide Convention, which was adopted by the United Nations General Assembly in 1948, gave rise to an important opinion of the ICJ on reservations under the law of treaties. The opinion was rendered in response to several questions submitted by the General Assembly concerning reservations to the 1948 Convention. The portion of the opinion set forth below also reflects the Court's views concerning the status under customary law of at least some principles underlying the Convention.

Reservations to the Convention on the Prevention and Punishment of the Crime of Genocide

International Court of Justice, 1951.
1951 I.C.J. 15 (May 28) (Advisory Opinion).

. . .

[The Court] must now determine what kind of reservations may be made and what kind of objections may be taken to them.

The solution of these problems must be found in the special characteristics of the Genocide Convention.... The origins of the Convention show that it was the intention of the United Nations to condemn and punish genocide as "a crime under international law" involving a denial of the right of existence of entire human groups, a denial which shocks the conscience of mankind and results in great losses to humanity, and which is contrary to moral law and to the spirit and aims of the United Nations (Resolution 96 (I) of the General Assembly, December 11th, 1946). The first consequence arising from this conception is that the principles underlying the Convention are principles which are recognized by civilized nations as binding on States, even without any conventional obligation. A second consequence is the universal character both of the condemnation of genocide and of the co-operation required "in order to liberate mankind from such an odious scourge" (Preamble to the Convention). The Genocide Convention was therefore intended by the General Assembly and by the contracting parties to be definitely universal in scope. It was in fact approved on December 9th, 1948, by a resolution which was unanimously adopted by fifty-six States.

The objects of such a convention must also be considered. The Convention was manifestly adopted for a purely humanitarian and civilizing purpose. It is indeed difficult to imagine a convention that might have this dual character to a greater degree, since its object on the one hand is to safeguard the very existence of certain human groups and on the other to confirm and endorse the most elementary principles of morality. In such a convention the contracting States do not have any interests of their own; they merely have, one and all, a common interest, namely, the accomplishment of those high purposes which are the *raison d'être* of the convention. Consequently, in a convention of this type one cannot speak of individual advantages or disadvantages to States, or of the maintenance of a perfect contractual balance between rights and duties. The high ideals which inspired the Convention provide, by virtue of the common will of the parties, the foundation and measure of all its provisions.

The foregoing considerations . . . lead to the following conclusions.

The object and purpose of the Genocide Convention imply that it was the intention of the General Assembly and of the State which adopted it that as many States as possible should participate. The complete exclusion from the Convention of one or more States would not only restrict the scope of its application, but would detract from the authority of the moral and humanitarian principles which are its basis. It is inconceivable that the contracting parties readily contemplated that an objection to a minor reservation should produce such a result. But even less could the contracting parties have intended to sacrifice the very object of the Convention in favour of a vain desire to secure as many participants as possible. The object and purpose of the convention thus limit both the freedom of making reservations and that of objecting to them. It follows that it is the compatibility of a reservation with the object and purpose of the Convention that must furnish the criterion for the attitude of a State in making the reservation on accession as well as for the appraisal by a State in objecting to the reservation. Such is the rule of conduct which must guide every State in the appraisal which it must make, individually and from its own standpoint, of the admissibility of any reservation.

Any other view would lead either to the acceptance of reservations which frustrate the purposes which the General Assembly and the contracting parties had in mind, or to recognition that the parties to the Convention have the power of excluding from it the author of a reservation, even a minor one, which may be quite compatible with those purposes.

. . .

Notes

1. The ICJ notes that the "principles underlying the [Genocide] Convention are principles which are recognized by civilized nations as binding on States, even without any conventional obligations." Which "principles underlying the Convention" embody principles of customary international law? Which do not?

2. What reservations would be permissible and impermissible in light of the ICJ's analysis? Consider the following possibilities:

    • State X enters a reservation to Article IX which provides that its consent to the jurisdiction of the International Court of Justice is required in each case.

    • When ratifying the Genocide Convention, State Y, which has a notorious history of persecuting members of Roma communities (often called "Gypsies," a term that is considered pejorative by many Roma), makes what it terms an "understanding" that "Roma are not a national, ethnical, racial or religious group as those terms are used in Article II of the Genocide Convention." Although the word "Roma" encompasses many diverse groups, Roma are widely considered to constitute a distinct ethnic group.

3. On reservations to treaties, and to human rights treaties in particular, see Chapter 2, Section A(1)(a) supra.

2. THE *BOSNIA v. YUGOSLAVIA* CASE

Although human rights issues have been addressed in several cases before the ICJ, alleged violations of a human rights convention have rarely constituted the central claim in contentious cases. The principal exception is a case instituted on March 20, 1993, when Bosnia and Herzegovina ("Bosnia") filed an Application against the Federal Republic of Yugoslavia ("Yugoslavia") alleging, inter alia, violations of the Genocide Convention. The applicant invoked Article IX of the Convention in support of the Court's jurisdiction.*

At the time this case was instituted, Bosnia was racked by armed conflict, triggered by its secession from the former Socialist Federal Republic of Yugoslavia (SFRY) in April 1992. Bosnia's secession was opposed by the armed forces of what remained of the SFRY, now named the Federal Republic of Yugoslavia, and by Bosnian Serb forces. Although the armed forces of Yugoslavia formally withdrew from Bosnia on May 19, 1992, they continued to provide various forms of support to Bosnian Serb forces until a peace agreement brought an end to the fighting in Bosnia in December 1995.

Serious violations of international humanitarian law were committed by all sides to the conflict,** but the overwhelming majority of documented atrocities were committed by Serb forces through a campaign that came to be known as "ethnic cleansing." These atrocities formed the basis of Bosnia's case against Yugoslavia. In its Application, Bosnia and Herzegovina requested the Court, inter alia, to adjudge and declare that Yugoslavia, through its agents and surrogates, "has killed, murdered, wounded, raped, robbed, tortured, kidnapped, illegally detained, and exterminated the citizens of Bosnia and Herzegovina" and that it must immediately cease this practice of "ethnic cleansing" and pay reparations.

---

* An earlier attempt to invoke this provision occurred in the early 1970s. India, which had intervened in a conflict between East and West Pakistan, handed over 95 Pakistani prisoners of war to Bangladesh for prosecution on charges including genocide. Pakistan instituted proceedings against India before the ICJ, claiming that, under the Genocide Convention, it had the exclusive right to try the defendants. The case was discontinued when the defendants were returned to Pakistan on the understanding that they would be prosecuted there. See Payam Akhavan, *Enforcement of the Genocide Convention: A Challenge to Civilization*, 8 Harv. Hum. Rts. J. 229, 249–50 (1995).

More recently, the Genocide Convention was invoked in ten related cases instituted by the Federal Republic of Yugoslavia on April 29, 1999. Although the Applicant's core claims involved allegations that a campaign of aerial bombardment undertaken by the North Atlantic Treaty Organization entailed the illegal use of force, Yugoslavia also alleged that the respondent states were committing violations of international humanitarian law and of the Genocide Convention. See Note 3 on p. 679 infra.

** During much of the conflict, Bosnian Muslims were allied with Bosnian Croats against Bosnian and Serbian Serb forces. But in mid–1993, armed conflict erupted between the formerly allied Croat and Muslim forces as well.

Immediately upon filing its Application, Bosnia also submitted a request for provisional measures (in effect, an interim injunction) pursuant to Article 41 of the ICJ's Statute. Article 41 provides:

1.   The Court shall have the power to indicate, if it considers that circumstances so require, any provisional measures which ought to be taken to preserve the respective rights of either party.

2.   Pending the final decision, notice of the measures suggested shall forthwith be given to the parties and to the Security Council.

In response, the Court adopted an order, portions of which follow, indicating provisional measures.

Case Concerning Application of the Convention on the Prevention and Punishment of the Crime of Genocide (Bosnia and Herzegovina v. Yugoslavia (Serbia and Montenegro))

International Court of Justice, 1993.
1993 I. C. J. 3 (Apr. 8) (Order on Request for the Indication of Provisional Measures)

. . .

1.   Whereas ... Bosnia–Herzegovina, basing the jurisdiction of the Court on Article IX of the Genocide Convention, recounts a series of events in Bosnia–Herzegovina from April 1992 up to the present day which, in its contention, amount to acts of genocide within the definition given in the Genocide Convention ...; and whereas Bosnia–Herzegovina claims that the acts complained of have been committed by former members of the Yugoslav People's Army (YPA) and by Serb military and paramilitary forces under the direction of, at the behest of, and with assistance from Yugoslavia; and whereas Bosnia–Herzegovina claims that Yugoslavia is therefore fully responsible under international law for their activities;

2.   Whereas on the basis of the facts alleged in the Application Bosnia–Herzegovina requests the Court to adjudge and declare as follows:

"*(a)* that Yugoslavia ... has breached, and is continuing to breach, its legal obligations toward the people and State of Bosnia and Herzegovina under Articles I, II*(a)*, II*(b)*, II*(c)*, II*(d)*, III*(a)*, III*(b)*, III*(c)*, III*(d)*, III*(e)*, IV, and V of the Genocide Convention;"

. . .

3.   Whereas by a request filed ... on 20 March 1993 ... Bosnia–Herzegovina, invoking Article 41 of the Statute of the Court ..., urgently requested that the Court indicate [enumerated] provisional measures to be in effect while the Court is seised of this case ...;

. . .

9.   Whereas in written observations, submitted to the Court on 1 April 1993, on the request for the indication of provisional measures, the Government of Yugoslavia [requested provisional measures instructing Bosnian

authorities to take various measures to cease alleged mistreatment of and atrocities against Serbs in Bosnia];

. . .

14.   Whereas on a request for provisional measures the Court need not, before deciding whether or not to indicate them, finally satisfy itself that it has jurisdiction on the merits of the case, yet it ought not to indicate such measures unless the provisions invoked by the Applicant or found in the Statute appear, prima facie, to afford a basis on which the jurisdiction of the Court might be established; . . .

. . .

19.   Whereas . . . if Bosnia–Herzegovina and Yugoslavia are both parties to the Genocide Convention, disputes to which Article IX [of that Convention] applies are . . . prima facie within the jurisdiction *ratione personae* of the Court [pursuant to Article 35(2) of its Statute];

[Despite some question about whether Bosnia had become a party to the Genocide Convention at the time necessary to support the Court's jurisdiction, the Court concluded that a prima facie case had been established that it had jurisdiction *ratione materiae* under Article IX of the Genocide Convention. It reached a preliminary conclusion rejecting Bosnia's claim that a letter dated June 8, 1992, which had been signed by the Presidents of Yugoslavia's two constituent republics, constituted a basis for jurisdiction over "all outstanding legal disputes" between Yugoslavia and Bosnia. Accordingly, it confined its examination of the request for provisional measures and the grounds asserted in support thereof "to those which fall within the scope of the Genocide Convention."]

. . .

40.   Whereas the Applicant has brought before the Court . . . accounts of military and paramilitary activities, including the bombing and shelling of towns and villages, the destruction of houses and forced migration of civilians, and of acts of violence, including execution, murder, torture, and rape which, in the circumstances in which they have occurred, show, in the view of the Applicant, that acts of genocide have been committed, and will continue to be committed against, in particular, the Muslim inhabitants of Bosnia–Herzegovina;

41.   Whereas Bosnia–Herzegovina claims in the Application that the acts there complained of have been committed by former members of the Yugoslav People's Army (YPA) and by Serb military and paramilitary forces under the direction of, at the behest of, and with assistance from Yugoslavia, and that Yugoslavia is therefore fully responsible under international law for their activities; and whereas in its request for the indication of provisional measures Bosnia–Herzegovina similarly contends that the facts stated in the Application show that Yugoslavia is committing acts of genocide, both directly and by means of its agents and surrogates, and that there is no reason to believe that Yugoslavia will voluntarily desist from this course of conduct while the case is pending before the Court;

42. Whereas Yugoslavia observes that the situation is not one of aggression by one State against another, but a civil war, and asserts that it has no soldiers in the territory of Bosnia–Herzegovina, that it does not militarily support any side in the conflict, and that it does not support or abet in any way the commission of crimes cited in the Application; that Yugoslavia and its subordinate bodies, including the military, have not committed and are not committing any of the acts to which Article III of the Genocide Convention refers . . . ;

43. Whereas Yugoslavia in its written observations on the request for the indication of provisional measures "requests the Court to establish the responsibility of the authorities" of Bosnia–Herzegovina for acts of genocide against the Serb people in Bosnia–Herzegovina, and indicates its intention to submit evidence to that effect; and whereas Yugoslavia claimed at the hearings that genocide and genocidal acts are being carried out against Serbs living in Bosnia–Herzegovina; whereas Bosnia–Herzegovina for its part contends however that there is no basis in fact or in law for the indication of provisional measures against it, there being no credible evidence that its Government has committed acts of genocide against anyone;

44. Whereas the Court, in the context of the present proceedings on a request for provisional measures, has in accordance with Article 41 of the Statute to consider the circumstances drawn to its attention as requiring the indication of provisional measures, but cannot make definitive findings of fact or of imputability, and the right of each Party to dispute the facts alleged against it, to challenge the attribution to it of responsibility for those facts, and to submit arguments in respect of the merits, must remain unaffected by the Court's decision;

45. Whereas Article I of the Genocide Convention provides that

"The Contracting Parties confirm that genocide, whether committed in time of peace or in time of war, is a crime under international law which they undertake to prevent and to punish"

Whereas all parties to the Convention have thus undertaken "to prevent and to punish" the crime of genocide; whereas in the view of the Court, in the circumstances brought to its attention and outlined above in which there is a grave risk of acts of genocide being committed, Yugoslavia and Bosnia–Herzegovina, whether or not any such acts in the past may be legally imputable to them, are under a clear obligation to do all in their power to prevent the commission of any such acts in the future;

46. Whereas the Court is not called upon, for the purpose of its decision on the present request for the indication of provisional measures, now to establish the existence of breaches of the Genocide Convention by either Party, but to determine whether the circumstances require the indication of provisional measures to be taken by the Parties for the protection of rights under the Genocide Convention; and whereas the Court is satisfied, taking into account the obligation imposed by Article I of the Genocide Convention, that the indication of measures is required for the

protection of such rights; and whereas Article 75, paragraph 2, of the Rules of Court recognizes the power of the Court, when a request for provisional measures has been made, to indicate measures that are in whole or in part other than those requested, or that ought to be taken or complied with by the party which has itself made the request;

. . .

48. Whereas in its request for the indication of provisional measures Bosnia–Herzegovina has also maintained that the Court should exercise its power to indicate provisional measures with a view to preventing the aggravation or extension of the dispute whenever it considers that circumstances so require; whereas from the information available to the Court it is satisfied that there is a grave risk of action being taken which may aggravate or extend the existing dispute over the prevention or punishment of the crime of genocide, or render it more difficult of solution;

49. Whereas the crime of genocide "shocks the conscience of mankind, results in great losses to humanity . . . and is contrary to moral law and to the spirit and aims of the United Nations", in the words of General Assembly resolution 96 (I) of 11 December 1946 on "the Crime of Genocide" . . . ;

50. Whereas in the light of the several considerations set out above, the Court finds that the circumstances require it to indicate provisional measures, as provided by Article 41 of the Statute of the Court;

51. Whereas the decision given in the present proceedings in no way prejudges the question of the jurisdiction of the Court to deal with the merits of the case, or any questions relating to the admissibility of the Application, or relating to the merits themselves, and leaves unaffected the right of the Governments of Bosnia–Herzegovina and Yugoslavia to submit arguments in respect of those questions;

52. For these reasons,

The Court,

Indicates, pending its final decision in the proceedings instituted on 20 March 1993 by the Republic of Bosnia and Herzegovina against the Federal Republic of Yugoslavia (Serbia and Montenegro), the following provisional measures

A. (1) Unanimously,

The Government of the Federal Republic of Yugoslavia (Serbia and Montenegro) should immediately, in pursuance of its undertaking in the Convention on the Prevention and Punishment of the Crime of Genocide of 9 December 1948, take all measures within its power to prevent commission of the crime of genocide;

(2) By 13 votes to 1,

The Government of the Federal Republic of Yugoslavia (Serbia and Montenegro) should in particular ensure that any military, paramilitary or irregular armed units which may be directed or supported by it, as well as any organizations and persons which may be subject to its control, direction or influence, do not commit any acts of genocide, of conspiracy to commit genocide, of direct and public incitement to commit genocide, or of complicity in genocide, whether directed against the Muslim population of Bosnia and Herzegovina or against any other national, ethnical, racial or religious group;

In Favour: *President* Sir Robert Jennings; Vice–President Oda; Judges Ago, Schwebel, Bedjaoui, Ni, Evensen, Guillaume, Shahabuddeen, Aguilar Mawdsley, Weeramantry, Ranjeva, Ajibola;

Against: *Judge* Tarassov;

B. Unanimously,

The Government of the Federal Republic of Yugoslavia (Serbia and Montenegro) and the Government of the Republic of Bosnia and Herzegovina should not take any action and should ensure that no action is taken which may aggravate or extend the existing dispute over the prevention or punishment of the crime of genocide, or render it more difficult of solution.

. . .

■ Declaration of JUDGE TARASSOV

The appalling atrocities which have taken place in the territory of the former State of Yugoslavia move me no less than they move my colleagues. Nevertheless I have not been able to join with them in voting for all the operative paragraphs of the Order, and I wish to say why.

I am generally in agreement with the consideranda and conclusions of the Order. . . . I support the provisional measures indicated by the Court in paragraph 52A(1) and paragraph 52B. I agree that the Government of the Federal Republic of Yugoslavia "should immediately . . . take all measures within its power to prevent commission of the crime of genocide"— meaning, of course, measures within its real power. In my opinion, the same measures should be taken under the same understanding in respect of the Government of the Republic of Bosnia and Herzegovina, which has responsibility over acts committed on its territory. Unfortunately, the Court did not find it necessary to so provide. . . .

. . . I regret that I have not been able to vote for the provision of paragraph 52A(2) that the Government of the Federal Republic of Yugoslavia should in particular "ensure" that any military, paramilitary or irregular armed units which "may" be directed or supported by it, and organizations or persons which "may be subject to its control, direction or influence" do not commit any acts of genocide, "of conspiracy to commit genocide", of incitement to genocide or of "complicity in genocide". In my view, these passages of the Order are open to the interpretation that the Court believes that the Government of the Federal Republic of Yugoslavia is indeed involved in such genocidal acts, or at least that it may very well be so involved. Thus, on my view, these provisions are very close to a prejudgment of the merits, despite the Court's recognition that, in an Order indicating provisional measures, it is not entitled to reach determinations of fact or law. Moreover, these passages impose practically unlimited, ill-defined and vague requirements for the exercise of responsibility by the Respondent in fulfilment of the Order of the Court, and lay the Respondent open to unjustifiable blame for failing to comply with this interim measure. . . .

Moreover, these objectionable provisions lack not only balance but practicality. Is it really within the realm of the practical for the Yugoslav Government to "ensure" that all persons who may claim to be subject to its influence do not conspire to commit genocide or incite genocide? Particularly when the persons who are accused of such acts are not its citizens and not within its territorial jurisdiction? Someone may affirm that he is under the influence of the Yugoslav Government without that being the fact. I am convinced that the Court should not imply that the Yugoslav Government may have responsibility for the commission of acts which in fact may be beyond its control.

Notes

1. Judge Tarassov faulted the majority for not indicating the same measures "under the same understanding in respect of the Government of the Republic of Bosnia and Herzegovina" that it indicated in respect of the Government of Yugoslavia. Could the Court have done so, as a matter of law? See paragraph 46 of its Order. Should it have done so? Note in this respect the Court's observation in paragraph 45 that "in the circumstances brought to its attention . . . in which there is a grave risk of acts of genocide being committed, Yugoslavia and Bosnia–Herzegovina, whether or not any such acts in the past may be legally imputable to them, are under a clear obligation to do all in their power to prevent the commission of any such acts in the future." Why, if Bosnia was "under a clear obligation to do all in [its] power to prevent the commission of any [acts of genocide] in the future," did the Court confine the indication of provisional measures set forth in Paragraph 52(A) to Yugoslavia?

2. Was Judge Tarassov correct in asserting that the indication of provisional measures set forth in Paragraph 52(A)(2) may be interpreted as suggesting "that the Court believes that the Government of the Federal Republic of Yugoslavia is indeed involved in . . . genocidal acts, or at least that it may very well be so involved"? If so, was the Court's action appropriate? Is there any merit in Judge Tarassov's criticism of Paragraph 52(A)(2) on the ground that its terms "impose practically unlimited, ill-defined and vague requirements for the exercise of responsibility by the Respondent in fulfilment of the Order of the Court, and lay the Respondent open to unjustifiable blame for failing to comply with this interim measure"?

3. Did the majority imply that indication of provisional measures is especially appropriate in light of the duty of States Parties to the Genocide Convention to "prevent" genocide? In light of the special gravity and

universal condemnation of the crime? Consider in particular its observations in paragraphs 46 and 49.

4.   Note that the basis of Bosnia–Herzegovina's allegation that Yugoslavia is responsible for breaching the Genocide Convention was that the acts alleged were "committed by former members of the Yugoslav People's Army . . . and by Serb military and paramilitary forces under the direction of, at the behest of, and with assistance from Yugoslavia, and that Yugoslavia is therefore fully responsible under international law for their activities. . . ." (Paragraph 41.) The extent to which conduct of Bosnian Serb forces could be imputed to Yugoslavia has also arisen in several cases before the International Criminal Tribunal for the former Yugoslavia (ICTY). Certain war crimes, known as "grave breaches" of the 1949 Geneva Conventions, can only occur in the context of inter-state armed conflict. In cases involving war crimes committed by one ethnic group in Bosnia against individuals belonging to a different ethnic group in Bosnia during what appeared to be essentially an internal armed conflict, the Prosecutor has sought to establish this element of internationality by proving that Yugoslav forces supported Bosnian Serb forces during the conflict. The Trial Chambers that have thus far rendered verdicts that turned, at least in part, on this issue have reached diverging conclusions. The first defendant tried before the ICTY, Duško Tadić, is a Bosnian Serb who was accused of committing various crimes, including grave breaches, against Bosnian Muslims. To prove that Tadić's conduct constituted grave breaches, the prosecution had to establish that, although armed forces of the Federal Republic of Yugoslavia (FRY) had officially withdrawn from Bosnia before the date of the relevant charges, Bosnian Serb forces nonetheless acted as agents of the FRY in their conduct toward Bosnian citizens. Holding that the relevant legal standard in this respect was one of "effective control" of Bosnian Serb forces by the FRY, a majority of the Trial Chamber—with its Presiding Judge dissenting—found that the prosecution had not adequately proved effective control. *Prosecutor v. Duško Tadić*, Case No. IT–94–1–T, Opinion and Judgment (May 7, 1997). The Trial Chamber that presided over the *Čelebići* case found that the FRY's withdrawal of armed forces from Bosnia "constituted a deliberate attempt to mask the continued involvement of the FRY in the conflict while its Government remained in fact the controlling force behind the Bosnian Serbs" at the time the alleged crimes occurred. It concluded that the armed conflict in which the alleged acts occurred was, therefore, international. *Prosecutor v. Zejnil Delalić et al.,* Case No. IT–96–21–T, Judgment (Nov. 16, 1998). As of mid-1999, appeals of both verdicts are still pending. See also *Tribunal Finds Croat Guilty of 1 of 3 Counts*, Int'l Herald Tribune, May 8–9, 1999 (reporting verdict dismissing grave breaches counts apparently due to failure to establish international element of charges).

Assuming that the ICJ case between Bosnia and Yugoslavia proceeds to judgment on the merits, to what extent, if at all, should the Court's determination of Yugoslav responsibility for acts committed in Bosnia by Bosnian Serb forces be influenced by the conclusions of the ICTY concerning the guilt of individual defendants charged with grave breaches? Note that the ICTY establishes individual responsibility for international crimes, while the ICJ establishes state responsibility for violations of international legal obligations.

5.   On July 27, 1993 Bosnia and Herzegovina filed a second request for provisional measures; Yugoslavia filed a request for provisional measures on August 10, 1993. In an Order dated September 18, 1993, the ICJ reaffirmed the measures indicated in its earlier Order, but declined to adopt more far-reaching measures sought by Bosnia. The Court observed that, since its Order of April 8, 1993, "great suffering and loss of life has been sustained by the population of Bosnia–Herzegovina in circumstances which shock the conscience of mankind and flagrantly conflict with moral law . . ." It declared that it was "not satisfied that all that might have been done has been done" to prevent genocide in Bosnia, and reminded the parties to the case that they were obliged to take the Court's provisional measures "seriously into account."

———

On July 11, 1996 the Court delivered a Judgment dismissing Yugoslavia's objection to its jurisdiction. While holding that it had jurisdiction to adjudge the dispute under the Genocide Convention, and thereby affirming its preliminary conclusion to this effect in its Order of April 8, 1993, the Court also affirmed its earlier preliminary conclusion rejecting other bases for jurisdiction put forth by Bosnia.

In the course of addressing Yugoslavia's objections to its jurisdiction, the Court had to resolve several key issues arising under the Genocide Convention. The following excerpt addresses the territorial scope of Contracting Parties' obligations under the Convention.

Case Concerning Application of the Convention on the Prevention and Punishment of the Crime of Genocide(Bosnia–Herzegovina v. Yugoslavia)

International Court of Justice, 1996.
1996 I. C. J. 595 (July 11).

Preliminary Objections

Judgment, July 11, 1996

. . .

27.   In order to determine whether it has jurisdiction to entertain the case on the basis of Article IX of the Genocide Convention, it remains for the Court to verify whether there is a dispute between the Parties that falls within the scope of that provision. . . .

30.   . . .

Yugoslavia disputes this. It contests the existence in this case of an "international dispute" within the meaning of the Convention, basing itself on two propositions: first, that the conflict occurring in certain parts of the Applicant's territory was of a domestic nature, Yugoslavia was not party to it and did not exercise jurisdiction over that territory at the time in question; and second, that State responsibility, as referred to in the requests of Bosnia–Herzegovina, was excluded from the scope of application of Article IX.

31. The Court will begin with a consideration of Yugoslavia's first proposition.

In doing so, it will start by recalling the terms of Article I of the Genocide Convention, worded as follows:

> "The Contracting Parties confirm that genocide, whether committed in time of peace or in time of war, is a crime under international law which they undertake to prevent and to punish."

The Court sees nothing in this provision which would make the applicability of the Convention subject to the condition that the acts contemplated by it should have been committed within the framework of a particular type of conflict. The contracting parties expressly state therein their willingness to consider genocide as "a crime under international law", which they must prevent and punish independently of the context "of peace" or "of war" in which it takes place. In the view of the Court, this means that the Convention is applicable, without reference to the circumstances linked to the domestic or international nature of the conflict, provided the acts to which it refers in Articles II and III have been perpetrated. In other words, irrespective of the nature of the conflict forming the background to such acts, the obligations of prevention and punishment which are incumbent upon the States parties to the Convention remain identical.

As regards the question whether Yugoslavia took part—directly or indirectly—in the conflict at issue, the Court would merely note that the Parties have radically differing viewpoints in this respect and that it cannot, at this stage in the proceedings, settle this question, which clearly belongs to the merits.

Lastly, as to the territorial problems linked to the application of the Convention, the Court would point out that the only provision relevant to this, Article VI, merely provides for persons accused of one of the acts prohibited by the Convention to "be tried by a competent tribunal of the State in the territory of which the act was committed ...". It would also recall its understanding of the object and purpose of the Convention, as set out in its Opinion of 28 May 1951, cited above:

> "The origins of the Convention show that it was the intention of the United Nations to condemn and punish genocide as 'a crime under international law' involving a denial of the right of existence of entire human groups, a denial which shocks the conscience of mankind and results in great losses to humanity, and which is contrary to moral law and to the spirit and aims of the United Nations (Resolution 96 (I) of

the General Assembly, December 11th 1946). The first consequence arising from this conception is that the principles underlying the Convention are principles which are recognized by civilized nations as binding on States, even without any conventional obligation. A second consequence is the universal character both of the condemnation of genocide and of the co-operation required 'in order to liberate mankind from such an odious scourge' (Preamble to the Convention).'' (I.C.J. Reports 1951, p. 23.)

It follows that the rights and obligations enshrined by the Convention are rights and obligations *erga omnes*. The Court notes that the obligation each State thus has to prevent and to punish the crime of genocide is not territorially limited by the Convention.

32.   The Court now comes to the second proposition advanced by Yugoslavia, regarding the type of State responsibility envisaged in Article IX of the Convention. According to Yugoslavia, that Article would only cover the responsibility flowing from the failure of a State to fulfil its obligations of prevention and punishment as contemplated by Articles V, VI and VII; on the other hand, the responsibility of a State for an act of genocide perpetrated by the State itself would be excluded from the scope of the Convention.

The Court would observe that the reference in Article IX to "the responsibility of a State for genocide or for any of the other acts enumerated in Article III", does not exclude any form of State responsibility.

Nor is the responsibility of a State for acts of its organs excluded by Article IV of the Convention, which contemplates the commission of an act of genocide by "rulers" or "public officials".

33.   In the light of the foregoing, the Court considers that it must reject the fifth preliminary objection of Yugoslavia. It would moreover observe that it is sufficiently apparent from the very terms of that objection that the Parties not only differ with respect to the facts of the case, their imputability and the applicability to them of the provisions of the Genocide Convention, but are moreover in disagreement with respect to the meaning and legal scope of several of those provisions, including Article IX. For the Court, there is accordingly no doubt that there exists a dispute between them relating to "the interpretation, application or fulfilment of the . . . Convention, including . . . the responsibility of a State for genocide . . .", according to the form of words employed by that latter provision. . . .

. . .

Notes

1.   Following the Court's July 11, 1996 ruling on jurisdiction, Yugoslavia filed a counter-claim asking the Court to adjudge that "Bosnia and Herzegovina is responsible for the acts of genocide committed against the Serbs in Bosnia and Herzegovina" and that it "has the obligation to punish the persons held responsible" for these acts. It also asked the Court to rule that

"Bosnia and Herzegovina is bound to take necessary measures so that the said acts would not be repeated" and "to eliminate all consequences of the violation" of the Genocide Convention. In an Order of Dec. 17, 1997 the Court held that Yugoslavia's counter-claims were "admissible as such" and that they formed "part of the current proceedings" in the case.

2. In contrast to most of the human rights conventions examined in this Chapter, the Genocide Convention does not specify its geographical scope of application. Article 29 of the Vienna Convention provides: "Unless a different intention appears from the treaty or is otherwise established, a treaty is binding upon each party in respect of its entire territory." Presumably with this general approach in mind, Yugoslavia challenged the ICJ's jurisdiction in the case instituted by Bosnia on the ground, inter alia, that Yugoslavia did not exercise jurisdiction over the territory where genocidal acts were allegedly committed. In response, the ICJ concluded that "the obligation each State thus has to prevent and to punish the crime of genocide is not territorially limited by the Convention." (Paragraph 31.) On what basis did the ICJ reach this conclusion? Does this mean that all States Parties to the Genocide Convention are required to intervene in another country to repress genocide? Could Bosnia bring a contentious case against the United States alleging that it breached its obligations as a Contracting Party to the Genocide Convention because the United States did not do enough to repress the genocide in Bosnia while it was occurring?

3. On April 29, 1999 the Federal Republic of Yugoslavia (FRY) filed applications against ten countries participating in a campaign of aerial bombardment by the North Atlantic Treaty Organization (NATO). On the same day, it requested the ICJ to indicate provisional measures ordering the respondent states to "cease immediately [their] acts of use of force" and to "refrain from any act of threat or use of force" against the FRY. One basis of jurisdiction invoked by the FRY was Article IX of the Genocide Convention. On June 2, 1999, the ICJ held that it manifestly lacked jurisdiction in respect of the cases instituted by Yugoslavia against Spain and the United States of America. In respect of the remaining cases, the Court found that it could not indicate provisional measures because it lacked prima facie jurisdiction, which is a prerequisite for the indication of provisional measures. See International Court of Justice, Press Communiqué 99/23, June 2, 1999.

With respect to Yugoslavia's allegations based upon the Genocide Convention, the Court's reasoning in respect of the case against Belgium is representative of its reasoning in each of the cases instituted by Yugoslavia against states that are parties to the Genocide Convention and which have not entered reservations to the Convention's compromissory clause:

> 37. ... [I]t is not disputed that both Yugoslavia and Belgium are parties to the Genocide Convention without reservation; ... Article IX of the Convention accordingly appears to constitute a basis on which the jurisdiction of the Court might be founded to the extent that the subject-matter of the dispute relates to "the interpretation, application or fulfilment" of the Convention, including disputes "relating to the

responsibility of a State for genocide or for any of the other acts enumerated in article II" of the said Convention;

38. ... [I]n order to determine, even prima facie, whether a dispute within the meaning of Article IX of the Genocide Convention exists, the Court cannot limit itself to noting that one of the Parties maintains that the Convention applies, while the other denies it; ... in the present case the Court must ascertain whether the breaches of the Convention alleged by Yugoslavia are capable of falling within the provisions of that instrument and whether, as a consequence, the dispute is one which the Court has jurisdiction *ratione materiae* to entertain pursuant to Article IX ...;

. . .

40. ... [I]t appears to the Court [from the definition of genocide set forth in Article II of the Genocide Convention] "that [the] essential characteristic [of genocide] is the intended destruction of 'a national, ethnical, racial or religious group' " ...; ... the threat or use of force against a State cannot in itself constitute an act of genocide within the meaning of Article II of the Genocide Convention; ... in the opinion of the Court, it does not appear at the present stage of the proceedings that the bombings which form the subject of the Yugoslav Application "indeed entail the element of intent, towards a group as such, required by the provision quoted above" ...;

41. ... [T]he Court is therefore not in a position to find, at this stage of the proceedings, that the acts imputed by Yugoslavia to the Respondent are capable of coming within the provisions of the Genocide Convention; ... Article IX of the Convention, invoked by Yugoslavia, cannot accordingly constitute a basis on which the jurisdiction of the Court could prima facie be founded in this case....

. . .

Case Concerning Legality of Use of Force (Yugoslavia v. Belgium), Request for the Indication of Provisional Measures, Order (June 2, 1999).

For discussion of the relevance of this case to the law of humanitarian intervention, see Section E(2)(c) infra.

3. ADVISORY OPINIONS ON U.N. HUMAN RIGHTS EXPERTS

Although the case between Bosnia and Yugoslavia was one of the few contentious cases before the ICJ based principally on allegations that the respondent state breached its obligations under a human rights convention, human rights concerns have been raised in other cases and in advisory opinions. For example, the Court has twice been asked to render "binding advisory opinions" in respect of situations involving a government's apparent harassment of United Nations human rights experts. These requests have arisen under the General Convention on the Privileges and Immunities of the United Nations ("General Convention"), which has a compromissory clause governing not only disputes between states parties, but also between the United Nations and states parties. Since contentious cases can be submitted only by and against states, the clause provides that if a difference arises between the United Nations on the one hand and a Member State on the other hand, "a request shall be made for an advisory opinion on any legal question involved," and that the opinion rendered by the Court "shall be accepted as decisive by the parties" (Section 30).

Relying on this provision, the Economic and Social Council (ECOSOC) of the United Nations asked the Court to provide an advisory opinion relating to a dispute that arose in the 1980s. In 1985, the Sub–Commission on Prevention of Discrimination and Protection of Minorities of the UN Commission on Human Rights asked one of its members, a Romanian national named Dumitru Mazilu, to write a report on human rights and youth. Mr. Mazilu did not appear at the 1987 session of the Sub–Commission. The Romanian government informed the United Nations that Mr. Mazilu could not attend the session for reasons of health. Mr. Mazilu later wrote the United Nations Information Centre in Bucharest that he had been hospitalized and forced to retire from Romanian government service, and that strong governmental pressure was being exerted on him. Invoking the General Convention, the UN Secretary–General asked the Romanian government to accord Mr. Mazilu all the necessary facilities to complete his report; the Romanian government replied that Mr. Mazilu was too ill to work.

Romania also challenged the Secretary–General's reliance on Article VI, Section 22 of the General Convention, which provides that "Experts on Missions for the United Nations" shall enjoy certain privileges and immunities "during the period of their missions." In its view, this provision did not cover special rapporteurs such as Mazilu. Further, the Romanian government argued that, even if special rapporteurs have the status of experts on mission, Section 22 applies only in the countries to which they are sent on mission or through which they transit, and only during the period of their mission.

In this setting, ECOSOC requested an advisory opinion on the applicability of Article VI, section 22 in the case of Mr. Mazilu. The Court's opinion found that this section did, in fact, cover human rights experts such as Mazilu whether or not they travel. Further, they enjoy the privileges and immunities established under this provision even "in their relations with the States of which they are nationals." *Applicability of Article VI, Section 22, of the Convention on the Privileges and Immunities of the United Nations (The Mazilu Case)*, 1989 I.C.J. 177, para. 51 (Advisory Opinion).

On August 5, 1998, ECOSOC once again requested an advisory opinion concerning the applicability of Article VI, Section 22 of the General Convention in respect of a human rights expert. The request concerned a difference that had arisen between the United Nations and the Government of Malaysia concerning the activities of Param Cumaraswamy, a Malaysian jurist who in 1994 was appointed by the UN Commission on

Human Rights as Special Rapporteur on the independence of judges and lawyers.

According to a note sent by UN Secretary–General Kofi Annan to ECOSOC in July 1998, Mr. Cumaraswamy at that time faced four lawsuits filed in Malaysian courts by different plaintiffs seeking damages totaling $112 million, following an interview that he gave in November 1995 to *International Commercial Litigation,* a magazine published in the United Kingdom and also circulated in Malaysia. In that interview, Mr. Cumaraswamy commented on certain litigations that had been carried out in Malaysian courts. The plaintiffs, among whom were commercial companies and a lawyer mentioned in the interview, claimed that they had been defamed by the words of Mr. Cumaraswamy.

After the first lawsuit was filed, the United Nations Legal Counsel, Hans Corell, acting on behalf of the Secretary–General, considered the circumstances of the interview and of the controverted passages of the article and determined that Mr. Cumaraswamy had spoken in his official capacity as Special Rapporteur. In his view, by virtue of Section 22 of Article VI of the Convention on the Privileges and Immunities of the United Nations, Mr. Cumaraswamy was immune from legal process. On January 15, 1997, Mr. Corell sent a note verbale to the Permanent Representative of Malaysia to the United Nations, requesting the competent Malaysian authorities "to promptly advise the Malaysia courts of the Special Rapporteur's immunity from legal process".

On March 7, 1997, the Secretary–General issued a note confirming that "the words which constitute the basis of plaintiffs' complaint in this case were spoken by the Special Rapporteur in the course of his mission" and that he was "immune from legal process with respect thereto". Identical certificates of the Special Rapporteur's immunity were issued later when new lawsuits were filed. On March 12, 1997, the Malaysian Ministry of Foreign Affairs filed a certificate with the trial court stating that Mr. Cumaraswamy enjoyed immunity "only in respect of words spoken or written and acts done by him in the course of the performance of his duties," but failing to note the position already taken by the Secretary—General.

In his July 1998 note to ECOSOC, Mr. Annan stated that he considered it "most important" that the principle be accepted that it is for the Secretary–General alone to determine, with conclusive effect, whether an expert on mission has spoken or written words or performed an act in the course of his mission. He contended that if national courts were to determine whether an expert enjoys immunity, this "would be certain to have a negative effect on the independence of officials and experts, who would then have to fear that at any time, whether they are still in office or after they had left it, they could be called to account in national courts, not necessarily their own, civilly or criminally, for their words spoken or written or acts performed as officials or experts".

On August 5, 1998 ECOSOC adopted a resolution calling for the Court to give, on a priority basis, an advisory opinion "on the legal question of the applicability of Article VI, Section 22, of the Convention on the Privileges and Immunities of the United Nations in the case of Dato' Param Cumaraswamy as Special Rapporteur of the Commission on Human Rights on the independence of judges and lawyers, taking into account the circumstances set out in paragraphs 1 to 15 of the note by the Secretary-General, and on the legal obligation of Malaysia in this case".

On April 29, 1999, the ICJ issued its Advisory Opinion in this case. The Court was of the opinion, by fourteen votes to one, that Article VI, Section 22 of the General Convention on the Privileges and Immunities of the United Nations was "applicable" in the case of Mr. Cumaraswamy and that he was "entitled to immunity from legal process of every kind for the words spoken by him" during the aforementioned interview. Concerning the first point, the Court reasoned: "It may be observed that Special Rapporteurs of the Commission usually are entrusted not only with a research mission but also with the task of monitoring human rights violations and reporting on them. But what is decisive is that they have been entrusted with a mission by the United Nations and are therefore entitled to the privileges and immunities provided for in Article VI, Section 22, that safeguard the independent exercise of their functions." *Difference Relating to Immunity from Legal Process of a Special Rapporteur of the Commission on Human Rights*, Advisory Opinion, para. 43 (April 29, 1999).

The Court concluded that the Government of Malaysia should have informed its national courts of the Secretary–General's finding and that the courts should have dealt with the question of Mr. Cumaraswamy's immunity as a preliminary issue to be decided expeditiously. Id., paras. 61–63. It unanimously stated that Mr. Cumaraswamy should be "held financially harmless for any costs imposed upon him by the Malaysian courts. . . . " Id., para. 67 (3).

Note on ICJ Clauses

The Genocide Convention (Article IX) includes a binding obligation on States Parties to submit to the jurisdiction of the International Court of Justice to resolve disputes between them relating to "the interpretation, application or fulfilment" of the Convention. There are modified ICJ Clauses in the Convention on the Elimination of All Forms of Discrimination Against Women (Article 29) and the Convention Against Torture (Article 30). The 1951 Convention Relating to the Status of Refugees did not permit reservations to its ICJ Clause (see Articles 38 and 42), and one of the important purposes of its 1967 Protocol was to authorize such reservations (see Articles IV and VII(1).) Why do other human rights conventions contain no ICJ clause?

There is no ICJ clause in either of the human rights Covenants. Suppose that a State Party alleged to be violating its obligations under one of the Covenants had made a declaration accepting the jurisdiction of the ICJ under the "optional clause" of the Court's Statute, Article 36(2). Could another State Party then institute a proceeding before the ICJ, charging a violation of the Covenant, pursuant to the "optional clause"? See Louis Henkin, International Law: Politics and Values 216–17 (1995).

E.   INTERNATIONAL POLITICAL IMPLEMENTATION AND ENFORCEMENT—THE UNITED NATIONS

In addition to the supervisory functions performed by various human rights treaty bodies (see Sections A and B supra), several Charter-based organs of the United Nations play important roles in the Organization's efforts to promote human rights. These include in particular the Commission on Human Rights, the Economic and Social Council (ECOSOC), the General Assembly and, occasionally, the Security Council. Similarly, political organs of regional organizations, such as the Committee of Ministers of the Council of Europe and the General Assembly of the Organization of American States, have played key roles in promoting human rights within member states.

In this section we examine the principal UN Charter-based mechanisms that promote human rights through non-coercive activities. In the section that follows, we consider the role of the UN Security Council in enforcing international human rights law through its coercive powers.

1.   PROMOTION AND IMPLEMENTATION BY U.N. CHARTER ORGANS

Louis Henkin, *International Law: Politics and Values*
217–18 (1995).

. . .

If law is politics, enforcement of law in the inter-state system is also heavily political. Political influence brought to bear in the organs and suborgans of the United Nations determined the enforcement machinery that found its way into covenants and conventions. (Political forces ... influenced also how that machinery has worked.) But United Nations bodies themselves have also been an arena for charges of human rights violations, sometimes evoking resolutions of condemnation and even sanctions.

The Members of the United Nations have been divided as to their readiness to address charges of specific human rights violations. Some states have resisted the airing of such charges on the ground that these were not the proper business of the Organization, which is forbidden "to intervene in matters which are essentially within the domestic jurisdiction of any state" (Art. 2 (7)). In fact, United Nations practice long ago rejected that objection, in effect reflecting the conclusion that human rights violations were not a matter of domestic jurisdiction, or that United Nations discussion of them is not intervention, or both. United Nations practice in this regard has been determined not according to legal principle but by negotiation and vote.

. . .

Tom J. Farer and Felice Gaer, *The UN and Human Rights: At the End of the Beginning*

in United Nations, Divided World 245 (Adam Roberts & Benedict Kingsbury, eds. 2d ed. 1993).*

. . .

At its inception, the United Nations seemed destined to be the engine of human rights. Article 1(3) of the Charter announces the UN's purposes to include "promoting and encouraging respect for human rights and ... fundamental freedoms for all without distinction as to race, sex, language, or religion". Article 13 mandates the General Assembly to "initiate studies and make recommendations for the purpose of ... assisting in the realization of human rights". Article 56, combined with Article 55, pledges all UN members "to take joint and separate action in cooperation with the Organization for the achievement of ... universal respect for, and observance of, human rights". Article 68 requires the Economic and Social Council to "set up commissions ... for the promotion of human rights".

To be sure, these provisions did not spring from a fierce, collective will to shatter the wall of national sovereignty wherever it sheltered some variety of oppression. John P. Humphrey, the first Director of the Division of Human Rights at the UN, reports that, but for the efforts of a few deeply committed delegates, and the representatives of some forty-two private organizations brought in as consultants by the United States, human rights would have received "only a passing reference". While in the end they obviously did much better than that, their subordination in the organization's hierarchy of purposes is evident, above all in the Charter's authorization of UN enforcement action only in case of "any threat to the peace, breach of the peace, or act of aggression",[20] language clearly intended to evoke images of inter-state conflict.

. . .

Events surrounding the adoption of the Charter and the UN's early life suggest that there was widespread ambivalence, if not towards human rights *per se*, then certainly to the prospect of their enforcement through the UN. The Soviet bloc quickly established the position to which it would thereafter cling, namely that UN activity should be confined to promulgating rights; enforcement, on the other hand, was a matter of purely domestic concern. But it was hardly alone in wishing to keep the UN out of the enforcement business. The colonial powers were hardly more enthusiastic at the prospect of UN "meddling" in their respective preserves.

. . .

20.   Chap. VII, Art. 39–51.

... **The Human Rights Machinery: Form**

. . .

The current system is composed mainly of commissions and one sub-commission, committees both regular and special, working groups, and special rapporteurs....

The General Assembly (GA) reigns, of course, at the apex of the institutional pyramid, with plenary authority to create subsidiaries for any purpose enumerated or implied in the Charter (used, for example, to establish the Office of the High Commissioner for Refugees in 1951 and the successive committees on apartheid beginning with the Special Committee of 1962), and free to act either through these subsidiaries or directly on any human rights issue that engages the concern of its members.

... [T]he GA remains a central actor in the human rights drama at the UN. It supervises all programmes in the field and ultimately determines what standards are adopted, what issues are addressed, and what proportion and kind of administrative and budgetary resources will be devoted to the UN's human rights machinery. Subject to the ultimate authority of the GA, the Economic and Social Council (ECOSOC) nominally directs and monitors the work of the organization's most active organ in the human rights field, that is, the Commission on Human Rights.

... The Council is a quintessentially political body, its fifty-four members, elected by the Assembly on the basis of so-called "equitable geographical distribution", being formal representatives of UN member states.

Equally political in its form is the Commission on Human Rights established by ECOSOC in 1946 to serve as the organization's principal *locus* for human rights activity.[43] Politicization of the Commission seems to have been a second thought, albeit one that came ever so quickly after the first. [In 1946, ECOSOC rejected a proposal of the Nuclear Commission that all members of the Commission should serve as non-governmental representatives], deciding instead that the Commission should consist of one representative from each of eighteen members of the UN selected by the Council.

The Commission has since grown to fifty-three state representatives elected, as has become customary in most parts of the UN, pursuant to precise understandings about the appropriate representation of every self-identified regional bloc....

In the performance of its several functions, ... the Commission employs working groups and special rapporteurs. Some have standard-setting or investigative mandates with respect to what are called "thematic issues", such as enforced or involuntary disappearances, arbitrary deten-

---

43. ECOSOC Res. 5 (I), first session, Feb. 1946 (establishing the Nuclear Commission); and Res. 9 (II), second session, June 1946 (laying down the basic structure and guide-lines in light of, but not consistent with, key elements in the Nuclear Commission's Report).

tion, and religious intolerance. Others are tasked to review human rights conditions in particular countries. The thematic and country-specific activities, designated "special procedures" by the Commission, are a relatively recent innovation, and have given the Commission a capacity for rapid and concrete action that would have been virtually unimaginable twenty years ago.

An additional flock of working groups and rapporteurs indirectly service the Commission through its principal subsidiary, the Sub–Commission on the Prevention of Discrimination and the Protection of Minorities ("the Sub–Commission"). In theory the twenty-six members of the Sub–Commission are elected as independent experts. However, in part because they must be nominated and re-nominated by states (in practice almost invariably their own state), many are no less instruments of their respective governments than their counterparts on the parent body. But at least until very recently, enough members have actually satisfied the formal requisites of independence and expertise to make this child considerably more adventurous than its parent. At the end of its 1992 session it had working groups on communications concerning patterns of gross violation of human rights (where the screening of "1503" communications, discussed below, begins), on contemporary forms of slavery, on indigenous populations, and on other subjects. It also had present or former members at work on some eighteen special studies or reports addressing not only various issues related to minorities, but also such topics as discrimination against persons infected with HIV virus, states of emergency, impunity for violators of human rights, harmful traditional health practices affecting women, the right to adequate housing, and human rights and the environment.

The Commission and the Sub–Commission are established as subsidiary bodies of UN Charter organs....

. . .

... The Human Rights Machinery: Praxis

. . .

The organs of the United Nations concerned with human rights ... have not, until recently, evinced much enthusiasm for [a] protective mission. Nor for much of their life were they vulnerable to the charge of impartiality.... As early as January 1947, when the members of the Commission on Human Rights gathered for their first regular session, the UN had already received a large number of letters containing allegations of human rights violations. In effect, the Commission was being petitioned for assistance in obtaining the redress of grievances against member states.

[I]t responded to this initial opportunity to define some protective role by concluding that it had none. In the words of the report of that first session summarizing the Commission's reaction to individual communications: "The Commission recognizes that it has no power to take any action in regard to any complaints concerning human rights."[68] In what seemed

---

68.   E/259 (1947), paras 21 and 22.

an effort to avoid even inadvertent pressure on governments accused of human rights violations, it also decided that communications containing such allegations would not be circulated to the individual members even on a confidential basis. Rather they would receive, but only in private meetings, a confidential list containing only a brief, presumably sanitized indication of the substance of these dangerous if not positively offensive epistles.

To one of the legal paladins of that day, the Cambridge don Hersch Lauterpacht, the Human Rights Commission's crippling act of self-denial was wholly unjustified, a view the Economic and Social Council was unable to share. At the first opportunity it explicitly endorsed the Commission's position. . . .

For more than twenty years thereafter the UN Commission on Human Rights remained an instrument of non-protection lounging under the protective wing of ECOSOC. As proof of its existence, it summoned the energy to draft soaring standards and issue occasional reports of a comfortably general character. . . .

. . .

In the mid–1960s, countries that were in the vanguard of anti-colonial and anti-racist struggles concluded that a non-treaty-based communications procedure could usefully bolster their efforts. As the following excerpt explains, their decision set in motion a series of steps that led the Commission and ECOSOC to abandon the ''no power to act'' doctrine described in the preceding selection.

Philip Alston, *The Commission on Human Rights*
in The United Nations and Human Rights: A Critical Appraisal (Philip Alston, ed. 1992)*

. . .

. . . It was on the initiative of the Special Committee on Decolonization, in 1965, that the attention of the Commission [on Human Rights] was drawn to petitions alleging human rights violations in southern Africa. The following year ECOSOC accordingly invited the Commission to consider urgently the question of the violation of human rights, including policies of racial discrimination and segregation and of apartheid in all countries, with particular reference to colonial and other dependent countries and territories, and to submit its recommendations on measures to halt those violations. In the Commission the view prevailed that an artificial restriction of such a mandate to only a single category of countries was not justified. As a result, the ambiguity of the Commission's original mandate was resolved by a General Assembly request that it give urgent consideration to ways and means of improving the capacity of the United Nations to put a stop to

* Reprinted by permission, © 1992 Oxford University Press.

violations of human rights *wherever they may occur*.[63] This latter phrase was to prove to be of vital importance, despite the clear desire of most of the resolution's key proponents to confine the focus to racist and colonialist situations.

These developments resulted in the adoption of what eventually turned out to be two separate procedures. The procedure established under ECO-SOC Resolution 1235 (XLII) established the principle that violations could be examined and responded to, and provided the necessary authorization for the Commission to engage in public debate on the issue each year. The procedure under ECOSOC Resolution 1503 (XLVIII) provided a carefully and deliberately constrained procedure by which situations which appear to reveal "a consistent pattern of gross and reliably attested violations of human rights" could be pursued with the governments concerned, but in private.

. . .

. . . The 1503 Procedure

[T]he 1503 procedure . . . is not properly called a "petition-redress" procedure since it offers no solace, or redress, to individual victims. It is better characterized as a "petition-information" system because its objective is to use complaints as a means by which to assist the Commission in identifying situations involving a "consistent pattern of gross and reliably attested violations". . . .

. . .

[As it evolved, the 1503 procedure entailed a four-stage process. A Working Group of the Sub–Commission reviews the complaints that have been received in the preceding year. The Working Group decides which "situations" should be forwarded to the Sub–Commission in plenary which, in turn, can decide to refer the country concerned to the Commission, drop the situation, or reconsider it the following year. The government concerned is invited to defend itself before the Commission, but the complainant is not even advised of the action taken. At the fourth stage the Commission considers all of the relevant material and then announces the names of the countries it has considered and those dropped from consideration. The Commission's chair does not provide information regarding the substance of the allegations or details about it has taken, except with respect to countries dropped from consideration altogether or transferred to the public 1235 procedure.]

Thus, in the absence of a decision to go public, the entire procedure is shrouded in secrecy, with each of its stages being accomplished in confidential sessions by the bodies concerned. Nevertheless, the details have invariably been leaked. . . .

. . . It can be said . . . that most of the available snapshots provide few grounds for optimism as to the procedure's effectiveness. Thus, for exam-

---

63. GA Res. 2144 A (XXI) (1966).

ple, the first attempt to put specific situations on the Commission's 1503 agenda, in 1972, rapidly became bogged down at the level of the Sub-Commission which was loath to act on its own Working Group's recommendation that the focus be on Greece, Iran and Portugal.... The Sub-Commission decided to do nothing for a year so that the governments concerned might be given more time to respond to the allegations if they so wished.... The Sub-Commission managed to defer any action [on Greece] until 1974, by which time the military government had been overthrown.

Another notorious case in the early years was that of Uganda under President Idi Amin. In 1974, confronted by allegations that Amin had killed 75,000 people since coming to power in 1970, the Sub-Commission placed the case on the Commission's agenda. But because Amin was then chairman of the Organization of African Unity, he had little difficulty in mobilizing the support need to have the case struck off the Commission's agenda. Although Uganda was again placed on the list, it was not until 1978 that the Commission finally sought to send an envoy to Amin, still on a confidential basis. But before this could have any effect Amin had been overthrown after an invasion by Tanzanian troops. Among the many troubling aspects of this case was the fact that a brutal regime had managed, by virtue of playing the 1503 game, to keep its case off the Commission's public agenda over a four-year period....

... In recent years, ... the record would not appear to be much better. In the late 1980s and in 1990 NGO observers have tended to be highly critical of the results obtained (or, rather, not obtained) by the procedure, both in general, and in specific cases such as China, Iraq, Somalia, Syria, Zaire, etc.

... *The 1235 Procedure*

... ECOSOC resolution 1235 (XLII) of 6 June 1967 established the procedure on the basis of which the Commission holds an annual public debate focusing on gross violations of human rights. It is in this context that it has developed an array of methods by which to investigate and apply pressure to individual states.... The ways in which violations are dealt with by the Commission in the 1990s, always under the rubric of "the 1235 procedure", bears only a passing resemblance to the actual procedure formally authorized by that resolution.

. . .

[One of the key steps in the previously-described reversal of the "no power to act" doctrine was the adoption in 1967 of resolution 8, which established that the Commission could] inscribe on its agenda an item entitled "Question of the violation of human rights and fundamental freedoms, including policies of racial discrimination and segregation and of apartheid, in all countries, with particular reference to colonial and other dependent countries and territories."[108] The same wording continues to be on the Commission's agenda almost a quarter of a century later.

108.   CHR Res.8 (XXIII) (1967).

... [This resolution, whose terms were later endorsed by ECOSOC resolution 1235, established the procedure for consideration of situations involving violations. The major aspects of the 1967 resolution] on which the Commission continues to draw are the authority: (1) to hold an annual public debate; and (2) to study and investigate situations, by whatever means the Commission may deem appropriate....

... [I]t is necessary to understand the political motivations of the principal actors involved in establishing and designing [the 1235 procedure]. In a nutshell, the Third World wanted action against violations in southern Africa and other colonial situations. The Eastern Europeans were happy with that focus since they had no colonies and were equally happy for racism in the West to be targeted. The West, well aware that it did not have the numbers to block action and in any event wary about appearing to condone racism, calculated that the resulting procedures would be applied in a far more balanced fashion if all states, as opposed to just those which might potentially be labelled racists and colonialists, were liable to be "indicted".

[During the early years of the 1235 procedure, the Commission appointed working groups in respect of only three countries—South Africa; the Occupied Territories [i.e., the West Bank and Gaza] (following the six-day war [in the Middle East in 1967]); and Chile, which became the focus of a working group in the wake of the 1973 coup by General Augusto Pinochet. Throughout the 1970s, the Commission failed to act under the 1235 procedure in response to major atrocities elsewhere. By the late 1970s, however, the political climate had changed, in part because of the public prominence given to human rights concerns by NGOs such as Amnesty International and by the U.S. government under the leadership of President Jimmy Carter.]

Although since 1979, country-specific special procedures have been set up in respect of only seventeen States,* this figure reflects only a small part of the overall number of situations debated by the Commission under the 1235 and related procedures. An enormous range of situations has been specifically discussed under the 1235 item, and in some of those cases, the mere expression of serious concern or the threat of a resolution has been sufficient to provoke a constructive response from the government concerned....

. . .

[Rapporteurs]

The implementation of special [country] procedures has been entrusted to a wide range of entities. While "working groups" and "special rapporteurs" were initially the favoured means of fact-finding, various other designations have been added over the years. They include: "rapporteurs",

---

* [This statement reflects the Commission's action through 1991.—Editors' Note.]

"envoys", "special representatives", "experts", "independent experts", "delegations", etc. . . .

. . .

. . . The terms used to describe the formal mandates given to country rapporteurs have varied considerably. But whether they have been asked to "study", "inquire into", "investigate", or "examine", most rapporteurs have tended to assume considerable flexibility and to approach each situation as they see fit.

. . . *The Thematic Procedures*

Just as the reinvigoration of the 1235 procedure resulted in part from the horrors of the 1970s and the accompanying unresponsiveness of the UN's human rights organs, so too did the evolution of various "thematic" procedures. The first of these procedures, the Working Group on Enforced or Involuntary Disappearances, was established in 1980 in response to developments in Argentina and Chile. In the latter case the Commission's rapporteur had devoted considerable attention not only to the phenomenon of disappearances but also to establishing the responsibility of the government for actions of which it denied all knowledge. In the case of Argentina, both the scale and the ramifications of the widespread disappearances had been known since 1976 but nothing had been done, largely because of the determined and highly professional lobbying efforts of that country's diplomatic representatives in Geneva [where the Human Rights Commission meets] and New York. By 1980 a major NGO campaign launched by Amnesty International was in full swing and UN action was virtually inevitable. At this point the Argentinians took a calculated gamble that an initiative which focused on a particular "theme" (i.e., disappearances) rather than on the general situation in one particular country (Argentina) would diffuse some of the heat that the resulting investigations might generate. Moreover, because a range of countries would be threatened by such a mechanism they could calculate that the Group's prospects of survival beyond a year or two were not great.

Once again, as with the opening up of the 1235 procedure after 1979, the establishment of the Disappearances Group served as a vital precedent that enabled other comparable initiatives to be taken in later years. Thus in 1982, a Special Rapporteur on Summary or Arbitrary Executions was appointed. . . . In 1985, . . . a Special Rapporteur on Torture was appointed. The following year the United States, at least partly motivated by a desire to focus the spotlight on Eastern Europe, was instrumental in the appointment of a Special Rapporteur on Religious Intolerance. . . .*

* [More recently, Special Rapporteurs have been appointed to address, inter alia, freedom of opinion and expression; racial discrimination and xenophobia; the sale of children, child prostitution and child pornography; internally displaced persons, the independence and impartiality of the judiciary, violence against women, and the effects of toxic and dangerous products on human rights.—Editors' Note.]

Notes

1. In December 1993, the General Assembly decided to establish the position of High Commissioner for Human Rights. The leading UN official with responsibility for human rights, the High Commissioner now heads the UN's Human Rights Centre in Geneva.

Almost immediately upon taking up his post, the first High Commissioner had to confront one of the greatest human rights tragedies since World War II:

> The first High Commissioner, José Ayala–Lasso, took up his post on 5 April 1994. The next day, genocide was unleashed in Rwanda. The High Commissioner visited Rwanda, and called for a special session of the Commission on Human Rights. [The Commission] mandated a special rapporteur on Rwanda, and requested the High Commissioner "to make the necessary arrangements for the Special Rapporteur to be assisted by a team of human rights field officers". Initially a small team was envisaged, but subsequently the High Commissioner appealed for funding for a team of 21, and during a second visit to Rwanda in late August he agreed with the government that as many as 147 officers would be deployed, corresponding to the 147 communes of the country.

Ian Martin, "The High Commissioner's Field Operations" (unpublished manuscript); see also Ian Martin, *A New Frontier: The Early Experience and Future of International Human Rights Field Operations*, 16 Neth. Q. Hum. Rts. 121 (1998). The United Nations had previously deployed several human rights field operations, but the Rwanda mission was the first such operation organized by the UN Human Rights Centre in Geneva.

Although human rights organizations had long campaigned for the establishment of the office of the High Commissioner for Human Rights, many advocates were critical of the United Nations' early steps in relation to the office. In a particularly critical assessment, a prominent human rights advocate wrote:

> If the world body's top human rights official were given such status [as the position of High Commissioner], Amnesty International and others argued, UN efforts would gain more visibility and clout. Instead, governments concerned that the high commissioner might point the finger at them took care that the office would have a tiny budget, $700,000 a year—a pittance if serious investigations of abuses are to be conducted. More important, they made it clear that they did not want anyone appointed to the post who would give them grief. In deference to such concerns, Secretary General Boutros Boutros–Ghali designated an Ecuadorian diplomat, José Ayala Lasso, to serve as high commissioner, though he had no background in human rights. With denunciation of those responsible for abuses the only means available for carrying out his mission, Ayala Lasso managed to go through his first

year in his post without publicly criticizing a single government anywhere in the world.

Aryeh Neier, War Crimes: Brutality, Genocide, Terror, and the Struggle for Justice 23–24 (1998). In 1997, UN Secretary–General Kofi Annan appointed former Irish president Mary Robinson to succeed Ayala Lasso in the post of High Commissioner. For a history of the creation of the post of High Commissioner, see Andrew Clapham, *Creating the High Commissioner for Human Rights: The Outside Story*, 5 Eur. J. Int'l L. 556 (1994).

2. What criteria are appropriate for evaluating the effectiveness of the UN Human Rights Commission? What criteria are implicit in the preceding selections by Professor Farer and Ms. Gaer, and Professor Alston, respectively? Consider, inter alia, the following criteria: the discernible impact of the Commission's activities on human rights practices of governments; the degree to which the Commission's decisions to address country conditions seem to be driven by political considerations; the transparency of the Commission's decision-making processes; the ability of the Commission's representatives to respond quickly in individual cases where serious abuse is threatened or being carried out; the ability of the Commission to respond in a timely fashion to major human rights disasters, such as "ethnic cleansing" in Bosnia in the early 1990s and the 1994 genocide in Rwanda; and the degree to which the Commission follows up on reports produced by its representatives.

3. Do the preceding readings provide any arguments for maintaining the 1503 procedure?

4. One of the noteworthy byproducts of the reports produced by special rapporteurs and other experts appointed by the Human Rights Commission and its Sub–Commission has been a rich, if uneven, body of jurisprudence interpreting international human rights standards. Some of the experts appointed to report on countries and thematic issues have been noted international law experts. For example, the first Special Rapporteur on Torture, Pieter Kooijmans, is now a Judge on the International Court of Justice. For an example of the impact that some of these experts' reports have had in advancing international human rights jurisprudence, see *Prosecutor v. Zejnil Delalić et al.*, Case No. IT–96–21–T, Judgment, para. 493 (Nov. 16, 1998) (citing the views expressed in the final report of a special rapporteur appointed by the Sub–Commission in support of an important aspect of a criminal judgment); see Chapter 2, Section F(3)(b) supra.

5. Especially during the Cold War, the political implementation of human rights by UN bodies was criticized as being heavily "politicized." In particular, implementation efforts were selective—addressing some violations but not others equally gross, or violations by a few countries and not by others.

Is UN enforcement since the end of the Cold War subject to similar criticism? Is implementation by political bodies unavoidably "politicized," targeting some countries and some violations but not others, rather than applying "neutral principles" fairly and equally? Can an effective UN High Commissioner for Human Rights alleviate that difficulty?

6. On the prospects for various contributions of the United Nations to the realization of human rights, see Stephen Marks, *The United Nations and Human Rights: The Promise of Multilateral Diplomacy and Action*, in The Future of International Human Rights 291 (Burns Weston & Stephen Marks eds. 1999).

2. ENFORCEMENT BY COERCIVE MEASURES—THE U.N. SECURITY COUNCIL

The Human Rights Commission, its Sub–Commission, ECOSOC and the General Assembly utilize diverse, flexible and increasingly innovative initiatives to induce states to respect human rights. As we have seen, these range from the "quiet diplomacy" of the Commission's 1503 procedure to the public denunciation of Rapporteurs' reports and Commission and Assembly resolutions.

But the techniques examined in the preceding section do not include measures of lawful coercion. For example, if a Special Rapporteur appointed by the Human Rights Commission seeks and is denied permission to visit a target country, she cannot lawfully force her way into its territory. Faced with governments' refusal to cooperate with their inquiries, some Rapporteurs have relied upon sources such as refugee testimonies and NGO reports, but they have not thought themselves entitled to flout the target government's denial of access to its territory. Nor are the Sub–Commission, the Commission, ECOSOC and the General Assembly able to impose mandatory sanctions on delinquent states or to compel compliance with such sanctions by other states. (As we note below, however, the General Assembly can invite Member States to observe voluntary sanctions, and did so in respect of South Africa beginning in the early 1960s.)

Under the law of the UN Charter, only the Security Council can impose mandatory coercive measures against a state, including military action.* The Council may authorize—and, occasionally, has authorized—military interventions aimed at alleviating essentially humanitarian disasters when it determines, pursuant to Article 39 of the Charter, that the situation presents a threat to or breach of international peace and security. (See sub-section 2(c) on Humanitarian Intervention, below.)

---

* The General Assembly cannot compel compliance with coercive measures, but in 1950 it adopted a resolution, known as the Uniting for Peace Resolution, which provides that the Assembly can make recommendations for collective measures, including the use of armed force, to maintain or restore international peace or security "if the Security Council, because of lack of unanimity of the permanent members, fails to exercise its primary responsibility for the maintenance of international peace and security in any case where there appears to be a threat to the peace, breach of the peace or act of aggression." G.A. Res. 377(V), 5 UN GAOR Supp. (No. 20) at 10, para. 1, UN Doc. A/1775 (1950).

The following materials examine the law and practice of the Security Council in authorizing coercive measures against states in response to serious violations of human rights. As these materials reflect, just as the anti-racist struggle spurred the UN Human Rights Commission to end its longstanding reluctance to act upon human rights violations, racist policies in southern Africa provided the impetus for the Security Council's earliest recourse to coercive sanctions against states that breached fundamental human rights.

a. UN ENFORCEMENT ACTION: NOTE ON CHAPTER VII

The UN Charter vests in the Security Council broad authority to address matters involving international peace and security. Article 24 provides, in pertinent part:

Article 24

1. In order to ensure prompt and effective action by the United Nations, its Members confer on the Security Council primary responsibility for the maintenance of international peace and security, and agree that in carrying out its duties under this responsibility the Security Council acts on their behalf.

2. In discharging these duties the Security Council shall act in accordance with the Purposes and Principles of the United Nations. The specific powers granted to the Security Council for the discharge of these duties are laid down in Chapters VI, VII, VIII, and XII.

It is only when the Council exercises its peace enforcement authority pursuant to Chapter VII, however, that it can impose or authorize coercive measures such as mandatory sanctions or military intervention. Article 2(7) of the UN Charter provides:

Article 2

. . .

7. Nothing contained in the present Charter shall authorize the United Nations to intervene in matters which are essentially within the domestic jurisdiction of any state or shall require the Members to submit such matters to settlement under the present Charter; but this principle shall not prejudice the application of enforcement measures under Chapter VII.

Chapter VII establishes a multilevel structure for responses by the Security Council to situations it deems a threat to or breach of the peace. Pursuant to Article 39, the first provision of Chapter VII, "The Security Council shall determine the existence of any threat to the peace, breach of the peace, or act of aggression and shall make recommendations, or decide what measures shall be taken in accordance with Articles 41 and 42, to maintain or restore international peace and security." Thus, a Security Council determination that a situation presents a threat to the peace, a breach of the peace or an act of aggression is the trip wire to enforcement measures under other provisions of Chapter VII. Articles 41 and 42 provide, respectively for non-military and military enforcement measures:

Article 41

The Security Council may decide what measures not involving the use of armed force are to be employed to give effect to its decisions, and it may call upon the Members of the United Nations to apply such measures. These may include complete or partial interruption of economic relations and of rail, sea, air, postal, telegraphic, radio, and other means of communication, and the severance of diplomatic relations.

Article 42

Should the Security Council consider that measures provided for in Article 41 would be inadequate or have proved to be inadequate, it may take such action by air, sea, or land forces as may be necessary to maintain or restore international peace and security. Such action may include demonstrations, blockade, and other operations by air, sea, or land forces of Members of the United Nations.

As used in Article 39, the concepts of a threat to and breach of "the peace" were intended to refer to international—or at least regional—peace and security. In principle, therefore, the Article 39 threshold determination presents a significant barrier to Security Council enforcement action in respect of human rights violations within a state.

Note that Article 39 contemplates two distinct types of response by the Security Council to situations that present a threat to or breach of the peace: It can make "recommendations," which by their nature are not legally binding, or it can "decide what measures shall be taken in accordance with Articles 41 and 42." Under the law of the Charter, "decide" is a term of art. Pursuant to Article 25, Member States are legally bound by Security Council "decisions":

Article 25

The members of the United Nations agree to accept and carry out the decisions of the Security Council in accordance with the present Charter.

. . .

It is often asserted or implied that what is distinctive about Security Council resolutions adopted under Chapter VII is that they are legally binding. But this interpretation of Charter law is misleading in two respects. First, as noted above, the Council can make recommendations as well as take decisions pursuant to its general Chapter VII authority.

Second, the Council may adopt legally binding decisions even outside the parameters of Chapter VII. This was affirmed by the International Court of Justice in a 1971 advisory opinion:

It has been contended that Article 25 of the Charter applies only to enforcement measures adopted under Chapter VII of the Charter. It is not possible to find in the Charter any support for this view. Article 25 is not confined to decisions in regard to enforcement action but applies to "the decisions of the Security Council" adopted in accordance with the Charter. Moreover, that Article is placed, not in Chapter VII, but immediately after Article 24 in that part of the Charter which deals with the functions and powers of the Security Council. If Article 25 had reference solely to decisions of the Security Council concerning enforcement action under Articles 41 and 42 of the Charter, that is to say, if it were only such decisions which had binding effect, then Article 25 would be superfluous, since this effect is secured by Articles 48 and 49 of the Charter.

Legal Consequences for States of the Continued Presence of South Africa in Namibia (South West Africa) Notwithstanding Security Council Resolution 276 (1970), 1971 I.C.J. 16, para. 113.

What, then, is distinctive about Chapter VII enforcement measures? A key part of the answer is found in Article 2(7) of the Charter; as noted above, this provision generally forbids the United Nations from intervening in matters that are essentially within the domestic jurisdiction of Member States, but makes clear that this prohibition is trumped by enforcement measures taken under Chapter VII.

In larger perspective, Chapter VII establishes the framework within which the Council operates when it imposes or authorizes *coercive* measures. In contrast, the Council can and does take a broad range of activities to foster pacific settlements of disputes through non-coercive "peacemaking" initiatives under Chapter VI. Such initiatives include the conduct of peace negotiations and the deployment of peacekeeping forces on the basis of consent by the host state.

b. NON–MILITARY ENFORCEMENT MEASURES

John Dugard, *Sanctions Against South Africa: An International Law Perspective*

in Sanctions Against Apartheid 113, 113–18 (Mark Orkin, ed. 1989).

[The following excerpt was written several years before South Africa ended its decades-long practice of apartheid. At the time this essay was written, South Africa remained subject to both mandatory and voluntary sanctions aimed at bringing an end to its practice of legalized racism.—Editors' Note.]

. . .

That South Africa has violated international law and the Charter of the United Nations by applying the policy of apartheid is no longer a subject of dispute. The international community, acting through the United Nations, has repeatedly rejected the argument of the South African government that its racial policies are a matter of exclusive domestic concern. Apartheid has been condemned as a violation of the provisions of the UN Charter, which oblige states to promote respect for human rights without distinctions based on race, by innumerable resolutions of the General Assembly and Security Council.... It has been held to be contrary to the purposes and principles of the UN Charter by the International Court of Justice. Moreover, apartheid has been labelled as an "international crime"—the most serious form of international delinquency—by the International Law Commission, the General Assembly, and the Convention on the Suppression and Punishment of the Crime of Apartheid. But the political organs of the United Nations are—and have been for many years—divided on the sanctions to be adopted to remedy the situation.

. . .

... In 1977 [the efforts of the sanctions lobby] were rewarded when the Security Council ordered the imposition of a mandatory arms embargo against South Africa. Attempts to obtain an extension of this embargo to include economic sanctions have failed because of the vetoes of the three Western powers....

. . .

Mandatory sanctions under the UN Charter

The legal framework

Chapter VII of the Charter of the United Nations authorises the Security Council to order enforcement action against a state whose conduct threatens international peace, if it finds that there is a "threat to the peace, breach of the peace, or act of aggression" under article 39 of the Charter. This is a political and not a judicial decision, but it is inconceivable that such a finding would be made in the absence of a violation of international law.

Once it has made a determination the Security Council may direct members of the United Nations to take "measures not involving the use of armed force" such as "complete or partial interruption of economic relations and of rail, sea, air, postal, telegraphic, radio and other means of communications and the severance of diplomatic relations" (article 41). If it considers that such measures are [or would be] inadequate, the Security Council "may take such action by air, sea or land forces" (article 42). As the United Nations has no permanent police or military force at its disposal the Secretary General is obliged to raise contingents from member states for the purpose of such an operation.[15] Decisions adopted under articles 41 and 42 are legally binding upon the ... member states of the United Nations.

15. The Charter contemplates the establishment of a permanent UN force under a UN Military Staff Committee (articles 43–7). Disagreement among the permanent members of the Security Council has, however, prevented such a force from being established. UN peacekeeping forces have therefore been established on an *ad hoc* basis for each operation.

The Charter prohibits the use of force by states in their international relations,[16] except where they act under the authority of the United Nations or in self-defence;[17] but it does not outlaw economic coercion[18] or the severance of diplomatic relations. However, it is widely held that economic coercion outside Chapter VII is contrary to customary international law unless taken in self-defence or to redress an international wrong.

. . .

The bite of the Security Council is to be found in Chapter VII. The bark is contained in Chapter VI, which states that the Security Council may *recommend* steps to remedy a situation that does not yet threaten international peace, but which is "likely to endanger" or "disturbs" international peace.... [M]ost Security Council resolutions on South Africa have been adopted under Chapter VI.

The General Assembly ... has a secondary role in the maintenance of international peace. Its powers are limited to recommendation....

South Africa and the Security Council

The Security Council first considered South Africa's racial polices in 1960 after Sharpeville.* It labelled the situation in South Africa as "one that has led to international friction and if continued might endanger international peace and security"—that is, not yet a threat to international peace under article 39—and merely called upon South Africa to abandon apartheid.[23] In 1963[24] and 1964[25] the Security Council went further and called on states to end the supply of arms and military equipment to South Africa. However, as the resolutions were based on the determination that the situation "seriously disturbed" international peace under Chapter VI, they were merely recommendatory.

... [In 1970 and 1972], the Council reaffirmed its non-mandatory calls regarding military equipment.[28]

Following the Soweto uprising of 1976–7 and the consequent repressive police action, in October 1977 the Security Council condemned the brutal action taken under the security laws; and in November it imposed a mandatory arms embargo against South Africa under Chapter VII, by means of Resolution 418. The preamble ... mentions Pretoria's "resort to massive violence against and killings of the African people", "military build up" and "persistent acts of aggression" against neighbouring states. The

---

16. Article 2(4).

17. Article 51.

18. Although the prohibition on the use of force in article 2(4) does not limit the prohibition to "armed force", there are indications in the Charter that this was the intention of the framers of the Charter. (See preamble and article 46.) While some states maintain that economic coercion is outlawed under article 2(4), this is not supported by state practice.

* [This reference is to a 1960 massacre by South African police of Black demonstrators who were protesting segregation laws.—Editors' Note.]

23. Resolution 134 (1960).

24. Resolutions 181 and 183 (1963).

25. Resolution 191 (1964).

28. Resolutions 282 (1970), 311 (1972).

resolution then "determines, having regard to the policies and acts of the South African Government, that the acquisition by South Africa of arms and related materiel constitutes a threat to the maintenance of international peace and security"; and provides "that all states shall cease forthwith" from providing such equipment or the means of manufacturing it.

This resolution was significant for a number of reasons. Firstly, it determined the situation to be a threat under article 39 and ordered states to take action under Chapter VII. Secondly, the Security Council had never previously ordered enforcement action to be taken against a member state. It had ordered such action to be taken against a non-member only—Rhodesia. Thirdly, it opened the door for further collective action under Chapter VII, as the major hurdle—a finding of a threat to the peace under article 39—had been cleared.

In 1977 it was widely believed that further mandatory sanctions would soon follow the imposition of the arms embargo. But the Reagan administration in the United States and the Thatcher government in Britain subsequently used their vetoes. Only non-binding resolutions were allowed to pass. . . .

After the declaration of a state of emergency in South Africa in 1985, the Security Council, by means of Resolution 569, called for the lifting of the state of emergency and urged member states to adopt measures such as the suspension of all new investments; prohibition of the sale of Kruger-rands; restriction of sports and cultural relations; suspension of guaranteed export loans; prohibition of all new contracts in the nuclear field; and prohibition of all sales of computer equipment for use by the South African Army and police.

However, this resolution was not preceded by a finding under article 39 and is not binding on states. Subsequent attempts to persuade the Security Council to impose mandatory sanctions have been vetoed by Britain and the United States[, whose vetoes] can be explained on two grounds. Firstly, these two states oppose sanctions as a means of bringing about political change in South Africa. (Although the US legislature now supports sanctions, the executive does not.*) Secondly, they fear that once sanctions have been imposed by the Security Council it will be difficult to terminate them in that the Soviet Union and China might then use *their* vetoes to block any resolution to lift sanctions before there had been a complete transfer of political power to an approved political movement.

Resolution 418 makes it clear from a legal point of view that South Africa's internal policies may be a threat to international peace under article 39. It is now only the political considerations that prevent the Security Council, and more particularly the Western powers, from resorting to mandatory, collective economic sanctions.

---

* [As noted in Chapter 4, Section D, in 1985 President Ronald Reagan adopted limited sanctions against South Africa to pre-empt more far-reaching congressional sanctions. In 1986, Congress nonetheless adopted the Comprehensive Anti–Apartheid Act.—Editors' Note.]

South Africa and the General Assembly

Apartheid was first placed on the agenda of the General Assembly in 1952. At first its resolutions were conciliatory, and consisted largely of appeals to South Africa to observe the human rights obligations contained in the Charter. After 1960, which saw the admission of a number of newly independent African states to the world body and the international outcry over Sharpeville, resolutions became more strident and action-oriented. In 1961 the General Assembly, by 95 votes to 1 (Portugal), requested states to consider taking separate and collective action against South Africa.[36] In the following year it called on states to break off diplomatic relations with South Africa, close their ports to South African ships, boycott all South African goods, refrain from exporting goods to South Africa, and refuse landing and passage facilities to all South African aircraft.[37] These suggested sanctions have since been endorsed and expanded to include a comprehensive trade boycott, and the severance of cultural, educational and sporting exchanges.

· · ·

Notes

1.   Discussing the legal principle supporting Security Council Resolution 418 (1977), which imposed a mandatory arms embargo against South Africa, Professor Dugard observed: "Resolution 418 makes it clear from a legal point of view that South Africa's internal policies may be a threat to international peace under article 39." What precisely, was the threat to the peace underlying the sanctions imposed by S. C. Resolution 418? Consider the following facts as well as the portions of Resolution 418 set forth below: The immediate impetus for this resolution was the South African government's action two weeks earlier banning 18 domestic civil rights organizations, shutting down two major black newspapers and arresting or banning at least 50 leaders of black or multiracial groups. The broader context of Resolution 418 included incursions by South African forces into Angola in pursuit of paramilitary forces of the Southwest People's Organization.

S.C. Res. 418 (1977)

The Security Council,

Recalling its resolution 392 (1976) strongly condemning the South African Government for its resort to massive violence against and killings of the African people, including schoolchildren and students and others opposing racial discrimination, and calling upon that Government urgently to end violence against the African people and take urgent steps to eliminate *apartheid* and racial discrimination,

36. Resolution 1598 (XV).   **37.** Resolution 1761 (XVII).

Recognizing that the military build-up and persistent acts of aggression by South Africa against the neighboring States seriously disturb the security of those States,

. . .

Gravely concerned that South Africa is at the threshold of producing nuclear weapons,

Strongly condemning the South African Government for its acts of repression, its defiant continuance of the system of *apartheid* and its attacks against neighboring independent States,

Considering that the policies and acts of the South African Government are fraught with danger to international peace and security,

. . .

Convinced that a mandatory arms embargo needs to be universally applied against South Africa in the first instance,

Acting therefore under Charter VII of the Charter of the United Nations,

1. *Determines*, having regard to the policies and acts of the South African Government, that the acquisition by South Africa of arms and related matériel constitutes a threat to the maintenance of international peace and security;

2. *Decides* that all States shall cease forthwith any provision to South Africa of arms and related matériel of all types, including the sale or transfer of weapons and ammunition, military vehicles and equipment, paramilitary police equipment, and spare parts for the aforementioned, and shall cease as well the provision of all types of equipment and supplies, and grants of licensing arrangements, for the manufacture or maintenance of the aforementioned.

. . .

4. *Further decides* that all States shall refrain from co-operation with South Africa in the manufacture and development of nuclear weapons;

5. *Calls upon* all States, including States non-members of the United Nations, to act strictly in accordance with the provisions of this resolution;

. . .

2. S.C. Resolution 418 (1977), like many other resolutions imposing mandatory arms embargoes, did not explicitly authorize states to use force to enforce the embargo (by, e.g., forcibly interdicting ships carrying arms to South Africa). Did the resolution nonetheless implicitly provide such authority? Consider first the text of Articles 41 and 42 of the UN Charter. Read together, do they shed light on this question?

3. In addition to its resolutions encouraging states to impose sanctions against South Africa, including a non-binding oil embargo adopted in a

1979 resolution, the UN General Assembly prevented the apartheid government from participating in the Assembly for many years. Although the Assembly had tried to expel South Africa from the UN, it needed the concurrence of the Security Council, which was blocked by the veto of three permanent members. The Assembly did succeed, however, in preventing South Africa from taking its seat in the General Assembly for some 20 years through the device of rejecting the government's credentials.

Evaluating the Sanctions Against South Africa

Throughout the long years of apartheid, many analysts judged the sanctions imposed against South Africa to be a manifest failure. But when South Africa's legally-sanctioned racism finally came to an end, many credited those same sanctions with playing a crucial role in the success of the anti-apartheid movement. Still, the long-term legacy of sanctions is complex, as the following article suggests.

Bill Keller, *South Africa's Sanctions May Have Worked, at a Price*

N.Y. Times, Sept. 12, 1993.

In the arsenal of diplomacy, economic sanctions are crude weapons, slow-acting and unpredictable. When they work, innocents suffer. The bad guys, after all, are usually the ones with the bunkers and gas masks—or, in this case, the power and cash—to endure a war of attrition.

But as the use of real force has become less politically palatable, the world has increasingly turned to the trade embargo, the investment ban, the credit blockade or the assets freeze as a way of punishing a misbehaving state. The United States now monitors official sanctions of one kind or another against a dozen countries. Do they work?

South Africa now presents one case study of sanctions that have run their course. With the white Government's agreement last week to submit to the oversight of a multiparty council in the months before next April's election, making the transition all but irreversible, the African National Congress is on the verge of calling off the economic penalties the world imposed against apartheid.

In hindsight, few now question that the sanctions had powerful consequences, but there is no consensus that the results were quite what the sponsors intended.

The United Nations imposed an arms embargo against South Africa in 1977 after a massacre of schoolchildren in Soweto, but the real economic siege of South Africa began in 1985 when Chase Manhattan Bank, under pressure to sever its ties with the apartheid rulers, called in its loans. Other banks in America and Europe followed suit. The following year Congress voted, over President Reagan's veto, to restrict trade, investment and lending by American companies in South Africa. Scores of state and local governments enacted their own anti-apartheid statutes.

It is impossible to isolate the effect of sanctions from the other pressures that finally drove the white Government towards surrender: the riots and nettlesome guerrilla war waged by the African National Congress, the ascent of a more sophisticated and pragmatic generation of Afrikaners like President F. W. de Klerk, the collapse of the Communist bogy man that so terrified South African whites, the shame of sports and cultural boycotts and, perhaps most of all, the sheer, self-defeating folly of an ideology that tried to make foreigners of the country's black laborers and customers.

The African National Congress contends, and some independent economists agree, that sanctions helped hasten the end of apartheid through a combination of psychological and economic pain.

. . .

Critics of sanctions counter that sanctions worked, but economic growth would have worked better, and would have left the next, democratic Government with a healthier country to run.

Such apartheid practices as reserving certain jobs for whites and forbidding blacks from living in cities, most experts agree, were abandoned because the state simply could not hold back the tide of job-seeking blacks. A booming economy, with more jobs, the critics argue, might have brought down those barriers faster.

. . .

Tight Money

The most devastating blow was the loss of easy credit from foreign banks. While most developing countries are big borrowers, South Africa became an exporter of capital, rationing out its cash to satisfy foreign creditors. Tight money helped push the country deeper into recession and, . . . economists are convinced, helped persuade Mr. de Klerk to reverse course in February 1990.

Critics of sanctions, including the Government and the Zulu-based Inkatha Freedom Party, contend that the main victims of this economic punishment were destitute blacks, who make up most of the country's nearly 50 percent unemployment rate. Poverty, in turn, bred violence.

. . .

Trevor Manuel, the head of the A.N.C. economics department, conceded that blacks shared in the suffering, but not disproportionately. In part because of sanctions, white South Africans, who were less accustomed to economic hardship, experienced a startling drop in their living standards, and newspapers began reporting the eye-opening novelty of whites lined up at soup kitchens.

The sanctions ricocheted with many unpredicted effects.

One, many economists agree, was that by slowing the most advanced economy in southern Africa, sanctions also retarded development in neighboring countries, including outspokenly anti-apartheid (but economically dependent) countries like Zimbabwe and Zambia.

. . .

Another was to convert many South African business executives into grudging lobbyists for political reform. Alarmed by the prospect of endless isolation, bankers and corporate executives privately urged Mr. de Klerk to move faster, and publicly entered into their own dialogue with black leaders.

Better to Stay or Go?

Some of the impetus came, paradoxically, from American companies like Colgate Palmolive and I.T.T. that decided, despite public vilification, to remain in South Africa. To justify their decision, they signed pledges that committed them to programs for black advancement, and a number of South African companies followed their example.

. . .

The stunted economy that sanctions helped create now becomes the inheritance of the A.N.C., assuming it wins elections next April. Blacks will take over an economy that is shrinking, that is not adept at competing in the world, that is lagging behind in research and modernization, that is inbred and dominated by a few corporate pyramids.

. . .

Notes

1. The unintended consequences of comprehensive economic sanctions have led many to question their morality as a tool for advancing human rights. While this critique has figured somewhat in evaluations of South Africa sanctions, the strong support by South African blacks for the various sanctions against the apartheid regime was widely viewed as decisive. Still, as the preceding article reflects, post-apartheid South Africa will long bear the social and economic costs of those sanctions. Are there policies or guidelines that the UN Security Council can and should follow when it imposes sanctions to mitigate their social costs?

2. For further reading on sanctions, see, e.g., Gary Clyde Hufbauer, Jeffrey J. Schott and Kimberly Ann Elliott, Economic Sanctions Reconsidered (1990); Economic Sanctions: Panacea or Peacebuilding in a Post–Cold War World? (David Cortright and George A. Lopez eds. 1995); Political Gain and Civilian Pain: Humanitarian Impacts of Economic Sanctions (Thomas G. Weiss et al. eds. 1997); Lori Fisler Damrosch, *The Civilian Impact of Economic Sanctions*, in Enforcing Restraint: Collective Intervention in Internal Conflicts (Damrosch ed. 1993); Lori Fisler Damrosch, *Enforcing International Law Through Non–Forcible Measures*, 269 Recueil des Cours (1997); Vojin Dimitrijević and Jelena Pejić, *UN Sanctions against Yugoslavia: Two Years Later*, in The United Nations in the New World

Order: The World Organization at Fifty (Dimitris Bourantonis and Jarrod Wiener eds. 1995).

c. HUMANITARIAN INTERVENTION

Under what circumstances may states lawfully use military force to try to repress grave and massive violations of human rights in another country? When, if ever, do states have a duty to intervene? These questions are the core concerns of the law of "humanitarian intervention"—a term we use in this section to refer to the coercive deployment of military forces by a state or states for the purpose of alleviating a humanitarian crisis in another state.

A key consideration is the distinction between unilateral intervention on the one hand and multilateral intervention on the other. In the legal literature on humanitarian intervention, the term "unilateral intervention" has been used to refer to an intervention undertaken by one or more states without authorization from the United Nations Security Council. The term "multilateral intervention" has been used to describe an armed intervention that has been authorized by the Security Council under Chapter VII of the UN Charter. Events in 1999 in Yugoslavia may have exemplified an intermediate category of "collective intervention" by an organized group of states, without prior authorization but with the arguably tacit acquiescence of the UN Security Council.

Beyond the law, the subject of humanitarian intervention raises vexing—and, at times, profoundly difficult—questions of international policy. When *should* states place their own troops in harm's way to alleviate a humanitarian crisis beyond their national borders? And how can states intervene effectively?

Pre–Charter Law and Practice

Although our principal focus is contemporary law, humanitarian intervention has a long and controversial history. The following excerpt summarizes the pre-Charter law, theory and practice of humanitarian intervention.

Michael J. Bazyler, *Reexamining the Doctrine of Humanitarian Intervention in Light of the Atrocities in Kampuchea and Ethiopia*

23 Stan. J. Int'l L. 547 (1987).

. . .

Pre–United Nations Foundations of the Doctrine [of Humanitarian Intervention]

The early writings of St. Thomas Aquinas, the great thirteenth-century religious scholar, make references to the proposition that one sovereign has the right to intervene in the internal affairs of another "when the latter greatly mistreats its subjects." Grotius, the "founding father" of international law, recognized the doctrine in the seventeenth century:

> There is also another question, whether a war for the subjects of another be just, for the purpose of defending them from injuries by their ruler. Certainly it is undoubted that ever since civil societies were formed, the ruler of each claimed some especial right over his own subjects.... [But i]f a tyrant ... practices atrocities towards his subjects, which no just man can approve, the right of human social connexion is not cut off in such case.

Vattel, another early international scholar, also accepted the doctrine: "[I]f the prince, attacking the fundamental laws, gives his people a legitimate reason to resist him, if tyranny becomes so unbearable as to cause the Nation to rise, any foreign power is entitled to help an oppressed people that has requested its assistance."

These scholars' pronouncements were based upon recognition of natural rights, which was then the basis of international law. In the nineteenth century, legal positivism replaced natural law as the foundation of international law; however, scholars still recognized the doctrine. Bernard, a British legal scholar, wrote: "The [positive] law ... prohibits intervention.... [However,] there may even be cases in which it becomes a positive duty to transgress [positive law]." ...

In the first part of the twentieth century, a majority of writers continued to recognize the doctrine of humanitarian intervention.... Oppenheim, whose work became one of the most authoritative and frequently cited treatises on international law, stated:

> [S]hould a State venture to treat its own subjects or a part thereof with such cruelty as would stagger humanity, public opinion of the rest of the world would call upon the Powers to exercise intervention for the purpose of compelling such a State to establish a legal order of things within its boundaries sufficient to guarantee to its citizens an existence more adequate to the ideas of modern civilization.

· · ·

Although a few scholars had rejected the doctrine, the humanitarian intervention doctrine was generally accepted for six hundred years....

· · ·

... Historical Uses and Non–Uses of the Doctrine

Religion provided the original motivation for humanitarian intervention by one state into the affairs of another state: one nation intervened to prevent religious persecution by the other nation. Interventions motivated by feelings of shared concern and reciprocal responsibility toward all humanity did not appear until the nineteenth century....

· · ·

In the early nineteenth century, major European powers began intervening in the affairs of other states to prevent the killing of foreigners living within those states. These interventions ... still had some religious motivation, since most were done to protect Christian minorities living in non-Christian states. The Turkish/Moslem Ottoman Empire, already declining in the nineteenth century, was frequently the object of such intervention, mostly because of its periodic abuses of Christian minorities living within its boundaries. Such interventions occurred throughout the nineteenth and early twentieth centuries: from 1827–1830, after a number of massacres of Christian Greeks; in 1860–1861, after a massacre of thousands of Christians in Syria; in 1866, following the Ottoman repression of a revolt by the Christian population of Crete; in 1877–1878, in support of Christian populations of Bosnia, Herzegovina and Bulgaria; and at the beginning of the twentieth century, following intense efforts by Turkey to convert the Christian population in Macedonia.

. . .

In hindsight, historians and international legal scholars examining these interventions have recognized that while the motives for intervening were not always pure, the motivations of the intervening powers were, in fact, humanitarian. In each instance, the governing power was either actively involved in the killings, or could not or did not prevent the massacres of many innocent nonbelligerents within their territorial domain. . . .

The pre–1945 period also exhibited a number of interventions where the humanitarian motives alleged were clearly spurious. These bogus "humanitarian interventions" illustrate the danger of an unbridled international law doctrine of humanitarian intervention.

. . .

Probably the most disconcerting for proponents of the doctrine is that Hitler used the excuse of humanitarian intervention both to annex Czechoslovakia and to attack Poland. In a letter to British Prime Minister Chamberlain on September 23, 1938, Hitler noted that ethnic Germans and "various nationalities in Czechoslovakia have been maltreated in the unworthiest manner, tortured, economically destroyed and, above all, prevented from realizing for themselves also the right of nations to self-determination." The ethnic Germans in Czechoslovakia, according to Hitler, "were subject to the 'brutal will to destruction of the Czechs[,]' whose behavior was 'madness' and had led to over 120,000 refugees being forced to flee the country in recent days while the 'security of more than 3,000,000 human beings' was at stake." Hitler also attempted to justify his subsequent invasion of Poland on September 1, 1939, on the ground that it was necessary to rescue ethnic Germans living in Poland whom the Poles were allegedly mistreating.

The opponents of [humanitarian intervention] cite the false humanitarian justifications for these naked and unjustified invasions of other nations as the major reason why international law should not recognize the doctrine. . . .

. . .

Post–Charter Law

L. Henkin, *Humanitarian Intervention*

in Human Rights: An Agenda for the Next Century 383, 384, 388–91, 398–401 (1993).*

. . .

. . . States have been reluctant to submit their human rights practices to scrutiny by others or to scrutinize the practices of others. All states have resisted forcible intervention, and international law has reinforced that resistance. Securing respect for the territorial integrity and political independence of states has been the principal purpose of the United Nations; Article 2(4) of the U.N. Charter prohibits the use of force by one state against another state, apparently on any ground for any purpose (except in self-defense). Exceptionally, the Charter contemplates collective use of force to maintain or restore international peace and security; there was no hint that collective force might be used for other purposes, even to terminate, prevent, punish or deter massive human rights violations.

. . .

Sources of U.N. authority

The basis for collective U.N. action must lie in the purposes of the Organization and in the authority conferred upon its organs. The principal purpose of the United Nations . . . is:

> To maintain international peace and security, and to that end: to take effective collective measures for the prevention and removal of threats to the peace, and for suppression of acts of aggression or other breaches of the peace, and to bring about by peaceful means . . . adjustments or settlements of international disputes or situations that might lead to a breach of the peace.

Authority to act to achieve that purpose comes from powers granted to the principal organs. In particular, under Chapter VI, the Security Council has authority to investigate "any situation which might lead to international friction or give rise to a dispute" (Art. 34); for those situations, the Council may "recommend appropriate procedures or methods of adjustment" (Art. 36). Under Chapter VII, the Security Council "shall determine the existence of any threat to the peace, breach of the peace, or act of aggression and shall make recommendations, or decide what measures shall be taken . . . to maintain or restore international peace and security." (Art. 39). Unlike its recommendations, Security Council decisions are binding on all U.N. members. The Council may decide on non-military measures pursuant to Article 41, or take military action under Article 42. The Council may undertake action itself or, presumably, it may authorize states to act.

The Charter appears to give the Security Council full authority to determine the existence of a threat to the peace and the measures to address such threat. The Charter includes no guidelines for determining whether a situation poses a threat to the peace; it makes no provision for review of the Security Council determinations or of measures it orders or recommends. In the traditional conception of "threat to the peace," even consistent patterns of gross human lights violations such as racial or gender discrimination, do not necessarily create such a threat. But killings, rape, other massive violence, or even massive hunger or the breakdown of social order, may well be found to be a threat to the peace, especially if they arouse world opinion and threaten reaction by other states. In some situations, surely, the Security Council would be obviously justified in determining that gross human rights violations have created a threat to the peace: atrocities may be so shocking or may otherwise incite reaction as to threaten international peace. That the threat to peace in particular circumstances may be due to the hostile reaction of neighbors does not diminish the threat to the peace, or the Security Council's authority to address it. Situations created by "ethnic cleansing," rape, and other atrocities in former Yugoslavia . . ., for example, fit readily within traditional conceptions of threat to peace, especially since they have accompanied military hostilities between entities claiming to be (and recognized as) independent states.

Those who favor collective responsibility and collective intervention in principle may be disposed to support it also in order to impose, maintain or restore democracy. Ordinarily, the failure to achieve or maintain democracy does not threaten international peace: the international system, including the United Nations Organization, is populated by states that are not authentically democratic. But political upheaval, accompanied by violence and wide disorder (as in Haiti in 1991–93) and the threat of forcible involvement by other states, might well constitute a threat to the peace justifying Security Council intervention. . . .

In other situations, the existence of a threat to the peace—by traditional conceptions—is less obvious. In 1992, the Security Council authorized United Nations Operations in Somalia (UNOSOM) to alleviate hunger and starvation (S.C. Res. 733). Then, the Secretary–General requested the Council to authorize military action to bring an end to violence against the relief effort by disarming various warring factions, irregular forces and gangs. On December 3, the Security Council found that the "magnitude of the human tragedy" together with obstacles to humanitarian assistance constituted a threat to international peace and security; the Council authorized the use of "military force" to establish "a secure environment for humanitarian relief operations in Somalia," [Resolution 794].

In Somalia, the Council acted on a conception of "threat to the peace" that included situations of mass starvation with the local government unwilling or unable to act to alleviate it. The Council asserted authority to meet that threat by the same means, including economic and military coercion, that might be used to address traditional threats to the peace. . . . That the Security Council has authority to determine that a breakdown of order, or massive hunger and serious health hazards, constitute threats to peace would not seem to be an extravagant interpretation.

In addition to a "threat to the peace," is there any other basis that might support humanitarian intervention under the authority of U.N. [organs]? It may be possible to distill justifications for some action from the other purposes of the United Nations. Article 1 of the Charter declares as one of the United Nations purposes:

> To achieve international cooperation in solving international problems of an economic, social, cultural or humanitarian character, and in promoting and encouraging respect for human lights and for fundamental freedoms for all . . .

Article 55 provides:

> With the view towards creation of stability and well-being which are necessary for peaceful and friendly relations among nations . . . the United Nations shall promote . . . universal respect for and observance of human rights and fundamental freedoms for all. . . .

In Article 56, Members pledge to take joint and separate action in cooperation with the United Nations to achieve those purposes.

These general provisions might lend additional support to the authority of the United Nations to respond to gross human rights violations. Arguably, even collective, coercive intervention might be justified as necessary to achieve that major U.N. purpose. But is such intervention within the authority conferred upon any U.N. [organ]? The General Assembly, for example, has authority to make recommendations "for the purpose of . . . assisting in the realization of human rights and fundamental freedoms" (Art. (13)(b)). As regards coercive action, however, there are strong arguments for limiting General Assembly recommendations (and even Security Council recommendations) to situations that can legitimately be called— and will be widely recognized—as threats to international peace.

. . .

Unilateral Intervention in the Post Cold War World

Humanitarian intervention by individual states is no longer restrained by the Cold War. However, it remains prohibited by the U.N. Charter. Unilateral intervention contravenes the target state's essential right to be let alone. The basic norm of the Charter and of international law is Article 2(4):

> All members shall refrain in their international relations from the threat or use of force against the territorial integrity or political independence of any state, or in any other manner inconsistent with the purposes of the United Nations.

The established interpretation of Article 2(4) is that the Charter prohibits any unilateral uses of force except in self-defense against much attack. The legal debate has been fairly summed up:[3]

---

3. Daniel Wolf, *Humanitarian Interven-*   40 (1988) (footnotes omitted).
tion, IX Mich. Y. B. Int'l Leg. Stud. 333, 339–

... [T]he prevailing view of the member states of the United Nations, as exemplified in General Assembly Resolutions, also strongly supports the view that the Charter prohibits all unilateral use of force except in self-defense.

There is nevertheless, a growing minority of writers which argues that because "humanitarian intervention seeks neither a territorial change nor a challenge to the political independence of the state involved," it is inaccurate to conclude it is precluded by Article 2(4). This analysis, however, contradicts both the plain meaning of Article 2(4)'s language and the intent of its drafters to prohibit absolutely the use of force except in self-defense.

... What matters is not the purpose of the violation, but the act of violating itself. An armed intervention, even if undertaken for the purpose of protecting human rights, violates the very essence of territorial integrity and, since it would necessarily require a change in authority structures to assure respect for human rights, would also be against the political independence of the target state.

The author nevertheless concludes that there "exists a compelling need for a contemporary and realistic interpretation of Article 2(4) based on state practice that recognizes an exception to the Charter when force is required to prevent mass slaughter." I do not know of any such practice or even state disposition to that effect. The international system is not likely to welcome reinterpretation of the Charter to permit unilateral action, which could easily be abused and which might give one activist state an enlarged, uncontrolled role in policing the world. Indeed, the improved prospects for collective action serve to reinforce resistance to unilateral action and to any reinterpretation of the Charter to permit it. One might have expected that grievous situations (such as "ethnic cleansing" in the former Yugoslavia) would make it tempting for some states to intervene and for others to tolerate such intervention; in fact, states have not rushed to intervene and have pursued collective action instead. . . .

Some states have claimed a right to intervene when the lives of their own nationals are threatened in a foreign state. In my view, the Charter does not permit intervention by force even in such circumstances. It is accepted that a state may invoke the "Entebbe principle" to use force necessary to extricate hostages (whether or not its own nationals); but it may not use threat to lives to justify invasion, to topple a regime, or to conquer territory. Whether in particular circumstances state-directed terrorist activities, targeted against nationals of a particular state, may constitute an armed attack against that state warranting it to use force in self-defense (Article 51) is an arguable, hypothetical question.

The Charter creates a sharp divide between intervention by an individual country on its own initiative and authority, and collective intervention by the Security Council or pursuant to its authority. During the years since the Charter was written, nearly all states have condemned virtually every unilateral use of force. They have rejected virtually every putative justification of a use of force other than in self-defense against armed attack. . . .

[N]ow that collective action is feasible, there is less reason than ever to support unilateral intervention by force.

Proponents of unilateral humanitarian intervention have asserted an analogy to a neighbor's intervention to prevent gross child abuse. But state neighbors cannot be trusted, and the risks and costs of permitting them to intrude are too great. State neighbors do not in fact intervene to safeguard human rights, though they may sometimes use that pretext. Oscar Schachter's warning against unilateral intervention holds true:

> The reluctance of governments to legitimize foreign invasion in the interest of humanitarianism is understandable in light of past abuses by powerful states. States strong enough to intervene and sufficiently interested in doing so tend to have political motives. They have a strong temptation to impose a political solution in their own national interest.[6]

In international political life, a neighbor aware of gross human rights violations should call the police—the Security Council. That is what states in the international system agreed and consented to; they did not consent to "citizens' actions" by individual states on their own authority. A state may be justified in resorting to non-forcible forms of response to human rights violations; it does not have authority to take action by force.

The principles of the Charter against unauthorized unilateral uses of force even against states guilty of consistent patterns of gross human rights violations must be reaffirmed.

. . .

Notes

1. The prevailing view of post-Charter law, as reflected in the preceding excerpt, is that it does not allow unilateral humanitarian intervention. Some scholars have argued, however, that the Charter did not alter existing customary international law concerning humanitarian intervention. As reflected in the excerpt by Professor Henkin, some proponents of this position have cited the text of Article 2(4) of the UN Charter which, in their view, prohibits the threat or use of force by UN Member States against another Member State only if the aim is territorial conquest or political domination. The drafting history of the Charter does not support this interpretation; it makes clear that Article 2(4) was meant to prohibit states from using force against other states for any reason other than self-defense.

Others have argued that, while drafters of the Charter intended to prohibit unilateral military intervention even for humanitarian purposes, this prohibition was based upon the premise that the UN system of collective security would operate effectively. Because the Cold War and

---

6. Schachter, International Law in Theory & Practice, General Course in Public International Law, The Hague Academy of International Law, 178 Recueil de Cours 144 (1982–V).

other sources of Security Council paralysis have more often than not blocked effective action by the Council, they argue, states must be permitted to act effectively when the Council fails to perform its role. Is this argument persuasive? What risks are associated with this approach? How, in this view, would it be possible to ensure that states do not abuse the right of humanitarian intervention? Is that risk worth taking in the face of massive atrocities on the order of the 1994 genocide in Rwanda?

2. On March 24, 1999, the North Atlantic Treaty Organization (NATO) began sustained aerial attacks against Yugoslav military targets with the express aim of repressing atrocities being committed by Yugoslav forces against separatist Albanians in Kosovo, a province of Yugoslavia. Although the UN Security Council had previously adopted several resolutions concerning the humanitarian crisis in Kosovo, it had not explicitly authorized Member States to use force to implement those resolutions. At first, NATO leaders argued that several resolutions adopted under Chapter VII provided sufficient authorization for the intervention. None of these resolutions had explicitly authorized Member States to use armed force, however. The argument that the NATO action was authorized by the Security Council was arguably bolstered when a resolution proposed by Russia demanding an immediate end to the NATO air strikes was defeated by a vote of 12–3. See Judith Miller, *Russia's Move to End Strikes Loses; Margin Is a Surprise*, N.Y. Times, Mar. 27, 1999. As the intervention neared the end of its first week and in the face of intensified repression by Yugoslav forces, some political leaders began to articulate another rationale for the NATO intervention: By severely repressing its own citizens in Kosovo, the government of Yugoslavia had, in effect, "forfeited" some measure of its sovereign rights in the region. Did the NATO intervention signify a new development in the law of humanitarian intervention? If so, what precedent was established? Was the intervention lawful? See pp. 733–737.

3. Henkin concluded in the reading above that unilateral humanitarian intervention by military force violates Article 2(4) of the UN Charter, but that, under Chapter VII of the Charter, the UN Security Council can authorize military force by one or more states if necessary to meet a threat to international peace and security. Does the Charter permit other *collective* military intervention to meet grave human rights violations? If so, what is necessary to render an intervention authentically "collective"?

Did the military intervention in Yugoslavia in effect "receive the blessing" of the Security Council when the Council overwhelmingly defeated a proposal to order the termination of the intervention? In what circumstances might tacit acquiescence of the Security Council, or failure of the Council to order termination of an intervention, render the intervention lawful, or not unlawful? Does it matter whether the opposing votes were cast by Big Powers which have a veto in the Security Council?

Can the Charter be interpreted to permit intervention by "regional bodies" under Article 53 of the Charter, at least where the Security Council does not adopt a decision to terminate the action? Does NATO now qualify as a regional body under Article 53?

UN Practice in the Aftermath of the Cold War

Freed from the political constraints that long inhibited it from performing its "primary role" under the Charter in assuring collective security, the Security Council became increasingly assertive in authorizing enforcement measures in the 1990s. Notably, in the final decade of the twentieth century various forms of humanitarian intervention figured prominently in the Security Council's Chapter VII resolutions.

Over the course of a brief period in the early 1990s, UN Security Council resolutions became increasingly forthright in their authorization of military force for explicitly humanitarian ends. But beneath the textual surface of these resolutions, a different trend emerged. Following a disastrous experience involving a UN operation in Somalia in October 1993, the Security Council became more restrained in its responses to humanitarian crises. In the early weeks of the 1994 genocide in Rwanda the Council, presented with the option of intervening to stop the violence, instead decided to withdraw the majority of UN forces that were already deployed in Rwanda.

Even before the debacle in Somalia, the Council evinced considerable ambivalence in its responses to the human tragedy unfolding in the former Yugoslavia. In some respects, the Council's responses seemed to break new ground in the evolving jurisprudence of humanitarian intervention under Chapter VII auspices. It was in respect of the former Yugoslavia that the Council first invoked Chapter VII to authorize a humanitarian relief operation (see S.C. Resolution 770, below). Less than one year later, again acting under Chapter VII, the Council declared six municipalities in Bosnia–Herzegovina—by then swollen with internally displaced persons—to be "safe areas." At first, however, the Council did not authorize states to use force to protect the safety of the designated areas, and they remained under siege. Although the Security Council later authorized military force in defense of the "safe areas," the UN Secretary–General hindered implementation of the relevant resolution.

The United Nations' recent practice thus raises fundamental questions of policy and implementation as well as of substantive legal standards governing humanitarian intervention. The following materials examine both dimensions of the UN's evolving approach to humanitarian intervention.

S.C. Res. 688 (1990): Iraqi Repression of Kurds and Shiites

The first significant Security Council resolution supporting humanitarian relief operations in the territory of a recalcitrant host state was adopted in the context of the Council's graduated responses to Iraq's invasion of Kuwait in August 1990. Within a day of the invasion, the Council adopted S.C. Resolution 660 (1990), which determined "that there exists a breach of international peace and security as regards the Iraqi invasion of Kuwait." "Acting under Articles 39 and 40 of the Charter," the Council demanded that Iraq withdraw immediately and unconditionally from Kuwait. Four days later the Council adopted S.C. Resolution 661 (1990), which imposed comprehensive economic sanctions against Iraq to secure compliance with S.C. Resolution 660. In short order, the Council adopted other resolutions, one of the most important of which, S.C. Resolution 678 (1990), authorized "Member States co-operating with the Government of Kuwait . . . to use all necessary means"—a Security Council term of art that generally encompasses military force—"to uphold and implement resolution 660 (1990) and all subsequent relevant resolutions and to restore international peace and security in the area . . ." unless Iraq fully withdrew from Kuwait by January 15, 1991. On January 16, 1991, coalition forces led by the United States began massive air attacks against Iraq.

In the immediate aftermath of the war and with encouragement from then U.S. President George W. Bush, Kurdish groups in the north of Iraq and Shiites in the south rose up against the government of Iraq. Their uprisings were forcibly repressed by Iraqi troops, instigating a massive exodus of Iraqi Kurds and Shiites to Turkey and Iran as well as to inaccessible areas within Iraq. Both Turkey and Iran sent letters to the United Nations expressing concern about the large numbers of Iraqis collecting on their borders and about the prospect that they would soon be forced across the borders. In this setting, the Security Council adopted Resolution 688.

Security Council Resolution 688

U.N. Doc. S/RES/688 (April 5, 1991).

The Security Council,

Mindful of its duties and its responsibilities under the Charter of the United Nations for the maintenance of international peace and security,

Recalling Article 2, paragraph 7, of the Charter of the United Nations,

Gravely concerned by the repression of the Iraqi civilian population in many parts of Iraq, including most recently in Kurdish populated areas which led to a massive flow of refugees towards and across international frontiers and to cross border incursions, which threaten international peace and security in the region,

. . .

Reaffirming the commitment of all Member States to the sovereignty, territorial integrity and political independence of Iraq and of all States in the area,

. . .

1. *Condemns* the repression of the Iraqi civilian population in many parts of Iraq, including most recently in Kurdish populated areas, the consequences of which threaten international peace and security in the region;

2. *Demands* that Iraq, as a contribution to removing the threat to international peace and security in the region, immediately end this repres-

sion and expresses the hope in the same context that an open dialogue will take place to ensure that the human and political rights of all Iraqi citizens are respected;

3. *Insists* that Iraq allow immediate access by international humanitarian organizations to all those in need of assistance in all parts of Iraq and to make available all necessary facilities for their operations;

4. *Requests* the Secretary–General to pursue his humanitarian efforts in Iraq . . .;

5. *Requests further* the Secretary–General to use all the resources at his disposal, including those of the relevant United Nations agencies, to address urgently the critical needs of the refugees and displaced Iraqi population;

6. *Appeals* to all Member States and to all humanitarian organizations to contribute to these humanitarian relief efforts;

7. *Demands* that Iraq cooperate with the Secretary–General to these ends;

. . .

Notes

1. Although Resolution 688 seemed to contemplate relief operations undertaken by UN agencies and "international humanitarian organizations," the urgency of the plight of the displaced Kurds in northern Iraq prompted three coalition countries to mount an emergency relief operation while other relief efforts were being organized. The United States, France and the United Kingdom sent armed forces into northern Iraq to provide emergency assistance and to establish a secure environment to which the Kurdish refugees could return. Was the relief operation mounted by coalition forces in northern Iraq authorized by Resolution 688? Does the legality of their intervention turn on the fact that the Council had already authorized the use of "all necessary means . . . to restore international peace and security in the area"—as the U.S. government argued?

The Secretary–General disputed the U.S. view, asserting said that a foreign military presence in Iraqi territory required either Iraqi consent or an express authorization of the Security Council. The coalition allies nonetheless persisted in their efforts to create a protected zone, and the Security Council effectively acquiesced. Then, the Iraqi government agreed to a UN presence in the northern zone for humanitarian purposes, signing a Memorandum of Understanding that allowed the UN to operate throughout Iraqi territory. The allied forces withdrew from Iraq after they had established a reasonably secure environment and lightly-armed UN guards had arrived in accordance with the agreement between the UN and Iraq.

2. In the view of the Legal Counsel to the UN, S.C. Resolution 688 was not adopted under Chapter VII of the UN Charter. Is this interpretation

plausible? What difference would it make if the decision were adopted under Chapter VII or, e.g., Articles 24 and 25 generally?

3. Whether or not Resolution 688 was adopted under Chapter VII, it established a precedent in respect of the factual circumstances that would or might justify Chapter VII enforcement action in response to an essentially humanitarian crisis. What precedent was established? Was massive repression in itself enough to justify an Article 39 (or pre-Article 39) determination? Or was more needed? If the latter, what additional factors were determinative?

4. What, precisely, did paragraphs 3 and 7 of Resolution 688 require of Iraq? Did these provisions implicitly authorize the use of force by those seeking to provide humanitarian assistance?

5. One of the curious aspects of Resolution 688 is the preambular language *"Recalling* Article 2, paragraph 7, of the Charter of the United Nations." In the context of Resolution 688, what did this mean? Three members of the Council (Cuba, Yemen and Zimbabwe) thought that the resolution was inconsistent with Article 2(7). Does Resolution 688 entail a new conception of Article 2(7)? Does it, for example, imply that Article 2(7) does not present a barrier to the type of humanitarian relief operation contemplated in Resolution 688? Does the answer depend on whether Resolution 688 was adopted under Chapter VII?

6. For analysis of the legal precedent established by S.C. Resolution 688, see Jane E. Stromseth, *Iraq's Repression of Its Civilian Population: Collective Responses and Continuing Challenges*, in Enforcing Restraint: Collective Intervention in Internal Conflicts (Lori Fisler Damrosch, ed. 1993).

Humanitarian Aid in Bosnia and Somalia

Resolution 688 broke new ground in its insistence that a sovereign state allow outside humanitarian relief providers into its territory. Although UN humanitarian organizations had frequently mounted major relief operations in the past, these had always been predicated upon the consent of the host state. Mindful of the pathbreaking nature of Resolution 688, the Council took care to ensure that the precedent was as modest as the circumstances permitted. To the extent Iraqi sovereignty was overridden, the incursion was authorized only to the degree necessary to provide emergency relief—not to protect the Kurds or Shiites from Iraqi repression.

The Council continued to follow this cautious path in its next series of resolutions authorizing humanitarian intervention. Adopted in respect of Somalia and Bosnia, those resolutions were more forthright in authorizing military force under Chapter VII. Still, at least initially this authorization was confined to a narrow purpose: providing humanitarian assistance.

S.C. Resolution 770 (1992), which is excerpted below, followed more than a dozen previous resolutions addressing various dimensions of the successive conflicts surrounding the dissolution of the former Yugoslavia, including a resolution imposing a mandatory arms embargo. At the time S.C. Resolution 770 was adopted, the former Yugoslav Republic of Bosnia and Herzegovina had formally seceded and had been admitted to UN membership. Since April 1992, the multi-ethnic but predominantly Muslim Bosnian government had been under assault by Serb forces from both Bosnia and the rump Yugoslavia, both of which opposed Bosnian independence. Relying on S.C. Resolution 770 (1992), the United States government organized a humanitarian airlift of relief supplies to Bosnia.

Security Council Resolution 770

U.N. Doc. S/RES/770 (August 13, 1992).

. . .

Recognizing that the situation in Bosnia and Herzegovina constitutes a threat to international peace and security and that the provision of humanitarian assistance in Bosnia and Herzegovina is an important element in the Council's effort to restore international peace and security in the area,

. . .

Dismayed by the continuation of conditions that impede the delivery of humanitarian supplies to destinations within Bosnia and Herzegovina and the consequent suffering of the people of that country,

. . .

Determined to establish as soon as possible the necessary conditions for the delivery of humanitarian assistance wherever needed in Bosnia and Herzegovina . . . ,

Acting under Chapter VII of the Charter of the United Nations,

1. *Reaffirms* its demand that all parties and others concerned in Bosnia and Herzegovina stop the fighting immediately;

2. *Calls upon* States to take nationally or through regional agencies or arrangements all measures necessary to facilitate in coordination with the United Nations the delivery by relevant United Nations humanitarian organizations and others of humanitarian assistance to Sarajevo and wherever needed in other parts of Bosnia and Herzegovina;

. . .

5. *Requests* all States to provide appropriate support for the actions undertaken in pursuance of this resolution;

6. *Demands* that all parties and others concerned take the necessary measures to ensure the safety of United Nations and other personnel engaged in the delivery of humanitarian assistance.

. . .

———

Several months after it adopted Resolution 770, the Security Council once again authorized states to use military force to provide humanitarian relief, this time in Somalia. This action was preceded by earlier, unsuccessful UN efforts to respond to mass starvation attending an internal armed conflict in Somalia. S.C. Resolution 767 (1992) authorized a humanitarian airlift and called upon all the factions in Somalia to facilitate the deployment of UN personnel who would deliver the aid. Armed gangs thwarted this relief effort, preventing or delaying ships bringing relief supplies from unloading and looting supplies that reached Somalia. In response to these developments and to a U.S. offer to send a substantial marine force to ensure delivery of supplies, the Council adopted Resolution 794.

Security Council Resolution 794

U.N. Doc. S/RES/794 (Dec. 3, 1992).

The Security Council,

. . .

Determining that the magnitude of the human tragedy caused by the conflict in Somalia, further exacerbated by the obstacles being created to the distribution of humanitarian assistance, constitutes a threat to international peace and security,

. . .

Responding to the urgent calls from Somalia for the international community to take measures to ensure the delivery of humanitarian assistance in Somalia,

. . .

Dismayed by the continuation of conditions that impede the delivery of humanitarian supplies to destinations within Somalia, and in particular reports of looting of relief supplies destined for starving people, attacks on aircraft and ships bringing in humanitarian relief supplies, and attacks on the Pakistani UNOSOM contingent in Mogadishu,

. . .

Noting the offer by Member States aimed at establishing a secure environment for humanitarian relief operations in Somalia as soon as possible,

. . .

2. *Demands* that all parties, movements and factions in Somalia take all measures necessary to facilitate the efforts of the United Nations, its specialized agencies and humanitarian organizations to provide urgent humanitarian assistance to the affected population in Somalia;

. . .

7. *Endorses* the recommendation by the Secretary–General in his letter of 29 November 1992 (S/24868) that action under Chapter VII of the Charter of the United Nations should be taken in order to establish a secure environment for humanitarian relief operations in Somalia as soon as possible;

8. *Welcomes* the offer by a Member State described in the Secretary–General's above mentioned letter concerning the establishment of an operation to create such a secure environment;

9. *Welcomes also* offers by other Member States to participate in that operation;

10. *Acting* under Chapter VII of the Charter of the United Nations, authorizes the Secretary–General and Member States cooperating to implement the offer referred to in paragraph 8 above to use all necessary means to establish as soon as possible a secure environment for humanitarian relief operations in Somalia;

11. *Calls* on all Member States which are in a position to do so to provide military forces and to make additional contributions, in cash or in kind, in accordance with paragraph 10 above and requests the Secretary–General to establish a fund through which the contributions, where appropriate, could be channelled to the States or operations concerned;

. . .

Notes

1. Some aspects of S.C. Resolution 794 (1992) are reminiscent of S.C. Resolution 688 (1991), such as the demand in paragraph 2 of the former that Somali parties cooperate with international relief efforts. But unlike Resolution 688, Resolution 794 was explicitly adopted under Chapter VII and authorized military force (through the term of art "all necessary means" in para. 10). What precedent(s) did Resolution 794 establish in the Council's evolving jurisprudence of humanitarian intervention under the framework of Chapter VII? What conditions supported the Security Council's Article 39 determination in Resolution 794? What precedent was established in respect of the aims for which force was authorized?

2. Pursuant to S.C. Resolution 794, the United Task Force (UNITAF), a US-led multinational force, was deployed in Somalia from December 1992 to April 1993, replacing the first United Nations Operation in Somalia (UNOSOM I). When it completed its mission, UNITAF was succeeded by a second United Nations force, known as UNOSOM II. The resolution authorizing the latter operation, S.C. Resolution 814 (1993), represented the high-water mark of the Security Council's robust approach to essentially humanitarian operations in the post-Cold War period, giving UNOSOM II an ambitious "nation-building" mandate.

The optimism reflected in this resolution came to an abrupt end as a result of an armed clash between UNOSOM II forces and one of the Somali factions in Mogadishu on October 3–4, 1993. Eighteen U.S. Army Rangers were killed during the clash.

The October 1993 clash in Mogadishu fundamentally altered the political environment in which humanitarian operations were deployed and commanded. Profoundly affected by U.S. casualties in Mogadishu, the Clinton Administration blocked UN intervention when the genocide in

Rwanda began six months later. The Mogadishu experience also cast a long shadow over the approach of the United Nations to the three and one-half year conflict in Bosnia. Explaining his reluctance to take more robust action there, Lt. Gen. Sir Michael Rose, then Commander of UN forces in Bosnia, explained that he did not want to "cross the Mogadishu line"—that is, trigger hostile fire against UN forces under his command.

3.   For analyses of the three operations in Somalia, see John L. Hirsch and Robert B. Oakley, Somalia and Operation Restore Hope: Reflections on Peacemaking and Peacekeeping (1995); Walter Clarke and Jeffrey Herbst, *Somalia and the Future of Humanitarian Intervention*, 75 Foreign Aff. 105 (March/April 1996); and Chester A. Crocker, *The Lessons of Somalia: Not Everything Went Wrong*, 74 Foreign Aff. 101 (May/June 1995).

"SAFE AREAS" IN BOSNIA

Systematic attacks against civilians were a fundamental feature of the conflicts that accompanied the breakup of Yugoslavia in the early 1990s and prompted the Security Council to adopt various resolutions addressing the humanitarian dimensions of the conflicts. On February 22, 1993, for example, the Council adopted a resolution signaling its intention to create the International Criminal Tribunal for the former Yugoslavia—an acknowledgment that the scale of the atrocities being committed in Bosnia warranted Nuremberg-type prosecutions.

In the meantime, a Serb assault on the Bosnian town of Srebrenica, by that time swollen with Bosnian Muslims who had fled Serb assaults in other towns, galvanized international attention and concern. In this setting, the Council adopted Resolution 819 "demanding" that "all parties and others concerned" treat Srebrenica as a "safe area." Less than a month later, the Council declared five other Bosnian municipalities, including its capital city of Sarajevo, "safe areas."

Security Council Resolution 819
U.N. Doc. S/RES/819 (Apr. 16,1993).

The Security Council,

. . .

Concerned by the pattern of hostilities by Bosnian Serb paramilitary units against towns and villages in eastern Bosnia and in this regard reaffirming that any taking or acquisition of territory by the threat or use of force, including through the practice of "ethnic cleansing", is unlawful and unacceptable,

Deeply alarmed at the information provided by the Secretary–General to the Security Council on 16 April 1993 on the rapid deterioration of the situation in Srebrenica and its surrounding areas, as a result of the continued deliberate armed attacks and shelling of the innocent civilian population by Bosnian Serb paramilitary units,

. . .

Aware that a tragic humanitarian emergency has already developed in Srebrenica and its surrounding areas as a direct consequence of the brutal actions of Bosnian Serb paramilitary units, forcing the large-scale displacement of civilians, in particular women, children and the elderly,

... *[A]cting* under Chapter VII of the Charter of the United Nations,

1. *Demands* that all parties and others concerned treat Srebrenica and its surroundings as a safe area which should be free from any armed attack or any other hostile act;

2. *Demands also* to that effect the immediate cessation of armed attacks by Bosnian Serb paramilitary units against Srebrenica and their immediate withdrawal from the areas surrounding Srebrenica;

. . .

4. *Requests* the Secretary–General, with a view to monitoring the humanitarian situation in the safe area, to take immediate steps to increase the presence of UNPROFOR in Srebrenica and its surroundings; *demands* that all parties and others concerned cooperate fully and promptly with UNPROFOR towards that end; and *requests* the Secretary–General to report urgently thereon to the Security Council;

. . .

8. *Demands* the unimpeded delivery of humanitarian assistance to all parts of the Republic of Bosnia and Herzegovina, in particular to the civilian population of Srebrenica and its surrounding areas and *recalls* that such impediments to the delivery of humanitarian assistance constitute a serious violation of international humanitarian law;

9. *Urges* the Secretary–General and the United Nations High Commissioner for Refugees to use all the resources at their disposal within the scope of the relevant resolutions of the Council to reinforce the existing humanitarian operations in the Republic of Bosnia and Herzegovina in particular Srebrenica and its surroundings;

. . .

Security Council Resolution 824

U.N. Doc. S/RES/824 (May 6, 1993).

The Security Council,

. . .

Deeply concerned at the continuing armed hostilities by Bosnian Serb paramilitary units against several towns in the Republic of Bosnia and Herzegovina and determined to ensure peace and stability throughout the country, most immediately in the towns of Sarajevo, Tuzla, Zepa, Gorazde, Bihac, as well as Srebrenica,

Convinced that the threatened towns and their surroundings should be treated as safe areas, free from armed attacks and from any other hostile acts which endanger the well-being and the safety of their inhabitants,

. . .

... *[A]cting* under Chapter VII of the Charter,

. . .

3. *Declares* that the capital city of the Republic of Bosnia and Herzegovina, Sarajevo, and other such threatened areas, in particular the towns of Tuzla, Zepa, Gorazde, Bihac, as well as Srebrenica, and their surroundings should be treated as safe areas by all the parties concerned and should be free from armed attacks and from any other hostile act;

4. *Further declares* that in these safe areas the following should be observed:

(*a*) The immediate cessation of armed attacks or any hostile act against these safe areas, and the withdrawal of all Bosnian Serb military or paramilitary units from these towns to a distance wherefrom they cease to constitute a menace to their security and that of their inhabitants to be monitored by United Nations military observers;

(*b*) Full respect by all parties of the rights of the United Nations Protection Force (UNPROFOR) and the international humanitarian agencies to free and unimpeded access to all safe-areas in the Republic of Bosnia and Herzegovina and full respect for the safety of the personnel engaged in these operations;

5. *Demands* to that end that all parties and others concerned cooperate fully with UNPROFOR and take any necessary measures to respect these safe areas;

6. *Requests* the Secretary–General to take appropriate measures with a view to monitoring the humanitarian situation in the safe areas and to that end, authorizes the strengthening of UNPROFOR by an additional 50 United Nations military observers, together with related equipment and logistical support; and in this connection, also *demands* that all parties and all others concerned cooperate fully and promptly with UNPROFOR;

7. *Declares* its readiness, in the event of the failure by any party to comply with the present resolution, to consider immediately the adoption of any additional measures necessary with a view to its full implementation, including to ensure respect for the safety of the United Nations personnel;

. . .

Security Council Resolution 836

U.N. Doc. S/RES/836 (June 4, 1993).

The Security Council,

. . .

Alarmed by the ... plight of the civilian population in the territory of the Republic of Bosnia and Herzegovina in particular in Sarajevo, Bihac, Srebrenica, Gorazde, Tuzla and Zepa,

. . .

Determined to ensure the protection of the civilian population in safe areas and to promote a lasting political solution,

. . .

Determining that the situation in the Republic of Bosnia and Herzegovina continues to be a threat to international peace and security,

Acting under Chapter VII of the Charter of the United Nations,

. . .

4. *Decides* to ensure full respect for the safe areas referred to in resolution 824 (1993);

5. *Decides* to extend to that end the mandate of UNPROFOR in order to enable it, in the safe areas referred to in resolution 824 (1993), to deter attacks against the safe areas, to monitor the cease-fire, to promote the withdrawal of military or paramilitary units other than those of the Government of the Republic of Bosnia and Herzegovina and to occupy some key points on the ground, in addition to participating in the delivery of humanitarian relief to the population as provided for in resolution 776 (1992) of 14 September 1992,

. . .

9. *Authorizes* UNPROFOR, in addition to the mandate defined in resolutions 770 (1992) of 13 August 1992 and 776 (1992), in carrying out the mandate defined in paragraph 5 above, acting in self-defence, to take the necessary measures, including the use of force, in reply to bombardments against the safe areas by any of the parties or to armed incursion into them or in the event of any deliberate obstruction in or around those areas to the freedom of movement of UNPROFOR or of protected humanitarian convoys;

10. *Decides* that, notwithstanding paragraph 1 of resolution 816 (1993), Member States, acting nationally or through regional organizations or arrangements, may take, under the authority of the Security Council and subject to close coordination with the Secretary–General and UNPROFOR, all necessary measures, through the use of air power, in and around the safe areas in the Republic of Bosnia and Herzegovina, to support UNPROFOR in the performance of its mandate set out in paragraph 5 and 9 above;

11. *Requests* the Members States concerned, the Secretary–General and UNPROFOR to coordinate closely on the measures they are taking to implement paragraph 10 above and to report to the Council through the Secretary–General;

. . .

Notes

1. Journalist Roy Gutman describes the events immediately preceding the Council's decision to declare Srebrenica a "safe area":

... After a Serbian offensive early in 1993 wiped out the tiny enclaves of Cerska and Konjevic Polje in eastern Bosnia, ... General Philippe Morillon of France, [the Commander of UNPROFOR], personally went to embattled Srebrenica. There, without previous authority, he promised U.N. protection to the city of 8,000 inhabitants, swollen by refugees to 60,000. "I will never abandon you," he said March 12. "You are now under the protection of the United Nations."

Morillon had uttered the words only when he had realized there was no other exit. In his 1993 account, *Croire et Oser*, he said that he had tried to escape Srebrenica earlier that night.... [H]e departed, alone, at 10:00 P.M. A U.N. vehicle was to link up with him outside of town but failed to materialize. At about 5:00 AM Morillon returned alone.... He went to bed, and on waking up knew he was trapped. Only then did he bestride the porch of the post office to declare his fidelity to the town.

Soon after Morillon's eventual departure, Srebrenica came under renewed attack, and the U.N. Security Council, under pressure by non-aligned states, responded in mid-April by proclaiming the town a "U.N. safe area." ...

Roy Gutman, *Bosnia: Negotiation and Retreat*, in Soldiers for Peace: Fifty Years of United Nations Peacekeeping (Barbara Benton, ed. 1996).

2.   What, precisely, did Resolutions 819 and 824 purport to do? In particular, did the resolutions authorize measures that would reasonably secure the safety of the municipalities declared to be "safe areas"? How, if at all, were the resolutions to be enforced? Note that the principal "enforcement" mechanism contemplated in S.C. Resolution 824 was the deployment of an additional 50 monitors for all six besieged enclaves. One of the so-called "safe areas," Gorazde, had first come under sustained attack by Serb forces in the late Spring of 1992. According to the New York *Times*, as of April 10, 1994 the UN had only 15 military observers in Gorazde, 11 of whom had arrived the previous week. Chuck Sudetic, *NATO Jets Bomb Serb Forces Assaulting Bosnian Haven; U.S. Warns of More Strikes*, N.Y. Times (Apr. 11, 1994).

3.   Paragraph 9 of S.C. Resolution 836 seems to imply that UNPROFOR was authorized to use force "in self-defence". This mandate was in keeping with the UN's longstanding approach to the use of force by its peacekeeping operations, which traditionally have been authorized to use force only in self defense. Classic peacekeeping operations are deployed only with the consent of the host state and therefore do not need a Chapter VII mandate. They have often been deployed as a buffer to help secure a cease fire or peace agreement that has already been reached between previously warring parties. In this setting, the self-restraint and impartiality of peacekeeping forces has been seen as essential to their effectiveness.

But although UNPROFOR in many respects functioned as a classic peacekeeping force, it operated under various peace enforcement (i.e.,

Chapter VII) mandates, including those established by S.C. Resolution 836. For what purposes and by whom was the use of force authorized by S.C. Resolution 836?

Implementation of S.C. Resolution 836 (1993)

Paragraph 10 of S.C. Resolution 836 (1993) authorized "Member States, acting . . . through regional . . . arrangements," to use air power in and around the "safe areas" "to support UNPROFOR in the performance of its mandate . . . ," but this authority was "subject to close coordination with the Secretary–General and UNPROFOR." The regional arrangement contemplated by this provision was the North Atlantic Treaty Organization (NATO). In practice, UN Secretary–General Boutros Boutros–Ghali was extremely reluctant to authorize NATO air strikes in support of the "safe areas." Seven months after S.C. Resolution 836 was adopted, the *New York Times* reported tensions between Mr. Boutros–Ghali and UNPROFOR commanders in Bosnia over the refusal of the Secretary–General to authorize air strikes. One UN commander quoted by the *Times* said, "I don't read the Security Council resolutions anymore because they don't help me. There is a fantastic gap between the resolutions of the Security Council, the will to execute those resolutions and the means available to commanders." The same article reported that NATO leaders had called for the use of NATO power to secure relief operations in Tuzla and other designated "safe areas," but said that NATO could provide such action only upon the request of the Secretary General and his field commanders. Roger Cohen, *Dispute Grows Over U.N.'s Troops in Bosnia*, N.Y. Times, Jan. 20, 1994.

The shelling of Sarajevo's central market, killing 68 civilians and wounding more than 200 others in February 1994, prompted the first substantial effort to utilize the authority for NATO air strikes granted by SC Resolution 836. In the wake of the attack, NATO set a ten-day deadline for Serb forces to withdraw their heavy weaponry from the Bosnian capital or face air strikes. Under this threat, Serb forces agreed on February 9, 1994, to meet the terms of the NATO ultimatum.

Over the ensuing months, the United Nations reverted to the practice of restraint. While the Secretary–General authorized NATO air strikes in April 1994 in response to a Serb offensive against the "safe area" of Gorazde, the attacks were modest.

The July 1995 assault on Srebrenica, described by contemporaneous news accounts as the single worst atrocity in Europe since World War II, spelled the end of the "safe area" policy.

Roy Gutman, *Bosnia: Negotiation and Retreat*

in Soldiers for Peace: Fifty Years of United Nations Peacekeeping (Barbara Benton, ed. 1996)*

. . .

... All the flaws of the U.N. mission [in Bosnia] combined into a single disaster....

. . .

The enclave fell on July 11, and as the heavily outnumbered Dutch [UNPROFOR] troops [stationed in Srebrenica] looked on, the Serb forces separated the population into two groups. They loaded the women, children, and old people onto buses and trucks, and sent the men and boys to unknown locations. Bosnian Serbs also captured thousands of men and boys who tried to flee overland to government-held territory with the remnants of the Bosnian army force in Srebrenica.

The Dutch troops failed to defend the town or even to alert the world to the slaughter of which they were witnesses. Serb forces had captured fifty-five Dutch troops at their observation posts, stripped them of their weapons and equipment in defiance of international law, and taken them hostage. On July 15, they bussed them out of Bosnia. En route to safety, the Dutch troops saw dozens of corpses piled on a truck-loading platform, and dozens more along the road near what turned out to be the main killing fields.... [T]hey should have reported such evidence of massive war crimes. But apart from answering questionnaires distributed by U.N. human-rights personnel, they kept their silence, waiting for 300 Dutch comrades to be released. They did not even inform Sarajevo headquarters. "The U.N. didn't ask for a debriefing," a Dutch spokesman said.

On July 19, ... the U.N. commander in Bosnia, General Rupert Smith of Britain, met the Bosnian–Serb commander, General Ratko Mladic, and asked him to give an account of the fall of Srebrenica. Mladic said the U.N. safe area had been "finished in a correct way." According to a memo of the meeting, Smith did not reply. The agreement made no direct mention of the 6,000 to 8,000 missing men and boys of Srebrenica, and said only that the International Red Cross would have access to "reception points" within twenty-four hours. Mladic reneged on the commitment. The reception points turned out to be mass graves. The Serb takeover of Srebrenica brought the U.N. presence in Bosnia to an ignominious end.

... In mid-December the U.N. closed down its peacekeeping operation in Bosnia.

Notes

1.   The assault on Srebrenica was the basis of genocide and other charges against General Ratko Mladić and the Bosnian Serb civilian leader, Radovan Karadzić, both of whom had already been indicted by the International Criminal Tribunal for the former Yugoslavia. As of July 1999, both suspects were still at large.

2.   The Srebrenica massacre had the effect of mobilizing concerted international action. In September 1995, NATO forces launched the "first serious bombing campaign against Serbian military installations" during the three and one-half year conflict in Bosnia. Gutman, supra, at 204. This

campaign, combined with a Croatian rout of Serb forces in Croatia in August 1995 and the long-term effects of sanctions against Serbia, finally brought Serb leaders to the negotiating table. U.S.-brokered negotiations in Dayton, Ohio concluded in a peace settlement, which was signed in Paris in mid-December 1995.

3.   What factors account for the failure of the "safe areas" policy? Was the policy itself misconceived, or was the principal failure in implementation? What would it have taken to make the policy work? Consider the views of Roy Gutman: "[T]he U.N. deployment in Bosnia, with no military force to back it up, had been untenable. Peacekeeping is not feasible during a raging war, nor is diplomacy, unless it is backed by force. While U.N. personnel doubtless saved many lives, their presence probably also prolonged the conflict." Gutman, supra, at 204. Could the "safe areas" policy have worked (only) if the U.N. did not also have vulnerable forces deployed and operating in essentially peacekeeping roles (though under peace enforcement mandates)? Or is it untenable to attempt to combine peacekeeping and peace enforcement? (On the distinction between peacekeeping and peace enforcement, see note 3 following the three Security Council Resolutions on "safe areas," above.)

4.   As noted earlier, when the UN Security Council began to authorize the use of force for essentially humanitarian ends in the 1990s, it was inclined to authorize narrow mandates, favoring the delivery of humanitarian assistance (see, for example, S.C. Resolution 770 and S.C. Resolution 794). In light of subsequent developments in Bosnia, does this cautious approach seem well conceived?

Developments in Bosnia and other countries recently racked by ethnic conflict prompted a wide-ranging debate about the legitimate goals of humanitarian interventions and appropriate criteria for the conduct of relief operations. In particular, many observers urged a re-examination of the fundamental ethos of many humanitarian organizations of providing aid to all sides in a conflict while remaining neutral in respect of the conflict itself. In Bosnia, some critics charged, this ethos seemed to demand moral neutrality in the face of crimes that may eventually be judged to constitute genocide: All sides to the conflict received humanitarian assistance, and United Nations and other personnel provided such assistance without taking sides in respect of the underlying conflict itself. Yet from a human rights perspective, it was argued, all sides were not equal. Although all parties to the conflict in Bosnia committed war crimes against civilians belonging to other parties to the conflict, the overwhelming majority of documented atrocities were committed by Serb forces.*

---

* As noted earlier, the three and one-half year conflict in Bosnia began as an assault by Serb forces against the government of Bosnia. For much of the war, the predominantly Muslim government forces were allied with Bosnian Croat forces. But in mid–1993, conflict erupted between these former allies. The International Criminal Tribunal for the former Yugoslavia has indicted individuals associated with all three parties to the conflict—Bosnian government, Serb and Croat forces—but the overwhelming majority of charges have been brought against Serbs.

In the wake of the UN's experience in Bosnia and other countries where similar issues were raised, one analyst concluded that "[t]here is no exit strategy for humanitarians if states do not take their humanitarian responsibilities seriously and use coercion to halt genocide and other massive abuses of civilians." Thomas G. Weiss, *Principles, Politics, and Humanitarian Action*, 13 Ethics & Int'l Aff. 1, 20 (1999). Another writer observed, "Inside the humanitarian international, the debate has largely revolved around the issue of whether it remains possible to go on adhering to the humanitarian movement's bedrock principles of neutrality and impartiality in an era in which most conflicts are internal and take place between irregular forces, target civilians for extermination or forcible migration, and rely all too often on child soldiers." David Rieff, *Moral Imperatives and Political Realities*, 13 Ethics & Int'l Aff. 35, 37 (1999). Is either or both of these views persuasive? Retrospectively, what implications would they have for the United Nations' approach to the humanitarian challenges presented by the conflict in Bosnia?

The Intervention That Did Not Occur: Genocide in Rwanda

One of the core questions raised by recent experiences with humanitarian interventions is when states, presented with numerous claims on their collective conscience, *should* intervene in another state. One consideration that might significantly affect this decision is whether military intervention is likely to be effective in bringing an end to the tragedy.

Considerations of efficacy aside, do some humanitarian tragedies by their nature compel an international response? In this respect, consider the 1948 Convention on the Prevention and Punishment of the Crime of Genocide, which imposes on Contracting Parties a duty not only to punish genocide, but also to prevent it (Article I). Pursuant to Article VIII, any Contracting Party "may call upon the competent organs of the United Nations to take such action under the Charter of the United Nations as they consider appropriate for the prevention and suppression of acts of genocide. . . . " Action to repress genocide might include military intervention, in which event the "competent organ" contemplated by this provision would be the UN Security Council.

The Security Council did not authorize a military intervention to halt the 1994 genocide of Rwandan Tutsis, although a UN peacekeeping force was already deployed in Rwanda when the genocide began. That force, known by the acronym "UNAMIR," arrived in Rwanda in November 1993 to monitor compliance with a recently-concluded peace accord between warring Rwandan factions. The explosion on April 6, 1994 of a plane carrying the President of Rwanda, Juvenal Habyarimana, along with the President of Burundi, triggered the violence that has since been judged a genocide. On April 7, 1994, Rwandan forces associated with the *genocidaires* killed 10 Belgian members of UNAMIR. One week later, Belgium withdrew from UNAMIR. On April 21, 1994, the Canadian commander of UNAMIR, Major General Romeo Dallaire, declared that with just five thousand well-equipped soldiers and the appropriate mandate, he could rapidly bring the genocide to an end. That same day, the UN Security Council adopted a resolution reducing UNAMIR by 90 percent, allowing only a token force of 270 troops to remain in Rwanda.

A chronicler of the tragedy in Rwanda concluded:

> The desertion of Rwanda by the UN force ... can be credited almost single-handedly to the United States. With the memory of the Somalia debacle still very fresh, the White House had just finished drafting a document called Presidential Decision Directive 25, which amounted to a checklist of reasons to avoid American involvement in UN peacekeeping missions. It hardly mattered that Dallaire's call for an expanded force and mandate would not have required American troops, or that the mission was not properly peacekeeping, but genocide prevention. PDD 25 also contained what Washington policymakers call "language" urging that the United States should persuade others not to undertake the missions that it wished to avoid. In fact, the Clinton [administration, represented by its] ambassador to the UN, Madeleine Albright, opposed leaving even the skeleton crew of two hundred seventy in Rwanda....

Philip Gourevitch, *We Wish to Inform You That Tomorrow We Will Be Killed With Our Families: Stories From Rwanda* 150 (1998).

On June 22, 1994, the Security Council endorsed a French proposal to send a humanitarian force to Rwanda. The next day, French troops entered Rwanda, initiating "Operation Turquoise." For a critical assessment of this controversial operation, see Gourevitch, supra, at 154–161 (concluding that it enabled the slaughter to continue for an additional month, and secured the escape of the leaders of the genocide into Zaire).

During a visit to Rwanda in March 1998, U.S. President Clinton acknowledged that the international community had failed to act quickly enough to halt the Rwandan genocide. "The international community, together with nations in Africa," he told a Rwandan audience, "must bear its share of responsibility for this tragedy. We did not act quickly enough after the killing began." Charles J. Hanley, *Looking Back at a Year of Genocide*, Associated Press, Mar. 25, 1998. Other countries have also reassessed their responsibilities—as well as that of the United Nations—in respect of the Rwandan genocide. The French National Assembly established a fact-finding mission, while a state investigation in Belgium disclosed that Belgian officials knew of the planned massacres as early as 1992. In March 1999, UN Secretary–General Kofi Annan wrote a letter to the President of the Security Council seeking the body's support for an independent inquiry into the UN's failure to prevent the Rwandan Genocide.

Notes

The preceding case studies highlight the pivotal role of dominant states—in particular, the United States—in shaping Security Council responses to humanitarian disasters. It was the United States that secured the resolution authorizing deployment of UNITAF to Somalia, and the United States blocked UN intervene to repress the genocide in Rwanda. A French proposal to send a force to Rwanda finally (and controversially) prompted the Security Council to deploy a force there. Without a standing UN force, perhaps it is inevitable that the Security Council will continue to be particularly disposed to authorize humanitarian operations with robust mandates in response to such offers. What risks might be associated with "sub-contracting" of UN operations to states such as the United States and France? Should the Council develop any guidelines for the deployment of humanitarian operations that might mitigate these risks? What principles should be included in such guidelines?

NATO Intervention in Kosovo

The 78–day aerial bombardment of Serb targets in the Federal Republic of Yugoslavia by the North Atlantic Treaty Organization (NATO) represented a major development in the postwar practice of humanitarian intervention. In contrast to the interventions in Somalia, Bosnia and Rwanda (by France *after* the 1994 genocide) that we examined in preceding sub-sections, the military campaign in Yugoslavia was not explicitly authorized by the Security Council. In the view of many legal experts and two permanent members of the Security Council—China and Russia—the NATO campaign represented a flagrant violation of international law. Others saw the war, which was justified by states participating in the NATO alliance squarely and explicitly on humanitarian grounds, as a watershed in the evolving law and practice of humanitarian intervention.

The military campaign was preceded by a series of unsuccessful efforts to achieve a negotiated settlement of the Yugoslav government's military campaign against separatist forces in the Yugoslav province of Kosovo. Key aims of various peacemaking initiatives included resolving the legal status of Kosovo and ending the severe repression of Kosovo's ethnic Albanians at the hands of military, paramilitary and police forces of the state of Yugoslavia and its dominant republic, Serbia. For more than a year before the NATO air strikes began, those forces had been engaged in armed conflict with the separatist Kosovo Liberation Army (KLA) and in a campaign of severe repression against the ethnic Albanians who constituted the vast majority of Kosovo's population.

One peace initiative, which was convened in Rambouillet, France in February 1999 under the auspices of the "Contact Group" comprising the United States, Russia, the United Kingdom, France, Germany and Italy, culminated in the adoption of a proposed settlement by the conference conveners. But although the KLA accepted the Rambouillet accords, Yugoslavia's President, Slobodan Milošević, rejected its terms.

With the failure of the Rambouillet effort, NATO forces began bombing Serb targets in Yugoslavia on March 24, 1999. Notably, leaders of the NATO alliance justified their military campaign on humanitarian grounds.

Although the Security Council had previously adopted several resolutions addressing the Kosovo crisis, including several that invoked Chapter VII, it had not explicitly authorized states to use force to implement its resolutions. For this reason, Russia and China argued that the military campaign constituted a fundamental breach of international law. But a draft resolution condemning the NATO attacks, introduced by Russia shortly after the military campaign began, was defeated by a vote of 12–3. See Judith Miller, *Russia's Move to End Strikes Loses; Margin Is a Surprise*, N.Y. Times, Mar. 27, 1999.

Yugoslavia challenged the legality of the NATO campaign in another forum, the International Court of Justice (ICJ). On April 26, 1999, the Yugoslav government deposited with the Secretary–General of the United Nations a declaration recognizing the Court's compulsory jurisdiction, subject to certain exceptions, "in all disputes arising or which may arise after the signature of the present Declaration, with regard to the situations or facts subsequent to this signature.... " On April 29, 1999, Yugoslavia filed applications against ten countries participating in the NATO air campaign. On the same day, it requested the Court to indicate provisional measures, essentially a form of interim injunction, ordering the respondent states to "cease immediately [their] acts of use of force" and to "refrain from any act of threat or use of force" against Yugoslavia.

On June 2, 1999, the ICJ held that it manifestly lacked jurisdiction in respect of the cases instituted by Yugoslavia against Spain and the United States of America. In respect of the remaining cases, the Court found that it could not indicate provisional measures because it lacked prima facie jurisdiction, which is a prerequisite for the indication of provisional measures. See International Court of Justice, Press Communiqué 99/23, June 2, 1999.

To the extent that the Court's June 2 orders dealt with Yugoslavia's allegations that the NATO campaign entailed unlawful use of force, they turned on technical questions of jurisdiction. (For discussion of the Court's response to Yugoslavia's allegations under the 1948 Genocide Convention, see pp. 679–80 supra.) But while these orders did not involve a determination of the merits of Yugoslavia's principal allegations, the Court made clear that it believed NATO's campaign raised serious issues of international law:

> 15. ... [T]he Court is deeply concerned with the human tragedy, the loss of life, and the enormous suffering in Kosovo which form the background of the present dispute, and with the continuing loss of life and human suffering in all parts of Yugoslavia;

> 16. ... [T]he Court is profoundly concerned with the use of force in Yugoslavia; ... under the present circumstances such use raises very serious issues of international law;

> 17. ... [T]he Court is mindful of the purposes and principles of the United Nations charter and of its own responsibilities in the

maintenance of peace and security under the Charter and the Statute of the Court;

18. ...[T]he Court deems it necessary to emphasize that all parties appearing before it must act in conformity with their obligations under the United Nations Charter and other rules of international law, including humanitarian law....

Case Concerning Legality of Use of Force (Yugoslavia v. United States of America), Order on Request for the Indication of Provisional Measures, June 2, 1999. (While the quoted text appears in the Court's order responding to Yugoslavia's request for the indication of provisional measures in its case against the United States, identical language appears in the Court's orders of June 2, 1999 vis-à-vis the other nine respondent states.)

The air strikes were suspended on June 10, 1999, following Yugoslavia's acceptance of NATO's conditions for ending its military campaign. That same day, the Security Council adopted a resolution that in effect endorsed the terms imposed by NATO and accepted by Yugoslavia. Invoking Chapter VII, S.C. Resolution 1244 (1999) demanded Yugoslavia's full cooperation in implementing those terms, "in particular that the Federal Republic of Yugoslavia put an immediate and verifiable end to violence and repression in Kosovo, and begin and complete verifiable phased withdrawal from Kosovo of all military, police and paramilitary forces according to a rapid timetable...." S.C. Resolution 1244, para. 3 (1999).

Consistent with the terms of the NATO–Yugoslavia accord, the resolution also authorized "the deployment in Kosovo, under United Nations auspices, of international civil and security presences." Id., para. 5. As elaborated in an annex to S.C. Resolution 1244, the Council authorized an "international security presence with substantial North Atlantic Treaty Organization participation" to be deployed in Kosovo "to establish a safe environment for all people" in the province "and to facilitate the safe return to their homes of all displaced persons and refugees." Id., Annex 2, para. 4.

In the days following the Security Council's action, Yugoslav forces withdrew from Kosovo as NATO forces moved in. Ethnic Albanians who had fled Kosovo began to stream back into the province, while thousands of others emerged from hiding within Kosovo. On June 20, 1999, the Secretary–General of NATO announced that, since Serbian troops and police had withdrawn from Kosovo in compliance with the previously-signed agreement, he was officially terminating NATO's bombing campaign.

Notes

1. Was the NATO intervention a violation of international law, as China, Russia and Yugoslavia charged? Does the above-quoted language of the ICJ in its orders dated June 2, 1999 shed any light on how the Court would answer this question if it were able to reach a judgment on the merits in any of the cases filed by Yugoslavia against NATO countries? What, if any,

legal relevance should be attached to the fact that the Security Council rejected by an overwhelming majority Russia's proposed resolution condemning the NATO attacks? What legal significance, if any, should be attached to the fact that, while not authorized prospectively by the UN Security Council, the military campaign was undertaken by a 19–member alliance, NATO? Does the fact that the Security Council adopted a resolution endorsing the terms of the settlement imposed by NATO as a condition to ending its military campaign retroactively legitimate the NATO campaign itself?

2.   On April 9, 1999, the UN Secretary–General, Kofi Annan, made a statement asserting that he was "deeply distressed by the humanitarian tragedy taking place in Kosovo and the region" and calling upon Yugoslav authorities to undertake the following commitments:

> — to end immediately the campaign of intimidation and expulsion of the civilian population;

> — to cease all activities of military and paramilitary forces in Kosovo and to withdraw these forces;

> — to accept unconditionally the return of all refugees and displaced persons to their homes;

> — to accept the deployment of an international military force to ensure a secure environment for the return of refugees and the unimpeded delivery of humanitarian aid; and

> — to permit the international community to verify compliance with the undertakings above.

The statement, which the Secretary–General transmitted to both the Security Council and Yugoslav President Slobodan Milošević, continued: "Upon the acceptance by the Yugoslav authorities of the above conditions, I urge the leaders of the North Atlantic Alliance to suspend immediately the air bombardments upon the territory of the Federal Republic of Yugoslavia." Letter Dated 9 April 1999 From the Secretary–General Addressed to the President of the Security Council, U.N. Doc. S/1999/402 (1999). Does this statement implicitly endorse the legality of the NATO air campaign?

3.   A significant aspect of the military campaign against Yugoslav forces was that NATO prosecuted the war through the use of aerial bombardment, avoiding a commitment of ground forces. This approach was undertaken to avoid NATO casualties and maintain unity among NATO's member states. In fact, not a single NATO soldier died in combat during the 78–day war and, despite disparate views among some NATO countries, the alliance held together throughout the war.

But while the NATO forces avoided combat fatalities, Yugoslav and Serbian forces intensified their persecution of Albanian Kosovars during the war with NATO. See Steven Erlanger, *NATO Bombing Sparked Butchery, Survivors Say; They Tell of Serb Rampage After Planes Struck*, Int'l Herald Tribune, June 21, 1999. In the estimation of a British official, Yugoslav and Serbian forces killed more than 10,000 people during the 11–

week NATO war against Yugoslavia, a number far exceeding the deaths attributed to Yugoslav forces before the NATO intervention. See *Kosovo Massacre Toll Is Estimated at 10,000; Advancing NATO Troops Learn of Graves; Kosovars Pour In, Defying Warning of Mines*, Int'l Herald Tribune, June 18, 1999.

In the view of many critics, the combined effect of NATO's aerial bombardment of Yugoslav targets and its decision to forego ground troops exposed Kosovar civilians to extraordinary risks, vitiating the humanitarian aims of the intervention. Consider, for example, the following critique:

> . . . The painful reality is that the bombing campaign has been conducted as if the human lives at stake should be priced at three different levels: The most precious lives are those of the NATO pilots, with military tactics explicitly designed to minimize their loss; next are those of Milosevic's officials, whose headquarters have been targeted only when empty; least valuable are the lives of the Kosovars themselves, on whose behalf no risks have been taken.

> . . . [T]o conduct a war in which no effort is made—even at some risk to one's own professional warriors—to protect the most defenseless is to deprive the undertaking itself of its higher moral purpose.

Zbigniew Brzezinski, *Compromise Over Kosovo Means Defeat*, Wall Street Journal Europe, May 25, 1999. What principles for future humanitarian interventions may be warranted in light of the Kosovo experience?

F.   IMPLEMENTATION BY NON-GOVERNMENTAL ORGANIZATIONS

It is difficult to identify any major advance in the development of substantive human rights law or its implementation in which non-governmental organizations (NGOs) have not played an important role. NGOs were largely responsible for launching the postwar human rights movement: They pressed governments to internationalize human rights and to develop an international law of human rights. They helped promote the human rights provisions in the UN Charter, the Universal Declaration of Human Rights, the UN Covenants and other conventions on human rights. And they continue to provide mobilizing force behind major advances in the substantive law of human rights and in the establishment and effective operation of international human rights institutions.

In many respects, NGOs have filled the vacuum in enforcement left by reluctant governments. As we have seen, under some international agreements and also under customary international law, the government of one state can challenge the human rights abuses of another state's government, but political leaders have proved unwilling to do so. In contrast, NGOs have made it their business to challenge abusive governments.

In this chapter, we examine both the contributions of, and controversies surrounding, the work of human rights NGOs. This material raises numerous issues, of which two have overarching significance: What explains the impact NGOs have had in the field of international human rights? How are NGOs themselves held accountable?

1.   THE ROLE OF NGOS

Kenneth Roth, *Human Rights Organizations: A New Force for Social Change**

I.

The fifty years since the adoption of the Universal Declaration of Human Rights have seen a transformation in the way that governments are expected to treat their people and each other. Although the language of the declaration has not been altered, its operational significance has changed dramatically. The role of governments, the scope of beneficiaries, and the strength of rights defenders are today dramatically different from what they were half a century ago. Indeed, they have evolved significantly in the past decade alone.

. . .

The expanded scope of human rights protection has largely been driven by another major development since the adoption of the Universal Declaration: the growth of the human rights movement itself—the many nongovernmental organizations (NGOs) devoted to developing and applying international standards on human rights. The movement did not begin with the declaration. Precursors can be found in the campaigns to abolish slavery, grant women the right to vote, and alleviate suffering in time of war. The earliest human rights groups might be said to be the Anti–Slavery Society, the International Woman Suffrage Alliance, or the International Committee of the Red Cross. Following World War II, NGOs lobbied for the inclusion of language on human rights in the U.N. Charter and for the adoption of the Universal Declaration. But there was little in the way of a formal human rights movement.

Since then, there has been a veritable explosion in the number and breadth of organizations devoted to human rights, particularly since the 1970s. That is when human rights groups began to emerge in Asia in response to repressive governments in Korea, Indonesia and the Philippines. The Helsinki accords of 1975, in affirming "the right of the individual to know and act upon his rights," helped launch the human rights movement in the Soviet bloc. Human rights groups emerged throughout Latin America in the 1970s and 1980s in response to death squads and "disappearances" under right-wing dictatorships. Much of Asia in the 1990s has seen a stunning proliferation of human rights groups. While

---

* Lecture, delivered at the John F. Kennedy School of Government, Harvard University, Nov. 4, 1998. That lecture, as edited, will appear in *Human Rights Policy: What Works*, Graham Allison and Samantha Powers, eds., for the Carr Center for Human Rights at the Kennedy School, publication 1999/2000.

growth has been slower in Africa and the Middle East, human rights organizations have established a firm presence in all but the most repressive countries. In many places, human rights defenders still face persecution, often severe. Twelve were killed for their work in 1998 alone. Yet, despite the danger, this growing movement has become a powerful new source of pressure to uphold human rights. It is the major reason why today the Universal Declaration has so much greater practical breadth and significance than it did fifty years ago.

In the process, the human rights movement has helped create a new kind of NGO. Many human rights organizations today serve not simply to amplify the voice of their members but also to collect and deploy information strategically. This role would not have been possible if human rights ideals did not speak so directly to the people of the world. It is only against the backdrop of popular values that human rights information has an impact. Yet because of these universal values, the human rights movement has an influence far beyond its numbers, since by uncovering human rights crimes it can expose their authors to public condemnation.

Moreover, in this decade, with the assistance of new communications technologies like the Internet, human rights organizations have gone beyond addressing countries one by one to launching global campaigns, such as those to ban landmines, establish an International Criminal Court (ICC), end the use of child soldiers, and curb the transfer of small arms. The coalitions assembled have transcended national boundaries and built a genuinely worldwide movement for human rights.

. . .

Notes

1. A wide range of organizations is potentially encompassed in the term "human rights NGO." Although some NGOs focus exclusively on human rights, for others this concern forms part of a broader mandate. A particularly important distinction among human rights NGOs is between those that operate on an international or regional basis on the one hand, and domestic NGOs—that is, organizations that address human rights concerns solely or principally within their own countries. Among the better known international human rights NGOs are the London-based Amnesty International and the New York-based Human Rights Watch. The diversity among human rights NGOs is also reflected in their institutional mandates, which we consider in sub-section 2.

As a legal matter, most NGOs are structured as non-profit corporations or trusts. Some, such as Amnesty International, have members; others do not. The organizations are typically run on a daily basis by a professional staff, with general oversight from a board of directors or similar body. Funding sources and practices vary widely. Some receive significant government support, while other refuse it entirely. Many solicit and receive substantial contributions from foundations. The John D. and Catherine T. MacArthur Foundation, the Ford Foundation and the Open Society Institute have been among the most generous supporters of human rights NGOs.

2. Although, as Kenneth Roth suggests, NGOs have a long history in human rights work, the explosion in their growth has primarily occurred in the last two decades:

> The human rights movement as we know it today is a post-World War II movement; in fact, it is a movement that began to gather momentum only in the 1970's, although there are some international human rights organizations with long and distinguished histories which predate the United Nations and the League of Nations—for example, the London-based Anti–Slavery Society for Human Rights was founded in 1838; the International Committee of the Red Cross was created in 1863; the French League for Human Rights was established in 1898 at the time of the Dreyfus Affair at the end of the Franco–Prussian War—this first generation of human rights NGO's were the precursors of the present human rights movement.

> However, by far the largest number of human rights NGO's, especially regional, national and local ones, but also international ones, emerged in the 1970's or later, and are thus between 15 and 20 years old. When we talk of the human rights movement today, we are thus talking of a phenomenon of the last two decades. Indeed, from the mid–1970's on, we have had an explosion in this area so that today there are literally thousands of non-governmental organizations.

Laurie S. Wiseberg, *Human Rights NGO's*, in The Role of Non–Governmental Organizations in the Promotion and Protection of Human Rights 24 (1990). Two events are particularly worthy of note: the creation of Amnesty International in 1961, and the establishment of the Helsinki Watch committees shortly after the 1975 Helsinki Final Act. See Virgina A. Leary, *The Right of the Individual to Know and Act Upon His Rights and Duties: Monitoring Groups and the Helsinki Final Act*, 13 Vanderbilt J. Transnational L. 375 (1980). For further reading on the early period of the contemporary human rights NGO movement, see William Korey, NGOs and the Universal Declaration of Human Rights: A Curious Grapevine (1998); David Weissbrodt, *The Role of International NonGovernmental Organizations in the Implementation of Human Rights*, 12 Texas Int'l L.J. 293 (1977).

3. Although influential for many years, NGOs became increasingly effective in the final decade of the twentieth century. What factors might account for their growing impact? Consider, in this regard, the views of one observer:

> [The recent] explosion in nongovernmental activity reflects the dramatically heightened permeability of national borders and improvements in communications that have allowed territorially dispersed individuals to develop common agendas and objectives at the international level.... Modern communication is much less dependent on location; increased travel, the fax, and perhaps most important the

Internet have created the possibility of a cohesion that is not tied to territory.... By providing institutional homes in the same way that states have accommodated nationalism, NGOs are the inevitable beneficiaries of the emergence of the new global communities.

Peter J. Spiro, *New Global Communities: Nongovernmental Organizations in International Decision–Making Institutions*, 18 Wash. Q. 45, 47–48 (1994).

2.   MANDATES AND AGENDAS

The rich diversity among NGOs is reflected in a number of distinctions among them. Substantively, some NGOs, such as the New York-based Human Rights Watch, address a broad range of civil and political rights on a universal basis. Others, such as the London-based African Rights, address a relatively broad range of human rights issues in a particular region. In contrast to organizations that address a wide range of human rights issues, some NGOs address particular types of human rights concerns, such as questions concerning religious liberty or the rights of women. Several NGOs focus on human rights issues of special concern to a particular professional community. Examples include the Committee to Protect Journalists, the Lawyers Committee for Human Rights and Physicians for Human Rights. (The Lawyers Committee has been an "all purpose" human rights NGO, but has also attended in particular to protecting lawyers and other human rights advocates, as well as to the independence of judges.)

The activities undertaken by NGOs to advance their substantive concerns also vary across a broad range. Possibilities include gathering information, publicizing abuses, meeting with governmental officials, advising victims and providing various forms of aid, organizing public responses such as letter writing and boycotts, attempting to secure action by domestic governments or international institutions through lobbying or litigation, and promoting the development of new legal standards and institutions.

The work an organization undertakes is determined both by its mandate and its agenda. The mandate is the constitutional purpose of the organization which limits the scope of its activity. It could be defined in a constitutive document such as charter, or it might be implicit in the organization's name, or otherwise the result of agreement by those who organized and run the NGO. The organization's agenda determines how, within the scope of its mandate, it focuses its resources and attention. The agenda might be set by a central governing body, or determined in a more decentralized way by groups or individuals working within the organization.

What principles should an NGO apply in determining its mandate? To whom is or should it be accountable in determining its agenda? What factors are likely to influence its decisions? To what extent are an NGO's funding sources and their priorities likely to be an important factor? When the activities of two or more NGOs overlap, to what extent should their agendas be coordinated? The following excerpt addresses these and other issues in the context of assessing fact-finding activities of NGOs, a subject we consider in greater depth in sub-section 3.

Hans Thoolen & Berth Verstappen, *Human Rights Missions: A Study of the Fact–Finding Practice of Nongovernmental Organizations*

137–40 (1986).

[The following extract is from a study by the Netherlands Institute of Human Rights on the quantitative aspects of NGO fact finding. The authors of the study evaluated NGO missions for the previous fifteen years on the basis of responses to a questionnaire. Although some of the authors' conclusions are dated, their critique and observations raise issues of enduring importance.]

[I]t can be concluded that in general there is a relatively large amount of missions to Latin America, compared with the number of missions going to Asia or Africa. This imbalance is demonstrated clearly by computing the average number of missions per country or region in the period 1970–1985. It turned out that Central America received in average more than 11 missions per country, while the average figure for Central Africa is 0.25 per country. A factor 44 times different!

. . .

Conclusions and Recommendations

. . .

The imbalance in geographical distribution of NGO missions is not surprising, but even stronger than expected.

However, before jumping to the conclusion that NGO's are good in selective indignation, it should be considered that the imbalance to some extent is caused by overlap of missions from different NGO's rather than biases within the same body.

. . .

It is when looking at all the categories of NGO's together that the impression of imbalance or selectiveness is strongest, the NGO's in the "middle" and "small" group add their few missions per organization to the already slightly imbalanced picture of the named NGO's.

The reason most likely to be offered by NGO's for not sending missions to other countries are that

1. the government does not give permission to enter the country,

2. the level of allegations of human-rights violations does not justify it, or

3. there is no money available to fund the mission.

Looking at the list of missions to specific countries, we cite the following examples of countries which received no mission at all or only one mission during the last fifteen years:

Africa: Algeria, Bourkina Fasso (Upper Volta), Burundi, Central African Republic, Ethiopia, Kenya, Liberia, Malawi, Nigeria, Sudan, Uganda;

Americas: Brazil, Ecuador, Guyana, Dominican Republic, Panama, Puerto Rico, United States, Venezuela;

Asia: Bangladesh, Burma, India, Indonesia, Jordan, Singapore, Syria, the whole of the Arab peninsula;

Europe: the Federal Republic of Germany, France, Greece, Italy, the Netherlands, Switzerland;

Oceania: New Zealand and almost all the Pacific Islands.

There is little reason to assume that permission would be denied consistently for all these countries, nor would it seem, at first sight, that there would be no allegations worthy of investigation. The lack of resources can only be a very partial explanation, as quite a number of countries mentioned in this list have equally distant neighbouring countries which did receive visits (with the exception perhaps of the Pacific Islands). Concerning the lack of resources, it has to be stated that the raising of funds and allocation of funds to priorities would seem to be the every essence of policy making, also with regard to sending missions.

We have the impression that other, less pronounced, considerations play an equally decisive role. It would seem that NGO's are also caught up in the complex mechanisms of public attention in the West, where certain situations for relatively short periods of time are in the limelight of the media's attention. The pressure from and through the membership to get involved in those situations, combined with the lack of coordination among NGO's may lead to quick decisions to engage in fact-finding missions without regard to existing reports and the impact of yet another mission on the overall balance.

We do not know to what extent NGO's have a desire to prevent overlap, and how strongly they feel about the public's impression that there is selective indignation on the side of the NGO community as a whole. We submit that it *should* be of concern to all NGO's engaging in fact-finding, and that mechanisms of coordination should be established by them in order to prevent at least unintended overlap.

The quest for more publicity, apparently expected from missions to certain countries, is not always stated as a reason, but would in our view, not be unjustified, as the mobilization of shame through public opinion is one of the few weapons in the arsenal of NGO's. However, whether amidst the abundance of missions and reports concerning some specific countries this goal is achieved remains doubtful. Would the 29 mission reports on El Salvador have in average the same or more impact than a single mission to, say, New Caledonia or Liberia?

Another explanation belonging to this category may be that (although not mentioned often in the report) many missions have to be paid out of special project funds provided by donors with specific wishes, who are equally caught up in the fabric of publicity.

The figures of the statistics combined with our reading of the reports lead us to believe that, in addition to the explanations given above, there are many other factors which determine whether a mission is sent to a certain country or region. Cultural, historical and linguistic links between the sending NGO and the receiving country seem to be of considerable importance. Language affinity, of course, does not only constitute an unconscious element but has also many practical aspects, such as the availability of suitable candidates for the delegation and the possibility to publish and distribute a report.

Whatever the explicit or hidden elements in the decision-making process may be, the overall impression remains that in quite a few instances the sending of a mission is determined not so much by the objectively assessed need of the human-rights situation elsewhere as by home-generated considerations. The presentation of reports in the cities where the NGO's are based and the absence of the language version of the country visited strengthens this impression.

We do not say that home-generated incentives are necessarily bad or not relevant to the protection and promotion of human rights abroad. E.g. many US-based NGO's, ... wanted to counter the semi-annual presidential statements about human-rights progress in El Salvador with well-documented, recent materials. This fact should also be borne in mind when considering the above-mentioned concentration of missions to particular countries.

Recommendations

NGO's should strive for a balance within their own fact-finding efforts, as well as, and perhaps even more, within the human-rights community as a whole.

A distinction has to be made between the unintended overlap, which is usually based on a lack of information, and conscious overlap, which is based on other considerations, such as the cumulative effect of several missions and a temporarily favourable public opinion.

With respect to the first situation, unintended overlap, it goes without saying that a faster and more complete circulation of recently published reports (or summaries and announcements of such reports) would be the right answer. Specialization in information and documentation work is being developed at present, but it is still insufficient. It would be in the interest of the whole NGO community if this development would be strengthened and stepped up. Information concerning planned and forthcoming missions better remains in the informal circuit, but also here decision-making should be based on recent information acquired through quick, informal consultation among the main actors.

With respect to the second type, the conscious overlap, the need for a better cooperation is also present. In-depth study of existing reports and, for forthcoming missions, better consultations would provide an opportunity to divide the work according to relative specializations, different places and focus on different topics.

In this context, it is advisable that the sending NGO's show that they were aware of previous missions and reports, and state explicitly the reasons why the country or case was selected.

Although the question of government permission remains a delicate and controversial subject among NGO's and researchers, we feel strongly that the present uncoordinated practice favours those countries which refuse permission formally as well as in fact. Concrete proposals to remedy this situation are difficult to make at this stage, but the direction has to be probably a double-track solution of giving on the one hand appropriate credit to those countries that are open to missions, and on the other a larger measure of negative publicity for countries with a record of constant refusal. Perhaps this could be done through a special mechanism of annual consultations among the major NGO's engaged in fact-finding; a listing of countries on this point should be established, which could be published every 10th December as a collective statement.

. . .

The preceding excerpt notes the extraordinary attention devoted by NGOs to human rights conditions in El Salvador and other Central American countries compared to other regions and countries during the period that was considered. The following excerpt addresses one of the key factors accounting for this imbalance on the part of U.S.-based NGOs.

Diane F. Orentlicher, *Bearing Witness: The Art and Science of Human Rights Fact-Finding*

3 Harv. Hum. Rts. Y.B. 83, 87–91 (1990).

. . .

While the underlying point of contention involved the evenhandedness . . . of the Reagan Administration's efforts to promote compliance with human rights standards, public disputes between the NGO community and the Administration increasingly focused on their respective characterizations of factual conditions. Critics accused the Administration of exaggerating the extent of abuses in countries like Nicaragua and Cuba to serve perceived geopolitical interests while understating the extent and severity of abuses committed by such strategic allies as Turkey and El Salvador. Administration officials responded in kind, charging that the Administration's most vocal critics distorted the facts in the opposite direction.

In the early years of President Reagan's first term, these battles focused primarily on the Administration's policy toward El Salvador. In the view of the Reagan Administration, the situation prevailing in El Salvador involved substantial foreign policy stakes . . . , and [it] was determined to "draw the line" in El Salvador against what it viewed as further Soviet expansionism in Central America.

This determination translated into a commitment to support the Salvadoran armed forces in their fight against [Marxist] insurgents. But the Salvadoran military's responsibility for massive human rights violations . . . generated intense public opposition to increased military aid for El Salvador.

Concern about the human rights situation in El Salvador ran high in Congress. Nevertheless, most members of Congress were reluctant to impose a blanket ban on aid . . . , perhaps because many of them sought to avoid taking responsibility for "losing El Salvador" in the event that the Salvadoran military was overpowered by Marxist insurgents. Congress resolved this dilemma by enacting legislation that required the President to provide, as a condition of continued United States aid to El Salvador, a biannual certification that certain human rights conditions had been met in the previous six-month period. . . .

Although this legislation purported to set forth specific preconditions for the continuation of aid to El Salvador, the terms of the conditions allowed wide latitude for interpretation. During a period of staggering human rights abuses by Salvadoran forces, the Administration certified every six months that the conditions had been satisfied. The certifications were disingenuous; privately, even Reagan Administration officials complained that the certification law, by posing an "all-or-nothing" choice with respect to Salvadoran aid, forced the Administration to mislead Congress.

Throughout the process, NGOs provided extensively documented reports of ongoing abuses to counter the Administration's certifications and provided testimony contradicting the Administration's findings at semiannual congressional hearings convened to review the presidential certifications. . . .

———

While fact-finding and reporting have traditionally been one of the core activities of human rights NGOs, in recent years some of the most influential organizations have increasingly broadened their agendas. The following report provides an overview of recent trends in this regard.

Human Rights Watch, *World Report 1999*

. . .

Will there come a time when the human rights movement can afford to "wither away"? That is no more likely than the possibility that police forces will solve the problem of crime. The temptation to violate rights will always be there. Vigilance and activism will always be necessary to counter that threat. This fiftieth anniversary marks a moment to celebrate the growing capacity of the human rights movement to mount that defense and protect the values embodied in the Universal Declaration.

A New Voice for Human Rights

The strength of this movement was nowhere more visible than in its recent efforts to establish new human rights laws and institutions. The successful campaign for a treaty to establish an International Criminal Court (ICC) demonstrated that the unprecedented partnership of NGOs and small and medium-sized states that had come together to ban antipersonnel landmines would be an ongoing force. Working at times in opposition to the major military and economic powers, including the United States, this partnership succeeded in harnessing what Canadian Foreign Minister Lloyd Axworthy calls "soft power"—a strong moral message coupled with active efforts to enlist the support of the general public. The combination transformed the diplomatic landscape.

The coalition of human rights and humanitarian groups behind the Mine Ban Treaty already had much to celebrate beyond its receipt of the 1997 Nobel Peace Prize. In December 1997 in Ottawa, an astounding 122 governments signed the treaty–a number that has since risen to 133.... In September 1998, Burkina Faso became the fortieth government to ratify the treaty, allowing it to take effect in March 1999—record speed for a major multilateral treaty . . . . .

A similar government-NGO partnership emerged to produce a treaty for the establishment of an International Criminal Court. Once sixty governments ratify the treaty, the ICC will be available to try those responsible for genocide, crimes against humanity, and war crimes, including crimes of gender and sexual violence, wherever these occur. Behind this victory was a broad international coalition of NGOs working closely with an alliance of more than sixty governments. Calling itself the "like-minded group," the governmental alliance cut across the regional groups that traditionally dominate international negotiations....

... In its fifty years, the Universal Declaration has also come to protect the rights of a far broader range of people. The declaration was deliberately written in sweeping language. Article 2, for example, affirms that "everyone" is entitled to the rights and freedoms set forth in the declaration. In fact, for many years, the international human rights movement generally understood its cause more narrowly. Although the declaration was born out of the horrors of the Nazi Holocaust, it was implemented at the height of the Cold War and, in its early years, was applied primarily for the benefit of political dissidents and opponents. It embraced the Soviet intellectual battling a Communist regime, the Latin American or Asian opposition figure struggling against a right-wing dictatorship, or the anti-apartheid activist. Yet it said little about the great mass of people who suffer violation of their rights not because of their immersion in politics but because of discrimination, police abuse, mistreatment in custody, indiscriminate warfare, and the like. The broad language of the Universal Declaration fairly embraces these people, but for many years it was not invoked for their defense. In this sense, the declaration was "universal" far more in the breadth of governments it addressed than in the range of people it protected.

Expanding the scope of human rights protection has not been easy. For example, when the human rights movement began to address the rights of women or to defend civilians from indiscriminate violence in time of war, some critics feared that this risked diluting the stigma of being called a human rights violator. They argued that taking on issues of violence against women, landmines, or the indiscriminate shelling of civilians might weaken the movement's ability to defend the jailed newspaper editor or the tortured opposition figure.

Today, it is far more possible to claim that the Universal Declaration indeed embraces "everyone." But the turning point came relatively recently. It was not until the World Conference on Human Rights of 1993 that many in the human rights movement genuinely endorsed the slogan that "women's rights are human rights." It was not until the horrors of the genocide in Bosnia that the movement broadly accepted that the Universal Declaration's assertion of the "right to life" could be understood to incorporate international humanitarian law and thus impose limits on military forces in time of war. It was not until the advent of the global economy that many international groups began defending the right of workers to organize. It was only in recent years that the international movement devoted serious attention to the rights of children, ethnic and religious minorities, common prisoners, and gays and lesbians, as well as to economic, social and cultural rights.

Notes

1.   To what extent should the monitoring and other activities of NGOs be shaped by such events as the semi-annual debate over El Salvador that was driven by congressional legislation during the 1980s? Is there a risk that participating in such debates may tarnish the reputation of NGOs as politically impartial monitors? On the other hand, can NGOs afford to sit on the sidelines during major debates of the type triggered by the 1980s legislation on El Salvador? Conversely, is it ever appropriate for NGOs to consider delaying the release of their reports to avoid distorting a major policy debate over one country's foreign policy vis-a-vis another?

Suppose, for example, that you worked for an organization that monitors human rights conditions in the Middle East. Your staff has prepared a report that addresses the organization's human rights concerns in areas of the West Bank and Gaza administered by the Palestinian Authority. At roughly the time the report is ready to be publicly released, long-stalled peace talks between the Palestinian Authority and the Israeli government revive, and a crucial set of negotiations is about to begin. In this setting, it seems likely that, if released now, 1) your report will receive substantially more press coverage than it otherwise would receive; and 2) media coverage will emphasize above all the report's implications for the peace talks themselves. In these circumstances, how would you recommend timing the release of your report? Note that it is not uncommon for NGOs to provide copies of their forthcoming reports to the authorities whose practices are examined on a private basis some weeks in advance of public release. Would you consider providing copies of your report on a private basis to officials of the Palestinian Authority while delaying public release? What would be the advantages and disadvantages to doing so or to publicly releasing the report just as peace talks were to resume? What is the professionally responsible course of action?

2.   On the issue of selective monitoring raised by Messrs. Thoolen and Verstappen, it should be noted that, during the period under evaluation, many human rights NGOs had substantially smaller professional and material resources than they do today. This necessarily limited the number of countries they could monitor—although, as the authors point out, this fact does not absolve NGOs from responsibility for the way that they allocate their limited resources. Their subsequent enlargement has enabled major NGOs such as Human Rights Watch to expand the scope of their monitoring activities and thereby diminish the selectivity noted by Messrs. Thoolen and Verstappen. Even so, should NGOs make greater efforts to coordinate their activities? What factors might explain why this does not always occur?

3.   Suppose that a human rights organization with a broadly defined mandate but limited resources is deciding on its activities for the next six months. Three projects have been proposed. One is country X, where there is good reason to believe that government troops are engaged in systematically terrorizing large segments of the minority population in order to encourage them to flee the country. Tactics include rapes and arbitrary executions, and numerous disappearances. The public, however, has shown relatively little interest in country X, and it seems doubtful whether publication of a report would produce a significant response by the media or by governments that could pressure Country X to improve its record. The second project concerns Country Y. Country Y is engaged in practices that systematically discriminate against women, including discrimination in educational and professional opportunities and wage scales. Country Y is interested in improving its image around the world. A negative report by a respected NGO would probably result in substantial action by Country Y to improve the situation, but there are indications that other NGOs are now seriously considering publishing reports on that situation. A third project involves Country Z, which has been known for some years to be violating the rights of certain religious minorities. Several other organizations have issued reports in the last few years, to little avail. A study by the organization would probably add little in the way of new information, but many of the organization's members and potential sources of funding take

a special interest in the situation in Z, and the issuance of a study would probably result in a significant increase in available funds. Those funds would enable the organization to undertake field work in several other countries where serious violations occur and which seem likely to respond to NGO advocacy, but which do not attract the interest of foundations in their own right.

Faced with these choices and sufficient resources for only one of the projects, which would you advocate and why?

4.   Some NGOs, for example the Lawyers Committee for Human Rights, have moved beyond monitoring for individual human rights violations to study of selected legal systems in order to identify systemic inadequacies and to promote change in such areas as the criminal justice system. Some programs with that purpose take the form of dialogue with foreign officials and scholars, and may involve comparative study of both deficiencies and remedies.

5.   The expansion of the activities of human rights NGOs into such areas as banning landmines raises the question whether, by moving well beyond their original, narrowly-defined concerns, influential NGOs risk diluting their influence. How does Human Rights Watch respond to this concern in its 1999 Annual Report?

6.   To what extent should NGOs regard themselves as representatives of the public? Do NGOs necessarily serve a democratic role? Consider the following statement:

> If significant implementation of international human rights is to be accomplished in the twenty-first century, a renewed effort by non-governmental actors must be made so that government actors fully understand and appreciate the will of the peoples whom they purport to represent and govern. The World Conference on Human Rights set the tone for this unprecedented private/public confrontation with the official participation of more than 800 non-governmental organizations ("NGOs"), collectively representing millions, if not billions of the world's people. If the present is indicative of the future, NGOs will continue to proliferate and participate in the renewed effort to maximize the implementation of international human rights law. Indeed, it is doubtful that governments will take the sometimes difficult measures necessary to comply with their treaty commitments without the pressure and the threat of condemnation, which only NGOs can provide on a non-political basis.

Neil H. Afran, *International Human Rights Law in the Twenty First Century: Effective Municipal Implementation or Paean to Platitudes*, 18 Fordham Int'l L.J. 1756, 1761 (1995). The writer is surely correct in suggesting that NGOs have played a unique role in pressuring governments to comply with their human rights commitments. But is it self-evident that NGOs participating in world conferences "represent[] millions, if not billions of the world's people"? How democratic are international NGOs?

Whom do they represent? Consider in this regard the following observations:

> [T]he representivity of NGOs, especially on a case-by-case basis, [is not] beyond question or above scrutiny. World conferences invariably face the problem of NGIs (nongovernmental individuals) and GONGOs (government-organized NGOs), and very few of even the larger international NGOs are operationally democratic, in the sense that members elect officers or direct policy on particular issues. (Amnesty International and the Sierra Club are notable exceptions.) Arguably, it is more often money than membership that determines influence, and money more often represents the support of centralized elites, such as the major foundations, than that of the true grass roots.

> But as they now stand, most international institutions are in formal terms themselves wildly undemocratic. In the General Assembly and other UN bodies, tiny San Marino (population 23,000) has the same vote as China (population 1.17 billion); the smallest 10 UN members have a total population less than that of Washington, D.C....

> If numbers are the benchmark of legitimacy, the NGO community easily passes the test. However imperfect the mechanisms of representation, environmentalist and human rights NGOs collectively speak for many times over the numbers represented by even medium-size states in the UN, and even narrowly defined NGOs would outrank the microstates. Memberships are attentive to an organization's general principles and in some cases its specific policies.... Funding more often follows success than the other way around, and the greater part of NGO coffers is filled by member contributions.

Peter J. Spiro, *New Global Communities: Nongovernmental Organizations in International Decision–Making Institutions*, 18 Wash. Q. 45, 52 (1994). Does the author's suggestion that NGOs are accountable to broad-based membership apply to organizations that are not, in his terms, "operationally democratic"? Why, in any case, is the democratic nature of NGOs relevant in assessing the legitimacy of their role in international conferences and other decision-making fora? Is there any plausible case to be made that it is not necessarily appropriate to apply a democratic paradigm in this context? Consider, in this regard, whether doing so could in some respects diminish the independence of NGOs. Is this a legitimate concern?

7. The preceding materials focus on mandate and other institutional issues from the perspective of international NGOs. To what extent should their mandates be affected by the concerns of domestic NGOs with whom they work? In considering this question, it may be helpful to understand the nature of the relationship between international and domestic NGOs. Kenneth Roth, Executive Director of Human Rights Watch, has summarized that relationship:

> A ... key factor in the growing success of the human rights cause has been the effective partnership forged between international and

local human rights organizations. Local organizations are best positioned to mobilize local opposition to human rights abuse and to insist on change. Given governments' preoccupation with maintaining power, these local voices tend to have the greatest resonance. The last thing an abusive government wants is to be denounced before its citizens or to have its disregard for human rights spark demonstrations and public protests. For that reason, many local activists have themselves become targets of abuse. Hundreds have been killed over the years, and many more have faced persecution.

Because of this danger, international human rights organizations are preoccupied foremost with trying to protect our colleagues on the front line of our movement. Any attack on a human rights monitor is met with fierce denunciations and intense pressure on the offending government. In this way, international human rights organizations help to create and maintain the political space that local activists need to function.

As local organizations are able to operate more freely, they, in turn, provide invaluable assistance to international groups. This ranges from logistical assistance in identifying witnesses and navigating difficult terrain, to strategic assistance in selecting topics for inquiry, shaping investigations, fashioning recommendations for policymakers, and planning advocacy campaigns. The partnership between local groups, with their superior knowledge of local conditions, and international groups, with their global perspective and access to the international press and policymakers, has been a powerful one.

Kenneth Roth, Human Rights Organizations: A New Force for Social Change, lecture delivered at the Kennedy School of Government, Harvard University, Nov. 4, 1998, publication forthcoming (see supra p. 738). For further discussion of the role of domestic NGOs and the risks that they face, see Lawyers Committee for Human Rights, *An Area of Neglect: The Treatment of Freedom of Association and Independent Human Rights Monitoring in the Country Reports*, in Critique: Review of the U.S. Department of State's Country Reports on Human Rights Practices for 1996.

During a 1989 retreat in which representatives of NGOs from around the world participated, some participants complained that international NGOs are often active "in parts of the world that are little consulted about their own priorities and toward which INGOs have no accountability." Henry J. Steiner, Diverse Partners: Non–Governmental Organizations in the Human Rights Movement 61 (1991). Does the nature of the "partnership" between international and domestic NGOs described by Roth carry with it any special responsibility on the part of international organizations to shape their mandates, at least in part, in a manner that is responsive to the chief concerns of their domestic partners? Note, in this regard, that United States NGOs have sometimes been accused of concentrating upon rights that are enshrined in the U.S. Constitution and viewing other matters as not involving "real rights" and being of lesser concern. See id. at 26. How broadly should "human rights concerns" be defined for purposes of establishing an international NGO's mandate? Does this depend at all or in substantial part upon the priorities of national NGOs with which an international NGO works closely?

3. MONITORING AND FACT-FINDING

Establishing and reporting the facts regarding human rights violations has traditionally been one of the most important functions performed by human rights NGOs. The preceding materials have raised some preliminary issues raised by these activities, including the question of how NGOs should decide which countries they will investigate. In this section we take a closer look at various issues relating to the methodology utilized to establish facts once NGOs have decided which countries they will monitor.

Diane F. Orentlicher, *Bearing Witness: The Art and Science of Human Rights Fact–Finding*

3 Harv. Hum. Rts. Y.B. 83, 84–85, 93–95 (1990).

. . .

A variety of factors account for the growing influence of the leading human rights NGOs, but their achievements rest, above all, on the quality of their work. And while NGOs undertake a range of activities to promote their concerns, perhaps none has been more influential than their efforts to document and publicize human rights violations. The premise of these efforts is straightforward: human rights professionals believe that no action is more effective in prompting governments to curb human rights violations than aiming the spotlight of public scrutiny on the depredations themselves.

The strategy—promoting change by reporting facts—is almost elegant in its simplicity. And there is growing evidence that it works. Governments frequently have adopted reforms in response to critical reports by NGOs.... Country reports prepared by the more prominent NGOs often receive front page news coverage abroad, and in the United States, such reports have prompted Congress to adopt legislation suspending foreign aid or conditioning future aid on a country's compliance with international human rights standards.

As the influence of NGO human rights reporting has grown, NGOs' underlying research methodology has come under heightened scrutiny and, at times, ... attack. In an age when acquiring the status of "human rights pariah" carries unprecedented costs internationally, governments whose rights violations are publicized frequently respond by challenging the credibility of the fact-finding methodology....

In this setting, perhaps no asset is more important to a human rights NGO than the credibility of its fact-finding and, in particular, its reputation for meticulous methodology. Despite the unprecedented attention to issues of human rights methodology, however, the leading NGOs have not adopted uniform methodological standards; most have not even adopted comprehensive, formal standards for use by their own [staff]. And while NGO reporting has drawn the close scrutiny of various parties, critiques of NGO methodology do not reflect a coherent set of commonly accepted standards.

. . .

[I]t is [nonetheless] possible to identify factors that figure prominently in public assessments of NGO fact-finding. The most frequently cited criteria fall into two categories. One relates to the integrity of an NGO's fact-finding methodology; the other takes account of various factors that are thought to indicate whether the NGO has an institutional bias ... that may taint the credibility of its conclusions....

A.   *Fact–Finding Methodology*

Several aspects of the methodology underlying country reports tend to make even the most meticulous NGOs vulnerable to credibility challenges.

. . .

First, the fact-finding activities of [many] NGOs tend to focus on violations of physical integrity, such as torture, extrajudicial executions, "disappearances," and arbitrary detention. The facts surrounding reported violations of this sort are rarely beyond dispute, in large part because the violations themselves are often deliberately shrouded in secrecy: military forces organize anonymous "death squads" to kill political opponents under cover of darkness; agents of the state seize suspected political opponents without judicial warrant and torture their victims in unauthorized, secret detention centers.

The obstacles to fact-finding posed by the state's nearly exclusive control of essential information are often compounded by other, related circumstances. In a context of widespread states lawlessness, for example, witnesses and victims often are afraid to provide testimony ... , fearing retaliation.... Moreover, a substantial number of countries in which gross violations are practiced on a systematic basis are closed to foreign investigators....

. . .

––––––

The following excerpt is taken from a pamphlet issued by Human Rights Watch, "Questions and Answers" (1996).

How does Human Rights Watch collect information?

Human Rights Watch sends frequent fact-finding missions to countries where abuses take place. In several countries, we maintain our own personnel to gather information on a continuing basis. We meet with government officials, opposition leaders, local human rights groups, church officials, labor leaders, journalists, scholars, lawyers, relief groups, doctors and others with information on human rights practices. Frequently, we interview victims, members of their families and witnesses to abuses. We attend court proceedings and examine court records.

In some places, not all of these methods can be pursued. Officials of some governments refuse to meet with us or allow us to examine court records. In such circumstances, we seek the best evidence we can find.

Human Rights Watch has established an extensive worldwide information-gathering network of persons or groups on the scene who assist us in our investigations. In addition, we examine information provided by governments under scrutiny, third-party governments, international agencies, other human rights groups, as well as the general and specialized press.

Participants in our fact-gathering are generally persons with a highly specialized knowledge of particular countries or particular kinds of human rights abuses. Some are members of our staff; others are members of our governing committees; still others are called upon because of their specialized knowledge.

Notes

1.   The preceding excerpt notes that some governments refuse to cooperate with human rights investigative efforts. Some governments have denied access to their countries altogether; others refuse to meet with NGO representatives and impose other obstacles to effective fact-finding. The former situation presents an evident dilemma: On the one hand, the government's action radically compromises the conditions for reliable fact-finding. On the other hand, if NGOs declined to report on conditions in "closed countries," governments responsible for especially serious abuses could escape scrutiny by virtue of their own recalcitrance. This dilemma brings into sharp focus an issue of general importance: What standard of proof should NGOs utilize in their reporting?

Consider, in this regard, the various aims of NGO reports. To the extent that NGOs seek to convince governments other than the one whose practices are examined to address the conditions described in their reports, what standard of proof would be persuasive? To the extent that they seek to persuade the government allegedly responsible for abuses to take corrective action, what level of proof seems appropriate? Consider the following observation: "[T]ypically, NGOs have acknowledged that they lack the capacity to verify every detail of accounts included in their reports, but have asserted that they have developed sufficient evidence of serious abuses to require the government to take appropriate action, including the institution of an impartial investigation. . . . If the NGO's methodology is persuasive, the government responsible for alleged violations is likely to face substantial pressure to 'answer for itself,' while the concerned public is unlikely to accept a bald denial as an adequate response." Diane F.

Orentlicher, supra, at 107–108. While the first part of the quoted text seems to provide "cover" for an NGO account of abuses that cannot be verified, the quoted text also implicitly acknowledges that such disclaimers will be credible only if and to the extent that the underlying methodology is itself persuasive. But how persuasive must NGOs' methodology be? In particular, should NGOs act in accordance with lower standards of proof in respect of closed countries than in respect of those where they have significant opportunities to corroborate allegations? Should they apply lower standards of proof when reporting on allegations concerning individuals who appear to be in immediate peril? What should an NGO do if, as happens from time to time, it discovers that an alleged violation it publicly reported as such did not, in fact, take place?

2. Suppose that a government or insurgent group grants an NGO permission to conduct an on-site investigation, but vetoes one member of the proposed team. Should the NGO decline to conduct the inquiry—even if it believes it can obtain valuable information operating within the constraints imposed by the authorities in question?

3. The account of the methodology of Human Rights Watch notes the diversity of sources upon which its staff rely and also seems to place special emphasis on the importance of court records. Why are diverse sources important? For what reasons and purposes would court records be especially relevant and probative? Why are interviews with government officials important?

4. Although there are no universally-accepted standards for NGOs' fact-finding methodology, there have been efforts to develop general guidelines, including a set developed by Human Rights Information and Documentation Systems, International (HURIDOCS). These efforts may provide especially useful guidance for relatively inexperienced NGOs. Given the diversity of NGO mandates, functions, resources and the situations in which they operate, do you think it is desirable to promote universal *adherence* to such a common set of fact-finding standards?

5. If you worked for an international NGO that monitored human rights conditions in Country X and were aware that the leading domestic human rights NGO produced politically-motivated, distorted accounts, what, if anything, would you do? Would you consider publicly criticizing the organization's methodology? Would your answer depend on whether the NGO in question operated in conditions of extreme risk to its staff? What criteria would you apply to evaluate the credibility of such an NGO? Consider the following letter to The New York *Times* by Aryeh Neier, then Executive Director of Human Rights Watch:

Not All Human Rights Groups Are Equal

To the Editor:

Two ... letters ("Why Both Sides Aren't the Same in Nicaragua") criticized your report of findings by Americas Watch, a component of Human Rights Watch.... Americas Watch had documented a pattern of summary executions by Nicaraguan Army and state security agents in which the victims were suspected contra collaborators in northern rural areas.

Blase Bonpane, director of the Office of the Americas, complained that, as far as Nicaragua was concerned, Americas Watch had "fallen into the trap of promoting the thesis that both sides are the same" and that the Nicaraguan Government's actions should be seen as a sovereign nation's attempt to defend itself against a "band of rapists, murderers and thieves."

Nina Shea, president of the Puebla Institute, on the other hand, complained of our finding that Sandinista executions of civilians now constitute a pattern, whereas during most of the war we had reported "sporadic" executions; instead, she asserts, "atrocities have been part of the Sandinista counterinsurgency strategy" since 1981.

Mr. Bonpane cites the findings of the National Commission for the Promotion and Protection of Human Rights, a Nicaraguan Government agency; Ms. Shea cites the findings of her own group, the Puebla Institute, an organization established by a Nicaraguan emigre, Humberto Belli.

A phenomenon that has concerned the human rights movement is the proliferation of groups claiming to speak in the name of the human rights cause but actually engaged in efforts to promote one or another side in a civil conflict. Nowhere has this been more of a factor than in Nicaragua. On both sides, the human rights issue has been a weapon to use against the enemy. It may be useful, accordingly, to suggest a few questions to raise in distinguishing partisan efforts from genuine efforts to promote human rights. These include:

- Is the organization funded by or otherwise linked to any party to the conflict?

- Is it impartial? If it is an international group, does it regularly criticize abuses by governments of all political persuasions and geopolitical alignments? In situations of sustained armed conflict, does it criticize violations of the laws of war by both sides according to the same criteria?

- Does it engage in systematic field research and does it avoid sweeping comments, except to the degree that these are sustained by its detailed findings through field research?

- Does it exercise care in the use of language? For example, does it refer to "torture" when the word "mistreatment" would be more appropriate? When does it allege "atrocities" as a "strategy"?

- Does it acknowledge contradictory evidence, such as a government's prosecutions of its own personnel for abuses, or the statements of one witness that cast doubt on the statements of another?

- Above all, of course, it is the record that an organization has compiled over time that indicates whether it deserves credence when it reports on human rights. . . .

Aryeh Neier, *Letter to the Editor*, N.Y. Times, May 27, 1989.

———

The preceding materials reflect the substantial challenges that are entailed in the process of gathering and substantiating reports of human rights violations. As the following excerpts suggest, the process of reporting the results of human rights inquiries raises another set of complex challenges.

Diane F. Orentlicher, *Bearing Witness: The Art and Science of Human Rights Fact-finding*

3 Harv. Hum. Rts. Y.B. 83, 95–97, 99–101 (1990).

. . . While it may be a truism that there are no "pure facts" and that any attempt to describe factual conditions entails substantial interpretation, the role of interpretation is particularly large in the context of human rights country reports. Because country reports aspire to describe broad patterns, the finder of fact must attempt not only to verify individual incidents of abuse, but also to reach more sweeping judgments about the extent of the violations, the nature of government (and, where relevant, insurgent) responsibility for the abuses, and the significance of apparent trends.

Consider, for example, a situation in which data show that a government, which in recent years has been responsible for several thousand political killings each year, now annually executes "only" several hundred victims. To be meaningful, an account of this trend must include an analysis of its underlying causes and significance. Otherwise the NGO's audience cannot assess whether the statistical decline reflects a genuine change in official policy, a decrease in opposition activity caused by governmental repression, or a shift in the geographical concentration of abuses to areas relatively inaccessible to human rights monitors. Similarly, a comparatively small number of political prisoners in a country may signify a low degree of political repression, or it may reflect a degree of governmental intimidation substantial enough to [deter] citizens from attempting dissident activity.

The point is that, however objective an NGO's methodology in ascertaining the "facts" about alleged human rights violations, its final conclusions draw upon qualitative interpretation of the data. While unavoidable, the substantial role of interpretation in human rights fact-finding leaves room for observers to reach different conclusions about the significance of even agreed upon facts.

Divergent conclusions about the "same" facts may also reflect differing judgments about a government's degree of moral culpability, or about the relative efficacy of alternative characterizations in promoting the institutional objectives of the fact-finding organization. Suppose, for example, that an NGO investigates conditions in a country that experienced staggering violations in the recent past. The fact-finder almost surely will find that the worst abuses have abated; the type of wholesale slaughter associated with Idi Amin's Uganda, Pol Pot's Cambodia, and East Timor in the years following Indonesia's invasion does not persist indefinitely. In reporting recent trends in such countries, the NGO might credit the government for improvement, while urging it to exert still greater efforts to end current violations. Or, the NGO could condemn the government for continuing abuses, perhaps recognizing that state violence has abated because the political opposition has been crushed, and that the government has undertaken earlier positive reforms only when prompted by international condemnation. Though different in tone, both approaches are consistent with the same "raw facts," and the choice between them may be determined, at least in part, by a calculation of their relative efficacy in promoting improvement.

... Governments that are the subject of scrutiny as well as other audiences often evaluate NGO reporting according to its "fairness" in a particular sense: whether it acknowledges contextual factors that place violations "in perspective." Thus, for example, the Israeli government is more likely to credit a report describing its violations in the West Bank and Gaza if the report acknowledges that human rights conditions are deplorable in other areas of the Middle East. Similarly, even if a human rights NGO's mandate does not extend to monitoring abuses committed by armed rebels, its account of a government's violations is likely to seem more credible to that government if the report acknowledges in a more-than-perfunctory fashion the threat posed by the insurgents....

While signaling that the NGO's motive in publicizing government abuses is not political, these types of "contextual" observations serve a separate function as well: they anticipate and address the target government's (or other target audiences') possible inclination to dismiss the NGO's reports as politically motivated, naive, inappropriate, or irrelevant....

Inclusion of [con]textual information to this end reflects a peculiar aspect of NGO reports: they form part of an ongoing dialogue with the target government and, often with other audiences. By acknowledging that the government has committed human rights violations as a response to circumstances that help explain its behavior, the NGO has anticipated the next stage in the dialogue—the government's response—and answered it.

A key point to be made here is that human rights reports are not merely abstract factual accounts. The reports are advocacy tools, designed to promote change in government practices. As such, their presentation of facts is designed to respond to factors likely to affect the report's impact.

Emerging standards used to judge institutional credibility place somewhat conflicting demands on NGOs concerned with maximizing the persuasive impact of their reports. In principle, the public judges NGO reporting as "fair" and "balanced" if the organization measures every government's record against the same, universal standards; in practice, however, the perceived fairness or balance of particular reports often depends upon the extent to which the report takes account of contextual factors that are peculiar to the country concerned. . . .

Kenneth Roth, *Human Rights Organizations: A New Force for Social Change**

. . .

The final important ingredient in the success of the human rights movement has been the growing professionalism of the movement itself. It has not been enough for human rights organizations simply to express outrage at abuse or to issue calls for others to rally to the cause. Outside the country where human rights violations are committed, the abuses are usually too distant from people's lives to be much of a priority. And even if motivated to address abuses, few people know what can be done to curtail them. Far more than most causes, the human rights movement has had to build and channel outrage. This has required an extraordinarily complex operation.

Generating outrage is, of course, not a matter of creating opinions out of thin air. As noted, the human rights ideal is built on widely shared values. But making potential outrage manifest can be complicated. Human rights activists must identify and speak with victims of abuse, analyze their plight under relevant standards, determine responsibility, suggest ways to improve the situation, and generate the political will to see these steps taken. This requires linguistic skills, familiarity with the country, competence in conducting investigations, knowledge of relevant human rights standards and issues, analysis of policy options in various capitals, experience in dealing with the press, and the ability to mobilize popular demands for action.

Take, for example, the problem of bonded child labor in India. Investigations must be conducted in the face of considerable resistance from local businesses and governments. Journalists must be convinced to write about an issue that may seem intractable and thus not "newsworthy." Only by enabling the general public to "meet" the children who are victims of this terrible practice can the human rights movement transform a general dislike of an abstract concept into active repulsion and a desire to do something about it. Even then, it is not obvious what should be done. Who can generate pressure on the Indian government to confront the problem?

* Lecture, delivered at the John F. Kennedy School of Government, Harvard University, Nov. 4, 1998, publication forthcoming (see supra p. 738).

How can remedies be devised that will not make the children worse off? Who will finance these remedies? How can external pressure be mobilized? In short, even after exposing a human rights violation, extensive policy research must be done to channel the outrage of the general public and sympathetic governments in useful directions.

To complicate matters further, a single investigation and report is rarely enough to make a difference. Often governments will decide simply to ride out a wave of bad publicity—until a second, third or fourth report is issued, and the government realizes that its public relations problem will not go away until it addresses the human rights problem at its core. Often governments will attack the messenger, which is why careful, scrupulously objective reporting is so important. Even when a government agrees to change, ongoing monitoring is needed to ensure that officials live up to their promises. And this scenario is repeated for each country and each issue that a human rights organization takes on.

Sustaining this effort is a complicated, expensive endeavor. It can be done only by attracting and training a staff of professionals willing to devote their talents to the cause. It also requires the financial support of those who recognize that it is not enough simply to add their voices on behalf of human rights, since without the professionalism of the modern human rights movement it would be difficult to channel their voices in an effective direction. In this way, the human rights movement has helped to create a new kind of NGO—not simply an organization that amplifies the voice of its members by enabling them to speak in unison, but an organization that allows its members and supporters to strategically collect and deploy information in a way that would have been beyond the capacity of any of them individually to undertake.

Some have asked whether, in contrast to an NGO that simply directs the voices of its members, a human rights-style NGO presents a problem of accountability. To whom is such an NGO accountable if not its members? The methodology of the modern human rights organization supplies the answer. Because such an organization can use the process of stigmatization only against the backdrop of broadly shared values, and because the stigmatization process must be highly visible to be effective, human rights NGOs cannot stray far from the basic values of the human rights cause without either losing their effectiveness or subjecting themselves to public criticism. Indeed, this highly public form of accountability is arguably stronger than the theoretical accountability exerted on a classic NGO by its members, many of whom may not have the time, inclination or knowledge to scrutinize lower-profile activities.

Notes

1.   We return again to the question of the accountability of human rights NGOs. Roth suggests that the methodology employed by NGOs, as well as their fidelity to universally-shared human values, is the principal source of their credibility. With respect to NGO methodology, should NGOs as a

general rule describe the methodology employed by their fact-finders? Consider the following recommendations:

> NGO's have no reason to be reluctant in providing detail, whether it is with regard to the programme (showing the purposefulness of the mission), with regard to the circumstances under which the facts were collected, the sources or the methods of checking that were used.
>
> Omissions of specific information on grounds of security are acceptable if done openly, and without making it a pretext for withholding other source relations.
>
> Desk research forms an important element in a reliable report, and ought to be recognizable as such. NGO's with weak supporting secretarial services should perhaps involve (voluntary) support of more research-orientated institutions. These links, when established, could also provide a solution to the question of how public records of the mission's findings could be maintained.

Hans Thoolen & Berth Verstappen, supra, at 135. The same authors recommend that NGOs hew closely to international standards in their reporting:

> References to legal standards, in particular international human-rights norms, should in fact be the basic normative framework for any human-rights mission. These should be stated in correct and unequivocal language and, where possible, refer to specific human-rights instruments.

Do you agree with this recommendation? Does the answer depend on whether a report is prepared by an international or a domestic human rights organization? What if serious violations of personal dignity do not seem to be covered by existing international standards?

2. While most NGOs that monitor states' compliance with international human rights standards consider publicity a powerful advocacy tool, some NGOs believe that "quiet diplomacy" can be effective. The International Committee of the Red Cross, which promotes compliance with international humanitarian law—i.e., the law of armed conflict—has an extensive program of visiting places of detention with the permission of the respective authorities. It provides details of its findings only to the authority concerned. It does, however, reserve the right to release its findings in the event that the recipient of these confidential reports publicly misrepresents the findings. Weissbrodt, supra, at 303–04.

4.   THE FORMAL STATUS OF NGOs

The impact of some NGOs has been notably disproportionate to any formal status they may enjoy. As the preceding materials make clear, the prestige of the most effective human rights NGOs stems above all from the quality of their work, as well as from the broad appeal of the ideals they advance. Still, to the extent that NGOs aspire to shape policy debates in legal, inter-governmental and other official institutions, certain kinds of formal status may enhance their efficacy. At the same time, proposals to enhance the status of NGOs in various fora may raise a new set of issues, as the following selections suggest.

Michael H. Posner & Candy Whittome, *The Status of Human Rights NGOs*

25 Colum. Hum. Rts. L. Rev. 269 (1994).

. . .

IV. NGO Access To The United Nations System

To be effective participants in the international debate on human rights, NGOs—local and international—need effective access to the key players in the U.N. system. Yet such access is still hard, if not almost impossible, to come by for most local NGOs.

Formal relations between the United Nations and NGOs are mandated by the United Nations Charter. Article 71 of the Charter provides: "The Economic and Social Council may make suitable arrangements for consultation with non-governmental organizations which are concerned with matters within its competence."

Today, ECOSOC Resolution 1296 governs relations between NGOs and the United Nations. To gain consultative status, an organization must be "of representative character and of recognized international standing; it shall represent a substantial proportion, and express the views of major sections of the population or of the organized persons within the particular field of competence, covering, where possible, a substantial number of countries in different regions of the world." National organizations are permitted only "after consultations with the Member State concerned in order to help achieve a balanced and effective representation of non-governmental organizations reflecting major interests of all regions and areas of the world, or where they have special experience upon which the Council may wish to draw."

The decision to award consultative status is made by the ECOSOC Committee on NGOs which meets biennially to review applications. NGOs awarded consultative status are placed in one of three categories: Category I, Category II or the Roster. The NGOs in Category I and II are permitted to attend public meetings of the Commissions and other subsidiary organs of ECOSOC as observers, while those on the Roster may attend "such meetings which are concerned with matters within their field of competence." NGOs in Categories I and II may submit written statements not exceeding 2,000 or 1,500 words respectively, which may then be circulated in full by the Secretariat. NGOs on the Roster may be invited to submit written statements. NGOs may also make oral presentations at the meetings they attend, at the invitation of the Chair. They are restricted to one such statement per agenda item, and usually have a time limit of ten minutes.

The implications of the current arrangements for formal NGO relations with the United Nations are significant. Two questions, in particular, arise: (1) does consultative status provide NGOs effective access to the United Nations system? and (2) how can the NGOs who do not have, or are not eligible for, consultative status, obtain effective access? Those with consultative status need to assess whether it grants them effective and meaningful participation in United Nations fora. For example, NGOs were excluded from the drafting sessions at the Vienna Conference where the final document, the Vienna Declaration and Programme of Action, was negotiated. Moreover, many of the "rights" granted are, in practice, less useful than they might at first appear. The right to make oral statements at the United Nations Commission on Human Rights, for example, is often rendered virtually useless because of the fact that the debate is so crowded, with so many governments and NGOs wanting to speak, that NGOs are frequently allotted the least popular time, late at night, when there are few government delegates to hear or respond to them.

Even this situation compares favorably with that of the majority of local NGOs that are unable to obtain consultative status at all. In most cases it is only if a local NGO is affiliated with an NGO with consultative status that is willing to let the local group speak or circulate documents under its name can a local group obtain even informal access to meetings such as those of the United Nations Commission on Human Rights. Attending such meetings simply to lobby delegates is not an option unless a national NGO can persuade an international one to give it accreditation.

On the other hand, NGOs do not need consultative status to participate in many of the other human rights activities of the United Nations. They may, for example, submit information to various thematic rapporteurs and treaty-monitoring bodies, and have been able to participate, to some extent, in major events such as the Vienna Conference on Human Rights....

The question of access to the United Nations is becoming increasingly important and complex as the number of local human rights groups continues to grow. At present there are over 900 NGOs in consultative status with the Economic and Social Council of the United Nations, and the great majority of these are international NGOs. Up until the early 1980s, when there were few local NGOs, the system could cope with the numbers. In recent years, the number of NGOs has increased dramatically—over 1500 NGOS were represented at the Vienna Conference alone. If all these groups were to be awarded consultative status and given the same rights and privileges as those with such status now enjoy, it is arguable that the system would collapse. There is simply not enough room for such large numbers of NGOs to attend United Nations meetings; there would not be time for each NGO to make an oral statement on every agenda item; there are not the resources within the United Nations NGO Liaison Office to deal with these vastly-expanded numbers. But this situation poses a challenge for NGOs and governments alike. How can the situation be remedied, with a greater number of NGOs be granted more effective access, without overloading the system to the breaking point?

. . .

... In the preparatory meetings leading up to the [Vienna] Conference, some governments attempted to restrict the rights of NGOs wishing to participate. The final agreement on NGO participation reflected a compromise between those who wished to open up the Conference to as many NGOs as possible (not just those with consultative status), and those who wanted to limit it at all costs. NGOs without consultative status were allowed to participate if they were "active in the field of human rights and/or development and have their headquarters in the concerned region, in prior consultation with the countries of the region." All NGOs which had participated in a preparatory meeting were permitted to attend the Vienna Conference itself. It is important that NGOs use their experience in Vienna to develop policies and strategies on NGO relations with the United Nations. . . .

The question of access to the United Nations system, however, is broader than that of consultative status alone. It includes the ability of NGOs—local and international—to make their voices heard by all parts of the United Nations system which relate to human rights, including the specialized agencies such as United Nations Development Plan (UNDP) and UNESCO, as well as entities such as the World Bank. Meaningful access would require outreach on the part of the United Nations to local groups, and incorporation of their concerns into in-country programs developed by the United Nations.

Conclusions

The problems addressed in this article need to be addressed on several levels. Internationally, the United Nations needs to undertake a broader review of its relationship with human rights advocates and to work more closely with them.

For example, United Nations human rights monitoring bodies should evaluate the ability of local human rights NGOs to operate freely and effectively as a key component in their evaluation of the human rights situation in particular countries. United Nations departments and agencies, such as UNDP and the World Bank, should take into account the concerns of local human rights NGOs in their planning and operations of in-country programs. United Nations bodies and agencies that deal with human rights issues should grant increased and more effective access to local and international human rights advocacy groups.

. . .

Peter J. Spiro, *New Global Communities: Nongovernmental Organizations in International Decision–Making Institutions*

18 Wash. Q. 45 (1994).

. . .

NGOs have emerged as prime movers on a broad range of global issues, framing agendas, mobilizing constituencies toward targeted results, and monitoring compliance as a sort of new world police force. International regimes protecting human rights ... would arguably amount to nothing without initial and continuing NGO pressure ...

. . .

At the same time as NGOs and the communities they represent emerge as serious international players, however, their impact is inadequately reflected in international law or in the formal structure of international institutions. In line with the doctrine of sovereignty and its conception of the state as the exclusive building block of international relations, international organizations have themselves made little room to formally acknowledge the significance of non-state communities, maintaining themselves for the most part as purely intergovernmental bodies. It may be time to reexamine this policy of exclusion. Bringing NGOs more deeply into the fold of international institutions—in the United Nations (UN), regional organizations, treaty-making bodies, international financial institutions ..., and the organs of world trade—could enhance the legitimacy of those institutions, as well as promote greater responsibility among the NGOs themselves.

. . .

In a tradition that dates to the 1932 World Disarmament Conference, issue-oriented intergovernmental summits are now uniformly shadowed by unofficial parallel NGO forums and are preceded by preparatory committee meetings at which NGOs appear in force....

NGO participation in these ad hoc standard-setting institutions has not been governed by uniform procedures. In addition to working the proverbial hallways in the same way that domestic interests lobby the Congress, NGOs have managed to insinuate themselves into decision-making contexts in three ways. As far back as the conference that led to the Peace of Paris, to which labor leader Samuel Gompers accompanied President Woodrow Wilson, nongovernmental leaders have been included in national delegations. This has become a routine phenomenon, with NGO representatives appearing as "public members" on national negotiating teams (mostly Western) in multilateral forums.... This may be a welcome development so long as it promotes transparency and allows NGOs a voice they would not otherwise enjoy. There looms, however, an inevitable danger of cooption, which explains a fairly consistent refusal on the part of human rights groups to accept such invitations.

NGOs have also participated in various informally constituted working groups associated with the development of protective regimes, especially when presiding officials have been sympathetically inclined. The Convention on the Rights of the Child ..., for example, came out of a working group in which representatives of Save the Children International and other NGOs were instrumental to the drafting process.... But inclusion of NGOs in such ad hoc decision making is at the whim of the chair and the sufferance of national delegations, and the NGOs must tread carefully to preserve privileges not procedurally protected.

Finally, there is the phenomenon of outright delegation capture.... Microstates lacking the resources to dispatch their own emissaries have in some cases effectively ceded their representation to NGOs.... Such infiltration, while affording select NGOs direct access to decision-making forums, is something in the nature of a fraud on other governments. NGO influence should not hinge on which groups happen best to ingratiate themselves to nation-state representatives.

The situation is not much better at standing UN institutions than in the ad hoc bodies. The UN Charter itself, in article 71, allows the Economic and Social Council (ECOSOC) to "make suitable arrangements for consultation with non-governmental organizations," and NGOs have been afforded some formal privileges in ECOSOC under a 1968 resolution that gave them a cumbersome and now anachronistic "consultative status." ... [I]n practice consultative status has amounted to little more than access passes and proverbial photocopying privileges. Nine hundred and seventy-eight NGOs currently have consultative status, up from 90 in 1949.

. . .

Existing avenues of access demonstrate that NGO influence will be felt, and there is a growing understanding that NGOs must be better integrated into decision-making processes. As a practical matter, that influence is likely to rise as NGOs mobilize constituencies with increasing effectiveness at the international level. International law should move to reflect and entrench this facet of the new global political dynamic, to the end of advancing the legitimacy of global institutions....

... [F]ormal recognition of nongovernmental actors [would not] be without important precedent. The [International Labor Organization (ILO)] operates under a tripartite structure in which governments, workers and employers have votes on a 2:1:1 ratio.... The ILO model could be readily transplanted to other contexts in which primary non-state communities are well-defined and have achieved some level of representivity.

In the context of world conferences, intergovernmental forums could allocate a number of seats—at the table—for each of these communities.... That number, although small, should be large enough to allow for reflection of the diversity among the NGOs and their constituencies. Liberally accredited by a secretariat office, the NGOs would then be left to decide on the composition of this representation. Although not seamlessly democratic, the exercise would likely result in the selection of legitimate and effective institutional leadership for NGO efforts in decision-making forums.

However visionary this may sound, it is not far from recent practice. Negotiation between NGOs and governmental delegations is already occurring outside of formal procedures....

... As lawmaking organs, both the world conferences and the standing multilateral institutions work more through negotiation and near-consensus than through legislative-type voting procedures. The further addition of, say, 5 or even 10 percent to the number of participants (on top of the numerous new national representatives of recent years) would not disrupt the decision-making process.

At the same time, such reform would pose important institutional benefits. As noted in the terms of reference for the Commission on Global Governance,

> a crucial factor in the effectiveness of organisations is their perceived legitimacy, [which] is linked to participation and transparency in their decision-making processes and to the representative nature of bodies that exercise authority.

To the extent individuals count themselves a part of non-state communities, formal participation in intergovernmental forums by the representatives of such communities would create an additional (and arguably more direct and responsive) uplink from the citizenry in a context where parliamentary-type representation remains impractical....

Institutionalizing the NGO role in global decision making would also strengthen the transnational ties that NGOs embody. This, too, would help stabilize government-to-government relationships, as genuine societal interdependence diminishes the possibilities for unbuffered national conflict and points toward the potential of a democratic peace. International recognition of NGOs would afford them some measure of protection from persecution by national governments. And entrenching the presence of the NGOs in international organizations would contribute to greater transparency because states would be less able to revert to their interests qua states in backroom deal-making.

Finally, NGOs would themselves become more open and accountable were they formally brought into the fold. The consequences of misbehavior would be magnified, in rather the same way that college sports teams are suspended for improper recruiting activities or that or that scientific research teams are subjected to rigorous peer review.... As a condition for participation in any UN body, NGOs might be required to subscribe to a code of conduct defining their basic mechanisms of accountability. This may imply some loss of independence, but that is the inevitable implication of power responsibly exercised.

. . .

Notes

1. The principal thrust of the article by Posner and Whittome is that more should be done to ensure NGO access to UN human rights fora. Yet they also note the explosive growth of NGOs seeking to participate in major UN conferences and the resulting problems that would be presented by unrestricted and equal access: "[O]ver 1500 NGOS were represented at the Vienna Conference alone. If all these groups were to be awarded consultative status and given the same rights and privileges as those with such

status now enjoy, it is arguable that the system would collapse. There is simply not enough room for such large numbers of NGOs to attend United Nations meetings; there would not be time for each NGO to make an oral statement on every agenda item; there are not the resources within the United Nations NGO Liaison Office to deal with these vastly-expanded numbers." How can this situation most productively be addressed? Should NGOs be required to "pool" their access to limited seats at major conferences, as Spiro suggests? Might this approach favor resource-rich international NGOs?

2.   Special conferences aside, in view of the influence that NGOs can have in the ongoing implementation activities of UN human rights bodies, how important is it to increase their ability to obtain formal status? NGOs have contributed to special studies on human rights issues conducted by the UN, and have been permitted to submit written or oral comments in other UN bodies. As Professor Weissbrodt has pointed out, " ... because many national delegations lack the resources to do thorough human rights research, NGOs often provide delegates with information and even draft documentation for use in UN bodies. Hence, NGOs are not dependent entirely upon their rights to make oral and written interventions. Their influence may be felt even more strongly in informal cooperation with governmental representatives." Weissbrodt, supra, at 308. Would formal access along the lines advocated by Spiro likely affect the substantive outcome of international decision-making processes? Even if this type of impact were minimal, are there nonetheless other persuasive reasons to enhance the formal status of NGOs in international decision-making processes? Are there any risks associated with the proposal Spiro advocates?

3.   For further reading on the contributions to and status of NGOs in various intergovernmental human rights fora and international litigation, see Elizabeth P. Barratt–Brown, *Building a Monitoring and Compliance Regime Under the Montreal Protocol*, 16 Yale J. Int'l L. 519 (1991); Dinah Shelton, *The Participation of Nongovernmental Organizations in International Judicial Proceedings*, 88 Am. J. Int'l L. 611 (1994); Cynthia Price Cohen, *Toward Adoption of the United Nations Convention on the Rights of the Child: A Policy–Oriented Overview*, 83 ASIL Proc. 155 (1989); Mona Zulficar, *From Human Rights to Program Reality: Vienna, Cairo, and Beijing in Perspective*, 44 Am. U.L. Rev. 1017 (1995); Karen Knop, *Symposium: Feminist Inquiries into International Law*, 3 Transnat'l L. & Contemp. Probs. 293 (1993).

CHAPTER 4

INTERNATIONAL HUMAN RIGHTS OBLIGATIONS OF THE UNITED STATES

A. INTERNATIONAL LAW AND THE LAW OF THE UNITED STATES: IN GENERAL

International human rights law is enforced and implemented in the United States, and remedies for violations are provided, within the framework for the creation, implementation and enforcement of international legal obligations generally. Despite the experience of 200 years, some uncertainties remain about the respective roles of the President, the Senate, the Congress, and the courts within that framework.

This section considers the relationship between international law and domestic law in the United States in respects that are particularly relevant to international human rights law. How does the United States incur treaty obligations, and what are the consequences of treaties and of customary international law within the U.S. domestic legal system?

Restatement (Third) of the Foreign Relations Law of the United States

§§ 111, 114, 115, 303, 312, 314 (1987).

§ 111. International Law and Agreements as Law of the United States

(1) International law and international agreements of the United States are law of the United States and supreme over the law of the several States.

(2) Cases arising under international law or international agreements of the United States are within the Judicial Power of the United States and, subject to Constitutional and statutory limitations and requirements of justiciability, are within the jurisdiction of the federal courts.

(3) Courts in the United States are bound to give effect to international law and to international agreements of the United States, except that a "non-self-executing" agreement will not be given effect as law in the absence of necessary implementation.

(4) An international agreement of the United States is "non-self-executing"

> (a) if the agreement manifests an intention that it shall not become effective as domestic law without the enactment of implementing legislation,
>
> (b) if the Senate in giving consent to a treaty, or Congress by resolution, requires implementing legislation, or
>
> (c) if implementing legislation is constitutionally required.

Comment:

. . .

h. Self-executing and non-self-executing international agreements. In the absence of special agreement, it is ordinarily for the United States to decide how it will carry out its international obligations. Accordingly, the intention of the United States determines whether an agreement is to be self-executing in the United States or should await implementation by legislation or appropriate executive or administrative action. If the international agreement is silent as to its self-executing character and the intention of the United States is unclear, account must be taken of any statement by the President in concluding the agreement or in submitting it to the Senate for consent or to the Congress as a whole for approval, and of any expression by the Senate or by Congress in dealing with the agreement. See § 314, Comments *b* and *d*; § 303, Comment *d*. After the agreement is concluded, often the President must decide in the first instance whether the agreement is self-executing, *i.e.*, whether existing law is adequate to enable the United States to carry out its obligations, or whether further legislation is required. Congress may also consider whether new legislation is necessary and, if so, what it should provide. Whether an agreement is to be given effect without further legislation is an issue that a court must decide when a party seeks to invoke the agreement as law. Whether an agreement is or is not self-executing in the law of another state party to the agreement is not controlling for the United States.

Some provisions of an international agreement may be self-executing and others non-self-executing. If an international agreement or one of its provisions is non-self-executing, the United States is under an international obligation to adjust its laws and institutions as may be necessary to give effect to the agreement. The United States would have a reasonable time to do so before it could be deemed in default. There can, of course, be instances in which the United States Constitution, or previously enacted legislation, will be fully adequate to give effect to an apparently non-self-executing international agreement, thus obviating the need of adopting new legislation to implement it.

. . .

§ 114. Interpretation of Federal Statute in Light of International Law or Agreement

Where fairly possible, a United States statute is to be construed so as not to conflict with international law or with an international agreement of the United States.

§ 115.   Inconsistency Between International Law or Agreement and Domestic Law: Law of the United States

(1) (a) An act of Congress supersedes an earlier rule of international law or a provision of an international agreement as law of the United States if the purpose of the act to supersede the earlier rule or provision is clear or if the act and the earlier rule or provision cannot be fairly reconciled.

(b) That a rule of international law or a provision of an international agreement is superseded as domestic law does not relieve the United States of its international obligation or of the consequences of a violation of that obligation.

(2) A provision of a treaty of the United States that becomes effective as law of the United States supersedes as domestic law any inconsistent preexisting provision of a law or treaty of the United States.

(3) A rule of international law or a provision of an international agreement of the United States will not be given effect as law in the United States if it is inconsistent with the United States Constitution.

. . .

Reporters' Notes

. . .

3. *President's power to supersede international law or agreement.* There is authority for the view that the President has the power, when acting within his constitutional authority, to disregard a rule of international law or an agreement of the United States, notwithstanding that international law and agreements are law of the United States and that it is the President's duty under the Constitution to "take care that the Laws be faithfully executed." Article II, Section 3. Compare the authority of the President to terminate international agreements on behalf of the United States, § 339. That the courts will not compel the President to honor international law may be implied in Supreme Court statements that courts will give effect to international law "where there is no treaty, and no controlling executive or legislative act or judicial decision," and "in the absence of any treaty or other public act of their own government in relation to the matter." The Paquete Habana, 175 U.S. 677, 700, 708 (1900)....

§ 303.   Authority to Make International Agreements: Law of the United States

Subject to § 302(2),

(1) the President, with the advice and consent of the Senate, may make any international agreement of the United States in the form of a treaty;

(2) the President, with the authorization or approval of Congress, may make an international agreement dealing with any matter that falls within the powers of Congress and of the President under the Constitution;

(3) the President may make an international agreement as authorized by treaty of the United States;

(4) the President, on his own authority, may make an international agreement dealing with any matter that falls within his independent powers under the Constitution.

Comment:

a. United States terminology as to international agreements. United States terminology as to international agreements differs from that employed in the Vienna Convention. See Introductory Note to this Part. The United States Constitution in Article II, Section 2, provides that the President "shall have Power, by and with the Advice and Consent of the Senate, to make Treaties, provided two-thirds of the Senators present concur." It is therefore necessary to use a term other than "treaty" to refer to agreements made by other processes. Such agreements are sometimes referred to collectively as "international agreements other than treaties" and specific categories are referred to as "Congressional–Executive agreements" (Subsection (2)), "executive agreements pursuant to treaty" (Subsection (3)), and "sole executive agreements." (Subsection (4)). However, the term "treaty" is not always restricted to the meaning signified in Article II, Section 2. It has been interpreted to include other international agreements in the provisions of the Constitution defining the Judicial Power of the United States (Article III, Section 2) and the Supremacy Clause (Article VI). A reference to a "treaty" in an act of Congress has in certain contexts been construed to include other international agreements.

. . .

d. Advice and consent of Senate. Under Article II, Section 2 of the Constitution, quoted in Comment *a*, it is the President who "makes" a treaty by ratifying or acceding to it (§ 312, Comment *d*), but he may do so only after the Senate consents. Even if a treaty has received the advice and consent of the Senate, the President has discretion whether to make the treaty.

The Senate often has given its consent subject to conditions. Sometimes the Senate consents only on the basis of a particular understanding of the meaning of the treaty, or on condition that the United States obtain a modification of its terms or enter a reservation to it. See § 314. The Senate may also give its consent on conditions that do not require change in the treaty but relate to its domestic application, *e.g.*, that the treaty shall not be self-executing (§ 111(4)); or that agreements or appointments made in implementation of the treaty shall require the Senate's advice and consent.

There is no accepted doctrine indicating limits on the conditions the Senate may impose. Surely, a condition that has no relation to the treaty would be improper, for example, a requirement that the President dismiss or appoint some cabinet officer. But a condition having plausible relation to the treaty, or to its adoption or implementation, is presumably not improper, and if the President proceeds to make the treaty he is bound by the condition. . . .

. . .

Reporters' Notes

3. *Senate advice and consent.* There is confusion about terminology in United States treaty practice. Properly speaking, the Senate does not ratify a treaty; the Senate gives its consent to ratification. The President makes, ratifies, or accedes to a treaty on behalf of the United States. The Senate cannot amend a treaty or enter reservations to it. It can, however, give its consent to a treaty on condition that it be modified, or, in the case of a multilateral agreement, that the United States enter one or more reservations. The President need not fulfill those conditions, but he cannot proceed to make the treaty unless they are met, whether they concern the terms of the treaty or its implementation in the United States.

The President may decline to make the treaty after the Senate has approved it. Comment *d*. Sometimes there has been a substantial delay between consent by the Senate and ratification. . . .

The Constitution gives the President power to make treaties "by and with the Advice and Consent of the Senate," but Senate advice, as distinguished from consent, is not necessary. Presidents since the early years of the nation's history generally have refrained from formally consulting the Senate prior to negotiating a treaty. However, there has been a practice of notification and exchange of information and views with Senate committees or selected members of the Senate, and sometimes with committees or selected members of the House of Representatives, especially where legislative implementation might be necessary, or where approval as a Congressional–Executive agreement was contemplated. Infrequently, the Senate has given formal advice. . . .

§ 312.   Entry into Force of International Agreements

[omitted]

Comment:

. . .

j. Entry into force for the United States. An international agreement made by the United States in the form of a treaty enters into force for the United States when the President, with the advice and consent of the Senate, has ratified it or otherwise given official notification of assent to it, provided the agreement is also in force internationally. If the United States has deposited its ratification or given other notification of assent but the required number of states have not, the agreement is not in force internationally and cannot be in force for the United States. A treaty can be brought into force for the United States only after the Senate has given consent to it, and only subject to any conditions imposed by the Senate. See § 303, Comment *d*. Although a treaty or other international agreement is in force for the United States, it will not be given effect as law of the

United States to the extent that it is inconsistent with the United States Constitution. See § 115(3).

An international agreement made by the United States other than as a treaty enters into force for the United States upon signature unless the circumstances indicate a contrary intent, provided the agreement is also in force internationally. The agreement, or the legislation or treaty authorizing it, may provide for another date. An agreement subject to approval by Congress normally takes effect when, following approval or authorization by Congress, the President ratifies it or otherwise gives official notice of assent.

§ 314. Reservations and Understandings: Law of the United States

(1) When the Senate of the United States gives its advice and consent to a treaty on condition that the United States enter a reservation, the President, if he makes the treaty, must include the reservation in the instrument of ratification or accession, or otherwise manifest that the adherence of the United States is subject to the reservation.

(2) When the Senate gives its advice and consent to a treaty on the basis of a particular understanding of its meaning, the President, if he makes the treaty, must do so on the basis of the Senate's understanding.

Comment:

a. United States reservations. The United States has adhered to a number of international agreements with reservations.... Many reservations entered by the United States were requested by the Senate, but the President may, of course, enter a reservation on his own initiative. Since such a reservation modifies the treaty, it, too, requires Senate consent. If the Senate objects to a reservation that the President would enter, he cannot make the treaty with that reservation; the President is free, however, not to proceed with ratification of or accession to the agreement.

· · ·

b. Conditions imposed by Senate. Since the President can make a treaty only with the advice and consent of the Senate, he must give effect to conditions imposed by the Senate on its consent. The President generally includes a verbatim recitation of any proposed reservation, statement of understanding, or other declaration relevant to the application or interpretation of the treaty contained in the Senate resolution of consent, both in the instrument notifying the other state or the depositary of United States ratification or accession and in the proclamation of the treaty. See § 312, Comment *k*. The President may also communicate a Senate qualification separately. The President may also decline to proceed with ratification of the treaty. See § 303, Comment *d*.

If a treaty is ratified or acceded to by the United States with a reservation effective under the principles stated in § 313, the reservation is part of the treaty and is law of the United States. See § 111.

· · ·

   d. Understandings. A treaty that is ratified or acceded to by the
United States with a statement of understanding becomes effective in
domestic law (§ 111) subject to that understanding. If no such statement is
made, indication that the President or the Senate ascribed a particular
meaning to the treaty is relevant to the interpretation of the treaty by a
United States court in much the same way that the legislative history of a
statute is relevant to its interpretation. . . .

Reporters' Notes

·   ·   ·

   4. *Withdrawal of reservation.* If the Senate consented to a treaty
subject to a reservation by the United States, the President must request
Senate consent to withdraw that reservation. See, *e.g.*, the request for
consent to the withdrawal of a reservation to the Patent Cooperation
Treaty, 28 U.S.T. 7645, T.I.A.S. No. 8733, reprinted at 78 Am.J. Int'l L.
889 (1984).

John H. Jackson, *Status of Treaties in Domestic Legal Systems: A Policy Analysis*

86 Am. J. Int'l L. 310, 323–29 (1992).*

[In this Article, Professor Jackson discusses generally the policy considerations relevant to whether treaty norms should be given "direct application" in the domestic legal system of a hypothetical state, without a further
"act of transformation" by the legislature. Jackson notes that the terms
"directly applicable" and "self-executing" are very similar, but are not
always used identically. The following excerpts concern possible arguments
against direct applicability.]

   Another consideration militating against direct application is that
legislatures may wish to tailor the act of transformation in certain ways,
perhaps by rewording the treaty to match domestic circumstances. The
most obvious example would be those agreements (usually multilateral
treaties) whose official language is not the (legal) language of the implementing nation. But even when the language is the same, certain nuances
of usage may differ and legislatures may wish to express the norms in
accordance with local usage. The legislators may also wish to elaborate on
the treaty provisions, which they may view as ambiguous. (In the United
States, for example, the ambiguity of some treaty language has caused
concern that its direct application to individuals might violate constitutional standards of due process.) Language in the act of transformation may
clarify some ambiguities (for use by domestic courts and other applications), or specify policy choices left open (implicitly or expressly) under the
terms of the treaty. All of these eventualities may occur in the context of a
good faith effort fully to apply the treaty norms.

   Legislatures may also have other policies in mind. They may desire to
place their interpretation of the treaty norm on record. Perhaps the treaty
is ambiguous or leaves room for interpretation. The act of transformation

can be used to impose an interpretation for domestic law. Such an act (and the domestic action under it) will constitute "practice" of a treaty party and may then become relevant to later international interpretation of the treaty. In some cases, however, the domestic interpretation may concern domestic law only, such as by indicating the allocation within a country of authority to make certain decisions or to take certain actions in connection with the implementation of the treaty. Indeed, the act of transformation sometimes becomes part of a purely *internal* power struggle, and may be used by certain governmental institutions to enhance their powers vis-a-vis other governmental entities. (*Per contra*, advocates of direct application may have similar motives, viewing it as a way to forestall the adoption of alternative policies or allocations of power, or as a way to have them determined in accordance with their preferences.) Some constitutions may require a form of lawmaking that is circumvented by direct application of a treaty. In these circumstances, one might conclude that this should be a matter for national decision and that direct application should generally be avoided.

Legislatures may have still other motives in opposing direct application. For example, they may wish to limit direct application to portions of the treaty, or to apply it in ways that may not fully conform to the international obligation. Or a legislature may find it politic to delay application to allow internal consensus and acceptance to develop (or to wait out an imminent election!). Some of these examples suggest less than full "good faith application"—and even, perhaps, that the legislature desires to preserve the *option to breach* the treaty in its method of application. Is this approach to policy making desirable or valid? Certainly, traditional internationalists will frown on it. Yet national sovereigns often have prerogatives enabling them to breach treaties; why (say some) take away one particular mode? Moreover, some breaches may be "minor" and therefore preferable to the alternative of refusing to join the treaty altogether.

.   .   .

A related consideration is that national officials may fear that direct application will result in court determinations that their government is acting in violation of the treaty. Such findings could embarrass that government and undercut its effectiveness if it should participate in an international proceeding where it is charged with breach of the treaty obligation. For this reason, it has been said that some domestic courts tend to avoid determining that their government has breached an international treaty.

.   .   .

Direct application also prompts an interesting question about interpretation. If a treaty is directly applicable, it can be argued that an international body's interpretation of a question of international law is definitive in domestic law as well. According to this view, since the domestic law consists of the international treaty applied directly, the international interpretations are binding on the domestic legal institutions, including the courts. In contrast, an act of transformation is an act of the domestic legal system, and thus can be interpreted by that system's institutions, including the courts, just as the courts would interpret other legislation or domestic legal acts. However, even in the case of a directly applicable treaty norm, domestic courts may believe that they have the power of interpretation. They certainly have that power preliminarily until a definitive interpretation under international law is set forth. The interesting question is: What happens when an international interpretation of the treaty norm clashes with an interpretation by a domestic legal institution, in a case where the treaty norm is directly applicable? There is at least a suspicion, or hint, that the domestic legal institutions will "strain" to apply their own interpretation, through one or another legal technique.

. . .

During the last several decades, the United States has seen an exercise of congressional authority regarding direct applicability. Congress (sometimes as a whole, and sometimes the Senate acting to give its advice and consent) participates in most of the treaty making of the United States Government. Congress in some important cases has expressed the intent, either in its statutory approval of a treaty or in the legislative history of that statute, that the treaty should not be directly applied. Thus, the domestic U.S. law implementing the treaty is the law of the statute as passed by the Congress, i.e., the act of transformation. To the knowledge of this author, there has been no indication that the courts, or other institutions of the U.S. Government, would try to contravene this expression of congressional intent. It seems safe to conclude that the U.S. constitutional practice and status is that the treaty-making officials, as a unilateral matter, will control the determination of "self-executing" in the domestic legal system. This is probably, on balance, a wise constitutional solution. It enables the democratic parliament to control some of the problems posed by direct applicability. . . .

Louis Henkin, *Foreign Affairs and the United States Constitution*

198–203 (2d ed. 1996).*

Self-executing and Non-self-executing Treaties

In some constitutional systems, treaties are only international obligations, without effect as domestic law; it is for the parliament to translate them into law, and to enact any domestic legislation necessary to carry out their obligations. The U.S. Constitution established a different regime. The Supremacy Clause (Article VI, clause 2) provides:

> This Constitution, and the Laws of the United States which shall be made in Pursuance thereof; and all Treaties made, or which shall be made, under the Authority of the United States, shall be the supreme Law of the Land; and the Judges in every State shall be bound thereby,

any Thing in the Constitution or Laws of any State to the Contrary notwithstanding.

That clause, designed principally to assure the supremacy of treaties to state law, was interpreted early to mean also that treaties are law of the land of their own accord and do not require an act of Congress to translate them into law. Chief Justice Marshall said:

A treaty is in its nature a contract between two nations, not a legislative act. It does not generally effect, of itself, the object to be accomplished, especially so far as its operation is infra-territorial; but is carried into execution by the sovereign power of the respective parties to the instrument.

In the United States a different principle is established. Our constitution declares a treaty to be the law of the land. It is, consequently, to be regarded in courts of justice as equivalent to an act of the legislature, whenever it operates of itself without the aid of any legislative provision....

Not all treaties, however, are in fact law of the land of their own accord. Marshall continued:

... But when the terms of the stipulation import a contract, when either of the parties engages to perform a particular act, the treaty addresses itself to the political, not the judicial department; and the legislature must execute the contract before it can become a rule for the Court.[94]

Marshall distinguished between a treaty that "operates of itself"—the normal treaty provision—and the exceptional treaty (or treaty provision) that promises "to perform a particular act." Both kinds of treaty contain "promises," undertakings by the United States, binding under international law. But in a treaty that operates of itself, the undertaking by the United States automatically has the quality of law: the Executive and the courts are to give effect to the treaty undertaking without awaiting any act by Congress. We denominate such a treaty "self-executing."

Marshall, however, felt obliged to read an exception into the Supremacy Clause. A treaty by which the United States promises "to perform a particular act," creates an obligation which the United States must carry out through the political branch that has the constitutional authority to perform the act promised.* Thus, if the United States has undertaken to enact a law, say to make genocide a crime, Congress has the obligation to enact such law; the courts cannot carry out the United States' promise to

---

94. Foster v. Neilson, 27 U.S. (2 Pet.) 253, 314 (1829)....

* Sometimes federal legislation adopted prior to the treaty (and even for other purposes) may be available to implement a treaty obligation; sometimes the President may have authority to carry out those obligations without Congressional authorization. State law may also serve to implement non-self-executing obligations. Strictly, if a treaty is not self-executing it is not the treaty but the implementing legislation that is effectively "law of the land." Sometimes the implementing legislation gives the treaty itself legal effect or incorporates it by reference. [Footnote in original]

enact a law; they cannot treat the treaty in which the United States promised to enact a law as itself the law promised. Similarly, if the United States undertakes to do a particular act that in the United States can only be done by a law—say, to appropriate and pay money—that undertaking has to be carried out by Congress, the political branch that has constitutional authority to appropriate money. The courts cannot consider the treaty itself as the equivalent of the act of Congress required by the Constitution.

By the Constitution, as Marshall recognized, treaty undertakings are generally, in principle, self-executing. Marshall, it appears, felt compelled to infer an exception for a treaty promise that by its character could not be self-executing. Whether a treaty promise is of that special character that cannot be self-executing often depends on how the treaty undertaking is couched. And sometimes the terms of the treaty are ambiguous so that it is not clear whether the undertaking by the United States was such that it could "operate of itself" (and be enforced by the courts), or whether the United States promised only "to perform a particular act" which, under the Constitution, only Congress can do, not the treaty itself.

What the treaty promised may have to be determined in the first instance by the Executive who must decide whether to proceed to "take care" that the treaty itself be faithfully executed as law, or whether the Executive is required to seek implementation by Congress. Or, the courts, asked to give effect to the treaty as law, may have to decide whether the treaty should be read as promising only that the United States would "perform a particular act," that the political branches (usually Congress) would enact a law that would provide the benefits promised. The courts have considered that to be a matter of interpretation of the agreement,[**] but agreements have often been drafted without attention to that question so that it may be difficult to determine what was contemplated. In particular instances, United States negotiators have been careful to make clear that the treaty will require Congressional implementation: in the North Atlantic Treaty, for example, it was accepted by all parties that no events would put the United States automatically at war; if war were called for, Congress would have to declare it.

The question whether a treaty is itself law or is promising to enact law becomes more difficult when the United States adheres to a multilateral treaty in the drafting of which it was only one participant, or did not participate at all. Such a treaty, intended for adherence by states having different constitutional jurisprudence as to treaties, might be drafted so as

---

** They will, therefore, give Executive views on the question "great weight."

It is sometimes said that whether a treaty is to be self-executing or not depends on the intent of the United States at the time the treaty is made. But the intent of the United States may not be the intent of the other party or parties. It is more accurate to say that the question is what the parties intended and what the United States promised and the other party (or parties) accepted. In the case of a multilateral treaty, in particular, what a party promised is determined by interpreting the provision, not by the intent of the party (unless communicated by reservation or understanding). [Footnote in original]

to make it self-executing for states whose jurisprudence contemplates such effect for treaties, and obligating others to execute the obligation promptly, but often the drafters do not have that problem in mind.

What seems clear, from the language of the Constitution and of John Marshall, is that in the United States the strong presumption should be that a treaty or a treaty provision is self-executing, and that a non-self-executing promise is highly exceptional. A tendency in the Executive Branch and in the courts to interpret treaties and treaty provisions as non-self-executing runs counter to the language, and spirit, and history of Article VI of the Constitution.

In recent years, the President, on his own initiative or at the behest of the U.S. Senate by declaration attached to its consent, has sometimes purported to declare non-self-executing treaties that by their terms and by their character are (or could well be) self-executing, could "operate of themselves" and be given effect as law of the land. The Executive branch and the Senate have pursued that practice in particular in relation to U.S. adherence to human rights covenants and conventions.

In my view, that recent practice, accepted without significant discussion, is "anti-Constitutional" in spirit and highly problematic as a matter of law.** In the Supremacy Clause, the Constitution declared treaties—generally, presumably all treaties—to be the law of the land. John Marshall read an exception into that Article in respect of treaties that by their character could not be self-executing; nothing in the Constitution, or in Chief Justice John Marshall's opinion, suggested that treaties which the Constitution declares to be law of the land need not be "faithfully executed" by the President, or enforced by the courts, because the President or the Senate (or both) so decided. If the treaty-makers thought it was necessary or desirable to include a role for Congress in special cases, such as in taking the United States into war pursuant to the North Atlantic Treaty, there was no suggestion—until the human rights conventions of recent date—that there was a general power for one or both of the treaty-makers to do so for any treaty, at will.

. . .

The difference between self-executing and non-self-executing treaties is commonly misunderstood. Whether a treaty is self-executing or not, it is legally binding on the United States. Whether it is self-executing or not, it is supreme law of the land. If it is not self-executing, Marshall said, it is not "a rule for the Court"; he did not suggest that it is not law for the President or for Congress. It is their obligation to see to it that it is faithfully implemented; it is their obligation to do what is necessary to make it a rule for the courts if the treaty requires that it be a rule for the

---

** . . .

Of course, every self-executing treaty might have been written as a promise to execute, but that requires the agreement of other parties, which might prove to be partic-ularly difficult in multilateral negotiations, and impossible when the United States joins a treaty already concluded. [Footnote in original]

courts, of if making it a rule for the courts is a necessary or proper means for the United States to carry out its obligation.

Notes on Self–Executing and Non–Self–Executing Treaties

1. In his article, Professor Jackson distinguishes between two aspects of the domestic application of treaty provisions, "direct applicability" and "invocability." Direct applicability concerns whether the treaty norm has been made a norm of the domestic legal system at all. Invocability concerns the particular circumstances in which parties have the ability to invoke or rely upon the treaty norm.

Professor Vázquez discerns four distinct aspects to the doctrine of "self-executing" treaties, and attributes much of the confusion surrounding that subject to the failure to distinguish among them:

> [There are] four grounds on which a court might legitimately conclude that legislative action is necessary to authorize it to enforce a treaty, notwithstanding the Supremacy Clause. First, legislative action is necessary if the parties to the treaty (or perhaps the U.S. treaty makers alone) intended that the treaty's object be accomplished through intervening acts of legislation. Second, legislative action is necessary if the norm the treaty establishes is "addressed" as a constitutional matter to the legislature. Third, legislative action is necessary if the treaty purports to accomplish what under our Constitution may be accomplished only by statute. Finally, legislation is necessary if no law confers a right of action on a plaintiff seeking to enforce the treaty.

Carlos Manuel Vázquez, *The Four Doctrines of Self–Executing Treaties*, 89 Am. J. Int'l L. 695, 696–97 (1995). See also Yuji Iwasawa, *The Doctrine of Self–Executing Treaties in the United States: A Critical Analysis*, 26 Va. J. Int'l L. 627 (1986).

2. Professor Jackson identifies a number of considerations for making treaty provisions not "directly applicable." Would any of these considerations justify the Senate in conditioning its consent to ratification of a multilateral treaty on a stipulation that the treaty would not be self-executing in the United States? Or would such a condition be inconsistent with the Supremacy Clause (or its spirit)? If such conditions are sometimes permissible, would any of the considerations identified by Professor Jackson justify the United States in stipulating that the entire ICCPR be non-self-executing (as the U.S. has in fact done)? In making particular provisions of the ICCPR non-self-executing?

3. Customary international law, including customary human rights law, is "self-executing" in the United States, in the sense that no statutory authorization is required before a U.S. court can apply it as domestic law. Many customary international law norms, however, create obligations only between governments, and do not create enforceable private rights for individuals. See Restatement § 111, Reporters' Note 4. Moreover, as reflected in Restatement § 115 and Reporters' Note 3, supra, courts will not

give effect to customary international law in the face of a superseding inconsistent act of Congress or a superseding inconsistent act of the President. This issue is further explored in *Garcia-Mir v. Meese*, and notes following, in Section C infra.

B.   UNITED STATES ADHERENCE TO HUMAN RIGHTS TREATIES

The United States played a leading part in the promulgation of the Universal Declaration of Human Rights and in converting the Declaration into the two principal human rights covenants, but as of July 1999 the United States is a party to only a few international human rights agreements. This section examines the U.S. record of adherence to human rights treaties, including the record of attaching qualifications to its adherence. The section focuses specifically on the reservations, understandings and declarations that accompanied the U.S. ratification of the ICCPR, and the position taken by the Human Rights Committee concerning the permissible scope of reservations to the ICCPR.

President Truman sought Senate consent to ratification of the Genocide Convention in 1949 but the Senate did not act. Between 1950 and 1955 Senator Bricker led a campaign to have the U.S. Constitution amended, in effect to prevent U.S. adherence to international human rights agreements. Recognizing that concern over the possible effects of such agreements within the United States had led to support for the Bricker Amendment, Secretary of State Dulles announced that President Eisenhower would not seek Senate approval of any of the principal human rights agreements.*

Subsequent Presidents slowly moved to a more affirmative policy. The first deviations from the Eisenhower policy came under President Kennedy. In 1963 President Kennedy obtained Senate consent to ratification of three human rights instruments: the **U.N. Supplementary Convention on the Abolition of Slavery, the Slave Trade and Institutions and Practices Similar to Slavery**; the **I.L.O. Convention for the Abolition of Forced Labor**, and the **U.N. Convention on the Political Rights of Women**.

The Senate gave consent and the United States ratified the **U.N. Protocol Relating to the Status of Refugees** in 1968, and the U.S. acceded to the **Convention on the Political Rights of Women** in 1976. In 1978 President Carter sent the following four instruments to the Senate for consent, although with important reservations: the **International Covenant on Civil and Political Rights (ICCPR)**; the **International Covenant on Economic, Social, and Cultural Rights (ICESCR)**; the

---

* See Treaties and Executive Agreements: Hearings on S.J. Res. 1 before a Subcomm. of the Sen. Comm. on the Judiciary, 83rd Cong., 1st Sess. 823–25 (1953) (statement of Secretary John Foster Dulles); Duane Tananbaum, The Bricker Amendment Controversy: A Test of Eisenhower's Political Leadership (1988). For some reasons why the U.S. refused to ratify human rights agreements, see Louis Henkin, The Age of Rights 74–78 (1989); Natalie Hevener Kaufman, Human Rights Treaties and the Senate: A History of Opposition (1990).

International Convention on the Elimination of All Forms of Racial Discrimination (CERD); and the **American Convention on Human Rights**. President Carter also requested Senate consent to the **International Convention on the Elimination of All Forms of Discrimination Against Women (CEDAW)** in 1980. The Senate took no action with respect to these instruments.

In 1984, President Reagan asked the Senate to consent to ratification of the **Genocide Convention**, and the Senate gave consent, accompanied by a package of reservations, understandings and declarations (RUDs), in 1986. Ratification was postponed until Congress had enacted implementing legislation; Congress passed the legislation in 1988, and the U.S. ratified the Convention later that year.

In 1990, the Senate gave consent to the ratification of the **U.N. Convention Against Torture and Other Cruel, Inhuman or Degrading Treatment or Punishment**. The consent was accompanied by RUDs, including a declaration that the Convention was not self-executing, and ratification was postponed until the enactment of implementing legislation. In 1992, Congress passed the Torture Victim Protection Act, discussed in Section D(2) infra, and in 1994 Congress passed the Torture Convention implementation legislation, 18 U.S.C. §§ 2340–2340B, whereupon the United States ratified the Convention.

In 1992, President Bush asked the Senate to consent to the **ICCPR**. The Senate gave consent with a series of RUDs, including a declaration that the Covenant was not self-executing. (These RUDs are reproduced below.) The U.S. deposited its instrument of ratification in June 1992. The Bush Administration indicated that it would not seek any implementing legislation, apparently because it held the view that none was necessary. As of July 1999, Congress has enacted no legislation designed to implement the Covenant.

In 1993, Secretary of State Warren Christopher announced that the Clinton Administration intended to seek Senate approval of **CERD, CEDAW**, the **American Convention**, and the **ICESCR**. In 1994, the Senate gave its consent to **CERD**, accompanied by RUDs including a declaration that the Convention was not self-executing. (The RUDs are reproduced at P. 1043 infra.) As of July 1999, Congress has passed no implementing legislation.

In 1994, the Senate Committee on Foreign Relations recommended Senate consent to **CEDAW**, subject to a series of RUDs, including a declaration that the Convention was not self-executing. As of July 1999, the full Senate has not acted on the Convention. (The proposed RUDs are reproduced supra, p. 364.) Also as of July 1999, there has been no Senate action on the **American Convention** or the **ICESCR**.

U.S. Reservations, Understandings and Declarations to the ICCPR

138 Cong. Rec. S4781–01 (1992).

I.   The Senate's advice and consent is subject to the following reservations:

(1) That Article 20 does not authorize or require legislation or other action by the United States that would restrict the right of free speech and association protected by the Constitution and laws of the United States.

(2) That the United States reserves the right, subject to its Constitutional constraints, to impose capital punishment on any person (other than a pregnant woman) duly convicted under existing or future laws permitting the imposition of capital punishment, including such punishment for crimes committed by persons below eighteen years of age.

(3) That the United States considers itself bound by Article 7 to the extent that "cruel, inhuman or degrading treatment or punishment" means the cruel and unusual treatment or punishment prohibited by the Fifth, Eighth and/or Fourteenth Amendments to the Constitution of the United States.

(4) That because U.S. law generally applies to an offender the penalty in force at the time the offense was committed, the United States does not adhere to the third clause of paragraph 1 of Article 15.

(5) That the policy and practice of the United States are generally in compliance with and supportive of the Covenant's provisions regarding treatment of juveniles in the criminal justice system. Nevertheless, the United States reserves the right, in exceptional circumstances, to treat juveniles as adults, notwithstanding paragraphs 2(b) and 3 of Article 10 and paragraph 4 of Article 14. The United States further reserves to these provisions with respect to individuals who volunteer for military service prior to age 18.

II.   The Senate's advice and consent is subject to the following understandings, which shall apply to the obligations of the United States under this Covenant:

(1) That the Constitution and laws of the United States guarantee all persons equal protection of the law and provide extensive protections against discrimination. The United States understands distinctions based upon race, colour, sex, language, religion, political or other opinion, national or social origin, property, birth or any other status—as those terms are used in Article 2, paragraph 1 and Article 26—to be permitted when such distinctions are, at minimum, rationally related to a legitimate governmental objective. The United States further understands the prohibition in paragraph 1 of Article 4 upon discrimination, in time of public emergency, based "solely" on the status of race, color, sex, language, religion or social origin not to bar distinctions that may have a disproportionate effect upon persons of a particular status.

(2) That the United States understands the right to compensation referred to in Articles 9(5) and 14(6) to require the provision of effective and enforceable mechanisms by which a victim of an unlawful arrest or detention or a miscarriage of justice may seek and, where justified, obtain compensation from either the responsible individual or the appropriate governmental entity. Entitlement to compensation may be subject to the reasonable requirements of domestic law.

(3) That the United States understands the reference to "exceptional circumstances" in paragraph 2(a) of Article 10 to permit the imprisonment of an accused person with convicted persons where appropriate in light of an individual's overall dangerousness, and to permit accused persons to waive their right to segregation from convicted persons. The United States further understands that paragraph 3 of Article 10 does not diminish the goals of punishment, deterrence, and incapacitation as additional legitimate purposes for a penitentiary system.

(4) That the United States understands that subparagraphs 3(b) and (d) of Article 14 do not require the provision of a criminal defendant's counsel of choice when the defendant is provided with court-appointed counsel on grounds of indigence, when the defendant is financially able to retain alternative counsel, or when imprisonment is not imposed. The United States further understands that paragraph 3(e) does not prohibit a requirement that the defendant make a showing that any witness whose attendance he seeks to compel is necessary for his defense. The United States understands the prohibition upon double jeopardy in paragraph 7 to apply only when the judgment of acquittal has been rendered by a court of the same governmental unit, whether the Federal Government or a constituent unit, as is seeking a new trial for the same cause.

(5) That the United States understands that this Convention shall be implemented by the Federal Government to the extent that it exercises legislative and judicial jurisdiction over the matters covered therein, and otherwise by the state and local governments; to the extent that state and local governments exercise jurisdiction over such matters, the Federal Government shall take measures appropriate to the Federal system to the end that the competent authorities of the state or local governments may take appropriate measures for the fulfillment of the Covenant.

III.   The Senate's advice and consent is subject to the following declarations:

(1) That the United States declares that the provisions of Articles 1 through 27 of the Covenant are not self-executing.

(2) That it is the view of the United States that States Party to the Covenant should wherever possible refrain from imposing any restrictions or limitations on the exercise of the rights recognized and protected by the Covenant, even when such restrictions and limitations are permissible under the terms of the Covenant. For the United States, Article 5, paragraph 2, which provides that fundamental human rights existing in any State Party may not be diminished on the pretext that the Covenant recognizes them to a lesser extent, has particular relevance to Article 19, paragraph 3, which would permit certain restrictions on the freedom of expression. The United States declares that it will continue to adhere to the requirements and constraints of its Constitution in respect to all such restrictions and limitations.

(3) That the United States declares that it accepts the competence of the Human Rights Committee to receive and consider communications

under Article 41 in which a State Party claims that another State Party is not fulfilling its obligations under the Covenant.

(4) That the United States declares that the right referred to in Article 47 may be exercised only in accordance with international law.

IV. The Senate's advice and consent is subject to the following proviso, which shall not be included in the instrument of ratification to be deposited by the President:

Nothing in this Covenant requires or authorizes legislation, or other action, by the United States of America prohibited by the Constitution of the United States as interpreted by the United States.

Notes on the U.S. Reservations, Understandings, and Declarations to the ICCPR

1. What are the consequences of the RUDs for

(a) The international responsibilities of the United States?

(b) The responsibility of the federal government and the states respectively for compliance with the Covenant?

(c) The enforcement of the Covenant in the courts of the United States and of the States?

Recall that, in international law, the character of a provision as a "reservation," an "understanding," or a "declaration" depends on its purported legal effect, not solely on the label applied by its authors. See Restatement of Foreign Relations Law § 313, supra p. 307.

2. Among the RUD's, the President and the Senate have attached a declaration that the treaty shall not be self-executing. See above; and compare the Torture Convention, and the proposed ratification of CEDAW. Such a declaration is not a reservation, since it does not modify the international obligation of the United States, and it concerns only the place of the treaty in U.S. law. See Restatement § 111(3), (4), Comments h, i, § 313 Comment g.

In the case of the Genocide Convention, the Senate avoided some of the controversy about declarations that a treaty be non-self-executing, by giving consent on condition that the instrument of U.S. ratification not be deposited until Congress had enacted necessary implementing legislation.

3. For more on RUDs and U.S. policy on the ratification of human rights conventions, see, e.g., Louis Henkin, *U.S. Ratification of Human Rights Conventions: The Ghost of Senator Bricker*, 89 Am. J. Int'l L. 341 (1995); *Symposium: The Ratification of the International Covenant on Civil and Political Rights*, 42 DePaul L. Rev. 1167 (1993). Consider also the following argument:

Human rights experts critical of the United States' reservations to the CCPR have described them as designed to ensure that the U.S. was taking on no new obligations, beyond what its constitution and laws already required. [citing Henkin, supra] This rhetoric should not be misunderstood. The U.S. certainly identified a series of respects in which the CCPR would have imposed new obligations, and sought to avoid them. But the reservations contain no systematic exclusion of new obligations, and the U.S. did not explicitly reserve against every aspect of the CCPR that went beyond existing law.

Gerald L. Neuman, *The Global Dimension of RFRA*, 14 Const. Commentary 33, 43 n.58 (1997).

Assume that a provision of the ICCPR imposes an obligation that is equivalent to an obligation already imposed by the U.S. Constitution, as currently interpreted, and that the United States has entered no reservation to that provision of the ICCPR. What is the legal significance of that provision of the ICCPR for the United States? If at a later date the Supreme Court changes its interpretation of the Constitution, and provides less protection for the right in question, what would the legal significance of that provision be then?

4.   On December 10, 1998, in connection with the commemoration of the fiftieth anniversary of the Universal Declaration, President Clinton issued an Executive Order on Implementation of Human Rights Treaties. Exec. Order No. 13107, 63 Fed. Reg. 68,991 (1998). The order declares the "policy and practice of the Government of the United States ... fully to respect and implement its obligations under the human rights treaties to which it is a party," including the ICCPR, the Convention Against Torture, and CERD. The order directs executive departments and agencies to perform their functions in a manner that respects relevant human rights obligations, and creates an Interagency Working Group on Human Rights Treaties to provide guidance, oversight and coordination in such matters. The order specifically includes in the Working Group representatives of the Assistant to the President for National Security Affairs (as chair), the State Department, the Justice Department, the Labor Department, the Defense Department, and the Joint Chiefs of Staff. The significance of the Executive Order and the Interagency Working Group remains to be seen. The order expressly states that it does not create any right or benefit enforceable by any party, or create any justiciable obligations.

How does the procedure created by this Executive Order compare with judicial enforcement as a vehicle for the implementation of the United States Government's human rights obligations?

Notes on the Human Rights Committee's Response to RUDs

1.   In its Consideration of Reports Submitted by States Parties Under Article 40 of the Covenant: Comments of the Human Rights Committee, 53d Sess., 1413th mtg., at 4, U.N. Doc. CCPR/C/79/Add.50 (1995), the Human Rights Committee criticized the extent of the U.S. RUDs, and asserted that some of them were incompatible with the object and purpose of the Covenant:

14.   The Committee regrets the extent of the State party's reservations, declarations and understandings to the Covenant. It believes that, taken together, they intended to ensure that the United States has accepted what is already the law of the United States. The Committee is also particularly concerned at reservations to article 6, paragraph 5, and article 7 of the Covenant, which it believes to be incompatible with the object and purpose of the Covenant.

. . .

16.   The Committee is concerned about the excessive number of offenses punishable by the death penalty in a number of States, the number of death sentences handed down by courts, and the long stay on death row which, in specific instances, may amount to a breach of article 7 of the Covenant. It deplores the recent expansion of the death penalty under federal law and the re-establishment of the death penalty in certain States. It also deplores provisions in the legislation of a number of States which allow the death penalty to be pronounced for crimes committed by persons under 18 and the actual instances where such sentences have been pronounced and executed. It also regrets that, in some cases, there appears to have been lack of protection from the death penalty of those mentally retarded.

. . .

27.   The Committee recommends that the State party review its reservations, declarations and understandings with a view to withdrawing them, in particular reservations to article 6, paragraph 5, and article 7 of the Covenant. . . .

2.   The Human Rights Committee's review of the U.S. Report under the ICCPR was preceded by the issuance of General Comment No. 24, General comment on issues relating to reservations made upon ratification or accession to the Covenant or the Optional Protocols thereto, or in relation to declarations under article 41 of the Covenant, U.N. Doc. CCPR/C/21/Rev.1/Add.6 (1994). In that General Comment, the Committee stated:

. . .

8.   Reservations that offend peremptory norms would not be compatible with the object and purpose of the Covenant. Although treaties that are mere exchanges of obligations between States allow them to reserve *inter se* application of rules of general international law, it is otherwise in human rights treaties, which are for the benefit of persons within their jurisdiction. Accordingly, provisions in the Covenant that represent customary international law (and *a fortiori* when they have the character of peremptory norms) may not be the subject of reservations. Accordingly, a State may not reserve the right to engage in slavery, to torture, to subject persons to cruel, inhumane or degrading treatment or punishment, to arbitrarily deprive persons of their lives, to arbitrarily arrest and detain persons, to deny freedom of thought, conscience and religion, to presume a person guilty unless he proves his innocence, to execute pregnant women or children, to permit the

advocacy of national, racial or religious hatred, to deny to persons of marriageable age the right to marry, or to deny to minorities the right to enjoy their own culture, profess their own religion, or use their own language. And while reservations to particular clauses of article 14 may be acceptable, a general reservation to the right to a fair trial would not be.

9.   Applying more generally the object and purpose test to the Covenant, the Committee notes that. . . . a reservation to the obligation to respect and ensure the rights, and to do so on a non-discriminatory basis (Article 2(1)) would not be acceptable. Nor may a State reserve an entitlement not to take the necessary steps at the domestic level to give effect to the rights of the Covenant (Article 2(2)).

. . .

11.   The Covenant consists not just of the specified rights, but of important supportive guarantees. These guarantees provide the necessary framework for securing the rights in the Covenant and are thus essential to its object and purpose. Some operate at the national level and some at the international level. Reservations designed to remove these guarantees are thus not acceptable. Thus, a State could not make a reservation to article 2, paragraph 3, of the Covenant, indicating that it intends to provide no remedies for human rights violations. Guarantees such as these are an integral part of the structure of the Covenant and underpin its efficacy. The Covenant also envisages, for the better attainment of its stated objectives, a monitoring role for the Committee. Reservations that purport to evade that essential element in the design of the Covenant, which is also directed to securing the enjoyment of the rights, are also incompatible with its object and purpose. A State may not reserve the right not to present a report and have it considered by the Committee. The Committee's role under the Covenant, whether under article 40 or under the Optional Protocol, necessarily entails interpreting the provisions of the Covenant and the development of a jurisprudence. Accordingly, a reservation that rejects the Committee's competence to interpret the requirements of any provisions of the Covenant would also be contrary to the object and purpose of that treaty.

. . .

17.   As indicated above, it is the Vienna Convention on the Law of Treaties that provides the definition of reservations and also the application of the object and purpose test in the absence of other specific provisions. But the Committee believes that its provisions on the role of State objections in relation to reservations are inappropriate to address the problem of reservations to human rights treaties. Such treaties, and the Covenant specifically, are not a web of inter-State exchanges of mutual obligations. They concern the endowment of individuals with rights. The principle of inter-State reciprocity has no place, save perhaps in the limited context of reservations to declarations on the Committee's competence under article 41. And because

the operation of the classic rules on reservations is so inadequate for the Covenant, States have often not seen any legal interest in or need to object to reservations. The absence of protest by States cannot imply that a reservation is either compatible or incompatible with the object and purpose of the Covenant. Objections have been occasional, made by some States but not others, and on grounds not always specified; when an objection is made, it often does not specify a legal consequence, or sometimes even indicates that the objecting party none the less does not regard the Covenant as not in effect as between the parties concerned. In short, the pattern is so unclear that it is not safe to assume that a non-objecting State thinks that a particular reservation is acceptable. In the view of the Committee, because of the special characteristics of the Covenant as a human rights treaty, it is open to question what effect objections have between States *inter se*. However, an objection to a reservation made by States may provide some guidance to the Committee in its interpretation as to its compatibility with the object and purpose of the Covenant.

18.   It necessarily falls to the Committee to determine whether a specific reservation is compatible with the object and purpose of the Covenant. This is in part because, as indicated above, it is an inappropriate task for States parties in relation to human rights treaties, and in part because it is a task that the Committee cannot avoid in the performance of its functions. In order to know the scope of its duty to examine a State's compliance under article 40 or a communication under the first Optional Protocol, the Committee has necessarily to take a view on the compatibility of a reservation with the object and purpose of the Covenant and with general international law. Because of the special character of a human rights treaty, the compatibility of a reservation with the object and purpose of the Covenant must be established objectively, by reference to legal principles, and the Committee is particularly well placed to perform this task. The normal consequence of an unacceptable reservation is not that the Covenant will not be in effect at all for a reserving party. Rather, such a reservation will generally be severable, in the sense that the Covenant will be operative for the reserving party without benefit of the reservation.

3.   General Comment 24 has proven controversial. The statement in paragraph 18 that "it necessarily falls to the Committee to determine whether a specific reservation is compatible with the object and purpose of the Covenant" was challenged by both the United States and the United Kingdom. The response of the United States included the following:

1.   Role of the Committee

The last sentence of paragraph 11 states that "a reservation that rejects the Committee's competence to interpret the requirements of any provisions of the Covenant would also be contrary to the object and purpose of that treaty."

. . .

In this regard, the analysis in paragraphs 16–20 regarding which body has the legal authority to make determinations concerning the permissibility of specific reservations, is of considerable concern. Here the Committee appears to reject the established rules of interpretation of treaties as set forth in the Vienna Convention on the Law of Treaties and in customary international law. The General Comment states, for example, that the established provisions of the Vienna Convention are "inappropriate to address the problem of reservations to human rights treaties ... [as to which] [t]he principle of inter-State reciprocity has no place, save perhaps in the limited context of reservations to declarations on the Committee's competence under article 41".

Moreover, the Committee appears to dispense with the established procedures for determining the permissibility of reservations and to divest States Parties of any role in determining the meaning of the Covenant, which they drafted and joined, and of the extent of their treaty obligations. In its view, objections from other States Parties may not "specify a legal consequence" and States with genuine objections may not always voice them, so that "it is not safe to assume that a non-objecting State thinks that a particular reservation is acceptable". Consequently, because "the operation of the classic rules on reservations is so inadequate for the Covenant, ...[i]t necessarily falls to the Committee to determine whether a specific reservation is compatible with the object and purpose of the Covenant".

The Committee's position, while interesting, runs contrary to the Covenant scheme and international law.

2. Acceptability of reservations: governing legal principles

The question of the status of the Committee's view is of some significance in light of the apparent lines of analysis concerning the permissibility of reservations in paragraphs 8–9. Those paragraphs reflects the view that reservations offending peremptory norms of international law would not be compatible with the object and purposes of the Covenant, nor may reservations be taken to Covenant provisions which represent customary international law.

It is clear that a State cannot exempt itself from a peremptory norm of international law by making a reservation to the Covenant. It is not at all clear that a State cannot choose to exclude one means of enforcement of particular norms by reserving against inclusion of those norms in its Covenant obligations.

The proposition that any reservation which contravenes a norm of customary international law is *per se* incompatible with the object and purpose of this or any other convention, however, is a much more significant and sweeping premise. It is, moreover, wholly unsupported by and is in fact contrary to international law. As recognized in the paragraph 10 analysis of non-derogable rights, an "object and purpose" analysis by its nature requires consideration of the particular treaty, right, and reservation in question.

. . .

Observations by the United States of America on General Comment No. 24 (52) U.N. GAOR, 50th Sess., at 131–32, U.N. Doc. A/50/40 (1995), Annex VI. See also Observations by the United Kingdom on General Comment No. 24, U.N. GAOR, 50th Sess., at 135–39, U.N. Doc. A/50/40 (1995), Annex VI.

The International Law Commission also responded to the assertion by the Human Rights Committee that it possessed the authority to determine the validity of a reservation, as follows:

. . .

5. The Commission also considers that where these treaties are silent on the subject, the monitoring bodies established thereby are competent to comment upon and express recommendations with regard, *inter alia*, to the admissibility of reservations by States, in order to carry out the functions assigned to them;

6. The Commission stresses that this competence of the monitoring bodies does not exclude or otherwise affect the traditional modalities of control by the contracting parties, on the one hand, in accordance with [articles 19–23] of the Vienna Conventions of 1969 and 1986 and, where appropriate, by the organs for settling any dispute that may arise concerning the interpretation or application of the treaties;

. . .

8. The Commission notes that the legal force of the findings made by monitoring bodies in the exercise of their power to deal with reservations cannot exceed that resulting from the powers given to them for the performance of their general monitoring role;

. . .

Report of the International Law Commission on the work of its forty-ninth session, U.N. GAOR, 52d Sess., Supp. No. 10, at 126, U.N. Doc. A/52/10 (1997).

4. Why does the Human Rights Committee interpret its powers in the manner described in General Comment 24? Is the Committee's interpretation of its powers persuasive? Is the Committee's interpretation of the limitations on the compatibility of particular categories of reservations with the object and purpose of the Covenant persuasive?

5. In 1996, Michael Domingues was sentenced to death pursuant to Nevada law for murders committed when he was 16 years old. He filed a motion for correction of illegal sentence on the grounds that the sentence violated Article 6 of the ICCPR, which prohibits execution for a crime committed by a person under 18. Although the United States had entered a reservation to that article, he argued that the reservation was invalid and therefore ineffective. The Nevada Supreme Court upheld the sentence. *Domingues v. Nevada*, 961 P.2d 1279 (Nev.1998). In June 1999, on petition

for certiorari, the Supreme Court invited the Solicitor General to file a brief in the case "expressing the views of the United States." *Domingues v. Nevada*, 119 S.Ct. 2044 (1999).

C.   JUDICIAL ENFORCEMENT OF INTERNATIONAL HUMAN RIGHTS OBLIGATIONS OF THE UNITED STATES

To the extent that domestic legal rights—constitutional, statutory, or common law—already exceed international human rights standards, reliance on international human rights as such may be unnecessary in the United States. Human rights litigation against state or federal officials is therefore likely to be concentrated in areas where international standards require more than domestic standards. In some instances, as we have seen, the United States has sought to avoid obligations to comply with higher international standards, by entering reservations to human rights treaties. In other instances, the United States has sought to avoid making its treaty obligations directly enforceable in court, by declaring them non-self-executing.

The cases in this section illustrate the efforts of litigants to invoke international human rights obligations against state and federal officials, and some of the questions that those efforts raise: when treaty provisions are self-executing in character, how a norm of customary international law can be proven, and when a "controlling executive or legislative act" supersedes customary international law.

Sei Fujii v. State
Supreme Court of California, 1952.
242 P.2d 617.

■ GIBSON, CHIEF JUSTICE.

Plaintiff, an alien Japanese who is ineligible to citizenship under our naturalization laws, appeals from a judgment declaring that certain land purchased by him in 1948 had escheated to the state. There is no treaty between this country and Japan which confers upon plaintiff the right to own land, and the sole question presented on this appeal is the validity of the California alien land law. [The statute provided that aliens who were ineligible to citizenship under the U.S. naturalization laws could not (inter alia) acquire any interest in real property within the state, unless a U.S. treaty provided otherwise. Property acquired in violation of the statute would escheat to the state. Japanese nationals were categorically ineligible for naturalization until 1952.]

United Nations Charter

It is first contended that the land law has been invalidated and superseded by the provisions of the United Nations Charter pledging the member nations to promote the observance of human rights and fundamental freedoms without distinction as to race. Plaintiff relies on statements in the preamble and in Articles 1, 55 and 56 of the Charter, 59 Stat. 1035.[2]

It is not disputed that the charter is a treaty, and our federal Constitution provides that treaties made under the authority of the United States are part of the supreme law of the land and that the judges in every state are bound thereby. U.S.Const., art. VI. A treaty, however, does not automatically supersede local laws which are inconsistent with it unless the treaty provisions are self-executing. In the words of Chief Justice Marshall: A treaty is "to be regarded in courts of justice as equivalent to an act of the Legislature, whenever it operates of itself, without the aid of any legislative provision. But when the terms of the stipulation import a contract—when either of the parties engages to perform a particular act, the treaty addresses itself to the political, not the judicial department; and the Legislature must execute the contract, before it can become a rule for the court." Foster v. Neilson, 1829, 2 Pet. 253.[3]

In determining whether a treaty is self-executing courts look to the intent of the signatory parties as manifested by the language of the instrument, and, if the instrument is uncertain, recourse may be had to the circumstances surrounding its execution. In order for a treaty provision to be operative without the aid of implementing legislation and to have the force and effect of a statute, it must appear that the framers of the treaty intended to prescribe a rule that, standing alone, would be enforceable in the courts.

2. The preamble recites that "We the peoples of the United Nations determined * * * to reaffirm faith in fundamental human rights * * * and for these ends * * * to employ international machinery for the promotion of the economic and social advancement of all peoples, have resolved to combine our efforts to accomplish these aims."

Article 1 states that "The Purposes of the United Nations are: * * * 3. To achieve international co-operation in solving international problems of an economic, social, cultural, or humanitarian character, and in promoting and encouraging respect for human rights and for fundamental freedoms for all without distinction as to race, sex, language, or religion; * * *."

Articles 55 and 56 appear in Chapter IX, entitled "International Economic and Social Cooperation." Article 55 provides: "With a view to the creation of conditions of stability and well-being which are necessary for peaceful and friendly relations among nations based on respect for the principle of equal rights and self-determination of peoples, the United Nations shall promote:

'a. higher standards of living, full employment, and conditions of economic and social progress and development;

'b. solutions of international economic, social, health, and related problems; and international cultural and educational cooperation; and

'c. universal respect for, and observance of, human rights and fundamental freedoms for all without distinction as to race, sex, language, or religion.' "

Article 56 provides: "All Members pledge themselves to take joint and separate action in cooperation with the Organization for the achievement of the purposes set forth in Article 55."

3. In Foster v. Neilson, certain treaty provisions were held not to be self-executing on the basis of construction of the English version of the document. Subsequently, upon consideration of the Spanish version, the provisions in question were held to be self-executing. United States v. Percheman, 7 Pet. 51. Chief Justice Marshall's language in the Foster case, however, has been quoted with approval in later cases.

It is clear that the provisions of the preamble and of Article 1 of the charter which are claimed to be in conflict with the alien land law are not self-executing. They state general purposes and objectives of the United Nations Organization and do not purport to impose legal obligations on the individual member nations or to create rights in private persons. It is equally clear that none of the other provisions relied on by plaintiff is self-executing. Article 55 declares that the United Nations "shall promote: * * * universal respect for, and observance of, human rights and fundamental freedoms for all without distinction as to race, sex, language, or religion," and in Article 56, the member nations "pledge themselves to take joint and separate action in cooperation with the Organization for the achievement of the purposes set forth in Article 55." Although the member nations have obligated themselves to cooperate with the international organization in promoting respect for, and observance of, human rights, it is plain that it was contemplated that future legislative action by the several nations would be required to accomplish the declared objectives, and there is nothing to indicate that these provisions were intended to become rules of law for the courts of this country upon the ratification of the charter.

The language used in Articles 55 and 56 is not the type customarily employed in treaties which have been held to be self-executing and to create rights and duties in individuals. For example, the treaty involved in Clark v. Allen, 331 U.S. 503, relating to the rights of a national of one country to inherit real property located in another country, specifically provided that "such national shall be allowed a term of three years in which to sell the [property] * * * and withdraw the proceeds * * *" free from any discriminatory taxation. In Nielsen v. Johnson, 279 U.S. 47, the provision treated as being self-executing was equally definite. There each of the signatory parties agreed that "no higher or other duties, charges, or taxes of any kind, shall be levied" by one country on removal of property therefrom by citizens of the other country "than are or shall be payable in each state, upon the same, when removed by a citizen or subject of such state respectively." In other instances treaty provisions were enforced without implementing legislation where they prescribed in detail the rules governing rights and obligations of individuals or specifically provided that citizens of one nation shall have the same rights while in the other country as are enjoyed by that country's own citizens. Bacardi Corp. v. Domenech,[4] 311 U.S. 150; Asakura v. City of Seattle, 265 U.S. 332.

It is significant to note that when the framers of the charter intended to make certain provisions effective without the aid of implementing legislation they employed language which is clear and definite and manifests that intention. For example, Article 104 provides: "The Organization shall enjoy in the territory of each of its Members such legal capacity as

---

4. It should be noted, however, that the treaty involved in the Bacardi case also contained a specific provision, not discussed by the court, that its terms "shall have the force of law in those States in which international treaties possess that character, as soon as they are ratified by their constitutional organs."

may be necessary for the exercise of its functions and the fulfillment of its purposes." Article 105 provides: "1. The Organization shall enjoy in the territory of each of its Members such privileges and immunities as are necessary for the fulfillment of its purposes. 2. Representatives of the Members of the United Nations and officials of the Organization shall similarly enjoy such privileges and immunities as are necessary for the independent exercise of their functions in connection with the Organization." In Curran v. City of New York, 77 N.Y.S.2d 206 [ ] these articles were treated as being self-executory. See, also, Balfour, Guthrie & Co. v. United States, D.C., 90 F.Supp. 831.

The provisions in the charter pledging cooperation in promoting observance of fundamental freedoms lack the mandatory quality and definiteness which would indicate an intent to create justiciable rights in private persons immediately upon ratification. Instead, they are framed as a promise of future action by the member nations. Secretary of State Stettinius, Chairman of the United States delegation at the San Francisco Conference where the charter was drafted, stated in his report to President Truman that Article 56 "pledges the various countries to cooperate with the organization by joint and separate action in the achievement of the economic and social objectives of the organization without infringing upon their right to order their national affairs according to their own best ability, in their own way, and in accordance with their own political and economic institutions and processes." The same view was repeatedly expressed by delegates of other nations in the debates attending the drafting of article 56. See U.N.C.I.O. Doc. 699, II/3/40, May 30, 1945, pp. 1–3; U.N.C.I.O. Doc. 684, II/3/38, May 29, 1945, p. 4; Kelsen, The Law of the United Nations (1950), footnote 9, pp. 100–102.

The humane and enlightened objectives of the United Nations Charter are, of course, entitled to respectful consideration by the courts and Legislatures of every member nation, since that document expresses the universal desire of thinking men for peace and for equality of rights and opportunities. The charter represents a moral commitment of foremost importance, and we must not permit the spirit of our pledge to be compromised or disparaged in either our domestic or foreign affairs. We are satisfied, however, that the charter provisions relied on by plaintiff were not intended to supersede existing domestic legislation, and we cannot hold that they operate to invalidate the alien land law.

[The court then went on to hold that the alien land law violated the Fourteenth Amendment.]

[Concurring and dissenting opinions omitted.]

Rodriguez Fernandez v. Wilkinson

United States District Court, District of Kansas, 1980.
505 F.Supp. 787, aff'd on other grounds, 654 F.2d 1382 (10th Cir.1981).

■ ROGERS, DISTRICT JUDGE.

[Pedro Rodriguez Fernandez, detained in the U.S. Penitentiary at Leavenworth, Kansas, filed a petition for writ of habeas corpus. The court's findings included the following:]

1.   Petitioner is a native and a citizen of Cuba who was incarcerated in a Cuban prison at the time he was given the opportunity to come to the United States.

2.   He was transported to this country by boat along with approximately 130,000 Cuban nationals who arrived at Key West, Florida, on or about June 2, 1980, seeking admission to this country.

3.   Completion of inspection of petitioner was deferred, and petitioner was temporarily removed into the United States in accordance with 8 U.S.C. § 1223.

4.   During the deferred primary interview on June 14, 1980, petitioner admitted in a sworn statement that he had been arrested and convicted of crimes in Cuba and that he had been imprisoned there prior to his arrival. The crimes and circumstances of those crimes admitted to were: theft of a suitcase in 1959 for which he was sentenced to and served two years in the Santa Clara Prison; theft of a suitcase in 1964 for which he was sentenced to eight years to serve in Francequita Prison, three years of which he served before he escaped; attempted burglary in 1973 for which he was sentenced to four years in Francequita Prison. A three-year sentence was attached to the latter term as a result of the escape. Petitioner claims that the theft convictions were not of a serious nature because conditions in Cuba force the citizens to steal, and that he did not commit the alleged, attempted burglary. Petitioner testified before this Court that he was convicted by military tribunals. He further stated that he intended to remain in the United States indefinitely and was not in possession of a valid immigration visa.

· · ·

9.   During exclusion proceedings, commencing July 21, 1980, an immigration judge determined that petitioner was excludable from the United States under 8 U.S.C. § 1182(a)(9) in that he admitted having been convicted of a crime involving moral turpitude, and under § 1182(a)(20) in that he was an immigrant not in possession of proper documents. The judge reconsidered and denied petitioner's application for asylum, determined that petitioner should be excluded from entry, and entered an order of deportation. The petitioner waived his statutory right to appeal this decision.

10.   The United States Penitentiary at Leavenworth is classified by the Bureau of Prisons as a maximum security institution. Petitioner has been confined in this prison for over half a year. He and approximately 230 other Cuban refugees are presently detained in a dormitory area supposedly separate from the general population of prison inmates, and are designated as on "holdover status." Petitioner testified that conditions in their detention area are more restrictive and privileges are fewer than for general population inmates at the prison.

11.   The INS and the Department of State are attempting to make necessary arrangements to return petitioner and the other excluded aliens to Cuba; however, Cuba has either not responded or responded negatively to six diplomatic notes transmitted by the United States. Thus, the Government has been unable to expeditiously carry out the order of deportation and cannot even speculate as to a date of departure. No other country has been contacted about possibly accepting petitioner.

[The court found that Rodriguez Fernandez's continued confinement at Leavenworth did not violate any of his rights under the U.S. Constitution, because of his status as an excludable alien.]

. . .

... [T]here is no indication in this case that petitioner is a threat to national security.[1] ...

We have declared that indeterminate detention of petitioner in a maximum security prison pending unforeseeable deportation constitutes arbitrary detention. Due to the unique legal status of excluded aliens in this country, it is an evil from which our Constitution and statutory laws afford no protection. ...

The Amicus Curiae in this case contends, and counsel for petitioner urges, that the continued detention of petitioner is in contravention of fundamental human justice as embodied in established principles of international law. Cited as legal authority are The Universal Declaration of Human Rights, U.N. Doc. A/801 (1948) and The American Convention of Human Rights, 77 Dept. of State Bulletin 28 (July 4, 1977), signed by President Carter on July 1, 1977. We agree that international law secures to petitioner the right to be free of arbitrary detention and that his right is being violated.

. . .

International rules are generally binding upon nations only in cases where either: (1) the nation concerned has expressly consented to be bound by such rules, as by ratification of a treaty containing the rules; or (2) where it can be established through evidence of a wide practice by states that a customary rule of international law exists.

The most important source of international law is international treaties. At present, the United States has ratified and is a party to only a few

---

1.   Respondents have never suggested to this Court that any interest implicating national security is latent within the circumstances of this case which might be jeopardized by judicial mandate. This is apparently the first case of record being decided on the issue of imprisoning these Cuban excludables with criminal backgrounds. Yet the State Department and immigration officials have proffered very little information to the Court. From this seeming lack of interest, the Court has deduced that we are faced here, not with a covert threat to national security, but quite simply, with a problematic situation for which the established immigration laws and regulations provide no direct solution and for which Congress and agency officials have failed, through a lack of either time or inclination, to formulate new, effective policy.

human rights treaties. Petitioner does not assert that his detention is in direct violation of any treaty to which the United States is a party.

. . .

One important document by which the United States is bound is the United Nations Charter. 1970 Yearbook of the U.N. 1001, 59 Stat. 1033 (1945). This document "stands as the symbol of human rights on an international scale." Stotzky, at 237. The Charter entered into force on October 24, 1945, and resolves to reaffirm faith in fundamental human rights and in the dignity of the human person. Almost all nations in the world are now parties to the U.N. Charter.

There are a great number of other international declarations, resolutions, and recommendations. While not technically binding, these documents establish broadly recognized standards. The most important of these is the Universal Declaration of Human Rights, adopted by the U.N. General Assembly in 1948. . . .

Richard Bilder, an international legal scholar, has suggested it may currently be argued that

> standards set by the Universal Declaration of Human Rights, although initially only declaratory and non-binding, have by now, through wide acceptance and recitation by nations as having normative effect, become binding customary law. Whatever may be the weight of this argument, it is certainly true that the Declaration is in practice frequently invoked as if it were legally binding, both by nations and by private individuals and groups.

Bilder, R., The Status of International Human Rights Law: An Overview. 1978 International Law and Practice 1, 8.

It is a jurist's opinion that

> although the affirmations of the Declaration are not binding qua international convention within the meaning of Article 38, paragraph 1(a) of the Statute of the Court, they can bind states on the basis of custom within the meaning of the same Article, whether because they constitute a codification of customary law as was said in respect of Article 6 of the Vienna Convention on the Law of Treaties, or because they have acquired the force of custom through a general practice accepted as law, in the words of Article 38, paragraph 1(b), of the Statute.

Separate Opinion of Vice–President Ammoun in Advisory Opinion on the continued presence of South Africa in Namibia (S.W. Africa) 1971 I.C.J. Reports 16, 76. Thus, it appears that the Declaration has evolved into an important source of international human rights law.

Articles 3 and 9 of the Declaration provide that "everyone has the right to life, liberty, and the security of person," and that "no one shall be subjected to arbitrary arrest, detention or exile."

The American Convention on Human Rights, cited by the Amicus Curiae, pertinently declares in Article 5 that "punishment shall not be extended to any person other than the criminal," and "all persons deprived of their liberty shall be treated with respect for the inherent dignity of the human person." In Article 7 of the Convention it is agreed:

1. Every person has the right to personal liberty and security.

2. No one shall be deprived of his physical liberty except for the reasons and under the conditions established beforehand by the Constitution of the State Party concerned or by a law established pursuant thereto.

3. No one shall be subject to arbitrary arrest or imprisonment.

Two other principal sources of fundamental human rights are the European Convention for the Protection of Human Rights and Fundamental Freedoms (Rome 1950), and the International Covenant on Civil and Political Rights, G. A. Res. 2200A(XXI) Dec. 16, 1966, U.N. Gen.Ass.Off. Rec., 21st Sess., Supp. No. 16(A/6316) p. 52. Although the United States is not bound by either of these documents, they are indicative of the customs and usages of civilized nations.

[The court goes on to quote Article 4 of the European Convention, and Articles 14(7), 9, 10(1), and 12(1) of the ICCPR.]

Members of our Congress and executive department have also recognized an international legal right to freedom from arbitrary detention. Congressman Donald M. Fraser as Chairman of the Subcommittee on International Organizations and the Commission on International Relations, House of Representatives, described prolonged detention without charges or trial as a gross violation of human rights:

> Congress has sought to write some general laws establishing standards for the granting or withholding of military and economic aid to nations in relation to the human rights issue. Generally we have said the military aid should be reduced or terminated to a country guilty of a consistent pattern of gross violations of internationally recognized human rights. We define gross violations as those involving the integrity of the person: torture, prolonged detention without charges or trial, and other cruel and inhuman treatment.

Fraser D., Human Rights and U.S. Foreign Policy—The Congressional Perspective, 1978 International Human Rights Law and Practice, 171,178. Patricia M. Derian, Assistant Secretary of State for Human Rights and Humanitarian Affairs, in discussing President Carter's policy on human rights stated:

> Our human rights concerns embrace those internationally recognized rights found in the United Nations Declaration of Human Rights. The specific focus of our policy is to seek greater observance by all governments of the rights of the person including freedom from torture and cruel and inhuman treatment, freedom from the fear of security forces breaking down doors and kidnapping citizens from their homes, and freedom from arbitrary detention.

Derian, P., Human Rights in U.S. Foreign Policy—The Executive Perspective, 1978; International Human Rights Law and Practice 183.

Tribunals enforcing international law have also recognized arbitrary detention as giving rise to a legal claim. The arbitrator in *France ex rel. Madame Julien Chevreau*, opined that the arbitrary arrest, detention or deportation of a foreigner may give rise to a claim under international law and that if detention is unnecessarily prolonged, a claim is justified. The arbitrator further stated that a claim is justified if the rule is not observed that the prisoner should be treated in a manner appropriate to his situation, and corresponding to the standard customarily accepted among civilized nations. M.S. Dept. of State, file no. 500. AIA/1197, cited in Whiteman, M., Damages in International Law (Washington 1937).

The cases cited earlier in [omitted portions of] this opinion which condemned protracted detention and detention beyond a reasonable time for deportation display our own judiciary's abhorrence of arbitrary detention.

Principles of customary international law may be discerned from an overview of express international conventions, the teachings of legal scholars, the general custom and practice of nations and relevant judicial decisions. Filartiga v. Pena–Irala, 630 F.2d 876 (2d Cir.1980). When, from this overview a wrong is found to be of mutual, and not merely several, concern among nations, it may be termed an international law violation, Id.

International law is a part of the laws of the United States which federal courts are bound to ascertain and administer in an appropriate case. The Nereide, 13 U.S. (9 Cranch) 388, 422 (1815); The Paquete Habana, 175 U.S. 677 (1900); Filartiga v. Pena–Irala, supra. Our review of the sources from which customary international law is derived clearly demonstrates that arbitrary detention is prohibited by customary international law. Therefore, even though the indeterminate detention of an excluded alien cannot be said to violate the United States Constitution or our statutory laws, it is judicially remedial as a violation of international law. Petitioner's continued, indeterminate detention on restrictive status in a maximum security prison, without having been convicted of a crime in this country or a determination having been made that he is a risk to security or likely to abscond, is unlawful; and as such amounts to an abuse of discretion on the part of the Attorney General and his delegates.

. . .

This Court has absolutely no desire to intrude upon matters of national security or executive decision-making and is not so arrogant as to feign expertise in the area of immigration law and policy. Such matters are wisely entrusted to a specialized agency. On this account, we have attempted to persuade respondent to instruct us as to potential solutions to the hard problem before us. We can only speculate that the INS and the State Department have been so overwhelmed handling the extraordinary assimilation of over 100,000 Cuban nationals into this country, not to mention pressing situations involving Iranian and Haitian aliens, as to have not had the available span of attention to perceive or counteract the possible violation of the fundamental human rights of less than two percent of the Cuban influx.

These rationalizations do not, however, assuage the extant violation of petitioner's fundamental human rights. Perpetuating a state of affairs which results in the violation of an alien's fundamental human rights is clearly an abuse of discretion on the part of the responsible agency officials. This Court is bound to declare such an abuse and to order its cessation. When Congress and the executive department decided to exclude certain aliens from entry into this country and thereafter allowed thousands to arrive upon our shores at once, it was their corollary responsibility to develop methods for processing this large influx of admissible and excludable aliens without offending any of their fundamental human rights. If, due solely to the morass created by these official decisions, some aliens who may not seem desirable have been caused to remain in the United States for attenuated periods of time, the courts cannot deny them protection from arbitrary governmental action.

For all the foregoing reasons, the Court declares that when an excluded alien is brought upon our lands to be detained in a maximum security prison facility pending effectuation of exclusion, that alien may be detained in such a facility only for a determinate period of time. Furthermore, the maximum limit of such term should be made known to the alien upon the commencement of his detention.

Respondent shall be granted ninety (90) days from the date of this Memorandum and Order in which to terminate the arbitrary detention of petitioner. This may be accomplished in one of a number of ways. Petitioner may be deported, or he may be released on parole under conditions specified by the Attorney General. Or the INS may conduct a procedurally-adequate hearing to determine whether further detention of petitioner is warranted on a finding that he is likely to abscond, is a threat to security, or is a serious and actual threat to the safety of the person or the property of the citizens of this nation. Petitioner might well be housed in a refugee camp rather than a federal prison. Respondent might even devise and implement his own resolution to the problem of petitioner's arbitrary detention. If the arbitrary detention of petitioner is not terminated to the satisfaction of this Court within the specified time, the Court shall, at the end of said ninety-day period, grant the writ of habeas corpus and order petitioner released on parole.

.   .   .

Garcia–Mir v. Meese

United States Court of Appeals, Eleventh Circuit, 1986.
788 F.2d 1446, cert. denied, 479 U.S. 889 (1986).

■ JOHNSON, CIRCUIT JUDGE:

These cases pose the question whether unadmitted aliens properly may claim the protection of the Due Process Clause of the United States

Constitution to secure parole revocation hearings. ... It is our opinion that, assuming that undocumented aliens may have actionable nonconstitutionally-based liberty interests, these particular aliens have not stated a viable claim for relief under the Due Process Clause. We also determine that customary international law does not afford these aliens a remedy in American courts.

. . .

This is an appeal and cross-appeal from the final decision of the trial court ordering the government to prepare and implement a plan to provide individual parole revocation hearings for unadmitted aliens.[1] The appellees-cross appellants ["appellees" or "aliens" or "Mariels"] are a certified class of Mariel Cuban refugees who were accorded a special immigration parole status by the Refugee Education Assistance Act of 1980. The district court has broken the class into two sub-classes. The "First Group" includes those who are guilty of crimes committed in Cuba before the boatlift or who are mentally incompetent. They have never been paroled into this country. The "Second Group" consists of all other Mariels—those who, because there was no evidence of criminal or mental defect, were paroled under the provisions of the general alien parole statute, 8 U.S.C.A. § 1182(d)(5) (1985), but whose parole was subsequently revoked. All are currently detained in the Atlanta Penitentiary.

This case is no stranger to this Court. In Garcia–Mir v. Smith, 766 F.2d 1478 (11th Cir.1985) ["Garcia–Mir I"], cert. denied sub nom. Marquez-Medina v. Meese, ___ U.S. ___ (1986), we considered the scope and effect of a Status Review Plan promulgated by the Attorney General and its effect on the parole of some class members. In Fernandez–Roque v. Smith, 671 F.2d 426 (11th Cir.1982) ["Fernandez I"], we considered the jurisdictional issues raised by the issuance of a temporary restraining order preventing the government from deporting the respondents. In Fernandez–Roque v. Smith, 734 F.2d 576 (11th Cir.1984) ["Fernandez II"], this Court reversed the trial court's finding that these aliens had a constitutionally-based liberty interest which could be denied only after full hearing. We withheld judgment on and remanded two other questions: whether there might be some nonconstitutionally-based but nonetheless actionable liberty interest; and whether the detention of these respondents was violative of the principles of public international law.

. . .

1. The complex factual posture of this case has been set forth amply in several earlier opinions by this Court. See, e.g., Garcia–Mir v. Meese, 781 F.2d 1450 (11th Cir. 1986); Garcia–Mir v. Smith, 766 F.2d 1478 (11th Cir.1985). The general circumstances leading to the "Freedom Flotilla," which re-sulted in the transporting of almost 125,000 Cuban refugees to the United States, are explained in United States v. Frade, 709 F.2d 1387 (11th Cir.1983). These facts need not be repeated here. Facts unique to this particular controversy will be provided as appropriate.

[The court then found that the plaintiffs had no nonconstitutionally-based liberty interest entitling them to a parole hearing.]

B.   International Law:

The public law of nations was long ago incorporated into the common law of the United States. The Paquete Habana, 175 U.S. 677, 700 (1900); The Nereide, 13 U.S. (9 Cranch) 388, 423 (1815); Restatement of the Law of Foreign Relations Law of the United States (Revised) § 131 comment d (Tent. Draft No. 6, 1985) [hereinafter cited as "Restatement 6"]. To the extent possible, courts must construe American law so as to avoid violating principles of public international law. Murray v. The Schooner Charming Betsy, 6 U.S. (2 Cranch) 64, 102, 118 (1804); Lauritzen v. Larsen, 345 U.S. 571, 578 (1953). But public international law is controlling only "where there is no treaty and no controlling executive or legislative act or judicial decision...." 175 U.S. at 700. Appellees argue that, because general principles of international law forbid prolonged arbitrary detention,[8] we should hold that their current detention is unlawful.

We have previously determined that the general deportation statute, 8 U.S.C.A. § 1227(a) (1985), does not *restrict* the power of the Attorney General to detain aliens indefinitely. Fernandez–Roque II, 734 F.2d at 580 n. 6. But this does not resolve the question whether there has been an *affirmative legislative grant* of authority to detain. As to the First Group there is sufficiently express evidence of congressional intent as to interdict the application of international law: Pub.L. No. 96–533, Title VII, § 716, 94 Stat. 3162 (1980), reprinted at 8 U.S.C.A. § 1522 note.[9]

The trial court found, correctly, that there has been no affirmative legislative grant to the Justice Department to detain the Second Group without hearings because 8 U.S.C.A. § 1227(c) does not expressly authorize indefinite detention. Fernandez–Roque v. Smith, 622 F.Supp. 887, 902 (N.D.Ga.1985). Thus we must look for a controlling executive act. The trial court found that there was such a controlling act in the Attorney General's termination of the status review plan and in his decision to incarcerate indefinitely pending efforts to deport. Id. at 903. The appellees and the

---

8. See, e.g., Restatement 6 § 702(e), comment h; Rodriguez–Fernandez v. Wilkinson, 654 F.2d 1382, 1388 (10th Cir.1981).

9. That enactment provides:

The Congress finds that the United States Government has already incarcerated recently arrived Cubans who are admitted criminals, are security threats, or have incited civil disturbances in Federal processing facilities. The Congress urges the Executive branch, consistent with United States law, to seek the deportation of such individuals.

Admittedly, the legislation encourages the Executive Branch to act in accordance with

United States law. That would implicitly incorporate international law prohibiting detention without a hearing, assuming for argument's sake that the international norm appellees invoke actually applies to circumstances of this sort. But the language suggests that Congress clearly anticipated that the First Group was being and would continue to be held until they could be deported. Congress made no attempt to undo what the Justice Department has already done. In fact they encouraged it to deport these persons. We hold that the First Group is subject to a controlling legislative enactment and hence unprotected by international law.

amicus challenge this by arguing that a controlling executive act can only come from an act by or expressly sanctioned by the President himself, not one of his subordinates. They rely for that proposition upon *The Paquete Habana* and upon the Restatement of the Law of Foreign Relations Law of the United States (Revised) § 131 comment c (Tent. Draft No. 1, 1980) [hereinafter cited as "Restatement 1"].

As to *The Paquete Habana*, that case involved the capture and sale as war prize of several fishing boats during the Spanish–American War. The Supreme Court found this contrary to the dictates of international law. The amicus characterizes the facts of the case such that the Secretary of the Navy authorized the capture and that the Supreme Court held that this did not constitute a controlling executive act because it was not ordered by the President himself. This is a mischaracterization. After the capture of the two vessels at issue, an admiral telegraphed the Secretary for permission to seize fishing ships, to which the Secretary responded that only those vessels " 'likely to aid enemy may be detained.' " 175 U.S. at 713. Seizing fishing boats aiding the enemy would be in obvious accord with international law. But the facts of *The Paquete Habana* showed the boats in question to be innocent of aiding the Spanish. The Court held that the ships were seized in violation of international law because they were used solely for fishing. It was the admiral who acted in excess of the clearly delimited authority granted by the Secretary, who instructed him to act only consistent with international law. Thus *The Paquete Habana* does not support the proposition that the acts of cabinet officers cannot constitute controlling executive acts. At best it suggests that lower level officials cannot by their acts render international law inapplicable. That is not an issue in this case, where the challenge is to the acts of the Attorney General.

As to the Restatement 1, the provision upon which amicus relies[11] has been removed in subsequent drafts. The most recent version of that provision notes that the President, "acting within his constitutional authority, may have the power under the Constitution to act in ways that constitute violations of international law by the United States." The Constitution provides for the creation of executive departments, U.S. Const. art. 2, § 2, and the power of the President to delegate his authority to those departments to act on his behalf is unquestioned. See, e.g., Jean v. Nelson, 472 U.S. 846 (1985). Likewise, in Restatement 6, § 135 Reporter's Note 3, the power of the President to disregard international law in service of domestic needs is reaffirmed. Thus we hold that the executive acts here evident constitute a sufficient basis for affirming the trial court's finding that international law does not control.

Even if we were to accept, arguendo, the appellees' interpretation of "controlling executive act," *The Paquete Habana* also provides that the reach of international law will be interdicted by a controlling judicial decision. In *Jean v. Nelson,* we interpreted the Supreme Court's decision in

---

11. Amicus cites to Restatement 1, § 131, Comment C to the effect that a controlling executive act within the meaning of *The Paquete Habana* can come only from the President himself.

Mezei to hold that even an indefinitely incarcerated alien "could not challenge his continued detention without a hearing." 727 F.2d at 974–75. This reflects the obligation of the courts to avoid any ruling that would "inhibit the flexibility of the political branches of government to respond to changing world conditions...." Mathews v. Diaz, 426 U.S. 67, 81 (1976). We find this decision sufficient to meet the test of *The Paquete Habana*.

.   .   .

For the reasons we have explained, we hold that the appellees are entitled to no relief on their claim of a nonconstitutionally-based liberty interest. To that extent, the judgment of the trial court is REVERSED. We also hold that the appellees have stated no basis for relief under international law because any rights there extant have been extinguished by controlling acts of the executive and judicial branches. To that extent the judgment of the trial court is AFFIRMED. The third claim, regarding the continued maintenance of this action in a class form, is DISMISSED AS MOOT.

.   .   .

Notes

1. In *Sei Fujii*, what human right did the California statute allegedly violate, and what was the textual basis in the U.N. Charter for finding that right enforceable? Should the court have found the right judicially enforceable? If the California statute still existed today, would it violate the obligations of the United States under the ICCPR? If so, and if a plaintiff sued in a U.S. court to invalidate it under the ICCPR, how would the court respond?

2. Note that the treaty discussion in *Sei Fujii* rests on the assumption that self-executing treaties are law binding on state courts as well as on federal courts. Indeed, one of the principal purposes of the Supremacy Clause of the Constitution was to make treaties of the United States binding on state judges. See *Asakura v. City of Seattle*, 265 U.S. 332, 341 (1924); *Martin v. Hunter's Lessee*, 14 U.S. (1 Wheat.) 304, 340–41 (1816).

3. The district court's decision in *Rodriguez Fernandez* was affirmed on statutory grounds by the Tenth Circuit Court of Appeals. The panel majority ruled that the immigration statute should be interpreted as not permitting the indefinite detention of an excludable alien whose home country would not take him back. The court maintained that construing the statute as authorizing indefinite detention would raise serious constitutional questions, and it noted that descriptions of congressional power in earlier cases rested on obsolete understandings of international law, which now embodied "the concept that human beings should be free from arbitrary imprisonment." *Rodriguez Fernandez v. Wilkinson*, 654 F.2d 1382, 1388 (10th Cir.1981). Rodriguez Fernandez was finally released in August 1981. See "4th Cuban Refugee Is Freed From Center by Court Order," N.Y. Times, Aug. 9, 1981, sec. 1, p. 38.

4. How did the district court in *Rodriguez Fernandez* determine that prolonged arbitrary detention violated customary international law? Why was the detention of Rodriguez Fernandez "arbitrary" within the meaning of customary international law? (Was it irrational? Unreasonable? Disproportionate to any valid interest served?) When did it become "prolonged" within the meaning of customary international law?

5. In *Garcia-Mir*, the Eleventh Circuit relied on controlling legislative, executive, and judicial acts that (in the court's view) superseded the customary international law prohibition on prolonged arbitrary detention.

(a) What legislative act was controlling with respect to the detention of the "First Group," and why?

(b) Given that Congress did not expressly authorize the detention of the "Second Group," why did the Attorney General's action prevent judicial enforcement of the international prohibition with regard to the "Second Group"? Should the personal authorization of the President have been necessary? Should the personal authorization of the President have been sufficient? If the Attorney General does have the authority to perform a "controlling executive act" that precludes judicial enforcement of international law, then how far down the chain of command in the Executive Branch does that authority extend?

Consider the following comment:

> In my opinion, *Garcia-Mir* misinterpreted and misapplied *The Paquete Habana*. The court of appeals apparently considered *any* act of the President to be "controlling", and extended that to include an act by the Attorney General.... There was no suggestion that the President, acting under his constitutional power, had by executive agreement or executive order, made law that superseded the rule of international law forbidding arbitrary detention as domestic law. There was no suggestion that the President ordered the detention in the valid exercise of some independent constitutional authority as "sole organ" or as Commander in Chief that might have effect as law of the United States.
>
> Only such Presidential acts, I believe, might constitute "controlling executive acts" permitting the courts to give them legal effect in disregard of international law as the law of the land....

Louis Henkin, Foreign Affairs and the U.S. Constitution 244–45 (2d ed. 1996).

For further discussion of these issues, see, e.g., *Agora, May the President Violate Customary International Law?*, 81 Am. J. Int'l L. 371, 912 (1987); Michael J. Glennon, *Raising the Paquete Habana: Is Violation of Customary International Law by the Executive Unconstitutional?*, 90 Nw. U. L. Rev. 321 (1985); Monroe Leigh, *Is the President Above Customary International Law?*, 86 Am. J. Int'l L. 757 (1992); Jordan J. Paust, International Law as Law of the United States (1996).

(c) In the alternative, the Eleventh Circuit cited as a controlling judicial act precedent indicating that detained excludable aliens had no constitutional right to challenge their detention. How can a ruling on the absence of a constitutional right amount to a controlling judicial act superseding customary international law?

6. A decade after the Garcia–Mir decision, a substantial number of Mariel Cubans remained in indefinite immigration detention, theoretically awaiting an eventual removal to Cuba. Courts have continued to follow the reasoning of Garcia–Mir in rejecting challenges to their detention on international law grounds. See, e.g., *Guzman v. Tippy*, 130 F.3d 64 (2d Cir.1997); *Barrera-Echavarria v. Rison*, 44 F.3d 1441 (9th Cir.), cert. denied, 516 U.S. 976 (1995); *Gisbert v. U.S. Attorney General*, 988 F.2d 1437 (5th Cir.1993).

7. In modern case law, customary international law, as incorporated into United States law, is generally viewed as a species of federal common law. See, e.g., *Filartiga v. Pena–Irala*, Section D(2) infra. Some commentators, however, have criticized this categorization, and sought alternative accounts of the status of customary international law in the domestic legal system. Some have argued that customary international law should not be regarded as hierarchically inferior to statutes, as common law rules are. See Louis Henkin, *The Constitution and United States Sovereignty: A Century of Chinese Exclusion and its Progeny*, 100 Harv. L. Rev. 853 (1987); Jules Lobel, *The Limits of Constitutional Power: Conflicts Between Foreign Policy and International Law*, 71 Va. L. Rev. 1071 (1985). On the other hand, some commentators have argued that characterizing customary international law as federal common law is too strong. See Phillip R. Trimble, *A Revisionist View of Customary International Law*, 33 U.C.L.A. L. Rev. 665 (1986) (arguing that courts do not treat customary international law as enforceable common law without the encouragement of the federal Executive Branch on a case-by-case basis); A.M. Weisburd, *State Courts, Federal Courts, and International Cases*, 20 Yale J. Int'l L. 1 (1995) (proposing new framework treating customary international law as analogous to the laws of a foreign sovereign to be applied in appropriate cases); Curtis A. Bradley and Jack L. Goldsmith, III, *The Current Illegitimacy of International Human Rights Litigation*, 66 Fordham L. Rev. 319 (1997) (arguing that federal courts should not have the power to incorporate rules of customary international law without explicit authorization by statute or treaty). For criticisms of the latter, see, e.g., Harold Hongju Koh, *Is International Law Really State Law?*, 111 Harv. L. Rev. 1824 (1998); Gerald L. Neuman, *Sense and Nonsense About Customary International Law: A Response to Professors Bradley and Goldsmith*, 66 Fordham L. Rev. 371 (1997); Beth Stephens, *The Law of Our Land, Customary International Law as Federal Law after Erie*, 66 Fordham L. Rev. 393 (1997).

8. In *United States v. Alvarez–Machain*, 504 U.S. 655 (1992), the Supreme Court held that the United States–Mexico Extradition Treaty did not require dismissal of a criminal prosecution against an accused Mexican national who had been abducted by U.S. agents from Mexican territory. The Court was willing to assume that the incursion violated the obligation of the United States to respect Mexico's territorial sovereignty under customary international law, but concluded that the Treaty did not itself

incorporate a prohibition against such abductions, and did not specify dismissal of a prosecution as a remedy for unlawful abduction. The Court noted that "Mexico has protested the abduction of respondent through diplomatic notes, ... and the decision of whether respondent should be returned to Mexico, as a matter outside of the Treaty, is a matter for the Executive Branch." 504 U.S. at 669. Three dissenting Justices would have interpreted the Treaty as incorporating the traditional prohibition against abduction. Does the majority opinion represent a refusal to recognize customary international law as part of the law of the United States, or a denial of the individual defendant's standing to assert a violation of customary international law, or the rejection of a particular remedy for a violation of customary international law?

9. In *Breard v. Greene*, 523 U.S. 371 (1998), the Government of Paraguay and a Paraguayan national sought to delay the latter's execution after a murder conviction in Virginia, on the ground that state officials had violated the obligations of the United States under the Vienna Convention on Consular Relations. That treaty requires arresting authorities to notify foreign nationals who are arrested of their right to contact their consulates. The Supreme Court held that Breard had procedurally defaulted his claims under the Convention by not raising them in state court, and that he could not raise them belatedly in habeas corpus proceedings, without a stronger showing of cause and prejudice than the facts of his case permitted. The Court also expressed doubt that either the Convention or federal statutes provided a foreign state a right of action in U.S. courts to set aside the conviction of one of its nationals as a remedy for a violation of the Convention. The case was complicated by the fact that Paraguay had brought proceedings against the United States on the Convention claim in the International Court of Justice, and the ICJ had issued an order on provisional measures indicating that the United States should not execute Breard during the pendency of the proceedings. The Supreme Court stated, without explanation, that it lacked the authority to direct the Governor of Virginia to comply with such an indication. Three Justices dissented. Later the same day, the Governor rejected a request from the Secretary of State to postpone the execution, and Angel Breard was executed.

An order indicating provisional measures is a form of interlocutory relief authorized by the Statute of the International Court of Justice, which is itself a treaty to which the United States is a party. Whether such an order is binding is a disputed issue of international law, and the federal government informed the Supreme Court of its view that the order was not binding. Among the issues raised by this case are the following: Assuming the ICJ's order creates a binding international obligation of the United States, should the Supreme Court have enforced it by granting a stay of execution? Assuming the order is binding, would any authority exist in the federal government to require Virginia to comply with it, and how could that authority be exercised? Assuming that the order is *not* binding, would authority exist in the federal government to require compliance, and how could that authority be exercised? And how should these questions be answered if the international effect of the order is uncertain? For further discussion, see *Agora: Breard*, 92 Am. J. Int'l L. 666 (1998).

10. For the possibility of enforcement of human rights norms against U.S. officials under the Alien Tort Statute, 28 U.S.C. § 1350, see infra p. 881.

D. U.S. ENFORCEMENT OF INTERNATIONAL HUMAN RIGHTS LAW AGAINST FOREIGN VIOLATORS

International law and treaties are commonly observed as a result of "horizontal enforcement": a potential violator is deterred by the anticipated response of the victim state(s). But "horizontal enforcement" has been manifestly inadequate in respect of international human rights law. The reasons are not difficult to discern; they inhere in the nature of international human rights law. In principle, a state's violation of human rights within its territory constitutes a breach of its international obligations toward other states. Human rights treaties are agreements among states parties, and customary human rights law establishes obligations for all states. The true "victim" of breaches of those obligations is not another state, however, but the individual who suffered the violation—the "third party beneficiary" of the interstate obligation.

States have been notably reluctant to invoke interstate complaint procedures in response to human rights violations committed by other states parties. (See Chapter 3, Sections A and B, above.) Collective implementation efforts through the human rights machinery of UN Charter organs, such as the Commission on Human Rights, has evolved from wholesale neglect in the Commission's early years to increasingly effective, but still inadequate, initiatives today. (See Chapter 3, Section E(1), above.) Exceptionally, as in the case of apartheid in South Africa, states have taken sustained collective action or, as in the case of the Rwandan genocide of 1994, have belatedly adopted extraordinary measures in response to mass atrocities.

Some states, notably including the United States, have been more willing to respond to human rights violations abroad through national policies. Although for many years unwilling to ratify most of the principal human rights treaties, the United States has long pursued a comparatively vigorous human rights agenda in its foreign policy. As the following materials make clear, the initial impetus for this dimension of U.S. foreign policy came from Congress, which has continued to press—sometimes compel—a reluctant Executive branch to respond to serious violations of fundamental rights abroad.

1. LEGISLATIVE/EXECUTIVE ENFORCEMENT

Louis Henkin, *Human Rights and United States Foreign Policy*

in The Age of Rights 65 (1990).

In the process that achieved the universalization and internationalization of human rights, the United States has played a major part. Yet the significance of international human rights in the policy of the United States has hardly been understood either abroad or at home, and indeed it has been riddled with apparent contradictions.

The United States is commonly acknowledged to be a principal ancestor of the contemporary idea of rights. Individual rights dominate its constitutional jurisprudence, and are the pride of its people, their banner to the world. President Franklin Roosevelt proclaimed human rights to be an aim of the Second World War; Eleanor Roosevelt was a major force in the development of the Universal Declaration of Human Rights. Other Americans labored for eighteen years to help conclude the human rights covenants as well as other human rights conventions; United States spokesmen continue to be prominent in all United Nations bodies addressing international human rights issues. The United States is party to the Helsinki Accord and has been most insistent on invoking its human rights provisions. United States laws forbid arms sales and foreign aid to nations guilty of gross violations of internationally recognized human rights. The United States Department of State has a human rights bureaucracy, sits in judgment and publishes annual reports on the condition of human rights around the world. President Carter made human rights a hallmark of his Administration. Congresses legislated and Presidents proclaimed human rights to be a "central feature"—"a principal goal"—of United States foreign policy.

And yet: [until recently, the United States was] the only major power, and one of the very few countries generally, that [had] not adhered to any of the major international human rights conventions. The United States has opposed many attempts to impose international sanctions against violators of human rights. Among allies or friends of the United States are highly repressive regimes, and most recent Presidents, Secretaries of State, and United States diplomats have acted as though generally the condition of human rights in other countries is hardly the business of the United States.

What is the human rights policy of the United States and what is the place of human rights in United States foreign policy generally? I suggest that the confusion of United States policy reflects not only, or principally, different policies at different times by different administrations, but, rather, more than one policy at any time—a Congressional policy and a different executive policy; one policy in respect of international human rights in some countries and another policy for other countries; one policy abroad and another at home.

EXECUTIVE AMBIVALENCE

Presidents (and Congresses) in the nineteenth century sometimes addressed the human condition in other countries, but only spasmodically, when moved by some dramatic egregious event, and responding to strong domestic outcry. Human rights did not achieve a prominent place in United States foreign policy until the Second World War. President Roosevelt proclaimed the Four Freedoms for all mankind, and subsequent Allied statements in effect adopted them as war aims. Human rights were included in the planning for the postwar order, and, with active United States support, they appeared in the Nuremberg Charter, in the United Nations Charter, and the Charter of the Organization of American States; the United States was in the forefront of the process that produced the Universal Declaration.

Ambivalence and tension in United States policy on human rights appeared early. Simply, one can attribute them to different influences in the foreign policy process, forces that combined to produce different "vector" in different times and contexts. There were differences among the active, front-line participants in the process—within the executive branch, between the President (and his advisers) and the Department of State, and within the Department of State. There were differences between Executive and Congress in their attitudes toward human rights in other countries, and to international concern with human rights in the United States.

Human rights in other countries was the particular preoccupation of "liberal," "idealistic" elements which had come into the "foreign policy establishment" during the war, and remained when the war was over. Amateur, activist, less bound by diplomatic traditions and niceties, they pursued the promises of wartime rhetoric and favored United States leadership for international cooperation, including the development of international human rights standards and effective institutions an procedures for implementing them. They were prepared to have the United States press other governments to accept those standards as well as "machinery" for their enforcement, and to have the United States scrutinize and criticize the actions of governments that violated these standards. They saw no reasons why, in order to further those ends, the United States should not subject itself to the same standards and the same scrutiny.

On the other hand, leading members of the traditional foreign policy establishment, notably the career foreign service, tended to find the new international human rights movement "unsophisticated," and at best a nuisance. They were inclined to consider human rights conditions in any other country that country's business, and active concern with these conditions by the United States, or by international institutions, to be meddlesome, officious, unprofessional, disturbing of "friendly relations" and disruptive of sound diplomacy. During war, they had seen no reason to resist rhetorical declarations that served the needs of morale and psychological warfare, but they looked with growing concern when the wartime spirit and the influence of its amateur supporters continued in the postwar years. They were skeptical of international institutions generally, and resisted particularly their involvement in the internal affairs of states, such as human rights.

"Idealists" and "realists" served the United States side-by-side, but they looked in different directions and saw United States interests differently. As the glow of victory and the "spirit of the United Nations" waned, the influence of the human rights contingent receded and traditional diplomats again dominated. They concerned themselves with other important things: security, alignments, military bases, trade. But the human rights movement continued to command wide support from church and other "do-good" bodies, and from particular ethnic constituencies, and therefore some support in Congress and even in the White House. It was a continuing activity of international organizations and therefore of those who represented the United States in those bodies, principally part-time citizen-diplomats at periodic meetings, and of the newfangled bureaus of the State Department. On the United Nations sidetrack, the United States joined and often led the human rights bandwagon. "Realists" in the State Department remained skeptical but were not disposed to challenge that program as long as it remained on the plane of rhetoric and was not allowed to disturb the sensibilities of particular states or roil relations with them. Therefore, they acquiesced or were indifferent when the United States supported multilateral programs that concentrated on developing standards and even implementing machinery; the Universal Declaration (the preoccupation of Eleanor Roosevelt, not of Dean Acheson), the Genocide Convention, the international human rights covenants and other conventions followed. But, under "realist" influence, the United States was disinclined to exert pressure on reluctant friendly foreign governments, sometimes even on less-friendly Communist governments; it resisted in particular "intrusive" scrutiny, criticism, and especially economic or military sanctions against governments for human rights violations.

CONGRESSIONAL HUMAN RIGHTS POLICY

In some respects the policies pursued by the executive branch reflected concern for Congressional opinion and anticipated Congressional reactions, particularly where international human rights policy had implications for United States trade or for life in the United States. For the most part, however, Congress did not attend seriously to the condition of human rights in other countries during the first twenty-five years of the postwar era and generally acquiesced in what the executive branch did. Congress had little occasion for formal involvement in the development of United States human rights policy. One or both Houses, at the behest of individual members responding particularly to constituencies sensitive to human rights violations in particular countries—the rights of Poles, of Greek minorities, of Soviet Jews, of Blacks in South Africa—sometimes expressed their sense of outrage or concern. Individual members of Congress occasionally participated in executive activities as a member of delegations to international organizations and conferences. The Senate, whose advice and consent is constitutionally required to human rights treaties as to others, had few occasions to consider agreements that aimed at the condition of rights in other countries. It consented to treaties that imposed human rights standards on defeated enemy countries in World War II. It consented to the UN Charter, including the provisions wherein the United States pledged to take joint and separate action in cooperation with the United Nations Organization to promote respect for human rights (Arts. 55 and 56).

An independent Congressional initiative to shape United States human rights policy developed in the early 1970's. Under influence of concerned liberal members of the House of Representatives, and responding to inadequacies in United Nations and other multilateral responses to human rights violations, Congress enacted a series of statutes declaring the promotion of respect for human rights to be a principal goal of United States foreign policy, and denying foreign aid, military assistance, and the sale of agricultural commodities to states guilty of gross violations of internationally recognized human rights. In addition, United States representatives were directed to act in international financial institutions so as to prevent or discourage loans to governments guilty of such violations. Congress also established a human rights bureau in the Department of State, and directed the department to report annually on the conditions of human rights in every country in the world.

The Congressional program, it should be clear, was directed not at deviations from democratic governance as practiced by the United States (and by its European allies) but against "consistent patterns of gross violations of internationally recognized human rights," those that nations publicly decried and that none claimed the right to do or admitted doing. Congress specified clearly the violations at which it aimed—"torture or cruel, inhuman or degrading treatment or punishment, prolonged detention without charges, causing the disappearance of persons by the abduction and clandestine detention of those persons, or other flagrant denial of the right to life, liberty or the security of person." Also, it should be clear, this general legislation was not aimed at Communism and the Communist states since they received neither arms nor aid from the United States, but at the non-Communist Third World. In addition, Congress addressed human rights in particular countries, e.g., denying various aid to Chile, Argentina, South Africa, Uganda and others, when the condition of human rights in those countries was particularly egregious. Later, Congress imposed various human rights conditions on assistance to particular countries in Central America. In 1986, Congress enacted the Comprehensive Anti–Apartheid Act.

The Congressional program was never popular with the executive branch (regardless of political party), particularly with those who reflected the dominant, traditional attitudes in the Department of State. That program limited executive autonomy in the conduct of foreign policy. It required embassies to collect information often critical of the countries in which they "lived"; it required the Department of State to publish information often critical of countries with which the United States had friendly relations. It injected into foreign policy elements that foreign governments, and many in the States Department, thought not to be United States business. It sometimes disturbed alliances and alignments, base agreements or trade arrangements, and friendly relations generally.

Congress made some concessions to executive branch resistance. It gave the Aid Administrator authority to disregard the statutory limitation when assistance "will directly benefit the needy people in such country." It authorized security assistance to a country guilty of gross violations if the President certified that "extraordinary circumstances exist warranting provision of such assistance" or if the President finds that "such a significant improvement in its human rights record has occurred as to warrant lifting the prohibition on furnishing such assistance in the national interest of the United States." United States representatives to international financial institutions were to oppose loans to gross violators "except where the President determines that the cause of international human rights is served more effectively by actions other than voting against such assistance or where the assistance is directed to programs that serve the basic needs of the impoverished majority of the country in question." The Anti–Apartheid Act was enacted despite resistance from the Reagan administration, but its terms took account of some executive objections.

In the main, the tension between Congress and the executive branch reflected not partisan or political differences, but the different positions and perspectives of the two branches. Congress was closer to popular sentiment in the United States, which was responsive to the human condition in other countries, and wished to do something about it or at least to dissociate the United States from repressive regimes in general or in particular countries. The executive branch, more removed from constituent influence in the United States, was closer to official sentiment in other countries with which it had to deal; it was not indifferent to, but less swayed by, moral concerns, more attuned to international political and diplomatic needs and mores. But these general differences between the two branches have not been impervious to political considerations. Congress, while sensing the need to induce a reluctant executive to attend to human rights, was also content to provide an avenue of escape from these restrictions in some cases if the President were prepared to assume the onus for taking it. For its part, the executive branch, or some elements in it, were often content to criticize or implement sanctions against human rights violators if they could attribute responsibility to Congress and could maintain executive helplessness to disregard the restrictions.

a.   U.S. IMPOSITION OF SANCTIONS FOR HUMAN RIGHTS VIOLATIONS

Selected U.S. Legislation Requiring or Imposing Sanctions on Countries That Violate Human Rights

As noted in the preceding essay, legislative activism in the human rights area was especially prominent between 1974 and 1980. It was during this period that the basic legislative framework for U.S. human rights policy abroad was established, principally under the leadership of Representative Donald Fraser, who served as Chairman of the Subcommittee on International Organizations and Movements of the House Committee on Foreign Affairs. In the legislation set forth below, Congress generally prohibited military and other forms of U.S. assistance to countries that engaged in a "consistent pattern of gross violations of internationally recognized human rights."

Congressional initiatives in the 1970s also included legislation establishing a human rights bureau in the Department of State and requiring the Secretary of State to prepare an annual report on human rights conditions in countries proposed to receive U.S. security assistance or development assistance. The reporting requirement was expanded in 1979 to apply to all states that are members of the United Nations.

The basic legislative framework established in the 1970s has been elaborated in subsequent years to reflect contemporary human rights concerns. For example, in 1990 Congress amended 22 U.S.C. § 2151n to bar assistance to "any government failing to take appropriate and adequate measures, within their means, to protect children from exploitation, abuse or forced conscription into military or paramilitary services." In 1998, Congress enacted the International Religious Freedom Act of 1998, which created an institutional framework to respond to violations of religious freedom in other countries.

Foreign Assistance Act of 1961, as Amended

22 U.S.C. § 2151n [Foreign Assistance Act § 116 "Harkin Amendment"]. Human rights and development assistance.

(a) *Violations barring assistance; assistance for needy people.* No assistance may be provided under subchapter I of this chapter to the government of any country which engages in a consistent pattern of gross violations of internationally recognized human rights, including torture or cruel, inhuman, or degrading treatment or punishment, prolonged detention without charges, causing the disappearance of persons by the abduction and clandestine detention of those persons, or other flagrant denial of the right to life, liberty, and the security of person, unless such assistance will directly benefit the needy people in such country.

(b) *Information to Congressional committees for realization of assistance for needy people; concurrent resolution terminating assistance.* In determining whether this standard is being met with regard to funds allocated under subchapter I of this chapter, the Committee on Foreign Relations of the Senate or the Committee on Foreign Affairs of the House of Representatives may require the Administrator primarily responsible for administering subchapter I of this chapter to submit in writing information demonstrating that such assistance will directly benefit the needy people in such country, together with a detailed explanation of the assistance to be provided (including the dollar amounts of such assistance) and an explanation of how such assistance will directly benefit the needy people in such country. If either committee or either House of Congress disagrees with the Administrator's justification it may initiate action to terminate assistance to any country by a concurrent resolution under section 2367 of this title.

(b)* *Protection of children from exploitation.* No assistance may be provided to any government failing to take appropriate and adequate measures,

---

* So in original. Two subsecs. (b) have been enacted.

within their means, to protect children from exploitation, abuse or forced conscription into military or paramilitary services.

(c) *Factors considered.* In determining whether or not a government falls within the provisions of subsection (a) of this section and in formulating development assistance programs under subchapter I of this chapter, the Administrator shall consider, in consultation with the Assistant Secretary of State for Democracy, Human Rights, and Labor and in consultation with the Ambassador at Large for International Religious Freedom—

> (1) the extent of cooperation of such government in permitting an unimpeded investigation of alleged violations of internationally recognized human rights by appropriate international organizations, including the International Committee of the Red Cross, or groups or persons acting under the authority of the United Nations or of the Organization of American States;

> (2) specific actions which have been taken by the President or the Congress relating to multilateral or security assistance to a less developed country because of the human rights practices or policies of such country; and

> (3) whether the government—

>> (A) has engaged in or tolerated particularly severe violations of religious freedom, as defined in [22 U.S.C. § 6402]; or

>> (B) has failed to undertake serious and sustained efforts to combat particularly severe violations of religious freedom ... when such efforts could have been reasonably undertaken.

(d) *Report to Speaker of House and Committee on Foreign Relations of the Senate.* The Secretary of State shall transmit to the Speaker of the House of Representatives and the Committee on Foreign Relations of the Senate, by February 25 of each year, a full and complete report regarding—

> (1) the status of internationally recognized human rights, within the meaning of subsection (a) of this section—

>> (A) in countries that receive assistance under subchapter I of this chapter, and

>> (B) in all other foreign countries which are members of the United Nations and which are not otherwise the subject of a human rights report under this chapter;

> (2) wherever applicable, practices regarding coercion in population control, including coerced abortion and involuntary sterilization;

> (3) the status of child labor practices in each country, including—

>> (A) whether such country has adopted policies to protect children from exploitation in the workplace, including a prohibition of forced and bonded labor and policies regarding acceptable working conditions; and

(B) the extent to which each country enforces such policies, including the adequacy of the resources and oversight dedicated to such policies;

(4) the votes of each member of the United Nations Commission on Human Rights on all country-specific and thematic resolutions voted on at the Commission's annual session during the period covered during the preceding year;

(5) the extent to which each country has extended protection to refugees, including the provision of first asylum and resettlement;

(6) the steps the Administrator has taken to alter United States programs under subchapter I of this chapter in any country because of human rights considerations; and

(7) wherever applicable, violations of religious freedom, including particularly severe violations of religious freedom. . . .

(e) *Promotion of civil and political rights.* The President is authorized and encouraged to use not less than $3,000,000 of the funds made available under this part and part IV of subchapter II of this chapter for each fiscal year for studies to identify, and for openly carrying out, programs and activities which will encourage or promote increased adherence to civil and political rights, including the right to free religious belief and practice, as set forth in the Universal Declaration of Human Rights, in countries eligible for assistance under this part or under part 10 of this subchapter, except that funds made available under part 10 of this subchapter may only be used under this subsection with respect to countries in sub-Saharan Africa. None of these funds may be used, directly or indirectly, to influence the outcome of any election in any country.

22 U.S.C. § 2304 [Foreign Assistance Act § 502B]. Human rights and security assistance

(a) *Observance of human rights as principal goal of foreign policy; implementation requirements.*

(1) The United States shall, in accordance with its international obligations as set forth in the Charter of the United Nations and in keeping with the constitutional heritage and traditions of the United States, promote and encourage increased respect for human rights and fundamental freedoms throughout the world without distinction as to race, sex, language, or religion. Accordingly, a principal goal of the foreign policy of the United States shall be to promote the increased observance of internationally recognized human rights by all countries.

(2) Except under circumstances specified in this section, no security assistance may be provided to any country the government of which engages in a consistent pattern of gross violations of internationally recognized human rights. Security assistance may not be provided to the police, domestic intelligence, or similar law enforcement forces of a country, and licenses may not be issued under the Export Administration Act of 1979 for the export of crime control and detection instru-

ments and equipment to a country, the government of which engages in a consistent pattern of gross violations of internationally recognized human rights unless the President certifies in writing to the Speaker of the House of Representatives and the chairman of the Committee on Foreign Relations of the Senate and the chairman of the Committee on Banking, Housing, and Urban Affairs of the Senate (when licenses are to be issued pursuant to the Export Administration Act of 1979) that extraordinary circumstances exist warranting provision of such assistance and issuance of such licenses. Assistance may not be provided under part V of this subchapter to a country the government of which engages in a consistent pattern of gross violations of internationally recognized human rights unless the President certifies in writing to the Speaker of the House of Representatives and the chairman of the Committee on Foreign Relations of the Senate that extraordinary circumstances exist warranting provision of such assistance.

(3) In furtherance of paragraphs (1) and (2), the President is directed to formulate and conduct international security assistance programs of the United States in a manner which will promote and advance human rights and avoid identification of the United States, through such programs, with governments which deny to their people internationally recognized human rights and fundamental freedoms, in violation of international law or in contravention of the policy of the United States as expressed in this section or otherwise.

(4) In determining whether the Government of a country engages in a consistent pattern of gross violations of internationally recognized human rights, the President shall give particular consideration to whether the Government—

(A) has engaged in or tolerated particularly severe violations of religious freedom...; or

(B) has failed to undertake serious and sustained efforts to combat particularly serious violations of religious freedom when such efforts could have been reasonably undertaken.

(b) *Report by Secretary of State on practices of proposed recipient countries; considerations.* The Secretary of State shall transmit to the Congress, as part of the presentation materials for security assistance programs proposed for each fiscal year, a full and complete report, prepared with the assistance of the Assistant Secretary of State for Democracy, Human Rights, and Labor and with the assistance of the Ambassador at Large for International Religious Freedom, with respect to practices regarding the observance of and respect for internationally recognized human rights in each country proposed as a recipient of security assistance. Wherever applicable, such report shall include information on practices regarding coercion in population control, including coerced abortion and involuntary sterilization. Such report shall also include, wherever applicable, information on violations of religious freedom, including particularly severe violations of religious freedom.... Each report under this section shall list the votes of each member of the United Nations Commission on Human Rights on all country-specific and thematic resolutions voted on at the Commission's annual session during the period covered during the preceding year. In determining whether a government falls within the provisions of subsection (a)(3) of this section and in the preparation of any report or statement required under this section, consideration shall be given to—

(1) the relevant findings of appropriate international organizations, including nongovernmental organizations, such as the International Committee of the Red Cross; and

(2) the extent of cooperation by such government in permitting an unimpeded investigation by any such organization of alleged violations of internationally recognized human rights.

(c) *Congressional request for information; information required; 30–day period; failure to supply information; termination or restriction of assistance.*

(1) Upon the request of the Senate or the House of Representatives by resolution of either such House, or upon the request of the Committee on Foreign Relations of the Senate or the Committee on Foreign Affairs of the House of Representatives, the Secretary of State shall, within thirty days after receipt of such request, transmit to both such committees a statement, prepared with the assistance of the Assistant Secretary of State for Democracy, Human Rights, and Labor, with respect to the country designated in such request, setting forth—

(A) all the available information about observance of and respect for human rights and fundamental freedom in that country, and a detailed description of practices by the recipient government with respect thereto;

(B) the steps the United States has taken to—

(i) promote respect for and observance of human rights in that country and discourage any practices which are inimical to internationally recognized human rights, and

(ii) publicly or privately call attention to, and disassociate the United states and any security assistance provided for such country from, such practices;

(C) whether, in the opinion of the Secretary of State, notwithstanding any such practices—

(i) extraordinary circumstances exist which necessitate a continuation of security assistance for such country, and, if so, a description of such circumstances and the extent to which such assistance should be continued (subject to such conditions as Congress may impose under this section), and

(ii) on all the facts it is in the national interest of the United States to provide such assistance; and

(D) such other information as such committee or such House may request.

: . .

(3) In the event a statement with respect to a country is requested pursuant to paragraph (1) of this subsection but is not transmitted in accordance therewith within thirty days after receipt of such request, no security assistance shall be delivered to such country except as may thereafter be specifically authorized by law from such country unless and until such statement is transmitted.

(4)(A) In the event a statement with respect to a country is transmitted under paragraph (1) of this subsection, the Congress may at any time thereafter adopt a joint resolution terminating, restricting, or continuing security assistance for such country. In the event such a joint resolution is adopted, such assistance shall be so terminated, so restricted, or so continued, as the case may be....

(d) *Definitions.* For the purposes of this section—

(1) the term "gross violations of internationally recognized human rights" includes torture or cruel, inhuman, or degrading treatment or punishment, prolonged detention without charges and trial, causing the disappearance of persons by the abduction and clandestine detention of those persons, and other flagrant denial of the right to life, liberty, or the security of person; and

(2) the term "security assistance" means—

(A) assistance under part II (military assistance) or part IV (economic support fund) or part V(military education and training) or part VI (peacekeeping operations) or part VIII (antiterrorism assistance) of this subchapter;

(B) sales of defense articles or services, extensions of credits (including participation in credits, and guaranties of loans under the Arms Export Control Act [22 U.S.C. § 2751 et seq.]); or

(C) any license in effect with respect to the export of defense articles or defense services to or for the armed forces, police intelligence, or other internal security forces of a foreign country under section 38 of the Arms Export Control Act [22 U.S.C. § 2778].

(e) *Removal of prohibition on assistance.* Notwithstanding any other provision of law, funds authorized to be appropriated under subchapter I of this chapter may be made available for the furnishing of assistance to any country with respect to which the President finds that such a significant improvement in its human rights record has occurred as to warrant lifting the prohibition on furnishing such assistance in the national interest of the United States.

(f) *Allocations concerned with performance record of recipient countries without contravention of other provisions.* In allocating the funds authorized to be appropriated by this chapter and the Arms Export Control Act [22 U.S.C. § 2751 et seq.], the President shall take into account significant improvements in the human rights records of recipient countries, except that such allocations may not contravene any other provision of law.

(g) *Report to Congress on use of certain authorities relating to human rights conditions.* Whenever the provisions of subsection (e) or (f) of this section are applied, the President shall report to the Congress before making any funds available pursuant to those subsections. The report shall specify the country involved, the amount and kinds of assistance to be provided, and the justifications for providing the assistance, including a description of the significant improvements which have occurred in the country's human rights record.

22 U.S.C. § 2420. Police training prohibition.

(a) *Effective date of prohibition.* On and after July 1, 1975, none of the funds made available to carry out this chapter, and none of the local currencies generated under this chapter, shall be used to provide training or advice, or provide any financial support, for police, prisons, or other law enforcement forces for any foreign government or any program of internal intelligence or surveillance on behalf of any foreign government within the United States or abroad.

(b) *Exception; qualification.* Subsection (a) of this section shall not apply—

(1) with respect to assistance rendered under section 3763 (c) of Title 42, with respect to any authority of the Drug Enforcement Administration or the Federal Bureau of Investigation which relates to crimes of the nature which are unlawful under the laws of the United States, or with respect to assistance authorized under section 2291a of this title; [or] . . .

(5) with respect to assistance, including training, relating to sanctions monitoring and enforcement; [or]

(6) with respect to assistance provided to reconstitute civilian police authority and capability in the post-conflict restoration of host nation infrastructure for the purposes of supporting a nation emerging from instability, and the provision of professional public safety training, to include training in internationally recognized standards of human rights, the rule of law, anti-corruption, and the promotion of civilian police roles that support democracy. . . .

(c) *Country with longstanding democratic tradition, etc.* Subsection (a) of this section shall not apply with respect to a country which has a long-standing democratic tradition, does not have standing armed forces, and does not engage in a consistent pattern of gross violations of internationally recognized human rights.

(d) *Assistance to Honduras or El Salvador.* Notwithstanding the prohibition contained in subsection (a) of this section assistance may be provided to Honduras or El Salvador for fiscal years 1986 and 1987 if, at least 30 days before providing assistance, the President notifies the [relevant House and Senate Committees] ...that he has determined that the government of the recipient country has made significant progress, during the preceding six months, in eliminating any human rights violations including torture, incommunicado detention, detention of persons solely for the nonviolent expression of their political views, or prolonged detention without trial. Any such notification shall include a full description of the assistance which is proposed to be provided and the purposes to which it is to be directed.

International Financial Institutions Act of 1977, as Amended

22 U.S.C. § 262d. Human Rights and United States Assistance policies with international financial institutions.

(a) *Policy goals.* The United States Government, in connection with its voice and vote in the International Bank for Reconstruction and Development, the International Development Association, the International Finance Corporation, the Inter–American Development Bank, the African Development Fund, the Asian Development Bank, the African Development Bank, the European Bank for Reconstruction and the International Monetary Fund, shall advance the cause of human rights, including by seeking to channel assistance toward countries other than those whose governments engage in—

(1) a pattern of gross violations of internationally recognized human rights, such as torture or cruel, inhumane, or degrading treatment or punishment, prolonged detention without charges, or other flagrant denial to life, liberty, and the security of person; or

(2) provide refuge to individuals committing acts of international terrorism by hijacking aircraft.

(b) *Policy considerations for Executive Directors of institutions in implementation of duties.* Further, the Secretary of the Treasury shall instruct each Executive Director of the above institutions to consider in carrying out his duties:

(1) specific actions by either the executive branch or the Congress as a whole on individual bilateral assistance programs because of human rights considerations;

(2) the extent to which the economic assistance provided by the above institutions directly benefit the needy people in the recipient country;

(3) whether the recipient country—

(A)is seeking to acquire unsafeguarded special nuclear material (as defined in section 830(8) of the Nuclear Proliferation Prevention Act of 1994) or a nuclear explosive device (as defined in section 830(4) of that Act);

(B) is not a State Party to the Treaty on the Non–Proliferation of Nuclear Weapons; or

(C) has detonated a nuclear explosive device; and

(4) in relation to assistance for the Socialist Republic of Vietnam, the People's Democratic Republic of Laos, Russia and other independent states of the former Soviet Union (as defined in section 5801 of this title), and Democratic Kampuchea (Cambodia), the responsiveness of the governments of such countries in providing a more substantial accounting of Americans missing in action.

. . .

(d) *Requirements of United States assistance through institutions for projects in recipient countries.* The United States Government, in connection with its voice and vote in the institutions listed in subsection (a) of this section, shall seek to channel assistance to projects which address basic human needs of the people of the recipient country.

(e) *Criteria for determination of gross violations of internationally recognized human rights standards.* In determining whether a country is in gross violation of internationally recognized human rights standards, as defined by the provisions of subsection (a) of this section, the United States Government shall give consideration to the extent of cooperation of such country in permitting an unimpeded investigation of alleged violations of internationally recognized human rights by appropriate international organizations including, but not limited to, the International Committee of the Red Cross, Amnesty International, the International Commission of Jurists, and groups or persons acting under the authority of the United Nations or the Organization of American States.

(f) *Opposition by United States Executive Directors of institutions to financial or technical assistance to violating countries.* The United States Executive Directors of the institutions listed in subsection (a) of this section are authorized and instructed to oppose any loan, any extension of financial assistance, or any technical assistance to any country described in subsection (a)(1) or (2) of this section, unless such assistance is directed specifically to programs which serve the basic human needs of the citizens of such country. . . .

Trade Act of 1974, as Amended

19 U.S.C. § 2432. Freedom of Emigration in East–West Trade [Jackson–Vanik Amendment]

(a) *Actions of nonmarket economy countries making them ineligible for most-favored-nation treatment programs of credits, credit guarantees, or investment guarantees, or commercial agreements.* To assure the continued dedication of the United States to fundamental human rights, and notwithstanding any other provision of law, on or after the January 3, 1975, products from any nonmarket economy country shall not be eligible to receive nondiscriminatory treatment (most-favored-nation treatment), such country shall not participate in any program of the Government of the United States which extends credits or credit guarantees or investment guarantees, directly, or indirectly, and the President of the United States shall not conclude any commercial agreement with any such country, during the period beginning with the date on which the President determines that such country—

(1) denies its citizens the right or opportunity to emigrate;

(2) imposes more than a nominal tax on emigration or on the visas or other documents required for emigration, for any purpose or cause whatsoever; or

(3) imposes more than a nominal tax, levy, fine, fee, or other charge on any citizen as a consequence of the desire of such citizen to emigrate to the country of his choice, and ending on the date on which the President determines that such country is no longer in violation of paragraph (1),(2), or (3).

(b) *Presidential determination and report to Congress that nation is not violating freedom of emigration.* After January 3, 1975, (A) products of a nonmarket economy country may be eligible to receive nondiscriminatory treatment (most-favored-nation treatment), (B) such country may participate in any program of the Government of the United States which extends credits or credit guarantees or investment guarantees, and (C) the President may conclude a commercial agreement with such country, only after the President has submitted to the Congress a report indicating that such country is not in violation of paragraph (1), (2), or (3) of subsection (a) of this section. Such report with respect to such country shall include information as to the nature and implementation of emigration laws and policies and restrictions or discrimination applied to or against persons wishing to emigrate. . . .

(c) *Waiver authority of President.*

(1) During the 18–month period beginning on January 3, 1975, the President is authorized to waive by Executive order the application of subsections (a) and (b) of this section with respect to any country, if he reports to the Congress that—

(A) he has determined that such waiver will substantially promote the objectives of this section; and

(B) he has received assurances that the emigration practices of that country will henceforth lead substantially to the achievement of the objectives of this section.

(2) During any period subsequent to the 18–month period referred to in paragraph (1), the President is authorized to waive by Executive order the application of subsections (a) and (b) of this section with respect to any country, if the waiver authority granted by this subsection continues to apply to such country pursuant to subsection (d) of this section, and if he reports to the Congress that—

(A) he has determined that such waiver will substantially promote the objectives of this section; and

(B) he has received assurances that the emigration practices of that country will henceforth lead substantially to the achievement of the objectives of this section.

(3) A waiver with respect to any country shall terminate on the day after the waiver authority granted by this subsection will substantially promote the objectives of this section, he may recommend further extensions of such authority for successive 12–month periods....

(d) *Extension of waiver authority.*

(1) If the President determines that the further extension of the waiver authority granted under subsection (c) of this section will substantially promote the objectives of this section, he may recommend further extensions of such authority for successive 12–month periods . . .

––––––

In addition to the statutes above, Congress has forbidden the United States to enter into agricultural trading agreements with countries engaging in a consistent pattern of gross human rights violations, 7 U.S.C. § 1733 (j)(1).

Congress has also over the years passed "country-specific" provisions that modify the general legislation above in respect to specific countries. See, e.g., 22 U.S.C. § 2420 (d) above (regarding aid to Honduras and El Salvador in the mid–1980's). Also during the 1980's, Argentina was exempted from some restrictions on assistance to human rights violators in light of its "significant progress in complying with international human rights," Pub. L. 97–113 § 725, 95 Stat. 1519 (1981); Pub. L. 101–162, Title V, 103 Stat. 1030 (1989). Congress has also in the past barred assistance to Chile, Uganda, and Cambodia.

In 1986, Congress passed the Comprehensive Anti–Apartheid Act, Pub. L. 99–440, 100 Stat. 1086 (1986), which, inter alia, banned new investment in South Africa, required all American nationals employing more than twenty-five South African nationals to adhere to a code of labor practices, and restricted trade in various commodities between the two nations. In 1993, Congress passed the South African Democratic Transition Support Act, repealing the Comprehensive Anti–Apartheid Act in light of "a new era" for South Africa "which presents a historic opportunity for a transition to a peaceful, stable, and democratic future." Pub. L. 103–149, 107 Stat. 1503 (1993).

In the 1990s, Congress established a trade embargo and other sanctions against Iraq, citing human rights violations against the Iraqi, Kuwaiti, and Kurdish populations. Pub. L. 101–513 §§ 586–586J, 107 Stat. 2047 (1990). Compare the Cuban Liberty and Democratic Solidarity Act of 1996, 22 U.S.C. §§ 6021–24.

––––––

As noted in the selection by Henkin, tensions between Congress and the Executive branch, as well as opposing perspectives within the latter, have been key factors shaping U.S. human rights policy vis-a-vis other countries. The following excerpt, written by one who had served as a Deputy Assistant Secretary of State in the Human Rights Bureau during the Administration of President Jimmy Carter, describes the impact of these tensions on U.S. human rights policy during the 1970s. Although some of the problems described in this article have been alleviated in subsequent years, the dynamics described by Professor Cohen continue to shape U.S. human rights policy.

Stephen B. Cohen, *Conditioning U.S. Security Assistance on Human Rights Practices*

76 Am. J. Int'l L. 246 (1982).*

. . .

... This article examines the legislation—in force since 1973—that conditions a foreign government's eligibility for United States military aid and arms sales on its human rights record.

. . .

The principal (although not exclusive) legislative enactment on human rights and military ties has been section 502B of the Foreign Assistance Act of 1961.[9] The key subsection of this statute, 502B(a)(2), provides a basic rule: military aid is not to be given and arms are not to be sold to "any country, the government of which engages in a consistent pattern of gross violations of internationally recognized human rights." An exception is allowed for cases where "extraordinary circumstances exist which necessitate a continuation of [military aid and arms sales] and . . . on all the facts it is in the national interest of the United States [to continue such assistance]."[11]

The history of the enactment and implementation of section 502B illuminates the obstacles encountered when Congress tries to influence executive decisions on foreign policy. It is not simply a question of enacting legislation that the Executive implements as a matter of course. A hostile administration may avoid implementation, as during the Nixon and Ford years. Even if high political officials seem sympathetic (as they did during the Carter administration), entrenched bureaucratic interests may actively resist the law, particularly where its subject is human rights and foreign policy. . . . The implementation of section 502B during the Carter years is a story of bureaucratic warfare of the most intense sort. The principal antagonists were the career Foreign Service, with responsibility for the day-to-day management of relations with other countries, and a newly created Department of State Bureau of Human Rights, staffed to a great degree by outsiders. . . .

---

9.   22 U.S.C. § 2304 (Supp. III 1979).

11.   Id. subsection (c)(1)(C). . . .

I. The Evolution of Section 502B

Congress enacted legislation on the subject of human rights and military ties for the first time in 1973. From the beginning, the legislation was openly disregarded by the Nixon and Ford administrations, primarily owing to the opposition of Secretary of State Henry Kissinger. Congress responded by regularly expanding and amending its initial product in an attempt to tighten the law and thus ensure that human rights concerns would be taken into account in executive branch decisions. During Kissinger's tenure, however, Congress was almost entirely unsuccessful in influencing the Executive to change its behavior. . . .

The absence of discernible impact resulted not only from the Executive's opposition to conditioning military aid and arms sales on human rights factors, but also from the fact that for this entire period the legislation was in a form that made it advisory. The statute became a binding legal requirement only in 1978, when Congress decided that earlier versions had not had a sufficient impact. . . .

The General Rule

Section 502B was not the first attempt by Congress to legislate on human rights and military relationships. It was preceded by section 32 of the Foreign Assistance Act of 1973. . . .

At about the same time that section 32 was first proposed, Representative Donald Fraser began a parallel effort, which eventually led to enactment of section 502B. During the fall of 1973, the House Subcommittee on International Organizations and Movements, under Fraser's leadership, began a series of extensive hearings on the subject of human rights and foreign policy and, in early 1974, issued a 54–page report emphasizing the existence of a body of international law that recognizes certain basic rights owed by all governments to their citizens. The report further stated that the United States was obligated not only to respect these rights within its own jurisdiction, but also to avoid supporting other governments engaged in violating them. The report concluded, however, that the United States had failed to meet its obligations:

> The human rights factor is not accorded the high priority it deserves in our country's foreign policy. Unfortunately, the prevailing attitude has led the United States into embracing governments which practice torture and unabashedly violate almost every human rights guarantee pronounced by the world community. . . . [C]onsideration for human rights in foreign policy is both morally imperative and practically necessary. . . . When charges of serious violations of human rights do occur, the most that the [State] Department is likely to do is make private inquiries and low-keyed appeals to the government concerned.[24]

. . .

24. [*International Protection of Human Rights, The Work of International Organiza-* *tions and the Role of U.S. Foreign Policy: Hearings Before the Subcomm. on Interna-*

In an effort to goad the Executive into taking account of human rights, Fraser proposed and Congress enacted the initial version of section 502B in December 1974. In its first incarnation, section 502B, like section 32, expressed the "sense of Congress" and was therefore merely advisory, rather than binding. It stated:

> It is the sense of the Congress that, except in extraordinary circumstances, the President shall substantially reduce or terminate security assistance to any government which engages in a consistent pattern of gross violations of internationally recognized human rights, including torture or cruel, inhuman, or degrading treatment or punishment; prolonged detention without charges; or other flagrant denials of the right to life, liberty, and the security of the person.[27]

It soon became apparent, however, that the Executive, just as it had ignored section 32, intended to give absolutely no effect to the sense of Congress as expressed in section 502B. In November 1975, the Under Secretary of State for Security Assistance . . . testified that in no case during the preceding year had military aid or arms sales been denied on human rights grounds. At the same time, the administration submitted to Congress a report on executive compliance with section 502B. Instead of providing the information required by the statute, the report attacked the policy enunciated by section 502B and clearly implied that the Executive had no intention of ever refusing military aid or arms sales to any government on human rights grounds.

One month later, frustrated by the blatant refusal of the Executive to implement section 502B, Congress attempted to transform the statute . . . into a mandatory requirement. In response to a proposal by Representative Fraser, Congress voted to delete the "sense of the Congress" language and make section 502B legally binding. . . .

President Ford vetoed the foreign aid authorization bill that contained these changes on May 7, 1976. In his veto message, he objected to the transformation of section 502B into a binding directive. Two months later, after a compromise was reached, President Ford signed a revised bill. The sense of the Congress language was replaced by an introduction stating that the section 502B standard was "the policy of the United States." . . .

In January 1977, the Carter administration entered office. [In contrast to the previous four years,] Congress refrained from attempting to strengthen the basic substantive rule of section 502B(a)(2) in order to allow the new Carter administration, publicly committed to renewed emphasis on human rights in foreign policy, an opportunity to implement the legislation as it existed. However, Congress did [provide] for the creation of the position of Assistant Secretary of State for Human Rights, with responsibility for participating in decisions on security assistance.[38] . . .

tional Organizations and Movements of the House Comm. on Foreign Affairs, 93d Cong., 1st Sess. (1974)] at 9–10.

27. Ibid.

38. Foreign Relations Authorization Act, Fiscal Year 1978, § 109, 91 Stat. 846 (1977). . . . [In 1994, the State Department Bureau of Human Rights and Humanitarian

... [I]n 1978 Congress resumed the process of strengthening section 502B by deleting the prefatory "it is the policy of the United States" language from subsection (a)(2). As a result, it directly states that, absent "extraordinary circumstances," "no security assistance may be provided to any country, the government of which engages in a consistent pattern of gross violations of internationally recognized human rights."[40]

. . .

II.   Resistance of the Career Bureaucracy Under Carter

The installation of the Carter administration in January 1977 produced a dramatic shift in attitudes of high political officials on the human rights issue.... Although [as a candidate Jimmy Carter] did not mention the specific issue of human rights and military ties or indicate his position on implementation of section 502B, his personal call for a human rights oriented foreign policy implied a promise to do considerably more than his predecessors to follow the legislation.

The executive branch, however, did not attempt to conform to the statute's requirements without a fierce internal struggle. Despite the change in attitudes at the highest political level (from opposition to section 502B to endorsement of its underlying principle), the Department of State's career bureaucracy remained implacably hostile and continued to resist implementation. The result was intense bureaucratic warfare between career officials, who resisted implementation, and the office of the newly established Assistant Secretary for Human Rights, who sought adherence to the law.

The Attitude of the Career Bureaucracy

. . .

The opposition of the Foreign Service ... was a logical consequence of its conception of its special role or of (what one student of the bureaucracy has labeled) its "organizational essence." The Foreign Service views its primary role or essence as the maintenance of smooth and cordial relations with other governments. It believes that military aid and arms sales are an indispensable means to achieving this goal. When provided, the other government is grateful and more inclined to get along with the United States. When refused, a cordial relationship may be harder to maintain, especially if the other government suspects that the reason for refusal is a judgment that it has mistreated its own citizens.

Keeping other governments happy becomes an end in itself. This phenomenon is often referred to as "clientism" because the Foreign Service views other governments as "clients" with whose interests it identifies,

Affairs was reorganized and renamed the Bureau of Human Rights and Democracy, Human Rights and Labor and the position established by the 1978 was renamed Assistant Secretary for Human Rights, Democracy and Labor.—Editors' Note.]

40.   22 U.S.C. § 2304(a)(2) (Supp. III 1979).

rather than as parties to be dealt with at arm's length according to the national interest of the United States.

. . .

. . . Even after the Carter administration entered office in 1997, the regional bureaus [of the State Department] vigorously fought nearly all attempts to apply section 502B to specific cases.... First, they tried to minimize the relevance of section 502B. During the first 2 years, they argued that it could be ignored because it was merely a statement of policy.... After it was made legally binding, they argued that the statutory rule was only one of several factors to be weighed in decisions on security assistance.

Second, the career bureaucracy attempted to distort information about human rights conditions in particular countries. The extent of abusive practices was consistently underreported.... In the case of Argentina, the Latin American Bureau argued that, at most, hundreds of individuals had been summarily executed by security forces. As the evidence became incontrovertible that the number was actually 6,500 or more, the bureau shifted gears and argued that only Marxist terrorists were the victims. When it was documented that most of the victims were neither Marxists nor terrorists, the bureau maintained that the abuses were the work of local military commanders whom the ruling junta was struggling to control.

As it minimized or concealed negative aspects of a "client's" human rights practices, the career bureaucracy exaggerated positive signs. Improvements were said to have occurred on the basis of insubstantial evidence or self-serving declarations of the government in power....

Third, the regional bureaus overstated the extent of U.S. interests at stake in particular cases and the damage that could possibly result from failure to approve proposed security assistance....

The Human Rights Bureau

Given the resistance of the career bureaucracy, ... implementation of section 502B during the Carter administration depended on the newly created Bureau of Human Rights, headed by an outsider who was personally committed to the policy of the statute and staffed, to a significant degree, by persons from outside the career bureaucracy.... It took the initiative in insisting that section 502B had to be satisfied before security assistance could be provided....

. . .

[The human rights office, newly strengthened by 1977 legislation,] inserted itself into the established Department of State procedures with vigor.... When it disagreed with the regional bureaus, which was quite frequent, it insisted that a decision paper—known formally as an action memorandum—be prepared and sent to the Secretary of State for resolution of the issue.

During the first 18 months of the Carter administration, individual proposals for both military aid and arms sales were continually at issue between the regional bureaus and the Bureau of Human Rights and therefore "litigated" through the action memorandum procedure. In some ways, this resembled a judicial process, for it was adversarial in nature....

. . .

III. Interpretation and Application of the Statute Under Carter

. . .

[A] careful examination of actual decisions under section 502B leads to [the conclusion that] the Carter administration exhibited a remarkable degree of tentativeness and caution.... Relatively few governments were considered to be "engaged in a consistent pattern of gross [human rights] violations." Security assistance was actually cut off to even fewer, because other U.S. interests were often found to outweigh human rights concerns under the exception for "extraordinary circumstances." Moreover, in some instances, the Carter administration adopted a highly strained reading of the statute which, although not contrary to its literal terms, produced a result contrary to congressional intent. In other cases, the language was simply disregarded, so that decisions violated even the letter of the law.

Fear of Finding

Perhaps the most remarkable evidence of the administration's conservative approach to section 502B was its policy never to determine formally, even in a classified decision, that a particular government was engaged in gross abuses. The primary reason for this policy was the belief that such a determination, even if classified, would inevitably be leaked to the press and become generally known. It was feared that each country named would then consider itself publicly insulted, with consequent damage to our bilateral relationship. In addition, there was concern that once such a finding was revealed, the freedom to alter it might be severely constrained by public political pressures. Any attempt to name a country as a "gross violator" would raise the ire of defense-minded conservatives who did not want military ties cut off. Any attempt to change the finding because a country had improved conditions would be subject to intense scrutiny by human rights partisans to determine whether the supposed improvements were cosmetic or genuine. Thus, maximum flexibility required that no country be formally found to be prohibited from receiving security assistance under section 502B.

In practice, the Secretary of State had to resist pressures both from Congress and within his own Department to make such findings. Administration representatives repeatedly refused congressional requests for a list of governments considered to be engaged in gross abuses, stating that it was administration policy not to draw up such a list. Within the Department, the Secretary of State sought to avoid explaining the reason for decisions on security assistance either in writing or even informally. When he resolved a dispute, he often communicated simply whether the request was approved or disapproved and little more. Particularly in cases of disapproval, the Secretary strenuously avoided ever stating that it was required by section 502B since such a statement would have meant that the government in question was considered to be engaged "in a consistent pattern of gross violations of human rights."

. . .

1. Gross Violations.

. . . Although no formal "hit" list of countries [deemed to be engaged in gross violations] was ever prepared, it could easily have been inferred from the pattern of decisions on specific security assistance issues raised in action memorandums. By the middle of Carter's term, the implied list would have looked more or less as follows:

Latin America: Argentina, Bolivia, El Salvador, Guatemala, Haiti, Nicaragua, Paraguay, Uruguay

East Asia: the Philippines, South Korea

The Middle East: Iran

Africa: Zaire

Changed circumstances in particular countries caused the implied list to be modified at certain points. For example, Bolivia was not on the list when elected civilian Governments were in power in 1977 and 1979, but was on it following military coups in 1978 and 1980. . . .

. . .

2. Extraordinary Circumstances.

The Carter administration always gave considerable weight to arguments that other U.S. interests might require continuation of security assistance, even when the government in question was thought to be a "gross violator." . . .

. . . Because of the liberal use made of the exception for "extraordinary circumstances," the number of countries subject to a section 502B cutoff was quite modest. In the end, human rights concerns resulted in the termination of security assistance to only eight countries, all in Latin America: Argentina, Bolivia, El Salvador, Guatemala, Haiti, Nicaragua, Paraguay, and Uruguay.

Extraordinary circumstances were found for all of the other countries considered to be gross violators. Thus Indonesia (although technically not on the list) was a key member of ASEAN (the pro-Western association of Southeast Asian countries) and important to countering Soviet and Vietnamese influence in the region. Iran was judged critical because it shared a long border with the Soviet Union, was a major supplier of oil to the West, and defended our strategic interests in the Persian Gulf. Military ties with South Korea were deemed essential to deterring the threat of an invasion from the north. Military bases in the Philippines were judged critical to the United States and a security assistance relationship essential to keeping the bases. Finally, Zaire, the third largest country by area in Africa, was the source of nearly all the West's cobalt, a material crucial to the performance of high-performance jet engines.

No claims of similar magnitude were made for United States interests in Latin American countries on the list. None supplied a critical resource, shared a border with the Soviets, or acted as a special surrogate to defend U.S. interests in the entire region. . . .

In all cases where a substantial interest was found, the administration assumed, mostly without question, that arms sales and military aid would automatically help secure it. In no case did the administration seriously consider that such approval might actually make the interest less attainable, particularly over the longer run. For example, during 1977 and 1978, the United States approved the sale of billions of dollars of sophisticated weaponry to Iran under the Shah. The enormous cost of these arms fed the Iranian belief that the country's oil wealth was being wasted to benefit U.S. defense companies, which reinforced anti-American feelings in Iran. Similarly, in 1978, the U.S. Government signed an agreement tripling military aid to the Philippines in order to make more secure its military bases there. But the net effect of this action was probably to make the bases less secure because it associated the United States with the unpopular, ineffective, and corrupt Marcos dictatorship.

. . .

IV. Conclusions

. . .

What are the lessons to be drawn for implementation by the Executive when Congress attempts to legislate foreign policy? The history of section 502B . . . underlines the need . . . for clearer directives, less discretion, and more assiduous congressional oversight. . . . [These observations] are especially apt when congressional objectives may require decisions that displease particular governments and that will therefore be resisted by the Foreign Service bureaucracy whose paramount interest is maintaining cordial relations. . . .

. . .

Congress has the most decisive impact when its directives allow the Executive no discretion at all. . . .

There are, perhaps, some drawbacks to statutes that deny all discretion, such as [country-specific legislation]. Once such a provision is enacted, the Executive lacks the flexibility to respond quickly to changed conditions. While Congress has a legitimate role to play in setting basic foreign policy goals, it may be less well equipped to make day-to-day decisions about how best to fulfill those goals in specific cases. . . .

For these reasons, a general rule that sets forth basic goals may be preferable to country-specific legislation. Yet the history of section 502B suggests that the creation or tightening of a general rule will produce, by itself, little change in executive behavior. Special implementing mechanisms are required if a substantive rule is to have a direct influence on decisions. Because the career bureaucracy can be expected to abuse the discretion allowed by a general rule, a countervailing center of bureaucratic influence is essential to implementation.

. . .

Notes

1.   Henkin and Cohen both identify sectors within the U.S. government that have opposed a vigorous human rights policy. What constituencies and considerations, then, help account for the important role that human rights has assumed in overall U.S. policy?

2.   As Henkin notes, "realists" serving in successive administrations tended to oppose making the advancement of human rights a key goal of U.S. foreign policy. To some extent, however, the differences between those who supported a human rights policy on essentially moral grounds and those who opposed it as an impediment to the advancement of U.S. security interests began to erode in the mid–1980s. During his second term in office, President Ronald Reagan, initially opposed to the human rights policy of his predecessor, became convinced that at least in some countries U.S. security interests would be advanced by promoting a strong human rights policy. See Diane F. Orentlicher, *The Power of an Idea: The Impact of United States Human Rights Policy*, 1 Transnat'l L. & Contemp. Probs. 43 (1991); Tamar Jacoby, *The Reagan Turnaround on Human Rights*, 64 Foreign Aff. 1066 (1986). See also note 7, below.

3.   Henkin notes that the principal human rights laws enacted in the 1970s as a result of Congressman Donald Fraser's leadership were not aimed at Communist states. But other legislation did target Communist states. Pursuant to the Jackson–Vanik amendment, enacted in 1975, the President may not extend most-favored-nation trade status to "nonmarket economy countries" that impede emigration of their citizens absent a presidential waiver (see pp. 825–827 above).

4.   In addition to the general legislation examined in the preceding article, Congress has enacted a number of country-specific laws imposing—or threatening to impose—military and other sanctions on countries engaged in serious violations of human rights. Some of these laws have specified preconditions that must be satisfied before aid can be appropriated; others have specified conditions that must be met in order for aid previously withheld on human rights grounds to be restored. In view of the option of applying sanctions that are tailored to a particular country's situations, is it desirable to maintain generally-applicable laws such as section 502B or its counterpart for non-military assistance, section 116? In the preceding excerpt, Cohen argues that generally applicable laws such as section 502B are preferable to country-specific legislation since they provide the Executive branch flexibility in its conduct of foreign affairs. But Cohen also writes that the "history of section 502B . . . underlines the need . . . for clearer directives, less discretion, and more assiduous oversight." What

approach does Cohen suggest for striking the proper balance between allowing the Executive appropriate discretion and risking abuse of that discretion?

5. Cohen describes the reluctance of senior State Department officials to find that a government was engaged in gross abuses. As he notes, the Secretary of State "strenuously avoided ever stating" that his decision to deny security assistance was required by section 502B "since such a statement would have meant that the government in question was considered to be engaged 'in a consistent pattern of gross violations of human rights.'" Did this approach defeat the purpose of section 502B—or did it represent an appropriate balance between Congress's objectives and the concerns of the State Department? Given that the State Department was already required to make a public assessment of each state's human rights record, what difference would a formal finding that a government was responsible for gross human rights violations have made?

6. In some instances the threat of country-specific legislation may prompt a reluctant Administration to adopt a more vigorous human rights policy as a preemptive measure. This happened in the mid–1980s with respect to South Africa. At the outset of his first term, President Reagan adopted a policy of "constructive engagement" toward the South African government, eschewing punitive sanctions. Substantial public pressure for a more aggressive human rights policy began to build in 1984 as opposition to apartheid escalated in South Africa and was met with violent repression. But when congressional legislation imposing a range of sanctions against South Africa seemed certain to pass, the Administration promulgated an executive order "Prohibiting Trade and Certain Other Transactions Involving South Africa." Exec. Order No. 12, 532, 50 Fed. Reg. 36,861 (Sept. 10, 1985). Two weeks later, President Reagan issued another order prohibiting imports of South African krugerrands. Exec. Order 12,535, 50 Fed. Reg. 40,325 (Oct. 1, 1985). (As previously noted, in 1986 Congress enacted the Comprehensive Anti–Apartheid Act.)

7. Writing in 1982, Cohen expressed the view that "the net effect" of the U.S. Government's action in 1978 in signing a military bases agreement with the Philippine government of Ferdinand Marcos "was probably to make the bases less secure because it associated the United States with the unpopular, ineffective, and corrupt Marcos dictatorship." Two years after he wrote this, the Reagan Administration, which entered office believing that human rights concerns in the Philippines should yield to overriding security interests, concluded that widespread human rights abuses by Philippine security forces were fueling the explosive growth of communist insurgency. The Administration was persuaded, therefore, that compelling national security interests required it to promote greater respect for human rights by Philippine security forces, and it began to pressure the government of Ferdinand Marcos to curb violations. Apparently responding to this pressure, President Marcos called a "snap" presidential election—which led to the end of his regime. See Tamar Jacoby, supra note 2.

As Cohen makes clear, security considerations, broadly conceived, have been among the most important counterweights to human rights objectives in U.S. foreign policy. Should speculative security considerations trump the basic goal underlying section 502B of terminating military aid to a government that consistently commits gross violations of human rights? Does the answer depend upon the gravity of the relevant security considerations? The gravity of the human rights violations? Whose assessment should prevail in the event there is a disagreement?

8.   To what end should sanctions be imposed in response to gross violations of human rights? How important, for example, is it for the United States to distance itself from atrocious conduct by other governments, even if sanctions are not likely to achieve improvement in the target state's human rights practices?

———

Some of the factors cited by Professor Cohen to explain Executive resistance to congressional human rights directives are no longer present, and others are no longer as influential. For one thing, the Human Rights Bureau, which originally did not fit easily into the established foreign policy bureaucracy, has become "institutionalized" since the period examined by Cohen. And although governments still resent being scolded about their human rights practices, they have become more accustomed to such criticism as the U.S. human rights policy launched in the early 1970s has gained length in years. (Still, many governments react intensely when their practices are critically assessed in the annual State Department report, which we consider in the following section.) Further, with the end of the Cold War, the most compelling security considerations that had long been invoked to block or blunt human rights policy initiatives are no longer pertinent.

Yet in many respects, public debate about the appropriate response to serious human rights violations continues to be characterized by the same underlying dynamic that has long shaped U.S. policy. Notably, Congress has continued to utilize its lawmaking authority to force a reluctant Administration to sanction countries that commit serious violations of fundamental rights. In contrast to the 1970s and 1980s, however, in the final years of the twentieth century the imperatives of U.S. competition in the global market emerged as a principal counterweight to U.S. human rights objectives.

Dana Priest, *New Human Rights Law Triggers Policy Debate*

Wash. Post, Dec. 31, 1998, p. A34.

The State Department this month rejected a request from defense giant General Dynamics Corp. for U.S. financing to help Turkey buy armored vehicles for police operating in provinces where state-sponsored torture "is a longstanding and pervasive practice," according to an internal State Department document. The decision marked the first serious test of a human rights law, passed by Congress in 1996 and expanded this year, that prohibits U.S. funds, in this case U.S. loan guarantees, from aiding units of foreign security forces that have been involved in human rights violations.

While the overall effect of the ruling was relatively modest—General Dynamics completed the deal with its own financing—the application of the law proved anything but simple. It ignited an angry dispute within the government, with opponents—including the U.S. ambassador to Turkey and a senator whose state manufactures the vehicles, as well as General Dynamics executives—arguing that the decision would increase Turkey's hostility to human rights and jeopardize U.S. business and national security interests.

State Department officials said they do not expect the law, which was sponsored by Sen. Patrick J. Leahy (D–Vt.), to drastically alter Washington's deep involvement with Turkey, a NATO ally to which the United States has sold or given more than $15 billion worth of weapons since 1980. But it is likely to cause future debate over policy in Turkey and other countries with controversial rights records, especially those, like Algeria, Colombia, Mexico, Indonesia, Rwanda and China, where the U.S. military is seeking to expand its relationships despite concerns about human rights.

In anticipation of future disputes, the State Department recently set up an interagency group to work out how to implement the Leahy law, which applies to most military assistance and, after its scope was expanded by Congress this year, to all military training activities funded by the Defense Department.

. . .

This year the State Department said it would not allow U.S. firms to sell attack helicopters to Turkey, which is considering bids for a $3.5 billion deal, unless there was a significant improvement of Turkey's human rights record. The State Department had found previously that some U.S. helicopters were used to force the evacuation of, or kill, noncombatants in Kurdish strongholds.

But Turkey has other military suppliers, and U.S. officials note that one of the benefits of Ankara's growing military relationship with Israel will be a new source for weaponry without strings attached. In 1996, Turkey canceled a planned purchase of 10 U.S. Super Cobra helicopters when Congress, concerned about human rights, delayed the deal.

Beyond arms deals, Turkey has perhaps the largest training program with the U.S. military of any country. . . .

But when it comes to deals such as those involving the armored vehicles, Turkey retains the ability to overcome U.S. conditions. Ankara turned down a compromise proposal offered by Washington that would have delayed the financing for six months until Turkey had met conditions laid out by Marc Grossman, assistant secretary of state for European affairs, including an agreement to investigate and prosecute police alleged to have used torture, to adopt the U.S. rules of engagement and to undergo anti-torture training. The compromise was eventually abandoned.

Levin believes the State Department went well beyond the letter of the law to satisfy human rights groups. He said the law should be narrowed to prohibit only equipment that is used directly for torture. "You have to hit the right target," he said in an interview this week. "You can't hit the whole national police force."

Leahy says the decision represents a small, but important victory that shows the State Department is resolved to take the law seriously. "There's no way we can do things that appear to condone torture," he said.

In this case, the vehicles will still go to the police groups in all of the provinces cited in the original deal. In areas where U.S. loan guarantees are prohibited, General Dynamics has agreed to finance the sale. "As a business, we would rather have the Ex–Im Bank finance all of the vehicles, but that's not possible," said General Dynamics spokesman Kendall Pease. "We're prepared to finance the deal because we have a commitment to our customer."

. . .

Notes

1.   Whereas Cold–War–related security concerns formerly provided the main counterweight to human rights concerns in U.S. foreign policy, in the late 1990s U.S. trade objectives emerged as a principal—arguably the most important—policy objective that served to temper or override human rights concerns. The Leahy amendment sought to strike a balance between U.S. trade and human rights policies by applying sanctions only with respect to units of foreign security forces involved in human rights abuses, thereby allowing U.S. financing for sales to other units of the same country. What are or should be the objectives of such a law? To deter actual abuses? To distance the United States symbolically from abuses that occur? Does the appropriateness of the Leahy law turn upon the seriousness of the alleged abuses?

2.   The tension between U.S. trade and human rights concerns dominated public debate concerning U.S. policy toward China in the 1990s. For several years, this debate centered on the annual renewal of China's most-favored-nation (MFN) trade status. In 1994, President Clinton put this debate to rest when he decided to de-link China's MFN status from its human rights record, thereby reversing a policy embodied in an Executive Order he had issued one year earlier. In doing so, President Clinton announced that he would instead promote a voluntary code of conduct governing the overseas practices of U.S. corporations. In this way, he suggested, U.S. investment in China (and other countries where human rights abuses are widespread) might serve to advance human rights. The Administration subsequently established a task force comprising representatives of business, human rights and labor communities, which developed a voluntary code of conduct

for corporations that source products from overseas facilities. The code of conduct established standards that adherents agreed to apply in respect of workplace conditions in overseas factories. Is this a better way of balancing U.S. trade and human rights interests than imposing trade sanctions? Should the code be mandatory? Should the Administration at least require companies to sign on to the code of conduct as a precondition to enjoying such privileges as participating in U.S. trade missions to countries like China?

3. *Sanctions by U.S. States against foreign violations of human rights.* States of the United States also imposed sanctions against South Africa during *apartheid.* More recently, a number of state and local governments have imposed sanctions against other violators, notably Myanmar (formerly Burma). For example, in 1995 Massachusetts enacted legislation prohibiting its public agencies from contracting with companies that do business in Myanmar. A Federal court of appeals ruled that the Massachusetts Burma Law was an unconstitutional invasion of the responsibility of the federal government to regulate U.S. foreign affairs; that it violated the Foreign Commerce clause; and that it was preempted by weaker federal sanctions against Myanmar. *National Foreign Trade Council v. Natsios,* 1999 WL 398414 (1st Cir. 1999) (citing *Zschernig v. Miller,* 389 U.S. 429 (1968)). The court distinguished *Board of Trustees v. Mayor of Baltimore,* 562 A.2d 720 (Md. 1989), which upheld a Baltimore ordinance that withdrew the city's investments from South Africa, on the ground that it and did not seek to control private commercial activities. How much authority should state and local governments have to respond to human rights violations in foreign countries? See, e.g., Daniel M. Price and John P. Hannah, *The Constitutionality of United States State and Local Sanctions,* 39 Harv. Int'l L.J. 443 (1998); Peter J. Spiro, *Foreign Relations Federalism,* 70 U. Colo. L. Rev. 1223 (1999).

b. HUMAN RIGHTS REPORTING

To help implement its human rights restrictions on U.S. aid, Congress directed the Department of State to report annually on the condition of human rights in foreign countries. Originally, these reports were to describe only countries receiving foreign assistance or which were proposed recipients of security assistance, which did not include the Soviet Bloc. Later, Congress extended the scope of the reporting obligation, requiring the Department of State to report on the human rights situation in all states that are members of the United Nations. (Currently, the Department of State also prepares reports on the few non-member states.)

Perhaps inevitably, country rights reports prepared by U.S. embassies or by the Department of State were colored by larger foreign policy attitudes and interests. Especially during the Cold War, the Department of State was sometimes inclined to temper criticism of human rights conditions in friendly and anti-Communist countries and to be harsh in its judgement of the friends and supporters of the Soviet Union. Non-governmental organizations interested in human rights undertook critical examinations of the country reports and called attention to perceived inadequacies.

Over time, the critics of the Country Reports have found less to criticize. For some years, in fact, the principal criticism voiced by U.S.-based human rights organizations has been that the U.S. government does not do enough to address the human rights violations it effectively documents. By the mid–1990s, the Lawyers Committee for Human Rights, which began to produce critiques of the State Department's Country Reports in 1978 (and for a time produced them jointly with organizations that now form constituent parts of Human Rights Watch), had narrowed the number of countries covered in its Critique to 25. The Committee explained: "In acknowledgment of the generally improved quality of the reports, the *Critique*, now in its 18th year of publication, has steadily narrowed its focus to a smaller list (25 this year) of countries that raise particular concerns." Lawyers Committee for Human Rights, Critique: Review of the U.S. Department of State's Country Reports on Human Rights Practices for 1996, pp. v–vi (July 1997). Two years later, the Committee decided to end its two-decades long project of critiquing the State Department's annual report; by then, the reports had improved to the point where the exercise of critiquing them no longer seemed necessary.

The following excerpts from 1985 Critique provide a benchmark of the problems that tended to characterize earlier State Department reporting. The 1994 Report and Critique reflect the substantial evolution in the quality of State Department reporting in the intervening years, as well as broader developments in respect of international human rights and U.S. policy.

Americas Watch Committee, The Helsinki Committee, & The Lawyers Committee for Human Rights, *Critique: Review of the Department of State's Country Reports on Human Rights Practices for 1984*

1–4, 25–31 & 71–73 (1985).

INTRODUCTION

This critique reviews the State Department's reporting on thirty-one countries where human rights conditions were a major concern during 1984. In the majority of the reports we reviewed, we found accurate information presented in such a way as to convey a fair impression of the human rights situation. Some flaws that we pointed out in previous critiques were corrected. In general, the State Department's annual report on human rights worldwide is an ever-more useful compendium of information. The Department deserves credit for the increasing professionalization of human rights monitoring that is reflected in most of the reports we examined.

Regrettably, as in the past, there are important exceptions to the generally high standard of reporting. The most striking are the reports dealing with four countries in Central America: El Salvador, Guatemala, Honduras and Nicaragua. In the case of the first three, the reports seem to make every effort to minimize abuses; in the case of Nicaragua, the report goes in the opposite direction, grossly exaggerating abuses. The effect is to paint an unrealistically rosy portrait of human rights conditions in those countries in the region supported by the United States and an unrealistically grim portrait of human rights conditions in the country opposed by the United States.

The reports on Central America have been colored by the United States' active engagement in civil wars in the region, at least in so far as El Salvador is concerned, where the United States supports government forces against her guerrilla antagonists, and in so far as Nicaragua is concerned, where the United States supports guerrilla forces against their government antagonist. However compelling the Administration perceives its interests to be in those countries, there can be no excuse for distorting a factual discussion of human rights conditions to further Administration policy in other spheres. We question whether it is possible for the State Department to carry out even-handed human rights monitoring in situations where the United States is at war, either directly or by all-out support for one side.

Of the remaining twenty-six country reports that we examined, four are very poor: the reports on Chile, Indonesia, Morocco and Uruguay. We call on the Department of State to review carefully our criticism of its reporting on these countries and to make changes. As matters stand, the Department is distorting the human rights situation in these countries.

Elsewhere, though we are critical of many particulars in the reports, a careful reader can obtain a generally accurate picture of the human rights situation.

Many of the comments in this critique focus on the terminology that is used to qualify information on abuses of human rights. Sometimes the State Department says that uses are "documented" or based on "credible" reports; other times, abuses are "alleged" or based on "claims." In fact, however, our examination makes it clear that the use of such terminology does not reflect consistent standards. Rather, it appears that the choice of terminology sometimes reflects the State Department's political biases. Again, this is most evident in the reports on the four Central American countries that we examined. At other times, the individual biases of the authors of the reports may be involved. There may also be times when the choice of qualifying term is merely quixotic. Whatever the reasons, the terms used to describe the evidence for a buses are important. It makes a great difference, for example, to report that "torture was documented" in one country and that there were "claims of torture" in another country even though the actual evidence with respect to torture may be similar in both cases.

To correct this problem, it would be useful for the Department of State to set forth the standard for using one or another qualifying term and to adhere to those standards.

Other comments in this critique focus on the summaries that preface each of the country's reports. This is where conclusory statements are made. Also, the summaries provide most of the quotable material. In the case of several governments that are supported by the United States, detailed information on abuses appears in the body of the report, but the summary statements addressing those issues convey a qualitatively different, and often misleading, impression. To correct this problem, we call on the Department of State to develop a standardized system of summarizing reports.

Again, despite our criticisms, we continue to believe that the country reports are an enormously valuable contribution to the cause of human rights and we congratulate those responsible for the improvements reflected in the reports for 1994.

. . .

EL SALVADOR

The Report on El Salvador thoroughly misrepresents the human rights situation in that country. . . .

Here are a few of the assertions in the Report on El Salvador and our responses:

. . .

Assertion: "The Armed Forces continue to be accused of human rights abuses, but the focus of these allegations has shifted primarily to the killing of noncombatants by gunfire or aerial bombardment. Most of these accusations, however, originate with the guerrillas themselves or from sources close to and sympathetic to the guerrillas."

Response: This assertion attempts to discredit both the accusations and those who have made them. In fact, the accusations that have attracted attention in the United States and internationally originate primarily with the human rights office of the Roman Catholic Archdiocese of San Salvador, Tutela Legal; or with Americas Watch and the Lawyers Committee for International Human Rights; or with U.S. newspapers covering El Salvador.

To deal just with the accounts by U.S. newspapers during 1984, *The New York Times*, *The Boston Globe* and *The Miami Herald* investigated the July massacre at Los Llanitos, Cabanas. At no point n the Country Report is this massacre even mentioned. Reuters and several U.S. journalists investigated the August massacre at the Gualsinga River, Chalatenango. At no point in the Country Report is this massacre even mentioned. *The Christian Science Monitor* regularly covered aerial attacks and ground sweeps against civilians. None of the episodes discussed in *The Monitor* articles is even mentioned. Instead these accounts are swept into the general assertion about accusations originating with the guerrillas and those sympathetic to them.

As to the accusations by Tutela Legal, the Americas Watch and the Lawyers Committee for International Human Rights, those are based on testimony from witnesses and family members that was recorded and published. Again, none of this is mentioned except insofar as the attempt is made to discredit it by attributing accusations to the guerrillas and their sympathizers.

. . .

NICARAGUA

The Country Report on Nicaragua is one of the most severely distorted in the 1984 volume. Major omissions, misleading statements and highly slanted reporting pervade the Report. Truth is distorted to serve the Administrations's policies toward Nicaragua.

A device consistently employed in the Report is the use of language implying certainty with regard to the reports of government abuses, and calling into question facts that are favorable to the government. Thus the former are reported as "documented" instances of abuse, even where unconfirmed reports are the basis of charges, while the latter are merely "claims" by the Nicaraguan government, even where such "claims" are confirmed by various neutral sources. . . .

———

U.S. Department of State, *Country Reports on Human Rights for 1994*

xi-xx, 1296–71 (1995).

PREFACE

. . .

This report is submitted to the Congress by the Department of State in compliance with sections 116 (d) and 502 (b) of the Foreign Assistance Act of 1961(FAA), as amended, and section 505 (c) of the Trade Act of 1974, as amended. . . .

HOW THE REPORTS ARE PREPARED

In August 1993, the Secretary of State moved to strengthen further the human rights efforts of our embassies. All sections in each embassy were asked to contribute information and to corroborate reports of human rights violations, and new efforts were made to link mission programming to the advancement of human rights and democracy. . . .

Our embassies, which prepared the initial drafts of the reports, gathered information throughout the year from a variety of sources across the political spectrum, including government officials, jurists, military sources, journalists, human rights monitors, academics, and labor activists. This information-gathering can be hazardous and U.S. Foreign Service Officers regularly go to great length, under trying and sometimes dangerous conditions, to investigate reports of human rights abuse, monitor elections, and come to the aid of individuals at risk, such as political dissidents and human rights defenders whose rights are threatened by their governments.

After the embassies completed their drafts, the texts were sent to Washington for careful review by the Bureau of Democracy, Human Rights, and Labor, in cooperation with other State Department offices. As they worked to corroborate, analyze, and edit the reports, the Department officers drew on their own sources of information. These included reports provided by U.S. and other human rights groups, foreign government officials, foreign representatives from the United Nations and other international and regional organizations and institutions, and experts from academia and the media. Officers also consulted with experts on worker rights issues, refugee issues, military and police matters, women's issues, and legal matters. The guiding principle was to ensure that all relevant information was assessed as objectively, thoroughly, and fairly as possible.

The reports in this volume will be used as a resource for shaping policy, conducting diplomacy, and making assistance, training, and other resource allocations. They will also serve as a basis for the U.S. Government's cooperation with private groups to promote the observance of internationally recognized human rights.

. . .

OVERVIEW

THE CHANGING NATURE OF HUMAN RIGHTS PROBLEMS

During the Cold War threats to human rights were seen as coming primarily from centralized authorities—strong governments ruling with an iron hand. In response, the human rights community developed the forms of advocacy with which we are now familiar—monitoring, reporting, publicizing cases, advocacy on behalf of individual victims of human rights abuse, and advocacy of sanctions against strong governments.

Today, in the post-Cold War world, much has changed. Human rights abuses are still committed by strong central governments. But we have become all too familiar with abuses in countries with weak or unresponsive governments, committed by ethnic, religious, and separatist extremists, as well as governments themselves, and in extreme cases fanned into genocide by cynical political leaders, and made harder to resist by enormous economic, environmental, an demographic pressures. These conflicts present us with a devastating array of new human rights problems.

At the same time, the post-Cold War environment offers opportunities for structural change both within countries and in the international community that could give internationally recognized human rights greater force than ever before. This is due in large part to the fall of Soviet

Communism, but also to a powerful global movement for human rights and democratic participation. . . .

. . .

Democracy is by definition a system which provides for the participation of ordinary citizens in governing their country, and depends for its success on the growth of democratic culture along with democratic institutions. Elections are one essential dimension of participation and accountability. Democracy's most stirring triumphs of the year were Nelson Mandela's election as President in South Africa and the restoration of President Jean–Bertrand Aristide and the democratically elected Government of Haiti.

In South Africa, concerted efforts by all sides eventually brought all parties into the political process, resulting in profound structural change that has ended institutional apartheid and sharply decreased the violence it engendered. In Haiti, President Aristide was peacefully returned to power through U.S. leadership and the international community's resolute stand against the violent usurpers who had disposed him and perpetrated massive human rights abuses on the people.

Away from the headlines, democracy has also make strides in little-noticed places:

In Malawi, voters defeated former President-for-Life H. Kamuzu Banda in free elections in May.

The countries of the former Soviet bloc continued their halting transitions from closed to open societies. The newly independent states of Kazakhstan, Kyrgyzstan, Tajikistan, and Uzbekistan held elections with varying degrees of freedom and fairness and in the shadow of continuing significant human rights abuse. The picture was brighter in the countries of Central Europe, through dimmed in some places by disturbing encroachments on freedom of speech and the press.

Democracy is not a one-time event but a process of governance and of history. As President Aristide said upon his return to Haiti, "The true test of a democracy is its second free election when power is transferred freely and constitutionally." These important milestones in democratic development were passed in a number of countries.

Several Latin American countries such as Uruguay, Chile, and Brazil, which were formerly ruled by the military, held new rounds of elections and inaugurated new presidents in 1994, further consolidating their democracies.

After Nepal's second parliamentary election since its democratic revolution in 1990, an opposition party formed a coalition government and peacefully assumed power.

There were significant setbacks for democracy as well. The long delayed return of democracy to Nigeria was again blocked by a military dictatorship's refusal to accept the outcome of elections. In Gambia, the military overthrew the elected civilian Government. In Burma, the military regime continued its refusal to abide by the results of the 1990 elections, keeping Nobel Peace Prize Winner Aung San Suu Kyi under house arrest and silencing all opposition.

CIVILIAN CONTROL OF THE MILITARY AND LAW ENFORCEMENT

As countries make the transition from authoritarian government to open societies, few issues become more crucial than the civilian control of the military and law enforcement authorities. Indeed, in many countries, human rights abuses and democratic setbacks resulted from the inability of civilian authorities to control armed forces and security services. In other countries, there were examples of progress.

In Argentina the Senate rejected the promotion of two navy commanders because of their admitted role in torture during the years of military rule. In Guatemala, the Congress held hearings on the killing of a student by security forces during rioting in November, marking a step forward in congressional oversight.

In Sri Lanka, the Government set up regional commissions to investigate allegations of disappearances and began prosecution proceedings against accused extrajudicial killers.

While members of Colombia's security forces and guerrilla groups continue to commit serous human rights abuses, the new administration has taken a number of steps aimed at reducing the incidence of official abuses and punishing those who commit them.

In Nigeria, on the other hand, the military regime that seized power after annulling the free and fair elections of 1993 continued to ride roughshod over the opposition and ruin hopes for political or economic progress.

. . .

John Shattuck
Assistant Secretary for
Democracy, Human Rights and
Labor.

APPENDIXES

———

Appendix A.—Notes on Preparation of the Reports

. . .

The following notes on specific categories of the report are not meant to be comprehensive descriptions of each category but to provide definitions of key terms used in the reports and to explain the organization of material within the format:

Political and Other Extrajudicial Killing—Includes killings in which there is evidence of government instigation without due process of law, or of political motivation by government or by opposition groups; also covers extrajudicial killings (e.g., other agents of the State whether against criminal suspects, detainee, prisoners, or others); excludes combat deaths and killings by common criminals, if the likelihood of political motivation can be ruled out (see also Section 1.g.).

Disappearance—Covers unresolved cases in which political motivation appears likely and in which the victims have not been found or perpetrators have not been identified; cases eventually classed as political killings are covered in the above category, those eventually identified as arrest or detention are covered under "Arbitrary Arrest, Detention, or Exile."

Torture and Other Cruel, Inhuman, or Degrading Treatment or Punishment—Torture is here defined as an extremely severe form of cruel, inhuman, or degrading treatment or punishment, committed by or at the instigation of government forces or opposition groups, with specific intent to cause extremely severe pain or suffering, whether mental or physical. Discussion concentrates on actual practices, not on whether they fit any precise definition and includes use of physical and other force that may fall short of torture but which is cruel, inhuman, or degrading.

Arbitrary Arrest, Detention or Exile—Covers cases in which detainees, including political detainees, are held in official custody without charges or, if charged, are denied a public preliminary judicial hearing within a reasonable period. Also discusses whether, and under what circumstances, governments exile citizens.

Denial of Fair Public Trial—Briefly describes the court system and evaluates whether there is an independent judiciary and whether trials are both fair and public (failure to hold any trial is noted in the category above); includes discussion of "political prisoners" (political detainees are covered above), defined as those imprisoned for essentially political beliefs or nonviolent acts of dissent or expression, regardless of actual charge.

Arbitrary Interference With Privacy, Family, Home, Correspondence—Discusses the "passive" right of individuals to noninterference by the State; includes the right to receive foreign publications, for example, while the right to publish is discussed under "Freedom of Speech and Press"; includes the right to be free from coercive population control measures, including coerced abortion and involuntary sterilization but does not include cultural or traditional practices, such as female genital mutilation, which are addressed in Section 5.

Use of Excessive Force and Violations of Humanitarian Law in Internal Conflicts—An optional subsection for use in describing abuses that occur in countries experiencing significant internal armed conflict. Includes indiscriminate, non-selective killings arising from excessive use of force, e.g., by police in putting down demonstrations (deliberate, targeted killing would be discussed in Section 1.a.). Also includes abuses against civilian noncombatants. For reports in which use of this section would be inappropriate, i.e., in which there is not significant internal conflict, lethal use of excessive force by security forces (which is herein defined as a form of extrajudicial killing) is discussed in Section 1.a.; nonlethal excessive force in Section 1.e.

Freedom of Speech and Press—Evaluates whether these freedoms exist and describes any direct or indirect restrictions. Includes discussion of academic freedom.

Freedom of Peaceful Assembly and Association—Evaluates the ability of individuals and groups (including political parties) to exercise these freedoms. Includes the ability of trade associations, professional bodies, and similar groups to maintain relations or affiliate with recognized international bodies in their fields. The right of labor to associate and to organize and bargain collectively is discussed under Section 6, Worker Rights (see Appendix B).

Freedom of Religion—Discusses whether the Constitution and/or laws provide for the right of citizens of whatever religious belief to worship free of government interference and whether the government respects that right. Includes the freedom to publish religious documents in foreign languages; addresses the treatment of foreign clergy and whether religious belief affects membership in a ruling party or a career in government.

Freedom of Movement Within the Country, Foreign Travel, Emigration, and Repatriation—Includes discussion of forced resettlement; "refugees" may refer to persons displaced by civil strife or natural disaster as well as persons who are "refugees" within the meaning of the Refugee Act of 1980, i.e., persons with a "well-founded fear of persecution" in their country of origin or, if stateless, in their country of habitual residence, on account of race, religion, nationality, membership in a particular social group, or political opinion.

Respect for Political Rights: The Right of Citizens to Change Their Government—Discusses the extent to which citizens have freedom of political choice and have the legal right and ability in practice to change the laws and officials that govern them; assesses whether elections are free and fair.

Governmental Attitude Regarding International and Non-governmental Investigation of Alleged Violations of Human Rights—Discusses whether the government permits the free functioning of local human rights groups (including the right to investigate and publish their findings on alleged human rights abuses) and whether they are subject to reprisal by government or other forces. Also discusses whether the government grants access to and cooperates with outside entities (including foreign human rights organizations, international organizations, and foreign governments) interested n human rights developments in the country.

Discrimination Based on Race, Sex, Religion, Disability, Language, or Social Status—Continuing the practice begun last year, every report contains a subheading on Women, Children, and People with Disabilities. As appropriate, some reports also include subheadings on Indigenous People, National/Racial/Ethnic Minorities, and Religious Minorities. Discrimination against groups not fitting one of the above subheadings is discussed in the introductory paragraphs of Section 5. In this section we address discrimination and abuses not discussed elsewhere in the report, focusing on laws, regulations, or state practices which are inconsistent with equal access to housing, employment, education, health care, or other governmental benefits by members of specific groups. (Abuses by government or opposition forces, such as killing, torture and other violence, or restriction of voting rights or free speech targeted against specific groups would be discussed under the appropriate preceding sections.) Government tolerance of societal violence or other abuse against women, e.g, "dowry deaths," wife beating, trafficking in women, is discussed under the subheading on women. We also discuss under this subheading the extent to which the law provides for, and the government enforces, equality of economic opportunity for women. Similarly, we discuss violence or other abuse against children under that subheading. Because female genital mutilation (circumcision) is most often performed on children, we discuss it under that subheading.

Worker Rights—See Appendix B.

———

Lawyers Committee for Human Rights, *Critique: Review of the U.S. Department of State's Country Reports on Human Rights Practices for 1994*

v-xix (1995).

The 1994 edition of the State Department's annual *Country Reports on Human Rights* Practices is a study in paradoxes. On one hand, the language of human rights is now more firmly than ever embedded in the discussion of public policy; on the other, an administration that came to office with the most vigorous rhetoric on international human rights in more than a decade now finds itself accused of abandoning its human rights pledges on all fronts, from China to the former Yugoslavia. On one hand, a newly reorganized Bureau of Democracy, Human Rights and Labor has demonstrated real seriousness of purpose in pursuing, through the vehicle of the *Country Reports*, its mandate of providing the primary documentary evidence on which decisions about foreign aid will be made; on the other, the Bureau has come to feel more and more orphan of the State Department, at times almost a non-governmental organization within the government, its findings increasingly hard to reconcile with the direction of US foreign policy. On one hand, the quality of the *Country Reports* has improved steadily over recent years; on the other, the reports now seem to have hit a frustrating ceiling, dogged by persistent shortcomings that prevent them from realizing their full potential as a policy resource.

The bulk of this year's Critique—the 16th to be published by the Lawyers Committee—is devoted as usual to an analysis of the individual *Country Reports*. This year we have narrowed our focus to 30 carefully selected countries—fewer than in past editions of the *Critique*, but still sufficient, we believe, to arrive at valid general conclusions about the strengths and weaknesses of the *Country Reports*. We freely acknowledge that they have many strengths. . . .

. . .

At the basic level of case-by-case, fact-by-fact accuracy, there is no doubt that the 1994 *Country Reports* sustain the steady trend of improvement that we have welcomed in recent years. Again, a number of countries show a notable change for the better. Perhaps the most striking of these is Haiti, which last year's *Critique* singled out for criticism as a result of its "omissions, understatements and mischaracterizations [which] severely distort[ed] the reality of human rights violations." The 1994 report on Haiti is virtually unrecognizable, particularly in its treatment of such previously neglected topics as the right-wing paramilitary group, the Revolutionary Front for the Advancement and Progress of Haiti (FRAPH), and the use of rape as a weapon of the military government that was forced from power in September 1994.

Other reports praised by our reviewers for significant improvement in 1994 include those on Argentina, India, Indonesia and Iraq. The report on Nicaragua seems finally to have shed the worst of the Cold War-era prejudices that so marred reporting on that country for more than a decade, while the report on Egypt—despite other failings that are detailed below—generally shows a welcome willingness to speak candidly about the frequent incidence of torture in the jails of a close US ally.

A handful of the reports studied, meanwhile, show movement in the opposite direction. Perhaps the main offender here is the report on the United Kingdom/Northern Ireland, which seriously fails to come to grips with the reality of several months of Republican and Loyalist cease-fires. In particular, the report does not recognize that there is no longer "a public emergency threatening the life of the nation"—the condition stipulated by the European Convention on Human Rights that would allow the United Kingdom to justify the maintenance of its emergency laws. The Northern Ireland report is also littered with errors and misinterpretations on points ranging from police accountability and torture to prison overcrowding and broadcasting restrictions.

Our intention in producing the *Critique*, however, is not to draw up a scorecard of improving and worsening *Country Reports*. It is to try and isolate the patterns of weaknesses—declining in number but still stubbornly present in many of the reports. In summary, the most striking weaknesses identified by our reviewers are as follows:

1.   *Even where they include generally accurate data on human rights violations, the Country Reports remain unwilling to condemn them in its own voice or to criticize the perpetrators directly. This is particularly true in reports dealing with "friendly" governments.*

. . .

2.   *On a related point, the Country Reports frequently cloud the issue of state responsibility for human rights violations by drawing an artificial*

distinction between governments and ostensibly independent groups beyond their control.

. . .

3. *The Country Reports still fail to adhere consistently to a single, universal standard for judging human rights violations. In many cases they display the influence of policy considerations that should be extraneous to the preparation of the Country Reports.*

The State Department's own instructions to those drafting the *Country Reports* state in unequivocal terms that: "We seek to apply a single worldwide standard to the reporting of human rights conditions." Governments of all political stripes are to be held to the same norms, and higher standards of proof should not be required "when evaluating allegations of abuse by friendly governments."

However, these ideals are not always complied with in practice. . . .

. . .

4. *The State Department's continuing difficulty in applying universal human rights standards is evident in a number of the chapters dealing with Islamic governments, or with countries in which political Islam is an influential force.*

. . .

5. *Like their predecessors, the 1994 Country Reports do not draw sufficiently on the findings of the various human rights mechanisms of the United Nations.*

The Lawyers Committee has repeated this complaint in a number of previous editions of the *Critique*. A number of UN mechanisms, and particularly the Special Rapporteurs and Working Groups appointed by the Commission on Human Rights, are an indispensable source of human rights documentation. This was recognized by the revised instructions issued by the State Department in August 1993 to embassies preparing the Country Reports, which stressed that: "Special attention is to be paid to reports by the various UN human rights mechanisms."

Inexplicably, the 1994 Country Reports appear to be even less mindful of this instruction than their predecessors. Time and again, they miss the opportunity to cite important data included in UN reports, or produce less forthright views on key violations than those contained in readily available UN materials. To cite just a few of the dozens of examples encountered in preparing this *Critique*:

- In the report on Bosnia, there are frequent glaring discrepancies between the State Department report and those of the UN Special Rapporteur. This is not just a matter of tone. Important events documented by the Special Rapporteur, such as the Bosnian Serb offensive against Gorazde, are omitted altogether from the State Department report. Other abuses, such as targeted sniper attacks against children, are described in great detail by the Special Rapporteur; the State Department report understates these, or denies that they occurred.

- The report on Colombia does not allude to the findings of the Special Rapporteur on Summary or Arbitrary Executions, which pointed directly at state culpability. The neglect of the rapporteur's findings is especially disturbing given the report's efforts to direct attention away from the Colombian government and toward paramilitary and other forces operating outside its control.

- While the State Department does cite the work of the UN Special Rapporteur on Iraq, it should also have explained that his work— and that of other independent human rights monitors—was impeded by refusal of the Iraqi authorities to allow him to travel to government-held areas. Similarly, the findings of MICIVIH, the joint UN/OAS monitoring mission in Haiti, are hard to comprehend without reference to the climate of threats and violence in which the mission was forced to operate.

- The *Country Reports'* discussion of discrimination against women would generally have been strengthened by clearer references to the Convention on the Elimination of Discrimination Against Women (CEDAW). The report on Guatemala is a case in point. The State Department merely notes that some domestic Guatemalan laws continued to discriminate against women in violation of constitutional guarantees. But it makes no reference to the much more strongly worded concern of the UN Committee on the Elimination of Discrimination Against Women about "the discrimination institutionalized in law" and "far-reaching legal discrimination."

6. *Despite explicit State Department instructions to the contrary, many of the Country Reports pay more attention to the claims and promises of governments than to their actual accomplishments. This is particularly true of governmental initiatives to protect and promote human rights. While the Country Reports continue to give excessive credence to the claims of government-sponsored human rights bodies, they continue at times to give inadequate regard to the views of local and international human rights NGOs.*

. . .

Notes

1. The annual release of the State Department's Country Reports typically generates extensive media coverage in many countries, and often prompts strongly-worded responses by government leaders abroad. See, e.g., *Serbia Assailed on Human Rights: Annual U.S. Report Also Accuses China, Turkey and the Tal[i]ban*, Int'l Herald Tribune, Feb. 27–28, 1999.

2. Apart from the impact of the Country Reports themselves, their preparation arguably produces a number of significant effects. As noted in the 1994 Country Reports, U.S. embassy personnel throughout the world make extensive contact with a diverse range of sources, including domestic

NGOs, to obtain information about human rights conditions. How might such outreach affect U.S. human rights practice and policy?

3. Judging by the selections included above, has the State Department been responsive to NGO critiques of the Country Reports? Do you detect any changes over time in the quality of the Critiques prepared by the Lawyers Committee for Human Rights?

4. One of the criticisms of both the 1984 and 1994 Country Reports reflected in the preceding materials was that the State Department obscured the issue of state responsibility for abuses by, in the words of the Lawyers Committee for Human Rights, "drawing an artificial distinction between governments and ostensibly independent groups beyond their control." Citing the entry on Guatemala, the Committee's 1994 Critique asserts that this report "makes a frankly astonishing separation between the government and its own security forces, treating the latter repeatedly as agencies unrelated to the government." Later, the same Critique faults the State Department for failing to present a "rounded, contextualized picture of the human rights situation." In this regard, the Critique asks, "How ... are policymakers to arrive at a sound judgment of the human rights situation in Russia without understanding the steady encirclement of the Yeltsin administration by undemocratic forces such as the Presidential Security Service—a phenomenon that is not mentioned in the 1994 report on Russia? A clear picture of the human rights situation may even demand much more imaginative reference to actors that have no formal jurisdiction in the country or territory in question." Is the Critique consistent in the standards it apparently applies in evaluating the State Department Country Reports? That aside, should the State Department's Country Reports recognize distinctions among various government branches in assessing a country's human rights record? Does the introduction to the 1994 Country Reports shed light on why the State Department might consider it appropriate to distinguish civilian and military activities in analyzing a country's human rights record?

5. In Appendix A to the 1994 Country Report, the State Department explains in respect of several categories of human rights violations that it uses certain terms to refer to specified practices by government forces "or opposition groups." See, for example, the Appendix's explanations of the categories of torture and discrimination. What is the basis in international human rights law for reporting on the conduct of "opposition groups"? To the extent that such groups are not directly regulated by international human rights standards, is it appropriate for the State Department to report upon their human rights records? Why does it do so?

6. The Lawyers Committee faults the 1994 Country Reports because they "do not draw sufficiently on the findings of the various human rights mechanisms of the United Nations." Is that a legitimate criterion for evaluating the Country Reports? Why might the Lawyers Committee regard it as relevant?

2. JUDICIAL ENFORCEMENT AGAINST FOREIGN VIOLATIONS

The federal courts have acquired a broader role than might have been expected in the enforcement of international human rights norms against violations in foreign countries. That role originated in 1980 with the *Filartiga* decision of the United States Court of Appeals for the Second Circuit, which found support for tort suits against violators of customary human rights norms in a provision enacted by the first U.S. Congress in 1789. The modern version of this provision, now known variously as the Alien Tort Statute, the Alien Tort Act, or the Alien Tort Claims Act, provides: "The district courts shall have original jurisdiction of any civil action by an alien for a tort only, committed in violation of the law of nations or a treaty of the United States." 28 U.S.C. § 1350.

The availability of a U.S. judicial forum in which private plaintiffs can litigate human rights disputes that arose in other countries, at least if the alleged violator comes within the jurisdictional reach of the U.S. courts, has provoked controversy. Nonetheless, the *Filartiga* approach has been confirmed and extended in the lower courts, and has been fortified by congressional legislation providing similar litigation opportunities to U.S. citizens who have been victims of human rights violations abroad, including the Torture Victim Protection Act .

Filartiga v. Pena–Irala

United States Court of Appeals, Second Circuit, 1980.
630 F.2d 876.

■ IRVING R. KAUFMAN, CIRCUIT JUDGE:

Upon ratification of the Constitution, the thirteen former colonies were fused into a single nation, one which, in its relations with foreign states, is bound both to observe and construe the accepted norms of international law, formerly known as the law of nations. Under the Articles of Confederation, the several states had interpreted and applied this body of doctrine as a part of their common law, but with the founding of the "more perfect Union" of 1789, the law of nations became preeminently a federal concern.

Implementing the constitutional mandate for national control over foreign relations, the First Congress established original district court jurisdiction over "all causes where an alien sues for a tort only (committed) in violation of the law of nations." Judiciary Act of 1789, ch. 20, § 9(b), 1 Stat. 73, 77 (1789), codified at 28 U.S.C. § 1350. Construing this rarely-invoked provision, we hold that deliberate torture perpetrated under color of official authority violates universally accepted norms of the international law of human rights, regardless of the nationality of the parties. Thus, whenever an alleged torturer is found and served with process by an alien within our borders, § 1350 provides federal jurisdiction. Accordingly, we reverse the judgment of the district court dismissing the complaint for want of federal jurisdiction.

I

The appellants, plaintiffs below, are citizens of the Republic of Paraguay. Dr. Joel Filartiga, a physician, describes himself as a longstanding opponent of the government of President Alfredo Stroessner, which has held power in Paraguay since 1954. His daughter, Dolly Filartiga, arrived in the United States in 1978 under a visitor's visa, and has since applied for permanent political asylum. The Filartigas brought this action in the Eastern District of New York against Americo Norberto Pena–Irala (Pena), also a citizen of Paraguay, for wrongfully causing the death of Dr. Filartiga's seventeen-year old son, Joelito. Because the district court dismissed the action for want of subject matter jurisdiction, we must accept as true the allegations contained in the Filartigas' complaint and affidavits for purposes of this appeal.

The appellants contend that on March 29, 1976, Joelito Filartiga was kidnapped and tortured to death by Pena, who was then Inspector General of Police in Asuncion, Paraguay. Later that day, the police brought Dolly Filartiga to Pena's home where she was confronted with the body of her brother, which evidenced marks of severe torture. As she fled, horrified, from the house, Pena followed after her shouting, "Here you have what you have been looking for for so long and what you deserve. Now shut up." The Filartigas claim that Joelito was tortured and killed in retaliation for his father's political activities and beliefs.

. . .

In July of 1978, Pena sold his house in Paraguay and entered the United States under a visitor's visa. He was accompanied by Juana Bautista Fernandez Villalba, who had lived with him in Paraguay. The couple remained in the United States beyond the term of their visas, and were living in Brooklyn, New York, when Dolly Filartiga, who was then living in Washington, D. C., learned of their presence. . . .

. . . Dolly caused Pena to be served with a summons and civil complaint at the Brooklyn Navy Yard, where he was being held pending deportation. The complaint alleged that Pena had wrongfully caused Joelito's death by torture and sought compensatory and punitive damages of $10,000,000. . . . The cause of action is stated as arising under "wrongful death statutes; the U. N. Charter; the Universal Declaration on Human Rights; the U. N. Declaration Against Torture; the American Declaration of the Rights and Duties of Man; and other pertinent declarations, documents and practices constituting the customary international law of human rights and the law of nations," as well as 28 U.S.C. § 1350, Article II, sec. 2 and the Supremacy Clause of the U. S. Constitution. Jurisdiction is claimed under the general federal question provision, 28 U.S.C. § 1331 and, principally on this appeal, under the Alien Tort Statute, 28 U.S.C. § 1350.

. . .

II

Appellants rest their principal argument in support of federal jurisdiction upon the Alien Tort Statute, 28 U.S.C. § 1350, which provides: "The district courts shall have original jurisdiction of any civil action by an alien for a tort only, committed in violation of the law of nations or a treaty of the United States." Since appellants do not contend that their action arises directly under a treaty of the United States, a threshold question on the jurisdictional issue is whether the conduct alleged violates the law of nations. In light of the universal condemnation of torture in numerous international agreements, and the renunciation of torture as an instrument of official policy by virtually all of the nations of the world (in principle if not in practice), we find that an act of torture committed by a state official against one held in detention violates established norms of the international law of human rights, and hence the law of nations.

The Supreme Court has enumerated the appropriate sources of international law. The law of nations "may be ascertained by consulting the works of jurists, writing professedly on public law; or by the general usage and practice of nations; or by judicial decisions recognizing and enforcing that law." . . .

The Paquete Habana, 175 U.S. 677 (1900), reaffirmed that

> where there is no treaty, and no controlling executive or legislative act or judicial decision, resort must be had to the customs and usages of civilized nations; and, as evidence of these, to the works of jurists and commentators, who by years of labor, research and experience, have made themselves peculiarly well acquainted with the subjects of which they treat. Such works are resorted to by judicial tribunals, not for the speculations of their authors concerning what the law ought to be, but for trustworthy evidence of what the law really is.

Modern international sources confirm the propriety of this approach.

Habana is particularly instructive for present purposes, for it held that the traditional prohibition against seizure of an enemy's coastal fishing vessels during wartime, a standard that began as one of comity only, had ripened over the preceding century into "a settled rule of international law" by "the general assent of civilized nations." Thus it is clear that courts must interpret international law not as it was in 1789, but as it has evolved and exists among the nations of the world today. See Ware v. Hylton, 3 U.S. (3 Dall.) 199 (1796) (distinguishing between "ancient" and "modern" law of nations).

The requirement that a rule command the "general assent of civilized nations" to become binding upon them all is a stringent one. Were this not so, the courts of one nation might feel free to impose idiosyncratic legal rules upon others, in the name of applying international law. Thus, in Banco Nacional de Cuba v. Sabbatino, 376 U.S. 398 (1964), the Court declined to pass on the validity of the Cuban government's expropriation of a foreign-owned corporation's assets, noting the sharply conflicting views on the issue propounded by the capital-exporting, capital-importing, socialist and capitalist nations.

The case at bar presents us with a situation diametrically opposed to the conflicted state of law that confronted the Sabbatino Court. Indeed, to paraphrase that Court's statement, there are few, if any, issues in international law today on which opinion seems to be so united as the limitations on a state's power to torture persons held in its custody.

The United Nations Charter (a treaty of the United States, see 59 Stat. 1033 (1945)) makes it clear that in this modern age a state's treatment of its own citizens is a matter of international concern. . . .

While this broad mandate has been held not to be wholly self-executing, this observation alone does not end our inquiry. For although there is no universal agreement as to the precise extent of the "human rights and fundamental freedoms" guaranteed to all by the Charter, there is at present no dissent from the view that the guaranties include, at a bare minimum, the right to be free from torture. This prohibition has become part of customary international law, as evidenced and defined by the Universal Declaration of Human Rights, General Assembly Resolution 217 (III)(A) (Dec. 10, 1948) which states, in the plainest of terms, "no one shall be subjected to torture." The General Assembly has declared that the Charter precepts embodied in this Universal Declaration "constitute basic principles of international law." G.A.Res. 2625 (XXV) (Oct. 24, 1970).

Particularly relevant is the Declaration on the Protection of All Persons from Being Subjected to Torture, General Assembly Resolution 3452, 30 U.N. GAOR Supp. (No. 34) 91, U.N.Doc. A/1034 (1975), . . . The Declaration expressly prohibits any state from permitting the dastardly and totally inhuman act of torture. Torture, in turn, is defined as "any act by which severe pain and suffering, whether physical or mental, is intentionally inflicted by or at the instigation of a public official on a person for such purposes as . . . intimidating him or other persons." The Declaration goes on to provide that "[w]here it is proved that an act of torture or other cruel, inhuman or degrading treatment or punishment has been committed by or at the instigation of a public official, the victim shall be afforded redress and compensation, in accordance with national law." This Declaration, like the Declaration of Human Rights before it, was adopted without dissent by the General Assembly.

These U.N. declarations are significant because they specify with great precision the obligations of member nations under the Charter. Since their adoption, "[m]embers can no longer contend that they do not know what human rights they promised in the Charter to promote." Sohn, "A Short History of United Nations Documents on Human Rights," in The United Nations and Human Rights, 18th Report of the Commission (Commission to Study the Organization of Peace ed. 1968). Moreover, a U.N. Declaration is, according to one authoritative definition, "a formal and solemn instrument, suitable for rare occasions when principles of great and lasting importance are being enunciated." 34 U.N. ESCOR, Supp. (No. 8) 15, U.N. Doc. E/CN.4/1/610 (1962) (memorandum of Office of Legal Affairs, U.N. Secretariat). Accordingly, it has been observed that the Universal Declaration of Human Rights "no longer fits into the dichotomy of 'binding treaty' against 'non-binding pronouncement,' but is rather an authoritative statement of the international community." E. Schwelb, Human Rights and the

International Community 70 (1964). Thus, a Declaration creates an expectation of adherence, and "insofar as the expectation is gradually justified by State practice, a declaration may by custom become recognized as laying down rules binding upon the States." 34 U.N. ESCOR, supra. Indeed, several commentators have concluded that the Universal Declaration has become, in toto, a part of binding, customary international law.

Turning to the act of torture, we have little difficulty discerning its universal renunciation in the modern usage and practice of nations. The international consensus surrounding torture has found expression in numerous international treaties and accords. E. g., American Convention on Human Rights, Art. 5, OAS Treaty Series No. 36 at 1, OAS Off. Rec. OEA/Ser 4 v/II 23, doc. 21, rev. 2 (English ed., 1975) ("No one shall be subjected to torture or to cruel, inhuman or degrading punishment or treatment"); International Covenant on Civil and Political Rights, U.N. General Assembly Res. 2200 (XXI)A, U.N. Doc. A/6316 (Dec. 16, 1966) (identical language); European Convention for the Protection of Human Rights and Fundamental Freedoms, Art. 3, Council of Europe, European Treaty Series No. 5 (1968), 213 U.N.T.S. 211 (semble). The substance of these international agreements is reflected in modern municipal i.e. national law as well. Although torture was once a routine concomitant of criminal interrogations in many nations, during the modern and hopefully more enlightened era it has been universally renounced. According to one survey, torture is prohibited, expressly or implicitly, by the constitutions of over fifty-five nations, including both the United States and Paraguay. Our State Department reports a general recognition of this principle:

> There now exists an international consensus that recognizes basic human rights and obligations owed by all governments to their citizens. . . . There is no doubt that these rights are often violated; but virtually all governments acknowledge their validity.

Department of State, Country Reports on Human Rights for 1979, published as Joint Comm. Print, House Comm. on Foreign Affairs, and Senate Comm. on Foreign Relations, 96th Cong. 2d Sess. (Feb. 4, 1980), Introduction at 1. We have been directed to no assertion by any contemporary state of a right to torture its own or another nation's citizens. Indeed, United States diplomatic contacts confirm the universal abhorrence with which torture is viewed:

> In exchanges between United States embassies and all foreign states with which the United States maintains relations, it has been the Department of State's general experience that no government has asserted a right to torture its own nationals. Where reports of torture elicit some credence, a state usually responds by denial or, less frequently, by asserting that the conduct was unauthorized or constituted rough treatment short of torture.

Memorandum of the United States as Amicus Curiae at 16 n.34.

Having examined the sources from which customary international law is derived the usage of nations, judicial opinions and the works of jurists we conclude that official torture is now prohibited by the law of nations. The prohibition is clear and unambiguous, and admits of no distinction between treatment of aliens and citizens. Accordingly, we must conclude that the dictum in Dreyfus v. Von Finck, [534 F.2d 24, 31 (2d Cir.), cert. denied, 429 U.S. 835 (1976)], to the effect that "violations of international law do not occur when the aggrieved parties are nationals of the acting state," is clearly out of tune with the current usage and practice of international law. The treaties and accords cited above, as well as the express foreign policy of our own government, all make it clear that international law confers fundamental rights upon all people vis-a-vis their own governments. While the ultimate scope of those rights will be a subject for continuing refinement and elaboration, we hold that the right to be free from torture is now among them. We therefore turn to the question whether the other requirements for jurisdiction are met.

III

Appellee submits that even if the tort alleged is a violation of modern international law, federal jurisdiction may not be exercised consistent with the dictates of Article III of the Constitution. The claim is without merit. Common law courts of general jurisdiction regularly adjudicate transitory tort claims between individuals over whom they exercise personal jurisdiction, wherever the tort occurred. Moreover, as part of an articulated scheme of federal control over external affairs, Congress provided, in the first Judiciary Act, § 9(b), 1 Stat. 73, 77 (1789), for federal jurisdiction over suits by aliens where principles of international law are in issue. The constitutional basis for the Alien Tort Statute is the law of nations, which has always been part of the federal common law.

It is not extraordinary for a court to adjudicate a tort claim arising outside of its territorial jurisdiction. A state or nation has a legitimate interest in the orderly resolution of disputes among those within its borders, and where the lex loci delicti commissi is applied, it is an expression of comity to give effect to the laws of the state where the wrong occurred. . . .

. . . Here, where in personam jurisdiction has been obtained over the defendant, the parties agree that the acts alleged would violate Paraguayan law, and the policies of the forum are consistent with the foreign law, state court jurisdiction would be proper. Indeed, appellees conceded as much at oral argument.

. . . [W]e proceed to consider whether the First Congress acted constitutionally in vesting jurisdiction over "foreign suits," alleging torts committed in violation of the law of nations. A case properly "aris[es] under the . . . laws of the United States" for Article III purposes if grounded upon statutes enacted by Congress or upon the common law of the United States. The law of nations forms an integral part of the common law, and a review of the history surrounding the adoption of the Constitution demonstrates that it became a part of the common law of the United States upon the adoption of the Constitution. Therefore, the enactment of the Alien Tort Statute was authorized by Article III.

. . .

As ratified, the judiciary article contained no express reference to cases arising under the law of nations. Indeed, the only express reference to that body of law is contained in Article I, sec. 8, cl. 10, which grants to the Congress the power to "define and punish ... offenses against the law of nations." Appellees seize upon this circumstance and advance the proposition that the law of nations forms a part of the laws of the United States only to the extent that Congress has acted to define it. This extravagant claim is amply refuted by the numerous decisions applying rules of international law uncodified in any act of Congress. E. g., Ware v. Hylton, 3 U.S. (3 Dall.) 199 (1796); The Paquete Habana, supra; Sabbatino, supra. A similar argument was offered to and rejected by the Supreme Court in United States v. Smith, supra, 18 U.S. (5 Wheat.) 153, 158–60 [(1820)], and we reject it today. As John Jay wrote in The Federalist No. 3, at 22 (1 Bourne ed. 1901), "Under the national government, treaties and articles of treaties, as well as the laws of nations, will always be expounded in one sense and executed in the same manner, whereas adjudications on the same points and questions in the thirteen states will not always accord or be consistent." Federal jurisdiction over cases involving international law is clear.

. . .

Although the Alien Tort Statute has rarely been the basis for jurisdiction during its long history, in light of the foregoing discussion, there can be little doubt that this action is properly brought in federal court. This is undeniably an action by an alien, for a tort only, committed in violation of the law of nations. The paucity of suits successfully maintained under the section is readily attributable to the statute's requirement of alleging a "violation of the law of nations" at the jurisdictional threshold. Courts have, accordingly, engaged in a more searching preliminary review of the merits than is required, for example, under the more flexible "arising under" formulation. Thus, the narrowing construction that the Alien Tort Statute has previously received reflects the fact that earlier cases did not involve such well-established, universally recognized norms of international law that are here at issue.

. . .

Since federal jurisdiction may properly be exercised over the Filartigas' claim, the action must be remanded for further proceedings. Appellee Pena, however, advances several additional points that lie beyond the scope of our holding on jurisdiction. Both to emphasize the boundaries of our holding, and to clarify some of the issues reserved for the district court on remand, we will address these contentions briefly.

IV

Pena argues that the customary law of nations, as reflected in treaties and declarations that are not self-executing, should not be applied as rules of decision in this case. In doing so, he confuses the question of federal jurisdiction under the Alien Tort Statute, which requires consideration of the law of nations, with the issue of the choice of law to be applied, which will be addressed at a later stage in the proceedings. The two issues are distinct. Our holding on subject matter jurisdiction decides only whether Congress intended to confer judicial power, and whether it is authorized to do so by Article III. The choice of law inquiry is a much broader one, primarily concerned with fairness; consequently, it looks to wholly different considerations. See Lauritzen v. Larsen, 345 U.S. 571 (1953). Should the district court decide that the *Lauritzen* analysis requires it to apply Paraguayan law, our courts will not have occasion to consider what law would govern a suit under the Alien Tort Statute where the challenged conduct is actionable under the law of the forum and the law of nations, but not the law of the jurisdiction in which the tort occurred.

Pena also argues that "[i]f the conduct complained of is alleged to be the act of the Paraguayan government, the suit is barred by the Act of State doctrine." This argument was not advanced below, and is therefore not before us on this appeal. We note in passing, however, that we doubt whether action by a state official in violation of the Constitution and laws of the Republic of Paraguay, and wholly unratified by that nation's government, could properly be characterized as an act of state. See Banco Nacional de Cuba v. Sabbatino, 376 U.S. 398 [(1964)]; Underhill v. Hernandez, 168 U.S. 250 (1897). Paraguay's renunciation of torture as a legitimate instrument of state policy, however, does not strip the tort of its character as an international law violation, if it in fact occurred under color of government authority.

· · ·

In the twentieth century the international community has come to recognize the common danger posed by the flagrant disregard of basic human rights and particularly the right to be free of torture. Spurred first by the Great War, and then the Second, civilized nations have banded together to prescribe acceptable norms of international behavior. From the ashes of the Second World War arose the United Nations Organization, amid hopes that an era of peace and cooperation had at last begun. Though many of these aspirations have remained elusive goals, that circumstance cannot diminish the true progress that has been made. In the modern age, humanitarian and practical considerations have combined to lead the nations of the world to recognize that respect for fundamental human rights is in their individual and collective interest. Among the rights universally proclaimed by all nations, as we have noted, is the right to be free of physical torture. Indeed, for purposes of civil liability, the torturer has become like the pirate and slave trader before him hostis humani generis, an enemy of all mankind. Our holding today, giving effect to a jurisdictional provision enacted by our First Congress, is a small but important step in the fulfillment of the ageless dream to free all people from brutal violence.

Tel–Oren v. Libyan Arab Republic

United States Court of Appeals, D.C. Circuit, 1984.
726 F.2d 774, cert. denied, 470 U.S. 1003 (1985).

[Plaintiffs, mostly Israeli citizens, included persons injured and representatives of persons murdered in an armed attack on a civilian bus in Israel. They sought compensatory and punitive damages against the Libyan Arab Republic, the Palestine Liberation Organization, and several organizations related to the PLO. The district court dismissed the action for lack of subject matter jurisdiction and on statute of limitations grounds. The plaintiffs appealed, and the court of appeals affirmed dismissal of the action, with each judge filing a separate opinion. Judge Edwards expressed approval of the interpretation of 28 U.S.C. § 1350 in *Filartiga*, but concluded that it was insufficiently clear that international law prohibited torture and murder by non-state actors such as the PLO. Both Judge Edwards and Judge Bork agreed that Libya was immune from suit under the Foreign Sovereign Immunities Act. Judge Robb concluded that the lawsuit presented nonjusticiable political questions. Excerpts from Judge Bork's opinion, critical of the *Filartiga* approach, follow:]

■ BORK, CIRCUIT JUDGE, concurring:

. . .

... I believe, as did the district court, that, in the circumstances presented here, appellants have failed to state a cause of action sufficient to support jurisdiction under either of the statutes on which they rely. 28 U.S.C. §§ 1331, 1350 (1976 & Supp. V 1981). Neither the law of nations nor any of the relevant treaties provides a cause of action that appellants may assert in courts of the United States. Furthermore, we should not, in an area such as this, infer a cause of action not explicitly given. In reaching this latter conclusion, I am guided chiefly by separation of powers principles, which caution courts to avoid potential interference with the political branches' conduct of foreign relations.

. . .

The question in this case is whether appellants have a cause of action in courts of the United States for injuries they suffered in Israel. Judge Edwards contends, and the Second Circuit in *Filartiga* assumed, that Congress' grant of jurisdiction also created a cause of action. That seems to me fundamentally wrong and certain to produce pernicious results. For reasons I will develop, it is essential that there be an explicit grant of a cause of action before a private plaintiff be allowed to enforce principles of international law in a federal tribunal. It will be seen below, however, that no body of law expressly grants appellants a cause of action; the relevant inquiry, therefore, is whether a cause of action is to be inferred. That inquiry is guided by general principles that apply whenever a court of the United States is asked to act in a field in which its judgment would necessarily affect the foreign policy interests of the nation.

. . .

The crucial element of the doctrine of separation of powers in this case is the principle that "[t]he conduct of the foreign relations of our Government is committed by the Constitution to the Executive and Legislative—'the political'—Departments." Oetjen v. Central Leather Co., 246 U.S. 297, 302 (1918). That principle has been translated into a limitation on judicial power in the international law area principally through the act of state and political question doctrines. Whether or not this case falls within one of these categories, the concerns that underlie them are present and demand recognition here.

. . .

Those principles counsel against recognition of a cause of action for appellants if adjudication of their claims would raise substantial problems of judicial interference with nonjudicial functions, such as the conduct of foreign relations. Appellants' complaint requires a determination, either at the jurisdictional stage or at the stage of defining and applying a rule of decision, whether international law has been violated. I am therefore guided in large measure by the Supreme Court's observation in [Banco Nacional de Cuba v. Sabbatino, 376 U.S. 398, 428 (1964),] that

> the greater the degree of codification or consensus concerning a particular area of international law, the more appropriate it is for the judiciary to render decisions regarding it, since the courts can then focus on the application of an agreed principle to circumstances of fact rather than on the sensitive task of establishing a principle not inconsistent with the national interest or with international justice. It is also evident that some aspects of international law touch more sharply on national nerves than do others; the less important the implications of an issue are for our foreign relations, the weaker the justification for exclusivity in the political branches.

There is no need to decide here under what circumstances considerations such as these might deprive an individual of a cause of action clearly given by a state, by Congress, by a treaty, or by international law. In the absence of such a cause of action, they lead to the conclusion that adjudication of appellants' claims would present grave separation of powers problems. It is therefore inappropriate to recognize a cause of action allowing appellants to bring this suit.

. . .

[A]ppellants' principal claim, that appellees violated customary principles of international law against terrorism, concerns an area of international law in which there is little or no consensus and in which the disagreements concern politically sensitive issues that are especially prominent in the foreign relations problems of the Middle East. Some aspects of terrorism have been the subject of several international conventions, such as those concerning hijacking, and attacks on internationally protected persons such as diplomats. But no consensus has developed on how properly to define "terrorism" generally. As a consequence, " '[i]nternational law and the rules of warfare as they now exist are inadequate to cope with this new mode of conflict.' '"'The dismal truth is that the international community has dealt with terrorism ambivalently and ineffectually."

Customary international law may well forbid states from aiding terrorist attacks on neighboring states. Although that principle might apply in a case like this to a state such as Libya (which is not a proper party here[13]), it does not, at least on its face, apply to a nonstate like the PLO. More important, there is less than universal consensus about whether PLO-sponsored attacks on Israel are lawful. . . .

There is, of course, no occasion here to state what international law should be. Nor is there a need to consider whether an extended and discriminating analysis might plausibly maintain that customary international law prohibits the actions alleged in the complaint. It is enough to observe that there is sufficient controversy of a politically sensitive nature about the content of any relevant international legal principles that litigation of appellants' claims would present, in acute form, many of the problems that the separation of powers principles inherent in the act of state and political question doctrines caution courts to avoid. The lack of clarity in, and absence of consensus about, the legal principles invoked by appellants, together with the political context of the challenged actions and the PLO's impingement upon American foreign relations, lead to the conclusion that appellants' case is not the sort that is appropriate for federal-court adjudication, at least not without an express grant of a cause of action.

. . .

Appellants, seeking to recover for a violation of international law, might look to federal statutes either for a grant of a cause of action or for evidence that a cause of action exists. These notions may be quickly dismissed. The only plausible candidates are the two jurisdictional statutes relied on by appellants, sections 1331 and 1350 of Title 28 of the United States Code. Neither of those statutes either expressly or impliedly grants a cause of action. Both statutes merely define a class of cases federal courts can hear; they do not themselves even by implication authorize individuals to bring such cases. . . .

Although the jurisdictional statutes relied on by appellants cannot be read to provide a cause of action, those statutes might conceivably provide evidence of Congress' recognition (as opposed to creation) of one. Appellants do not suggest that section 1331 is evidence of any such recognition, as nothing in its language or history could support such a reading. Rather, appellants focus on section 1350, which is concerned expressly and only with international law (treaties and customary international law) and therefore might suggest that Congress understood, when providing jurisdiction through section 1350, that some individuals would be able to take

---

13. Libya must be dismissed from the case because the Foreign Sovereign Immunities Act, 28 U.S.C. §§ 1330, 1602–1611 (1976), plainly deprives us of jurisdiction over Libya. . . . [relocated footnote]

advantage of that jurisdiction because they had causes of action for torts committed in violation of the law of nations.

The broadest reading of section 1350 as evidence of congressional recognition of such a cause of action is that it merely requires that a plaintiff prove that the actions complained of violated international law. If that jurisdictional prerequisite is met, according to appellants, the plaintiff has a cause of action for tort damages, as he would for any tort. This approach is adopted by the Second Circuit in *Filartiga*, as well as by Judge Edwards. I believe, nonetheless, that this construction of section 1350 must be rejected for several reasons.

. . .

Historical research has not as yet disclosed what section 1350 was intended to accomplish. The fact poses a special problem for courts. A statute whose original meaning is hidden from us and yet which, if its words are read incautiously with modern assumptions in mind, is capable of plunging our nation into foreign conflicts, ought to be approached by the judiciary with great circumspection. It will not do simply to assert that the statutory phrase, the "law of nations," whatever it may have meant in 1789, must be read today as incorporating all the modern rules of international law and giving aliens private causes of action for violations of those rules. It will not do because the result is contrary not only to what we know of the framers' general purposes in this area but contrary as well to the appropriate, indeed the constitutional, role of courts with respect to foreign affairs.

What little relevant historical background is now available to us indicates that those who drafted the Constitution and the Judiciary Act of 1789 wanted to open federal courts to aliens for the purpose of avoiding, not provoking, conflicts with other nations. The Federalist No. 80 (A. Hamilton). A broad reading of section 1350 runs directly contrary to that desire. . . .

. . .

Though it is not necessary to the decision of this case, it may be well to suggest what section 1350 may have been enacted to accomplish, if only to meet the charge that my interpretation is not plausible because it would drain the statute of meaning. The phrase "law of nations" has meant various things over time. It is important to remember that in 1789 there was no concept of international human rights; neither was there, under the traditional version of customary international law, any recognition of a right of private parties to recover. That problem is not avoided by observing that the law of nations evolves. It is one thing for a case like *The Paquete Habana* to find that a rule has evolved so that the United States may not seize coastal fishing boats of a nation with which we are at war. It is another thing entirely, a difference in degree so enormous as to be a difference in kind, to find that a rule has evolved against torture by government so that our courts must sit in judgment of the conduct of foreign officials in their own countries with respect to their own citizens.

The latter assertion raises prospects of judicial interference with foreign affairs that the former does not. A different question might be presented if section 1350 had been adopted by a modern Congress that made clear its desire that federal courts police the behavior of foreign individuals and governments. But section 1350 does not embody a legislative judgment that is either current or clear and the statute must be read with that in mind.

What kinds of alien tort actions, then, might the Congress of 1789 have meant to bring into federal courts? According to Blackstone, a writer certainly familiar to colonial lawyers, "the principal offences against the law of nations, animadverted on as such by the municipal laws of England, [were] of three kinds; 1. Violation of safe-conducts; 2. Infringement of the rights of embassadors; and 3. Piracy." One might suppose that these were the kinds of offenses for which Congress wished to provide tort jurisdiction for suits by aliens in order to avoid conflicts with other nations.

. . .

Under the possible meaning I have sketched, section 1350's current function would be quite modest, unless a modern statute, treaty, or executive agreement provided a private cause of action for violations of new international norms which do not themselves contemplate private enforcement. Then, at least, we would have a current political judgment about the role appropriate for courts in an area of considerable international sensitivity.

Notes

1. Should the phrase "the law of nations" in the Alien Tort Statute be construed as referring to the content of the law of nations as it existed in the eighteenth-century when the statute was originally enacted, or to the current content of international law?

What benefits result from the interpretation given to the statute in *Filartiga*? Benefits to victims of past human rights violations? Deterrence of future human right violations? Deterrence of future visits to the United States by human rights violators? Benefits to the system of protecting human rights more generally?

What dangers, if any, are presented by the broad *Filartiga* interpretation of the statute? Does judicial adjudication of human rights disputes interfere with the prerogatives of the political branches in elaborating the content of human rights? Does providing judicial enforcement of human rights norms against foreign violators commit the United States to a greater degree of consistency than its foreign policy interests might allow? Are there means available for mitigating those dangers?

2. Before a court can provide a remedy for a tort committed in violation of customary international law, the court must determine what customary international law requires. From what sources did the *Filartiga* court conclude that customary international law prohibits official torture? In determining the content of international law, how much weight should the

court give to positions taken by the United States in its conduct of international relations? How much weight to positions taken by the United States in submissions to the court in that very lawsuit?

3. *Filartiga* has been praised for emphasizing conventions and declarations in the face of contrary state practice. Critics, however, maintain that by relying on such documents, the court attributes legislative powers to the international bodies such as the United Nations that formulated these agreements. Is that a valid characterization? What consequences might this method of identifying customary international law have for the United States? What consequences might it have on the ability of international organizations to forge such agreements in the future? See Dean Rusk, *A Comment on Filartiga v. Pena–Irala*, 11 Ga. J. Int'l & Comp. L. 311 (1981).

It has been estimated that the governments of over one-third of all countries permitted, if not ordered, the use of torture in the 1980s. See Karl R. Moor & Alan H. Nichols, *Combating Torture in the 90s*, 17 Hum. Rts. 28 (Spring 1990). Does that fact belie any general assent given in conventions and declarations, and indicate that torture has not yet risen to the level of a violation of customary international law? For the purpose of establishing customary international law, is there an argument for placing less emphasis on what states do, and more on what they say, in the field of human rights than in other areas of international law? See Restatement of Foreign Relations Law § 701, Reporters' Notes 1 & 2.

4. Although the *Filartiga* opinion makes clear that torture must be a violation of the "law of nations" in order to bring the claim under the Alien Tort Statute, it also indicates the possibility that the governing law in the tort action might be the law of Paraguay. What arguments might favor, or disfavor, the application of Paraguayan law under these circumstances? If Paraguayan law should not be applied, what law should be? New York state law? Law created by the federal courts pursuant to authority delegated by the statute?

5. As recognized in *Tel–Oren*, foreign states enjoy sovereign immunity from suit in both federal and state courts in the United States. This subject is codified in the Foreign Sovereign Immunities Act, 28 U.S.C. §§ 1330, 1602–1611. The Supreme Court has confirmed that the rules of immunity set out in the FSIA apply to actions under the Alien Tort Statute. See *Argentine Republic v. Amerada Hess Shipping Corp.*, 488 U.S. 428 (1989); cf. *Saudi Arabia v. Nelson*, 507 U.S. 349 (1993) (detention and torture of U.S. citizen employee by Saudi police in connection with dispute arising from his employment would not come within "commercial activity" exception to immunity under FSIA). (Congress has, however, amended the FSIA to deny the defense of sovereign immunity in certain actions for personal injury or death brought by U.S. nationals (not by aliens) against foreign states that have been designated as state sponsors of terrorism by the U.S. State Department. 28 U.S.C. § 1605(a)(7); see, e.g., *Cicippio v. Islamic Republic of Iran*, 18 F. Supp. 2d 62 (D.D.C.1998); *Alejandre v. Republic of Cuba*, 996 F.Supp. 1239 (S.D.Fla.1997).)

6.   The court in *Filartiga* rejected another proposed defense, the act of state doctrine. Under that judicially created doctrine, "[i]n the absence of a treaty or other unambiguous agreement regarding controlling legal principles, courts in the United States will generally refrain from examining the validity of a taking by a foreign state of property within its own territory, or from sitting in judgment on other acts of a governmental character done by a foreign state within its own territory and applicable there." Restatement of Foreign Relations Law § 443(1); *Banco Nacional de Cuba v. Sabbatino*, 376 U.S. 398 (1964). The Restatement further observes: "A claim arising out of an alleged violation of fundamental human rights—for instance, a claim on behalf of a victim of torture or genocide—would (if otherwise sustainable) probably not be defeated by the act of state doctrine, since the accepted international law of human rights is well established and contemplates external scrutiny of such acts." § 443 comment c. Might some human rights claims involve sufficient uncertainty, regarding the existence of the norm or its application to the facts alleged, that the act of state doctrine would nonetheless apply if the foreign state confirmed its responsibility for the defendant's conduct?

7.   Defendants in Alien Tort actions frequently default, and frequently lack the means to pay the large default judgments entered against them. On remand in *Filartiga*, the district court awarded $385,364 in compensatory damages and $10,000,000 in punitive damages. See *Filartiga v. Pena-Irala*, 577 F.Supp. 860 (E.D.N.Y.1984). The judgment was not collected. There may be a greater likelihood of collecting a substantial judgment against former high officials who have fled their country. A class action against former Philippine dictator Ferdinand Marcos led, after lengthy litigation, to awards of over $750 million in compensatory damages and $1.2 billion in corrective damages for nearly 10,000 victims. See *Hilao v. Estate of Marcos*, 103 F.3d 767 (9th Cir.1996); Joan Fitzpatrick, *The Future of the Alien Tort Claims Act of 1789: Lessons from In re Marcos Human Rights Litigation*, 67 St. John's L. Rev. 491 (1993); Ralph G. Steinhardt, *Fulfilling the Promise of Filartiga: Litigating Human Rights Claims Against the Estate of Ferdinand Marcos*, 20 Yale J. Int'l L. 65 (1995). As of 1999, it remains to be seen whether any of the award will be collected. In light of the Marcos litigation, does the *Filartiga* interpretation further the cause of human rights, or does it complicate human rights diplomacy, by preventing the United States from offering sanctuary in the United States as an incentive for dictators to relinquish power?

8.   For a once-obscure statute, the Alien Tort Statute has generated a considerable literature. See, e.g., Curtis A. Bradley and Jack L. Goldsmith, III, *The Current Illegitimacy of International Human Rights Litigation*, 66 Fordham L. Rev. 319 (1997); Anne–Marie Burley, *The Alien Tort Statute and the Judiciary Act of 1789: A Badge of Honor*, 83 Am. J. Int'l L. 461 (1989); William R. Casto, *The Federal Courts' Protective Jurisdiction Over Torts Committed in Violation of the Law of Nations*, 18 Conn. L. Rev. 467 (1986); Anthony D'Amato, *The Alien Tort Statute and the Founding of the Constitution*, 82 Am. J. Int'l L. 62 (1988); William S. Dodge, *The Historical Origins of the Alien Tort Statute: A Response to the "Originalists,"* 19

Hastings Int'l & Comp. L. Rev. 221 (1996); Harold Hongju Koh, *Transnational Public Law Litigation*, 100 Yale L.J. 2347 (1991); Kenneth C. Randall, *Federal Jurisdiction over International Law Claims: Inquiries into the Alien Tort Statute*, 18 N.Y.U. J. Int'l L. & Pol. 1 (1985); Kenneth C. Randall, *Further Inquiries into the Alien Tort Statute and a Recommendation*, 18 N.Y.U. J. Int'l L. & Pol. 473 (1986); Joseph Modeste Sweeney, *A Tort Only in Violation of the Law of Nations*, 18 Hastings Int'l & Comp. L. Rev. 445 (1995); John M. Walker, Jr., *Domestic Adjudication of International Human Rights Violations under the Alien Tort Statute*, 41 St. Louis U. L. J. 539 (1997); see also Beth Stephens & Michael Ratner, International Human Rights Litigation in U.S. Courts (1996).

9. The doubts expressed in Judge Bork's opinion about the availability of a cause of action for torture, and the fact that the Alien Tort Statute authorizes federal jurisdiction over suits brought by aliens but not by U.S. citizens, ultimately led to enactment of the Torture Victim Protection Act ("of 1991," but actually enacted in 1992), expressly providing a federal cause of action in cases of torture or extrajudicial killing. The TVPA includes a definition of "torture" based upon the definition contained in the package of reservations, understandings and declarations that accompanied the U.S. ratification of the Torture Convention. What other limitations does the TVPA contain? What implications does the TVPA have for the availability of redress under the Alien Tort Statute?

Torture Victim Protection Act

Pub. L. 102–256, 106 Stat. 73 (codified at 28 U.S.C. § 1350 note).

Sec. 1. Short Title.

This Act may be cited as the "Torture Victim Protection Act of 1991".

Sec. 2 . Establishment of civil action.

(a) Liability.—An individual who, under actual or apparent authority, or color of law, of any foreign nation—

(1) subjects an individual to torture shall, in a civil action, be liable for damages to that individual; or

(2) subjects an individual to extrajudicial killing shall, in a civil action, be liable for damages to the individual's legal representative, or to any person who may be a claimant in an action for wrongful death.

(b) Exhaustion of remedies.—A court shall decline to hear a claim under this section if the claimant has not exhausted adequate and available remedies in the place in which the conduct giving rise to the claim occurred.

(c) Statute of limitations.—No action shall be maintained under this section unless it is commenced within 10 years after the cause of action arose.

Sec. 3. Definitions.

(a) Extrajudicial killing.—For the purposes of this Act, the term "extrajudicial killing" means a deliberate killing not authorized by a previous judgment pronounced by a regularly constituted court affording all the judicial guarantees which are recognized as indispensable by civilized peoples. Such term, however, does not include any such killing that, under international law, is lawfully carried out under the authority of a foreign nation.

(b) Torture.—For the purposes of this Act—

(1) the term "torture" means any act, directed against an individual in the offender's custody or physical control, by which severe pain or suffering (other than pain or suffering arising only from or inherent in, or incidental to, lawful sanctions), whether physical or mental, is intentionally inflicted on that individual for such purposes as obtaining from that individual or a third person information or a confession, punishing that individual for an act that individual or a third person has committed or is suspected of having committed, intimidating or coercing that individual or a third person, or for any reason based on discrimination of any kind; and

(2) mental pain or suffering refers to prolonged mental harm caused by or resulting from—

(A) the intentional infliction or threatened infliction of severe physical pain or suffering;

(B) the administration or application, or threatened administration or application, of mind altering substances or other procedures calculated to disrupt profoundly the senses or the personality;

(C) the threat of imminent death; or

(D) the threat that another individual will imminently be subjected to death, severe physical pain or suffering, or the administration or application of mind altering substances or other procedures calculated to disrupt profoundly the senses or personality.

Kadic v. Karadzic

United States Court of Appeals, Second Circuit, 1995.
70 F.3d 232, cert. denied, 518 U.S. 1005 (1996).

■ JON O. NEWMAN, CHIEF JUDGE:

Most Americans would probably be surprised to learn that victims of atrocities committed in Bosnia are suing the leader of the insurgent Bosnian–Serb forces in a United States District Court in Manhattan. Their claims seek to build upon the foundation of this Court's decision in Filartiga v. Pena–Irala, 630 F.2d 876 (2d Cir.1980), which recognized the important principle that the venerable Alien Tort Act, 28 U.S.C. § 1350

(1988), enacted in 1789 but rarely invoked since then, validly creates federal court jurisdiction for suits alleging torts committed anywhere in the world against aliens in violation of the law of nations. The pending appeals pose additional significant issues as to the scope of the Alien Tort Act: whether some violations of the law of nations may be remedied when committed by those not acting under the authority of a state; [and] if so, whether genocide, war crimes, and crimes against humanity are among the violations that do not require state action....

. . .

The plaintiffs-appellants are Croat and Muslim citizens of the internationally recognized nation of Bosnia–Herzegovina, formerly a republic of Yugoslavia. Their complaints, which we accept as true for purposes of this appeal, allege that they are victims, and representatives of victims, of various atrocities, including brutal acts of rape, forced prostitution, forced impregnation, torture, and summary execution, carried out by Bosnian–Serb military forces as part of a genocidal campaign conducted in the course of the Bosnian civil war. Karadzic, formerly a citizen of Yugoslavia and now a citizen of Bosnia–Herzegovina, is the President of a three-man presidency of the self-proclaimed Bosnian–Serb republic within Bosnia–Herzegovina, sometimes referred to as "Srpska," which claims to exercise lawful authority, and does in fact exercise actual control, over large parts of the territory of Bosnia-Herzegovina. In his capacity as President, Karadzic possesses ultimate command authority over the Bosnian–Serb military forces, and the injuries perpetrated upon plaintiffs were committed as part of a pattern of systematic human rights violations that was directed by Karadzic and carried out by the military forces under his command. The complaints allege that Karadzic acted in an official capacity either as the titular head of Srpska or in collaboration with the government of the recognized nation of the former Yugoslavia and its dominant constituent republic, Serbia.

. . .

In early 1993, Karadzic was admitted to the United States on three separate occasions as an invitee of the United Nations. According to affidavits submitted by the plaintiffs, Karadzic was personally served with the summons and complaint in each action during two of these visits while he was physically present in Manhattan. . . .

. . .

Though the District Court dismissed for lack of subject-matter jurisdiction, the parties have briefed not only that issue but also the threshold issues of personal jurisdiction and justiciability under the political question doctrine. Karadzic urges us to affirm on any one of these three grounds. We consider each in turn.

I. Subject–Matter Jurisdiction

. . .

A.   The Alien Tort Act

1.   General Application to Appellants' Claims

... Our decision in *Filartiga* established that this statute confers federal subject-matter jurisdiction when the following three conditions are satisfied: (1) an alien sues (2) for a tort (3) committed in violation of the law of nations (i.e., international law). The first two requirements are plainly satisfied here, and the only disputed issue is whether plaintiffs have pleaded violations of international law.

. . .

[The district judge] accepted Karadzic's contention that "acts committed by non-state actors do not violate the law of nations," and considered him to be a non-state actor. The Judge appears to have deemed state action required primarily on the basis of cases determining the need for state action as to claims of official torture, without consideration of the substantial body of law, discussed below, that renders private individuals liable for some international law violations.

We do not agree that the law of nations, as understood in the modern era, confines its reach to state action. Instead, we hold that certain forms of conduct violate the law of nations whether undertaken by those acting under the auspices of a state or only as private individuals. An early example of the application of the law of nations to the acts of private individuals is the prohibition against piracy. In The Brig Malek Adhel, 43 U.S. (2 How.) 210, 232 (1844), the Supreme Court observed that pirates were "hostis humani generis" (an enemy of all mankind) in part because they acted "without ... any pretense of public authority." Later examples are prohibitions against the slave trade and certain war crimes.

... The Executive Branch has emphatically restated in this litigation its position that private persons may be found liable under the Alien Tort Act for acts of genocide, war crimes, and other violations of international humanitarian law. See Statement of Interest of the United States at 5–13.

The Restatement (Third) of the Foreign Relations Law of the United States (1986) ("Restatement (Third)") proclaims: "Individuals may be held liable for offenses against international law, such as piracy, war crimes, and genocide." Restatement (Third) pt. II, introductory note. The Restatement is careful to identify those violations that are actionable when committed by a state, Restatement (Third) § 702, and a more limited category of violations of "universal concern," id. § 404,[4] partially overlapping with those listed in section 702. Though the immediate focus of section 404 is to identify those offenses for which a state has jurisdiction to punish without regard to territoriality or the nationality of the offenders, cf. id.

---

4. Section 404 provides:

A state has jurisdiction to define and prescribe punishment for certain offenses recognized by the community of nations as of universal concern, such as piracy, slave trade, attacks on or hijacking of aircraft, genocide, war crimes, and perhaps certain acts of terrorism, even where [no other basis of jurisdiction] is present.

§ 402(1)(a), (2), the inclusion of piracy and slave trade from an earlier era and aircraft hijacking from the modern era demonstrates that the offenses of "universal concern" include those capable of being committed by non-state actors. Although the jurisdiction authorized by section 404 is usually exercised by application of criminal law, international law also permits states to establish appropriate civil remedies, id. § 404 cmt. b, such as the tort actions authorized by the Alien Tort Act. ...

. . .

Karadzic also contends that Congress intended the state-action requirement of the Torture Victim Act to apply to actions under the Alien Tort Act. We disagree. Congress enacted the Torture Victim Act to codify the cause of action recognized by this Circuit in *Filartiga*, and to further extend that cause of action to plaintiffs who are U.S. citizens. See H.R.Rep. No. 367, 102d Cong., 2d Sess., at 4 (1991), reprinted in 1992 U.S.C.C.A.N. 84, 86 (explaining that codification of *Filartiga* was necessary in light of skepticism expressed by Judge Bork's concurring opinion in *Tel-Oren*). At the same time, Congress indicated that the Alien Tort Act "has other important uses and should not be replaced," because

> Claims based on torture and summary executions do not exhaust the list of actions that may appropriately be covered [by the Alien Tort Act]. That statute should remain intact to permit suits based on other norms that already exist or may ripen in the future into rules of customary international law.

Id. The scope of the Alien Tort Act remains undiminished by enactment of the Torture Victim Act.

2. Specific Application of Alien Tort Act to Appellants' Claims

In order to determine whether the offenses alleged by the appellants in this litigation are violations of the law of nations that may be the subject of Alien Tort Act claims against a private individual, we must make a particularized examination of these offenses, mindful of the important precept that "evolving standards of international law govern who is within the [Alien Tort Act's] jurisdictional grant." In making that inquiry, it will be helpful to group the appellants' claims into three categories: (a) genocide, (b) war crimes, and (c) other instances of inflicting death, torture, and degrading treatment.

(a) Genocide. In the aftermath of the atrocities committed during the Second World War, the condemnation of genocide as contrary to international law quickly achieved broad acceptance by the community of nations. In 1946, the General Assembly of the United Nations declared that genocide is a crime under international law that is condemned by the civilized world, whether the perpetrators are "private individuals, public officials or statesmen." G.A.Res. 96(I), 1 U.N.GAOR, U.N. Doc. A/64/Add.1, at 188–89 (1946). ...

The Convention on the Prevention and Punishment of the Crime of Genocide, 78 U.N.T.S. 277, entered into force Jan. 12, 1951, for the United States Feb. 23, 1989 (hereinafter "Convention on Genocide"), provides a more specific articulation of the prohibition of genocide in international law. ... Especially pertinent to the pending appeal, the Convention makes clear that "[p]ersons committing genocide ... shall be punished, whether they are constitutionally responsible rulers, public officials or private individuals." ...

The applicability of this norm to private individuals is also confirmed by the Genocide Convention Implementation Act of 1987, 18 U.S.C. § 1091 (1988), which criminalizes acts of genocide without regard to whether the offender is acting under color of law, see id. § 1091(a) ("[w]hoever" commits genocide shall be punished), if the crime is committed within the United States or by a U.S. national, id. § 1091(d). Though Congress provided that the Genocide Convention Implementation Act shall not "be construed as creating any substantive or procedural right enforceable by law by any party in any proceeding," id. § 1092, the legislative decision not to create a new private remedy does not imply that a private remedy is not already available under the Alien Tort Act. Nothing in the Genocide Convention Implementation Act or its legislative history reveals an intent by Congress to repeal the Alien Tort Act insofar as it applies to genocide, and the two statutes are surely not repugnant to each other. Under these circumstances, it would be improper to construe the Genocide Convention Implementation Act as repealing the Alien Tort Act by implication. ...

Appellants' allegations that Karadzic personally planned and ordered a campaign of murder, rape, forced impregnation, and other forms of torture designed to destroy the religious and ethnic groups of Bosnian Muslims and Bosnian Croats clearly state a violation of the international law norm proscribing genocide, regardless of whether Karadzic acted under color of law or as a private individual. The District Court has subject-matter jurisdiction over these claims pursuant to the Alien Tort Act.

(b) War crimes. Plaintiffs also contend that the acts of murder, rape, torture, and arbitrary detention of civilians, committed in the course of hostilities, violate the law of war. Atrocities of the types alleged here have long been recognized in international law as violations of the law of war. See In re Yamashita, 327 U.S. 1, 14 (1946). Moreover, international law imposes an affirmative duty on military commanders to take appropriate measures within their power to control troops under their command for the prevention of such atrocities. Id. at 15–16.

. . .

The offenses alleged by the appellants, if proved, would violate the most fundamental norms of the law of war ..., which bind[] parties to internal conflicts regardless of whether they are recognized nations or roving hordes of insurgents. The liability of private individuals for committing war crimes has been recognized since World War I and was confirmed at Nuremberg after World War II, and remains today an important aspect of international law. The District Court has jurisdiction pursuant to the Alien Tort Act over appellants' claims of war crimes and other violations of international humanitarian law.

(c) Torture and summary execution. In *Filartiga*, we held that official torture is prohibited by universally accepted norms of international law, and the Torture Victim Act confirms this holding and extends it to cover summary execution. Torture Victim Act §§ 2(a), 3(a). However, torture and summary execution—when not perpetrated in the course of genocide or war crimes—are proscribed by international law only when committed by state officials or under color of law. . . .

. . . It suffices to hold at this stage that the alleged atrocities are actionable under the Alien Tort Act, without regard to state action, to the extent that they were committed in pursuit of genocide or war crimes, and otherwise may be pursued against Karadzic to the extent that he is shown to be a state actor. . . .

B. The Torture Victim Protection Act

. . .

By its plain language, the Torture Victim Act renders liable only those individuals who have committed torture or extrajudicial killing "under actual or apparent authority, or color of law, of any foreign nation." Legislative history confirms that this language was intended to "make[ ] clear that the plaintiff must establish some governmental involvement in the torture or killing to prove a claim," and that the statute "does not attempt to deal with torture or killing by purely private groups." H.R.Rep. No. 367, 102d Cong., 2d Sess., at 5 (1991), reprinted in 1992 U.S.C.C.A.N. 84, 87. In construing the terms "actual or apparent authority" and "color of law," courts are instructed to look to principles of agency law and to jurisprudence under 42 U.S.C. § 1983, respectively. Id.

. . .

II. Service of Process and Personal Jurisdiction

[The court held that Karadzic had been properly served with process. It held that he was not immune from service under the UN Headquarters Agreement, because he was outside the defined "headquarters district" at the time he was served, and was not a designated representative of any member of the United Nations. The court declined to imply an additional immunity for United Nations invitees beyond the terms of the Headquarters Agreement, either as a matter of interpretation of that Agreement or as a rule of federal common law.]

III. Justiciability

We recognize that cases of this nature might pose special questions concerning the judiciary's proper role when adjudication might have implications in the conduct of this nation's foreign relations. We do not read *Filartiga* to mean that the federal judiciary must always act in ways that risk significant interference with United States foreign relations. To the contrary, we recognize that suits of this nature can present difficulties that implicate sensitive matters of diplomacy historically reserved to the jurisdiction of the political branches. See First National Bank v. Banco Nacional de Cuba, 406 U.S. 759, 767 (1972). We therefore proceed to consider whether, even though the jurisdictional threshold is satisfied in the pending cases, other considerations relevant to justiciability weigh against permitting the suits to proceed.

Two nonjurisdictional, prudential doctrines reflect the judiciary's concerns regarding separation of powers: the political question doctrine and the act of state doctrine. It is the " 'constitutional' underpinnings" of these doctrines that influenced the concurring opinions of Judge Robb and Judge Bork in *Tel–Oren*. Although we too recognize the potentially detrimental effects of judicial action in cases of this nature, we do not embrace the rather categorical views as to the inappropriateness of judicial action urged by Judges Robb and Bork. Not every case "touching foreign relations" is nonjusticiable, see Baker v. Carr, 369 U.S. 186, 211 (1962), and judges should not reflexively invoke these doctrines to avoid difficult and somewhat sensitive decisions in the context of human rights. We believe a preferable approach is to weigh carefully the relevant considerations on a case-by-case basis. This will permit the judiciary to act where appropriate in light of the express legislative mandate of the Congress in section 1350, without compromising the primacy of the political branches in foreign affairs.

Karadzic maintains that these suits were properly dismissed because they present nonjusticiable political questions. We disagree. Although these cases present issues that arise in a politically charged context, that does not transform them into cases involving nonjusticiable political questions. "[T]he doctrine 'is one of "political questions," not one of "political cases." ' "

· · ·

... [O]ur decision in *Filartiga* established that universally recognized norms of international law provide judicially discoverable and manageable standards for adjudicating suits brought under the Alien Tort Act, which obviates any need to make initial policy decisions of the kind normally reserved for nonjudicial discretion. Moreover, the existence of judicially discoverable and manageable standards further undermines the claim that such suits relate to matters that are constitutionally committed to another branch.

· · ·

In the pending appeal, we need have no concern that interference with important governmental interests warrants rejection of appellants' claims. After commencing their action against Karadzic, attorneys for the plaintiffs in Doe wrote to the Secretary of State to oppose reported attempts by Karadzic to be granted immunity from suit in the United States; a copy of plaintiffs' complaint was attached to the letter. Far from intervening in the case to urge rejection of the suit on the ground that it presented political questions, the Department responded with a letter indicating that Karadzic was not immune from suit as an invitee of the United Nations. After oral argument in the pending appeals, this Court wrote to the Attorney General to inquire whether the United States wished to offer any further views concerning any of the issues raised. In a "Statement of Interest," signed by the Solicitor General and the State Department's Legal Adviser, the United States has expressly disclaimed any concern that the political question doctrine should be invoked to prevent the litigation of these lawsuits: "Although there might be instances in which federal courts are asked to issue rulings under the Alien Tort Statute or the Torture Victim Protection Act that might raise a political question, this is not one of them." Statement of Interest of the United States at 3. Though even an assertion of the political question doctrine by the Executive Branch, entitled to respectful consideration, would not necessarily preclude adjudication, the Government's reply to our inquiry reinforces our view that adjudication may properly proceed.

As to the act of state doctrine, the doctrine was not asserted in the District Court and is not before us on this appeal. Moreover, the appellee has not had the temerity to assert in this Court that the acts he allegedly committed are the officially approved policy of a state. Finally, as noted, we think it would be a rare case in which the act of state doctrine precluded suit under section 1350. [The Supreme Court's decision in Banco Nacional de Cuba v. Sabbatino, 376 U.S. 398, 428–30 (1964),] was careful to recognize the doctrine "in the absence of ... unambiguous agreement regarding controlling legal principles," such as exist in the pending litigation, and applied the doctrine only in a context—expropriation of an alien's property—in which world opinion was sharply divided.

Finally, we note that at this stage of the litigation no party has identified a more suitable forum, and we are aware of none. Though the Statement of the United States suggests the general importance of considering the doctrine of forum non conveniens, it seems evident that the courts of the former Yugoslavia, either in Serbia or war-torn Bosnia, are not now available to entertain plaintiffs' claims, even if circumstances concerning the location of witnesses and documents were presented that were sufficient to overcome the plaintiffs' preference for a United States forum.

. . .

The judgment of the District Court dismissing appellants' complaints for lack of subject-matter jurisdiction is reversed, and the cases are remanded for further proceedings in accordance with this opinion.

Notes

1. The court in *Kadic* concludes that the grant of a cause of action for official torture under the TVPA, and the express refusal to grant a cause of action in the Genocide Convention Implementation Act, do not impliedly repeal the availability of relief under the Alien Tort Statute for torture in connection with genocide or war crimes by non-state actors. Does the TVPA imply any limits on a court's authority to grant relief under the Alien Tort Statute? Could the Alien Tort Statute be used to circumvent the exhaustion requirement or the statute of limitations in the TVPA? Could it

be used to reach mistreatment that does not satisfy the TVPA's definition of "torture," or deprivations of life that do not satisfy the TVPA's definition of "extrajudicial killing"?

2.   The conclusion that the TVPA supplements, and does not replace, the Alien Tort Statute means that courts can continue to recognize causes of action under the Alien Tort Statute for violations of other customary international human rights norms, such as prolonged arbitrary detention, *Martinez v. City of Los Angeles*, 141 F.3d 1373 (9th Cir.1998); *Eastman Kodak v. Kavlin*, 978 F.Supp. 1078 (S.D.Fla.1997); forced labor, *Doe v. Unocal Corp.*, 963 F.Supp. 880 (C.D.Cal.1997); *Doe v. Islamic Salvation Front*, 993 F.Supp. 3 (D.D.C.1998), and cruel, inhuman or degrading treatment, *Abebe-Jira v. Negewo*, 72 F.3d 844 (11th Cir.), cert. denied, 519 U.S. 830 (1996); *Xuncax v. Gramajo*, 886 F.Supp. 162 (D.Mass.1995).

3.   *Kadic* identifies some of the circumstances under which modern international law binds private individuals and supports liability under the Alien Tort Statute. Note also the conclusion that cooperation between Karadzic and the government of Yugoslavia might render him a state actor engaged in activities "under color of law" for purposes of either the Alien Tort Statute or the TVPA. Some TVPA or Alien Tort Statute actions have been brought against U.S. or foreign corporations that allegedly acted in concert with foreign regimes. See, e.g., *Doe v. Unocal Corp.*, 963 F.Supp. 880 (C.D.Cal.1997) (action against U.S. oil company alleging torture and slavery in Burma); *Eastman Kodak Co. v. Kavlin*, 978 F.Supp. 1078 (S.D.Fla.1997) (action against Bolivian individual and corporation for causing prolonged arbitrary detention of Kodak representative); but cf. *Beanal v. Freeport–McMoRan, Inc.*, 969 F.Supp. 362 (E.D.La.1997) (corporation is not "individual" within meaning of TVPA).

4.   The *Kadic* court finds personal jurisdiction based on service of process while Karadzic was temporarily present in Manhattan. The Supreme Court has upheld such "transient jurisdiction" as consistent with the requirements of due process. *Burnham v. Superior Court*, 495 U.S. 604 (1990). Does Karadzic's temporary presence justify the provision of a U.S. forum to the plaintiffs? Does it assure the fairness of subjecting Karadzic to adjudication in the United States? Note the court's reference to the doctrine of forum non conveniens, which authorizes dismissal of a lawsuit that could more appropriately be brought in another location, and the court's skepticism that plaintiffs have an adequate forum available in former Yugoslavia. When might it be appropriate for TVPA or Alien Tort Statute action to be dismissed on forum non conveniens grounds?

5.   The *Kadic* court refers expressly to the positions taken by the Executive Branch on the legal merits of the case and on the desirability of its proceeding in a U.S. forum. What role should the views of the Executive play in a court's resolution of issues of international law, or in deciding whether plaintiffs should be permitted to proceed in a U.S. court?

6.   If Karadzic had been president of a recognized state, he would presumably have been protected by the doctrine of head-of-state immunity. In *Lafontant v. Aristide*, 844 F.Supp. 128 (E.D.N.Y.1994), the President of

Haiti asserted head-of-state immunity in a TVPA action, although he had fled to the United States after a successful military coup and the military regime had attempted to waive the immunity. The court held, however, that he retained immunity because the U.S. Executive Branch recognized him as the only legitimate leader of Haiti. The court stated, "Recognition of a government and its officers is the exclusive function of the Executive Branch. ...[T]he courts must defer to the Executive determination." See also Restatement of Foreign Relations Law § 464 comments f & i, & Reporters' Note 14 (discussing head of state immunity and Executive suggestion of immunity). Does the practice reflected in this decision leave the TVPA at the mercy of the current U.S. Administration's political agenda?

On the scope of immunity for heads of state, compare the House of Lords decision denying the immunity of General Pinochet as a former head of state from extradition for acts of torture committed under his government. See *Regina v. Bow Street Metropolitan Stipendiary Magistrate ex parte Pinochet Ugarte (No. 3)*, [1999] 2 W.L.R. 827 (H.L. 1999) (U.K.) discussed at pp. 658–664 supra.

7. Liability under the TVPA is expressly limited to individuals acting under authority or color of law of a *foreign* nation. The Alien Tort Statute has no such limitation, and its history suggests that it was originally designed to deal with violations of international law that might have implicated the responsibility of the United States. Thus far, the statute has rarely been employed against persons acting under color of U.S. law, perhaps because of the availability of less esoteric remedies. But see *Jama v. U.S. I.N.S.*, 22 F. Supp. 2d 353 (D.N.J.1998) (allowing immigration detainees to bring claims under Alien Tort Statute against private corrections contractor for cruel, inhuman or degrading treatment).

*

PART IV

SELECTED RIGHTS COMPARED

The international law of human rights derived largely from national legal systems, including that of the United States. Inevitably, the international character of international human rights law, and the international processes that produce it, have required it to draw on the law of other cultures and other rights systems, principally in Europe and in the Americas but also in other countries around the world. National human rights may differ in conception or in detail because of several factors, including cultural or religious values, political and economic conditions, government structure and legal traditions. As a result, international human rights, while striving for a common denominator, differ in more or less significant respects from rights in any particular national system.

Students in the United States may be particularly interested to determine in what respects international human rights law has diverged from its U.S. antecedents. The rights jurisprudence of the United States is rooted in the Eighteenth Century, was updated after the Civil War, and has been developed by judicial interpretation largely since the Second World War, but it has not wholly shed its Eighteenth Century origins and limitations. Constitutional and legal systems that have been established since the Second World War, even some that reflect substantial U.S. influence, e.g., Germany, have sometimes become preferred models for new constitutional systems and for international human rights standards. Most striking, perhaps, has been the development of international economic and social rights, which have become solidly entrenched in international human rights law, e.g., in the Universal Declaration and the Covenant on Economic, Social and Cultural Rights. However, in the United States, most economic and social rights lack constitutional foundations, and at the end of the Twentieth Century, their support in U.S. law is being eroded. Even as regards civil and political rights, the United States has resisted moving to international standards where they are higher; witness U.S. reservations to the Civil and Political Rights Covenant and the Race Convention, and the proposed reservations to the Women's Convention.

Some of the differences between human rights under U.S. law and international human rights law reflect not only their different ages but their different ideology, history, and political development. Rights in the United States still show their natural rights origins, although judges often avoid reference to philosophical assumptions. International human rights law must forge consensus across an even wider range of ideologies than U.S. law, and has largely eschewed theory other than that reflected in its commitment to "human dignity." Rights in the United States have been shaped by judicial review and judicial supremacy, as reflected in exercises of intense judicial scrutiny and the protection of unenumerated rights. The emphasis on judicial review also produces the conviction that claims that are ill-suited to judicial enforcement should not be regarded as constitutionally protected. Additional differences between U.S. rights and international rights may be due to differences between national and international political processes and to the structural features of U.S. constitutionalism, federalism and separation of powers.

In this Part we have selected for detailed comparison important rights as to which U.S. constitutional law and international human rights law differ significantly. In several instances, where the jurisprudence of another national system enriches the comparison, we have included it as well. As will become evident, U.S. law offers greater protection to some rights than international law; international law offers greater protection to other rights; and in some contexts the systems strike a different balance between conflicting rights. If time and space permitted, other enlightening examples could have been explored, such as freedom of religion, rights in criminal procedure, family rights, and the rights of children.

The international and national materials illustrate differing conceptions of a particular human right in different legal systems. They also illustrate the methods employed by international human rights tribunals in response to claims that one nation's needs justify greater intrusions on human rights than elsewhere, whether because of cultural differences or because of varying local conditions. The materials further exhibit interpretive techniques utilized by international human rights tribunals, and some of the common doctrinal structures they have adopted for implementing particular rights.

CHAPTER 1

CIVIL RIGHTS

The distinction between civil rights and political rights reflects both historical developments and conceptual differences. Rights to life, liberty and property achieved recognition earlier than citizens' rights to participate in governing themselves and each other. While civil rights restrict the application of laws that affect particular protected interests, political rights confer an opportunity to contribute to the determination of the laws in general. At the same time, in a democratic society some civil rights are so closely related to the effective exercise of political rights that the distinction may appear artificial. Freedom of speech, for example, and freedom of association, usually characterized as civil rights, are often employed in criticism of government or in election campaigns.

It is also difficult to maintain a sharp distinction between civil rights and economic and social rights. Civil rights are often conceived as negative or defensive rights, rights not to be subjected to certain invasions of natural liberty, rather than positive or affirmative rights, rights to the assistance of the state in achieving important human goals. But even in U.S. constitutional law, civil rights may have positive implications. For example, the right to counsel requires government to provide legal representation to indigent criminal defendants, and the right to due process requires medical services for detained persons; the right to civil jury trial requires the government to make expensive procedures available to plaintiffs who have taken the initiative in bringing suit. Moreover, the positive aspect of civil rights receives greater emphasis in international human rights law than in U.S. constitutional law. Finally, some economic and social rights, such as the right to form trade unions, can be understood either as an instance of the civil right to freedom of association or as part of a structure of economic and social rights protecting the wages and working conditions of workers. (Compare ICCPR art. 22(1) with ICESCR art. 8(1)(a).)

The list of civil rights in the ICCPR, however, derives primarily from the classic liberal rights that protect individuals and their interactions in civil society from the intrusions of the state. We examine civil rights under four headings: life, together with the right to be free of cruel, inhuman or degrading punishment; autonomy and privacy; freedom of expression; and equality.

A. THE RIGHT TO LIFE, AND CAPITAL PUNISHMENT

The Universal Declaration and the Covenant on Civil and Political Rights each begins its list of individual rights with the right to life. It has often been said that the right to life is the most fundamental, and that no other right can exist without it. What, however, does the right to life entail? This Section first sets forth the Human Rights Committee's General Comment on the right to life under Article 6 of the Covenant, discussing some of the ramifications of a state's obligation to respect and ensure the right to life.

One conceivable consequence of a right to life is the right not to be deprived of life as punishment for a criminal offense. Article 6 of the Covenant articulates a series of limitations on the imposition of capital punishment, and encourages states to move toward its abolition. But Article 6 does not prohibit capital punishment altogether. The subsequent Second Optional Protocol to the Covenant does require abolition of capital punishment; it entered into force in 1991, and had 35 States Parties as of January 1, 1999.*

The U.S. Constitution does not address a right to life as such. But the Fifth Amendment provides that no person shall be deprived of life without due process of law, and the Fourteenth Amendment protects life similarly against deprivation by the States. In its original conception, the due process clause protected life against deprivation except pursuant to law and with due process of law. With the birth of substantive due process, see Part II, Chapter 1(D)(1), the Constitution came to protect against official deprivation of life pursuant to laws that were irrational or unreasonable.

An alternative objection to capital punishment, under some or all circumstances, may be that it is "cruel and unusual," or "cruel, inhuman or degrading." The Constitutional Court of South Africa invalidated that state's death penalty statutes in 1995, under a clause of its interim constitution forbidding "cruel, inhuman or degrading treatment or punishment." The objection that capital punishment is "cruel and unusual" within the meaning of the Eighth Amendment to the U.S. Constitution, directly or as subsumed in the Fourteenth Amendment, has been raised with mixed success in the United States. Some Justices have concluded that capital punishment is inherently cruel and unusual, but Eighth Amendment challenges have succeeded only on narrower grounds since *Furman v. Georgia*, 408 U.S. 238 (1972).

Meanwhile, the European Court of Human Rights and some national courts have held that, even if capital punishment is not prohibited, the period of waiting prior to execution may itself produce a form of inhuman

---

* In addition, the Sixth Protocol to the European Human Rights Convention also requires abolition of the death penalty; some European states are parties to this Protocol but not to the Second Optional Protocol to the Covenant.

and degrading treatment or punishment. The consequences of that conclusion affect not only states that impose capital punishment, but also states that are requested to extradite fugitive offenders.

Finally, the section briefly examines capital punishment in China, a state that (as of January 1, 1999) has not yet ratified the Covenant.

Article 6 ICCPR

1. Every human being has the inherent right to life. This right shall be protected by law. No one shall be arbitrarily deprived of his life.

2. In countries which have not abolished the death penalty, sentence of death may be imposed only for the most serious crimes in accordance with the law in force at the time of the commission of the crime and not contrary to the provisions of the present Covenant and to the Convention on the Prevention and Punishment of the Crime of Genocide. This penalty can only be carried out pursuant to a final judgement rendered by a competent court.

3. When deprivation of life constitutes the crime of genocide, it is understood that nothing in this article shall authorize any State Party to the present Covenant to derogate in any way from any obligation assumed under the provisions of the Convention on the Prevention and Punishment of the Crime of Genocide.

4. Anyone sentenced to death shall have the right to seek pardon or commutation of the sentence. Amnesty, pardon or commutation of the sentence of death may be granted in all cases.

5. Sentence of death shall not be imposed for crimes committed by persons below eighteen years of age and shall not be carried out on pregnant women.

6. Nothing in this article shall be invoked to delay or to prevent the abolition of capital punishment by any State Party to the present Covenant.

Human Rights Committee, General Comment 6

U.N. Doc. HRI/GEN/1 at 5.

THE RIGHT TO LIFE (ARTICLE 6) (1982)

1. The right to life enunciated in article 6 of the Covenant has been dealt with in all State reports. It is the supreme right from which no derogation is permitted even in time of public emergency which threatens the life of the nation (art. 4). However, the Committee has noted that quite often the information given concerning article 6 was limited to only one or other aspect of this right. It is a right which should not be interpreted narrowly.

2. The Committee observes that war and other acts of mass violence continue to be a scourge of humanity and take the lives of thousands of innocent human beings every year. Under the Charter of the United Nations the threat or use of force by any State against another State,

except in exercise of the inherent right of self-defence, is already prohibited. The Committee considers that States have the supreme duty to prevent wars, acts of genocide and other acts of mass violence causing arbitrary loss of life. Every effort they make to avert the danger of war, especially thermonuclear war, and to strengthen international peace and security would constitute the most important condition and guarantee for the safeguarding of the right to life. In this respect, the Committee notes, in particular, a connection between article 6 and article 20, which states that the law shall prohibit any propaganda for war (para. 1) or incitement to violence (para. 2) as therein described.

3.   The protection against arbitrary deprivation of life which is explicitly required by the third sentence of article 6 (1) is of paramount importance. The Committee considers that States parties should take measures not only to prevent and punish deprivation of life by criminal acts, but also to prevent arbitrary killing by their own security forces. The deprivation of life by the authorities of the State is a matter of the utmost gravity. Therefore, the law must strictly control and limit the circumstances in which a person may be deprived of his life by such authorities.

4.   States parties should also take specific and effective measures to prevent the disappearance of individuals, something which unfortunately has become all too frequent and leads too often to arbitrary deprivation of life. Furthermore, States should establish effective facilities and procedures to investigate thoroughly cases of missing and disappeared persons in circumstances which may involve a violation of the right to life.

5.   Moreover, the Committee has noted that the right to life has been too often narrowly interpreted. The expression "inherent right to life" cannot properly be understood in a restrictive manner, and the protection of this right requires that States adopt positive measures. In this connection, the Committee considers that it would be desirable for States parties to take all possible measures to reduce infant mortality and to increase life expectancy, especially in adopting measures to eliminate malnutrition and epidemics.

6.   While it follows from article 6 (2) to (6) that States parties are not obliged to abolish the death penalty totally they are obliged to limit its use and, in particular, to abolish it for other than the "most serious crimes". Accordingly, they ought to consider reviewing their criminal laws in this light and, in any event, are obliged to restrict the application of the death penalty to the "most serious crimes". The article also refers generally to abolition in terms which strongly suggest (paras. 2 (2) and (6)) that abolition is desirable. The Committee concludes that all measures of abolition should be considered as progress in the enjoyment of the right to life within the meaning of article 40, and should as such be reported to the Committee. The Committee notes that a number of States have already abolished the death penalty or suspended its application. Nevertheless, States' reports show that progress made towards abolishing or limiting the application of the death penalty is quite inadequate.

7. The Committee is of the opinion that the expression "most serious crimes" must be read restrictively to mean that the death penalty should be a quite exceptional measure. It also follows from the express terms of article 6 that it can only be imposed in accordance with the law in force at the time of the commission of the crime and not contrary to the Covenant. The procedural guarantees therein prescribed must be observed, including the right to a fair hearing by an independent tribunal, the presumption of innocence, the minimum guarantees for the defence, and the right to review by a higher tribunal. These rights are applicable in addition to the particular right to seek pardon or commutation of the sentence.

State v. Makwanyane

Constitutional Court of South Africa, 1995.
1995(3) South Africa Law Reports 391.

[In this case, the Constitutional Court unanimously invalidated the death penalty as a violation of the interim South African Constitution of 1993. The excerpts that follow are primarily from the opinion of the President of the court, holding that the death penalty violated the constitutional prohibition on cruel, inhuman or degrading punishments. Each Justice wrote an opinion with differing emphases, and some of these opinions relied directly on the constitutional guarantee of the right to life. Paragraphs are numbered as in the original.]

■ CHASKALSON, P.

(8) Chapter 3 of the Constitution sets out the fundamental rights to which every person is entitled under the Constitution and also contains provisions dealing with the way in which the chapter is to be interpreted by the Courts. It does not deal specifically with the death penalty, but in section 11(2), it prohibits "cruel, inhuman or degrading treatment or punishment". There is no definition of what is to be regarded as "cruel, inhuman or degrading" and we therefore have to give meaning to these words ourselves.

(10) ... [S]ection 11(2) of the Constitution must not be construed in isolation, but in its context, which includes the history and background to the adoption of the Constitution, other provisions of the Constitution itself and, in particular, the provisions of Chapter 3 of which it is part. It must also be construed in a way which secures for "individuals the full measure" of its protection. Rights with which section 11(2) is associated in Chapter 3 of the Constitution, and which are of particular importance to a decision on the constitutionality of the death penalty are included in section 9, "every person shall have the right to life", section 10, "every person shall have the right to respect for and protection of his or her dignity", and section 8, "every person shall have the right to equality before the law and to equal protection of the law".. . .

(26) ... Death is a cruel penalty and the legal processes which necessarily involve waiting in uncertainty for the sentence to be set aside or carried

out, add to the cruelty. It is also an inhuman punishment for it "...
involves, by its very nature, a denial of the executed person's humanity",
and it is degrading because it strips the convicted person of all dignity and
treats him or her as an object to be eliminated by the State. The question is
not, however, whether the death sentence is a cruel, inhuman or degrading
punishment in the ordinary meaning of these words but whether it is a
cruel, inhuman or degrading punishment within the meaning of section
11(2) of our Constitution. The accused, who rely on section 11(2) of the
Constitution, carry the initial onus of establishing this proposition.

(33) The death sentence is a form of punishment which has been used
throughout history by different societies. It has long been the subject of
controversy. As societies became more enlightened, they restricted the
offences for which this penalty could be imposed. The movement away from
the death penalty gained momentum during the second half of the present
century with the growth of the abolitionist movement. In some countries it
is now prohibited in all circumstances, in some it is prohibited save in times
of war, and in most countries that have retained it as a penalty for crime,
its use has been restricted to extreme cases. According to Amnesty International, 1831 executions were carried out throughout the world in 1993 as a
result of sentences of death, of which 1419 were in China, which means
that only 412 executions were carried out in the rest of the world in that
year. Today, capital punishment has been abolished as a penalty for murder
either specifically or in practice by almost half of the countries of the world
including the democracies of Europe and our neighbouring countries,
Namibia, Mozambique and Angola. In most of those countries where it is
retained, as the Amnesty International statistics show, it is seldom used.

(34) ... The international and foreign authorities are of value because
they analyse arguments for and against the death sentence and show how
courts of other jurisdictions have dealt with this vexed issue. ... They may
also have to be considered because of their relevance to section 35(1) of the
Constitution, which states:

> "In interpreting the provisions of this Chapter a court of law shall
> promote the values which underlie an open and democratic society
> based on freedom and equality and shall, where applicable, have regard
> to public international law applicable to the protection of the right
> entrenched in this Chapter, and may have regard to comparable
> foreign case law."

(36) Capital punishment is not prohibited by public international law. ...

(37) Comparative "bill of rights" jurisprudence will no doubt be of importance, particularly in the early stages of the transition when there is no
developed indigenous jurisprudence in this branch of the law on which to
draw. Although we are told by section 35(1) that we "may" have regard to
foreign case law, it is important to appreciate that this will not necessarily
offer a safe guide to the interpretation of Chapter 3 of our Constitution.
This ... is implicit in the injunction given to the Courts in section 35(1),
which in permissible terms allows the Courts to "have regard to" such law.
There is no injunction to do more than this.

(38) When challenges to the death sentence in international or foreign courts and tribunals have failed, the constitution or the international instrument concerned has either directly sanctioned capital punishment or has specifically provided that the right to life is subject to exceptions sanctioned by law. The only case to which we were referred in which there were not such express provisions in the constitution, was the decision of the Hungarian Constitutional Court. There the challenge succeeded and the death penalty was declared to be unconstitutional.*

(87) The attorney-general argued that what is cruel, inhuman or degrading depends to a large extent upon contemporary attitudes within society, and that South African society does not regard the death sentence for extreme cases of murder as a cruel, inhuman or degrading form of punishment. . . .

(88) Public opinion may have some relevance to the enquiry, but in itself, it is no substitute for the duty vested in the Courts to interpret the Constitution and to uphold its provisions without fear or favour. If public opinion were to be decisive there would be no need for constitutional adjudication. . . .

(94) Proportionality is an ingredient to be taken into account in deciding whether a penalty is cruel, inhuman or degrading. . . . The wilful taking of an innocent life calls for a severe penalty, and there are many countries which still retain the death penalty as a sentencing option for such cases. Disparity between the crime and the penalty is not the only ingredient of proportionality; factors such as the enormity and irredeemable character of the death sentence in circumstances where neither error nor arbitrariness can be excluded, the expense and difficulty of addressing the disparities which exist in practice between accused persons facing similar charges, and which are due to factors such as race, poverty, and ignorance, and the other subjective factors which have been mentioned, are also factors that can and should be taken into account in dealing with this issue. It may possibly be that none alone would be sufficient under our Constitution to justify a finding that the death sentence is cruel, inhuman or degrading. But these factors are not to be evaluated in isolation. They must be taken together, and in order to decide whether the threshold set by section 11(2) has been crossed they must be evaluated with other relevant factors, including the two fundamental rights on which the accused rely, the right to dignity and the right to life.

(95) The carrying out of the death sentence destroys life, which is protected without reservation under section 9 of our Constitution, it annihilates human dignity which is protected under section 10, elements of arbitrariness are present in its enforcement and it is irremediable. Taking these factors into account, as well as the assumption that I have made in regard to public opinion in South Africa, and giving the words of section 11(2) the broader meaning to which they are entitled at this stage of the enquiry,

---

* [A translation of the 1990 decision of the Hungarian Constitutional Court, invalidating capital punishment as an unconstitutional deprivation of life and human dignity, appears at 1 East Eur. Case Rep. Const. L. 177 (1994).—Editors' Note.]

rather than a narrow meaning, I am satisfied that in the context of our Constitution the death penalty is indeed a cruel, inhuman and degrading punishment.

(96) The question that now has to be considered is whether the imposition of such punishment is nonetheless justifiable as a penalty for murder in the circumstances contemplated by [the statute].

(97) It is difficult to conceive of any circumstances in which torture, which is specifically prohibited under section 11(2), could ever be justified. But that does not necessarily apply to capital punishment. Capital punishment, unlike torture, has not been absolutely prohibited by public international law. It is therefore not inappropriate to consider whether the death penalty is justifiable under our Constitution as a penalty for murder. . . .

(98) Section 33(1) of the Constitution provides, in part, that:

> "The rights entrenched in this Chapter may be limited by law of general application, provided that such limitation
>
> > (a) shall be permissible only to the extent that it is
> >
> > > (i) reasonable; and
> > >
> > > (ii) justifiable in an open and democratic society based on freedom and equality;
> >
> > and
> >
> > (b) shall not negate the essential content of the right in question."

(99) Section 33(1)(b) goes on to provide that the limitation of certain rights, including the rights referred to in section 10 and section 11 "shall, in addition to being reasonable as required in paragraph (a)(i), also be necessary".

(104) The limitation of constitutional rights for a purpose that is reasonable and necessary in a democratic society involves the weighing up of competing values, and ultimately an assessment based on proportionality.[130] This is implicit in the provisions of section 33(1). The fact that different rights have different implications for democracy, and in the case of our Constitution, for "an open and democratic society based on freedom and equality", means that there is no absolute standard which can be laid down for determining reasonableness and necessity. Principles can be established, but the application of those principles to particular circumstances can only be done on a case by case basis. This is inherent in the requirement of proportionality, which calls for the balancing of different interests. In the balancing process, the relevant considerations will include the nature of the right that is limited, and its importance to an open and democratic society based on freedom and equality; the purpose for which

---

130. A proportionality test is applied to the limitation of fundamental rights by the Canadian courts, the German Federal Constitutional Court and the European Court of Human Rights. Although the approach of these Courts to proportionality is not identical, all recognise that proportionality is an essential requirement of any legitimate limitation of an entrenched right. Proportionality is also inherent in the different levels of scrutiny applied by United States courts to governmental action.

the right is limited and the importance of that purpose to such a society; the extent of the limitation, its efficacy, and particularly where the limitation has to be necessary, whether the desired ends could reasonably be achieved through other means less damaging to the right in question. In the process regard must be had to the provisions of section 33(1), and the underlying values of the Constitution, bearing in mind that, as a Canadian Judge has said, "the role of the Court is not to second-guess the wisdom of policy choices made by legislators".

(111) "Every person" is entitled to claim the protection of the rights enshrined in Chapter 3, and "no" person shall be denied the protection that they offer. Respect for life and dignity which are at the heart of section 11(2) are values of the highest order under our Constitution. The carrying out of the death penalty would destroy these and all other rights that the convicted person has, and a clear and convincing case must be made out to justify such action.

(116) The attorney-general attached considerable weight to the need for a deterrent to violent crime. He argued that the countries which had abolished the death penalty were on the whole developed and peaceful countries in which other penalties might be sufficient deterrents. We had not reached that stage of development, he said. If in years to come we did so, we could do away with the death penalty....

(117) The need for a strong deterrent to violent crime is an end the validity of which is not open to question. The State is clearly entitled, indeed obliged, to take action to protect human life against violation by others.... Without law, society cannot exist. Without law, individuals in society have no rights. The level of crime in our country has reached alarming proportions. It poses a threat to the transition to democracy, and the creation of development opportunities for all, which are primary goals of the Constitution. ... But the question is not whether criminals should go free and be allowed to escape the consequences of their anti-social behaviour.... The question is whether the death sentence for murder can legitimately be made part of that law. And this depends on whether it meets the criteria prescribed by section 33(1).

(127) It was accepted by the attorney-general that [the deterrent effect] is a much disputed issue in the literature on the death sentence. He contended that it is common sense that the most feared penalty will provide the greatest deterrent, but accepted that there is no proof that the death sentence is in fact a greater deterrent than life imprisonment for a long period. ... It is, however, a major obstacle in the way of the attorney-general's argument, for he has to satisfy us that the penalty is reasonable and necessary, and the doubt which exists in regard to the deterrent effect of the sentence must weigh heavily against his argument. "A punishment as extreme and as irrevocable as death cannot be predicated upon speculation as to what the deterrent effect might be ...."....

(128) Prevention is another object of punishment. The death sentence ensures that the criminal will never again commit murders, but it is not the only way of doing so....

(130) Retribution ought not to be given undue weight in the balancing process. The Constitution is premised on the assumption that ours will be a constitutional state founded on the recognition of human rights. The concluding provision on national unity and reconciliation contains the following commitment:

> "The adoption of this Constitution lays the secure foundation for the people of South Africa to transcend the divisions and strife of the past, which generated gross violations of human rights, the transgression of humanitarian principles in violent conflicts and a legacy of hatred, fear, guilt and revenge. These can now be addressed on the basis that there is a need for understanding but not for vengeance, a need for reparation but not for retaliation, a need for *ubuntu* but not for victimisation."*

(131) Although this commitment has its primary application in the field of political reconciliation, it is not without relevance to the enquiry we are called upon to undertake in the present case. To be consistent with the value of *ubuntu* ours should be a society that "wishes to prevent crime . . . (not) to kill criminals simply to get even with them".

Conclusion

(144) The rights to life and dignity are the most important of all human rights, and the source of all other personal rights in Chapter 3. By committing ourselves to a society founded on the recognition of human rights we are required to value these two rights above all others. And this must be demonstrated by the State in everything that it does, including the way it punishes criminals. This is not achieved by objectifying murderers and putting them to death to serve as an example to others in the expectation that they might possibly be deterred thereby.

(145) In the balancing process the principal factors that have to be weighed are on the one hand the destruction of life and dignity that is a consequence of the implementation of the death sentence, the elements of arbitrariness and the possibility of error in the enforcement of capital punishment, and the existence of a severe alternative punishment (life imprisonment) and, on the other, the claim that the death sentence is a greater deterrent to murder, and will more effectively prevent its commis-

---

* [The concept of *ubuntu* was explained in the opinion of Justice Mokgoro in this case as follows:

Generally, *ubuntu* translates as humaneness. In its most fundamental sense, it translates as personhood and morality. Metaphorically, it expresses itself in *umuntu ngumuntu ngabantu*, describing the significance of group solidarity on survival issues so central to the survival of communities. While it envelops the key values of group solidarity, compassion, respect, human dignity, conformity to basic norms and collective unity, in its fundamental sense it denotes humanity and morality. Its spirit emphasises respect for human dignity, marking a shift from confrontation to conciliation. In South Africa *ubuntu* has become a notion with particular resonance in the building of a democracy. It is part of our "rainbow" heritage, though it might have operated and still operates differently in diverse community settings.

(Editors' Note.)]

sion, than would a sentence of life imprisonment, and that there is a public demand for retributive justice to be imposed on murderers, which only the death sentence can meet.

(146) Retribution cannot be accorded the same weight under our Constitution as the rights to life and dignity, which are the most important of all the rights in Chapter 3. It has not been shown that the death sentence would be materially more effective to deter or prevent murder than the alternative sentence of life imprisonment would be. Taking these factors into account, as well as the elements of arbitrariness and the possibility of error in enforcing the death penalty, the clear and convincing case that is required to justify the death sentence as a penalty for murder, has not been made out. The requirements of section 33(1) have accordingly not been satisfied, and it follows that the provisions of [the statute] must be held to be inconsistent with section 11(2) of the Constitution. In the circumstances, it is not necessary for me to consider whether the section would also be inconsistent with sections 8, 9 or 10 of the Constitution if they had been dealt with separately and not treated together as giving meaning to section 11(2).

■ MAHOMED, J. [concurring]:

(267) ... I am satisfied that the death penalty as a form of punishment violates crucial sections of the Constitution and that it is not saved by the limitations permitted in terms of section 33....

(268) In the first place, it offends section 9 of the Constitution which prescribes in peremptory terms that "every person shall have the right to life". What does that mean? What is a "person"? When does "personhood" and "life" begin? Can there be a conflict between the "right to life" in section 9 and the right of a mother to "personal privacy" in terms of section 13 and her possible right to the freedom and control of her body? Does the "right to life", within the meaning of section 9, preclude the practitioner of scientific medicine from withdrawing the modern mechanisms which mechanically and artificially enable physical breathing in a terminal patient to continue, long beyond the point, when the "brain is dead" and beyond the point when a human being ceases to be "human" although some unfocussed claim to qualify as a "being" is still retained? If not, can such a practitioner go beyond the point of passive withdrawal into the area of active intervention? When? Under what circumstances?

(269) It is, for the purposes of the present case, unnecessary to give to the word "life" in section 9 a comprehensive legal definition, which will accommodate the answer to these and other complex issues, should they arise in the future, it is possible to approach the constitutionality of the death sentence by a question with a sharper and narrower focus, thus:

> "Does the right to life guaranteed by section 9, include the right of every person, not to be deliberately killed by the State, through a systematically planned act of execution sanctioned by the State as a mode of punishment and performed by an executioner remunerated for this purpose from public funds?"

The answer to that question, is in my view: "Yes, every person has that right". It immediately distinguishes that right from some other obvious rights referred to in argument, such as for example the right of a person in life-threatening circumstances to take the life of the aggressor in self-defence or even the acts of the State, in confronting an insurrection or in the course of war.

(270) The deliberate annihilation of the life of a person, systematically planned by the State, as a mode of punishment, is wholly and qualitatively different. It is not like the act of killing in self-defence, an act justifiable in the defence of the clear right of the victim to the preservation of his life. It is not performed in a state of sudden emergency, or under the extraordinary pressures which operate when insurrections are confronted or when the State defends itself during war. It is systematically planned long after sometimes years after the offender has committed the offence for which he is to be punished, and whilst he waits impotently in custody, for his date with the hangman. . . .

Gregg v. Georgia

Supreme Court of the United States, 1976.
428 U.S. 153.

■ Judgment of the Court, and opinion of MR. JUSTICE STEWART, MR. JUSTICE POWELL, and MR. JUSTICE STEVENS, announced by MR. JUSTICE STEWART.

[Gregg was convicted of armed robbery and murder on the basis of evidence that he had killed and robbed two men. He was then sentenced to death.]

. . .

We address initially the basic contention that the punishment of death for the crime of murder is, under all circumstances, "cruel and unusual" in violation of the Eighth and Fourteenth Amendments of the Constitution. . . .

The Court on a number of occasions has both assumed and asserted the constitutionality of capital punishment. In several cases that assumption provided a necessary foundation for the decision, as the Court was asked to decide whether a particular method of carrying out a capital sentence would be allowed to stand under the Eighth Amendment. But until *Furman v. Georgia*, 408 U.S. 238 (1972), the Court never confronted squarely the fundamental claim that the punishment of death always, regardless of the enormity of the offense or the procedure followed in imposing the sentence, is cruel and unusual punishment in violation of the Constitution. Although this issue was presented and addressed in *Furman*, it was not resolved by the Court. Four Justices would have held that capital punishment is not unconstitutional per se; two Justices would have reached the opposite conclusion; and three Justices, while agreeing that the statutes then before the Court were invalid as applied, left open the question whether such punishment may ever be imposed. We now hold that the punishment of death does not invariably violate the Constitution. . . .

. . .

[T]he Court has not confined the prohibition embodied in the Eighth Amendment to "barbarous" methods that were generally outlawed in the 18th century. Instead, the Amendment has been interpreted in a flexible and dynamic manner. . . .

. . .

. . . As Mr. Chief Justice Warren said, in an oft-quoted phrase, "[t]he Amendment must draw its meaning from the evolving standards of decency that mark the progress of a maturing society." Thus, an assessment of contemporary values concerning the infliction of a challenged sanction is relevant to the application of the Eighth Amendment. As we develop below more fully, . . . this assessment does not call for a subjective judgment. It requires, rather, that we look to objective indicia that reflect the public attitude toward a given sanction.

But our cases also make clear that public perceptions of standards of decency with respect to criminal sanctions are not conclusive. A penalty also must accord with "the dignity of man," which is the "basic concept underlying the Eighth Amendment." This means, at least, that the punishment not be "excessive." When a form of punishment in the abstract (in this case, whether capital punishment may ever be imposed as a sanction for murder) rather than in the particular (the propriety of death as a penalty to be applied to a specific defendant for a specific crime) is under consideration, the inquiry into "excessiveness" has two aspects. First, the punishment must not involve the unnecessary and wanton infliction of pain. Second, the punishment must not be grossly out of proportion to the severity of the crime.

. . .

Of course, the requirements of the Eighth Amendment must be applied with an awareness of the limited role to be played by the courts. . . .

. . .

[I]n assessing a punishment selected by a democratically elected legislature against the constitutional measure, we presume its validity. We may not require the legislature to select the least severe penalty possible so long as the penalty selected is not cruelly inhumane or disproportionate to the crime involved. And a heavy burden rests on those who would attack the judgment of the representatives of the people.

This is true in part because the constitutional test is intertwined with an assessment of contemporary standards and the legislative judgment weighs heavily in ascertaining such standards. "[I]n a democratic society legislatures, not courts, are constituted to respond to the will and consequently the moral values of the people." . . .

. . .

The imposition of the death penalty for the crime of murder has a long history of acceptance both in the United States and in England. The common-law rule imposed a mandatory death sentence on all convicted murderers. And the penalty continued to be used into the 20th century by most American States, although the breadth of the common-law rule was diminished, initially by narrowing the class of murders to be punished by death and subsequently by widespread adoption of laws expressly granting juries the discretion to recommend mercy.

. . .

Four years ago, the petitioners in *Furman* and its companion cases predicated their argument primarily upon the asserted proposition that standards of decency had evolved to the point where capital punishment no longer could be tolerated. The petitioners in those cases said, in effect, that the evolutionary process had come to an end, and that standards of decency required that the Eighth Amendment be construed finally as prohibiting capital punishment for any crime regardless of its depravity and impact on society. This view was accepted by two Justices. Three other Justices were unwilling to go so far; focusing on the procedures by which convicted defendants were selected for the death penalty rather than on the actual punishment inflicted, they joined in the conclusion that the statutes before the Court were constitutionally invalid.

The petitioners in the capital cases before the Court today renew the "standards of decency" argument, but developments during the four years since *Furman* have undercut substantially the assumptions upon which their argument rested. Despite the continuing debate, dating back to the 19th century, over the morality and utility of capital punishment, it is now evident that a large proportion of American society continues to regard it as an appropriate and necessary criminal sanction.

The most marked indication of society's endorsement of the death penalty for murder is the legislative response to *Furman*. The legislatures of at least 35 States have enacted new statutes that provide for the death penalty for at least some crimes that result in the death of another person. And the Congress of the United States, in 1974, enacted a statute providing the death penalty for aircraft piracy that results in death.... [T]he post-*Furman* statutes make clear that capital punishment itself has not been rejected by the elected representatives of the people.

In the only statewide referendum occurring since *Furman* and brought to our attention, the people of California adopted a constitutional amendment that authorized capital punishment, in effect negating a prior ruling by the Supreme Court of California ... that the death penalty violated the California Constitution.

The jury also is a significant and reliable objective index of contemporary values because it is so directly involved.... [T]he actions of juries in many States since *Furman* are fully compatible with the legislative judgments, reflected in the new statutes, as to the continued utility and necessity of capital punishment in appropriate cases. At the close of 1974 at least 254 persons had been sentenced to death since *Furman*, and by the end of March 1976, more than 460 persons were subject to death sentences.

As we have seen, however, the Eighth Amendment demands more than that a challenged punishment be acceptable to contemporary society. The Court also must ask whether it comports with the basic concept of human dignity at the core of the Amendment. Although we cannot "invalidate a category of penalties because we deem less severe penalties adequate to serve the ends of penology," the sanction imposed cannot be so totally without penological justification that it results in the gratuitous infliction of suffering.

The death penalty is said to serve two principal social purposes: retribution and deterrence of capital crimes by prospective offenders.[28]

In part, capital punishment is an expression of society's moral outrage at particularly offensive conduct. This function may be unappealing to many, but it is essential in an ordered society that asks its citizens to rely on legal processes rather than self-help to vindicate their wrongs. ... "Retribution is no longer the dominant objective of the criminal law," but neither is it a forbidden objective nor one inconsistent with our respect for the dignity of men. Indeed, the decision that capital punishment may be the appropriate sanction in extreme cases is an expression of the community's belief that certain crimes are themselves so grievous an affront to humanity that the only adequate response may be the penalty of death.

Statistical attempts to evaluate the worth of the death penalty as a deterrent to crimes by potential offenders have occasioned a great deal of debate. The results simply have been inconclusive....

. . .

Although some of the studies suggest that the death penalty may not function as a significantly greater deterrent than lesser penalties, there is no convincing empirical evidence either supporting or refuting this view....

. . .

In sum, we cannot say that the judgment of the Georgia Legislature that capital punishment may be necessary in some cases is clearly wrong. Considerations of federalism, as well as respect for the ability of a legislature to evaluate, in terms of its particular State, the moral consensus concerning the death penalty and its social utility as a sanction, require us to conclude, in the absence of more convincing evidence, that the infliction of death as a punishment for murder is not without justification and thus is not unconstitutionally severe.

Finally, we must consider whether the punishment of death is disproportionate in relation to the crime for which it is imposed. There is no question that death as a punishment is unique in its severity and irrevoca-

---

28. Another purpose that has been discussed is the incapacitation of dangerous criminals and the consequent prevention of crimes that they may otherwise commit in the future.

bility.... But we are concerned here only with the imposition of capital punishment for the crime of murder, and when a life has been taken deliberately by the offender, we cannot say that the punishment is invariably disproportionate to the crime. It is an extreme sanction, suitable to the most extreme of crimes.

We hold that the death penalty is not a form of punishment that may never be imposed, regardless of the circumstances of the offense, regardless of the character of the offender, and regardless of the procedure followed in reaching the decision to impose it....

. . .

[Opinions of Justice White, Chief Justice Burger, Justice Rehnquist, and Justice Blackmun, concurring in the judgment, omitted.]

■ MR. JUSTICE BRENNAN, dissenting.

. . .

... Death for whatever crime and under all circumstances "is truly an awesome punishment. The calculated killing of a human being by the State involves, by its very nature, a denial of the executed person's humanity.... An executed person has indeed 'lost the right to have rights.' " Death is not only an unusually severe punishment, unusual in its pain, in its finality, and in its enormity, but it serves no penal purpose more effectively than a less severe punishment; therefore the principle inherent in the Clause that prohibits pointless infliction of excessive punishment when less severe punishment can adequately achieve the same purposes invalidates the punishment.

The fatal constitutional infirmity in the punishment of death is that it treats "members of the human race as nonhumans, as objects to be toyed with and discarded. [It is] thus inconsistent with the fundamental premise of the Clause that even the vilest criminal remains a human being possessed of common human dignity." As such it is a penalty that "subjects the individual to a fate forbidden by the principle of civilized treatment guaranteed by the [Clause]." I therefore would hold, on that ground alone, that death is today a cruel and unusual punishment prohibited by the Clause....

■ MR. JUSTICE MARSHALL, dissenting.

. . .

... [T]he death penalty is constitutionally invalid for two reasons. First, the death penalty is excessive. And second, the American people, fully informed as to the purposes of the death penalty and its liabilities, would in my view reject it as morally unacceptable.

... [I]f the constitutionality of the death penalty turns, as I have urged, on the opinion of an informed citizenry, then even the enactment of new death statutes cannot be viewed as conclusive. In *Furman*, I observed that the American people are largely unaware of the information critical to a judgment on the morality of the death penalty, and concluded that if they were better informed they would consider it shocking, unjust, and unacceptable....

Even assuming, however, that the post-*Furman* enactment of statutes authorizing the death penalty renders the prediction of the views of an informed citizenry an uncertain basis for a constitutional decision, the enactment of those statutes has no bearing whatsoever on the conclusion that the death penalty is unconstitutional because it is excessive....

The two purposes that sustain the death penalty as nonexcessive in the Court's view are general deterrence and retribution....

. . .

... The evidence I reviewed in *Furman* remains convincing, in my view, that "capital punishment is not necessary as a deterrent to crime in our society." The justification for the death penalty must be found elsewhere.

... The notion that retribution can serve as a moral justification for the sanction of death finds credence in the opinion of my Brothers Stewart, Powell, and Stevens, and that of my Brother White....

. . .

... As my Brother Brennan stated in *Furman*, "[t]here is no evidence whatever that utilization of imprisonment rather than death encourages private blood feuds and other disorders." It simply defies belief to suggest that the death penalty is necessary to prevent the American people from taking the law into their own hands.

. . .

... The mere fact that the community demands the murderer's life in return for the evil he has done cannot sustain the death penalty, for as Justices Stewart, Powell, and Stevens remind us, "the Eighth Amendment demands more than that a challenged punishment be acceptable to contemporary society." To be sustained under the Eighth Amendment, the death penalty must "compor[t] with the basic concept of human dignity at the core of the Amendment." The objective in imposing it must be "[consistent] with our respect for the dignity of [other] men." Under these standards, the taking of life "because the wrongdoer deserves it" surely must fall, for such a punishment has as its very basis the total denial of the wrong-doer's dignity and worth.

Notes

1. The Human Rights Committee's attention to disappearances in its General Comment on the right to life reflects what is, unfortunately, a major category of international human rights violation. Examples from the caselaw of the Committee itself, the Inter–American Court of Human Rights and the European Court of Human Rights appear at pp. 506, 525, and 580 supra.

2. The Committee's General Comment emphasizes both the responsibility of the state to refrain from depriving individuals of life and the responsibility of the state to adopt positive measures for the protection of the right to life. The derivation of positive state obligations from classic civil rights is a characteristic feature of modern international human rights law. In the context of the ICCPR, the existence of both negative and positive obligations is often attributed to the dual obligation under Article 2(1) "to respect and to ensure" the rights recognized in the Covenant.

In the United States, in contrast, the Constitution does not usually oblige the federal government and the states to protect individual rights against infringement by private actors (although there are some exceptions). See p. 152 supra (discussing the "state action" doctrine). The leading modern case is *DeShaney v. Winnebago County Department of Social Services*, 489 U.S. 189 (1989). The Supreme Court rejected an action against social workers and other local officials for failing to protect a young child from ongoing physical abuse by his father, which ultimately resulted in severe brain damage. The majority explained:

> [N]othing in the language of the Due Process Clause itself requires the State to protect the life, liberty, and property of its citizens against invasion by private actors. The Clause is phrased as a limitation on the State's power to act, not as a guarantee of certain minimal levels of safety and security. It forbids the State itself to deprive individuals of life, liberty, or property without "due process of law," but its language cannot fairly be extended to impose an affirmative obligation on the State to ensure that those interests do not come to harm through other means. Nor does history support such an expansive reading of the constitutional text.

The majority distinguished particular situations in which the state, by depriving individuals of liberty (for example as prisoners or as involuntarily committed patients), prevented them from protecting themselves, and acquired an affirmative duty to care for them. *DeShaney* may be contrasted with such cases as the decision of the European Court of Human Rights in *A. v. United Kingdom* (1998), p. 576 supra, and the German Constitutional Court's abortion decision, p. 938 infra.

3. In *Callins v. Collins*, 510 U.S. 1141 (1994), the Supreme Court denied certiorari in a death penalty case. Justice Blackmun dissented from the denial of certiorari, with an opinion that included the following:

> Twenty years have passed since this Court declared that the death penalty must be imposed fairly, and with reasonable consistency, or not at all, and, despite the effort of the States and courts to devise legal formulas and procedural rules to meet this daunting challenge, the death penalty remains fraught with arbitrariness, discrimination, caprice, and mistake. This is not to say that the problems with the death penalty today are identical to those that were present 20 years ago. Rather, the problems that were pursued down one hole with procedural rules and verbal formulas have come to the surface somewhere else, just as virulent and pernicious as they were in their original form.

Experience has taught us that the constitutional goal of eliminating arbitrariness and discrimination from the administration of death, can never be achieved without compromising an equally essential component of fundamental fairness—individualized sentencing.

. . .

From this day forward, I no longer shall tinker with the machinery of death. For more than 20 years I have endeavored—indeed, I have struggled—along with a majority of this Court, to develop procedural and substantive rules that would lend more than the mere appearance of fairness to the death penalty endeavor. Rather than continue to coddle the Court's delusion that the desired level of fairness has been achieved and the need for regulation eviscerated, I feel morally and intellectually obligated simply to concede that the death penalty experiment has failed. It is virtually self-evident to me now that no combination of procedural rules or substantive regulations ever can save the death penalty from its inherent constitutional deficiencies. The basic question—does the system accurately and consistently determine which defendants "deserve" to die?—cannot be answered in the affirmative. It is not simply that this Court has allowed vague aggravating circumstances to be employed, relevant mitigating evidence to be disregarded, and vital judicial review to be blocked. The problem is that the inevitability of factual, legal, and moral error gives us a system that we know must wrongly kill some defendants, a system that fails to deliver the fair, consistent, and reliable sentences of death required by the Constitution.

Justice Scalia replied to Justice Blackmun's dissent in a concurrence including the following:

Justice Blackmun dissents from the denial of certiorari in this case with a statement explaining why the death penalty "as currently administered," is contrary to the Constitution of the United States. That explanation often refers to "intellectual, moral and personal" perceptions, but never to the text and tradition of the Constitution. It is the latter rather than the former that ought to control. The Fifth Amendment provides that "[n]o person shall be held to answer for a capital . . . crime, unless on a presentment or indictment of a Grand Jury, . . . nor be deprived of life . . . without due process of law." This clearly permits the death penalty to be imposed, and establishes beyond doubt that the death penalty is not one of the "cruel and unusual punishments" prohibited by the Eighth Amendment.

. . . [S]ince 1972 this Court has attached to the imposition of the death penalty two quite incompatible sets of commands: the sentencer's discretion to impose death must be closely confined, but the sentencer's discretion not to impose death (to extend mercy) must be unlimited. These commands were invented without benefit of any textual or historical support; they are the product of just such "intellectual, moral, and personal" perceptions as Justice Blackmun expresses today. . . .

. . . [A]t least one of these judicially announced irreconcilable commands which cause the Constitution to prohibit what its text explicitly permits must be wrong.

Convictions in opposition to the death penalty are often passionate and deeply held. That would be no excuse for reading them into a Constitution that does not contain them, even if they represented the convictions of a majority of Americans. Much less is there any excuse for using that course to thrust a minority's views upon the people. Justice Blackmun begins his statement by describing with poignancy the death of a convicted murderer by lethal injection. He chooses, as the case in which to make that statement, one of the less brutal of the murders that regularly come before us—the murder of a man ripped by a bullet suddenly and unexpectedly, with no opportunity to prepare himself and his affairs, and left to bleed to death on the floor of a tavern. The death-by-injection which Justice Blackmun describes looks pretty desirable next to that. It looks even better next to some of the other cases currently before us which Justice Blackmun did not select as the vehicle for his announcement that the death penalty is always unconstitutional—for example, the case of the 11–year-old girl raped by four men and then killed by stuffing her panties down her throat. How enviable a quiet death by lethal injection compared with that! If the people conclude that such more brutal deaths may be deterred by capital punishment; indeed, if they merely conclude that justice requires such brutal deaths to be avenged by capital punishment; the creation of false, untextual and unhistorical contradictions within "the Court's Eighth Amendment jurisprudence" should not prevent them.

4. In *Thompson v. Oklahoma*, 487 U.S. 815 (1988), the Supreme Court considered the constitutionality of executing a defendant for a murder committed when he was 15 years old. A plurality of four Justices concluded that imposing the death penalty for a crime committed as a juvenile was unacceptable. Justice Stevens maintained that the "assumptions we make about our children when we legislate on their behalf tell us that it is likely cruel, and certainly unusual, to impose on a child a punishment that takes as its predicate the existence of a fully rational, choosing agent, who may be deterred by the harshest of sanctions and toward whom society may legitimately take a retributive stance." He observed: "The conclusion that it would offend civilized standards of decency to execute a person who was less than 16 years old at the time of his or her offense is consistent with the views that have been expressed by respected professional organizations, by other nations that share our Anglo–American heritage, and by the leading members of the Western European community," adding in a footnote, "We have previously recognized the relevance of the views of the international community in determining whether a punishment is cruel and unusual." 487 U.S. at 830–31 & n.31 (citing *Trop v. Dulles*, 356 U.S. 86 (1958); *Coker v. Georgia*, 433 U.S. 584 (1977); and *Enmund v. Florida*, 458 U.S. 782

(1982)). Justice Scalia's dissent argued that individualized consideration of a particular defendant's maturity and responsibility sufficed, and rejected the relevance of the international comparisons:

> The plurality's reliance upon Amnesty International's account of what it pronounces to be civilized standards of decency in other countries is totally inappropriate as a means of establishing the fundamental beliefs of this Nation. That 40% of our States do not rule out capital punishment for 15–year-old felons is determinative of the question before us here, even if that position contradicts the uniform view of the rest of the world. We must never forget that it is a Constitution for the United States of America that we are expounding. The practices of other nations, particularly other democracies, can be relevant to determining whether a practice uniform among our people is not merely a historical accident, but rather so "implicit in the concept of ordered liberty" that it occupies a place not merely in our mores but, text permitting, in our Constitution as well. But where there is not first a settled consensus among our own people, the views of other nations, however enlightened the Justices of this Court may think them to be, cannot be imposed upon Americans through the Constitution. In the present case, therefore, the fact that a majority of foreign nations would not impose capital punishment upon persons under 16 at the time of the crime is of no more relevance than the fact that a majority of them would not impose capital punishment at all, or have standards of due process quite different from our own.

487 U.S. at 869 n.4 (Scalia, J., joined by Rehnquist, C.J., and White, J., dissenting). Justice Scalia reiterated this rejection of comparative data, writing for a majority of the Court, in *Stanford v. Kentucky*, 492 U.S. 361, 369 n. 1 (1989) (upholding imposition of capital punishment for murders committed at the age of 16 years plus 6 months, and 17 years plus four months).

When the United States ratified the ICCPR, which prohibits imposition of the death penalty for crimes committed by persons below eighteen years of age (Article 6(5)), the United States specifically entered a reservation against this prohibition. See supra p. 785.

5.   Does the right to life absolutely prohibit deprivation of life? Compare its character under the U.S. and interim South African Constitutions with the formulations in the Universal Declaration, the Covenant on Civil and Political Rights, and the regional conventions.

6.   Is the right not to be subjected to "cruel, inhuman or degrading" punishment (or its variants) absolute? What role does (or should) the concept of proportionality play in evaluating claims that such rights have been violated?* If proportionality is an important factor, then should the consequences of the right vary from time to time and from place to place?

---

* In the United States context, see also *Harmelin v. Michigan*, 501 U.S. 957 (1991) (debating role of proportionality in Eighth Amendment challenge to life imprisonment without possibility of parole).

7.   The Fifth Amendment to the U.S. Constitution provides that no person shall "be deprived of life, liberty, or property, without due process of law." Does this demonstrate that the death penalty cannot be a per se violation of the Eighth Amendment? The Fifth Amendment provides that no person shall "be subject for the same offence to be twice put in jeopardy of life or limb." Does this demonstrate that amputation of limbs cannot be a per se violation of the Eighth Amendment?

8.   Where can a court look to determine "the evolving standards of decency that mark the progress of a maturing society" for Eighth Amendment purposes? Federal legislation? State legislation? Jury decisions? Public opinion polls? Sermons and philosophical dissertations? If a small minority of states impose a punishment that other states do not, then what conclusion should a court draw?

Are the practices of other nations relevant to the inquiry? Are international treaties to which the United States is not a party? Are international treaties to which the United States *is* a party?

Why might South African judges approach such questions differently than United States judges?

"The Death Row Phenomenon"

Soering v. United Kingdom

European Court of Human Rights, 1989.
161 Eur. Ct. H.R. (ser. A), 11 E.H.R.R. 439.

[Jens Soering was an 18–year old West German student attending the University of Virginia when he and his girlfriend carried out a plan to kill her parents. The pair then fled to the United Kingdom, where they were arrested for other offenses, and the United States requested extradition for trial on capital murder charges in Virginia.]

80.   The applicant alleged that the decision by the Secretary of State for the Home Department to surrender him to the authorities of the United States of America would, if implemented, give rise to a breach by the United Kingdom of Article 3 of the Convention, which provides:

No one shall be subjected to torture or to inhuman or degrading treatment or punishment.

81.   The alleged breach derives from the applicant's exposure to the so-called "death row phenomenon." This phenomenon may be described as consisting in a combination of circumstances to which the applicant would be exposed if, after having been extradited to Virginia to face a capital murder charge, he were sentenced to death.

85.   As results from Article 5(1)(f), which permits "the lawful ... detention of a person against whom action is being taken with a view to ... extradition," no right not to be extradited is as such protected by the Convention. Nevertheless, in so far as a measure of extradition has consequences adversely affecting the enjoyment of a Convention right, it may,

assuming that the consequences are not too remote, attract the obligations of a Contracting State under the relevant Convention guarantee. (See, mutatis mutandis, Abdulaziz, Cabales and Balkandali v. United Kingdom, [94 Eur. Ct. H.R. (ser. A) (1985)]—in relation to rights in the field of immigration.) What is at issue in the present case is whether Article 3 can be applicable when the adverse consequences of extradition are, or may be, suffered outside the jurisdiction of the extraditing State as a result of treatment or punishment administered in the receiving State.

86.   Article 1 of the Convention, which provides that "the High Contracting parties shall secure to everyone within their jurisdiction the rights and freedoms defined in Section I," sets a limit, notably territorial, on the reach of the Convention. In particular, the engagement undertaken by a Contracting State is confined to "securing" ("reconnaitre" in the French text) the listed rights and freedoms to persons within its own "jurisdiction." Further, the Convention does not govern the actions of States not parties to it, nor does it purport to be a means of requiring the Contracting States to impose Convention standards on other States. Article 1 cannot be read as justifying a general principle to the effect that, notwithstanding its extradition obligations, a Contracting State may not surrender an individual unless satisfied that the conditions awaiting him in the country of destination are in full accord with each of the safeguards of the Convention. Indeed, as the United Kingdom Government stressed, the beneficial purpose of extradition in preventing fugitive offenders from evading justice cannot be ignored in determining the scope of application of the Convention and of Article 3 in particular.

. . .

These considerations cannot, however, absolve the Contracting Parties from responsibility under Article 3 for all and any foreseeable consequences of extradition suffered outside their jurisdiction.

87.   In interpreting the Convention regard must be had to its special character as a treaty for the collective enforcement of human rights and fundamental freedoms. (See Ireland v. United Kingdom, [25 Eur. Ct. H.R. (ser. A) (1978)].) Thus, the object and purpose of the Convention as an instrument for the protection of individual human beings require that its provisions be interpreted and applied so as to make its safeguards practical and effective. (See, inter alia, Artico v. Italy, [37 Eur. Ct. H.R. (ser. A) (1980).]) In addition, any interpretation of the rights and freedoms guaranteed has to be consistent with "the general spirit of the Convention, an instrument designed to maintain and promote the ideals and values of a democratic society." (See Kjeldsen, Busk Madsen and Pedersen v. Denmark, [23 Eur. Ct. H.R. (ser. A) (1976)]).

88.   Article 3 makes no provision for exceptions and no derogation from it is permissible under Article 15 in time of war or other national emergency. This absolute prohibition on torture and on inhuman or degrading treatment or punishment under the terms of the Convention shows that Article 3 enshrines one of the fundamental values of the democratic societies making up the Council of Europe. It is also to be found in similar

terms in other international instruments such as the 1966 International Covenant on Civil and Political Rights and the 1969 American Convention on Human Rights and is generally recognized as an internationally accepted standard.

The question remains whether the extradition of a fugitive to another State where he would be subjected or be likely to be subjected to torture or to inhuman or degrading treatment or punishment would itself engage the responsibility of a Contracting State under Article 3. That the abhorrence of torture has such implications is recognised in Article 3 of the United Nations Convention Against Torture and Other Cruel, Inhuman or Degrading Treatment or Punishment, which provides that "no State Party shall ... extradite a person where there are substantial grounds for believing that he would be in danger of being subjected to torture." The fact that a specialised treaty should spell out in detail a specific obligation attaching to the prohibition of torture does not mean that an essentially similar obligation is not already inherent in the general terms of Article 3 of the European Convention. It would hardly be compatible with the underlying values of the Convention, that "common heritage of political traditions, ideals, freedom and the rule of law" to which the Preamble refers, were a Contracting State knowingly to surrender a fugitive to another State where there were substantial grounds for believing that he would be in danger of being subjected to torture, however heinous the crime allegedly committed. Extradition in such circumstances, while not explicitly referred to in the brief and general wording of Article 3, would plainly be contrary to the spirit and intendment of the Article, and in the Court's view this inherent obligation not to extradite also extends to cases in which the fugitive would be faced in the receiving State by a real risk of exposure to inhuman or degrading treatment or punishment proscribed by that Article.

91.   In sum, the decision by a Contracting State to extradite a fugitive may give rise to an issue under Article 3, and hence engage the responsibility of that State under the Convention, where substantial grounds have been shown for believing that the person concerned, if extradited, faces a real risk of being subjected to torture or to inhuman or degrading treatment or punishment in the requesting country. The establishment of such responsibility inevitably involves an assessment of conditions in the requesting country against the standards of Article 3 of the Convention. Nonetheless, there is no question of adjudicating on or establishing the responsibility of the receiving country, whether under general international law, under the Convention or otherwise. In so far as any liability under the Convention is or may be incurred, it is liability incurred by the extraditing Contracting State by reason of its having taken action which has a direct consequence the exposure of an individual to proscribed ill-treatment.

[The Court then concluded that Soering ran "a real risk of a death sentence and hence of exposure to the 'death row phenomenon'" in Virginia.]

Whether in the circumstances the risk of exposure to the "death row phenomenon" would make extradition a breach of Article 3

100.   As is established in the Court's case law, ill-treatment, including punishment, must attain a minimum level of severity if it is to fall within the scope of Article 3. The assessment of this minimum is, in the nature of things, relative; it depends on all the circumstances of the case, such as the nature and context of the treatment or punishment, the manner and method of its execution, its duration, its physical or mental effects and, in some instances, the sex, age and state of health of the victim.

Treatment has been held by the Court to be both "inhuman" because it was premeditated, was applied for hours at a stretch and "caused, if not actual bodily injury, at least intense physical and mental suffering," and also "degrading" because it was "such as to arouse in [its] victims feelings of fear, anguish and inferiority capable of humiliating and debasing them and possibly breaking their physical or moral resistance." In order for a punishment or treatment associated with it to be "inhuman" or "degrading," the suffering or humiliation involved must in any event go beyond that inevitable element of suffering or humiliation connected with a given form of legitimate punishment. In this connection, account is to be taken not only of the physical pain experienced but also, where there is a considerable delay before execution of the punishment, of the sentenced person's mental anguish of anticipating the violence he is to have inflicted on him.

101.   Capital punishment is permitted under certain conditions by Article 2(1) of the convention, which reads:

Everyone's right to life shall be protected by law. No one shall be deprived of his life intentionally save in the execution of a sentence of a court following his conviction of a crime for which this penalty is provided by law.

. . .

In view of this wording, the applicant did not suggest that the death penalty per se violated Article 3. He, like the two Government Parties, agreed with the Commission that the extradition of a person to a country where he risks the death penalty does not in itself raise an issue under either Article 2 or Article 3. On the other hand, Amnesty International in their written comments argued that the evolving standards in Western Europe regarding the existence and use of the death penalty required that the death penalty should now be considered as an inhuman and degrading punishment within the meaning of Article 3.

102.   Certainly, "the Convention is a living instrument which . . . must be interpreted in the light of present-day conditions"; and, in assessing whether a given treatment or punishment is to be regarded as inhuman or degrading for the purposes of Article 3, "the Court cannot but be influenced by the developments and commonly accepted standards in the penal policy of the member States of the Council of Europe in this field." (See Tyrer v. United Kingdom, [26 Eur. Ct. H.R. (ser. A) (1978)].) De facto the death penalty no longer exists in time of peace in the contracting States to the Convention. In the few Contracting States which retain the death

penalty in law for some peacetime offences, death sentences, if ever imposed, are nowadays not carried out. This "virtual consensus in Western European legal systems that the death penalty is, under current circumstances, no longer consistent with regional standards of justice," to use the words of Amnesty International, is reflected in Protocol No. 6 to the Convention, which provides for the abolition of the death penalty in time of peace. Protocol No. 6 was opened for signature in April 1983, which in the practice of the Council of Europe indicates the absence of objection on the part of any of the Member States of the Organisation; it came into force in March 1985 and to date has been ratified by 13 Contracting States to the Convention, not however including the United Kingdom.

Whether these marked changes have the effect of bringing the death penalty per se within the prohibition of ill-treatment under Article 3 must be determined on the principles governing the interpretation of the Convention.

103.   The Convention is to be read as a whole and Article 3 should therefore be construed in harmony with the provisions of Article 2. (See, mutatis mutandis, Klass v. Germany, [28 Eur. Ct. H.R. (ser. A) (1978)].) On this basis Article 3 evidently cannot have been intended by the drafters of the Convention to include a general prohibition of the death penalty since that would nullify the clear wording of Article 2(1). . . .

104.   That does not mean however that circumstances relating to a death sentence can never give rise to an issue under Article 3. The manner in which it is imposed or executed, the personal circumstances of the condemned person and a disproportionality to the gravity of the crime committed, as well as the conditions of detention awaiting execution, are examples of factors capable of bringing the treatment or punishment received by the condemned person within the proscription under Article 3. . . .

(i) Length of detention prior to execution

106.   The period that a condemned prisoner can expect to spend on death row in Virginia before being executed is on average six to eight years. This length of time awaiting death is, as the Commission and the United Kingdom Government noted, in a sense largely of the prisoner's own making in that he takes advantage of all avenues of appeal which are offered to him by Virginia law. . . .

Nevertheless, just as some lapse of time between sentence and execution is inevitable if appeal safeguards are to be provided to the condemned person, so it is equally part of human nature that the person will cling to life by exploiting those safeguards to the full. However well-intentioned and even potentially beneficial is the provision of the complex of post-sentence procedures in Virginia, the consequence is that the condemned prisoner has to endure for many years the conditions on death row and the anguish and mounting tension of living in the ever-present shadow of death.

(ii) Conditions on death row

107.   . . . [Although the] stringency of the custodial regime in Mecklenburg [prison might well] be justifiable in principle, the severity of a special regime such as that operated on death row in Mecklenburg is compounded by the fact of inmates being subject to it for a protracted period lasting on average six to eight years.

(iii) The applicant's age and mental state

108.   At the time of the killings, the applicant was only 18 years old and there is some psychiatric evidence, which was not contested as such, that he "was suffering from [such] an abnormality of mind . . . as substantially impaired his mental responsibility for his acts."

Unlike Article 2 of the Convention, Article 6 of the 1966 International Covenant on Civil and Political Rights and Article 4 of the 1969 American Convention on Human Rights expressly prohibit the death penalty from being imposed on persons aged less than 18 at the time of commission of the offence. Whether or not such a prohibition be inherent in the brief and general language of Article 2 of the European Convention, its explicit enunciation in other, later international instruments, the former of which has been ratified by a large number of States Parties to the European Convention, at the very least indicates that as a general principle the youth of the person concerned is a circumstance which is liable, with others, to put in question the compatibility with Article 3 of measures connected with a death sentence. . . .

(iv) Possibility of extradition to the Federal Republic of Germany

110.   . . . [S]ending Mr. Soering to be tried in his own country would remove the danger of a fugitive criminal going unpunished as well as the risk of intense and protracted suffering on death row. It is therefore a circumstance of relevance for the overall assessment under Article 3 in that it goes to the search for the requisite fair balance of interests and to the proportionality of the contested extradition decision in the particular case.

111.   For any prisoner condemned to death, some element of delay, between imposition and execution of the sentence and the experience of severe stress in conditions necessary for strict incarceration are inevitable. . . . However, in the Court's view, having regard to the very long period of time spent on death row in such extreme conditions, with the ever-present and mounting anguish of awaiting execution of the death penalty, and to the personal circumstances of the applicant, especially his age and mental state at the time of the offence, the applicant's extradition to the United States would expose him to a real risk of treatment going beyond the threshold set by Article 3. A further consideration of relevance is that in the particular instance the legitimate purpose of extradition could be achieved by another means which would not involve suffering of such exceptional intensity or duration.

Accordingly, the Secretary of State's decision to extradite the applicant to the United States would, if implemented, give rise to a breach of Article 3.

. . .

■ Concurring Opinion of JUDGE DE MEYER

... [T]he most important issue in this case is not "the likelihood of the feared exposure of the applicant to the 'death row phenomenon,' " but the very simple fact that his life would be put in jeopardy by the extradition.

. . .

The second sentence of Article 2(1) of the Convention was adopted, nearly forty years ago, in particular historical circumstances, shortly after the Second World War. In so far as it still may seem to permit, under certain conditions, capital punishment in time of peace, it does not reflect the contemporary situation, and is now overridden by the development of legal conscience and practice....

Such punishment is not consistent with the present state of European civilisation.

. . .

No State party to the Convention can in that context, even if it has not yet ratified the Sixth Protocol, be allowed to extradite any person if that person thereby incurs the risk of being put to death in the requesting State.

Notes

1. Initially, several formal features of the Court's reasoning deserve attention. First, note the Court's practice, similar to that of a common law court, of citing its own opinions. The Court does not, however, follow a formal rule of stare decisis. Second, note the following aspects of the Court's interpretive practice in *Soering*:

> (a) the emphases in paragraph 87 on interpreting human rights treaties in light of their object and purpose, and on making their safeguards effective (the principle of effectiveness, or *effet utile*);

> (b) the reference in paragraph 103 to interpretation of the Convention "as a whole," construing individual provisions in light of other provisions;

> (c) the emphasis in paragraph 102 on the character of the Convention as a "living instrument";

> (d) the use in paragraph 102 of current trends in European legislation to shed light on the evaluation of a treatment or punishment;

> (e) the use in paragraphs 88 and 108 of other human rights treaties to shed light on the Convention.

2. Recall that, under the European Convention, the decisions of the European Court of Human Rights are binding on the parties. Ultimately, Soering was extradited after the United States gave assurances that the death penalty would not be imposed; he was convicted of both murders and sentenced to two terms of life imprisonment. See *Va. Court Upholds*

Murder Convictions, Wash. Post, Mar. 17, 1992, at D7; *Soering v. Deeds*, 499 S.E.2d 514 (Va.1998) (denying petition for habeas corpus).

3.   The Court's interpretation of Article 3 imposes a broader prohibition against the return of an individual to a country where he fears mistreatment than the prohibition contained in Article 3 of the Torture Convention, which applies only to torture, or Article 33 of the Refugee Convention, which applies only to persecution on specified grounds. Since *Soering*, the Court has applied its interpretation of Article 3 to a variety of situations. See, e.g., *Chahal v. United Kingdom*, 1996–V Eur. Ct. H.R. 1831, 23 E.H.R.R. 413 (1996) (Sikh militant suspected of terrorism would face danger of serious ill-treatment by security forces if returned to India); *Ahmed v. Austria*, 1996–V Eur. Ct. H.R. 2195, 24 E.H.R.R. 278 (1996) (member of one clan would face danger of execution or mistreatment by rival clan in Somalia); *D. v. United Kingdom*, 1997–III Eur. Ct. H.R. 777, 24 E.H.R.R. 423 (1997) (criminal dying of AIDS would face degrading treatment if returned to St. Kitts due to inadequacy of medical facilities).

4.   *Soering-type cases in the Human Rights Committee.* The Human Rights Committee has considered a number of individual communications raising objections under the ICCPR to extradition from Canada to the United States. (Canada, unlike the United States, is a party to the First Optional Protocol to the ICCPR.)

In *Kindler v. Canada*, U.N. Doc. CCPR/48/D/470/1991 (1993), the individual had escaped to Canada after his conviction for first-degree murder and kidnapping in Pennsylvania. A majority of the Committee expressed the view that returning him to face execution and possible exposure to the "death row phenomenon" would not violate Canada's obligations under ICCPR arts. 6 and 7. Article 6 did not require the abolition of the death penalty, nor forbid states that had abolished the death penalty to extradite fugitives to states that maintained the death penalty in the manner contemplated by Article 6. It would violate Article 7 to extradite an individual to a state where he would be exposed to a real risk of cruel, inhuman or degrading treatment or punishment, but Kindler had not shown that he faced such treatment. Absent special circumstances, prolonged incarceration on death row while a defendant availed himself of appellate remedies would not constitute cruel, inhuman or degrading treatment. Several members of the Committee dissented, arguing that since Canada was a state that had abolished the death penalty, it could not rely on Article 6(2) as a basis for extraditing a defendant to the United States without obtaining assurances that the death penalty would not be imposed.

In *Ng v. Canada*, U.N. Doc. A/49/40, vol. II, at 189 (1993), a majority of the Committee held that Canada had violated Article 7 by extraditing an accused murderer to California, where he faced the likelihood of execution by cyanide gas asphyxiation. On the limited record before it, the majority concluded that this method of execution "may cause prolonged suffering and agony and does not result in death as swiftly as possible, as asphyxiation by cyanide gas may take over 10 minutes." Some members of the Committee dissented from this finding; others continued to maintain that

Article 6 should be interpreted as prohibiting the extradition, regardless of the anticipated method of execution.

See also *Cox v. Canada*, U.N. Doc. CCPR/C/52/D/539/1993 (1994) (finding no violation in extradition of accused murderer to United States); *Gomez v. United States District Court*, 503 U.S. 653 (1992) (Stevens, J., and Blackmun, J., dissenting) (dissenting from refusal on procedural grounds to hear case concerning the compatibility of California's gas chambers with the Eighth Amendment).

The Human Rights Committee has continued to reject the argument that a lengthy period of incarceration under a sentence of death would amount to cruel, inhuman or degrading treatment or punishment merely because of its length. See, e.g., *Johnson v. Jamaica*, U.N. Doc. CCPR/C/56/D/588/1994 (1996). In the United Kingdom, however, the Judicial Committee of the Privy Council, which has operated as an appellate tribunal for Jamaica and other Commonwealth countries, has held that excessive delay in the execution of a death sentence would render the punishment "inhuman." See *Pratt v. Attorney General for Jamaica*, [1994] 2 App. Cas. 1 (1993) (applying Jamaican Constitution). In the *Pratt* case, the Privy Council stated that a delay of five years after sentence, including the time occupied by proceedings before the UN Human Rights Committee, was presumptively inhuman. As part of efforts to expedite the enforcement of the death penalty, Jamaica withdrew from the First Optional Protocol to the ICCPR in 1997; in 1998, Trinidad and Tobago first denounced the Protocol and then reratified it subject to a reservation barring the consideration of communications "relating to any prisoner who is under sentence of death." See, e.g., Natalia Schiffrin, *Jamaica Withdraws the Right of Individual Petition under the International Covenant on Civil and Political Rights*, 92 Am. J. Int'l L. 563 (1998); Report of the Human Rights Committee, U.N. Doc. A/53/40, para. 78 (1998); *Sudden Spate of Executions is Sweeping Caribbean*, N.Y. Times, June 9, 1999, at A7.

5.   In paragraph 85 of its *Soering* opinion, the European Court explains that, although the European Convention does not recognize a right against extradition as such, the extradition process is subject to constraints based on the rights recognized by the Convention. The Court rejects the notion that international obligations created by extradition treaties prevail over human rights obligations. Moreover, some foreseeable violations of rights in a non-European receiving state would implicate obligations of a European extraditing state. Which other foreseeable violations of rights in the receiving state should have that consequence? For one attempt to provide an answer, see John Dugard and Christine Van Den Wyngaert, *Reconciling Extradition with Human Rights*, 92 Am. J. Int'l L. 187 (1998) (recommending denial of extradition where requested state concludes that accused would face real risk of torture, cruel, inhuman or degrading treatment, or flagrant denial of fair trial rights). What constraints do human rights place on the process by which a state, acting outside its own territory, acquires custody of an accused criminal? See, e.g., *Saldías de López v. Uruguay*, (Human Rights Comm. 1981), U.N. Doc. CCPR/C/OP/1 at 88 (concluding

that Uruguay's abduction of its own national from Argentina violated ICCPR Article 9, and that mistreating him in Argentine territory violated Article 7); *Alvarez-Machain v. United States*, 107 F.3d 696 (9th Cir. 1996), cert. denied, 118 S.Ct. 60 (1997) (tort claims arising out of abduction from Mexico and allegations of accompanying mistreatment).

6. In United States extradition practice, federal magistrates or judges are assigned the task of determining whether a foreign government's request for extradition of an accused meets the requirements of the governing extradition treaty. In proceedings pursuant to most extradition treaties, however, the judges follow a rule of "noninquiry" into the fairness or humaneness of the treatment awaiting the accused. The Secretary of State has discretion to refuse extradition on humanitarian grounds, but the exercise of this discretion is not subject to judicial review. Might the Constitution require the Secretary of State to deny extradition in some situations, even if the decision were not judicially reviewable? Might there be circumstances, as some dicta indicate, in which the accused would be "subject to procedures or punishment so antipathetic to a federal court's sense of decency" as to require an exception to the rule of noninquiry? See *United States v. Lui Kin–Hong*, 110 F.3d 103, 112 (1st Cir.) (quoting *Gallina v. Fraser*, 278 F.2d 77, 79 (2d Cir.1960), and reserving the question), cert. denied, 520 U.S. 1206 (1997). The Supreme Court has never addressed whether the Constitution would require the United States to refuse extradition if an egregiously unfair trial or barbaric punishment would ensue. Nonconstitutional grounds, including nonrefoulement obligations under human rights treaties, may nonetheless oblige the Secretary of State to withhold extradition. See, e.g., Andreas F. Lowenfeld, *Ahmad: Profile of an Extradition Case*, 23 N.Y.U. J. Int'l L. & Pol. 723 (1991); Jacques Semmelman, *Federal Courts, The Constitution, and the Rule of Non–Inquiry in International Extradition Proceedings*, 76 Cornell L. Rev. 1198 (1991).

Alan W. Lepp, *Note, The Death Penalty in Late Imperial, Modern, and Post-Tiananmen China*

11 Mich. J. Int'l L. 987, 1000–03, 1011–20, 1036–37 (1990).

Since the demonstrations of spring 1989, there have been at least forty officially announced death sentences and executions of individuals associated with the pro-democracy movement. Numerous unannounced executions are also believed to have taken place. Many of those executed were convicted of crimes against property, such as burning vehicles, obstructing traffic, and setting fire to trains. For instance, three were executed in Shanghai on June 22 for allegedly burning a train. In addition, seven persons were executed in Beijing on June 22 for allegedly "setting fire to military trucks, stealing military goods, and assaulting soldiers," and two more were executed in Chengdu in July, allegedly for arson. In late October a Jinan factory worker was sentenced to death for allegedly setting ablaze a car during one of the June demonstrations. In November, three persons from Chengdu were given death sentences for burning a cinema during the period June 4–6. In December, two persons in Beijing were sentenced for beating a policeman to death on the morning of June 4.

The reappearance of old customs from the Cultural Revolution years suggests that the legal reforms of the Dengist years have yet to stabilize themselves. The atmosphere of intimidation carried out by the police, the public humiliation of offenders with heads shaven and placards hung around their necks, indicating their names and crimes, the use of ideological terms such as "thugs" and "ruffians" who staged the "counterrevolutionary rebellion" once again demonstrate the power of the state. . . .

. . .

The political nature of the death penalty in Communist China underscores these alternating cycles of Party policy over the past six decades. In China, the death penalty has been used extensively to liquidate political enemies, often labeled as "counterrevolutionaries," a very severe criminal charge clearly containing political overtones. This display of political power has been achieved through streamlined and truncated judicial procedures, such as in the case of mass trials, or through the circumvention or evasion of formal processes entirely, such as when the leadership deliberately sanctions killing either by specific prior instructions or by collaboration with other government organs. While the basic aims of such actions are the traditional ones of deterrence and retribution, they take on a different significance in a political context. When the aging Chinese leadership decided to use lethal force against the mass protests on June 4 and subsequently to employ the death penalty less restrictively, it demonstrated the extent of the political power it was willing to expend in order to quash threats to its authority.

. . .

Since 1984, the Chinese authorities have publicly countered the negative international coverage of their use of the death penalty and other punishments. Although they continue to insist that their legal system and human rights record is an internal matter into which the international arena should not intrude, they have begun to respond to their critics. . . .

Both deterrence and retribution have been the primary motivations in China's use of the death penalty over the years. In describing the purposes that punishment may serve, or may be perceived to serve, in the Chinese context, the edges between the different justifications are not easy to separate. The Chinese leadership continues to resort to draconian measures to instill fear in the populace.

At present, deterrence seems to be the main justification for capital punishment in China. According to this doctrine, the death penalty aims to deter both actual and potential offenders from the commission of crimes. The severity of the punishment should not be greater than that which is necessary to prevent crime. This emphasis on the deterrent function of the death penalty has consistently been a central feature of criminal law throughout Chinese history. . . .

. . .

For the threat of capital punishment to be effective, communications networks and propaganda is essential. The death penalty has been widely publicized in the belief that its emotional effect would be strongest if more people witnessed or heard about trials and executions. Frequently, authorities have sought to capture the attention of a threatened audience by making examples of select lawbreakers. The severe sentencing of offenders is intended to send to potential criminals a powerful message that will result in general deterrence. As Liu Yunfeng, president of the Beijing High People's Court, explained, "We sentence people to death not to seek revenge but to educate others—by killing one we educate one hundred."

The importance of publicizing negative examples reflects both the underlying traditional Chinese belief in the malleability of man and Mao Zedong's great faith in "mass line" governance. Thus, for many trials and executions, the masses have been mobilized to observe and learn. Almost all cases are heard in public, often held in large stadiums, and are generally open to people with admission tickets distributed through organizations designated by the authorities. Adopted by the Chinese Communists during the Soviet period of 1927–1934, mass trials are envisioned as a means to involve the populace directly in the legal process. Cases of important propaganda value have been carefully staged to inspire fear and class hatred, and to endorse government decisions against the accused. The size of a mass sentencing rally has totaled as many as 100,000 people.

In addition to mass trials, modern technology and the media—in particular, television, radio, and the press—have been utilized to disseminate news of executions to a wider audience. Occasionally, the announcement of death sentences at mass trials and even executions have been shown on Chinese television. On January 30, 1986, the Shenyang City Intermediate People's Court sentenced fourteen criminals to death, while more than 200,000 people throughout the city listened to the live relay at some 150 assembly sites. Despite the message of article 155 of the new Law of Criminal Procedure, stating that "the condemned should not be exposed to the public," some executions continue to be carried out in public and some corpses still remain exposed afterwards. Furthermore, prior to execution, condemned prisoners are often paraded in public with their heads bowed and placards proclaiming their crimes hung around their necks, a practice particularly widespread during the Cultural Revolution.

. . . Chinese newspapers still continue to cover executions as a form of popular education and general deterrence of crime. In a commentary about a former Communist Party official who was executed for taking more than $29,000 worth of goods seized from smugglers, the Yangcheng Evening News of Guangzhou wrote, "Execute one as a warning to a hundred."

If capital punishment is to serve as a deterrent, then executions should be frequent rather than scarce and sporadic. When China experienced a significant jump in its crime rate during the early post-Mao period, the Chinese leaders increased the use of the death penalty in 1979–80. As the number of serious crimes continued to rise, in large part due to the increasing liberalization of Chinese society, the government launched an anti-crime campaign in 1981 and again resorted to more frequent use of the death penalty. *Beijing Review* commented, "anyone without bias who is really concerned with the welfare of the people in this part of the word will feel pleased that China is cracking down on crime."

A wave of mass executions immediately followed the launching of the anti-crime campaign of August, 1983. Foreign press reports estimated that more than 5,000 executions were carried out during the first three months of the campaign. Within five months, some one hundred persons had been put to death in Beijing and at least 120 others had been executed in the more remote city of Guiyang. The rate of executions reported during this time was the highest in China since the early 1970's. Between 1983 and 1987, Western estimates of the number of executions ranged from 7,000 to as many as 14,000.

A substantial drop in the number of crimes during the first six months of 1986 was announced in early 1987, reportedly as a result of the successfully waged anti-crime campaign. . . .

During the first half of 1988, however, serious crime increased thirty-five percent over the same six-month period in 1987. The government's response in controlling this disorder was an uncompromising policy of severe punishment, including the continued convening of large "mass sentencing rallies" and frequent use of the death penalty.

The question of whether China's public and frequent use of the death penalty constitutes a more effective deterrent than other forms of punishment, such as life imprisonment, has been left unanswered due to the unavailability of statistics and the political sensitivity of researching the Party's criminal justice policy. . . .

Retributive justice has also been one of the primary purposes for China's frequent use of the death penalty. According to this theory, the crime itself justifies the punishment, and the punishment is intended solely to be imposed as the legal consequence of guilt. . . .

[Conclusion]

One explanation for China's evolving policies toward the death penalty can be traced to domestic or social factors, such as Marxist–Leninist ideology, historical legacy, or traditional attitudes towards the function of the criminal law. Reflecting the perceived needs of the state, these factors have strongly influenced the state's determinations about what type of policies would most effectively implement its desired goals. . . .

. . .

Another explanation for the shifts in China's administration of criminal justice and use of the death penalty can be found in the various external pressures impinging upon the regime's power. Such exogenous pressures might include political or economic instability, military threats, geographic constraints, or even international condemnation. These pressures often coincided with and determined changes in China's use of the death penalty. During times of stability, China's leadership has been more likely to lean towards a more formalized criminal process with more lenient punishment. During periods of internal turmoil or stress, however, adherence to laws and procedures has been undermined by the regime's need to consolidate control or promote its political policies.

China's use of the death penalty reflects not only state ideology or the extent to which the state perceives challenges to its power, but also the basic aims of penological theory—those of deterrence and retribution. Over the centuries, the state has exploited the deterrence function by carrying out brutal methods of execution, widely publicizing death sentences and executions, and altering the frequency of such sentences in order to meet its needs through campaigns or other movements. The Chinese use of capital punishment has also been marked by retribution, whether expressed through notions of vengeance and anger or through the principle of just requital.

The continuities with the past associated with China's implementation of the death penalty are revealed in a number of indigenous traditions. First, China's penchant for hierarchy, which has long been viewed as natural and cosmological, is reflected in the intricate review process that aimed to prevent arbitrariness and capriciousness. Second, the concept of elite privilege has resonated throughout Chinese history, having been both formally codified and informally observed in the legal process. Third, the notion of amnesty, reflected most recently in the form of the death sentence with a two-year [probationary] reprieve, exemplifies the Chinese faith in the re-educability of man. Deeply rooted in China's traditional political culture, these practices and preferences endure, even amidst China's continued efforts at legal reform.

U.S. Department of State, Country Reports on Human Rights Practices for 1997

105th Cong., 2d Sess. 715–19 (1998).

CHINA

There were reports of a number of extrajudicial killings related to separatist activity in the Xinjiang region. In February police dispersed a crowd of women in Yining during the Ramadan Festival. In subsequent protests of this action, police killed at least 10, and perhaps as many as 70, Uyghur demonstrators. On April 24, in Yining security forces killed two protesters when they opened fire on a crowd that had surrounded a bus carrying individuals convicted of involvement in the February riots.

There is no reliable information about the number of extrajudicial killings nationwide. There continued to be numerous executions carried out after summary trials. These trials can occur under circumstances where the lack of due process protections borders on extrajudicial killing. . . .

. . .

The effects of the lack of due process are particularly egregious in death penalty cases. A 1995 law raised the number of capital offenses from 26 to 65, and included financial crimes such as counterfeiting currency, passing fake negotiable notes and letters of credit, and illegal "pooling" of funds. In May 1996, the Supreme Court ruled that crimes resulting in death should be punished by death regardless of extenuating circumstances. Amnesty International (AI) reported in August, based on a review of Chinese press accounts, that in 1996 China sentenced more than 6,100 convicts to death and carried out 4,367 executions. More summary executions were reported as officials continued to promote the "strike-hard," national anticrime campaign. A high court nominally reviews all death sentences, but the time between arrest and execution is often days, and reviews have consistently resulted in a confirmation of sentence. The AI report included one case in which a man was convicted on May 13, 1996 and executed on May 19, 1996. According to a Chinese newspaper, the Shijiazhuang Intermediate People's Court held a public sentencing on June 26, at which seven previously convicted criminals were given the death penalty. The convicts were "escorted to the execution ground and executed by shooting after the meeting." No executions for political offenses are known to have occurred in 1997.

In recent years, credible reports have alleged that organs from some executed prisoners were removed, sold, and transplanted. Officials have confirmed that executed prisoners are among the sources of organs for transplant, but maintain that consent is required from prisoners or their relatives before organs are removed. There is no national law governing organ donations, but a Ministry of Health directive explicitly states that buying and selling human organs and tissues is not allowed.

Notes

1. Does the existence of the Sixth Protocol to the European Human Rights Convention demonstrate that the death penalty does not violate Article 3 of the original convention? Does the existence of the Second Optional Protocol to the Covenant on Civil and Political Rights demonstrate that the death penalty does not violate Article 7 of the Covenant?

2. Suppose that Canada, having abolished the death penalty, refuses to extradite fugitives to the United States without receiving assurances that the death penalty will not be imposed. What would the practical consequences of such a practice be? Do Articles 6 and 7 of the Covenant oblige Canada to adopt such a practice?

3. In *Lackey v. Texas*, 514 U.S. 1045 (1995), Justice Stevens filed a concurring memorandum to a denial of certiorari, in which he observed that the question whether it would violate the Eighth Amendment to

execute the petitioner, who had already spent 17 years on death row, was novel and important. Since then, several lower courts have rejected similar claims. See, e.g., *White v. Johnson*, 79 F.3d 432 (5th Cir.1996); *Chambers v. Bowersox*, 157 F.3d 560 (8th Cir.1998); *McKenzie v. Day*, 57 F.3d 1461 (9th Cir.1995), cert. denied, 514 U.S. 1104 (1995); *Stafford v. Ward*, 59 F.3d 1025 (10th Cir.1995), cert. denied, 515 U.S. 1173 (1995).

The Antiterrorism and Effective Death Penalty Act, Pub. L. 104–132, 110 Stat. 1214 (1996), substantially contracted the availability of federal postconviction relief for prisoners in the United States, including those convicted of capital offenses. Among other things, it established a short statute of limitations, accelerated judicial consideration of challenges to convictions, and created barriers to second or further challenges. Does decreasing prisoners' access to the courts alleviate the "death row phenomenon," and elevate the level of human rights protection in the United States?

4.   As noted in Part III, Chapter 4(B) supra, the United States ratification of human rights treaties in the 1990s has been accompanied by packages of reservations, understandings and declarations designed to preserve certain U.S. practices. The death penalty and the *Soering* decision motivated several of these provisions. When the United States ratified the Convention Against Torture and Other Cruel, Inhuman or Degrading Treatment or Punishment, one of the reservations specified:

> That the United States considers itself bound by the obligation under Article 16 to prevent "cruel, inhuman or degrading treatment or punishment," only insofar as the term "cruel, inhuman or degrading treatment or punishment" means the cruel, unusual and inhumane treatment or punishment prohibited by the Fifth, Eighth and/or Fourteenth Amendments to the Constitution of the United States.

The package also included the so-called "*Soering* understanding" prompted by European criticism of the "death row phenomenon":

> That the United States understands that international law does not prohibit the death penalty, and does not consider this Convention to restrict or prohibit the United States from applying the death penalty consistent with the Fifth, Eighth and/or Fourteenth Amendments to the Constitution of the United States, including any constitutional period of confinement prior to the imposition of the death penalty.

Correspondingly, U.S. ratification of the Covenant on Civil and Political Rights included reservations preserving the right of the United States to impose capital punishment in accordance with its Constitution, and placing a similar limitation on the meaning of the phrase "cruel, inhuman or degrading treatment or punishment."

5.   As of 1998, China had not ratified the Covenant on Civil and Political Rights. If it had, would its death penalty practice, as described in the foregoing excerpts, violate the Covenant? Does that practice violate customary international law?

In October 1998, China signed the Covenant, but as of mid–1999 had not yet taken steps to ratify it. That raises the further question whether continuation of its death penalty practices would be consistent with the obligation of a state that has signed but not yet ratified a treaty "to refrain from acts that would defeat the object and purpose of the agreement." See Restatement (Third) of the Foreign Relations Law of the United States § 312(3) & comment i (1987).

6. Further Reading. See, e.g., Amnesty International, When the State Kills: The Death Penalty, a Human Rights Issue (1989); Roger Hood, The Death Penalty: A World–Wide Perspective (2d ed. 1996); William Schabas, The Death Penalty as Cruel Treatment and Torture: Capital Punishment Challenged in the World's Courts (1996); William Schabas, The Abolition of the Death Penalty in International Law (2d ed. 1997); Ernest van den Haag & John P. Conrad, The Death Penalty: A Debate (1983); Welsh S. White, The Death Penalty in the Nineties: An Examination of the Modern System of Capital Punishment (1991); The Death Penalty in America: Current Controversies (Hugo Adam Bedau ed. 1997).

B.   AUTONOMY AND PRIVACY

John Stuart Mill maintained that no society was free if its government did not, on the whole, respect "liberty of tastes and pursuits; of framing the plan of our life to suit our own character; of doing as we like, subject to such consequences as may follow: without impediment from our fellow-creatures, so long as what we do does not harm them, even though they should think our conduct foolish, perverse, or wrong." Essay on Liberty (1859), supra p. 42. Justice Louis Brandeis wrote in praise of "the right to be let alone—the most comprehensive of rights and the right most valued by civilized men." *Olmstead v. United States*, 277 U.S. 438, 478 (1928) (Brandeis, J., dissenting).

The Universal Declaration expresses no such comprehensive right to autonomy. But it does declare particular rights to spheres of privacy, including protection against "arbitrary interference with [one's] privacy, family, home or correspondence" (Article 12), more fully elaborated protection of the family (Article 16), and freedom of thought and opinion (Articles 18 and 19). The Universal Declaration omits the classical liberal right of freedom of contract, the autonomy in the economic sphere that appeared more genuine to thinkers of the Nineteenth Century than to those of the 1940s. The ICCPR and the European and American regional conventions follow the Universal Declaration in linking privacy with family, home and correspondence, rather than subsuming it in a general right to autonomy.

Earlier, as discussed in Part II above, the United States Supreme Court had interpreted the word "liberty" in the due process clauses of the Fifth and Fourteenth Amendments as protecting individual freedom of action, particularly in economic matters. The Court abandoned the aggressive use of this "substantive due process" doctrine in the field of economic regulation in the 1930s, and today in most contexts due process condemns only wholly arbitrary deprivations of liberty to engage in economic transactions. Instead, the doctrine of substantive due process has been employed in recent decades to recognize a right of privacy guaranteeing autonomy in respect of certain intimate matters such as marriage and reproductive rights. Both the methodology of substantive due process and some of the results achieved by its means have been controversial in the United States.

This section compares national and international responses to claims for autonomy in two spheres of arguably private conduct: termination of pregnancy and consensual sexual activity between persons of the same sex.

1.   ABORTION

Neither the United States Constitution nor the constitution (*Grundgesetz* or "Basic Law") of the Federal Republic of Germany explicitly addresses abortion. Nonetheless, in the 1970s, both the U.S. Supreme Court and the German Federal Constitutional Court invalidated abortion legislation, on diametrically opposed grounds. The U.S. court struck down legislation because it infringed a woman's right to terminate a pregnancy, and the German court struck down legislation because it gave women too much freedom to terminate a pregnancy. These contrasting decisions reflect conflicting perspectives about the issues of morality and human rights at stake in the abortion context. The conflict of perspective exists not only between the United States and Germany but also within each of the countries, and within the European and American regional systems. Given the diversity of national views, international tribunals have not insisted on a single approach to abortion. This sub-section therefore begins with the leading national decisions of the 1970s, as well as their subsequent modifications in the 1990s, before turning to the responses of the regional tribunals.

Roe v. Wade

Supreme Court of the United States, 1973.
410 U.S. 113.

■ MR. JUSTICE BLACKMUN delivered the opinion of the Court.

This [case presents] constitutional challenges to state criminal abortion legislation. The Texas statutes under attack here are typical of those that have been in effect in many States for approximately a century....

We forthwith acknowledge our awareness of the sensitive and emotional nature of the abortion controversy, of the vigorous opposing views, even among physicians, and of the deep and seemingly absolute convictions that the subject inspires. One's philosophy, one's experiences, one's exposure to the raw edges of human existence, one's religious training, one's attitudes toward life and family and their values, and the moral standards one establishes and seeks to observe, are all likely to influence and to color one's thinking and conclusions about abortion.

In addition, population growth, pollution, poverty, and racial overtones tend to complicate and not to simplify the problem.

Our task, of course, is to resolve the issue by constitutional measurement, free of emotion and of predilection. We seek earnestly to do this, and, because we do, we have inquired into, and in this opinion place some emphasis upon, medical and medical-legal history and what that history reveals about man's attitudes toward the abortion procedure over the centuries....

. . .

The Texas statutes that concern us here.... make it a crime to "procure an abortion," as therein defined, or to attempt one, except with respect to "an abortion procured or attempted by medical advice for the purpose of saving the life of the mother." Similar statutes are in existence in a majority of the States. ...

. . .

The principal thrust of appellant's attack on the Texas statutes is that they improperly invade a right, said to be possessed by the pregnant woman, to choose to terminate her pregnancy. Appellant would discover this right in the concept of personal "liberty" embodied in the Fourteenth Amendment's Due Process Clause; or in personal, marital, familial, and sexual privacy said to be protected by the Bill of Rights or its penumbras, or among those rights reserved to the people by the Ninth Amendment. Before addressing this claim, we feel it desirable briefly to survey, in several aspects, the history of abortion, for such insight as that history may afford us, and then to examine the state purposes and interests behind the criminal abortion laws.

It perhaps is not generally appreciated that the restrictive criminal abortion laws in effect in a majority of States today are of relatively recent vintage. Those laws, generally proscribing abortion or its attempt at any time during pregnancy except when necessary to preserve the pregnant woman's life, are not of ancient or even of common-law origin. Instead, they derive from statutory changes effected, for the most part, in the latter half of the 19th century....

. . .

... It is undisputed that at common law, abortion performed before "quickening"—the first recognizable movement of the fetus *in utero*, appearing usually from the 16th to the 18th week of pregnancy—was not an indictable offense. The absence of a common-law crime for pre-quickening abortion appears to have developed from a confluence of earlier philosophical, theological, and civil and canon law concepts of when life begins. These disciplines variously approached the question in terms of the point at which the embryo or fetus became "formed" or recognizably human, or in terms of when a "person" came into being, that is, infused with a "soul" or "animated." A loose consensus evolved in early English law that these events occurred at some point between conception and live birth. This was "mediate animation." Although Christian theology and the canon law came to fix the point of animation at 40 days for a male and 80 days for a female, a view that persisted until the 19th century, there was otherwise little agreement about the precise time of formation or animation. There was agreement, however, that prior to this point the fetus was to be regarded as part of the mother, and its destruction, therefore, was not homicide. Due to continued uncertainty about the precise time when animation occurred, to the lack of any empirical basis for the 40–80–day view, and perhaps to Aquinas' definition of movement as one of the two first principles of life, Bracton focused upon quickening as the critical point. The significance of quickening was echoed by later common-law scholars and found its way into the received common law in this country.

Whether abortion of a quick fetus was a felony at common law, or even a lesser crime, is still disputed. Bracton, writing early in the 13th century, thought it homicide. But the later and predominant view, following the great common-law scholars, has been that it was, at most, a lesser offense. . . .

. . .

. . . In this country, the law in effect in all but a few States until mid–19th century was the pre-existing English common law. . . . By 1840, when Texas had received the common law, only eight American States had statutes dealing with abortion. It was not until after the War Between the States that legislation began generally to replace the common law. Most of these initial statutes dealt severely with abortion after quickening but were lenient with it before quickening. . . .

Gradually, in the middle and late 19th century the quickening distinction disappeared from the statutory law of most States and the degree of the offense and the penalties were increased. By the end of the 1950's, a large majority of the jurisdictions banned abortion, however and whenever performed, unless done to save or preserve the life of the mother. . . . In the past several years, however, a trend toward liberalization of abortion statutes has resulted in adoption, by about one-third of the States, of less stringent laws, most of them patterned after the ALI Model Penal Code, § 230.3. . . .

. . . .

Three reasons have been advanced to explain historically the enactment of criminal abortion laws in the 19th century and to justify their continued existence.

It has been argued occasionally that these laws were the product of a Victorian social concern to discourage illicit sexual conduct. Texas, however, does not advance this justification in the present case, and it appears that no court or commentator has taken the argument seriously. . . .

A second reason is concerned with abortion as a medical procedure. When most criminal abortion laws were first enacted, the procedure was a hazardous one for the woman. This was particularly true prior to the development of antisepsis. . . .

. . .

The third reason is the State's interest—some phrase it in terms of duty—in protecting prenatal life. Some of the argument for this justification rests on the theory that a new human life is present from the moment of conception. The State's interest and general obligation to protect life then extends, it is argued, to prenatal life. Only when the life of the pregnant mother herself is at stake, balanced against the life she carries within her, should the interest of the embryo or fetus not prevail. Logically, of course, a legitimate state interest in this area need not stand or fall on acceptance of the belief that life begins at conception or at some other point prior to live birth. In assessing the State's interest, recognition may be given to the less rigid claim that as long as at least *potential* life is involved, the State may assert interests beyond the protection of the pregnant woman alone.

. . .

The Constitution does not explicitly mention any right of privacy. In a line of decisions, however, going back perhaps as far as [1891], the Court has recognized that a right of personal privacy, or a guarantee of certain areas or zones of privacy, does exist under the Constitution. In varying contexts, the Court or individual Justices have, indeed, found at least the roots of that right in the First Amendment, in the Fourth and Fifth Amendments, in the penumbras of the Bill of Rights, in the Ninth Amendment, or in the concept of liberty guaranteed by the first section of the Fourteenth Amendment. These decisions make it clear that only personal rights that can be deemed "fundamental" or "implicit in the concept of ordered liberty," are included in this guarantee of personal privacy. They also make it clear that the right has some extension to activities relating to marriage, Loving v. Virginia, 388 U.S. 1 (1967); procreation, Skinner v. Oklahoma, 316 U.S. 535 (1942); contraception, Eisenstadt v. Baird, 405 U.S. [438 (1972)]; family relationships, Prince v. Massachusetts, 321 U.S. 158 (1944); and child rearing and education, Pierce v. Society of Sisters, 268 U.S. 510 (1925), Meyer v. Nebraska, [262 U.S. 390 (1923)].

This right of privacy, whether it be founded in the Fourteenth Amendment's concept of personal liberty and restrictions upon state action, as we feel it is, or, as the District Court determined, in the Ninth Amendment's reservation of rights to the people, is broad enough to encompass a woman's decision whether or not to terminate her pregnancy. The detriment that the State would impose upon the pregnant woman by denying this choice altogether is apparent. Specific and direct harm medically diagnosable even in early pregnancy may be involved. Maternity, or additional offspring, may force upon the woman a distressful life and future. Psychological harm may be imminent. Mental and physical health may be taxed by child care. There is also the distress, for all concerned, associated with the unwanted child, and there is the problem of bringing a child into a family already unable, psychologically and otherwise, to care for it. In other cases, as in this one, the additional difficulties and continuing stigma of unwed motherhood may be involved. All these are factors the woman and her responsible physician necessarily will consider in consultation.

On the basis of elements such as these, appellant and some amici argue that the woman's right is absolute and that she is entitled to terminate her pregnancy at whatever time, in whatever way, and for whatever reason she alone chooses. With this we do not agree. Appellant's arguments that Texas either has no valid interest at all in regulating the abortion decision, or no interest strong enough to support any limitation upon the woman's sole determination, are unpersuasive. The Court's decisions recognizing a right of privacy also acknowledge that some state regulation in areas protected by that right is appropriate. As noted above, a State may properly assert important interests in safeguarding health, in maintaining medical standards, and in protecting potential life. At some point in pregnancy, these respective interests become sufficiently compelling to sustain regulation of the factors that govern the abortion decision. The privacy right involved, therefore, cannot be said to be absolute. In fact, it is not clear to us that the claim asserted by some amici that one has an unlimited right to do with one's body as one pleases bears a close relationship to the right of privacy previously articulated in the Court's decisions. The Court has refused to recognize an unlimited right of this kind in the past. Jacobson v. Massachusetts, 197 U.S. 11 (1905) (vaccination); Buck v. Bell, 274 U.S. 200 (1927) (sterilization).

. . .

Where certain "fundamental rights" are involved, the Court has held that regulation limiting these rights may be justified only by a "compelling state interest," and that legislative enactments must be narrowly drawn to express only the legitimate state interests at stake. . . .

. . .

The appellee and certain amici argue that the fetus is a "person" within the language and meaning of the Fourteenth Amendment. In support of this, they outline at length and in detail the well-known facts of fetal development. If this suggestion of personhood is established, the appellant's case, of course, collapses, for the fetus' right to life would then be guaranteed specifically by the Amendment. The appellant conceded as much on reargument. On the other hand, the appellee conceded on reargument that no case could be cited that holds that a fetus is a person within the meaning of the Fourteenth Amendment.

The Constitution does not define "person" in so many words. Section 1 of the Fourteenth Amendment contains three references to "person.". . . . "Person" is used in other places in the Constitution. . . . But in nearly all these instances, the use of the word is such that it has application only postnatally. None indicates, with any assurance, that it has any possible prenatal application.[54]

54. When Texas urges that a fetus is entitled to Fourteenth Amendment protec-

tion as a person, it faces a dilemma. Neither in Texas nor in any other State are all abor-

All this, together with our observation that throughout the major portion of the 19th century prevailing legal abortion practices were far freer than they are today, persuades us that the word "person," as used in the Fourteenth Amendment, does not include the unborn. This is in accord with the results reached in those few cases where the issue has been squarely presented.

. . .

The pregnant woman cannot be isolated in her privacy. She carries an embryo and, later, a fetus, if one accepts the medical definitions of the developing young in the human uterus. The situation therefore is inherently different from marital intimacy, or bedroom possession of obscene material, or marriage, or procreation, or education, with which *Eisenstadt* and *Griswold, Stanley, Loving, Skinner* and *Pierce* and *Meyer* were respectively concerned. As we have intimated above, it is reasonable and appropriate for a State to decide that at some point in time another interest, that of health of the mother or that of potential human life, becomes significantly involved. The woman's privacy is no longer sole and any right of privacy she possesses must be measured accordingly.

Texas urges that, apart from the Fourteenth Amendment, life begins at conception and is present throughout pregnancy, and that, therefore, the State has a compelling interest in protecting that life from and after conception. We need not resolve the difficult question of when life begins. When those trained in the respective disciplines of medicine, philosophy, and theology are unable to arrive at any consensus, the judiciary, at this point in the development of man's knowledge, is not in a position to speculate as to the answer.

It should be sufficient to note briefly the wide divergence of thinking on this most sensitive and difficult question. There has always been strong support for the view that life does not begin until live birth. This was the belief of the Stoics. It appears to be the predominant, though not the unanimous, attitude of the Jewish faith. It may be taken to represent also the position of a large segment of the Protestant community, insofar as that can be ascertained; organized groups that have taken a formal position on the abortion issue have generally regarded abortion as a matter for the conscience of the individual and her family. As we have noted, the common

tions prohibited. Despite broad proscription, an exception always exists. The exception contained in Art. 1196, for an abortion procured or attempted by medical advice for the purpose of saving the life of the mother, is typical. But if the fetus is a person who is not to be deprived of life without due process of law, and if the mother's condition is the sole determinant, does not the Texas exception appear to be out of line with the Amendment's command?

There are other inconsistencies between Fourteenth Amendment status and the typi-cal abortion statute. It has already been pointed out that in Texas the woman is not a principal or an accomplice with respect to an abortion upon her. If the fetus is a person, why is the woman not a principal or an accomplice? Further, the penalty for criminal abortion specified by Art. 1195 is significantly less than the maximum penalty for murder prescribed by Art. 1257 of the Texas Penal Code. If the fetus is a person, may the penalties be different?

law found greater significance in quickening. Physicians and their scientific colleagues have regarded that event with less interest and have tended to focus either upon conception, upon live birth, or upon the interim point at which the fetus becomes "viable," that is, potentially able to live outside the mother's womb, albeit with artificial aid. Viability is usually placed at about seven months (28 weeks) but may occur earlier, even at 24 weeks. The Aristotelian theory of "mediate animation," that held sway throughout the Middle Ages and the Renaissance in Europe, continued to be official Roman Catholic dogma until the 19th century, despite opposition to this "ensoulment" theory from those in the Church who would recognize the existence of life from the moment of conception. The latter is now, of course, the official belief of the Catholic Church. As one brief amicus discloses, this is a view strongly held by many non-Catholics as well, and by many physicians. Substantial problems for precise definition of this view are posed, however, by new embryological data that purport to indicate that conception is a "process" over time, rather than an event, and by new medical techniques such as menstrual extraction, the "morning-after" pill, implantation of embryos, artificial insemination, and even artificial wombs.

. . .

In view of all this, we do not agree that, by adopting one theory of life, Texas may override the rights of the pregnant woman that are at stake. We repeat, however, that the State does have an important and legitimate interest in preserving and protecting the health of the pregnant woman, whether she be a resident of the State or a non-resident who seeks medical consultation and treatment there, and that it has still *another* important and legitimate interest in protecting the potentiality of human life. These interests are separate and distinct. Each grows in substantiality as the woman approaches term and, at a point during pregnancy, each becomes "compelling."

With respect to the State's important and legitimate interest in the health of the mother, the "compelling" point, in the light of present medical knowledge, is at approximately the end of the first trimester. This is so because of the now-established medical fact that until the end of the first trimester mortality in abortion may be less than mortality in normal childbirth. . . .

. . .

With respect to the State's important and legitimate interest in potential life, the "compelling" point is at viability. This is so because the fetus then presumably has the capability of meaningful life outside the mother's womb. State regulation protective of fetal life after viability thus has both logical and biological justifications. If the State is interested in protecting fetal life after viability, it may go so far as to proscribe abortion during that period, except when it is necessary to preserve the life or health of the mother.

Measured against these standards, Art. 1196 of the Texas Penal Code, in restricting legal abortions to those "procured or attempted by medical

advice for the purpose of saving the life of the mother," sweeps too broadly.
. . .

. . .

Affirmed in part and reversed in part.

■ MR. JUSTICE STEWART, concurring.

. . .

"In a Constitution for a free people, there can be no doubt that the meaning of 'liberty' must be broad indeed." Board of Regents v. Roth, 408 U.S. 564 (1972). The Constitution nowhere mentions a specific right of personal choice in matters of marriage and family life, but the "liberty" protected by the Due Process Clause of the Fourteenth Amendment covers more than those freedoms explicitly named in the Bill of Rights.

As Mr. Justice Harlan once wrote: "[T]he full scope of the liberty guaranteed by the Due Process Clause cannot be found in or limited by the precise terms of the specific guarantees elsewhere provided in the Constitution. This 'liberty' is not a series of isolated points pricked out in terms of the taking of property; the freedom of speech, press, and religion; the right to keep and bear arms; the freedom from unreasonable searches and seizures; and so on. It is a rational continuum which, broadly speaking, includes a freedom from all substantial arbitrary impositions and purposeless restraints . . . and which also recognizes, what a reasonable and sensitive judgment must, that certain interests require particularly careful scrutiny of the state needs asserted to justify their abridgment." Poe v. Ullman, 367 U.S. 497 [(1961)] (opinion dissenting from dismissal of appeal). In the words of Mr. Justice Frankfurter, "Great concepts like . . . 'liberty' . . . were purposely left to gather meaning from experience. For they relate to the whole domain of social and economic fact, and the statesmen who founded this Nation knew too well that only a stagnant society remains unchanged." National Mutual Ins. Co. v. Tidewater Transfer Co., 337 U.S. 582 [(1949)] (dissenting opinion).

Several decisions of this Court make clear that freedom of personal choice in matters of marriage and family life is one of the liberties protected by the Due Process Clause of the Fourteenth Amendment. . . .

. . .

■ MR. JUSTICE REHNQUIST, dissenting.

. . .

. . . I have difficulty in concluding, as the Court does, that the right of "privacy" is involved in this case. Texas, by the statute here challenged, bars the performance of a medical abortion by a licensed physician on a plaintiff such as Roe. A transaction resulting in an operation such as this is not "private" in the ordinary usage of that word. Nor is the "privacy" that the Court finds here even a distant relative of the freedom from searches and seizures protected by the Fourth Amendment to the Constitution, which the Court has referred to as embodying a right to privacy. Katz v. United States, 389 U.S. 347 (1967).

If the Court means by the term "privacy" no more than that the claim of a person to be free from unwanted state regulation of consensual transactions may be a form of "liberty" protected by the Fourteenth Amendment, there is no doubt that similar claims have been upheld in our earlier decisions on the basis of that liberty. I agree with the statement of Mr. Justice Stewart in his concurring opinion that the "liberty," against deprivation of which without due process the Fourteenth Amendment protects, embraces more than the rights found in the Bill of Rights. But that liberty is not guaranteed absolutely against deprivation, only against deprivation without due process of law. The test traditionally applied in the area of social and economic legislation is whether or not a law such as that challenged has a rational relation to a valid state objective. Williamson v. Lee Optical Co., 348 U.S. 483 (1955). The Due Process Clause of the Fourteenth Amendment undoubtedly does place a limit, albeit a broad one, on legislative power to enact laws such as this. If the Texas statute were to prohibit an abortion even where the mother's life is in jeopardy, I have little doubt that such a statute would lack a rational relation to a valid state objective under the test stated in *Williamson* supra. But the Court's sweeping invalidation of any restrictions on abortion during the first trimester is impossible to justify under that standard, and the conscious weighing of competing factors that the Court's opinion apparently substitutes for the established test is far more appropriate to a legislative judgment than to a judicial one.

. . .

Planned Parenthood of Southeastern Pennsylvania v. Casey

Supreme Court of the United States, 1992.
505 U.S. 833.

[This decision involved a challenge to a Pennsylvania statute regulating abortion. Much of the argument in the case concerned whether *Roe v. Wade* should be either overruled or modified. The following passages come from the Joint Opinion of Justices O'Connor, Kennedy and Souter, which both reaffirmed the fundamental right of a woman to terminate her pregnancy and modified the standard by which regulations of the exercise of that right would be evaluated. The portions of this Opinion reaffirming the right were also joined by Justices Blackmun and Stevens, who dissented from the portions modifying the standard. Chief Justice Rehnquist and Justices White, Scalia and Thomas dissented from the Court's failure to overrule *Roe v. Wade* altogether.]

Our law affords constitutional protection to personal decisions relating to marriage, procreation, contraception, family relationships, child rearing, and education. Our cases recognize "the right of the *individual*, married or single, to be free from unwarranted governmental intrusion into matters so fundamentally affecting a person as the decision whether to bear or beget a child." Our precedents "have respected the private realm of family life which the state cannot enter.'' These matters, involving the most intimate and personal choices a person may make in a lifetime, choices central to personal dignity and autonomy, are central to the liberty protected by the Fourteenth Amendment. At the heart of liberty is the right to define one's own concept of existence, of meaning, of the universe, and of the mystery of human life. Beliefs about these matters could not define the attributes of personhood were they formed under compulsion of the State.

These considerations begin our analysis of the woman's interest in terminating her pregnancy but cannot end it, for this reason: though the abortion decision may originate within the zone of conscience and belief, it is more than a philosophic exercise. Abortion is a unique act. It is an act fraught with consequences for others: for the woman who must live with the implications of her decision; for the persons who perform and assist in the procedure; for the spouse, family, and society which must confront the knowledge that these procedures exist, procedures some deem nothing short of an act of violence against innocent human life; and, depending on one's beliefs, for the life or potential life that is aborted. Though abortion is conduct, it does not follow that the State is entitled to proscribe it in all instances. That is because the liberty of the woman is at stake in a sense unique to the human condition and so unique to the law. The mother who carries a child to full term is subject to anxieties, to physical constraints, to pain that only she must bear. That these sacrifices have from the beginning of the human race been endured by woman with a pride that ennobles her in the eyes of others and gives to the infant a bond of love cannot alone be grounds for the State to insist she make the sacrifice. Her suffering is too intimate and personal for the State to insist, without more, upon its own vision of the woman's role, however dominant that vision has been in the course of our history and our culture. The destiny of the woman must be shaped to a large extent on her own conception of her spiritual imperatives and her place in society.

It should be recognized, moreover, that in some critical respects the abortion decision is of the same character as the decision to use contraception, to which *Griswold v. Connecticut, Eisenstadt v. Baird*, and *Carey v. Population Services International* afford constitutional protection. We have no doubt as to the correctness of those decisions. They support the reasoning in *Roe* relating to the woman's liberty because they involve personal decisions concerning not only the meaning of procreation but also human responsibility and respect for it. As with abortion, reasonable people will have differences of opinion about these matters. One view is based on such reverence for the wonder of creation that any pregnancy ought to be welcomed and carried to full term no matter how difficult it will be to provide for the child and ensure its well-being. Another is that the inability to provide for the nurture and care of the infant is a cruelty to the child and an anguish to the parent. These are intimate views with infinite variations, and their deep, personal character underlay our decisions in *Griswold, Eisenstadt*, and *Carey*. The same concerns are present when the woman confronts the reality that, perhaps despite her attempts to avoid it, she has become pregnant. It was this dimension of personal liberty that *Roe* sought to protect, and its holding invoked the reasoning and the tradition of the precedents we have discussed, granting protection to substantive liberties of the person. *Roe* was, of course, an extension of those cases and, as the decision itself indicated, the separate States could act in some degree to further their own legitimate interests in protecting prenatal life. The extent to which the legislatures of the States might act to outweigh the interests of the woman in choosing to terminate her pregnancy was a subject of debate both in *Roe* itself and in decisions following it.

[The Joint Opinion included a lengthy analysis of why considerations of stare decisis favored reaffirmation of *Roe v. Wade*, regardless of whether one thought it had been correctly decided as an original matter. This analysis included the following passages further explaining the right protected.]

[To discount reliance on the continued existence of the right] would be simply to refuse to face the fact that for two decades of economic and social developments, people have organized intimate relationships and made choices that define their views of themselves and their places in society, in reliance on the availability of abortion in the event that contraception should fail. The ability of women to participate equally in the economic and social life of the Nation has been facilitated by their ability to control their reproductive lives.

. . .

It will be recognized, of course, that *Roe* stands at an intersection of two lines of decisions, but in whichever doctrinal category one reads the case, the result for present purposes will be the same. The *Roe* Court itself placed its holding in the succession of cases most prominently exemplified by *Griswold v. Connecticut*, 381 U.S. 479 (1965). When it is so seen, *Roe* is clearly in no jeopardy, since subsequent constitutional developments have neither disturbed, nor do they threaten to diminish, the scope of recognized protection accorded to the liberty relating to intimate relationships, the family, and decisions about whether or not to beget or bear a child.

Roe, however, may be seen not only as an exemplar of *Griswold* liberty but as a rule (whether or not mistaken) of personal autonomy and bodily integrity, with doctrinal affinity to cases recognizing limits on governmental power to mandate medical treatment or to bar its rejection. If so, our cases since *Roe* accord with *Roe's* view that a State's interest in the protection of life falls short of justifying any plenary override of individual liberty claims. *Cruzan v. Director, Mo. Dept. of Health*,497 U.S. 261 (1990) [(concerning right to refuse life-sustaining treatment)]; cf., e.g., *Riggins v. Nevada*, 504 U.S. 127 (1992) [(concerning criminal defendant's right to refuse antipsychotic medication)]; *Washington v. Harper*, 494 U.S. 210 (1990) [(concerning prisoner's right to refuse antipsychotic medication)]; see also, e.g., *Rochin v. California*, 342 U.S. 165 (1952) [(concerning violation of criminal suspect's rights by violent pumping of his stomach)];

Jacobson v. Massachusetts, 197 U.S. 11 (1905) [(concerning compulsory vaccination)].

. . .

[Having reaffirmed the fundamentality of the right to terminate a pregnancy, the Joint Opinion then turned to the standards for evaluating interferences with that right:]

From what we have said so far it follows that it is a constitutional liberty of the woman to have some freedom to terminate her pregnancy. We conclude that the basic decision in *Roe* was based on a constitutional analysis which we cannot now repudiate. The woman's liberty is not so unlimited, however, that from the outset the State cannot show its concern for the life of the unborn, and at a later point in fetal development the State's interest in life has sufficient force so that the right of the woman to terminate the pregnancy can be restricted.

That brings us, of course, to the point where much criticism has been directed at *Roe*, a criticism that always inheres when the Court draws a specific rule from what in the Constitution is but a general standard. We conclude, however, that the urgent claims of the woman to retain the ultimate control over her destiny and her body, claims implicit in the meaning of liberty, require us to perform that function. Liberty must not be extinguished for want of a line that is clear. And it falls to us to give some real substance to the woman's liberty to determine whether to carry her pregnancy to full term.

We conclude the line should be drawn at viability, so that before that time the woman has a right to choose to terminate her pregnancy. We adhere to this principle for two reasons. First, as we have said, is the doctrine of stare decisis. Any judicial act of line-drawing may seem somewhat arbitrary, but *Roe* was a reasoned statement, elaborated with great care. We have twice reaffirmed it in the face of great opposition [in the *Thornburgh* and *Akron I* cases]. Although we must overrule those parts of *Thornburgh* and *Akron I* which, in our view, are inconsistent with *Roe's* statement that the State has a legitimate interest in promoting the life or potential life of the unborn, the central premise of those cases represents an unbroken commitment by this Court to the essential holding of *Roe*. It is that premise which we reaffirm today.

The second reason is that the concept of viability, as we noted in *Roe*, is the time at which there is a realistic possibility of maintaining and nourishing a life outside the womb, so that the independent existence of the second life can in reason and all fairness be the object of state protection that now overrides the rights of the woman. Consistent with other constitutional norms, legislatures may draw lines which appear arbitrary without the necessity of offering a justification. But courts may not. We must justify the lines we draw. And there is no line other than viability which is more workable. To be sure, as we have said, there may be some medical developments that affect the precise point of viability, but this is an imprecision within tolerable limits given that the medical community and all those who must apply its discoveries will continue to explore the matter. The viability line also has, as a practical matter, an element of fairness. In some broad sense it might be said that a woman who fails to act before viability has consented to the State's intervention on behalf of the developing child.

. . .

Though the woman has a right to choose to terminate or continue her pregnancy before viability, it does not at all follow that the State is prohibited from taking steps to ensure that this choice is thoughtful and informed. Even in the earliest stages of pregnancy, the State may enact rules and regulations designed to encourage her to know that there are philosophic and social arguments of great weight that can be brought to bear in favor of continuing the pregnancy to full term and that there are procedures and institutions to allow adoption of unwanted children as well as a certain degree of state assistance if the mother chooses to raise the child herself. " '[T]he Constitution does not forbid a State or city, pursuant to democratic processes, from expressing a preference for normal childbirth.' " It follows that States are free to enact laws to provide a reasonable framework for a woman to make a decision that has such profound and lasting meaning. This, too, we find consistent with *Roe*'s central premises, and indeed the inevitable consequence of our holding that the State has an interest in protecting the life of the unborn.

We reject the trimester framework, which we do not consider to be part of the essential holding of *Roe*. Measures aimed at ensuring that a woman's choice contemplates the consequences for the fetus do not necessarily interfere with the right recognized in *Roe*, although those measures have been found to be inconsistent with the rigid trimester framework announced in that case. A logical reading of the central holding in *Roe* itself, and a necessary reconciliation of the liberty of the woman and the interest of the State in promoting prenatal life, require, in our view, that we abandon the trimester framework as a rigid prohibition on all previability regulation aimed at the protection of fetal life. The trimester framework suffers from these basic flaws: in its formulation it misconceives the nature of the pregnant woman's interest; and in practice it undervalues the State's interest in potential life, as recognized in *Roe*.

[The Joint Opinion rejected *Roe*'s holding that all restrictions on the right to terminate a pregnancy must be necessary to the achievement of a compelling government interest, proposing instead an "undue burden" standard:]

A finding of an undue burden is a shorthand for the conclusion that a state regulation has the purpose or effect of placing a substantial obstacle in the path of a woman seeking an abortion of a nonviable fetus. A statute with this purpose is invalid because the means chosen by the State to further the interest in potential life must be calculated to inform the woman's free choice, not hinder it. And a statute which, while furthering the interest in potential life or some other valid state interest, has the effect of placing a substantial obstacle in the path of a woman's choice cannot be considered a permissible means of serving its legitimate ends. To the extent that the opinions of the Court or of individual Justices use the undue burden standard in a manner that is inconsistent with this analysis, we set out what in our view should be the controlling standard.

. . .

Some guiding principles should emerge. What is at stake is the woman's right to make the ultimate decision, not a right to be insulated from all others in doing so. Regulations which do no more than create a structural mechanism by which the State, or the parent or guardian of a minor, may express profound respect for the life of the unborn are permitted, if they are not a substantial obstacle to the woman's exercise of the right to choose. Unless it has that effect on her right of choice, a state measure designed to persuade her to choose childbirth over abortion will be upheld if reasonably related to that goal. Regulations designed to foster the health of a woman seeking an abortion are valid if they do not constitute an undue burden.

Basic Law (Grundgesetz) of the Federal Republic of Germany, Articles 1 and 2

Article 1

(1) Human dignity shall be inviolable. To respect and to protect it shall be the duty of all state authority.

(2) The German people therefore acknowledge inviolable and inalienable human rights as the basis of every community, of peace and of justice in the world.

(3) The following basic rights shall bind the legislature, the executive, and the judiciary as directly enforceable law.

Article 2

(1) Everyone shall have the right to the free development of his personality in so far as he does not violate the rights of others or offend against the constitutional order or the moral code.

(2) Everyone shall have the right to life and to inviolability of his person. The liberty of the individual shall be inviolable. These rights may be encroached upon only pursuant to statute.

David P. Currie, Lochner Abroad: Substantive Due Process and Equal Protection in the Federal Republic of Germany

1989 Sup. Ct. Rev. 333, 358–61 (1990).

"Free development of personality" (die freie Entfaltung der Persönlichkeit) is no more self-defining in German than it is in English. Literally it seems to suggest something akin to a right of privacy, an intimate sphere of autonomy into which the state is forbidden to intrude. Various aspects of privacy are indeed embraced within Article 2(1), but any such limiting construction was firmly rejected in the seminal *Elfes* case in 1957. The free development of personality, the Court argued, could not be limited to "that central area of personality that essentially defines a human person as a spiritual-moral being, for it is inconceivable how development within this core area could offend the moral code, the rights of others, or even the constitutional order...." Rather the Court construed the provision to guarantee a "general right of freedom of action" (allgemeine Handlungs freiheit)—citing the debates of the constitutional convention for the conclusion that "linguistic rather than legal considerations prompted the framers to substitute the current language for the original proposal" that "[e]very person is free to do or not to do what he wishes." Casting Article 2(1) loose from its restrictive terminology—like the [U.S. Supreme Court's] freeing of "liberty" in the Fourteenth Amendment from its history in *Allgeyer v. Louisiana*—opened the door to judicial review of all restrictive government action.

What this review would produce in practice depended upon interpretation of the three limits Article 2(1) places upon freedom of action, "the rights of others, ... the constitutional order, [and] the moral code." The first and last are easy enough to understand, if not always to apply.... More difficult to determine was the meaning of the second limitation, which leaves unprotected those activities which "offend against the constitutional order."

This term or something very like it appears in several other articles in connection with constitutional limitations on subversive activities. In those articles, in order not unduly to encroach upon legitimate political opposition, it has been given a restrictive meaning. In the quite different context of Article 2(1), "the constitutional order" has been interpreted more broadly. The general right to freedom of action, the Court stated in *Elfes*, was limited both by the Basic Law itself and "by every legal norm that conforms procedurally and substantively with the Constitution."

This interpretation ... provoked the question whether Article 2(1) added anything at all. At a minimum, as the cases have shown, it provided affected individuals with standing to attack laws passed without legislative authority or delegating excessive rulemaking power to the executive. More important and interesting was the reminder in the *Elfes* case that a law qualified as part of the constitutional order only if it conformed with "the principles of the rule of law and the social welfare state."

... [T]he rule of law [Rechtsstaat] has given Article 2(1) much of its bite. [E]ven in the absence of express provisions such as those applicable to bodily restraint, condemnation, and occupational freedom, the Rechtsstaat principle has been held to permit restrictions of liberty only in accordance with a statute, and limitations on general freedom of action lacking a sufficient legal basis have been struck down. The Rechtsstaat principle also contains a significant limitation on delegation of policymaking authority that ... requires fair warning and fair procedure, and imposes meaningful limitations on retroactivity. Most important, ... the German conception of the rule of law embodies the pervasive principle of proportionality. It is this principle, in connection with the broad interpretation of "personality" in *Elfes*, that has enabled the German Court to act as censor of the reasonableness of all government action.

As in the United States during the *Lochner* era, most challenged measures have passed muster. National security was held to justify the law limiting issuance of passports in *Elfes*; price regulations were upheld because they were reasonable. At the same time, a number of restrictions on the general freedom of action have been struck down for want of proportionality. The state may not prohibit intermediaries from seeking to match willing drivers with people who were looking for rides. A person in pretrial custody may not be denied a typewriter. As noted in connection with the human dignity provision, persons who have undergone sex change operations are entitled to have birth records corrected to reflect their new gender. Parents may not be given power to bind minor children by contract; the filing of criminal charges in good faith may not be treated as a tort. In one of the best known cases of this nature the Constitutional Court found it unreasonable to require those who sought to hunt with falcons to demonstrate competence in the use of firearms. Not only did the required skills have "no connection either with the care of falcons or with the practice of falconry," but any hunter who discharged a weapon during the chase would frighten away his own falcon.

Article 2(1) and the proportionality principle have also been employed on a number of occasions to secure a general right of "informational self-determination" (informationelle Selbstbestimmung), or freedom from unwarranted publicity. First elaborated in the *Microcensus* case in 1969, this right has been held to limit divulgence of divorce files, medical records, and private recordings of conversations. More recently it has led the Court to require greater restraint and confidentiality in connection with both the census and legislative investigations, and even to forbid general dissemination of the names of individuals who had been stripped of contracting authority as spendthrifts—although one might have though publicity essential to protection of those with whom the spendthrift might deal. In this as in so many other respects the German Court has gone beyond its American counterpart; while freedom from certain disclosures is afforded in this country by the First, Fourth, and Fifth Amendments, we have as yet no general right to informational privacy—much less a governmental duty to prevent private revelations of past crimes, such as the German Court established in the *Lebach* case in 1973.

First Abortion Decision*

Federal Constitutional Court of Germany, First Senate, 1975.
39 BVerfGE 1.

[In 1974, the German federal legislature amended the Criminal Code to liberalize its treatment of abortion. Under new Section 218a of the Crimi-

---

* Translation adapted from Donald P. Kommers, The Constitutional Jurisprudence of the Federal Republic of Germany, 2d ed. Copyright 1997, Duke University Press. All

nal Code, an abortion would no longer be punished if performed by a licensed physician with the consent of the pregnant woman during the first twelve weeks of pregnancy. Prior to seeking an abortion, however, the woman was legally obliged to seek advice from a physician or counseling agency concerning available public and private assistance for pregnant women, mothers, and children. Criminal penalties would continue to be enforced, as before, with respect to abortions performed after the third month of pregnancy except in those instances where medical, eugenic, or ethical (i.e., in cases of rape or incest) indications would justify the fetus's destruction. The statute was brought before the Federal Constitutional Court for review of its constitutionality under the Basic Law.]

Section 218a of the Criminal Code [as amended] is incompatible with Article 2 (2)(1) in conjunction with Article 1(1) of the Basic Law and is void insofar as it exempts termination of pregnancy from punishment in cases where no reasons exist which—within the meaning of the [present] decisional grounds—have priority over the value order contained in the Basic Law....

I.   1. Article 2 (2)(1) of the Basic Law protects the life developing within the mother's womb as an independent legal interest.

(a) [T]he categorical inclusion of the inherently self-evident right to life in the Basic Law may be explained principally as a reaction to the "destruction of life unworthy to live," the "final solution," and "liquidations" that the National Socialist regime carried out as government measures. Article 2 (2) (1) of the Basic Law implies, as does the repeal of the death penalty by Article 102 of the Basic Law, "an affirmation of the fundamental value of human life and of a state concept which emphatically opposes the views of a political regime for which the individual life had little significance and therefore which practiced unlimited abuse in the name of the arrogated right over life and death of the citizen."

(b) In interpreting Article 2 (2)(1) of the Basic Law, one must proceed from its wording: "Everyone shall have the right to life...." Life in the sense of the developmental existence of a human individual begins, according to established biological-physiological findings, on the fourteenth day after conception (implantation, individuation). The developmental process thus begun is a continuous one which manifests no sharp demarcation and does not permit any precise delimitation of the various developmental stages of the human life. Nor does it end with birth; for instance, the phenomena of consciousness specific to human personality do not appear until some time after birth. Therefore [we] may not limit the protection of Article 2 (2)(1) of the Basic Law either to the "completed" human being after birth or to the independently viable *nasciturus*. [Article 2 (2)(1)] guarantees the right of life to everyone who "lives"; no distinction can be made between individual stages of the developing life before birth or

rights reserved. Reprinted with permission. Another translation, of the full text of the decision, appears in John D. Gorby and Robert E. Jonas, *West German Abortion Decision: A Contrast to Roe v. Wade*, 9 John Marshall J. Prac. & Proc. 551, 605–84 (1976).

between prenatal and postnatal life. "Everyone" within the meaning of Article 2 (2)(1) of the Basic Law is "every living human being," or, expressed otherwise, every human individual possessing life; "everyone" therefore also includes the yet-unborn human being....

2.   Therefore, [we] derive the obligation of the state to protect all human life directly from Article 2(2)(1) of the Basic Law. Additionally, [this obligation] follows from the express provision of Article 1(1) of the Basic Law; for the developing life also enjoys the protection which Article 1 (1) accords to human dignity. Wherever human life exists it merits human dignity; whether the subject of this dignity is conscious of it and knows how to safeguard it is not of decisive moment. The potential capabilities inherent in human existence from its inception are adequate to establish human dignity.

3.   ... According to established precedent of the Federal Constitutional Court, the constitutional norms contain not only an individual's subjective defensive rights against the state. [T]hey also represent an objective order of values that serves as a basic constitutional decision for all areas of the law and provides guidelines and impulses for legislative, administrative, and judicial practice ....

II.   1. The obligation of the state to furnish protection is comprehensive.... Human life represents a supreme value within the constitutional order that needs no further justification; it is the vital basis of this human dignity and the prerequisite of all other basic rights.

2.   The obligation of the state to take the developing life under its protection also exists in principle with regard to the mother. Undoubtedly, the natural union of the prenatal life with the mother establishes a special type of relationship for which there is no parallel in any other factual situation in life. Pregnancy belongs to the intimate sphere of the woman that is constitutionally protected by Article 2 (1) in conjunction with Article 1 (1) of the Basic Law. If [one] were to regard the embryo only as a part of the maternal organism, the termination of pregnancy would remain within the sphere of [a woman's] private life into which the legislator may not intrude. Because the *nasciturus* is an independent human being under the protection of the Constitution, termination of pregnancy has a social dimension which makes it accessible to and in need of state regulation. It is true that the right of a woman freely to develop her personality also lays claim to recognition and protection. [This right] includes freedom of action in its comprehensive meaning and consequently also embraces the woman's responsible decision against parenthood and its attendant duties. But this right is not given without limitation—the rights of others, the constitutional order, and moral law limit it. It can never confer *a priori* the authority to intrude upon the protected legal sphere of another without a justifiable reason, much less the authority to destroy [this sphere] as well as a life, especially because a special responsibility exists precisely for this life.

No compromise is possible that would both guarantee the protection of the unborn life and concede to the pregnant woman the freedom of terminating the pregnancy because termination of pregnancy always means destruction of the prenatal life. In the ensuing balancing process, "both constitutional values must be perceived in their relation to human dignity as the center of the Constitution's value system." When using Article 1(1) as a guidepost, the decision must come down in favor of the preeminence of protecting the fetus's life over the right of self-determination of the pregnant woman. Pregnancy, birth, and child-rearing may impair the woman's [right of self-determination] as to many personal developmental potentialities. The termination of pregnancy, however, destroys prenatal life. Pursuant to the principle of carefully balancing competing constitutionally protected positions, and considering the fundamental concept behind Article 19 (2) of the Basic Law, [the state] must give the protection of the *nasciturus*'s life priority.* In principle, this preeminence lasts for the entire duration of the pregnancy and may not be questioned for any particular phase....

3. [We] may deduce the basic position that the Constitution requires of the legal order from the [aforementioned discussion]. The legal order may not use the woman's right of self-determination as the sole guideline for its regulations. Basically, the state must assume [that a woman has] the duty to carry the pregnancy to term and must consequently consider its termination as a wrong. [It] must clearly express its disapproval of the termination of pregnancy. [The state] must avoid the false impression that terminating a pregnancy involves the same social course of events as, for instance, a trip to the doctor to have an illness healed or even a legally neutral alternative to contraception....

III. It is incumbent principally upon the legislature to decide how the state is to fulfill its obligation effectively to protect the developing life.

1. ... It is therefore the state's task to use sociopolitical means as well as public assistance to safeguard the developing life. The legislature is largely responsible for organizing what assistance can be effectuated and how these measures are to be implemented in detail. The Constitutional Court generally may not review these decisions. [The legislature's] primary concern will be to strengthen the willingness of the expectant mother to accept the pregnancy as her own responsibility and to bring the fetus to full term. Regardless of how the state fulfills its obligation to protect human life, [we] must not forget that nature has entrusted the protection of the developing life to the mother. The principal goal of the state's endeavor to protect life should be to reawaken and, if required, to strengthen the maternal will to protect [the unborn child] where it has been lost....

[After noting that the legislature is not obligated to protect unborn life in the same way that it protects born life, the court continues:]

2. (a) From time immemorial it has been the task of the criminal law to protect the elementary values of community life. In the preceding passages [we] established that the life of every individual human being is

---

* [Under Article 19(2) of the Basic Law, even where limitation of a basic right is permissible, the limitation must not encroach upon the essential content of the right.—Editors' Note.]

among the most important legal values. The termination of a pregnancy irrevocably destroys human life that has come into being. [I]t is an act of killing.... [T]he use of criminal law to punish "acts of abortion" is undoubtedly legitimate; it is the law in force in most civilized states—under variously formulated conditions—and is particularly in keeping with the German legal tradition.

(b) However, punishment should never be an end in itself. Basically, its use is subject to the decision of the legislature. Nothing prevents the legislature from expressing the constitutionally required disapprobation of abortion by means other than the threat of penal sanctions. What is determinative is whether the totality of those measures serving to protect prenatal life, whether classifiable as measures of private, public, or, more particularly, of social or criminal law, in fact guarantee protection commensurate with the importance of the legal interest to be safeguarded....

3. As has been shown, the obligation of the state to protect the developing life also exists with respect to the mother. Here, however, the use of criminal law gives rise to special problems which result from the singular situation of the pregnant woman. The incisive effects of pregnancy upon a woman's physical and mental condition are immediately apparent and require no further exposition. They often mean a considerable change in her entire lifestyle and a limitation of potential personal development. This burden is not always not fully compensated by the fact that the woman finds new fulfillment in her task as a mother and that the pregnant woman can claim assistance from the community. In individual cases difficult and even life-threatening situations of conflict may arise. The unborn's right to life may place a substantially greater burden on the woman than that normally connected with a pregnancy. Thus [we] are confronted with the question of what she may reasonably be expected to endure; in other words, whether the state, even in these cases, may compel her to carry the child to term by means of criminal sanctions. Respect for the unborn life conflicts with the woman's right not to be forced to sacrifice her own values beyond reasonable expectations. The legislature must show particular restraint in a situation of conflict which, generally, permits no clear moral evaluation and in which a decision to terminate the pregnancy may be a question of conscience worthy of respect. If in these cases the legislature does not consider the conduct of the pregnant women deserving of punishment and forgoes the imposition of criminal sanctions, then this decision must be accepted constitutionally as the result of a judgment incumbent upon the legislature....

It would appear unreasonable to expect [a woman] to continue her pregnancy if the termination proves to be necessary to "avert a danger to the life" of the pregnant woman "or the danger of a grave injury to her health" (section 218b(1), Criminal Code [as amended]). In this case her own "right to life and physical inviolability" (Article 2(2)(1) of the Basic Law) are at stake, and she cannot be expected to sacrifice it for the unborn life. In addition, the legislature may refrain from imposing penal sanctions for abortions in other cases where pregnancy would subject the woman to extraordinary burdens which, from the viewpoint of what may [reasonably] be expected of her, are as oppressive as those listed in section 218b(1). Special reasons for termination of a pregnancy include those based on eugenic, ethical (criminological), and social [considerations]. ... The decisive point in these cases is that another interest equally worthy of constitutional protection asserts itself with such urgency that the state's legal order cannot require the pregnant woman always to defer to the right of the unborn.

The legislature may also include [termination of pregnancy] for reasons of general necessity (social reasons) in this [list of reasons]. For the general social situation of the pregnant woman and her family may produce conflicts of such gravity that sacrifices in favor of the unborn life cannot be exacted by the instrumentalities of criminal law. In regulating this case, the legislature must describe the statutory elements of the offense which will not be subject to punishment so that the gravity of the social conflict to be presumed here is clearly recognizable and so that—viewed from the standpoint of what the state may [reasonably] expect [of the parties involved]—congruence of this case with the other reasons [for termination] is assured. In removing genuine cases of this kind of conflict from the protection of penal law, the legislature does not violate its duty to protect life. Even in cases [of real conflict] the state may not be content with merely examining whether the legal prerequisites exist for exempting an abortion from punishment and certifying that they exist, where appropriate. Rather, [we] expect the state to offer counseling and assistance so as to remind the pregnant woman of her fundamental duty to respect the unborn's right to life, to encourage her to go through with the pregnancy, and to support her—particularly in cases of social need—with practical assistance.

In all other cases the termination of pregnancy remains a wrong deserving of punishment; for here the destruction of a legal interest of the highest order is subject to the uncontrolled discretion of another and is not motivated by any necessity. If the legislature had wanted to dispense with criminal sanctions, this [decision] would only have been compatible with the protective command of Article 2(2)(1) of the Basic Law under the condition that another, equally effective, legal sanction was at its command which would permit the clear recognition of this act as a wrong (disapprobation by the legal order) and which would prevent abortions as effectively as a penal provision.

[In the concluding section of its opinion, the Constitutional Court applied these standards to the revision of the Criminal Code, and found that it fell short of constitutional standards in several particulars.]

[Justice Rupp-von Brünneck, the only woman on the Court at the time, and Justice Simon filed a dissenting opinion. They agreed with the majority's starting point: "The life of every single human being is, of course, a central value of the legal order. It is indisputable that the constitutional obligation to protect this life also encompasses its preliminary state before birth." They disagreed, however, with the majority's decision to require criminal sanctions for the purpose of achieving this protection, rather than giving more deference to the legislature's choice of means.]

Note on German Abortion Law After Unification

The unification of Germany in 1990 posed a dilemma regarding abortion law, because West German law, pursuant to the decision of the Federal Constitutional Court, permitted abortions only if certain criteria were met (serious danger to the life or physical or mental health of the pregnant woman, severe birth defects, pregnancy resulting from rape or certain related crimes, or such serious hardship that the woman cannot reasonably be expected to continue with the pregnancy), while East German law permitted abortion at the woman's option during the first trimester. A compromise was negotiated permitting East German laws to remain in effect pending new regulation by the united legislature.

In July 1992, after protracted political controversy, the German legislature adopted a new "Statute for the Protection of Prenatal Life, the Promotion of a Society More Hospitable to Children, Assistance in Pregnancy Conflict Situations, and the Regulation of Termination of Pregnancy." This statute once more removed the criminal penalties for abortion within the first twelve weeks after conception, subject to a requirement of mandatory counseling. The statute also increased to some degree the public assistance available to women who bear children; due to the fiscal difficulties resulting from unification, these subsidies were not as generous as had originally been proposed by those who hoped that the Federal Constitutional Court could accept a system of public assistance and mandatory counseling as an adequate substitute for the current [West] German abortion laws. The Federal Constitutional Court preliminarily enjoined the statute from taking effect, pending final decision.

In May 1993, the Second Senate of the Federal Constitutional Court invalidated the 1992 abortion legislation. Its new decision partly reaffirmed and partly modified the principles of the 1975 decision. The major consequences of the decision were (1) to permit decriminalization of first trimester abortions, subject to a counseling requirement; (2) to make the counseling process more intrusive; and (3) to prohibit state reimbursement for the cost of counseled abortions through the statutory health insurance system.*

Two judges dissented from the invalidation of the legislation; a third judge dissented in limited part.

The following is a translation of the relevant portions of the court's official syllabus of decision:

1.   The Constitution obliges the state to protect human life, including the unborn. This duty of protection has its basis in Article 1, Para-

---

* More precisely, reimbursement was prohibited to the extent that the abortion had been based on a free decision of the pregnant woman following mandatory counseling, without any determination of the presence of an "indication." See paragraph 16 of the syllabus.

graph 1 of the Constitution. Unborn human life already possesses human dignity. The legal order must secure the legal prerequisites of its development, which means a right to life of the unborn. This right to life does not depend on acceptance by the mother.

2.   The duty to protect unborn life relates to individual lives, not merely to human life in general.

3.   The unborn is entitled to legal protection even with respect to its mother. Such protection is possible only if the legislature prohibits abortion as a general principle, and imposes on her a legal duty, as a general principle, to carry the child to term. The prohibition in principle of abortion and the duty in principle to carry the child to term are two inseparably linked elements of the protection required by the Constitution.

4.   Abortion must be seen as, in principle, wrongful for the entire duration of the pregnancy, and accordingly must be legally forbidden. The right to life of the unborn cannot, even for a limited time, be left up to the legally unconstrained decision of a third party, even the mother herself.

5.   The reach of the duty to protect unborn human life is to be determined with regard to the significance and vulnerability of the legal interest to be protected on the one hand, and the conflicting legal interests on the other hand. The legal interests that come into consideration as affected by the right to life of the unborn include—proceeding from the pregnant woman's right to protection and respect for her human dignity—above all her right to life and bodily integrity and also her right to personality. The woman cannot, however, claim a fundamental right to the killing of the unborn through abortion under Article 4, Paragraph 1 of the Constitution [freedom of conscience].

6.   For the fulfillment of its duty of protection, the state must adopt sufficient normative and practical measures—taking into account the conflicting legal interests—leading to an appropriate and to that degree effective protection. (Prohibition of insufficiency.) For this purpose a model of protection that combines elements of prevention and punishment is necessary.

7.   Fundamental rights of the woman do not in general outweigh the legal duty to carry the child to term. The fundamental rights of the woman do, however, lead to the conclusion that it is permissible in certain exceptional situations (and might even be required in some of these cases) not to impose such a legal duty. It is the task of the legislature to specify more fully such exceptional factual circumstances according to the criterion of "unreasonable demands" [Unzumutbarkeit]. To meet this standard the burdens imposed must require a greater degree of sacrifice of the woman's own life values than can be expected from her.

8.   The prohibition of insufficiency does not permit the state to dispense at will with the utilization of the criminal law and its resulting protective effects for human life.

9.   The state's duty of protection also includes protection against dangers to unborn human life that arise from the influence of the familial or broader social environment of the pregnant woman, or from the present and foreseeable actual life circumstances of the woman and her family, that diminish her readiness to carry the child to term.

10.   The duty of protection also obliges the state, to preserve and to vivify in the public's sense of justice the legal claim of unborn life to protection.

11.   The legislature is not precluded by the Constitution from employing a model for the protection of unborn life that, in the first stage of pregnancy, focuses on counseling of the pregnant woman, in order to win her over to the carrying of the child to term, and dispenses with the threat of punishment for abortions that do not meet certain criteria ["indications"] and the determination of these criteria by a third party.

12.   Such a counseling model requires a framework that creates favorable preconditions for the woman's action to benefit the unborn life. The state is fully responsible for the implementation of the counseling procedure.

13.   The state's duty of protection requires that the participation of the physician, which is necessary in the interest of the woman, simultaneously contribute to the protection of unborn life.

14.   The constitutional inviolability of human dignity precludes a legal characterization of the existence of a child as a source of damages. It is therefore prohibited to conceive of the duty of support for a child as damages.*

15.   Abortions that are performed in accordance with the counseling legislation, but without the determination of an "indication," may not be declared justified (not unlawful). According to indispensable principles of the rule of law, an exceptional circumstance can have the effect of justification only if the presence of its factual predicates is determined by authority derived from the state.

16.   The Constitution does not permit the provision of benefits from the statutory health insurance program for the performance of an abortion whose lawfulness has not been determined. But the provision

* [The corresponding portion of the opinion broadly rejected the case law of the German civil courts authorizing damage awards for "wrongful birth" against physicians whose malpractice had led to the birth of an unintended or medically defective child. The First Senate of the Federal Constitutional Court later characterized this broad discussion as dictum, and upheld the doctrine of tort damages for "wrongful birth" in connection with failed sterilizations or erroneous genetic counseling as constitutionally proper, over the protest of the Second Senate. See Judgment of November 12, 1997, 96 BVerfGE 375.—Editors' Note.]

of welfare benefits for decriminalized abortions performed in accordance with the counseling legislation in cases of inability to pay is not constitutionally objectionable; nor is the mandatory continuation of wages [during absence from work due to such an abortion.]

. . .

Judgment of May 28, 1993, 88 BVerfGE 203. For commentaries in English on the decision, and its aftermath, see, e.g., Peter E. Quint, The Imperfect Union: Constitutional Structures of German Unification 154–165 (1997); Nanette Funk, *Abortion Counselling and the 1995 German Abortion Law*, 12 Conn. J. Int'l L. 33 (1996); Donald P. Kommers, *The Constitutional Law of Abortion in Germany: Should Americans Pay Attention?*, 10 J. Contemp. Health L. & Pol'y 1 (1994); Gerald L. Neuman, *Casey in the Mirror: Abortion, Abuse and the Right to Protection in the United States and Germany*, 43 Am. J. Comp. L. 273 (1995); Christina P. Schlegel, *Landmark in German Abortion Law: the German 1995 Compromise Compared with English Law*, 11 Int'l J. L. Pol'y & Family 36 (1997); Susanne Walther, *Thou Shalt Not (But Thou Mayest): Abortion After the German Constitutional Court's 1993 Landmark Decision*, 36 German Yb. Int'l L. 387 (1993); Rosemarie Will, *German Unification and the Reform of Abortion Law*, 3 Cardozo Women's L.J. 399 (1996).

Note on Abortion Decisions in Regional Human Rights Systems

A.   The European Human Rights System

1.   After the German Federal Constitutional Court's first abortion decision in 1975 had been implemented by legislation, two German women challenged the legislation under the European Convention. *Brüggemann and Scheuten v. Federal Republic of Germany*, 10 Eur. Comm'n H.R. 100, 3 E.H.R.R. 244 (1977). Their principal argument was that the legislation violated the right to respect for private life under Article 8 of the Convention. Article 8 provides:

1.   Everyone has the right to respect for private and family life, his home and his correspondence.

2.   There shall be no interference by a public authority with the exercise of this right except such as is in accordance with the law and is necessary in a democratic society in the interests of national security, public safety or the economic well-being of the country, for the prevention of disorder or crime, for the protection of health or morals, or for the protection of the rights and freedoms of others.

The majority of the Commission rejected the women's argument, denying that the legislation constituted an interference with the right to respect for private life. It reasoned:

55.   The right to respect for private life is of such a scope as to secure to the individual a sphere within which he can freely pursue the development and fulfilment of his personality. To this effect, he must

also have the possibility of establishing relationships of various kinds, including sexual, with other persons. In principle, therefore, whenever the State sets up rules for the behaviour of the individual within this sphere, it interferes with the respect for private life and such interference must be justified in the light of Article 8 (2).

56.   However, there are limits to the personal sphere. While a large proportion of the law existing in a given State has some immediate or remote effect on the individual's possibility of developing his personality by doing what he wants to do, not all of these can be considered to constitute an interference with private life in the sense of Article 8 of the Convention. In fact, as the earlier jurisprudence of the Commission has already shown, the claim to respect for private life is automatically reduced to the extent that the individual himself brings his private life into contact with public life or into close connection with other protected interests.

57.   Thus, the Commission has held that the concept of private life in Article 8 was broader than the definition given by numerous Anglo–Saxon and French authors, namely, the "right to live as far as one wishes, protected from publicity", in that it also comprises, "to a certain degree, the right to establish and to develop relationships with other human beings, especially in the emotional field for the development and fulfilment of one's own personality". But it denied "that the protection afforded by Article 8 of the Convention extends to relationships of the individual with his entire immediate surroundings". It thus found that the right to keep a dog did not pertain to the sphere of private life of the owner because "the keeping of dogs is by the very nature of that animal necessarily associated with certain interferences with the life of others and even with public life" . . . .

59.   The termination of an unwanted pregnancy is not comparable with the situation in any of the above cases. However, pregnancy cannot be said to pertain uniquely to the sphere of private life. Whenever a woman is pregnant, her private life becomes closely connected with the developing foetus.

60.   The Commission does not find it necessary to decide, in this context, whether the unborn child is to be considered as "life" in the sense of Article 2 of the Convention, or whether it could be regarded as an entity which under Article 8(2) could justify an interference "for the protection of others". There can be no doubt that certain interests relating to pregnancy are legally protected, e.g. as shown by a survey of the legal order in 13 High Contracting Parties. This survey reveals that, without exception, certain rights are attributed to the conceived but unborn child, in particular the right to inherit. The Commission also notes that Article 6 (5) of the United Nations Covenant on Civil and Political Rights prohibits the execution of death sentences on pregnant women.

61.   The Commission therefore finds that not every regulation of the termination of unwanted pregnancies constitutes an interference with

the right to respect for the private life of the mother. Article 8 (1) cannot be interpreted as meaning that pregnancy and its termination are, as a principle, solely a matter of the private life of the mother. In this respect the Commission notes that there is not one member State of the Convention which does not, in one way or another, set up legal rules in this matter. The applicants complain about the fact that the Constitutional Court declared null and void the Fifth Criminal Law Reform Act, but even this Act was not based on the assumption that abortion is entirely a matter of the private life of the pregnant woman. It only provided that an abortion performed by a physician with the pregnant woman's consent should not be punishable if no more than 12 weeks had elapsed after conception.

64.   Furthermore, the Commission has had regard to the fact that, when the European Convention of Human Rights entered into force, the law on abortion in all member States was at least as restrictive as the one now complained of by the applicants. In many European countries the problem of abortion is or has been the subject of heated debates on legal reform since. There is no evidence that it was the intention of the Parties to the Convention to bind themselves in favour of any particular solution under discussion—e.g. a solution of the kind set out in the Fifth Criminal Law Reform Act (Fristenlösung—time limitation) which was not yet under public discussion at the time the Convention was drafted and adopted.

Three members of the Commission, Messrs. Opsahl, Norgaard and Kellberg, concurred. They first stated their personal view "that laws regulating abortion ought to leave the decision to have it performed in the early stage of pregnancy to the woman concerned." They added, however:

> Nevertheless, we must admit that such a view cannot easily be read into the terms of Article 8. The problem is not a new one and traditional views of the interpretation and application of this Article have to be taken into account, notwithstanding the rapid development of views on abortion in many countries. We are aware that the reality behind these traditional views is that the scope of protection of private life has depended on the outlook which has been formed mainly by men, although it may have been shared by women as well.

Mr. Fawcett dissented, stating that he:

> [was not] able to follow the Commission in holding, if I understand its reasoning correctly, that there are certain inherent limits to treating pregnancy and its termination as part of private life. Such limits, beyond those mentioned, at least in the form of intervention by legislation, must be found and justified in Article 8 (2): in the absence of such limits, the decision to terminate a pregnancy remains a free part of private life.

He found that the legislation was not justified as necessary to the achievement of any of the goals specifically listed in Article 8(2). For example:

> The intervention of the legislator in sexual morality may here have the purpose of preventing abortion being often reduced simply to a

form of contraception, or of inducing a sense of moral responsibility in the commencement of pregnancy, but it is not shown how the new legislation, as distinct from what it replaces, will achieve these purposes. On the contrary, the statistics and other evidence quoted in the minority judgment in the Federal Constitutional Court demonstrate the ineffectiveness of the earlier restrictive law in achieving these purposes.... Even though the new legislation is less restrictive of termination of pregnancy than the old law, it has not in my view been shown, in relation to the earlier Article 218a, that it is "necessary" under Article 8 (2) for the protection of morals.

There remains "the protection of the rights and freedoms of others" and the question how far this can cover the unborn child. The Convention does not expressly extend the right to life, protected by Article 2, to an unborn child; but that is not I think conclusive. However, it would serve no purpose for me to try to answer so controversial a question at any length here and I can only say that I am unable to attribute rights and freedoms under the convention to an unborn child not yet capable of independent life, that Article 218a did not extend the permitted termination of pregnancy beyond 12 weeks from conception, and that the elimination of that section of the Act was therefore not "necessary" for the protection of the rights and freedoms of others.

2.   The Commission has considered the abortion issue from other perspectives in rejecting claims raised by men who object to termination of a pregnancy by their wives or partners. See *H. v. Norway*, 73 Eur. Comm'n H.R. 155 (1992); *Paton v. United Kingdom*, 19 Eur. Comm'n H.R. 244, 3 E.H.R.R. 408 (1980). The Commission observed that the limitations on the right to life contained in Article 2(2) address only the situation of persons who are already born. Without resolving whether Article 2(1) might *ever* require the state to afford protection to a fetus, the Commission has concluded that such a right would have to be subject to implied limitations. In *Paton*, the Commission concluded that, even if Article 2 applied, the medically indicated abortion during the initial stage of pregnancy would be within the scope of an implied limitation.

In *H. v. Norway*, the Commission similarly rejected an objection to an abortion in the fourteenth week of pregnancy based on the more controversial "social indication," after a third-party determination that "the pregnancy, birth or care for the child may place the woman in a difficult situation of life." The Commission majority stated:

As the present case shows, there are different opinions as to whether such an authorisation strikes a fair balance between the legitimate need to protect the foetus and the legitimate interests of the woman in question. However, having regard to [the] Norwegian legislation, its requirements for the termination of pregnancy as well as the specific circumstances of the present case, the Commission does not find that the respondent State has gone beyond its discretion which the Commission considers that it has in this sensitive area of abortion.

73 Eur. Comm'n H.R. at 168–69.

In both cases, the Commission also rejected the potential father's claims under Article 8 based on a right to respect for *his* private or family life, finding that any interference with that right was justified under Article 8(2) as necessary for the protection of the rights of the wife.

3.   The European Court of Human Rights has considered abortion regulation in the context of limitations on information. In *Open Door and Dublin Well Woman v. Ireland*, 246 Eur. Ct. H.R. (ser. A), 15 E.H.R.R. 244 (1992), the Court found by a vote of 15 to 8 that an injunction against the provision within Ireland of information concerning the availability of abortions outside Ireland violated the right to receive and impart information under Article 10 of the Convention.

The majority concluded that the injunction was not necessary in a democratic society for the prevention of disorder or crime, for the protection of health or morals, or for the protection of the reputation or rights of others, as required by Article 10(2). It stated:

> The Court cannot accept that the restrictions at issue pursued the aim of the prevention of crime since ... neither the provision of the information question nor the obtaining of an abortion outside the jurisdiction involved any criminal offence. However, it is evident that the protection afforded under Irish law to the right to life of the unborn is based on profound moral values concerning the nature of life which were reflected in the stance of the majority of the Irish people against abortion as expressed in the 1983 referendum [which added a provision guaranteeing the "right to life of the unborn" in the Irish Constitution]. The restriction thus pursued the legitimate aim of the protection of morals of which the protection in Ireland of the right to life of the unborn is one aspect. It is not necessary in the light of this conclusion to decide whether the term "others" under Article 10(2) extends to the unborn.

The majority found the injunction overbroad and disproportionate in view of a variety of factors, including the fact that Irish law did not criminalize extraterritorial abortions; that the injunction also covered the limited circumstances in which abortion would have been lawful even in Ireland; that the organizations subject to the injunction did not advocate or encourage abortion, but merely informed women of their options; that some of the information was available through other channels in Ireland; and that the injunction created a risk to the health of those women who did not have access to the information. Having found a violation of Article 10, the Court declined to examine whether there had been a violation of the right to respect for private life contrary to Article 8 of the Convention.

The majority rejected Ireland's argument that no violation of Article 10 could be found because, under Article 60, the Convention should not be construed as limiting or derogating from human rights more greatly protected under national law. The majority concluded that the failure of Irish law to prevent travel abroad for abortion purposes, not the majority's interpretation of Article 10, was responsible for the current level of abortions obtained by Irish women abroad.

B. The Inter–American Human Rights System

The *"Baby Boy" Case, White and Potter v. United States, Case 2141, Inter–Am. C.H.R. 25, OEA ser.L./V/II.54, doc. 9 rev.1 (1981),* arose out of a petition to the Inter–American Commission on Human Rights seeking a declaration that the United States had violated the American Declaration of the Rights and Duties of Man by permitting the killing of unborn children by abortion. Petitioners focused on the Massachusetts Supreme Judicial Court's reversal of a conviction for manslaughter for an abortion performed on an arguably viable fetus. The Commission majority first observed that the phrasing of the right to life in Article I of the American Declaration did not specify when life begins. It then examined the drafting history of the American Declaration, and concluded that a proposal to define life as beginning from the moment of conception had been rejected because of its inconsistency with the abortion laws of a majority of the American States. The Commission next turned to the argument that the American Declaration should be construed in connection with the American Convention, which provides that the right to life "shall be protected by law and, in general, from the moment of conception." The majority concluded that the qualifying phrase, "in general," was intended to accommodate the legality of abortion, as in the American Declaration. Moreover, even if the American Convention did require prohibition of abortion, the United States was not a party to the American Convention, and that Convention should not be used to change the meaning of the American Declaration: "it would be impossible to impose upon the United States Government or that of any Member State of the OAS, by means of 'interpretation,' an international obligation based upon a treaty that such State has not duly accepted or ratified."*

Two members of the Commission, Dr. Monroy Cabra and Dr. Tinoco Castro, dissented. Dr. Monroy Cabra argued that, since the text of the American Declaration was not explicit, it should be given "the interpretation most in accord with the genuine protection of the right to life[,] that this protection begins at conception rather than at birth." He wrote:

> Life is the primary right of every individual. It is the fundamental right and the condition for existence of all other rights. If human existence is not recognized, there is no subject upon which to predicate the other rights. It is a right that antecedes other rights and exist by the mere fact of being, with no need for the state to recognize it as such. It is not up to the state to decide whether that right shall be recognized in one case and not in another....

United Nations, Dept. For Economic and Social Information and Policy Analysis, Population Division, *Reproductive Rights and Reproductive Health: A Concise Report*

U.N. Doc. ST/ESA/SER.A/157, 25–28 (1996).

Approximately 25 million legal abortions were performed worldwide around 1990, or one legal abortion for every six births. This estimate must be considered the minimum number, as no attempt has been made to estimate the magnitude of unreported legal abortions. In addition, WHO has estimated that some 20 million unsafe abortions are performed each year, or one unsafe abortion for every seven births.

Induced abortion has attained high public visibility in many countries, both developed and developing. In some cases, public concern has been voiced primarily because of the alarmingly high levels of maternal mortality and morbidity that have resulted from unsafe abortion. In others, the visibility has resulted more from public debate concerning the moral and legal status of abortion and the role that the State should play in permitting or denying access to safe abortion.

. . .

Induced abortion is one of the oldest methods of fertility control and one of the most widely used. It is practised both in remote rural societies and in large modern urban centers and in all regions of the world, although with differing consequences. When performed by appropriately qualified practitioners under hygienic circumstances, induced abortions generally pose a relatively small threat to women's reproductive health. Where abortion is illegal, however, it is usually performed in medically substandard and unsanitary conditions, leading to a high incidence of complications and resulting in chronic morbidity and often death. Indeed, WHO has estimated that approximately 76,000 women die annually as a result of complications arising from unsafe abortion. Moreover, long-term consequences of unsafe abortion may include chronic pelvic pain, pelvic inflammatory disease, tubal occlusion, secondary infertility and increased risk of spontaneous abortion in subsequent pregnancies.

. . .

Based on information available for 193 countries, the overwhelming majority of countries (98 per cent) permit abortions to be performed to save the pregnant woman's life. In a number of those countries, criminal law specifically allows abortion on this ground. In others, however, one must look to other laws or court decisions to determine whether there are exceptions to a general prohibition of abortion. For example, in Honduras, the Code of Medical Ethics permits abortion to save the woman's life; in Nepal, the rules of the Medical Council have been interpreted to permit abortion in various situations; and in Ireland the Supreme Court has ruled that an abortion can be performed to preserve the life of the pregnant woman. In yet other countries, such as the Central African Republic, the Dominican Republic, Egypt and the Philippines, the criminal law principle of necessity can be invoked to exempt from punishment the performance of an abortion to save a pregnant woman's life.

Abortion to preserve the woman's physical health is permitted in 119 countries (62 per cent). Fewer countries (95, or 50 per cent) allow abortion to preserve the woman's mental health, and 81 countries (42 per cent) permit it when pregnancy has resulted from rape or incest. The number declines to 78 countries (40 per cent) when there is the possibility of foetal impairment and to 55 countries (29 per cent) when the reasons are economic or social. Lastly, in 41 countries (21 per cent), abortion is available on request.

An examination of abortion policies in terms of population discloses that 96 per cent of the world population live in countries that permit abortion to save the woman's life, 75 per cent live in countries permitting abortion to preserve the woman's physical health, 69 per cent in countries where abortion is legal to preserve the woman's mental health and 72 per cent in countries where abortions is allowed when the pregnancy results from rape or incest. The percentage declines to 64 when there is the possibility of foetal impairment and to 44 in countries that permit abortion for economic or social reasons. Lastly, abortion is available on request to 38 per cent of the world population.

Notes

1. Disputes over abortion involve, among other things, conflict between asserted interests of the woman who wishes to terminate her pregnancy and the asserted interests in the life of the fetus. In each of the foregoing cases, how is the conflict framed in terms of rights and interests, by the majority and by the dissent? Whose rights or interests? Which rights or interests? What degree of protection do these rights or interests receive?

2. How is the right recognized in *Roe* and *Casey* best described? In terms of "privacy"? "Liberty"? "Bodily integrity"? "Autonomy"? "Freedom of action"? Does the German court not recognize the relevant right, or does it recognize it, but draw different conclusions about its limits? Do the United States dissenters not recognize the relevant right?

3. In the United States context, what is the constitutional status of a state interest in potential life? Is this an interest that the state *may* assert? *Must* assert? Does the United States answer differ from the German answer? Why?

4. When does an individual human being's life begin? Is this an empirical or normative question? Where do the cases derive their answers to this question, and how do they deal with uncertainty about the answer?

5. To what extent is a fetus treated as a human being with rights under each of the constitutions and treaties in these decisions?

6. How do the U.S. Supreme Court and the German Federal Constitutional Court deal with the diversity of moral views about abortion within their respective societies? How do the international tribunals deal with the diversity of moral and legal views among their member states?

7. To what extent have or should have the regional tribunals' decisions been guided by (a) the text of the human rights treaties, (b) the drafting history of the treaties, (c) the status quo in national laws at the time of the adoption of the treaties, (d) the status quo in national laws at the time of decision?

8.   What results would each of the analyses of abortion rights imply for an analysis of legislation prohibiting contraception? For legislation imposing mandatory sterilization?

9.   Further Reading. See, e.g., Mary Ann Glendon, Abortion and Divorce in Western Law (1987); United Nations Dept. for Economic and Social Information and Policy Analysis, Abortion Policies: A Global Review (1992–95); Abortion and the Protection of the Human Fetus: Legal Problems in a Cross–Cultural Perspective (George Cole & Stanislaw Frankowski eds. 1987); International Handbook on Abortion (Paul Sachdev ed. 1988).

2.   SEXUAL AUTONOMY

Although European societies remain sharply divided on the morality of abortion, most have achieved a broader political consensus that the criminal law should not be used to enforce traditional moral objections to physical intimacies between consenting adults of the same sex. That consensus has been reflected in the interpretation by the European Court of Human Rights of the right to respect for private life as protecting such intimacies, and that interpretation has in turn influenced the Human Rights Committee's understanding of the Covenant on Civil and Political Rights. In the United States, however, the Supreme Court has refused to construe the right to privacy as encompassing sexual activities between persons of the same sex. This sub-section contrasts the U.S. and international approaches, which may come into conflict now that the U.S. is a party to the Covenant. It then concludes with a brief discussion of other dimensions of the international protection of private life, family life, home and correspondence.

Dudgeon v. United Kingdom

European Court of Human Rights, 1981.
45 Eur. Ct. H.R. (ser. A), 4 E.H.R.R. 149.

[Jeffrey Dudgeon, a 35–year-old shipping clerk resident in Belfast, Northern Ireland, contended that his rights under Article 8 of the European Convention were violated by the existence in Northern Ireland of laws which had the effect of making certain sexual acts between consenting adult males criminal offences. Article 8 provides:

1.   Everyone has the right to respect for private and family life, his home and his correspondence.

2.   There shall be no interference by a public authority with the exercise of this right except such as is in accordance with the law and is necessary in a democratic society in the interests of national security, public safety or the economic well-being of the country, for the prevention of disorder or crime, for the protection of health or morals, or for the protection of the rights and freedoms of others.]

39.   Although it is not homosexuality itself which is prohibited but the particular acts of gross indecency between males and buggery, there can be

no doubt but that male homosexual practices whose prohibition is the subject of the applicant's complaints come within the scope of the offences punishable under the impugned legislation; it is on that basis that the case has been argued by the Government, the applicant and the Commission. Furthermore, the offences are committed whether the act takes place in public or in private, whatever the age or relationship of the participants involved, and whether or not the participants are consenting. It is evident from Mr. Dudgeon's submissions, however, that his complaint was in essence directed against the fact that homosexual acts which he might commit in private with other males capable of valid consent are criminal offences under the law of Northern Ireland.

The existence of an interference with an Article 8 right

41. [T]he maintenance in force of the impugned legislation constitutes a continuing interference with the applicant's right to respect for his private life (which includes his sexual life) within the meaning of Article 8(1). In the personal circumstances of the applicant, the very existence of this legislation continuously and directly affects his private life: either he respects the law and refrains from engaging (even in private with consenting male partners) in prohibited sexual acts to which he is disposed by reason of his homosexual tendencies, or he commits such acts and thereby becomes liable to criminal prosecution.

It cannot be said that the law in question is a dead letter in this sphere. It was, and still is, applied so as to prosecute persons with regard to private consensual homosexual acts involving males under 21 years of age. Although no proceedings seem to have been brought in recent years with regard to such acts involving only males over 21 years of age, apart from mental patients, there is no stated policy on the part of the authorities not to enforce the law in this respect. Furthermore, apart from prosecution by the Director of Public Prosecutions, there always remains the possibility of a private prosecution.

Moreover, the police investigation in January 1976 was, in relation to the legislation in question, a specific measure of implementation (albeit short of actual prosecution) which directly affected the applicant in the enjoyment of his right to respect for his private life. As such, it showed that the threat hanging over him was real.

The existence of a justification for the interference found by the Court

42. In the Government's submission, the law in Northern Ireland relating to homosexual acts does not give rise to a breach of Article 8, in that it is justified by the terms of Article 8(2). This contention was disputed by both the applicant and the Commission.

43. An interference with the exercise of an Article 8 right will not be compatible with Article 8(2) unless it is "in accordance with the law", has an aim or aims that is or are legitimate under that paragraph and is "necessary in a democratic society" for the aforesaid aim or aims.

44. It has not been contested that the first of these three conditions was met. [T]he interference is plainly "in accordance with the law" since it

results from the existence of certain provisions in the 1861 and 1885 Acts and the common law.

45. It next falls to be determined whether the interference is aimed at "the protection of ... morals" or "the protection of the rights and freedoms of others", the two purposes relied on by the Government.

46. The 1861 and 1885 Acts were passed in order to enforce the then prevailing conception of sexual morality. Originally they applied to England and Wales, to all Ireland, then unpartitioned, and also, in the case of the 1885 Act, to Scotland. In recent years the scope of the legislation has been restricted in England and Wales (with the 1967 Act) and subsequently in Scotland (with the 1980 Act): with certain exceptions it is no longer a criminal offence for two consenting males over 21 years of age to commit homosexual acts in private. In Northern Ireland, in contrast, the law has remained unchanged. The decision announced in July 1979 to take no further action in relation to the proposal to amend the existing law was, the Court accepts, prompted by what the United Kingdom Government judged to be the strength of feeling in Northern Ireland against the proposed change, and in particular the strength of the view that it would be seriously damaging to the moral fabric of Northern Irish society. This being so, the general aim pursued by the legislation remains the protection of morals in the sense of moral standards obtaining in Northern Ireland.

47. Both the Commission and the Government took the view that, in so far as the legislation seeks to safeguard young persons from undesirable and harmful pressures and attentions, it is also aimed at "the protection of the rights and freedoms of others". The Court recognises that one of the purposes of the legislation is to afford safeguards for vulnerable members of society, such as the young, against the consequences of homosexual practices. However, it is somewhat artificial in this context to draw a rigid distinction between "protection of the rights and freedoms of others" and "protection of ... morals". The latter may imply safeguarding the moral ethos or moral standards of a society as a whole, but may also, as the Government pointed out, cover protection of the moral interests and welfare of a particular section of society, for example schoolchildren. (See Handyside v United Kingdom [24 Eur. Ct. H.R. (ser. A) (1976)], in relation to Art 10(2).) Thus, "protection of the rights and freedoms of others" when meaning the safeguarding of the moral interests and welfare of certain individuals or classes of individuals who are in need of special protection for reasons such as lack of maturity, mental disability or state of dependence, amounts to one aspect of "protection of ... morals". The Court will therefore take account of the two aims on this basis.

48. [T]he cardinal issue arising under Article 8 in this case is to what extent, if at all, the maintenance in force of the legislation is "necessary in a democratic society" for these aims.

49. There can be no denial that some degree of regulation of male homosexual conduct, as indeed of other forms of sexual conduct, by means of the criminal law can be justified as "necessary in a democratic society". The overall function served by the criminal law in this field is, in the words

of the Wolfenden report,* "to preserve public order and decency [and] to protect the citizen from what is offensive or injurious". Furthermore, this necessity for some degree of control may even extend to consensual acts committed in private, notably where there is call:

> to provide sufficient safeguards against exploitation and corruption of others, particularly those who are specially vulnerable because they are young, weak in body or mind, inexperienced, or in a state of special physical, official or economic dependence.

In practice there is legislation on the matter in all the member States of the Council of Europe, but what distinguishes the law in Northern Ireland from that existing in the great majority of the member-States is that it prohibits generally gross indecency between males and buggery whatever the circumstances. It being accepted that some form of legislation is "necessary" to protect particular sections of society as well as the moral ethos of society as a whole, the question in the present case is whether the contested provisions of the law of Northern Ireland and their enforcement remain within the bounds of what, in a democratic society, may be regarded as necessary in order to accomplish those aims.

50.   A number of principles relevant to the assessment of the "necessity", in a democratic society, of a measure taken in furtherance of an aim that is legitimate under the Convention have been stated by the Court in previous judgments.

51.   First, "necessary" in this context does not have the flexibility of such expressions as "useful", "reasonable", or "desirable", but implies the existence of a "pressing social need" for the interference in question. (See Handyside v United Kingdom [supra].)

52.   In the second place, it is for the national authorities to make the initial assessment of the pressing social need in each case; accordingly, a margin of appreciation is left to them. (See Handyside v United Kingdom [supra].) However, their decision remains subject to review by the Court. [Id.]

As was illustrated by The Sunday Times judgment ([3 Eur. Ct. H.R. (ser. A) (1979)]), the scope of the margin of appreciation is not identical in respect of each of the aims justifying restrictions on a right. The Government inferred from the Handyside judgment that the margin of appreciation will be more extensive where the protection of morals is in issue. It is an indisputable fact, as the Court stated in the Handyside judgment, that: "the view taken . . . of the requirements of morals varies from time to time and from place to place, especially in our era," and that

> By reason of their direct and continuous contact with the vital forces of their countries, State authorities are in principle in a better position

---

* [The Wolfenden Report, more formally, *Departmental Committee on Homosexual Offences and Prostitution, Report to the Secretary of State for the Home Department* (1957), recommended decriminalization of homosexual behavior between consenting adults in private. The report triggered the famous debate between Lord Devlin and H.L.A. Hart on the purposes of the criminal law, mentioned in Judge Walsh's dissent infra.—Editors' Note.]

than the international judge to give an opinion on the exact content of those requirements.

However, not only the nature of the aim of the restriction but also the nature of the activities involved will affect the scope of the margin of appreciation. The present case concerns a most intimate aspect of private life. Accordingly, there must exist particularly serious reasons before interferences on the part of the public authorities can be legitimate for the purposes of Article 8(2).

53. Finally, in Article 8 as in several other Articles of the Convention, the notion of "necessity" is linked to that of a "democratic society". According to the Court's case-law, a restriction on a Convention right cannot be regarded as "necessary in a democratic society" (two hallmarks of which are tolerance and broadmindedness) unless, amongst other things, it is proportionate to the legitimate aim pursued. (See Handyside v. United Kingdom [supra]; and Young, James and Webster v United Kingdom [44 Eur. Ct. H.R. (ser. A) (1981).]

54. The Court's task is to determine on the basis of the aforestated principles whether the reasons purporting to justify the "interference" in question are relevant and sufficient under Article 8(2). The Court is not concerned with making any value-judgment as to the morality of homosexual relations between adult males.

55. It is convenient to begin by examining the reasons set out by the Government in their arguments contesting the Commission's conclusion that the penal prohibition of private consensual homosexual acts involving male persons over 21 years of age is not justified under Article 8(2).

56. In the first place, the Government drew attention to what they described as profound differences of attitude and public opinion between Northern Ireland and Great Britain in relation to questions of morality. Northern Ireland society was said to be more conservative and to place greater emphasis on religious factors, as was illustrated by more restrictive laws even in the field of heterosexual conduct.

Although the applicant qualified this account of the facts as grossly exaggerated, the Court acknowledges that such differences do exist to a certain extent and are a relevant factor....

The fact that similar measures are not considered necessary in other parts of the United Kingdom or in other member-States of the Council of Europe does not mean that they cannot be necessary in Northern Ireland. Where there are disparate cultural communities residing within the same State, it may well be that different requirements, both moral and social, will face the governing authorities.

57. As the Government correctly submitted, it follows that the moral climate in Northern Ireland in sexual matters, in particular as evidenced by the opposition to the proposed legislative change, is one of the matters which the national authorities may legitimately take into account in exercising their discretion....

58.   The Government argued that this conclusion is further strengthened by the special constitutional circumstances of Northern Ireland....

In the present circumstances of direct rule, the need for caution and
for sensitivity to public opinion in Northern Ireland is evident. However,
the Court does not consider it conclusive....

59.   Without any doubt, faced with these various considerations, the
United Kingdom Government acted carefully and in good faith.... Nevertheless, this cannot of itself be decisive as to the necessity for the interference with the applicant's private life resulting from the measures being
challenged. Notwithstanding the margin of appreciation left to the national
authorities, it is for the Court to make the final evaluation whether the
reasons it has found to be relevant were sufficient in the circumstances, in
particular whether the interference complained of was proportionate to the
social need claimed for it.

60.   The Convention right affected by the impugned legislation protects an essentially private manifestation of the human personality.

As compared with the era when that legislation was enacted, there is
now a better understanding, and in consequence an increased tolerance, of
homosexual behaviour to the extent that in the great majority of the
member-States of the Council of Europe it is no longer considered to be
necessary or appropriate to treat homosexual practices of the kind now in
question as in themselves a matter to which the sanctions of the criminal
law should be applied; the Court cannot overlook the marked changes
which have occurred in this regard in the domestic law of the member-
States. In Northern Ireland itself, the authorities have refrained in recent
years from enforcing the law in respect of private homosexual acts between
consenting males over the age of 21 years capable of valid consent. No
evidence has been adduced to show that this has been injurious to moral
standards in Northern Ireland or that there has been any public demand
for stricter enforcement of the law.

It cannot be maintained in these circumstances that there is a "pressing social need" to make such acts criminal offences, there being no
sufficient justification provided by the risk of harm to vulnerable sections
of society requiring protection or by the effects on the public. On the issue
of proportionality, the Court considers that such justifications as there are
for retaining the law in force unamended are outweighed by the detrimental effects which the very existence of the legislative provisions in question
can have on the life of a person of homosexual orientation like the
applicant. Although members of the public who regard homosexuality as
immoral may be shocked, offended or disturbed by the commission by
others of private homosexual acts, this cannot on its own warrant the
application of penal sanctions when it is consenting adults alone who are
involved.

61.   Accordingly, the reasons given by the Government, although
relevant, are not sufficient to justify the maintenance in force of the
impugned legislation in so far as it has the general effect of criminalising

private homosexual relations between adult males capable of valid consent. In particular, the moral attitudes towards male homosexuality in Northern Ireland and the concern that any relaxation in the law would tend to erode existing moral standards cannot, without more, warrant interfering with the applicant's private life to such an extent. "Decriminalisation" does not imply approval and a fear that some sectors of the population might draw misguided conclusions in this respect from reform of the legislation does not afford a good ground for maintaining it in force with all its unjustifiable features.

To sum up, the restriction imposed on Mr. Dudgeon under Northern Ireland law, by reason of its breadth and absolute character, is, quite apart from the severity of the possible penalties provided for, disproportionate to the aims sought to be achieved.

62. In the opinion of the Commission, the interference complained of by the applicant can, in so far as he is prevented from having sexual relations with young males under 21 years of age, be justified as necessary for the protection of the rights of others. This conclusion was accepted and adopted by the Government, but disputed by the applicant who submitted that the age of consent for male homosexual relations should be the same as that for heterosexual and female homosexual relations, that is, 17 years under current Northern Ireland law.

The Court has already acknowledged the legitimate necessity in a democratic society for some degree of control over homosexual conduct notably in order to provide safeguards against the exploitation and corruption of those who are specially vulnerable by reason, for example, of their youth. However, it falls in the first instance to the national authorities to decide on the appropriate safeguards of this kind required for the defence of morals in their society and, in particular, to fix the age under which young people should have the protection of the criminal law.

For these reasons, THE COURT holds ... by 15 votes to four, that there is a breach of Article 8 of the Convention....

■ Dissenting Opinion of JUDGE ZEKIA.

. . .

After taking all relevant facts and submissions made in this case into consideration, I have arrived at a conclusion opposite to the one of the majority....

1. Christian and Moslem religions are all united in the condemnation of homosexual relations and of sodomy. Moral conceptions to a great degree are rooted in religious beliefs.

2. All civilised countries until recent years penalised sodomy and buggery and similar unnatural practices.

In Cyprus, criminal provisions similar to those embodied in the Acts of 1861 and 1885 in the North of Ireland are in force. ...

While on the one hand I may be thought biased for being a Cypriot judge, on the other hand I may be considered to be in a better position in forecasting the public outcry and the turmoil which would ensue if such laws are repealed or amended in favour of homosexuals either in Cyprus or in Northern Ireland. Both countries are religious-minded and adhere to moral standards which are centuries old.

3.   While considering the respect due to the private life of a homosexual under Article 8(1), we must not forget and must bear in mind that respect is also due to the people holding the opposite view, especially in a country populated by a great majority of such people who are completely against unnatural immoral practices. Surely the majority in a democratic society are also entitled under Articles 8, 9 and 10 of the Convention and Article 2 of Protocol No. 1 to respect for their religious and moral beliefs and entitled to teach and bring up their children consistently with their own religious and philosophical convictions.

. . .

4.   If a homosexual claims to be a sufferer because of physiological, psychological or other reasons and the law ignores such circumstances, his case might then be one of exculpation or mitigation if his tendencies are curable or incurable. Neither of these arguments has been put forward or contested. . . .

. . .

Much has been said about the scarcity of cases coming to court under the prohibitive provisions of the Acts we are discussion. It was contended that this fact indicates the indifference of the people in Northern Ireland to the non-prosecution of homosexual offences committed. The same fact, however, might indicate the rarity of homosexual offences having been perpetrated and also the unnecessariness and the inexpediency of changing the law.

. . .

■ Partially Dissenting Opinion of JUDGE WALSH . . . .

8.   . . . This [case] raises the age-old philosophical question of what is the purpose of law. Is there a realm of morality which is not the law's business or is the law properly concerned with moral principles? In the context of United Kingdom jurisprudence and the true philosophy of law this debate in modern times has been between Professor H.L.A. Hart and Lord Devlin. Generally speaking the former accepts the philosophy propounded in the last century by John Stuart Mill while the latter contends that morality is properly the concern of the law. Lord Devlin argues that as the law exists for the protection of society it must not only protect the individual from injury, corruption and exploitation but it—

> must protect also the institutions and the community of ideas, political and moral, without which people cannot live together. Society cannot ignore the morality of the individual any more than it can his loyalty; it flourishes on both and without either it dies.

He claims that the criminal law of England not only "has from the very first concerned itself with moral principles but continues to concern itself with moral principles''. Among the offences which he pointed to as having been brought within the criminal law on the basis of moral principle, notwithstanding that it could be argued that they do not endanger the public, were euthanasia, the killing of another at his own request, suicide pacts, duelling, abortion, incest between brother and sister. These are acts which he viewed as ones which could be done in private and without offence to others and need not involve the corruption or exploitation of others. Yet, as he pointed out, no one has gone so far as to suggest that they should all be left outside the criminal law as matters of private morality.

11. ... [T]he Court accepts that some form of legislation is necessary to protect not only particular sections of society but also the moral ethos of society as a whole. However, experience has shown that exploitation and corruption of others is not confined to persons who are young, weak in body or mind or inexperienced or in a state of physical, moral or economic dependence.

12. The fact that a person consents to take part in the commission of homosexual acts is not proof that such person is sexually orientated by nature in that direction. A distinction must be drawn between homosexuals who are such because of some kind of innate instinct or pathological constitution judged to be incurable and those whose tendency comes from a lack of normal sexual development or from habit or from experience or from other similar causes but whose tendency is not incurable. So far as the incurable category is concerned, the activities must be regarded as abnormalities or even as handicaps and treated with the compassion and tolerance which is required to prevent those persons from being victimised in respect of tendencies over which they have no control and for which they are not personally responsible. However, other considerations are raised when these tendencies are translated into activities. The corruption for which the Court acknowledges need for control and the protection of the moral ethos of the community referred to by the Court may be closely associated with the translation of such tendencies into activities. Even assuming one of the two persons involved has the incurable tendency, the other may not. It is known that many male persons who are heterosexual or pansexual indulge in these activities not because of any incurable tendency but for sexual excitement. However, it is to be acknowledged that the case for the applicant was argued on the basis of the position of a male person who is by nature homosexually predisposed or orientated. The Court, in the absence of evidence to the contrary, has accepted this as the basis of the applicant's case and in its Judgment rules only in respect of males who are so homosexually orientated.

13. If it is accepted that the State has a valid interest in the prevention of corruption and in the preservation of the moral ethos of its society, then the State has a right to enact such laws as it may reasonably think necessary to achieve these objects. The rule of law itself depends on a moral consensus in the community and in a democracy the law cannot afford to ignore the moral consensus of the community. If the law is out of

out of touch with the moral consensus of the community, whether by being either too far below it or too far above it, the law is brought into contempt. Virtue cannot be legislated into existence but non-virtue can be if the legislation renders excessively difficult the struggle after virtue. Such a situation can have an eroding effect on the moral ethos of the community in question. The ultimate justification of law is that it serves moral ends. It is true that many forms of immorality which can have a corrupting effect are not the subject of prohibitory or penal legislation. However such omissions do not imply a denial of the possibility of corruption or of the erosion of the moral ethos of the community but acknowledge the practical impossibility of legislating effectively for every area of immorality. Where such legislation is enacted it is a reflection of the concern of the "prudent legislator".

15.   In my view the Court's reference to the fact that in most countries in the Council of Europe homosexual acts in private between adults are no longer criminal does not really advance the argument. The 21 countries making up the Council of Europe extend geographically from Turkey to Iceland and from the Mediterranean to the Arctic Circle and encompass considerable diversities of culture and moral values. The Court states that it cannot overlook the marked changes which have occurred in the laws regarding homosexual behaviour throughout the member-States. It would be unfortunate if this should lead to the erroneous inference that a Euro-norm in the law concerning homosexual practices has been or can be evolved.

19.   The law has a role in influencing moral attitudes and if the respondent Government is of the opinion that the change sought in the legislation would have a damaging effect on moral attitudes then in my view it is entitled to maintain the legislation it has. The judgment of the Court does not constitute a declaration to the effect that the particular homosexual practices which are subject to penalty by the legislation in question virtually amount to fundamental human rights. However, that will not prevent it being hailed as such by those who seek to blur the essential difference between homosexual and heterosexual activities.

22.   It is to be noted that Article 8(1) of the Convention speaks of "private and family life". If the ejusdem generis rule is to be applied, then the provision should be interpreted as relating to private life in that context as, for example, the right to raise one's children according to one's own philosophical and religious tenets and generally to pursue without interference the activities which are akin to those pursued in the privacy of family life and as such are in the course of ordinary human and fundamental rights. No such claim can be made for homosexual practices.

Notes

1. Several formal features of the Court's reasoning deserve attention. First, observe that unlike Article 3 of the European Convention, which articulates the right against torture or inhuman or degrading treatment or

punishment without mention of limitations, Article 8 identifies rights in its first paragraph and then identifies permissible limitations on the right in its second paragraph. Articles 9, 10, and 11 have a similar structure. Under Article 8(2), an interference with the rights listed in Article 8(1) is permitted if it "is in accordance with the law and is necessary in a democratic society" for one of several enumerated purposes. In analyzing the case, the Court asks first whether there is an interference with an Article 8(1) right; then whether the interference is authorized by law; then whether it pursues an enumerated aim; and finally whether it is "necessary in a democratic society" for the accomplishment of that aim. This latter criterion involves both the existence of a "pressing social need" and the requirement that the restriction be proportionate to its legitimate aim.

2. Second, note the Court's explication of the phrase "necessary *in a democratic society*" as implying tolerance and broadmindedness. Why should this phrase in Article 8 be interpreted as reflecting a substantive conception of a democratic society as characterized by tolerance and broadmindedness, rather than a purely procedural conception of a democratic society as one in which the laws implement values chosen by the majority of the community? The phrase "in a democratic society" also appears in Article 29 of the Universal Declaration and in several limitation provisions of the ICCPR; should it also be interpreted in those documents as implying tolerance and broadmindedness?

3. Third, observe the Court's emphasis on the state's "margin of appreciation" in evaluating the need for the restriction. (See the discussion of the margin of appreciation in Part III Chapter 3(B)(2)(b) supra.) To what extent does the margin of appreciation (a) give effect to the state's superior knowledge of local conditions and of its own legal system; (b) accommodate cultural diversity; (c) help the Court to avoid issuing decisions with which states will not comply?

4. The Court observes that it "cannot overlook" the changes in the law of the member states, the great majority of which no longer consider it appropriate to criminalize sexual relations between consenting adults of the same sex. Is the Court saying that the question whether a law in one member state violates the European Convention should be determined by comparing it to the laws currently prevailing in the great majority of member states? What would be the content of Convention rights under such a methodology? Are there other elements in the Court's analysis that point in a different direction?

In this respect, consider Judge Macdonald's observations:

> The recommendation that the scope of the margin of appreciation be narrowed by the recognition of "common European standards" is best understood as part of [a] pragmatic gradualist project. On this view, the gradual refining of an originally expansive margin of appreciation reflects the increasing legitimacy of the Convention organs in the European legal order. . . .

[W]hile it has the obvious attraction that it provides an easy justification for bringing wayward countries up to a supposed European minimum prevailing in most other Contracting States, it also illustrates well the dangers of selective justification which pragmatism condones. For on another occasion the Court may find itself confronted with a widely tolerated practice which is clearly in breach of the Convention's standards. If the Court were to embrace the common European standards approach, it would forfeit its aspirational role by tying itself to a crude, positivist conception of "standards." The approach advocated here, by contrast, could enable the Court instead to decide questions of appropriateness by open reference to the standards of an ideal European democratic society.

R. St. J. Macdonald, *The Margin of Appreciation*, in The European System for the Protection of Human Rights, at 123–24 (R. St. J. Macdonald, F. Matscher and H. Petzold eds. 1993).

Bowers v. Hardwick

Supreme Court of the United States, 1986.
478 U.S. 186.

■ JUSTICE WHITE delivered the opinion of the Court.

[Hardwick was arrested for violating a Georgia statute criminalizing sodomy* after police entered his home and found him in bed with another man. He brought suit to have the statute declared unconstitutional. The District Court dismissed the action for failure to state a claim, but the court of appeals reversed, finding that the statute impinged upon a fundamental right protected by the Due Process Clause of the Fourteenth Amendment. It remanded the case to give the state the opportunity to demonstrate that the prohibition was necessary for the achievement of a compelling government interest.]

This case does not require a judgment on whether laws against sodomy between consenting adults in general, or between homosexuals in particular, are wise or desirable. It raises no question about the right or propriety of state legislative decisions to repeal their laws that criminalize homosexual sodomy, or of state-court decisions invalidating those laws on state constitutional grounds. The issue presented is whether the Federal Constitution confers a fundamental right upon homosexuals to engage in sodomy and hence invalidates the laws of the many States that still make such conduct illegal and have done so for a very long time. The case also calls for some judgment about the limits of the Court's role in carrying out its constitutional mandate.

We first register our disagreement with the Court of Appeals and with respondent that the Court's prior cases have construed the Constitution to

---

* The statute defined sodomy as "perform[ing] or submit[ting] to any sexual act involving the sex organs of one person and the mouth or anus of another."

confer a right of privacy that extends to homosexual sodomy and for all intents and purposes have decided this case. . . .

. . . [W]e think it evident that none of the rights announced in those cases bears any resemblance to the claimed constitutional right of homosexuals to engage in acts of sodomy that is asserted in this case. No connection between family, marriage, or procreation on the one hand and homosexual activity on the other has been demonstrated, either by the Court of Appeals or by respondent. Moreover, any claim that these cases nevertheless stand for the proposition that any kind of private sexual conduct between consenting adults is constitutionally insulated from state proscription is unsupportable. . . .

Precedent aside, however, respondent would have us announce, as the Court of Appeals did, a fundamental right to engage in homosexual sodomy. This we are quite unwilling to do. It is true that despite the language of the Due Process Clauses of the Fifth and Fourteenth Amendments, which appears to focus only on the processes by which life, liberty, or property is taken, the cases are legion in which those Clauses have been interpreted to have substantive content, subsuming rights that to a great extent are immune from federal or state regulation or proscription. Among such cases are those recognizing rights that have little or no textual support in the constitutional language. *Meyer, Prince*, and *Pierce* fall in this category, as do the privacy cases from *Griswold* to *Carey*.

Striving to assure itself and the public that announcing rights not readily identifiable in the Constitution's text involves much more than the imposition of the Justices' own choice of values on the States and the Federal Government, the Court has sought to identify the nature of the rights qualifying for heightened judicial protection. In Palko v. Connecticut, 302 U.S. 319 (1937), it was said that this category includes those fundamental liberties that are "implicit in the concept of ordered liberty," such that "neither liberty nor justice would exist if [they] were sacrificed." A different description of fundamental liberties appeared in Moore v. East Cleveland, 431 U.S. 494, 503 (1977) (opinion of Powell, J.), where they are characterized as those liberties that are "deeply rooted in this Nation's history and tradition."

It is obvious to us that neither of these formulations would extend a fundamental right to homosexuals to engage in acts of consensual sodomy. Proscriptions against that conduct have ancient roots. Sodomy was a criminal offense at common law and was forbidden by the laws of the original thirteen States when they ratified the Bill of Rights. In 1868, when the Fourteenth Amendment was ratified, all but 5 of the 37 States in the Union had criminal sodomy laws. In fact, until 1961,[7] all 50 States outlawed sodomy, and today, 24 States and the District of Columbia continue to provide criminal penalties for sodomy performed in private and between consenting adults. Against this background, to claim that a right

---

7. In 1961, Illinois adopted the American Law Institute's Model Penal Code, which decriminalized adult, consensual, private, sexual conduct. . . .

to engage in such conduct is "deeply rooted in this Nation's history and tradition" or "implicit in the concept of ordered liberty" is, at best, facetious.

Nor are we inclined to take a more expansive view of our authority to discover new fundamental rights imbedded in the Due Process Clause. The Court is most vulnerable and comes nearest to illegitimacy when it deals with judge-made constitutional law having little or no cognizable roots in the language or design of the Constitution. That this is so was painfully demonstrated by the face-off between the Executive and the Court in the 1930's, which resulted in the repudiation of much of the substantive gloss that the Court had placed on the Due Process Clauses of the Fifth and Fourteenth Amendments. There should be, therefore, great resistance to expand the substantive reach of those Clauses, particularly if it requires redefining the category of rights deemed to be fundamental. Otherwise, the Judiciary necessarily takes to itself further authority to govern the country without express constitutional authority. The claimed right pressed on us today falls far short of overcoming this resistance.

· · ·

Even if the conduct at issue here is not a fundamental right, respondent asserts that there must be a rational basis for the law and that there is none in this case other than the presumed belief of a majority of the electorate in Georgia that homosexual sodomy is immoral and unacceptable. This is said to be an inadequate rationale to support the law. The law, however, is constantly based on notions of morality, and if all laws representing essentially moral choices are to be invalidated under the Due Process Clause, the courts will be very busy indeed. Even respondent makes no such claim, but insists that majority sentiments about the morality of homosexuality should be declared inadequate. We do not agree, and are unpersuaded that the sodomy laws of some 25 States should be invalidated on this basis.

. . . [R]eversed.

■ Chief Justice Burger, concurring.

· · ·

As the Court notes, the proscriptions against sodomy have very "ancient roots." Decisions of individuals relating to homosexual conduct have been subject to state intervention throughout the history of Western civilization. Condemnation of those practices is firmly rooted in Judeo–Christian moral and ethical standards. . . . To hold that the act of homosexual sodomy is somehow protected as a fundamental right would be to cast aside millennia of moral teaching. . . .

■ Justice Powell, concurring.

I join the opinion of the Court. I agree with the Court that there is no fundamental right—i.e., no substantive right under the Due Process Clause—such as that claimed by respondent Hardwick, and found to exist by the Court of Appeals. This is not to suggest, however, that respondent may not be protected by the Eighth Amendment of the Constitution. The Georgia statute at issue in this case authorizes a court to imprison a person for up to 20 years for a single private, consensual act of sodomy. In my view, a prison sentence for such conduct—certainly a sentence of long duration—would create a serious Eighth Amendment issue. . . .

■ JUSTICE BLACKMUN, with whom JUSTICE BRENNAN, JUSTICE MARSHALL, and JUSTICE STEVENS join, dissenting.

. . .

The Court concludes today that none of our prior cases dealing with various decisions that individuals are entitled to make free of governmental interference "bears any resemblance to the claimed constitutional right of homosexuals to engage in acts of sodomy that is asserted in this case." While it is true that these cases may be characterized by their connection to protection of the family, the Court's conclusion that they extend no further than this boundary ignores the warning in Moore v. East Cleveland, 431 U.S. 494, 501 (1977) (plurality opinion), against "clos[ing] our eyes to the basic reasons why certain rights associated with the family have been accorded shelter under the Fourteenth Amendment's Due Process Clause." We protect those rights not because they contribute, in some direct and material way, to the general public welfare, but because they form so central a part of an individual's life. "[T]he concept of privacy embodies the 'moral fact that a person belongs to himself and not others nor to society as a whole.' " . . . .

Only the most willful blindness could obscure the fact that sexual intimacy is "a sensitive, key relationship of human existence, central to family life, community welfare, and the development of human personality." The fact that individuals define themselves in a significant way through their intimate sexual relationships with others suggests, in a Nation as diverse as ours, that there may be many "right" ways of conducting those relationships, and that much of the richness of a relationship will come from the freedom an individual has to choose the form and nature of these intensely personal bonds. . . .

. . .

The Court's failure to comprehend the magnitude of the liberty interests at stake in this case leads it to slight the question whether petitioner, on behalf of the State, has justified Georgia's infringement on these interests. I believe that neither of the two general justifications for [the statute] that petitioner has advanced warrants dismissing respondent's challenge for failure to state a claim.

First, petitioner asserts that the acts made criminal by the statute may have serious adverse consequences for "the general public health and welfare," such as spreading communicable diseases or fostering other criminal activity. Inasmuch as this case was dismissed by the District Court on the pleadings, it is not surprising that the record before us is barren of any evidence to support petitioner's claim. . . .

The core of petitioner's defense of [the statute], however, is that respondent and others who engage in the conduct prohibited by [the statute] interfere with Georgia's exercise of the " 'right of the Nation and of the States to maintain a decent society,' " Essentially, petitioner argues, and the Court agrees, that the fact that the acts described in [the statute] "for hundreds of years, if not thousands, have been uniformly condemned as immoral" is a sufficient reason to permit a State to ban them today.

. . .

The assertion that "traditional Judeo–Christian values proscribe" the conduct involved cannot provide an adequate justification for [the statute]. That certain, but by no means all, religious groups condemn the behavior at issue gives the State no license to impose their judgments on the entire citizenry. The legitimacy of secular legislation depends instead on whether the State can advance some justification for its law beyond its conformity to religious doctrine. . . .

Nor can [the statute] be justified as a "morally neutral" exercise of Georgia's power to "protect the public environment." Certainly, some private behavior can affect the fabric of society as a whole. Reasonable people may differ about whether particular sexual acts are moral or immoral, but "we have ample evidence for believing that people will not abandon morality, will not think any better of murder, cruelty and dishonesty, merely because some private sexual practice which they abominate is not punished by the law." H.L.A. Hart, Immorality and Treason, reprinted in The Law as Literature 220, 225 (L. Blom–Cooper ed. 1961). Petitioner and the Court fail to see the difference between laws that protect public sensibilities and those that enforce private morality. Statutes banning public sexual activity are entirely consistent with protecting the individual's liberty interest in decisions concerning sexual relations: the same recognition that those decisions are intensely private which justifies protecting them from governmental interference can justify protecting individuals from unwilling exposure to the sexual activities of others. But the mere fact that intimate behavior may be punished when it takes place in public cannot dictate how States can regulate intimate behavior that occurs in intimate places.

This case involves no real interference with the rights of others, for the mere knowledge that other individuals do not adhere to one's value system cannot be a legally cognizable interest, let alone an interest that can justify invading the houses, hearts, and minds of citizens who choose to live their lives differently. . . .

[Dissenting opinion of Justice Stevens omitted.]

Note: Developments Since Bowers v. Hardwick

1. Although *Bowers v. Hardwick* denies the existence of a fundamental privacy right to engage in "homosexual conduct," other litigation has continued to challenge statutes and policies discriminating against gays and lesbians on the basis of the Equal Protection Clause of the Fourteenth

Amendment and its federal equivalent. One such case reached the Supreme Court, *Romer v. Evans*, 517 U.S. 620 (1996). In that case, Colorado voters had adopted by referendum an amendment to the state constitution, prohibiting both state and local governments in Colorado from adopting laws or policies protecting any person against discrimination on grounds of "homosexual, lesbian or bisexual orientation, conduct, practices or relationships." Justice Kennedy's majority opinion found that the amendment effected a sweeping and comprehensive change in the status of gays and lesbians, and inflicted upon them "immediate, continuing, and real injuries that outrun and belie any legitimate justification that may be claimed for it." It concluded that the amendment "classifies homosexuals not to further a proper legislative end but to make them unequal to everyone else." As such, it violated the Equal Protection Clause. The majority opinion did not mention *Bowers v. Hardwick*.

Justice Scalia filed a dissent, joined by Chief Justice Rehnquist and Justice Thomas. He maintained that it followed from *Bowers v. Hardwick* that if a state could criminalize sexual conduct between people of the same sex, it could also adopt measures that disfavored such conduct, and could "deny special favor and protection to those with a self-avowed tendency or desire to engage in the conduct."

Commentators have offered a variety of interpretations of *Romer*. Some construe it as implicitly discarding the Court's prior assumption that the state has a legitimate interest in enforcing majority views on the morality of homosexuality. Others see *Romer* as the first step toward a recognition of sexual orientation as a suspect classification. Still others regard *Romer* as depending crucially on the vast scope of the discrimination imposed by the amendment. See, e.g., Daniel Farber & Suzanna Sherry, *The Pariah Principle*, 13 Const. Comment. 257 (1996); Thomas C. Grey, *Bowers v. Hardwick Diminished*, 68 U. Colo. L. Rev. 373 (1997); Roderick M. Hills, Jr., *Is Amendment 2 Really a Bill of Attainder?*, 95 Mich. L. Rev. 236 (1996); Andrew Koppelman, *Romer v. Evans and Invidious Intent*, 6 Wm. & Mary Bill of Rights J. 89 (1997); Cass R. Sunstein, *Foreword: Leaving Things Undecided*, 110 Harv. L. Rev. 4, 53–71 (1996).

2.   Subsequent to *Bowers v. Hardwick*, some state courts have found that prohibition of private consensual sexual conduct between adults of the same sex violates express or implied constitutional rights to privacy under their state constitutions. See, e.g., *Gryczan v. State*, 942 P.2d 112 (Mont. 1997) (express constitutional right to privacy); *Campbell v. Sundquist*, 926 S.W.2d 250 (Tenn.Ct.App.) (implied constitutional right to privacy), appeal denied (1996); *Commonwealth v. Wasson*, 842 S.W.2d 487 (Ky.1992) (implied right to privacy and equal protection).

Notes

1.   In *Dudgeon*, the Judges of the European Court agreed that Dudgeon's conduct was included within the concept of private life under Article 8(1), but disagreed over the justifiability of the state's interference with that

conduct. In *Bowers v. Hardwick*, the Justices of the Supreme Court were divided over whether Hardwick's conduct implicated a constitutionally recognized liberty protected by anything more stringent than the rational basis test. Why did the Supreme Court majority reject the dissent's interpretation of the right to privacy? Was the dissent's interpretation in *Bowers v. Hardwick* any less persuasive than the majority's interpretation in *Roe v. Wade*, supra p. 923?

2. How important to the decision in *Bowers v. Hardwick* is the fact that the right to privacy has been implied under the due process clause? Is the Supreme Court's legitimacy more greatly at risk in substantive due process cases than in equal protection or free speech cases or cases about federalism? Did the *Dudgeon* decision reflect similar concerns about legitimacy in applying the express right to respect for private life?

3. If the majority in *Bowers v. Hardwick* had been willing to recognize a right to privacy as broad as the one favored by the dissent, would it inevitably have followed that Hardwick had a right not to be prosecuted for his conduct? Or could the majority have found the interference with this right to be justified, as the dissenting Judges in *Dudgeon* did?

4. What assumptions, if any, about human sexuality inform the various opinions in *Dudgeon* and *Bowers v. Hardwick*? The European Court states in *Dudgeon* (paragraph 60) that "there is now a better understanding, and in consequence an increased tolerance, of homosexual behaviour." Does the majority of that Court have a particular better understanding of human sexuality in mind? (For example that sexual behavior is varied and unpredictable; or that it is a matter of conscious choice; or that a fixed sexual orientation is biologically determined at birth; or that it is psychodynamically determined by early childhood experiences; or that it develops over a lifetime in response to external factors; or that no single explanation accounts for everyone?) Do the dissenters share the majority's understanding(s)? On what basis does (or can) the Court choose among rival explanations of human sexuality?

5. The *Dudgeon* Court also states that it "is not concerned with making any value-judgment as to the morality of homosexual relations between adult males." Can the Court decide the case without making any such judgment? Does the *Dudgeon* decision represent an endorsement of the positions of J.S. Mill and H.L.A. Hart on the enforcement of morality? Would such an endorsement be consistent with Article 8(2) of the European Convention? The Supreme Court majority in *Bowers v. Hardwick* rejects the dissent's invocation of Hart. Is that rejection an exceptional event in a constitutional jurisprudence that otherwise follows Mill's approach, or does U.S. constitutional doctrine permit the enforcement of morals in other contexts?

Note: Developments Since Dudgeon

1. Does the *Dudgeon* case rest on a specific conclusion about the circumstances prevailing in Northern Ireland? Might the Court conclude that a

similar prohibition was "necessary" in a different European state? In *Norris v. Ireland*, 142 Eur. Ct. H.R. (ser. A), 13 E.H.R.R. 186 (1988), the Court found that Ireland had "adduced no evidence which would point to the existence of factors justifying the retention of the impugned laws which are additional to or are of greater weight than those present in [*Dudgeon*]," and accordingly found that Ireland's prohibition of private sexual relations between consenting male adults violated Article 8. In *Modinos v. Cyprus*, 259 Eur. Ct. H.R. (ser. A), 16 E.H.R.R. 485 (1993), the government conceded that its statute was unjustified and inconsistent with the Convention. It argued only that there was no violation because, under the Constitution of Cyprus, treaties prevail over inconsistent domestic law, and there was therefore no possibility that the statute would be enforced. The Court found sufficient uncertainty about future enforcement to amount to a violation of Article 8. In March 1998, a representative of Cyprus informed the Human Rights Committee that repeal of the statute had not yet been accomplished, because the repeal bill "had been misinterpreted as promoting or legalizing certain forms of sexual activity to which public opinion and religious authorities were opposed." See Human Rights Committee, Summary Record of the 1648th Meeting, U.N. Doc. CCPR/C/SR.1648, para. 32 (1998). (Compare these developments regarding Cyprus with Judge Zekia's dissent in *Dudgeon*.)

2. While finding a violation of Article 8 in the regulation of conduct among consenting adults, the European Court of Human Rights rejected Dudgeon's complaint that the age of consent was set higher for conduct between men than for conduct between men and women. What assumptions about human psychology and sexuality underlie that decision? The European Commission on Human Rights had previously made the following observations in rejecting a challenge to German legislation criminalizing homosexual relations with men under the age of 21:

> The purpose of the German legislature ... is to prevent homosexual acts with adults having an unfortunate influence on the development of heterosexual tendencies in minors. In particular it was feared that on account of the social reprobation with which homosexuality is still frequently regarded a minor involved in homosexual relationships with an adult might in fact be cut off from society and seriously affected in his psychological development....

> [T]he action of the German legislature was clearly inspired by the need to protect the rights of children and adolescents and enable them to achieve true autonomy in sexual matters.

X v. Germany, 3 Eur. Comm'n H.R. 46, 50–51 (1975); see also *Johnson v. United Kingdom*, 47 Eur. Comm'n H.R. 72, 9 E.H.R.R. 386 (1986). In 1997, however, the Commission determined that setting the age of consent for homosexual activities at 18, when the age of consent for heterosexual activities was 16, violated Article 14 of the Convention in connection with Article 8. (Article 14 prohibits sex discrimination with regard to rights protected by the Convention.) *Sutherland v. United Kingdom*, 24 E.H.R.R. CD22 (Eur. Comm'n H.R. 1997). The Commission majority stated:

> [C]urrent medical opinion is to the effect that sexual orientation is fixed in both sexes by the age of 16 and that men aged 16–21 are not in need of special protection because of the risk of their being "recruited" into homosexuality. [T]he risk posed by predatory older men would appear to be as serious whether the victim is a man or woman and does not justify a differential age of consent. Even if, as claimed in the Parliamentary debate, there may be certain young men for whom homosexual experience after the age of 16 will have influential and potentially disturbing effects and who may require protection, the Commission is unable to accept that it is a proportionate response to the need for protection to expose to criminal sanctions not only the older man who engages in homosexual acts with a person under the age of 18 but the young man himself who is claimed to be in need of such protection.
>
> [A]s to the second ground relied on—society's claimed entitlement to indicate disapproval of homosexual conduct and its preference for a heterosexual lifestyle—the Commission cannot accept that this could in any event constitute an objective or reasonable justification for inequality of treatment under the criminal law.

Id. paras. 64–65.

Rather than defend the case in the European Court, the British government agreed to revise the law. As of July 1999, a bill lowering the age of consent to 16 had been passed by the House of Commons, but blocked temporarily by the House of Lords, and the government was expected to insist upon its enactment.

3. The European Court has not construed Article 8 as prohibiting all regulation of sexual behavior among consenting adults. In *Laskey, Jaggard and Brown v. United Kingdom*, 1997–I Eur. Ct. H.R. 120, 24 E.H.R.R. 39 (1997), the Court unanimously rejected complaints against convictions for intentional infliction of bodily harm arising from a series of consensual sado-masochistic encounters. It distinguished prior cases on the ground that the activities involved a significant degree of injury, and concluded that the government could prohibit these activities despite the consent of those injured, for the protection of health. The Court left open whether the prohibition could also have been justified on the ground of protection of morals.

4. Article 12 of the European Convention provides that "Men and women of marriageable age have the right to marry and to found a family, according to the national laws governing the exercise of this right." The majority of the Court has construed Article 12 itself as limited to "the traditional marriage between persons of opposite biological sex." *Rees v. United Kingdom*, 106 Eur. Ct. H.R. (ser. A), para. 49, 9 E.H.R.R. 56 (1986). In *Rees*, and again in *Cossey v. United Kingdom*, 184 Eur. Ct. H.R. (ser. A), 13 E.H.R.R. 622 (1990), the Court held that transsexuals who had been

surgically reassigned from one gender to another could not claim a right under Article 12 to marry persons of their former gender. *But see Cossey* at 22, 42 (dissenting opinions of Judge Martens and Judges Palm, Foighel and Pekkanen) (post-operative transsexuals should be classified under their new gender for purposes of Article 12); see also *B. v. France*, 232–C Eur. Ct. H.R. (ser. A), 16 E.H.R.R. 1 (1992) (finding that multiple consequences of France's refusal to give legal recognition to new sexual identity of transsexual amounted to violation of right to respect for private life under Article 8). Does Article 12 have any relevance to the interpretation of Article 8? The European Court has held that the concept of "family life" under Article 8 includes more than just those families founded in accordance with Article 12. See, e.g., *Marckx v. Belgium*, 31 Eur. Ct. H.R. (ser. A), 2 E.H.R.R. 330 (1979) (protecting inheritance rights of nonmarital child under Article 8).

5.   While the *Dudgeon* decision construed the protection of "private and family life" under Article 8 of the European Convention, similar questions can be asked about the scope of protection of "privacy [and] family" under Article 12 of the Universal Declaration and Article 17 of the Covenant on Civil and Political Rights, and the protection of "private life [and] family" under Article 11 of the American Convention. ICCPR Article 17(1) provides: "No one shall be subjected to arbitrary or unlawful interference with his privacy, family, home or correspondence, nor to unlawful attacks on his honour and reputation."

The Human Rights Committee has had occasion to construe Article 17 of the Covenant in relation to consensual sexual activity. *Toonen v. Australia*, U.N. Doc. CCPR/C/50/D/488/1992 (Human Rights Comm. 1994), concerned the criminal provisions in Tasmania, the only Australian state that still prohibited sexual acts between consenting male adults. The Australian government submitted Tasmania's justifications for its statutes, but expressed its own view that Article 17 had been violated. The Human Rights Committee reasoned:

> 8.2   Inasmuch as article 17 is concerned, it is undisputed that adult consensual sexual activity in private is covered by the concept of "privacy", and that Mr. Toonen is actually and currently affected by the continued existence of the Tasmanian laws. The Committee considers that Sections 122(a), (c) and 123 of the Tasmanian Criminal Code "interfere" with the author's privacy, even if these provisions have not been enforced for a decade. In this context, it notes that the policy of the Department of Public Prosecutions not to initiate criminal proceedings in respect of private homosexual conduct does not amount to a guarantee that no actions will be brought against homosexuals in the future, particularly in the light of undisputed statements of the Director of Public Prosecutions of Tasmania in 1988 and those of members of the Tasmanian Parliament. The continued existence of the challenged provisions therefore continuously and directly "interferes" with the author's privacy.

8.3 The prohibition against private homosexual behaviour is provided for by law, namely, Sections 122 and 123 of the Tasmanian Criminal Code. As to whether it may be deemed arbitrary, the Committee recalls that pursuant to its General Comment 16[32] on article 17, the "introduction of the concept of arbitrariness is intended to guarantee that even interference provided for by the law should be in accordance with the provisions, aims and objectives of the Covenant and should be, in any event, reasonable in the circumstances". The Committee interprets the requirement of reasonableness to imply that any interference with privacy must be proportional to the end sought and be necessary in the circumstances of any given case.

8.4 While the State party acknowledges that the impugned provisions constitute an arbitrary interference with Mr. Toonen's privacy, the Tasmanian authorities submit that the challenged laws are justified on public health and moral grounds, as they are intended in part to prevent the spread of HIV/AIDS in Tasmania, and because, in the absence of specific limitation clauses in article 17, moral issues must be deemed a matter for domestic decision.

8.5 As far as the public health argument of the Tasmanian authorities is concerned, the Committee notes that the criminalization of homosexual practices cannot be considered a reasonable means or proportionate measure to achieve the aim of preventing the spread of AIDS/HIV. The Australian Government observes that statutes criminalizing homosexual activity tend to impede public health programmes "by driving underground many of the people at the risk of infection". Criminalization of homosexual activity thus would appear to run counter to the implementation of effective education programmes in respect of the HIV/AIDS prevention. Secondly, the Committee notes that no link has been shown between the continued criminalization of homosexual activity and the effective control of the spread of the HIV/AIDS virus.

8.6 The Committee cannot accept either that for the purposes of article 17 of the Covenant, moral issues are exclusively a matter of domestic concern, as this would open the door to withdrawing from the Committee's scrutiny a potentially large number of statutes interfering with privacy. It further notes that with the exception of Tasmania, all laws criminalizing homosexuality have been repealed throughout Australia and that, even in Tasmania, it is apparent that there is no consensus as to whether Sections 122 and 123 should not also be repealed. Considering further that these provisions are not currently enforced, which implies that they are not deemed essential to the protection of morals in Tasmania, the Committee concludes that the provisions do not meet the "reasonableness" test in the circumstances of the case, and that they arbitrarily interfere with Mr. Toonen's right under article 17, paragraph 1.

8.7 The State party has sought the Committee's guidance as to whether sexual orientation may be considered an "other status" for the purposes of article 26. The same issue could arise under article 2, paragraph 1, of the Covenant. The Committee confines itself to noting, however, that in its view the reference to "sex" in articles 2, paragraph 1, and 26 is to be taken as including sexual orientation.

One concurring member argued that the Tasmanian law violated Article 26 of the Covenant because it discriminated on grounds of sexual orientation, and that the finding of a violation of Article 17 should be based on this discrimination rather than on the Committee's analysis.

Are the Human Rights Committee's interpretations of the Covenant in *Toonen* persuasive? (Recall that the legal effect of the Committee's views is unresolved; see Part III, Chapter 3(A)(1).) How important are the differences in phrasing between Article 17 of the Covenant and Article 8 of the European Convention? How important is the absence of a reference to "democratic society" in Article 17? After substantial controversy within Tasmania and between Tasmania and the Australian federal government, Tasmania repealed the offending legislation in 1997.

Are there any circumstances in which a country could show that a prohibition of private sexual relations between consenting adult males was reasonable and proportional to the end sought?

When the United States submitted its first report to the Human Rights Committee under Article 40 of the Covenant in 1994, the Committee's Concluding Observations contained the following paragraph:

> The Committee is concerned at the serious infringement of private life in some states which classify as a criminal offence sexual relations between adult consenting partners of the same sex carried out in private, and the consequences thereof for their enjoyment of other human rights without discrimination.

Human Rights Committee, Concluding Observations: United States of America, U.N. Doc. CCPR/C/79/Add.50; A/50/40, para. 287 (1995). It may be recalled that the United States's reservations to the Covenant do not include any provision addressed to Article 8.

The Human Rights Committee has also criticized sodomy laws and other forms of discrimination on grounds of sexual orientation in Zimbabwe. See Human Rights Committee, Summary Record of the 1651st Meeting, U.N. Doc. CCPR/C/SR.1651, paras. 41, 45 (1998); Human Rights Committee, Concluding Observations: Zimbabwe, U.N. Doc. CCPR/C/79/Add.89, para. 24 (1998). In that country, leading politicians have engaged in well-publicized condemnations of homosexuality as a European import inconsistent with traditional African values, and as a sin denounced by Christian beliefs. See, e.g., Oliver Phillips, *Zimbabwe*, in Sociological Control of Homosexuality: A Multi–Nation Comparison 43 (Donald J. West & Richard Green eds. 1997).

6.   In contrast to Zimbabwe, the Constitutional Court of South Africa held in October 1998 that the common law offense of sodomy and related statutory provisions were unconstitutional. The court invoked not only the equality guarantee of the 1996 Constitution, which provides that the state

may not "unfairly discriminate directly or indirectly against anyone" on specified grounds including "sexual orientation," but also the right to dignity and the right to privacy. See *National Coalition for Gay and Lesbian Equality v. Minister of Justice*, 1998 (12) BCLR 1517 (CC). The court observed:

> Just as apartheid legislation rendered the lives of couples of different racial groups perpetually at risk, the sodomy offence builds insecurity and vulnerability into the daily lives of gay men. There can be no doubt that the existence of a law which punishes a form of sexual expression for gay men degrades and devalues gay men in our broader society. As such it is a palpable invasion of their dignity and a breach of section 10 of the Constitution.

Id. ¶ 28. On the question whether the infringement could be justified, the court noted:

> The issues in this case touch on deep convictions and evoke strong emotions. It must not be thought that the view which holds that sexual expression should be limited to marriage between men and women with procreation as its dominant or sole purpose, is held by crude bigots only. On the contrary, it is also sincerely held, for considered and nuanced religious and other reasons, by persons who would not wish to have the physical expression of sexual orientation differing from their own proscribed by the law. It is nevertheless equally important to point out, that such views, however honestly and sincerely held, cannot influence what the Constitution dictates in regard to discrimination on grounds of sexual orientation.

Id. ¶ 38. In invalidating the criminal prohibitions, the court held that nonconsensual and inappropriately public sexual activities should be prosecuted in the future only under nondiscriminatory laws.

7.   Further Reading. In addition to the volume edited by West & Green, supra, see, e.g., William N. Eskridge, Jr. & Nan D. Hunter, Sexuality, Gender, and the Law (1997); Eric Heinze, Sexual Orientation: A Human Right (1995); William B. Rubinstein, Sexual Orientation and the Law (2d ed. 1997); Robert Wintemute, Sexual Orientation and Human Rights: The United States Constitution, the European Convention, and the Canadian Charter (1995); Homosexuality: A European Community Issue (Kees Waaldijk & Andrew Clapham, eds. 1993); The Third Pink Book: A Global View of Lesbian and Gay Liberation (Rob Tielman et al. eds. 1993).

Note: Some Additional Dimensions of Article 8

As previously mentioned, Article 8 of the European Convention guarantees to everyone "the right to respect for his private and family life, his home and his correspondence." Each of these four elements, as well as broader notions of privacy derived from their conjunction, has figured in the European Court's case law.

Under the rubric of respect for family life, the Court has considered a range of issues arising in family law, including separation, the rights of nonmarital children, and parental rights. See, e.g., *Airey v. Ireland*, 32 Eur. Ct. H.R. (ser. A), 2 E.H.R.R.305 (1979) (judicial separation); *Marckx v. Belgium*, 31 Eur. Ct. H.R. (ser. A), 2 E.H.R.R. 330 (1979) (nonmarital children); *Kroon v. Netherlands*, 297–C Eur. Ct. H.R. (ser. A), 19 E.H.R.R. 263 (1994) (relationship between biological father and child born during mother's marriage to another); *Johansen v. Norway*, 1996–III Eur. Ct. H.R. 979, 23 E.H.R.R. 33 (1996) (termination of parental rights). The Court has also deduced from these rights some limits on the state's power to deny residence permits to aliens whose close relatives reside lawfully within the state's territory, or to deport resident aliens whose family members reside lawfully in the territory. See, e.g., *Berrehab v. Netherlands*, 138 Eur. Ct. H.R. (ser. A), 11 E.H.R.R. 322 (1988); *Moustaquim v. Belgium*, 193 Eur. Ct. H.R. (ser. A), 13 E.H.R.R. 802 (1991); *Nasri v. France*, 324 Eur. Ct. H.R. (ser. A), 21 E.H.R.R. 458 (1995). Cf. *Fiallo v. Bell*, 430 U.S. 787 (1977) (applying extremely limited judicial review to immigration law provisions preventing reunification of fathers and their nonmarital children), discussed in Part II, Chapter 1(F)(2) supra.

Under the rubric of respect for the home, the Court has considered physical searches of residences that would be analyzed in the United States under Fourth Amendment doctrine. See, e.g., *Chappell v. United Kingdom*, 152–A Eur. Ct. H.R. (ser. A), 12 E.H.R.R. 1 (1989); *Funke v. France*, 256–A Eur. Ct. H.R. (ser. A), 16 E.H.R.R. 297 (1993). Searches of business offices also give rise to issues under Article 8, either through broad interpretation of the term "home" ("*domicile*" in the French version of the Convention) or under the rubric of respect for private life. See *Niemietz v. Germany*, 251–B Eur. Ct. H.R. (ser. A), 16 E.H.R.R. 97 (1992); *Miailhe v. France*, 256–C Eur. Ct. H.R. (ser. A), 16 E.H.R.R. 332 (1993).

Under the rubric of respect for correspondence, the Court has evaluated practices regarding censorship and surveillance of mail to and from prisoners. See, e.g., *Golder v. United Kingdom*, 18 Eur. Ct. H.R. (ser. A), 1 E.H.R.R. 524 (1975); *Pfeifer and Plankl v. Austria*, 227 Eur. Ct. H.R. (ser. A), 14 E.H.R.R. 692 (1992); *Schönenberger and Durmaz v. Switzerland*, 137 Eur. Ct. H.R. (ser. A), 11 E.H.R.R. 202 (1988). The protection of "correspondence" also extends to telephone calls, thus limiting the state's discretion to wiretap. See *Kruslin v. France*, 176–B Eur. Ct. H.R. (ser. A), 12 E.H.R.R. 547 (1990); *Lüdi v. Switzerland*, 238 Eur. Ct. H.R. (ser. A), 15 E.H.R.R. 173 (1992).

The Court has also found Article 8 applicable in situations involving more general interferences with privacy. For example, state interferences with an individual's choice of a name implicate Article 8. See, e.g., *Burghartz v Switzerland*, 280–B Eur. Ct. H.R. (ser. A), 18 E.H.R.R. 101 (1994) (finding violation); *Guillot v. France*, 1996–V Eur. Ct. H.R. 1593 (no violation). The adequacy of the state's remedial response to private sexual abuse implicates Article 8. See *X & Y v. Netherlands*, 91 Eur. Ct. H.R. (ser. A), 8 E.H.R.R. 235 (1985) (finding violation); *Stubbings v. United Kingdom*, 1996–IV Eur. Ct. H.R. 1487, 23 E.H.R.R. 213 (1996) (no violation). The state's maintenance of a file collecting information about an individual's private life implicates Article 8. See *Leander v. Sweden*, 116 Eur. Ct. H.R. (ser. A), 9 E.H.R.R. 433 (1987) (no violation). Under some circumstances, the state's failure to give an individual access to the file implicates Article 8. See *Gaskin v. United Kindom*, 160 Eur. Ct. H.R. (ser. A), 12 E.H.R.R. 36 (1989) (denial of access to applicant's foster care records violated Article 8). The state's disclosure of private information to third parties implicates Article 8. See *Z v. Finland*, 1997–I Eur. Ct. H.R. 323, 25 E.H.R.R. 371 (1997) (finding violation in public disclosure of wife's HIV-positive status to the public in course of criminal proceedings against her husband). The state's failure to protect nearby residents against industrial activity that endangers their health can also implicate Article 8. See *Lopez Ostra v. Spain*, 303–C Eur. Ct. H.R. (ser. A), 20 E.H.R.R. 277 (1994) (finding violation of right to respect for private and family life and home); *Guerra v. Italy*, 1998–I Eur. Ct. H.R. 210, 26 E.H.R.R. 357 (1998) (finding violation of right to respect for private and family life). On the other hand, the European Court has denied that a disabled person's claim to "access to the beach and the sea at a place distant from his normal place of residence during his holidays" was within the scope of Article 8. *Botta v. Italy*, 1998–I Eur. Ct. H.R. 412, 26 E.H.R.R. 241 (1998).

Do these interpretations suggest comparable scope for the similarly worded provisions of the Universal Declaration, the Covenant on Civil and Political Rights, and the American Declaration? Consider the following excerpts from the Human Rights Committee's General Comment on Article 17 of the Covenant.

Human Rights Committee, General Comment 16

U.N. Doc. HRI/GEN/1 at 20.

The right to respect of privacy, family, home and correspondence, and protection of honour and reputation (Article 17) (1988)

1.   Article 17 provides for the right of every person to be protected against arbitrary or unlawful interference with his privacy, family, home or correspondence as well as against unlawful attacks on his honour and reputation. In the view of the Committee this right is required to be guaranteed against all such interferences and attacks whether they emanate from State authorities or from natural or legal persons. The obligations imposed by this article require the State to adopt legislative and other measures to give effect to the prohibition against such interferences and attacks as well as to the protection of this right.

. . .

4.   The expression "arbitrary interference" is also relevant to the protection of the right provided for in article 17. In the Committee's view the expression "arbitrary interference" can also extend to interference provided for under the law. The introduction of the concept of arbitrariness is intended to guarantee that even interference provided for by law should be in accordance with the provisions, aims and objectives of the Covenant and should be, in any event, reasonable in the particular circumstances.

5. Regarding the term "family", the objectives of the Covenant require that for purposes of article 17 this term be given a broad interpretation to include all those comprising the family as understood in the society of the State party concerned. The term "home" in English, "manzel" in Arabic, "zhùzhái" in Chinese, "domicile" in French, "zhilische" in Russian and "domicilio" in Spanish, as used in article 17 of the Covenant, is to be understood to indicate the place where a person resides or carries out his usual occupation. In this connection, the Committee invites States to indicate in their reports the meaning given in their society to the terms "family" and "home".

. . .

7. As all persons live in society, the protection of privacy is necessarily relative. However, the competent public authorities should only be able to call for such information relating to an individual's private life the knowledge of which is essential in the interests of society as understood under the Covenant. Accordingly, the Committee recommends that States should indicate in their reports the laws and regulations that govern authorized interferences with private life.

8. Even with regard to interferences that conform to the Covenant, relevant legislation must specify in detail the precise circumstances in which such interferences may be permitted. A decision to make use of such authorized interference must be made only by the authority designated under the law, and on a case-by-case basis. Compliance with article 17 requires that the integrity and confidentiality of correspondence should be guaranteed de jure and de facto. Correspondence should be delivered to the addressee without interception and without being opened or otherwise read. Surveillance, whether electronic or otherwise, interceptions of telephonic, telegraphic and other forms of communication, wire-tapping and recording of conversations should be prohibited. Searches of a person's home should be restricted to a search for necessary evidence and should not be allowed to amount to harassment. So far as personal and body search is concerned, effective measures should ensure that such searches are carried out in a manner consistent with the dignity of the person who is being searched. Persons being subjected to body search by State officials, or medical personnel acting at the request of the State, should only be examined by persons of the same sex.

. . .

10. The gathering and holding of personal information on computers, data banks and other devices, whether by public authorities or private individuals or bodies, must be regulated by law. Effective measures have to be taken by States to ensure that information concerning a person's private life does not reach the hands of persons who are not authorized by law to receive, process and use it, and is never used for purposes incompatible with the Covenant. In order to have the most effective protection of his private life, every individual should have the right to ascertain in an intelligible form, whether, and if so, what personal data is stored in automatic data files, and for what purposes. Every individual should also be

able to ascertain which public authorities or private individuals or bodies control or may control their files. If such files contain incorrect personal data or have been collected or processed contrary to the provisions of the law, every individual should have the right to request rectification or elimination.

. . .

C.   FREEDOM OF EXPRESSION

U.S. readers may be surprised that freedom of expression appears so late in the Universal Declaration, and in the ICCPR and the regional conventions. U.S. lawyers are accustomed to the formal and substantive priority of the First Amendment,* and to judicial assertions of the fundamentality of freedom of speech. There are obvious historical explanations for the fact that freedom of speech textually precedes equality and freedom from involuntary servitude: the Bill of Rights was adopted at a time when the Constitution protected slavery, not universal human freedom. But Justice Cardozo offered a theoretical justification for the fundamentality of "freedom of thought, and speech" in *Palko v. Connecticut*, 302 U.S. 319, 327 (1937): "Of that freedom one may say that it is the matrix, the indispensable condition, of nearly every other form of freedom. With rare aberrations a pervasive recognition of that truth can be traced in our history, political and legal." For which other individual human rights is freedom of speech essential?

Besides making important contributions to individual self-determination, freedom of speech is also essential to democratic governance. Both U.S. law and international human rights law recognize the fundamental role of freedom of expression for public evaluation of ideas, criticism of government, and electoral competition. This recognition sometimes leads to an emphasis on protection of political speech as the core of freedom of expression.

But if free expression can support other individual rights and can mobilize political power, it can also threaten the rights and interests of others. Even in the United States, freedom of speech is not absolute, and may need to yield to compelling government interests. Still, the strong attachment to freedom of speech in the United States contrasts with other societies in which other values—e.g., human dignity, or traditional morality—receive priority. The regional and universal human rights instruments reflect a compromise among the perspectives of different societies, and offer less rigid protection for freedom of speech than U.S. law currently affords.

This section first compares the international and U.S. approaches to regulation of political speech, and then turns to the particular problems raised by the regulation of "hate speech."

---

* They may sometimes forget, however, that within the First Amendment, freedom of speech comes *after* the prohibition on establishment of religion and the right of free exercise.

1.   POLITICAL SPEECH

Governments react strongly to political movements that challenge their legitimacy and that encourage disobedience to their laws. Governments may also have difficulty distinguishing criticism from advocacy of illegal conduct and distinguishing advocacy from incitement to violence or crime. As a result, a central problem in free speech law has been the proper limits on regulation of the politically motivated advocacy of illegal conduct. Given that the government can punish actual violations of law, at what stage (if any) in the discussion, advocacy, or planning of resistance to its laws should the government be permitted to intervene with criminal sanctions?

This sub-section begins by contrasting the approaches of the European Court of Human Rights and the United States Supreme Court to the (alleged) advocacy of political violence. The U.S. approach itself has varied over the course of the Twentieth Century, and therefore the section illustrates both the weaker protection in the early Cold War years (*Dennis v. United States*) and the stronger protection adopted later (*Brandenburg v. Ohio*). The section then turns to a different form of regulation of political speech, laws protecting the "honor" of government institutions against verbal attack.

Zana v. Turkey

European Court of Human Rights, 1997.
1997–VII Eur. Ct. H.R. 2533.

AS TO THE FACTS

9.   Mr. Mehdi Zana, a Turkish citizen born in 1940, is a former mayor of Diyarbakir, where he currently lives.

10.   Since approximately 1985 serious disturbances have raged in south-east Turkey between the security forces and members of the PKK (Workers' Party of Kurdistan). According to the Government, the conflict has so far claimed the lives of 4,036 civilians and 3,884 members of the security forces.

11.   At the time of the Court's consideration of the case, ten of the eleven provinces of south-east Turkey had since 1987 been subjected to emergency rule.

12.   In August 1987, while serving several sentences in Diyarbakir military prison, the applicant made the following remarks in an interview with journalists:

"I support the PKK national liberation movement; on the other hand, I am not in favour of massacres. Anyone can make mistakes, and the PKK kill women and children by mistake. . . . "

That statement was published in the national daily newspaper Cumhuriyet on 30 August 1987.

26. In a judgment of 26 March 1991 the Diyarbakir National Security Court sentenced the applicant to twelve months' imprisonment for having "defended an act punishable by law as a serious crime" and "endangering public safety". In accordance with the Act of 12 April 1991, he would have to serve one-fifth of the sentence (two months and twelve days) in custody and four-fifths on parole.

31. The relevant provisions of the Criminal Code at the material time [included the following:]

Article 312

It shall be an offence, punishable by six months' to two years' imprisonment and a "heavy" (agir) fine of 6,000 to 30,000 liras publicly to praise or defend an act punishable by law as a serious crime or to urge the people to disobey the law. . . .

AS TO THE LAW

38. Mr. Zana maintained that his conviction by the Diyarbakir National Security Court on account of his statement to journalists had infringed his right to freedom of expression. He relied on Article 10 of the Convention, which provides:

"1.   Everyone has the right to freedom of expression. This right shall include freedom to hold opinions and to receive and to impart information and ideas without interference by public authority and regardless of frontiers. This Article shall not prevent States from requiring the licensing of broadcasting, television or cinema enterprises.

2.   The exercise of these freedoms, since it carries with it duties and responsibilities, may be subject to such formalities, conditions, restrictions or penalties as are prescribed by law and are necessary in a democratic society, in the interests of national security, territorial integrity or public safety, for the prevention of disorder or crime, for the protection of health or morals, for the protection of the reputation or rights of others, for preventing the disclosure of information received in confidence, or for maintaining the authority and impartiality of the judiciary."

45. [T]he applicant's conviction and sentence by the Turkish courts for remarks made to journalists indisputably amounted to an "interference" with his freedom of expression. . . .

46. The interference contravened Article 10 unless it was "prescribed by law", had one or more of the legitimate aims referred to in paragraph 2 of Article 10 and was "necessary in a democratic society" for achieving such an aim or aims.

47. The Court notes that the applicant's conviction and sentence were based on Articles 168 and 312 of the Turkish Criminal Code and accordingly considers that the impugned interference was "prescribed by law". . . .

50. The Court notes that in the interview he gave the journalists the applicant indicated that he supported "the PKK national liberation move-

ment" and, as the Commission noted, the applicant's statement coincided with the murders of civilians by PKK militants.

That being so, it considers that at a time when serious disturbances were raging in south-east Turkey such a statement—coming from a political figure well known in the region—could have an impact such as to justify the national authorities' taking a measure designed to maintain national security and public safety. The interference complained of therefore pursued legitimate aims under Article 10 § 2.

51.   The Court reiterates the fundamental principles which emerge from its judgments relating to Article 10:

(i) Freedom of expression constitutes one of the essential foundations of a democratic society and one of the basic conditions for its progress and for each individual's self-fulfilment. Subject to paragraph 2, it is applicable not only to "information" or "ideas" that are favourably received or regarded as inoffensive or as a matter of indifference, but also to those that offend, shock or disturb. Such are the demands of that pluralism, tolerance and broadmindedness without which there is no "democratic society". As set forth in Article 10, this freedom is subject to exceptions, which must, however, be construed strictly, and the need for any restrictions must be established convincingly.

(ii) The adjective "necessary", within the meaning of Article 10 § 2, implies the existence of a "pressing social need". The Contracting States have a certain margin of appreciation in assessing whether such a need exists, but it goes hand in hand with European supervision, embracing both the legislation and the decisions applying it, even those given by an independent court. The Court is therefore empowered to give the final ruling on whether a "restriction" is reconcilable with freedom of expression as protected by Article 10.

(iii) In exercising its supervisory jurisdiction, the Court must look at the impugned interference in the light of the case as a whole, including the content of the remarks held against the applicant and the context in which he made them. In particular, it must determine whether the interference in issue was "proportionate to the legitimate aims pursued" and whether the reasons adduced by the national authorities to justify it are "relevant and sufficient". In doing so, the Court has to satisfy itself that the national authorities applied standards which were in conformity with the principles embodied in Article 10 and, moreover, that they based themselves on an acceptable assessment of the relevant facts.

52.   Mr. Zana submitted that his conviction and sentence were wholly unjustified. An activist in the Kurdish cause since the 1960s, he had always spoken out against violence. In maintaining that he was supporting the PKK's armed struggle, the Government had, he argued, misinterpreted what he had said. In reality he had told the journalists that he supported the national liberation movement but was opposed to violence, and he had condemned the massacres of women and children. At all events, he was not

a member of the PKK and had been imprisoned for belonging to the "Path of Freedom" organisation, which had always advocated non-violent action.

55.   The Court considers that the principles set out in paragraph 51 above also apply to measures taken by national authorities to maintain national security and public safety as part of the fight against terrorism. In this connection, it must, with due regard to the circumstances of each case and a State's margin of appreciation, ascertain whether a fair balance has been struck between the individual's fundamental right to freedom of expression and a democratic society's legitimate right to protect itself against the activities of terrorist organisations.

56.   In the instant case the Court must consequently assess whether Mr. Zana's conviction and sentence answered a "pressing social need" and whether they were "proportionate to the legitimate aims pursued". To that end, it considers it important to analyse the content of the applicant's remarks in the light of the situation prevailing in south-east Turkey at the time.

57.   The Court takes as a basis the applicant's statement as published in the national daily newspaper Cumhuriyet on 30 August 1987, which the applicant did not contest in substance. The statement comprises two sentences. In the first of these the applicant expresses his support for the "PKK national liberation movement", while going on to say that he is not "in favour of massacres". In the second he says "Anyone can make mistakes, and the PKK kill women and children by mistake."

58.   Those words could be interpreted in several ways but, at all events, they are both contradictory and ambiguous. They are contradictory because it would seem difficult simultaneously to support the PKK, a terrorist organisation which resorts to violence to achieve its ends, and to declare oneself opposed to massacres; they are ambiguous because whilst Mr. Zana disapproves of the massacres of women and children, he at the same time describes them as "mistakes" that anybody could make.

59.   The statement cannot, however, be looked at in isolation. It had a special significance in the circumstances of the case, as the applicant must have realised. As the Court noted earlier, the interview coincided with murderous attacks carried out by the PKK on civilians in south-east Turkey, where there was extreme tension at the material time.

60.   In those circumstances the support given to the PKK—described as a "national liberation movement"—by the former mayor of Diyarbakir, the most important city in south-east Turkey, in an interview published in a major national daily newspaper, had to be regarded as likely to exacerbate an already explosive situation in that region.

61.   The Court accordingly considers that the penalty imposed on the applicant could reasonably be regarded as answering a "pressing social need" and that the reasons adduced by the national authorities are "relevant and sufficient"; at all events, the applicant served only one-fifth of his sentence in prison.

62. Having regard to all these factors and to the margin of appreciation which national authorities have in such a case, the Court considers that the interference in issue was proportionate to the legitimate aims pursued. There has consequently been no breach of Article 10 of the Convention.

■ Dissenting Opinion of JUDGE THÓR VILHJÁLMSSON

... The plain meaning of [the applicant's] words is that the applicant has the same opinion as the PKK on the question of the status of the territory where Kurds live in Turkey but he disapproves of the methods used by this organisation. I have to believe that this public statement is in breach of Turkish law. However, I do not see how these words, published in a newspaper in Istanbul, can be taken as a danger to national security or public safety or territorial integrity, let alone that they endorse criminal activities.

Accordingly, I am of the opinion that the restrictions and the penalty imposed did not pursue a legitimate aim and were not necessary in a democratic society....

■ Partly Dissenting Opinion of JUDGE VAN DIJK, Joined by JUDGES PALM, LOIZOU, MIFSUD BONNICI, JAMBREK, KURIS and LEVITS

. . .

Even if one accepts–and in view of the circumstances prevailing in south-east Turkey at the relevant time I am prepared to do so–that the maintenance of national security and public safety constituted a legitimate aim for the purpose of taking measures in respect of the statement made by the applicant, his conviction and twelve-month prison sentence for making that statement cannot, in my opinion, be held to be proportionate to those aims, considering the content of the statement. If the Government were of the opinion that the statement constituted a threat to national security and public safety, they could have taken more effective and less intrusive measures to prevent or restrict such harm. The fact that the applicant had to serve only one-fifth of his sentence in prison does not suffice to persuade me to a different view, since I would also find a sentence of two months' imprisonment disproportionate in the circumstances of the case....

... I have to grant the majority that the applicant's statement as recorded in the Cumhuriyet is partly contradictory and ambiguous. However–and this is my main point of disagreement with the majority–the Court should have taken into consideration that the Turkish court which ultimately examined the charges against the applicant and convicted and sentenced him, did not offer him any opportunity to explain what he had actually said and had meant to say and against what background the statement had to be interpreted....

... Finally, the statement having been made by "the former mayor of Diyarbakir, the most important city in south-east Turkey" (see paragraph 60 of the judgment), the Court should, in order to determine the possible effect the statement might have had in the "already explosive situation in that region", have expressly indicated what weight it attached to the fact that the interview was with a former mayor who, moreover, was in prison at the relevant time.

These considerations lead me to the conclusion that the interference with the applicant's freedom of expression was not proportionate and amounted to a breach of Article 10. I therefore do not find it possible to concur with the majority in this part of the judgment.

Dennis v. United States

Supreme Court of the United States, 1951.
341 U.S. 494.

[Plurality opinion of Chief Justice Vinson, joined by Justices Reed, Burton, and Minton.]

[Petitioners were leading officials of the Communist Party of the United States. They were indicted in July, 1948 for conspiring to violate Section 2 of the Smith Act, 54 Stat. 671 (current version at 18 U.S.C. § 2385), whose relevant provisions made it unlawful:

(1) to knowingly or willfully advocate, abet, advise, or teach the duty, necessity, desirability, or propriety of overthrowing or destroying any government in the United States by force or violence, or by the assassination of any officer of any such government;

(3) to organize or help to organize any society, group, or assembly of persons who teach, advocate, or encourage the overthrow or destruction of any government in the United States by force or violence; or to be or become a member of, or affiliate with, any such society, group, or assembly of persons, knowing the purposes thereof.]

The indictment charged the petitioners with wilfully and knowingly conspiring (1) to organize as the Communist Party of the United States of America a society, group and assembly of persons who teach and advocate the overthrow and destruction of the Government of the United States by force and violence, and (2) knowingly and wilfully to advocate and teach the duty and necessity of overthrowing and destroying the Government of the United States by force and violence. . . .

[T]he statute requires as an essential element of the crime proof of the intent of those who are charged with its violation to overthrow the Government by force and violence. . . .

The obvious purpose of the statute is to protect existing Government, not from change by peaceable, lawful and constitutional means, but from change by violence, revolution and terrorism. That it is within the power of the Congress to protect the Government of the United States from armed rebellion is a proposition which requires little discussion. Whatever theoretical merit there may be to the argument that there is a "right" to rebellion against dictatorial governments is without force where the existing structure of the government provides for peaceful and orderly change. We reject any principle of governmental helplessness in the face of preparation for revolution, which principle, carried to its logical conclusion, must lead to anarchy. No one could conceive that it is not within the power of Congress to prohibit acts intended to overthrow the Government by force and violence. The question with which we are concerned here is not whether Congress has such power, but whether the means which it has employed conflict with the First and Fifth Amendments to the Constitution.

One of the bases for the contention that the means which Congress has employed are invalid takes the form of an attack on the face of the statute on the grounds that by its terms it prohibits academic discussion of the merits of Marxism–Leninism, that it stifles ideas and is contrary to all concepts of a free speech and a free press. . . .

The very language of the Smith Act negates the interpretation which petitioners would have us impose on that Act. It is directed at advocacy, not discussion. Thus, the trial judge properly charged the jury that they could not convict if they found that petitioners did "no more than pursue peaceful studies and discussions or teaching and advocacy in the realm of ideas." . . .

But although the statute is not directed at the hypothetical cases which petitioners have conjured, its application in this case has resulted in convictions for the teaching and advocacy of the overthrow of the Government by force and violence, which, even though coupled with the intent to accomplish that overthrow, contains an element of speech. For this reason, we must pay special heed to the demands of the First Amendment marking out the boundaries of speech.

. . . [T]he basis of the First Amendment is the hypothesis that speech can rebut speech, propaganda will answer propaganda, free debate of ideas will result in the wisest governmental policies. It is for this reason that this Court has recognized the inherent value of free discourse. An analysis of the leading cases in this Court which have involved direct limitations on speech, however, will demonstrate that both the majority of the Court and the dissenters in particular cases have recognized that this is not an unlimited, unqualified right, but that the societal value of speech must, on occasion, be subordinated to other values and considerations. . . .

The rule we deduce from [prior] cases is that where an offense is specified by a statute in nonspeech or nonpress terms, a conviction relying upon speech or press as evidence of violation may be sustained only when the speech or publication created a "clear and present danger" of attempting or accomplishing the prohibited crime, e.g., interference with enlistment. . . .

In this case we are squarely presented with the application of the "clear and present danger" test, and must decide what that phrase imports. We first note that many of the cases in which this Court has reversed convictions by use of this or similar tests have been based on the fact that the interest which the State was attempting to protect was itself too insubstantial to warrant restriction of speech. . . . Overthrow of the Government by force and violence is certainly a substantial enough interest for the Government to limit speech. Indeed, this is the ultimate value of any society, for if a society cannot protect its very structure from armed internal attack, it must follow that no subordinate value can be protected. If, then, this interest may be protected, the literal problem which is presented is what has been meant by the use of the phrase "clear and present danger" of the utterances bringing about the evil within the power of Congress to punish.

Obviously, the words cannot mean that before the Government may act, it must wait until the putsch is about to be executed, the plans have been laid and the signal is awaited. If Government is aware that a group aiming at its overthrow is attempting to indoctrinate its members and to commit them to a course whereby they will strike when the leaders feel the circumstances permit, action by the Government is required. The argument that there is no need for Government to concern itself, for Government is strong, it possesses ample powers to put down a rebellion, it may defeat the revolution with ease needs no answer. For that is not the question. Certainly an attempt to overthrow the Government by force, even though doomed from the outset because of inadequate numbers or power of the revolutionists, is a sufficient evil for Congress to prevent. The damage which such attempts create both physically and politically to a nation makes it impossible to measure the validity in terms of the probability of success, or the immediacy of a successful attempt. In the instant case the trial judge charged the jury that they could not convict unless they found that petitioners intended to overthrow the Government "as speedily as circumstances would permit." This does not mean, and could not properly mean, that they would not strike until there was certainty of success. What was meant was that the revolutionists would strike when they thought the time was ripe. We must therefore reject the contention that success or probability of success is the criterion. . . .

Chief Judge Learned Hand, writing for the majority below, interpreted the phrase as follows: "In each case [courts] must ask whether the gravity of the 'evil,' discounted by its improbability, justifies such invasion of free speech as is necessary to avoid the danger." We adopt this statement of the rule. As articulated by Chief Judge Hand, it is as succinct and inclusive as any other we might devise at this time. It takes into consideration those factors which we deem relevant, and relates their significances. More we cannot expect from words.

Likewise, we are in accord with the court below, which affirmed the trial court's finding that the requisite danger existed. The mere fact that from the period 1945 to 1948 petitioners' activities did not result in an attempt to overthrow the Government by force and violence is of course no answer to the fact that there was a group that was ready to make the attempt. The formation by petitioners of such a highly organized conspiracy, with rigidly disciplined members subject to call when the leaders, these petitioners, felt that the time had come for action, coupled with the inflammable nature of world conditions, similar uprisings in other countries, and the touch-and-go nature of our relations with countries with whom petitioners were in the very least ideologically attuned, convince us that their convictions were justified on this score. And this analysis disposes of the contention that a conspiracy to advocate, as distinguished from the advocacy itself, cannot be constitutionally restrained, because it comprises only the preparation. It is the existence of the conspiracy which creates the danger. If the ingredients of the reaction are present, we cannot bind the Government to wait until the catalyst is added. . . .

[Concurring opinions of Justices Frankfurter and Jackson and dissenting opinions of Justices Black and Douglas omitted.]

Brandenburg v. Ohio

Supreme Court of the United States, 1969.
395 U.S. 444.

■ PER CURIAM.

The appellant, a leader of a Ku Klux Klan group, was convicted under the Ohio Criminal Syndicalism statute for "advocat[ing] . . . the duty, necessity, or propriety of crime, sabotage, violence, or unlawful methods of terrorism as a means of accomplishing industrial or political reform" and for "voluntarily assembl[ing] with any society, group, or assemblage of persons formed to teach or advocate the doctrines of criminal syndicalism." Ohio Rev. Code Ann. § 2923.13. He was fined $1,000 and sentenced to one to 10 years' imprisonment. The appellant challenged the constitutionality of the criminal syndicalism statute under the First and Fourteenth Amendments to the United States Constitution. . . .

The record shows that a man, identified at trial as the appellant, telephoned an announcer-reporter on the staff of a Cincinnati television station and invited him to come to a Ku Klux Klan "rally" to be held at a farm in Hamilton County. With the cooperation of the organizers, the reporter and a cameraman attended the meeting and filmed the events. Portions of the films were later broadcast on the local station and on a national network.

The prosecution's case rested on the films and on testimony identifying the appellant. . . .

One film showed 12 hooded figures, some of whom carried firearms. They were gathered around a large wooden cross, which they burned. No one was present other than the participants and the newsmen who made the film. Most of the words uttered during the scene were incomprehensible when the film was projected, but scattered phrases could be understood that were derogatory of Negroes and, in one instance, of Jews. Another scene on the same film showed the appellant, in Klan regalia, making a speech. The speech, in full, was as follows:

This is an organizers' meeting. We have had quite a few members here today which are—we have hundreds, hundreds of members throughout the State of Ohio. I can quote from a newspaper clipping from the Columbus, Ohio Dispatch, five weeks ago Sunday morning. The Klan has more members in the State of Ohio than does any other organization. We're not a revengent organization, but if our President, our Congress, our Supreme Court, continues to suppress the white, Caucasian race, it's possible that there might have to be some revengeance taken.

We are marching on Congress July the Fourth, four hundred thousand strong. From there we are dividing into two groups, one group to march on St. Augustine, Florida, the other group to march into Mississippi. Thank you.

The second film showed six hooded figures one of whom, later identified as the appellant, repeated a speech very similar to that recorded on the first film. The reference to the possibility of "revengeance" was omitted, and one sentence was added: "Personally, I believe the nigger should be returned to Africa, the Jew returned to Israel." Though some of the figures in the films carried weapons, the speaker did not.

The Ohio Criminal Syndicalism Statute was enacted in 1919. From 1917 to 1920, identical or quite similar laws were adopted by 20 States and two territories. In 1927, this Court sustained the constitutionality of California's Criminal Syndicalism Act, the text of which is quite similar to that of the laws of Ohio. Whitney v. California, 274 U.S. 357 (1927). The Court upheld the statute on the ground that, without more, "advocating" violent means to effect political and economic change involves such danger to the security of the State that the State may outlaw it. But *Whitney* has been thoroughly discredited by later decisions. See Dennis v. United States, 341 U.S. 494, 507 (1951). These later decisions have fashioned the principle that the constitutional guarantees of free speech and free press do not permit a State to forbid or proscribe advocacy of the use of force or of law violation except where such advocacy is directed to inciting or producing imminent lawless action and is likely to incite or produce such action.[2] As we said in Noto v. United States, 367 U.S. 290, 297–98 (1961), "the mere abstract teaching * * * of the moral propriety or even moral necessity for a resort to force and violence, is not the same as preparing a group for violent action and steeling it to such action." A statute which fails to draw this distinction impermissibly intrudes upon the freedoms guaranteed by the First and Fourteenth Amendments. It sweeps within its condemnation speech which our Constitution has immunized from governmental control.

Measured by this test, Ohio's Criminal Syndicalism Act cannot be sustained. The Act punishes persons who "advocate or teach the duty, necessity, or propriety" of violence "as a means of accomplishing industrial or political reform"; or who publish or circulate or display any book or

---

2. It was on the theory that the Smith Act embodied such a principle and that it had been applied only in conformity with it that this Court sustained the Act's constitutionality. That this was the basis for Dennis was emphasized in Yates v. United States, 354 U.S. 298, 320–24 (1957), in which the Court overturned convictions for advocacy of the forcible overthrow of the Government under the Smith Act, because the trial judge's instructions had allowed conviction for mere advocacy, unrelated to its tendency to produce forcible action.

paper containing such advocacy; or who "justify" the commission of violent acts "with intent to exemplify, spread or advocate the propriety of the doctrines of criminal syndicalism"; or who "voluntarily assemble" with a group formed "to teach or advocate the doctrines of criminal syndicalism." Neither the indictment nor the trial judge's instructions to the jury in any way refined the statute's bald definition of the crime in terms of mere advocacy not distinguished from incitement to imminent lawless action.

Accordingly, we are here confronted with a statute which, by its own words and as applied, purports to punish mere advocacy and to forbid, on pain of criminal punishment, assembly with others merely to advocate the described type of action.[4] Such a statute falls within the condemnation of the First and Fourteenth Amendments. The contrary teaching of Whitney v. California, supra, cannot be supported, and that decision is therefore overruled.

■ MR. JUSTICE BLACK, concurring.

I agree with the views expressed by Mr. Justice Douglas in his concurring opinion in this case that the "clear and present danger" doctrine should have no place in the interpretation of the First Amendment. I join the Court's opinion, which, as I understand it, simply cites Dennis v. United States, 341 U.S. 494 (1951), but does not indicate any agreement on the Court's part with the "clear and present danger" doctrine on which *Dennis* purported to rely.

■ MR. JUSTICE DOUGLAS, concurring.

While I join the opinion of the Court, I desire to enter a caveat.

The "clear and present danger" test was adumbrated by Mr. Justice Holmes in a case arising during World War I.... [T]he defendant was charged with attempts to cause insubordination in the military and obstruction of enlistment. The pamphlets that were distributed urged resistance to the draft, denounced conscription, and impugned the motives of those backing the war effort. The First Amendment was tendered as a defense. Mr. Justice Holmes in rejecting that defense said:

> The question in every case is whether the words used are used in such circumstances and are of such a nature as to create a clear and present danger that they will bring about the substantive evils that Congress has a right to prevent. It is a question of proximity and degree.

. . .

Whether the war power—the greatest leveler of them all—is adequate to sustain that doctrine is debatable. The dissents in [later cases] show how easily "clear and present danger" is manipulated to crush what Brandeis called "[t]he fundamental right of free men to strive for better conditions

---

4. Statutes affecting the right of assembly, like those touching on freedom of speech, must observe the established distinctions between mere advocacy and incitement to imminent lawless action, for as Chief Justice Hughes wrote in De Jonge v. Oregon, [299 U.S. 353, 364 (1937)]: "The right of peaceable assembly is a right cognate to those of free speech and free press and is equally fundamental."

through new legislation and new institutions" by argument and discourse even in time of war. Though I doubt if the "clear and present danger" test is congenial to the First Amendment in time of a declared war, I am certain it is not reconcilable with the First Amendment in days of peace....

The line between what is permissible and not subject to control and what may be made impermissible and subject to regulation is the line between ideas and overt acts.

The example usually given by those who would punish speech is the case of one who falsely shouts fire in a crowded theatre.

This is, however, a classic case where speech is brigaded with action. They are indeed inseparable and a prosecution can be launched for the overt acts actually caused. Apart from rare instances of that kind, speech is, I think, immune from prosecution. Certainly there is no constitutional line between advocacy of abstract ideas ... and advocacy of political action.... The quality of advocacy turns on the depth of the conviction; and government has no power to invade that sanctuary of belief and conscience.

Notes

1. Assume that Mr. Zana's quoted remarks should be interpreted as the majority of the European Court interprets them. Are the speech acts in the *Zana* and *Brandenburg* cases comparable? Which, if either, poses the greater danger of violence? Why would either of them deserve protection at all? Because all speech is protected? Because it makes valuable contributions to the "free debate of ideas" that produces the "wisest government policies"? Because it permits the self-expression of the speaker? Because the elements worthy of protection and those unworthy of protection are too intertwined to separate? Because government should not be trusted to judge the value of speech?

2. As the European Court explains in *Zana*, Article 10 of the European Convention provides that limitations on the right to freedom of expression must be "necessary in a democratic society" for achieving enumerated aims such as national security and public safety. What does "necessary" mean in this context? Does defining "necessary" in terms of "proportionate" lead to a standard similar to the one employed by the Supreme Court in *Dennis*?

The *Brandenburg* standard, providing that political advocacy may be criminalized only when it "is directed to inciting or producing imminent lawless action *and* is likely to incite or produce such action" (emphasis added), is understood to be the operative test in the United States today. Can the *Brandenburg* test be justified as postponing suppression of speech until speech can no longer rebut speech, and suppression is absolutely necessary? Does it protect too much speech? Too little?

3. If a "democratic society" is characterized by "pluralism, tolerance, and broadmindedness," then should that tolerance extend to those who advo-

cate change by nondemocratic methods? Should it extend to those who express approval of others who seek change by violence?*

If Article 312 of the Turkish Criminal Code could be challenged on its face, would it be consistent with Article 10 of the European Convention? Would such a statute be consistent with the First Amendment?

4. Is punishing Mr. Zana for his remarks "necessary in a democratic society" under the European Court's understanding of that standard? Is the majority saying that Mr. Zana can be punished merely for expressing dangerous ideas in an explosive situation? Note that Article 15 of the European Convention permits derogation from rights under Article 10 in certain emergencies, but that Turkey had not taken steps to invoke the derogation procedure.

Would the remarks be punishable under the *Brandenburg* test? Under the standard employed in *Dennis*? If the United States were already engaged in a military struggle against a violent separatist movement in a substantial portion of its territory, which of those tests would the Supreme Court employ?

5. The *Zana* decision should be compared with the thirteen cases concerning convictions on security grounds in Turkey decided by the European Court of Human Rights on 8 July 1999. Most of the cases involved charges of disseminating propaganda against the indivisibility of the state. The Court found violations of Article 10 in eleven cases, e.g., *Ceylan v. Turkey*, No. 23556/94 (Eur. Ct. H.R. 8 July 1999); *Arslan v. Turkey*, No. 23462/94 (Eur. Ct. H.R. 8 July 1999), and no violation in two cases, *Sürek v. Turkey (no. 1)*, No. 26682/95 (Eur. Ct. H.R. 8 July 1999), and *Sürek v. Turkey (no. 3)*, No. 24735/94 (Eur. Ct. H.R. 8 July 1999). The majority of the Court asserted that "where . . . remarks incite to violence against an individual or a public official or a sector of the population, the state authorities enjoy a wider margin of appreciation when examining the need for an interference with freedom of expression," but drew its own conclusions as to whether the remarks in each case constituted an incitement to violence. See, e.g., *Arslan v. Turkey*, paras. 47–48.

Grigoriades v. Greece

European Court of Human Rights, 1997.
1997–VII Eur. Ct. H.R. 2575, 27 E.H.R.R. 464.

. . .

10. The applicant was a conscripted probationary reserve officer holding the rank of second lieutenant.

11. In the course of his military service, the applicant claimed to have discovered a number of abuses committed against conscripts and came into

* We will return to the question of democratic toleration of nondemocratic move- ments in Chapter 2 of Part IV.

conflict with his superiors as a result. Criminal and disciplinary proceedings were instituted against him. The former ended with his acquittal. However, a disciplinary penalty was imposed on him, as a result of which he had to serve additional time in the army.

13. On 10 May 1989 the applicant sent a letter to his unit's commanding officer through a taxi driver.

[The full text of the letter is omitted here because of its length; key phrases are quoted in paragraph 19 infra.]

15. A fellow reserve officer testified . . . that the applicant gave him a copy of the letter on 10 May 1989. It has not been alleged that any further copies were circulated.

16. Taking the view that the content of the letter constituted an insult to the armed forces, the commanding officer instituted further criminal proceedings against the applicant under Article 74 of the Military Criminal Code (see paragraph 26 below).

19. At the close of the hearing the president of the court formulated a series of questions which the members of the court had to address before deciding on the applicant's guilt. The questions relating to the insult charge [included] the following:

> "(a) Did the accused commit the offence of insulting the Greek army when, on 10 May 1989, while a reserve officer on probation, he sent a two-page typed personal statement to the commanding officer of the X unit, which came to the latter's knowledge on the same day and which contained, inter alia, the following expressions contemptuous of, and disparaging, the authority of the army: '. . . The army is an apparatus opposed to man and society . . . the army remains a criminal and terrorist apparatus which, by creating an atmosphere of intimidation and reducing to tatters the spiritual welfare of the radical youth, clearly aims at transforming people to mere parts of an apparatus of domination which ruins human nature and transforms human relations from relations of friendship and love to relations of dependence, through a hierarchy of fear guided by an illiberal and oppressive set of Standing Orders (No. 20–1), records of political beliefs, etc. . . .'. In so doing, did he wilfully insult the Greek Army as a constitutionally entrenched institution of the Nation?"

. . .

20. In a judgment delivered the same day the Tribunal, by a unanimous vote, answered the first question in the affirmative. . . .

22. [T]he applicant lodged an appeal on points of law to the Court of Cassation (Arios Pagos), on the ground that Article 74 of the Military Criminal Code had not been correctly construed and applied. He argued, inter alia, that general criticism of the armed forces could not be considered an insult. He claimed in addition that the provision in question violated the Constitution. . . .

24. [T]he plenary Court of Cassation considered that Article 74 of the Code sufficiently circumscribed the elements of the offence, namely the insult and the intention of the culprit. Elaborating on this point, the court held that

> "[t]he concept of 'insult' includes every show of contempt damaging the esteem, and respect for, and the reputation of, the protected value. To qualify as an insult, such expression must convey contempt, taunt and denigration; it is not sufficient merely to call into question the protected value. This value is the armed forces and, more particularly, not the army or air force and the navy individually, but the armed forces in their entirety as an idea and an institution entrusted with defending the freedom and independence of the country and the necessary training of Greeks who are able to bear arms. . . ."

[T]he plenary Court of Cassation upheld the applicant's conviction.

26. Article 74 of the Military Criminal Code provides:

> "Insults to the flag or the armed forces
>
> A member of the armed forces who insults the flag, the armed forces or an emblem of their command shall be punished by a term of imprisonment of at least six months. If he is an officer, he shall also be stripped of his rank."

27. A corresponding civilian offence is defined by Article 181 of the Criminal Code, which provides as follows:

> "Insults to authorities and to symbols
>
> 1. Any person shall be punished with imprisonment for up to two years who:
>
> a) publicly insults the Prime Minister of the country, the Government, the Greek Parliament, the Chairman of Parliament, the leaders of the political parties recognised by the Rules of Parliament and the judicial authorities;
>
> b) insults or, as a display of hatred or contempt, damages or disfigures an emblem or symbol of State sovereignty or the President of the Republic.
>
> 2. Criticism in itself shall not constitute an insult of an authority."

AS TO THE LAW

33. It was common ground that the applicant's conviction of insulting the army, and the sentence of three months imposed on him, constituted an interference with his freedom of expression, guaranteed by paragraph 1 of Article 10. . . .

41. The Court has no doubt that an effective military defence requires the maintenance of an appropriate measure of discipline in the armed forces and accordingly finds that the interference complained of pursued at any rate the legitimate aims of protecting national security and public safety invoked by the Government.

45.   Article 10 does not stop at the gates of army barracks. It applies to military personnel as to all other persons within the jurisdiction of the Contracting States. Nevertheless, as the Court has previously indicated, it must be open to the State to impose restrictions on freedom of expression where there is a real threat to military discipline, as the proper functioning of an army is hardly imaginable without legal rules designed to prevent servicemen from undermining it (see the Vereinigung demokratischer Soldaten Österreichs and Gubi v Austria judgment [302 Eur. Ct. H.R. (ser. A) (1994)]). It is not, however, open to the national authorities to rely on such rules for the purpose of frustrating the expression of opinions, even if these are directed against the army as an institution.

46.   In the present case the applicant had a letter delivered to his commanding officer which the latter considered insulting to the armed forces.
. . .

47.   It is true that the contents of the letter included certain strong and intemperate remarks concerning the armed forces in Greece. However, the Court notes that those remarks were made in the context of a general and lengthy discourse critical of army life and the army as an institution. The letter was not published by the applicant or disseminated by him to a wider audience—apart from one other officer who apparently had been given a copy of it—and it has not been alleged that any other person had knowledge of it. Nor did it contain any insults directed against either the recipient of the letter or any other person. Against such a background the Court considers the objective impact on military discipline to have been insignificant.

48.   The Court accordingly considers that the prosecution and conviction of the applicant cannot be justified as "necessary in a democratic society" within the meaning of paragraph 2 of Article 10. There has thus been a violation of that Article.

■ Concurring Opinion of JUDGE JAMBREK

1.   The key reasons for the finding of a violation in the present case are to be found in § 47 of the judgment. There, the point was made, that critical remarks were made "in the context" (of a general and lengthy discourse critical of army life and the army as an institution), that they were not published or disseminated to a wider audience, that they were not directed against the recipient or any other person, and that therefore their impact on military discipline was insignificant. It is the aim of this opinion to amend and elaborate on these reasons in some respects.

2.   A number of remarks made by the applicant and described in the judgment as "strong", "intemperate" or "insulting" may be characterised as "opinions", i.e., subjective attitudes whereby facts and ideas are assessed, in contrast to factual claims. The protection of "opinions" by Article 10 of the Convention relates both to their substance and to their form; the fact that their wording is offensive, shocking, disturbing or polemical does not take them outside the scope of protection.

3. In the proceedings in the Greek courts the impugned remarks were characterised as "insults". The Court notes that they were not directed against the recipient commanding officer, and that he himself considered them "insulting to the armed forces". The legal concept of an "insult" protects mainly personal honour. State institutions, and the army in particular, do not possess "personal honour" to be protected as a personality right. In this sense, the legitimate aim of the interference with the applicant's freedom of expression could hardly be the "protection of the rights and freedoms of others".

4. The remarks made by the applicant come close to the concept of a "collective insult" which is not directed at any individual. In the present case the critical and even derogatory remarks were directed at the army as a national institution, respect for which is protected by Greek law. According to the Court of Cassation judgment of 22 September 1993, the protected value is not only the army as an organisation, but also the army as an idea, thus symbolically related to "the defence of the freedom and independence of the country".

5. Defamation of the military may of course have an objective impact on military discipline. For that reason the army should also be protected against "insults" which aim at degrading its public acceptance and may thereby undermine fulfilment of its functions. On the other hand, the army, like other state institutions, should not be shielded from criticism. Nor may permissible criticism on relevant issues be prevented by fear of punishment (compare the judgment of the German Constitutional Court, BVerfGE 93, 266, "Soldiers are murderers").

6. I also agree, in general terms, with the logic of the American "flag burning" cases where, inter alia, the public interest to show proper respect for the national emblem could not justify government interference with the symbolic act of casting contempt upon the American flag. This act may be considered analogous to a "collective insult", directed at highly respected national values (see the following judgments of the United States Supreme Court: Street v. New York, 394 U.S. 576 (1969), Texas v. Johnson, 491 U.S. 397 (1989), United States v. Eichman, 496 U.S. 310 (1990)). "Symbolic speech", offensive even to the supreme national values, in my view deserves, mutatis mutandis, protection under Article 10 of the Convention whenever an interference is not proportional and necessary in a democratic society.

7. I would also suggest, as an obiter dictum, that limitations of the Convention, restricting the exercise of the right to freedom of expression, should be applied—and here I quote from the opinion of Mr. Justice Jackson in Board of Education v. Barnette, 319 U.S. 624 (1943)—"with no fear that freedom to be intellectually and spiritually diverse or even contrary will disintegrate the social organisation ... Freedom to differ is not limited to things that do not matter much. That would be a mere shadow of freedom. The test of its substance is the right to differ as to things that touch the heart of the existing order" (Quoted in Street v. New York, 394 U.S. 576 (1969).)

■ Dissenting Opinion of Sir John Freeland, Joined by Judges Russo, Valticos, Loizou and Morenilla

1.   We are unable to agree that there has been a violation of Article 10 of the Convention in this case.

3.   As the Court pointed out in its Vereinigung demokratischer Soldaten Österreichs and Gubi v. Austria judgment, Article 10 applies to servicemen just as it does to other persons within the jurisdiction of the contracting States, but " 'the proper functioning of an army is hardly imaginable without legal rules designed to prevent servicemen from undermining military discipline' ".

4.   The primary purpose of military discipline is to ensure that in all circumstances, including situations of extreme stress, lawful orders from a superior in rank are unquestioningly and immediately carried out by the serviceman to whom they are addressed. The rigidity with which military discipline is enforced, and the nature of the legal rules adopted to ensure that it is not undermined, differ from time to time and from State to State. They are no doubt conditioned by a variety of factors, including national characteristics and military traditions as well as the extent of military readiness considered necessary at the relevant time by the State concerned.

7.   Whether or not the aim of the applicant throughout his letter was, as he claimed, that of "improving the living conditions of soldiers and creating the prerequisites for a more humane army", there can surely be no doubt that some of the language which he used could reasonably be regarded by the military authorities as calling into question the legitimacy of the army as an institution and hence the extent of his willingness to obey orders emanating within it—in short, as being the language of insubordination rather than that of permissible criticism. More than that, it could reasonably be regarded as being, if left unpunished, a possible encouragement to other soldiers to waver in their duty of obedience—a consideration which gained in importance because of the disclosure of a copy of the letter to a fellow officer and the risk that knowledge of its contents would go further.

8.   In the circumstances, and having regard to the margin of appreciation left to the national authorities, we consider that there was sufficient justification for treating the actions of the applicant as having a significant potential for undermining military discipline and the maintenance of order in the army.

■ Dissenting Opinion of Judge Casadevall

. . .

2.   It is true that freedom of expression constitutes one of the fundamental pillars of any democratic society and for that reason the States' margin of appreciation must be delimited as strictly as possible. However, paragraph 2 of Article 10 provides that the exercise of freedom of expression, which also carries with it duties and responsibilities, may be subject to such formalities, conditions, restrictions or penalties as are prescribed by law and are necessary for the protection of certain legal interests.

3.   Freedom of expression must include freedom to criticise, provided that the criticism is couched in terms that are not excessive and strike a fair balance with regard to the rights of others, order and morals. Certain remarks in the applicant's letter to his superior, such as "The army remains a criminal and terrorist apparatus ..." to quote but one example, clearly constitute an insult, and even an outrage, to a State institution.

4.   Since the case concerned the Greek Army, in which the applicant was a probationary reserve officer with the rank of second lieutenant, there could be no difficulty in justifying the applicant's conviction by one of the legitimate aims set out in the second paragraph of Article 10 such as "the prevention of disorder"—because it was an offence which discredited a State institution ("prevention of disorder" in the wider sense given to it by the Court in the Engel and Others v. the Netherlands judgment, [22 Eur. Ct. H.R. (ser. A) (1976)])—and by the fact that "... the functioning of an army is hardly imaginable without legal rules designed to prevent service-men from undermining military discipline, for example by writings" (ibid., § 100).

5.   Over and above the fact that the applicant was a member of the armed forces, insulting or offending State institutions (the army, judiciary, parliament or even emblems) constitutes a punishable offence under the ordinary law in most member States of the Council of Europe and the criminal law provisions concerned are, in my opinion, compatible with the Convention and in particular freedom of expression.

■ Joint dissenting opinion of JUDGES GÖLCÜKLÜ AND PETTITI

. . .

It has always been accepted that military and prison discipline come within the sphere of public order and require rules that differ from those normally applying.

Every civilised State with an army has a military code on its statute book. Such codes have never been outlawed by any international instrument. They are based on the discipline to which soldiers and particularly officers in active service or in reserve are subject for so long as they have service obligations.

In all States it is an offence to insult the army. In every European State, the State, the army and patriotic public opinion demand that respect be shown for the nation's army, at least by its officers....

It is not ... possible to compare the freedom of expression of a citizen who is no longer in the army with the more limited freedom of expression of a soldier required to respect rank while doing national service. On the other hand, historians are totally free to criticise the army. ...

Yet it is accepted in Europe that discipline is essential to maintain the authority of the army and that the army is essential to ensure that democracy is protected from subversion, in accordance with one of the major objectives of the European Convention on Human Rights. The positive results obtained by the international forces in Bosnia emphasise the need to ensure respect for their professional code of ethics, especially as they have for a number of years agreed to incorporate teaching on human rights.

Notes

1. The judges in *Grigoriades* all confirm that members of the armed forces enjoy the right to freedom of expression, but that the needs of military discipline may justify particular limitations on that right. They then disagree in their assessment of the effect of Grigoriades's letter on military discipline. United States law reflects similar general principles— that members of the armed forces enjoy First Amendment protection, but that military discipline may justify greater restrictions on their rights, both as speakers and as listeners. See, e.g., *Goldman v. Weinberger*, 475 U.S. 503, 507–08 (1986); *Brown v. Glines*, 444 U.S. 348 (1980); *Greer v. Spock*, 424 U.S. 828 (1976); *Parker v. Levy*, 417 U.S. 733 (1974).

2. The criminal statutes discussed in *Grigoriades* include not only restrictions on speech by members of the armed forces, but also restrictions on speech by civilians. Are statutes protecting the armed forces as an institution from "insult," or protecting the state, the head of state, or the flag from "insult," necessary in a democratic society? If such statutes are as common in Europe as the dissenting judges in *Grigoriades* indicate, then on what basis could the Court find them disproportionate?

3. Judge Jambrek's concurrence in *Grigoriades* invokes the recent U.S. cases invalidating convictions for burning the American flag. *See United States v. Eichman*, 496 U.S. 310 (1990); *Texas v. Johnson*, 491 U.S. 397 (1989). In both cases, the Supreme Court held by five-to-four vote that the criminal statutes sought impermissibly to suppress a form of expressive conduct because of disagreement with the message it communicated. In his comparative analysis of flag desecration cases in the United States and Germany, Professor Peter Quint emphasizes that:

> neither of the dissenters in *Johnson* and *Eichman* relies on the view that the state's interest in prohibiting flag-burning is its interest in preserving the nation. Neither Rehnquist nor Stevens argues that the flag as a symbol should remain "unimpaired" because it represents the essence of the nation and because its impairment might weaken the power of the state and lead to overthrow of the government or rejection of its underlying principles. Thus, none of the Justices defends flag desecration statutes on the ground that attacking the flag amounts to attacking and weakening the government; even in the views of the dissenters, flag desecration is not equivalent to seditious libel.

The reasons the dissenters avoided any theory of seditious libel are clear enough—they lie in the history and development of First Amendment doctrine. The initial series of First Amendment cases in the Supreme Court dealt with problems of "sedition," and the Court's doctrine in this area ultimately came to require a "clear and present danger" of violent attempts to overthrow the government before seditious speech could be penalized. Of course, nothing that approaches violent overthrow (or even attempted violent overthrow) is evident in any of the flag-burning cases.

The Supreme Court clarified and reinforced its views on seditious libel in *New York Times v. Sullivan*, decided in 1964.[*] In that case the Court engaged in a retrospective consideration of the Sedition Act of 1798, a Federalist Era statute that prohibited verbal attacks on the government or government officials. The Court concluded that the Sedition Act was unconstitutional and emphasized that the "central meaning of the first amendment" protects the ability of citizens to direct verbal attacks against government officials and the government itself. Any acknowledgment that the government has a legitimate interest in penalizing individuals who criticize its basic principles—whatever the means of expression employed—would contravene that fundamental First Amendment doctrine, at least when there is no clear and present danger of violent action.

Peter Quint, *The Comparative Law of Flag Desecration: The United States and the Federal Republic of Germany*, 15 Hastings Comp. & Int'l L. Rev. 613 (1992). In contrast, Professor Quint continues, a decision of the German Federal Constitutional Court analyzing a conviction under the flag desecration provision, Section 90a of the German Criminal Code, found that the statute rested on:

> "the right of the state to use such symbols in its self-representation" for the purpose of "appealing to the state-feeling (Staatsgefühl) of the citizens." Indeed, "as a free state, the Federal Republic is dependent on the identification of its citizens with the basic values symbolized by the flag," and the colors of the flag "stand for the free democratic basic order." From this analysis, the point of the countervailing constitutional value incorporated into section 90a becomes clear: "As the flag serves as an important means of [political] integration through the principal state goals which it incorporates," it follows that defaming the flag "can injure the authority of the state which is necessary for internal peace."

Thus, the countervailing interest recognized by the Court is the interest of the state in being free from attack on its basic principles and "authority," a freedom from a form of seditious libel that would "injure the authority of the state" and endanger "internal peace." In theory at least, this value might disfavor not only destruction or defacement of the flag but even verbal attacks on the flag. Indeed, the nature of the government's interest in punishing desecration of the flag—its interest in punishing a form of seditious libel—is underscored by the fact that the provision penalizing "defamation" of the flag is

---

* [Excerpts from the *New York Times* supra.—Editors' Note.]
decision appear in Part II, Chapter 1(E)(4)

immediately preceded by a subsection that penalizes anyone who "insults or maliciously casts into contempt the Federal Republic of Germany or one of its states or its constitutional order." ...

Quint also quotes a German academic's reminder that "[i]n light of the multifarious aggressions that increasingly force our political system onto the defensive, it should not be forgotten that the Weimar State was doomed to ruin as a result of constant attacks on its continued existence—as expressed, not least, in contempt for the symbols of that era." Id. at 633 n.113 (translating from Thomas Wurtenberger, *Kunst, Kunstfreiheit and Staatsverunglimpfung (§ 90a StGB)*, 1979 Juristische Rundschau 309, 313).

4.   Judge Jambrek's concurrence also refers to the German Federal Constitutional Court's decision concerning the categorical defamation of soldiers as "murderers." See Judgment of October 10, 1995, 93 BVerfGE 266, translated in 17 Human Rts. L.J. 140 (1996). In that decision, the Constitutional Court explained that defamation law protects the "personal honour" of individual soldiers and groups of soldiers, but that it also protects

> authorities or other agencies carrying out tasks of the public administration. [In this regard] the norm cannot be justified from the viewpoint of personal honour, since State institutions neither have "personal" honour nor are bearers of the universal right of personality. ... Without a minimum of social acceptance, State institutions cannot carry out their functions. They may therefore in principle be protected against verbal attacks that threaten to undermine these requirements. Protection by the criminal law may not however lead to the position of protecting State institutions against criticism, even in some circumstances in sharp forms, that ought to be especially guaranteed by the fundamental right of freedom of opinion.

The Constitutional Court observed, however, that characterizing *all* soldiers as murderers, rather than particular soldiers or the soldiers of the contemporary German army, could be understood as the expression of a general moral view directed against war as an activity. Whether the use of the slogan "soldiers are murderers" could be punished as an unlawful insult would depend on the context in which the statement was made. The Constitutional Court's five-to-three decision, overturning convictions of pacifists who had employed the slogan "soldiers are murderers" in a variety of contexts, was widely regarded in Germany as affording soldiers insufficient protection against grave attacks on their honor. See Donald P. Kommers, The Constitutional Jurisprudence of the Federal Republic of Germany 392–95 (2d ed. 1997); Edward J. Eberle, *Public Discourse in Contemporary Germany*, 47 Case W. Res. L. Rev. 797, 878–89 (1997). How would the U.S. Supreme Court respond to the criminal conviction of a civilian demonstrator for carrying a sign that said "Soldiers Are Murderers"?

5.   Further reading. See, e.g., Eric Barendt, Freedom of Speech (1985); Sandra Coliver, The Article 19 Freedom of Expression Handbook: International and Comparative law, Standards and Procedures (1993); Internation-

al Media Liability: Civil Liability in the Information Age (Christian Campbell ed. 1997); Press Law in Modern Democracies: A Comparative Study (Pnina Lahav, ed. 1985); Free Speech and National Security (Shimon Shetreet ed. 1991).

2. HATE SPEECH

One of the strongest contrasts between international human rights law and U.S. constitutional law concerns the treatment of racial hate speech. Part of this contrast is evident on the face of the international treaties, some of which include provisions that expressly require the prohibition of specific categories of racist speech. In the wake of World War II, international lawyers were acutely aware of the effective employment of modern propaganda techniques by the Nazi regime in Germany. Furthermore, the drafters of the universal human rights treaties included representatives of Communist governments that were opposed to granting freedom of speech to Fascist movements, and representatives of Third World peoples who had been victimized by ideologies of European racial supremacy.

The Genocide Convention of 1948 includes as one of the punishable acts "[d]irect and public incitement to commit genocide" (Article III(c)). The phrasing of this provision reflected an accommodation with U.S. constitutional concerns. The Convention on the Elimination of All Forms of Racial Discrimination of 1965 goes considerably further, requiring States Parties to make punishable "all dissemination of ideas based on racial superiority or hatred, incitement to racial discrimination, as well as all acts of violence or incitement to such acts against any race or group of persons of another colour or ethnic origin, and also the provision of any assistance to racist activities, including the financing thereof" (CERD Article 4(a)). The International Covenant on Civil and Political Rights of 1966 provides that "[a]ny advocacy of national, racial or religious hatred that constitutes incitement to discrimination, hostility or violence shall be prohibited by law" (ICCPR Article 20(2)).

When the United States finally became a party to these conventions, the broader provisions of CERD and the ICCPR prompted specific reservations limiting United States obligations to adopting prohibitions consistent with the First Amendment. Any doubts about the scope of the incitement provision of the Genocide Convention were covered by a general reservation limiting United States obligations to those it could undertake under its Constitution. (The United States is not the only country to be troubled by ICCPR Article 20. A dozen other Western states have entered reservations against either Article 20(2) or Article 20(1) (requiring prohibition of "propaganda for war") or both.) The U.S. implementing legislation for the Genocide Convention criminalizes incitement only when the speaker "urges another to engage imminently in [genocidal] conduct in circumstances under which there is a substantial likelihood of imminently causing such conduct." See 18 U.S.C. §§ 1091(c), 1093(3).

Jersild v. Denmark

European Court of Human Rights, 1994.
298 Eur. Ct. H.R. (ser. A); 19 E.H.R.R. 1.

9.   Mr. Jens Olaf Jersild, a Danish national, is a journalist and lives in Copenhagen. He was at the time of the events giving rise to the present case, and still is, employed by Danmarks Radio (Danish Broadcasting Corporation, which broadcasts not only radio but also television programmes), assigned to its Sunday News Magazine (Sondagsavisen). The latter is known as a serious television programme intended for a well-informed audience, dealing with a wide range of social and political issues, including xenophobia, immigration and refugees.

10.   On 31 May 1985 the newspaper Information published an article describing the racist attitudes of members of a group of young people, calling themselves "the Greenjackets" ("gronjakkerne") at Osterbro in Copenhagen. In the light of this article, the editors of the Sunday News Magazine decided to produce a documentary on the Greenjackets. Subsequently the applicant contacted representatives of the group, inviting three of them together with Mr. Per Axholt, a social worker employed at the local youth centre, to take part in a television interview. During the interview, which was conducted by the applicant, the three Greenjackets made abusive and derogatory remarks about immigrants and ethnic groups in Denmark. . . .

11.   The applicant subsequently edited and cut the film of the interview down to a few minutes. On 21 July 1985 this was broadcast by Danmarks Radio as a part of the Sunday News Magazine. . . .

12.   . . . [T]he Public Prosecutor instituted criminal proceedings in the City Court of Copenhagen against the three youths interviewed by the applicant, charging them with a violation of Article 266(b) of the Penal Code. . . .*

14.   On 24 April 1987 the City Court convicted the three youths, one of them for having stated that "niggers" and "foreign workers" were "animals", and two of them for their assertions in relation to drugs and "Perkere"**. The applicant was convicted of aiding and abetting them, as was Mr. Jensen, in his capacity as programme controller; they were sentenced to pay day-fines (dagsboder) totalling 1,000 and 2,000 Danish kroner, respectively, or alternatively to five days imprisonment (hoefte).

27.   It is common ground that the measures giving rise to the applicant's case constituted an interference with his right to freedom of expression.

---

* [The Court provides the following translation of the Penal Code section:

Any person who, publicly or with the intention of disseminating it to a wide circle of people, makes a statement, or other communication, threatening, insulting or degrading a group of persons on account of their race, colour, national or ethnic origin or be-

lief shall be liable to a fine or to simple detention or to imprisonment for a term not exceeding two years.—Editors' Note.]

** [The Court defines this term as "a very derogatory word in Danish for immigrant workers."—Editors' Note]

It is moreover undisputed that this interference was "prescribed by law", the applicant's conviction being based on Articles 266(b) and 23(1) of the Penal Code....

Finally it is uncontested that the interference pursued a legitimate aim, namely the "protection of the reputation or rights of others".

The only point in dispute is whether the measures were "necessary in a democratic society" ...

30. The Court would emphasise at the outset that it is particularly conscious of the vital importance of combating racial discrimination in all its forms and manifestations. It may be true, as has been suggested by the applicant, that as a result of recent events the awareness of the dangers of racial discrimination is sharper today than it was a decade ago, at the material time. Nevertheless, the issue was already then of general importance, as is illustrated for instance by the fact that the UN Convention [on the Elimination of All Forms of Racial Discrimination] dates from 1965. Consequently, the object and purpose pursued by the UN Convention are of great weight in determining whether the applicant's conviction, which—as the Government have stressed—was based on a provision enacted in order to ensure Denmark's compliance with the UN Convention, was "necessary" within the meaning of Article 10(2).... The Court is however of the opinion that its interpretation of Article 10 of the European Convention in the present case is compatible with Denmark's obligations under the UN Convention....

31. ... The Court reiterates that freedom of expression constitutes one of the essential foundations of a democratic society and that the safeguards to be afforded to the press are of particular importance. Whilst the press must not overstep the bounds set, inter alia, in the interest of "the protection of the reputation and right of others", it is nevertheless incumbent on it to impart information and ideas of public interest. Not only does the press have the task of imparting such information and ideas: the public also has a right to receive them. Were it otherwise, the press would be unable to play its vital role of "public watchdog". Although formulated primarily with regard to the print media, these principles doubtless apply also to the audio-visual media.

In considering the "duties and responsibilities" of a journalist, the potential impact of the medium concerned is an important factor and it is commonly acknowledged that the audio-visual media have often a much more immediate and powerful effect than the print media. The audio-visual media have means of conveying through images meanings which the print media are not able to impart.

At the same time, the methods of objective and balanced reporting may vary considerably, depending among other things on the media in question. It is not for this Court, nor for the national courts for that matter, to substitute their own views for those of the press as to what technique of reporting should be adopted by journalists. In this context the Court recalls that Article 10 protects not only the substance of the ideas and information expressed, but also the form in which they are conveyed. . . .

32.   The national courts laid considerable emphasis on the fact that the applicant had himself taken the initiative of preparing the Greenjackets feature and that he not only knew in advance that racist statements were likely to be made during the interview but also had encouraged such statements. He had edited the programme in such a way as to include the offensive assertions. Without his involvement, the remarks would not have been disseminated to a wide circle of people and would thus not have been punishable. . . .

33.   On the other hand, as to the contents of the Greenjackets item, it should be noted that the TV presenter's introduction started by a reference to recent public discussion and press comments on racism in Denmark, thus inviting the viewer to see the programme in that context. He went on to announce that the object of the programme was to address aspects of the problem, by identifying certain racist individuals and by portraying their mentality and social background. There is no reason to doubt that the ensuing interviews fulfilled that aim. Taken as a whole, the feature could not objectively have appeared to have as its purpose the propagation of racist views and ideas. On the contrary, it clearly sought—by means of an interview—to expose, analyse and explain this particular group of youths, limited and frustrated by their social situation, with criminal records and violent attitudes, thus dealing with specific aspects of a matter that already then was of great public concern. . . .

34.   . . . Admittedly the item did not explicitly recall the immorality, dangers and unlawfulness of the promotion of racial hatred and of ideas of superiority of one race. However, in view of the above-mentioned counter-balancing elements and the natural limitations on spelling out such elements in a short item within a longer programme as well as the journalist's discretion as to the form of expression used, the Court does not consider the absence of such precautionary reminders to be relevant.

35.   . . . There can be no doubt that the remarks in respect of which the Greenjackets were convicted were more than insulting to members of the targeted groups and did not enjoy the protection of Article 10. However, even having regard to the manner in which the applicant prepared the Greenjackets item, it has not been shown that, considered as a whole, the feature was such as to justify also his conviction of, and punishment for, a criminal offence under the Penal Code. . . .

37.   Having regard to the foregoing, the reasons adduced in support of the applicant's conviction and sentence were not sufficient to establish convincingly that the interference thereby occasioned with the enjoyment of his right to freedom of expression was "necessary in a democratic society"; in particular the means employed were disproportionate to the aim of protecting "the reputation or rights of others". Accordingly the measures gave rise to a breach of Article 10 of the Convention. . . .

For these reasons, THE COURT [h]olds by 12 votes to seven that there has been a violation of Article 10 of the Convention. . . .

■ Joint dissenting opinion of JUDGES RYSSDAL, BERNHARDT, SPIELMAN and LOIZOU

1.   This is the first time that the Court has been concerned with a case of dissemination of racist remarks which deny to a large group of persons the quality of "human beings". In earlier decisions the Court has—in our view, rightly—underlined the great importance of the freedom of the press and the media in general for a democratic society, but it has never had to consider a situation in which "the reputation or rights of others" (Art 10, para 2) were endangered to such an extent as here.

2.   We agree with the majority that the Greenjackets themselves "did not enjoy the protection of Article 10". The same must be true of journalists who disseminate such remarks with supporting comments or with their approval. This can clearly not be said of the applicant. Therefore it is admittedly difficult to strike the right balance between the freedom of the press and the protection of others. But the majority attributes much more weight to the freedom of the journalist than to the protection of those who have to suffer from racist hatred.

3.   Neither the written text of the interview nor the video film we have seen makes it clear that the remarks of the Greenjackets are intolerable in a society based on respect for human rights. The applicant has cut the entire interview down to a few minutes, probably with the consequence or even the intention of retaining the most crude remarks. That being so, it was absolutely necessary to add at least a clear statement of disapproval. The majority of the Court sees disapproval in the context of the interview, but this is an interpretation of cryptic remarks. Nobody can exclude that certain parts of the public found in the television spot support for their racist prejudices.

And what must be the feelings of those whose human dignity has been attacked, or even denied, by the Greenjackets? Can they get the impression that seen in context the television broadcast contributes to their protection? A journalist's good intentions are not enough in such a situation, especially in a case in which he has himself provoked the racist statements. . . .

. . . We are convinced that the Danish courts acted inside the margin of appreciation which must be left to the Contracting States in this sensitive area. Accordingly, the findings of the Danish courts cannot be considered as giving rise to a violation of Article 10 of the Convention.

[Dissenting opinions of three other Judges omitted.]

As with other categories of speech, the U.S. Supreme Court's approach to racial hate speech has evolved over the latter half of the Twentieth Century. In 1952, the Supreme Court upheld by five-to-four vote a group libel law, which prohibited any publication that "portrays depravity, criminality, unchastity, or lack of virtue of a class of citizens, of any race, color, creed or religion [and] exposes [them] to contempt, derision or obloquy." *Beauharnais v. Illinois*, 343 U.S. 250 (1952). The majority analogized the statute to traditional criminal libel laws that punished defamation of individuals, observing that libel was one of the exceptional categories of speech (along with obscenity and "fighting words") regarded in the Court's jurisprudence as outside the protection of the First Amendment. Justices Black and Douglas dissented, arguing that the expansion of the libel exception beyond defamation of individuals permitted the state to censor debate on broad political issues. The dissents of Justices Reed and Jackson accepted the possibility that a narrowly drafted group libel statute might be constitutional, but found the Illinois statute too broad in several respects.

The reasoning of *Beauharnais* was undermined in the 1960s when the Supreme Court began to develop First Amendment limits on state libel laws in order to respect "the principle that debate on public issues should be uninhibited, robust, and wide-open." *New York Times v. Sullivan*, 376 U.S. 254, 270 (1964) (see Part II, Chapter 1(E)(4) supra). The narrowing of exceptions to constitutional protection made it likely that claims of racial superiority, and pseudo-factual assertions alleged to support them, would be regarded as protected political ideas, however repulsive, and not as beyond the reach of the First Amendment. The Supreme Court addressed the implications of the First Amendment for legislation restricting racist speech in the following case.

R.A.V. v. City of St. Paul

Supreme Court of the United States, 1992.
505 U.S. 377.

■ JUSTICE SCALIA delivered the opinion of the Court.

In the predawn hours of June 21, 1990, petitioner and several other teenagers allegedly assembled a crudely-made cross by taping together broken chair legs. They then allegedly burned the cross inside the fenced yard of a black family that lived across the street from the house where petitioner was staying. Although this conduct could have been punished under any of a number of laws, one of the two provisions under which respondent city of St. Paul chose to charge petitioner (then a juvenile) was the St. Paul Bias–Motivated Crime Ordinance, St. Paul, Minn. Legis. Code § 292.02 (1990), which provides:

> Whoever places on public or private property a symbol, object, appellation, characterization or graffiti, including, but not limited to, a burning cross or Nazi swastika, which one knows or has reasonable grounds to know arouses anger, alarm or resentment in others on the basis of race, color, creed, religion or gender commits disorderly conduct and shall be guilty of a misdemeanor.

Petitioner moved to dismiss this count on the ground that the St. Paul ordinance was substantially overbroad and impermissibly content-based and therefore facially invalid under the First Amendment. The trial court granted this motion, but the Minnesota Supreme Court reversed. That court rejected petitioner's overbreadth claim because, as construed in prior Minnesota cases, the modifying phrase "arouses anger, alarm or resentment in others" limited the reach of the ordinance to conduct that amounts to "fighting words," i.e., "conduct that itself inflicts injury or tends to incite immediate violence ...," (citing Chaplinsky v. New Hampshire, 315 U.S. 568, 572 (1942)), and therefore the ordinance reached only expression "that the first amendment does not protect." The court also concluded that the ordinance was not impermissibly content-based because, in its view, "the ordinance is a narrowly tailored means toward accomplishing the compelling governmental interest in protecting the community against bias-motivated threats to public safety and order." We granted certiorari.

I

.... Assuming, arguendo, that all of the expression reached by the ordinance is proscribable under the "fighting words" doctrine, we nonetheless conclude that the ordinance is facially unconstitutional in that it prohibits otherwise permitted speech solely on the basis of the subjects the speech addresses.

The First Amendment generally prevents government from proscribing speech, or even expressive conduct, because of disapproval of the ideas expressed. Content-based regulations are presumptively invalid. From 1791 to the present, however, our society, like other free but civilized societies, has permitted restrictions upon the content of speech in a few limited areas, which are "of such slight social value as a step to truth that any benefit that may be derived from them is clearly outweighed by the social interest in order and morality." *Chaplinsky*, supra, at 572. We have recognized that "the freedom of speech" referred to by the First Amendment does not include a freedom to disregard these traditional limitations. See, e.g., Roth v. United States, 354 U. S. 476 (1957) (obscenity); Beauharnais v. Illinois, 343 U. S. 250 (1952) (defamation); Chaplinsky v. New Hampshire, supra, ("fighting words"). Our decisions since the 1960's have narrowed the scope of the traditional categorical exceptions for defamation, and for obscenity, but a limited categorical approach has remained an important part of our First Amendment jurisprudence.

We have sometimes said that these categories of expression are "not within the area of constitutionally protected speech," or that the "protection of the First Amendment does not extend" to them. Such statements must be taken in context, however, and are no more literally true than is the occasionally repeated shorthand characterizing obscenity "as not being speech at all." What they mean is that these areas of speech can, consistently with the First Amendment, be regulated because of their constitutionally proscribable content (obscenity, defamation, etc.)—not that they are categories of speech entirely invisible to the Constitution, so that they may be made the vehicles for content discrimination unrelated to their distinctively proscribable content. Thus, the government may proscribe libel; but it may not make the further content discrimination of proscribing only libel critical of the government....

Even the prohibition against content discrimination that we assert the First Amendment requires is not absolute. It applies differently in the context of proscribable speech than in the area of fully protected speech. The rationale of the general prohibition, after all, is that content discrimination "rais[es] the specter that the Government may effectively drive certain ideas or viewpoints from the marketplace." But content discrimination among various instances of a class of proscribable speech often does not pose this threat.

When the basis for the content discrimination consists entirely of the very reason the entire class of speech at issue is proscribable, no significant danger of idea or viewpoint discrimination exists. Such a reason, having been adjudged neutral enough to support exclusion of the entire class of speech from First Amendment protection, is also neutral enough to form the basis of distinction within the class. To illustrate: A State might choose to prohibit only that obscenity which is the most patently offensive in its prurience—i.e., that which involves the most lascivious displays of sexual activity. But it may not prohibit, for example, only that obscenity which includes offensive political messages. And the Federal Government can criminalize only those threats of violence that are directed against the President, see 18 U. S. C. § 871—since the reasons why threats of violence are outside the First Amendment (protecting individuals from the fear of violence, from the disruption that fear engenders, and from the possibility that the threatened violence will occur) have special force when applied to the person of the President. See Watts v. United States, 394 U.S. 705, 707 (1969) (upholding the facial validity of § 871 because of the "overwhelmin[g] interest in protecting the safety of [the] Chief Executive and in allowing him to perform his duties without interference from threats of physical violence"). But the Federal Government may not criminalize only those threats against the President that mention his policy on aid to inner cities....

Another valid basis for according differential treatment to even a content-defined subclass of proscribable speech is that the subclass happens to be associated with particular "secondary effects" of the speech, so that the regulation is "justified without reference to the content of the ... speech." ... A State could, for example, permit all obscene live performances except those involving minors. Moreover, since words can in some circumstances violate laws directed not against speech but against conduct (a law against treason, for example, is violated by telling the enemy the nation's defense secrets), a particular content-based subcategory of a proscribable class of speech can be swept up incidentally within the reach of a statute directed at conduct rather than speech. Thus, for example, sexually derogatory "fighting words," among other words, may produce a violation of Title VII's general prohibition against sexual discrimination in employment practices, 42 U.S.C. § 2000e–2; 29 CFR § 1604.11 (1991). Where the government does not target conduct on the basis of its expressive content, acts are not shielded from regulation merely because they express a discriminatory idea or philosophy.

These bases for distinction refute the proposition that the selectivity of the restriction is "even arguably 'conditioned upon the sovereign's agreement with what a speaker may intend to say.' " There may be other such bases as well. Indeed, to validate such selectivity (where totally proscribable speech is at issue) it may not even be necessary to identify any particular "neutral" basis, so long as the nature of the content discrimination is such that there is no realistic possibility that official suppression of ideas is afoot. (We cannot think of any First Amendment interest that would stand in the way of a State's prohibiting only those obscene motion pictures with blue-eyed actresses.) Save for that limitation, the regulation of "fighting words," like the regulation of noisy speech, may address some offensive instances and leave other, equally offensive, instances alone.

II

Applying these principles to the St. Paul ordinance, we conclude that, even as narrowly construed by the Minnesota Supreme Court, the ordinance is facially unconstitutional. Although the phrase in the ordinance, "arouses anger, alarm or resentment in others," has been limited by the Minnesota Supreme Court's construction to reach only those symbols or displays that amount to "fighting words," the remaining, unmodified terms make clear that the ordinance applies only to "fighting words" that insult, or provoke violence, "on the basis of race, color, creed, religion or gender." Displays containing abusive invective, no matter how vicious or severe, are permissible unless they are addressed to one of the specified disfavored topics. Those who wish to use "fighting words" in connection with other ideas—to express hostility, for example, on the basis of political affiliation, union membership, or homosexuality—are not covered. The First Amendment does not permit St. Paul to impose special prohibitions on those speakers who express views on disfavored subjects.

In its practical operation, moreover, the ordinance goes even beyond mere content discrimination, to actual viewpoint discrimination. Displays containing some words—odious racial epithets, for example—would be prohibited to proponents of all views. But "fighting words" that do not themselves invoke race, color, creed, religion, or gender—aspersions upon a person's mother, for example—would seemingly be usable ad libitum in the placards of those arguing in favor of racial, color, etc. tolerance and equality, but could not be used by that speaker's opponents. One could hold up a sign saying, for example, that all "anti-Catholic bigots" are misbegotten; but not that all "papists" are, for that would insult and provoke violence "on the basis of religion." St. Paul has no such authority to license one side of a debate to fight freestyle, while requiring the other to follow Marquis of Queensbury Rules.

What we have here, it must be emphasized, is not a prohibition of fighting words that are directed at certain persons or groups (which would be facially valid if it met the requirements of the Equal Protection Clause); but rather, a prohibition of fighting words that contain (as the Minnesota Supreme Court repeatedly emphasized) messages of "bias-motivated" hatred and in particular, as applied to this case, messages "based on virulent notions of racial supremacy." One must wholeheartedly agree with the Minnesota Supreme Court that "[i]t is the responsibility, even the obligation, of diverse communities to confront such notions in whatever form they appear," but the manner of that confrontation cannot consist of selective limitations upon speech. St. Paul's brief asserts that a general "fighting words" law would not meet the city's needs because only a content-specific measure can communicate to minority groups that the "group hatred" aspect of such speech "is not condoned by the majority." The point of the First Amendment is that majority preferences must be expressed in some fashion other than silencing speech on the basis of its content.

Despite the fact that the Minnesota Supreme Court and St. Paul acknowledge that the ordinance is directed at expression of group hatred, Justice Stevens suggests that this "fundamentally misreads" the ordinance. It is directed, he claims, not to speech of a particular content, but to particular "injur[ies]" that are "qualitatively different" from other injuries. This is word-play. What makes the anger, fear, sense of dishonor, etc. produced by violation of this ordinance distinct from the anger, fear, sense of dishonor, etc. produced by other fighting words is nothing other than the fact that it is caused by a distinctive idea, conveyed by a distinctive message. The First Amendment cannot be evaded that easily. It is obvious that the symbols which will arouse "anger, alarm or resentment in others on the basis of race, color, creed, religion or gender" are those symbols that communicate a message of hostility based on one of these characteristics. . . .

The content-based discrimination reflected in the St. Paul ordinance comes within neither any of the specific exceptions to the First Amendment prohibition we discussed earlier, nor within a more general exception for content discrimination that does not threaten censorship of ideas. It assuredly does not fall within the exception for content discrimination based on the very reasons why the particular class of speech at issue (here, fighting words) is proscribable. As explained earlier, the reason why fighting words are categorically excluded from the protection of the First Amendment is not that their content communicates any particular idea, but that their content embodies a particularly intolerable (and socially unnecessary) mode of expressing whatever idea the speaker wishes to convey. St. Paul has not singled out an especially offensive mode of expression—it has not, for example, selected for prohibition only those fighting words that communicate ideas in a threatening (as opposed to a merely obnoxious) manner. Rather, it has proscribed fighting words of whatever manner that communicate messages of racial, gender, or religious intolerance. Selectivity of this sort creates the possibility that the city is seeking to handicap the expression of particular ideas. That possibility would alone be enough to render the ordinance presumptively invalid, but St. Paul's comments and concessions in this case elevate the possibility to a certainty. . . .

It hardly needs discussion that the ordinance does not fall within some more general exception permitting all selectivity that for any reason is beyond the suspicion of official suppression of ideas. The statements of St. Paul in this very case afford ample basis for, if not full confirmation of, that suspicion.

Finally, St. Paul and its amici defend the conclusion of the Minnesota Supreme Court that, even if the ordinance regulates expression based on hostility towards its protected ideological content, this discrimination is nonetheless justified because it is narrowly tailored to serve compelling state interests. Specifically, they assert that the ordinance helps to ensure the basic human rights of members of groups that have historically been subjected to discrimination, including the right of such group members to live in peace where they wish. We do not doubt that these interests are compelling, and that the ordinance can be said to promote them. But the "danger of censorship" presented by a facially content-based statute, requires that that weapon be employed only where it is "necessary to serve the asserted [compelling] interest." The existence of adequate content-neutral alternatives thus "undercut[s] significantly" any defense of such a statute, casting considerable doubt on the government's protestations that "the asserted justification is in fact an accurate description of the purpose and effect of the law." The dispositive question in this case, therefore, is whether content discrimination is reasonably necessary to achieve St. Paul's compelling interests; it plainly is not. An ordinance not limited to the favored topics, for example, would have precisely the same beneficial effect. In fact the only interest distinctively served by the content limitation is that of displaying the city council's special hostility towards the particular biases thus singled out. That is precisely what the First Amendment forbids. The politicians of St. Paul are entitled to express that hostility— but not through the means of imposing unique limitations upon speakers who (however benightedly) disagree.

* * *

Let there be no mistake about our belief that burning a cross in someone's front yard is reprehensible. But St. Paul has sufficient means at its disposal to prevent such behavior without adding the First Amendment to the fire.

The judgment of the Minnesota Supreme Court is reversed. . . .

■ JUSTICE WHITE, with whom JUSTICE BLACKMUN and JUSTICE O'CONNOR join, and with whom JUSTICE STEVENS joins except as to Part I(A), concurring in the judgment.

I agree with the majority that the judgment of the Minnesota Supreme Court should be reversed. However, our agreement ends there.

This case could easily be decided within the contours of established First Amendment law by holding, as petitioner argues, that the St. Paul ordinance is fatally overbroad because it criminalizes not only unprotected expression but expression protected by the First Amendment.

I

A

This Court's decisions have plainly stated that expression falling within certain limited categories so lacks the values the First Amendment was designed to protect that the Constitution affords no protection to that expression.... Today, however, the Court announces that earlier Courts did not mean their repeated statements that certain categories of expression are "not within the area of constitutionally protected speech." ... To the contrary, those statements meant precisely what they said: The categorical approach is a firmly entrenched part of our First Amendment jurisprudence....

[T]he Court's insistence on inventing its brand of First Amendment underinclusiveness puzzles me. The overbreadth doctrine has the redeeming virtue of attempting to avoid the chilling of protected expression, ... but the Court's new "underbreadth" creation serves no desirable function. Instead, it permits, indeed invites, the continuation of expressive conduct that in this case is evil and worthless in First Amendment terms, until the city of St. Paul cures the underbreadth by adding to its ordinance a catch-all phrase such as "and all other fighting words that may constitutionally be subject to this ordinance."

Any contribution of this holding to First Amendment jurisprudence is surely a negative one, since it necessarily signals that expressions of violence, such as the message of intimidation and racial hatred conveyed by burning a cross on someone's lawn, are of sufficient value to outweigh the social interest in order and morality that has traditionally placed such fighting words outside the First Amendment. Indeed, by characterizing fighting words as a form of "debate," the majority legitimates hate speech as a form of public discussion....

II

Although I disagree with the Court's analysis, I do agree with its conclusion: The St. Paul ordinance is unconstitutional. However, I would decide the case on overbreadth grounds....

In construing the St. Paul ordinance, the Minnesota Supreme Court drew upon the definition of fighting words that appears in *Chaplinsky*— words "which by their very utterance inflict injury or tend to incite an immediate breach of the peace." However, the Minnesota court was far from clear in identifying the "injur[ies]" inflicted by the expression that St. Paul sought to regulate. Indeed, the Minnesota court emphasized (tracking the language of the ordinance) that "the ordinance censors only those displays that one knows or should know will create anger, alarm or resentment based on racial, ethnic, gender or religious bias." I therefore understand the court to have ruled that St. Paul may constitutionally prohibit expression that "by its very utterance" causes "anger, alarm or resentment."

Our fighting words cases have made clear, however, that such generalized reactions are not sufficient to strip expression of its constitutional protection. The mere fact that expressive activity causes hurt feelings, offense, or resentment does not render the expression unprotected....

■ JUSTICE STEVENS, with whom JUSTICE WHITE and JUSTICE BLACKMUN join as to Part I, concurring in the judgment.

I

... As I understand [the majority opinion], Congress may choose from the set of unprotected speech (all threats) to proscribe only a subset (threats against the President) because those threats are particularly likely to cause "fear of violence," "disruption," and actual "violence."

Precisely this same reasoning, however, [would compel] the conclusion that St. Paul's ordinance is constitutional. Just as Congress may determine that threats against the President entail more severe consequences than other threats, so St. Paul's City Council may determine that threats based on the target's race, religion, or gender cause more severe harm to both the target and to society than other threats. This latter judgment—that harms caused by racial, religious, and gender-based invective are qualitatively different from that caused by other fighting words—seems to me eminently reasonable and realistic....

[Opinion of Justice Blackmun, concurring in the judgment, omitted]

ICCPR, Articles 19 and 20(2)

Article 19

1. Everyone shall have the right to hold opinions without interference.

2. Everyone shall have the right to freedom of expression; this right shall include freedom to seek, receive and impart information and ideas of all kinds, regardless of frontiers, either orally, in writing or in print, in the form of art, or through any other media of his choice.

3. The exercise of the rights provided for in paragraph 2 of this article carries with it special duties and responsibilities. It may therefore be subject to certain restrictions, but these shall only be such as are provided by law and are necessary:

(a) For respect of the rights or reputations of others;

(b) For the protection of national security or of public order (*ordre public*), or of public health or morals.

Article 20(2)

Any advocacy of national, racial, or religious hatred that constitutes incitement to discrimination, hostility or violence shall be prohibited by law.

Faurisson v. France

Human Rights Committee, 1996.
U.N. Doc. CCPR/C/58/D/550/1993.

1. The author of the communication, dated 2 January 1993, is Robert Faurisson, born in the United Kingdom in 1929 and with dual French/British citizenship, currently residing in Vichy, France. He claims to be a victim of violations of his human rights by France. . . .

2.1 The author was a professor of literature at the Sorbonne University in Paris until 1973 and at the University of Lyon until 1991, when he was removed from his chair. Aware of the historical significance of the Holocaust, he has sought proof of the methods of killings, in particular by gas asphyxiation. While he does not contest the use of gas for purposes of disinfection, he doubts the existence of gas chambers for extermination purposes ("chambres à gaz homicides") at Auschwitz and in other Nazi concentration camps.

2.3 On 13 July 1990, the French legislature passed the so-called "Gayssot Act", which amends the law on the Freedom of the Press of 1881 by adding an article 24 bis; the latter makes it an offence to contest the existence of the category of crimes against humanity as defined in the London Charter of 8 August 1945, on the basis of which Nazi leaders were tried and convicted by the International Military Tribunal at Nuremberg in 1945–1946. The author submits that, in essence, the "Gayssot Act" promotes the Nuremberg trial and judgment to the status of dogma, by imposing criminal sanctions on those who dare to challenge its findings and premises. Mr. Faurisson contends that he has ample reason to believe that the records of the Nuremberg trial can indeed be challenged and that the evidence used against Nazi leaders is open to question, as is, according to him, the evidence about the number of victims exterminated at Auschwitz.

2.5 Shortly after the enactment of the "Gayssot Act", Mr. Faurisson was interviewed by the French monthly magazine Le Choc du Mois, which published the interview in its Number 32 issue of September 1990. Besides expressing his concern that the new law constituted a threat to freedom of research and freedom of expression, the author reiterated his personal conviction that there were no homicidal gas chambers for the extermination of Jews in Nazi concentration camps. Following the publication of this interview, eleven associations of French resistance fighters and of deportees to German concentration camps filed a private criminal action against Mr. Faurisson and Patrice Boizeau, the editor of the magazine Le Choc du Mois. By judgment of 18 April 1991, the 17th Chambre Correctionnelle du Tribunal de Grande Instance de Paris convicted Messrs. Faurisson and Boizeau of having committed the crime of "contestation de crimes contre l'humanité" and imposed on them fines and costs amounting to FF 326,832.

2.6 The conviction was based, inter alia, on the following Faurisson statements:

"... No one will have me admit that two plus two make five, that the earth is flat, or that the Nuremberg Tribunal was infallible. I have excellent reasons not to believe in this policy of extermination of Jews or in the magic gas chamber...."

"I would wish to see that 100 per cent of all French citizens realize that the myth of the gas chambers is a dishonest fabrication ('est une gredinerie'), endorsed by the victorious powers of Nuremberg in 1945–46 and officialized on 14 July 1990 by the current French Government, with the approval of the 'court historians' ''.

9.2   The Committee takes note of public debates in France, including negative comments made by French parliamentarians on the Gayssot Act, as well as of arguments put forward in other, mainly European, countries which support and oppose the introduction of similar legislations.

9.3   Although it does not contest that the application of the terms of the Gayssot Act, which, in their effect, make it a criminal offence to challenge the conclusions and the verdict of the International Military Tribunal at Nuremberg, may lead, under different conditions than the facts of the instant case, to decisions or measures incompatible with the Covenant, the Committee is not called upon to criticize in the abstract laws enacted by States parties. The task of the Committee under the Optional Protocol is to ascertain whether the conditions of the restrictions imposed on the right to freedom of expression are met in the communications which are brought before it.

9.4   Any restriction on the right to freedom of expression must cumulatively meet the following conditions: it must be provided by law, it must address one of the aims set out in paragraph 3 (a) and (b) of article 19, and must be necessary to achieve a legitimate purpose.

9.5   The restriction on the author's freedom of expression was indeed provided by law i.e. the Act of 13 July 1990. It is the constant jurisprudence of the Committee that the restrictive law itself must be in compliance with the provisions of the Covenant. In this regard the Committee concludes, on the basis of the reading of the judgment of the 17th Chambre correctionnelle du Tribunal de grande instance de Paris that the finding of the author's guilt was based on his following two statements: "... I have excellent reasons not to believe in the policy of extermination of Jews or in the magic gas chambers ... I wish to see that 100 per cent of the French citizens realize that the myth of the gas chambers is a dishonest fabrication". His conviction therefore did not encroach upon his right to hold and express an opinion in general, rather the court convicted Mr. Faurisson for having violated the rights and reputation of others. For these reasons the Committee is satisfied that the Gayssot Act, as read, interpreted and applied to the author's case by the French courts, is in compliance with the provisions of the Covenant.

9.6   To assess whether the restrictions placed on the author's freedom of expression by his criminal conviction were applied for the purposes provided for by the Covenant, the Committee begins by noting, as it did in its

General Comment 10 that the rights for the protection of which restrictions on the freedom of expression are permitted by article 19, paragraph 3, may relate to the interests of other persons or to those of the community as a whole. Since the statements made by the author, read in their full context, were of a nature as to raise or strengthen anti-semitic feelings, the restriction served the [right] of the Jewish community to live free from fear of an atmosphere of anti-semitism. The Committee therefore concludes that the restriction of the author's freedom of expression was permissible under article 19, paragraph 3 (a), of the Covenant.

9.7 Lastly the Committee needs to consider whether the restriction of the author's freedom of expression was necessary. The Committee noted the State party's argument contending that the introduction of the Gayssot Act was intended to serve the struggle against racism and anti-semitism. It also noted the statement of a member of the French Government, the then Minister of Justice, which characterized the denial of the existence of the Holocaust as the principal vehicle for anti-semitism. In the absence in the material before it of any argument undermining the validity of the State party's position as to the necessity of the restriction, the Committee is satisfied that the restriction of Mr. Faurisson's freedom of expression was necessary within the meaning of article 19, paragraph 3, of the Covenant.

■ Statement by MR. THOMAS BUERGENTHAL

As a survivor of the concentration camps of Auschwitz and Sachsenhausen whose father, maternal grandparents and many other family members were killed in the Nazi Holocaust, I have no choice but to recuse myself from participating in the decision of this case.

■ Individual opinion by ELIZABETH EVATT and DAVID KRETZMER, co-signed by ECKART KLEIN (concurring)

1. While we concur in the view of the Committee that in the particular circumstances of this case the right to freedom of expression of the author was not violated, given the importance of the issues involved we have decided to append our separate, concurring, opinion.

4. Every individual has the right to be free not only from discrimination on grounds of race, religion and national origins, but also from incitement to such discrimination. This is stated expressly in article 7 of the Universal Declaration of Human Rights. It is implicit in the obligation placed on States parties under article 20, paragraph 2, of the Covenant to prohibit by law any advocacy of national, racial or religious hatred that constitutes incitement to discrimination, hostility or violence. The crime for which the author was convicted under the Gayssot Act does not expressly include the element of incitement, nor do the statements which served as the basis for the conviction fall clearly within the boundaries of incitement, which the State party was bound to prohibit, in accordance with article 20, paragraph 2. However, there may be circumstances in which the right of a person to be free from incitement to discrimination on grounds of race, religion or national origins cannot be fully protected by a narrow, explicit law on incitement that falls precisely within the boundaries of article 20, para-

graph 2. This is the case where, in a particular social and historical context, statements that do not meet the strict legal criteria of incitement can be shown to constitute part of a pattern of incitement against a given racial, religious or national group, or where those interested in spreading hostility and hatred adopt sophisticated forms of speech that are not punishable under the law against racial incitement, even though their effect may be as pernicious as explicit incitement, if not more so.

7. The Committee correctly points out, as it did in its General Comment 10, that the right for the protection of which restrictions on freedom of expression are permitted by article 19, paragraph 3, may relate to the interests of a community as a whole. This is especially the case in which the right protected is the right to be free from racial, national or religious incitement. The French courts examined the statements made by the author and came to the conclusion that his statements were of a nature as to raise or strengthen anti-semitic tendencies. It appears therefore that the restriction on the author's freedom of expression served to protect the right of the Jewish community in France to live free from fear of incitement to anti-semitism. This leads us to the conclusion that the State party has shown that the aim of the restrictions on the author's freedom of expression was to respect the right of others, mentioned in article 19, paragraph 3. The more difficult question is whether imposing liability for such statements was necessary in order to protect that right.

9. The Gayssot Act is phrased in the widest language and would seem to prohibit publication of bona fide research connected with matters decided by the Nuremburg Tribunal. Even if the purpose of this prohibition is to protect the right to be free from incitement to anti-semitism, the restrictions imposed do not meet the proportionality test. They do not link liability to the intent of the author, nor to the tendency of the publication to incite to anti-semitism. Furthermore, the legitimate object of the law could certainly have been achieved by a less drastic provision that would not imply that the State party had attempted to turn historical truths and experiences into legislative dogma that may not be challenged, no matter what the object behind that challenge, nor its likely consequences. In the present case we are not concerned, however, with the Gayssot Act, in abstracto, but only with the restriction placed on the freedom of expression of the author by his conviction for his statements in the interview in Le Choc du Mois . . . .

. . .

■ Individual opinion by RAJSOOMER LALLAH (concurring)

1. I have reservations on the approach adopted by the Committee in arriving at its conclusions. I also reach the same conclusions for different reasons.

11. I conclude . . . that the creation of the offence provided for in the Gayssot Act, as it has been applied by the Courts to the author's case, falls more appropriately, in my view, within the powers of France under article

20, paragraph 2, of the Covenant. The result is that there has, for this reason, been no violation by France under the Covenant.

13.   Recourse to restrictions that are, in principle, permissible under article 19, paragraph 3, bristles with difficulties, tending to destroy the very existence of the right sought to be restricted. The right to freedom of opinion and expression is a most valuable right and may turn out to be too fragile for survival in the face of the too frequently professed necessity for its restriction in the wide range of areas envisaged under paragraphs (a) and (b) of article 19, paragraph 3.

[Concurring opinions of other members omitted.]

Notes

1.   In *Jersild*, the European Court observes that the racist remarks of the Greenjackets "did not enjoy the protection of Article 10" (para. 35). Is the Court saying (like the concurring opinions in *R.A.V.*) that the particular forms of speech lie entirely outside the scope of freedom of expression, or rather (like the majority in *R.A.V.*) that it is clearly permissible to suppress those forms of speech by appropriately drafted legislation? Would Article 17 of the European Convention, denying the existence of any right to engage in activity aimed at the destruction of the rights of others, apply to the remarks of the Greenjackets?

After *Jersild*, what must a journalist do in order to be entitled under the European Convention to cover stories about racism and xenophobia?

2.   Why does the majority in *R.A.V.* conclude that legislation must treat racial epithets and epithets directed at racial bigots evenhandedly? Why does the Fourteenth Amendment's commitment to racial equality not permit the state to coordinate its opposition to racial discrimination with its regulation of "fighting words"? Why is it incorrect to say that the St. Paul ordinance prohibits the most offensive of the "fighting words"?

Despite their disagreements on particular issues, all the Justices in *R.A.V.* agreed that the St. Paul ordinance violated the First Amendment. The concurring Justices concluded that the ordinance was substantially overbroad, that is, that its prohibition covered too broad a range of constitutionally protected speech whose suppression could not be justified under normal First Amendment standards.

How would the Supreme Court be likely to rule if the Illinois statute upheld in *Beauharnais* were challenged before it today? How would the Court rule if Congress adopted legislation implementing Article 20(2) of the ICCPR?

3.   In *Faurisson*, the Human Rights Committee concludes that Mr. Faurisson's conviction was necessary to protect the rights and reputation of others. Whose rights and/or reputations were threatened by Mr. Faurisson's contentions: (a) the deceased victims of the concentration camps, (b) the persons accused of fabricating the existence of the Holocaust, (c) the people who would be harmed if disbelief in the Holocaust led to an increase

in antisemitism? Under the Committee's reasoning, when if ever would it be permissible for someone other than Mr. Faurisson to publish statements questioning the occurrence of the Holocaust? Would the Committee's reasoning also support statutes making it a crime to deny other events in world history?

4.   Other European countries have also enforced statutes prohibiting denial of the occurrence of the Holocaust. In one case, the Federal Constitutional Court of Germany quoted the following explanation by the Federal Court of Justice:

> The historical fact itself, that human beings were singled out according to the criteria of the so-called "Nuremberg Laws" and robbed of their individuality for the purpose of extermination, puts Jews living in the Federal Republic in a special, personal relationship vis-à-vis their fellow citizens; what happened [then] is also present in this relationship today. It is part of their personal self-perception to be understood as part of a group of people who stand out by virtue of their fate and in relation to whom there is a special moral responsibility on the part of all others, and that this is part of their dignity. Respect for this self-perception, for each individual, is one of the guarantees against repetition of this kind of discrimination and forms a basic condition of their lives in the Federal Republic. Whoever seeks to deny these events denies vis-à-vis each individual the personal worth of [Jewish persons]. For the person concerned, this is continuing discrimination against the group to which he belongs and, as part of the group, against him.

Judgment of April 13, 1994, 90 BVerfGE 241 (upholding denial of permission to hold a meeting at which revisionist historian would argue against occurrence of the Holocaust) (as translated in Donald P. Kommers, The Constitutional Jurisprudence of the Federal Republic of Germany 386 (2d ed. 1997)). Does this provide a different justification for the suppression of Holocaust denial? A better one? For a comparative analysis of an earlier version of the German prohibition, see Eric Stein, *History against free speech: German Law in European and American Perspective*, in Verfassungsrecht und Völkerrecht: Gedächtnisschrift für Wilhelm Karl Geck 831 (Wilfried Fielder & Georg Ress eds. 1989)

5.   In *Lehideux and Isorni v. France*, 1998–VII Eur. Ct. H.R. 2864 (1998), the European Court found by vote of fifteen to six that France had violated Article 10 by punishing two individuals who had placed an advertisement extolling Marshal Pétain, the head of the collaborationist Vichy regime during World War II. The two authors were convicted of publicly defending crimes of collaboration. The majority of the Court maintained that the issue addressed by the advertisement—whether Pétain had collaborated with the Nazis in order to spare France worse treatment under the occupation, rather than because he shared their goals—did not "belong to the category of clearly established historical facts—such as the Holocaust—whose negation or revision would be removed from the protection of Article 10 by Article 17." The majority also emphasized that the advertisement itself referred to "Nazi atrocities and persecution" and "German omnipo-

tence and barbarism." The dissenting judges argued that the polemical advertisement did not make a serious historical contribution, and that the Court should defer to the French authorities' assessment of the effects that would result from public praise of the racist Vichy regime.

6. In *Regina v. Keegstra*, [1990] 3 S.C.R. 697, the Supreme Court of Canada upheld (by 4–3 vote) the conviction a high school teacher who had been dismissed for teaching antisemitic views to his students. The court found that the criminal statute, which prohibited the wilful promotion of hatred, other than in private conversation, towards any section of the public distinguished by color, race, religion or ethnic origin, placed justified limitations on the right to freedom of expression under the Canadian Charter of Rights and Freedoms. The majority summarized the purpose of the statute as follows:

> Parliament has recognized the substantial harm that can flow from hate propaganda, and in trying to prevent the pain suffered by target group members and to reduce racial, ethnic and religious tension in Canada has decided to suppress the wilful promotion of hatred against identifiable groups. The nature of Parliament's objective is supported not only by the work of numerous study groups, but also by our collective historical knowledge of the potentially catastrophic effects of the promotion of hatred. Additionally, the international commitment to eradicate hate propaganda and the stress placed upon equality and multiculturalism in the Charter strongly buttress the importance of this objective.

The majority also held that the Charter permitted the legislature to make the truth of the defendant's statements an affirmative defense on which he would bear the burden of proof. See also *Regina v. Andrews*, [1990] 3 S.C.R. 870; *Canadian Human Rights Commission v. Taylor*, [1990] 3 S.C.R. 892; *Attis v. Board of School Trustees*, [1996] 1 S.C.R. 825.

Subsequently, in *Zundel v. The Queen*, [1992] 2 S.C.R 731 (1992), the Supreme Court overturned (also by 4–3 vote) a conviction for Holocaust denial, because of the excessive breadth of the "false news" statute under which the defendant had been prosecuted. The statute, which derived from a Thirteenth Century English act, criminalized "wilfully publish[ing] a statement, tale or news that he knows is false and that causes or is likely to cause injury or mischief to a public interest." The majority concluded that the statute prohibited too broad and amorphous a category of falsehoods, and threatened those who disagreed with prevailing public opinion.

7. Could the U.S. Congress adopt a statute prohibiting denial of the Holocaust? The greatest source of dissemination of Holocaust denial literature is Southern California. As a result, U.S. tolerance for racist speech creates significant challenges for other countries that seek to enforce stricter laws; the challenges have increased with the advent of the Internet. See *Anti-Semitic Site Tests Canada Law*, Int'l Herald Tribune, Aug. 3, 1998, p. 11; Comment, *More than a River in Egypt: Holocaust Denial, the Internet, and International Freedom of Expression Norms*, 33 Gonz. L. Rev. 241 (1997–98). Could Congress adopt a statute prohibiting publications that

promote pseudoscientific theories of racial inferiority? If not, why not? Do such publications pose less danger in the United States than antisemitic publications do in Canada and Europe?

8.   Article 20(2) of the ICCPR requires states to prohibit "advocacy of national, racial, or religious hatred that constitutes incitement to discrimination, hostility or violence." It does not mention gender. Although CERD Article 4(a) requires states to "punish all dissemination of ideas based on racial superiority or hatred [and] incitement to racial discrimination," CEDAW does not contain a corresponding provision. Why might that be?

9.   Pornography as hate speech. In *Regina v. Butler*, [1992] 1 S.C.R. 452, the Supreme Court of Canada upheld a conviction under an obscenity statute, prohibiting the sale of publications a dominant characteristic of which was the undue exploitation of sex. The court identified two major categories of undue exploitation as sex coupled with violence and explicit sex that is degrading or dehumanizing. The court observed that "if true equality between male and female persons is to be achieved, we cannot ignore the threat to equality resulting from exposure to audiences of certain types of violent and degrading material. Materials portraying women as a class as objects for sexual exploitation and abuse have a negative impact on 'the individual's sense of self-worth and acceptance.' "

The Canadian approach may be contrasted with the earlier decision in *American Booksellers Association v. Hudnut*, 771 F.2d 323 (7th Cir.1985), aff'd mem., 475 U.S. 1001 (1986). In that case, the court invalidated a city ordinance that banned "pornography," defined in terms of categories of "graphic sexually explicit subordination of women, whether in pictures or in words." The court held that the ordinance violated the First Amendment precisely because it made the ideas conveyed by pornographic materials the basis for prohibiting them. The Supreme Court summarily affirmed the court of appeals decision.

10.   Further Reading. See, e.g., Henry Louis Gates, Jr., et al., Speaking of Race, Speaking of Sex: Hate Speech, Civil Rights, and Civil Liberties (1994); Thomas David Jones, Human Rights: Group Defamation, Freedom of Expression, and the Law of Nations (1998); Mari J. Matsuda et al., Words That Wound: Critical Race Theory, Assaultive Speech, and the First Amendment (1993); The Price We Pay: The Case Against Racist Speech, Hate Propaganda, and Pornography (Laura J. Lederer & Richard Delgado eds. 1995); Striking a Balance: Hate Speech, Freedom of Expression and Nondiscrimination (Sandra Coliver, ed. 1992); Under the Shadow of Weimar: Democracy, Law, and Racial Incitement in Six Countries (Louis Greenspan and Cyril Levitt eds. 1993).

D.   EQUALITY, NON-DISCRIMINATION AND AFFIRMATIVE ACTION

The principle of equality is implicit in the concept of human rights, as belonging to all human beings, and therefore to all equally. The assurance of equality in the enjoyment of rights occupies a central place in international human rights law, as well as in the constitutional law of many states. This section begins by illustrating the range of manifestations of the equality principle in international human rights law, and the long tradition of attention to both formal equality and equality in fact. It then turns to race discrimination and gender discrimination as particularly important concerns in human rights law, and concludes with a discussion of "special measures" or affirmative action.

1.   EQUALITY, EQUAL RIGHTS AND EQUAL PROTECTION

The principle of equality is recognized in the UN Charter, which affirms that one of the Organization's purposes is to "achieve international co-operation ... in promoting and encouraging respect for human rights and for fundamental freedoms for all without distinction as to race, sex, language, or religion" (Article 1 (3); see also Articles 13(b) and 55(c)), as well as in the Universal Declaration of Human Rights (Article 2), and in all of the comprehensive human rights conventions. The norm of non-discrimination is further elaborated in such specialized treaties as the Convention on the Elimination of All Forms of Racial Discrimination and the Convention on the Elimination of All Forms of Discrimination Against Women, as well as in UN Declarations addressing non-discrimination on grounds of race and religion, respectively.

The Universal Declaration and the International Covenant on Civil and Political Rights (ICCPR) include, in addition to the basic guarantee of equality in the enjoyment of rights enumerated therein, separate assurances of the right to equality before the law and equal protection of the law. See Universal Declaration, art. 7; ICCPR, art. 26. In contrast, the European Convention assures non-discrimination only in respect of rights enumerated in the convention. Article 14 provides:

> The enjoyment of the rights and freedoms set forth in this Convention shall be secured without discrimination on any ground such as sex, race, colour, language, religion, political or other opinion, national or social origin, association with a national minority, property, birth or other status.

A proposed protocol to the European Convention now under consideration would expand the protection against discrimination beyond the context of rights enumerated in the treaty. As of early 1999, a text for this protocol had not yet been approved.

Like the ICCPR, the American Convention on Human Rights and the African Charter on Human and Peoples' Rights assure both non-discrimination in the enjoyment of rights enumerated in those treaties and the right to equal protection of the law. See American Convention, arts. 1(1) & 24; African Charter, arts. 2 & 3. The African Charter further addresses equality of "peoples," providing: "All peoples shall be equal; they shall enjoy the same respect and shall have the same rights. Nothing shall justify the domination of a people by another" (Article 18). At least certain forms of discrimination violate customary international law (see subsection 2).

Although the prohibition of discrimination enjoys a pride of place in international human rights law, not all distinctions on such grounds as race, gender and religion violate this prohibition. The European Court of Human Rights has held that a distinction on one of the grounds proscribed by Article 14 of the European Convention may be permissible if it pursues a legitimate aim and utilizes proportionate means to achieve that aim. In the *Belgian Linguistics Case*, the Court, "following the principles which may be extracted from the legal practice of a large number of democratic States," held that

> the principle of equality of treatment is violated if the distinction has no objective and reasonable justification. The existence of such a justification must be assessed in relation to the aim and effects of the measure under consideration, regard being had to the principles which normally prevail in democratic societies. A difference in treatment in the exercise of a right laid down in the Convention must not only pursue a legitimate aim: Article 14 is likewise violated when it is clearly established that there is no reasonable relationship of proportionality between the means employed and the aim sought to be realised.

Case Relating to Certain Aspects of the Laws on the Use of Languages in Education in Belgium ("Belgian Linguistics Case"), 6 Eur. Ct. H.R. (ser. A) 34, 1 E.H.R.R. 252 (1968).

Similarly, the Human Rights Committee has expressed its view that "not every differentiation of treatment will constitute discrimination, if the criteria for such differentiation are reasonable and objective and if the aim is to achieve a purpose which is legitimate under the Covenant." General Comment No. 18, para. 13 (1989), in U.N. Doc. A/45/40 at 173 (1990); see also *Zwaan-de Vries v. Netherlands*, U.N. Doc. CCPR/C/OP/2 at 209, para. 13 (Hum. Rts. Comm. 1990) (finding discrimination between men and women in standard for receipt of unemployment benefits "not reasonable").

These interpretations of postwar human rights conventions build upon a rich jurisprudence interpreting the meaning of equality under other principles and sources of international law. The Permanent Court of International Justice (PCIJ), the predecessor to the International Court of Justice, elucidated the meaning of the right to equality assured by various minorities treaties during the interwar period* in an advisory opinion, *Minority Schools in Albania*. The dissenting opinion of Judge Tanaka in the *South West Africa Cases*, written some three decades later, includes a classic statement of distinctions that are consistent with international law's prohibition of discrimination.

---

* The interwar minority rights regime is discussed in Part III, Chapter 2(H)(1)(b)(i).

Minority Schools in Albania

Permanent Court of International Justice, 1935.
1935 P.C.I.J. (ser. A–B) No. 64 (Advisory Opinion).

[The case was based on a Declaration made by Albania before the Council of the League of Nations in 1921. Article 5 of the Declaration provided:

> Albanian nationals who belong to racial, religious or linguistic minorities will enjoy the same treatment and security in law and in fact as other Albanian nationals. In particular they shall have an equal right to maintain, manage and control at their own expense or to establish in the future, charitable, religious and social institutions, schools and other educational establishments, with the right to use their own language and to exercise their religion freely therein.

This Declaration was allegedly infringed by the following provisions in the Albanian Constitution of 1933:

> The instruction and education of Albanian subjects are reserved to the State and will be given in State schools. Primary education is compulsory for all Albanian nationals and will be given free of charge. Private schools of all categories at present in operation will be closed.

The PCIJ expressed the view that the Declaration accepted by Albania "was a regime of minority protection substantially the same as that which had been already agreed upon with other States" subject to the interwar minorities rights regime. Accordingly, the PCIJ would interpret the 1921 Declaration in light of "the general principles of the treaties for the protection of minorities."]

The contention of the Albanian Government is that [Article 5 of the 1921 Declaration] imposed no other obligation upon it, in educational matters, than to grant to its nationals belonging to racial, religious, or linguistic minorities a right equal to that possessed by other Albanian nationals. Once the latter have ceased to be entitled to have private schools, the former cannot claim to have them either. . . . [The Albanian Government argues that] any interpretation which would compel Albania to respect the private minority schools would create a privilege in favour of the minority and run counter to the essential idea of the law governing minorities. . . .

According to the explanations furnished to the Court by the Greek Government, . . . the application of the same regime to a majority as to a minority, whose needs are quite different, would only create an apparent equality, whereas the Albanian Declaration, consistently with ordinary minority law, was designed to ensure a genuine and effective equality, not merely a formal equality.

. . .

The idea underlying the treaties for the protection of minorities is to secure for certain elements incorporated in a State, the population of which differs from them in race, language or religion, the possibility of living peaceably alongside that population and co-operating amicably with it, while at the same time preserving the characteristics which distinguish them from the majority, and satisfying the ensuing special needs.

In order to attain this object, two things were regarded as particularly necessary, and have formed the subject of provisions in these treaties.

The first is to ensure that nationals belonging to racial, religious or linguistic minorities shall be placed in every respect on a footing of perfect equality with the other nationals of the State.

The second is to ensure for the minority elements suitable means for the preservation of their racial peculiarities, their traditions and their national characteristics.

These two requirements are indeed closely interlocked, for there would be no true equality between a majority and a minority if the latter were deprived of its own institutions, and were consistently compelled to renounce that which constitutes the very essence of its being as a minority.

. . .

Article 4 [of the 1921 Declaration] only relates to Albanian nationals and stipulates on their behalf equality before the law and the enjoyment of the same civil and political rights, without distinction as to race, language or religion. It also defines certain of these rights, with the same object of preventing differences of race, language or religion from becoming a ground of inferiority in law or an obstacle in fact to the exercise of the rights in question.

. . .

. . . [T]he Declaration goes on to make special provision for Albanian nationals belonging to minorities of race, language or religion. That is the subject dealt with in paragraph 1 of Article 5, the provision which is expressly referred to in the first question put to the Court, and with which the court must now occupy itself more particularly.

. . .

It has already been remarked that paragraph 1 of Article 5 consists of two sentences, the second of which is linked to the first by the words *in particular*: for a right apprehension of the second part, it is therefore first necessary to determine the meaning and the scope of the first sentence.

This sentence is worded as follows:

"Albanian nationals who belong to racial, linguistic or religious minorities, will enjoy the same treatment and security in law and in fact as other Albanian nationals."

The question that arises is what is meant by the *same treatment and security in law and in fact*.

. . .

[As] Article 4 stipulates equality before the law for all Albanian nationals, while Article 5 stipulates the "same treatment and security in law and in fact" for Albanian nationals belonging to racial, religious or linguistic minorities as compared with other Albanian nationals, it is natural to conclude that the "same treatment and security in law and in fact" implies a notion of equality which is peculiar to the relations between the majority and minorities.

This special conception finds expression in the idea of an equality in fact which in Article 5 supplements equality in law. All Albanian nationals enjoy the equality in law stipulated in Article 4; on the other hand the equality between members of the majority and of the minority must, according to the terms of Article 5, be an equality in law and in fact.

It is perhaps not easy to define the distinction between the notions of equality in fact and equality in law; nevertheless, it may be said that the former notion excludes the idea of a merely formal equality....

Equality in law precludes discrimination of any kind; whereas equality in fact may involve the necessity of different treatment in order to attain a result which establishes an equilibrium between different situations.

It is easy to imagine cases in which equality of treatment of the majority and of the minority, whose situation and requirements are different, would result in inequality in fact; treatment of this description would run counter to the first sentence of paragraph 1 of Article 5. The equality between members of the majority and of the minority must be an effective, genuine equality; that is the meaning of this provision.

The second sentence of this paragraph provides as follows:

"In particular they shall have an equal right to maintain, manage and control at their own expense or to establish in the future, charitable, religious and social institutions, schools and other educational establishments, with the right to use their own language and to exercise their religion freely therein."

This sentence of the paragraph being linked to the first by the words "in particular", it is natural to conclude that it envisages a particularly important illustration of the application of the principle of identical treatment in law and in fact that is stipulated in the first sentence of the paragraph. For the institutions mentioned in the second sentence are indispensable to enable the minority to enjoy the same treatment as the majority, not only in law but also in fact. The abolition of these institutions, which alone can satisfy the special requirements of the minority groups, and their replacement by government institutions, would destroy this equality of treatment, for its effect would be to deprive the minority of the institutions appropriate to its needs, whereas the majority would continue to have them supplied in the institutions created by the State.

Far from creating a privilege in favour of the minority, as the Albanian Government avers, this stipulation ensures that the majority shall not be given a privileged situation as compared with the minority.

. . .

If the object and effect of the second sentence of [paragraph 1 of Article 5] is to ensure that Albanian nationals belonging to racial, linguistic or religions minorities shall in fact enjoy the same treatment as other Albanian nationals, it is clear that the expression "equal right" must be construed on the assumption that the right stipulated must always be accorded to the members of the minority. The idea embodied in the expression "equal right" is that the right thus conferred on the members of the minority cannot in any case be inferior to the corresponding right of other Albanian nationals. In other words, the members of the minority must always enjoy the right stipulated in the Declaration, and, in addition, any more extensive rights which the State may accord to other nationals. The right provided by the Declaration is in fact the minimum necessary to guarantee effective and genuine equality as between the majority and the minority; but if the members of the majority should be granted a right more extensive than that which is provided, the principle of equality of treatment would come into play and would require that the more extensive right should also be granted to the members of the minority.

. . .

Dissenting Opinion of Judge Tanaka, *South West Africa Cases*

(Ethiopia v. South Africa; Liberia v. South Africa).
International Court of Justice, 1966.
1966 I.C.J. Rep. 6, 248 (July 18) (Tanaka, J., dissenting).

[The applicant states, Ethiopia and Liberia, brought a contentious case against South Africa alleging that it had violated the terms of its Mandate for South West Africa (now Namibia) by maintaining the system of *apartheid* there. Among the violations alleged was a breach of Article 2, paragraph 2, of the Mandate, which required the Mandatory to "promote to the utmost the material and moral well-being and the social progress of the inhabitants of the territory." Although the International Court of Justice did not reach the merits of this case, certain aspects of the merits were addressed in the dissenting opinion of Judge Tanaka.

Turning first to multilateral treaties as a source of international legal obligation, Judge Tanaka concluded that the United Nations Charter contains a legal norm of equality before the law and the principle of non-discrimination on grounds of race and color and that this norm is applicable to South Africa's Mandate over South West Africa. He then concluded, on the basis of numerous resolutions, declarations and treaties, that "the norm of non-discrimination or non-separation on the basis of race has become a rule of customary international law...."]

... Although the existence of [the principle of equality before the law] is universally recognized as we have seen above, its precise content is not very clear.

This principle has been recognized as one of the fundamental principles of modern democracy and government based on the rule of law. Judge Lauterpacht puts it:

> "The claim to equality before the law is in a substantial sense the most fundamental of the rights of man. It occupies the first place in most written constitutions. It is the starting point of all other liberties." (Sir Hersch Lauterpacht, *An International Bill of the Rights of Man*, 1945, p. 115.)

Historically, this principle was derived from the Christian idea of the equality of all men before God. All mankind are children of God, and, consequently, brothers and sisters, notwithstanding their natural and social differences, namely man and woman, husband and wife, master and slave, etc. The idea of equality of man is derived from the fact that human beings "by the common possession of reason" distinguish themselves "from other living beings." (Lauterpacht, *op.cit.*, p. 116.) This idea existed already in the Stoic philosophy, and was developed by the scholastic philosophers and treated by natural law scholars and encyclopedists of the seventeenth and eighteenth centuries. It received legislative formulation however, at the end of the eighteenth century first by the Bill of Rights of some American states, next by the Declaration of the French Revolution, and then in the course of the nineteenth century the equality clause, as we have seen above, became one of the common elements of the constitutions of modern European and other countries.

Examining the principle of equality before the law, we consider that it is philosophically related to the concepts of freedom and justice. The freedom of individual persons, being one of the fundamental ideas of law, is not unlimited and must be restricted by the principle of equality allotting to each individual a sphere of freedom which is due to him. In other words the freedom can exist only under the premise of the equality principle.

In what way is each individual allotted his sphere by the principle of equality? What is the content of this principle? The principle is that what is equal is to be treated equally and what is different is to be treated differently, namely proportionately to the factual difference. This is what was indicated by Aristotle as *justitia commutativa* and *justitia distributiva*.

The most fundamental point in the equality principle is that all human beings as persons have an equal value in themselves, that they are the aim itself and not means for others, and that, therefore, slavery is denied. The idea of equality of men as persons and equal treatment as such is of a metaphysical nature. It underlies all modern, democratic and humanitarian law systems as a principle of natural law. This idea, however, does not exclude the different treatment of persons from the consideration of the differences of factual circumstances such as sex, age, language, religion, economic condition, education, etc. To treat different matters equally in a mechanical way would be as unjust as to treat equal matters differently.

. . .

We can say ... that the principle of equality before the law does not mean the absolute equality, namely equal treatment of men without regard to individual, concrete circumstances, but it means the relative equality, namely the principle to treat equally what are equal and unequally what are unequal.

The question is, in what case equal treatment or different treatment should exist. If we attach importance to the fact that no man is strictly equal to another and he may have some particularities, the principle of equal treatment could be easily evaded by referring to any factual and legal differences and the existence of this principle would be virtually denied. A different treatment comes into question only when and to the extent that it corresponds to the nature of the difference. To treat unequal matters differently according to their inequality is not only permitted but required. The issue is whether the difference exists. Accordingly, not every different treatment can be justified by the existence of differences, but only such as corresponds to the differences themselves, namely that which is called for by the idea of justice—"the principle to treat equal equally and unequal according to its inequality, constitutes an essential content of the idea of justice" (Goetz Hueck, *Der Grundsatz der Gleichmässigen Behandlung in Privatrecht*, 1958, p. 106) *[translation]*.

. . .

Briefly, a different treatment is permitted when it can be justified by the criterion of justice. One may replace justice by the concept of reasonableness generally referred to by the Anglo–American school of law.

Justice or reasonableness as a criterion for the different treatment logically excludes arbitrariness. The arbitrariness which is prohibited, means the purely objective fact and not the subjective condition of those concerned. Accordingly, the arbitrariness can be asserted without regard to his motive or purpose.

. . .

The Respondent for the purpose of justifying its policy of apartheid or separate development quotes many examples of different treatment such as minorities treaties, public conveniences (between man and woman), etc. Nobody would object to the different treatment in these cases as a violation of the norm of non-discrimination or non-separation....

. . .

In the case of the minorities treaties the norm of non-discrimination as a reverse side of the notion of equality before the law prohibits a State to exclude members of a minority group from participating in rights, interests and opportunities which a majority population group can enjoy. On the other hand, a minority group shall be guaranteed the exercise of their own religious and education activities. This guarantee is conferred on members of a minority group, for the purpose of protection of their interests and not from the motive of discrimination itself....

In any event, in case of a minority, members belonging to this group, enjoying the citizenship on equal terms with members of majority groups, have conferred on them the possibility of cultivating their own religious, educational or linguistic values as a recognition of their fundamental human rights and freedoms.

The spirit of the minorities treaties, therefore, is not negative and prohibitive, but positive and permissive.

. . .

In the case of apartheid, we cannot deny the existence of reasonableness in some matters that diverse ethnic groups should be treated in certain aspects differently from one another. As we have seen above, differentiation in law and politics is one of the most remarkable tendencies of the modern political society. This tendency is in itself derived from the concept of justice, therefore it cannot be judged as wrong. . . .

. . .

. . . [W]hether a racial or ethnic group can be treated in the same way as categories such as minors, disabled persons, men and women, is doubtful. Our conclusion on this point is negative. The reasons therefor are that the scientific and clear-cut definition of race is not established; that what man considers as a matter of common-sense as criteria to distinguish one race from the other, are the appearance, particularly physical characteristics such as colour, hair, etc., which do not constitute in themselves relevant factors as the basis for different political or legal treatment; and that, if there exists the necessity to treat one race differently from another, this necessity is not derived from the physical characteristics or other racial qualifications but other factors, namely religious, linguistic, educational, social, etc., which in themselves are not related to race or colour.

Briefly, in these cases it is possible that the different treatment in certain aspects is reasonably required by the differences of religion, language, education, custom, etc., not by reason of race or colour. Therefore, the Respondent tries in some cases to justify the different treatment of population groups by the concept of cultural population groups. The different treatment would be justified if there really existed the need for it by reason of cultural differences. The different treatment, however, should be condemned if cultural reasons are referred to for the purpose of dissimulating the underlying racial intention.

. . .

The important question is whether there exists, from the point of view of the requirements of justice, any necessity for establishing an exception to the principle of equality, and the Respondent must prove this necessity, namely the reasonableness of different treatment.

On the aspect of "reasonableness" two considerations arise. The one is the consideration whether or not the individual necessity exists to establish an exception to the general principle of equality before the law and equal opportunity. In this sense the necessity may be conceived as of the same nature as in the case of minorities treaties of which the objectives are protective and beneficial. The other is the consideration whether the different treatment does or does not harm the sense of dignity of individual persons.

For instance, if we consider education, on which the Parties argued extensively, we cannot deny the value of vernacular as the medium of instruction and the result thereof would be separate schooling as between children of diverse population groups, particularly between the Whites and the Natives. In this case separate education and schooling may be recognized as reasonable. This is justified by the nature of the matter in question. But even in such a case, by reason of the matter which is related to a delicate racial and ethnic problem, the manner of dealing with this matter should be extremely careful. But, so far as the public use of such facilities as hotels, buses, etc., justification of discriminatory and separate treatment by racial groups cannot be found in the same way as separation between smokers and non-smokers in a train.

. . .

One of the characteristics of the policy of apartheid is marked by its restrictive tendency on the basis of racial distinction. . . .

. . .

Finally, we wish to make the following conclusive and supplementary remarks on the matter of the Applicants' Submissions Nos. 3 and 4.

1. The principle of equality before the law requires that what are equal are to be treated equally and what are different are to be treated differently. The question arises: what is equal and what is different.

2. All human beings, notwithstanding the differences in their appearance and other minor points, are equal in their dignity as persons. Accordingly, from the point of view of human rights and fundamental freedoms, they must be treated equally.

3. The principle of equality does not mean absolute equality, but recognizes relative equality, namely different treatment proportionate to concrete individual circumstances. Different treatment must not be given arbitrarily; it requires reasonableness, or must be in conformity with justice, as in the treatment of minorities, different treatment of the sexes regarding public conveniences, etc. In these cases, the differentiation is aimed at the protection of those concerned, and it is not detrimental and therefore not against their will.

4. Discrimination according to the criterion of "race, colour, national or tribal origin" in establishing the rights and duties of the inhabitants of the territory is not considered reasonable and just. Race, colour, etc., do not constitute in themselves factors which can influence the rights and duties of the inhabitants as in the case of sex, age, language, religion, etc. If differentiation be required, it would be derived from the difference of language, religion, custom, etc., not from the racial difference itself. In the policy of apartheid the necessary logical and material link between differ-

ence itself and different treatment, which can justify such treatment in the case of sex, minorities, etc., does not exist.

We cannot imagine in what case the distinction between Natives and White, namely racial distinction apart from linguistic, cultural or other differences, may necessarily have an influence on the establishment of the rights and duties of the inhabitants of the territory.

5.   Consequently, the practice of apartheid is fundamentally unreasonable and unjust. The unreasonableness and injustice do not depend upon the intention or motive of the Mandatory, namely its *mala fides*. Distinction on a racial basis is in itself contrary to the principle of equality which is of the character of natural law, and accordingly illegal.

The above-mentioned contention of the Respondent that the policy of apartheid has a neutral character, as a tool to attain a particular end, is not right. If the policy of apartheid is a means, the axiom that the end cannot justify the means can be applied to this policy.

. . .

Notes

1.   In its advisory opinion in the *Minority Schools in Albania* case, the PCIJ distinguished between equality in law, which it interpreted as formal equality or nondiscrimination, and equality in fact (or substantive equality). The PCIJ explained that the minorities treaties required both. Is there a tension between these two principles? In Judge Tanaka's dissent in the *South West Africa* case, he stated that "[t]he principle of equality before the law requires that what are equal are to be treated equally and what are different are to be treated differently." Does his opinion imply that equality before the law had come to include equality in fact?

2.   The PCIJ observed that the abolition of "[charitable, religious and social institutions, schools and other educational establishments], which alone can satisfy the special requirements of the minority groups, . . . would destroy . . . equality of treatment, for its effect would be to deprive the minority of the institutions appropriate to its needs, whereas the majority would continue to have them supplied in the institutions created by the State." Does the Court's reasoning have any implications for multi-ethnic countries where no distinct group constitutes a majority—or where the minority claiming a right to maintain its own institutions is a *dominant* minority, such as South African whites under apartheid?

Consider the situation in Bosnia and Hercegovina following the 1992–95 inter-ethnic conflict in that country. In 1997, the Education Ministry decreed that all children in the area of Bosnia jointly controlled by Bosnian Croats and Muslims must declare their ethnicity; students would then be separated into separate classes with different lectures and perhaps entirely different curricula. This practice was criticized internationally on the ground that it perpetuated ethnic hatred, and the policy was formally reversed. See Lee Hockstader, *In Bosnia, Classes Open on School Segrega-*

tion; Separate Curricula Based on Ethnicity Raise Questions, Wash. Post, Oct. 19, 1997. Under what circumstances are separate schools established for children belonging to a specific ethnic, racial, religious or national group consistent with the equality principle? Under what circumstances—if any—does the equality principle mandate state support for separate educational institutions for groups that are ethnically, racially, nationally or religiously distinct? For a critical analysis of the Bosnian effort to establish separate classes for different ethnic groups, see International Human Rights Law Group, Action Alert: Segregation in Federation Schools (Oct. 6, 1997).

3.   The basic approach toward separate educational and other minority institutions embodied in the minorities treaties as interpreted by the Permanent Court of International Justice in the *Minority Schools in Albania* case is enjoying a resurgence in contemporary practice, particularly in Europe. For example, the Framework Convention for the Protection of National Minorities, opened for signature Feb. 1, 1995, E.T.S. No. 157, provides that "the Parties shall recognise that persons belonging to a national minority have the right to set up and to manage their own private educational and training establishments." Id., art. 13(1). The Convention, which was adopted under the auspices of the Council of Europe, makes clear that "[t]he exercise of this right shall not entail any financial obligation for the Parties." Id., art. 13(2). For an example of national legislation supporting minority education institutions, see Act LXXVII on the Rights of National Minorities, which the Hungarian Parliament adopted in 1993. Pursuant to Article 18(3), "Minority communities" have the right to:

> a) initiate the creation of the necessary conditions for kindergarten, primary, secondary and higher education in the mother tongue or "bilingually" (i.e. in the mother tongue and in Hungarian);
>
> b) establish a national educational ... structure of their own within the boundaries of existing laws.

This legislation also requires government authorities to provide education in minority students' mother tongue at state institutions under certain circumstances. Pursuant to Article 43(2), "[i]n accordance with the decision of their parents or guardian, children will be and may be educated in their mother tongue, 'bilingually' (in their mother tongue and in Hungarian), or in Hungarian." At the request of the parents or legal representatives of at least eight students belonging to the same minority group, "it is compulsory to establish and run a minority class or group". Id., para. 4.

4.   Under the analysis set forth in Judge Tanaka's dissenting opinion, can race itself ever provide a permissible basis for a distinction in legal rights and duties? If not, is this because racial characteristics are never relevant to legitimate public objectives, or because the use of racial distinctions inflicts harm on the dignity of individual persons, or for some combination of these reasons?

Does membership in an ethnic group ever provide a permissible basis for a distinction in legal rights and duties? What does Judge Tanaka mean by membership in an "ethnic group," and how does this differ from race? In Judge Tanaka's analysis, are ethnic distinctions the same as cultural diversity, which Judge Tanaka describes as a legitimate basis for distinctions in legal rights and duties? How does Judge Tanaka reconcile the minorities treaties with the norm of non-discrimination?

5. According to Judge Tanaka's dissenting opinion, what is the relevance, if any, of motive in determining whether a distinction based upon race is compatible with international law? Is it possible to reconcile Judge Tanaka's statement that the "unreasonableness and injustice [of apartheid] do not depend upon the intention or motive of the Mandatory, namely its *mala fides*" with his emphasis on the fact that the interwar minorities treaties established special rights for members of minority groups "for the purpose of protection of their interests and not from the motive of discrimination itself"?

6. Judge Tanaka asserted that the idea of equality "does not exclude the different treatment of persons from the consideration of the differences of factual circumstances such as sex...." What "factual circumstances" relating to one's sex would justify different treatment in, e.g., employment?

2. RACIAL DISCRIMINATION

As the dissenting opinion of Judge Tanaka in the *South West Africa Cases* concludes, "the norm of non-discrimination or non-separation on the basis of race has become a rule of customary international law." His opinion also concluded that the norm of non-discrimination on the basis of race is contained in the UN Charter. A subsequent advisory opinion by the International Court of Justice similarly concluded that South Africa's policy of apartheid, as practiced in Namibia, violated the UN Charter:

> Under the Charter of the United Nations, the former Mandatory [i.e., South Africa] had pledged itself to observe and respect, in a territory having an international status, human rights and fundamental freedoms for all without distinction as to race. To establish instead, and to enforce, distinctions, exclusions, restrictions and limitations exclusively based on grounds of race, colour, descent or national or ethnic origin which constitute a denial of fundamental rights is a flagrant violation of the purposes and principles of the Charter.

Legal Consequences for States of the Continued Presence of South Africa in Namibia (South West Africa) Notwithstanding Security Council Resolution 276 (1970), 1971 I.C.J. 16, 57, ¶ 131 (Advisory Opinion of June 21). According to the Restatement of Foreign Relations Law, systematic racial discrimination is a violation of customary international law if practiced, encouraged or condoned as a matter of state policy. Restatement § 702.

As noted earlier, various conventions prohibit discrimination in the enjoyment of enumerated rights on the basis of race or color, and also ensure equal protection of the laws. These rights are further elaborated in a specialized convention, the International Convention on the Elimination of All Forms of Racial Discrimination, 660 U.N.T.S. 195.

States Parties' compliance with the Race Convention is supervised by the Committee on the Elimination of Racial Discrimination ("CERD"). The Convention provides for both an interstate complaint procedure (Articles 11–13) and a procedure enabling CERD to receive communications from individuals or groups of individuals within the jurisdiction of states that have recognized its competence in this regard (Article 14). In practice, however, the Committee's principal supervisory mechanism is its review, pursuant to Article 9, of States Parties' reports on measures they have taken to give effect to the Convention. Records of CERD's questions and comments when reviewing these reports have at times received substantial public attention, and its comments are often cited for the insights they provide into the meaning of the Convention's substantive provisions. See, e.g., *Jersild v. Denmark*, 298 Eur. Ct. H.R. (ser. A), para. 21, 19 E.H.R.R. 1 (1994). Article 9 also authorizes CERD to make "general recommendations" in its reports to the General Assembly. In recent years, CERD has increasingly used that authority to issue interpretations of the Convention. See Compilation of General Recommendations, U.N. Doc. CERD/C/365 (1999).

Theodor Meron, *The Meaning and Reach of the International Convention on the Elimination of All Forms of Racial Discrimination*

79 Am. J. Int'l L. 283 (1985).*

. . .

Article 1(1) [of the International Convention on the Elimination of All Forms of Racial Discrimination (the Convention)] defines racial discrimination as

> any distinction, exclusion, restriction or preference based on race, colour, descent, or national or ethnic origin which has the purpose or effect of nullifying or impairing the recognition, enjoyment or exercise, on an equal footing, of human rights and fundamental freedoms in the political, economic, social, cultural or any other field of public life.

Unlike Article 2(1) of the International Covenant on Civil and Political Rights (Political Covenant), which only addresses distinctions in the enjoyment of the rights recognized by the Covenant, Article 1(1) extends to all human rights and fundamental freedoms, whatever their source.

This definition of racial discrimination is different from the statement of the right to equality before the law, which appears in Article 5 of the Convention, but the notion of equality before the law must be taken into account in interpreting the definition. It has been suggested that equality and nondiscrimination can be seen as affirmative and negative statements of the same principle. But what does "equality" mean? In the U.S. fair employment laws, there is tension between equality in the sense of equal treatment (obligation of means) and equality in the sense of equal achievement (equality of result). The goal of equal achievement, of course, has a

---

redistributive quality.... The Committee [that monitors States Parties' compliance with the Race Convention] appears to regard equality of result as the principal object of the Convention....

. . .

That the goal of de facto equality is central to the interpretation of the Convention is supported by references in the Preamble to enjoyment of certain rights "without distinction of any kind" and to "discrimination between human beings on the grounds of race," as well as by the reference in Article 5 to equality before the law. Moreover, the phrase "on an equal footing" in Article 1(1), considered in conjunction with the exception created in Article 1(4) allowing distinctions for the purpose of affirmative action, "to ensure ... groups or individuals equal enjoyment or exercise of human rights," and the obligation imposed by Article 2(2) to take certain affirmative action indicate that the Convention promotes racial equality, not merely color-neutral values.... Of particular importance in this context is Article 2(1)(c), which requires states to take policy measures and to amend, rescind or nullify any laws or regulations that have the effect of creating or perpetuating racial discrimination.

Past acts of discrimination have created systemic patterns of discrimination in many societies. The present effects of past discrimination may be continued or even exacerbated by facially neutral policies or practices that, though not purposely discriminatory, perpetuate the consequences of prior, often intentional discrimination....

. . .

Whether the provisions of the Convention apply not only to public, but also to private, or partly private, action presents particular difficulties of interpretation. Article 1(1) defines racial discrimination as certain distinctions "in the political, economic, social, cultural or any other field of *public life*" (emphasis added). This suggests that only public action is targeted by the Convention, including the activities of organizations that, though legally autonomous, perform functions of a public nature. But without explicitly addressing the possible conflict with Article 1(1), Article 2(1)(d) obligates state parties to "prohibit and bring to an end, by all appropriate means, including legislation as required by circumstances, racial discrimination by any persons, group or organization." ... Interpreted in the context of Article 1(1), Article 2(1)(d) appears to mean that racially discriminatory action that occurs in public life is prohibited even if it is taken by a person, group or organization. But how does one determine what "public life" is? To which areas does the prohibition of discrimination apply? When does the duty to accord equal treatment prevail?

. . .

... "[P]ublic life" is not synonymous with governmental action but is the opposite of "private life," which would thus not be reached by the Convention. But to apply this concept to concrete situations is difficult. The legislative history reveals concern that freedom of thought and expression may be jeopardized and the private life of individuals invaded.

Perhaps a rationale for at least some distinction between public and private life can be developed by reference to the right of association. That right is recognized in Article 5(d)(ix).... Although freedom of association is recognized in the Convention only in [this] limited context ..., that right is widely stated in other human rights instruments, including Article 22 of the Political Covenant, which establishes (Art. 22(2)) strict limits on any restrictions that may be imposed on its exercise. In accordance with the rule stated in Article 31(3)(c) of the Vienna Convention on the Law of Treaties,* the right of association—as a recognized principle of international human rights law—may therefore be taken into account in the interpretation of the Convention so as to protect strictly personal relations from its reach.

. . .

The dichotomy between the public and private realms also arises in the context of Article 2(1)(b), which forbids state parties to "sponsor, defend or support racial discrimination by any persons or organizations." Arguably, "support" encompasses not only the extension of benefits as a positive action, but also the failure to impose obligations that are required of other persons or organizations....

Article 4 imposes the following obligations on state parties: to penalize the dissemination of ideas based on racial superiority or hatred, incitement to racial discrimination, all acts of violence or incitement to such acts against any race or group of persons of another color or ethnic origin, and the provision of any assistance to racist activities, including the financing of such activities ...; to declare illegal and prohibit organizations and all other propaganda activities that promote and incite racial discrimination, and participation in such organizations or activities ...; and to prohibit public authorities or institutions from promoting or inciting racial discrimination....

. . .

Both racist groups as organizations and individuals who participate in such groups in violation of the prohibitions stated in Article 4 are subject to criminal sanctions. The opening paragraph of Article 4 identifies the eradication of all incitement to or acts of racial discrimination as the objective underlying the obligations enumerated....

The offenses set forth in Article 4 go beyond the definition of racial discrimination given in Article 1(1). The latter encompasses only such prohibited distinctions as lead to the denial of human rights on an equal footing. The former prohibits certain organizations and activities, including the dissemination of opinion and thought (ideas based on racial hatred or superiority), regardless of whether or not they lead to a denial of human rights....

. . .

* [Art. 31(c)(3) provides that a treaty shall be interpreted in light of "any relevant rules of international law applicable in the relations between the parties."–Editors' Note.]

Article 4 explicitly mandates legislative action to implement its provisions. The Committee has insisted that reporting states have a duty to legislate irrespective of whether the prohibited activities actually occur in them, except where legislation that fully satisfies the provisions of Article 4 is already in place.... [This] is consistent with the prophylactic purposes of the Convention as indicated by the definition of racial discrimination, the wide scope of the obligations of the parties and the various educational measures mentioned in Article 7. The Committee has emphasized, correctly, that "[f]ar from being concerned solely with combating acts of racial discrimination after they have been perpetrated, the national policies of the State parties must also provide for preventive programmes, which seek to remove the sources from which those acts might spring—be they subjective prejudices or objective socio-economic conditions." ...

Organizations that promote racial discrimination, and not merely their specific activities which have that purpose or effect, are prohibited. During the drafting debates, an amendment inserting the words "or the activities of such organizations" after the word "organizations" in paragraph (b) was not adopted, perhaps because the very existence of such organizations was felt to be destructive of the aims of the Convention.

. . .

Committee on the Elimination of Racial Discrimination, General Recommendation XIV

U.N. Doc. A/48/18, at 114 (1993).

1. Non-discrimination, together with equality before the law and equal protection of the law without any discrimination, constitutes a basic principle in the protection of human rights. The Committee wishes to draw the attention of States parties to certain features of the definition of racial discrimination in article 1, paragraph 1, of the International Convention on the Elimination of All Forms of Racial Discrimination. It is of the opinion that the words "based on" do not bear any meaning different from "on the grounds of" in preambular paragraph 7. A distinction is contrary to the Convention if it has either the purpose or the effect of impairing particular rights and freedoms. This is confirmed by the obligation placed upon States parties by article 2, paragraph 1 (c), to nullify any law or practice which has the effect of creating or perpetuating racial discrimination.

2. The Committee observes that a differentiation of treatment will not constitute discrimination if the criteria for such differentiation, judged against the objectives and purposes of the Convention, are legitimate or fall within the scope of article 1, paragraph 4, of the Convention. In considering the criteria that may have been employed, the Committee will acknowledge that particular actions may have varied purposes. In seeking to determine whether an action has an effect contrary to the Convention, it will look to see whether that action has an unjustifiable disparate impact upon a group distinguished by race, colour, descent, or national or ethnic origin.

3. Article 1, paragraph 1, of the Convention also refers to the political, economic, social and cultural fields; the related rights and freedoms are set up in article 5.

Notes

1. The United States signed the Race Convention in 1966, but did not ratify it until 1994. It did so subject to the following:

Upon signature:

> The Constitution of the United States contains provisions for the protection of individual rights, such as the right of free speech, and nothing in the Convention shall be deemed to require or to authorize legislation or other action by the United States of America incompatible with the provisions of the Constitution of the United States of America.

Upon ratification:

> I.   The Senate's advice and consent is subject to the following reservations:
>
> (1) That the Constitution and laws of the United States contain extensive protections of individual freedom of speech, expression and association. Accordingly, the United States does not accept any obligation under this Convention, in particular under articles 4 and 7, to restrict those rights, through the adoption of legislation or any other measures, to the extent that they are protected by the Constitution and laws of the United States.
>
> (2) That the Constitution and laws of the United States establish extensive protections against discrimination, reaching significant areas of non-governmental activity. Individual privacy and freedom from governmental interference in private conduct, however, are also recognized as among the fundamental values which shape our free and democratic society. The United States understands that the identification of the rights protected under the Convention by reference in article 1 to fields of "public life" reflects a similar distinction between spheres of public conduct that are customarily the subject of governmental regulation, and spheres of private conduct that are not. To the extent, however, that the Convention calls for a broader regulation of private conduct, the United States does not accept any obligation under this Convention to enact legislation or take other measures under paragraph (1) of article 2, subparagraphs (1) (c) and (d) of article 2, article 3 and article 5 with respect to private conduct except as mandated by the Constitution and laws of the United States.
>
> (3) That with reference to article 22 of the Convention, before any dispute to which the United States is a party may be submitted to the jurisdiction of the International Court of Justice under this article, the specific consent of the United States is required in each case.

II. the Senate's advice and consent is subject to the following understanding, which shall apply to the obligations of the United States under this Convention:

That the United States understands that this Convention shall be implemented by the Federal Government to the extent that it exercises jurisdiction over the matters covered therein, and otherwise by the state and local governments. To the extent that state and local governments exercise jurisdiction over such matters, the Federal Government shall, as necessary, take appropriate measures to ensure the fulfilment of this Convention.

III. The Senate's advice and consent is subject to the following declaration:

That the United States declares that the provisions of the Convention are not self-executing.

For critical analyses of the United States package of reservations, understandings and declarations, see International Human Rights Law Group, U.S. Ratification of the International Convention on the Elimination of All Forms of Racial Discrimination (1994); Gay J. McDougall, *Toward a Meaningful International Regime: The Domestic Relevance of International Efforts to Eliminate All Forms of Racial Discrimination*, 40 Howard L.J. 571 (1997), and other articles in this symposium volume on the Race Convention. For general accounts of the Race Convention, see, e.g., Michael Banton, International Action Against Racial Discrimination (1996); Natan Lerner, The U.N. Convention on the Elimination of All Forms of Racial Discrimination (2d ed. 1980).

2. As Professor Meron observes, the Race Convention requires States Parties to "prohibit and bring to an end, by all appropriate means, ... racial discrimination by any persons, group or organization," Article 2(1)(c). Thus the Convention clearly requires States Parties to address conduct by private parties. The Convention also defines racial discrimination in terms of distinctions that have the purpose or effect of nullifying or impairing the enjoyment, on an equal footing, of rights "in the political, economic, social, cultural or any other field of public life." If a state were a party to the Race Convention, would its government be required to address the following situations?

• Owners of private houses who rent a room in the house to strangers frequently choose roomers of the same race as themselves.

• Students at a private college are allowed to select their roommates after the first year. Students consistently choose roommates of the same race as themselves.

• Census records show that citizens of the country virtually always marry people of the same race as themselves. Assume that the relevant country is racially diverse.

The United States sought to avoid taking on obligations it deemed unduly intrusive by means of its second reservation, which limits regulation to the sphere of "public conduct," as opposed to "private conduct." The legislative history of the reservation suggests that this distinction was intended to correspond to the state action doctrine in U.S. constitutional law. See Sen. Exec. Rep. 103–29, 103d Cong., 2d Sess. 21–24 (1994) (explaining proposed reservation). Was such a broad reservation needed to avoid undue interference with legitimate interests in the private sphere?

3. Under Article 2(1)(a) of the Race Convention, states undertake not to engage in any act or practice of racial discrimination, and Article 1 defines the term "racial discrimination." Is all differential treatment on the basis of "race, colour, descent, or national or ethnic origin" that comes within this definition unlawful under the Convention? Does the second paragraph of General Comment XIV suggest that a form of intentional differential treatment that is covered by the definition in Article 1 may nonetheless be permissible if its purpose is legitimate? Are the standards for judging the lawfulness of differential treatment on the basis of race under the Race Convention more stringent or less stringent than the standard of "objective and reasonable justification" employed under Article 26 of the ICCPR and Article 14 of the European Convention?

Under U.S. constitutional law, intentional distinctions on the basis of race may be employed by the federal and state governments only if the reliance on race is shown to be necessary to the achievement of a compelling government interest. See supra Part II; *Adarand Constructors, Inc. v. Pena*, infra subsection 4. How does this standard of justification compare with the standards employed under the Race Convention, the ICCPR, and the European Convention?

When the United States ratified the ICCPR, the package of RUDs included an "understanding" containing the following passage:

> The United States understands distinctions based upon race, colour, sex, language, religion, political or other opinion, national or social origin, property, birth or any other status—as those terms are used in Article 2, paragraph 1 and Article 26—to be permitted when such distinctions are, at minimum, rationally related to a legitimate governmental objective.

What purpose or purposes does this "understanding" serve? (For further discussion, see Chapter 3(C) infra, pp. 1173–1176.) Does it reduce the obligations of the United States under Article 26 to the level of insignificance? Why did the RUDs accompanying the U.S. ratification of the Race Convention contain no comparable understanding?

4. Do the same standards apply under the Race Convention for evaluating intentional distinctions based on race and intentional distinctions based on ethnic origin? If so, then are institutional regimes for the benefit of national minorities and indigenous peoples, such as those described at pp. 440–457 above, incompatible with the Race Convention? See also Note 7 on p. 1064 below.

5. The U.S. RUDs do not address the question of facially neutral government policies that have unintended discriminatory effects. Does the phras-

ing of the definition of discrimination in Article 1(1) support the interpretation of the Convention as requiring both formal and substantive equality? Does the CERD Committee's General Recommendation XIV resolve the issue, and does it do so persuasively?*

In U.S. constitutional law, facially neutral policies with unintended discriminatory effects are not treated as racially discriminatory, and are generally upheld if any rational basis can be conceived to support them. In *Washington v. Davis*, 426 U.S. 229, 248 (1976), the Supreme Court explained:

> A rule that a statute designed to serve neutral ends is nevertheless invalid, absent compelling justification, if in practice it benefits or burdens one race more than another would be far-reaching and would raise serious questions about, and perhaps invalidate, a whole range of tax, welfare, public service, regulatory, and licensing statutes that may be more burdensome to the poor and to the average black than to the more affluent white.
>
> . . . [I]n our view, extension of the rule beyond those areas where it is already applicable by reason of statute, such as in the field of public employment, should await legislative prescription.

As this passage indicates, some U.S. antidiscrimination statutes do address practices with unintended discriminatory effects; for example, Title VII of the Civil Rights Act of 1964 prohibits employment practices with disparate impact by race or gender unless they are justified by "business necessity." See 42 U.S.C. § 2000e–2. Does adherence to the Race Convention require the United States to apply a disparate impact standard to the wide "range of tax, welfare, public service, regulatory and licensing" practices of the state and federal governments? Does General Recommendation XIV clarify the standard to be applied in determining whether an action had an "unjustifiable disparate impact" on a group distinguished by race?

3. GENDER DISCRIMINATION

Like race and color, a person's sex or gender is an impermissible basis in international human rights law for adverse distinctions in the enjoyment of fundamental rights and the protection of law. As noted earlier, the UN Charter provides that one of the Organization's purposes is to "achieve international co-operation . . . in promoting and encouraging respect for human rights and for fundamental freedoms for all without distinction as to race, *sex*, language, or religion" (Article 1 (3), emphasis added). Article 2 of the Universal Declaration provides that "Everyone is entitled to all the rights and freedoms set forth in this Declaration, without distinction of any kind, such as . . . sex. . . ." Similarly, both the ICCPR and the Covenant on Economic, Social, and Cultural Rights assure the enjoyment of rights

---

* Similar issues arise under Articles 2 and 26 of the ICCPR, see Human Rights Committee, General Comment 18, paras. 6, 7, 10. The "understanding" attached to the U.S. ratification of the ICCPR, however, discussed in Note 3, may make those aspects of equality under the ICCPR inapplicable to the United States.

enumerated therein without distinction on any ground, including sex (Article 2 of both covenants). In addition, both covenants include a separate article explicitly requiring States Parties to ensure "the equal right of men and women" to the enjoyment of rights set forth therein (Article 3 of both covenants), while Article 26 of the ICCPR provides the further assurance of equality before the law:

> All persons are equal before the law and are entitled without discrimination to the equal protection of the law. In this respect, the law shall prohibit any discrimination and guarantee to all persons equal and effective protection against discrimination on any ground such as . . . sex. . . . **

Interpreting these provisions in response to communications under the Optional Protocol, the Human Rights Committee has found distinctions between men and women in matters of immigration and naturalization,*** unemployment benefits**** and matrimonial property***** to be impermissible forms of discrimination.

Although not identical to the provisions set forth in the ICCPR, the regional human rights conventions each contain assurances of gender equality in the enjoyment of enumerated rights. In applying its test for discrimination in violation of Article 14 of the European Convention, which seeks a "reasonable relationship of proportionality between the means employed and the aim sought to be realised," the European Court of Human Rights has stated that

> the advancement of the equality of the sexes is today a major goal in the Member States of the Council of Europe. This means that very weighty reasons would have to be advanced before a difference of treatment on the ground of sex could be regarded as compatible with the Convention.

Abdulaziz, Cabales and Balkandali v. United Kingdom, 94 Eur. Ct. H.R. (ser. A) 38, 7 E.H.R.R. 471 (1985); but see *Petrovic v. Austria*, 1998–II Eur. Ct. H.R. 579 (1998) (upholding failure in 1989 to provide parental leave subsidy for fathers, while providing parental leave subsidy for mothers, as

---

** In addition to these general guarantees, both covenants include provisions reiterating the right to equality in the enjoyment of particular rights. See, e.g., Article 7 of the Covenant on Economic, Social and Cultural Rights (recognizing the right to just and favorable conditions of work, entailing, inter alia, "[f]air wages and equal remuneration for work of equal value without distinction of any kind, in particular women being guaranteed conditions of work not inferior to those enjoyed by men, with equal pay for equal work", and Articles 23 and 24 of the Political Covenant (assuring equality of men and women in respect of marriage and assuring

children the right to appropriate measures of protection "without discrimination as to . . . sex . . .").

*** *Aumeeruddy–Cziffra v. Mauritius*, U.N. Doc. CCPR/C/OP/1 at 67 (Hum. Rts. Comm. 1981).

**** *Zwaan–de Vries v. Netherlands*, U.N. Doc. CCPR/C/OP/2 at 209 (Hum. Rts. Comm. 1987); *Broeks v. Netherlands*, U.N. Doc. CCPR/C/OP/2 at 196 (Hum. Rts. Comm. 1987).

***** *Ato del Avellanal v. Peru*, U.N. Doc. A/44/40 at 196 (Hum. Rts. Comm. 1989).

within legislature's margin of appreciation in adapting policy to social change).

To implement these guarantees more fully, a separate convention was drafted dealing exclusively with gender discrimination—the Convention on the Elimination Against all Forms of Discrimination Against Women, which we examine in Part III, Chapter 2, Section F(1).

United States v. Virginia

Supreme Court of the United States, 1996.
518 U.S. 515.

■ JUSTICE GINSBURG delivered the opinion of the Court.

Virginia's public institutions of higher learning include an incomparable military college, Virginia Military Institute (VMI). The United States maintains that the Constitution's equal protection guarantee precludes Virginia from reserving exclusively to men the unique educational opportunities VMI affords. We agree.

I

Founded in 1839, VMI is today the sole single-sex school among Virginia's 15 public institutions of higher learning. VMI's distinctive mission is to produce "citizen-soldiers," men prepared for leadership in civilian life and in military service.... The school's graduates leave VMI with heightened comprehension of their capacity to deal with duress and stress, and a large sense of accomplishment for completing the hazardous course.

VMI has notably succeeded in its mission to produce leaders; among its alumni are military generals, Members of Congress, and business executives. The school's alumni overwhelmingly perceive that their VMI training helped them to realize their personal goals....

Neither the goal of producing citizen-soldiers nor VMI's implementing methodology is inherently unsuitable to women. And the school's impressive record in producing leaders has made admission desirable to some women. Nevertheless, Virginia has elected to preserve exclusively for men the advantages and opportunities a VMI education affords.

. . .

IV

We note, once again, the core instruction of this Court's pathmarking decisions in J. E. B. v. Alabama ex rel. T. B., 511 U.S. 127 (1994), and Mississippi Univ. for Women [v. Hogan, 458 U.S. 718 (1982)]: Parties who seek to defend gender-based government action must demonstrate an "exceedingly persuasive justification" for that action.

Today's skeptical scrutiny of official action denying rights or opportunities based on sex responds to volumes of history. As a plurality of this Court acknowledged a generation ago, "our Nation has had a long and unfortunate history of sex discrimination." Frontiero v. Richardson, 411 U.S. 677 (1973). Through a century plus three decades and more of that history, women did not count among voters composing "We the People"; not until 1920 did women gain a constitutional right to the franchise.... And for a half century thereafter, it remained the prevailing doctrine that government, both federal and state, could withhold from women opportunities accorded men so long as any "basis in reason" could be conceived for the discrimination. See, e. g., Goesaert v. Cleary, 335 U.S. 464 (1948) (rejecting challenge of female tavern owner and her daughter to Michigan law denying bartender licenses to females—except for wives and daughters of male tavern owners; Court would not "give ear" to the contention that "an unchivalrous desire of male bartenders to ... monopolize the calling" prompted the legislation).

In 1971, for the first time in our Nation's history, this Court ruled in favor of a woman who complained that her State had denied her the equal protection of its laws. Reed v. Reed, 404 U.S. 71 [(1971)] (holding unconstitutional Idaho Code prescription that, among " 'several persons claiming and equally entitled to administer [a decedent's estate], males must be preferred to females' "). Since *Reed*, the Court has repeatedly recognized that neither federal nor state government acts compatibly with the equal protection principle when a law or official policy denies to women, simply because they are women, full citizenship stature—equal opportunity to aspire, achieve, participate in and contribute to society based on their individual talents and capacities. See, e. g., Kirchberg v. Feenstra, 450 U.S. 455 (1981) (affirming invalidity of Louisiana law that made husband "head and master" of property jointly owned with his wife, giving him unilateral right to dispose of such property without his wife's consent); Stanton v. Stanton, 421 U.S. 7 (1975) (invalidating Utah requirement that parents support boys until age 21, girls only until age 18).

Without equating gender classifications, for all purposes, to classifications based on race or national origin,[6] the Court, in post-*Reed* decisions, has carefully inspected official action that closes a door or denies opportunity to women (or to men). To summarize the Court's current directions for cases of official classification based on gender: Focusing on the differential treatment or denial of opportunity for which relief is sought, the reviewing court must determine whether the proffered justification is "exceedingly persuasive." The burden of justification is demanding and it rests entirely on the State. The State must show "at least that the [challenged] classification serves 'important governmental objectives and that the discriminatory means employed' are 'substantially related to the achievement of those objectives.' " The justification must be genuine, not hypothesized or invented post hoc in response to litigation. And it must not rely on overbroad

---

6. The Court has thus far reserved most stringent judicial scrutiny for classifications based on race or national origin, but last Term observed that strict scrutiny of such classifications is not inevitably "fatal in fact." Adarand Constructors, Inc. v. Pena, 515 U.S. 200, 237 (1995).

generalizations about the different talents, capacities, or preferences of males and females.

The heightened review standard our precedent establishes does not make sex a proscribed classification. Supposed "inherent differences" are no longer accepted as a ground for race or national origin classifications. See Loving v. Virginia, 388 U.S. 1 (1967). Physical differences between men and women, however, are enduring: "The two sexes are not fungible; a community made up exclusively of one [sex] is different from a community composed of both." Ballard v. United States, 329 U.S. 187, 193 (1946).

"Inherent differences" between men and women, we have come to appreciate, remain cause for celebration, but not for denigration of the members of either sex or for artificial constraints on an individual's opportunity. Sex classifications may be used to compensate women "for particular economic disabilities [they have] suffered," to "promote equal employment opportunity," to advance full development of the talent and capacities of our Nation's people.[7] But such classifications may not be used, as they once were, to create or perpetuate the legal, social, and economic inferiority of women.

Measuring the record in this case against the review standard just described, we conclude that Virginia has shown no "exceedingly persuasive justification" for excluding all women from the citizen-soldier training afforded by VMI. We therefore affirm the Fourth Circuit's initial judgment, which held that Virginia had violated the Fourteenth Amendment's Equal Protection Clause. Because the remedy proffered by Virginia—the Mary Baldwin VWIL program—does not cure the constitutional violation, i.e., it does not provide equal opportunity, we reverse the Fourth Circuit's final judgment in this case.

· · ·

[Concurring opinion of Chief Justice Rehnquist and dissenting opinion of Justice Scalia omitted.]

Notes

1. The Supreme Court's opinion in *United States v. Virginia* has been seen as raising the standard of justification required for gender discrimina-

---

7. Several amici have urged that diversity in educational opportunities is an altogether appropriate governmental pursuit and that single-sex schools can contribute importantly to such diversity. Indeed, it is the mission of some single-sex schools "to dissipate, rather than perpetuate, traditional gender classifications." We do not question the Commonwealth's prerogative evenhandedly to support diverse educational opportunities. We address specifically and only an educational opportunity recognized by the District Court and the Court of Appeals as "unique," an opportunity available only at Virginia's premier military institute, the Commonwealth's sole single-sex public university or college. Cf. Mississippi Univ. For Women v. Hogan, 458 U.S. 718, 720, n. 1 (1982) ("Mississippi maintains no other single-sex public university of college. Thus, we are not faced with the question of whether States can provide 'separate but equal' undergraduate institutions for males and females.").

tion higher than some earlier formulations of a "substantial relationship" to an "important government objective," and closer to the strict scrutiny applied to racial discrimination. Why does the Court not adopt strict scrutiny as the standard for gender discrimination as well? Does discrimination on grounds of gender inflict less severe injury than discrimination on grounds of race? Are legislatures and government officials less likely to act on the basis of gender stereotypes or prejudice against women than they are to act on the basis of racial stereotypes or racial prejudice? Are there other reasons for allowing governments to employ gender classifications that are not strictly necessary?

Note the Court's observation that "[s]upposed 'inherent differences' are no longer accepted as a ground for race or national origin classifications," but that physical differences between men and women are "enduring" and "cause for celebration." Are differences between men and women more genuine than cultural differences between ethnic groups? Might the correct answer to that question vary from country to country?

For an argument that the decision in *United States v. Virginia* actually does raise the standard for gender discrimination to strict scrutiny, see Candace Saari Kovacic–Fleischer, United States v. Virginia's *New Gender Equal Protection Analysis with Ramifications for Pregnancy, Parenting, and Title VII*, 50 Vand. L. Rev. 845 (1997).

2.   How does the Supreme Court's standard for evaluating gender discrimination under the Equal Protection Clause compare with the standard applicable, for example, under the European Convention?

3.   European Community law has played an important role in regulating gender discrimination in the sphere of employment in the Member States of the European Union. When the European Economic Community was established in 1957, the founding Treaty of Rome included a provision requiring Member States to apply "the principle that men and women should receive equal pay for equal work." (Art. 119.) Although Article 119 was initially intended to protect the economic interests of Member States whose national laws already respected that principle, protection against discrimination based on sex subsequently came to be viewed as a fundamental right within Community law. See Case 149/77, *Defrenne v. Sabena*, 1978 E.C.R. 1365.

The consequences of the gender equality principle have also been given more specific form in a series of Directives, a form of secondary legislation binding on the Member States. In 1976, protection was extended from equal pay to equal treatment in the employment sphere by Council Directive 76/207/EEC, on the implementation of the principle of equal treatment for men and women as regards access to employment, vocational training and promotion, and working conditions. The Directive prohibits both direct discrimination and indirect discrimination on grounds of sex (or, in U.S. parlance, both intentional disparate treatment and unjustified actions having disparate impact on the basis of sex). Article 2 of the Directive provides:

1. For the purposes of the following provisions, the principle of equal treatment shall mean that there shall be no discrimination whatsoever on grounds of sex either directly or indirectly by reference in particular to marital or family status.

2. This Directive shall be without prejudice to the right of Member States to exclude from its field of application those occupational activities and, where appropriate, the training leading thereto, for which, by reason of their nature or the context in which they are carried out, the sex of the worker constitutes a determining factor.

3. This Directive shall be without prejudice to provisions concerning the protection of women, particularly as regards pregnancy and maternity.

4. This Directive shall be without prejudice to measures to promote equal opportunity for men and women, in particular by removing existing inequalities which affect women's opportunities in the areas referred to in Article 1(1) [i.e., access to employment, including promotion, working conditions, and social security].

Recent case law of the European Court of Justice interpreting Article 2(4) of this Directive is discussed in sub-section 4, below.

European Community law will place greater emphasis on issues of gender equality by means of provisions of the Amsterdam Treaty, a wide-ranging revision of the foundational treaties of the European Union. See, e.g., Evelyn Ellis, *Recent developments in European Community sex equality law*, 35 Comm. Mkt. L. Rev. 379 (1998). The Amsterdam Treaty, which entered into force on 1 May 1999, gives the European Community institutions new legislative powers to promote gender equality in the workplace. It amends former Article 119 in order to embody in the treaty itself "the principle of equal opportunities and equal treatment of men and women in matters of employment and occupation" (new Article 141(3)).

4. Special Measures (Affirmative Action)

International law's prohibition of discrimination in the enjoyment of human rights does not preclude "special measures"—measures that would be called "affirmative action" programs in a U.S. context—designed to accelerate de facto equality, as long as those measures are temporary. Article 1(4) of the Race Convention provides:

Special measures taken for the sole purpose of securing adequate advancement of certain racial or ethnic groups or individuals requiring such protection as may be necessary in order to ensure such groups or individuals equal enjoyment or exercise of human rights and fundamental freedoms shall not be deemed racial discrimination, provided, however, that such measures do not, as a consequence, lead to the maintenance of separate rights for different racial groups and that they shall not be continued after the objectives for which they were taken have been achieved.

Moreover, Article 2(2) of the Race Convention *requires* the adoption of special measures under certain conditions:

> States Parties shall, when circumstances so warrant, take, in the social, economic, cultural and other fields, special and concrete measures to ensure the adequate development and protection of certain racial groups or individuals belonging to them, for the purpose of guaranteeing them the full and equal enjoyment of human rights and fundamental freedoms. These measures shall in no case entail as a consequence the maintenance of unequal or separate rights for different racial groups after the objectives for which they were taken have been achieved.

Article 4(1) of the Women's Convention provides:

> Adoption by States Parties of temporary special measures aimed at accelerating *de facto* equality between men and women shall not be considered discrimination as defined in this Convention, but shall in no way entail, as a consequence, the maintenance of unequal or separate standards; these measures shall be discontinued when the objectives of equality of opportunity and treatment have been achieved.

The ICCPR does not include a similar provision, but the Human Rights Committee has taken the position that special measures are compatible with the Covenant "as long as such action is needed to correct discrimination in fact." In these instances, special measures entail "legitimate differentiation under the Covenant." General Comment 18, para. 10. Indeed, the Committee has asserted that in some circumstances affirmative action measures may be required:

> ... [T]he principle of equality sometimes requires States parties to take affirmative action in order to diminish or eliminate conditions which cause or help to perpetuate discrimination prohibited by the Covenant. For example, in a State where the general conditions of a certain part of the population prevent or impair their enjoyment of human rights, the State should take specific action to correct those conditions. Such action may involve granting for a time to the part of the population concerned certain preferential treatment in specific matters as compared with the rest of the population....

Id.

In European Community law, the question of special measures to promote gender equality has been governed by Council Directive 76/207/EEC, which is set forth in Note 3, above. Article 2(4) of the Directive permits but does not require certain forms of affirmative action. In the decades since its adoption Member States of the European Union have differed in their approaches to affirmative action (also known in Europe as "positive discrimination"). In 1995, the European Court of Justice decided its first case involving a challenge to affirmative action as unlawful discrimination. Case C–450/93, *Kalanke v. Freie Hansestadt Bremen*, [1995] E.C.R. I–3051, [1996] 1 C.M.L.R. 175, involved the Bremen Law on Equal Treatment of Men and Women in the Public Service. That law provided that whenever a man and a woman competing for the same position had equal qualifications, and women were underrepresented in the sector in question, the woman was automatically to be given priority. The European Court of Justice observed that Article 2(4) operated as a derogation from the individual right to equal treatment, and should therefore be interpreted strictly. It held that granting automatic priority in all cases of equal qualification went beyond promoting equal opportunities and amounted to imposing equal results, and therefore fell outside the scope of the authorization in Article 2(4). Commentators offered sharply divergent interpretations of *Kalanke*, from a prohibition of all preferences in hiring and promotion to a rejection of only the most rigid forms of quota system. The Court clarified, or modified, its position in the following case:

Marschall v. Land Nordrhein–Westfalen

Court of Justice of the European Communities, 1997.
Case C–409/95, 1997 E.C.R. I–6363, [1998] 1 C.M.L.R. 547.

Judgment

1.   By order of 21 December 1995, received at the Court on 29 December 1995, the Verwaltungsgericht (Administrative Court) Gelsenkirchen referred to the Court for a preliminary ruling under Article 177 of the EC Treaty a question on the interpretation of Article 2(1) and (4) of Council Directive 76/207/EEC of 9 February 1976 on the implementation of the principle of equal treatment for men and women as regards access to employment, vocational training and promotion, and working conditions (OJ 1976 L 39, p. 40, hereinafter "the Directive").

2.   That question has been raised in proceedings between Hellmut Marschall and *Land* Nordrhein–Westfalen (*Land* of North Rhine–Westphalia, hereinafter "the *Land*") concerning his application for a higher grade post at the Gesamtschule (comprehensive school) Schwerte in Germany.

3.   The ... Law on Civil Servants of the *Land* ... provides:

"Where, in the sector of the authority responsible for promotion, there are fewer women than men in the particular higher grade post in the career bracket, women are to be given priority for promotion in the event of equal suitability, competence and professional performance, unless reasons specific to an individual male candidate tilt the balance in his favour."

4.   According to the observations of the *Land*, the rule of priority laid down by that provision introduced an additional promotion criterion, that of being a female, in order to counteract the inequality affecting female candidates as compared with male candidates applying for the same post: where qualifications are equal, employers tend to promote men rather than women because they apply traditional promotion criteria which in practice put women at a disadvantage, such as age, seniority and the fact that a male candidate is a head of household and sole breadwinner for the household.

5.   In providing that priority is to be given to the promotion of women "unless reasons specific to an individual male candidate tilt the balance in his favour", the legislature deliberately chose, according to the *Land*, a legally imprecise expression in order to ensure sufficient flexibility and, in particular, to allow the administration latitude to take into account any reasons which may be specific to individual candidates. Consequently, notwithstanding the rule of priority, the administration can always give preference to a male candidate on the basis of promotion criteria, traditional or otherwise.

[Mr. Marschall was a tenured teacher working for the *Land*, with salary in career bracket A 12. He applied for promotion to an A 13 post. After an evaluation of the qualifications of the candidates, he was informed that the authorities intended to appoint a female candidate, because he and the female candidate had equal qualifications, and there were fewer women than men in career bracket A 13. He brought legal proceedings in the Administrative Court, claiming that he had been subjected to discrimination on grounds of sex, and that the civil service law of the *Land* was incompatible with the Directive, as interpreted in the *Kalanke* decision.]

13.   The [Administrative Court then] decided to stay proceedings and to refer the following question to the Court for a preliminary ruling:

"Does Article 2(1) and (4) of Council Directive 76/207/EEC of 9 February 1976 on the implementation of the principle of equal treatment for men and women as regards access to employment, vocational training and promotion, and working conditions, preclude a rule of national law which provides that, in sectors of the public service in which fewer women than men are employed in the relevant higher grade post in a career bracket, women must be given priority where male and female candidates for promotion are equally qualified (in terms of suitability, competence and professional performance), unless reasons specific to an individual male candidate tilt the balance in his favour ...?"

· · ·

21.   The Court observes that the purpose of the Directive, as is clear from Article 1(1), is to put into effect in the Member States the principle of equal treatment for men and women as regards, inter alia, access to employment, including promotion. Article 2(1) states that the principle of equal treatment means that "there shall be no discrimination whatsoever on grounds of sex either directly or indirectly."

22.   According to Article 2(4), the Directive is to "be without prejudice to measures to promote equal opportunity for men and women, in particular by removing existing inequalities which affect women's opportunities in the areas referred to in Article 1(1)".

23.   In paragraph 16 of its judgment in *Kalanke*, the Court held that a national rule which provides that, where equally qualified men and women are candidates for the same promotion in fields where there are fewer women than men at the level of the relevant post, women are automatically to be given priority, involves discrimination on grounds of sex.

24. However, unlike the provisions in question in *Kalanke*, the provision in question in this case contains a clause ("Öffnungsklausel", hereinafter "saving clause") to the effect that women are not to be given priority in promotion if reasons specific to an individual male candidate tilt the balance in his favour.

25. It is therefore necessary to consider whether a national rule containing such a clause is designed to promote equality of opportunity between men and women within the meaning of Article 2(4) of the Directive.

26. Article 2(4) is specifically and exclusively designed to authorize measures which, although discriminatory in appearance, are in fact intended to eliminate or reduce actual instances of inequality which may exist in the reality of social life (Case 312/86 *Commission v France* 1988 ECR 6315, paragraph 15, and *Kalanke*, paragraph 18).

27. It thus authorizes national measures relating to access to employment, including promotion, which give a specific advantage to women with a view to improving their ability to compete on the labour market and to pursue a career on an equal footing with men (*Kalanke*, paragraph 19).

28. As the Council stated in the third recital in the preamble to Recommendation 84/635/EEC of 13 December 1984 on the promotion of positive action for women (OJ 1984 L 331, p. 34), "existing legal provisions on equal treatment, which are designed to afford rights to individuals, are inadequate for the elimination of all existing inequalities unless parallel action is taken by governments, both sides of industry and other bodies concerned, to counteract the prejudicial effects on women in employment which arise from social attitudes, behaviour and structures" (*Kalanke*, paragraph 20).

29. As the *Land* and several governments have pointed out, it appears that even where male and female candidates are equally qualified, male candidates tend to be promoted in preference to female candidates particularly because of prejudices and stereotypes concerning the role and capacities of women in working life and the fear, for example, that women will interrupt their careers more frequently, that owing to household and family duties they will be less flexible in their working hours, or that they will be absent from work more frequently because of pregnancy, childbirth and breastfeeding.

30. For these reasons, the mere fact that a male candidate and a female candidate are equally qualified does not mean that they have the same chances.

31. It follows that a national rule in terms of which, subject to the application of the saving clause, female candidates for promotion who are equally as qualified as the male candidates are to be treated preferentially in sectors where they are under-represented may fall within the scope of Article 2(4) if such a rule may counteract the prejudicial effects on female candidates of the attitudes and behaviour described above and thus reduce actual instances of inequality which may exist in the real world.

32. However, since Article 2(4) constitutes a derogation from an individual right laid down by the Directive, such a national measure specifically

favouring female candidates cannot guarantee absolute and unconditional priority for women in the event of a promotion without going beyond the limits of the exception laid down in that provision (*Kalanke*, paragraphs 21 and 22).

33.   Unlike the rules at issue in *Kalanke*, a national rule which, as in the case in point in the main proceedings, contains a saving clause does not exceed those limits if, in each individual case, it provides for male candidates who are equally as qualified as the female candidates a guarantee that the candidatures will be the subject of an objective assessment which will take account of all criteria specific to the individual candidates and will override the priority accorded to female candidates where one or more of those criteria tilts the balance in favour of the male candidate. In this respect, however, it should be remembered that those criteria must not be such as to discriminate against female candidates.

34.   It is for the national court to determine whether those conditions are fulfilled on the basis of an examination of the scope of the provision in question as it has been applied by the *Land*.

35.   The answer to be given to the national court must therefore be that a national rule which, in a case where there are fewer women than men at the level of the relevant post in a sector of the public service, and both female and male candidates for the post are equally qualified in terms of their suitability, competence and professional performance, requires that priority be given to the promotion of female candidates unless reasons specific to an individual male candidate tilt the balance in his favour is not precluded by Article 2(1) and (4) of the Directive, provided that:

– in each individual case the rule provides for male candidates who are equally as qualified as the female candidates a guarantee that the candidatures will be the subject of an objective assessment which will take account of all criteria specific to the individual candidates and will override the priority accorded to female candidates where one or more of those criteria tilts the balance in favour of the male candidate, and

– such criteria are not such as to discriminate against the female candidates.

Notes

1.   Does *Marschall* persuasively distinguish *Kalanke*? How does the *Land*'s law serve the goal of equality of opportunity rather than equality of result?

2.   What does it mean for two job candidates to have equal qualifications? How much effect will an affirmative action program have if it operates only in cases where male and female candidates are equally qualified?

3.   How do the "traditional promotion criteria" of age, seniority, and preference for a "sole breadwinner" disadvantage women? Are they discriminatory in intent? In impact? Would giving female candidates priority in promotion in order to compensate for these factors be permissible under Article 2(4)? Does Article 2(4) permit an employer to exclude these factors

from consideration under a "savings clause" on the grounds that they are discriminatory?

4.   The *Kalanke* decision excited considerable discussion in the European Union, and a draft Directive was proposed that would have amended Directive 76/207 to clarify the scope of permissible special measures. Instead, the issue was addressed in the negotiation of the Amsterdam Treaty. See, e.g., Evelyn Ellis, *Recent developments in European Community sex equality law*, 35 Comm. Mkt. L. Rev. 379 (1998); Albertine Veldman, *The Lawfulness of Women's Priority Rules in the EC Labour Market*, 5 Maastricht J. Eur. & Comp. L. 403 (1998). New Article 141(4) provides:

> With a view to ensuring full equality in practice between men and women in working life, the principle of equal treatment shall not prevent any Member State from maintaining or adopting measures providing for specific advantages in order to make it easier for the underrepresented sex to pursue a vocational activity or to prevent or compensate for disadvantages in professional careers.

This new provision will require interpretation; how does the treaty language adopted in October 1997 compare with the *Marschall* court's interpretation of the Directive in November 1997?

Adarand Constructors, Inc. v. Pena

Supreme Court of the United States, 1995.
515 U.S. 200.

■ JUSTICE O'CONNOR announced the judgment of the Court and delivered an opinion with respect to Parts I, II, III–A, III–B, III–D, and IV, which is for the Court except insofar as it might be inconsistent with the views expressed in JUSTICE SCALIA'S concurrence....

Petitioner Adarand Constructors, Inc., claims that the Federal Government's practice of giving general contractors on government projects a financial incentive to hire subcontractors controlled by "socially and economically disadvantaged individuals," and in particular, the Government's use of race-based presumptions in identifying such individuals, violates the equal protection component of the Fifth Amendment's Due Process Clause. The Court of Appeals rejected Adarand's claim. We conclude, however, that courts should analyze cases of this kind under a different standard of review than the one the Court of Appeals applied. We therefore vacate the Court of Appeals' judgment and remand the case for further proceedings. . . .

III

. . .

Adarand's claim arises under the Fifth Amendment to the Constitution, which provides that "No person shall . . . be deprived of life, liberty, or property, without due process of law." Although this Court has always understood that Clause to provide some measure of protection against arbitrary treatment by the Federal Government, it is not as explicit a guarantee of equal treatment as the Fourteenth Amendment, which provides that "No State shall . . . deny to any person within its jurisdiction the equal protection of the laws." Our cases have accorded varying degrees of significance to the difference in the language of those two Clauses. We think it necessary to revisit the issue here. . . .

B

Most of the cases discussed above involved classifications burdening groups that have suffered discrimination in our society. In 1978, the Court confronted the question whether race-based governmental action designed to benefit such groups should also be subject to "the most rigid scrutiny." . . .

The Court's failure to produce a majority opinion in [Regents of Univ. of California v.] Bakke, 438 U.S. 265 (1978), Fullilove [v. Klutznick, 448 U.S. 448 (1980)], and Wygant [v. Jackson Board of Ed., 476 U.S. 267 (1986),] left unresolved the proper analysis for remedial race-based governmental action. . . .

The Court resolved the issue, at least in part, in 1989. Richmond v. J.A. Croson Co., 488 U.S. 469 (1989), concerned a city's determination that 30% of its contracting work should go to minority-owned businesses. A majority of the Court in *Croson* held that "the standard of review under the Equal Protection Clause is not dependent on the race of those burdened or benefited by a particular classification," and that the single standard of review for racial classifications should be "strict scrutiny." As to the classification before the Court, the plurality agreed that "a state or local subdivision . . . has the authority to eradicate the effects of private discrimination within its own legislative jurisdiction," but the Court thought that the city had not acted with "a 'strong basis in evidence for its conclusion that remedial action was necessary.' " The Court also thought it "obvious that [the] program is not narrowly tailored to remedy the effects of prior discrimination." With *Croson*, the Court finally agreed that the Fourteenth Amendment requires strict scrutiny of all race-based action by state and local governments. . . .

. . . [T]he Court's cases through *Croson* had established three general propositions with respect to governmental racial classifications. First, skepticism: " '[a]ny preference based on racial or ethnic criteria must necessarily receive a most searching examination.' " Second, consistency: "the standard of review under the Equal Protection Clause is not dependent on the race of those burdened or benefited by a particular classification," i.e., all racial classifications reviewable under the Equal Protection Clause must be strictly scrutinized. And third, congruence: "[e]qual protection analysis in the Fifth Amendment area is the same as that under the Fourteenth Amendment." Taken together, these three propositions lead to the conclusion that any person, of whatever race, has the right to demand that any governmental actor subject to the Constitution justify any racial classification subjecting that person to unequal treatment under the strictest judicial scrutiny. Justice Powell's defense of this conclusion bears repeating here:

> If it is the individual who is entitled to judicial protection against classifications based upon his racial or ethnic background because such distinctions impinge upon personal rights, rather than the individual only because of his membership in a particular group, then constitutional standards may be applied consistently. Political judgments regarding the necessity for the particular classification may be weighed in the constitutional balance, but the standard of justification will remain constant. This is as it should be, since those political judgments are the product of rough compromise struck by contending groups within the democratic process. When they touch upon an individual's race or ethnic background, he is entitled to a judicial determination that the burden he is asked to bear on that basis is precisely tailored to serve a compelling governmental interest. The Constitution guarantees that right to every person regardless of his background....

A year later, however, the Court took a surprising turn. Metro Broadcasting, Inc. v. FCC, 497 U.S. 547 (1990), involved a Fifth Amendment challenge to two race-based policies of the Federal Communications Commission. In *Metro Broadcasting*, the Court [held] that "benign" federal racial classifications need only satisfy intermediate scrutiny, even though *Croson* had recently concluded that such classifications enacted by a State must satisfy strict scrutiny. "[B]enign" federal racial classifications, the Court said, "—even if those measures are not 'remedial' in the sense of being designed to compensate victims of past governmental or societal discrimination—are constitutionally permissible to the extent that they serve important governmental objectives within the power of Congress and are substantially related to achievement of those objectives."

The Court did not explain how to tell whether a racial classification should be deemed "benign," other than to express "confiden[ce] that an 'examination of the legislative scheme and its history' will separate benign measures from other types of racial classifications."

... By adopting intermediate scrutiny as the standard of review for congressionally mandated "benign" racial classifications, *Metro Broadcasting*.... turned its back on *Croson*'s explanation of why strict scrutiny of all governmental racial classifications is essential:

> Absent searching judicial inquiry into the justification for such race-based measures, there is simply no way of determining what classifications are "benign" or "remedial" and what classifications are in fact motivated by illegitimate notions of racial inferiority or simple racial politics. Indeed, the purpose of strict scrutiny is to "smoke out" illegitimate uses of race by assuring that the legislative body is pursuing a goal important enough to warrant use of a highly suspect tool. The test also ensures that the means chosen "fit" this compelling goal so closely that there is little or no possibility that the motive for the classification was illegitimate racial prejudice or stereotype.

We adhere to that view today, despite the surface appeal of holding "benign" racial classifications to a lower standard, because "it may not always be clear that a so-called preference is in fact benign." ...

. . .

The three propositions [of skepticism, consistency and congruence] all derive from the basic principle that the Fifth and Fourteenth Amendments to the Constitution protect persons, not groups. It follows from that principle that all governmental action based on race—a group classification long recognized as "in most circumstances irrelevant and therefore prohibited,"—should be subjected to detailed judicial inquiry to ensure that the personal right to equal protection of the laws has not been infringed. These ideas have long been central to this Court's understanding of equal protection, and holding "benign" state and federal racial classifications to different standards does not square with them. "[A] free people whose institutions are founded upon the doctrine of equality," should tolerate no retreat from the principle that government may treat people differently because of their race only for the most compelling reasons. Accordingly, we hold today that all racial classifications, imposed by whatever federal, state, or local governmental actor, must be analyzed by a reviewing court under strict scrutiny. In other words, such classifications are constitutional only if they are narrowly tailored measures that further compelling governmental interests. To the extent that *Metro Broadcasting* is inconsistent with that holding, it is overruled.

. . .

Justice Stevens chides us for our "supposed inability to differentiate between 'invidious' and 'benign' discrimination," because it is in his view sufficient that "people understand the difference between good intentions and bad." But, as we have just explained, the point of strict scrutiny is to "differentiate between" permissible and impermissible governmental use of race. And Justice Stevens himself has already explained in his dissent in *Fullilove* why "good intentions" alone are not enough to sustain a supposedly "benign" racial classification:

[E]ven though it is not the actual predicate for this legislation, a statute of this kind inevitably is perceived by many as resting on an assumption that those who are granted this special preference are less qualified in some respect that is identified purely by their race. Because that perception—especially when fostered by the Congress of the United States—can only exacerbate rather than reduce racial prejudice, it will delay the time when race will become a truly irrelevant, or at least insignificant, factor. Unless Congress clearly articulates the need and basis for a racial classification, and also tailors the classification to its justification, the Court should not uphold this kind of statute.

Perhaps it is not the standard of strict scrutiny itself, but our use of the concepts of "consistency" and "congruence" in conjunction with it, that leads Justice Stevens to dissent. According to Justice Stevens, our view of consistency "equate[s] remedial preferences with invidious discrimination," and ignores the difference between "an engine of oppression" and an effort "to foster equality in society," or, more colorfully, "between a 'No Trespassing' sign and a welcome mat". It does nothing of the kind. The principle of consistency simply means that whenever the government treats any person unequally because of his or her race, that person has suffered an injury that falls squarely within the language and spirit of the Constitution's guarantee of equal protection. It says nothing about the ultimate validity of any particular law; that determination is the job of the court applying strict scrutiny. The principle of consistency explains the circumstances in which the injury requiring strict scrutiny occurs. The application of strict scrutiny, in turn, determines whether a compelling governmental interest justifies the infliction of that injury.

Consistency does recognize that any individual suffers an injury when he or she is disadvantaged by the government because of his or her race, whatever that race may be. This Court clearly stated that principle in *Croson*. Justice Stevens does not explain how his views square with *Croson*, or with the long line of cases understanding equal protection as a personal right. . . .

D

. . .

Finally, we wish to dispel the notion that strict scrutiny is "strict in theory, but fatal in fact." The unhappy persistence of both the practice and the lingering effects of racial discrimination against minority groups in this country is an unfortunate reality, and government is not disqualified from acting in response to it. As recently as 1987, for example, every Justice of this Court agreed that the Alabama Department of Public Safety's "pervasive, systematic, and obstinate discriminatory conduct" justified a narrowly tailored race-based remedy. When race-based action is necessary to further a compelling interest, such action is within constitutional constraints if it satisfies the "narrow tailoring" test this Court has set out in previous cases.

. . .

■ JUSTICE SCALIA, concurring in part and concurring in the judgment.

I join the opinion of the Court, . . . except insofar as it may be inconsistent with the following: In my view, government can never have a "compelling interest" in discriminating on the basis of race in order to "make up" for past racial discrimination in the opposite direction. Individuals who have been wronged by unlawful racial discrimination should be made whole; but under our Constitution there can be no such thing as either a creditor or a debtor race. That concept is alien to the Constitution's focus upon the individual, and its rejection of dispositions based on race, or based on blood. To pursue the concept of racial entitlement—even for the most admirable and benign of purposes—is to reinforce and preserve for future mischief the way of thinking that produced race slavery, race privilege and race hatred. In the eyes of government, we are just one race here. It is American. It is unlikely, if not impossible, that the challenged program would survive under this understanding of strict scrutiny, but I am content to leave that to be decided on remand.

■ JUSTICE STEVENS, with whom JUSTICE GINSBURG joins, dissenting.

. . .

. . . . There is no moral or constitutional equivalence between a policy that is designed to perpetuate a caste system and one that seeks to eradicate racial subordination. Invidious discrimination is an engine of oppression, subjugating a disfavored group to enhance or maintain the power of the majority. Remedial race-based preferences reflect the opposite impulse: a desire to foster equality in society. No sensible conception of the Government's constitutional obligation to "govern impartially," should ignore this distinction. . . .

[Dissenting opinion of Justice Ginsburg, joined by Justice Breyer, omitted.]

Notes

1. The Supreme Court in *Adarand* denies that it can identify "benign" racial preferences without first subjecting them to strict scrutiny. What characteristics distinguish non-benign racial preferences that favor a racial minority group? How does strict scrutiny filter out the non-benign preferences? Is strict scrutiny likely to invalidate many benign measures, and is that an appropriate price to pay for preventing the occurrence of non-benign measures?

2. Do international human rights treaties and their interpretations by international bodies reflect less insecurity about the ability to identify legitimate special measures on behalf of a racial group than the Supreme Court expresses in *Adarand*? If so, what accounts for this difference?

3. Does *Adarand* reflect a different resolution of the tension between formal equality and equality in fact than the resolution reflected in the Race Convention? How do each of these compare with the resolution of that tension in *Marschall*?

4. Does *Adarand* reflect a different approach to the conflict between individual rights and group rights than the approach reflected in the Race Convention? How do each of these compare with the approach to this conflict reflected in *Marschall*?

5. Is a comparison between *Adarand* and *Marschall* complicated by the fact that the former involves a race-based preference and the latter involves a gender-based preference? Should gender-based preferences provoke less "skepticism" than race-based preferences? Is it relevant that the Supreme Court appears committed to denying the existence of inherent differences between racial groups, but to "celebrating" the inherent differences between women and men?

6. Do the strict limits imposed on affirmative action by the Supreme Court's opinion in *Adarand* place the United States in conflict with its obligations under Article 2(2) of CERD? Do any of the RUDs affect the answer to this question?

In 1996, voters in California adopted an amendment to the California state constitution, Proposition 209, which provides that "[t]he state shall not discriminate against, or grant preferential treatment to, any individual or group on the basis of race, sex, color, ethnicity, or national origin in the operation of public employment, public education, or public contracting." Proposition 209 absolutely forbids race-based (as well as gender-based) affirmative action, even in circumstances where state officials conclude that such action would be necessary for the achievement of the state's compelling interest in remedying past discrimination. See *Coalition for Economic Equity v. Wilson*, 122 F.3d 718 (9th Cir. 1997) (upholding Proposition 209 against equal protection challenge), cert. denied, 118 S.Ct. 397 (1997). Does Proposition 209 place the United States in conflict with its obligations under Article 2(2) of CERD? Do any of the RUDs affect the answer to this question?

For discussion of these issues, see Connie de la Vega, *Civil Rights During the 1990s: New Treaty Could Help Immensely*, 65 U. Cin. L. Rev. 423 (1997); Jordan J. Paust, *Race-Based Affirmative Action and International Law*, 18 Mich. J. Int'l L. 659 (1997).

7. Article 1(4) of the Race Convention provides that special measures will not be deemed racial discrimination "provided . . . that such measures do not, as a consequence, lead to the maintenance of separate rights for different racial groups and that they shall not be continued after the objectives for which they were taken have been achieved." Does this mean that the Race Convention prohibits "the devolution of power to ethnic federal and regional sub-units, electoral adjustments, and other consociational and quasi-consociational mechanisms" designed for the protection of national minorities or indigenous peoples, if they are intended to be permanent? See David Wippman, *Practical and Legal Constraints on Internal Power Sharing*, in International Law and Ethnic Conflict 211, 232–33 (D. Wippman ed. 1998) (arguing that such arrangements should be accepted under General Recommendation XIV if they are based on reasonable and objective criteria, aim to achieve a legitimate purpose, and are proportionate to the ends sought).

CHAPTER 2

POLITICAL RIGHTS

Political rights overlap with, but differ from, civil rights. Political rights guarantee the positive liberty to contribute to the process of self-government. They directly involve the structure of the state and the distribution of political power, and therefore are of great concern to all governments.

The Universal Declaration of Human Rights proclaims popular sovereignty, universal and equal suffrage in genuine elections, the right to take part in government, and equal access to public service. Article 25 of the ICCPR articulates political rights as follows:

> Every citizen shall have the right and the opportunity, without any of the distinctions mentioned in article 2 and without unreasonable restrictions:
>
> (a) To take part in the conduct of public affairs, directly or through freely chosen representatives;
>
> (b) To vote and to be elected at genuine periodic elections which shall be by universal and equal suffrage and shall be held by secret ballot, guaranteeing the free expression of the will of the electors;
>
> (c) To have access, on general terms of equality, to public service in his country.

How much or how little political participation do these rights guarantee?

The United States Constitution invokes the principle of popular sovereignty in its Preamble, consistent with the emphasis on the consent of the governed in the Declaration of Independence. But the Framers created a form of representative government with limited opportunities for political participation. Of all the branches of the federal government, only the House of Representatives was directly elected; and even for that House suffrage was open only to those who had been given the right to vote by each state. In most states eligibility to vote extended only to white males, and many of those were excluded by property qualifications. Later amendments to the Constitution indirectly extended the enjoyment of voting rights by prohibiting discriminatory denial on particular grounds: the grounds of race (Amendment XV), gender (Amendment XIX), and age for those over 18 (Amendment XXVI). Conditioning the right to vote in federal elections on payment of a poll tax or other tax was also forbidden (Amendment XXIV). In the 1960s, finally, the Supreme Court derived a right to universal suffrage in most elections from the Fourteenth Amendment's guarantee of the equal protection of the laws. The U.S. Senate has been directly elected since 1913 (Amendment XVII), but popular electoral participation in the choice of the President and Vice President rests on tradition and statutory law rather than on any constitutional provision.

As this history illustrates, political rights involve both individual claims for inclusion or equality within existing political processes, and claims that systems of governance should be structured so as to provide opportunities for political participation. This chapter examines the specific formulations of political rights in the European Convention and in the ICCPR, and the scope of political participation that they guarantee. It also addresses an area of potential conflict between one person's political rights and the rights of others—the exclusion of extremist political parties from electoral competition.

Mathieu–Mohin and Clerfayt v. Belgium

European Court of Human Rights, 1987.
113 Eur. Ct. H.R. (ser. A), 10 E.H.R.R. 1.

[The case concerned complex institutional arrangements in Belgium for the accommodation of the interests of speakers of the two major languages, Dutch and French. In accordance with a Special Act of 1980, on a transitional basis, members of the Senate and the House of Representatives also served as members of councils that represented the interests of the language communities and the interests of the regions where those languages were predominantly spoken. Mathieu–Mohin and Clerfayt were French-speaking legislators residing in Halle–Vilvoorde, a district in the Flemish (Dutch-speaking) region with a substantial French-speaking population. As legislators, they faced a dilemma: under existing rules, if they took the parliamentary oath in French they would be assigned to the French Community Council, which had no power over regional matters in Halle–Vilvoorde, and if they took the oath in Dutch they would be assigned to the Flemish Council, and would lose the right to vote on certain matters affecting the French-speaking community. They argued that this system denied the French-speaking residents of Halle–Vilvoorde the full electoral rights enjoyed by the Dutch-speaking residents of Halle–Vilvoorde, in violation of Article 3 of Protocol 1 of the European Convention, either alone or in conjunction with the prohibition on discrimination in Article 14.

Article 3 of Protocol No. 1 provides:

> The High Contracting Parties undertake to hold free elections at reasonable intervals by secret ballot, under conditions which will ensure the free expression of the opinion of the people in the choice of the legislature.

Article 14 of the Convention provides:

> The enjoyment of the rights and freedoms set forth in this Convention shall be secured without discrimination on any ground such as sex, race, colour, language, religion, political or other opinion, national

or social origin, association with a national minority, property, birth or other status.]

A.   Interpretation of Article 3 of Protocol No. 1

47.   According to the Preamble to the Convention, fundamental human rights and freedoms are best maintained by "an effective political democracy". Since it enshrines a characteristic principle of democracy, Article 3 of Protocol No. 1 is accordingly of prime importance in the Convention system.

51.   As to the nature of the rights thus enshrined in Article 3, the view taken by the Commission has evolved. From the idea of an "institutional" right to the holding of free elections, the Commission has moved to the concept of "universal suffrage" and then, as a consequence, to the concept of subjective rights of participation—the "right to vote" and the "right to stand for election to the legislature". The Court approves this latter concept.

52.   The rights in question are not absolute. Since Article 3 recognises them without setting them forth in express terms, let alone defining them, there is room for implied limitations. (See, mutatis mutandis, Golder v United Kingdom[, 18 Eur. Ct. H.R. (ser. A) (1975)].) In their internal legal orders the Contracting States make the rights to vote and to stand for election subject to conditions which are not in principle precluded under Article 3. (Collected Edition of the Travaux Préparatoires, vol. III p. 264 and vol. IV p. 24.) They have a wide margin of appreciation in this sphere, but it is for the Court to determine in the last resort whether the requirements of Protocol No. 1 have been complied with; it has to satisfy itself that the conditions do not curtail the rights in question to such an extent as to impair their very essence and deprive them of their effectiveness; that they are imposed in pursuit of a legitimate aim; and that the means employed are not disproportionate. (See, amongst other authorities and mutatis mutandis, Lithgow v United Kingdom [102 Eur. Ct. H.R. (ser. A) (1986).]) In particular, such conditions must not thwart "the free expression of the opinion of the people in the choice of the legislature".

53.   Article 3 applies only to the election of the "legislature", or at least of one of its chambers if it has two or more. (Travaux Préparatoires, vol. VIII pp. 46, 50 and 52.) The word "legislature" does not necessarily mean only the national parliament, however; it has to be interpreted in the light of the constitutional structure of the State in question.

The Court notes at the outset that the 1980 reform vested the Flemish Council with competence and powers wide enough to make it, alongside the French Community Council and the Walloon Regional Council, a constituent part of the Belgian "legislature" in addition to the House of Representatives and the Senate; those appearing before the Court were agreed on this point.

54.   As regards the method of appointing the "legislature", Article 3 provides only for "free" elections "at reasonable intervals", "by secret

ballot" and "under conditions which will ensure the free expression of the opinion of the people". Subject to that, it does not create any "obligation to introduce a specific system" (Travaux Préparatoires, vol. VII pp. 130, 202 and 210 and vol. VIII p. 14) such as proportional representation or majority voting with one or two ballots.

Here too the Court recognises that the Contracting States have a wide margin of appreciation, given that their legislation on the matter varies from place to place and from time to time.

Electoral systems seek to fulfil objectives which are sometimes scarcely compatible with each other; on the one hand, to reflect fairly faithfully the opinions of the people, and on the other, to channel currents of thought so as to promote the emergence of a sufficiently clear and coherent political will. In these circumstances the phrase "conditions which will ensure the free expression of the opinion of the people in the choice of the legislature" implies essentially—apart from freedom of expression (already protected under Article 10 of the Convention)—the principle of equality of treatment of all citizens in the exercise of their right to vote and their right to stand for election.

It does not follow, however, that all votes must necessarily have equal weight as regards the outcome of the election or that all candidates must have equal chances of victory. Thus no electoral system can eliminate "wasted votes".

For the purposes of Article 3 of Protocol No. 1, any electoral system must be assessed in the light of the political evolution of the country concerned; features that would be unacceptable in the context of one system may accordingly be justified in the context of another, at least so long as the chosen system provides for conditions which will ensure the "free expression of the opinion of the people in the choice of the legislature".

B. Application of Article 3 of Protocol No. 1 in the instant case

55.   The Court has to consider the applicants' complaints from the point of view of Article 3 thus interpreted.

56.   The Government pointed out that nothing prevented the French-speaking electors in the district of Halle–Vilvoorde from knowingly voting for a candidate who was likewise French-speaking but willing to take his parliamentary oath in Dutch; once elected, such a candidate would sit on the Flemish Council as of right and represent his constituents.

This argument is not decisive. Admittedly, electors cannot be defined wholly in terms of their language and culture; political, economic, social, religious and philosophical considerations also influence their votes. Linguistic preferences, however, are a major factor affecting the way citizens vote in a country like Belgium, especially in the case of the residents of a "sensitive" area, such as the municipalities on the outskirts of Brussels. An elected representative who took his parliamentary oath in Dutch would not belong to the French-language group in the House of Representatives or the Senate; and these groups, like the Dutch-language groups, play an important role in those areas in which the Constitution requires special majorities.

57.   The 1980 Special Act, however, fits into a general institutional system of the Belgian State, based on the territoriality principle. The system covers the administrative and political institutions and the distribution of their powers. The reform, which is not yet complete, is designed to achieve an equilibrium between the Kingdom's various regions and cultural communities by means of a complex pattern of checks and balances. The aim is to defuse the language disputes in the country by establishing more stable and decentralised organisational structures. This intention, which is legitimate in itself, clearly emerges from the debates in the democratic national Parliament and is borne out by the massive majorities achieved in favour—notably—of the Special Act, including section 29.

In any consideration of the electoral system in issue, its general context must not be forgotten. The system does not appear unreasonable if regard is had to the intentions it reflects and to the respondent State's margin of appreciation within the Belgian parliamentary system—a margin that is all the greater as the system is incomplete and provisional. One of the consequences for the linguistic minorities is that they must vote for candidates willing and able to use the language of their region. A similar requirement is found in the organisation of elections in a good many States. Experience shows that such a situation does not necessarily threaten the interests of the minorities. This is particularly true, in respect of a system which makes concessions to the territoriality principle, where the political and legal order provide safeguards against inopportune or arbitrary changes—by requiring, for example, special majorities.

The French-speaking electors in the district of Halle–Vilvoorde enjoy the right to vote and the right to stand for election on the same legal footing as the Dutch-speaking electors. They are in no way deprived of these rights by the mere fact that they must vote either for candidates who will take the parliamentary oath in French and will accordingly join the French-language group in the House of Representatives or the Senate and sit on the French Community Council, or else for candidates who will take the oath in Dutch and so belong to the Dutch-language group in the House of Representatives or the Senate and sit on the Flemish Council. This is not a disproportionate limitation such as would thwart "the free expression of the opinion of the people in the choice of the legislature."

The Court accordingly finds that there has been no breach of Article 3 of Protocol No. 1 taken alone.

[For the same reasons, the court also found that there was no violation of Article 14 of the Convention taken together with Article 3 of Protocol No. 1.]

■ Concurring Opinion of JUDGE PINHEIRO FARINHA

... I concurred in the result but [the wording of paragraph 53] causes me great difficulty. . . .

. . .

In my opinion, we should say "or at least of one of its chambers if it has two or more, on the twofold condition that the majority of the membership of the legislature is elected and that the chamber or chambers whose members are not elected does or do not have greater powers than the chamber that is freely elected by secret ballot".

■ Joint dissenting opinion of Judges Cremona, Bindschedler-Robert, Bernhardt, Spielmann and Valticos

To our regret we are unable to share the opinion of the majority of the Court, since it appears to us that in law the position in which the French-speaking electorate and the French-speaking elected representatives of the administrative district of Halle–Vilvoorde are placed is not compatible with Belgium's obligations under Article 3 of Protocol No. 1, whether taken by itself or together with Article 14 of the Convention.

... [T]he members of the House of Representatives and the Senate elected in the district of Halle–Vilvoorde cannot, if they take the parliamentary oath in French, sit on the Flemish Council (a body which indisputably has legislative powers) and are therefore unable to defend their Region's interests in a number of important fields (such as regional planning, environment, housing, economic policy, energy and employment), whereas elected representatives who take the oath in Dutch are automatically members of the Flemish Council. . . .

. . .

In our opinion, such a situation, excluding, as it does in practice, representation of the French-speaking electorate of Halle–Vilvoorde at regional level, does not ensure "the free expression of the opinion of the people in the choice of the legislature" as stipulated in Article 3 of Protocol No. 1, and it creates a language-based distinction contrary to Article 14 of the Convention.

None of the reasons put forward to justify this incompatibility appears to us to be convincing.

. . .

Lastly, it cannot be said that the state of affairs submitted to the Court represents the only conceivable solution of the problem; indeed, the very fact that it is regarded as transitional indicates that other acceptable arrangements are contemplated or are at least not being ruled out. Merely by way of example and without in any way claiming to offer practical proposals (which we are not qualified to do), one could imagine allowing the various French-speaking elected representatives of the Halle–Vilvoorde district to belong to the Flemish Council even if they have taken the parliamentary oath in French—which does not preclude their speaking Dutch in the Flemish Council. Or again, one might envisage holding separate elections at regional level and national level, on the understanding that the representatives elected at regional level would have to be able to be members of the relevant regional Council. But obviously it is for the Government themselves to find the best means of solving the problem.

Reynolds v. Sims

Supreme Court of the United States, 1964.
377 U.S. 533.

■ CHIEF JUSTICE WARREN delivered the Opinion of the Court.

[The plaintiffs were Alabama voters who filed suit in 1961, complaining that the apportionment of seats in the state legislature had not been changed since 1903, despite the uneven population growth since the census of 1900. They argued that the resulting underrepresentation of the more populous districts violated their rights under the Equal Protection Clause of the Fourteenth Amendment.]

A predominant consideration in determining whether a State's legislative apportionment scheme constitutes an invidious discrimination violative of rights asserted under the Equal Protection Clause is that the rights allegedly impaired are individual and personal in nature. ...While the result of a court decision in a state legislative apportionment controversy may be to require the restructuring of the geographical distribution of seats in a state legislature, the judicial focus must be concentrated upon ascertaining whether there has been any discrimination against certain of the State's citizens which constitutes an impermissible impairment of their constitutionally protected right to vote. Like Skinner v. Oklahoma, 316 U.S. 535, such a case "touches a sensitive and important area of human rights," and "involves one of the basic civil rights of man," presenting questions of alleged "invidious discriminations . . . against groups or types of individuals in violation of the constitutional guaranty of just and equal laws." Undoubtedly, the right of suffrage is a fundamental matter in a free and democratic society. Especially since the right to exercise the franchise in a free and unimpaired manner is preservative of other basic civil and political rights, any alleged infringement of the right of citizens to vote must be carefully and meticulously scrutinized. . . .

Legislators represent people, not trees or acres. Legislators are elected by voters, not farms or cities or economic interests. As long as ours is a representative form of government, and our legislatures are those instruments of government elected directly by and directly representative of the people, the right to elect legislators in a free and unimpaired fashion is a bedrock of our political system. It could hardly be gainsaid that a constitutional claim had been asserted by an allegation that certain otherwise qualified voters had been entirely prohibited from voting for members of their state legislature. And, if a State should provide that the votes of citizens in one part of the State should be given two times, or five times, or 10 times the weight of votes of citizens in another part of the State, it could hardly be contended that the right to vote of those residing in the disfavored areas had not been effectively diluted. . . . Of course, the effect of state legislative districting schemes which give the same number of representatives to unequal numbers of constituents is identical. . . .

. . .

[R]epresentative government is in essence self-government through the medium of elected representatives of the people, and each and every citizen has an inalienable right to full and effective participation in the political processes of his State's legislative bodies. Most citizens can achieve this participation only as qualified voters through the election of legislators to represent them. Full and effective participation by all citizens in state government requires, therefore, that each citizen have an equally effective voice in the election of members of his state legislature. Modern and viable state government needs, and the Constitution demands, no less.

Logically, in a society ostensibly grounded on representative government, it would seem reasonable that a majority of the people of a State could elect a majority of that State's legislators. To conclude differently, and to sanction minority control of state legislative bodies, would appear to deny majority rights in a way that far surpasses any possible denial of minority rights that might otherwise be thought to result. Since legislatures are responsible for enacting laws by which all citizens are to be governed, they should be bodies which are collectively responsive to the popular will. And the concept of equal protection has been traditionally viewed as requiring the uniform treatment of persons standing in the same relation to the governmental action questioned or challenged. With respect to the allocation of legislative representation, all voters, as citizens of a State, stand in the same relation regardless of where they live. Any suggested criteria for the differentiation of citizens are insufficient to justify any discrimination, as to the weight of their votes, unless relevant to the permissible purposes of legislative apportionment. Since the achieving of fair and effective representation for all citizens is concededly the basic aim of legislative apportionment, we conclude that the Equal Protection Clause guarantees the opportunity for equal participation by all voters in the election of state legislators. Diluting the weight of votes because of place of residence impairs basic constitutional rights under the Fourteenth Amendment just as much as invidious discriminations based upon factors such as race, or economic status. Our constitutional system amply provides for the protection of minorities by means other than giving them majority control of state legislatures. And the democratic ideals of equality and majority rule, which have served this Nation so well in the past, are hardly of any less significance for the present and the future.

. . .

We hold that, as a basic constitutional standard, the Equal Protection Clause requires that the seats in both houses of a bicameral state legislature must be apportioned on a population basis. Simply stated, an individual's right to vote for state legislators is unconstitutionally impaired when its weight is in a substantial fashion diluted when compared with votes of citizens living on other parts of the State. Since, under neither the existing apportionment provisions nor either of the proposed plans was either of the houses of the Alabama Legislature apportioned on a population basis, the District Court correctly held that all three of these schemes were constitutionally invalid. . . .

. . .

Since neither of the houses of the Alabama Legislature, under any of the three plans considered by the District Court, was apportioned on a population basis, we would be justified in proceeding no further. However, one of the proposed plans, that contained in the so-called 67–Senator Amendment, at least superficially resembles the scheme of legislative representation followed in the Federal Congress. Under this plan, each of Alabama's 67 counties is allotted one senator, and no counties are given more than one Senate seat. Arguably, this is analogous to the allocation of two Senate seats, in the Federal Congress, to each of the 50 States, regardless of population. . . .

. . .

The system of representation in the two Houses of the Federal Congress is one ingrained in our Constitution, as part of the law of the land. It is one conceived out of compromise and concession indispensable to the establishment of our federal republic. Arising from unique historical circumstances, it is based on the consideration that in establishing our type of federalism a group of formerly independent States bound themselves together under one national government. Admittedly, the original 13 States surrendered some of their sovereignty in agreeing to join together "to form a more perfect Union." But at the heart of our constitutional system remains the concept of separate and distinct governmental entities which have delegated some, but not all, of their formerly held powers to the single national government. The fact that almost three-fourths of our present States were never in fact independently sovereign does not detract from our view that the so-called federal analogy is inapplicable as a sustaining precedent for state legislative apportionments. The developing history and growth of our republic cannot cloud the fact that, at the time of the inception of the system of representation in the Federal Congress, a compromise between the larger and smaller States on this matter averted a deadlock in the Constitutional Convention which had threatened to abort the birth of our Nation. . . .

Political subdivisions of States—counties, cities, or whatever—never were and never have been considered as sovereign entities. Rather, they have been traditionally regarded as subordinate governmental instrumentalities created by the State to assist in the carrying out of state governmental functions. . . . The relationship of the States to the Federal Government could hardly be less analogous.

Thus, we conclude that the plan contained in the 67–Senator Amendment for apportioning seats in the Alabama Legislature cannot be sustained by recourse to the so-called federal analogy. Nor can any other inequitable state legislative apportionment scheme be justified on such an asserted basis. This does not necessarily mean that such a plan is irrational or involves something other than a "republican form of government." We conclude simply that such a plan is impermissible for the States under the Equal Protection Clause, since perforce resulting, in virtually every case, in submergence of the equal-population principle in at least one house of a state legislature.

. . .

By holding that as a federal constitutional requisite both houses of a state legislature must be apportioned on a population basis, we mean that the Equal Protection Clause requires that a State make an honest and good faith effort to construct districts, in both houses of its legislature, as nearly of equal population as is practicable. We realize that it is a practical impossibility to arrange legislative districts so that each one has an identical number of residents, or citizens, or voters. Mathematical exactness or precision is hardly a workable constitutional requirement.

. . .

History indicates . . . that many States have deviated, to a greater or lesser degree, from the equal-population principle in the apportionment of seats in at least one house of their legislatures. So long as the divergences from a strict population standard are based on legitimate considerations incident to the effectuation of a rational state policy, some deviations from the equal-population principle are constitutionally permissible with respect to the apportionment of seats in either or both of the two houses of a bicameral state legislature. But neither history alone, nor economic or other sorts of group interests, are permissible factors in attempting to justify disparities from population-based representation. Citizens, not history or economic interests, cast votes. Considerations of area alone provide an insufficient justification for deviations from the equal-population principle. Again, people, not land or trees or pastures, vote. Modern developments and improvements in transportation and communications make rather hollow, in the mid–1960's, most claims that deviations from population-based representation can validly be based solely on geographical considerations. Arguments for allowing such deviations in order to insure effective representation for sparsely settled areas and to prevent legislative districts from becoming so large that the availability of access of citizens to their representatives is impaired are today, for the most part, unconvincing.

A consideration that appears to be of more substance in justifying some deviations from population-based representation in state legislatures is that of insuring some voice to political subdivisions, as political subdivisions. . . . Local governmental entities are frequently charged with various responsibilities incident to the operation of state government. In many States much of the legislature's activity involves the enactment of so-called local legislation, directed only to the concerns of particular political subdivisions. And a State may legitimately desire to construct districts along political subdivision lines to deter the possibilities of gerrymandering. . . . But if, even as a result of a clearly rational state policy of according some legislative representation to political subdivisions, population is submerged as the controlling consideration in the apportionment of seats in the particular legislative body, then the right of all of the State's citizens to cast an effective and adequately weighted vote would be unconstitutionally impaired.

. . .

■ HARLAN, J., dissenting

. . .

... Stripped of aphorisms, the Court's argument boils down to the assertion that appellees' right to vote has been invidiously "debased" or "diluted" by systems of apportionment which entitle them to vote for fewer legislators than other voters, an assertion which is tied to the Equal Protection Clause only by the constitutionally frail tautology that "equal" means "equal."

Had the Court paused to probe more deeply into the matter, it would have found that the Equal Protection Clause was never intended to inhibit the States in choosing any democratic method they pleased for the apportionment of their legislatures. This is shown by the language of the Fourteenth Amendment taken as a whole, by the understanding of those who proposed and ratified it, and by the political practices of the States at the time the Amendment was adopted. It is confirmed by numerous state and congressional actions since the adoption of the Fourteenth Amendment, and by the common understanding of the Amendment as evidenced by subsequent constitutional amendments and decisions of this Court before Baker v. Carr, [369 U.S. 186], made an abrupt break with the past in 1962.

. . .

Kramer v. Union Free School Dist. No. 15

Supreme Court of the United States, 1969.
395 U.S. 621.

■ WARREN, C.J.

In this case we are called on to determine whether § 2012 of the New York Education Law, is constitutional. The legislation provides that in certain New York school districts residents who are otherwise eligible to vote in state and federal elections may vote in the school district election only if they (1) own (or lease) taxable real property within the district, or (2) are parents (or have custody of) children enrolled in the local public schools. Appellant, a bachelor who neither owns nor leases taxable real property, filed suit in federal court claiming that § 2012 denied him equal protection of the laws in violation of the Fourteenth Amendment. ...

New York law provides basically three methods of school board selection. In some large city districts, the school board is appointed by the mayor or city council. On the other hand, in some cities, primarily those with less than 125,000 residents, the school board is elected at general or municipal elections in which all qualified city voters may participate. Finally, in other districts such as the one involved in this case, which are primarily rural and suburban, the school board is elected at an annual meeting of qualified school district voters.

. . .

. . . "[S]ince the right to exercise the franchise in a free and unimpaired manner is preservative of other basic civil and political rights, any alleged infringement of the right of citizens to vote must be carefully and meticulously scrutinized." Reynolds v. Sims, 377 U.S. 533, 562 (1964). This careful examination is necessary because statutes distributing the franchise constitute the foundation of our representative society. Any unjustified discrimination in determining who may participate in political affairs or in the selection of public officials undermines the legitimacy of representative government.

. . .

[T]he deference usually given to the judgment of legislators does not extend to decisions concerning which resident citizens may participate in the election of legislators and other public officials. Those decisions must be carefully scrutinized by the Court to determine whether each resident citizen has, as far as is possible, an equal voice in the selections. Accordingly, when we are reviewing statutes which deny some residents the right to vote, the general presumption of constitutionality afforded state statutes and the traditional approval given state classifications if the Court can conceive of a "rational basis" for the distinctions made are not applicable. The presumption of constitutionality and the approval given "rational" classifications in other types of enactments are based on an assumption that the institutions of state government are structured so as to represent fairly all the people. However, when the challenge to the statute is in effect a challenge of this basic assumption, the assumption can no longer serve as the basis for presuming constitutionality. And, the assumption is no less under attack because the legislature which decides who may participate at the various levels of political choice is fairly elected. Legislation which delegates decision making to bodies elected by only a portion of those eligible to vote for the legislature can cause unfair representation. Such legislation can exclude a minority of voters from any voice in the decisions just as effectively as if the decisions were made by legislators the minority had no voice in selecting.

The need for exacting judicial scrutiny of statutes distributing the franchise is undiminished simply because, under a different statutory scheme, the offices subject to election might have been filled through appointment. . . .

. . .

Appellees argue that it is necessary to limit the franchise to those "primarily interested" in school affairs because "the ever increasing complexity of the many interacting phases of the school system and structure make it extremely difficult for the electorate fully to understand the whys and wherefores of the detailed operations of the school system." . . . . [A]ssuming, arguendo, that New York legitimately might limit the franchise in these school district elections to those "primarily interested in school affairs," close scrutiny of the [statutory] classifications demonstrates that they do not accomplish this purpose with sufficient precision to justify denying appellant the franchise. ... The classifications ... permit inclusion of many persons who have, at best, a remote and indirect interest, in school affairs and, on the other hand, exclude others who have a distinct and direct interest in the school meeting decisions.[15]

[Dissenting opinion of Justice Stewart, joined by Justices Harlan and Black, omitted.]

Igartua de la Rosa v. United States

United States Court of Appeals, First Circuit, 1994.
32 F.3d 8, cert. denied, 514 U.S. 1049 (1995).

■ PER CURIAM.

Appellant residents of Puerto Rico allege that their inability to vote in the United States presidential election violates their constitutional rights.... The district court dismissed appellants' request for declaratory and injunctive relief for failure to state a claim upon which relief could be granted. We summarily affirm.

. . .

While appellants are citizens of the United States, the Constitution does not grant citizens the right to vote directly for the President. Instead, the Constitution provides that the President is to be chosen by electors who, in turn, are chosen by "each state ... in such manner as the Legislature thereof may direct." U.S. Const. art. II, § 1, cl. 2. Pursuant to Article II, therefore, only citizens residing in states can vote for electors and thereby indirectly for the President. Since Puerto Rico is concededly not a state, it is not entitled under Article II to choose electors for the President, and residents of Puerto Rico have no constitutional right to participate in that election.

The only jurisdiction, not a state, which participates in the presidential election is the District of Columbia, which obtained that right through the twenty-third amendment to the Constitution. Such a constitutional amendment was necessary precisely "because the Constitution ha[d] restricted th[e] privilege [of voting in national elections] to citizens who reside[d] in States." H.R.Rep. No. 1698, 86th Cong., 2d Sess. 2 (1960), reprinted in 1960 U.S.Code Cong. & Ad.News 1459, 1460. Only a similar constitutional amendment or a grant of statehood to Puerto Rico, therefore, can provide appellants the right to vote in the presidential election which they seek.[1]

. . .

15. For example, appellant resides with his parents in the school district, pays state and federal taxes and is interested in and affected by school board decisions; however, he has no vote. On the other hand, an uninterested unemployed young man who pays no state or federal taxes, but who rents an apartment in the district, can participate in the election.

1. Appellants' contention that their right to vote in the presidential election is secured by Article 25 of the International

Appellants' request for oral argument is denied. The dismissal of appellants' claims is affirmed.

Notes

1. In *Mathieu-Mohin*, the European Court emphasizes that Protocol 1, Article 3 does not dictate a particular electoral system. It is compatible with winner-take-all district elections of the Anglo–American type, with pure proportional representation, and with hybrid systems that combine local district elections with proportional representation. It also permits proportional representation to be qualified by a threshold percentage that prevents splinter parties from impairing the functioning of the legislature. See *Magnago and Südtiroler Volkspartei v. Italy*, 85 Eur. Comm'n H.R. 112 (1996) (rejecting challenge to 4% threshold in hybrid system). Do all of these systems equally "ensure the free expression of the opinion of the people in the choice of the legislature"? Do they equally ensure that the composition of the legislature reflects the opinions thus expressed? Or is that more than Article 3 requires?

Because Article 3 addresses only legislative elections, it is compatible with parliamentary systems in which the legislature chooses the chief executive, and with presidential systems in which the chief executive is directly elected. It is compatible with both republics and constitutional monarchies. Do Article 3 and the rest of the European Convention imply any limitations on the quantity of governing power that can be vested in a hereditary monarch? Finally, the European Court interpreted Article 3, in light of its travaux préparatoires and obvious political realities, as not precluding a nonelected upper house such as the British House of Lords. Should human rights instruments permit executive or legislative powers to be held on a hereditary basis?

2. Note that the European Court observes (paragraph 53) that the word "legislature" must "be interpreted in the light of the constitutional structure of the State in question," and concludes that the powers vested in the various Councils were wide enough to make them constituent parts of the "legislature." This reasoning illustrates the practice of autonomous interpretation of the Convention—where a term used in the Convention has different formal definitions in the legal systems of the different states, it may be necessary to adopt an independent conception of the term and apply that conception to the different national systems. See F. Matscher, *Methods of Interpretation of the Convention*, in The European System for the Protection of Human Rights 63, 70–73 (R. St. J. Macdonald et al. eds. 1993).

Covenant on Civil and Political Rights, 6 I.L.M. 368 (1967) (entered into force Sept. 8, 1992), is without merit. Even if Article 25 could be read to imply such a right, Articles 1 through 27 of the Covenant were not self-executing, see 138 Cong.Rec. S4784 (daily ed. Apr. 2, 1992), and could not therefore give rise to privately enforceable rights under United States law. ... Nor could the Covenant override the constitutional limits discussed above. See *Reid v. Covert*, 354 U.S. 1, 15–16 (1957) (plurality opinion).

In an important recent decision, the European Court held that, given the present state of development of the European Union, the European Parliament also counts as the "legislature" within the meaning of Article 3 of Protocol No. 1. The European Parliament is directly elected, and plays an increasingly significant role in the lawmaking procedure of the European Union, but not to the same degree as a national parliament. See *Matthews v. United Kingdom*, No. 24833/94 (Eur. Ct. H.R. 18 Feb. 1999) (finding, by fifteen votes to two, violation in denial of voting rights to residents of Gibraltar in elections for European Parliament).

3.   What elections, if any, does the U.S. Constitution *require* state and federal governments to hold? Does Article I, Section 2, defining the qualifications for elections to the House of Representatives in terms of the "Qualifications requisite for Electors of the most numerous Branch of the State Legislature" imply a constitutional requirement that each state must have a legislature and that at least the more numerous branch of that legislature must be popularly elected, or does it merely reflect a factual assumption based on the structure of existing state legislatures in 1787? What requirements flow from Article IV, Section 4, providing that "[t]he United States shall guarantee to every State in this Union a Republican Form of Government"? Note that the Supreme Court has usually treated issues arising under the Guarantee Clause as nonjusticiable. See, e.g., *Pacific States Telephone & Telegraph Co. v. Oregon*, 223 U.S. 118 (1912); *Luther v. Borden*, 48 U.S. (7 How.) 1 (1849).

4.   The Supreme Court insists in *Reynolds* that a majority of the voters ought to be able to elect a majority of the legislature. But the usual American system of winner-take-all elections in geographically defined districts does not guarantee that result. If the supporters of one party are geographically concentrated (whether by happenstance or because they have been deliberately "packed" into their districts by the the lawmakers who designed the districts), then some of their votes will be "wasted," and they will elect less than their proportionate share of the legislators.

Could it therefore be said that the Supreme Court in *Reynolds* gives the states leeway to structure their legislatures in order to facilitate the representation of geographically defined interest groups, but not economic or social interest groups? If so, then why does that approach reflect the proper understanding of democracy?

In later cases, however, the Supreme Court has recognized a category of special purpose public agencies whose governing boards may be elected by segments of the public particularly affected by their activities, on a basis other than one-person, one vote. See, e.g., *Salyer Land Co. v. Tulare Lake Basin Water Storage District*, 410 U.S. 719 (1973) (upholding election of board of water storage district by local landowners on a one-acre, one-vote basis).

5.   Why does the Supreme Court in *Reynolds* reject the analogy between representation in a state senate and representation in the federal Senate? Is the unequal representation of U.S. citizens in the Senate an invidious discrimination that is shielded from equal protection attack by the text of

the Constitution? Recall that the less populous states are also dispropor-tionately represented in the formula for electoral votes that determines the choice of the President and Vice President. Do these features of the U.S. electoral system violate the "democratic ideals" that the Court invokes in *Reynolds*? Or are they justified by historical factors or sociological factors distinguishing the United States from a unitary state? If such factors do justify the U.S. system, then what other historical or sociological factors might justify deviations from formal equality in an electoral system?

6.   The Supreme Court has relied on a right to nondiscrimination in the distribution of the franchise, rather than an affirmative constitutional right to vote, as the basis for achieving universal suffrage. The Court's case law has progressed beyond the specific prohibitions contained in the Fifteenth, Nineteenth, Twenty-fourth and Twenty-sixth Amendments to strict equal protection scrutiny of voter qualifications. States may nonetheless deny voting rights to noncitizens, nonresidents, convicted felons, minors, and persons lacking mental competence. As *Kramer* illustrates, the Supreme Court has enforced this egalitarian vision not only in the election of the state legislature, but also in optional elections at the local level. (Note, however, that it follows from the cases on special-purpose agencies that some narrowly focused elections need not be held on the basis of universal suffrage.) Why does equality, or democracy, require universal suffrage for subordinate governmental units that could have been appointed? Why should a popularly chosen legislature be prohibited from experimenting with electoral structures in these subunits?

Contrast the more limited scope of the right to vote under Protocol 1, Article 3 of the European Convention, as construed in *Mathieu-Mohin*. What is the scope of the right to "universal and equal suffrage" in Article 21 of the Universal Declaration, Article 25 of the ICCPR and Article 23 of the American Convention? (Note that this phrase is not repeated in the European Convention or in Article 13 of the African Charter.) How might *Kramer* be decided if each of these instruments provided the governing standard?

7.   The European Court in *Mathieu-Mohin* upheld Belgium's complex institutional structure for ensuring the representation of the distinct inter-ests of the French-speaking and Dutch-speaking communities, despite their particular effects on the substantial French minority population of a predominantly Dutch-speaking district. The Court accepted the legitimacy of structuring the legislative process for this purpose, despite the prohibi-tion in Article 14 against discrimination on grounds of language in the enjoyment of enumerated rights and freedoms. In the United States, would legislative restructuring to afford specific representation to ethnic minori-ties be constitutionally permissible? In recent years, the Supreme Court has heightened its scrutiny of legislative districting schemes designed to ensure the representation of *racial* minorities. In *Shaw v. Reno*, 509 U.S. 630 (1993), the Court condemned a legislative district that was "so extremely irregular on its face that it rationally can be viewed only as an effort to segregate the races for purpose of voting." The majority warned that

"[r]acial gerrymandering, even for remedial purposes, may balkanize us into competing racial factions; it threatens to carry us further from the goal of a political system in which race no longer matters...." The Court has since extended strict scrutiny to invalidate redistricting legislation in which it found that race was the predominant factor in drawing district boundaries. See, e.g., *Bush v. Vera*, 517 U.S. 952 (1996); *Miller v. Johnson*, 515 U.S. 900 (1995). It is currently unclear what the Court would count as a compelling interest that would justify such use of race. Should or would the Supreme Court treat district boundaries drawn on the basis of ethnicity any differently from district boundaries drawn on the basis of race? Do the differences between the European Court's approach in *Mathieu-Mohin* and the Supreme Court's recent approach reflect (a) the difference between race discrimination and language discrimination, (b) the difference between the current international and U.S. approaches to affirmative action, (c) different assumptions about the legitimate role of group affiliations in politics? Cf. Chapter 1(D), supra.

8. On what grounds does the First Circuit Court of Appeals in *Igartua* reject the claim under Article 25 of the Covenant? Do the facts in *Igartua* demonstrate that the United States has violated its obligations under Article 25? Or is the United States saved from a violation by one of its reservations to the Covenant?

   Putting aside the reservations, would it be sufficient under Article 25 that the citizens of Puerto Rico elect their own legislature and Governor, even if they cannot participate in federal elections? Does the status of Puerto Rico as an overseas territory of the United States justify its exclusion from presidential and congressional elections? Compare *X v. United Kingdom*, 28 Eur. Comm'n. H.R. 99 (1982) (rejecting claim of residents of Island of Jersey to representation in U.K. Parliament), with *Matthews v. United Kingdom*, No. 24833/94 (Eur. Ct. H.R. 18 Feb. 1999) (finding violation in denial of voting rights to residents of Gibraltar in elections for European Parliament). If overseas territories present special situations, then how should the denial of representation in Congress to the District of Columbia be evaluated under Article 25?

The Right to Political Participation Under the ICCPR

Bwalya v. Zambia

Human Rights Committee, 1993.
U.N. Doc. CCPR/C/48/D/314/1988.

The facts as submitted by the author:

1. The author of the communication is Peter Chiiko Bwalya, a Zambian citizen born in 1961 and currently chairman of the People's Redemption Organization, a political party in Zambia. He claims to be a victim of violations of the International Covenant on Civil and Political Rights by Zambia.

2.1 In 1983, at the age of 22, the author ran for a parliamentary seat in the Constituency of Chifubu, Zambia. He states that the authorities prevented him from properly preparing his candidacy and from participating in the electoral campaign. The authorities' action apparently helped to increase his popularity among the poorer strata of the local population, as the author was committed to changing the Government's policy towards, in particular, the homeless and the unemployed. He claims that in retaliation for the propagation of his opinions and his activism, the authorities subjected him to threats and intimidation, and that in January 1986 he was dismissed from his employment. The Ndola City Council subsequently expelled him and his family from their home, while the payment of his father's pension was suspended indefinitely.

2.2 Because of the harassment and hardship to which he and his family were being subjected, the author emigrated to Namibia, where other Zambian citizens had settled. Upon his return to Zambia, however, he was arrested and placed in custody....

2.3 The author notes that by September 1988 he had been detained for 31 months, on charges of belonging to the People's Redemption Organization an association considered illegal under the terms of the country's one-party Constitution and for having conspired to overthrow the Government of the then President Kenneth Kaunda. On an unspecified subsequent date, he was released....

2.4 On 25 March 1990, the author sought the Committee's direct intercession in connection with alleged discrimination, denial of employment and refusal of a passport. By letter of 5 July 1990, the author's wife indicated that her husband had been rearrested on 1 July 1990 and taken to the Central Police Station in Ndola, where he was reportedly kept for two days. Subsequently, he was transferred to Kansenshi prison in Ndola....

5.1 In a submission dated 28 January 1992, the State party indicates that "Mr. Peter Chiiko Bwalya has been released from custody and is a free person now". No information on the substance of the author's allegations, nor copies of his indictment or any judicial orders concerning the author, have been provided by the State party, in spite of reminders addressed to it on 9 January and 21 May 1992.

5.2 In a letter dated 3 March 1992, the author confirms that he was released from detention but requests the Committee to continue consideration of his case. He adds that the change in the Government has not changed the authorities' attitude towards him.

6.1 The Committee has considered the communication in the light of all the information provided by the parties. It notes with concern that, with the exception of a brief note informing the Committee of the author's release, the State party has failed to cooperate on the matter under consideration. It further recalls that it is implicit in article 4, paragraph 2, of the Optional Protocol that a State party examine in good faith all the allegations brought against it, and that it provide the Committee with all the information at its disposal, including all available judicial orders and decisions. The State party has not forwarded to the Committee any such information. In the circumstances, due weight must be given to the author's allegations, to the extent that they have been substantiated.

6.2 In respect of issues under article 19, the Committee considers that the uncontested response of the authorities to the attempts of the author to express his opinions freely and to disseminate the political tenets of his party constitute a violation of his rights under article 19.

6.6 As to the alleged violation of article 25 of the Covenant, the Committee notes that the author, a leading figure of a political party in opposition to the former President, has been prevented from participating in a general election campaign as well as from preparing his candidacy for this party. This amounts to an unreasonable restriction on the author's right to "take part in the conduct of public affairs" which the State party has failed to explain or justify. In particular, it has failed to explain the requisite conditions for participation in the elections. Accordingly, it must be assumed that Mr. Bwalya was detained and denied the right to run for a parliamentary seat in the Constituency of Chifubu merely on account of his membership in a political party other than that officially recognized; in this context, the Committee observes that restrictions on political activity outside the only recognized political party amount to an unreasonable restriction of the right to participate in the conduct of public affairs.

8. Pursuant to article 2 of the Covenant, the State party is under an obligation to provide Mr. Bwalya with an appropriate remedy. The Committee urges the State party to grant appropriate compensation to the author. The State party is under an obligation to ensure that similar violations do not occur in the future.

9. The Committee would wish to receive information, within 90 days, on any relevant measures taken by the State party in respect of the Committee's Views.

Human Rights Committee, General Comment 25

U.N. Doc. A/51/40, Annex V (1997)

The right to participate in public affairs, voting rights and the right of equal access to public service (Article 25) (1996)

1. Article 25 of the Covenant recognizes and protects the right of every citizen to take part in the conduct of public affairs, the right to vote and to be elected and the right to have access to public service. Whatever form of constitution or government is in force, the Covenant requires States to adopt such legislative and other measures as may be necessary to ensure that citizens have an effective opportunity to enjoy the rights it protects. Article 25 lies at the core of democratic government based on the consent of the people and in conformity with the principles of the Covenant.

2. The rights under article 25 are related to, but distinct from, the right of peoples to self-determination. By virtue of the rights covered by article 1(1),

peoples have the right to freely determine their political status and to enjoy the right to choose the form of their constitution or government. Article 25 deals with the right of individuals to participate in those processes which constitute the conduct of public affairs. Those rights, as individual rights, can give rise to claims under the first Optional Protocol.

. . .

5.   The conduct of public affairs, referred to in paragraph (a), is a broad concept which relates to the exercise of political power, in particular the exercise of legislative, executive and administrative powers. It covers all aspects of public administration, and the formulation and implementation of policy at international, national, regional and local levels. The allocation of powers and the means by which individual citizens exercise the right to participate in the conduct of public affairs protected by article 25 should be established by the constitution and other laws.

6.   Citizens participate directly in the conduct of public affairs when they exercise power as members of legislative bodies or by holding executive office. This right of direct participation is supported by paragraph (b). Citizens also participate directly in the conduct of public affairs when they choose or change their constitution or decide public issues through a referendum or other electoral process conducted in accordance with paragraph (b). Citizens may participate directly by taking part in popular assemblies which have the power to make decisions about local issues or about the affairs of a particular community and in bodies established to represent citizens in consultation with government. Where a mode of direct participation by citizens is established, no distinction should be made between citizens as regards their participation on the grounds mentioned in article 2, paragraph 1, and no unreasonable restrictions should be imposed.

7.   Where citizens participate in the conduct of public affairs through freely chosen representatives, it is implicit in article 25 that those representatives do in fact exercise governmental power and that they are accountable through the electoral process for their exercise of that power. It is also implicit that the representatives exercise only those powers which are allocated to them in accordance with constitutional provisions. Participation through freely chosen representatives is exercised through voting processes which must be established by laws that are in accordance with paragraph (b).

8.   Citizens also take part in the conduct of public affairs by exerting influence through public debate and dialogue with their representatives or through their capacity to organize themselves. This participation is supported by ensuring freedom of expression, assembly and association.

9.   Paragraph (b) of article 25 sets out specific provisions dealing with the right of citizens to take part in the conduct of public affairs as voters or as candidates for election. Genuine periodic elections in accordance with paragraph (b) are essential to ensure the accountability of representatives for the exercise of the legislative or executive powers vested in them. Such elections must be held at intervals which are not unduly long and which

ensure that the authority of government continues to be based on the free expression of the will of electors. The rights and obligations provided for in paragraph (b) should be guaranteed by law.

10.   The right to vote at elections and referenda must be established by law and may be subject only to reasonable restrictions, such as setting a minimum age limit for the right to vote. It is unreasonable to restrict the right to vote on the ground of physical disability or to impose literacy, educational or property requirements. Party membership should not be a condition of eligibility to vote, nor a ground of disqualification.

. . .

12.   Freedom of expression, assembly and association are essential conditions for the effective exercise of the right to vote and must be fully protected. Positive measures should be taken to overcome specific difficulties, such as illiteracy, language barriers, poverty, or impediments to freedom of movement which prevent persons entitled to vote from exercising their rights effectively. Information and materials about voting should be available in minority languages. Specific methods, such as photographs and symbols, should be adopted to ensure that illiterate voters have adequate information on which to base their choice. States parties should indicate in their reports the manner in which the difficulties highlighted in this paragraph are dealt with.

. . .

14.   In their reports, States parties should indicate and explain the legislative provisions which would deprive citizens of their right to vote. The grounds for such deprivation should be objective and reasonable. If conviction for an offence is a basis for suspending the right to vote, the period of such suspension should be proportionate to the offence and the sentence. Persons who are deprived of liberty but who have not been convicted should not be excluded from exercising the right to vote.

. . .

17.   The right of persons to stand for election should not be limited unreasonably by requiring candidates to be members of parties or of specific parties. If a candidate is required to have a minimum number of supporters for nomination this requirement should be reasonable and not act as a barrier to candidacy. Without prejudice to paragraph (1) of article 5 of the Covenant, political opinion may not be used as a ground to deprive any person of the right to stand for election.

. . .

19.   In conformity with paragraph (b), elections must be conducted fairly and freely on a periodic basis within a framework of laws guaranteeing the effective exercise of voting rights. Persons entitled to vote must be free to vote for any candidate for election and for or against any proposal submitted to referendum or plebiscite, and free to support or to oppose government, without undue influence or coercion of any kind which may distort or inhibit the free expression of the elector's will. Voters should be able to

form opinions independently, free of violence or threat of violence, compulsion, inducement or manipulative interference of any kind. Reasonable limitations on campaign expenditure may be justified where this is necessary to ensure that the free choice of voters is not undermined or the democratic process distorted by the disproportionate expenditure on behalf of any candidate or party. The results of genuine elections should be respected and implemented.

. . .

21. Although the Covenant does not impose any particular electoral system, any system operating in a State party must be compatible with the rights protected by article 25 and must guarantee and give effect to the free expression of the will of the electors. The principle of one person, one vote, must apply, and within the framework of each State's electoral system, the vote of one elector should be equal to the vote of another. The drawing of electoral boundaries and the method of allocating votes should not distort the distribution of voters or discriminate against any group and should not exclude or restrict unreasonably the right of citizens to choose their representatives freely.

. . .

25. In order to ensure the full enjoyment of rights protected by article 25, the free communication of information and ideas about public and political issues between citizens, candidates and elected representatives is essential. This implies a free press and other media able to comment on public issues without censorship or restraint and to inform public opinion. It requires the full enjoyment and respect for the rights guaranteed in articles 19, 21 and 22 of the Covenant, including freedom to engage in political activity individually or through political parties and other organizations, freedom to debate public affairs, to hold peaceful demonstrations and meetings, to criticize and oppose, to publish political material, to campaign for election and to advertise political ideas.

26. The right to freedom of association, including the right to form and join organizations and associations concerned with political and public affairs, is an essential adjunct to the rights protected by article 25. Political parties and membership in parties play a significant role in the conduct of public affairs and the election process. States should ensure that, in their internal management, political parties respect the applicable provisions of article 25 in order to enable citizens to exercise their rights thereunder.

27. Having regard to the provision of article 5, paragraph 1, of the Covenant, any rights recognized and protected by article 25 may not be interpreted as implying a right to act or as validating any act aimed at the destruction or limitation of the rights and freedoms protected by the Covenant to a greater extent than what is provided for in the present Covenant.

Notes

1. Note the Human Rights Committee's broad interpretation of the right to participate in public affairs under Article 25(a), and its explanation of

the relationship between Article 25(a) and Article 25(b). How much participation does Article 25(a) guarantee? What would constitute a violation of Article 25(a)? To what degree does the United States afford its own citizens the right guaranteed by Article 25(a)?

Consider the following characterization of Article 25:

> [T]he right to political participation can be better understood as sharing the programmatic character of many economic and social rights. So understood, it nourishes a vital ideal and serves important purposes. I mean, to be sure, a programmatic right of a distinct character from the typical economic rights. Moreover, my characterization applies to the "take part" clause of the international norms rather than to the "elections" clause. . . .

> . . .

> As societies change—through industrialization or urbanization, evolving relations between public and private sectors, reorganization of political and economic life, ideological shifts—the content of the right must be open to experimental reformulation The notion of what it requires of governments will change significantly with ongoing national experiences. New needs and possibilities will emerge.

> The clearer if still open-textured character of the "elections" clause, together with the programmatic character of the "take part" clause, nourish the argument that Article 25 now expresses some "positive law," but also contains an aspirational or hortatory element which distinguishes it from most provisions of the [ICCPR]. The aspirations that it expresses are of course shaped by the different strands of political theory and the different national practices with which the world is familiar. But this rich historical deposit of ideas and practices cannot exhaust the ways of understanding or institutionalizing an ideal of political participation.

Henry J. Steiner, *Political Participation as a Human Right*, 1 Harv. Hum. Rts. Yb. 77, 130–32 (1988).

2.   In both the General Comment (paragraph 17) and the *Bwalya* case, the Human Rights Committee appears to reject as unreasonable per se the limitation of the electoral system to one political party. That conclusion may seem unremarkable in the United States, but it would not have been politically feasible for the Committee to adopt it before the collapse of the Communist system in the Soviet Union and Eastern Europe. Communist states usually permitted only one party, and insisted that elections genuinely reflecting the true will of the people were possible only under its auspices. They contended that electoral competition in liberal democracies was illusory, because the major parties served similar class interests, and the working class was denied the resources to compete effectively. Numerous African states also adopted one-party systems, arguing that Western models of party competition were inferior to traditional African modes of consensus building, that maintaining multiple parties misallocated resources and energies needed for economic development, and that multiple

parties would tend to divide along ethnic lines, undermining the essential task of nation-building after decolonization. See, e.g., International Commission of Jurists, Human Rights in a One–Party State (1978); The One Party State and Democracy: The Zimbabwe Debate (Ibbo Mandaza and Lloyd Sachikonye eds. 1991). These arguments evidently enjoy less popularity in the 1990s. Are all of them demonstrably wrong?

3.   An influential article by Professor Thomas Franck has argued more broadly that a customary international law norm requiring democratic governance is in the process of emerging. A customary international law norm would bind even countries that are not parties to the ICCPR. Professor Franck wrote:

> . . . The failure of the August [1991] coup in the Soviet Union, an event of inestimable human, political and historic import, demonstrates—for those sensitive to trends—that democracy is beginning to be seen as the sine qua non for validating governance. While President Boris Yeltsin of the Russian Republic and many Soviet citizens deserve primary credit for this triumph, it also derived considerable impetus from the new global climate, as evidenced by the vigor with which leaders of other democracies around the world aligned themselves against the coup's leaders. Equally significant is the reaction of governments in the Organization of American States and the United Nations General Assembly to the overthrow, in September 1991, of the elected President of Haiti, Jean-Bertrand Aristide, by a military coup. On October 11, the Assembly unanimously, without vote, approved a ground-breaking resolution demanding the return of Aristide to office, full application of the Haitian Constitution and full observance of human rights in Haiti. The OAS, a week earlier, had unanimously recommended that its member states take "action to bring about the diplomatic isolation of those who hold power illegally in Haiti" and "suspend their economic, financial, and commercial ties" with the country until constitutional rule is restored.
>
> In both the Soviet and the Haitian cases, the leaders of states constituting the international community vigorously asserted that only democracy validates governance. This dramatic statement attains even more potency if, as in the Haitian case, it is transposed from political philosophy, where it is "mere" moral prescription, to law, where a newly recognized "democratic entitlement" was used in both the OAS and the UN General Assembly to impose new and important legal obligations on states. The OAS resolution, for one, stated that "the solidarity of the American states and the high aims which are sought through it require the political organization of those states on the basis of the effective exercise of representative democracy." Undeniably, a new legal entitlement is being created, based in part on custom and in part on the collective interpretation of treaties.
>
> This newly emerging "law"—which requires democracy to validate governance—is not merely the law of a particular state that, like the United States under its Constitution, has imposed such a precondition

on national governance. It is also becoming a requirement of international law, applicable to all and implemented through global standards, with the help of regional and international organizations.

The transformation of the democratic entitlement from moral prescription to international legal obligation has evolved gradually. In the past decade, however, the tendency has accelerated. . . . As of late 1991, there are more than 110 governments, almost all represented in the United Nations, that are legally committed to permitting open, multiparty, secret-ballot elections with a universal franchise. Most joined the trend in the past five years. While a few, arguably, are democracies more in form than in substance, most are, or are becoming, genuinely open to meaningful political choice. Many of these new regimes want, indeed need, to be validated by being seen to comply with global standards for free and open elections.

. . .

The almost-complete triumph of the democratic notions of Hume, Locke, Jefferson and Madison—in Latin America, Africa, Eastern Europe and, to a lesser extent, Asia—may well prove to the most profound event of the twentieth century and, in all likelihood, the fulcrum on which the future development of global society will turn. It is the unanswerable response to those who have said that free, open, multiparty, electoral parliamentary democracy is neither desired nor desirable outside a small enclave of western industrial states.

Thomas M. Franck, *The Emerging Right to Democratic Governance*, 86 Am. J. Int'l L. 46, 46–49 (1992).* For a more skeptical view of the evidence several years later, and criticism of the Human Rights Committee's interpretation, consider the following:

Given the extent of ideological contestation at the time of the adoption of the ICCPR, it is difficult to justify an interpretation of Article 25 that simply excludes the openly espoused understandings of non-liberal-democratic signatories. To be sure, states cannot eviscerate the meaning of a treaty's terms simply by announcing Orwellian interpretations in the course of negotiation, ratification or performance. . . .[The usual] touchstones of interpretation clearly establish that the ICCPR sought to oblige states to conform their practices to certain common standards, not to leave states the authority to adopt self-serving interpretations that render the obligations illusory.

Yet with respect to Article 25, all of the [usual] bases of interpretation can be understood in conflicting ways. Many, perhaps most, of the signatories would have refused to ratify a Covenant that committed them to liberal-democratic institutions of rule or even to specifically liberal-democratic criteria for the evaluation of their existing core institutions. . . . The evidently intentional choices not to specify multiparty processes and not to include such UDHR terms as "basis of authority" and "democratic society" in the ICCPR seem to have been calculated to avoid controversy over institutional requisites, while still asserting a universal human interest in political participation that states are bound to satisfy in some manner.

The initial indeterminacy of the meaning of fundamental aspects of Article 25 does not preclude the emergence over time of a more determinate meaning. According to the Vienna Convention [on Treaties], treaty interpretation may take into account "any subsequent practice in the application of the treaty which establishes the agreement of the parties regarding its interpretation." With respect to multilateral treaties, however, this rule is difficult to apply, as practice and *opinio juris* tend to indicate the agreement of some, but not all, states parties.

. . .

With the end of the Cold War period has come a shift in the patterns of international division regarding participatory rights. The most robust challenge to the liberal-democratic approach, the concept of revolutionary-democratic dictatorship that held sway in the Socialist and in much of the Non–Aligned bloc, has been crippled by the ignominious collapse of the Soviet and Eastern European regimes and the fading away of revolutionary nationalist regimes and movements in the Third World. Of the remaining regimes of revolutionary origin, some, like China and Vietnam, have reversed their programmatic course so thoroughly as to render invocations of revolutionary struggle implausible, while others, like Cuba and North Korea, have seen their revolutionary programs' claims to social welfare gains for the popular classes discredited by economic catastrophe. As a result, revolutionary regimes' earlier proclamations of the universal superiority of their forms of government have given way to defensive claims of exceptionalism and to pro-sovereignty alliances in intergovernmental bodies with non-revolutionary—often rightist and Islamist—dictatorships.

. . .

The argument for the universal applicability of liberal-democratic norms is today no longer confronted by a similarly universalist alternative. Rather, opposition takes the form of appeals to cultural differences, traditional modes of governance, and special circumstances.

. . .

Although most of the international community is now disposed to regard Article 25 as imposing some concrete obligation to allow for challenges to the established government, the right to political participation remains subject to a very wide range of interpretation. Even beyond the core of states that persistently object to any specification of criteria for participatory mechanisms as an intrusion into "matters essentially within the domestic jurisdiction," there are a great many that oppose any detailed specification of requisites. General Assembly resolutions demonstrate large majorities both for the proposition that "determining the will of the people requires an electoral process that provides an equal opportunity for all citizens to become candidates and put forward their political views, individually and in co-operation with others," and for the proposition that "there is no single political system or single model for electoral processes equally suited to all nations and their peoples, and that political systems and electoral processes are subject to historical, political, cultural, and religious factors."

Brad R. Roth, Governmental Illegitimacy in International Law 332–37 (1999).* After the decline of Communist ideology, would an interpretation of the right to "genuine periodic elections ... guaranteeing the free expression of the will of the electors" that permits a state to hold *no* elections, or only single-party elections, necessarily be disingenuous (or "Orwellian")?

4.   In paragraph 14 of its General Comment, the Committee insists that disenfranchisement after conviction for crime should be only for a period "proportionate to the offence and the sentence." Does the term "unreasonable restrictions" in Article 25 incorporate a proportionality requirement? Recall that proportionality is not the usual judicial methodology in U.S. equal protection cases, most of which employ a sharp dichotomy between strict scrutiny (a very demanding standard) and the rational basis test (an exceedingly lenient one). The U.S. Supreme Court has held that the Fourteenth Amendment permits the states to disenfranchise convicted felons for life. *Richardson v. Ramirez*, 418 U.S. 24 (1974) (relying on reference to disenfranchisement "for participation in rebellion, or other crime" in Section 2 of the Fourteenth Amendment); but cf. *Hunter v. Underwood*, 471 U.S. 222 (1985) (invalidating criminal disqualification provision that was openly designed to disenfranchise African–Americans). Does U.S. adherence to the Covenant require the states to reevaluate their criminal disenfranchisement rules?

5.   What justifies the Committee's disapproval of literacy or educational requirements for voting in paragraph 10, and its solicitude for linguistic minorities in paragraph 12? Who is likely to be disenfranchised by literacy requirements in the United States? In other countries? The U.S. Supreme Court upheld an English literacy requirement for voting in *Lassiter v. Northampton County Board of Elections*, 360 U.S. 45 (1959), but has not directly reexamined *Lassiter* since the advent of strict scrutiny of voter qualifications in the 1960s. The Court has, however, upheld federal voting rights statutes prohibiting the use of literacy tests. See, e.g., *Oregon v. Mitchell*, 400 U.S. 112 (1970). Federal law also requires the provision of ballot materials in languages other than English. See 42 U.S.C. '1973b(f). Some proposals to enshrine English as the official language of the United States would replace this requirement with a mandate that ballot materials be available only in English. Would such a policy violate Article 25?

6.   Note that article 25 is the only article of the ICCPR that is framed expressly as a right of *citizens*, not as a right of *persons*. See also African Charter Article 13 ("Every citizen"); American Convention Article 23 ("Every citizen"), and compare the more ambiguous phrasings in Universal Declaration Article 21 ("of his country"); European Convention, Protocol 1,

---

* Reprinted with permission, © 1999 Oxford University Press.

Article 3 ("of the people"); but cf. European Convention Article 16 (contemplating "restrictions on the political activity of aliens."). Is the category of "citizens" coextensive with the nationals of the state? Or may it be narrower, or broader? Assuming the two categories are coextensive, why should aliens residing permanently in a state have civil rights but not political rights? Is that distinction inherent in the very definition of citizenship? Is limiting political rights to citizens required by the theory of popular sovereignty, or by the right to self-determination?

In fact, states do not always limit the right to vote to their own nationals. Historically, the enfranchisement of resident aliens was a widespread practice in the United States in the nineteenth century; the Constitution neither requires nor forbids it. Since 1992, the Maastricht Treaty on European Union has required member states of the European Union to permit nationals of other member states who reside within their borders to vote in municipal elections, though not in national elections. Some member states also permit nationals of non-European Union states to vote. New Zealand permits resident aliens to vote in national elections. See *Minor v. Happersett*, 88 U.S. (21 Wall.) 162 (1874); Carlos Closa, T*he Concept of Citizenship in the Treaty on European Union*, 29 Common Market L. Rev. 1137 (1992); Gerald L. Neuman, *"We are the People": Alien Suffrage in German and American Perspective*, 13 Mich. J. Int'l L. 259 (1992); Jamin B. Raskin, *Legal Aliens, Local Citizens: The Historical, Constitutional and Theoretical Meanings of Alien Suffrage*, 141 U. Pa. L. Rev. 1391 (1993).

7. Note the reminder in paragraph 27 of the General Comment about Article 5 of the Covenant. Article 25 does not protect an exercise of political rights that is "aimed at the destruction of any of the rights and freedoms recognized herein or at their limitation to a greater extent than is provided for in the present Covenant." Thus, although Article 25 may protect competition among political parties, it does not require states to tolerate all political parties regardless of their goals. The next readings address that subject.

Exclusion of Extremist Parties

Recall that in *Dennis v. United States*, 341 U.S. 494 (1951), Chapter 1(C)(1) supra, the U.S. Supreme Court upheld the conviction of leaders of the Communist Party for conspiring to advocate the overthrow of the U.S. government by force and violence. The Court's reasoning emphasized the finding that the defendants planned to seize power by violent means and not to transform the U.S. government through the peaceful use of the electoral process. In some countries, however, political parties whose goals conflict sufficiently with the nation's constitutional order may be banned from the political process, even if they seek to accomplish these goals though peaceful persuasion.

Gregory H. Fox and Georg Nolte, *Intolerant Democracies*

36 Harv. Int'l L.J. 1 (1995).

. . .

1.   Substantive Democracy in France

In contrast to the American system, the French constitution of 1958 explicitly provides that, "[t]he republican form of government shall not be subject to amendment." A further substantive limit on traditional democratic principles appears in article 4 of the French constitution. This article provides that all political parties must respect the principles of national sovereignty and democracy. This principle originated from concern over the threat posed by the French Communist party. At one point it was even suggested that the constitution should explicitly allow the government, upon application to the Haute Cour de Justice, to dissolve a political party which violated its constitutional duties. Although this proposal was ultimately defeated, French constitutional law still seems to pose no obstacles to the banning of political parties on the basis of an act of parliament. . . .

The evolution of the right of association in France, including the right to form political parties, provides a good example of how civil rights are protected. Like its United States counterpart, none of the various French constitutions have explicitly guaranteed the right of association. But unlike the United States, the French legislature proclaimed this right—and specifically defined its limitations—by statute in 1901. Article 3 of this 1901 law states that any association which "intends to infringe on the republican form of government is null and void," as pronounced *ex officio* by a civil court. In practice, however, a prohibition under the law of 1901 has never taken place, in part because the law applies only to officially registered associations and not to more informal political groups.

The same is not true of a 1936 law that gives the President of the Republic the power to dissolve groups that: (1) provoke armed demonstrations, (2) are of a paramilitary nature, or (3) have as their goal the dismemberment of the territorial state, the forceful overthrow of the republican form of government, the instigation of racial or other group discrimination, or the dissemination of propaganda promoting such discrimination. This rather imprecisely worded statute has frequently been invoked by French Presidents against small groups on the political fringe, even though it is clear that the law of 1936 could also be applied against major political parties.

The highest French administrative court, the Conseil d'Etat, is empowered to review the President's action. The court has interpreted the 1936 law rather broadly. For instance, the court has held that a group need not pose a threat of actual violent behavior to apply the law if, for example, its platform or published views question the integrity of the national territory. Accordingly, the Conseil d'Etat has affirmed the dissolution of parties and groups based solely on their secessionist goals.[141] Groups that merely

---

141. Judgment of Oct. 8, 1975 (Association Enbata), Conseil d'etat, Lebon 494 (Fr.) (affirming the dissolution of Basque separatists); Judgment of Jan. 9, 1959 (Sieurs Hoang Xuan Man), Conseil d'etat, Lebon 25 (Fr.) (dissolving group for propaganda hostile to French sovereignty over Indochina); Judgment of July 15, 1964 (Dame Tapua et autres), Conseil d'etat, Lebon 407 (Fr.) (dissolv-

express support for other violent groups may also be prohibited.[142] The court has reversed only two prohibition decisions—one for lack of good cause and the other because the government failed to meet its burden of proof.

While there appears to be meaningful judicial review of party prohibition orders under the 1901 and 1936 laws, the French parliament retains the power to enact more restrictive legislation, subject to a challenge under a landmark 1971 decision of the Conseil Constitutionnel requiring that no act of parliament infringe certain core civil rights principles ("principes fondamentaux"). The precise impact of the 1971 rule is not entirely clear. Nevertheless, because political parties owe a constitutional duty to respect the principle of democracy (article 4), it appears that behavior threatening the democratic process would not be protected by the Conseil Constitutionnel as an element of the right of association.[144]

. . .

[2.] Militant Substantive Democracy in Germany

When the West German constitution (the "Basic Law," now the constitution of the unified Germany) was drafted in 1948–49, two overarching factors influenced its content: the fresh memory of the Nazi regime and the aggressive communist dictatorship then consolidating power in the East. These experiences fostered a strongly anti-totalitarian mindset in the framers of the Grundgesetz. The Grundgesetz contains several provisions collectively described by the Federal Constitutional Court (Bundesverfassungsgericht) as expressing the principle of "militant democracy."[164] A close look at these provisions, however, reveals that on their face they do not go much further than French law: several core principles (including that of democracy) are unalterable even by constitutional amendment, and all associations whose purposes or activities violate criminal law or are directed against the constitutional order may be prohibited.

A group to which a dissolution order is addressed must challenge that act in court. If, however, the group is a political party, the dissolution order is initiated by the federal government filing an application with the Bundesverfassungsgericht. The Court will order dissolution upon a finding that parties "by reason of their aims or the behavior of their adherents,

ing political party in Tahiti seeking to found an independent Polynesian republic).

142. Judgment of Feb. 5, 1965 (Association Comite d'entente pour l'Algerie francaise), Conseil d'etat, Lebon 73 (Fr.).

144. Jean–Paul Jaque, L'abus des Droits Fondamentaux et la Lutte contre les Ennemis de la Democratie—en Droit International et en Droit interne Francais, in Ilioupoulos–Strangas, Der Missbrauch von Grundrechten in der Demokratie 129, 137 (1989). This view seems to be confirmed by a deci-

sion of the Conseil Constitutionnel holding that under article 4, political parties are granted no privileges beyond the general right of association. Receuil des Decisions du Conseil Constitutionnel 78 (1984). See also Marcel Prelot & Jean Boulois, Institutions Politiques et Droit Constitutionnel 669 (11th ed. 1990).

164. See Communist Party Case, 5 BVerfGE 85, 139 (1956), translated in Donald Kommers, The Constitutional Jurisprudence of the Federal Republic of Germany 223.

seek to impair or abolish the free democratic basic order or to endanger the existence of the Federal Republic of Germany." A similar procedure appears in article 18. Upon application by the federal government to the Bundesverfassungsgericht, individuals may forfeit certain fundamental rights if they have used those rights to combat the "free democratic basic order."[169]

Yet, the most important differences between the French and German systems lie not in the written law but in their interpretation and application. In post-war France, no association or political party has been dissolved without a showing that it either posed a threat of violent behavior or pursued secessionist goals. In Germany, by contrast, two prominent and (until then) non-violent parties were declared unconstitutional by the Bundesverfassungsgericht: the Nazi-like Sozialistische Reichspartei in 1952,[170] and the German Communist Party in 1956. In the second case the court adopted a higher standard of proof, requiring that the party adopt "a fixed purpose constantly and resolutely to combat the free democratic basic order" and manifest this purpose "in political action according to a fixed plan of action." This seemingly objective standard, although formulated in terms of actual danger to the democratic system, does not require evidence of imminent harm. The focus is on a party's attitude as revealed by its conduct. Proof of a "concrete undertaking" to that end, or evidence of an actual danger to the democratic system, is not necessary.

The instruments of "militant democracy" continued to play a role in Germany after the prohibition of the Communist Party. In the 1960s, the federal government brought applications for the forfeiture of fundamental rights against two individuals. In the 1970s, the principle of militant democracy played an important role in a debate over disloyal public servants. Today, the rise of right-wing violence following reunification has prompted the federal government to dissolve several organizations under article 9(2) of the Grundgesetz. In addition, proceedings have been instituted before the Bundesverfassungsgericht to dissolve three neo-Nazi parties and to divest two right-wing individuals of their free speech rights.

[3.]   Militant Substantive Democracy in Israel

Like the United Kingdom, Israel does not possess a formal constitution. However, the Israeli Knesset has passed several so-called Basic Laws, which do not rank higher than ordinary laws but have some constitutional significance. According to Section 7A of the Basic Law: The Knesset, a party "shall not participate in elections to the Knesset if its objectives or actions entail, explicitly or implicitly, one of the following: (1) a denial of the existence of the State of Israel as the State of the Jewish nation, (2) a denial of the democratic character of the state, (3) incitement to racism."

---

169. The European Commission on Human Rights upheld a similar Belgian procedure under the European Convention on Human Rights, while invalidating its application in the instant case. De Becker Case, Application No. 214/56, Eur. Comm'n H.R., Ser. B 123–29 (1962).

170. Sozialistische Reichspartei Case, 2 BVerfGE 1 (1952), translated in Kommers, supra note 164, at 509.

Although this rule excludes political parties only from elections, and not from political life altogether, its essential feature is a loosely phrased test focusing on the goals or organizing principles of a party. This attitude-based standard thus mirrors article 21(2) of the German Grundgesetz. Section 7A was enacted in response to a 1984 decision of the Israeli Supreme Court which had found no legal basis for the Israeli Election Commission's decision to bar two political parties from participating in the Knesset elections that year. When the Election Commission, this time acting under the new section 7A, decided to exclude the same two political parties from the next elections, the Israeli court affirmed the exclusion of one of the two parties.[180] In so doing, the court adhered to its general practice of interpreting narrowly statutes which restrict fundamental rights. Not unlike the German Bundesverfassungsgericht in the Communist Party case, the Israeli court focussed on party goals as shown through concrete action: it held that in order to meet its burden, the government must prove beyond any doubt, and by clear and unequivocal evidence, that (1) a party has as its dominant and central objective one of the proscribed goals set out in the statute; and (2) that it intends to implement this goal in a concrete manner.

This standard was held to be satisfied by the right-wing Kach Party, whose objectives and activities were found to be clearly racist in the sense contemplated by the statute. The test was not satisfied by the other party, which advocated a form of Palestinian nationalism. Thus, the Court seems to have tightened the requirements of the statute by rejecting exclusion of a party solely on the basis of its platform.

· · ·

[4.]   Militant Substantive Democracies in Other Countries

In brief, the laws of several other established democracies also permit restrictions on anti-democratic actors. Both the Italian and Spanish constitutions contain a clause prohibiting the reestablishment of the fascist party. The Portuguese constitution prohibits all paramilitary associations which adhere to a fascist ideology. In Finland, a group can only register as a political party if it demonstrates, by its actions, a respect for democratic principles. Austria makes it a criminal offense to found an association dedicated to endangering national independence or the constitutionally mandated form of government. And the Greek constitution prohibits the abusive exercise of fundamental rights.

In addition, the model provided by the German Grundgesetz has been adopted by several of the new and nascent Central and Eastern European democracies, including Croatia, Lithuania, Poland, Romania and Slovenia. In Russia the former Constitutional Court affirmed President Yeltsin's dissolution of the Communist Party. However, in Bulgaria the Constitutional Court refused to declare unconstitutional a party supported mainly

---

180. Election Appeal 1/88, Naiman v. Chairman of the Central Appeal Committee of the Twelfth Knesset, 42(4) P.D. 177 (1988).

by the Turkish minority population. This decision is surprising, given that article 11(4) of the Bulgarian constitution expressly prohibits the formation of ethnically or religiously based political parties.

United Communist Party of Turkey v. Turkey

European Court of Human Rights, 1998.
1998–I Eur. Ct. H.R. 1, 26 E.H.R.R. 121 (1998).

[Shortly after the United Communist Party of Turkey (TBKP) was formed in 1990, proceedings were initiated before the Constitutional Court of Turkey to dissolve it. The Court issued an order dissolving the party in 1991. The TBKP, its Chairman and its General Secretary applied to the European Convention organs, complaining of a violation of their rights, including rights under Article 11 of the Convention, which provides:

1.   Everyone has the right to freedom of peaceful assembly and to freedom of association with others, including the right to form and to join trade unions for the protection of his interests.

2.   No restrictions shall be placed on the exercise of these rights other than such as are prescribed by law and are necessary in a democratic society in the interests of national security or public safety, for the prevention of disorder or crime, for the protection of health or morals or for the protection of the rights and freedoms of others. This Article shall not prevent the imposition of lawful restrictions on the exercise of these rights by members of the armed forces, of the police or of the administration of the State.

The dissolution decision relied in part on passages in the TBKP's official statement of its program, including the following:

The Kurdish problem is a political one arising from the denial of the Kurdish people's existence, national identity and rights. It therefore cannot be resolved by oppression, terror and military means. Recourse to violence means that the right to self-determination, which is a natural and inalienable right of all peoples, is not exercised jointly, but separately and unilaterally. The remedy for this problem is political. If the oppression of the Kurdish people and discrimination against them are to end, Turks and Kurds must unite.

The TBKP will strive for a peaceful, democratic and fair solution of the Kurdish problem, so that the Kurdish and Turkish peoples may live together of their free will within the borders of the Turkish Republic, on the basis of equal rights and with a view to democratic restructuring founded on their common interests.]

11.   At the material time the relevant provisions of the Constitution [included the following:]

Article 2

"The Republic of Turkey is a democratic, secular and social State based on the rule of law, respectful of human rights in a spirit of social peace, national solidarity and justice, adhering to the nationalism of Atatürk and resting on the fundamental principles set out in the Preamble.''

Article 3 § 1

"The State of Turkey constitutes with its territory and nation, an indivisible whole. The official language is Turkish.''

Article 14 § 1

"None of the rights and freedoms referred to in the Constitution shall be exercised with a view to undermining the territorial integrity of the State and the unity of the nation, jeopardising the existence of the Turkish State or Republic, abolishing fundamental rights and freedoms, placing the control of the State in the hands of a single individual or group, ensuring the domination of one social class over other social classes, introducing discrimination on the grounds of language, race, religion or membership of a religious sect, or establishing by any other means a political system based on any of the above concepts and opinions.''

.   .   .

12.   The relevant provisions of Law no. 2820 on the regulation of political parties [included the following:]

Section 78

"Political parties

(a) shall not aim, strive or incite third parties to change: the republican form of the Turkish State; the ... provisions concerning the absolute integrity of the Turkish State's territory, the absolute unity of its nation, its official language, its flag or its national anthem; . . . .''

.   .   .

Section 81

"Political parties shall not

(a) assert that there exist within the territory of the Turkish Republic any national minorities based on differences relating to national or religious culture, membership of a religious sect, race or language; or

(b) aim to destroy national unity by proposing, on the pretext of protecting, promoting or disseminating a non-Turkish language or culture, to create minorities on the territory of the Turkish Republic or to engage in similar activities ...''

Section 96(3)

"No political party shall be formed with the name 'communist', 'anarchist', 'fascist', 'theocratic' or 'national socialist', the name of a religion, language, race, sect or region, or a name including any of the above words or similar ones.''

. . .

19.   The Government submitted that [w]here in its constitution or programme a party attacked a State's constitutional order, the Court should declare the Convention to be inapplicable *ratione materiae* or apply Article 17, rather than apply Article 11.* . . .

20.   [According to the Government, the] constitution and programme of the TBKP were clearly incompatible with Turkey's fundamental constitutional principles. By choosing to call itself ''communist'', the TBKP perforce referred to a subversive doctrine and a totalitarian political goal that undermined Turkey's political and territorial unity and jeopardised the fundamental principles of its public law, such as secularism. ''Communism'' invariably presupposed seizing power and aimed to establish a political order that would be unacceptable, not just in Turkey but also in the other member States of the Council of Europe. . . . In any event, whatever the intentions of the TBKP and its leaders in choosing the name ''communist'' in 1990 (after the fall of the Berlin Wall) may have been, that name could not, in the Government's view, be considered devoid of political meaning.

21.   Furthermore, if the TBKP were able to achieve its political aims, Turkey's territorial and national integrity would be seriously undermined. By drawing a distinction in its constitution and programme between Turks and Kurds, referring to the Kurds' ''national'' identity, requesting constitutional recognition of ''the existence of the Kurds'', describing the Kurds as a ''nation'' and asserting their right to self-determination, the TBKP had opened up a split that would destroy the basis of citizenship, which was independent of ethnic origin. As that was tantamount to challenging the very principles underpinning the State, the Constitutional Court had had to review the constitutionality of that political aim. . . .

In the Government's submission, the States Parties to the Convention had at no stage intended to submit their constitutional institutions, and in particular the principles they considered to be the essential conditions of their existence, to review by the Strasbourg institutions. For that reason, where a political party such as the TBKP had called those institutions or principles into question, it could not seek application of the Convention or its Protocols.

At the very least, Article 17 of the Convention should be applied in respect of the TBKP since the party had called into question both the bases of the Convention and the freedoms it secured. In a context of vicious terrorism such as Turkey was experiencing, the need to preclude improper use of the Convention by applying Article 17 was even more obvious, as the Turkish

---

* [Article 17 of the Convention provides:
Nothing in this Convention may be interpreted as implying for any State, group or person any right to engage in any activity or perform any act aimed at the destruction of any of the rights and freedoms set forth herein or at their limitation to a greater extent than is provided for in the Convention.—Editors' Note.]

authorities had to prohibit the use of "expressions" and the formation of "associations" that would inevitably incite violence and enmity between the various sections of Turkish society.

26.   As to the Government's allegation that the TBKP had called Turkey's constitutional order into question and the inferences that were to be drawn from that fact, it should be said at the outset that at this stage the Court does not have to decide whether that allegation is true. . . .

27.   The Court notes on the other hand that an association, including a political party, is not excluded from the protection afforded by the Convention simply because its activities are regarded by the national authorities as undermining the constitutional structures of the State and calling for the imposition of restrictions. As the Court has said in the past, while it is in principle open to the national authorities to take such action as they consider necessary to respect the rule of law or to give effect to constitutional rights, they must do so in a manner which is compatible with their obligations under the Convention and subject to review by the Convention institutions.

29.   The Court points out, moreover, that Article 1 requires the States Parties to "secure to everyone within their jurisdiction the rights and freedoms defined in Section 1 of th[e] Convention". . . . It makes no distinction as to the type of rule or measure concerned and does not exclude any part of the member States' jurisdiction from scrutiny under the Convention. It is, therefore, with respect to their jurisdiction as a whole—which is often exercised in the first place through the Constitution—that the States Parties are called on to show compliance with the Convention.

30.   The political and institutional organisation of the member States must accordingly respect the rights and principles enshrined in the Convention. It matters little in this context whether the provisions in issue are constitutional or merely legislative. From the moment that such provisions are the means by which the State concerned exercises its jurisdiction, they are subject to review under the Convention.

32.   It does not, however, follow that the authorities of a State in which an association, through its activities, jeopardises that State's institutions are deprived of the right to protect those institutions. In this connection, the Court points out that it has previously held that some compromise between the requirements of defending democratic society and individual rights is inherent in the system of the Convention. For there to be a compromise of that sort any intervention by the authorities must be in accordance with paragraph 2 of Article 11, which the Court considers below. Only when that review is complete will the Court be in a position to decide, in the light of all the circumstances of the case, whether Article 17 of the Convention should be applied.

[The Court found that the dissolution of the TBKP was in accordance with Turkish law, and that it "pursued at least one of the 'legitimate aims' set out in Article 11: the protection of 'national security'." It turned next to whether the dissolution was "necessary in a democratic society" for the achievement of that aim.]

(i) General principles

42. The Court reiterates that notwithstanding its autonomous role and particular sphere of application, Article 11 must, in the present case, also be considered in the light of Article 10. The protection of opinions and the freedom to express them is one of the objectives of the freedoms of assembly and association as enshrined in Article 11.

43. That applies all the more in relation to political parties in view of their essential role in ensuring pluralism and the proper functioning of democracy.

As the Court has said many times, there can be no democracy without pluralism. It is for that reason that freedom of expression as enshrined in Article 10 is applicable, subject to paragraph 2, not only to "information" or "ideas" that are favourably received or regarded as inoffensive or as a matter of indifference, but also to those that offend, shock or disturb. The fact that their activities form part of a collective exercise of freedom of expression in itself entitles political parties to seek the protection of Articles 10 and 11 of the Convention.

44. [T]he Court [has] described the State as the ultimate guarantor of the principle of pluralism. In the political sphere that responsibility means that the State is under the obligation, among others, to hold, in accordance with Article 3 of Protocol No. 1, free elections at reasonable intervals by secret ballot under conditions which will ensure the free expression of the opinion of the people in the choice of the legislature. Such expression is inconceivable without the participation of a plurality of political parties representing the different shades of opinion to be found within a country's population. By relaying this range of opinion, not only within political institutions but also—with the help of the media—at all levels of social life, political parties make an irreplaceable contribution to political debate, which is at the very core of the concept of a democratic society

46. Consequently, the exceptions set out in Article 11 are, where political parties are concerned, to be construed strictly; only convincing and compelling reasons can justify restrictions on such parties' freedom of association. In determining whether a necessity within the meaning of Article 11 § 2 exists, the Contracting States possess only a limited margin of appreciation, which goes hand in hand with rigorous European supervision embracing both the law and the decisions applying it, including those given by independent courts. . . .[S]uch scrutiny is all the more necessary where an entire political party is dissolved and its leaders banned from carrying on any similar activity in the future.

(ii) Application of the principles to the present case

47. When the Court carries out its scrutiny, its task is not to substitute its own view for that of the relevant national authorities but rather to review under Article 11 the decisions they delivered in the exercise of their discretion. This does not mean that it has to confine itself to ascertaining

whether the respondent State exercised its discretion reasonably, carefully and in good faith; it must look at the interference complained of in the light of the case as a whole and determine whether it was "proportionate to the legitimate aim pursued" and whether the reasons adduced by the national authorities to justify it are "relevant and sufficient". In so doing, the Court has to satisfy itself that the national authorities applied standards which were in conformity with the principles embodied in Article 11 and, moreover, that they based their decisions on an acceptable assessment of the relevant facts.

51.   The Court notes at the outset that the TBKP was dissolved even before it had been able to start its activities and that the dissolution was therefore ordered solely on the basis of the TBKP's constitution and programme, which however—as is for that matter apparent from the Constitutional Court's decision—contain nothing to suggest that they did not reflect the party's true objectives and its leaders' true intentions (see paragraph 58 below). Like the national authorities, the Court will therefore take those documents as a basis for assessing whether the interference in question was necessary.

53.   [First,] it was alleged that the TBKP had included the word "communist" in its name, contrary to section 96(3) of Law no. 2820.

54.   ... The Court ... attaches much weight to the Constitutional Court's finding that the TBKP was not seeking, in spite of its name, to establish the domination of one social class over the others, and that, on the contrary, it satisfied the requirements of democracy, including political pluralism, universal suffrage and freedom to take part in politics. In that respect, the TBKP was clearly different from the German Communist Party, which was dissolved on 17 August 1956 by the German Constitutional Court.

Accordingly, in the absence of any concrete evidence to show that in choosing to call itself "communist", the TBKP had opted for a policy that represented a real threat to Turkish society or the Turkish State, the Court cannot accept that the submission based on the party's name may, by itself, entail the party's dissolution.

55.   The second submission accepted by the Constitutional Court was that the TBKP sought to promote separatism and the division of the Turkish nation. By drawing a distinction in its constitution and programme between the Kurdish and Turkish nations, the TBKP had revealed its intention of working to achieve the creation of minorities which ... posed a threat to the State's territorial integrity. It was for that reason that self-determination and regional autonomy were both proscribed by the constitution.

56.   The Court notes that although the TBKP refers in its programme to the Kurdish "people" and "nation" and Kurdish "citizens", it neither describes them as a "minority" nor makes any claim—other than for recognition of their existence—for them to enjoy special treatment or rights, still less a right to secede from the rest of the Turkish population.

On the contrary, the programme states: "The TBKP will strive for a peaceful, democratic and fair solution of the Kurdish problem, so that the Kurdish and Turkish peoples may live together of their free will within the borders of the Turkish Republic, on the basis of equal rights and with a view to democratic restructuring founded on their common interests." With regard to the right to self-determination, the TBKP does no more in its programme than deplore the fact that because of the use of violence, it was not "exercised jointly, but separately and unilaterally", adding that "the remedy for this problem is political" and that "[i]f the oppression of the Kurdish people and discrimination against them are to end, Turks and Kurds must unite".

The TBKP also said in its programme: "A solution to the Kurdish problem will only be found if the parties concerned are able to express their opinions freely, if they agree not to resort to violence in any form in order to resolve the problem and if they are able to take part in politics with their own national identity."

57.   The Court considers one of the principal characteristics of democracy to be the possibility it offers of resolving a country's problems through dialogue, without recourse to violence, even when they are irksome. Democracy thrives on freedom of expression. From that point of view, there can be no justification for hindering a political group solely because it seeks to debate in public the situation of part of the State's population and to take part in the nation's political life in order to find, according to democratic rules, solutions capable of satisfying everyone concerned. To judge by its programme, that was indeed the TBKP's objective in this area. That distinguishes the present case from those referred to by the Government.

58.   Admittedly, it cannot be ruled out that a party's political programme may conceal objectives and intentions different from the ones it proclaims. . . . In the present case, the TBKP's programme could hardly have been belied by any practical action it took, since it was dissolved immediately after being formed and accordingly did not even have time to take any action.

59.   The Court is also prepared to take into account the background of cases before it, in particular the difficulties associated with the fight against terrorism. In the present case, however, it finds no evidence to enable it to conclude, in the absence of any activity by the TBKP, that the party bore any responsibility for the problems which terrorism poses in Turkey.

60.   Nor is there any need to bring Article 17 into play as nothing in the constitution and programme of the TBKP warrants the conclusion that it relied on the Convention to engage in activity or perform acts aimed at the destruction of any of the rights and freedoms set forth in it.

61.   Regard being had to all the above, a measure as drastic as the immediate and permanent dissolution of the TBKP, ordered before its activities had even started and coupled with a ban barring its leaders from discharging any other political responsibility, is disproportionate to the aim

pursued and consequently unnecessary in a democratic society. It follows that the measure infringed Article 11 of the Convention.

63. The applicants submitted that the effects of the TBKP's dissolution—its assets were confiscated and transferred to the Treasury, and its leaders were banned from taking part in elections—entailed a breach of Articles 1 and 3 of Protocol No. 1 . . . .

64. The Court notes that the measures complained of by the applicants were incidental effects of the TBKP's dissolution, which the Court has held to be a breach of Article 11. It is consequently unnecessary to consider these complaints separately.

Notes

1. How does the European Court respond to Turkey's argument that Article 11 does not protect associations directed at undermining its constitutional order?

2. What is the scope of Article 17 of the Convention, and what are its consequences when it is applicable? If the European Court had found that the TBKP's ultimate aim was the establishment of a Communist dictatorship, would Article 11 become inapplicable, and would Turkey be permitted to ban the party without any inquiry into the necessity or proportionality of the prohibition? Would Turkey be permitted to subject members of the party to inhuman or degrading treatment?*

Does Article 17 entail that the right to freedom of expression under Article 10 is inapplicable to:

(a) the advocacy of the establishment of a Communist dictatorship?

(b) the advocacy of abolishing a statutory right to compensation for victims of unlawful arrest (see Article 5(5))?

(c) the advocacy of criminalization of private homosexual conduct between consenting adults (see the *Dudgeon* case supra)?

(d) the advocacy of amendments to the Convention?

(e) criticism of the Court's judgments?

Note that Article 5(1) of the ICCPR is substantially identical in wording to Article 17 of the European Convention. See also Article 30 of the Universal Declaration, Article 29 of the American Convention, and Article 5(1) of the ICESCR.

3. Note the European Court's factual assumption that the TBKP did not pursue secessionist goals. If the TBKP had been dedicated to the accomplishment of the independence of a Kurdish province through peaceful democratic means, then how should the case have been decided?

---

* The answer to this last question is no: Article 17 precludes reliance on a Convention right to engage in certain activities, but does not provide that persons who engage in such activities forfeit all their Convention rights. See *Lawless v. Ireland*, 3 Eur. Ct. H.R. (ser. A), 1 E.H.H.R. 15 (1961) (suspected terrorist retains rights under Articles 5 and 6).

4.   Does the European Court's analysis reflect a purely positivistic inquiry into the scope of the protection provided by the Convention? Or does it imply a value judgment favoring the provisions of the European Convention over the provisions of the Turkish Constitution? Would such a value judgment be justified? What light does the answer to this question shed on the extent of the Convention's protection of human rights?

5.   How would the United States probably react to a decision of an international tribunal ruling against it, if that decision included the language of paragraphs 27–30 as quoted above? Would the reaction be justified?

CHAPTER 3

Economic and Social Rights

In broad terms, the distinction between civil and political rights on the one hand and economic and social rights on the other hand, reflects the shift from the minimal state advocated by classical liberalism to the modern activist state that promotes the well-being of all its members out of social solidarity. The United States adopted the vision of an activist state guaranteeing economic and social entitlements in the New Deal of the 1930s, and President Franklin D. Roosevelt emphasized the fundamentality of "freedom from want" in his famous "Four Freedoms" Speech, excerpted below. The Universal Declaration expresses a right to positive government in Article 22, the prelude to its catalogue of economic and social rights:

> Everyone, as a member of society, has the right to social security and is entitled to realization, through national effort and international co-operation and in accordance with the organization and resources of each State, of the economic, social and cultural rights indispensable for his dignity and the free development of his personality.

When the time came, however, to embody the aspirations of the Universal Declaration in binding international treaties, disputes arose over the desirability of including some or all of the rights characterized as economic or social. These disputes reflected a number of substantive and political factors: disagreement over whether the mechanisms for implementation of positive rights should differ from those for implementation of negative rights; disagreement over the relative importance of particular rights; Cold War rivalries; and the emergence of Third World states that perceived a link between economic and social rights and their striving for economic development. The disputes also mirrored disagreements among political thinkers, as we have seen in Part I supra, pp. 81–86, over the existence of human rights to the fulfillment of economic and social needs. Ultimately, the solution adopted was the division of the treaty project into two separate Covenants, the ICCPR and the ICESCR. At the same time, the General Assembly affirmed that both sets of rights were "interconnected and interdependent." That proposition has been reaffirmed, with variations in wording, on numerous occasions.

This chapter examines in comparative context three types of economic and social rights that serve human dignity and the free development of the human personality. The chapter begins with an introductory discussion concerning economic and social rights and their character. The second section then considers the right to provide well-being through private initiative, including economic rights to property and freedom of enterprise. The third section turns to a category of social rights for which political support has weakened in the United States, the social welfare rights by

1106

which the state acts as the ultimate guarantor of a minimum standard of living for those whom the market has failed. The fourth section contrasts a social right more firmly anchored in the United States, the right to education.

A.   ECONOMIC AND SOCIAL RIGHTS AS RIGHTS

Franklin D. Roosevelt, *The "Four Freedoms" Address*

87 Cong. Rec. 44, 46–47 (1941).

. . .

As men do not live by bread alone, they do not fight by armaments alone. Those who man our defenses, and those behind them who build our defenses, must have the stamina and courage which come from an unshakable belief in the manner of life which they are defending. The mighty action which we are calling for cannot be based on a disregard of all things worth fighting for.

The Nation takes great satisfaction and much strength from the things which have been done to make its people conscious of their individual stake in the preservation of democratic life in America. Those things have toughened the fiber of our people, have renewed their faith and strengthened their devotion to the institutions we make ready to protect.

Certainly this is no time to stop thinking about the social and economic problems which are the root cause of the social revolution which is today a supreme factor in the world.

There is nothing mysterious about the foundations of a healthy and strong democracy. The basic things expected by our people of their political and economic systems are simple. They are:

Equality of opportunity for youth and for others.

Jobs for those who can work.

Security for those who need it.

The ending of special privilege for the few.

The preservation of civil liberties for all.

The enjoyment of the fruits of scientific progress in a wider and constantly rising standard of living.

These are the simple and basic things that must never be lost sight of in the turmoil and unbelievable complexity of our modern world. The inner and abiding strength of our economic and political systems is dependent upon the degree to which they fulfill these expectations.

Many subjects connected with our social economy call for immediate improvement.

As examples:

We should bring more citizens under the coverage of old-age pensions and unemployment insurance.

We should widen the opportunities for adequate medical care.

We should plan a better system by which persons deserving or needing gainful employment may obtain it.

I have called for personal sacrifice. I am assured of the willingness of almost all Americans to respond to that call.

A part of the sacrifice means the payment of more money in taxes. In my Budget message I recommend that a greater portion of this great defense program be paid for from taxation than we are paying today. No person should try, or be allowed, to get rich out of this program; and the principle of tax payments in accordance with ability to pay should be constantly before our eyes to guide our legislation.

If the Congress maintains these principles, the voters, putting patriotism ahead of pocketbooks, will give you their applause.

In the future days, which we seek to make secure, we look forward to a world founded upon four essential human freedoms.

The first is freedom of speech and expression everywhere in the world.

The second is freedom of every person to worship God in his own way everywhere in the world.

The third is freedom from want, which, translated into world terms, means economic understandings which will secure to every nation a healthy peacetime life for its inhabitants everywhere in the world.

The fourth is freedom from fear—which, translated into the world terms, means a world-wide reduction of armaments to such a point and in such a thorough fashion that no nation will be in a position to commit an act of physical aggression against any neighbor—anywhere in the world.

That is no vision of a distant millennium. It is a definite basis for a kind of world attainable in our own time and generation. That kind of world is the very antithesis of the so-called new order of tyranny, which the dictators seek to create with the crash of a bomb.

To that new order we oppose the greater conception—the moral order. A good society is able to face schemes of world domination and foreign revolutions alike without fear.

Since the beginning of our American history we have been engaged in change—in a perpetual peaceful revolution—a revolution which goes on steadily, quietly adjusting itself to changing conditions—without the concentration camp or the quicklime in the ditch. The world order which we seek is the cooperation of free countries, working together in a friendly, civilized society.

This Nation has placed its destiny in the hands and heads and hearts of its millions of free men and women; and its faith in freedom under the guidance of God. Freedom means the supremacy of human rights everywhere. Our support goes to those who struggle to gain those rights or keep them. Our strength is in our unity of purpose.

To that high concept there can be no end save victory.

Notes

Roosevelt further elaborated the concept of economic and social rights in his call for an Economic Bill of Rights in his State of the Union address of 1944:

> We have come to a clear realization of the fact that true individual freedom cannot exist without economic security and independence. "Necessitous men are not freemen." People who are hungry and out of a job are the stuff of which dictatorships are made.
>
> In our day these economic truths have become accepted as self-evident. We have accepted, so to speak, a second Bill of Rights under which a new basis of security and prosperity can be established for all— regardless of station, race, or creed.
>
> Among these are:
>
> The right to a useful and remunerative job in the industries, or shops or farms or mines of the Nation;
>
> The right to earn enough to provide adequate food and clothing and recreation;
>
> The right of every farmer to raise and sell his products at a return which will give him and his family a decent living;
>
> The right of every businessman, large and small, to trade in an atmosphere of freedom from unfair competition and domination by monopolies at home or abroad;
>
> The right of every family to a decent home;
>
> The right to adequate medical care and the opportunity to achieve and enjoy good health;
>
> The right to adequate protection from the economic fears of old age, sickness, accident, and unemployment;
>
> The right to a good education.
>
> All of these rights spell security. And after this war is won, we must be prepared to move forward, in the implementation of these rights, to new goals of human happiness and well-being.

90 Cong. Rec. 55, 57 (1944). Which of these rights received later articulation in the Universal Declaration or in the ICESCR? Were any of these rights omitted? Are the omitted rights implied by rights that were included, or were they excluded altogether?

Vratislav Pechota, *The Development of the Covenant on Civil and Political Rights*

in The International Bill of Rights: The Covenant on Civil and Political Rights 32, 41–43. (Louis Henkin ed., 1981).

The notion that the social and economic security of man is part of the common fund of human rights, and indeed is an essential condition of his freedom, has been current for decades and was given most eloquent expression in the Universal Declaration. Yet the integration of these rights into one document with civil and political rights became a burning question [in the process of drafting the Covenants], both in its own right and because it had been proposed with urgency by governments which sought to strengthen their international influence and questioned by others that feared how that influence might be used.

The Commission [on Human Rights] initially prepared a draft covering civil and political rights only, as the first of a series of covenants. But in response to a request for guidance from the General Assembly, the Commission was asked "to include in the draft covenant a clear expression of economic, social and cultural rights in a manner which relates them to the civil and political freedoms proclaimed by the draft covenant."[16]

This decision was a clear victory for those who had regarded the inclusion of economic, social, and cultural rights as a major balancing factor in the international approach toward human rights. Evidently, they suspected the motives of those Western states that had proposed separate covenants. In the General Assembly, the socialist and most of the developing countries opposed this division; they called it "erroneous, illegal and unjustified" on the ground that it defied the earlier (1948) decision of the General Assembly "to draw up a single covenant closely connected with the Universal Declaration of Human Rights, to which it had to give legal expression" (USSR). In their view, "an incomplete covenant would destroy the value of the Universal Declaration by opening the way to the argument that, inasmuch as only the provisions contained in the Covenant were binding, any part of the Declaration which was not included in the covenant was of no importance" (Mexico). It was observed that the absence of economic, social and cultural rights was unacceptable since "those rights had become an essential part of the structure of civilized society" (Egypt), and the accusation was made that "the general public would find there a proof of the organized resistance of persons who wished to perpetuate obvious inequalities" (Poland). In an obvious allusion to public statements by the United States delegation that its government would find it difficult to accept a treaty containing economic, social and cultural rights because they went beyond those guaranteed by the Constitution and were therefore not enforceable by the courts, one delegation bluntly suggested that "no great harm would be done if some countries used the inclusion of articles on economic, social, and cultural rights as a pretext not to ratify the covenant" (Iraq).

These suspicions had been prompted in part by the proponents of the division [into two Covenants] themselves. They may have overemphasized the essential difference between the two sets of rights by suggesting that the covenant could not contain rights that "might be regarded as advantages, either material or psychological, conferred upon the individual by a social system" and that "might properly be the subject of a declaration but

---

16. G.A. Res. 421–E, 5 GAOR Supp. 20,
UN Doc. A/1775 at 43 (1950).

not, in the existing state of international law, of an international instrument with legal force" (Canada). The argument that "in the existing circumstances it would be much more useful to allow immediate promulgation of the first covenant already drafted" (United Kingdom), as "much time and effort would be needed before any agreement was reached on the definition of the rights and the means of bringing them into effect" (New Zealand), was seen as little more than a delaying tactic.

The atmosphere was poisoned by the political tensions of the Korean War period. Thus, it is small wonder that little attention was paid to the fact that the controversy derived from a difference of approach rather than of purpose. It took another year and much diplomacy to diminish the suspicions. Meanwhile, at its seventh session in 1951, the Commission drafted articles on economic, social, and cultural rights, and the Economic and Social Council invited the General Assembly to reconsider its decision that economic and social rights should be included in the same covenant.

This time, the arguments concentrated more on the merits and disadvantages of the proposed division. Its proponents defined the difference between the two categories of rights in terms of their applicability: while civil and political rights were immediately applicable, economic, social, and cultural rights often called for progressive implementation. While the former protected the individual against unlawful and unjust action of the authorities, the latter would have to be promoted by the positive action of states; and they would also require different methods of international implementation. Opponents of the division advanced no less cogent views: human rights could not be so simply divided, nor could they be compared and classified according to their respective value.

As often happens with issues of principle, the resolution approving two covenants, which emerged after a long debate in the General Assembly, justified neither all the hopes nor all the fears expressed prior to its adoption. It reaffirmed the propositions of the earlier decision that "the enjoyment of civil and political freedoms and of economic, social and cultural rights are interconnected and interdependent" and that "when deprived of economic, social and cultural rights, man does not represent the human person whom the Universal Declaration regards as the ideal of the free man," and it provided that the two covenants should be prepared and opened for signature simultaneously, in order to emphasize their unity of purpose.

In practical terms, the decision to prepare two instruments had both advantages and disadvantages. On the positive side, the separation made it possible to maintain the absolute character of civil and political rights and to strengthen their international implementation while encouraging a bolder approach than might otherwise have been feasible toward the formulation of economic, social, and cultural rights, notably by admitting that they could be implemented progressively. On the negative side, the division created uncertainty about the equal standing of the two categories of rights and led to duplication of a number of provisions in the covenants, raising problems of interpretation. However, the common ground and the identity of purpose, as well as the similarity of many provisions in the final drafts, make the covenants complementary and mutually reinforcing. The two covenants attained a normative unity as, together with other conventions adopted by the United Nations and its specialized agencies, they form a single body of new international law of human rights.

Notes on the United States and the ICESCR

1.   As of July 1999, the United States had not ratified the International Covenant on Economic, Social, and Cultural Rights, and it appeared unlikely that the Senate would give its advice and consent to ratification in the foreseeable future. Administration policies have varied over the years. President Carter signed both the ICESCR and the ICCPR on behalf of the United States in October 1977, and transmitted them to the Senate for its advice and consent. At that time, President Carter proposed the following reservations, understanding and declarations for adoption as part of the ratification of the ICESCR:

a.   With respect to Article 2(1): "The United States understands paragraph (1) of Article 2 as establishing that the provisions of Articles 1 through 15 of this Covenant describe goals to be achieved progressively rather than through immediate implementation."

b.   With respect to Article 2(3) and Article 25: "The United States declares that nothing in the Covenant derogates from the equal obligation of all States to fulfill their responsibilities under international law. The United States understands that under the Covenant everyone has the right to own property alone as well as in association with others, and that no one shall be arbitrarily deprived of his property."

c.   With respect to Article 5(1): "The Constitution of the United States and Article 19 of the International Covenant on Civil and Political Rights contain provisions for the protection of individual rights, including the right to free speech, and nothing in this Covenant shall be deemed to require or to authorize legislation or other action by the United States which would restrict the right of free speech protected by the Constitution, laws, and practice of the United States."

d.   With respect to Article 28: "The United States shall progressively implement all the provisions of the Covenant over whose subject matter the Federal Government exercises legislative and judicial jurisdiction; with respect to the provisions over whose subject matter constituent units exercise jurisdiction, the Federal Government shall take appropriate measures, to the end that the competent authorities of the constituent units may take appropriate measures for the fulfillment of this Covenant."

e.   With respect to Articles 1 through 15: "The United States declares that the provisions of Articles 1 through 15 of this Covenant are not self-executing."

S. Exec. Docs. C, D, E and F, 95th Cong., 2d Sess. viii-xi (1978). (These reservations, understanding and declarations may be compared with those ultimately adopted when the United States ratified the ICCPR in 1992, see supra Part III, Chapter 4(B).) The Senate was unwilling to give advice and consent to either of the Covenants at that time.

2. The election of President Reagan in 1980 led to the reversal of many human rights policies of the Carter administration, including Executive support for the ICESCR. Consistent with President Reagan's attacks on New Deal social policies in the domestic sphere, the State Department called into question the concept of economic and social rights. Philip Alston has described this reversal:

> In the early days of the Reagan administration, an internal memorandum of the Department of State on human rights policy was leaked to the press and reprinted in full in the New York Times. The memorandum, which was apparently approved by then Secretary of State Alexander Haig, has subsequently been shown to have had a major impact on U.S. policy. It dealt with a variety of issues and, although it exhibited a degree of subtlety and caution on most of them, it nevertheless endorsed the unqualified rejection of economic, social and cultural "rights" as rights. Human rights were to be explicitly defined for the purposes of future U.S. policy as "meaning political rights and civil liberties." To entrench this highly restrictive definition, the memorandum urged that the administration "move away from 'human rights' as a term, and begin to speak of 'individual rights,' 'political rights' and 'civil liberties.'"
>
> This strategy of simply defining economic rights out of existence was rapidly put into place by deleting the sections dealing with "economic and social rights" from the first of the State Department's annual Country Reports on Human Rights Practices submitted to Congress by the Reagan administration in February 1982. This deletion was strongly defended by Assistant Secretary of State Elliott Abrams in a congressional hearing to review the report.[31] His arguments were buttressed by both pragmatic and philosophical considerations. The former, which [were] repeated in [subsequent issues] of the Country Reports, consisted of two strands. The first was that recognition of economic and social rights "tends to create a growing confusion about priorities in the human rights area and a growing dispersion of energy in ending human rights violations." The second was that the rights in question are "easily exploited to excuse violations of civil and political rights." ...
>
> Abrams's historical and political arguments, however, constitute the most significant obstacle to acceptance of the very concept of economic and social rights and hence to [U.S.] ratification of the Covenant. In brief, Abrams invoked the public/private distinction: "The great men who founded the modern concern for human rights ... established

---

31. Review of State Department Country Reports on Human Rights Practices for 1981: Hearing Before the Subcomm. on Human Rights and International Organizations of the House Comm. on Foreign Affairs, 97th Cong., 2d Sess. 7 (1982) (statement of Elliott Abrams, Assistant Secretary of State, Bureau of Human Rights and Humanitarian Affairs)....

separate spheres of public and private life.... Social, economic and cultural life was left in the private sphere...." Without so labeling them, Abrams used the distinction between positive and negative categories of rights and concluded that "the rights that no government can violate [i.e., civil and political rights] should not be watered down to the status of rights that governments should do their best to secure [i.e., economic, social and cultural rights]." This interpretation of the philosophical underpinnings of human rights owes much to the Founding Fathers of the United States and nothing at all to the drafters of the Universal Declaration of Human Rights or the International Covenants. ....

. . .

After 1986, the language of rejection became even more straightforward, and unquestionably consistent. Thus, to take but one example, the U.S. representative told the Third Committee of the UN General Assembly in November 1988 that responsible adults select their own careers, obtain their own housing, and arrange for their own medical care. It is true that the state must establish a legal framework which encourages fairness and prohibits fraud; but, having done so, the state must then get out of the way and permit individuals to live their own lives as they see fit.[38] She went on to criticize UN bodies for departing from the "traditional concern for civil and political rights" and having "from time to time ... decreed the existence of so-called social and economic rights." ...

Philip Alston, *U.S. Ratification of the Covenant on Economic, Social and Cultural Rights: The Need for an Entirely New Strategy*, 84 Am. J. Int'l L. 365, 372–75 (1990).*

38.   Statement by Ambassador Patricia M. Byrne to the Third Committee of the UN General Assembly, Nov. 9, 1988, Dep't of State Press Release USUN 129–(88), at 1. . . .

* Reproduced with permission from 84 AJIL 365 (1990) © The American Society for International Law.

Alston further comments:

Another strand in the arguments used against economic and social rights in recent years by U.S. officials has been to portray the issue as one of East versus West. This argument has been expressed by Assistant Secretary Schifter in the following terms:

Critics of the Western democracies used to contend that, while emphasizing free speech and a free press, the democracies ignored such basic needs as food, jobs, housing and medical care. These critics, particularly those affiliated with the Soviet bloc, stressed that their governments guaranteed citizens the right to obtain these basic needs. Supporters in democracies responded that, people needed, not guarantees of food, jobs, housing and medical care, but delivery of these benefits.

But the "critics" of whom he speaks have not assailed "the Western democracies" in general, since, with the sole exception of the United States, all the Western democracies have accepted the validity and equal importance of economic, social and cultural human rights, at least in principle. For example: the Australians had championed those rights even before the UN Charter was adopted in 1945; Dutch courts have applied the provisions of the Covenants in domestic cases; the Dutch, Greek, Portuguese, Spanish, Swedish and Swiss Constitutions all explicitly recognize at least some economic and social rights; and the Scandinavians have consistently accorded

3.   Although, as Alston describes, economic and social rights were eliminated from the Country Reports, since 1984 Congress has required the administration to report on a limited number of "workers' rights," pursuant to a provision of the Generalized System of Preferences Renewal Act of 1984 (current version codified at 19 U.S.C. § 2464). Discussions of these workers' rights, including the right of association, the right to organize and bargain collectively, prohibition of forced or compulsory labor, minimum age for employment of children, and acceptable working conditions, are also included in the Country Reports. Indeed, in 1994, the unit in the State Department that prepares the Country Reports was renamed from the Bureau of Human Rights and Humanitarian Affairs to the Bureau of Human Rights, Democracy and Labor.

4.   In 1993, at the World Conference on Human Rights in Vienna, the United States joined in efforts to rebut the claim, made by China and some other states, that human rights were not universal but rather represented culturally specific Western values. As a result, the Conference adopted the Vienna Declaration and Programme of Action, in which one key paragraph both reaffirms the universality of human rights and emphasizes their indivisibility:

> All human rights are universal, indivisible and interdependent and interrelated. The international community must treat human rights globally in a fair and equal manner, on the same footing, and with the same emphasis. While the significance of national and regional particularities and various historical, cultural and religious backgrounds must be borne in mind, it is the duty of States, regardless of their political, economic and cultural systems, to promote and protect all human rights and fundamental freedoms.

Vienna Declaration and Programme of Action, ¶ I.5, reprinted in 32 I.L.M. 1661, 1665 (1993).

Secretary of State Warren Christopher announced at the Vienna Conference that President Clinton would seek Senate consent to ratify the Convention on the Elimination of all Forms of Racial Discrimination, and then the Convention on the Elimination of all Forms of Discrimination Against Women, the American Convention on Human Rights, and the ICESCR. See 4 U.S. Dept. of State Dispatch 441 (1993) (reprinting Sec. Christopher's address). The United States ratified the CERD convention in 1994, but the Administration was unable to persuade the Senate to agree to the ratification of CEDAW, and has not pressed for ratification of the ICESCR.

Asbjørn Eide, *Economic, Social and Cultural Rights as Human Rights*

in Economic, Social and Cultural Rights: A Textbook 21, 36–39 (Asbjørn Eide et al. eds. 1995).

A widely spread misunderstanding has been that all economic, social and cultural rights must be provided by the State, and that they are costly

prominence to those rights in the context
of their domestic political agendas.

and lead to an overgrown state apparatus. This view results from a very narrow understanding of these rights and of the corresponding state obligations; consequently, some words about their nature is required.

Fundamental to a realistic understanding of state obligations is that the individual is the active subject of all economic and social development, as stated in the Declaration on the Right to Development (Article 2).[47] The individual is expected, whenever possible through his or her own efforts and by use of own resources, to find ways to ensure the satisfaction of his or her own needs, individually or in association with others. Use of his or her own resources, however, requires that the person has resources that can be used—typically land or other capital, or labour. This could include the shared right to use communal land, and the land rights held by indigenous peoples. Furthermore, the realization of economic, social and cultural rights of an individual will usually take place within the context of a household as the smallest economic unit, although aspects of female and male division of labour and control over the production, as well as various forms of wider kinship arrangements may present alternative alliances.

State obligations must be seen in this light. States must, at the primary level, *respect* the resources owned by the individual, her or his freedom to find a job of preference and the freedom to take the necessary actions and use the necessary resources—alone or in association with others—to satisfy his or her own needs. It is in regard to the latter that *collective* or group rights become important: the resources belonging to a collective of persons, such as indigenous populations, must be respected in order for them to be able to satisfy their needs. Consequently, as part of the obligation to respect these resources the State should take steps to recognize and register the land rights of indigenous peoples and land tenure of smallholders whose title is uncertain. By doing so, the State will have assisted them in making use of their resources in greater safety in their pursuit to maintain an adequate standard of living. Similarly, the rights of peoples to exercise permanent sovereignty over their natural resources may be essential for them to be able, through their own collective efforts, to satisfy the needs of the members of that group.

State obligations consist, at a secondary level, of, for example, the protection of the freedom of action and the use of resources against other, more assertive or aggressive subjects—more powerful economic interests, protection against fraud, against unethical behaviour in trade and contractual relations, against the marketing and dumping of hazardous or dangerous products. This protective function of the State is the most important aspect of state obligations also with regard to economic, social and cultural

---

47. General Assembly resolution 41/128 of 4 December 1986. Article 2 reads, in part:

1. The human being is the central subject of development and should be the active participant and beneficiary of the right to development.

2. All human beings have a responsibility for development, individually and collectively. . . .

rights, and it is similar to the role of the State as protector of civil and political rights.

Significant components of the obligation to *protect* are spelled out in existing law. Such legislation becomes manageable for judicial review, and therefore belies the argument that economic and social rights are inherently non-justiciable. Legislation of this kind must, of course, be contextual— that is, it must be based on the specific requirements of the country concerned. To take one example: legislation requiring that land can be owned only by the tiller of the land is essential where agriculture is the major basis of income, but may be much less relevant in highly industrialized technological societies where only a small percentage of the population lives off the land. For groups of people whose culture requires a close link to the use of land, protection of that land is even more important as an obligation to realize the right to food—again, the indigenous peoples serve as the clearest example.

At the tertiary level, the State has the obligations to assist and to fulfill the rights of everyone under economic, social and cultural rights. The obligation to assist takes many forms, some of which are spelled out in the relevant instruments. For example, under CESCR (Article 11(2)), the State shall take measures to improve measures of production, conservation and distribution of food by making full use of technical and scientific knowledge and by developing or reforming agrarian systems. The obligation to fulfill could consist of the direct *provisions* of basic needs, such as food or resources which can be used as food (direct food aid, or social security) when no other possibility exists, such as, for example: (1) when unemployment sets in (such as under recession); (2) for the disadvantaged, and the elderly; (3) during sudden situations of crisis or disaster ...; and (4) for those who are marginalized (for example, due to structural transformations in the economy and production).

It may now have become clearer why the allegation that economic and social rights differ from the civil and political is that the former requires the use of resources by the State, while the obligation for States to ensure the enjoyment of civil and political rights does not require resources. This is a gross oversimplification. The argument is tenable only in situations where the focus on economic and social rights is on the tertiary level (the obligation to fulfil), while civil and political rights are observed on the primal level (the obligation to respect). This scenario is, however, arbitrary. Some civil rights require state obligations at all levels—also the obligation to provide direct assistance, when there is a need for it.[50] Economic and social rights, on the other hand, can in many cases best be safeguarded

---

50.   General Comment 6 on the right to life, adopted by the Human Rights Committee ... refers, *inter alia*, to widespread and serious malnutrition leading to extensive child mortality, as a non-fulfillment of the right to life. Remedies to counteract child malnutrition often require government organized provisions. In a field more well-known to lawyers, equal access to justice (which is essential for the protection of civil and political rights) requires legal aid to those in the lowest income brackets, another illustration that the state may have to be a provider in order to complete its range of obligations also in regard to civil and political rights.

through non-interference by the State with the freedom and use of resources possessed by individuals. In light of the complexity of the issue, and the need for flexibility to respond to different situations, it now becomes understandable that the basic provisions (CESCR, Articles 2 and 11) were drafted more in the form of *obligations of result* rather than *obligations of conduct*. It is also understandable that these obligations, taken at their highest and most general level, cannot easily be made justiciable (manageable by third party judicial settlement). Nevertheless, the obligations exist and can in no way be neglected.

B.   Rights to Property and Freedom of Enterprise

In the characterization of rights as civil-political or economic-social-cultural, economic-social rights were conceived as "welfare" rights, *i.e.*, those declared in Articles 22–27 of the Universal Declaration. Within that division in the Universal Declaration, the right to own property and not to be deprived of one's property appears among the civil rights—where John Locke put it, together with life and liberty, as moral rights in the state of nature, before society. See Universal Declaration Article 17. Freedom of private economic enterprise is not mentioned in the Universal Declaration or in either Covenant, instruments designed to be universal, applying to state socialist societies as well as capitalist societies.

1.   Rights to Property

The right to own, acquire, maintain, use, and dispose of property was a fundamental right for John Locke and at common law, and is recognized generally in all developed societies. For Blackstone, *supra* Part II, Chapter 1(A)(1), the "third absolute right" inherent in every Englishman was that of property, which consisted "in the free use, enjoyment, and disposal of all his acquisitions, without any control or diminution, save only by the laws of the land."

Developed societies have regulated the acquisition of both personal property and real property, whether by inheritance, by gift, or by sale. Property could be taken for public use ("eminent domain") if not exercised arbitrarily or discriminatorily, upon payment of just compensation.

The right to own property implies the right to use it, but use can be regulated to safeguard the rights of others, of other property owners, or to prevent public nuisance. See *Euclid v. Ambler Realty Co., supra* p. 202. The right to accumulate property might be subject to regulation; the right to dispose of it may also be regulated, for example by laws prohibiting restrictive covenants and other racial discrimination.

All states have imposed limitations on the acquisition of certain kinds of property, for example arms and nuclear weapons. In strictly socialist economies, such as the former Soviet Union, the "means of production" were reserved to the state and, by implication, individuals were prohibited from acquiring properties designed for production. With the essential disappearance of state socialism, the right to own property may no longer be encumbered by such exceptions or limitations, but property rights are subject to limitations by the police power generally. See *supra* p. 196.

a. PROPERTY RIGHTS UNDER THE U.S. CONSTITUTION

The right to own, maintain, and dispose of property is an economic right explicitly protected by the U.S. Constitution against deprivation without due process of law, and against taking for public use without just compensation. The right to acquire, retain, maintain, and dispose of property may be seen also as a "liberty" protected against arbitrary interference by the doctrine of "substantive due process." See *supra* pp. 183–184.

In general, the right to property is protected against unreasonable searches and seizures by the Fourth Amendment; against deprivation or interference with the use of one's property by "substantive due process"; by limitations on the taking of property other than for public use, and by the requirement of just compensation. See U.S. Constitution Amendments IV and V. In recent years, the U.S. Supreme Court has increasingly been finding regulations of the use of property to constitute a taking of property requiring compensation. See Part II, p. 176.

When property has been taken for a public use, the usual standard for "just compensation" is the fair market value of the property, not its special or subjective value to the owner:

> The Court has repeatedly held that just compensation normally is to be measured by "the market value of the property at the time of the taking contemporaneously paid in money." Olson v. United States, 292 U.S. 246, 255 (1934). "Considerations that may not reasonably be held to affect market value are excluded." Deviation from this measure of just compensation has been required only "when market value has been too difficult to find, or when its application would result in manifest injustice to owner or public."

United States v. 50 Acres of Land, 469 U.S. 24, 29 (1984).

b. PROPERTY RIGHTS UNDER INTERNATIONAL LAW

i. *Human Rights Law*

International law of human rights addressed rights to property in Article 17 of the Universal Declaration, recognizing the right to own property alone as well as in association with others, but that clause was not developed in either of the Covenants.

Universal Declaration of Human Rights, Article 17

1. Everyone has the right to own property alone as well as in association with others.

2. No one shall be arbitrarily deprived of his property.

The Universal Declaration does not elaborate on the right "to own property" or on the right not to be deprived of one's property "arbitrarily."

The right to property is not mentioned in the Covenants but is guaranteed by the European Convention. See *infra* p. 1125. The failure to include that right in the Covenant may reflect not rejection of property in principle, but political controversy during that period over foreign investments and the asserted right to expropriate such property even without full compensation. See Part III, p. 323.

ii.   Special Rights of Foreign Nationals

Long before the emergence of an international law of human rights, international law developed a doctrine that a state had obligations to foreign nationals which included prohibition of denying them "justice."

Restatement (Third) of the Foreign Relations Law of the United States

§ 711 and comment d, and § 712 and comments (1987).

§ 711.   State Responsibility for Injury to Nationals of Other States

A state is responsible under international law for injury to a national of another state caused by an official act or omission that violates

(a) a human right that, under § 701, a state is obligated to respect for all persons subject to its authority;

(b) a personal right that, under international law, a state is obligated to respect for individuals of foreign nationality; or

(c) a right to property or another economic interest that, under international law, a state is obligated to respect for persons, natural or juridical, of foreign nationality, as provided in § 712.

Comment:

d.   Right to property as human right. Article 17 of the Universal Declaration of Human Rights declares: [quotation omitted.]

There is lack of agreement on the scope of this right and permissible limitations on it, but the right of an individual to own some property and not to be deprived of it arbitrarily is recognized as a human right. See § 702, Comment *k*. Under this section, clause (a), therefore, a state is responsible for violation of that right with respect to an individual who is a national of a foreign state. Customary international law accords additional protection to the property and other economic interests of foreign nationals, as provided in clause (c) and in § 712. For limitations on the right of aliens to acquire property or bring it into the state, see § 712, Comment *i*, and § 722, Comment *g*.

. . .

§ 712.   State Responsibility for Economic Injury to Nationals of Other States

A state is responsible under international law for injury resulting from:

(1) a taking by the state of the property of a national of another state that

    (a) is not for a public purpose, or

    (b) is discriminatory, or

    (c) is not accompanied by provision for just compensation;

For compensation to be just under this Subsection, it must, in the absence of exceptional circumstances, be in an amount equivalent to the value of the property taken and be paid at the time of taking, or within a reasonable time thereafter with interest from the date of taking, and in a form economically usable by the foreign national;

(2) a repudiation or breach by the state of a contract with a national of another state

    (a) where the repudiation or breach is (i) discriminatory; or (ii) motivated by noncommercial considerations, and compensatory damages are not paid; or

    (b) where the foreign national is not given an adequate forum to determine his claim of repudiation or breach, or is not compensated for any repudiation or breach determined to have occurred; or

(3) other arbitrary or discriminatory acts or omissions by the state that impair property or other economic interests of a national of another state.

Comment:

    a. Responsibility under general principles of international law. This section sets forth the responsibility of a state under customary international law for certain economic injury to foreign nationals. A state may have additional obligations under international agreements to which it is party. . . .

    b. Expropriation of alien property under international law. Subsection (1) states the traditional rules of international law on expropriation of alien properties and takes essentially the same substantive positions as the previous Restatement, §§ 187–90. These rules have been challenged in recent years, but this Restatement reaffirms that they continue to be valid and effective principles of international law. In particular, international law requires that when foreign properties are expropriated there must be compensation and such compensation must be just. See Comments *c* and *d.*

    c. Requirement and standard of compensation. International law requires that a taking of the property of a foreign national, whether a natural or juridical person, be compensated. There are authoritative declarations that under international law the compensation to be paid must be "appropriate." This Restatement maintains the view that compensation must also be "just." Compare the Fifth Amendment to the United States Constitution: "nor shall private property be taken for public use, without just compensation." See Comment *d.*

The United States Government has consistently taken the position in diplomatic exchanges and in international fora that under international law compensation must be "prompt, adequate and effective," and those terms have been included in United States legislation. See Reporters' Note 2. That formulation has met strong resistance from developing states and has not made its way into multilateral agreements or declarations or been universally utilized by international tribunals, but it has been incorporated into a substantial number of bilateral agreements negotiated by the United States as well as by other capital-exporting states both among themselves and with developing states.

d. Just compensation. The elements constituting just compensation are not fixed or precise, but, in the absence of exceptional circumstances, compensation to be just must be equivalent to the value of the property taken and must be paid at the time of taking or with interest from that date and in an economically useful form.

— There must be payment for the full value of the property, usually "fair market value" where that can be determined. Such value should take into account "going concern value," if any, and other generally recognized principles of valuation.

— Provision for compensation must be based on value at the time of taking; as in United States domestic law, if compensation is not paid at or before the time of taking but is delayed pending administrative, legislative, or judicial processes for fixing compensation, interest must be paid from the time of the taking.

— Compensation should be in convertible currency without restriction on repatriation, but payment in bonds may satisfy the requirement of just compensation if they bear interest at an economically reasonable rate and if there is a market for them through which their equivalent in convertible currency can be realized.

. . .

In exceptional circumstances, some deviation from the standard of compensation set forth in Subsection (1) might satisfy the requirement of just compensation. Whether circumstances are so exceptional as to warrant such deviation, and whether in the circumstances the particular deviation satisfies the requirement of just compensation, are questions of international law. An instance of exceptional circumstances that has been specifically suggested and extensively debated, but never authoritatively passed upon by an international tribunal, involves national programs of agricultural land reform. See Reporters' Note 3. A departure from the general rule on the ground of such exceptional circumstances is unwarranted if (i) the property taken had been used in a business enterprise that was specifically authorized or encouraged by the state; (ii) the property was an enterprise taken for operation as a going concern by the state; (iii) the taking program did not apply equally to nationals of the taking state; or (iv) the taking itself was otherwise wrongful under Subsection (1)(a) or (b).

Exceptional circumstances that would permit deviation from the standard of compensation set forth in subsection (1) might include takings of alien property during war or similar exigency. As to alien enemies in time of war, see § 711, Comment *h*.

When, by an international agreement, a state has undertaken not to expropriate the properties of nationals of another state, or has agreed that in the event of such expropriation it will provide compensation in accordance with a particular standard, any claim of a right to terminate, suspend, or modify that obligation on grounds of special circumstances is governed by the law of international agreements, including the principle of *rebus sic stantibus*. See § 336.

e. Taking for public purpose. The requirement that a taking be for a public purpose is reiterated in most formulations of the rules of international law on expropriation of foreign property. That limitation, however, has not figured prominently in international claims practice, perhaps because the concept of public purpose is broad and not subject to effective re-examination by other states. Presumably, a seizure by a dictator or oligarchy for private use could be challenged under this rule.

f. Discriminatory takings. Formulations of the rules on expropriation generally include a prohibition of discrimination, implying that a program of taking that singles out aliens generally, or aliens of a particular nationality, or particular aliens, would violate international law. Where discrimination is charged, or where the public purpose is challenged, Comment *e*, there is often also a failure to pay just compensation, and a program of takings that did not meet the requirements of equal treatment and public purpose but did provide just compensation under Subsection (1) might not in fact be successfully challenged.

Discrimination implies unreasonable distinction. Takings that invidiously single out property of persons of a particular nationality would be unreasonable; classifications, even if based on nationality, that are rationally related to the state's security or economic policies might not be unreasonable. Discrimination may be difficult to determine where there is no comparable enterprise owned by local nationals or by nationals of other countries, or where nationals of the taking state are treated equally with aliens but by discrete actions separated in time.

Whether a state can take the property of private persons in response to a violation of international law by their state of nationality, even in retaliation for unlawful takings of private property by that state, is doubtful. See previous Restatement § 200. For other forms of response to a violation of international law, see § 905, Comments *b* and *f* and Reporters' Note 2. As to the taking of the property of enemy aliens during war, see § 711, Comment *h*.

g. Expropriation or regulation. Subsection (1) applies not only to avowed expropriations in which the government formally takes title to property, but also to other actions of the government that have the effect of "taking" the property, in whole or in large part, outright or in stages ("creeping expropriation"). A state is responsible as for an expropriation of property under Subsection (1) when it subjects alien property to taxation, regulation, or other action that is confiscatory, or that prevents, unreasonably interferes with, or unduly delays, effective enjoyment of an alien's property or its removal from the state's territory. Depriving an alien of control of his property, as by an order freezing his assets, might become a taking if it is long extended. A state is not responsible for loss of property or for other economic disadvantage resulting from bona fide general taxation, regulation, forfeiture for crime, or other action of the kind that is commonly accepted as within the police power of states, if it is not discriminatory, Comment *f*, and is not designed to cause the alien to abandon the property to the state or sell it at a distress price. As under United States constitutional law, the line between "taking" and regulation is sometimes uncertain. See Reporters' Note 6.

. . .

Notes

The Restatement was published in 1987. Might the standard of justice that protects foreign nationals now extend as a principle of customary law of human rights to all persons subject to a state's jurisdiction, including the state's own nationals?

Comment *k* to Restatement § 702, which addressed the customary international law of human rights, observed that there was "wide disagreement among states as to the scope and content of [the right to property], which weighs against the conclusion that a human right to property generally has become a principle of customary law. All states have accepted a limited core of rights to private property, and violation of such rights, as state policy, may already be a violation of customary law."

c. PROPERTY RIGHTS UNDER REGIONAL HUMAN RIGHTS CONVENTIONS

The right to property is protected as a human right in the African, the American, and the European Conventions.

i.   *The African Charter*

African Charter on Human and Peoples' Rights, Article 14

The right to property shall be guaranteed. It may only be encroached upon in the interest of public need or in the general interest of the community and in accordance with the provisions of appropriate laws.

ii. *The American Convention*

American Convention on Human Rights, Article 21

1.   Everyone has the right to the use and enjoyment of his property. The law may subordinate such use and enjoyment to the interest of society.

2.   No one shall be deprived of his property except upon payment of just compensation, for reasons of public utility or social interest, and in the cases and according to the forms established by law.

3.   Usury and any other form of exploitation of man by man shall be prohibited by law.

Notes

No known complaints had been filed under Article 14 of the African Charter, as of January 1, 1999.

Although the Inter–American Court of Human Rights has not issued a substantive ruling on Article 21 of the American Convention, several violations have been found by the Inter–American Commission on Human Rights. See, e.g., *Comadres v. El Salvador*, Case 10.948, Inter–Am. Comm'n H.R. 101, OEA/ser.L./V./II.91 doc. 7 rev. (1996) (government of El Salvador responsible for violations of property rights for pillaging offices and explosive attacks on organization established to support mothers and families of disappeared persons); *Marín et al. v. Nicaragua*, Case 10.770, Inter–Am. Comm'n H.R. 293, OEA/ser. L/V/II.85, doc. 9 rev. (1994) (de facto confiscation of family's real estate without legal proceedings or compensation violated Article 21(2)); *Thebaud v. Haiti*, Case 3405, Inter–Am. Comm'n H.R. 46, OEA/ser. L/V/II.63, doc. 10 rev. (1983) (pillaging of lawyer's home and office, in connection with beating and imprisoning him, violated Article 21).

iii.   The European Convention

European Convention for the Protection of Human Rights and Fundamental Freedoms, Protocol No. 1, Article 1 (1952)

Every natural or legal person is entitled to the peaceful enjoyment of his possessions. No one shall be deprived of his possessions except in the public interest and subject to the conditions provided for by law and by the general principles of international law.

The preceding provisions shall not, however, in any way impair the right of a State to enforce such laws as it deems necessary to control the use of property in accordance with the general interest or to secure the payment of taxes or other contributions or penalties.

Notes

1.   Article 1 of Protocol No. 1 has been the focus of a substantial body of case law in the European system. The European Court of Human Rights interprets Article 1 of Protocol 1 as comprising three distinct rules:

The first, which is expressed in the first sentence of the first paragraph and is of a general nature, lays down the principle of the peaceful enjoyment of possessions. The second, in the second sentence of the same paragraph, covers deprivation of possessions and makes it subject to certain conditions. The third, contained in the second paragraph, recognises that the Contracting States are entitled to control the use of property in accordance with the general interest or to secure the payment of taxes or other contributions or penalties.

However, the three rules are not "distinct" in the sense of being unconnected: the second and third rules are concerned with particular interferences with the right to peaceful enjoyment of property and should therefore be construed in the light of the general principle enunciated in the first rule.

National & Provincial Building Society v. United Kingdom, 1997–VII Eur. Ct. H.R. 2325, para. 78, 25 E.H.R.R. 127 (1997).

2.　Note that Article 1 of Protocol No. 1 protects the property right of "every legal person" as well as a "natural person," the only express safeguard of the rights of legal persons in a treaty devoted to "human rights." The individual complaint procedures (both prior to and after the merger of the Court and the Commission) have permitted applications from "any person, non-governmental organization or group of individuals claiming to be the victim of a violation. . . . " See Article 25 of the original Convention; Article 34 of the Convention as revised by Protocol No. 11. Should corporations be recognized as having human rights? Or are there valid instrumental reasons for conferring the equivalent of human rights on corporations? Under the European Convention, it is well settled that "[a] corporate body has some but not all of the rights of individuals; thus it has the right to a fair trial under Article 6, to protection of its correspondence under Article 8, and is expressly granted property rights under Article 1 of the first Protocol, but it does not have the right to education under Article 2." Francis G. Jacobs and Robin C.A. White. The European Convention on Human Rights 350 (2d ed. 1996).

3.　In *Loizidou v. Turkey*, below, the Court addressed the right of a refugee "to peaceful enjoyment" of her property in northern Cyprus to which she was denied access for over sixteen years. The case arose against the background of the 1974 invasion of northern Cyprus by Turkey after violence between the Greek Cypriot and Turkish Cypriot communities. Turkey has remained in continuous occupation of northern Cyprus since that period. An attempt to declare an independent "Turkish Republic of Northern Cyprus" ("TRNC") in 1983 was condemned by the UN Security Council, and rejected by the Committee of Ministers of the Council of Europe.

Loizidou v. Turkey

European Court of Human Rights, 1996.
1996–VI Eur. Ct. H.R. 2216, 23 E.H.R.R. 513.

. . .

11.　The applicant, a Cypriot national, grew up in Kyrenia in northern Cyprus. In 1972 she married and moved with her husband to Nicosia.

12.   She claims to be the owner of plots of land ... in Kyrenia in northern Cyprus and she alleges that prior to the Turkish occupation of northern Cyprus on 20 July 1974, work had commenced on plot no. 5390 for the construction of flats, one of which was intended as a home for her family....

. . .

13.   On 19 March 1989 the applicant participated in a march organised by a women's group ("Women Walk Home" movement) in the village of Lymbia ... in the occupied area of northern Cyprus. The aim of the march was to assert the right of Greek Cypriot refugees to return to their homes. Leading a group of fifty marchers she advanced up a hill towards the Church of the Holy Cross in the Turkish-occupied part of Cyprus passing the United Nations' guard post on the way. When they reached the churchyard they were surrounded by Turkish soldiers and prevented from moving any further.

14.   She was eventually detained by members of the Turkish Cypriot police force and brought by ambulance to Nicosia....

. . .

48.   The applicant contended that the continuous denial of access to her property in northern Cyprus and the ensuing loss of all control over it is imputable to the Turkish Government and constitutes a violation of Article 1 of Protocol No. 1....

. . .

59.   For the Turkish Government and the Commission the case only concerns access to property, and the right to the peaceful enjoyment of possessions does not include as a corollary a right to freedom of movement.

The Turkish Government further submitted that if the applicant was held to have absolute freedom of access to her property, irrespective of the de facto political situation on the island, this would undermine the intercommunal talks, which were the only appropriate way of resolving this problem.

. . .

63.   [A]s a consequence of the fact that the applicant has been refused access to the land since 1974, she has effectively lost all control as well as all possibilities to use and enjoy her property. The continuous denial of access must therefore be regarded as an interference with her rights under Article 1 of Protocol No. 1. Such an interference cannot, in the exceptional circumstances of the present case [i.e., the de facto control of northern Cyprus by Turkey rather than the legitimate government of Cyprus], be regarded as either a deprivation of property or a control of use within the meaning of the first and second paragraphs of Article 1 of Protocol No. 1. However, it clearly falls within the meaning of the first sentence of that provision as an interference with the peaceful enjoyment of possessions. In

this respect the Court observes that hindrance can amount to a violation of the Convention just like a legal impediment. . . .

64.   Apart from a passing reference to the doctrine of necessity as a justification for the acts of the "TRNC" and to the fact that property rights were the subject of intercommunal talks, the Turkish Government has not sought to make submissions justifying the above interference with the applicant's property rights which is imputable to Turkey.

It has not, however, been explained how the need to rehouse displaced Turkish Cypriot refugees in the years following the Turkish intervention in the island in 1974 could justify the complete negation of the applicant's property rights in the form of a total and continuous denial of access and a purported expropriation without compensation.

Nor can the fact that property rights were the subject of intercommunal talks involving both communities in Cyprus provide a justification for this situation under the Convention.

In such circumstances, the Court concludes that there has been and continues to be a breach of Article 1 of Protocol No. 1.

. . .

Notes

1.   The Court's decision in *Loizidou* is significant also for the impact it could have on the number of claims brought against Turkey by refugees and property owners from northern Cyprus. At least 160,000 Greek Cypriots were displaced when Turkey invaded northern Cyprus in 1974, and several thousand have already filed lawsuits at the European Court of Human Rights. See Charles Spies, *European Court of Human Rights Rules Turkey Responsible for Refugees' Property in Turkish–Occupied Northern Cyprus*, 11 Geo. Immigr. L.J. 663, 665–66 (1997). "Should the Court refrain from [opening the door to a new category of cases] if its judgment entails the possibility that thousands of similar complaints will be lodged with the Convention organs and threaten the effectiveness of human rights protections within the Council of Europe?" Beate Rudolf, *International Decision: European Convention on Human Rights*, 91 Am. J. Int'l L. 532, 537 (1997).

2.   In *Loizidou*, the European Court held Turkey responsible for human rights violations committed outside its own national territory. Under Article 1 of the European Convention, states agree to "secure to everyone within their jurisdiction the rights and freedoms" defined by the Convention. Confirming its prior decision rejecting Turkey's preliminary objections, the Court reiterated:

> that under its established case law the concept of "jurisdiction" under Article 1 of the Convention is not restricted to the national territory of the Contracting States. Accordingly, the responsibility of Contracting States can be involved by acts and omissions of their authorities which produce effects outside their own territory.

Loizidou, para. 52. Under the particular circumstances of the case, Turkey exercised effective control over northern Cyprus, and was obliged to secure the rights and freedoms set out in the Convention there. Compare the discussion of extraterritorial responsibility under other human rights treaties in Part III, pp. 323, 425–426 supra.

3.   In *Loizidou*, given the nature of the Turkish occupation, the Court refused to consider the property in question as having been lawfully expropriated. In the following decision, the Court discussed the consequences of Article 1 of Protocol No. 1 in cases of formal expropriation of property belonging to a state's own nationals.

Lithgow and Others v. United Kingdom

European Court of Human Rights, 1986.
102 Eur. Ct. H.R. (ser. A), 8 E.H.R.R. 329.

[The cases arose from the nationalization of the British shipbuilding and aircraft industries. Former owners challenged the compensation paid for their interests on a variety of grounds, including the use of share values rather than asset values, use of hypothetical share values for untraded shares, the choice of the valuation period, and the absence of a control premium. The Court first discussed the standard by which the compensation should be judged under Article 1 of Protocol No. 1.]

C.   "General principles of international law"

111.   The applicants argued that the reference in the second sentence of Article 1 to "the general principles of international law" meant that the international law requirement of, so they asserted, prompt, adequate and effective compensation for the deprivation of property of foreigners also applied to nationals.

113.   In the first place, purely as a matter of general international law, the principles in question apply solely to non-nationals. They were specifically developed for the benefit of non-nationals. As such, these principles did not relate to the treatment accorded by States to their own nationals.

114.   In support of their argument, the applicants relied first on the actual text of Article 1. In their submission, since the second sentence opened with the words "No one", it was impossible to construe that sentence as meaning that whereas everyone was entitled to the safeguards afforded by the phrases "in the public interest" and "subject to the conditions provided for by law", only non-nationals were entitled to the safeguards afforded by the phrase "subject to the conditions provided for ... by the general principles of international law".…

Whilst there is some force in the applicants' argument as a matter of grammatical construction, there are convincing reasons for a different interpretation. Textually the Court finds it more natural to take the reference to the general principles of international law in Article 1 of Protocol No. 1 to mean that those principles are incorporated into that

Article, but only as regards those acts to which they are normally applicable, that is to say acts of a State in relation to non-nationals. . . .

115.   The applicants also referred to arguments to the effect that, on the [proposed] interpretation, the reference in Article 1 to the general principles of international law would be redundant since non-nationals already enjoyed the protection thereof.

The Court does not share this view. The inclusion of the reference can be seen to serve at least two purposes. Firstly, it enables non-nationals to resort directly to the machinery of the Convention to enforce their rights on the basis of the relevant principles of international law, whereas otherwise they would have to seek recourse to diplomatic channels or to other available means of dispute settlement to do so. Secondly, the reference ensures that the position of non-nationals is safeguarded, in that it excludes any possible argument that the entry into force of Protocol No. 1 has led to a diminution of their rights. . . .

116.   . . . .

Especially as regards a taking of property effected in the context of a social reform or an economic restructuring, there may well be good grounds for drawing a distinction between nationals and non-nationals as far as compensation is concerned. To begin with, non-nationals are more vulnerable to domestic legislation: unlike nationals, they will generally have played no part in the election or designation of its authors nor have been consulted on its adoption. Secondly, although a taking of property must always be effected in the public interest, different considerations may apply to nationals and non-nationals and there may well be legitimate reason for requiring nationals to bear a greater burden in the public interest than non-nationals.

117.   Confronted with a text whose interpretation has given rise to such disagreement, the Court considers it proper to have recourse to the travaux préparatoires as a supplementary means of interpretation.

Examination of the travaux préparatoires reveals that the express reference to a right to compensation contained in earlier drafts of Article 1 was excluded, notably in the face of opposition on the part of the United Kingdom and other States. The mention of the general principles of international law was subsequently included and was the subject of several statements to the effect that they protected only foreigners. . . .

. . .

118.   Finally, it has not been demonstrated that, since the entry into force of Protocol No. 1, State practice has developed to the point where it can be said that the parties to that instrument regard the reference therein to the general principles of international law as being applicable to the treatment accorded by them to their own nationals. The evidence adduced points distinctly in the opposite direction.

119.   For all these reasons, the Court concludes that the general principles of international law are not applicable to a taking by a State of the property of its own nationals.

D.   Entitlement to compensation

120.   The question remains whether the availability and amount of compensation are material considerations under the second sentence of the first paragraph of Article 1, the text of the provision being silent on the point. . . .

. . . [T]he Court observes that under the legal systems of the Contracting States, the taking of property in the public interest without payment of compensation is treated as justifiable only in exceptional circumstances not relevant for present purposes. As far as Article 1 is concerned, the protection of the right of property it affords would be largely illusory and ineffective in the absence of any equivalent principle.

In this connection, the Court recalls that not only must a measure depriving a person of his property pursue, on the facts as well as in principle, a legitimate aim "in the public interest", but there must also be a reasonable relationship of proportionality between the means employed and the aim sought to be realised. This latter requirement was expressed in other terms in [Sporrong and Lönnroth v. Sweden, 52 Eur. Ct. H.R. (ser. A), 5 E.H.R.R. 35 (1982),] by the notion of the "fair balance" that must be struck between the demands of the general interest of the community and the requirements of the protection of the individual's fundamental rights. The requisite balance will not be found if the person concerned has had to bear "an individual and excessive burden".

Although the Court was speaking in that judgment in the context of the general rule of peaceful enjoyment of property enunciated in the first sentence of the first paragraph, it pointed out that "the search for this balance is . . . reflected in the structure of Article 1" as a whole.

Clearly, compensation terms are material to the assessment whether a fair balance has been struck between the various interests at stake and, notably, whether or not a disproportionate burden has been imposed on the person who has been deprived of his possessions.

E.   Standard of compensation

121.   The Court further accepts the Commission's conclusion as to the standard of compensation: the taking of property without payment of an amount reasonably related to its value would normally constitute a disproportionate interference which could not be considered justifiable under Article 1. Article 1 does not, however, guarantee a right to full compensation in all circumstances, since legitimate objectives of "public interest", such as pursued in measures of economic reform or measures designed to achieve greater social justice, may call for less than reimbursement of the full market value.

. . .

[The Court went on to rule against the former owners' claims by a large majority. Five Judges dissented from the finding that the compensation was adequate; one Judge dissented from the conclusion that Article 1 required compensation at all in cases where the property of nationals was lawfully expropriated.]

Notes

1. Given that Article 1 of Protocol No. 1 does not expressly require compensation for expropriation of the property of nationals, why should the Court infer a compensation requirement? If the inference of a compensation requirement is justified, then why should the standard under human rights law for nationals differ from the standard for non-nationals?

2. Other decisions by the European Court of Human Rights on Article 1 of Protocol No. 1 include the following:

"peaceful enjoyment of possessions" : *Phocas v. France*, 1996–II Eur. Ct. H.R. 519 (scheme to improve crossroads which prohibited development of applicant's property did not infringe right to peaceable enjoyment of property given the states' "wide margin of appreciation in order to implement their town-planning policy"); *Selçuk & Asker v. Turkey*, 1998–IT Eur. Ct. H.R. 891, 26 E.H.R.R. 477 (1998) (burning of applicants' homes constituted "particularly grave and unjustified interferences with the applicants' ... peaceful enjoyment of their possessions"); *Sporrong and Lönnroth v. Sweden*, 52 Eur. Ct. H.R. (ser. A), 5 E.H.R.R. 35 (1982) (long pendency of threatened expropriation, which was never completed, and resulting prohibition on construction unjustifiably interfered with owners' rights to peaceful enjoyment of possessions); *Matos e Silva, LDA v. Portugal*, 1996–IV Eur. Ct. H.R. 1092, 24 E.H.R.R. 573 (1996) (preliminary steps to expropriation and thirteen-year ban on building greatly reduced applicants' ability to deal with and use their possessions and state's failure to pay or offer compensation "upset the fair balance that must be struck between the requirements of the general interest and the protections of the right to the peaceful enjoyment of one's possessions").

"right not to be deprived of possessions" : *Holy Monasteries v. Greece*, 301–A Eur. Ct. H.R. (ser. A), 20 E.H.R.R. 1 (1994) ("taking of property without payment of an amount reasonably related to its value will normally constitute a disproportionate interference and a total lack of compensation can be considered justifiable under Article 1 only in exceptional circumstance"); *James and Others v. United Kingdom*, 98 Eur. Ct. H.R. (ser. A), 8 E.H.R.R. 123 (1986) (state's determination of "public interest" regarding compulsory transfer of landlords' property upon payment of less than full value was not "manifestly unreasonable" and actions were not "arbitrary"); *Akkus v. Turkey*, 1997–IV Eur. Ct. H.R. 1300 (payment for land expropriated to build a hydro-electric plant was inadequate due to seventeen month delay in payment, high monetary inflation, and low statutory rate of interest).

"control the use of property in accordance with the general interest or to secure the payment of taxes" : *Air Canada v. United Kingdom*, 316–A Eur. Ct. H.R. (ser. A), 20 E.H.R.R. 150 (1995) (seizure of Air Canada aircraft used to smuggle 331 kilograms of marijuana following a series of Air Canada security lapses struck a fair balance between the community's general interest and the airline's property rights, as aircraft was returned on the day of the seizure and payment of a penalty); *Raimondo v. Italy,* 281–A Eur. Ct. H.R. (ser. A),18 E.H.R.R. 237 (1994) (provisional confiscation of possessions representing proceeds from unlawful activities was justified by the general interest and was "effective and necessary" and "not disproportionate to the aim pursued" given the "extremely dangerous economic power of an 'organisation' like the Mafia"); *Gasus Dosier- und Fördertechnik GmbH v. Netherlands*, 306–B Eur. Ct. H.R. (ser. A), 20 E.H.R.R. 403 (1995) (tax authority's seizure and sale of concrete mixer in which applicant held a security interest was not an unjustified interference with property rights given states' wide margin of appreciation to enact laws to enforce tax debts); *National & Provincial Building Society v. United Kingdom*, 1997–VII Eur. Ct. H.R. 2325, 25 E.H.R.R. 127 (1997) (tax measures with retrospective effect were not "manifestly without reasonable foundation").

3.   On the protection of property rights in European Community law, see Fiona Campbell–White, *Property Rights: A Forgotten Issue Under the Union*, in The European Union and Human Rights 249 (Neuwahl & Rosas eds., 1995).

2.   FREEDOM OF ENTERPRISE

Rights of free enterprise were recognized at common law, as an aspect of the inherent liberty of the individual, subject to the police power. In the second half of the Nineteenth Century, the U.S. Supreme Court recognized freedom of enterprise as a liberty protected by due process of law, and the Due Process Clause became a guardian of *laissez-faire*, subject only to certain limitations for narrow purposes under the police power narrowly conceived. See *Lochner v. New York, infra.*

The *Lochner* era ended in 1937 and there is no evidence that it may be reborn. (But compare the recent tendency to consider some regulations as constituting a taking requiring compensation.)

International human rights law guarantees particular liberties, for example freedom of press, freedom of association, freedom of religion, and the protection of private life; it contains no explicit guarantee of freedom of enterprise or of "liberty" generally. International human rights law, developed during the heyday of socialism, and designed to have universal appeal—to socialists as well as to free-enterprise societies—does not address freedom of enterprise; and no such freedom is explicitly recognized in either the Universal Declaration or in the Covenants. But some right to freedom of enterprise may be implied in the right to own property "alone as well as in association with others," in the rights to work and to leisure, and perhaps even in the scheme of economic and social rights generally.

Some constitutional systems contain stronger protections for freedom of enterprise than does the United States. Compare the use of the principle of "proportionality" in evaluating restrictions on the exercise of an occupation in German constitutional law, discussed *infra* pp. 1144–1147.

a.   FREEDOM OF ENTERPRISE UNDER THE U.S. CONSTITUTION

Amendment V (1791)

No person shall ... be deprived of life, liberty, or property, without due process of law; nor shall private property be taken for public use, without just compensation.

Amendment XIV (1868)

No State shall ... deprive any person of life, liberty or property without due process of law.

Allgeyer v. Louisiana

Supreme Court of the United States, 1897.
165 U.S. 578, 589.

The liberty mentioned in [the fourteenth] amendment means not only the right of the citizen to be free from the mere physical restraint of his person, as by incarceration, but the term is deemed to embrace the right of the citizen to be free in all his faculties; to be free to use them in all lawful ways; to live and work where he will; to earn his livelihood by any lawful calling; to pursue any livelihood or avocation, and for that purpose to enter into all contracts which may be proper, necessary, and essential to his carrying out to a successful conclusion the purposes above mentioned.

Lochner v. New York

Supreme Court of the United States, 1905.
198 U.S. 45.

■ Mr. Justice Peckham ... delivered the opinion of the court.

... [T]he plaintiff in error violated the labor law of the state of New York, in that he wrongfully and unlawfully required and permitted an employee working for him to work more than sixty hours in one week.... The mandate of the statute, that "no employee shall be required or permitted to work," is the substantial equivalent of an enactment that "no employee shall contract or agree to work," more than ten hours per day; and, as there is no provision for special emergencies, the statute is mandatory in all cases. It is not an act merely fixing the number of hours which shall constitute a legal day's work, but an absolute prohibition upon the employer permitting, under any circumstances, more than ten hours' work to be done in his establishment. The employee may desire to earn the extra money which would arise from his working more than the prescribed time, but this statute forbids the employer from permitting the employee to earn it.

The statute necessarily interferes with the right of contract between the employer and employees, concerning the number of hours in which the latter may labor in the bakery of the employer. The general right to make a contract in relation to his business is part of the liberty of the individual protected by the 14th Amendment of the Federal Constitution. Allgeyer v. Louisiana, 165 U. S. 578. Under that provision no state can deprive any person of life, liberty, or property without due process of law. The right to purchase or to sell labor is part of the liberty protected by this amendment, unless there are circumstances which exclude the right. There are, however, certain powers, existing in the sovereignty of each state in the Union, somewhat vaguely termed police powers ... [Those powers] relate to the safety, health, morals, and general welfare of the public. Both property and liberty are held on such reasonable conditions as may be imposed by the governing power of the state in the exercise of those powers, and with such conditions the 14th Amendment was not designed to interfere.

. . .

It must, of course, be conceded that there is a limit to the valid exercise of the police power by the state. There is no dispute concerning this general proposition. Otherwise the 14th Amendment would have no efficacy and the legislatures of the states would have unbounded power, and it would be enough to say that any piece of legislation was enacted to conserve the morals, the health, or the safety of the people; such legislation would be valid, no matter how absolutely without foundation the claim might be. The claim of the police power would be a mere pretext,—become another and delusive name for the supreme sovereignty of the state to be exercised free from constitutional restraint. This is not contended for. In every case that comes before this court, therefore, where legislation of this character is concerned, and where the protection of the Federal Constitution is sought, the question necessarily arises: Is this a fair, reasonable, and appropriate exercise of the police power of the state, or is it an unreasonable, unnecessary, and arbitrary interference with the right of the individual to his personal liberty, or to enter into those contracts in relation to labor which may seem to him appropriate or necessary for the support of himself and his family? Of course the liberty of contract relating to labor includes both parties to it. The one has as much right to purchase as the other to sell labor.

. . .

The question whether this act is valid as a labor law, pure and simple, may be dismissed in a few words. There is no reasonable ground for interfering with the liberty of person or the right of free contract, by determining the hours of labor, in the occupation of a baker. There is no contention that bakers as a class are not equal in intelligence and capacity to men in other trades or manual occupations, or that they are not able to assert their rights and care for themselves without the protecting arm of the state, interfering with their independence of judgment and of action. They are in no sense wards of the state. Viewed in the light of a purely labor law, with no reference whatever to the question of health, we think that a law like the one before us involves neither the safety, the morals, nor the welfare, of the public, and that the interest of the public is not in the slightest degree affected by such an act. The law must be upheld, if at all, as a law pertaining to the health of the individual engaged in the occupation of a baker. It does not affect any other portion of the public than those who are engaged in that occupation. Clean and wholesome bread does not depend upon whether the baker works but ten hours per day or only sixty hours a week. The limitation of the hours of labor does not come within the police power on that ground.

. . .

We think that there can be no fair doubt that the trade of a baker, in and of itself, is not an unhealthy one to that degree which would authorize the legislature to interfere with the right to labor, and with the right of free contract on the part of the individual, either as employer or employee. . . . Some occupations are more healthy than others, but we think there are none which might not come under the power of the legislature to supervise and control the hours of working therein, if the mere fact that the occupation is not absolutely and perfectly healthy is to confer that right upon the legislative department of the government. . . .

It is also urged, pursuing the same line of argument, that it is to the interest of the state that its population should be strong and robust, and therefore any legislation which may be said to tend to make people healthy must be valid as health laws, enacted under the police power. If this be a valid argument and a justification for this kind of legislation, it follows that the protection of the Federal Constitution from undue interference with liberty of person and freedom of contract is visionary, wherever the law is sought to be justified as a valid exercise of the police power. Scarcely any law but might find shelter under such assumptions, and conduct, properly so called, as well as contract, would come under the restrictive sway of the legislature. . . .

. . .

It is manifest to us that the limitation of the hours of labor as provided for in this section of the statute under which the indictment was found, and the plaintiff in error convicted, has no such direct relation to, and no such substantial effect upon, the health of the employee, as to justify us in regarding the section as really a health law. It seems to us that the real object and purpose were simply to regulate the hours of labor between the master and his employees (all being men, *sui juris*), in a private business, not dangerous in any degree to morals, or in any real and substantial degree to the health of the employees. Under such circumstances the freedom of master and employee to contract with each other in relation to their employment, and in defining the same, cannot be prohibited or interfered with, without violating the Federal Constitution.

. . .

Reversed.

■ MR. JUSTICE HOLMES dissenting:

. . .

This case is decided upon an economic theory which a large part of the country does not entertain. If it were a question whether I agreed with that theory, I should desire to study it further and long before making up my mind. But I do not conceive that to be my duty, because I strongly believe that my agreement or disagreement has nothing to do with the right of a majority to embody their opinions in law. It is settled by various decisions of this court that state constitutions and state laws may regulate life in many ways which we as legislators might think as injudicious, or if you like as tyrannical, as this, and which, equally with this, interfere with the liberty to contract. Sunday laws and usury laws are ancient examples. A more modern one is the prohibition of lotteries. The liberty of the citizen to do as he likes so long as he does not interfere with the liberty of others to do the same, which has been a shibboleth for some well-known writers, is interfered with by school laws, by the Post Office, by every state or municipal institution which takes his money for purposes thought desirable, whether he likes it or not. The 14th Amendment does not enact Mr. Herbert Spencer's Social Statics. The other day we sustained the Massachusetts vaccination law. Jacobson v. Massachusetts ... Some of these laws 07 embody convictions or prejudices which judges are likely to share. Some may not. But a Constitution is not intended to embody a particular economic theory, whether of paternalism and the organic relation of the citizen to the state or of laissez faire. It is made for people of fundamentally differing views, and the accident of our finding certain opinions natural and familiar, or novel, and even shocking, ought not to conclude our judgment upon the question whether statutes embodying them conflict with the Constitution of the United States.

General propositions do not decide concrete cases. The decision will depend on a judgment or intuition more subtle than any articulate major premise. But I think that the proposition just stated, if it is accepted, will carry us far toward the end. Every opinion tends to become a law. I think that the word "liberty," in the 14th Amendment, is perverted when it is held to prevent the natural outcome of a dominant opinion, unless it can be said that a rational and fair man necessarily would admit that the statute proposed would infringe fundamental principles as they have been understood by the traditions of our people and our law. It does not need research to show that no such sweeping condemnation can be passed upon the statute before us. A reasonable man might think it a proper measure on the score of health. Men whom I certainly could not pronounce unreasonable would uphold it as a first instalment of a general regulation of the hours of work. Whether in the latter aspect it would be open to the charge of inequality I think it unnecessary to discuss.

[Justice Harlan, joined by Justice White and Justice Day, dissented on the ground that the New York statute imposed reasonable limitations on liberty of contract in order to protect the health of the employees.]

Nebbia v. New York

Supreme Court of the United States, 1934.
291 U.S. 502.

■ MR. JUSTICE ROBERTS delivered the opinion of the Court.

The Legislature of New York established ... a Milk Control Board with power, among other things to "fix minimum and maximum * * * retail prices to be charged by * * * stores to consumers for consumption off the premises where sold." ...

The question for decision is whether the Federal Constitution prohibits a state from so fixing the selling price of milk. We first inquire as to the occasion for the legislation and its history.

During 1932 the prices received by farmers for milk were much below the cost of production. The decline in prices during 1931 and 1932 was much greater than that of prices generally. The situation of the families of dairy producers had become desperate and called for state aid similar to that afforded the unemployed, if conditions should not improve.

· · ·

... [The] question is whether, in light of the conditions disclosed, the enforcement of section 312(e) denied the appellant the due process secured to him by the Fourteenth Amendment....

Under our form of government the use of property and the making of contracts are normally matters of private and not of public concern. The general rule is that both shall be free of governmental interference. But neither property rights nor contract rights are absolute; for government cannot exist if the citizen may at will use his property to the detriment of his fellows, or exercise his freedom of contract to work them harm. Equally fundamental with the private right is that of the public to regulate it in the common interest. ...

· · ·

The Fifth Amendment, in the field of federal activity, and the Fourteenth, as respects state action, do not prohibit governmental regulation for the public welfare. They merely condition the exertion of the admitted power, by securing that the end shall be accomplished by methods consistent with due process. And the guaranty of due process, as has often been held, demands only that the law shall not be unreasonable, arbitrary, or capricious, and that the means selected shall have a real and substantial relation to the object sought to be attained. It results that a regulation valid for one sort of business, or in given circumstances, may be invalid for another sort, or for the same business under other circumstances, because the reasonableness of each regulation depends upon the relevant facts.

. . .

The Constitution does not guarantee the unrestricted privilege to engage in a business or to conduct it as one pleases. Certain kinds of business may be prohibited; and the right to conduct a business, or to pursue a calling, may be conditioned. Regulation of a business to prevent waste of the state's resources may be justified. And statutes prescribing the terms upon which those conducting certain businesses may contract, or imposing terms if they do enter into agreements, are within the state's competency.

Legislation concerning sales of goods, and incidentally affecting prices, has repeatedly been held valid. In this class fall laws forbidding unfair competition by the charging of lower prices in one locality than those exacted in another, by giving trade inducements to purchasers, and by other forms of price discrimination. The public policy with respect to free competition has engendered state and federal statutes prohibiting monopolies, which have been upheld. . . .

The milk industry in New York has been the subject of long-standing and drastic regulation in the public interest. The legislative investigation of 1932 was persuasive of the fact that for this and other reasons unrestricted competition aggravated existing evils and the normal law of supply and demand was insufficient to correct maladjustments detrimental to the community. The inquiry disclosed destructive and demoralizing competitive conditions and unfair trade practices which resulted in retail price cutting and reduced the income of the farmer below the cost of production. We do not understand the appellant to deny that in these circumstances the Legislature might reasonably consider further regulation and control desirable for protection of the industry and the consuming public. . . . In the light of the facts the order appears not to be unreasonable or arbitrary, or without relation to the purpose to prevent ruthless competition from destroying the wholesale price structure on which the farmer depends for his livelihood, and the community for an assured supply of milk.

But we are told that because the law essays to control prices it denies due process. Notwithstanding the admitted power to correct existing economic ills by appropriate regulation of business, even though an indirect result may be a restriction of the freedom of contract or a modification of charges for services or the price of commodities, the appellant urges that direct fixation of prices is a type of regulation absolutely forbidden. His position is that the Fourteenth Amendment requires us to hold the challenged statute void for this reason alone. The argument runs that the public control of rates or prices is per se unreasonable and unconstitutional, save as applied to businesses affected with a public interest; that a business so affected is one in which property is devoted to an enterprise of a sort which the public itself might appropriately undertake, or one whose owner relies on a public grant or franchise for the right to conduct the business, or in which he is bound to serve all who apply; in short, such as is commonly called a public utility; or a business in its nature a monopoly. The milk industry, it is said, possesses none of these characteristics, and, therefore, not being affected with a public interest, its charges may not be controlled by the state. Upon the soundness of this contention the appellant's case against the statute depends.

We may as well say at once that the dairy industry is not, in the accepted sense of the phrase, a public utility. We think the appellant is also right in asserting that there is in this case no suggestion of any monopoly or monopolistic practice. It goes without saying that those engaged in the business are in no way dependent upon public grants or franchises for the privilege of conducting their activities. But if, as must be conceded, the industry is subject to regulation in the public interest, what constitutional principle bars the state from correcting existing maladjustments by legislation touching prices? We think there is no such principle.... Thus understood, "affected with a public interest" is the equivalent of "subject to the exercise of the police power"; and it is plain that nothing more was intended by the expression....

. . .

It is clear that there is no closed class or category of businesses affected with a public interest, and the function of courts in the application of the Fifth and Fourteenth Amendments is to determine in each case whether circumstances vindicate the challenged regulation as a reasonable exertion of governmental authority or condemn it as arbitrary or discriminatory.... These decisions must rest, finally, upon the basis that the requirements of due process were not met because the laws were found arbitrary in their operation and effect. But there can be no doubt that upon proper occasion and by appropriate measures the state may regulate a business in any of its aspects, including the prices to be charged for the products or commodities it sells.

. . .

Tested by these considerations we find no basis in the due process clause of the Fourteenth Amendment for condemning the provisions of the Agriculture and Markets Law here drawn into question.

The judgment is affirmed.

■ Separate opinion of MR. JUSTICE MCREYNOLDS

. . .

Not only does the statute interfere arbitrarily with the rights of the little grocer to conduct his business according to standards long accepted—complete destruction may follow; but it takes away the liberty of 12,000,000 consumers to buy a necessity of life in an open market. It imposes direct and arbitrary burdens upon those already seriously impoverished with the alleged immediate design of affording special benefits to others. To him with less than 9 cents it says: You cannot procure a quart of milk from the grocer although he is anxious to accept what you can pay and the demands of your household are urgent! A superabundance; but no child can purchase from a willing storekeeper below the figure appointed by three men at headquarters! And this is true although the storekeeper himself may have bought from a willing producer at half that rate and must sell quickly or lose his stock through deterioration. The fanciful scheme is to protect the farmer against undue exactions by prescribing the price at which milk disposed of by him at will may be resold! . . .

. . .

Mr. Justice Van Devanter, Mr. Justice Sutherland, and Mr. Justice Butler authorize me to say that they concur in this opinion.

Day–Brite Lighting, Inc. v. Missouri

Supreme Court of the United States, 1952.
342 U.S. 421.

■ MR. JUSTICE DOUGLAS delivered the opinion of the Court.

Missouri has a statute, Mo.Rev.Stat., 1949, first enacted in 1897, which was designed to end the coercion of employees by employers in the exercise of the franchise. It provides that an employee may absent himself from his employment for four hours between the opening and closing of the polls without penalty, and that any employer who among other things deducts wages for that absence is guilty of a misdemeanor.

. . . November 5, 1946, was a day for general elections in Missouri, the polls being open from 6 A.M. to 7 P.M. One Grotemeyer, an employee of appellant, was on a shift that worked from 8 A.M. to 4:30 P.M. each day, with thirty minutes for lunch. His rate of pay was $1.60 an hour. He requested four hours from the scheduled work day to vote on November 5, 1946. That request was refused; but Grotemeyer and all other employees on his shift were allowed to leave at 3 P.M. that day, which gave them four consecutive hours to vote before the polls closed.

Grotemeyer left his work at 3 P.M. in order to vote and did not return to work that day. He was not paid for the hour and a half between 3 P.M. and 4:30 P.M. Appellant was found guilty and fined for penalizing Grotemeyer in violation of the statute. The judgment was affirmed by the Missouri Supreme Court over the objection that the statute violated the Due Process and the Equal Protection Clauses of the Fourteenth Amendment and the Contract Clause of Art. I, § 10.

The liberty of contract argument pressed on us is reminiscent of the philosophy of *Lochner v. State. of New York*, 198 U.S. 45, which invalidated a New York law prescribing maximum hours for work in bakeries; *Coppage v. State of Kansas*, 236 U.S. 1, which struck down a Kansas statute outlawing "yellow dog" contracts; *Adkins v. Children's Hospital of District of Columbia*, 261 U.S. 525, which held unconstitutional a federal statute fixing minimum wage standards for women in the District of Columbia, and others of that vintage. Our recent decisions make plain that we do not sit as a super-legislature to weigh the wisdom of legislation nor to decide whether the policy which it expresses offends the public welfare. The legislative power has limits, as *Tot v. United States*, 319 U.S. 463 holds. But the state legislatures have constitutional authority to experiment with new techniques; they are entitled to their own standard of the public welfare; they may within extremely broad limits control practices in the business-labor field, so long as specific constitutional prohibitions are not violated and so long as conflicts with valid and controlling federal laws are avoided. That is the essence of *West Coast Hotel Co. v. Parrish*, 300 U.S. 379; *Nebbia v. People of State of New York*, 291 U.S. 502.

West Coast Hotel Co. v. Parrish, overruling *Adkins v. Children's Hospital*, held constitutional a state law fixing minimum wages for women. The present statute contains in form a minimum wage requirement. There is a difference in the purpose of the legislation. Here it is not the protection of the health and morals of the citizen. Missouri by this legislation has sought to safeguard the right of suffrage by taking from employers the incentive and power to use their leverage over employees to influence the vote. But the police power is not confined to a narrow category; it extends, as stated in *Noble State Bank v. Haskell*, 219 U.S. 104, 111, to all the great public needs. The protection of the right of suffrage under our scheme of things is basic and fundamental.

The only semblance of substance in the constitutional objection to Missouri's law is that the employer must pay wages for a period in which the employee performs no services. Of course many forms of regulation reduce the net return of the enterprise; yet that gives rise to no constitutional infirmity. Most regulations of business necessarily impose financial burdens on the enterprise for which no compensation is paid. Those are part of the costs of our civilization. Extreme cases are conjured up where an employer is required to pay wages for a period that has no relation to the legitimate end. Those cases can await decision as and when they arise. The present law has no such infirmity. It is designed to eliminate any penalty for exercising the right of suffrage and to remove a practical obstacle to getting out the vote. The public welfare is a broad and inclusive concept. The moral, social, economic, and physical well-being of the community is one part of it; the political well-being, another. The police power which is adequate to fix the financial burden for one is adequate for the other. The judgment of the legislature that time out for voting should cost the employee nothing may be a debatable one. It is indeed conceded by the opposition to be such. But if our recent cases mean anything, they leave debatable issues as respects business, economic, and social affairs to legislative decision. We could strike down this law only if we returned to the philosophy of the *Lochner*, *Coppage*, and *Adkins* cases.

Affirmed.

■ MR. JUSTICE FRANKFURTER concurs in the result.

■ MR. JUSTICE JACKSON, dissenting.

. . .

Appellant employed one Grotemeyer, under a union contract, on an hourly basis at $1.60 per hour for each hour worked. He demanded a four-hour leave of absence, with full pay, on election day to do campaigning and to get out the vote. It is stipulated that his residence was 200 feet from the polling place and that it actually took him about five minutes to vote. Appellant closed the day's work for all employees one and one-half hours earlier than usual, which gave them the statutory four hours before the polls closed. For failure to pay something less than $3 for this hour and a half which Grotemeyer did not work and for which his contract did not provide that he should be paid, the employer is convicted of crime under the statute set forth in the Court's opinion.

To sustain this statute by resort to the analogy of minimum wage laws seems so farfetched and unconvincing as to demonstrate its weakness rather than its strength. Because a State may require payment of a minimum wage for hours that are worked it does not follow that it may compel payment for time that is not worked. To overlook a distinction so fundamental is to confuse the point in issue.

The Court, by speaking of the statute as though it applies only to industry, sinister and big, further obscures the real principle involved. The statute plainly requires farmers, small service enterprises, professional offices, housewives with domestic help, and all other employers, not only to allow their employees time to vote, but to pay them for time to do so. It does not, however, require the employee to use any part of such time for that purpose. Such legislation stands in a class by itself and should not be uncritically commended as a mere regulation of "practices in the business-labor field."

. . .

It undoubtedly is the right of every union negotiating with an employer to bargain for voting time without loss of pay. It is equally the right of any individual employee to make that part of his hire. I have no reason to doubt that a large number of voters already have voluntary arrangements which make their absence for voting without cost. But a constitutional philosophy which sanctions intervention by the State to fix terms of pay without work may be available tomorrow to give constitutional sanction to state-imposed terms of employment less benevolent.

b. FREEDOM OF ENTERPRISE UNDER INTERNATIONAL HUMAN RIGHTS LAW

International human rights law contains no general right to "liberty" or freedom of enterprise. The Universal Declaration and the Covenants contain no reference to freedom of enterprise, but such a freedom may be implied or assumed among the rights recognized in the Universal Declaration. Does "the right to own property alone as well as in association with others" and the right not to "be arbitrarily deprived" of property imply or assume a right of free enterprise? See Article 17. Is freedom to found an enterprise included within the freedom of association (Article 20)? Is freedom of enterprise one of the "economic, social and cultural rights indispensable for [one's] dignity and the free development of [one's] personality" (Article 22)? Is it included in the "free choice of employment" (Article 23(1)), or derived from "the right to a standard of living adequate for the health and well-being of [oneself] and [one's] family" (Article 25)? Is it implied by the right to "[t]echnical and professional education" (Article 26(1))? Are some aspects of freedom of enterprise fortified by "the right to the protection of the moral *and material interests* resulting from any scientific, literary or artistic production of which [one] is the author" (Article 27(2))?

The implications and assumptions of freedom of enterprise in the various guarantees in the Universal Declaration and other international human rights instruments may suggest a basic principle of free enterprise as a matter of customary international law. Any such principle presumably would be subject to the limitations of Article 29, clauses 2–3 of the Universal Declaration:

> 2.   In the exercise of his rights and freedoms, everyone shall be subject only to such limitations as are determined by law solely for the purpose of securing due recognition and respect for the rights and freedoms of others and of meeting just requirements of morality, public order and the general welfare in a democratic society.

> 3.   These rights and freedoms may in no case be exercised contrary to the purposes and principles of the United Nations

c.   FREEDOM OF ENTERPRISE UNDER CONTEMPORARY CONSTITUTIONS

Contemporary constitutions guarantee or assume freedom of enterprise subject to general police power limitations. Compare Article 12 of the Basic Law of Germany.

David P. Currie, *Lochner Abroad: Substantive Due Process and Equal Protection in the Federal Republic of Germany*

1989 Sup. Ct. Rev. 333, 347–50 (1990).

Article 12(1) [of the German Basic Law (*Grundgesetz*)] codifies the occupational freedom recognized by the [U.S.] Supreme Court in such cases as *Lochner*:

> All Germans shall have the right freely to choose their trade, occupation, or profession, their place of work and their place of training. The practice of trades, occupations, and professions may be regulated by or pursuant to statute.

Like the right to property, occupational freedom is taken very seriously in Germany as an element of individual autonomy and an essential basis of other freedoms. The right extends to preparation for—as well as exercise of—an occupation. Like property, it may be limited basically only in accordance with statute. Even statutory limitations, moreover, have been subjected to sometimes demanding scrutiny under the pervasive proportionality principle, and quite a number of them have been struck down.

The leading case remains the seminal 1958 *Pharmacy* decision,[113] which established varying degrees of judicial review (Stufentheorie) according to the severity of the intrusion. To begin with, regulation of how a profession is practiced is easier to justify than limitation of entry into the profession itself:

> The practice of an occupation may be restricted by reasonable regulations predicated on considerations of the common good. The freedom to choose an occupation, however, may be restricted only insofar as an especially important public interest compellingly requires . . .—[and] only to the extent that the protection cannot be accomplished by a lesser restriction on freedom of choice.

Moreover, entry limitations such as educational requirements designed to protect the public from unqualified practitioners are easier to justify than those irrelevant to individual ability; and the desire to protect existing practitioners from competition, the Court said, could "never" justify an entry restriction. On the basis of this calculus the Constitutional Court has achieved results reminiscent of those reached by the Supreme Court during the *Lochner* period.

As under the reign of *Lochner*, a great many limitations of occupational freedom have been upheld—some of them rather intrusive. Compulsory retirement ages may be set for chimney sweeps and midwives. The sale of headache remedies may be restricted to pharmacists, and the latter may be forbidden to own more than one store. Shops may be required to close on Saturday afternoons, Sundays, holidays, and in the evening; nocturnal baking may be prohibited. The legislature may outlaw the erection or expansion of flour mills and limit the amount of flour produced. The state may monopolize building insurance and employment agencies. It may require employers to hire the handicapped, limit the number of notaries, and require them to serve welfare applicants without charge.

At the same time, throughout its history the Constitutional Court has struck down as unwarranted infringements on occupational freedom an impressive array of restrictions that would pass muster without question in the United States today. The state may not limit the number of drugstores on the ground that there are already enough of them or license taxicabs only in cases of special need. It may not require vending machines to be shut down after stores are closed or require barbers who close on Saturday afternoon to shut down on Monday morning too. It may ban neither door-to-door sales of veterinary medicines nor C.O.D. shipments of live animals. It may not require that retailers be competent to practice their trade, forbid doctors to specialize in more than one field or to perform services outsider their specialties, or ban the collection of dead birds for scientific purposes. Finally, in perfect contrast to the decision that sealed the death of economic due process in the United States, it may not forbid the

---

113.   7 BVerfGE 377 (1958).

manufacture and sale of healthful food products on the ground that they might be confused with chocolate.[139]

Here too, ... there are strong indications that the Basic Law may impose affirmative duties on government. The most notable decision is that in the so-called *Numerus Clausus* case,[140] where, despite insisting that it was not deciding whether Article 12(1) required the state to set up institutions of higher learning, the Constitutional Court flatly declared that the right to obtain a professional education was worthless if the state did not provide one, and therefore that access to public education was not a matter of legislative grace. ...

Chocolate Candy Case

Federal Constitutional Court of Germany, First Senate, 1980.
53 BVerfGE 135.*

[A federal consumer-protection statute banned the sale of foodstuffs that might be confused with products made of chocolate. The statute was successfully invoked against a producer of Christmas and Easter candy made of puffed rice and coated with chocolate. The company brought the constitutional complaint grounded on Article 12(1) against a decision of the Federal High Court of Justice sustaining the ban as applied.]

. . .

II.   The constitutional complaint is justified.

I.   Section 14(2) of the Chocolate Products Act of June 30, 1975, is incompatible with Article 12(1) to the extent that it imposes an absolute ban on the sale of the designated product. The provision under discussion regulates the practice of an occupation. Under Article 12(1), a regulation may be imposed only by law or pursuant to a law. If an administrative decree regulates the practice of an occupation, it must be rooted in a delegated power authorized by the Basic Law and adhere to the confines of this delegated power. Reasonable concerns for the common good must justify the regulation, and the means chosen [to implement the regulation] must be necessary and proper for the achievement of its purpose. Section 14(2) of the Chocolate Products Act satisfies this requirement only in part....

(C) (aa) In deciding whether a regulation [which limits] the practice of a trade is consistent with the principle of proportionality, we must take into account the discretion which the legislature has—within the frame-

---

139. 53 BVerfGE 135, 145–47 (1980). Cf. Carolene Products Co. v. United States, 323 U.S. 18 (1944)....

... None of this is to say that there is actually more occupational freedom in West Germany than in the United States. Notwithstanding the lack of judicial interest in the area, legislators in this country seem somewhat less inclined to inhibit such freedom than their German counterparts, as Americans seem more mistrustful of government in general....

140. 33 BVerfGE 303 (1972).

work of its authority—in the sphere of commercial activity. The Basic Law grants the legislature wide latitude in setting economic policy and devising the means necessary to implement it. In the instant case, however, the legislature has exceeded the proper bounds of its discretion, for less restrictive means can easily achieve the purpose of the statute.... Statutes like those involved here are designed to protect the consumer from confusion when purchasing food and from threats to his health.... Section 14(2) of the Chocolate Products Act is designed to protect the consumer from deception. This protection is undoubtedly in the public interest and justifies restrictions on the practice of a trade.

To achieve this purpose the legislature has not only required proper labeling but also prohibited the sale of the product. Prohibiting [the sale of a product], however, is one of the most drastic means imaginable of protecting the consumer from confusion and deceptive trade practices. [The regulator] can ordinarily avert these threats to the public interest just as effectively and efficiently by mandating proper labeling. It may indeed be true that a consumer bases his decision to purchase a product not on a careful scrutiny of the product but rather on its external appearance. But this does not justify the presumption that [the regulator] must ban the sale of every form of food product described in section 14(2) of the statute in order to protect the "flighty" consumer. Nor do other considerations justify the competitive edge given here to pure chocolate products. If a case involves possible confusion between milk and margarine products, then the legislature may indeed adopt measures in the public interest for maintaining a productive farm economy—thus serving a purpose beyond the immediate goal of consumer protection. In the instant case, however, no justifiable grounds exist for [imposing] a broader restriction than is needed to safeguard the consumer from false labeling. Thus [the regulator] should only take measures which are necessary for the protection of the consumer. To accomplish this end it would have been enough to require proper labeling.

Notes

1. Why are the economic rights described in *Allgeyer* and protected by the Supreme Court during the *Lochner* era no longer favored in U.S. constitutional law? Because they lack a textual basis in the U.S. Constitution? Because they are not plausibly considered as fundamental human rights? Because they are tainted by their association with laissez faire economic policy? Because they are not vulnerable to mistreatment in a democratic political process (cf. the *Carolene Products* footnote, supra p. 221)?

Justice Holmes stated in his celebrated dissent in *Lochner* that "a Constitution is not intended to embody a particular economic theory." Is this statement true as a general matter, or true of the U.S. Constitution specifically? Although it might not have been possible to embody a particular economic theory in a human rights treaty during the Cold War, would it be objectionable to do so today?

2.   Is the right to free choice of trade, occupation or profession, protected by Article 12 of the German constitution, also protected by the U.S. Constitution? Should it be? Are state legislatures free to create unreasonable barriers to entry into particular occupations? Are they free to assign individuals to particular occupations? Cf. *Kotch v. Board of River Port Pilot Commissioners*, 330 U.S. 552 (1947) (upholding restrictions on entry to profession of port pilot despite resulting pattern of nepotism).

3.   Should there be a human right to practice one's trade as one sees fit, without being subjected to "unreasonable" or "disproportional" limitations? As the *Chocolate Candy* case illustrates, the German constitutional court enforces this economic right under its national constitution. German constitutional law has also influenced the broader use of proportionality as a limitation on economic regulation in European Community law, enforced by the European Court of Justice. See Note on the European Court of Justice as a Human Rights Tribunal, supra Part III, Chapter 3(B)(2).

4.   Despite the U.S. Supreme Court's abandonment of economic due process, a minority of state supreme courts continue to apply more substantial review under the due process clauses (or their equivalents) of state constitutions. See Robert F. Williams, State Constitutional Law 256–65 (2d ed. 1993); *Developments in the Law–Interpretation of State Constitutional Rights*, 95 Harv. L. Rev. 1324, 1463–93 (1982).

5.   Does a right to freedom of enterprise include a right to compete freely, without undue restraint by private anticompetitive conduct or government-granted monopoly? The common law tradition disfavored private restraint of trade, and limited the authority of the Executive to grant monopolies. In 1873, the four dissenting Justices in the *Slaughter-House Cases*, 83 U.S. (16 Wall.) 36 (1872), agreed that the privileges and immunities of citizens of the United States under the Fourteenth Amendment included the right to engage in common occupations without the obstruction of state-granted monopolies.

Modern antitrust law was launched by the Sherman Act of 1890, which condemned combinations in restraint of trade and monopolization of markets. Historically, U.S. antitrust law reflected the fear of multiple dangers—not only exploitation of consumers, but also curtailing opportunities of small businessmen, and the acquisition of political power by massive corporations. See Herbert Hovenkamp, Federal Antitrust Policy 51–52 (1994). The Sherman Act has not, however, been interpreted as prohibiting state governments from granting local monopolies or coordinating anticompetitive arrangements among producers. Id. at 670–74. Nor does the statute prevent other federal statutes from authorizing anticompetitive arrangements at the national level.

Since the 1980s, U.S. antitrust policy has tended to adopt a more limited economic orientation, focusing on the harm that certain anticompetitive arrangements pose to consumers, and deemphasizing the protection of the freedom of enterprise of competitors. Id. 69–70.

During the same period, antitrust policy under the rubric of "competition policy" has gained wider attention in Europe. Initially, European Community competition policy had emphasized breaking down private barriers to the creation of a unified market within the community, complementing the dismantling of tariffs and other governmental barriers to intracommunity trade. More recently, however, European competition policy has adopted a broader focus on competition per se, and preventing the abuse of power over competitors. The European Community has also targeted public monopolies in particular sectors. See, e.g., Giuliano Amato, Antitrust and the Bounds of Power (1997); Per Jebsen & Robert Stevens, *Assumptions, Goals and Dominant Undertakings: The Regulation of Competition under Article 86 of the European Union*, 64 Antitrust L.J. 443 (1996). (A related assault on traditional public monopolies has occurred in the context of broadcasting, where the European Court of Human Rights has found that a public broadcasting monopoly violated Article 10 of the European Convention. See *Informationsverein Lentia v. Austria*, 276 Eur. Ct. H.R. (ser. A), 17 E.H.R.R. 93 (1993); cf. *Elliniki Radiophonia Tileorassi AE v. Dimotiki Etairia Piliroforissis*, 1991 E.C.R. I–2925, [1994] 4 C.M.L.R. 540 (1991) (finding broadcasting monopoly incompatible with EC law).)

Should the greater international attention to anticompetitive conduct be seen as an instrumentally justified economic policy, or should it also be understood as reflecting a human right to freedom of competition? If the latter, then who is the holder of the right—consumers, entrepreneurs, shareholders, or corporations as such?

On the difficulty of finding common global agreement on competition policy, see Eleanor M. Fox, *Toward World Antitrust and Market Access*, 91 Am. J. Int'l L. 1 (1997).

C.   SOCIAL WELFARE RIGHTS

The most basic social right is the right to the means of subsistence. A minimum level of subsistence is necessary for human life to continue at all; respect for human dignity has been thought to require assurance of a higher standard of living than that bare minimum. Article 25(1) of the Universal Declaration provides:

> Everyone has the right to a standard of living adequate for the health and well-being of himself and of his family, including food, clothing, housing and medical care and necessary social services, and the right to security in the event of unemployment, sickness, disability, widowhood, old age or other lack of livelihood in circumstances beyond his control.

If the state must act as the ultimate guarantor of the standard of living of those for whom the private sector does not adequately provide, then what level of well-being should it protect? Must everyone be guaranteed sufficient resources, either in cash or in kind, to ensure both "his dignity and the free development of his personality" (cf. UDHR art. 22)?

Article 9 of the ICESCR recognizes "the right of everyone to social security, including social insurance." That terminology reflects a distinction commonly drawn between "social insurance" and "social assistance" as forms of social security. Social insurance programs often aim at replacing income lost by workers and their families as a consequence of unemployment, disability, retirement or death; the financial support for these programs often includes specific contributions from covered workers or their employers. Social assistance programs, in contrast, often respond to actual need without regard to prior work history or contributions, and are funded from general tax revenues. Social insurance programs often provide higher benefit levels than social assistance programs, and may correlate with the worker's prior level of earnings, whereas social assistance benefits may be designed to provide a minimum acceptable level of support.

To what extent should social assistance, or social insurance, be understood as a right, and if so, how should such a right be legally embodied? Should the formulation of social security policies be entrusted exclusively to the legislature, or are social security rights deserving of constitutional protection? Is a right to social assistance judicially enforceable? Is it worthy of some form of constitutional recognition even if it is not ordinarily enforceable by judicial means?

This section first considers the right to subsistence as an example of a "minimum core obligation" immediately binding on States Parties to the ICESCR. Next, it examines contrasting approaches to the recognition—or nonrecognition—of social assistance rights within national constitutional systems (including the contrasting approaches of different states within the United States). Third, the section briefly addresses the implications of international protection of civil rights, such as equality or fair procedure, for social welfare programs. It closes with a hypothetical note, asking the reader to juxtapose trends in U.S. welfare policy with international standards.

Note on Obligations Under the ICESCR

The obligations accepted in the ICESCR must be interpreted in light of two preliminary Articles. First, the undertaking clause in Article 2(1) provides: "Each State Party to the present Covenant undertakes to take steps, individually and through international assistance and cooperation, especially economic and technical, to the maximum of its available resources, with a view to achieving progressively the full realization of the rights recognized in the present Covenant by all appropriate means, including particularly the adoption of legislative measures." Second, unlike the ICCPR (which includes limitations clauses in particular articles, but not a general limitations clause applicable to all articles in the Covenant), the ICESCR contains a general limitations clause, Article 4, providing that, "in the enjoyment of those rights provided by the State in conformity with the present Covenant, the State may subject such rights only to such limitations as are determined by law only in so far as this may be compatible with the nature of these rights and solely for the purpose of promoting the general welfare in a democratic society."

The implementation procedures of the ICESCR do not create a mechanism for the binding resolution of disputes over states' compliance with their obligations. The implementation procedures require the States Parties to submit reports to the Economic and Social Council of the United Nations (ECOSOC), and allows ECOSOC to make recommendations of a general nature. ICESCR arts. 16–21.

In 1985, however, ECOSOC created a body of outside experts, the Committee on Economic, Social and Cultural Rights, to review reports submitted by States Parties. This Committee was designed as an analogue to the Human Rights Committee expressly created by the ICCPR, reflecting the perceived success of the Human Rights Committee. The Economic, Social and Cultural Rights Committee has adopted some of the techniques employed by the Human Rights Committee for communicating its understanding of its Covenant, such as making Concluding Observations after the examination of individual country reports, and issuing General Comments of an interpretive character. The following General Comment, offering the Committee's perspective on the nature of the obligations imposed by the ICESCR, is particularly relevant to the provisions regarding social welfare rights.

Committee on Economic, Social and Cultural Rights, General Comment 3 (1990)

U.N. Doc. HRI/GEN/1/Rev. 1 at 45.

The nature of States parties' obligations (art. 2, para. 1 of the Covenant).

1.   Article 2 is of particular importance to a full understanding of the Covenant and must be seen as having a dynamic relationship with all of the other provisions of the Covenant. It describes the nature of the general legal obligations undertaken by States parties to the Covenant. Those obligations include both what may be termed (following the work of the International Law Commission) obligations of conduct and obligations of result. While great emphasis has sometimes been placed on the difference between the formulations used in this provision and that contained in the equivalent article 2 of the International Covenant on Civil and Political Rights, it is not always recognized that there are also significant similarities. In particular, while the Covenant provides for progressive realization and acknowledges the constraints due to the limits of available resources, it also imposes various obligations which are of immediate effect. Of these, two are of particular importance in understanding the precise nature of States parties obligations. One of these, which is dealt with in a separate General Comment, and which is to be considered by the Committee at its sixth session, is the "undertaking to guarantee" that relevant rights "will be exercised without discrimination ...".

2.   The other is the undertaking in article 2 (1) "to take steps", which in itself, is not qualified or limited by other considerations. The full meaning of the phrase can also be gauged by noting some of the different language versions. In English the undertaking is "to take steps", in French it is "to act" ("s'engage à agir") and in Spanish it is "to adopt measures" ("a adoptar medidas"). Thus while the full realization of the relevant rights may be achieved progressively, steps towards that goal must be taken within a reasonably short time after the Covenant's entry into force for the States concerned. Such steps should be deliberate, concrete and targeted as clearly as possible towards meeting the obligations recognized in the Covenant.

3.   The means which should be used in order to satisfy the obligation to take steps are stated in article 2 (1) to be "all appropriate means, including particularly the adoption of legislative measures". The Committee recognizes that in many instances legislation is highly desirable and in some cases may even be indispensable. For example, it may be difficult to combat discrimination effectively in the absence of a sound legislative foundation for the necessary measures. In fields such as health, the protection of children and mothers, and education, as well as in respect of the matters dealt with in articles 6 to 9, legislation may also be an indispensable element for many purposes.

4.   The Committee notes that States parties have generally been conscientious in detailing at least some of the legislative measures that they have taken in this regard. It wishes to emphasize, however, that the adoption of legislative measures, as specifically foreseen by the Covenant, is by no means exhaustive of the obligations of States parties. Rather, the phrase "by all appropriate means" must be given its full and natural meaning. While each State party must decide for itself which means are the most appropriate under the circumstances with respect to each of the rights, the "appropriateness" of the means chosen will not always be self-evident. It is therefore desirable that States parties' reports should indicate not only the measures that have been taken but also the basis on which they are considered to be the most "appropriate" under the circumstances. However, the ultimate determination as to whether all appropriate measures have been taken remains one for the Committee to make.

5.   Among the measures which might be considered appropriate, in addition to legislation, is the provision of judicial remedies with respect to rights which may, in accordance with the national legal system, be considered justiciable. The Committee notes, for example, that the enjoyment of the rights recognized, without discrimination, will often be appropriately promoted, in part, through the provision of judicial or other effective remedies. Indeed, those States parties which are also parties to the International Covenant on Civil and Political Rights are already obligated (by virtue of arts. 2 (paras. 1 and 3), 3 and 26) of that Covenant to ensure that any person whose rights or freedoms (including the right to equality and non-discrimination) recognized in that Covenant are violated, "shall have an effective remedy" (art. 2 (3) (a)). In addition, there are a number of

other provisions in the International Covenant on Economic, Social and Cultural Rights, including articles 3, 7 (a) (i), 8, 10 (3), 13 (2) (a), (3) and (4) and 15 (3) which would seem to be capable of immediate application by judicial and other organs in many national legal systems. Any suggestion that the provisions indicated are inherently non-self-executing would seem to be difficult to sustain.

6.   Where specific policies aimed directly at the realization of the rights recognized in the Covenant have been adopted in legislative form, the Committee would wish to be informed, inter alia, as to whether such laws create any right of action on behalf of individuals or groups who feel that their rights are not being fully realized. In cases where constitutional recognition has been accorded to specific economic, social and cultural rights, or where the provisions of the Covenant have been incorporated directly into national law, the Committee would wish to receive information as to the extent to which these rights are considered to be justiciable (i.e. able to be invoked before the courts). The Committee would also wish to receive specific information as to any instances in which existing constitutional provisions relating to economic, social and cultural rights have been weakened or significantly changed.

7.   Other measures which may also be considered "appropriate" for the purposes of article 2 (1) include, but are not limited to, administrative, financial, educational and social measures.

8.   The Committee notes that the undertaking "to take steps ... by all appropriate means including particularly the adoption of legislative measures" neither requires nor precludes any particular form of government or economic system being used as the vehicle for the steps in question, provided only that it is democratic and that all human rights are thereby respected. Thus, in terms of political and economic systems the Covenant is neutral and its principles cannot accurately be described as being predicated exclusively upon the need for, or the desirability of a socialist or a capitalist system, or a mixed, centrally planned, or laisser-faire economy, or upon any other particular approach. In this regard, the Committee reaffirms that the rights recognized in the Covenant are susceptible of realization within the context of a wide variety of economic and political systems, provided only that the interdependence and indivisibility of the two sets of human rights, as affirmed inter alia in the preamble to the Covenant, is recognized and reflected in the system in question. The Committee also notes the relevance in this regard of other human rights and in particular the right to development.

9.   The principal obligation of result reflected in article 2 (1) is to take steps "with a view to achieving progressively the full realization of the rights recognized" in the Covenant. The term "progressive realization" is often used to describe the intent of this phrase. The concept of progressive realization constitutes a recognition of the fact that full realization of all economic, social and cultural rights will generally not be able to be achieved in a short period of time. In this sense the obligation differs significantly from that contained in article 2 of the International Covenant on Civil and

Political Rights which embodies an immediate obligation to respect and ensure all of the relevant rights. Nevertheless, the fact that realization over time, or in other words progressively, is foreseen under the Covenant should not be misinterpreted as depriving the obligation of all meaningful content. It is on the one hand a necessary flexibility device, reflecting the realities of the real world and the difficulties involved for any country in ensuring full realization of economic, social and cultural rights. On the other hand, the phrase must be read in the light of the overall objective, indeed the raison d'être, of the Covenant which is to establish clear obligations for States parties in respect of the full realization of the rights in question. It thus imposes an obligation to move as expeditiously and effectively as possible towards that goal. Moreover, any deliberately retrogressive measures in that regard would require the most careful consideration and would need to be fully justified by reference to the totality of the rights provided for in the Covenant and in the context of the full use of the maximum available resources.

10.   On the basis of the extensive experience gained by the Committee, as well as by the body that preceded it, over a period of more than a decade of examining States parties' reports the Committee is of the view that a minimum core obligation to ensure the satisfaction of, at the very least, minimum essential levels of each of the rights is incumbent upon every State party. Thus, for example, a State party in which any significant number of individuals is deprived of essential foodstuffs, of essential primary health care, of basic shelter and housing, or of the most basic forms of education is, prima facie, failing to discharge its obligations under the Covenant. If the Covenant were to be read in such a way as not to establish such a minimum core obligation, it would be largely deprived of its raison d'être. By the same token, it must be noted that any assessment as to whether a State has discharged its minimum core obligation must also take account of resource constraints applying within the country concerned. Article 2 (1) obligates each State party to take the necessary steps "to the maximum of its available resources". In order for a State party to be able to attribute its failure to meet at least its minimum core obligations to a lack of available resources it must demonstrate that every effort has been made to use all resources that are at its disposition in an effort to satisfy, as a matter of priority, those minimum obligations.

11.   The Committee wishes to emphasize, however, that even where the available resources are demonstrably inadequate, the obligation remains for a State party to strive to ensure the widest possible enjoyment of the relevant rights under the prevailing circumstances. Moreover, the obligations to monitor the extent of the realization, or more especially of the non-realization, of economic, social and cultural rights, and to devise strategies and programmes for their promotion, are not in any way eliminated as a result of resource constraints. The Committee has already dealt with these issues in its General Comment 1 (1989).

12.   Similarly, the Committee underlines the fact that even in times of severe resources constraints whether caused by a process of adjustment, of

economic recession, or by other factors the vulnerable members of society can and indeed must be protected by the adoption of relatively low-cost targeted programmes. In support of this approach the Committee takes note of the analysis prepared by UNICEF entitled "Adjustment with a human face: protecting the vulnerable and promoting growth," the analysis by UNDP in its Human Development Report 1990 and the analysis by the World Bank in the World Development Report 1990.

13.   A final element of article 2 (1), to which attention must be drawn, is that the undertaking given by all States parties is "to take steps, individually and through international assistance and cooperation, especially economic and technical . . .". The Committee notes that the phrase "to the maximum of its available resources" was intended by the drafters of the Covenant to refer to both the resources existing within a State and those available from the international community through international cooperation and assistance. Moreover, the essential role of such cooperation in facilitating the full realization of the relevant rights is further underlined by the specific provisions contained in articles 11, 15, 22 and 23. With respect to article 22 the Committee has already drawn attention, in General Comment 2 (1990), to some of the opportunities and responsibilities that exist in relation to international cooperation. Article 23 also specifically identifies "the furnishing of technical assistance" as well as other activities, as being among the means of "international action for the achievement of the rights recognized . . .".

14.   The Committee wishes to emphasize that in accordance with Articles 55 and 56 of the Charter of the United Nations, with well-established principles of international law, and with the provisions of the Covenant itself, international cooperation for development and thus for the realization of economic, social and cultural rights is an obligation of all States. It is particularly incumbent upon those States which are in a position to assist others in this regard. The Committee notes in particular the importance of the Declaration on the Right to Development adopted by the General Assembly in its resolution 41/128 of 4 December 1986 and the need for States parties to take full account of all of the principles recognized therein. It emphasizes that, in the absence of an active programme of international assistance and cooperation on the part of all those States that are in a position to undertake one, the full realization of economic, social and cultural rights will remain an unfulfilled aspiration in many countries. In this respect, the Committee also recalls the terms of its General Comment 2 (1990).

Notes

1.   Is the Committee's interpretation of the obligation to take steps with a view to achieving progressively the full realization of the right recognized in the Covenant persuasive? How does the Committee justify the conclusion that this obligation has certain immediate consequences for some states?

Consider the Committee's listing in paragraph 5 of provisions that appear to be capable of immediate judicial enforcement. To what extent are those provisions sufficiently well-defined? To what extent is their enforcement independent of resource constraints? Do these provisions illustrate the overlapping nature of civil and political rights and economic, social and cultural rights?

Consider the Committee's illustrative list of minimum core obligations in paragraph 10. Does the Covenant require states to make every effort to satisfy these minimum obligations, as a matter of priority, on an immediate basis (as the Committee asserts)? What considerations would justify a state in failing to assure minimum essential levels of foodstuffs, health care, or basic shelter and housing to a substantial segment of its population?

Should these minimum obligations also have been included as obligations capable of judicial enforcement?

2.   President Carter's proposal for "understandings" to be adopted in the course of ratifying the ICESCR included the statement that: "The United States understands paragraph (1) of Article 2 as establishing that the provisions of Articles 1 through 15 of this Covenant describe goals to be achieved progressively rather than through immediate implementation." How does that interpretation compare with the Committee's interpretation? Under the Committee's interpretation, if the United States were to ratify the ICESCR without entering any reservations, what would the immediate consequences be with respect to "minimum core obligations"?

3.   The Committee adopted General Comment 3 in 1990. Since that time, it has further elaborated its views on the methods of implementation of the Covenant in General Comment 9 (The domestic application of the Covenant), U.N. Doc. E/C.12/1998/24 (1998), and General Comment 10 (The role of national human rights institutions in the protection of economic, social and cultural rights) U.N. Doc. E/C.12/1998/25 (1998). The Committee states in paragraph 5 of General Comment 9:

> The Covenant does not stipulate the specific means by which it is to be implemented in the national legal order. And there is no provision obligating its comprehensive incorporation or requiring it to be accorded any specific type of status in national law. Although the precise method by which Covenant rights are given effect in national law is a matter for each State party to decide, the means used should be appropriate in the sense of producing results which are consistent with the full discharge of its obligations by the State party. The means chosen are also subject to review as part of the Committee's examination of the State party's compliance with its obligations under the Covenant.

The General Comment "strongly encourages formal adoption or incorporation of the Covenant in national law" (¶ 8); urges establishment of judicial remedies for the enforcement of Covenant rights, at least in their "justiciable dimensions" (¶ 10); and invokes the generally accepted rule that domestic courts should construe domestic law, as far as possible, in a manner that conforms to a state's international legal obligations (¶ 15).

4.   The Committee's fullest exploration of a particular right in the Covenant concerns the right to adequate housing, as reflected in General Comment 4 (The right to adequate housing (art. 11.1 of the Covenant)) (1991), HRI/GEN/1/Rev.1 at 53, and General Comment 7 (on forced evictions), E/C.12/1997/4 (1997).

5.   In addition to the Committee's General Comments, other attempts have been made to elaborate the consequences of states' undertakings under the ICESCR. In 1986, a symposium convened in association with the International Commission of Jurists produced The Limburg Principles on the Implementation of the International Covenant on Economic, Social and Cultural Rights, reprinted with supporting papers at 9 Hum. Rts. Q. 121–286 (1987). A decade later, a follow-up conference produced The Maastricht Guidelines on Violations of Economic, Social and Cultural Rights, reprinted with commentary in 20 Hum. Rts.Q. 691–730 (1998).

The following four cases address the *constitutional* status of social welfare rights, in one foreign country and three U.S. jurisdictions. To what extent do constitutional analyses of social welfare rights turn upon different societies' fundamental understandings of the claims that human beings can make on government and on each other, and to what extent do they turn on institutional considerations concerning the proper role of a constitution and of the judiciary?

V. v. Municipality X. and Council of the Canton of Bern

Federal Court of Switzerland, 1995.
BGE 122 I 367.

[The three brothers V. fled to Switzerland from Czechoslovakia with their mother in 1980, and were recognized as refugees. In 1990, after a criminal conviction, the brothers were deported to Czechoslovakia (political conditions there having changed in 1989). They returned to Switzerland illegally in 1991, and lived at the home of their mother, who had become a Swiss citizen, in municipality X. Renewed attempts to deport them failed, because the Czech Republic took the position that they had been deprived of Czech nationality and had not reacquired it.

Being unauthorized to work in Switzerland after their reentry, the brothers sought social assistance from municipality X. Assistance was denied on the grounds that the brothers were not lawfully resident in Switzerland, that if they applied for reacquisition of their Czech nationality they could be deported to the Czech Republic and would be able to work there, and that therefore they were responsible for creating their own situation of need. The brothers brought a constitutional complaint to the Federal Court.

The Court began by observing that the newly revised constitution of the canton of Bern included an express constitutional right to security of livelihood, but that this provision was inapplicable at the time when the case arose. Accordingly, the case would be decided under the Swiss Federal Constitution.]

2.-a) The Federal Constitution ... does not expressly provide a basic right to security of livelihood (*Existenzsicherung*). There are however also unwritten constitutional rights to be derived from the Constitution. An unwritten constitutional guarantee of liberty rights not named in the Constitution has been assumed by the Federal Court in relation to those freedoms that are the prerequisites for the exercise of other liberty rights named in the Constitution or that otherwise appear as indispensable elements of the legal order of the Confederation as a state based on democracy and the rule of law. In order not to overstep the limits of the judicial role, the Federal Court has always also examined whether the asserted guarantee reflects widespread constitutional practice in the cantons and is supported by a general consensus. Thus the Federal Court has recognized the right to property, freedom of expression, personal freedom, freedom of language, and freedom of assembly as unwritten federal constitutional rights, but has not recognized, for example, a right to free design of grave monuments, a right to education, or a freedom to demonstrate extending beyond the content of freedom of expression and freedom of assembly.

b) The security of elemental human necessities like food, clothing and shelter is *the* precondition for human existence and development. It is simultaneously an indispensable element of a community based on democracy and the rule of law. Therefore security of livelihood satisfies the requirements for being guaranteed as an unwritten constitutional right.

The further question then arises whether such a fundamental right is supported by a general consensus. This consensus is not to be measured exclusively by the written constitutional law of the cantons, which is incomplete. It can also arise from actual practice and constitutional scholarship or from other sources. As far as written cantonal constitutional law is concerned, the constitutions of the canton of Basel and the new constitution of the canton of Bern (not yet applicable to the present case) guarantee explicitly a fundamental right to security of livelihood. The same is true for the proposed new constitution of the canton of Appenzell.... Other cantonal constitutions have included social assistance in the form of a provision on governmental goals or tasks for the legislature. Although in the newer constitutions of the cantons of Aargau, Uri, Solthurn, Thurgau and Glarus, it was deliberately decided not to anchor an individual legal right to security of livelihood, this decision was not based on an objection in principle, but rather on the consideration that public social assistance has a subsidiary character, and that the cooperation of the Confederation, cantons and municipalities in the area of social security necessarily requires statutory regulation. At the level of legislation all the cantons proceed from the assumption that assistance is to be provided to the needy, whether or not in the form of an individual right, if the relevant criteria are satisfied. The principle that a citizen who falls into economic need must be supported (by his home municipality) has long been known to Swiss law; it dates back to the Sixteenth Century. The Federal Court for its part has explained in older decisions on the subject of intercantonal disputes over care of the poor that it is both a humanitarian obligation and a duty inherent in the purpose of the modern state to preserve persons found within its territory against physical ruin when necessary. [Citing cases from 1925 and 1914.]

In scholarly writings a fundamental right to security of livelihood is almost unanimously recognized. [Citing as foundational J. P. Müller, *Soziale Grundrechte in der Verfassung?*, 92 Zeitschrift für Schweizerisches Recht (n.s) 896 (1973), as well as later writings.] The view primarily expressed in scholarship is that it involves an unwritten constitutional right. Various other constitutional starting points have also been invoked: the constitutional principle of human dignity, which guarantees to every person what she may expect from the community by virtue of her humanity; the right to life as the core of personal freedom, which would no longer be preserved if the most minimal prerequisites of survival were not ensured; personal freedom in its form as a guarantee of all fundamental manifestations of the development of the personality; the principle of equality, which also performs the function of guaranteeing minimal substantive justice; and finally the constitutional provision of Art. 48(1) BV, according to which the needy are to be supported by the canton in which they reside, which could also be understood as a claim of fundamental right.*

c) If accordingly it can be assumed that the guarantee of a constitutional right to security of livelihood is supported by a widespread consensus, the further question arises whether such a right is sufficiently justiciable. While defensive claims of fundamental right do not create problems in this respect, claims to benefits presuppose that they are normatively sufficiently determinate and can be made concrete and enforced by judges using the procedures and means available to them. In this connection, judges must respect the functional limits of their jurisdiction. In view of the scarcity of public resources, they do not have the authority to set the priorities for distribution of funds. Therefore only a minimum of public benefits can be directly required by fundamental rights and enforceable by judges.

The fundamental right to security of livelihood satisfies these criteria for justiciability. It is inherently addressed to a minimum required by fundamental right (assistance in situations of need). The governmental tasks connected therewith are recognized in the cantons as a result of the

---

* [Article 48 of the Federal Constitution (BV), added in 1975, provides:

   1. The needy are supported by the Canton in which they reside. The costs of support are borne by the Canton of residence.

2. The Confederation may regulate claims of the Canton of residence against a former Canton of residence or the Canton of origin.

(Editors' Note).]

legislation on social assistance; they require no additional basic decision of budgetary policy. What represents the indispensable prerequisites of a life consistent with human dignity is sufficiently clearly recognizable and accessible to investigation in a judicial proceeding. A guaranteed minimum income is not however at issue. All that the Constitution requires is what is indispensable for an existence consistent with human dignity, and what can shield a person from the indignity of life as a beggar. It is primarily the task of the relevant community to determine on the basis of its legislation the type and extent of services necessary in a particular case. For this purpose monetary benefits and also in-kind benefits come into consideration. Direct invocation of the constitutional right only becomes necessary if the results of the ordinary legislation cannot satisfy the constitutional minimum standard. In the present case, it is not appropriate to discuss that standard in further detail, because the type and extent of the benefits are not disputed, but rather the only question is whether the plaintiffs may be denied support altogether.

d) The plaintiffs are, however, not Swiss citizens.

To the extent that a fundamental right is based on human rights, it is available both to Swiss citizens and to aliens. The Federal Court has emphasized the human rights component of livelihood in the previously cited older decisions, when it stated that it was both a humanitarian obligation and a duty inherent in the purpose of the modern state to preserve the persons found within its territory against physical ruin when necessary. ... The domain of application of the fundamental right to security of livelihood is therefore not limited only to Swiss citizens; it extends also to aliens, regardless of their legal residence status. This does not, of course, preclude drawing distinctions: One who has settled in Switzerland (as a citizen or an alien) has different requirements for support than one who has fallen into need during a short-term visit or one for whom it is not yet determined whether he can remain in Switzerland or not (e.g. an asylum applicant).

e) In summary, the Court holds that the plaintiffs can rely upon the constitutional right to security of livelihood ...

[The court went on to find that the reasons relied upon by the local agencies did not justify denial of social assistance to the plaintiffs, who were legally prohibited from supporting themselves through employment.]

Dandridge v. Williams

Supreme Court of the United States, 1970.
397 U.S. 471.

■ Mr. Justice Stewart delivered the opinion of the Court.

This case involves the validity of a method used by Maryland, in the administration of an aspect of its public welfare program, to reconcile the demands of its needy citizens with the finite resources available to meet those demands....

The operation of the Maryland welfare system is not complex. By statute the State participates in the [federal Aid to Families with Dependent Children (AFDC)] program. It computes the standard of need for each eligible family based on the number of children in the family and the circumstances under which the family lives. In general, the standard of need increases with each additional person in the household, but the increments become proportionately smaller. The regulation here in issue imposes upon the grant that any single family may receive an upper limit of $250 per month in certain counties and Baltimore City, and of $240 per month elsewhere in the State. The appellees all have large families, so that their standards of need as computed by the State substantially exceed the maximum grants that they actually receive under the regulation. The appellees urged in the District Court that the maximum grant limitation operates to discriminate against them merely because of the size of their families, in violation of the Equal Protection Clause of the Fourteenth Amendment....

. . .

Although a State may adopt a maximum grant system in allocating its funds available for AFDC payments without violating the Act, it may not, of course, impose a regime of invidious discrimination in violation of the Equal Protection Clause of the Fourteenth Amendment. Maryland says that its maximum grant regulation is wholly free of any invidiously discriminatory purpose or effect, and that the regulation is rationally supportable on at least four entirely valid grounds. The regulation can be clearly justified, Maryland argues, in terms of legitimate state interests in encouraging gainful employment, in maintaining an equitable balance in economic status as between welfare families and those supported by a wage-earner, in providing incentives for family planning, and in allocating available public funds in such a way as fully to meet the needs of the largest possible number of families. The District Court, while apparently recognizing the validity of at least some of these state concerns, nonetheless held that the regulation "is invalid on its face for overreaching."—that it violates the Equal Protection Clause "[b]ecause it cuts too broad a swath on an indiscriminate basis as applied to the entire group of AFDC eligibles to which it purports to apply,...."

If this were a case involving government action claimed to violate the First Amendment guarantee of free speech, a finding of "overreaching" would be significant and might be crucial. For when otherwise valid governmental regulation sweeps so broadly as to impinge upon activity protected by the First Amendment, its very overbreadth may make it unconstitutional.... But the concept of "overreaching" has no place in this case. For here we deal with state regulation in the social and economic field, not affecting freedoms guaranteed by the Bill of Rights, and claimed to violate the Fourteenth Amendment only because the regulation results in some disparity in grants of welfare payments to the largest AFDC families. For this Court to approve the invalidation of state economic or social regulation as "overreaching" would be far too reminiscent of an era when the Court thought the Fourteenth Amendment gave it power to strike down state laws "because they may be unwise, improvident, or out of harmony with a particular school of thought." That era long ago passed into history.

In the area of economics and social welfare, a State does not violate the Equal Protection Clause merely because the classifications made by its laws are imperfect. If the classification has some "reasonable basis," it does not offend the Constitution simply because the classification "is not made with mathematical nicety or because in practice it results in some inequality." "The problems of government are practical ones and may justify, if they do not require, rough accommodations—illogical, it may be, and unscientific." "A statutory discrimination will not be set aside if any state of facts reasonably may be conceived to justify it."

To be sure, the cases cited, and many others enunciating this fundamental standard under the Equal Protection Clause, have in the main involved state regulation of business or industry. The administration of public welfare assistance, by contrast, involves the most basic economic needs of impoverished human beings. We recognize the dramatically real factual difference between the cited cases and this one, but we can find no basis for applying a different constitutional standard.[17] It is a standard that has consistently been applied to state legislation restricting the availability of employment opportunities. And it is a standard that is true to the principle that the Fourteenth Amendment gives the federal courts no power to impose upon the States their views of what constitutes wise economic or social policy.

Under this long-established meaning of the Equal Protection Clause, it is clear that the Maryland maximum grant regulation is constitutionally valid. We need not explore all the reasons that the State advances in justification of the regulation. It is enough that a solid foundation for the regulation can be found in the State's legitimate interest in encouraging employment and in avoiding discrimination between welfare families and the families of the working poor. By combining a limit on the recipient's grant with permission to retain money earned, without reduction in the amount of the grant, Maryland provides an incentive to seek gainful employment. And by keying the maximum family AFDC grants to the minimum wage a steadily employed head of a household receives, the State maintains some semblance of an equitable balance between families on welfare and those supported by an employed breadwinner.[19]

It is true that in some AFDC families there may be no person who is employable.[20] It is also true that with respect to AFDC families whose

17. It is important to note that there is no contention that the Maryland regulation is infected with a racially discriminatory purpose or effect such as to make it inherently suspect.

19. The present federal minimum wage is $52—$64 per 40-hour week....

20. It appears that no family members of any of the named plaintiffs in the present case are employable.

determined standard of need is below the regulatory maximum, and who therefore receive grants equal to the determined standard, the employment incentive is absent. But the Equal Protection Clause does not require that a State must choose between attacking every aspect of a problem or not attacking the problem at all. It is enough that the State's action be rationally based and free from invidious discrimination. The regulation before us meets that test.

We do not decide today that the Maryland regulation is wise, that it best fulfills the relevant social and economic objectives that Maryland might ideally espouse, or that a more just and humane system could not be devised. Conflicting claims of morality and intelligence are raised by opponents and proponents of almost every measure, certainly including the one before us. But the intractable economic, social, and even philosophical problems presented by public welfare assistance programs are not the business of this Court. The Constitution may impose certain procedural safeguards upon systems of welfare administration. But the Constitution does not empower this Court to second-guess state officials charged with the difficult responsibility of allocating limited public welfare funds among the myriad of potential recipients.

The judgment is reversed.

■ MR. JUSTICE MARSHALL, whom MR. JUSTICE BRENNAN joins, dissenting.

. . . . The cases relied on by the Court, in which a "mere rationality" test was actually used, are most accurately described as involving the application of equal protection reasoning to the regulation of business interests. The extremes to which the Court has gone in dreaming up rational bases for state regulation in that area may in many instances be ascribed to a healthy revulsion from the Court's earlier excesses in using the Constitution to protect interests that have more than enough power to protect themselves in the legislative halls. This case, involving the literally vital interests of a powerless minority—poor families without breadwinners—is far removed from the area of business regulation, as the Court concedes. Why then is the standard used in those cases imposed here? We are told no more than that this case falls in "the area of economics and social welfare," with the implication that from there the answer is obvious.

In my view, equal protection analysis of this case is not appreciably advanced by the a priori definition of a "right," fundamental or otherwise.[14] Rather, concentration must be placed upon the character of the

---

14. ... [T]he Court's insistence that equal protection analysis turns on the basis of a closed category of "fundamental rights" involves a curious value judgment. It is certainly difficult to believe that a person whose very survival is at stake would be comforted by the knowledge that his "fundamental" rights are preserved intact.

On the issue of whether there is a "right" to welfare assistance, see generally Graham, Public Assistance: The Right To Receive; the Obligation To Repay, 43 N.Y.U.L.Rev. 451 (1968); Harvith, Federal Equal Protection and Welfare Assistance, 31 Albany L.Rev. 210 (1967); Note, Welfare Due Process: The Maximum Grant Limitation on the Right To Survive, 3 Ga.L.Rev. 459 (1969). See also Universal Declaration of Human Rights, Art. 25.

classification in question, the relative importance to individuals in the class discriminated against of the governmental benefits that they do not receive, and the asserted state interests in support of the classification.

It is the individual interests here at stake that, as the Court concedes, most clearly distinguish this case from the "business regulation" equal protection cases. AFDC support to needy dependent children provides the stuff that sustains those children's lives: food, clothing, shelter. . . .

Appellees are not a gas company or an optical dispenser; they are needy dependent children and families who are discriminated against by the State. The basis of that discrimination—the classification of individuals into large and small families—is too arbitrary and too unconnected to the asserted rationale, the impact on those discriminated against—the denial of even a subsistence existence—too great, and the supposed interests served too contrived and attenuated to meet the requirements of the Constitution. In my view Maryland's maximum grant regulation is invalid under the Equal Protection Clause of the Fourteenth Amendment.

[Concurring opinions and dissenting opinion of Justice Douglas omitted.]

Tucker v. Toia

New York Court of Appeals, 1977.
371 N.E.2d 449.

[Plaintiffs were three individuals under the age of 21 who applied for "home relief" payments, a form of public assistance, from the State of New York. Their applications were rejected for the sole reason that they had not obtained a final decision in a court proceeding for support against their fathers. In two cases, the father's whereabouts were unknown; in another, the father was living in a distant state; in all three cases a suit for support would take from several months to a year before producing a final decision. The absence of a final decision in a support proceeding made them ineligible for home relief under a new statute, replacing an earlier system under which the state had provided home relief to individuals under age 21, and then sought to recover the money by suing the parents. The plaintiffs claimed that the new statute violated the New York State Constitution.]

In New York State, the provision for assistance to the needy is not a matter of legislative grace; rather, it is specifically mandated by our Constitution. Section 1 of article XVII of the New York State Constitution declares: "The aid, care and support of the needy are public concerns and shall be provided by the state and by such of its subdivisions, and in such manner and by such means, as the legislature may from time to time determine." This provision was adopted in 1938, in the aftermath of the great depression, and was intended to serve two functions: First, it was felt to be necessary to sustain from constitutional attack the social welfare programs first created by the State during that period; and, second, it was intended as an expression of the existence of a positive duty upon the State to aid the needy.

The legislative history of the Constitutional Convention of 1938 is indicative of a clear intent that State aid to the needy was deemed to be a fundamental part of the social contract. For example, the report of the Committee on Public Welfare, the group which drafted what became section 1 of article XVII of our Constitution, specifically states that one purpose of the amendment was to "recognize the responsibility of the State for the aid, care and support of persons in need". . . .

. . .

In view of this legislative history, as well as the mandatory language of the provision itself, it is clear that section 1 of article XVII imposes upon the State an affirmative duty to aid the needy. Although our Constitution provides the Legislature with discretion in determining the means by which this objective is to be effectuated, in determining the amount of aid, and in classifying recipients and defining the term "needy", it unequivocally prevents the Legislature from simply refusing to aid those whom it has classified as needy. Such a definite constitutional mandate cannot be ignored or easily evaded in either its letter or its spirit.

We find that [the challenged statute] is unconstitutional in that it contravenes the letter and spirit of section 1 of article XVII of the Constitution. The effect of the questioned statute is plain: it would effectively deny public assistance to persons under the age of 21 who are concededly needy, often through no fault of their own, who meet all the criteria developed by the Legislature for determining need, solely on the ground that they have not obtained a final disposition in a support proceeding. Certainly, the statute is in furtherance of a valid State objective, for it is intended to prevent unnecessary welfare expenditures by placing the burden of supporting persons under 21 upon their legally responsible relatives. This valid purpose, however, cannot be achieved by methods which ignore the realities of the needy's plight and the State's affirmative obligation to aid all its needy.

In *Matter of Barie v. Lavine*, 357 N.E.2d 349 [(1976)], we were presented with a somewhat similar challenge to a social services regulation providing for the temporary suspension of recipients who unjustifiably refuse to accept employment. We summarily dismissed the constitutional arguments proffered in *Barie*, stating: "The Legislature may in its discretion deny aid to employable persons who may properly be deemed not to be needy when they have wrongfully refused an opportunity for employment." In that case we were concerned with a reasonable legislative determination that such individuals were not needy. The present case, in contradistinction, presents a very different question: may the Legislature deny all aid to certain individuals who are admittedly needy, solely on the basis of criteria having nothing to do with need? Today, we hold that it may not. As the chairman of the Constitutional Convention's Committee on Social Welfare indicated, although the Legislature is given great discretion in this area, it cannot simply "shirk its responsibility which ... is as fundamental as any responsibility of government."

[Judgment affirmed.]

Moore v. Ganim

Supreme Court of Connecticut, 1995.
660 A.2d 742.

[The plaintiffs challenged a revision of Connecticut's general assistance laws that limited the entitlement of recipients who were "employable" to nine months out of each year. General assistance is a state-run public assistance program that provides support to needy persons who do not qualify under federal categorical assistance programs, or whose assistance under the federal programs is inadequate. The nine-month limitation was designed "to reinforce the principle that general assistance was, as a matter of policy, intended as a temporary program for employable persons and had been instituted in order to provide an incentive for people to find employment." The plaintiffs argued that the limitation violated a provision of Connecticut's state constitution of 1818 by abrogating a common law right to support that had existed in 1818, and that it violated an unenumerated fundamental right to minimum subsistence. A four-justice majority rejected both arguments and denied the existence of a state constitutional right to subsistence. Chief Justice Peters concurred, concluding that an unenumerated right to subsistence did exist, but had not been violated. Two justices dissented. The following are excerpts from the majority opinion.]

For the purposes of this opinion, we assume that the framers [of the 1818 state constitution] believed that individuals would continue to possess certain natural rights even if those rights were not enumerated in the written constitution. On the basis of this assumption, we will not draw firm conclusions from the silence of the constitutional text. The mere fact that the framers intended some unenumerated natural rights to survive the drafting of the written constitution, however, does not give us carte blanche to recognize new constitutional rights as inherent in natural law. Rather, in determining whether unenumerated rights were incorporated into the constitution, we must focus on the framers' understanding of whether a particular right was part of the natural law, i.e., on the framers' understanding of whether the particular right was so fundamental to an ordered society that it did not require explicit enumeration. ...

The plaintiffs argue that Connecticut's history and tradition of caring for the indigent, taken as a whole, supports a conclusion that the framers believed that the state had an inherent duty to provide subsistence benefits to the needy, and therefore we must recognize under our state constitution an unenumerated duty to provide such support. The plaintiffs concede that the state's duty was minimal. They argue, however, that both the writings of our principal eighteenth century jurists and our 350 year history of enacting statutes to provide for the indigent demonstrate that the state had a duty at least to provide "a warm, secure place to sleep at night, adequate food, minimal clothing and personal effects, and some level of medical care." We conclude, to the contrary, that the historical record is not properly read to create such a duty.

The writings of jurists in temporal proximity to the adoption of the 1818 constitution provide the strongest basis for the plaintiffs' argument for an unenumerated constitutional obligation derived from principles of natural law. In particular, both Chief Justice Zephaniah Swift and Judge Jesse Root referred to an obligation of the government to support the indigent. For example, Chief Justice Swift wrote: "The selectmen are bound to provide necessaries for all the inhabitants of the town, who are incapable of supporting themselves. Towns are obliged to support their respective inhabitants, whether living in the town to which they belong, or any other town, either with or without a certificate, who may need relief.... [T]he law has made provision for support of the poor, so that every one may know where to call for his bread in the hour of want." Similarly, Judge Root stated: "The poor and indigent in all countries, call not only for private charity, but for support and assistance from the government, and to give scope to the exercise of benevolence, the most noble and godlike virtue.... It is the duty of every government to protect and to provide for the poor; the laws of the state therefore humanely enact and ordain ... that every town shall take care of, provide for and maintain, its own poor." In interpreting our state constitution, the statements of both jurists are entitled to significant weight.

Although both Swift and Root believed that the government had an obligation to support the indigent, neither jurist's writings can be read to entitle the plaintiffs to relief. Swift and Root provided only the faintest outlines of what they considered to be the government's obligation. They did not delimit the various means by which the government could choose to fulfill that obligation. Beyond referring to the "necessaries" of life, they did not explain what level of support had to be provided. Indeed, they did not even establish who was to be considered one of "the poor." Their silence on each of these issues implies what the remainder of the historical sources suggests: that the historical record, taken in its entirety, is too ambiguous and contradictory to provide a basis from which we, with any reasonable degree of confidence, can infer an implied unenumerated fundamental constitutional obligation to provide minimal subsistence.

Connecticut's first statute relating to assistance to the poor was included in the Ludlow Code of 1650, the first recorded code of laws of our state. Statutory language regarding maintenance of the poor thereafter can be traced through the colonial laws of 1672 and 1702, the first statutes of the state of Connecticut in 1784, the 1808 statutory revisions and the post-constitution statutes of 1821, to today's current statutes. While Connecticut's 350 year statutory history obviously demonstrates a longstanding policy of assisting the indigent, the mere existence of a 350 year statutory history does not necessarily show that the framers intended to incorporate that policy in our constitution as a fundamental constitutional right. Notably absent from the statutes is any evidence that there was an inherent obligation on the part of the towns, other than that mandated by the colonial government, to care for the indigent. These statutes failed to provide a clear articulation of the basis of such a duty, and they fail to provide specific guidance as to the extent of the government's obligation. In particular, the statutes show that in the entire period before the constitution of 1818, local elected officials had wide discretion to decide the nature of, amount of and eligibility criteria for receiving such assistance. ... Moreover, the towns were required to support only those persons who were settled in a town.

Indeed, although Connecticut has a long history of supporting its indigent, the main purpose of many of the preconstitutional poor relief statutes may have been to relieve others of the social problems caused by paupers by isolating and punishing the indigent, rather than to meet any fundamental constitutional obligation to the indigent. For example, selectmen had the power to bind out children as apprentices or servants if the children "live idly, or mispend their time ... loitering," or where a family "cannot, or do[es] not provide competently for [its] children." General Statutes (1808 Rev.) tit. CXXX, § 5.

In addition, indigent persons could be confined to workhouses or could be contracted out as laborers for the benefit of the town. ...

In workhouses, the "masters or keepers" of the house could punish the indigent by "putting fetters or shackles upon them, and by moderate whipping, not exceeding ten stripes at one time ... and from time to time, in case they be stubborn, disorderly or idle ... [the master or keeper] may abridge them of their food ... until they be reduced to better order and obedience...." General Statutes (1808 Rev.) tit. CLXXVI, c. 1, § 21. Not only would these poor laws undoubtedly violate contemporary civilized standards of decency, but they would also arguably violate several federal constitutional provisions.

. . .

Thus, we conclude that the historical record merely begs the question of what the intended reach of these statutes was; it does not define who should be considered indigent, nor does it elucidate what level of services would amount to minimal subsistence. Such an undefined and discretionary grant of support is insufficient to provide a basis for defining the modern personal right or state affirmative obligation that the plaintiffs claim. Without an objective referent to guide the definition of such a right and obligation and without further support that the framers intended to impose a constitutional obligation on the state, we are unprepared to translate a longstanding policy regarding the poor into an affirmative constitutional obligation.

Sarah Ramsey & Daan Braveman, *"Let Them Starve": Government's Obligation to Children in Poverty*
68 Temp. L. Rev. 1607, 1622–29 (1995).

The constitutions of at least twenty states include language relating to the care of the needy or the protection of the health of residents. In this respect, those state constitutions differ significantly from the United States Constitution and might well be interpreted more broadly, thereby imposing a duty on the states to aid poor children. . . .

The texts of these documents can be divided into three categories. The first includes those constitutions that make a statement of principle about the care of the less fortunate.[119] On the most general level, the Hawaii Constitution states in its Preamble that government should have "an understanding and compassionate heart toward all the peoples of the earth." The Preamble to the Illinois Constitution is more specific, stating that its constitution was intended and founded, among other reasons, to "eliminate poverty and inequality; assure legal, social and economic justice; [and] provide opportunity for the fullest development of the individual."

The second category includes those constitutions that authorize the state, or a local entity, to provide for the poor or for the health of the state citizens.[122] The Oklahoma Constitution, for example, authorizes the legislature and the people through initiatives "to provide by appropriate legislation for the relief and care of needy, aged persons who are unable to provide for themselves, and other needy persons who, on account of immature age, physical infirmity, disability, or other cause, are unable to provide or care for themselves."

Finally, a third category includes constitutions that do not explicitly authorize assistance, but instead make reference to a governmental duty to care for the needy.[124] The North Carolina Constitution states: "Beneficent provision for the poor, the unfortunate, and the orphan is one of the first

---

119. See Haw. Const. pmbl.; Ill. Const. pmbl; and S.C. Const. art. XII, § 1. . . .

122. See Cal. Const. art. XVI, § 11 (authorizing legislature to enact laws relating to relief administration); Ga. Const. art. IX, § 3, cl. 1 (authorizing local governments to contract with public entities for the care of its indigent sick); Ind. Const. art. IX, § 3 (authorizing county boards to establish farms for those who have claims upon the aid of society); La. Const. art XII, § 8 (authorizing legislature to establish welfare and unemployment compensation, as well as public health system); Miss. Const. art. XIV, § 262 (authorizing board of supervisors to provide homes or farms to those who have claims upon the aid of society); Mont. Const. art. XII, § 3(3) (permitting legislature to provide economic assistance to those in need); N.M. Const. art. IX, § 14 (authorizing state and local governments to make provisions relating to the care of sick and indigent persons); Okla. Const. art. XXV, § 1 (authorizing legislature to provide for the relief and care of aged and needy); Tex. Const. art. III, § 51–a (authorizing payment of assistance to needy).

124. See Ala. Const. art. IV, § 88 (imposing duty upon legislature to "require the several counties of this state to make adequate provision for the maintenance of the poor"); Alaska Const. art. VII, § 5 (stating that "legislature shall provide for public welfare"); Kan. Const. art. VII, § 4 (imposing duty upon counties to provide for those inhabitants who "may have claims upon the aid of society"); Mich. Const. art. IV, § 51 (stating that "legislature shall pass suitable laws for the protection and promotion of public health"); Mo. Const. art. IV, § 37 (establishing department of social services charged with "promoting improved health and other social services to the citizens of the state"); N.Y. Const. art. XVII, §§ 1, 3 (stating that aid, care, and support of the needy shall be provided by State); N.C. Const. art. XI, § 4 (stating that the General Assembly "shall provide for and define the duties of a board of public welfare"); Wyo. Const. art. VII, § 20 (defining duty of legislature to provide for "health and morality of the people").

duties of a civilized and a Christian state. Therefore the General Assembly shall provide for and define the duties of a board of public welfare." Similarly, the Alabama Constitution affirms that "[it] shall be the duty of the legislature to require the several counties of this state to make adequate provision for the maintenance of the poor."

. . .

New York has been the most aggressive in developing an independent state constitutional analysis of welfare issues. . . .

. . .

The Montana experience in defining the scope of the constitutional duty to the poor is quite revealing. In *Butte Community Union v. Lewis* ("*Butte II*"),[153] the Montana Supreme Court considered the constitutionality of a provision of the general assistance program that granted only two months of aid in any one year to needy, able-bodied persons without children. Plaintiffs framed the challenge as an unconstitutional distinction between needy, able-bodied persons without children and those with children (and eligible for benefits). At the time of the decision, the Montana Constitution stated: "The legislature shall provide such economic assistance and social and rehabilitative services as may be necessary for those inhabitants who, by reason of age, infirmities, or misfortune may have need for the aid of society."

The *Butte II* court did not declare that this provision creates a constitutional right to public assistance, but instead ruled that, because of the explicit constitutional language, the challenged law must be subjected to a heightened level of scrutiny. The *Butte II* court adopted a test similar to the one proposed by Justice Marshall in his dissent in *Dandridge*, requiring first a determination of whether the classification is reasonable, and then a balancing of the state's interest in making the classification against the individual's interest in obtaining the benefits. The *Butte II* court concluded that the factual record supported the finding that the statutory classification was unreasonable under the first prong of the test, and thus violated the state constitution.

Butte II did not end the Montana story, however. The Montana legislature responded by adopting a proposed constitutional amendment giving the legislature much greater discretion in providing assistance to the needy. Specifically, the amendment substituted "may provide" for "shall provide," and gave the legislature discretion to determine who is needy. The amendment was approved at the general election in 1988 and became effective on January 1, 1989. As amended, Article XII, Section 3(3) of the Montana Constitution now states: "The legislature may provide such economic assistance and social and rehabilitative services for those who, by reason of age, infirmities, or misfortune are determined by the legislature to be in need."

---

153. 745 P.2d 1128 (Mont.1987).

Notes on Constitutional Protection of Social Welfare Rights

1. The Swiss Federal Court maintains that security of elemental human necessities such as food, clothing and shelter is an indispensable element of a community based on democracy and the rule of law. Why so? What other bases does the Court identify for constitutional recognition of a right to security of livelihood, and are they persuasive?

2. The argument that a right to security of livelihood can be derived from the principle of human dignity reflects a similar interpretation of the postwar German Constitution. Article 1(1) of that Constitution provides: "Human dignity shall be inviolable. To respect and to protect it shall be the duty of all state authority." An early decision of the Federal Administrative Court construed this principle of human dignity as requiring that provisions for the support of the poor be available as a matter of enforceable individual right, not merely as a matter of administrative policy. Judgment of June 24, 1954, 1 BVerwGE 159. The Federal Constitutional Court subsequently adopted the position that Article 1(1), in conjunction with the principle that the Federal Republic of Germany is a "social state" (Article 20(1)), implied a guarantee of security of livelihood. The Constitutional Court has further concluded that income tax legislation must provide an exemption for the minimum level of income necessary to ensure an existence consistent with human dignity for the taxpayer's family. Judgment of June 12, 1990, 82 BVerfGE 198.

3. Why does the U.S. Supreme Court in *Dandridge* regard social welfare legislation as entitled to the same degree of judicial deference as business regulation? What is Maryland's justification for applying its maximum grant rule to the plaintiffs' families? Does the majority opinion imply that the states have no federal constitutional obligation to feed starving citizens?

    Should the arguments identified by the Swiss Federal Court be persuasive as arguments for recognition of a constitutional right to security of livelihood in the United States? Are the arguments for recognition of an unenumerated right to security of livelihood less persuasive within the U.S. context than the arguments for recognition of an unenumerated right to abortion? Does one right have more fundamental importance than the other? Is one right more easily analogized to other rights enumerated in the Constitution than the other? Does one right have more historical support than the other? Should great weight be placed on the positive or negative character of each right?

4. The Swiss Federal Court mentions three methods by which a constitution can provide for security of livelihood. It can be guaranteed as a human right, it can be assigned to the legislature as an obligatory task, or it can be stated aspirationally as a governmental goal. How might these methods differ in their consequences for legislative deliberations on budgetary priorities and social assistance policy? How might they differ in terms of the availability of judicial enforcement? Which of these methods does the

language of Article 48(1) of the Swiss Federal Constitution suggest? Which does the language of Article XVII § 1 of the New York State Constitution suggest? Taken within the context of the ICESCR, does the right to an adequate standard of living (Article 11(1)) function as a goal, an obligatory task, or a right?

The discussion of the history of relief of the poor in Connecticut in *Moore v. Ganim* illustrates another potential difference between understanding social assistance as a legislative task and understanding it as a right. Advocates of welfare rights maintain that the poor are entitled to public assistance, and that receipt of public assistance should not be stigmatizing or accompanied by harsh conditions. Some opponents of welfare rights maintain that public assistance should not be configured as a right, but rather as a privilege dependent on unpredictable factors of compassion and resources, in order to preserve important incentives for people to support themselves and to insure themselves against risks of future disability.

5. The Constitution of India offers both a prominent illustration of the distinction between individual rights and legislative tasks, and an indication of its potential instability. Part III of the Constitution (Articles 12 through 35) guarantees a series of "Fundamental Rights," primarily but not exclusively civil and political rights. Part IV of the Constitution (Articles 36 through 51) sets out a series of "Directive Principles of State Policy," most of which address economic and social policies, and some of which expressly aim at securing rights.* Article 37 states that "[t]he provisions contained in this Part shall not be enforceable by any court, but the principles therein laid down are nevertheless fundamental in the governance of the country and it shall be the duty of the State to apply these principles in making laws."

Since the adoption of the Constitution in 1950, courts in India have attributed increasing significance to these Directive Principles. Although these Principles cannot be directly enforced, they guide the interpretation of statutes. Directive Principles can supply justifications for the limitation of Fundamental Rights, and Fundamental Rights have been construed in a manner that harmonizes them with the Directive Principles. Since the 1980s, the Supreme Court of India has gone further and has interpreted Fundamental Rights such as the rights to "life [and] personal liberty" in Article 21 as implying a right "to live with human dignity" that incorporates elements of economic and social rights derived from the Directive Principles. See, e.g., Sujata V. Manohar, *Judiciary and Human Rights*, 36 Indian J. Int'l L. 39, 43–45 (Apr.-June 1996); Mahendra P. Singh, V.N. Shukla's Constitution of India 164–69, 297–302 (9th ed. 1994); Craig Scott & Patrick Macklem, *Constitutional Ropes of Sand or Justiciable Guaran-*

---

* See Art. 39(a) ("The State shall, in particular, direct its policy towards securing ... that the citizens, men and women equally, have the right to an adequate means of livelihood"); Art. 41 ("Right to work, to education and to public assistance in certain cases").

tees? Social Rights in a New South African Constitution, 141 U. Pa. L. Rev. 1, 114–31 (1992) (reviewing Indian experience).

For discussions of the forms taken by economic and social rights in other national constitutions, see, e.g., Mary Ann Glendon, *Rights in Twentieth–Century Constitutions*, 59 U. Chi. L. Rev. 519 (1992); Shadrack B. O. Gutto, *Beyond Justiciability: Challenges of Implementing/Enforcing Socio–Economic Rights in South Africa*, 4 Buff. Hum. Rts. L. Rev. 79 (1998); George S. Katrougalos, *The Implementation of Social Rights in Europe*, 2 Colum. J. Eur. L. 277 (1996); Wiktor Osiatynski, *Rights in New Constitutions of East Central Europe*, 26 Colum. Hum. Rts. L. Rev. 111 (1994).

6. The Swiss Federal Court observes that the right to public social assistance in a canton has a subsidiary character. It comes into play only if private resources do not meet the individual's need. Moreover, given the federal character of the Swiss political system, assistance at one level of government is necessary only if other levels of government do not provide it. How might these observations affect the drafting of constitutional provisions on social assistance in a federal system?

7. Note the concerns of the Swiss, New York, and Connecticut courts as to whether rights to social assistance can be defined with sufficient clarity and specificity to be justiciable. Why are the Swiss Federal Court and the New York Court of Appeals persuaded that this requirement has been met? Do their decisions nonetheless avoid undue rigidity in setting social assistance policy? Why is the Connecticut Supreme Court not persuaded?

8. If the United States were a party to the ICESCR and had entered no relevant reservation, then would the Maryland maximum grant rule involved in *Dandridge* and the Connecticut nine-month rule involved in *Moore* be consistent with the obligations of the United States under the Covenant, as the Committee on Economic, Social and Cultural Rights interprets them in General Comment 3 (see especially paragraph 10)?

9. Does the absence of federal protection for welfare rights in *Dandridge* reflect a general lack of belief in social rights in the United States? A practical concern that social rights should not be constitutionally rigidified? The antiquity of the U.S. Constitution?

Notes on Civil Rights Implications of Social Welfare Programs

1. As the *Dandridge* case exemplifies, disputes over denials of social assistance or social insurance within an existing program may also be framed in terms of equal protection. Thus social rights may also have implications within systems for the protection of civil and political rights. Cases from the Human Rights Committee (discussed in this Note) and from the European Court of Human Rights (discussed in the next Note) further illustrate this aspect of social rights.

For example, in *Danning v. The Netherlands*, (1987), U.N. Doc. CCPR/C/OP/2 at 205, the Human Rights Committee confronted a challenge under ICCPR art. 26 to provisions of Dutch social insurance law that treated married couples and cohabiting but unmarried couples differently in setting benefit levels when one of the partners became disabled.* The Committee explained the applicability of the prohibition of discrimination in Article 26 as follows:

12.1. The State party contends that there is considerable overlapping of the provisions of article 26 with the provisions of article 2 of the International Covenant on Economic, Social and Cultural Rights. The Committee is of the view that the International Covenant on Civil and Political Rights would still apply even if a particular subject-matter is referred to or covered in international instruments, for example, the International Convention on the Elimination of All Forms of Racial Discrimination, the Convention on the Elimination of All Forms of Discrimination against Women, or, as in the present case, the International Covenant on Economic Social and Cultural Rights. Notwithstanding the interrelated drafting history of the two Covenants, it remains necessary for the Committee to apply fully the terms of the International Covenant on Civil and Political Rights. The Committee observes in this connection that the provisions of article 2 of the International covenant on Economic, Social and Cultural Rights do not detract from the full application of article 26 of the International Covenant on Civil and Political Rights.

12.2. The Committee has also examined the contention of the State party that article 26 of the International Covenant on Civil and Political Rights cannot be invoked in respect of a right which is specifically provided for under article 9 of the International Covenant on Economic, Social and Cultural Rights (social security, including social insurance). In so doing, the Committee has perused the *travaux préparatoires* of the International Covenant on Civil and Political Rights, namely the summary records of the discussion that took place in the Commission on Human Rights in 1948, 1949, 1950 and 1952 and in the Third Committee of the General Assembly in 1961, which provide a "supplementary means of interpretation" (art. 32 of the Vienna Convention on the Law of Treaties). The discussions, at the time of drafting concerning the question whether the scope of article 26 extended to rights not otherwise guaranteed by the Covenant, were inconclusive and cannot alter the conclusion arrived at by the ordinary means of interpretation referred to in paragraph 12.3 below.

12.3. For the purpose of determining the scope of article 26, the Committee has taken into account the "ordinary meaning" of each element in the article in its context and in light of its object and purpose (art. 31 of the Vienna Convention on the Law of Treaties). The

---

* ICCPR art. 26, as discussed in Part IV, Chapter 1(D) supra, provides:

All persons are equal before the law and are entitled without any discrimination to the equal protection of the law. In this respect, the law shall prohibit any discrimination and guarantee to all persons equal and effective protection against discrimination on any ground such as race, colour, sex, language, religion, political or other opinion, national or social origin, property, birth or other status.

Committee begins by noting that article 26 does not merely duplicate the guarantees already provided for in article 2. It derives from the principle of equal protection of the law without discrimination, as contained in article 7 of the Universal Declaration of Human Rights, which prohibits discrimination in law or in practice in any field regulated and protected by public authorities. Article 26 is thus concerned with the obligations imposed on States with regard to their legislation and the application thereof.

12.4. Although article 26 requires that legislation should prohibit discrimination, it does not of itself contain any obligation with respect to the matters that may be provided for by legislation. Thus it does not, for example, require any State to enact legislation to provide for social security. However, when such legislation is adopted in the exercise of a State's sovereign power, then such legislation must comply with article 26 of the Covenant.

12.5. The Committee observes in this connection that what is at issue is not whether or not social security should be progressively established in the Netherlands but whether the legislation providing for social security violates the prohibition against discrimination contained in article 26 of the International Covenant on Civil and Political Rights and the guarantee given therein to all persons regarding equal and effective protection against discrimination.

The Committee then concluded that the differentiation between married and unmarried couples in the Dutch legislation on disability benefits was based on reasonable and objective criteria, and did not violate Article 26.

In a subsequent case, also involving differentiations based on marital status in Dutch social welfare legislation, three members of the Human Rights Committee appended a concurring statement that included the following passage:

> [It is] necessary to take into account the reality that the socio-economic and cultural needs of society are constantly evolving, so that legislation—in particular in the field of social security—may well, and often does, lag behind developments. Accordingly, article 26 of the Covenant should not be interpreted as requiring absolute equality or non-discrimination in that field at all times; instead, it should be seen as a general undertaking on the part of the States parties to the Covenant to regularly review their legislation in order to ensure that it corresponds to the changing needs of society. In the field of civil and political rights, a State party is required to respect Covenant rights such as the right to a fair trial, to freedom of expression and freedom of religion, immediately from the date of entry into force of the Covenant, and to do so without discrimination. On the other hand, with regard to rights enshrined in the International Covenant on Economic, Social and Cultural Rights, it is generally understood that States parties may need time for the progressive implementation of these rights and to adapt relevant legislation in stages; moreover, constant efforts are needed to ensure that distinctions that were

reasonable and objective at the time of enactment of a social security provision are not rendered unreasonable and discriminatory by the socio-economic evolution of society. Finally, we recognize that legislative review is a complex process entailing consideration of many factors, including limited financial resources, and the potential effects of amendments on other existing legislation.

Individual opinion of Members Nisuke Ando, Kurt Herndl and Birame Ndiaye, *Sprenger v. The Netherlands*, U.N. Doc. CCPR/C/44/D/395/1990 (1992).

Is the Human Rights Committee's interpretation of Article 26 in *Danning* consistent with the separation of the two Covenants and the different character of state obligations under them? How deeply does the requirement of an "objective and reasonable" basis for distinctions in social welfare legislation on enumerated grounds or "other status" intrude upon the state's discretion to set social policy?

In light of *Danning*, what implications does Article 26 of the ICCPR have for the obligations of the United States with respect to social welfare legislation? Are any of the U.S. reservations, understandings and declarations relevant to answering this question?

2. In *Gaygusuz v. Austria*, 1996–IV Eur. Ct. H.R. 1129, 23 E.H.R.R. 364 (1996), the European Court of Human Rights confronted a claim of nationality discrimination in the grant of emergency assistance benefits to workers who had lost their employment. Unlike ICCPR art. 26, which provides a free-standing prohibition of discrimination, Article 14 of the European Convention forbids discrimination only with respect to rights and freedoms otherwise set forth in the Convention.* The European Court concluded, however, that the right to emergency assistance under the Austrian legislation was a form of property protected under Article 1 of Protocol No. 1.** The Court reasoned:

39. The Court notes that at the material time emergency assistance was granted to persons who had exhausted their entitlement to unemployment benefit and satisfied the other statutory conditions laid down in section 33 of the 1977 Unemployment Insurance Act.

---

*Article 14, as discussed in Part IV, Chapter 1(D) supra, provides:

The enjoyment of the rights and freedoms set forth in the Convention shall be secured without discrimination on any ground such as sex, race, colour, language, religion, political or other opinion, national or social origin, association with a national minority, property, birth or other status.

**Article 1 of Protocol No. 1, as discussed in Section A supra, provides:

Every natural or legal person is entitled to the peaceful enjoyment of his possessions. No one shall be deprived of his possessions except in the public interest and subject to the conditions provided for by law and by the general principles of international law.

The preceding provisions shall not, however, in any way impair the right of a State to enforce such laws as it deems necessary to control the use of property in accordance with the general interest or to secure the payment of taxes or other contributions or penalties.

Entitlement to this social benefit is therefore linked to the payment of contributions to the unemployment insurance fund, which is a precondition for the payment of unemployment benefit. It follows that there is no entitlement to emergency assistance where such contributions have not been made.

40.   In the instant case it has not been argued that the applicant did not satisfy that condition; the refusal to grant him emergency assistance was based exclusively on the finding that he did not have Austrian nationality and did not fall into any of the categories exempted from that condition.

41.   The Court considers that the right to emergency assistance—in so far as provided for in the applicable legislation—is a pecuniary right for the purposes of Article 1 of Protocol No. 1. That provision is therefore applicable without it being necessary to rely solely on the link between entitlement to emergency assistance and the obligation to pay "taxes or other contributions".

Accordingly, as the applicant was denied emergency assistance on a ground of distinction covered by Article 14, namely his nationality, that provision is also applicable.

The Court then found that the denial of emergency assistance solely on grounds of nationality to a legally resident worker who had paid contributions to the unemployment assistance fund on the same basis as Austrian nationals was not based on any "objective and reasonable justification," and violated Article 14.

Should the contested benefits be regarded as "possessions" within the meaning of Article 1 of Protocol No. 1 because they are pecuniary rights conditioned on prior contributions? Or merely because they are pecuniary rights? Is the Court's interpretation of Article 14, in conjunction with the protection of "possessions," as applying to discrimination in the initial grant of social benefits persuasive? Given that the decisions of the European Court of Human Rights are binding on the parties, how deeply does the requirement of an "objective and reasonable justification" for status-based discriminations intrude upon the state's discretion to set social policy?

3.   The *Gaygusuz* decision rejected discrimination on the basis of nationality (which it includes within "national origin"), at least with regard to emergency assistance to a legal resident alien who has contributed to a social insurance fund. The Swiss Federal Court in *V. v. Municipality X. and Council of the Canton of Bern*, supra, invalidated discrimination on grounds of nationality in the provision of emergency assistance to aliens who were not lawfully resident. U.S. constitutional law has developed complex equal protection doctrine with regard to discrimination against aliens in social welfare legislation. When federal legislation discriminates against aliens with regard to eligibility for benefits, the Supreme Court applies only the rational basis test, in light of a perceived connection to the plenary federal power over immigration. *Mathews v. Diaz*, 426 U.S. 67 (1976). When, however, state legislation denies social benefits to aliens who have been

admitted as lawful permanent residents by the federal government, the Supreme Court's modern precedents require strict equal protection scrutiny, on the theory that aliens are a discrete and insular class of residents vulnerable to mistreatment by a political process in which they are not represented. See *Graham v. Richardson*, 403 U.S. 365 (1971); *Bernal v. Fainter*, 467 U.S. 216 (1984). This jurisprudence may undergo further evolution in response to policies adopted by Congress in welfare reform legislation enacted in 1996. See, e.g., Recent Legislation: Welfare Reform—Treatment of Legal Immigrants, 110 Harv. L. Rev. 1191 (1997).

4.   Another important example of the interaction of social and economic rights with civil rights concerns the procedures employed in the resolution of disputes over the denial of benefits. Article 6(1) of the European Convention entitles everyone to certain elements of fair procedure "[i]n the determination of his civil rights and obligations." The European Court of Human Rights has held that both social insurance and social assistance schemes may create civil rights that trigger the applicability of Article 6(1). See, e.g., *Feldbrugge v. Netherlands*, 99 Eur. Ct. H.R. (ser. A), 8 E.H.R.R. 425 (1986) (social insurance); *Salesi v. Italy*, 257–E Eur. Ct. H.R. (ser. A), 26 E.H.R.R. 187 (1993) (social assistance). In the latter case, the European Court stated:

> despite the public law features pointed out by the Government, Mrs. Salesi was not affected in her relations with the administrative authorities as such, acting in the exercise of discretionary powers; she suffered an interference with her means of subsistence and was claiming an individual, economic right flowing from specific rules laid down in a statute. . . .

Similarly, the United States Supreme Court held in *Goldberg v. Kelly*, 397 U.S. 254 (1970), that procedural due process required the state to provide a welfare recipient an evidentiary hearing before the termination of her benefits on disputed grounds of ineligibility. The Supreme Court observed:

> Such benefits are a matter of statutory entitlement for persons qualified to receive them. Their termination involves state action that adjudicates important rights. The constitutional challenge cannot be answered by an argument that public assistance benefits are " 'a privilege' and not a 'right.' " Relevant constitutional constraints apply as much to the withdrawal of public assistance benefits as to disqualification for unemployment compensation; or to denial of a tax exemption; or to discharge from public employment.

The Supreme Court's rejection of the right-privilege distinction as the basis for determining the applicability of procedural due process resulted in a "due process revolution" affecting both social welfare law and administrative law more generally. See, e.g., Jerry L. Mashaw, Due Process in the Administrative State (1985); Cynthia R. Farina, *On Misusing "Revolution" and "Reform": Procedural Due Process and the New Welfare Act*, 50 Admin. L. Rev. 591 (1998).

5. Further Reading. See, e.g., Matthew C.R. Craven, The International Covenant on Economic, Social and Cultural Rights: A Perspective on its Development (1995); Economic, Social and Cultural Rights: A Textbook (Asbjørn Eide et al. eds. 1995); The Protection of Fundamental Social Rights in the European Union (Lammy Betten and Delma Mac Devitt eds. 1996). In the U.S. context, compare, e.g., Frank I. Michelman, *Foreword: On Protecting the Poor Through the Fourteenth Amendment*, 83 Harv. L. Rev. 7 (1969), with Ralph K. Winter, Jr., *Poverty, Economic Equality, and the Equal Protection Clause*, 1972 Sup. Ct. Rev. 41 (1973).

Note: *The ICESCR and Welfare Reform*

In 1996, the U.S. federal government enacted the Personal Responsibility and Work Opportunity Reconciliation Act, Pub. L. 104–193, 110 Stat. 2105 (1996) ("PRWORA"). The statute was designed to "end welfare as we know it." As one of its central features, PRWORA abolished the federal Aid to Families with Dependent Children program, which had provided a federal entitlement to subsistence aid for eligible families under joint federal-state administration. PRWORA replaced AFDC with the Temporary Assistance to Needy Families (TANF) program, under which the federal government would neither guarantee assistance to all eligible families nor require the states to do so. The provisions of PRWORA are complex; how they would operate in the long-term if unamended is uncertain as of this writing; some of the provisions were modified after enactment, and further amendments may also be enacted in the future. Nonetheless, juxtaposition of this radical revision of U.S. social welfare policy with the ICESCR provides a useful vehicle for examining the meaning of economic and social rights.

Consider the following characterizations of features of the PRWORA and the principles it incorporates. Make the counterfactual assumptions that the United States is a party to the ICESCR, and has entered no relevant reservations. Which if any of these features of PRWORA would be incompatible with the obligations of the United States under the ICESCR, and which could be justified within the framework of the ICESCR?

(a) Under PRWORA benefits are not guaranteed to all eligible recipients, but rather are contingent on the relationship between the number of applicants and the limits of the appropriations, even while billions of dollars are being spent for unnecessary programs such as exploration of outer space.

(b) PRWORA requires most recipients to work if they are receiving benefits. (See 42 U.S.C. § 607.) Assume that a state program implements this policy by requiring recipients to accept whatever job it offers them, and cancels their benefits if they decline. Could such a program be justified under the ICESCR?

(c) PRWORA makes anyone who is convicted of a state or federal felony relating to illegal possession, use, or distribution of a controlled substance permanently ineligible for benefits. (See 21 U.S.C. § 862a.)

(d) PRWORA imposes a 5–year lifetime limit on benefits for most recipients. (See 42 U.S.C. § 608(a)(7).)

(e) PRWORA constitutes a deliberate retrogression in the assurance of subsistence benefits to families in need. (Cf. General Comment 3, ¶ 9.)

D. THE RIGHT TO EDUCATION

The right to receive an education, as a right to receive instructional services at public expense, may be characterized as a social right. Educational policy raises a variety of complex issues, however, and aspects of educational policy addressing the content of education, the provision of private educational services, and choice among available educational options may also be viewed as implicating civil, economic, and cultural rights. This section focuses primarily on education as a social right. After discussing the dimensions of education addressed by international human rights instruments, it turns to the more limited guarantee of the right to education in the European Convention. It then contrasts the right to education under the European Convention with the treatment of the right to education under the U.S. Constitution, and the more robust guarantees of some state constitutions.

Note: Rights to Education in International Human Rights Instruments

Article 26 of the Universal Declaration of Human Rights addresses a number of different aspects of education at substantial length. It provides:

1. Everyone has the right to education. Education shall be free, at least in the elementary and fundamental stages. Elementary education shall be compulsory. Technical and professional education shall be made generally available and higher education shall be equally accessible to all on the basis of merit.

2. Education shall be directed to the full development of the human personality and to the strengthening of respect for human rights and fundamental freedoms. It shall promote understanding, tolerance and friendship among all nations, racial or religious groups, and shall further the activities of the United Nations for the maintenance of peace.

3. Parents have a prior right to choose the kind of education that shall be given to their children.

The two Covenants add further detail to the provisions of Article 26. Education is mentioned explicitly in the ICCPR in connection with freedom of conscience. Article 18(4) provides:

The States Parties to the present Covenant undertake to have respect for the liberty of parents and, when applicable, legal guardians to ensure the religious and moral education of their children in conformity with their own convictions.

The ICESCR devotes two articles to education:

Article 13

1.   The States Parties to the present Covenant recognize the right of everyone to education. They agree that education shall be directed to the full development of the human personality and the sense of its dignity, and shall strengthen the respect for human rights and fundamental freedoms. They further agree that education shall enable all persons to participate effectively in a free society, promote understanding, tolerance and friendship among all nations and all racial, ethnic or religious groups, and further the activities of the United Nations for the maintenance of peace.

2.   The States Parties to the present Covenant recognize that, with a view to achieving the full realization of this right:

(a) Primary education shall be compulsory and available free to all;

(b) Secondary education in its different forms, including technical and vocational secondary education, shall be made generally available and accessible to all by every appropriate means, and in particular by the progressive introduction of free education;

(c) Higher education shall be made equally accessible to all, on the basis of capacity, by every appropriate means, and in particular by the progressive introduction of free education;

(d) Fundamental education shall be encouraged or intensified as far as possible for those persons who have not received or completed the whole period of their primary education;

(e) The development of a system of schools at all levels shall be actively pursued, an adequate fellowship system shall be established, and the material conditions of teaching staff shall be continuously improved.

3.   The States Parties to the present Covenant undertake to have respect for the liberty of parents and, when applicable, legal guardians to choose for their children schools, other than those established by the public authorities, which conform to such minimum educational standards as may be laid down or approved by the State and to ensure the religious and moral education of their children in conformity with their own convictions.

4.   No part of this article shall be construed so as to interfere with the liberty of individuals and bodies to establish and direct educational institutions, subject always to the observance of the principles set forth in paragraph 1 of this article and to the requirement that the education given in such institutions shall conform to such minimum standards as may be laid down by the State.

Article 14

Each State Party to the present Covenant which, at the time of becoming a Party, has not been able to secure in its metropolitan territory or other territories under its jurisdiction compulsory primary education, free of charge, undertakes, within two years, to work out and adopt a detailed plan of action for the progressive implementation, within a reasonable number of years, to be fixed in the plan, of the principle of compulsory education free of charge for all.

Within the ICESCR's design for progressive achievement of the full realization of rights, the specification of time limits in Article 14 is unique. Note also the repeated requirements that primary (or elementary) education be compulsory. Why is it consistent with the character of rights to frame compulsory education as a human *right*?

Note further the curious formulation of Article 13(4), which does not guarantee a liberty to establish private schools. Can such a liberty be derived from elsewhere in the ICESCR, or from the ICCPR? If not, does ICESCR Article 13(3) recognize the right of parents to choose private schooling for their children only if the state already permits such schools to exist? (In the United States, the Supreme Court has recognized a substantive due process right of parents to send their children to private schools, and invalidated a state statute requiring all children to attend public schools. *Pierce v. Society of Sisters*, 268 U.S. 510 (1925); *see also Meyer v. Nebraska*, 262 U.S. 390 (1923) (recognizing right of parents to have their children taught a foreign language)).

The Convention on the Rights of the Child devotes two articles to education, Articles 28 and 29; Article 29 stipulates additional goals for education, including cultural goals and "development of respect for the natural environment." Article 10 of the Convention on the Elimination of All Forms of Discrimination Against Women addresses a series of issues regarding education of women as well as gender stereotyping within education.

The Committee on Economic, Social and Cultural Rights held a Day of General Discussion on the Right to Education under Articles 13 and 14 of the ICESCR on November 30, 1998. Days of general discussion are a technique that the Committee has used to deepen its understanding of particular issues, and have sometimes been precursors to the issuance of a General Comment. The 1998 general discussion focused on a number of aspects of the right to education, among which were the many millions of children who attend no schools at all; the severe gender disparity in access to education in some countries; and cooperation with UN specialized agencies in order to agree on indicators for monitoring the realization of the right to education. In May 1999, the Committee adopted General Comment No. 11, addressing Article 14. U.N. Doc. E/C.12/1999/4.

Note: The Right to Education under the European Convention and the Belgian Linguistics Case

Article 2 of Protocol No. 1 to the European Convention protects the right to education in the following terms·

No person shall be denied the right to education. In the exercise of any functions which it assumes in relation to education and to teaching, the State shall respect the right of parents to ensure such education and teaching in conformity with their own religious and philosophical convictions.

The European Court of Human Rights interpreted this provision in one of its earliest cases, the *Case Relating to Certain Aspects of the Laws on the Use of Languages in Education in Belgium*, 6 Eur. Ct. H.R. (ser. A), 1 E.H.R.R. 252 (1968) (the "Belgian Linguistics Case"). The case was brought by French-speaking parents residing in areas of Belgium in which their children were required to attend schools in which Dutch was the language of instruction. The Court found that most of the rules to which the parents objected were consistent with the European Convention, but a majority of the Court concluded that the rules governing access to French-language and Dutch-language schools in certain districts in the vicinity of Brussels constituted unjustifiable discrimination on the basis of language, and therefore violated Article 14 of the Convention in conjunction with Article 2 of Protocol No. 1. In the course of its analysis, the Court provided the following explanation of Article 2:

3.   By the terms of the first sentence of this Article, "no person shall be denied the right to education".

In spite of its negative formulation, this provision uses the term "right" and speaks of a "right to education". Likewise the preamble to the Protocol specifies that the object of the Protocol lies in the collective enforcement of "rights and freedoms". There is therefore no doubt that Article 2 does enshrine a right.

It remains however to determine the content of this right and the scope of the obligation which is thereby placed upon States.

The negative formulation indicates, as is confirmed by the preparatory work ... that the Contracting Parties do not recognise such a right to education as would require them to establish at their own expense, or to subsidise, education of any particular type or at any particular level. However, it cannot be concluded from this that the State has no positive obligation to ensure respect for such a right as is protected by Article 2 of the Protocol. As a "right" does exist, it is secured, by virtue of Article 1 of the Convention, to everyone within the jurisdiction of a Contracting State.

To determine the scope of the "right to education", within the meaning of the first sentence of Article 2 of the Protocol, the Court must bear in mind the aim of this provision. It notes in this context that all member States of the Council of Europe possessed, at the time of the opening of the Protocol to their signature, and still do possess, a general and official education system. There neither was, nor is now, therefore, any question of requiring each State to establish such a system, but merely of guaranteeing to persons subject to the jurisdiction of the Contracting Parties the right, in principle, to avail themselves of the means of instruction existing at a given time.

The Convention lays down no specific obligations concerning the extent of these means and the manner of their organisation or subsidisation. In particular, the first sentence of Article 2 does not specify the language in which education must be conducted in order that the right to education should be respected. It does not contain precise provisions similar to those which appear in Articles 5 (2) and 6 (3) (a) and (e). However, the right to education would be meaningless if it did not imply, in favour of its beneficiaries, the right to be educated in the national language or in one of the national languages, as the case may be.

4.   The first sentence of Article 2 of the Protocol consequently guarantees, in the first place, a right of access to educational institutions existing at a given time, but such access constitutes only a part of the right to education. For the "right to education" to be effective, it is further necessary that, inter alia, the individual who is the beneficiary should have the possibility of drawing profit from the education received, that is to say, the right to obtain, in conformity with the rules in force in each State, and in one form or another, official recognition of the studies which he had completed. . . .

5.   The right to education guaranteed by the first sentence of Article 2 of the Protocol by its very nature calls for regulation by the State, regulation which may vary in time and place according to the needs and resources of the community and of individuals. It goes without saying that such regulation must never injure the substance of the right to education nor conflict with other rights enshrined in the Convention.

The Court considers that the general aim set for themselves by the Contracting Parties through the medium of the European Convention on Human Rights was to provide effective protection of fundamental human rights, and this, without doubt, not only because of the historical context in which the Convention was concluded, but also of the social and technical developments in our age which offer to States considerable possibilities for regulating the exercise of these rights. The Convention therefore implies a just balance between the protection of the general interest of the community and the respect due to fundamental human rights while attaching particular importance to the latter.

6.   The second sentence of Article 2 of the Protocol does not guarantee a right to education; this is clearly shown by its wording. . . .

This provision does not require of States that they should in the sphere of education or teaching, respect parents' linguistic preferences, but only their religious and philosophical convictions. To interpret the terms "religious" and "philosophical" as covering linguistic preferences would amount to a distortion of their ordinary and usual meaning and to read into the Convention something which is not there. Moreover the preparatory work confirms that the object of the second sentence of Article 2 was in no way to secure respect by the State of a right for parents to have education conducted in a language other than that of the country in question; indeed in June 1951 the Committee of Experts which had the task of drafting the Protocol set aside a proposal put forward in this sense. Several members of the Committee believed that it concerned an aspect of the problem of ethnic minorities and that it consequently fell outside the scope of the Convention. The second sentence of Article 2 is therefore irrelevant to the problems raised in the present case.

Campbell and Cosans v. United Kingdom

European Court of Human Rights, 1982.
48 Eur. Ct. H.R. (ser. A), 4 E.H.R.R. 293.

8. Both Mrs. Campbell and Mrs. Cosans live in Scotland.* Each of them had one child of compulsory school age at the time when she applied to the Commission. The applicants' complaints concern the use of corporal punishment as a disciplinary measure in the State schools in Scotland attended by their children. For both financial and practical reasons, the applicants had no realistic and acceptable alternative to sending their children to State schools.

10. Mrs. Cosans's son Jeffrey, who was born on 31 May 1961, used to attend Beath Senior High School in Cowdenbeath which is situated in the Fife Region Education Authority area. On 23 September 1976, he was told to report to the Assistant Headmaster on the following day to receive corporal punishment for having tried to take a prohibited short cut through a cemetery on his way home from school. On his father's advice, Jeffrey duly reported, but refused to accept the punishment. On that account, he was immediately suspended from school until such time as he was willing to accept the punishment.

11. On 1 October 1976, Jeffrey's parents were officially informed of his suspension. On 18 October, they had an inconclusive meeting with the Senior Assistant Director of Education of the Fife Regional Council during which they repeated their disapproval of corporal punishment. On 14 January 1977, the day after a further meeting, that official informed Mr. and Mrs. Cosans by letter that he had decided to lift the suspension in view of the fact that their son's long absence from school constituted punishment enough; however, he added the condition that they should accept, inter alia, that "Jeffrey will obey the rules, regulations or disciplinary requirements of the school". However, Mr. and Mrs. Cosans stipulated that if their son were to be readmitted to the school, he should not receive corporal punishment for any incident while he was a pupil. The official replied that this constituted a refusal to accept the aforesaid condition.

* [The discussion of Mrs. Campbell and her son is omitted.—Editors' Note.]

Accordingly, Jeffrey's suspension was not lifted and his parents were warned that they might be prosecuted for failure to ensure his attendance at school.

In the event, Jeffrey never returned to school after 24 September 1976. He ceased to be of compulsory school age on 31 May 1977, his sixteenth birthday.

13.   In the two schools concerned, corporal chastisement takes the form of striking the palm of the pupil's hand with a leather strap called a "tawse". For misconduct in the class-room, punishment is administered there and then, in the presence of the class; for misconduct elsewhere and for serious misconduct, it is administered by the Headmaster, or his deputy, in his room.

The Commission noted that, on the facts of the case, it could not be established that the applicants' children had suffered any adverse psychological or other effects which could be imputed to the use of corporal punishment in their schools.

18.   ...   The Government remain committed to a policy aimed at abolishing corporal punishment as a disciplinary measure in Scottish schools, but they take the view that that policy is best implemented by seeking to secure progress in this direction by consensus of all concerned rather than by statute. A working group established in 1979 by the convention of Scottish Local Authorities has been considering, inter alia, the introduction of alternative sanctions and there are, in fact, some schools in which the use of corporal punishment has ceased or will soon be abandoned. However, its continued use by teachers is apparently, according to a recent opinion survey, favoured by a large majority of Scottish parents and, according to the Pack Committee's report, by pupils, who even prefer it to some other forms of punishment.

[The Court found that Jeffrey Cosans and his mother could not raise the issue of the compatibility of corporal punishment with Article 3 of the European Convention (prohibiting inhuman or degrading treatment or punishment), because Jeffrey had never been subjected to corporal punishment.]

II.   THE ALLEGED VIOLATION OF THE SECOND SENTENCE OF ARTICLE 2 OF PROTOCOL NO. 1

32.   ...   Mrs. Cosans alleged that [her] rights under the second sentence of this Article were violated on account of the existence of corporal punishment as a disciplinary measure in the [school attended by her child]. . . .

33.   The Government maintained in the first place that functions relating to the internal administration of a school, such as discipline, were ancillary and were not functions in relation to "education" and to "teaching", within the meaning of Article 2, these terms denoting the provision of facilities and the imparting of information, respectively.

The Court would point out that the education of children is the whole process whereby, in any society, adults endeavour to transmit their beliefs, culture and other values to the young, whereas teaching or instruction refers in particular to the transmission of knowledge and to intellectual development.

... Moreover, as the Court pointed out in Kjeldsen, Busk Madsen and Pedersen [v. Denmark, 23 Eur. Ct. H.R. (ser. A), 1 E.H.R.R. 711 (1976)], the second sentence of Article 2 is binding upon the contracting States in the exercise of "each and every" function that they undertake in the sphere of education and teaching, so that the fact that a given function may be considered to be ancillary is of no moment in this context.

36. The Government also contested the conclusion of the majority of the Commission that the applicants' view on the use of corporal punishment amounted to "philosophical convictions", arguing, inter alia, that the expression did not extend to opinions on internal school administration, such as discipline, and that, if the majority were correct, there was no reason why objections to other methods of discipline, or simply to discipline in general, should not also amount to "philosophical convictions".

. . .

Having regard to the Convention as a whole, including Article 17, the expression "philosophical convictions" in the present context denotes, in the Court's opinion, such convictions as are worthy of respect in a "democratic society" and are not incompatible with human dignity; in addition, they must not conflict with the fundamental right of the child to education, the whole of Article 2 being dominated by its first sentence.

The applicants' views relate to a weighty and substantial aspect of human life and behaviour, namely the integrity of the person, the propriety or otherwise of the infliction of corporal punishment entails. They are views which satisfy each of the various criteria listed above; it is this that distinguishes them from opinions that might be held on other methods of discipline or on discipline in general.

37. The Government pleaded, in the alternative, that the obligation to respect the applicants' convictions had been satisfied by the adoption of a policy of gradually eliminating corporal chastisement. They added that any other solution would be incompatible with the necessity of striking a balance between the opinions of supporters and opponents of this method of discipline and with the terms of the reservation of Article 2 made by the United Kingdom at the time of signing the Protocol, which reads:

... in view of certain provisions of the Education Acts in force in the United Kingdom, the principle affirmed in the second sentence of Article 2 is accepted by the United Kingdom only so far as it is compatible with the provision of efficient instruction and training, and the avoidance of unreasonable public expenditure.

The Court is unable to accept these submissions.

(a) Whilst the adoption of the policy referred to clearly foreshadows a move in the direction of the position taken by the applicants, it does not amount to "respect" for their convictions. As is confirmed by the fact that, in the course of the drafting of Article 2, the words "have regard to" were replaced by the word "respect" (See Document CDH (67) 2, p 163), the latter word means more than "acknowledge" or "take into account"; in addition to a primarily negative undertaking, it implies some positive obligation on the part of the State. This being so, the duty to respect parental convictions in this sphere cannot be overridden by the alleged necessity of striking a balance between the conflicting views involved, nor is the Government's policy to move gradually towards the abolition of corporal punishment in itself sufficient to comply with this duty.

(b) As regards the United Kingdom reservation, the Court . . .

. . . accepts that certain solutions canvassed—such as the establishment of a dual system whereby in each sector there would be separate schools for the children of parents objecting to corporal punishment—would be incompatible, especially in the present economic situation, with the avoidance of unreasonable public expenditure. However, the Court does not regard it as established that other means of respecting the applicants' convictions, such as a system of exemption for individual pupils in a particular school, would necessarily be incompatible with "the provision of efficient instruction and training, and the avoidance of unreasonable public expenditure".

38. . . . Mrs. Cosans [has] accordingly been [a victim] of a violation of the second sentence of Article 2 of Protocol No. 1.

III.   THE ALLEGED VIOLATION OF THE FIRST SENTENCE OF ARTICLE 2 OF PROTOCOL NO 1.

39. Mrs. Cosans alleged that, by reason of his suspension from school (see para 10–11 above), her son Jeffrey had been denied the right to education, contrary to the first sentence of Article 2. . . .

40. The Court considers that it is necessary to determine this issue. Of course, the existence of corporal punishment as a disciplinary measure in the school attended by her son Jeffrey underlay both of Mrs. Cosans's allegations concerning Article 2, but there is a substantial difference between the factual basis of her two claims. In the case of the second sentence, the situation complained of was attendance at a school where recourse was had to a certain practice, whereas, in the case of the first sentence, it was the fact of being forbidden to attend; the consequences of the latter situation are more far-reaching than those of the former. Accordingly, a separate complaint, and not merely a further legal submission or argument, was involved.

Again, Article 2 constitutes a whole that is dominated by its first sentence, the right set out in the second sentence being an adjunct of the fundamental right to education.

Finally, there is also a substantial difference between the legal basis of the two claims, for one concerns a right of a parent and the other a right of a child.

The issue arising under the first sentence is therefore not absorbed by the finding of a violation of the second.

41.   The right to education guaranteed by the first sentence of Article 2 by its very nature calls for regulation by the State, but such regulation must never injure the substance of the right nor conflict with other rights enshrined in the Convention or its Protocols.

The suspension of Jeffrey Cosans—which remained in force for nearly a whole school year—was motivated by his and his parents' refusal to accept that he receive or be liable to corporal chastisement (see paras 10–11 above). His return to school could have been secured only if his parents had acted contrary to their convictions, convictions which the United Kingdom is obliged to respect under the second sentence of Article 2 (see paras 35–36 above). A condition of access to an educational establishment that conflicts in this way with another right enshrined in Protocol No. 1 cannot be described as reasonable and in any event falls outside the State's power of regulation under Article 2.

There has accordingly also been, as regards Jeffrey Cosans, breach of the first sentence of that Article.

. . .

■ Partly Dissenting Opinion of JUDGE SIR VINCENT EVANS

. . .

3.   In the previous two cases in which the application of Article 2 has been in issue, the Court has found it indispensable to have recourse to the negotiating history of the Article as an aid to the interpretation of what is undeniably a very difficult text. ... In the Kjeldsen, Busk Madsen and Pedersen case (in which parents sought unsuccessfully to have their children exempted from sex education in state schools on the ground that it was contrary to their beliefs as Christian parents) this was that the State is forbidden to pursue an aim of indoctrination that might be considered as not respecting parents' religious and philosophical convictions. "That", said the Court, "is the limit that must not be exceeded" and consequently it was held that legislation which "in no way amount[ed] to an attempt at indoctrination aimed at advocating a specific kind of sexual behaviour" did not offend the applicants' religious and philosophical convictions to the extent forbidden by the second sentence of Article 2. In the Belgian Linguistic case it was held that this provision did not require of States that they should, in the sphere of education and teaching, respect parents' linguistic preferences, but only their religious and philosophical convictions and that to interpret the terms "religious" and "philosophical" as covering linguistic preferences would amount to a distortion of their ordinary and usual meaning and read into the convention something that was not there.

4. . . . [M]y understanding of the second sentence of Article 2 is that it is concerned with the content of information and knowledge imparted to the child through education and teaching and the manner of imparting such information and knowledge and that the views of parents on such matters as the use of corporal punishment are as much outside the intended scope of the provision as are their linguistic preferences. If there had been any intention that it should apply to disciplinary measures, and to the use of corporal punishment in particular, it is inconceivable that the implications of this would not have been raised in the course of the lengthy debates that preceded its adoption.

6.   However, even if the wider interpretation of the second sentence of Article 2 adopted by the Court in the present case were correct, it would be my opinion that there has been no violation of this provision in view of the reservation made by the United Kingdom on signature of the Protocol. . . . [T]he obligation thereunder to respect the right of parents has been assumed by the United Kingdom only so far as this can be done compatibly with the provision of efficient instruction and training and the avoidance of unreasonable public expenditure.

7. . . . In the course of the proceedings, only three possible solutions have been canvassed which, apart from the reservation, which sufficiently comply with the State's obligation as interpreted by the Court. These are—

1. that separate schools should be provided within the State educational system for children of parents who object to corporal punishment.

2. that separate classes within the same school should be provided for such children;

3. that a system should be established in which children in the same class should be treated differently according to the views and wishes of their parents.

The Court accepts that the first solution would be incompatible with the avoidance of unreasonable public expenditure, especially in the present economic situation. The second solution too would surely involve unreasonable expense and hardly be compatible with the provision of efficient instruction and training. . . . There remains the third possible solution referred to above. The Court was informed at the oral hearing that at least some members of the Commission held the view that this would, for many reasons, not be a practical solution. I agree with this view. It seems to me essential that any system of discipline in a school should be seen to be fair and capable of being fairly administered, otherwise a sense of injustice will be generated with harmful consequences both for the upbringing of the individual and for harmonious relations within the group. It will also place the teacher in an impractical position to administer discipline fairly if children in the same class have to be treated differently according to the views of their parents. It has been pointed out that, where corporal punishment is used, exceptions are in any event made in respect of girls and children suffering from a disability. I believe that children will readily understand the reasons for this, but I think they are likely to regard it as arbitrary and unjust if Johnny is exempted simply because his Mum or Dad says so.

San Antonio Independent School District v. Rodriguez

Supreme Court of the United States, 1973.
411 U.S. 1.

[The plaintiffs were schoolchildren residing in "property-poor" school districts in the state of Texas. They alleged that, because Texas law relied heavily on local property taxes to finance public education, the funds available and the resulting quality of education varied widely with the wealth of the district. They argued that this discrimination violated the Equal Protection Clause of the Fourteenth Amendment. A majority of the Supreme Court denied their claim, applying only rational basis scrutiny. In the following passage, the majority rejected the argument that unequal distribution of educational services should be strictly scrutinized because education was a fundamental right.]

... It is not the province of this Court to create substantive constitutional rights in the name of guaranteeing equal protection of the laws. Thus, the key to discovering whether education is "fundamental" is not to be found in comparisons of the relative societal significance of education as opposed to subsistence or housing. Nor is it to be found by weighing whether education is as important as the right to travel. Rather, the answer lies in assessing whether there is a right to education explicitly or implicitly guaranteed by the Constitution.

Education, of course, is not among the rights afforded explicit protection under our Federal Constitution. Nor do we find any basis for saying it is implicitly so protected. As we have said, the undisputed importance of education will not alone cause this Court to depart from the usual standard for reviewing a State's social and economic legislation. It is appellees' contention, however, that education is distinguishable from other services and benefits provided by the State because it bears a peculiarly close relationship to other rights and liberties accorded protection under the Constitution. Specifically, they insist that education is itself a fundamental personal right because it is essential to the effective exercise of First Amendment freedoms and to intelligent utilization of the right to vote. In asserting a nexus between speech and education, appellees urge that the right to speak is meaningless unless the speaker is capable of articulating his thoughts intelligently and persuasively. The "marketplace of ideas" is an empty forum for those lacking basic communicative tools. Likewise, they argue that the corollary right to receive information becomes little more than a hollow privilege when the recipient has not been taught to read, assimilate, and utilize available knowledge.

A similar line of reasoning is pursued with respect to the right to vote. Exercise of the franchise, it is contended, cannot be divorced from the educational foundation of the voter. The electoral process, if reality is to conform to the democratic ideal, depends on an informed electorate: a voter cannot cast his ballot intelligently unless his reading skills and thought processes have been adequately developed.

We need not dispute any of these propositions. The Court has long afforded zealous protection against unjustifiable governmental interference with the individual's rights to speak and to vote. Yet we have never presumed to possess either the ability or the authority to guarantee to the citizenry the most effective speech or the most informed electoral choice. That these may be desirable goals of a system of freedom of expression and of a representative form of government is not to be doubted. These are indeed goals to be pursued by a people whose thoughts and beliefs are freed from governmental interference. But they are not values to be implemented by judicial intrusion into otherwise legitimate state activities.

Even if it were conceded that some identifiable quantum of education is a constitutionally protected prerequisite to the meaningful exercise of either right, we have no indication that the present levels of educational expenditures in Texas provide an education that falls short. Whatever merit appellees' argument might have if a State's financing system occasioned an absolute denial of educational opportunities to any of its children, that argument provides no basis for finding an interference with fundamental rights where only relative differences in spending levels are involved and where—as is true in the present case—no charge fairly could be made that the system fails to provide each child with an opportunity to acquire the basic minimal skills necessary for the enjoyment of the rights of speech and of full participation in the political process.

Furthermore, the logical limitations on appellees' nexus theory are difficult to perceive. How, for instance, is education to be distinguished from the significant personal interests in the basics of decent food and shelter? Empirical examination might well buttress an assumption that the ill-fed, ill-clothed, and ill-housed are among the most ineffective participants in the political process, and that they derive the least enjoyment from the benefits of the First Amendment. If so, appellees' thesis would cast serious doubt on the authority of Dandridge v. Williams, [397 U.S. 471 (1970) (denying existence of fundamental right to welfare benefits)] and Lindsey v. Normet, [405 U.S. 56 (1972) (denying existence of fundamental right to housing)].

We have carefully considered each of the arguments supportive of the District Court's finding that education is a fundamental right or liberty and have found those arguments unpersuasive. In one further respect we find this a particularly inappropriate case in which to subject state action to strict judicial scrutiny. The present case, in another basic sense, is significantly different from any of the cases in which the Court has applied strict scrutiny to state or federal legislation touching upon constitutionally protected rights. Each of our prior cases involved legislation which "deprived," "infringed," or "interfered" with the free exercise of some such fundamental personal right or liberty. A critical distinction between those cases and the one now before us lies in what Texas is endeavoring to do with respect to education. . . .

Every step leading to the establishment of the system Texas utilizes today—including the decisions permitting localities to tax and expend locally, and creating and continuously expanding the state aid—was implemented in an effort to extend public education and to improve its quality. Of course, every reform that benefits some more than others may be criticized for what it fails to accomplish. But we think it plain that, in substance, the thrust of the Texas system is affirmative and reformatory and, therefore, should be scrutinized under judicial principles sensitive to the nature of the State's efforts and to the rights reserved to the States under the Constitution.

Notes

1. In the U.S. context, are the arguments for an unenumerated constitutional right to education, rejected by the Supreme Court's 1973 decision in *Rodriguez*, less persuasive or more persuasive than the arguments for an unenumerated constitutional right to abortion, accepted by the Supreme Court's 1973 decision in *Roe v. Wade*? Does one right have more fundamental importance than the other? Is one right more easily analogized to other rights enumerated in the Constitution than the other? Does one right have more historical support than the other? Should great weight be placed on the positive or negative character of each right?

2. Should *Rodriguez* be read as leaving open the possibility of a federal constitutional right not to be denied an education altogether? In *Plyler v. Doe*, 457 U.S. 202 (1982), a five-Justice majority invalidated on equal protection grounds a Texas statute that denied undocumented alien children a free public education. The majority opinion gave the following reasons for intensifying its scrutiny of the statute:

> Public education is not a ''right'' granted to individuals by the Constitution. San Antonio Independent School Dist. v. Rodriguez, 411 U.S. 1, 35 (1973). But neither is it merely some governmental ''benefit'' indistinguishable from other forms of social welfare legislation. Both the importance of education in maintaining our basic institutions, and the lasting impact of its deprivation on the life of the child, mark the distinction. The ''American people have always regarded education and [the] acquisition of knowledge as matters of supreme importance.'' We have recognized ''the public schools as a most vital civic institution for the preservation of a democratic system of government,'' and as the primary vehicle for transmitting ''the values on which our society rests.'' ''[A]s . . . pointed out early in our history, . . . some degree of education is necessary to prepare citizens to participate effectively and intelligently in our open political system if we are to preserve freedom and independence.'' And these historic ''perceptions of the public schools as inculcating fundamental values necessary to the maintenance of a democratic political system have been confirmed by the

observations of social scientists." In addition, education provides the basic tools by which individuals might lead economically productive lives to the benefit of us all. In sum, education has a fundamental role in maintaining the fabric of our society. We cannot ignore the significant social costs borne by our Nation when select groups are denied the means to absorb the values and skills upon which our social order rests.

In addition to the pivotal role of education in sustaining our political and cultural heritage, denial of education to some isolated group of children poses an affront to one of the goals of the Equal Protection Clause: the abolition of governmental barriers presenting unreasonable obstacles to advancement on the basis of individual merit. Paradoxically, by depriving the children of any disfavored group of an education, we foreclose the means by which that group might raise the level of esteem in which it is held by the majority. But more directly, "education prepares individuals to be self-reliant and self-sufficient participants in society." Illiteracy is an enduring disability. The inability to read and write will handicap the individual deprived of a basic education each and every day of his life. The inestimable toll of that deprivation on the social economic, intellectual, and psychological well-being of the individual, and the obstacle it poses to individual achievement, make it most difficult to reconcile the cost or the principle of a status-based denial of basic education with the framework of equality embodied in the Equal Protection Clause. . . .

. . .

These well-settled principles allow us to determine the proper level of deference to be afforded [to the Texas statute]. Undocumented aliens cannot be treated as a suspect class because their presence in this country in violation of federal law is not a "constitutional irrelevancy." Nor is education a fundamental right; a State need not justify by compelling necessity every variation in the manner in which education is provided to its population. See San Antonio Independent School Dist. v. Rodriguez, supra. But more is involved in these cases than the abstract question whether [the statute] discriminates against a suspect class, or whether education is a fundamental right. [The statute] imposes a lifetime hardship on a discrete class of children not accountable for their disabling status. The stigma of illiteracy will mark them for the rest of their lives. By denying these children a basic education, we deny them the ability to live within the structure of our civic institutions, and foreclose any realistic possibility that they will contribute in even the smallest way to the progress of our Nation. In determining the rationality of [the statute], we may appropriately take into account its costs to the Nation and to the innocent children who are its victims. In light of these countervailing costs, the discrimination contained in [the statute] can hardly be considered rational unless it furthers some substantial goal of the State.

Justice Powell, the author of the *Rodriguez* decision, concurred. Should *Plyler* be read as recognizing a constitutional right not be denied an education altogether?

The Supreme Court may have an opportunity to reaffirm or modify the *Plyler* decision in the wake of California's adoption in 1994 of Proposition 187, an initiative that included a provision deliberately inconsistent with *Plyler*. See *League of United Latin American Citizens v. Wilson*, 997 F.Supp. 1244 (C.D.Cal.1997).

Leandro v. State of North Carolina

Supreme Court of North Carolina, 1997.
488 S.E.2d 249.

■ MITCHELL, CHIEF JUSTICE.

[Plaintiffs were students and parents from several North Carolina counties. They alleged that, as a result of North Carolina's system for funding education partly from local resources and partly from state resources, the students were receiving an inadequate education, and were not receiving an equal education in comparison with students in other North Carolina counties. The allegations regarding some districts focused on the insufficiency of the tax base; the allegations regarding other districts focused on the disproportionate concentration of students with special educational needs.]

It has long been understood that it is the duty of the courts to determine the meaning of the requirements of our Constitution. When a government action is challenged as unconstitutional, the courts have a duty to determine whether that action exceeds constitutional limits. Therefore, it is the duty of this Court to address plaintiff-parties' constitutional challenge to the state's public education system. ...

. . .

The right to a free public education is explicitly guaranteed by the North Carolina Constitution: "The people have a right to the privilege of education, and it is the duty of the State to guard and maintain that right." N.C. Const. art. I, § 15.* The Constitution also provides:

> The General Assembly shall provide by taxation and otherwise for a general and uniform system of free public schools, which shall be maintained at least nine months in every year, and wherein equal opportunities shall be provided for all students.

Id. art. IX, § 2(1). The principal question presented by this argument is whether the people's constitutional right to education has any qualitative content, that is, whether the state is required to provide children with an education that meets some minimum standard of quality. We answer that question in the affirmative and conclude that the right to education

---

* [This provision derives verbatim from N.C. Const. of 1868, art. I, § 27. The original North Carolina Constitution of 1776 had no corresponding provision.—Editors' Note.]

provided in the state constitution is a right to a sound basic education. An education that does not serve the purpose of preparing students to participate and compete in the society in which they live and work is devoid of substance and is constitutionally inadequate.

. . . .

This Court has long recognized that there is a qualitative standard inherent in the right to education guaranteed by this state's constitution. In Board of Educ. v. Board of Comm'rs of Granville County, 93 S.E. 1001 (N.C.1917), for example, we stated:

> [I]t is manifest that these constitutional provisions were intended to establish a system of public education adequate to the needs of a great and progressive people, affording school facilities of recognized and ever-increasing merit to all the children of the State, and to the full extent that our means could afford and intelligent direction accomplish.

93 S.E. at 1002.

The General Assembly also seems to have recognized the constitutional right to a sound basic education and to have embraced that right in chapter 115C of the General Statutes. For example, in a statute governing the use of funds under the control of the State Board of Education, the General Assembly has stated:

> (a) It is the policy of the State of North Carolina to create a public school system that graduates good citizens with the skills demanded in the marketplace, and the skills necessary to cope with contemporary society, using State, local and other funds in the most cost-effective manner. . . .

> (b) To insure a quality education for every child in North Carolina, and to assure that the necessary resources are provided, it is the policy of the State of North Carolina to provide from State revenue sources the instructional expenses for current operations of the public school system as defined in the standard course of study.

N.C.G.S. § 115C–408 (1994). In addition, the legislature has required local boards of education "to provide adequate school systems within their respective local school administrative units, as directed by law." N.C.G.S. § 115C–47(1) (Supp.1996).

We conclude that Article I, Section 15 and Article IX, Section 2 of the North Carolina Constitution combine to guarantee every child of this state an opportunity to receive a sound basic education in our public schools. For purposes of our Constitution, a "sound basic education" is one that will provide the student with at least: (1) sufficient ability to read, write, and speak the English language and a sufficient knowledge of fundamental mathematics and physical science to enable the student to function in a complex and rapidly changing society; (2) sufficient fundamental knowledge of geography, history, and basic economic and political systems to enable the student to make informed choices with regard to issues that affect the student personally or affect the student's community, state, and nation; (3) sufficient academic and vocational skills to enable the student to successfully engage in post-secondary education or vocational training; and (4) sufficient academic and vocational skills to enable the student to compete on an equal basis with others in further formal education or gainful employment in contemporary society. See generally Rose v. Council for Better Educ., Inc., 790 S.W.2d 186, 212 (Ky.1989); Pauley v. Kelly, 255 S.E.2d 859, 877 (W.Va.1979).

. . .

By other arguments, plaintiff-parties contend that the Court of Appeals erred in holding that the alleged disparity in the educational opportunities offered by the different school districts in the state does not violate their right to equal opportunities for education. They contend that Article IX, Section 2(1), requiring a "general and uniform system" in which "equal opportunities shall be provided for all students," mandates equality in the educational programs and resources offered the children in all school districts in North Carolina.

Plaintiffs and plaintiff-intervenors make somewhat different arguments in support of their purported rights to equal educational opportunities. Specifically, plaintiffs contend that inequalities in the facilities, equipment, student-teacher ratios, and test results between their poor districts and the wealthy districts compel the conclusion that students in their poor districts are denied equal opportunities for education. Plaintiffs contend that such inequalities arise from great variations in per-pupil expenditures from district to district.

. . .

Article IX, Section 2(2) of the North Carolina Constitution expressly authorizes the General Assembly to require that local governments bear part of the costs of their local public schools. Further, it expressly provides that local governments may add to or supplement their school programs as much as they wish.

> The General Assembly may assign to units of local government such responsibility for the financial support of the free public schools as it may deem appropriate. The governing boards of units of local government with financial responsibility for public education may use local revenues to add to or supplement any public school or post-secondary school program.

N.C. Const. art. IX, § 2(2).

. . .

Because the North Carolina Constitution expressly states that units of local governments with financial responsibility for public education may provide additional funding to supplement the educational programs provided by the state, there can be nothing unconstitutional about their doing so or in any inequality of opportunity occurring as a result. . . .

Further, as the North Carolina Constitution so clearly creates the likelihood of unequal funding among the districts as a result of local supplements, we see no reason to suspect that the framers intended that substantially equal educational opportunities beyond the sound basic education mandated by the Constitution must be available in all districts. A constitutional requirement to provide substantial equality of educational opportunities in every one of the various school districts of the state would almost certainly ensure that no matter how much money was spent on the schools of the state, at any given time some of those districts would be out of compliance. If strong local public support in a given district improved the educational opportunities of that district to the point that they were substantially better than those of any other district, the children of all the other school districts by definition would be denied substantially equal educational opportunities. The result would be a steady stream of litigation which would constantly interfere with the running of the schools of the state and unnecessarily deplete their human and fiscal resources as well as the resources of the courts.

Substantial problems have been experienced in those states in which the courts have held that the state constitution guaranteed the right to a sound basic education. See generally Horton v. Meskill, 486 A.2d 1099 (1985) (describing changes in the Connecticut public schools since the Connecticut Supreme Court had struck down an earlier financing system); Edgewood Indep. Sch. Dist. v. Meno, 917 S.W.2d 717 (Tex.1995) (a 5–4 decision upholding the state's school financing plan after the Texas Supreme Court had struck down three state plans for funding public education in Texas); State ex rel. Bds. of Educ. v. Chafin, 376 S.E.2d 113 (1988) (describing changes in the public schools since the Supreme Court of West Virginia had struck down the school financing system); William E. Thro, The Third Wave: The Impact of the Montana, Kentucky, and Texas Decisions on the Future of Public School Finance Reform Litigation, 19 J.L. & Legal Educ. 219 (1990) (describing the difficulty in understanding and implementing the mandates of the courts); James S. Liebman, Implementing Brown in the Nineties: Political Reconstruction, Liberal Recollection, and Litigatively Enforced Legislative Reform, 76 Va.L.Rev. 349, 392–93 (1990) (arguing that changes in Connecticut schools after successful litigation had failed to improve student performance); Note, Unfulfilled Promises: School Finance Remedies and State Courts, 104 Harv.L.Rev. 1072, 1075–78 (1991) (describing the lack of an adequate remedy in New Jersey). We believe that even greater problems of protracted litigation resulting in unworkable remedies would occur if we were to recognize the purported right to equal educational opportunities in every one of the state's districts. See generally Abbott v. Burke, 693 A.2d 417 (1997) (decision of a divided Court striking down the most recent efforts of the New Jersey legislature and for the third time declaring the funding system for the schools of that state to be in violation of the state constitution). We conclude that the framers of our Constitution did not intend to set such an impractical or unattainable goal. Instead, their focus was upon ensuring that the children of the state have the opportunity to receive a sound basic education.

For the foregoing reasons, we conclude that Article IX, Section 2(1) of the North Carolina Constitution requires that all children have the opportunity for a sound basic education, but it does not require that equal educational opportunities be afforded students in all of the school districts of the state. . . .

[The court concluded, however, that the plaintiffs should be permitted to present evidence that the existing system distributed funds from state sources to local school districts in an arbitrary and capricious manner unrelated to educational objectives, in violation of the equal protection and due process guarantees of the state constitution.]

. . .

In conclusion, we reemphasize our recognition of the fact that the administration of the public schools of the state is best left to the legislative and executive branches of government. Therefore, the courts of the state must grant every reasonable deference to the legislative and executive branches when considering whether they have established and are administering a system that provides the children of the various school districts of the state a sound basic education. A clear showing to the contrary must be made before the courts may conclude that they have not. Only such a clear showing will justify a judicial intrusion into an area so clearly the province, initially at least, of the legislative and executive branches as the determination of what course of action will lead to a sound basic education.

But like the other branches of government, the judicial branch has its duty under the North Carolina Constitution. If on remand of this case to the trial court, that court makes findings and conclusions from competent evidence to the effect that defendants in this case are denying children of the state a sound basic education, a denial of a fundamental right will have been established. It will then become incumbent upon defendants to establish that their actions denying this fundamental right are "necessary to promote a compelling governmental interest." If defendants are unable to do so, it will then be the duty of the court to enter a judgment granting declaratory relief and such other relief as needed to correct the wrong while minimizing the encroachment upon the other branches of government.

. . .

[Opinion of Justice Orr, dissenting in part and concurring in part, omitted.]

Brigham v. State of Vermont

Supreme Court of Vermont, 1997.
692 A.2d 384.

■ PER CURIAM.

In this appeal, we decide that the current system for funding public education in Vermont, with its substantial dependence on local property taxes and resultant wide disparities in revenues available to local school districts, deprives children of an equal educational opportunity in violation of the Vermont Constitution. In reaching this conclusion, we acknowledge the conscientious and ongoing efforts of the Legislature to achieve equity in educational financing and intend no intrusion upon its prerogatives to define a system consistent with constitutional requirements. In this context, the Court's duty today is solely to define the impact of the State Constitution on educational funding, not to fashion and impose a solution. The remedy at this juncture properly lies with the Legislature.

When we consider the evidence in the record before us, and apply the Education and Common Benefits Clauses of the Vermont Constitution to that evidence, see Vt. Const. ch. I, art. 7 and ch. II, § 68,* the conclusion becomes inescapable that the present system has fallen short of providing every school-age child in Vermont an equal educational opportunity. . . .

. . .

A.   The Right to Education in Vermont

From its earliest days, Vermont has recognized the obligation to provide for the education of its youth. That obligation begins with the Education Clause in the Vermont Constitution. A provision for the establishment of public schools was contained in the first Vermont Constitution of 1777. That section, in part, provided: "A school or schools shall be established in each town, by the legislature, for the convenient instruction of youth.... " Vt. Const. of 1777, ch. II, § 40. The clause was amended in 1786 as part of a comprehensive constitutional revision. The amendment modified the language of the section and combined it with the so-called "Virtue" Clause which followed the Education Clause in the original Constitution....

. . .

The important point is not simply that public education was mentioned in the first Constitution. It is, rather, that education was the only governmental service considered worthy of constitutional status. The framers were not unaware of other public needs. Among the first statutes enacted by the General Assembly in 1779 were two separate acts for the maintenance and support of the poor and infirm. . . .

Despite the obvious public concern for those least able to care for themselves, the framers made no provision in the Constitution for public

---

* [The Education Clause provides:

Laws for the encouragement of virtue and prevention of vice and immorality ought to be constantly kept in force, and duly executed; and a competent number of schools ought to be maintained in each town unless the general assembly permits other provisions for the convenient instruction of youth.

The Common Benefit Clause, which has been interpreted as an equal protection guarantee, provides:

That government is, or ought to be, instituted for the common benefit, protection, and security of the people, nation, or community, and not for the particular emolument or advantage of any single person, family, or set of persons, who are a part only of that community....

(Editors' Note)]

welfare or "poor relief" as it was then known. Indeed, many essential governmental services such as welfare, police and fire protection, transportation, and sanitation receive no mention whatsoever in our Constitution. Only one governmental service—public education—has ever been accorded constitutional status in Vermont.

. . .

In 1786, as noted, the Virtue and Education Clauses were combined to form a single section. Nothing could be more indicative of the close connection in the minds of the framers between virtue and all that that implied—civic responsibility, ethical values, industry, self-restraint—and public education than this textual union within the Constitution. No explanation for the 1786 modification survives, but the logical connection is self-evident. The amalgamation was perfectly consistent with the commonly held view of the framers that virtue was essential to self-government, and that education was the primary source of virtue. . . .

The State places great store in the fact that the 1786 amendment which combined the virtue and education sections also modified the text of the Education Clause from its original "schools shall be established" to its current "ought to be maintained." From this it infers that the framers intended to relegate education to a mere discretionary ideal. The framers, however, drew no distinction between "ought" and "shall" in defining rights and duties. . . .

The State also suggests that placement of the Education Clause in Chapter II, setting forth the "Frame of Government," rather than Chapter I, which contained the Declaration of Rights, implies that education was not considered by the framers to be an individual right. The argument is equally unpersuasive. Chapter II of the original Constitution enumerated any number of individual rights besides education, including the right to trial by jury, the right to bail, and the right to hold and acquire land. . . .

Apart from its prominence in the Constitution, the importance of education to self-government and the state's duty to ensure its proper dissemination have been enduring themes in the political history of Vermont. . . .

. . .

B. The Right to Equal Educational Opportunities

It is against the foregoing legal and historical backdrop that the sharp disparities among school districts in per-pupil spending, and the resultant inequities in educational opportunities, must be constitutionally evaluated. We have held that the Common Benefits Clause in the Vermont Constitution, see ch. I, art. 7, is generally coextensive with the equivalent guarantee in the United States Constitution, and imports similar methods of analysis.

. . .

This is not a case, however, that turns on the particular constitutional test to be employed. Labels aside, we are simply unable to fathom a legitimate governmental purpose to justify the gross inequities in educational opportunities evident from the record. The distribution of a resource as precious as educational opportunity may not have as its determining force the mere fortuity of a child's residence. It requires no particular constitutional expertise to recognize the capriciousness of such a system.

The principal rationale offered by the State in support of the current financing system is the laudable goal of local control. Individual school districts may well be in the best position to decide whom to hire, how to structure their educational offerings, and how to resolve other issues of a local nature. The State has not explained, however, why the current funding system is necessary to foster local control. Regardless of how the state finances public education, it may still leave the basic decision-making power with the local districts. Moreover, insofar as "local control" means the ability to decide that more money should be devoted to the education of children within a district, we have seen—as another court once wrote—that for poorer districts "such fiscal freewill is a cruel illusion." Serrano v. Priest, 487 P.2d 1241, 1260 (Cal.1971). We do not believe that the voters of Londonderry necessarily care more about education than their counterparts in Lowell simply because they spend nearly twice as much per student ($6005 as compared to $3207 in fiscal year 1995). On the contrary, if commitment to learning is measured by the rate at which residents are willing to tax themselves, then Lowell, with a property base of less than one-third per student than that of Londonderry, and a property tax nearly twice as high, should be considered the more devoted to education.

. . .

Finally, the State contends that the Common Benefits Clause is simply not offended by the unequal treatment of public schoolchildren residing in different districts so long as all are provided a minimally "adequate" education. The basis for such an argument is not entirely clear. We find no authority for the proposition that discrimination in the distribution of a constitutionally mandated right such as education may be excused merely because a "minimal" level of opportunity is provided to all. . . .

. . .

. . . [W]e emphasize that absolute equality of funding is neither a necessary nor a practical requirement to satisfy the constitutional command of equal educational opportunity. As plaintiffs readily concede, differences among school districts in terms of size, special educational needs, transportation costs, and other factors will invariably create unavoidable differences in per-pupil expenditures. Equal opportunity does not necessarily require precisely equal per-capita expenditures, nor does it necessarily prohibit cities and towns from spending more on education if they choose, but it does not allow a system in which educational opportunity is necessarily a function of district wealth. Equal educational opportunity cannot be achieved when property-rich school districts may tax low and property-poor districts must tax high to achieve even minimum standards. Children who live in property-poor districts and children who live in property-rich districts should be afforded a substantially equal opportunity to have access to similar educational revenues. Thus, as other state courts have done, we hold only that to fulfill its constitutional obligation the state must ensure substantial equality of educational opportunity throughout Vermont.

Finally, we underscore the limited reach of our holding. Although the Legislature should act under the Vermont Constitution to make educational opportunity available on substantially equal terms, the specific means of discharging this broadly defined duty is properly left to its discretion.

Peter Enrich, *Leaving Equality Behind: New Directions in School Finance Reform*

48 Vand. L. Rev. 101, 105–110 (1995).

State constitutions vary widely, but they typically include two types of provisions that have provided the primary ammunition for post-*Rodriguez* education funding litigation.[5] First, most state constitutions contain one or more provisions that either parallel the federal Equal Protection Clause or have been interpreted to impose substantially the same limitations. Second, every state, with the arguable exception of Mississippi, includes in its constitution an "education clause" that assigns to the state the responsibility for establishment of a public school system.[16] A number of these education clauses obligate the state legislatures to provide for "a thorough and efficient system" of public schools,[17] while others use a broad variety of other formulations.[18] All of the clauses, however, impose an express duty on the state government to make provision for a system of public education.

5. [As of January 1995], state constitutional litigation challenging locally funded education systems has resulted in final determinations that the systems were unconstitutional in fourteen states (Alabama, Arizona, Arkansas, California, Connecticut, Kentucky, Massachusetts, Montana, New Jersey, Tennessee, Texas, Washington, West Virginia, and Wyoming), whereas in another eighteen (Colorado, Georgia, Idaho, Illinois, Maryland, Michigan, Minnesota, Nebraska, New York, North Carolina, North Dakota, Ohio, Oklahoma, Oregon, Pennsylvania, South Carolina, Virginia, and Wisconsin) the systems have survived constitutional challenges (although in some of the latter group, subsequent suits seeking to revive the constitutional claims are currently pending). ... [(relocated footnote)]

16. ... The education clauses are collected in an appendix to Allen Hubsch, Note, The Emerging Right to Education Under State Constitutional Law, 65 Temp. L. Rev. 1325, 1343 (1992). Mississippi presents a complex case. In 1960, in response to the threat of desegregation, Mississippi amended

its constitution to replace its education clause with a provision that allowed the legislature "in its discretion" to provide for public schools. See 1960 Miss. Acts ch. 547 (amending Miss. Const., Art. VII, § 201). This provision was subsequently amended in 1987, to direct the legislature to "provide for the establishment, maintenance and support of free public schools upon such conditions and limitations as the Legislature may prescribe." See 1987 Miss. Acts ch. 671. ...

17. See, for example, N. J. Const., Art. VIII, § 4, para. 1; Ohio Const., Art. VI, § 3. Compare Colo. Const., Art. 9, § 2 (requiring "a thorough and uniform system of free public schools").

18. See, for example, Mass. Const., Pt. II, ch. V, § 2 (stating that "[w]isdom and knowledge, as well as virtue, diffused generally among the body of the people, being necessary for the preservation of their rights and liberties ..., it shall be the duty of Legislators and Magistrates, in all future periods ..., to cherish the interests of literature and the sciences, and all seminaries of

These two types of clauses provide the foundations for a range of different arguments attacking property-tax based systems for financing public schools. One class of arguments builds solely on the state's equal protection clause, contending that the state clause, unlike its federal parallel, should be construed to bar distinctions, grounded in differences in property wealth, in the fiscal capacity of different school systems in the state. . . .

A second class of arguments rests on the two clauses taken together. Such arguments rely on the presence of the state's education clause as the justification for reaching a different result under the state equal protection clause than under its federal counterpart. . . .

A third class of arguments builds exclusively on the state constitution's education clause. The precise form of these arguments may vary with the specific language of the state's constitutional provision, but in general they assert that the state's duty to provide for a system of public schools has not been satisfied, and perhaps cannot be satisfied, by a financing structure that is heavily reliant on highly variable local property wealth. . . .

. . .

[I]n the third class of arguments, the claimed right is a substantive right to a particular category of governmental services—public schooling. This reorientation opens the way to a crucial shift of focus, away from educational equality and toward educational adequacy. Adequacy arguments, instead of asking comparative questions about the differences in the resources or opportunities available to children in different districts, look directly at the quality of the educational services delivered to children in disadvantaged districts and ask evaluative questions about whether those services are sufficient to satisfy the state's constitutional obligations.

Not all arguments resting exclusively on education clauses focus on issues of adequacy. In fact, a significant subclass of education clause arguments seek to derive a commitment to educational equality from the use of terms like "uniform" or "efficient" or "system" in the education clause. . . . [T]he New Jersey Supreme Court, which played a leading role in identifying educational adequacy as the primary constitutional standard in issue, has more recently fallen back upon equality of resources and opportunities as the appropriate way to give content to standards of adequacy.

them; especially the . . . public schools and grammar schools in the towns"); Wash. Const., Art. 9, § 1 (stating that "[i]t is the paramount duty of the state to make ample provision for the education of all children residing within its borders").

A number of recent articles have relied on a typology, originated in Erica Grubb, Breaking the Language Barrier: The Right to Bilingual Education, 9 Harv. C.R.-C.L. L. Rev. 52, 66–70 (1974), which sorts education clauses into four categories, ostensibly reflecting the intensity with which they express a commitment to education. . . . See also Molly McUsic, The Use of Education Clauses in School Finance Reform Litigation, 28 Harv. J. Leg. 307, 319–26 (1991) (offering an alternative typology of education clauses, focusing on the contrast between "equity" and "minimum standards" approaches).

Nonetheless, arguments grounded in state constitutional education clauses have the capacity to reframe the debate in education funding litigation from issues of equality to issues of adequacy. Such adequacy arguments have played an occasional role from relatively early in the history of education funding litigation. In recent years, as an increasing share of education finance cases have come to focus primarily on education clauses, issues of adequacy show signs of assuming an increasingly central role in the way that both courts and litigants cast the constitutional debate.

Notes

1. The European Court's decision in *Campbell and Cosans* confirms that the Court will scrutinize the reasons for excluding individual students from existing educational institutions. Note the Court's distinction between the first sentence of Article 2 of Protocol No. 1, which confers a right on the child, with the second sentence, which confers a right on the parents. Should human rights in the educational process be understood as rights of the children or rights of the parents? Is the Court's conclusion that respect for the parents' philosophical convictions necessitates an exemption for their children from corporal punishment, rather than an acknowledgment of the morally debated character of corporal punishment, persuasive? Is it possible that the Court's decision reflects its own reservations about corporal punishment? Compare *Campbell and Cosans* with *Tyrer v. United Kingdom*, 26 Eur. Ct. H.R. (ser. A), 2 E.H.R.R. 1 (1978) (finding that corporal punishment of *adults* violated article 3); *Costello-Roberts v. United Kingdom*, 247–C Eur. Ct. H.R. (ser. A), 19 E.H.R.R. 112 (1993) (finding that particular instance of corporal punishment of student was insufficiently severe to rise to level of article 3 violation). In the United States, the Supreme Court has upheld infliction of corporal punishment on schoolchildren as not even amounting to "punishment" within the meaning of the Eighth Amendment (which prohibits only "cruel and unusual punishment"). *Ingraham v. Wright*, 430 U.S. 651 (1977).

2. The opinions in *Campbell and Cosans* cite the earlier case of *Kjeldsen, Busk Madsen, and Pedersen v. Denmark*, 23 Eur. Ct. H.R. (ser. A), 1 E.H.R.R. 711 (1976), in which a majority of the court rejected claims by parents that compulsory sex education in public primary schools violated their rights under Article 2 of Protocol No. 1 to have their children educated in conformity with their own religious convictions. The majority explained that, so long as the option of private schooling also existed, respect for the parents' rights required the state only to "take care that information or knowledge included in the curriculum is conveyed in an objective, critical and pluralistic manner. The State is forbidden to pursue an aim of indoctrination that might be considered as not respecting parents' religious and philosophical convictions." Does this standard sufficiently accommodate the child's right of access to public education and the parents' right to "ensure such education and teaching in conformity with their own religious ... convictions"? See also *Valsamis v. Greece*, 1996–VI Eur. Ct. H.R. 2312, 24 E.H.R.R. 294 (1996) (upholding one-day suspension

of Jehovah's Witness from school for refusing to take part in a parade that she and her parents regarded as militaristic).

The *Kjeldsen* case may be compared with cases in the United States in which parents have sought to exempt their children from elements of public school education that are inconsistent with the parents' religious beliefs. So long as the parents choose to send their children to public school, constitutional objections to secular materials have not succeeded. See, e.g., *Brown v. Hot, Sexy and Safer Productions, Inc.*, 68 F.3d 525 (1st Cir.1995), cert. denied, 516 U.S. 1159 (1996) (rejecting religious objections to sexually explicit AIDS education); *Mozert v. Hawkins County Board of Education*, 827 F.2d 1058 (6th Cir.1987), cert. denied, 484 U.S. 1066 (1988) (holding that public schools' refusal to exempt children from reading textbooks deemed offensive to their religious beliefs did not violate First Amendment guarantee of free exercise of religion); *Fleischfresser v. Directors of School District 200*, 15 F.3d 680 (7th Cir.1994) (similar to *Mozert*); Nomi Maya Stolzenberg, *"He Drew a Circle That Shut Me Out": Assimilation, Indoctrination, and the Paradox of a Liberal Education*, 106 Harv. L. Rev. 581 (1993) (using *Mozert* case to analyze claims of liberal "neutrality" in education). Exceptionally, the Supreme Court upheld the claim of Amish parents to exempt their children from compulsory education laws after the eighth grade. *Wisconsin v. Yoder*, 406 U.S. 205 (1972).

The relatively rigid separation of church and state under the clause of the First Amendment prohibiting any "law respecting an establishment of religion" has afforded greater success to parents and children who object to religious instruction or official practice of religion within the public schools. See, e.g., *Lee v. Weisman*, 505 U.S. 577 (1992) (finding Establishment Clause violation in official prayer at middle school graduation ceremony); *Stone v. Graham*, 449 U.S. 39 (1980) (invalidating state statute that required posting of the Ten Commandments in every public classroom); *Edwards v. Aguillard*, 482 U.S. 578 (1987) (invalidating state statute requiring public schools to teach "creation science" whenever they taught the theory of evolution). International human rights treaties do not impose a requirement of separation of church and state comparable to the U.S. Establishment Clause, although they do include protections for both religious and nonreligious dissenters. See, e.g., ICCPR art. 18; European Convention art. 9.

3. The U.S. Constitution contains neither an education clause nor a clause providing for support of the poor. Every state constitution contains an education clause, and some state constitutions contain clauses providing for support of the poor. What accounts for this pattern? Is education a more fundamental human right than subsistence? Is provision of education institutionally more complex or simpler than provision of relief to the poor? Is free public education more consistent with fundamental U.S. values than a social safety net? Or do these differences reflect historical contingencies of U.S. federalism?

4. The North Carolina Constitution (quoted in *Leandro*) expressly phrases education as a right; the Vermont Constitution (quoted in *Brigham*) does

not. Why does the Vermont Supreme Court interpret the Vermont Education Clause as recognizing an individual right rather than an obligatory task for the legislature? Why does each court interpret the right as judicially enforceable?

Should a right to education be understood as a right to a particular level of adequate education, and if so, how should a court (or a legislature) go about defining that level? Once a student has been guaranteed an adequate education, should any further education be regarded as a discretionary benefit rather than a right? Does the prospect of competition in the job market among graduates of public schools of differing quality suggest that the right should be understood in terms of equality, and not merely in terms of adequacy? How does the North Carolina court's vision of an adequate education compare with the visions of education expressed in international human rights treaties?

Are obligations to provide equal educational opportunity (as in Vermont), or an adequate education (as in North Carolina), more suitable to judicial enforcement than obligations to provide subsistence benefits to the poor?

5. If equality of educational opportunity is a constitutional right, should it be understood as requiring equality only among students attending public schools? Or also between students attending public schools and students attending private schools? If private schools are outside the scope of the constitutional obligation, then does the right of parents to send their children to private schools have implications for the effectiveness of efforts to equalize educational opportunity among public schools?

Should the human right to education be understood as including a right to equality of educational opportunity? If so, would that right include equality as between students attending public schools and students attending private schools?

6. If free public education is a fundamental right, then should courts closely scrutinize the reasons given for expulsion of individual students from the public schools as in *Campbell and Cosans*? Compare *McDuffy v. Secretary of the Executive Office of Education*, 615 N.E.2d 516 (Mass.1993) (holding that state had violated its obligation under the Massachusetts Constitution of 1780 to provide an adequate education) with *Doe v. Superintendent of Schools*, 653 N.E.2d 1088, 1095 (Mass.1995) (rejecting argument "that a student's right to an education is a 'fundamental right' which would trigger strict scrutiny analysis whenever school officials determine, in the interest of safety, that a student's misconduct warrants expulsion").

7. Further Reading. John E. Coons, William H. Clune III, and Stephen D. Sugarman, Private Wealth and Public Education (1970); Molly S. McUsic, *The Law's Role in the Distribution of Education: The Promises and Pitfalls of School Finance Litigation*, in Law and School Reform: Six Strategies for Promoting Educational Equity (Jay P. Heubert ed. 1999); Education and the Law: International Perspectives (Witold Tulasiewicz & Gerald Strowbridge eds. 1994).

8.   Concluding Note: The Right to Human Rights Education. Article 26(2) of the Universal Declaration urges that "Education shall be directed to . . . the strengthening of respect for human rights and fundamental freedoms." Article 13(1) of the ICESCR repeats this mission in slightly different phrasing, as does Article 29(1)(b) of the Convention on the Rights of the Child. Consider also the provision of the (nonbinding) Helsinki Accords, confirming "the right of the individual to know and act upon his rights and duties in [the] field [of human rights]." What content do these provisions require educators to communicate? Is it sufficient to teach respect for the concept of human rights and fundamental freedoms? For the rights and freedoms protected within the national constitutional system? Or should education also convey information about international formulations of human rights and fundamental freedoms, and explore divergences between the local and the international conceptions? Is this a mandate for political correctness, or a spur to critical thinking? See, e.g., Gudmundur Alfredsson, *The Right to Human Rights Education*, in Economic, Social and Cultural Rights: A Textbook 21, 36–39 (Asbjørn Eide et al. eds. 1995); Jost Delbrück, *The Right to Education as an International Human Right*, 35 German Yb. Int'l L. 92 (1992); Theodor Meron, *Teaching Human Rights: An Overview*, in Human Rights in International Law: Legal and Policy Issues (Theodor Meron ed. 1984).

EPILOGUE
—Louis Henkin

I. RHETORIC AND REALITY*

In 1998, the world celebrated the fiftieth anniversary of the Universal Declaration, and did so with enthusiasm and with little dissent. During 1998, also—and before, and since—the Press carried reports of horrendous acts of genocide (sometimes euphemized as "ethnic cleansing"), of torture and disappearances and prolonged arbitrary detention in various parts of the world, of floods of refugees and displaced persons. Less dramatically, governments, non-governmental organizations and international bodies found systemic failures in constitutionalism and the rule of law, as well as innumerable particular violations of civil and political rights in many countries; chronic poverty and under-development, with consequent defaults in realizing economic and social rights; rampant discrimination against women, and denials of the rights of children.

What did the world celebrate? And what is the human rights reality?

The Rhetoric: What We Celebrate

Celebrating the Universal Declaration celebrated the birth and growth of universal and international Human Rights.

In 1948, the Declaration revived the idea of inherent individual rights, converted it into an ideology, and effectively rendered it the ideology of the post-War World. The Universal Declaration "universalized" the idea of human rights, gave it a firm foundation in "human dignity," and established it as a fundamental—perhaps *the* fundamental—human value in our time.

The Universal Declaration also launched the international human rights movement, internationalized the human rights idea and ideology, and rendered them of legitimate international concern. It placed human rights on the international political agenda and made it the subject of a growing corpus of international covenants, conventions and other treaties, and of an expanding customary international law of human rights. The Universal Declaration, and the national constitutional laws and the international law that it engendered, converted an easy colloquialism—"human rights"—into a catalogue of specific, defined rights—civil and political and economic and social. The international law and politics of human rights bred international institutions, and committed them as well as governments, non-governmental organizations, and innumerable individuals to

* Adapted and updated from Louis Henkin, *The Age of Rights* 26–29 (1990), and from "Human Rights: Ideology and Aspiration, Reality and Prospect," a paper delivered at the John F. Kennedy School of Government, Harvard University, November 1998. That paper, as edited, will appear in *Human Rights Policy: What Works?*, Graham Allison and Samantha Power, eds., published for The Carr Center for Human Rights Policy at the Kennedy School, 1999/2000.

the human rights ideology, and to promoting and ensuring respect for human rights for real people in real places.

The international norms and institutions that constitute international human rights have helped achieve, slowly, imperceptibly, an international culture of human rights, as well as a culture of human rights and constitutionalism within national societies. The edifice of norms and institutions has confirmed a significant erosion of state "sovereignty," and has established that how a state treats its inhabitants is not its own business only, but is of legitimate international concern. As a result, every human being—every one of more than six billion human beings—has a recognized, justified, claim to these rights, a claim upon his or her society and upon the international political system, to recognize, respect and ensure his or her human rights.

Reality: Has It Made a Difference?

What difference has half a century of international human rights wrought in the lives of human beings? Are human rights more respected and better ensured for more human beings than they were a half-century ago?

There have been differences—large and small, some immediate, some long-term; some concrete and demonstrable, some subtle and difficult to prove. Some important international human rights "successes" have been undramatic. In numerous countries on every continent, human rights are respected and ensured where they were not respected and ensured before the Second World War; hundreds of millions of human beings in Western Europe are now enjoying human rights they did not know fifty years ago. Constitutionalism and human rights have come to Eastern and Central Europe, to many countries in Latin America, to parts of Asia and Africa. Some constitutional systems, for example that of post-war Germany, rising from the ashes of the Holocaust and unconditional surrender in World War, have become models of constitutionalism, providing examples for other countries in Europe, and beyond. South Africa, throwing off the shame of apartheid, has developed a new constitution and a new constitutional court explicitly incorporating international human rights.

The growing mound of international human rights norms and institutions has changed the map of international law and international organizations. It is more than an act of faith to declare that they have importantly improved how people live. Nearly 200 governments, many thousands of national and international officials, scores of NGO's and thousands of citizens, have devoted energies and resources to the creation and implementation of human rights norms and institutions. They have done so in the belief that norms and institutions will promote respect for human rights and improve the human rights condition of human beings in significant measure.

International human rights principles and obligations influence how governments behave in ways different from the influence of other international law and institutions. "Horizontal enforcement" of international norms—compliance induced by fear of retaliation—does not operate effectively in the law of human rights. But respect for human rights obligations is enhanced by international monitoring and international criticism and various sanctions, as well as by criticism at home invoking international standards. International human rights norms and institutions deter violations and promote change.

Some realizations of the human rights ideology are clear and indisputable. The most dramatic realization of respect for human rights in our day has been the end of *apartheid* in South Africa, in important part in response to the force of international norms and actions. Many credit international human rights also with a role in ending the Cold War and bringing the seeds of democracy and human rights to the former Soviet Union and to the former Soviet Empire. Less directly, massive killings in Cambodia, "dirty war" in Argentina, disappearances and extra-judicial killings in Chile, El Salvador and Guatemala, ended in substantial measure through international human rights influence. A UN tribunal has convicted a former prime minister of genocide and related crimes in Rwanda; a UN tribunal has indicted persons for genocide, crimes against humanity, and war crimes in the former Yugoslavia. In October 1998, the United Kingdom arrested General Augusto Pinochet, former Head of State of Chile, for extradition to Spain to stand trial for the murder of Spanish citizens as well as others. In these and other cases, the influence of international human rights is beyond doubt.

International human rights have been established in Europe pursuant to the European Convention on Human Rights. Powerful "sovereign states," *e.g.*, the United Kingdom, have been called to account, and where found in default have discontinued violations and reformed laws and practices. There have been successes in the Inter–American Human Rights Court and Commission. There is increased human rights activity and attention in Africa. The Human Rights Committee (under the Covenant on Civil and Political Rights) has acted on individual complaints in some two hundred cases, and governments found to be in violation have frequently responded and provided remedies. And more countries are submitting to the Committee's jurisdiction.

In October 1998, China signed the International Covenant on Civil and Political Rights; it may be long before China ratifies the Covenant, and if it ratifies, it will doubtless do so with reservations that may be crippling. Chinese citizens are a long way from enjoying a full measure of human rights by international standards, but now one billion Chinese are under the mantle of international human rights, China is answerable for gross violations of their human rights, and international institutions and other governments react to such violations.

Intergovernmental and governmental policies and actions combine with those of NGO's and the media to mobilize and maximize "public shame,"—a not-ineffectual system of human rights "enforcement." Why does China go to lengths, and invest diplomatic capital, to avoid having the UN Human Rights Commission designate a *rapporteur* to investigate the condition of human rights in China? Why do more than one hundred countries sign and ratify conventions, obligate themselves to report on human rights conditions, respond to criticism by international bodies, by non-governmental organizations and by "the Press"? Indeed, the influence of international human rights obligations and institutions is reflected when countries—including the United States—refrain from assuming international human rights obligations, rather than court criticism and obloquy for violating obligations they have assumed.

Alas, there is another aspect to the human rights reality. The past half century—the age of rights—has not been free of genocide, crimes against humanity, war crimes, massive floods of refugees. Constitutionalism has not come to all countries in all corners of the world, and repressive regimes continue to jail opponents and suppress freedoms. Economic and social rights have not flourished for all, even in affluent societies. International norms have not prevented or deterred other violations; international institutions and powerful states have failed to respond promptly and adequately. But international human rights can be credited with what response there has been, however late and however inadequate. International human rights imbue all the continuing efforts to address the terrible violations. Notably, the efforts to bring peace in the former Yugoslavia, and the outcome of Kosovo, have large human rights elements. In the former Yugoslavia and Rwanda, Haiti, Iraq, and other human rights trouble spots, gross violations of human rights were declared "threats to international peace and security," became a responsibility of the UN Security Council, and led to international sanctions and even military intervention.

In other contexts in recent decades, governments have invoked international human rights standards and produced known results. President Jimmy Carter helped ameliorate, and ultimately end, the "dirty war" in Argentina, contributing to the end of killings and disappearances and the release of political detainees. The U.S. Department of State's "country reports" have provided a framework for discussion by U.S. diplomats with foreign governments; as a result of such conversations, one foreign government discontinued police torture; several foreign governments cleaned up security prisons.

There have been massive human rights failures; there will no doubt be human rights failures in the new century. The human rights idea and the human rights ideology are largely helpless in the face of terrible violations of human life and human welfare during wars (including civil wars), and before horrendous abuses by mobs and terrorists. Human rights norms and institutions can address only violations for which stable societies and their governments can be held responsible, and which governments can strive to prevent, to terminate, and to remedy. But even in chaotic situations such as the former Yugoslavia, or in "failed states," the international community cannot deny concern and avoid involvement.

In sum, half a century after the Universal Declaration, the international human rights movement has established international human rights, essentially as declared in the Declaration, as a universal ideology. Every political society now must, in some way, attend to the rights of its people in its constitution, its laws and institutions. Every political society must answer for its human rights conditions to its own citizenry, to other governments, to the world. Many more societies than before 1948 have human rights systems, with fewer patterns of gross violation, and with institutions that help deter, prevent, remedy. Societies where these are absent or deficient are "abnormal," "under emergency," and are under continuing pressures to remedy. Where human rights systems become established, instances of retrogression are infrequent—"The Greek Colonels," the "dirty war" in Argentina, Nigeria—and perpetrators are under continuing pressure to recant and reform.

The condition of human rights leaves something to be desired in every society; in some societies human rights are grossly violated. But the idea and the ideology prevail. All human beings in all countries have claims to rights they did not have before the human rights movement. Hundreds of millions of human beings enjoy respect for their human rights because governments and societies have committed themselves to the idea and, perhaps, because they are monitored, shamed and deterred from violating human rights. No country can now say that the human rights of any human being subject to its jurisdiction are no one else's business. The world and its institutions may or may not respond, but they remain responsible.

II. PROSPECT

A. *A Human Rights Agenda for the Next Century*

International human rights are here to stay; they need serious attention.

Taking stock at the threshold of its second half-century, participants in the human rights movement have noted its achievements, but then have also sought to identify failures and obstacles to progress, and to plan for the century ahead.* The challenges faced by the human rights movement

---

* In 1994 a group of activists and scholars, under the auspices of the American Society of International Law, prepared a volume entitled, *Human Rights: An Agenda for the Next Century.* The table of contents is instructive:

Part I. Rights Protected

Section A. Strengthening the Human Rights Standards

Chapters: Minorities, Indigenous Peoples, and Self–Determination (Hurst Hannum); International Protection for Internally Displaced Persons (Roberta Cohen); Refugees: An Agenda for Reform (Arthur C. Helton); Democracy as a Human Right (Thomas M. Franck).

Section B. Making Principles a Reality

Chapters: Women's Human Rights: Making the Theory a Reality (Marsha A. Freeman & Avonne S. Fraser); Economic and Social Rights (Philip Alston); Development and Human Rights (Danilo Türk); Rights of Children and the Family (Marta Santos Pais).

Part II. Implementing and Enforcing Human Rights

Chapters: Protection against Abuse of the Concept of "Emergency" (Joan Fitzpatrick); Making the Human Rights Treaties Work (Anne F. Bayefsky); Improving UN Human Rights Structures (Reed Brody); Possibilities for Development of New International Judicial Mechanisms (Richard B. Bilder); Enforc-

include: maintaining the universality of human rights; strengthening recognized human rights standards; realizing human rights that have been accepted in principle; protecting minority rights and addressing ethnic hostility; facing the incessant floods of refugees and other displaced persons; and improving international human rights implementation and enforcement.

1.   Maintaining the Universality of Human Rights

"Cultural relativism" will doubtless continue to be a battle cry in the next century. Despite a half-century of the human rights movement, governments not yet fully committed to constitutionalism at home remain resistant to change, and reluctant to be monitored and judged. But human rights is not Western "cultural imperialism." The human rights ideology may have been developed in the West (and borrowed its forms and terminology), but, in fact, all cultures and all religions lay claim to the ideas of justice and fairness and respect for human dignity that underlie the human rights idea. No political or religious or cultural representative has purported to justify slavery, or torture, or extrajudicial killings, as religiously or culturally legitimate. Some particular practices claiming cultural authority—female genital mutilation, amputation as punishment—run afoul of contemporary human rights standards, and the international human rights community has not yielded to clamors of "cultural relativism" but has declared such practices unacceptable. That was the lesson brought home to successive regimes in South Africa as regards systematic racial discrimination (*apartheid*); it is a lesson slowly being learned as regards the suppression and degradation of women. Surely, cultural differences cannot justify genocide and ethnic cleansing and crimes against humanity.

No doubt repressive regimes will continue to invoke cultural relativism to support resistance to change, and will wave the banner of state "sovereignty" to support resistance to effective human rights monitoring and enforcement. Overcoming that resistance is a standing item on the human rights agenda.

2.   Strengthening Human Rights Standards

The decades since the UN Charter and the Universal Declaration have revealed some lacunae and some ambiguities in the catalogue of rights.

Some of the omissions were perhaps the inevitable consequence of attempting to achieve consensus while the world was ideologically divided

---

ing Human Rights through International Criminal Law and through an International Criminal Tribunal (M. Cherif Bassiouni); Humanitarian Intervention (Louis Henkin); The Establishment of the Right of Non–Governmental Human Rights Groups to Operate (Michael H. Posner); Addressing Gross Human Rights Abuses: Punishment and Victim Compensation (Diane F. Orentlicher); Enforcing International Human Rights Law in the United States (Paul L. Hoffman & Nadine Strossen).

See also The Future of International Human Rights (Burns H. Weston and Stephen P. Marks, eds. 1999).

and engaged in Cold War. It was necessary to overcome the cleavage between the Western concern for the individual implicit in the idea of human rights, and Communist insistence on submerging the individual in perceived societal needs. As a result, ideological differences prevented recognition of some rights and achieved only specious recognition of some others. For example: the Universal Declaration recognized particular liberties but is silent on "liberty," on individual autonomy and freedom of choice generally. The Declaration recognized a right to property, but that right failed to find a place in the Covenants. The right to work meant different things in different economic systems, and the implication of various economic, social and cultural rights are ambiguous. There is an allusion to democracy, but it is undefined. The Declaration recognizes a right to seek and enjoy asylum but no obligation to grant it; millions of persons displaced inside their own countries remain largely without recognized rights.

The international instruments remain impressive achievements, and it may not be possible, or desirable, to tamper with them. Some improvement can doubtless be achieved by interpretation, in the ideologically less-riven world since the end of the Cold War. Some improvement can be achieved by supplemental agreements, international or regional, some by incorporation in national constitutions, laws and jurisprudence, some by learned enlightened practice. But the definition of human rights is not accomplished and the human rights agenda ought not neglect it.

Human Rights and Democracy

The relation between human rights and democracy (and popular sovereignty, and the rule of law, and constitutionalism) is an intricate conceptual inquiry, as well as a continuing source of human rights dilemmas. The Universal Declaration barely alludes to "democracy" (Article 29(2)). Popular sovereignty is declared in the Declaration (Article 21(3)), but the International Covenant on Civil and Political Rights (Article 25(3)) seeks to guarantee only "the free expression of the will" of citizen electors.

The human right to live in a representative democracy, we know, does not imply that the majority may oppress minorities, or violate the human dignity of individuals. But the forms and limits of representation and suffrage run from permissible and progressive within the spirit of popular sovereignty, to inauthentic and abusive, masks for maintaining oligarchy.

Democracy and its relations to human rights ask to be better defined.

Human Rights and Globalization

Globalization of the economy and of communication may be transforming the political-legal context in which human rights are to be claimed and enjoyed in the new century. Already there are rumblings that globalization may be eroding state control of multinational companies, weakening state responsibility for the condition of human rights, without effectively lodging responsibility elsewhere.

Immediately, the consequences of globalization do not appear devastating. The state is not yet "withering away", and every "actor" among the globalizing forces is subject to some control by one or more states. Evidence of violation of human rights by such companies, or of their complicity in gross violations by states, has raised the need to determine their responsibility under international law, including responsibility under the principal covenants and conventions.

3.   Making Principles a Reality

The new century will have to attend to basic rights which have been accepted in principle but which want realization. For example, the international system has not yet done for freedom of religion and religious equality what it has done for racial equality when it developed the Convention on the Elimination of all Forms of Racial Discrimination. In the Universal Declaration, economic and social rights are recognized equally with civil and political rights, and many states have adhered to the Covenant on Economic, Social, and Cultural Rights, but those rights suffer in most countries, as a result of economic underdevelopment.

The Rights of Women

The international human rights movement succeeded in obtaining general recognition of a right to gender equality and wide agreement on eliminating discrimination against women, but agreement has been less than authentic and its implementation not impressive. The Convention on the Elimination of All Forms of Discrimination Against Women, modeled after the Convention on the Elimination of All Forms of Racial Discrimination, is a progressive instrument, but it could not avoid ambiguity of text, and could not fend off reservations which "patriarchal" societies might exploit for the continued subordination of women. Resistance to authentic gender equality is deeply rooted in some religions and cultures. But human rights means rights for all human beings of both sexes, and gender equality is a cardinal principle of the human rights ideology. It is also essential for authentic democracy, for political development, for economic development, and for population control for the next century.

The Rights of Children

Children are human and have human rights, but the International Bill of Rights has treated them largely as "appendages," and mentions them only occasionally and incidentally.

The Convention on the Rights of the Child recognizes children as human beings of young age with their own rights, including rights independent of those of parents and family, even rights against parents and family not to be abused or neglected. The new century has much to learn about, and to do for, the child.

Economic and Social Rights and Economic and Social Development

Debates at the World Conference on Human Rights (1993), reanimated the divisions of the Cold War as to the relation between civil/political and economic/social rights, and between human rights and economic and political development. It is necessary to reaffirm—as did the Vienna Declaration and Programme of Action adopted by the Conference—what should never have been questioned: that human rights are indivisible and interdependent; that so-called generations of rights are a historic but artificial construct; that one category of rights should have neither priority nor preference to the other; that, if development is essential to respect for human rights, respect for rights is indispensable to development, and need not, and may not, be sacrificed to its alleged needs. The lesson has yet to be fully learned and doubtless will have to be relearned in the coming decades.

4. Minority Rights and Ethnic Hostility

Understandably, the human rights agenda must begin with the urgent. The final decade of the twentieth century brought the end to minority racial rule in South Africa, the most divisive racial issue of the second half of this century. But elsewhere differences of race or ethnicity, and sometimes related religious differences, have signaled new, sometimes terrible, consequences for human rights. The fragmentation of Yugoslavia revealed ethnic "fault lines" and brought terrible blows to human rights along ethnic lines—ethnic differences were exploited to promote ethnic war, resulting in killing, rape, and massive expulsions. Political/ethnic divisions in the former U.S.S.R.; continued fighting along ethnic lines in Sri Lanka; religious-ethnic differences threatening explosion in India; long-festering tribal animosities in Africa; and tensions between dominant groups and indigenous populations in other parts of the world—all have given new urgency to minority protection and issues of minority rights.

"Humanitarian Intervention": after Kosovo

Since Kosovo, surely, there has been a need to clarify the international norms and the responsibility and authority of states and of international institutions, in respect of "humanitarian intervention." Kosovo persuaded many that the need for humanitarian intervention may sometimes be compelling, and international human rights law and institutions must find a way.

The United Nations Charter prohibits the threat or use of force against the political independence or territorial integrity of another state. That, it has been generally agreed, prohibits intervention in another state for whatever purpose. But the prohibition of unilateral intervention does not reflect a conclusion that the "sovereignty" of the target state stands higher in the scale of values of contemporary international society than do the human rights of its inhabitants to be safe from genocide and crimes against humanity. The law against unilateral intervention, rather, reflects the conclusion that the need for intervention may be ambiguous, may involve uncertainties of fact and motive, and difficult questions of degree; the law against unilateral intervention reflects, above all, the moral-political conclusion that no state can be trusted with the authority to judge and determine wisely that the need to intervene is compelling.

The prohibition of unilateral intervention, however, requires, and may command, the development of responsible, trustworthy means for collective humanitarian intervention. The U.N. Security Council has sometimes authorized intervention for humanitarian reasons when deemed necessary to meet threats to international peace and security. But even after the Cold War ended, the Security Council has not proved to be unfailingly responsive. States have sometimes been unwilling to rouse the Council to responsibility, or to intervene even when authorized by the Council.

In Kosovo, NATO intervened by military force for humanitarian purposes, without authorization in advance by the Security Council, though, it later appeared, with the acquiescence or even the tacit blessing of a large majority of the members of the Council. But Kosovo did not resolve the issues of the law and of the politics of intervention; it has not eliminated the need to clarify the law and develop institutional arrangements for responsible, trustworthy, collective intervention by responsible forces acting in the common interest.

In today's world (and tomorrow's) responsible collective intervention depends on the Security Council. But Kosovo revealed its deficiencies. There is no sign of movement towards establishing standing UN forces by agreements between the Security Council and member states (as contemplated by Article 43 of the UN Charter). Humanitarian intervention, therefore, would require *ad hoc* voluntary commitments by states to provide forces and unified command. The example of NATO at Kosovo suggests the possibility of authorizing bodies such as the new NATO, and perhaps other responsible bodies, perhaps "regional bodies," as contemplated by Chapter VIII in Articles 52–53 of the UN Charter.

But intervention pursuant to Security Council authorization depends on Big Power unanimity and can be frustrated by the veto of even a single Permanent Member. Might Kosovo also lead to Big Power forbearance in the use of the veto to frustrate humanitarian intervention by responsible, collective bodies, especially when such intervention is seen as necessary by a majority of the members of the Council?

5.   Refugees and Displaced Persons

Refugees are on the front pages and the television screens but for long they were the forgotten people of the international human rights movement. Many millions of people have been driven from their homes; many have exercised their human right to leave their country, but no one recognized for them a right to a haven, and a right to enter a new social contract with a new society. When refugees find a country of first asylum they may enjoy few human rights there; and they have no assurance that even first asylum will last, or that they will find a permanent haven there or elsewhere. States Parties to the Convention relating to the Status of Refugees are bound not to return a refugee to a country where his/her life or freedom would be in danger (*non-refoulement*), but even that right has been constricted, and no country is obligated to accept such a refugee for permanent residence.

Many millions of other persons are displaced from their homes but they are not recognized as international refugees, if only because they remain inside their own country. Measures to ensure their economic/social as well as their civil/political rights, and measures to anticipate and prevent or prepare for their displacement, require new norms, new institutions, and new resources.

Refugees cry for a prominent place on the human rights agenda.

6. Improving International Human Rights Implementation and Enforcement

All states have committed themselves to respect human rights standards, but many states have not been prepared to see them effectively implemented or enforced, to accept community scrutiny of the condition of human rights in their own countries, to scrutinize others, to establish effective monitoring bodies, or to accept and respond to non-governmental monitoring,

That is a major human rights task facing the international system. Treaty bodies have been proving themselves but they require greater authority, greater resources. A network of national and international non-governmental organizations is committed to help all human beings in the world know and act upon their rights, to monitor the condition of human rights everywhere, to intercede with governments and to shame them into compliance. But NGOs themselves are commonly harassed and repressed and need international protection urgently. The international community should hold every society, its leaders and its citizens, accountable for massive gross violations, if necessary by criminal prosecution, if necessary before international tribunals. The international system should help assure the punishment of gross violators, and assure remedies for the victims even in the face of claims to impunity and immunity. As a last resort, the international system should be prepared to prevent or terminate massive gross violations by international sanctions, economic and even military.

After half a century of quiet activity, the international community has adopted a treaty to establish an international criminal court, with jurisdiction to bring to trial those who commit genocide, crimes against humanity, war crimes. As of mid–1999, many States have signed the proposed ICC treaty, but there has been some strong opposition (notably by the United States) which may harm the court's effectiveness.

B. An Agenda for the United States

The Human Rights agenda implies also an agenda for the United States.

Since the Second World War, the United States has repeatedly declared human rights to be an important element in its foreign policy, including its relations to important countries (*e.g.*, China). In principle and in general, the United States has paid a decent respect to the human rights of its own inhabitants and has helped promote human rights for others elsewhere. But the United States has seen international human rights as essentially for others. It has been reluctant to adhere to international human rights agreements and the few it has ratified have been saddled with reservations. By reservations it has refused to accept international standards where U.S.

standards fall short, for example, in its insistence on reserving the right to impose (and to allow its States to impose) capital punishment for crimes committed by juveniles under 18 years of age. There have been no apparent steps towards ratification of the International Covenant on Economic, Social, and Cultural Rights, or to bring the Women's Convention, approved in Committee, to the Senate floor. The Federal Government appears not to have done enough to remind the States that they are subject to the international obligations of the United States, including obligations in human rights agreements and under the customary international law of human rights.

The United States has to clarify, and reaffirm, its commitment to economic and social rights. It may be that the economic and social condition of the inhabitants of the United States is not less favorable than it would be if the U.S. adhered to the Covenant on Economic, Social, and Cultural Rights without reservations, and carried out its terms in good faith. But failure to adhere to that Covenant is seen the world over as rejection of such rights as rights, and as a rejection of rights dear to the developing world and an affront to their hopes and aspirations. It is seen as a continuing confusion of ideological communism (which almost all are now prepared to reject) with commitment to the welfare of individual human beings (to which virtually all states are now committed in principle and, in differing measures, in fact).

The United States needs to reconsider its policy of ratifying conventions with reservations even when they are not required by the U.S. Constitution. It needs to reconsider its policy of declaring human rights conventions which it ratifies to be "non-self-executing": if a convention is non-self-executing, the United States is obligated to act promptly to adopt legislation or take other official action to execute the treaty and to assure U.S. compliance with its international undertakings. Executive Order 13107* could be an important step toward developing institutional structures, procedures, and practices to assure compliance with the human rights obligations of the United States. That will require coordination within the Executive Branch as well as guidance to State governments.

Human Rights are a hallmark of U.S. society and international human rights should be a keystone of U.S. foreign policy. Unless the United States moves to the forefront of the Human Rights movement by adhering to the principal covenants and conventions, by abandoning reservations, by submitting to international scrutiny, it will not lead others to respect human rights and to impose respect for human rights on recalcitrant states. It will not earn leadership in human rights in the world of the next century.

The United States has as much interest as any country, and the inhabitants of the United States have as great interest as any people in constitutionalism and rights at home, and in international human rights. That interest should determine and shape the human agenda for the next century, for the United States, and for the world.

The themes for that agenda are scattered through this volume, including "Eternal vigilance is the price of liberty," and "Necessitous men are not free men."

* See p. 788 supra.

INDEX

References are to pages